The
Municipal
Year
Book

1995

The authoritative
source book of
urban data and
developments

International
City/County
Management
Association

ICMA

The Municipal Year Book

1995

Washington, DC

For eighty-one years ICMA has been the professional association of appointed administrators serving local governments. Its primary goals include strengthening the quality of local government through professional management and developing and disseminating new concepts and approaches to management through a wide range of information services, training programs, and publications.

As an educational and professional association, ICMA is interested in the dissemination and application of knowledge for better local government management. To further these ends, the association supports a comprehensive research, data collection, and information dissemination program to facilitate reference and research by local government officials, university professors and students, researchers, and others concerned with local affairs.

Comprehensive Research, Data Collection, and Information Dissemination Program

The Municipal Year Book

Urban Data Service
　Special Data Issues
　Survey data resources
Management Information Service
　Monthly management reports
　Inquiry service
　Special reports

Research Projects and Publications

Copyright © 1995 by the International City/County Management Association, 777 North Capitol Street, N.E., Suite 500, Washington, D.C. 20002-4201. All rights reserved.

Volume 62, 1995

ISBN: 0-87326-970-5
ISSN: 0077-2186

Library of Congress Catalog Card Number:
34-27121

Printed in the United States of America

The views expressed in this *Year Book* are those of individual authors and are not necessarily those of the International City/County Management Association.

Suggested citation for use of material in this *Year Book*: Jane S. Author [and John N. Other], ''Title of Article,'' in *The Municipal Year Book 1995* (Washington, DC: International City/County Management Association, 1995), 00–000.

Table of Contents

A Management Issues and Trends

D

Directories

E

References

Acknowledgments

The Municipal Year Book, which provides local government officials with information on local government management, represents an important part of ICMA's extensive research program. Each year, ICMA surveys local officials on a variety of topics, and the data derived from their responses constitute the primary information source for the *Year Book.* Authors from local, state, and federal government agencies; universities; public interest groups; and ICMA staff prepare articles that describe the data collected and examine trends and developments affecting local governments.

We would like to express our appreciation to the thousands of city and county managers, clerks, finance officers, personnel directors, police chiefs, fire chiefs, and other officials who patiently and conscientiously responded to ICMA questionnaires. It is only because of their time-consuming efforts that we are able to provide the information in this volume.

Barbara H. Moore is the director of publications, Evelina R. Moulder is the editor of *The Municipal Year Book.* Other ICMA staff members who contributed to this publication are Haywood J. Tal- cove, director of survey design and evaluation; Lisa Huffman, research associate; Aubrey Charles, director of data processing; Dawn Leland, director of publications production; Brian Derr, assistant director of publications production; and Gwen Hall, publications assistant.

William H. Hansell, Jr.
Executive Director
ICMA

Inside the Year Book

The future of local government is linked to information. High performance local governments will have access to the right information at the right time. They will know how to use the information to gain the competitive edge in economic development, to negotiate health care benefits for employees, to make the budget process work for them, and to deliver services more efficiently and effectively than ever before.

Congress is sending the message that state and local governments, not the federal, must be in charge of programs that have heretofore been orchestrated at the federal level. This proposed shifting of responsibility will bring promises and costs, opportunities and challenges. In order to meet these challenges and benefit from the opportunities, local governments will need access to information as it becomes available. *The 1995 Municipal Year Book* provides some of the most important and timely local government information available.

Management Issues and Trends
Knowledge of the issues is crucial to local government decision makers who want to control the increasing cost of health care benefits for employees. In ''Municipal Employee Health Care Benefits'' (A/1), Joseph Cayer uses the results of ICMA's survey on health care benefits for municipal employees to examine types of health care plans and the financial implications of retiree coverage, employee contributions to premiums, health insurance consortia, self-insurance, and other issues.

New technology and the reduction in trade barriers position local governments to compete for new business and investment. A team of experts from the consulting firm Deloitte & Touche uses the results of a recent ICMA survey to explore trends and issues in local economic development. The article, ''Local Economic Development: Trends and Prospects'' (A/2), also describes directions that local governments can take to achieve optimum performance.

Under the council-manager form of government an appointed city manager serves at the pleasure of the council. A key component of the

council's role is conducting the city manager's performance evaluation. In ''Council Evaluation of the City Manager's Performance'' (A/3), Craig Wheeland examines that process and suggests ways in which it could be improved to achieve the best results for managers and councils.

Advances in telecommunications promise to change how local governments operate, how they approach economic development, and how they interact with citizens. The issues and possibilities are endless and the role of local government is significant as the Information Superhighway links businesses and communities around the corner and around the globe. In ''Telecommunications in Local Government: Preparing for an Uncertain Future'' (A/4), Anthony Cahill describes advances in technology, regulatory and fiscal issues, and the importance of telecommunications to high performance local governments.

Survey results described in Glen Cope's ''Budgeting for Performance in Local Government'' (A/5) show that local government budgeting processes have changed to accommodate management improvement processes. This article covers performance measurement, quality improvement, benchmarking, and other techniques that have been used in the budget process to improve budgeting, productivity, and management processes.

The Intergovernmental Dimension
David Berman, in ''State-Local Relations: Patterns, Problems, and Partnerships'' (B/1) looks at the overall pattern of state and local relations—focusing in particular on state aid, local authority, mandates, education, and the environment.

Twenty-six cases that were decided in the 1993–94 term of the U.S. Supreme Court significantly affect local government. In ''Recent Supreme Court Cases Affecting Local Governments'' (B/2), Rosemary O'Leary and Charles Wise examine the major holdings of these cases in the important areas of property rights, environmental law, sexual harassment, taxes and user

fees, public schools, voting rights, free speech, criminal law, and medicare reimbursement.

Among the many pieces of legislation examined in ''Congressional Actions Affecting Local Governments'' (B/3), by Eugene Boyd, are the Crime Bill, the School-to-Work Opportunities Act, Goals 2000: Educate America Act, Head Start, and the numerous significant bills that were introduced addressing welfare reform, housing and community development, and health care.

Staffing and Compensation
One of the most basic managerial concerns is compensation. This section provides salary data for a variety of positions held by local officials.

In ''Salaries of Municipal Officials for 1994,'' Evelina Moulder looks at the salaries of 21 municipal officials (C/1). The article is based on the results of the salary survey conducted by ICMA in July 1994.

Gwen Hall uses the salary survey results to evaluate the salaries of 12 county managerial positions in ''Salaries of County Officials for 1994'' (C/2).

''Police and Fire Personnel and Expenditures, 1994'' presents the following in tabular form: total personnel, the number of uniformed personnel, hours worked per week, entrance and maximum salaries, information on longevity pay, and a breakdown of departmental expenditures (C/3). Tari Renner compares the 1994 data with the results of the 1993 survey.

Directories
The directories section (D/1/1 through D/1/10) encourages *Year Book* users to turn to sources beyond the *Year Book*—state municipal leagues, state agencies for community affairs, state management associations, and colleagues in other municipalities, counties, and regional councils—to exchange information and set up informal networks. *The Year Book* directories provide the names of nearly 70,000 contacts in United States local governments and a means of getting in touch with them—a phone number and in some cases an address.

A special directory in the *Year Book* is "Professional, Special Assistance, and Educational Organizations Serving Local and State Governments" (D/2). The organizations included in this directory provide educational and research services to members or others on a cost-of-service basis and in this way strengthen professionalism in government administration.

References

The "Sources of Information" (E/1), prepared by Anne Maura English, provides bibliographic listings of the latest books and periodicals in 2 basic reference categories and 15 functional area categories: basic references; basic statistical resources; emergency management; environment and energy; fire protection; housing; human resources and services; information technologies; intergovernmental relations; law enforcement and criminal justice; local government organization and management; personnel and labor relations; planning and development; public finance; public works and utilities; recreation and leisure; and transportation and roads. Online data sources are included.

PROFESSIONAL MUNICIPAL MANAGEMENT

Professional municipal management in the United States and Canada has its roots in the council-manager plan, as does ICMA. The first appointment to a position similar to a city manager was 87 years ago, in 1908, in Staunton, Virginia, where a "general manager" was employed to oversee the administrative functions of the municipality. The first adoption of the council-manager plan in the United States is usually considered to have been in Sumter, South Carolina, in 1912, and in Canada during the next year at Westmount, Québec. Dayton, Ohio, in 1914, was the first community of substantial size to adopt the council-manager plan, and in 1930 Durham County, North Carolina, became the first county to institute professional management.

The council-manager plan grew steadily from 1914, slowed only as a result of the difficulties of war and depression. By 1918 there were 98 council-manager municipalities. In 1930 the total had increased to 418, and by 1945, it had reached 622. By the end of 1969, 2,252 municipalities in the United States and Canada were using the council-manager plan. Since that time the number of places using the plan has increased by 843 so that by December 1994 ICMA had verified the existence of the plan in 2,962 cities and counties in the United States and 133 in Canada, for a total of 3,095.

During the 1960s, the profile of local government had begun to show significant changes. Not only were there new problems, but variations in organization and structure became evident. Many cities, towns, and counties began providing for an appointed official responsible for overall administrative affairs without adopting the council-manager plan as it was originally conceived. Similarly, the development of councils of governments and regional councils

brought new and innovative structures to local government. It became obvious to ICMA that, in many cities, professional management positions were being developed that did not vary significantly from the role of the traditional city and county manager positions provided for in the council-manager plan.

Therefore, in July 1969, the International City Managers' Association changed its name to the International City Management Association and provided for full professional recognition of these positions. To distinguish these municipalities from those recognized as council-manager municipalities, they were designated "general management municipalities." Criteria were established for recognition, and the incumbents in these positions were made eligible for Corporate (voting) Membership in ICMA. Similarly, ICMA began recognizing state municipal leagues in the spring of 1986. In 1991, ICMA changed its name to the International City/County Management Association.

Between June 1969 and December 1994 ICMA recognized 1,428 governments in the United States and Canada under the general management criteria. Included in this total are 1,057 municipalities, 210 counties, 143 councils of governments, and 18 leagues.

Figure 1 shows the numbers of council-manager and general management recognitions since 1984. The numbers include recognitions in the United States and Canada.

Recognized Municipalities

All management executives are selected by municipalities on the basis of relevant education and experience. Although professional management is defined by a common set of functions, the association has not sought to control entrance into the profession by requiring comple-

tion of a specified education program. The primary emphasis has been on demonstrated competence in a position with significant management responsibility and authority.

These professional positions are defined by a set of criteria describing the characteristics of overall professional management. The present criteria provide for recognition of a position in the council-manager form of government and a position of general management that applies to a wide variety of governmental forms, councils of government, and state municipal leagues.

Table 1 indicates, by ICMA regions, the number of municipalities in which there is a recognized professional manager. ICMA regions are determined by the Executive Board in accordance with the relative number of corporate members in the various geographic areas. The ICMA regions are *Northeast*: Connecticut, Delaware, the District of Columbia, Maine, Maryland, Massachusetts, New Hampshire, New Jersey, New York, Pennsylvania, Rhode Island, and Vermont; *Southeast*: Alabama, Florida, Georgia, Kentucky, Mississippi, North Carolina, South Carolina, Tennessee, Virginia, and West Virginia; *Midwest*: Illinois, Indiana, Iowa, Michigan, Minnesota, Missouri, Ohio, and Wisconsin; *Mountain-Plains*: Arizona, Arkansas, Colorado, Idaho, Kansas, Louisiana, Montana, Nebraska, New Mexico, North Dakota, Oklahoma, South Dakota, Texas, Utah, and Wyoming; *West Coast*: Alaska, California, Hawaii, Nevada, Oregon, and Washington. The Canadian information is reported as for an independent region. (Although all members in countries outside of North America are currently represented in the association through a region which includes Canada, data for these countries are excluded from the table.) Further information on these recognized places, including legal basis,

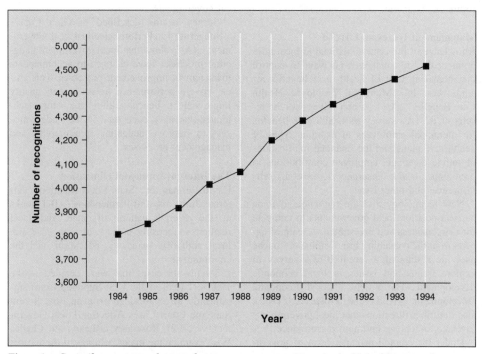

Figure 1   *Council-manager and general management recognitions in the United States and Canada, 1984–1994*

Table 1   RECOGNIZED LOCAL GOVERNMENTS, COUNCILS OF GOVERNMENTS, AND LEAGUES BY ICMA REGION[1]

	Council-manager (CM)			General management (GM)					Total CM and GM
ICMA region	Cities, towns, etc.	Counties	Total CM	Cities, towns, etc.	Counties	COGs	State municipal leagues	Total GM	
Northeast	591	6	597	342	28	10	4	384	981
Southeast	608	83	691	116	93	39	6	254	945
Midwest	553	14	567	326	35	27	3	391	958
Mountain-Plains	569	12	581	161	16	40	3	220	801
West Coast	509	17	526	82	36	24	2	144	670
U.S. total	2,830	132	2,962	1,027	208	140	18	1,393	4,355
Canada total	127	6	133	30	2	3	0	35	168
Grand total	2,957	138	3,095	1,057	210	143	18	1,428	4,523

[1]Data in this table are as of 30 December 1994.

title of position, form of government, and year of recognition, is presented in the annual ICMA publication, *Who's Who in Local Government Management*.

Organizational Goals

Beginning in the fall of 1983, the association underwent an extensive self-analysis and strategic planning process that resulted in a revision of ICMA's organizational goals. Adopted by the executive board in January 1985, these goals, the framework for ICMA services, are as follows:

1. To provide professional development programs and publications for local government professionals that improve their skills, increase their knowledge of local government, and strengthen their commitment to the values and ideals of professional management.
2. To support professional management in all forms of local government and specifically to encourage local governments in the United States and in other countries to adopt and retain the council-manager or the general management plan.
3. To improve the recruiting process for professional local government administrators, in order to ensure the future of the profession and increase professional management opportunities for women and minorities.
4. To serve as a national and international clearinghouse for the collection, analysis, and dissemination of local government-related information and to conduct research and offer contractual technical consulting services in areas that address local government needs.
5. To promote professional local government management by working in cooperation with and serving as a resource for public interest groups directly involved in the formulation of public policy.
6. To offer services and programs and to provide a communications network to respond to personal, professional, and family needs of members.

ORGANIZATION OF DATA

Most of the tabular data for *The Municipal Year Book 1994* were obtained from public officials through questionnaires developed and administered by the ICMA. ICMA's Municipal Data Service maintains a computer-based information file of all data collected through ICMA surveys.

Every city[1] of 2,500 and over in population, all recognized places under 2,500 population, and all counties 2,500 and over were surveyed by questionnaire for sections C1, C2, and D1/9 and D1/10 of this *Year Book*. However, not every city and county were surveyed for each local government function and activity included in the other sections. Questionnaires are reviewed by local authorities and pretested before they are prepared in final form. All governments surveyed for each study receive a mail questionnaire; if they do not respond to the first mailing, a second request is sent.

All survey questionnaires are edited to eliminate respondent errors and to assure that questionnaire responses are keypunched as accurately as possible for computer tabulation. *Year Book* authors determine the analysis and the tables required from the computer as the basis for their articles.

Government Definitions

At the beginning of 1987, there were 83,237 governments in the United States. Fifty-one of these are nonlocal governments; the remainder are all local governments—counties, municipalities, townships, school districts, and special districts.

A municipality, by census definition, is a "political subdivision within which a municipal corporation has been established to provide general local government for a specific population concentration in a defined area." This definition includes all active governmental units officially designated as cities, boroughs (except in Alaska), villages, or towns (except in Minnesota, New York, New England, and Wisconsin). The definition generally includes all places incorporated under the procedures established by the several states.

Counties are the primary political administrative divisions of the state. In Louisiana these units are called parishes. Alaska has county-type governments called boroughs. There are certain unorganized areas of some states that are not included in the *Year Book* data base, which have a county designation from the Census Bureau for strictly administrative purposes. These comprise 12 areas in Alaska; 2 areas in South Dakota; 5 areas in Rhode Island; 8 areas in Connecticut; and 1 area in Montana.[3]

Year Book Data Base

Unless otherwise noted, this edition of the *Year Book* uses the 1990 Census Bureau figures for placing local governments in the United States into population groups for tabular presentation.

Using the 1990 census data, it is possible to show information for 6,608 cities and other urban places 2,500 and over in population and 592 council-manager and general management places under 2,500 population. Although the selection of cities 2,500 and over in population largely corresponds to the criteria established by the Bureau of the Census, there are some variations. Selection of council-manager and general management places under 2,500 population is based on recognition by ICMA. *The Year Book* data base shows 3,043 counties.

City Classification

Table 2 details the distribution of all municipalities of 2,500 and over in population (and all municipalities udner 2,500 recognized by ICMA as providing for the council-manager plan or providing for a position of overall general management) by population, geographic region and division, metro status, and form of government.

Population

The population categories are self-explanatory.

Geographic Classification

Nine geographic divisions and four regions are used by the Bureau of the Census (Figure 2). The nine divisions are *New England*: Connecticut, Maine, Massachusetts, New Hampshire, Rhode Island, and Vermont; *Mid-Atlantic*: New Jersey, New York, and Pennsylvania; *East North Central*: Illinois, Indiana, Michigan, Ohio, and Wisconsin; *West North Central*: Iowa, Kansas, Minnesota, Missouri, Nebraska, North Dakota, and South Dakota; *South Atlantic*: Delaware, the District of Columbia, Florida, Georgia, Maryland, North Carolina, South Carolina, Virginia, and West Virginia; *East South Central*: Alabama, Kentucky, Mississippi, and Tennessee; *West South Central*: Arkansas, Louisiana, Oklahoma, and Texas; *Mountain*: Arizona, Colorado, Idaho, Montana, New Mexico, Nevada, Utah, and Wyoming; and *Pacific Coast*: Alaska, California, Hawaii, Oregon, and Washington.

For *The Year Book* the regions are further consolidated as follows: *Northeast*: Connecticut, Maine, Massachusetts, New Hampshire, New Jersey, New York, Pennsylvania, Rhode Island, and Vermont; *North Central*: Illinois, Indiana, Iowa, Kansas, Michigan, Minnesota,

Table 2   CUMULATIVE DISTRIBUTION OF U.S. MUNICIPALITIES

Classification	All cities	Cities 2,500 & over	Cities 5,000 & over	Cities 10,000 & over	Cities 25,000 & over	Cities 50,000 & over	Cities 100,000 & over	Cities 250,000 & over	Cities 500,000 & over	Cities over 1,000,000
Total, all cities	7,231	6,623	4,622	2,817	1,215	533	195	64	25	8
Population group										
Over 1,000,000	8	8	8	8	8	8	8	8	8	8
500,000–1,000,000	17	17	17	17	17	17	17	17	17	
250,000–499,999	39	39	39	39	39	39	39	39		
100,000–249,999	131	131	131	131	131	131	131			
50,000–99,999	338	338	338	338	338	338				
25,000–49,999	682	682	682	682	682					
10,000–24,999	1,602	1,602	1,602	1,602						
5,000–9,999	1,805	1,805	1,805							
2,500–4,999	2,001	2,001								
Under 2,500[1]	608									
Geographic region										
Northeast	1,998	1,844	1,347	782	282	97	24	6	3	2
North Central	2,104	1,919	1,280	782	310	125	40	14	6	2
South	2,103	1,905	1,250	728	292	138	65	24	9	2
West	1,036	955	745	525	331	173	66	20	7	2
Geographic division										
New England	798	708	529	327	128	46	10	1	1	0
Mid-Atlantic	1,190	1,136	818	455	154	51	14	5	2	2
East North Central	1,365	1,274	890	558	224	89	25	8	6	2
West North Central	739	645	390	224	86	36	15	6	0	0
South Atlantic	887	783	522	314	141	65	29	9	3	0
East South Central	470	430	284	149	47	15	11	4	2	0
West South Central	746	692	444	265	104	58	25	11	4	2
Mountain	373	328	225	129	71	38	15	7	1	0
Pacific Coast	663	627	520	396	260	135	51	13	6	2
Metro status										
Central	515	515	515	514	484	326	160	64	25	8
Suburban	3,882	3,685	2,777	1,709	610	202	35			
Independent	2,834	2,423	1,330	594	121	5				
Form of government										
Mayor-council	3,555	3,294	2,038	1,118	440	201	83	36	20	6
Council-manager	3,030	2,738	2,173	1,468	722	319	106	26	5	2
Commission	163	156	118	81	26	9	6	2		
Town meeting	411	364	233	105	7	0				
Rep. town meeting	72	71	60	45	20	4				

[1]Municipalities recognized by ICMA as providing for the council-manager plan or providing for a position of overall general management. Also includes municipalities with populations that dropped below 2,500 between the 1980 and 1990 U.S. censuses.

Missouri, Nebraska, North Dakota, South Dakota, and Wisconsin; *South*: Alabama, Arkansas, Delaware, the District of Columbia, Florida, Georgia, Kentucky, Louisiana, Maryland, Mississippi, North Carolina, Oklahoma, South Carolina, Tennessee, Texas, Virginia, and West Virginia; and *West*: Alaska, Arizona, California, Colorado, Hawaii, Idaho, Montana, Nevada, New Mexico, Oregon, Utah, Washington, and Wyoming.

Metro Status
Metro status refers to the status of a municipality within the context of the U.S. Office of Management and Budget definition of a metropolitan statistical area. The criteria allow for three levels of classification: metropolitan statistical areas, primary metropolitan statistical areas, and consolidated statistical areas.

Metropolitan Statistical Areas (MSAs) These areas have either a city of at least 50,000 population or a Bureau of the Census urbanized area of at least 50,000 *and* a total metropolitan statistical area population of at least 100,000. Each MSA has at least one central city and one central county and may include outlying counties with economic and social ties to the central

components of the area. Outlying counties must also meet requirements relating to community level and ''urban character'' to be included in an MSA.

MSAs are not closely associated with other metropolitan statistical areas and are surrounded by nonmetropolitan counties.

Primary Metropolitan Statistical Areas (PMSAs) Metropolitan statistical areas of over 1,000,000 population can be designated as primary metropolitan statistical areas. There must be local support for separate recognition and at least 60% of the area's population must be urban; less than 50% of its residents are permitted to commute to jobs outside the country for it to be considered a PMSA.

If any area within a metropolitan statistical area is recognized as a primary metropolitan statistical area, the remaining area of that statistical area is designated as a separate primary metropolitan statistical area.

Consolidated Metropolitan Statistical Areas (CMSAs) A metropolitan statistical area in which primary statistical areas have been identified is designated as a consolidated metropolitan statistical area. If no primary metropolitan statistical areas are identified within an MSA, the term metropolitan statistical area applies.

In New England, the city and town are administratively more important than the county, and a wide range of data is compiled locally for such entities. Here, towns and cities are the units used in defining metropolitan statistical areas. Because cities and towns are generally smaller in area than counties, the total MSA population requirement is lower in the six New England states (75,000) than in the other states (100,000).

The Office of Management and Budget currently identifies 353 metropolitan areas. Of this number 262 are MSAs, and 71 are PMSAs. There are 20 CMSAs.

Central cities are the core cities of an MSA and must have a population of at least 25,000 and meet two commuting requirements: At least 50% of the employed residents of the city must work within the city, and there must be at least 75 jobs for each 100 residents who are employed. Cities between 15,000 and 25,000 population may also be considered central cities if they are at least one-third the size of the MSA's largest city and meet the commuting requirements. Suburban cities are the other cities, towns, and incorporated places in an MSA. Independent cities are incorporated places not located in an MSA.

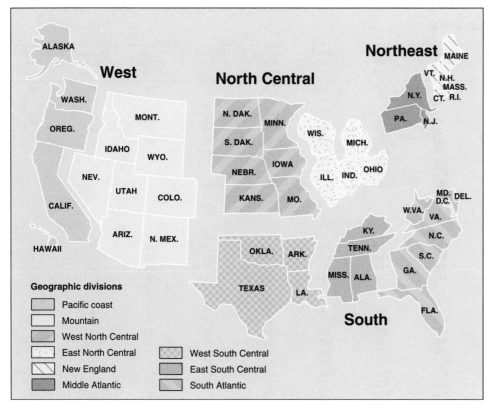

Figure 2   *U.S. Bureau of the Census geographic regions and divisions*

Form of Government

Form of government relates primarily to the organization of the legislative and executive branches of municipalities and townships. In the *mayor-council form*, an elected mayor generally acts as the chief executive officer with the amount of administrative authority dependent on state law and variations in local organization. These variations include the scope of the powers of the elected council and the delegation of some authority to appointed professional administrators, to special boards, and to commissions.

Many cities with a mayor-council form of government have an appointed city administrator. These officials are appointed by the elected representatives (council) and are responsible to them for the execution of their duties. However, their administrative authority is limited—they often do not directly appoint department heads or other key city personnel, and their responsibility for budget preparation and administration, although significant, is subordinate to that of the elected officials.

Under the *council-manager form*, a manager is appointed by and responsible to an elected council to serve as chief administrative officer to oversee personnel, development of the budget, proposing policy alternatives, and general implementation of policies and programs adopted by the council.

The *commission form* of government operates with an elected commission performing both legislative and executive functions, generally with departmental administration divided among the commissioners.

The *town meeting form* of government is a system in which all qualified voters of a municipality meet annually (or more often if necessary) to set policy and choose selectmen to carry out the basic policies they have established.

Under the *representative town meeting form* of government, the voters select a large number of citizens to represent them at the meeting(s). All citizens can participate in the meeting(s), but only the representatives actually have a direct vote.

County Classification

Counties are the primary political administrative divisions of the states. The county-type governments in Alaska are called boroughs. Table 3 details the distribution of counties thoughout the nation, using the same categories as Table 3. The population categories are self-explanatory, and the geographic regions are described in the discussion of Table 3.

Metropolitan Status

For counties, metro status refers to the status of a county within the context of the U.S. Office of Management and Budget definition of a metropolitan statistical area (MSA). "Metro" means a county is located within an MSA; "nonmetro" indicates that it is located outside of the boundaries of an MSA.

Counties that are located in an MSA are classified in a way similar to that for cities. Central counties are those in which central cities are located. Suburban counties are the other coun-

ties located within an MSA. Counties not located in an MSA are considered independent.

Form of Government

For counties, form of government relates to structural organizations of the legislative and executive branches of counties; counties are classified as being with or without an administrator. There are three basic forms of county government: commission, council-administrator, and council-elected executive.

The *commission form* of county government is characterized by a governing board that shares the administrative and, to an extent, legislative responsibilities with several independently elected functional officials. Counties with this form of government are designated as being without an administrator.

Counties with the *council-administrator form*, in which an administrator is appointed by, and responsible to, the elected council to carry out directives, are designated under form of government as "with administrator." The *council-elected executive form* features two branches of government: the executive and the legislative. The independently elected executive is considered the formal head of the county. This form of government is also included in the designation "with administrator."

The use of varying types of local government is an institutional response to the needs, requirements, and articulated demands of citizens at the local level. Within each type of local government, structures are developed to provide adequate services. These structural adaptations are a partial result of the geographic location, population, metropolitan status, and form of government of the jurisdiction involved.

USES OF STATISTICAL DATA

The Municipal Year Book uses primary and secondary data sources. ICMA collects and publishes the primary source data. Secondary source data refers to data collected by another organization. Most of the primary source data are collected through survey research. ICMA develops questionnaires on a variety of subjects during a given year and then pretests and refines them to increase the validity of each survey instrument. Once completed, the surveys are sent to officials in all cities above a given population level (i.e., 2,500 and above, 10,000 and above, etc.). Surveys are sent to the appropriate officials. For example, city managers or chief administrative officers receive the *Organizational Structure and Decision Making* survey, and finance officers receive the *Police and Fire Personnel and Expenditures* survey.

ICMA conducts the city, county, and councils of governments salary surveys and the *Police and Fire Personnel and Expenditures* survey every year. The other research projects are conducted every several years, and some are one-time efforts to provide information on subjects of current interest.

Table 3   CUMULATIVE DISTRIBUTION OF U.S. COUNTIES

Classification	All counties	Counties 2,500 & over	Counties 5,000 & over	Counties 10,000 & over	Counties 25,000 & over	Counties 50,000 & over	Counties 100,000 & over	Counties 250,000 & over	Counties 500,000 & over	Counties over 1,000,000
Total, all counties	3,043	2,928	2,752	2,315	1,408	796	418	174	80	25
Population group										
Over 1,000,000	25	25	25	25	25	25	25	25	25	25
500,000–1,000,000	55	55	55	55	55	55	55	55	55	
250,000–499,999	94	94	94	94	94	94	94	94		
100,000–249,999	244	244	244	244	244	244	244			
50,000–99,999	378	378	378	378	378	378				
25,000–49,999	612	612	612	612	612					
10,000–24,999	907	907	907	907						
5,000–9,999	437	437	437							
2,500–4,999	176	176								
Under 2,500[1]	115									
Geographic region										
Northeast	196	196	195	190	180	134	87	43	20	4
North Central	1,053	1,009	918	740	417	208	112	38	16	5
South	1,374	1,344	1,299	1,111	637	329	145	54	24	6
West	420	379	340	274	174	125	74	39	20	10
Geographic division										
New England	52	52	52	50	46	28	20	8	5	1
Mid-Atlantic	144	144	143	140	134	106	67	35	15	3
East North Central	436	435	432	403	282	153	84	29	13	4
West North Central	617	574	486	337	135	55	28	9	3	1
South Atlantic	545	540	532	461	296	172	85	32	13	2
East South Central	362	360	357	312	156	65	19	7	3	0
West South Central	467	444	410	338	185	92	41	15	8	4
Mountain	276	242	206	153	76	49	23	11	4	1
Pacific Coast	144	137	134	121	98	76	51	28	16	9
Metro status										
Central	336	336	336	336	336	327	277	134	63	24
Suburban	347	347	347	344	303	212	107	40	17	1
Independent	2,360	2,245	2,069	1,635	769	257	34			
Form of government										
Without administrator	2,335	2,224	2,050	1,643	882	404	165	51	22	6
With administrator	708	704	702	672	526	392	253	123	58	19

[1]Includes recognized counties and those with populations that dropped below 2,500 between the 1980 and 1990 censuses.

LIMITATIONS OF THE DATA

Regardless of the subject or type of data presented, they should be read cautiously. All policy, political, and social data have strengths and limitations. These factors should be considered in any analysis and application. Statistics are no magic guide to perfect understanding and decision-making, but they can shed light on particular subjects and questions in lieu of haphazard and subjective information. They can clarify trends in policy expenditures, processes, and impacts, and consequently, assist in evaluating the equity and efficiency of alternative courses of action. Statistical data are most valuable when one remembers their imperfections, both actual and potential, while drawing conclusions.

For example, readers should examine the response bias for each survey. Surveys may be sent to all municipalities above a certain population threshold, but not all of them are necessarily returned. Jurisdictions that fail to respond are rarely mirror images of those that do. ICMA reduces the severity of this problem by maximizing the opportunities to respond through second and (sometimes) third requests. But although this practice mitigates the problem, response bias invariably appears. Consequently, ICMA always includes a "Survey Response" table in each article that analyzes a particular survey. This allows the reader to examine the patterns and degrees of response bias through a variety of demographic and structural variables.

Other possible problems can occur with survey data. Local governments have a variety of record-keeping systems. Therefore, some of the data (particularly those on expenditures) may lack uniformity. In addition, no matter how carefully a questionnaire is refined, problems such as divergent interpretations of directions, definitions, and specific questions invariably arise. However, when inconsistencies or apparently extreme data are reported, every attempt is made to verify these responses through follow-up telephone calls.

TYPES OF STATISTICS

There are basically two types of statistics: descriptive and inferential.

Descriptive

Most of the data presented in this volume are purely descriptive. Descriptive statistics summarize some characteristics of a group of numbers. A few numbers represent many. If you want to find out something about the age of a city's work force, for example, it would be quite cumbersome to read a list of several hundred numbers (each representing the age of individual employees). It would be much easier to have a few summary descriptive statistics such as the mean (average) or the range (the highest value minus the lowest value). These two "pieces" of information would not convey all of the details of the entire data set, but they can help and are much more useful and understandable than complete numerical lists.

There are essentially two types of descriptive statistics: measures of central tendency and measures of dispersion.

Measures of Central Tendency These types of statistics indicate the most common or typical value of a data set. The most popular examples are the mean and median. The mean is simply the arithmetic average. It is calculated by summing the items in a data set and dividing by the total number of items. For example, given the salaries of $15,000, $20,000, $25,000, $30,000 and $35,000, the mean is $25,000 ($125,000 divided by 5).

The mean is the most widely used and intuitively obvious measure of central tendency. However, it is sensitive to extreme values. A few large or small numbers in a data set can produce a mean that is not representative of the "typical" value. Consider the example of the five salaries above. Suppose the highest value was not $35,000 but $135,000. The mean of the data set would now be $45,000 ($225,000 divided by 5). This figure, however, is not representative of this group of numbers because it is substantially greater than four of the five values and is $90,000 below the high score. A data set such as this is "positively skewed" (it has one or more extremely high scores). Under these circumstances (or when the data set is "negatively skewed," with extremely low scores), it is more appropriate to use the median as a measure of central tendency.

The median is the middle score of a data set that is arranged in order of increasing magnitude. Theoretically, it represents the point that is equivalent to the 50th percentile. For a data set with an odd number of items, the median has the same number of observations above and below it (i.e., the third value in a data set of five or the eighth value in a data set of fifteen). With an even number of cases, the median is the average of the middle two scores (i.e., the second and third values in a data set of four or the seventh and eighth values in a data set of fourteen). In the example of the five salaries used above, the median is $25,000 regardless of whether the largest score is $35,000 or $135,000. When the mean exceeds the median, the data set is positively skewed. If the median exceeds the mean, then it is negatively skewed.

Measures of Dispersion This form of descriptive statistics indicates how widely scattered or spread out the numbers are in a data set. Some common measures of dispersion are the range and the interquartile range. The range is simply the highest value minus the lowest value. For the numbers 3, 7, 50, 80, and 100, the range is 97 (100 − 3 = 97). For the numbers 3, 7, 50, 80, and 1,000, it is 997 (1,000 − 3 = 997). The interquartile range is the value of the third quartile minus the value of the first quartile. Quartiles divide a data set into four equal parts similar to the way percentiles divide a data set into 100 equal parts. Consequently, the third quartile is equivalent to the 75th percentile, and the first quartile is equivalent to the 25th percentile. The interquartile range is essentially the range of the middle 50% of the data.

Inferential

Inferential statistics permit the social and policy researcher to make inferences about whether or not a correlation exists between two (or more) variables in a population based on data from a sample. Specifically, inferential statistics provide the probability that the sample results could have occurred by chance if there were really no relationship between the variables in the population as a whole. If the probability of random occurrence is sufficiently low (below the researcher's preestablished significance level), then the null hypothesis, that there is no association between the variables, is rejected. This lends indirect support to the research hypothesis that a correlation does exist. If they can rule out chance factors (the null hypothesis), then researchers conclude that they have found a "statistically significant" relationship between the two variables under examination.

Significance tests are those statistics that permit inferences about whether or not variables are correlated but provide nothing directly about the strength of such correlations. Measures of association, on the other hand, indicate how strong relationships are between variables.

These statistics range from a high of +1.0 (for a perfect positive correlation), to zero (indicating no correlation), to a low of −1.0 (for a perfect negative correlation).

Some common significance tests are the Chi Square and difference-of-means tests. Some common measures of association are Yule's Q, Sommer's Gamma, Lambda, Cramer's V, Pearson's C, and the correlation coefficient. Consult any major statistics textbook for further information on these tests and measures.[2]

Inferential statistics are used less frequently in this volume than descriptive statistics. However, whenever possible, the data have been presented so that the user can calculate inferential statistics whenever appropriate.

SUMMARY

All social, political, and economic data are collected with imperfect techniques in an imperfect world. Therefore, users of such data should be continuously cognizant of the strengths and weaknesses of the information from which they are attempting to draw conclusions. Readers should note the limitations of the data published in this volume. Particular attention should be paid to the process of data collection and potential problems such as response bias.

[1]The terms *city* and *cities*, as used in this volume, refer to cities, villages, towns, townships, and boroughs.
[2]For additional information on statistics see Tari Renner's *Statistics Unraveled: A Practical Guide to Using Data in Decision Making* (Washington, D.C.: International City/County Management Association, 1988).

A Management Issues and Trends

A 1

Municipal Employee Health Care Benefits

Joseph N. Cayer
Arizona State University

Findings

Nearly all responding municipalities (98.8%) offer health insurance to some or all of their employees. All cities with populations of 25,000 or more provide benefits.

The majority of the cities reporting (78.4%) expect employee health care benefit costs to increase over the next three years, 19.0% expect costs to remain the same, and 2.6% expect decreases.

Traditionally, local governments have provided relatively generous health care benefits to employees. The provision of benefits evolved from a sense of concern about the welfare of employees and their families, collective bargaining agreements, and the realization that healthy employees are productive employees. As in the private sector, health benefits programs in local government started with health insurance through a private insurance carrier. These plans, usually referred to as indemnity plans, cover most health problems, and employees have the discretion to choose any provider. Limits often are imposed on the total dollar value of benefits available, and in most cases employees have to cover a part of the costs. Plans vary with respect to whether the employer pays all premiums or whether such costs are shared by employer and employee.

As the costs of health care have risen and, with them, premium costs, employers have searched for ways to provide benefits in a more cost-efficient manner. Thus many employers have begun to experiment with health maintenance organizations (HMOs) or preferred provider organizations (PPOs) as a way of controlling costs. Over time, changes have been made to the way in which the benefits are financed and what levels of benefits are available. Health care reform debate at the national level has reflected health care concerns of both employers and employees. Local governments, under continuing pressures to provide more and better services with fewer resources, have had to consider very carefully the costs of providing health care benefits for employees, and thus have engaged in policy changes. This article provides an overview of the types and levels of benefits provided by local governments.

METHODOLOGY

In 1994, ICMA conducted a survey of municipalities—cities, towns, townships, villages, and boroughs—to gather information about their practices, experiences, and policies relative to employee health-care benefits. A total of 7,135

surveys were mailed to personnel directors or chief appointed officials in all U.S. municipalities 2,500 and over in population and to those under 2,500 that are recognized by ICMA.[1] A total of 3,301 surveys were returned, for a response rate of 46.3%. Table 1/1 summarizes the responses by population, geographic division, and metro status.

The survey contained questions about whether health care benefits were provided and, if so, to whom. It also included questions about the administration of the program, the type of programs available (indemnity, HMO, PPO), the benefits offered, cost, and demographics. This article discusses these data with reference to the literature on health care benefits and the current debate about implications of health care reform for employer provided health care benefits.

GENERAL POLICIES

Virtually all responding municipalities (98.8%) offer some type of health care to some or all of their employees (not shown). All cities 25,000 and above in population report providing these benefits. Not surprisingly, lack of health care benefits is reported by only the smaller cities. Even then, 93.6% of the cities under 2,500 in population report health care benefits for their employees. There are no significant variations by geographic division or metro status.

Types of Plans

As Table 1/2 shows, there is variation in the types of plans available to employees. Approximately half the cities reporting offer an indemnity plan for employees, although there is variation by size of city and geographic location. For example, 88.9% of cities with populations from 500,000 to 1,000,000 report that they offer an indemnity plan, while only 44.3% of those under 2,500 report doing so. There is a gradual increase in the prevalence of indemnity plans among cities beginning with those in the population group of 10,000 to 24,999, with 49.7% reporting indemnity plans and continu-

ing to 66.7% of cities with populations over 1,000,000. As the numbers in Table 1/2 indicate, some municipalities offer employees more

Table 1/1 SURVEY RESPONSE

Classification	No. surveyed (A)	No. reporting	% of (A)
Total	7,135	3,301	46.3
Population group			
Over 1,000,000	8	3	37.5
500,000–1,000,000 ..	16	9	56.3
250,000–499,999	40	24	60.0
100,000–249,999	131	68	51.9
50,000–99,999	334	173	51.8
25,000–49,999	674	346	51.3
10,000–24,999	1,590	787	49.5
5,000–9,999	1,794	767	42.8
2,500–4,999	1,989	859	43.2
Under 2,500	559	265	47.4
Geographic division[1]			
New England	793	298	37.6
Mid-Atlantic	1,180	391	33.1
East North Central ...	1,349	667	49.4
West North Central ..	719	433	60.2
South Atlantic	868	448	51.6
East South Central ..	470	186	39.6
West South Central ..	746	325	43.6
Mountain	367	204	55.6
Pacific Coast	643	349	54.3
Metro status[2]			
Central	509	261	51.3
Suburban	3,825	1,738	45.4
Independent	2,801	1,302	46.5

[1]Geographic divisions: *New England*—the states of Connecticut, Maine, Massachusetts, New Hampshire, Rhode Island, and Vermont; *Mid-Atlantic*—the states of New Jersey, New York, and Pennsylvania; *East North Central*—the states of Illinois, Indiana, Michigan, Ohio, and Wisconsin; *West North Central*—the states of Iowa, Kansas, Minnesota, Missouri, Nebraska, North Dakota, and South Dakota; *South Atlantic*—the states of Delaware, Florida, Georgia, Maryland, North Carolina, South Carolina, Virginia, West Virginia, and the District of Columbia; *East South Central*—the states of Alabama, Kentucky, Mississippi, and Tennessee; *West South Central*—the states of Arkansas, Louisiana, Oklahoma, and Texas; *Mountain*—the states of Arizona, Colorado, Idaho, Montana, Nevada, New Mexico, Utah, and Wyoming; *Pacific Coast*—the states of Alaska, California, Hawaii, Oregon, and Washington.

[2]Metro status: *Central*—core city of an MSA; *Suburban*—incorporated city located within an MSA; *Independent*—city located outside of an MSA.

than one plan. Geographic division seems to have little effect on the offering of indemnity plans, although cities in the New England states are a little more likely to offer them (70.5%), with a gradual decrease to 46.0% of the Pacific Coast cities and then a drop to 32.8% of the East South Central cities. Metro status appears to have even less effect than geography.

HMO plans are offered by 36.9% of the cities reporting. The prevalence of HMOs is comparatively high in the larger cities, with 100% of those with populations over 1,000,000 offering this option; HMO coverage tapers off gradually as population size decreases, to the point where only 20.3% of cities under 2,500 in population report offering it. Some variation exists in use of HMOs across geographic divisions, with the Pacific Coast cities reporting them most often (60.3%) followed by Mid-Atlantic cities, 46.0% of which offer an HMO option to employees. The lowest incidence of HMOs is found in the East South Central cities (19.5%), followed closely by the West South Central (21.3%). Metro status does appear to have an effect on the availability of HMOs, with only 15.0% of independent cities offering them, while 51.2% of central cities and 50.7% of suburban cities provide HMO options. Independent cities, by definition, are in nonmetropolitan areas and thus are unlikely to have the concentration of medical professionals that makes an HMO possible.

PPO plans are available in 38.7% of the cities, with the highest percentage (66.2%) of cities offering this plan in the population group from 100,000 to 249,999. The 28.0% of those under 2,500 offering PPOs is not much smaller than the 33.3% of cities over 1,000,000 and cities in the 250,000 to 499,999 population ranges pro-

viding the same option. The Pacific Coast cities lead in offering PPOs at 55.5%, followed by East South Central cities (44.8%), East North Central (44.2%), West South Central (42.3%), South Atlantic (42.2%), and the Mountain states (42.1%). New England cities are least likely to offer the PPO option (18.9%), while the Mid-Atlantic (28.2%) and West North Central (28.9%) are slightly more likely to do so. In offering the PPO option, central and suburban cities are relatively close at 45.7% and 44.7% respectively, while only 29.1% of independent cities offer them.

It is clear from these data that there is a great deal of variety among cities in their offering of health care benefits. Most cities offer more than one plan so that employees may select the one that best meets their needs. Probably cities are experimenting with various options in an effort to contain health care benefit costs.

Coverage for Part-Time and Retired Employees

While health care benefits are generous for full-time employees, there are limits to what is extended to part-time and retired employees. Only 24.4% of the cities surveyed extend the benefit to part-time employees, with the availability of the benefit generally increasing with the size of the city (not shown). Almost 67% of the cities with populations from 500,000 to 1,000,000 provide such coverage, while under 20% of the cities with populations under 5,000 do so. New England (45.9%) and Pacific Coast (42.8%) cities are more likely than other geographic divisions to offer health care benefits to part-time employees. East South Central cities (11.0%) are least likely to do so. Central cities (43.8%)

provide health care benefits to part-time employees more frequently than suburban (24.0%) and independent cities (20.9%).

Retirees enjoy health care benefits from 59.8% of the cities, with the larger population cities being more likely to offer the benefit. Significantly, 84.7% of the cities offer the same level of benefits to retirees that they offer to current employees; however, 83.6% of reporting municipalities do not provide coverage for dependents of retirees. The 617 cities that provided figures on the amount they spend on retiree benefits each year report an average annual expenditure of $325,698, although the actual figure varies greatly by size of the jurisdiction. Retired employees pay an average of 90% of the premium themselves. Costs of health care benefits to retirees in the private sector have caused some employers, to reduce or eliminate such benefits. So far, the public sector does not reflect this trend.

ADMINISTRATION OF THE HEALTH CARE PROGRAM

Clearly, cities believe that the costs of health care benefits will increase and will be a significant issue to deal with in the immediate future. The majority (78.4%) reported that they expect their jurisdictions' health care costs to increase over the next three years (not shown). Only 2.6% expect decreases in such costs, and the remaining 19% expect costs to remain about the same. Cities did not vary much by population, geographic division, or metro status in their expectations regarding costs. With health care costs rising nationally from about $250 billion to $600 billion in the ten years from 1980 to 1990,[2] it is no surprise that city officials expect such increases.

Cafeteria benefit plans, in which the employee may pick and choose among benefits, have become popular in the private sector in recent years as the needs of the work population change. Individuals have different needs and needs vary as responsibilities and life-styles change. Only 20.9% of those responding indicate that they offer them. One of the three (33.3%) cities over 1,000,000 offers a cafeteria benefits plan, which is the highest percentage in any of the population groups, and the lowest percentage (11.7%) of cities offering cafeteria plans are under 2,500 in population. By geographic division, the proportions of cities range from a low of 10.0% (Mid-Atlantic) to a high of 33.3% (South Atlantic) offering such options for employees. There is little variation by metro status. The reason for so few cities offering cafeteria plans may relate to the perception that administering them creates additional work. Among those cities which offer cafeteria benefit plans, 47.9% reported greater administrative difficulty than they experienced without the plans (not shown).

Slightly over one-third of the cities (35.0%) report that they offer employees a pretax payroll deduction for coverage of out-of-pocket medical expenses (not shown). Smaller cities tend to be

Table 1/2   TYPE OF HEALTH PLAN OFFERED

Classification	No. reporting (A)	HMO		PPO		Indemnity/ commercial plan		Other	
		No.	% of (A)	No.	% of (A)	No.	% of (A)	No.	% of (A)
Total	3,220	1,188	36.9	1,246	38.7	1,583	49.2	475	14.8
Population group									
Over 1,000,000	3	3	100.0	1	33.3	2	66.7	1	33.3
500,000–1,000,000	9	8	88.9	5	55.6	8	88.9	2	22.2
250,000–499,999	24	23	95.8	8	33.3	15	62.5	3	12.5
100,000–249,999	68	51	75.0	45	66.2	38	55.9	6	8.8
50,000–99,999	173	109	63.0	95	54.9	100	57.8	15	8.7
25,000–49,999	345	188	54.5	164	47.5	198	57.4	30	8.7
10,000–24,999	773	326	42.2	308	39.8	384	49.7	112	14.5
5,000–9,999	754	236	31.3	274	36.3	352	46.7	120	15.9
2,500–4,999	825	194	23.5	277	33.6	377	45.7	136	16.5
Under 2,500	246	50	20.3	69	28.0	109	44.3	50	20.3
Geographic division									
New England	285	112	39.3	54	18.9	201	70.5	42	14.7
Mid-Atlantic	383	176	46.0	108	28.2	220	57.4	83	21.7
East North Central	656	245	37.3	290	44.2	309	47.1	97	14.8
West North Central	426	133	31.2	123	28.9	197	46.2	56	13.1
South Atlantic	436	137	31.4	184	42.2	195	44.7	63	14.4
East South Central	174	34	19.5	78	44.8	57	32.8	30	17.2
West South Central	310	66	21.3	131	42.3	145	46.8	52	16.8
Mountain	202	75	37.1	85	42.1	99	49.0	16	7.9
Pacific Coast	348	210	60.3	193	55.5	160	46.0	36	10.3
Metro status									
Central	258	132	51.2	118	45.7	154	59.7	34	13.2
Suburban	1,711	868	50.7	764	44.7	775	45.3	219	12.8
Independent	1,251	188	15.0	364	29.1	654	52.3	222	17.7

the least likely to offer this benefit, with 18.3% of those under 2,500 and 20.5% of those from 2,500 to 4,999 doing so, in contrast to 75.0% of those in the 100,000 to 249,999 population range. The percentages among the geographic divisions do not vary much, except that only 8.2% of the Mid-Atlantic cities offer this option. The others range from a low of 24.9% in the East South Central division to a high of 52.0% in the Mountain division. Sixty-three percent of the central cities offer pretax payroll deductions for out-of-pocket medical expenses, while only 33.4% of the suburban and 31.4% of the independent cities do so.

HEALTH MAINTENANCE ORGANIZATIONS

Health Maintenance Organizations (HMOs) have emerged as one way of attempting to control costs of health care. Employers contract with HMOs for health care services for their employees at a fixed cost for the term of the contract. Usually employees pay some small fee for each service and the HMO guarantees services to all who participate.

Use of Consortia
In securing HMO services, most cities responding (76.1%) contract individually; approximately one-third participate in a consortium of two or more public entities that contract as a whole for the services (Table 1/3). A small number of cities contract both as an individual entity and as part of a consortium, most likely because they offer more than one HMO alternative to employees. The smaller cities are slightly more

likely than larger cities to contract as part of a consortium as their sole way of offering HMOs or to combine that method with contracting as an individual entity. Consortia are more likely to give smaller entities a bargaining power that they would not otherwise have.

Geographic division does not seem to affect the way cities contract for HMO services, except that Pacific Coast cities appear more likely to participate in consortia (54.6%), while Mountain cities fall way behind, with only 12.2% doing so. The number of Mountain cities reporting is very small, however, thus the value of the statistic is limited. The dispersion of the population in the Mountain states probably makes it more difficult to establish consortia. By metro status, central cities are least likely to participate in a consortium (18.6%), while 34.9% of suburbs and 45.6% of independent cities do so. This variation probably is related to size; central cities generally are larger in population, followed by suburbs and then independent cities. Larger cities have sufficient employee participants for bargaining purposes and thus have less need for a consortium.

Premium Payment
Employees pay part of the premium for HMO coverage in a little more than half the cities reporting (53.3%); the percentage in which employees contribute to the cost of the premium gradually increases with city size (not shown). New England cities require employees to contribute to the premium more often than cities in other geographic divisions (84.8%). Proportionately, the Mid-Atlantic cities least often require employee contributions toward the premium (25.1%), followed by the West South Central at

37.3% and East North Central at 44.9%. There is little variation by metro status, as it ranges from 50.7% of suburban cities requiring employee contribution to premiums to 58.2% for independent cities and 64.3% for central cities.

In virtually all cities, the portion of premium paid by employees for HMO services is independent of salary and constitutes an average of 24.4% of the total premium. There is not much variation in the average portion of the premium paid based on population, geographic division, or metro status.

Copayment, Second Opinions, and Approved Hospital Admissions
Copayment by employees for HMO services (such as a fixed minimum fee for office visits) is required by 83.9% of the cities reporting (Figure 1/1). There are no discernible trends in the requirement of copayment based on population, geographic division, or metro status (not shown).

A majority of cities (59.7%) report that their HMO plans do not require second opinions before surgery (Figure 1/1), with cities under 2,500 in population being most likely to require a second opinion (63.4%) and the largest cities least likely to do so (not shown). Among the geographic divisions, there is little variation in the requirement of a second opinion, except among jurisdictions in the West North Central division, where only 18.6% report the need for a second surgical opinion.

Seventy-seven percent of those reporting have a prehospitalization certification requirement (Figure 1/1). This figure does not vary greatly by population group except among the cities with populations of 500,000 and over, which

Table 1/3   USE OF CONSORTIA TO PURCHASE HEALTH PLANS

Classification	HMO			PPO			Indemnity		
	No. reporting (A)	Individual contract (% of A)	Consortium (% of A)	No. reporting (B)	Individual contract (% of B)	Consortium (% of B)	No. reporting (C)	Individual contract (% of C)	Consortium (% of C)
Total	1,136	76.1	34.7	1,166	61.3	38.7	1,489	66.9	33.1
Population group									
Over 1,000,000	3	100.0	0.0	1	100.0	0.0	2	100.0	0.0
500,000–1,000,000	7	85.7	42.9	4	100.0	0.0	7	85.7	14.3
250,000–499,999	23	95.7	13.0	8	87.5	12.5	13	92.3	7.7
100,000–249,999	50	84.0	30.0	44	79.5	20.5	31	74.2	25.8
50,000–99,999	107	83.2	26.2	90	76.7	23.3	92	83.7	16.3
25,000–49,999	187	75.9	32.1	153	63.4	36.6	189	74.6	25.4
10,000–24,999	317	78.9	30.3	293	62.1	37.9	359	71.6	28.4
5,000–9,999	224	68.3	42.4	256	59.0	41.0	338	60.1	39.9
2,500–4,999	173	74.6	41.0	251	54.2	45.8	357	63.6	36.4
Under 2,500	45	62.2	51.1	66	50.0	50.0	101	47.5	52.5
Geographic division									
New England	111	77.5	28.8	50	40.0	60.0	195	48.7	51.3
Mid-Atlantic	169	74.6	29.6	100	57.0	43.0	213	64.8	35.2
East North Central	231	87.0	29.9	274	70.8	29.2	296	77.0	23.0
West North Central	125	72.8	39.2	112	69.6	30.4	188	81.4	18.6
South Atlantic	134	83.6	32.8	169	65.1	34.9	183	60.7	39.3
East South Central	30	63.3	43.3	77	51.9	48.1	52	84.6	15.4
West South Central	57	86.0	28.1	123	65.9	34.1	132	75.8	24.2
Mountain	74	95.9	12.2	80	68.8	31.3	84	78.6	21.4
Pacific Coast	205	53.2	54.6	181	44.2	55.8	146	41.8	58.2
Metro status									
Central	129	93.0	18.6	110	80.0	20.0	142	85.2	14.8
Suburban	836	74.8	34.9	722	61.2	38.8	728	64.4	35.6
Independent	171	69.6	45.6	334	55.4	44.6	619	65.6	34.4

show percentages well below average requiring pre-hospitalization approval (not shown). In the East South Central division, only one city does not require precertification for hospitalization, and in the South Atlantic division, all but 9.8% of cities require pre-certification.

Trends in Costs

Over the fiscal years of 1990, 1991, and 1992, HMO rates increased gradually. Table 1/4 shows the average increase in HMO rates for all cities reporting. The information on decreases in rates that was provided by a few cities is not included in these calculations. While the average increase has declined slightly from 12.7% in 1990 to 10.5% in 1992, these increases are substantial, at least partially reflecting the rising cost of health care generally. The rate increases for the largest cities have been significantly reduced, while those of the smallest cities have remained approximately level. The larger cities have greater numbers of employees and thus can bargain on that basis; they also are likely to have access to alternative HMO providers, and thus competition may drive costs down. The jurisdictions in the New England, West South Central, and Pacific Coast divisions show rate increases of under 10% in 1992. Among metro types, central cities show a 1992 increase that is three percentage points lower than the 1990 rate of increase for HMO plans.

The overall cost of health care to the cities has not decreased dramatically with use of HMOs either (Table 1/5). Of the cities reporting, 37.4% indicate no cost reduction; 17.8%, minimal reduction; and 33.4%, moderate reduction. Only 4.0% report significant reduction. There appear to be no significant trends in cost reduction by population, geographic division, or metro status.

Participation in a consortium does not necessarily lead to cost reduction either (not shown). Over half (60.8%) the cities that contract with HMOs through consortia indicate that costs have increased for health care benefits; 14.9% report that the increase has been significant. Only 15.3% report a decrease in costs while about a quarter (23.9%) report costs remaining about the same. Obviously, with the escalating costs of health care generally, it is quite possible that costs would have increased even more without the movement to HMOs and use of a consortium as a way of providing the benefit.

Three of the ten cities in the East South Central division that are in consortia indicate a significant decrease in cost, which may be attributable to a switch from another type of plan to an HMO.

The data on the benefits provided through consortia indicate that benefits have not increased overall with the increasing costs (not shown). Two-thirds (66.4%) of the cities report that the benefits have remained about the same, while 19.5% indicate that they have decreased and only 14.2% report increases in benefits with the HMO. These data are fairly consistent across cities of different population, geographic division, and metro status.

Specialty Services

HMOs provide a variety of specialized services for enrollees. Comparisons of the specialized services offered by the three types of plans will be made later in this article. Dental care is offered by 21.2% of the cities with HMOs, mental health benefits by 87.0%, fitness programs by 27.9%, eye care by 55.7%, substance abuse programs by 76.1%, prescription drugs by 92.1%, screening for such things as high blood pressure

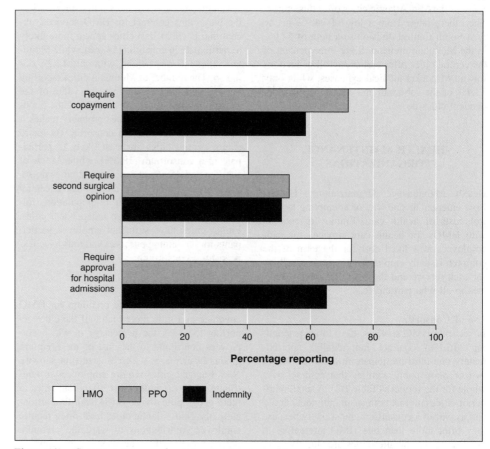

Figure 1/1   *Copayments, second opinions, and approved hospital admissions*

Table 1/4   HMO RATE INCREASES

Classification	FY 1990 Increase		FY 1991 Increase		FY 1992 Increase	
	No. reporting	Average (%)	No. reporting	Average (%)	No. reporting	Average (%)
Total	624	12.7	684	11.6	742	10.5
Population group						
Over 1,000,000	2	18.0	2	15.5	2	6.0
500,000–1,000,000	5	14.6	5	10.2	5	7.8
250,000–499,999	19	12.4	20	12.8	19	9.7
100,000–249,999	39	12.9	40	9.8	43	9.5
50,000–99,999	64	11.1	66	9.2	72	9.6
25,000–49,999	117	13.0	124	11.1	126	10.1
10,000–24,999	174	12.9	192	11.8	204	10.4
5,000–9,999	117	12.7	133	12.2	148	10.7
2,500–4,999	71	13.6	83	13.8	100	12.3
Under 2,500	16	10.0	19	11.4	23	10.2
Geographic division						
New England	73	12.8	76	12.1	86	9.2
Mid-Atlantic	87	13.5	96	12.7	108	12.2
East North Central	124	12.3	129	11.6	146	10.0
West North Central	77	14.4	87	11.5	89	11.6
South Atlantic	69	12.6	82	12.0	81	12.6
East South Central	12	10.7	14	12.3	14	11.5
West South Central	24	11.3	29	11.0	37	9.3
Mountain	42	13.0	44	11.6	48	10.4
Pacific Coast	116	11.9	127	10.4	133	8.6
Metro status						
Central	95	12.4	100	10.8	98	9.4
Suburban	451	12.7	501	11.6	546	10.4
Independent	78	13.1	83	12.6	98	12.0

Table 1/5   HMOs AND COST REDUCTION

Classification	No. reporting (A)	No reduction		2		Moderate reduction		4		Significant reduction	
		No.	% of (A)	No.	% of (A)	No.	% of (A)	No.	% of (A)	No.	% of (A)
Total	996	373	37.4	177	17.8	333	33.4	73	7.3	40	4.0
Population group											
Over 1,000,000	3	1	33.3	0	0.0	1	33.3	0	0.0	1	33.3
500,000–1,000,000	5	3	60.0	0	0.0	1	20.0	1	20.0	0	0.0
250,000–499,999	21	4	19.0	5	23.8	9	42.9	2	9.5	1	4.8
100,000–249,999	48	16	33.3	11	22.9	13	27.1	5	10.4	3	6.3
50,000–99,999	98	32	32.7	18	18.4	33	33.7	10	10.2	5	5.1
25,000–49,999	165	54	32.7	31	18.8	61	37.0	12	7.3	7	4.2
10,000–24,999	269	99	36.8	49	18.2	92	34.2	21	7.8	8	3.0
5,000–9,999	200	75	37.5	35	17.5	74	37.0	10	5.0	6	3.0
2,500–4,999	150	70	46.7	25	16.7	39	26.0	10	6.7	6	4.0
Under 2,500	37	19	51.4	3	8.1	10	27.0	2	5.4	3	8.1
Geographic division											
New England	100	26	26.0	21	21.0	43	43.0	7	7.0	3	3.0
Mid-Atlantic	152	62	40.8	17	11.2	64	42.1	5	3.3	4	2.6
East North Central	200	78	39.0	39	19.5	61	30.5	15	7.5	7	3.5
West North Central	107	46	43.0	18	16.8	34	31.8	4	3.7	5	4.7
South Atlantic	123	44	35.8	22	17.9	37	30.1	13	10.6	7	5.7
East South Central	27	12	44.4	1	3.7	12	44.4	1	3.7	1	3.7
West South Central	42	9	21.4	7	16.7	20	47.6	6	14.3	0	0.0
Mountain	66	23	34.8	15	22.7	16	24.2	9	13.6	3	4.5
Pacific Coast	179	73	40.8	37	20.7	46	25.7	13	7.3	10	5.6
Metro status											
Central	120	40	33.3	24	20.0	41	34.2	9	7.5	6	5.0
Suburban	733	272	37.1	132	18.0	248	33.8	52	7.1	29	4.0
Independent	143	61	42.7	21	14.7	44	30.8	12	8.4	5	3.5

Note: Respondents ranked the extent of cost reduction on a scale of "1" to "5", with 1 indicating *no reduction* and 5 indicating *significant reduction*.

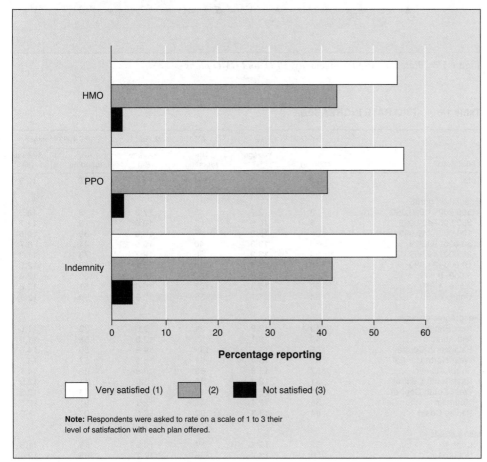

Percentage reporting

☐ Very satisfied (1)   ▨ (2)   ■ Not satisfied (3)

Note: Respondents were asked to rate on a scale of 1 to 3 their level of satisfaction with each plan offered.

Figure 1/2   *Level of satisfaction with plans*

and cholesterol by 69.7%, and women's wellness programs by 60.5%. There appears to be little major variation in extent of services by population, geographic division, or metro status.

Level of Satisfaction
Although respondents indicate overall satisfaction with the HMOs (Figure 1/2), when asked if employees have made specific complaints, of the 1,038 cities that provided information, 44.6% indicated that employees complain about choice of doctors, and 23.7% reported complaints about location of doctors. This complaint about doctors is consistent with the conventional wisdom about HMOs, that limited choice in the doctor patients see leads to a less personal relationship with the doctor and thus complaints. On location of doctors, payment and reimbursement, response to complaints, and various other matters, the vast majority of cities reported no complaints by employees enrolled in HMOs.

PREFERRED PROVIDER ORGANIZATIONS

Cities also use preferred provider organizations (PPOs) in an attempt to control costs of health care. With PPOs, employees are offered benefits through medical personnel who contract with the employer, much like the HMO, to provide services at an agreed upon rate. The employee chooses from a list of those identified as preferred providers.

Use of Consortia
As with the HMO option, most cities (61.3%) report contracting individually for PPO services rather than participating in a consortium (38.7%) (Table 1/3). As the size of cities decreases, there is an increase in the likelihood of participation in a consortium. Although 50% of the cities under 2,500 participate in consortia for PPOs, none of the cities with populations 500,000 and above do so. Ability to negotiate individual contracts with providers is probably the most significant factor in this disparity, as small cities do not have the numbers of employees to leverage good agreements on their own.

Premium Payment
Employees are slightly less likely to pay part of the premium for PPOs (43.7%) than for HMOs (53.3%). As with the HMOs, the employee contribution is not based on salary. Patterns are also similar between the two types of plans in the proportion of the premium paid by the employee. Employees pay an average of 26.5% of the premium for PPO plans versus 24.5% for HMOs (not shown). Unlike the HMO option, where little variation by population occurs, contribution to the PPO premium increases appreciably as size of city decreases. Thus, in cities under 2,500 population, employees have to pay an average of 34.6% of the premium, and in

cities with populations from 500,000 to 1,000,000, the percentage is 12.0%.

Variations among geographic divisions are slight, and independent cities tend to require higher contributions from employees (35.8% of premium) than suburban (23.4%) or central (23.2%) cities.

Copayment, Second Opinions, and Approved Hospital Admissions

PPO plans of most cities (72.1%) require a co-payment for services (Figure 1/1). The figure is relatively consistent across the variables noted in this study. Under PPOs, employees are more often required to get second opinions before surgery (53.8%) than with HMOs (40.3%). The increased incidence of the requirement appears in all categories of cities. Certification before entering the hospital for nonemergency matters is required in 80.6% of the cities using PPOs, and again, there is little variation across categories of cities. The figure is similar to that of cities with HMO plans (77.0%).

Trends in Costs

Over the 1990, 1991, and 1992 fiscal years, average rate increases for PPOs in all cities have been slightly higher than the HMO increases (Figure 1/3). In FY 1990, the average rate increase for PPOs was 14.2%, with the average for each population group ranging from 10.6% to 15.9% (Table 1/6). From 1991 to 1992, the average rate of increase dropped slightly from 13.6% to 12.5%. This downward trend did not hold for those cities reporting with populations from 500,000 to 1,000,000, because their average rates steadily increased. Municipalities in a few other population groups experienced slight increases. The most significant reduction in average increase was reported by cities with populations from 50,000 to 99,999—a difference of four percentage points from 1990 to 1992.

Although cities in the Pacific Coast division show a drop of 4.4 percentage points in the percentage of increase from 1990 to 1992, the other divisions show that generally municipalities had either a slight increase or a slight decrease.

Health care costs appear to be reduced somewhat by the use of PPOs. Overall 53.5% of the cities reported that health care costs have been reduced with the use of PPOs (Table 1/7). Of those reporting cost reductions, 4.9% indicate that costs have been reduced significantly. These percentages are higher than for HMOs, where 44.7% reported reductions with 4.0% indicating significant cost reductions. Except for cities in the two largest population categories, health care cost reduction appears to increase with use of PPOs as population increases. Except for the three cities with populations over 1 million, the smaller cities realize the least in savings from PPOs. Cities in the New England division show the highest percentage (65.0%) reporting some cost reduction, compared with the low of 35.3% of cities in the Mid-Atlantic division. Central cities seem to fare the best in realizing cost advantages from PPOs.

When answering a question about whether purchasing through consortia had affected the

cost of the PPO, 53.8% of the cities report cost increases, with 10.0% indicating those increases are significant. These figures compare to 60.8% and 14.9% respectively for HMOs. Costs remained about the same in 31.5% of the cities with PPOs reporting, as opposed to 23.9% on HMOs. Significant variations do not appear to be related to the classifications of cities identified for the survey. Under the PPO consortia plan, benefits either remain about the same (61.3%) or decrease slightly (14.0%). These results are similar to those describing HMO benefit levels.

Specialty Services

Many specialty services are offered through the PPO plans, with a high preponderance of cities offering mental health care, prescription drugs, and substance abuse programs (Figure 1/4). About half offer screening services and women's wellness programs. A little less than a third offer dental care and eye care services. Only 8.7%

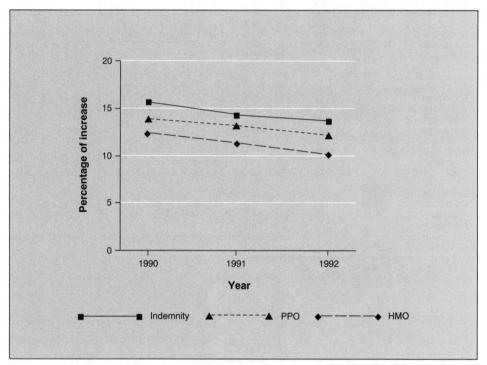

Figure 1/3 *Rate increase for indemnity, PPO, and HMO plans*

Table 1/6 PPO RATE INCREASES

Classification	FY 1990 Increase		FY 1991 Increase		FY 1992 Increase	
	No. reporting	Average (%)	No. reporting	Average (%)	No. reporting	Average (%)
Total	472	14.2	554	13.6	628	12.5
Population group						
500,000–1,000,000	3	12.7	3	17.3	3	18.3
250,000–499,999	5	10.6	5	10.6	3	11.7
100,000–249,999	26	15.9	27	13.3	30	10.6
50,000–99,999	39	13.3	40	10.5	41	8.7
25,000–49,999	54	13.9	66	12.7	73	11.9
10,000–24,999	118	13.4	140	13.1	153	12.6
5,000–9,999	87	15.3	110	14.0	135	12.8
2,500–4,999	106	15.3	127	15.6	151	13.8
Under 2,500	34	11.7	36	12.5	39	12.7
Geographic division						
New England	19	12.8	21	9.6	23	11.0
Mid-Atlantic	49	13.1	52	12.8	58	11.9
East North Central	109	15.1	135	14.8	150	14.6
West North Central	51	15.4	61	15.5	67	14.3
South Atlantic	57	16.8	68	13.8	82	14.1
East South Central	31	12.2	36	13.9	41	12.9
West South Central	37	13.5	43	12.7	49	10.3
Mountain	35	12.4	46	12.3	51	12.5
Pacific Coast	84	13.3	92	12.6	107	8.9
Metro status						
Central	52	13.8	57	12.5	55	11.5
Suburban	280	13.7	336	12.7	385	12.0
Independent	140	15.4	161	15.9	188	13.9

offer fitness programs. PPOs appear to offer fewer preventive medicine programs than HMOs; thus, they are much less likely to provide for fitness, eye care, screening, and women's wellness programs. HMOs have a vested interest in keeping people healthy so that they do not use the more expensive health care services, which would decrease the profit margin. PPOs do not have the same incentives because the payments are based on medical services and procedures rather than on a fixed cost for providing services overall.

Level of Satisfaction

According to the reports of the cities, employees seem to have few complaints with the PPO programs (Figure 1/5). Three-quarters and more of the cities report no complaints about doctors, location of services, payment and reimbursement, or any other aspects of the PPOs. This information is consistent with the overall level of satisfaction shown in Figure 1/2.

INDEMNITY PLANS

Indemnity plans for health care represent the traditional approach to employee health care insurance. Plans are offered through commercial carriers/insurance companies. Typically, benefits are provided with an annual and lifetime limit on the dollar amount. In recent years, it has been common to establish a standard dollar amount for any given medical service or procedure, sometimes referred to as a prospective payment system or reasonable and customary charges. Any cost above this predetermined amount will be borne by the patient, although some plans attempt to limit the fees medical professionals can actually charge. About half (1,583) of the cities responding to the survey offer the indemnity plan; its availability increases with city size.

Use of Consortia

One third (33.1%) of cities with indemnity plans participate in a consortium. This level of participation roughly approximates the percentages of cities that are in HMO and PPO consortia. Not surprisingly, smaller cities tend to join indemnity consortia more than large cities do. Although the majority of cities contract individually for indemnity programs, fewer than half (47.5%) of the cities under 2,500 in population do so (Table 1/3). Small cities are likely to band together to add to their numbers and bring rates down as much as possible. Cities in the New England and the Pacific Coast divisions show the highest percentage participating in consortia. Central cities (14.8%) are less likely to participate in consortia than suburban (35.6%) or independent (34.4%) cities. These patterns are similar to those for HMOs and PPOs.

Premium Payment

Employees pay a portion of the premium for indemnity plans in less than half the cities (43.9%) which is about the same as for PPOs (43.7%) (not shown). Cities appear to be providing incentives for employees to join HMOs because slightly over half (53.3%) the cities do not require employees to pay part of the premium for HMOs. As with the other plans, employees in larger cities are more likely to have to pay part of the premium than those in smaller cities. There are no discernible patterns by geographic division, but central cities report a higher incidence of employee contribution to

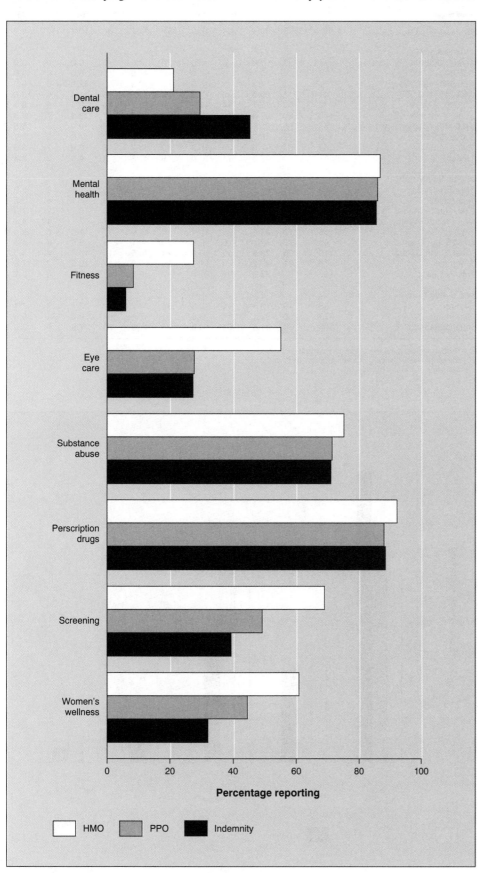

Figure 1/4   *Specialty services offered by the plans*

the premium (64.9%) than suburban (42.2%) and independent cities (41.0%). As with the other options, salary is not the determining factor in the level of premium paid by the employee. The portion of the indemnity plan premium (24.2%) paid by employees is about the same as it is for HMO and PPO plans.

Copayment, Second Opinions, and Approved Hospital Admissions

With indemnity plans, employees are less likely to have to make copayments than with the other options (Figure 1/1). Only 58.3% of the cities report that copayments are required under the indemnity plans, as opposed to 83.9% for HMO and 72.1% for PPO alternatives. Generally, the smaller the city, the more likely employees are to make copayments under indemnity plans (not shown). Independent (56.5%) and suburban (57.7%) cities are slightly less likely to require copayments than central cities (69.1%).

Indemnity plans are comparable to PPOs in requiring second opinions before surgery (51.2% and 53.8%, respectively), whereas HMOs require it in 40.3% of the cities. Precertification for admission to a hospital is required more often. Survey results show that 65.7% of cities have indemnity plans that include approval before hospitalization.

Trends in Costs

Rates for indemnity plans have risen much faster than those for either PPOs or HMOs, thus justifying those other options as cost containment strategies, at least as compared to indemnity plans (Figure 1/3). Although the differences in rate increases are narrowing, clearly indemnity plans are more costly both in initial rates and in the level of increase in rates. Larger cities generally sustain moderately higher increases in rates for indemnity plans than smaller cities (Table 1/8).

Over half (54.1%) the cities report that indemnity plans have not helped reduce health care costs (Figure 1/5). Moderate to significant cuts in costs are reported by 28.9% of the cities, but only 2.7% report significant cost reductions. Fifty percent of the cities in the population range of 500,000 to 1,000,000 report cost reductions (Table 1/9), probably reflecting their ability to negotiate with insurers because of the size of their labor force and because of competition from HMOs and, to a lesser extent, PPOs. Otherwise, there appears to be little variation in responses across the categories of cities.

The percentage of increase in cost appears higher for cities that purchase indemnity plans through consortia than for those that purchase either HMO or PPO plans through consortia (not shown). Overall, 69.2% of the consortia cities report that indemnity costs increased compared with 60.8% in HMO consortia and 53.8% in PPO consortia. The percentage reporting significant cost increases in indemnity plans is most dramatic at 22.5%. Comparable figures are 14.9% for HMOs and 10.0% for PPOs. Slightly higher percentages of smaller cities tend to report increases than do larger cities. There seems to be no clear geographic pattern except in the

Table 1/7   PPOs AND COST REDUCTION

Classification	No. reporting (A)	No reduction		2		Moderate reduction		4		Significant reduction	
		No.	% of (A)	No.	% of (A)	No.	% of (A)	No.	% of (A)	No.	% of (A)
Total	1,024	313	30.6	164	16.0	391	38.2	106	10.4	50	4.9
Population group											
Over 1,000,000	1	1	100	0	0.0	0	0.0	0	0.0	0	0.0
500,000–1,000,000	4	0	0.0	2	50.0	1	25.0	1	25.0	0	0.0
250,000–499,999	7	1	14.3	0	0.0	3	42.9	3	42.9	0	0.0
100,000–249,999	44	13	29.5	5	11.4	15	34.1	5	11.4	6	13.6
50,000–99,999	72	12	16.7	14	19.4	26	36.1	14	19.4	6	8.3
25,000–49,999	128	35	27.3	20	15.6	49	38.3	17	13.3	7	5.5
10,000–24,999	255	65	25.5	43	16.9	100	39.2	33	12.9	14	5.5
5,000–9,999	219	73	33.3	32	14.6	89	40.6	17	7.8	8	3.7
2,500–4,999	233	87	37.3	37	15.9	89	38.2	13	5.6	7	3.0
Under 2,500	61	26	42.6	11	18.0	19	31.1	3	4.9	2	3.3
Geographic division											
New England	40	8	20.0	6	15.0	19	47.5	5	12.5	2	5.0
Mid-Atlantic	85	43	50.6	12	14.1	21	24.7	6	7.1	3	3.5
East North Central	234	67	28.6	34	14.5	91	38.9	25	10.7	17	7.3
West North Central	98	24	24.5	20	20.4	43	43.9	7	7.1	4	4.1
South Atlantic	155	42	27.1	25	16.1	65	41.9	17	11.0	6	3.9
East South Central	68	22	32.4	6	8.8	30	44.1	6	8.8	4	5.9
West South Central	110	26	23.6	19	17.3	44	40.0	15	13.6	6	5.5
Mountain	72	21	29.2	8	11.1	29	40.3	12	16.7	2	2.8
Pacific Coast	162	60	37.0	34	21.0	49	30.2	13	8.0	6	3.7
Metro status											
Central	98	19	19.4	16	16.3	34	34.7	22	22.4	7	7.1
Suburban	623	200	32.1	97	15.6	231	37.1	61	9.8	34	5.5
Independent	303	94	31.0	51	16.8	126	41.6	23	7.6	9	3.0

Note: Respondents ranked the extent of cost reduction on a scale of "1" to "5", with 1 indicating *no reduction* and 5 indicating *significant reduction*.

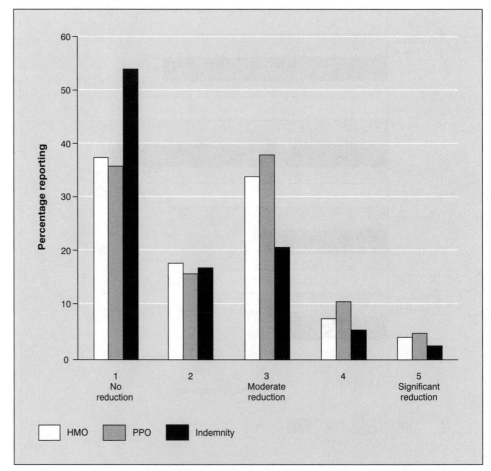

Figure 1/5   *Health plans and cost reduction*

Mountain division, where 58.9% of cities report that their costs remained the same or decreased. At the same time, benefits appear to have remained constant across cities of different population, geographic division, and metro status.

Specialty Services

As with HMOs and PPOs, cities with indemnity plans offer a variety of specialized services (Figure 1/4). Most often, the services are traditional health care programs and focus less on prevention than treatment. As with PPOs, the primary focus of indemnity plans is on payment for medical services and procedures. There is little incentive for prevention built into the contracts. Thus, mental health care, substance abuse programs, and prescription drugs are provided

for by the vast majority of cities. Nearly half the cities (45.2%) provide dental coverage in their indemnity plan; coverage drops off to 39.6% for screening, 32.2% for women's wellness, and 27.1% for eye care. Only 5.9% of the cities offer fitness programs under their indemnity plans.

Level of Satisfaction

As with other plans, cities report that employees show little dissatisfaction with services under indemnity plans. The complaints they receive deal primarily with payment and reimbursement and response to complaints (Figure 1/6). Not surprisingly, there are virtually no complaints about doctors, because patients are able to choose their own.

SUMMARY

Health care costs have become a major issue in American public policy discussions. The U.S. Congress spent much of 1993 and 1994 debating how to respond to what many characterize as a health care crisis. Election-year politics doomed health care reform in 1994, but the issue is certain to arise in the next Congress. Issues such as universal coverage, mandating employer health care benefits, and finding ways of cutting costs dominated much of the debate. All those issues are important to cities as they deal with their benefits packages and ever-increasing costs. Health care benefits are a large part of municipal expenditures, and controlling costs will provide relief for the overall costs of government.

The data reported here have relevance to the universal coverage issue. According to the information provided by the survey respondents, approximately 742,000 of the nearly 1,100,000 employees of these municipal governments are covered by employer health care benefits. That means that 67.5% of employees have health care coverage, leaving 32.5% without it. Of course, it is impossible to know how many of these employees have coverage through their spouse's employer. Nonetheless, the figure 32.5% represents a large portion of the workforce and is more than double the 15% of the population many members of Congress claimed were not covered in the population as a whole during the 1994 debates over health care reform.

Mandating provision of health care benefits by employers would add significantly to the health care costs of cities if all employees not now covered had to be included. The alternative is to find ways of cutting costs by reducing benefits or requiring a greater employee contribution to the financing of health care benefits, such as through paying a higher share of the premiums or through more copayment requirements. The private sector already is implementing some of these measures; General Motors recently began requiring nonunion employees to pay part of their premiums for health care benefits.

According to the expenditure information provided by respondents, retirees represent a major portion of the health care expenditures of cities. The cities report that, on average, local health care expenditures for municipalities that cover retirees are four times those of municipalities that do not provide coverage for retirees. These figures might cause local governments to look at making changes in retiree health care benefits, as some private sector industries are doing.

The evidence in this survey is that some cost containment strategies are working. For example, use of HMOs and PPOs seems to result in lower rates of increase in health care premiums for employers. Costs have continued to increase, but at a lower rate for HMOs and PPOs than for indemnity plans. HMOs in particular seem to have a significant effect on keeping rate increases down. Municipalities options to employees who can choose among plans, knowing

Table 1/8   INDEMNITY PLAN RATE INCREASES

Classification	FY 1990 Increase		FY 1991 Increase		FY 1992 Increase	
	No. reporting	Average (%)	No. reporting	Average (%)	No. reporting	Average (%)
Total	916	16.0	979	14.7	996	14.0
Population group						
Over 1,000,000	1	23.0	1	29.0	1	7.0
500,000–1,000,000	6	18.8	6	22.8	6	21.2
250,000–499,999	12	11.9	13	14.2	12	13.6
100,000–249,999	26	14.1	24	13.3	25	9.6
50,000–99,999	65	16.1	67	14.9	68	14.1
25,000–49,999	128	16.6	124	15.2	127	14.9
10,000–24,999	202	17.7	224	14.9	229	14.4
5,000–9,999	210	16.4	234	15.5	228	13.7
2,500–4,999	200	14.6	216	13.7	229	13.9
Under 2,500	66	14.0	70	13.1	71	13.0
Geographic division						
New England	131	15.7	137	14.0	141	12.2
Mid-Atlantic	134	17.0	142	14.9	145	14.0
East North Central	184	15.8	203	14.6	215	14.9
West North Central	118	15.8	126	15.3	122	14.8
South Atlantic	102	18.0	106	16.2	117	15.4
East South Central	27	15.6	31	17.4	25	16.7
West South Central	72	16.9	72	14.5	68	12.6
Mountain	53	14.5	57	14.2	57	15.8
Pacific Coast	95	13.8	105	13.0	106	11.2
Metro status						
Central	106	15.8	106	16.3	104	15.3
Suburban	424	16.4	468	14.5	479	13.6
Independent	386	15.7	405	14.5	413	14.1

Table 1/9   INDEMNITY PLANS AND COST REDUCTION

Classification	No. reporting (A)	No reduction		2		Moderate reduction		4		Significant reduction	
		No.	% of (A)	No.	% of (A)	No.	% of (A)	No.	% of (A)	No.	% of (A)
Total	1,310	709	54.1	223	17.0	270	20.6	73	5.6	35	2.7
Population group											
Over 1,000,000	2	2	100	0	0.0	0	0.0	0	0.0	0	0.0
500,000–1,000,000	6	3	50.0	0	0.0	2	33.3	0	0.0	1	16.7
250,000–499,999	14	6	42.9	3	21.4	3	21.4	1	7.1	1	7.1
100,000–249,999	30	15	50.0	6	20.0	3	10.0	4	13.3	2	6.7
50,000–99,999	88	39	44.3	20	22.7	22	25.0	4	4.5	3	3.4
25,000–49,999	168	81	48.2	31	18.5	47	28.0	6	3.6	3	1.8
10,000–24,999	315	167	53.0	54	17.1	65	20.6	20	6.3	9	2.9
5,000–9,999	298	154	51.7	54	18.1	59	19.8	21	7.0	10	3.4
2,500–4,999	300	186	62.0	40	13.3	52	17.3	16	5.3	6	2.0
Under 2,500	89	56	62.9	15	16.9	17	19.1	1	1.1	0	0.0

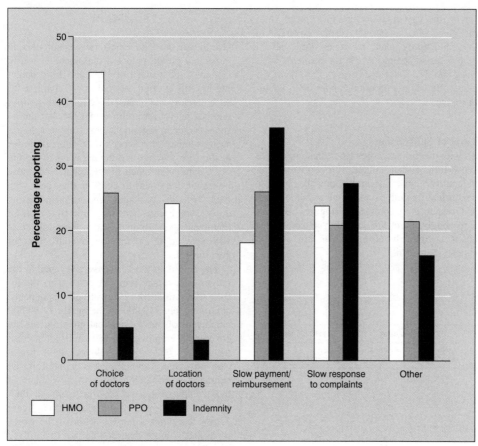

Figure 1/6   *Employee dissatisfaction by plan type*

the costs and benefits of each. Cafeteria plans allowing such choices are becoming increasingly popular.

Another strategy for lowering or containing costs is joining a consortium. Consortia were used in each type of health care benefit plan reported on by the cities in this survey. While the evidence presented here does not demonstrate that consortia help reduce or contain costs, the data do not permit any definitive conclusions on the matter. It is impossible to know what would have happened to costs without consortia, especially in the smaller cities.

The 1994 survey indicates that health care benefits are a major cost item for local governments and that cities are searching for ways to address such costs. Small jurisdictions, in particular, need to find innovative ways of providing these benefits, as they often are at a disadvantage in dealing with providers. Any health care reform will certainly affect local government health care benefits.

[1] The term *recognition* refers to a formal process whereby ICMA ascertains that a local government provides for an appointed professional manager.

[2] Fred Luthans and Elaine David, ''The Healthcare Cost Crisis: Causes and Containment,'' *Personnel* 67 (February), p. 24.

2

Council Evaluation of the City Manager's Performance

Craig M. Wheeland
Villanova University

Findings

Eighty-five percent of city councils evaluate their managers; 62% are required to do so.

Training in conducting evaluations is provided to only 21% of councils according to managers responding to the survey.

Survey results suggest that although city managers know of the council's expectations of their performance, managers must take the initiative to find out about these expectations because they are not directly communicated.

The council-manager plan creates a council-centered form of government. Under the council-manager form of government citizens elect a council that typically has from five to nine members who exercise both legislative and executive powers. The council delegates its executive power to a professional city manager who is appointed by the council a serve as head of a unified administrative structure. The city manager serves at the pleasure of the council and is supervised by the council.[1] Although many structural features—the number of council-members, the selection of the mayor, and the method of electing councilmembers—of the council-manager plan have changed since it was originally proposed in the early 1900s, the council's power to hire and fire the manager remains a central tenet. Much of the literature concludes that the supervisory role helps preserve the democratic character of the council-manager form even when the city manager emerges as the dominant participant in the governing process.[2]

Evaluating the city manager's performance is a key part of the supervisory role. It contributes to the ongoing effort made by the council to keep the city manager informed of its expectations regarding his or her performance. Evaluation is also that part of the supervisory responsibility that most clearly reveals that the city manager is the employee of the council. The evaluation responsibility derives from the council's authority to hire and terminate the manager. Previous research suggests that the manager evaluation has not been performed as well as it could be.[3] This article describes the results of a national survey on the council's performance in evaluating the manager. The evaluation methods used by city councils in the United States are described, the quality of the council's performance is assessed, and ways to improve the council's effort are identified.

METHODOLOGY

In May 1993, the author mailed a four-page questionnaire to city managers working in ICMA-recognized council-manager municipalities in the United States with populations of 20,000 and above. The questionnaire is a revision of one the author used in 1992 to study the council's evaluation of the manager's performance in council-manager municipalities in Pennsylvania.[4]

Of the 829 city managers surveyed, 495 returned the questionnaire, for a response rate of 60%. Thirteen questionnaires were not usable for any of these reasons: (1) the city no longer had the council-manager form of government, (2) an interim manager was employed, or (3) the city manager had served less than three months. Eliminating these 13 cases reduced the total number of cases analyzed in this article to 482, for an adjusted response rate of 59%.

PROFILE OF CITIES

Data on three characteristics of the cities in this study are presented in Table 2/1. The data on population size indicate no population size is over-represented among cities returning the questionnaire. The mean population size for responding cities is 56,522 and the median population size is 37,000 (not shown).

City managers estimated the level of conflict among council members in their cities compared with cities of similar population size. The mean level of conflict is 3.39 on a seven point scale from "1" (*very low*) to "7" (*very high*). The standard deviation is 1.64, which shows wide variation in responses across cities. The impact that level of conflict has on the evaluation activity is explored later in this article.

Turnover among managers is another possible measure of a turbulent political context. Cities employing several managers within the five-year period preceding the completion of this survey may be cities in which the evaluation process has unique characteristics. The data in Table 2/1 indicate a pattern of stability for a majority of cities. Only 9.6% of the cities had three or more managers from 1988 to 1993.

Table 2/1   PROFILE OF RESPONDENTS' CITIES

Characteristics	No. of cities surveyed		No. of cities responding	
	n=829	(% of n)	n=482	(% of n)
Population size				
500,000 and above	7	0.8	2	0.4
250,000–499,999	16	1.9	9	1.9
100,000–249,999	79	9.5	37	7.7
50,000–99,999	194	23.4	114	23.7
20,000–49,999	533	64.3	320	66.4
Estimated level of council conflict (n=481)				
Level 1 (very low)	...		63	13.1
Level 2	...		107	22.2
Level 3	...		91	18.9
Level 4 (moderate)	...		94	19.5
Level 5	...		70	14.6
Level 6	...		37	7.7
Level 7 (very high)	...		19	4.0
Number of managers in past five years (n=479)				
One (no turnover)	...		245	51.1
Two	...		188	39.2
Three	...		34	7.1
Four	...		9	1.9
Five	...		3	0.6

Note: In this and the following tables missing cases are excluded from all calculations. A case is missing usually because the manager did not answer the question. Leaders (...) indicate data not applicable. The number in parentheses (n =   ) is the number of respondents that answered the question.

PROFILE OF CITY MANAGERS

Over three-fourths of the managers report having a graduate degree, which is usually an MPA (Table 2/2). The mean length of service is 6.4 years and the median length of service is 5.0 years, so the majority of city managers responding have served their cities for six years or less. Almost two-thirds of those reporting were employed as city managers before they took their current job. The large majority changed jobs for professional advancement. Fewer than 10% of the managers reported being fired or pressured to resign, and only 5% "fled council conflict." Ninety-five percent of the city managers report membership in ICMA, and almost half have served on an ICMA task force or committee. Thirty-two percent of the city managers have held office in ICMA or in a state association.

The city manager profile suggested by the survey data matches the profiles described in other research on city managers—another indicator of the representativeness of the respondents.[5]

FEATURES OF EVALUATION METHODS

Several ICMA publications, including handbooks and articles, offer advice to public officials on the evaluation method. In keeping with its tradition of not approaching issues that affect the council-manager relationship with a "there is one best way to solve it" mentality, ICMA has recommended that councils and their managers jointly design the evaluation method. A method based on mutual acceptance and ownership is the cornerstone of any successful evaluation. The following list of eight recommendations for a successful evaluation method has been compiled from various ICMA publications that offer assistance to councils and managers in designing their own process:[6]

1. If the city council has several years of experience conducting manager evaluations and the manager has many years of service, an annual evaluation of the manager is recommended. A six-month evaluation of the manager is recommended for city councils just beginning to conduct performance evaluations or having a newly hired manager.
2. Include in an employment agreement the frequency and method of the manager's evaluation. When an evaluation is formally required, an incentive exists for the evaluation to occur according to an agreed upon format.
3. Presenting the evaluation in executive session to secure the candor of the participants by protecting their confidentiality.
4. Separate the evaluation from the budget process, especially the decision about the manager's salary, to avoid focusing on such issues as tax rates and budget constraints, which could turn the activity into a negotiation instead of an opportunity to communicate.
5. Use a form with numerical rating scales and a space for written comments to document the evaluation and to help focus on the agreed-upon criteria.
6. Educate the participants by providing training in the evaluation process, perhaps by using a consultant/facilitator to help overcome inexperience, discomfort, and other obstacles.
7. Conduct a two-way evaluation in which the council evaluates the manager and the manager evaluates the council. This approach helps all participants improve their performance.
8. Use a retreat, especially when first designing the method, in order to provide a setting away from daily routines that distract the participants.

Table 2/2   PROFILE OF RESPONDENTS

Characteristics	No. reporting	(% of n)
Graduate degree (n=482)	381	79.0
Master of Public Administration (n=381)	236	62.0
Master of Arts (or Science) (n=381)	85	22.3
Doctorate (n=381)	9	2.3
Other (n=381)	51	13.4
Length of service in current job (n=480)		
one to three years	176	36.7
four to six years	128	26.7
seven to nine years	85	17.7
ten to twelve years	35	7.3
thirteen to fifteen years	24	5.0
sixteen to eighteen years	12	2.5
nineteen or more years	20	4.2
ICMA relationship		
Member (n=482)	459	95.2
Served on task force/ committee (n=476)	219	46.0
Held national or state office (n=478)	154	32.2
Changed jobs as city manager (n=482)	311	64.5
Reason for leaving last appointment (n=302)		
Career advancement	214	71.0
Fired or pressured to resign	24	8.0
Fled council conflict	16	5.0
Family or personal reasons	12	4.0
Other	36	12.0

Note: 482 managers responded.

Definitions of Evaluation Techniques

Graphic rating scales
Definition: The evaluation is based on a set of traits and the degree to which they describe your performance.

Example: "In carrying out the many responsibilities of the office, how does the manager rank on the following personal attributes as they affect his or her performance? (Note: "F" indicates failure; "N" indicates no response.)

a. Innovation	*A*	*B*	*C*	*D*	*F*	*N*
b. Initiative	*A*	*B*	*C*	*D*	*F*	*N*
c. Sense of humor	*A*	*B*	*C*	*D*	*F*	*N*
d. Self-confidence	*A*	*B*	*C*	*D*	*F*	*N*

Critical Incidents
Definition: The council documents negative and positive events.

Example: The buildings are well-maintained. The budget document and presentation were outstanding. You and your department heads need to give us more mid-year progress reports.

Management by Objectives
Definition: You and the council jointly set goals and objectives, and your performance is rated upon the achievement of those targets.

Example: 1. Complete the North Ridge Street renovation.
2. Implement phase two of the strategic plan.
3. Establish an intergovernmental agreement providing police services to neighboring townships.

Behaviorally Anchored Rating Scales
Definition: Council reads a set of statements describing aspects of a city manager's performance and rates your performance of those activities.

The data in Table 2/3 document the use of these eight recommendations. Eighty-five percent of city councils evaluate their city managers, and the great majority of councils use an annual evaluation. Sixty-two percent of the respondents report that councils are required to evaluate the manager. Almost 55% of city councils report the results of the evaluation to the manager in an executive session, and close to three-fourths of councils link the evaluation to decisions about the manager's salary. Sixty percent of city councils use a form to document the evaluation, with a slight majority (55.2%) using graphic rating scales. It is clear from the percentages that often more than one evaluation technique is used.

Training in conducting evaluations is provided to only 21% of the councils, usually by the city manager and/or consultants. A two-way evaluation occurs in less than 19% of the cities, and retreats are rarely used. The results show that training programs, two-way evaluations, and retreats are not used to the extent recommended by ICMA, and the popularity of linking the evaluation to salary decisions also goes against ICMA's recommendation.

Evaluation forms can be constructed using several different techniques; often more than one technique is used. Six of the most well-known techniques were listed and defined in the questionnaire; their definitions were based on discussions found in several sources.[7] The six definitions are presented in the accompanying sidebar as they appeared in the questionnaire and are followed by examples of how they are used. Before examining the list, two cautionary comments are in order.

First, because the need for brevity on the survey instrument required short definitions, the definition of Behavioral Anchored Rating Scales (BARS) appears not to have been precise enough. By examining copies of evaluation forms returned with some of the questionnaires and interviewing several managers subsequently, it is clear that the use of BARS is overestimated. Behavioral statements describing an aspect of the manager's performance were used (see example below), but statements were not prepared for every level of the scale, which would be the case in a fully-developed BARS approach. The examples presented for BARS fit the manager's interpretation of the brief definition.

Second, few managers reported that their councils use direct indexes, and no examples were provided by the 20 who did. Therefore, the examples of direct indexes listed are not necessarily used in evaluations by any particular city and are offered only to illustrate the technique. The information conveyed by the indexes is often used as data in oral and written reports provided to the council, even if it is not formally part of the evaluation form.[8]

Although some features of a performance review—requiring an evaluation, conducting an annual evaluation, completing a form, and having the council report the results in an executive session—are practiced by a majority of cities, the general pattern suggests that the majority of cities do not use a process that includes most

Table 2/3 MAIN FEATURES IN THE EVALUATION METHOD

Features	No. reporting	% of n
Council evaluates the manager (n=482)	407	84.4
Annually (n=407)	350	86.0
Six months (n=407)	41	10.0
Other (n=407)	16	4.0
Evaluation required by law (n=481)	301	62.4
Annually (n=301)	267	89.0
Six months (n=301)	31	10.3
Other (n=301)	3	1.0
Reporting of results (n=402)		
Council in executive session	221	54.9
Mayor in one-on-one meeting	58	14.4
Council in public meeting	22	5.5
Mayor in one-on-one meeting and council in executive session	17	4.2
Council committee in executive session	14	3.5
Council president in one-on-one meeting	7	1.7
Other	63	15.6
Linked to salary decisions (n=405)	298	73.6
Form used to document decisions (n=406)	247	60.8
Graphic rating scales (n=247)	137	55.2
Behaviorally anchored rating scales (n=247)	97	39.1
Management by objectives (n=247)	78	31.7
Critical incidents (n=247)	75	30.2
Narrative essay (n=247)	72	29.0
Direct indexes (n=247)	20	8.1
Training for council members (n=406)	86	21.1
City manager (n=85)	20	23.5
Consultant (n=85)	15	17.6
City manager and consultant (n=85)	12	14.1
Staff (n=85)	6	7.1
Professional association (n=85)	6	7.1
University institute (n=85)	6	7.1
Other (n=85)	20	23.5
Two-way evaluation (n=405)	76	18.8
Retreat used as the setting (n=403)	32	7.9

Definitions of Evaluation Techniques *continued*

Example: rating scale

Exceeds expectations	*Meets expectations*	*Needs improvement*	*Needs substantial improvement*

Example: behavioral statements
1. *Anticipates future community issues and citizen needs*
2. *Maintains open and honest communication, both oral and written, with governing body members*
3. *Encourages the training and development of employees*

Narrative Essay
Definition: Council members write essays discussing your performance

Example: leading questions
1. *How do you view the manager's performance in handling finance and administration and labor relations?*
2. *Does the city manager do appropriate research, develop options, and present them clearly?*
3. *Does the city manager coordinate city operations with those of other governmental agencies in the area?*
4. *I would like the city manager to give more emphasis to the following:*

Direct Indexes
Definition: Council sets specific, quantifiable measures or standards, and you are evaluated against these standards

Example:
1. *10% reduction in overtime cost for public works department*
2. *15% increase in collection of personal property tax revenue*
3. *100% completion of sidewalk reconstruction in the downtown business district*
4. *25% reduction in the number of refuse collection crews receiving more than five complaints per month*

Table 2/4   METHODS COUNCILS USE TO EVALUATE THE CITY MANAGER

Features	Fourteen methods													
	1	2	3	4	5	6	7	8	9	10	11	12	13	14
Total reporting	10 (3%)	32 (8%)	4 (1%)	45 (11%)	19 (5%)	4 (1%)	10 (3%)	78 (19%)	15 (4%)	13 (3%)	3 (1%)	7 (2%)	9 (2%)	2 (0.5%)
Annual evaluation	X	X	X	X	X	X	X	X	X	X	X	X	X	X
Linked to salary	–	X	–	X	X	X	X	X	X	X	X	X	X	X
Required	–	–	X	X	–	X	X	X	X	X	X	X	X	X
Form used	–	–	–	–	X	–	–	X	X	X	–	X	X	X
Training provided	–	–	–	–	–	X	–	–	X	–	X	–	X	X
Two-way evaluation	–	–	–	–	–	–	X	–	–	X	X	–	X	X
Retreat used	–	–	–	–	–	–	–	–	–	–	–	X	–	X

Note: The entries in parentheses are percentages based on the 402 cities reporting on the features used by councils. The 14 methods cover 251 of the 402 cities or 63%.

of ICMA's recommendations. Indeed, cities have combined the eight features in many different ways. The data in Table 2/4 help reveal the large variety of methods used by councils in council-manager forms of government in the United States.

When the features used in each reporting city's evaluation process are examined, numerous combinations of features emerge. Table 2/4 shows 14 combinations used by 251 cities or 63% of the 402 cities reporting on the features used in the method to evaluate the manager. There are more than 14 combinations, but to list each of them would be cumbersome. In addition, some of the additional combinations are used by so few cities the information is insignificant. (Table 2/4 shows seven of the eight features listed in Table 2/3; the way councils report the results of the evaluation to their managers is omitted in Table 2/4. This was done because to include that feature would further reduce the number of cities included in the table.)

The main conclusion emerging from the data in Table 2/3 and Table 2/4 is that about 85% of the cities have followed ICMA's two key recommendations: (1) do an evaluation of the manager at least annually, and (2) design a method using the features appropriate for your city. When designing a method, the majority of cities use at least four of the eight features, and the annual evaluation is usually one of them. When other features are added to the annual evaluation, it is clear that no method predominates in the United States. The combination reported most often is Method 8, which consists of requiring an evaluation, conducting it annually, linking the evaluation to decisions about the manager's salary, and completing a form to document the review. Yet, even Method 8 is used in only about one in five cities.

PERSONAL DISCUSSIONS

ICMA stresses that an evaluation is primarily a "communications process," in which continuous "feedback improves communication and helps to avoid misunderstandings."[9] Personal discussions between a council member and the city manager about the manager's performance offer one way for continuous feedback to occur. Previous research suggests that personal discus-

Table 2/5   PERFORMANCE DISCUSSIONS BETWEEN A COUNCILMEMBER AND THE MANAGER

Frequency of discussions	Before council meetings (%)	After council meetings (%)	During office visits (%)	During phone calls (%)
Level 1 (Never)	45.3	38.0	14.6	25.5
Level 2 (Rarely)	33.2	34.9	34.4	33.2
Level 3 (Sometimes)	16.7	21.5	40.9	33.8
Level 4 (Often)	4.0	5.0	9.4	6.7
Level 5 (Always)	0.8	0.6	0.6	0.8
Mean level	1.8	2.0	2.5	2.2
Mean of "personal"	2.1*			

Note: There are three missing cases, so n = 479. *The variable named "personal" is an index created for each manager by averaging his or her responses for the four settings.

sions about the manager's performance occur rarely, so they are no substitute for a council evaluation.[10] The data in Table 2/5 confirm this conclusion.

City managers estimated the frequency of personal discussions about their performance on a scale from "1" (*never*) to "5" (*always*). The discussions could occur before council meetings, after council meetings, during office visits, or during phone calls. Respondents were asked to indicate the frequency of any discussions they had with council members about their performance as managers. Using the 1 to 5 scale for all four settings and calculating an average frequency for discussions results in a mean of 2.1, which suggests such discussions are rare. The most likely place for a personal discussion between the city manager and a council member to occur is during an office visit, and the mean of 2.5 indicates that they occur more than *rarely*, but less than *sometimes*. If city managers are to obtain "continuous feedback," they will need to find ways to encourage more personal discussions.

COVERAGE OF THE EVALUATION

The quality of the council's evaluation depends partially on the comprehensiveness of the review. Does the council evaluate the manager's performance using criteria that cover the breadth of the manager's job? City managers reported on the number of subjects personally discussed with them and the number of subjects

included in the council's evaluation of their performance. The data are presented in Table 2/6.

The median number of subjects reviewed during personal discussions is 3.0, which indicates that when personal discussions take place, they are not comprehensive. Council members tend to discuss the manager's skills in communicating with the council, managing finances, and maintaining good relations with the council. The limited focus of most personal discussions is another reason that they are no substitute for a council evaluation.

In contrast, the council evaluation is much more comprehensive. Of the 13 subjects listed in Table 2/6, 70% or more of the managers report that 8 of them are covered by council in evaluations. The median number of subjects covered in evaluations is 9.5, or 73% of the 13 subjects related to the manager's job. Councils most often evaluate the manager's personal qualities/leadership style, fiscal management skill, skill at maintaining good relations with the council, ability to execute policies, council communication, and achievement of goals. The comprehensiveness of these council evaluations is one reason why they are an important tool for enhancing communication between the council and the manager.

ASSESSING THE COUNCIL'S PERFORMANCE

The results of three survey questions are used to assess the council's performance of its supervisory responsibility:

Table 2/6 SUBJECTS REVIEWED IN THE MANAGER'S EVALUATION

Subject	Personal discussion (% reporting)	Rank	Council discussion (% reporting)	Rank
Council communication	49.5	1	77.0	5
Fiscal management	41.2	2	81.4	2
Council relations	40.5	3	81.1	3
Personal qualities	36.7	4	86.0	1
Execution of Policies	36.7	5	79.3	4
Citizen relations	36.2	6	71.2	8
Personnel management	35.1	7	68.6	9
Intergovernmental relations	22.9	8	54.8	11
Goal achievement	21.3	9	76.0	6
Planning/organization	20.6	10	71.4	7
Media relations	20.4	11	50.3	12
Program development	18.1	12	60.2	10
Other subjects	5.0	13	11.5	13
Median number of subjects	3.0		9.5	

Note: The n is 442 for "Personal" and 467 for "Council." The ranks are based on the percentage of managers reporting that the subject is reviewed.

Table 2/8 MULTIPLE LINEAR REGRESSION ANALYSIS

	Dependent variables		
Independent variables	Knowledge of council expectations	Satisfaction with council effort	Effectiveness of council communication
Constant	2.96*** (.10)	.779*** (.13)	3.90*** (.26)
Effectiveness	.241*** (.02)	.771*** (.03)	. . .
Length of service	.013 (.01)	.028*** (.01)	. . .
Council conflict	. . .	. . .	−.30*** (.04)
Comprehensiveness I	. . .	. . .	.06** (.02)
Comprehensiveness II	. . .	. . .	.05* (.02)
F	50.54***	357.10***	26.62***
Multiple R	.42	.78	.39
R²	.18	.60	.15
N	473	473	366

Note: The entries are unstandardized regression coefficients with the standard errors reported in the parentheses.

Comprehensiveness I refers to the number of subjects that council members personally discuss with the manager.

Comprehensiveness II refers to the number of subjects re-viewed by the council. Both scales range from "1" (no subjects) to "14" (all 13 subjects).

***p ≤ .001, two-tailed test.
**p ≤ .01, two-tailed test;
*p ≤ .05, two-tailed test;

Table 2/7 CITY MANAGER'S ASSESSMENT OF THE COUNCIL'S METHOD

Criteria	No. reporting	Mean	Standard Deviation
Knowledge of council expectations	478	3.9	0.87
Satisfaction with council's effort	478	3.7	1.5
Effectiveness of council's communication	478	3.6	1.4

Note: The knowledge scale is "1" = poor, "2" = fair, "3" = average, "4" = good, and "5" = excellent. The satisfaction scale ranges from "1" (very unsatisfied) to "7" (very satisfied) with "4" indicating satisfied.
The effectiveness scale ranges from "1" (very ineffective) to "7" (very effective) with "4" indicating effective.

1. How would you rate your level of knowledge of the council's expectations regarding your performance?
2. How effectively does your council communicate with you about your performance?
3. How satisfied are you with your council's effort to evaluate your performance?

Respondents used 5-point scales to answer these questions. As shown in Table 2/7, the mean for the rating of knowledge of the council's expectations is 3.91. The standard deviation of 0.87 indicates that the managers' self-ratings cluster closely about the mean. Although reluctance to award oneself a low rating may help explain the high knowledge ratings, the high mean and low standard deviation serve as indirect evidence that councils are communicating their expectations. Do both councils and managers contribute to this flow of information?

Satisfaction ratings and effectiveness ratings are more direct measures of the council's contribution. The mean ratings on the seven-point scales for satisfaction and effectiveness are 3.7 and 3.6, respectively. The standard deviations for each scale are 1.5 and 1.4, respectively, which suggests that the quality of the council's performance varies widely on these two measures.

Although city managers provide above average ratings on knowledge of council's expectations, they report that they are less than satisfied with the council's effort to evaluate their performances and that the council's effort to communicate performance expectations for the manager is less than effective. This pattern suggests that many managers think they must make the effort to discover the council's expectations, because they cannot rely on the council to directly communicate its expectations.

IMPROVING THE COUNCIL'S PERFORMANCE

A statistical analysis that seeks to explain the variation in the knowledge, satisfaction, and ef-fectiveness ratings can identify ways to achieve high ratings on all three scales. Multiple linear regression can identify the separate effects of several independent variables on a dependent variable. The dependent variables are the ratings on the knowledge, satisfaction, and effectiveness scales.

The knowledge ratings are positively related to the effectiveness of council communication; the manager's length of service in his or her current position does not effect the knowledge ratings (Table 2/8). This finding suggests that city managers cannot rely on the years served in the city to learn about council expectations. The city managers who think they are knowledgeable about their council's expectations are the ones who gave their councils high ratings on effectiveness of communication. Therefore, finding ways to increase the effectiveness of council communication about its expectations regarding the manager's performance can raise the manager's level of knowledge about expectations.

Two independent variables—effectiveness of council communications and length of service in current position—are positively related to the city manager's satisfaction ratings. The effectiveness of council communication has a much greater impact on the level of satisfaction than does the length of service. Although managers who have served a longer period of time report more satisfaction with the council's effort to evaluate his or her performance, in order to identify ways to raise satisfaction ratings the focus should be on what makes the council effectively communicate its expectations of the manager's performance.

Three independent variables remained in the equation explaining the city manager's effectiveness ratings. The effectiveness of the council's communication is negatively related to the estimated level of council conflict, positively related to the comprehensiveness of the personal discussions between a council member and the manager about the manager's performance, and positively related to the comprehensiveness of the council's evaluation of the manager's performance. This analysis suggests three ways to increase the effectiveness of council communication about its expectations regarding the manager's performance.

First, managers can encourage the use of

team-building techniques to reduce the level of conflict among council members or at least to help council members learn to use conflict constructively. Principled bargaining, integrative bargaining, and other variations of collaborative decisionmaking can help councils learn to constructively work through differences.[11] As the main suppliers of information to councils, managers are in a strong position to supply councilmembers with literature on collaborative decisionmaking. One desirable effect of a council that works through conflict more skillfully may be an improved ability to effectively communicate its expectations to the manager.

Second, managers can find ways to increase

Table 2/9   T-TEST ANALYSIS OF FEATURES IN METHOD

Features in method	Comprehensiveness II	Effectiveness
Evaluation required		
Yes	10.1*** (n=283)	3.7 (n=298)
No	8.7 (n=108)	3.5 (n=180)
Evaluation occurs		
Yes	9.7 (n=392)	3.7** (n=403)
No	0.0 (n=75)	3.1 (n=75)
Form used to document		
Yes	10.7*** (n=241)	3.8* (n=244)
No	8.0 (n=151)	3.5 (n=158)
Training for council		
Yes	11.1*** (n=83)	4.1** (n=85)
No	9.3 (n=309)	3.6 (n=317)
Two-way evaluation		
Yes	10.8** (n=74)	4.0* (n=75)
No	9.4 (n=317)	3.6 (n=326)
Linked to salary		
Yes	9.7 (n=288)	3.7 (n=295)
No	9.7 (n=103)	3.5 (n=106)
Retreat used as setting		
Yes	10.0 (n=31)	3.7 (n=31)
No	9.7 (n=358)	3.7 (n=368)

Note: The entries are means for each scale.
***p ≤ .001, two-tailed test.
**p ≤ .01, two-tailed test;
*p ≤ .05, two tailed test;

the comprehensiveness of their councils' evaluations. Use of several ICMA-endorsed features in the council's method of evaluation can raise the comprehensiveness of the council's evaluation. The statistical tests reported in Table 2/9 reveal the effect several features in the evaluation method have on the comprehensiveness of the council's evaluation and on the effectiveness ratings. Requiring an evaluation and/or conducting the evaluation annually, using a form, training the council, and using a two-way evaluation are features that produce significantly higher means on the comprehensiveness scale. Conducting an annual evaluation, using a form, training the council, and using a two-way evaluation are four features that also directly produce significantly higher means on the effectiveness scale. Although requiring an evaluation does not directly produce a statistically significant higher mean on the effectiveness scale, it does make it more likely that an evaluation will occur at least annually.[12]

Third, managers also can encourage more personal discussions. More personal discussions help because councils whose members more frequently discuss the manager's performance with the manager also tend to discuss more job-related subjects with the manager. As the regression analysis has shown, more comprehensive personal discussions are associated with more effective council efforts to communicate its expectations regarding the manager's performance. The strong positive relationship between personal discussions about the manager's performance and the comprehensiveness of these discussions is evident from the .53 Pearson correlation coefficient reported in Table 2/10.

Several other relationships between variables in Table 2/10 deserve explanation. There are two weak, positive relationships between (1) conflict among council members and the number of managers who served the city between 1988 and 1993 and (2) conflict among council members and the length of the manager's service in his or her current position. Although the large majority of city managers who changed jobs did so for career advancement, a small percentage changed because of council conflict and/or being fired, so this weak, positive relationship is not surprising. Also expected is the strong, negative relationship between the number of managers and the manager's length of service. As the number of managers increases within the five-year period, the manager's length of service should decline. Finally, there

is a weak, positive relationship between the frequency of personal discussions and the number of managers and a weak, negative relationship between the frequency of personal discussions and the length of the manager's service. At the risk of making too much of these weak relationships, perhaps the most likely explanation for this pattern is that when a managerial change occurs, council members are more likely to personally discuss the manager's performance in order to become better acquainted and to clarify their expectations. In light of the contribution personal discussions make to the overall effectiveness of the council's communication about the manager's performance, the task for managers is to encourage council members to continue these personal discussions with them even after they have served the council for several years.

IDENTIFYING THE KEYS TO IMPROVED EVALUATION EFFORTS

Table 2/11 shows the 14 combinations of evaluation methods presented in Table 2/4 and the mean ratings on the knowledge, effectiveness, satisfaction, comprehensiveness II, and conflict scales. The data illustrate some of the findings from the statistical analysis and help identify the key features that can improve the council's evaluation effort. There are four main observations.

First, the higher (and therefore more desirable) means for knowledge, satisfaction, effectiveness, and comprehensiveness II tend to be to the right-side of Table 2/11, which indicates generally that the more ICMA-endorsed features used, the better the ratings.

Second, by comparing the means for Methods 1 through 4, the limited value of requiring the evaluation becomes evident. The means for satisfaction and effectiveness are actually lower for Method 3, which is distinguished by its reliance on a required evaluation, in comparison to Methods 1, 2, and 4. The main benefit in requiring the evaluation is that the evaluation is more likely to occur. Improving council performance, however, depends on using other features.

Third, there are three features that strengthen the council's performance of the evaluation function: use of a form, training, and two-way evaluations. By comparing the means for Methods 5 and 8 to 9, Method 7 to 11, and noting the means for Method 6, it is clear that training councilmembers is especially important. Councils use the form and engage in a two-way evaluation more effectively when they have been trained to use these tools.

Fourth, the importance of the level of conflict, as well as the value of using a form, training councilmembers, and using a two-way evaluation, is reinforced by examining Methods 1 and 2 and comparing them to the other methods, especially Methods 8 through 12. The low levels of conflict in Methods 1 and 2 help explain why the informal evaluation method can approach being satisfactory and effective. Less

Table 2/10   PEARSON CORRELATION COEFFICIENT MATRIX FOR SELECTED VARIABLES

	Conflict	Personal	No. of managers	City population	Comprehensiveness I	Length of service
Conflict	1.000	.0586	.1636**	.0203	−.0774	−.1096*
Personal		1.000	.1108**	−.0183	.5300**	−.1232**
No. of managers			1.000	.0413	.0787	−.5749**
City population				1.000	.0432	−.0672
Comprehensiveness I ...					1.000	−.1112*
Length service						1.000

Note: *p ≤ .05, two-tailed test; **p ≤ .01, two-tailed test.
The variable named "Personal" is an index created for each manager by averaging his or her responses for the four settings in which a personal discussion between the council member and manager could occur (see Table 2/4).

Table 2/11   METHODS COUNCILS USE TO EVALUATE THE MANAGER WITH MEANS FOR SELECTED SCALES

Features	Fourteen Methods													
	1	2	3	4	5	6	7	8	9	10	11	12	13	14
Total reporting	10 (3%)	32 (8%)	4 (1%)	45 (11%)	19 (5%)	4 (1%)	10 (3%)	78 (19%)	15 (4%)	13 (3%)	3 (1%)	7 (2%)	9 (2%)	2 (0.5%)
Annual evaluation	X	X	X	X	X	X	X	X	X	X	X	X	X	X
Linked to salary	–	X	–	X	X	X	X	X	X	X	X	X	X	X
Required by law	–	–	X	X	–	X	X	X	X	X	X	X	X	X
Form used	–	–	–	–	X	–	–	X	X	X	–	X	X	X
Training provided	–	–	–	–	–	X	–	–	X	–	X	–	X	X
Two-way evaluation	–	–	–	–	–	–	X	–	–	X	X	–	X	X
Retreat used	–	–	–	–	–	–	–	–	–	–	–	X	–	X
Mean Knowledge	3.5	3.8	4.0	3.8	3.9	4.8	3.9	3.9	4.1	4.0	4.3	4.1	3.8	4.0
Mean Satisfaction	3.8	3.8	3.3	3.4	3.7	4.3	2.9	3.7	4.8	4.5	3.7	3.6	4.2	4.5
Mean Effectiveness	3.5	3.9	2.8	3.5	3.6	5.0	2.7	3.7	4.1	4.7	3.7	3.6	4.1	5.0
Mean Conflict	2.5	2.9	2.5	3.5	3.0	2.3	3.6	3.5	3.7	3.3	5.0	3.4	3.0	2.5
Mean Comprehensiveness II	5.0	7.0	7.0	8.0	10.0	8.0	8.0	11.0	12.0	11.0	12.0	9.0	12.0	11.0

Note: The entries in parentheses are percentages based on
the 402 cities reporting on the features used by councils.
The 14 methods cover 251 of the 402 cities or 62%.

conflict among council members may make it easier for the council to communicate its expectations to the manager through an informal method. The higher levels of conflict in Methods 8 through 12 appear to be controlled or moderated by the use of the three key features in the evaluation method. A more formal evaluation method may be most useful in cities experiencing a moderate to high level of conflict among council members.

These four observations must be tempered with a word of caution. The number of cities using each of the 14 methods varies widely. The most reliable means are those based on the larger number of cities, such as those for Methods 2, 4, and 8. In addition, only 62% of the 402 cities reporting on the features used by the council are covered by the 14 methods in Table 2/11. In spite of the need for caution in interpreting the data, the four observations are valuable because they are based on the more complete and rigorous statistical analysis presented in Tables 2/8, 2/9, and 2/10.

The effectiveness and satisfaction ratings could be biased by personal and professional influences.[13] If this is the case, then the previous analysis would be suspect. City managers with graduate degrees, particularly in public administration, could have offered higher ratings if the council's method used features that were endorsed in their course work, such as in a public personnel management course. City managers who changed jobs because they were fired or fled council conflict may have exaggerated their current council's effectiveness. The bias also could have worked in the other direction; that is, these city managers could have underestimated their current council's effectiveness and underestimated their satisfaction with their current council due to lingering effects of their recent bad experience. City managers also could have been influenced to give higher ratings to councils that used evaluation features suggested in ICMA publications and lower ratings to councils whose methods lacked these features. Perhaps a stronger commitment to profession-

alism will lead managers to judge more severely those methods that lack certain ICMA-endorsed features. Since 95% of the managers returning the survey are ICMA members, the two best measures of a possible professional bias are (1) having held an office in the ICMA and (2) having served on an ICMA task force or committee. The statistical analysis presented in Table 2/12 indicates that none of these biases significantly influenced the mean ratings for effectiveness and satisfaction. The main findings of this research appear to be secure.

CONCLUSION

One of the main responsibilities of the council's supervisory function is to evaluate the performance of the manager. The large majority of councils in the United States complete this task at least once per year using a wide variety of methods. While there are a few exceptions to the general rule, the majority of councils could improve their efforts to evaluate their manager's performance.

This study has identified some of the features that can improve the council's evaluation effort by making the evaluation method more comprehensive and systematic. Four features are especially useful: (1) requiring an evaluation to ensure that one occurs, (2) using a form to document the evaluation, (3) training the council members to do an evaluation, and (4) using a two-way evaluation. City managers also could encourage more personal discussions about their performances with individual council members in order to promote a more comprehensive and more frequent flow of information.

No single evaluation method predominates in the United States. Cities continue to experiment with different combinations of features. No particular method will serve as a panacea to solve all the problems that may prevent a council from evaluating the manager thoroughly and communicating the results clearly. Ultimately, it is the people using the method that make it

Table 2/12   T-TEST ANALYSIS OF POSSIBLE PERSONAL AND PROFESSIONAL BIASES

Biases	Effectiveness	Satisfaction
Graduate degree		
Yes	3.6 (n=378)	3.7 (n=378)
No	3.7 (n=100)	3.9 (n=100)
Public administration major		
Yes	3.5 (n=269)	3.7 (n=270)
No	3.7 (n=208)	3.8 (n=207)
Fled council conflict		
Yes	3.5 (n=16)	3.7 (n=16)
No	3.6 (n=283)	3.7 (n=284)
Fired or pressured		
Yes	3.7 (n=24)	3.7 (n=24)
No	3.6 (n=275)	3.7 (n=276)
Held ICMA national office/state office		
Yes	3.6 (n=152)	3.7 (n=154)
No	3.6 (n=322)	3.8 (n=320)
Served on ICMA task force or committee		
Yes	3.6 (n=215)	3.8 (n=217)
No	3.6 (n=257)	3.7 (n=255)

Note: The entries are means for each scale.

work in any particular city. Examples of success can be found among a wide variety of methods. Yet, this study has identified several features that can increase the chances of success. Adopting a more systematic method that embraces many of ICMA's recommendations offers councils and city managers the best chance for each to acquire the kind of information they need to be effective public officials.

[1]The explanation of the supervisory role is developed by J. H. Svara in *Official Leadership in the City* (New York: Oxford University Press, 1990).

[2]See for example, H. A. Stone, D. K. Price, and K. H. Stone, *City Manager Government in the United States* (Chicago: Public Administration Service, 1940); R. O. Loveridge, *City Managers in Legislative Politics* (Indianapolis: Bobbs-Merrill, 1971); R. J. Stillman, *The Rise of The City Manager Profession* (Albuquerque: University of New Mexico Press, 1974); J. Nalbandian, *Professionalism in Local Government* (San Francisco: Jossey-Bass, 1991); Svara, 1990.

[3]See for example, C. M. Wheeland, "Performance Evaluation of City Managers in Four Pennsylvania Municipalities," *Southeastern Political Review*, vol. 21, no. 4 (Winter 1993): 59–78; C. M. Wheeland, "Evaluating the City Manager's Performance: Pennsylvania Managers Report on the Methods Used by Their Councils," *State and Local Government Review* (Fall 1994); J. H. Svara, "The Complimentary Roles of Officials in Council-Manager Government," in *The Municipal Year Book 1988* (Washington, DC: International City Management Association, 1988): 22–23.

[4]Wheeland, 1994 (or 1995).

[5]See for example, T. Renner, "Appointed Local Government Managers: Stability and Change," *The Municipal Year Book 1990* (Washington, DC: International City Management Association, 1990), 46–47; R. E. Green, *The Profession of Local Government Management: Management Expertise and The American Community* (New York: Praeger, 1989), 92–92.

[6]See for example, L. Hopper, "Laying the Groundwork for Evaluation," *Public Management*, vol. 70, no. 2 (February 1988): 10–12; L. J. Sumek, "Evaluate or Not? This is Not the Question," *Public Management*, vol. 70, no. 2 (February 1988): 2–9; C. Schwarz, "Council Evaluation: State of the Art," *Public Management*, vol. 58, no. 5 (May 1976): 2–7; C. S. Becker, *Evaluating the Chief Administrator* (Washington, DC: International City Management Association, 1977); C. S. Becker, *Performance Evaluation: An Essential Management Tool* (Washington, DC: International City Management Association, 1988). See also these two ICMA handbooks, *Employment Agreements for Managers: Guidelines for Local Government Managers* (1992) and *Elected Officials Handbooks: Handbook 1, Setting Goals for Action*, 3d Ed. (1988).

[7]See D. L. Dresang, *Public Personnel Management and Public Policy*, 2d ed. (New York: Longman, 1991), 136–140; N. P. Lovrich, "Performance Appraisal," in S. W. Hays and R. C. Kearney, eds., *Public Personnel Administration: Problems and Prospects*, 2d ed. (Englewood Cliffs, NJ: Prentice-Hall, 1990), 92–99.

[8]For an excellent discussion of performance measurement that offers many examples, see P. D. Epstein, *Using Performance Measurement in Local Government* (New York: National Civic League Press, 1988). Also, see the articles in the September 1994 issue of *Public Management* in the Special Section: Benchmarks of Performance, on pages S1 to S23.

[9]Hopper, 1988, 12.

[10]Wheeland, 1993; 1994.

[11]There is an extensive literature on collaborative decision making. Two popular books are: Roger Fisher and William Ury (and Bruce Patton). *Getting to Yes: Negotiating Agreement Without Giving In*. 2d Ed. (New York: Penguin Books, 1991) and Lawrence Susskind and Jeffrey Cruikshank. *Breaking the Impasse: Consensual Approaches to Resolving Public Disputes* (New York: Basic Books, 1987).

[12]The crosstabulation between two dichotomous variables *required* (yes or no) and *evaluate* (yes or no) produced a Chi-Square value of 97.1, which is significant at the .001 level, and a Phi of .45 indicating a moderately strong relationship. Indeed, 97% of the councils in cities with a required evaluation did at least an annual evaluation. The fact that 63% of the councils that did not require the evaluation also did an evaluation at least annually is why the measure of association (Phi) is not higher.

[13]The reasoning supporting these possible biases was first developed in another article using the data from Pennsylvania managers. The findings here confirm the conclusions reached in that article. See Wheeland 1994.

A3

Local Economic Development: Trends and Prospects

Adam J. Prager
Deloitte & Touche LLP
Chicago, Illinois

Philip Benowitz
Deloitte & Touche LLP
Parsippany, New Jersey

Robert Schein
Deloitte & Touche LLP
Parsippany, New Jersey

Findings

Although over 70% (1,133) of reporting jurisdictions identify manufacturing as the focus of their economic development efforts, few jurisdictions expect to register substantial gains in this area in the future.

Local governments are extremely optimistic about their prospects: 82% believe they will experience some amount of growth over the next five years.

Nearly 87% of the respondents surveyed indicate that they use local government revenues to fund their economic development programs.

Local economic development has made considerable strides over the last few decades. Whereas formal, professional efforts to influence local economic direction and growth were once primarily the domain of states and major cities, today economic development programs can be found in virtually every level of government and throughout the private sector.

Although certain economic development programs around the country have evolved in a systematic fashion, the majority in United States have developed in response to economic change. As a result, two commonalities can be found among most programs, regardless of their sophistication or geographic orientation. First, economic development programs are considerably more reactive than proactive. They tend to respond to the shifts in local or regional economies and attempt to alter or enhance economic trends. Second, economic development professionals today are more in tune with the needs of the end-user, or target audience, than in the past.

At one time economic development programs were dedicated primarily to the attraction of industry, with little thought given to industry retention or expansion. Furthermore, government-dominated programs emphasized the resources and location advantages that they could readily offer rather than those of most importance to their target audiences. The work of today's economic development professionals is rapidly becoming market driven, with programs and delivery mechanisms implemented that are responsive to the demands and desires of the business community.

Economic development today offers much more of a continuum of services than previously, with the provision of services carrying over after the local business investment has been made. Responsive stand-alone programs dedicated solely to existing industry are relatively rare today at the local level; however,

they are evolving faster than any other facet of the economic development profession. Additionally, with considerable private sector influence, economic development programs have become more flexible and customer-driven than in the past, offering services that are requested rather than merely those readily available or easily accessible.

ICMA conducted an economic development survey to understand better the level of commitment and focus of local government economic development programs. This article uses the survey results to describe economic development funding, staffing, and participation levels; program planning and direction; and use of performance measures. It provides insight into economic development program variations by community size and geographic location within the United States.

SURVEY METHODOLOGY

In 1994, ICMA conducted a mail survey on local government economic development. In May 1994, the survey questionnaire was sent to all cities and counties with populations 2,500 and over and to those cities and counties under 2,500 that are recognized by ICMA as providing for an appointed position of professional management. In July 1994, a second mailing was sent to those local governments that did not respond to the first mailing. Of the 7,135 cities surveyed, 20% responded; 12% of the 3,108 counties responded (Table 3/1).

Approximately 80% of the more than 1,700 survey respondents are from municipalities; the rest are from counties. Approximately half the local governments responding have populations between 5,000 and 25,000, which reflects the overall survey universe. Only 7% of the respondents are from communities with populations over 100,000, which also mirrors the survey universe (Table 3/2).

All geographic divisions throughout the United States are well represented by the survey respondents, with the greatest representation from communities in the North Central and South Atlantic divisions. Central cities account for 10% of total respondents, with suburban and independent locations accounting for 46% and 44%, respectively.

ECONOMIC OVERVIEW

Successful development strategies are contingent upon a strong grasp of the current economic climate as well as on an ability to anticipate future changes and trends. For example, the decision to invest funds in a campaign to promote tourism must be predicated upon certain assumptions about future spending patterns by population segments in different markets. The long-term outlook is an essential part of any examination of economic development policies at the local level. The way local governments understand present conditions and anticipate future trends provides insight into the rationale behind many economic development policies. Three important elements in those policies are the commitment of a locality to a particular industry or sector of the economy, the economic outlook of the locality, and particularly relevant national trends or policies that may have an impact on the economy of a locality.

Primary Economic Base

Survey respondents were asked to identify the economic base of their local government over the last five years and to predict the economic base for the next five years. Residential and manufacturing economic foundations have supported the economy for 24% and 23% of the respondents, respectively, followed by combined retail/service economies (18%). The survey results suggest that many local areas believe that agriculture will no longer occupy a position of prominence in their communities (Table 3/3).

Over the last five years, this sector has been the primary economic base for 17% of survey respondents. However, only 12% of the communities in the survey indicate that agriculture will retain this position during the next five years.

These trends are also reflected across population groups. With only one or two negligible exceptions, fewer cities and counties of all sizes anticipate that either manufacturing or agriculture will be the core of their economic base during the next five years. Similarly, almost all population groups show an increase in the number of localities where either the tourism/hospitality or the retail/service sector is expected to be the main source of economic activity over the next five years. It is anticipated that the decline in the agricultural base will be felt nationwide because the percentage of jurisdictions listing agriculture as the main sector of their economy dropped in all population groups and geographic divisions.

Several developments are worth noting. Among cities and counties with populations from 100,000 to 500,000, the prominence of manufacturing is expected to decline dramatically. Whereas 30% of those localities indicate that manufacturing was their primary economic base over the last five years, only 18% predict that the sector will have such a status during the next five years. Meanwhile, 49% of these local governments expect that retail/service will be their top industry in the next five years, up from 35% during the previous period.

The survey suggests that the retail/service and tourism/hospitality sectors will see increased activity as more and more jurisdictions rely upon them to be growth engines for their economies. The retail/service segment is expected to be the largest portion of the economy for 21% of localities in the next five years, up from 18% over the previous period. Tourism/ hospitality will be the top industry in the economies of 8% of the cities and counties during that period compared to 5% over the last five years. These changes are likely to occur in all geographic divisions of the country.

Among the other sectors of the economy, differing geographic trends are evident. Overall, the percentage of cities and counties that expect manufacturing to be their primary economic base for the next five years is slightly lower than the percentage that relied on manufacturing during the previous five years. Manufacturing is expected to lose its prominence in a number of New England and Mid-Atlantic jurisdictions but maintain its position elsewhere. It should be noted that although manufacturing is expected to slip overall, more than 46% of respondents pick this sector as the one they would most like to attract in the future.

Though the manufacturing industry may be the most economically desirable, it is apparently one of the most difficult to attract. Although over 70% (1,133) of reporting jurisdictions identify manufacturing as the focus of their economic development efforts (the highest of all sectors), few jurisdictions expect to register substantial gains in this area in the future. A significant amount of resources and effort are

necessary simply to keep existing companies from relocating. Companies' willingness to shift the location of their operations has been previously demonstrated by the movement of many manufacturers from large urban industrial centers to the cheaper land of the suburbs. Given the mobility of this sector, the 23% of localities that listed manufacturing as their primary economic base for the next five years may find themselves struggling to meet their expectations for future economic growth.

One surprising result of the survey is the relative stability in the institutional category, which comprises government, military, and

Table 3/1 SURVEY RESPONSE

Classification	No of cities surveyed (A)	No. responding	% of (A)	No. of counties surveyed (B)	No. responding	% of (B)
Total	7,135	1,407	19.7	3,108	357	11.5
Population group						
Over 1,000,000	8	1	12.5	27	6	22.2
500,000–1,000,000	16	4	25.0	65	11	16.9
250,000–499,999	40	17	42.5	98	10	10.2
100,000–249,999	131	43	32.8	255	39	15.3
50,000–99,999	334	87	26.1	380	49	12.9
25,000–49,999	674	165	24.5	619	64	10.3
10,000–24,999	1,590	355	22.3	922	104	11.3
5,000–9,999	1,794	316	17.6	449	44	9.8
2,500–4,999	1,989	331	16.6	178	18	10.1
Under 2,500	559	88	15.7	115	12	10.4
Geographic division						
New England	793	141	17.8	54	5	9.3
Mid-Atlantic	1,180	133	11.3	146	15	10.3
East North Central	1,349	313	23.2	437	47	10.8
West North Central	719	206	28.7	618	76	12.3
South Atlantic	868	203	23.4	590	121	20.5
East South Central	470	40	8.5	364	22	6.0
West South Central	746	121	16.2	470	20	4.3
Mountain	367	82	22.3	280	31	11.1
Pacific Coast	643	168	26.1	149	20	13.4
Metro status						
Central	509	131	25.7	367	48	13.1
Suburban	3,825	761	19.9	359	53	14.8
Independent	2,801	515	18.4	2,382	256	10.8

Table 3/2 REPRESENTATIVENESS OF SURVEY RESPONSE

Classification	No. of cities and counties surveyed (A)	% of total (A)	No. responding (B)	% of total (B)	% of (A)
Total	10,243	...	1,764	...	17.2
Population group					
Over 1,000,000	35	0.3	7	0.4	20.0
500,000–1,000,000	81	0.8	15	0.9	18.5
250,000–499,999	138	1.3	27	1.5	19.6
100,000–249,999	386	3.8	82	4.6	21.2
50,000–99,999	714	7.0	136	7.7	19.1
25,000–49,999	1,293	12.6	229	13.0	17.7
10,000–24,999	2,512	24.5	459	26.0	18.3
5,000–9,999	2,243	21.9	360	20.4	16.1
2,500–4,999	2,167	21.2	349	19.8	16.1
Under 2,500	674	6.7	100	5.7	14.8
Geographic division					
New England	847	8.0	146	8.3	17.2
Mid-Atlantic	1,326	12.9	148	8.4	11.2
East North Central	1,786	17.4	360	20.4	20.2
West North Central	1,337	13.1	282	16.0	21.1
South Atlantic	1,458	14.2	324	18.4	22.2
East South Central	834	8.1	62	3.5	7.4
West South Central	1,216	11.9	141	8.0	11.6
Mountain	647	6.3	113	6.4	17.5
Pacific Coast	792	7.7	188	10.7	23.7
Metro status					
Central	876	8.6	179	10.1	20.4
Suburban	4,184	40.8	814	46.1	19.5
Independent	5,183	50.6	771	43.7	14.9

nonprofit organizations. Six percent of respondents describe their economic base as institutional during the last five years. This percentage dropped only slightly, to a little more than 5%, for the next five years. Given the difficult fiscal conditions local governments face across the country and the widespread acceptance of the need to adjust the size of the workforce at all levels of government, a more significant decline in this category may have been expected. Several factors may be at work. First, the number of respondents affected by military base closings was relatively small (4%). Second, future reductions in the governmental labor force may be offset by increases in employment in the not-for-profit community as the nongovernmental sector assumes a greater responsibility for "public sector" services. Finally, if the composite term *institutional* had not been used and separate categories for *military, nonprofit,* and *government* had been established instead, a sharp decline in government employment and an increase in nonprofit employment could probably have been traced.

Overall Economic Growth

It remains to be seen if the shift away from agriculture to more service-related sectors will put communities in a stronger economic position. Most of the respondents seem to think that their economies will improve in the future. In fact, local governments are extremely optimistic about their prospects: 82% believe they will experience some amount of growth over the next five years, even though only 68% registered any growth during the past five years. This optimism is exhibited in all geographic divisions of the country. Nevertheless it is somewhat surprising given the fiscal difficulties that localities have faced in the past few years and the generally conservative nature of their economic forecasting as influenced by bond-rating agencies. In this case, survey respondents may have perceived dire economic predictions to be self-defeating and therefore decided to err on the side of optimism.

The number of medium- to large-size cities projecting future economic growth is staggering. Ninety-two percent of large cities and counties (250,000 and over in population) predict some amount of growth during the next five years. Forty-six percent of jurisdictions in this population category expect growth of 10% or more. Slightly over 93% of medium-size jurisdictions (from 50,000 to 250,000 in population) are forecasting growth for the upcoming period.

There is substantial disparity among geographic divisions as to overall economic outlook. In five geographic divisions—East North Central, South Atlantic, East South Central, West South Central, and Mountain—at least half the localities predict economic growth of more than 10%. The survey indicates that localities in the East South Central division are in much better shape than their counterparts elsewhere in the country. This area had the largest number of rapid and moderate growth areas over the past five years and is expected to maintain a similar status during the next five years. The West South Central division respondents expect to have the greatest increase in economic growth, with 83% of the local governments forecasting growth in the upcoming period, whereas only 62% experienced such gains over the past five years.

The Mid-Atlantic and New England Divisions lag far behind, with only 25% and 26%, respectively, of localities in these divisions forecasting moderate to rapid expansion (rate of 10% and above). Jurisdictions in these areas have the least amount of land area zoned for commercial, industrial, and manufacturing uses. Conversely, jurisdictions in the Mid-Atlantic and New England divisions have the greatest percentage of land available for residential use. The percentage of localities focusing on manufacturing in their economic development efforts is also the smallest in these divisions. Such factors suggest that in their effort to overcome a relatively bleak economic outlook, the New England and Mid-Atlantic divisions should at least reexamine their land-use policies.

IMPACT OF NAFTA

If survey respondents have the ability accurately to predict the twists and turns of their local economies, then a period of economic expansion is imminent. Local governments will have to be well prepared for many of the negative implications of growth, however, especially those that expect moderate or rapid growth. Depending upon the sectors driving economic resurgence, governments may experience greater strains on their already limited resources for infrastructure repair and expansion, pollution control, and public safety. The public sector faces

Table 3/3 PRIMARY ECONOMIC BASE

Classification	No. reporting Last five years (A)	Next five years (B)	Agriculture Last five years % of (A)	Next five years % of (B)	Manufacturing Last five years % of (A)	Next five years % of (B)	Retail/Service Last five years % of (A)	Next five years % of (B)	Institutional Last five years % of (A)	Next five years % of (B)	Residential community Last five years % of (A)	Next five years % of (B)	Tourism/ hospitality Last five years % of (A)	Next five years % of (B)	Warehousing/ distribution Last five years % of (A)	Next five years % of (B)	Other Last five years % of (A)	Next five years % of (B)
Total	1,520	1,486	17.2	11.8	23.1	22.6	17.7	21.0	5.93	5.4	24.1	23.5	5.0	8.0	1.3	2.4	5.7	5.3
Population group																		
Over 1,000,000	7	5	0.0	0.0	14.3	20.0	28.6	20.0	14.3	0.0	14.3	0.0	28.6	60.0	0.0	0.0	0.0	0.0
500,000–1,000,000	12	12	0.0	0.0	16.7	25.0	33.3	33.3	16.7	16.7	0.0	0.0	16.7	16.7	0.0	0.0	16.7	8.3
250,000–499,999	22	22	0.0	0.0	31.8	9.1	54.5	72.7	9.1	9.1	0.0	0.0	4.5	4.5	0.0	4.5	0.0	0.0
100,000–249,999	67	67	4.5	3.0	29.9	20.9	28.4	41.8	10.4	6.0	9.0	6.0	4.5	6.0	3.0	3.0	10.4	13.4
50,000–99,999	112	110	8.0	3.6	31.3	31.8	28.6	33.6	8.9	5.5	13.4	12.7	3.6	4.5	2.7	4.5	3.6	3.6
25,000–49,999	192	185	11.5	7.0	22.4	22.7	28.1	30.3	9.4	9.2	17.7	14.6	6.3	10.8	1.0	2.2	3.6	3.2
10,000–24,999	403	398	17.1	11.8	21.8	22.1	16.4	20.1	6.0	4.5	27.8	26.4	3.2	6.3	2.0	3.0	5.7	5.8
5,000–9,999	315	306	18.7	13.4	23.8	24.5	12.1	13.1	5.1	6.9	28.3	27.8	5.1	7.8	0.6	1.3	6.3	5.2
2,500–4,999	302	297	21.2	14.8	22.5	21.2	12.3	14.5	3.0	2.7	29.5	31.0	5.0	8.8	1.0	2.4	5.6	4.7
Under 2,500	88	84	39.8	28.6	13.6	15.5	5.7	8.3	1.1	2.4	22.7	26.2	9.1	10.7	0.0	1.2	8.0	7.1
Geographic division																		
New England	132	128	3.8	1.6	25.8	20.3	11.4	14.1	4.5	3.1	40.9	43.0	6.1	8.6	1.5	3.1	6.1	6.3
Mid-Atlantic	135	133	4.4	2.3	15.6	8.3	14.8	18.8	4.4	6.0	51.9	51.9	3.0	6.0	3.0	3.0	3.0	3.8
East North Central	323	316	8.0	4.1	35.0	35.8	17.0	18.4	2.8	2.8	30.7	29.1	1.2	3.8	1.5	2.5	3.7	3.5
West North Central	240	234	37.9	31.2	18.8	20.5	16.3	17.9	4.6	5.1	15.0	14.5	1.7	2.6	1.7	2.6	4.2	5.6
South Atlantic	270	261	15.6	8.4	25.6	26.1	22.6	26.1	8.1	7.7	15.2	14.6	6.7	9.2	1.1	2.7	5.2	5.4
East South Central	53	52	15.1	13.5	34.0	36.5	13.2	21.2	7.5	5.8	17.0	13.5	3.8	5.8	0.0	3.8	1.9	0.0
West South Central	123	120	27.6	20.0	15.4	17.5	17.1	20.0	8.9	9.2	19.5	18.3	0.8	4.2	0.8	2.5	9.8	8.3
Mountain	90	90	21.1	17.8	10.0	8.9	18.9	21.1	11.1	7.8	4.4	5.6	23.3	27.8	0.0	1.1	11.1	10.0
Pacific Coast	154	152	16.9	9.9	14.9	14.5	22.1	30.9	7.1	3.9	18.8	17.8	9.1	16.4	0.6	0.7	10.4	5.9
Metro status																		
Central	145	141	1.4	0.7	34.5	29.1	30.3	35.5	16.6	12.8	2.8	2.1	6.9	9.9	0.7	2.8	6.9	7.1
Suburban	720	711	4.3	2.3	16.1	15.5	23.5	27.0	3.9	3.5	43.9	40.9	2.4	3.8	2.4	3.4	3.6	3.7
Independent	655	634	34.8	24.9	28.2	29.2	8.5	11.0	5.8	5.8	7.0	8.7	7.5	12.3	0.3	1.3	7.8	6.8

the challenge of channeling growth into areas that maximize local tax bases but create minimal demands for costly enhancement of services.

Last year, a controversial treaty ratified by Congress was the North American Free Trade Agreement (NAFTA), which reduces trade barriers among the United States, Canada, and Mexico. During consideration of the NAFTA legislation, one of the most heated issues was the eventual impact of NAFTA on American jobs. This debate was largely conducted at a national level, and its focus was on the effect of the agreement on the country as a whole. Given the disparity of opinions on this issue, it seemed that an examination of NAFTA from a local angle might provide new insight and reveal what changes, if any, city and county governments expect it to bring.

The survey shows that the majority of responding local governments (55%) believe that NAFTA will not affect their jurisdictions (Table 3/4). To the extent that NAFTA is expected to have an impact on localities, that impact is generally considered positive—either through job creation or increased revenues from U.S. exports. Furthermore, a greater percentage of large- and medium-size cities and counties believe they will be in a position to reap economic benefits from NAFTA than do their smaller counterparts.

Predictably, some of the most interesting variations in the survey data are geographic. Local governments in the West South Central and Mountain divisions believe they will be the prime beneficiaries of NAFTA as it pertains to employment. Of localities in the West South Central division, 48% report NAFTA will create jobs in their areas, compared with 4% indicating it will cause job losses. In the Mountain division, 37% of the respondents indicate NAFTA will increase the number of jobs, while 7% predict that

it will cost jobs. The East South Central division is the only area where the percentage of localities forecasting job loss as a result of NAFTA (25%) exceeds the percent expecting increases in employment (19%).

Although most localities do not believe that NAFTA will have an impact on them, the survey also indicates that many areas stand to gain from it. All this suggests that many local economies are not positioned to take advantage of the liberalization of trade restrictions NAFTA contains. The facts that respondents in West South Central division jurisdictions see themselves as the primary beneficiaries of job creation through NAFTA; that 37 out of the 137 jurisdictions responding from this division report moderate or rapid growth for the last five years, and that 70 of the 137 expect moderate or rapid growth for the next five years may be no coincidence. Certainly proximity (to Mexico) of the states in this division gives them a locational advantage, but no more so than those several geographic divisions that share borders with Canada.

Theoretically, the parts of the country that should benefit most are those that were doing business with these two countries prior to the enactment of NAFTA. During the next few years, it will be worth watching the localities in divisions that have either Canada or Mexico as neighbors to see if their economies change substantially in response to NAFTA. Finally, the ability of large- and medium-size cities to benefit from NAFTA further confirms the importance of foreign linkages and diversity in economic holdings in the pursuit of economic growth.

Economic Forecasting

The survey data raise significant questions about the nature of economic forecasting in the public sector. State-of-the-art long-term eco-

nomic development strategies are often predicated on developments in the economy that never materialize or trends that are short-lived. Yet plans that appear to be revenue winners in the short term are often criticized as being too shortsighted. Local governments that are surprised by changes in the economy are chastised as being unprepared.

Economic forecasting has never been a precise science. In the next five years localities will be confronted with changes in their economies that even the most sophisticated economists could not have predicted. Therefore, these entities must be flexible and make their best judgments about economic development policies based upon limited information. Such flexibility is dependent upon, among other things, discretion in land use, favorable political climates, and the willingness and resolve to enter into short-term agreements with businesses. Based upon the survey results, many areas would best be served by closely examining policies regarding land use and subsidies for manufacturing operations while exploring ways to modify their economies in light of certain national trends and developments—especially NAFTA.

FACTORS INFLUENCING ECONOMIC DEVELOPMENT

Each community confronts a unique set of economic circumstances that vary in impact and importance. The ways in which they choose to respond are as different as the circumstances themselves. Economic development programs, while still more reactive than proactive in nature, are a method by which communities can influence their own destiny and, if necessary, alter the course of their economic evolution. When conducted in a comprehensive fashion, an economic development program addresses

---

Table 3/4   EFFECT OF NAFTA ON LOCAL GOVERNMENT OVER THE NEXT FIVE YEARS

Classification	No. reporting (A)	Job loss No.	% of (A)	Decrease in export revenues No.	% of (A)	Decrease in illegal immigration No.	% of (A)	No effect No.	% of (A)	Job creation No.	% of (A)	Increase in export revenues No.	% of (A)	Other No.	% of (A)
Total	1,667	170	10.2	60	3.6	45	2.7	915	54.9	449	26.9	384	23.0	94	5.6
Population group															
Over 1,000,000	6	2	33.3	2	33.3	0	0.0	1	16.7	2	33.3	3	50.0	0	0.0
500,000–1,000,000 ..	15	2	13.3	0	0.0	0	0.0	3	20.0	10	66.7	7	46.7	2	13.3
250,000–499,999	26	3	11.5	0	0.0	1	3.8	1	3.8	19	73.1	21	80.8	1	3.8
100,000–249,999	76	10	13.2	4	5.3	2	2.6	20	26.3	43	56.6	35	46.1	6	7.9
50,000–99,999	132	11	8.3	3	2.3	3	2.3	52	39.4	52	39.4	46	34.8	7	5.3
25,000–49,999	215	21	9.8	7	3.3	8	3.7	114	53.0	61	28.4	55	25.6	12	5.6
10,000–24,999	441	40	9.1	12	2.7	14	3.2	245	55.6	126	28.6	105	23.8	22	5.0
5,000–9,999	340	32	9.4	10	2.9	6	1.8	193	56.8	79	23.2	69	20.3	21	6.2
2,500–4,999	323	40	12.4	19	5.9	7	2.2	228	70.6	43	13.3	29	9.0	15	4.6
Under 2,500	93	9	9.7	3	3.2	4	4.3	58	62.4	14	15.1	14	15.1	8	8.6
Geographic division															
New England	136	14	10.3	9	6.6	3	2.2	79	58.1	30	22.1	32	23.5	7	5.1
Mid-Atlantic	132	13	9.8	3	2.3	1	0.8	92	69.7	23	17.4	14	10.6	8	6.1
East North Central ...	343	26	7.6	9	2.6	3	0.9	206	60.1	83	24.2	71	20.7	17	5.0
West North Central ...	262	18	6.9	4	1.5	8	3.1	144	55.0	65	24.8	70	26.7	14	5.3
South Atlantic	307	58	18.9	19	6.2	10	3.3	151	49.2	79	25.7	72	23.5	17	5.5
East South Central ...	57	14	24.6	1	1.8	0	0.0	30	52.6	11	19.3	9	15.8	2	3.5
West South Central ..	138	6	4.3	1	0.7	9	6.5	58	42.0	66	47.8	40	29.0	9	6.5
Mountain	111	8	7.2	8	7.2	2	1.8	52	46.8	41	36.9	28	25.2	11	9.9
Pacific Coast	181	13	7.2	6	3.3	9	5.0	103	56.9	51	28.2	48	26.5	9	5.0

issues that go well beyond the economy itself. Physical, social, and environmental issues that are inherent in the economic development process are often included.

At the end of most decades, economic development pundits proclaim that a dramatic shift is occurring in focus and that the upcoming decade will emphasize different industry sectors, with new technologies and initiatives. In truth, although the thrust of economic development today is different from that of yesterday, programmatic transformations have been gradual and are a result of a myriad of factors both within and outside the control of the economic development practitioner.

Shifting Economic Base

Perhaps the greatest external factor influencing economic development has been the steady shift away from manufacturing-dominated economies. In five of the nine geographic divisions, the combined retail and service sectors are anticipated by respondents to equal, if not surpass, manufacturing over the next several years. The gap is narrowing between the percentage of respondents who report economies based in the manufacturing and retail/service sectors during the last five years (23% and 18%, respectively) and those who predict such a base in the next five years (22% predict manufacturing and 21%, retail/service).

This shift away from manufacturing-dominated economies has forced localities to rethink the ways in which economic development services are packaged and provided. Many location-based attractions that may appeal to a manufacturing audience are often quite different from those of interest to the service or retail sectors. While factors such as market access, local resource procurement, and cost sensitivity may be of central importance to each target audience, the degree to which they influence location decisions and help ensure facility operating success varies considerably, not only between these sectors, but within them as well.

A clear indication of shifting focus is in the name of the field itself. As recently as the 1970s, the term *industrial development* was most often applied to the attraction and retention of facility investment. Today, *economic development* is the most widely accepted term, and *industrial development* refers primarily to the provision of manufacturing-specific services.

Competition

Another trend that has greatly influenced the economic development field is the shift away from central-city dependence and the "suburbanization" or "exurbanization" of the American economy. Ever-expanding transportation routes, reliance on telecommunications, and the migration of desirable labor to less costly surroundings have, in combination, had a dramatic impact on decisions to expand or relocate facilities. This phenomenon is particularly evident in the manufacturing sector. No longer do companies need to be within large cities to access the amenities necessary for operating viability. In many instances, the benefits of the operating climate in suburban or exurban locations far outweigh those of large cities.

Perhaps surprisingly, while the threat of suburban or exurban business competition is great, according to survey results, central locations do not fear this competition any more than they fear competition from locations in surrounding states (Table 3/5). By comparison, suburban locations appear most sensitive to competition in immediately surrounding areas, and independent locations focus most on in-state competition.

On average, only 9% of local governments report foreign countries as a source of competition for the attraction of investment. Foreign competition is feared the most in high-cost areas, such as New England, and in those geographic divisions where proximity and access to foreign markets is great, such as in the South Atlantic and Pacific Coast divisions. Central cities and counties are more sensitive to the influence of foreign competition than their suburban or independent counterparts, though far less so than they are to competition within the United States.

Several reasons can be cited to explain why concern over foreign competition is low among local economic developers. First, it is only fairly recently that the importance of globalization has entered into the consciousness of local economic development professionals, excluding those within the nation's largest cities. Second, inland communities and those that do not border other countries generally have had little international exposure. Even today, international linkages in local economic development programs often are limited to the relatively small presence of multinational companies within the jurisdictions.

Barriers to Economic Development

While by no means a new phenomenon, efforts on the part of business to reduce ongoing op-

Table 3/5 COMPETITION IN ATTRACTING INVESTMENT

	No. reporting (A)	Nearby local governments		Other local governments within the state		Local governments in surrounding states		Other states		Foreign countries		Other	
		No.	% of (A)	No.	% of (A)	No.	% of (A)	No.	% of (A)	No.	% of (A)	No.	% of (A)
Total	1669	1241	74.4	1162	69.6	749	44.9	755	45.2	155	9.3	57	3.4
Population group													
Over 1,000,000	7	3	42.9	5	71.4	3	42.9	6	85.7	2	28.6	0	.0
500,000–1,000,000	15	10	66.7	10	66.7	11	73.3	12	80.0	5	33.3	1	6.7
250,000–499,999	26	17	65.4	13	50.0	22	84.6	20	76.9	4	15.4	2	7.7
100,000–249,999	81	54	66.7	56	69.1	49	60.5	56	69.1	10	12.3	1	1.2
50,000–99,999	136	93	68.4	109	80.1	68	50.0	88	64.7	16	11.8	4	2.9
25,000–49,999	220	165	75.0	158	71.8	103	46.8	107	48.6	19	8.6	7	3.2
10,000–24,999	446	343	76.9	314	70.4	208	46.6	198	44.4	41	9.2	14	3.1
5,000–9,999	335	246	73.4	230	68.7	142	42.4	130	38.8	22	6.6	12	3.6
2,500–4,999	314	247	78.7	208	66.2	114	36.3	112	35.7	26	8.3	12	3.8
Under 2,500	89	63	70.8	59	66.3	29	32.6	26	29.2	10	11.2	4	4.5
Geographic division													
New England	138	103	74.6	89	64.5	53	38.4	76	55.1	18	13.0	8	5.8
Mid-Atlantic	123	96	78.0	68	55.3	27	22.0	46	37.4	6	4.9	11	8.9
East North Central	343	272	79.3	235	68.5	153	44.6	147	42.9	27	7.9	7	2.0
West North Central	269	188	69.9	190	70.6	150	55.8	133	49.4	19	7.1	11	4.1
South Atlantic	311	227	73.0	239	76.8	161	51.8	145	46.6	32	10.3	10	3.2
East South Central	58	41	70.7	33	56.9	33	56.9	27	46.6	5	8.6	1	1.7
West South Central	134	97	72.4	98	73.1	58	43.3	45	33.6	13	9.7	1	.7
Mountain	108	69	63.9	91	84.3	44	40.7	45	41.7	8	7.4	4	3.7
Pacific Coast	185	148	80.0	119	64.3	70	37.8	91	49.2	27	14.6	4	2.2
Metro status													
Central	176	114	64.8	123	69.9	116	65.9	121	68.8	25	14.2	8	4.5
Suburban	763	664	87.0	470	61.6	263	34.5	279	36.6	66	8.7	30	3.9
Independent	730	463	63.4	569	77.9	370	50.7	355	48.6	64	8.8	19	2.6

erating costs continue to influence decisions about location and, correspondingly, influence the efforts of economic development professionals. Indigenous cost variations between locations are often the driving force in a company's decision to uproot or expand in one community rather than another. But where cost comparisons were once based primarily on easily quantifiable measures (such as labor, real estate, utilities, and taxes), today's sophisticated site seeker looks at many indirect or ancillary factors that often have a pronounced short-term and long-term impact on their bottom line. Government responsiveness, flexibility of regulatory and permit functions, labor quality and dependability, property and infrastructure readiness, quality of life, and community appeal for labor recruitment are but a few of the critical issues that are difficult to quantify but factor heavily into a company's ultimate operating cost structure. When asked to indicate what they believe to be the greatest barriers to economic development in their respective locations, the top four answers of survey respondents were lack of capital, availability of land, cost of land, and a lack of skilled labor (Figure 3/1).

In addition to cost cutting through facility location, facility investment decisions and organization reengineering are having a noticeable impact on local economic development. In efforts to improve the capacity, utilization, and efficiency of their existing facilities (particularly those that are manufacturing related), many companies are going through the exercise of facility consolidation, often at the expense of older facilities in more expensive locations. Such actions are reflected in the fact that survey respondents within urban locations expect manufacturing presence to drop appreciably over the next five years, whereas in suburban and independent locations they expect a range from relative stagnation to a modest increase.

PROGRAM FUNDING

Needless to say, a locality's capacity to fund economic development has a direct impact on its ability to attract investment and provide meaningful, lasting services to its existing business community. The most effective and most common economic development programs and

initiatives are long term in nature. As the need for steady and controlled economic development continues to gain importance, so does the community's financial commitment to its economic development programs.

Although the funding of local economic development programs has come a long way in recent years, it is still hampered by common procedures that limit long-term program stability and continuity. First, local economic development programs tend to be funded, like most government programs, on an annual basis. Thus their funding cycles often do not coincide with the implementation periods of the programs that they are intended to fund. Further, although overall funding may continue from year to year, the funding levels often fluctuate greatly and are influenced by political considerations. Second, funding, especially as a result of fund-raising, is often specific to a particular economic development activity and not designated for discretionary use within the broader program. Targeted funding tends to discourage joint or leveraged activities and eliminate beneficial economies of scale that may otherwise occur. Third, financial contributions for local eco-

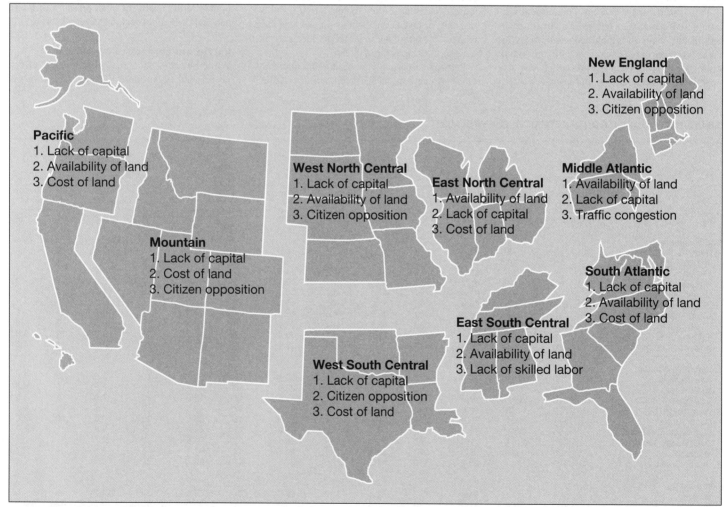

Figure 3/1   *Top barriers to local economic development*

nomic development are derived mostly from public sector sources, with private sector funding often considered supplemental. This imbalance tends to lessen private sector ownership in the economic development process. It also ties program funding to considerable public scrutiny and to the uncertainty of a local government's annual budget.

Local Government Economic Development Budgets

A rough correlation exists between community population size and the existence and amount of economic development budgets. All responding local governments 250,000 and over in population have funds dedicated exclusively to economic development (not shown). The percentage of communities with dedicated economic development budgets declines steadily as population size decreases. Additionally, according to survey results, annual economic development budgets for the largest communities, those 250,000 and over in population, averaged over $3 million in 1994. By comparison, communities with populations under 25,000 show average economic development budgets below $250,000. Economic development funding in central cities and counties averages six to twelve times that of suburban and independent locations, respectively. One explanation for this disparity is that programs within large cities tend to emphasize public sector contributions tied to relatively balanced tax revenue generation. Smaller, less urbanized communities may be hampered by a tax base that is both smaller and more reliant on residential taxpayers than on higher paying commercial or industrial taxpayers.

A comparison of funding levels among the

Table 3/6 FY 1994 ECONOMIC DEVELOPMENT BUDGET

	FY 1994	
	No. reporting	Average ($)
Total	1,251	316,346
Population group		
Over 1,000,000	5	3,724,000
500,000–1,000,000 ..	14	2,347,857
250,000–499,999	25	3,421,354
100,000–249,999	71	797,046
50,000–99,999	119	516,222
25,000–49,999	178	283,042
10,000–24,999	341	137,212
5,000–9,999	242	104,289
2,500–4,999	204	41,595
Under 2,500	52	188,649
Geographic division		
New England	85	53,036
Mid-Atlantic	58	277,202
East North Central ...	264	272,589
West North Central ...	227	302,097
South Atlantic	249	341,181
East South Central ...	41	369,501
West South Central ..	94	158,023
Mountain	90	275,165
Pacific Coast	143	663,638
Metro status		
Central	152	1,378,440
Suburban	518	227,880
Independent	581	117,355

geographic divisions indicates that economic development programs in the New England and West South Central divisions are woefully underrepresented and that programs that do exist tend to be underfunded relative to their counterparts. According to survey results, FY 1994 economic development funding averaged a scant $53,000 per local government in New England, and $158,000 in the West South Central division jurisdictions, compared with a national average of $316,000 (Table 3/6). Only 65% of New England locations report having any funds dedicated to economic development, compared to 73% for the West South Central division and the national survey average of 79%. In New England, one of the most significant impediments to public sector funding for economic development programs is citizen opposition. Almost 46% of survey respondents from New England jurisdictions listed this as an economic development barrier, compared with an average of only 34% of respondents nationally.

The Mid-Atlantic division has the lowest percentage of locations funding economic development (47%), but the average economic development budget is $277,000. The South Atlantic division possesses the highest percentage of communities with economic development budgets (86%) as well as the highest level of funding. The Mountain division actually has slightly higher percentages of communities with economic development programs; however, the funding level per program is on average more than $65,000 behind that of the South Atlantic division.

Private sector financial contributions to local government economic development marketing efforts are reported by 385 survey respondents (not shown). Of those 385 jurisdictions, 278 provided information on the amount of the contributions, with the average contribution approximately $55,000 per locality. The average private sector contribution is highest in jurisdictions with populations from 500,000 to 1,000,000 ($535,000), in central jurisdictions (approximately $178,000), and in the South Atlantic division ($98,000).

On average, almost half those surveyed expect their economic development budgets to increase over the next five years; only 6% expect budget cuts. South Atlantic division respondents, already laying claim to the second highest average budget, show the highest percentage of respondents (55%) expecting an increase in their economic development budget over the next five years. Local governments in the Mid-Atlantic division, where average 1994 budgets are among the lowest, are least optimistic about receiving additional economic development funding in the next five years.

Funding Sources

Public sector funding is most commonly derived from local tax revenues (Table 3/7). However, funding from outside sources differs greatly by geographic division and population group. Economic development programs in the Mid-Atlantic and East South Central divisions rely heavily on outside funding from federal and state sources. North Central locations, as

well as those in the Pacific division, are far more likely than their counterparts to utilize user-driven programs, such as tax-increment financing and special assessment districts. Further, revenue from bond issues (either general obligation or revenue bonds) is more widely used to fund economic development in the eastern than in the western United States. The use of bonds for economic development is also considerably more common among larger communities. At least 38% of those with populations 250,000 and over use some type of bond, whereas in communities under 25,000 in population, less than 10% do so. Conversely, with the exception of communities 500,000 and over in population, the smallest communities are most likely to use state-level funding for their economic development programs. On average, the larger the community, the more balanced its use of funding sources. Urban locations, for instance, are far more likely to combine many sources of funding for local economic development than is customary among their suburban or independent counterparts.

PROGRAM STAFFING

The level of program funding is typically a good determinant of economic development staff size. Governments in the New England and West South Central divisions have both the smallest economic development budgets and the smallest number of individuals dedicated principally to local economic development. Conversely, the Pacific Coast and East South Central divisions possess, on average, both the highest budgets and the largest economic development staffs.

Population size, which frequently influences funding level, is a critical factor in economic development staffing. Although the average number of economic development staff in reporting jurisdictions is 2.8, the largest communities, those with populations 250,000 and over, on average have 15 or more employees who dedicate at least 70% of their time to economic development (not shown). In contrast, economic development programs in communities under 50,000 population average fewer than two staff members with 70% of their time dedicated to economic development. Similarly, central jurisdictions average over twice as many economic development professionals as suburban locations and almost four times as many as independent locations. Although size of professional staff often determines the amount of effort that an economic development organization is able to put forth, this is not always the case. Certain program activities are far more labor intensive than others. For instance, economic development organizations that use a sizable portion of their funds for the leveraging or for the capacity building of other programs may function quite effectively with only a skeleton crew. Programs with a large contingent of private sector involvement often rely heavily upon volunteer assistance, frequently on an ad hoc basis in lieu of the availability of full-time individuals.

Table 3/7   FUNDING ECONOMIC DEVELOPMENT

	No. reporting (A)	Local revenues/ general fund % of (A)	Federal grants-in-aid % of (A)	State grants-in-aid % of (A)	General obligation bonds % of (A)	Revenue bonds % of (A)	Tax increment financing districts % of (A)	Special assessment districts % of (A)	Other % of (A)
Total	1,558	86.5	28.1	39.6	8.0	11.4	24.7	8.7	14.7
Population group									
Over 1,000,000	7	85.7	57.1	71.4	14.3	42.9	28.6	14.3	42.9
500,000–1,000,000	15	86.7	53.3	46.7	26.7	46.7	26.7	13.3	13.3
250,000–499,999	26	92.3	57.7	38.5	7.7	38.5	46.2	11.5	7.7
100,000–249,999	81	91.4	37.0	32.1	12.3	12.3	24.7	9.9	23.5
50,000–99,999	130	86.2	33.8	26.9	8.5	25.4	36.9	14.6	14.6
25,000–49,999	210	88.1	26.7	36.2	7.6	11.0	25.2	9.5	16.2
10,000–24,999	411	85.9	28.0	38.0	8.0	9.2	25.5	9.5	16.1
5,000–9,999	309	86.1	26.5	46.0	7.1	9.1	21.0	8.1	14.6
2,500–4,999	292	87.3	21.2	42.5	6.5	6.8	20.9	4.1	9.6
Under 2,500	77	77.9	28.6	46.8	9.1	7.8	19.5	7.8	14.3
Geographic division									
New England	129	88.4	33.3	43.4	5.4	1.6	8.5	3.1	12.4
Mid-Atlantic	103	79.6	37.9	52.4	8.7	9.7	6.8	4.9	12.6
East North Central	327	85.9	26.0	37.3	12.5	11.9	42.8	13.8	10.7
West North Central	264	86.0	27.3	48.5	6.8	14.8	41.3	9.8	14.8
South Atlantic	287	92.0	25.4	38.0	8.4	17.1	6.3	4.2	17.1
East South Central	56	92.9	33.9	60.7	16.1	16.1	3.6	5.4	12.5
West South Central	120	82.5	16.7	24.2	5.8	9.2	6.7	2.5	25.8
Mountain	101	93.1	34.7	33.7	3.0	8.9	16.8	8.9	6.9
Pacific Coast	171	78.9	30.4	29.8	4.1	5.8	42.7	16.4	18.7
Metro status									
Central	175	88.6	53.1	41.1	13.1	22.3	33.7	13.1	19.4
Suburban	687	85.7	18.3	29.4	7.1	9.3	27.1	9.9	13.0
Independent	696	86.8	31.5	49.3	7.6	10.8	20.1	6.3	15.2

Table 3/8   PARTICIPANTS IN ECONOMIC DEVELOPMENT STRATEGY

Classification	No. reporting (A)	City % of (A)	County % of (A)	Chamber of commerce % of (A)	Private business % of (A)	Citizen advisory board/ commission % of (A)	Public/ private partnership % of (A)	Private economic development foundation % of (A)	Utility % of (A)	State government % of (A)	Federal government % of (A)	Other % of (A)
Total	1,670	86.5	49.2	70.5	49.2	51.2	26.4	22.3	30.5	32.8	7.1	8.8
Population group												
Over 1,000,000	7	85.7	100.0	85.7	85.7	71.4	71.4	14.3	57.1	42.9	28.6	42.9
500,000–1,000,000 ..	15	86.7	86.7	80.0	86.7	66.7	80.0	33.3	46.7	20.0	13.3	13.3
250,000–499,999	26	100.0	65.4	92.3	76.9	57.7	57.7	34.6	42.3	11.5	0.0
100,000–249,999	81	82.7	65.4	75.3	59.3	45.7	40.7	30.9	33.3	27.2	11.1	4.9
50,000–99,999	131	84.7	55.7	78.6	58.0	50.4	34.4	23.7	35.9	32.8	9.9	8.4
25,000–49,999	8.8	87.6	51.2	76.5	49.8	61.3	32.3	21.7	32.3	32.7	6.9	8.8
10,000–24,999	444	87.6	47.7	75.0	53.2	55.6	23.9	21.4	30.4	32.9	6.1	9.2
5,000–9,999	336	86.9	50.3	67.6	49.7	46.4	22.3	21.4	29.8	34.8	6.5	9.2
2,500–4,999	319	85.3	40.8	61.8	36.4	44.8	20.4	20.7	26.6	32.6	6.0	8.2
Under 2,500	94	83.0	39.4	51.1	33.0	45.7	16.0	22.3	26.6	29.8	6.4	11.7
Geographic division												
New England	136	79.4	11.8	51.5	46.3	66.2	25.7	19.9	11.0	34.6	5.9	16.2
Mid-Atlantic	126	57.1	54.0	55.6	34.9	32.5	24.6	14.3	23.0	40.5	7.9	19.0
East North Central ...	346	90.8	41.3	68.2	47.1	50.3	28.3	21.1	31.8	28.6	7.2	6.9
West North Central ...	272	94.5	53.3	71.7	48.5	52.2	25.4	34.9	37.5	39.3	7.7	7.0
South Atlantic	305	79.0	74.1	72.5	54.4	52.8	26.9	14.1	28.9	35.4	5.2	6.9
East South Central ...	59	98.3	66.1	72.9	45.8	42.4	23.7	10.2	27.1	44.1	15.3	11.9
West South Central ..	135	93.3	37.0	82.2	44.4	48.9	15.6	31.9	35.6	23.0	2.2	5.2
Mountain	108	88.0	52.8	75.0	57.4	55.6	30.6	25.0	37.0	26.9	5.6	7.4
Pacific Coast	183	94.5	42.6	82.0	56.8	52.5	31.7	21.9	33.3	27.3	10.9	8.2
Metro status												
Central	176	94.3	61.4	81.3	60.2	51.7	50.6	34.1	33.5	32.4	14.2	10.8
Suburban	758	85.1	35.5	66.4	48.8	51.8	22.4	13.9	23.0	27.3	4.5	7.5
Independent	736	86.0	60.5	72.1	46.9	50.4	24.7	28.1	37.5	38.6	8.0	9.6

PRIVATE SECTOR INVOLVEMENT

The drive to ensure long-term economic vitality has prompted the private sector to play an active role in economic development planning and implementation. Though private sector participation in economic development is not a prerequisite for success, a program that lacks private sector input risks failure. As such, the multidisciplinary nature of economic development demands that those involved in the process possess a broad understanding of critical private sector issues and the acumen to respond to problems and opportunities quickly and effectively.

The economic development function has changed immeasurably from the early days of industrial attraction, or "smokestack chasing." Where once the primary responsibility of the organization was simply to provide timely and accurate information on the local business climate, economic developers today wear many hats, ranging from consultant to negotiator to ombudsman. The economic development professional often serves as the prospective business's advocate. This is especially important when dealing with regulatory, permit, training, or financial issues.

Changing demands of the end-user have brought a change in the economic development organization's structure. Today's typical program is an amalgamation of private and public sector resources and individuals working in tandem for the common good of the local economy. While the public sector still dominates the economic development landscape, few local programs can be found today that are not heavily influenced by, if not partnered with, the private sector.

Perhaps the greatest problem with the inclusion of the private sector is one of coordination. In many communities, private sector economic development programs have grown independently from those in the public sector, and periodically they two compete or conflict with one another. But programs that include the private sector in the economic development process have certain distinct advantages over those that are exclusively government operated. Private sector involvement often

1. increases and stabilizes long-term program funding,
2. provides expertise and direction from the end-user perspective, and
3. offers the potential for business-to-business marketing, which can greatly enhance program credibility.

Chambers of commerce provide input into the local economic development process of over 70% of reporting local governments (Table 3/8). Perhaps the fastest evolving private sector participants are utilities. In several southeastern and midwestern states, the capabilities of the largest public utility rival those of the state's economic development organization. Utilities, and often chambers of commerce, are typically regional, and can thus address issues that transcend local political boundaries.

Perhaps surprisingly, respondents on average consider citizens and private businesses more active participants in local economic development planning than state agencies. While state economic development organizations typically possess the financial resources and skills to supplement local efforts, some communities fear that state involvement will dilute local initiative and bring in potential in-state competitors who would otherwise have been excluded. Local governments in the Mid-Atlantic and East South Central divisions report relatively active state economic development agencies, with those least active in the western United States.

A steadily evolving role of many state-level organizations is local capacity building. Rather than dedicate funds to an additional, often duplicative, marketing staff, state-level organizations financially support the educational and training infrastructure, and economic development efforts of local communities. State economic development agencies have considerable resources at their disposal, especially information, funds, personnel, and technology. The agencies that provide the greatest value to local economic developers are highly networked with other state agencies and regulatory bodies and are able to share and dedicate resources from many sources. While macro policy- and direction-setting is an important function of these entities, ability to support instead of compete with local development activities is typically the state agency's preferred role.

Private sector participation is far more common among large communities than among small ones. Several factors may contribute to this phenomenon, including the smaller communities' lack of a sizable base of corporate decision-makers and other parties likely to contribute to local programs. Private sector involvement, whether it be through individual businesses, chambers of commerce, or public/private partnerships, is far more common in urban areas than in suburban or independent locations.

Private sector participation takes a variety of forms. Many communities utilize the expertise of their business leadership to address issue-specific concerns that existing and prospective companies may have. One strategy that is becoming more popular is executive loan programs, where companies dedicate experts in specific fields on a part-time basis to support their local government's economic development programs. Under this program, banks may provide financial analysts or grant packagers, corporate or divisional headquarters may loan staff with marketing and promotional expertise, and real-estate companies may dedicate individuals to assist with industrial property development.

Educational systems and institutions are fast emerging as contributors to economic development programs. Vocational/technical establishments have long been key to the economic development process, but primary educational systems and local universities and colleges have not participated until fairly recently. Given the emphasis that businesses place on the availability of skilled and dependable labor, these en-

tities can play a vital role in a community's economic development success. In addition to providing labor and coordinating future educational programs with local businesses, institutions of higher learning are beginning to provide valuable research and technology transfer services and leadership in a host of other critical areas.

Among the entities that remain woefully underutilized in most local economic development programs are labor unions, public libraries, and certain service sector businesses, such as accounting and legal services. In assembling active participants in the economic development process, the most savvy communities recognize the value of focusing on, and gaining the involvement of, their primary "stakeholder" organizations—those that have a stake in the community's economic future and can contribute to its progress. A partial list of local public and private stakeholder groups would include:

Chambers of commerce
Civic organizations
Economic development organizations
Educational organizations (primary and secondary)
Financial institutions
Government officials, regulators, and planners
Industry and service sector leaders
Public libraries
Real-estate developers and builders
Training institutions
Unions
Utilities

ECONOMIC DEVELOPMENT PLANS

The principal role of an economic development organization is to influence the direction of its local economy by fostering stability and growth. The intent of strategic planning within economic development is to ensure that the process is conducted in a logical and systematic fashion, emphasizing efficiency and effectiveness, in the context of predefined community goals and objectives. Whether the focus is singular in nature—stressing stability, diversity, or expansion—or multidirectional, the emphasis should be placed on applying the right level and mix of resources to enhance the location's economic climate and quality of life.

Strategic economic development planning is the only formal process that encourages participants to concentrate on critical issues, leverage support in a systematic fashion, implement a controlled set of targeted action steps, measure and monitor program effectiveness, and alter activities and emphasis in response to changing circumstances.

Given the undeniable value that planning adds to total economic development, one would expect an economic development plan to be at the core of every community's program; however, this is not the case. While most local leaders tout the virtues of strategic planning, only 41% of all cities and counties report the use of a formal, written economic development plan (Figure 3/2). Economic development planning is far more common in local governments with populations 250,000 and above and in the Pacific Coast and Mountain divisions. Localities in the Mid-Atlantic and West South Central divisions are among the least likely to carry out economic development planning, a fact that could hamper their ability to enhance their respective economies.

Approximately two-thirds of all suburban locations surveyed do not utilize economic development plans, as compared to urban and independent locations, where economic development planning is considerably more common. Substantial economic growth in many suburban locations has occurred primarily as a result of proximity to more costly, perhaps less desirable, urban hubs and a position that enables them to capture investment from outmigrating businesses. But the lack of economic development planning for some suburban locations has resulted in severe labor shortages, congestion, and other problems associated with an inability to control or manage this rapid growth.

Loosely defined, strategic planning for economic development comprises three distinct yet mutually dependent phases: formulation, implementation, and evaluation. Although all phases are critical, economic development agencies routinely emphasize implementation, often to the virtual exclusion of the other two phases. Strategic plans should be updated regularly and treated as functional documents that facilitate establishment of priorities, confrontation of difficult choices, and regular self-examination.

Highly effective local economic development plans are those that are customized to address and capitalize on unique locational characteristics and operating circumstances. At the foundation of all economic development programs should be a keen understanding of a location's position relative to key competitors and, from the perspective of the target audience, whether

the audience is existing or prospective businesses. All too often economic development plans prescribe a course of action with little basis in either community capabilities or the needs of the end-user. These are the plans that produce minimal, if any, positive results.

The participants in the planning process are as important as the plan itself. Those involved at the inception of the planning process are typically the ones who develop the strongest sense of ownership and remain the plan's staunchest supporters. Formal public-private partnerships are prime examples of this phenomenon. Economic development programs in communities where the public-private sector bond has been forged during plan formulation are typically

characterized by broad business and government involvement, smoother coordination, less duplication of effort, and a longer-term vision for the future.

Increasingly, inclusion of the general public in the formulation phase of the plan is a way in which communities garner widespread economic development awareness and support. In general, if the desires of the citizenry are reflected in the plan, the community in the aggregate is more likely to back its ongoing implementation. However, excessive community involvement can tend to slow or impede the planning process. It also can provide added opportunity for criticism and opposition. This is no more evident than in New England, where

The most successful economic development plans are those that possess the same basic elements as corporate business plans. At a minimum, they include:

1. *well-researched situation or competitor analyses,*
2. *opportunity analyses,*
3. *realistic and measurable goals and objectives,*
4. *logical action steps,*
5. *task-specific budgets and staffing models,*
6. *performance monitoring and measuring mechanisms,*
7. *avenues for plan adjustment or realignment.*

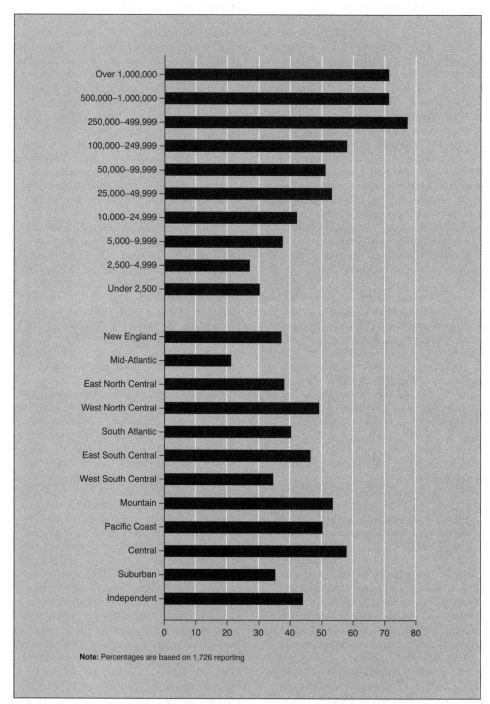

Note: Percentages are based on 1,726 reporting

Figure 3/2   *Local governments with written economic development plans*

citizen advisory boards are the second greatest participants (beyond city government) in developing economic development strategy and are among the most frequently cited impediments to economic development success.

Once community issues and desires are clearly understood, organizational goals and objectives can be formed. It is not uncommon to see goals and objectives mentioned interchangeably in a strategic plan, though actually they are quite different. Goals reflect the aspirations of program participants and stakeholders. Objectives are targets that provide a framework and preferably a means for measuring specific actions.

Historically, the most common objectives among economic development organizations have been to create jobs and to generate tax revenue. Today, however, many communities are more concerned with labor shortages, outmigration of their best, brightest, and most educated residents, and fragility of economies too heavily dependent upon one industry sector or one institution. As such, objectives may have additional qualifiers, such as the quality or skill level of the job created, or the type of company attracted and its potential compatibility with existing companies, suppliers, and consumers.

While all objectives should be measurable, even if subjectively, economic development programs that state their targets in absolute terms often run the risk of undue scrutiny and failure. For instance, if the success of a program is measured solely by its ability to attract a certain number of firms or create a certain number of jobs, failure to achieve these numbers could result in unmet community expectations and, quite possibly, a reduction in funding. Furthermore, although effective economic development organizations have the ability to influence company decision-making, they neither control the ultimate decision nor the magnitude of the investment. In fact, careful scrutiny of apparent economic development "successes" in many high-growth communities may reveal that market trends and natural industry migration patterns are the driving location forces rather than the influence of local economic development programs. Still, the most astute organizations know how to leverage these forces and use them to their advantage.

Implementing the Economic Development Plan

The success of any economic development program is contingent upon its ability to identify realistic strategic actions that satisfy the demands of the targeted audience and at the same time comply with the prescribed objectives of the community. Among the difficulties in devising a game plan is matching available resources with local demands. Local economic development organizations often make the mistake of allowing community desires to dictate the strategies selected. The end result may be the selection of far more strategies than a city or county has resources to implement.

In an attempt to simplify the process, communities often distinguish between programs devised to assist their existing industry base versus those devised to entice new facility locations and accompanying location investment. In actuality, these efforts are inseparable because one of the most critical site selection factors is a community's ability to satisfy business needs once the move has taken place. In addition, many of the same principles, methods, and resources applied to one activity are directly transferable to the other.

Only 344 local governments report a written *business attraction* plan, and slightly fewer indicate *written retention* plans (297). Similarly, 1,337 local governments indicate the methods they use to attract business, and slightly fewer (1,204) provide information on their retention methods. On average, attraction programs are still more widely utilized than retention programs, though the gap is clearly narrowing.

Business Retention

Formal business retention programs are typically, and understandably, more common in older economies that are characterized by real or perceived compelling locational disadvantages that contribute to the pronounced outmigration of their businesses, particularly their manufacturers. For instance, while the Mid-Atlantic and New England divisions' resource dedication to business retention is, on average, less than that of other divisions, it is greater than that which they dedicate to business attraction (Figure 3/3). The greatest disparity between retention and attraction is, however, found in the South Atlantic and Mountain divisions jurisdictions, where, on average, the latter focus receives considerably more emphasis.

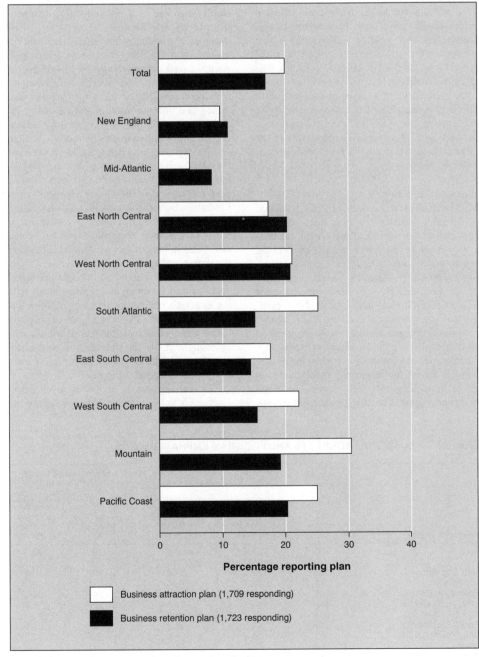

Figure 3/3 *Business attraction and retention plans*

Existing industry programs, also known as retention programs, have seen a marked increase in popularity over the last two decades. The intent of these programs is to stimulate or support local economic development through efforts that help existing industry enhance its competitiveness and increase sales, employment, and profitability.

Effective existing industry programs are becoming increasingly important to local economic development efforts. Competition over the attraction of industry is more fierce than ever, and the frequency of company expansion through new facility development, especially within manufacturing, is considerably less than it once was. On average, over 75% of a community's job growth is generated from companies already residing within its boundaries. Against a backdrop of increased competition, decreased facility attraction opportunities, and ever-increasing foreign competition for U.S. company investment, many economic development agencies are turning their attention inward to tend to those businesses of most importance to their long-term viability.

As the name suggests, retention programs are heavily skewed toward preventing local firms from relocating. While most retention efforts tend to be reactive in nature, it is those that are preventive that stand the greatest chance of success. Once a firm decides to relocate, more often than not this decision is unchangeable. The local economic development challenge is to help foster a business climate that satisfies the needs of the business base and an array of existing industry programs and resources that lessen the temptation to move elsewhere.

The primary goals of most retention programs are to promote company stability, longevity and, where possible, growth. While typically not as critical for retention as for business attraction programs, increased jobs and tax revenue generation for the local community are often retention objectives. The success of retention programs may be measured by the number of jobs and amount of tax revenue prevented from leaving the local community. Calculating this can be tricky because it is difficult to establish links between economic development efforts and existing businesses that have not relocated.

When conducted in a comprehensive fashion, retention programs can serve as an accurate barometer of a location's business climate. Eliciting the input and opinion of a community's own businesses is the most effective mechanism for learning about important operating issues or problems that they may be experiencing. But determining the extent of local business satisfaction must be done with caution. A business leader's perspective, exposure to competing locations, facility working conditions, and a myriad of other issues can skew impressions of a local operating environment.

Strong retention programs are excellent complements to business attraction efforts. The importance of local government attention and customized service to a prospective investor cannot be overstated. In addition to the testi-

monial value that can be realized by having satisfied businesses, a solid working relationship between retention and attraction speaks volumes about the way in which the prospect will be treated once the decision to locate has been made.

The benefits of a successful retention program far outweigh its costs, but costs do exist. On average, retention related activities are considerably more time and labor intensive than those dedicated to attraction. In the latter, the focus is often skewed toward promoting and generating the awareness of a location's business climate advantages. With the former, however, considerable personal attention becomes the norm. All-consuming projects for local businesses, such as regulatory assistance, trade development aid, skill enhancement, and infrastructure improvement measures can quickly convert a retention professional into an extension of the client company's staff.

A problem commonly voiced by retention professionals, particularly those whose task is fund-raising and program justification, is that retention efforts are perceived to lack "sex appeal." Whereas the attraction of a large labor-intensive company is a newsworthy event and often credited to local economic development efforts, the retention of a company already in existence may be viewed as merely a temporary measure with no net gain. Ironically, it is the latter success that is usually far more beneficial to the local economy.

Business Attraction
Marketing cities and counties for the attraction of desirable industry has long been, and will continue to be, a vital element of local economic development. The basic premise behind business attraction programs is that communities are seen as products. As the consumer, corporate site seekers will shop for the most advantageous, highest quality, lowest cost product that is responsive to their long-term needs.

Given the magnitude and steady proliferation of competition for the attraction of businesses, communities are constantly striving for unique ways in which to "package" themselves and create a uniquely appealing identity. Evidence of this packaging is readily apparent in the ways

communities describe themselves and the messages they attempt to convey.

Although no business attraction program can offer guaranteed results, if properly focused, supported, and implemented, the benefits of such a program can be substantial. While some question the value and effectiveness of expending substantial resources to attract businesses, much anecdotal evidence indicates that, if carried out properly, such programs can be quite beneficial. Communities that poll their newly located businesses to learn their reasons for choosing the new location occasionally learn that it was a particular promotional activity that sparked a prospect's interest and led to further investigation.

The marketing of a location has led to an all-out war between communities dueling for a limited number of facility locations. As the survey results indicate, cities and counties are no longer simply competing with jurisdictions of similar character and proximity. The competitive playing field for many of even the smallest locations has widened into other states and divisions, and for large locations, competition stretches well beyond the country's borders.

When applied to local marketing campaigns, the term *competitive advantage* is overused and, more often than not, used improperly. Most locations will flaunt as their competitive advantages a high-quality workforce, central location, and pro-business attitude. These are hollow expressions when not supported by meaningful, quantifiable evidence and placed in the proper context. Often a location's true competitive advantage, whether it be a characteristic of the physical, economic, or political environment, is either only partially recognized, masked behind other, less important factors, or directed toward the wrong audience.

It is the act of identifying the right marketing audience and matching its operating needs with the location's operating climate capabilities that is the linchpin of a business attraction program. Given the range of location options and the specific nature of site selector needs, a generic approach to marketing may do little more than confuse its intended audience.

The challenge for the economic development marketer is to learn the specific needs of the site

Table 3/9   BUSINESS PROSPECTS AND PROGRAM EMPHASIS

Geographic division	No. reporting (A)	Current business prospects		Emphasis on attracting nonmanufacturing business	
		Manufacturing % of (A)	Nonmanufacturing % of (A)	No. reporting (B)	More than moderate emphasis % of (B)
Total	935	37.8	62.2	1,396	26.7
New England	73	34.2	65.8	107	17.8
Mid-Atlantic	70	21.4	78.6	91	29.7
East North Central	194	46.4	53.6	295	25.1
West North Central	156	44.9	55.1	229	22.7
South Atlantic	173	41.6	58.4	261	29.5
East South Central	32	43.8	56.2	51	21.6
West South Central	85	36.5	63.5	122	23.8
Mountain	60	25.0	75.0	91	24.2
Pacific Coast	92	22.8	77.2	149	40.9

selector and then craft a direct response to satisfying them. This is the intent of a well-thought-out target marketing campaign. By dissecting and evaluating the typical needs of potential industry groups, the economic developer will be better able to focus only on those sectors most suited to what the location has to offer. By doing so, use of marketing resources can be limited to those industries and companies with the greatest likelihood of investing locally.

In the past, the primary rationale for communities to engage in business attraction efforts was to boost local employment. A secondary rationale was typically to expand and diversify the local tax base. While these are still important goals, they are by no means the only ones. Some communities may turn to business attraction as a means to fill a local supplier or consumer gap to benefit an existing industry. Others may do so to introduce new technologies or to capitalize better on available workforce skills, underutilized economic development potential, or job training programs. Regardless of the rationale, the ultimate goal of business attraction is to match the needs and capabilities of the community with those of the prospective business investor and to foster a relationship in which both benefit from what the other has to offer.

Investment Targeting

Economic development organizations have been very slow to alter their target focus in response to economic shifts. Although manufacturing is no longer the sole focus of the economic development profession, the emphasis of business attraction programs is still on the manufacturing sector. Survey responses to questions about business prospects show that 62% of all business prospects today are generated from sectors other than manufacturing (Table 3/9). In three divisions, the Mid-Atlantic, Pacific, and Mountain, nonmanufacturing prospect activity exceeds 75% of the total activity. This suggests that although the *focus* of business attraction is on the manufacturing sector, the *successes* are derived from other sectors. The greatest amount of manufacturing prospect activity is found in the East North Central division. However, even in this division, nonmanufacturing prospects exceed half the total. The percent of nonmanufacturing prospect activity tends to be highest in the northeast and western United States, as manufacturing continues its migration to the southeastern and central sections of the United States.

Even with the overwhelming evidence that manufacturing activity is declining in prominence, local economic development efforts remain heavily skewed in favor of the attraction of companies in this sector. Only 27% of all respondents put more than moderate emphasis on nonmanufacturing businesses in their business attraction programs. The Pacific Coast division respondents show the second highest percentage reporting current business prospects in nonmanufacturing activity and place the greatest emphasis on attracting business outside

the manufacturing sector. Approximately 41% of jurisdictions responding from the Pacific Coast division emphasize nonmanufacturing in their attraction efforts, compared with 24% of localities responding from the neighboring Mountain division.

Although numerous opportunities remain for economic growth through manufacturing-sector development, the sector as a whole has expanded little in the last 20 years. In contrast, the service sector has virtually doubled during this period.

Economic development organizations have begun to take notice of the benefits of focusing on the service sector, but to many of them, identifying viable targets within this rapidly expanding audience remains a mystery. Whereas manufacturing targets break down neatly along industry lines, the service sector is much more difficult to segment. Standard Industrial Classification (SIC) codes that precisely categorize industries by product are of limited value in evaluating service industries. Segmentation of service industries along functional lines, such as information processing or telemarketing, will enable economic development organizations to understand better the factors that influence service sector location decisions. This, in turn, will allow them to position and market themselves accordingly.

Tourism and hospitality development may, in fact, be the next wave of economic development within the service sector. Successful strategies designed to enhance local tourism and hospitality industries often result in the attraction of such business amenities as hotels, restaurants, and conference centers that are of importance to the corporate decision-maker. Although the jobs created tend to be lower paying than those within traditional manufacturing or office settings, the multiplier benefits that ripple through the local economy can be sizable. Only 6% of the survey respondents report tourism/hospitality companies as active business prospects, but over 48% state that this sector is a focus of their economic development programs. Not surprisingly, in the Mountain, South Atlantic, and Pacific Coast divisions, where the tourism and hospitality industries are already an economic staple, the percentage of localities focusing on these industries is considerably higher than in other divisions.

PERFORMANCE MEASUREMENT

Establishing and monitoring performance objectives is critical to a local government's effectiveness. Today there is a renewed interest in performance measurement at all levels of government. Spurred in part by tough economic conditions and taxpayer skepticism about service quality, public officials are becoming increasingly committed to demonstrating what is being accomplished with public dollars.

Performance measures play an integral role in the three administrative functions of nearly every government program—planning, budgeting, and management. Planning involves for-

mulating program goals and objectives, defining action steps, projecting revenues and expenses, etc. To develop and utilize performance measures in the planning function, agencies must have plans. Only 41% of the survey respondents have written economic development plans, 17% have written business retention plans, and 20% have written business attraction plans. As previously discussed, the importance of such planning cannot be overstated, and survey respondents themselves support this point. As the survey data indicate, organizations that have had written economic development, business retention, and business attraction plans in place have experienced stronger growth in their economic bases over the past five years than those agencies without plans (Figure 3/4). Similarly, local governments that have plans in place today expect stronger growth in their economic bases over the next five years than those that do not. Although there is no concrete evidence that having an economic development plan guarantees success, survey respondents from localities with these plans have experienced and anticipate future programmatic achievements.

The budgeting function allocates financial resources among competing programs and services. As an example, the survey found that only 47% of the respondents conduct cost/benefit analyses before offering business incentives, and only 28% conduct cost/benefit analyses after offering business incentives (Figure 3/5). Again, although perhaps not surprising, this finding is disturbing. At a minimum, one would expect that the same number of agencies that conduct cost/benefit analyses before offering incentives would conduct analyses afterward to determine the effectiveness of the incentives and the accuracy of their original estimates. Such information would certainly be useful for making similar decisions in the future.

The management function typically focuses on the implementation of programs and the dedication of resources intended to achieve program objectives. According to survey results, only 17% of respondents use performance measures to assess and manage their economic development programs. Although unfortunate, given the amount of dollars involved and the importance of economic development programs, this finding is not surprising. It is generally consistent among most government programs because there are so many obstacles involved in establishing and maintaining meaningful performance measurement systems. Developing and implementing a system of performance measures is not easy. Data collection and integrity, staff resistance, and the types of measures to use are just a few of the challenges. Each of these problems is discussed below.

Performance measures require a consistent flow of reliable operational and financial data. Many economic development organizations lack the organizational and technical infrastructure required to provide such information. Even with such systems, data must be periodically audited to ensure integrity and accuracy. Since investments in operational and financial systems can be costly, governments must strike a compromise between the benefits of a high-quality performance measurement system and the costs of data collection and integrity.

The use of performance measures may be challenged and resisted by economic development managers and staff. Managers may feel threatened by measures for a variety of reasons. First and foremost is the increased accountability and capacity to be held to specific standards that often follow the implementation of performance measures. Such resistance can be valid, however, when the performance being measured is not within the direct control of the manager. But resistance can be entirely or partially overcome through the participation of staff in the selection and development of performance measures and the use of explanatory or qualitative data to explain external data or deviations from goals.

In general, there are four types of performance measures:

1. *Input measures* focus on resources needed to provide a program or service (e.g. expenditures, full-time equivalent personnel).
2. *Output measures* gauge the level of activity in providing a program or service (e.g. workload measures).
3. *Efficiency measures* gauge the cost (in dollars or personnel hours) per unit of output or outcome.
4. *Outcome measures* focus of whether a program or service is meeting its goals; used most often to evaluate program quality and effectiveness.

Of the respondents who use performance measures, 34% use input measures, 63% use output measures, and 62% use efficiency measures. In assessing the effectiveness of business incentives, for instance, many respondents measure the amount of job creation and local facility and labor investment provided by the targeted business

Most organizations plan, budget, and manage their resources based on input, output, and efficiency data. Ideally, however, outcome information should be used, since such information relates directly to program objectives and priorities. But if resources are to be allocated based on program results, reliable outcome data must be collected. This is a difficult task for several reasons. First, there is often disagreement among stakeholders regarding the objectives of the programs or services. Unless consensus can be achieved, there likely will be different interpretations of performance outcome data. Second, outcomes tend to be difficult and expensive to measure compared to inputs and outputs. In situations where there are complementary or related programs, it is often unclear which program has produced the actual outcome. In addition, economic development outcomes often do not occur for several years, making it difficult to link them back to financial resources for budgeting purposes. Finally, whether or not an outcome has been achieved is often deter-

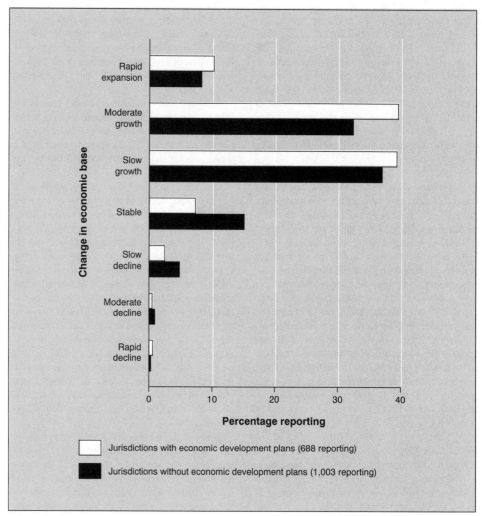

Figure 3/4   *Projected change in economic base in jurisdictions with and without economic development plans*

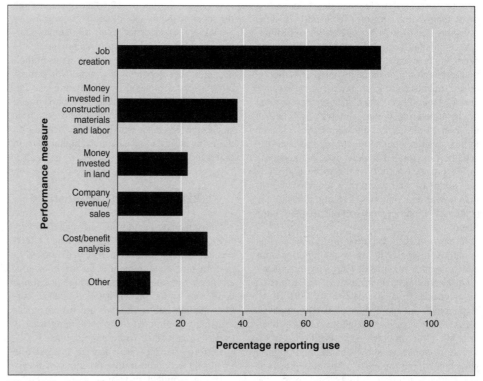

Figure 3/5   *Methods of measuring effectiveness of business incentives*

mined by public perceptions, changes in public behavior, or other qualitative indicators.

Nearly 87% of the respondents surveyed indicate that they use local government revenues to fund their economic development programs. As the public clamors for increasing accountability and improved services, performance measures will become more and more popular or, at a minimum, necessary evils. For measures to lead to program and service improvements, however, they must become integral parts of the planning, budgeting, and management functions and processes.

CONCLUSION

The changing nature of the economic development landscape is making it more difficult for professionals in this field to satisfy the needs of their respective communities. Businesses are demanding a higher and more customized level of government service. Funding sources and levels are inconsistent at best, with widespread budget cuts continuing to impede long-term program development and continuity. Competition for the attraction of desirable business investment is quite high and growing; increasing globalization of local and national economics is only exacerbating this condition. These constraints are coming at a time when the call for economic development program justification, demonstrable results, and accountability has never been louder.

The challenges facing economic development programs are further complicated by the relatively poor state of economic development planning at the local level. Fewer than half the survey respondents indicate they possess a formal written economic development plan to guide their efforts. Such plans are critical for well-focused, sustainable approaches. Without formal plans, local governments are far more likely to waste precious resources attempting to attract or retain industries that are not particularly well suited to their environments. In addition, few communities with economic development programs use meaningful performance measures. They therefore lack the ability to determine whether their efforts are satisfactorily achieving their prime objectives.

Survey respondents remain optimistic about the future economic growth of their communities. However, limitations and obstacles that they face suggest that these individuals may encounter difficulty in properly positioning their communities and directing this growth. Ultimately they may fall short of meeting their high expectations.

Local economic development practitioners are well advised to adapt their programs to the environment in which they operate. They should play to the unique strengths of their communities by focusing on those opportunities with the highest probability of success, rather than simply pursuing those that offer the greatest economic reward. Economic developers should expand their focus by incorporating information about international conditions and linkages into their existing activities. Given the high level of competition for investment as well as the multijurisdictional benefits associated with industry attraction and retention, more localities should develop cooperative agreements with neighboring communities to foster economic growth. Better ways to garner private funding and to encourage participation in the local economic development process should be sought. Finally, economic development professionals will see greater, more predictable returns on investments if they systematically plan their economic development strategies, cultivate useful ways to measure performance, and adjust accordingly.

A **4**

Telecommunications in Local Government: Preparing for an Uncertain Future

Anthony G. Cahill
University of Maine

E. Sam Overman
University of Colorado at Denver

Findings

Nearly three-quarters of survey respondents believe that telecommunications advances will have a positive effect on economic development and citizen involvement with government.

Fifty percent of jurisdictions report access to state government databases. Much less common is access to the Internet and use of commercial on-line services.

Local governments feel strongly that they should continue to play a regulatory role in cable television services in their jurisdictions.

In 1990, an article in *The Municipal Year Book* predicted that "by the turn of the century, computers will be ubiquitous [in local governments]."[1] In retrospect, this prediction was far too pessimistic; it became reality in 1994. Data collected by ICMA as well as other groups and organizations have documented the phenomenal growth of computing hardware, software, and applications in local governments of all sizes throughout the United States.[2] In the 14 years since IBM introduced the first mass-market personal computer, the computer revolution has come and gone, superseded by the technology revolution. We have seen a movement away from centralized batch-style computing on large systems, performed upon request by technical-information-systems staff, to decentralized end-user computing. Stand-alone computers are gradually giving way to computers linked by local area and wide area networks and to distributed computing, in which jobs are routed to computers that have processing capacity available, and "massively parallel" computing, in which one PC has five chips that can be used simultaneously to process different jobs.[3] These technologies allow PCs to handle processing that previously would have required a mainframe.

The technology revolution has also affected the *applications* that are used:

The first "computer revolution" was a revolution only in the sense that it consisted of new ways to do what was already being done. Typing correspondence or reports, maintaining financial records, keeping lists of homeowners, or producing mailing labels were the essential but unglamorous tasks to which computers were (and of course still are) put. The second stage of the revolution . . . allowed local governments to consider doing tasks in ways which had not, practically speaking, been possible before [such as] powerful geographic information systems which provide land use planners and zoning officers with . . . information about everything from population density [to] flood plain information . . . .[4]

Despite the enormous impact that computing has had to date, the telecommunications advances now taking place are most likely to affect local governments into the twenty-first century. Telecommunications advances are poised to change radically several aspects of local governments. These advances can best be explained within the context of technological *convergence*. In short, current distinctions among types of technologies will become increasingly blurred. Over the next several years, technology industry leaders and government planners have as their goal the joining of currently separate forms of technology, including communication devices and capabilities. The computer, television, telephone, video, VCR, recorder, and fax will reside in one machine and will carry voice, live and static images, and text. This hybrid machine, which can already be seen in computers that include fax and modem capabilities, will combine processing power and communications abilities.

Another factor contributing to advances in telecommunications and technological convergence is new software that is changing our notion of computing. Common software protocols and operating systems have been developed that allow information sharing over different types of computing/telecommunications devices, including electronic bulletin boards, the Internet, and various commercial on-line services. In addition, these systems enable direct access to thousands of databases across the country and around the globe.

What are some of the uses that local governments will have for telecommunications? The list is long, and it is growing daily. In general, however, advances in telecommunications offer three major uses for local governments:

1. To change the way local governments operate (government functions)
2. To change the way local governments approach the issues of economic development
3. To change the relationship between local government and its citizens

In terms of government functions, advances in telecommunications are already having a significant impact on the way that local governments do business. These advances include accessing information in databases maintained by many jurisdictions and levels of government, transmitting information to and from the field to central computers, video-conferencing, giving citizens the opportunity to use on-line services to apply for permits or pay bills and fines, and communicating via electronic mail.

Technology and telecommunications give American business and industry the option to locate some personnel and facilities anywhere in the country. Local governments can use this mobility to attract industry. Often localities that can offer overhead and a cost of living lower than those in metropolitan areas have been at a disadvantage because they are removed from major centers of commerce. Telecommunication systems are the ally of economic development departments in these localities because of the tremendous flexibility they make possible.

Finally, telecommunications holds the promise of enhancing the links between citizens and their governments. In the electronic village, citizens will no longer be confined to face-to-face interactions with government employees. They will be able to communicate directly with elected and appointed officials through electronic mail. Citizens will be able to listen to forums for candidates for local offices, to question candidates interactively, and to vote electronically. They will be able to check on the availability of books and other sources of information from their local library, which will be connected to libraries across the country and to the Library of Congress. Finally, from their living rooms, residents will be able to communicate effortlessly with their neighbors and friends across the street, across town, or across the globe.

THE NATIONAL CONTEXT

These rapid advances in telecommunications and technology have been recognized by other levels of government, especially the federal government. Both the executive and legislative branches are systematically creating policies to encourage the use of existing telecommunications technologies and to create additional technologies. In 1991, the High Performance Computing Act, sponsored by then-Senator Gore, established the High Performance Computing and Communication (HPCC) Program in the President's Office of Science and Technology Policy. The goal of the HPCC is to develop computing, communications, and software technologies for the twenty-first century and to foster the rapid development and use of high-performance computers and networks throughout the United States.

There are five integrated components to the HPCC Program:

1. The High Performance Computing Systems Program (HPCS) is charged with developing parallel and distributed common computing systems capable of supporting all levels of users–from those at individual workstations, including users of portable computers, through users of the largest-scale highest-performance systems.
2. The National Research and Education Network (NREN) Program supports research and development in computer communications within the research and education community. NREN is to provide support for computer communications and access to high-performance computing centers located across the country and to accelerate the development of networking technologies within the telecommunications industry.
3. The Advanced Software and Technology Algorithms Program is developing prototype solutions to what are called "Grand Challenge" problems in such areas as forecasting weather, improving environmental quality, and building energy-efficient machines.
4. The Information Infrastructure Technology and Applications (IITA) Program supports the application of new computing and communications technologies to such areas as manufacturing, libraries and education, and health care. This program demonstrates how people can use new data and information management technologies—including user interfaces, virtual reality, and image processing—to accomplish their jobs.
5. The Basic Research and Human Resources Program supports research, training, and education in computer science and engineering that will prepare students to develop and use the information highway. This program has established or participated in education opportunities at all levels, such as SuperQuest, Earth Vision, the National High School Honors Program, and Adventures in Supercomputing.

Soon after the passage of this act, the National Information Infrastructure Initiative (NII) was created in 1993, under the direction of Vice President Gore. The NII has a number of major policy goals, including:

1. To promote private-sector investment in the emerging hardware, software, and telecommunications systems across the country
2. To make the resources of the information highway available to all citizens
3. To promote technological innovation in both the private and public sectors
4. To promote seamless, interactive user-driven operations so that the maximum number of individuals without specialized training are able to use the resources of the highway
5. To ensure that information carried over the highway is secure and that the network accurately and reliably carries information
6. To improve the management of the radio-frequency spectrum, which is increasingly the medium of choice for transmission of data over the highway, as well as for traditional radio, television, and similar communications
7. To protect the intellectual property rights of individuals and organizations that choose to transmit over the highway information that they own
8. To coordinate efforts of the national government with other levels of government in the United States as well as with other nations
9. To provide citizens with regular access to information collected by the government and/or contained in government databases

The importance of these developments is that the telecommunications revolution is being managed and directed by the federal government in combination with private industry, largely without the close consultation or involvement of local governments. At a national teleconference on local governments and the information highway, which was held in September 1994, a member of the National Information Infrastructure Initiative Taskforce reported that the taskforce includes only one member from local government, an appointee from the city of Los Angeles.

The telecommunications future envisioned by the federal government includes local governments as full partners, regardless of whether local governments have decided to participate, are prepared to participate, or have even considered participation.

THE CHALLENGES FOR LOCAL GOVERNMENT

Given these technological and governmental factors operating in the environment, how well are local governments preparing to meet the challenges brought by the next phase of the technology revolution? To what extent are local governments using telecommunications technology and applications?

Most evidence about telecommunications in local government has been anecdotal. Municipalities that have begun "cutting-edge" telecommunications projects, such as Blacksburg, Virginia, and Palo Alto, California, have re-

Table 4/1 SURVEY RESPONSE

Classification	No of cities and counties surveyed (A)	No. responding	% of (A)
Total	10,243	1,111	10.9
Population group			
Over 1,000,000	35	0	0.0
500,000–1,000,000	81	2	2.5
250,000–499,999	138	11	8.0
100,000–249,999	386	25	6.5
50,000–99,999	714	49	6.9
25,000–49,999	1,293	88	6.8
10,000–24,999	2,512	150	6.0
5,000–9,999	2,243	251	11.2
2,500–4,999	2,167	231	10.7
Under 2,500	674	304	45.1
Geographic division[1]			
New England	847	103	12.2
Mid-Atlantic	1,326	91	6.9
East North Central	1,786	220	12.3
West North Central	1,337	174	13.0
South Atlantic	1,458	174	11.9
East South Central	834	46	5.5
West South Central	1,216	98	8.1
Mountain	647	89	13.8
Pacific Coast	792	124	15.7
Metro status			
Central	876	122	13.9
Suburban	4,184	496	11.9
Independent	5,183	501	9.7

[1]Geographic divisions: *New England*—the states of Connecticut, Maine, Massachusetts, New Hampshire, Rhode Island, and Vermont; *Mid-Atlantic*—the states of New Jersey, New York, and Pennsylvania; *East North Central*—the states of Illinois, Indiana, Michigan, Ohio, and Wisconsin; *West North Central*—the states of Iowa, Kansas, Minnesota, Missouri, Nebraska, North Dakota, and South Dakota; *South Atlantic*—the states of Delaware, Florida, Georgia, Maryland, North Carolina, South Carolina, Virginia, West Virginia, and the District of Columbia; *East South Central*—the states of Alabama, Kentucky, Mississippi, and Tennessee; *West South Central*—the states of Arkansas, Louisiana, Oklahoma, and Texas; *Mountain*—the states of Arizona, Colorado, Idaho, Montana, Nevada, New Mexico, Utah, and Wyoming; *Pacific Coast*—the states of Alaska, California, Hawaii, Oregon, and Washington.

ceived extensive, well-deserved positive publicity. News about other jurisdictions initiating telecommunications-related projects appears regularly in *Government Technology* and publications by ICMA, Public Technology, Inc., and others. Are these municipalities typical? What can be said about the majority of local governments?

To address these issues, ICMA, in conjunction with Public Technology, Inc. (PTI), the National League of Cities (NLC), and the National Association of Counties (NACo), developed a comprehensive survey of telecommunications-related issues and mailed it to 10,243 cities and counties across the United States during the summer of 1994. Responses were received from 1,111 local governments, for a response rate of 10.9% (Table 4/1). The survey focused on current and planned telecommunications applications, on the extent to which municipalities are aware of telecommunications issues within their jurisdictions, and on current and planned policy development relative to telecommunications.

Local governments responding to the survey are uniformly optimistic concerning the impact that the telecommunications revolution will have on government operations and functions, economic development, and the link between the citizen and government. By large margins, responding jurisdictions believe that advances in telecommunications will have a positive impact on the quality and efficiency of service delivery, and particularly on the variety of services delivered (Table 4/2). Nearly three-quarters believe that it will have a positive impact on economic development (72.1%) and citizen involvement with government (72.1%); almost 40% believe it will positively affect the rate of employment.

To what extent are these rosy predictions about telecommunications based on experience? Based on the survey respondents' experience with telecommunications-related applications, it would appear that the hopes and expectations of local governments are based more on unbridled optimism than on experience. For purposes of this discussion, telecommunications applications can be divided into three major categories: applications used within the local government itself, government information offered to citizens on-line, and general information applications used by both citizens and government employees. In all three cases, the use of telecommunication applications by responding local governments is fairly low.

Local Government Use of Telecommunications Applications

Slightly over 56% of responding local governments report using no on-line communications services or databases (Table 4/3), although more respondents indicate that they do plan to begin utilizing these services within the next two years (Table 4/4). Interesting variations appear across local governments of different size and geographic location. As might be expected, larger jurisdictions use on-line services and databases more frequently (particularly in municipalities of 100,000 and above) and confirm

plans to develop these applications within the next two years. In terms of geographic location, interesting East-West differences appear. Although not a hard-and-fast rule, telecommunication use appears to be lowest in the East and then to increase across the country, with the Pacific Coast division enjoying the highest level of use (63.6%). A final variation in use is especially revealing. Enormous differences exist in the use of on-line services and databases among different metropolitan classifications. Central jurisdictions report by far the highest level of use (71%), compared with suburban (40.6%) and independent (34.5%) localities. The same variation holds true for planned use. Nearly 69% of central jurisdictions report plans to introduce access to on-line services and databases for employees within two years, while only 23.9% of suburban jurisdictions and 22.8% of independent jurisdictions plan to do so.

What types of on-line services and databases are local governments using? As Table 4/5 shows, the most common application, reported by 50% of jurisdictions, is access to state government databases. Access to databases maintained by other levels of government or government associations is reported by approximately one-quarter of those using either on-line services or databases. This finding is especially revealing in that access to databases (particularly those maintained by other governments) receives far less attention in the popular and trade press than access to on-line communications services. Contrary to the conventional wisdom, use of these services was quite low: 29.3% reported access to the Internet, while of the commercial on-line services, CompuServe was the most popular, with 23% reporting use. In terms of local government employees, this suggests that telecommunications applications are

Table 4/2   IMPACT OF ADVANCES IN TELECOMMUNICATIONS

	No. reporting (A)	Positive 1	2	None 3	4	Negative 5
		% of (A)	% of (A)	% of (A)	% of (A)	% of (A)
On quality of service delivery	973	35.4	43.7	20.0	0.8	0.1
On citizen involvement	969	25.9	46.2	25.7	2.0	0.2
On the rate of unemployment	961	13.5	24.8	57.8	3.7	0.2
On economic development	975	29.4	42.7	26.6	1.2	0.1
On the variety of services in your jurisdiction	980	45.3	40.3	14.1	0.2	0.1
On the efficiency of service delivery	970	37.1	43.2	18.9	0.7	0.1

Note: Respondents used a 5 point scale, with "1" representing a positive impact and "5," a negative impact.

Table 4/3   ON-LINE SERVICES/DATABASES FOR EMPLOYEE USE

		On-line services/databases provided for local government employees					
	No. reporting (A)	Yes		No		Not sure	
Classification		No.	% of (A)	No.	% of (A)	No.	% of (A)
Total	1,093	451	41.3	616	56.4	26	2.4
Population group							
Over 1,000,000	2	2	100	0	0.0	0	0.0
500,000–1,000,000	11	9	81.8	2	18.2	0	0.0
250,000–499,999	24	18	75.0	6	25.0	0	0.0
100,000–249,999	49	41	83.7	8	16.3	0	0.0
50,000–99,999	88	54	61.4	31	35.2	3	3.4
25,000–49,999	148	76	51.4	68	45.9	4	2.7
10,000–24,999	247	107	43.3	136	55.1	4	1.6
5,000–9,999	228	80	35.1	141	61.8	7	3.1
2,500–4,999	226	48	21.2	171	75.7	7	3.1
Under 2,500	70	16	22.9	53	75.7	1	1.4
Geographic division							
New England	102	32	31.4	68	66.7	2	2.0
Mid-Atlantic	87	30	34.5	56	64.4	1	1.1
East North Central	216	80	37.0	132	61.1	4	1.9
West North Central	169	66	39.1	96	56.8	7	4.1
South Atlantic	171	76	44.4	91	53.2	4	2.3
East South Central	46	10	21.7	34	73.9	2	4.3
West South Central	93	37	39.8	53	57.0	3	3.2
Mountain	88	43	48.9	43	48.9	2	2.3
Pacific Coast	121	77	63.6	43	35.5	1	0.8
Metro status							
Central	121	86	71.1	34	28.1	1	0.8
Suburban	485	197	40.6	277	57.1	11	2.3
Independent	487	168	34.5	305	62.6	14	2.9

primarily used to access needed information in specific government-maintained and controlled databases, not the general-purpose information sources provided by the Internet or, especially, by the commercial on-line services.

Citizen Access to Government Information
Responding jurisdictions appear to be even further behind the level of anecdotal use reported in the press when it comes to providing citizen access to government information using telecommunications. Only 193, or 17.9% of 1,076 jurisdictions responding to this question, report providing such access. As can be seen in Table 4/6, the type of information most frequently available to the public on-line is that concerning property assessments, followed by information on tax bills and payments and council meetings.

Of the 101 respondents to the question about charging for on-line information, most provide access free of charge. When asked who should pay the cost of providing this type of on-line information, 70.1% of the 938 jurisdictions indicate that citizens who use these services should pay to do so. While the issue of how much to charge for such information in "value-added" (on-line) form was not addressed, this issue is one that will confront local governments more often in the years ahead. The question (although not the answer) is simple: Should citizens be charged only the incremental cost of "producing" one more copy of a particular piece of information (analogous to the cost of photocopying a form in paper format), or should charges be levied at a rate designed to recoup a jurisdiction's costs of developing and maintaining the electronic database and the telecommunications infrastructure that supports it?

General Telecommunications Applications
Table 4/7 shows general telecommunications applications used and planned within the next three years by local governments. The application most frequently reported in use is a public-access channel. Although just under half the survey respondents report this application, the figure is somewhat misleading because public-access channels are most frequently provided by the private-sector cable company that services the municipality. Thus, it may not be the most

Table 4/4 PLANNED ON-LINE SERVICES/DATABASES

| | No. reporting (A) | Planned on-line services and databases | | | |
| | | Yes | | No | |
		No.	% of (A)	No.	% of (A)
Total	555	144	25.9	411	74.1
Population					
500,000–1,000,000	2	2	100.0	0	0.0
250,000–499,999	6	5	83.3	1	16.7
100,000–249,999	8	4	50.0	4	50.0
50,000–99,999	28	13	46.4	15	53.6
25,000–49,999	61	26	42.6	35	57.4
10,000–24,999	119	36	30.3	83	69.7
5,000–9,999	131	26	19.8	105	80.2
2,500–4,999	151	27	17.9	124	82.1
Under 2,500	49	5	10.2	44	89.8
Geographic division					
New England	61	21	34.4	40	65.6
Mid-Atlantic	51	7	13.7	44	86.3
East North Central	125	33	26.4	92	73.6
West North Central	86	18	20.9	68	79.1
South Atlantic	82	30	36.6	52	63.4
East South Central	31	5	16.1	26	83.9
West South Central	47	7	14.9	40	85.1
Mountain	36	10	27.8	26	72.2
Pacific Coast	36	13	36.1	23	63.9
Metro status					
Central	32	22	68.8	10	31.3
Suburban	251	60	23.9	191	76.1
Independent	272	62	22.8	210	77.2

Note: Jurisdictions with populations over one million have these services.

Table 4/6 TYPES OF ON-LINE INFORMATION AVAILABLE TO THE PUBLIC

Type of information	Reporting use (%)
Property assessments	42.2
Tax bill payment information	32.4
Council meeting information	31.8
Local government employment information	24.3
Parks and recreation activities	23.1
Permit information	22.0
Court docket information	15.0
Requests for proposals	8.1
Other	35.3

Note: The percent reporting is based on 193 responding to the question.

Table 4/7 TELECOMMUNICATIONS APPLICATIONS

Application	Jurisdictions with application (No.)	Jurisdictions planning (No.)
Public access channel	415	116
On-line library	240	149
Voice mail	232	188
Fax-back service	174	110
Two-way video services	30	85
Public kiosk	25	136

Note: The percentages are based on 1,090 jurisdictions reporting.

Table 4/5 TYPES OF ON-LINE SERVICES/DATABASES IN USE

Population group	No. reporting (A)	America Online % of (A)	Prodigy % of (A)	GEnie % of (A)	CompuServe % of (A)	Internet % of (A)	State league database % of (A)	Local government database % of (A)	State databases % of (A)	Federal databases % of (A)	Other % of (A)
Total	444	5.4	10.4	0.7	23.0	29.3	22.3	28.4	50.0	15.1	14.2
Over 1,000,000	2	.0	0.0	0.0	0.0	50.0	0.0	50.0	100.0	100.0	50.0
500,000–1,000,000	9	.0	11.1	0.0	22.2	77.8	33.3	33.3	66.7	44.4	22.2
250,000–499,999	18	.0	11.1	0.0	44.4	44.4	11.1	50.0	66.7	11.1	16.7
100,000–249,999	40	2.5	10.0	2.5	37.5	37.5	17.5	27.5	52.5	20.0	17.5
50,000–99,999	53	7.5	17.0	0.0	32.1	41.5	32.1	26.4	47.2	11.3	13.2
25,000–49,999	76	6.6	14.5	1.3	26.3	35.5	18.4	21.1	44.7	14.5	9.2
10,000–24,999	105	5.7	8.6	1.0	19.0	25.7	21.0	35.2	52.4	11.4	16.2
5,000–9,999	79	5.1	6.3	0.0	17.7	11.4	20.3	27.8	41.8	17.7	10.1
2,500–4,999	47	6.4	8.5	0.0	10.6	19.1	29.8	23.4	55.3	14.9	12.8
Under 2,500	15	6.7	6.7	0.0	6.7	33.3	26.7	13.3	53.3	6.7	33.3

accurate measure of the extent to which the jurisdictions replying to the survey are actually involved in providing telecommunications applications.

The figures for the remaining applications are most likely a more accurate reflection of the level of general telecommunications application use: the second most frequently used application, on-line access to library catalogues, was reported by under a quarter of responding jurisdictions. In the same vein, jurisdictions reporting on planned additions to telecommunications applications in the next three years reveal only relatively modest plans to add to their list of uses. Voice mail was the application most frequently mentioned as a planned addition, followed by on-line library, public kiosks, public access channels, fax back services, and two-way video services.

Nearly all reporting jurisdictions use wireless communication services such as telephones and mobile radios; 91.6% of 1,087 jurisdictions report using these devices. This is not surprising, given the relatively low and decreasing cost and widespread availability of these popular devices.

REGULATORY AND FISCAL ISSUES

In addition to their role as actual or potential users of telecommunications, local governments will play two other roles that will become increasingly important in the years ahead. First, as regulators and policy makers–managing and controlling telecommunications in their jurisdictions. Most local governments (86.4%) have a statutory relationship with cable television companies in their jurisdictions that enables them to issue licenses or franchises, and over half (57.5%) have authority to regulate cable (not shown). Moreover, local governments feel strongly that they should continue to play a regulatory role in cable television services in their jurisdictions; nearly three-quarters (74.9%) feel that local governments need regulatory status in order to protect their interests. In the same vein, 73.7% feel that losing their role would result in a "major" problem or "somewhat" of a problem relative to the collection of franchise fees (Figure 4/1).

Events on Capitol Hill over the last year, however, moved in the opposite direction, threatening the ability of jurisdictions to retain any existing regulatory role or to collect franchise fees. Two bills introduced in the last session of Congress would significantly change the relationship between local governments and cable telecommunications providers, particularly cable television operators. The National Communications Competition and Information Infrastructure Act of 1993 (HR 3636), passed by the House Energy and Commerce Committee, would have lifted current ownership restrictions on cable and telephone company businesses provided that a number of safeguards to ensure competition were in place. Other provisions in the House bill, as well as in the Senate bill, would have had an even greater impact. The

first provision would have barred state and local governments from forbidding any communications company from providing any type of communications services within their jurisdictions—all applicants would have to be approved. In many or most jurisdictions, this would end the jurisdiction's ability to select one communications provider. Given that cross-ownership of cable and telephone companies would also be allowed, this could effectively mean the end of local government control of cable television services.

The second provision would have mandated that local governments impose franchising or license fees equally—that is, charging the same franchise fees to all telecommunications service providers in the new open market. This would most likely entail imposing new charges on telecommunications providers that do not now pay franchise or license fees. While this may sound potentially attractive to local governments, the opposition to the imposition of such charges from businesses and citizens alike could be fierce.

In terms of their ability to play a regulatory or policy role in future advances in telecommunications, local governments are facing a long uphill battle and a decidedly uncertain future. The regulatory environment in Washington, which will be the source of telecommuni-

cations policy affecting all governments, is changing. The bills discussed above did not pass in the session of Congress recently concluded. This was not because of some inherent problem with the bills, but because Congress became caught up in other issues, including health care and the midterm election. Regardless of their final form, these bills will be reintroduced and will move the country closer to an open-markets and open-services perspective. Telecommunication services that have traditionally been offered by separate industries (e.g., telephone, computing, and cable television companies), using separate technology and operating under relatively strict control of the national government, will in all likelihood be offered on a seamless, integrated basis by multiple service providers in a competitive manner.

On a national level, the issue is whether the traditional model of the regulated monopoly will survive. Given the sentiments in both Congress and the executive branch over the last two years, it is unlikely that it will. The November 1994 elections will only provide impetus to deregulation and privatization. The corporate players include telephone companies, the entertainment and media industries, and companies developing and manufacturing hardware and software. The increasing power of telecommunications technology and the blurring of tech-

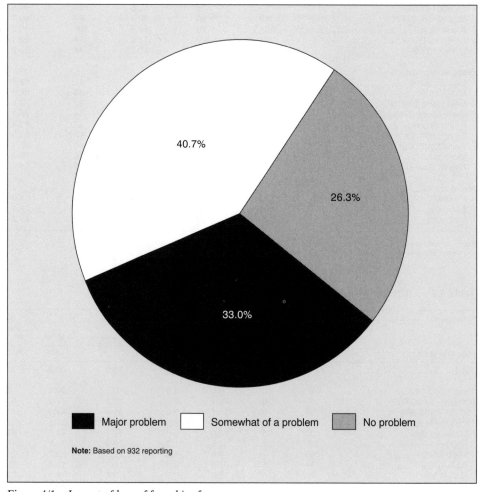

40.7%

26.3%

33.0%

■ Major problem □ Somewhat of a problem ▨ No problem

Note: Based on 932 reporting

Figure 4/1 *Impact of loss of franchise fee revenue*

Table 4/8 TECHNICAL ASSISTANCE USEFUL TO LOCAL GOVERNMENTS

Population group	No. reporting (A)	Sample policies and procedures % of (A)	Sample ordinances % of (A)	Sample right-of-way agreements % of (A)	Sample franchise agreements % of (A)	Education and training of staff % of (A)	Education and training of citizens % of (A)	Action at local level % of (A)	Model RFP for public/ private partnerships % of (A)	Inventory of infrastructure % of (A)	Peer matches % of (A)	Other % of (A)	Other % of (A)
Total	955	83.6	77.7	55.9	65.5	82.2	64.2	54.5	54.3	47.3	26.4	4.5	1.0
Over 1,000,000	2	0.0	0.0	0.0	0.0	100.0	100.0	0.0	50.0	50.0	50.0	0.0	0.0
500,000–1,000,000	11	81.8	45.5	27.3	36.4	81.8	63.6	45.5	81.8	54.5	9.1	0.0	0.0
250,000–499,999	22	77.3	59.1	45.5	50.0	68.2	63.6	50.0	50.0	40.9	22.7	4.5	0.0
100,000–249,999	47	78.7	68.1	51.1	61.7	78.7	72.3	53.2	66.0	53.2	19.1	0.0	0.0
50,000–99,999	82	81.7	70.7	50.0	63.4	81.7	68.3	64.6	62.2	56.1	29.3	9.8	1.2
25,000–49,999	137	83.2	75.9	59.9	62.8	89.1	71.5	52.6	58.4	53.3	30.7	5.1	1.5
10,000–24,999	217	82.9	77.9	56.7	65.0	82.0	63.6	54.4	64.5	50.2	30.4	5.5	0.9
5,000–9,999	195	84.6	82.1	52.8	67.7	83.6	61.5	52.8	45.6	40.5	24.1	3.1	0.5
2,500–4,999	185	86.5	82.7	61.1	70.8	81.1	61.6	54.6	43.2	44.3	23.8	3.8	2.2
Under 2,500	57	86.0	84.2	61.4	70.2	73.7	52.6	56.1	47.4	38.6	22.8	3.5	0.0

nologies, markets, and corporate structures of the businesses involved are forcing the national government to come to grips with a basic issue: Who will lead the next phase of the telecommunications revolution?

While not directly addressed in the telecommunications survey, two other issues related to the impact of telecommunications must be mentioned briefly. The first is the issue of forgone revenues in addition to cable television franchise fees. Local governments that now collect sales taxes and business and individual income taxes stand to suffer tremendous losses of those revenues to shopping services that function over the electronic highway. This issue is far more important than many local governments realize. It is not simply the Home Shopping Network; it is the ability of consumers to use software programs called "agents." These programs receive purchasing instructions from consumers and then identify the businesses across the country that offer the goods or services at the lowest price. The technology to accomplish this exists today; the agent programs are being fine tuned, and businesses across the country are gearing up to compete in this new marketplace.

Second, where will the revenue come from to support the investments in hardware, software, and trained personnel to take full advantage of the opportunities presented by telecommunications advances? Although prices of hardware and software are falling dramatically, setting up and establishing the coordinated, integrated systems of hardware, software, and trained personnel necessary will always involve costs. The two jurisdictions that have received national attention for their comprehensive "electronic villages," Palo Alto, California, and Blacksburg, Virginia, are currently having much of the cost paid by private industry and/or nearby universities under demonstration agreements. How will these services be paid for when the agreements end?

Preparing for the Telecommunications Revolution

How will local governments prepare themselves to take advantage of the opportunities that will be provided by the telecommunications revolution? The survey results provide information on three different aspects of this issue. The first is the extent to which local governments have prepared written telecommunications plans outlining their telecommunications goals (both application and policy oriented) as well as methods to achieve those goals. The results here are discouraging. Only 5.6% of the 996 jurisdictions responding to this question report a written telecommunications plan, and few local governments have knowledge of the "telecommunications pathways" in their jurisdiction—the various wires, fiber-optic cables, microwave signals, and satellite linkages that are the backbone, or infrastructure, of any new developments in telecommunications.

On the positive side, however, nearly all jurisdictions seem aware of and interested in the types of technical assistance that would bring them "up to speed" on telecommunications issues. As Table 4/8 indicates, responding jurisdictions believe that several types of technical assistance would be useful. All jurisdictions, regardless of size, respond favorably to such things as sample policies and procedures, education and training of municipal staff, and, to a lesser degree, assistance in creating an agenda for action. As might be expected, larger jurisdictions see less value in assistance with sample ordinances and rights-of-way and franchise agreements. Smaller jurisdictions see less value in model requests for proposals for public-private partnerships and methodologies for conducting an inventory of the telecommunications infrastructures in their jurisdiction.

Despite the rapid progress being made in technological advances, the next phase of the computing and technological revolution is still in its infancy. This is also true of research on and documentation of the impact of telecommunications in local governments. While it seems hard to believe, it was only a decade ago that the major topics of interest to researchers were such things as counting the number of microcomputers in jurisdictions and listing the various software programs used. Technology, in the form of computing devices and applications, has indeed become ubiquitous. The same evolution is now beginning to occur in the field of telecommunications. It would be foolhardy to predict the speed with which upcoming advances in telecommunications will begin to have a significant, widespread impact on local governments. The first two phases of the computing revolution were accomplished far more quickly than most government officials and researchers anticipated. However, it appears safe to say that, by the turn of the century, sophisticated telecommunications applications will have become ubiquitous in local governments as well.

[1]Mary Ann Young, "Local Government Use of Communication and Information Technologies for Citizen Participation," in *The Municipal Year Book 1990* (Washington, DC: International City/County Management Association, 1990), 8.

[2]See Kenneth L. Kraemer and Donald F. Norris, "Computers in Local Government," in *The Municipal Year Book 1994* (Washington: DC: International City/County Management Association, 1994), 3–13. Donald F. Norris and Kenneth L. Kraemer, *Leading Edge Computer Use in U.S. Municipalities*, Special Data Issue (Washington, DC: International City/County Management Association, 1994).

[3]In distributed computing, jobs are routed to computers that have processing capacity available. In massively parallel computing, one PC has many chips that can be used simultaneously to process different jobs.

[4]A. G. Cahill and E. S. Overman, *A Guide to the Information Highway* (Washington, DC: ICMA and Public Technology, Inc., 1995), CD-ROM.

A 5

Budgeting for Performance in Local Government

Glen Hahn Cope
Lyndon B. Johnson School of Public Affairs
The University of Texas at Austin

Findings

The majority (57.9%) of local governments report a combined operating and capital budget process.

Program measures are developed by department/division staff in 87% of responding jurisdictions.

Approximately 21% of local governments indicate that performance measurement has enhanced productivity and efficiency.

Budgeting practices in local governments have undergone significant changes in the twentieth century. The need for good local government budget practices was recognized in the late 1800s, when muckrakers like Ida Tarbell, Ray Stannard, and Lincoln Steffans wrote about municipal corruption in big cities, including inadequate control over finances. In 1899, the National Municipal League (now the National Civic League) published a model city charter that included a proposal that the executive budget be prepared under the direct control of the mayor in order to provide for greater accountability. One result was the establishment, in 1906, of the New York City Bureau of Municipal Research and the publication, in 1907, of its first report, *Making a Municipal Budget.* Shortly thereafter, the ''good government'' movement proposed that cities adopt the council-manager form of government, which included an executive budget system. Attention to budget processes and systems became intense during the ''roaring twenties,'' when many local governments suffered fiscal stress because Prohibition had eliminated an important revenue source—the excise tax on the sale of alcoholic beverages. Since then, often as a result of fiscal stress, U.S. cities and counties have continued to change and improve their budget systems and processes in order to serve the needs of elected officials, appointed staff, and citizens.

METHODOLOGY

Data for this project were collected by a survey of the finance directors of 3,564 cities and counties in the United States, using the ICMA mailing list. These included all 2,657 finance directors from cities and counties with popula-

tions of 25,000 or more and a sample of 907 finance directors from cities and counties with populations between 2,500 and 25,000. Smaller cities and counties were not surveyed. If a finance director did not respond within approximately 30 days of the first mailing, a second survey was sent. In some cases, respondents received follow-up phone calls. Usable responses were received from 1,396 finance directors, for a response rate of 39% (Table 5/1). A higher proportion of finance directors (or their staffs) from large jurisdictions responded than did their counterparts from smaller ones, which is understandable, because larger governments are more likely to have staff available to complete a questionnaire.

BUDGET FORMATS

Budget formats and systems have many purposes: (1) to allocate funds to particular organizational units; (2) to propose plans for the use of those funds; (3) to provide a forum for approval (and funding) of new programs and continuation of old ones; (4) to inform citizens of government policy and funding decisions and priorities; and (5) to provide information on the costs and activities of government organizations. Based on this information, decision makers can determine how much money is needed from taxes and other revenue sources and how that money should be spent on particular government programs and activities. Depending on the purpose most important to a particular jurisdiction, budgets may take different forms and include different types of information. Each format has strengths and weaknesses.

The 1994 budget process survey asked finance officers to identify which formats they use, either alone or in combination with others, to present the budget to their legislative bodies for decision making; the results show a variety of formats (Table 5/2).

Line-Item Budget

The traditional line-item budget, which allocates funds according to object-of-expenditure

categories, is most useful if the goal of the budget is control over expenditure details or input costs.[1] Line-item budgets provide decision makers with detailed information about the operational expenses of government agencies. They are easy to create with computerized accounting systems, but they offer little information about the activities being performed or the results achieved for the money spent.

The traditional line-item budget, which is used by over 79% of the responding jurisdictions, remains most popular. Smaller governments use line-item budgets more frequently than larger cities and counties. For example, over 80% of the jurisdictions with populations under 50,000 use line-item formats, while less than half those with populations over one million do. Line-item budgets are used most by jurisdictions in the Mid-Atlantic states (93%) and least by those on the Pacific Coast (64%). More counties use line-item budgets (86%) than do cities (74%). Many jurisdictions that use a line-item format do so in conjunction with another type of budget format, especially a performance or program budget.

Program Budgeting

Planning-Programming-Budgeting (PPB) formats provide decision makers with information

Table 5/1   SURVEY RESPONSE

Population group	No. cities and counties surveyed (A)	No. responding	% of (A)
Total	3,564	1,396	39
Over 1,000,000	35	21	60
500,000–1,000,000 .	80	42	53
250,000–499,999 ...	138	61	44
100,000–249,999 ...	386	180	47
50,000–99,999	718	318	44
25,000–49,999	1,300	443	34
10,000–24,999	328	116	35
5,000–9,999	295	115	39
2,500–4,999	284	100	35

Note: Percentages are rounded.

The author wishes to acknowledge financial assistance from the Mike Hogg Urban Studies endowment of the Lyndon B. Johnson School of Public Affairs. She also wishes to thank David Bluestein for his invaluable research assistance on this project and the other LBJ School students who assisted with data entry for this project.

about the broad goals and programs of governments and their total costs, but provide few details about specific expenditures. PPB was developed in the 1950s and 1960s primarily for use in the Department of Defense, but was implemented in all federal departments and agencies in 1965 by executive order of President Lyndon B. Johnson. PPB subsequently was adopted by many state and local governments, in part because federal funding was provided to them for training in PPB methods.[2] Although PPB in its original form was short-lived in the federal government,[3] it was soon modified by local governments to meet their need for more informative budget submissions and public documents. As a result, "program budgeting" became a popular budget format.[4] Program budgeting formats provide information on the programmatic activities of government agencies through use of a few broad expenditure categories (e.g., salaries, fringe benefits, equipment, supplies and materials, contractual services, travel) and inclusion of narrative descriptions, written program justifications, and measures of program achievement, goal attainment, outputs, and outcomes.

Program budgets provide more programmatic and output information to decision makers than line-item formats do, and tend to focus the attention of decision makers on programmatic achievement of goals. For these reasons, program budgets may foster expenditure and program growth. Line-item budgets provide much more expenditure detail than program budgets do, tend to focus attention on inputs and expenditure control, and lend themselves best to incremental decision making.

The versatile program budget format has been modified and adapted from its original PPB structure many times over the years, for use by both cities and counties to meet the information and decision making needs of their councils, commissions, boards, and town meetings. Approximately 35% of all jurisdictions use program formats, either alone or in combination with one or more other formats. This includes over three quarters of the cities and counties with populations over one million people and only 11% of the jurisdictions with populations between 2,500 and 4,999. Over half of all responding jurisdictions with populations of 250,000 or above use program budgets, and nearly half of those in the next smaller population category of 100,000 to 249,999 also use them. Among the jurisdictions reporting, program formats are most popular in the Pacific Coast division (62%) and are also frequently used in both the South Atlantic and Mountain divisions (43%). They are used least often in New England (23%). Central jurisdictions use program budgets more than independent and suburban jurisdictions, and they are also used more frequently in municipalities than in counties.

Performance Budgeting

One of the oldest budget formats—performance budgeting—has also become popular in the 1990s. Although performance budgeting was introduced in New York City by the Bureau of Municipal Research soon after the city adopted a formal budgeting system, its modern popularity dates from its inclusion in the 1949 report of the first Hoover Commission, the Commission on Organization of the Executive Branch of the Government.[5]

Performance budgets include measurements of the efficiency, effectiveness, outputs, outcomes, unit costs, workloads, and productivity of a government agency, activity, or service. Typically, performance budgets have backup line-item detail information, but the emphasis is on efficiency and productivity rather than on specific expenditure details. Performance budgeting has always been relatively popular in cities and counties, in part because most local governments have limited resources and are accountable to citizens who want to see their tax and fee dollars spent wisely and efficiently.

In the 1990s, performance budgeting has enjoyed a resurgence fueled in part by the quality improvement, total quality management, reengineering, and reinventing government movements.[6] Several new "entrepreneurial budgeting" systems were proposed by David Osborne and Ted Gaebler in their popular book, *Reinventing Government,* which suggested providing more budget flexibility to government managers and measuring performance of government agencies in order to support a mission-driven, customer-oriented government.[7] Their proposals include mission-driven budgets that are results oriented and therefore measure outputs and outcomes as well as costs, and focus on service to the customer. Other recent advocates of performance budgeting have been proponents of strategic planning, who suggest linking strategic plans to budget outcomes (reminiscent of both PPB and performance budgets) and advocates of the quality improvement movement, who suggest that the organizational

Table 5/2   BUDGET FORMATS

Classification	No. reporting (A)	Line item		Performance		Program		Zero-base		Target-base		Other	
		No.	% of (A)	No.	% of (A)	No.	% of (A)	No.	% of (A)	No.	% of (A)	No.	% of (A)
Total	1,396	1,109	79.4	256	18.3	492	35.2	90	6.4	243	17.4	77	5.5
Population group													
Over 1,000,000	21	10	47.6	7	33.3	16	76.2	2	9.5	8	38.1	1	4.8
500,000–1,000,000 .	42	26	61.9	14	33.3	24	57.1	6	14.3	10	23.8	4	9.5
250,000–499,999 ...	61	35	57.4	22	36.1	35	57.4	3	4.9	14	23.0	10	16.4
100,000–249,999 ...	180	119	66.1	46	25.6	85	47.2	13	7.2	25	13.9	9	5.0
50,000–99,999	318	251	78.9	66	20.8	124	39.0	26	8.2	60	18.9	22	6.9
25,000–49,999	443	373	84.2	76	17.2	150	33.9	25	5.6	70	15.8	17	3.8
10,000–24.999	116	98	84.5	12	10.3	33	28.4	5	4.3	20	17.2	7	6.0
5,000–9,999	115	106	92.2	10	8.7	14	12.2	5	4.3	19	16.5	4	3.5
2,500–4,999	100	91	91.0	3	3.0	11	11.0	5	5.0	17	17.0	3	3.0
Geographic division													
New England	80	70	87.5	10	12.5	18	22.5	8	10.0	7	8.8	3	3.8
Mid-Atlantic	129	120	93.0	16	12.4	36	27.9	17	13.2	25	19.4	7	5.4
East North Central ...	225	187	83.1	30	13.3	54	24.0	8	3.6	44	19.6	13	5.8
West North Central ..	171	133	77.8	24	14.0	58	33.9	8	4.7	36	21.1	10	5.8
South Atlantic	228	173	75.9	65	28.5	97	42.5	19	8.3	30	13.2	13	5.7
East South Central ..	72	62	86.1	9	12.5	17	23.6	1	1.4	11	15.3	3	4.2
West South Central ..	186	156	83.9	31	16.7	43	23.1	10	5.4	43	23.1	6	3.2
Mountain	106	81	76.4	23	21.7	46	43.4	11	10.4	21	19.8	7	6.6
Pacific Coast	199	127	63.8	48	24.1	123	61.8	8	4.0	26	13.1	15	7.5
Metro status													
Central	365	240	65.8	104	28.5	183	50.1	30	8.2	68	18.6	26	7.1
Suburban	490	386	78.8	106	21.6	186	38.0	31	6.3	83	16.9	27	5.5
Independent	541	483	89.3	46	8.5	123	22.7	29	5.4	92	17.0	24	4.4
Type													
Municipalities	764	567	74.2	170	22.3	322	42.1	51	6.7	116	15.2	38	5.0
Counties	632	542	85.8	86	13.6	170	26.9	39	6.2	127	20.1	39	6.2

changes usually incorporated in TQM imply changes in the budgeting system as well.

Performance budgeting's emphasis on measurements and the adaptability of those measurements to new uses may be its main advantage in the 1990s. The same characteristics can be drawbacks, however, because measuring outputs, outcomes, and productivity can be difficult and costly unless the government already has the necessary data collection and analysis capabilities in place.

Performance budgets, including measures of efficiency, productivity, and performance, are used by 18% of the responding jurisdictions. About a third of the jurisdictions with populations of 250,000 or more prepare performance budgets, often in conjunction with line-item or other formats. Only about 10% or less of the smallest jurisdictions, with populations under 25,000, use performance formats. The most frequent users of performance budgets are in the South Atlantic (29%), the Pacific Coast (24%), and Mountain (22%) geographic divisions. Performance formats also are more popular in central jurisdictions (29%) than in suburban (22%) or independent (9%) localities and in municipalities (22%) more than in counties (14%).

Zero-Base Budgeting

Zero-base budgeting (ZBB) was first developed by the U.S. Department of Agriculture in the 1960s.[8] In the late 1960s, the private sector developed an industry version to help companies cut costs and improve operational efficiency.[9] The industry version was adapted for use by Georgia and by other state and local governments that were experiencing fiscal stress and revenue stagnation or decline.[10]

Like PPB, ZBB was popularized by a president, Jimmy Carter, and implemented in the federal government by executive order in 1976. State and local governments eagerly embraced the concept of looking at all aspects of the budget from a ''zero-base,'' but quickly adapted the format to their purposes. They streamlined the process by reducing the paperwork and using particular percentages of the previous year's base as the starting point instead of building from zero every year. They retained the idea of ranking agency priorities and specifically measuring the efficiency of organizational units and programmatic activities.

Zero-base budgets are prepared by only a few of the responding jurisdictions (6%). Of the 90 governments that use ZBB in some form, over half are in the population ranges between 25,000 and 100,000, but they represent less than 10% of those population groups. Both municipalities and counties use ZBB in about the same proportion, just over 6%.

Target-Base Budgeting

Target-base budgeting (TBB) was developed in local governments in the early 1980s for reasons similar to ZBB development: fiscal stress and revenue stagnation or decline.[11] TBB is based on the relative stability of the budget shares allocated to local government functions. Each government department is assigned a base

amount—usually the same as or below the amount allocated in the previous year—and asked to prepare its base budget within that amount. The remainder of the total available revenue is then allocated on the basis of specific proposals for enhancement, program growth, efficiency or productivity efforts, and specific needs. In this way, only a small amount of scrutiny needs to be given to the base budgets, because most local government functions are necessities and change little from one year to the next. With TBB, most of the attention of

budgetary decision makers is focused on requests for funding above the base, because these represent the portion of the budget where most discretion is possible.

Both ZBB and TBB are suited for jurisdictions experiencing fiscal stress from revenue stagnation or decline. Both focus attention on decisions at the margins rather than on the base budgets. ZBB is more concerned with measurements of efficiency and ranking of program priorities in the budget process and is best suited for cutback situations. TBB is a streamlined

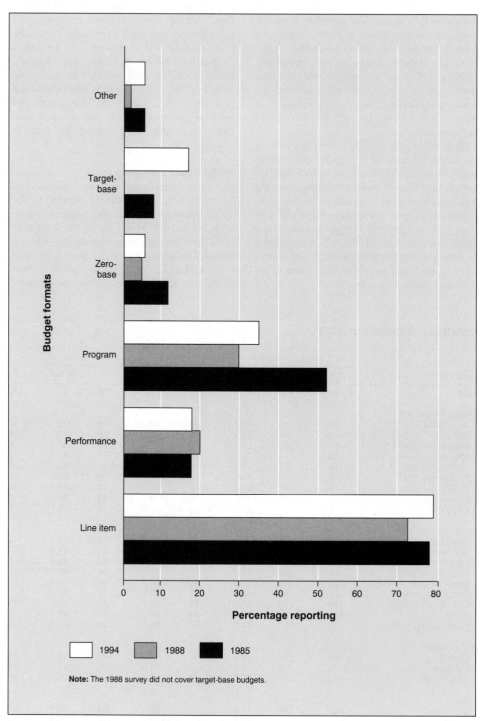

Figure 5/1 *Budget Formats—1985, 1988, and 1994*

process that assumes a stable and efficient base, with little need for budgetary scrutiny, and allows for some changes at the margins. While ZBB can be used at all levels of government, TBB is probably best used by local governments in which there is a general consensus about the basic functions that need to be performed and the level of service required. Target-base budgets, developed especially for local governments with stagnant or declining revenues, are used by only 17% of the responding local governments. More of the jurisdictions with populations of over one million people use TBB (38%) than do smaller governments, although over 20% of those with populations between 250,000 and one million also use this format. More counties prepare target-base budgets (20%) than municipalities (15%).

Other Formats

Some jurisdictions (6%) use budget formats other than those identified in Table 5/2, including combination formats that did not fit the survey categories and unique formats developed for a particular jurisdiction. Many of these were supplemental forms used in conjunction with one or more of the other formats mentioned, most often a line-item budget.

Changes Over Time

Overall local government budgeting patterns have not changed significantly over the past decade, but some differences have occurred. Figure 5/1 compares budget-format use in 1985, 1988, and 1994. Data for 1985 and 1988 are from the budget-process surveys conducted by the author in those years and published in ICMA *Baseline Data Reports*.[12] Budgeting patterns are fairly consistent over the three time periods, although the 1994 data include both municipalities and counties and the 1985 and 1988 data cover only municipalities. The line-item budget has been the format most widely reported. The second most popular format continues to be the program budget, although a considerably smaller percentage of jurisdictions reported program budgets in 1994 (35%) than reported them in 1985 (52%). Use of performance budgets has been quite consistent; 18% of the jurisdictions that responded to both the 1985 and 1994 surveys use performance budgets, and about 20% of the 1988 respondents did so. Zero-base budget usage has fallen in popularity since 1985, from 12% in 1985 to 6% in 1994; target-base budgets, on the other hand, are used somewhat more frequently in 1994 (17%) than they were in 1985 (8%). (Target-

base budgets were not separately identified in the 1988 survey.) In all three years, a few jurisdictions have used other formats not easily categorized.

COMPUTER USE IN BUDGETING

One factor that contributes to the ease of preparation, the data used, and the format is the availability of computer resources for data collection, processing, and analysis. In 1994, 95% of the jurisdictions responding to this survey report using computers in their budget processes (Table 5/3). All local governments with populations over one million use computers in their budget processes, and nearly all (98% or more) of those with populations of 50,000 or more use them. Most smaller jurisdictions also use computers in their budget processes, including over 93% of those with populations from 10,000 to 49,999, and 85% or more of those with populations from 2,500 to 9,999. These results are consistent with the survey findings reported in *The Municipal Year Book 1994*, that all municipalities with populations of 50,000 or more used computers for some city functions (the survey did not include counties).[13]

Table 5/3 USE OF COMPUTERS IN THE BUDGET PROCESS

	No. reporting (A)	Use of computers		Mainframe	Minicomputer	Microcomputer	Network	File server	Laptops	Other
Classification		No. reporting (B)	% of (A)	% of (B)	% of (B)	% of (B)	% of (B)	% of (B)	% of (B)	% of (B)
Total	1,396	1,328	95.1	53.1	22.2	66.0	40.1	19.2	12.6	1.3
Population group										
Over 1,000,000	21	21	100.0	66.7	19.0	71.4	57.1	47.6	28.6	0.0
500,000–1,000,000	42	41	97.6	82.9	12.2	80.5	58.5	41.5	24.4	7.3
250,000–499,999	61	61	100.0	77.0	19.7	80.3	62.3	39.3	32.8	3.3
100,000–249,999	180	178	98.9	69.1	16.3	69.7	50.6	30.3	19.1	1.7
50,000–99,999	318	312	98.1	58.7	23.1	68.3	39.1	16.3	12.8	2.2
25,000–49,999	443	420	94.8	51.9	27.9	63.8	33.6	13.3	8.8	0.2
10,000–24,999	116	108	93.1	34.3	25.9	59.3	33.3	13.9	3.7	0.9
5,000–9,999	115	102	88.7	29.4	15.7	60.8	37.3	14.7	8.8	0.0
2,500–4,999	100	85	85.0	22.4	14.1	57.6	36.5	15.3	8.2	0.0
Geographic division										
New England	80	76	95.0	34.2	27.6	57.9	48.7	23.7	11.8	0.0
Mid-Atlantic	129	124	96.1	48.4	14.5	58.1	48.4	25.0	13.7	1.6
East North Central	225	208	92.4	54.8	22.6	63.9	29.3	13.5	10.1	0.5
West North Central	171	160	93.6	56.9	20.0	68.1	33.8	13.1	8.8	0.6
South Atlantic	228	219	96.1	62.1	20.5	69.4	44.3	22.8	15.1	1.8
East South Central	72	68	94.4	47.1	23.5	60.3	26.5	10.3	10.3	0.0
West South Central	186	175	94.1	48.0	16.0	71.4	31.4	11.4	9.7	1.7
Mountain	106	101	95.3	54.5	25.7	67.3	41.6	22.8	16.8	2.0
Pacific Coast	199	197	99.0	54.3	31.5	67.5	54.8	28.9	16.2	2.0
Metro status										
Central City	365	363	99.5	69.4	18.5	75.2	46.8	26.4	20.9	2.8
Suburban	490	471	96.1	44.6	24.8	71.6	42.7	21.4	10.6	1.1
Independent	541	494	91.3	49.2	22.5	54.0	32.6	11.7	8.3	0.4
Type										
Municipalities	764	739	96.7	32.9	24.9	72.5	39.4	5.5	12.7	0.8
Counties	632	599	94.8	61.8	18.5	56.9	40.2	1.7	12.2	1.8
Budget format										
Line-item	1,109	1,058	95.4	51.3	20.6	63.0	37.2	16.2	10.0	1.2
Performance	256	252	98.4	65.5	23.4	74.2	52.0	21.8	18.7	1.6
Program	492	478	97.2	61.1	26.4	76.4	48.3	25.5	18.8	1.5
Zero-base	90	89	98.9	60.7	25.8	67.4	46.1	21.3	9.0	2.2
Target-base	243	232	95.5	58.6	23.7	63.8	45.3	22.4	14.7	0.4
Other	77	74	96.1	55.4	29.7	71.6	37.8	27.0	20.3	5.4

As might be expected from the concentration of computer and software firms located there, the Pacific Coast division shows the highest percentage (99%) of jurisdictions using computers in their budget process. Over 92% of the counties and municipalities in all geographical divisions use computers for budgeting, however. Nearly all central cities use computers (almost 100%), as do most suburban (96%) and independent (91%) jurisdictions. Municipalities use computers slightly more frequently (97%) than counties (95%).

Computer use varies slightly among the jurisdictions surveyed according to the types of budget formats used. The most commonly used budget format, line-item, is easy to develop using computer linkages to the accounting system, but can be produced without computers specifically dedicated to the budget process if the necessary line-item object-of-expenditure data are available. Other budget formats also can be easier to use if computers are available for data collection and analysis. Of the responding jurisdictions that prepare line-item budgets, 95% use computers in their budget processes (Table 5/3). Similarly, 98% of those who develop performance budgets and 97% of those who have program budgets also use computers in their preparation. Computers are also used by 99%

of the jurisdictions using zero-base budgets and 96% of those preparing target-base budgets. These results are consistent with the finding that 95% of the total jurisdictions use computers, and seem to indicate that there is not a great advantage in using computers for one type of budget format over another.

Slightly over half the responding jurisdictions report using mainframe computers for budget preparation. Even more (66%) now use microcomputers or personal computers (PCs) for budgeting. About one-fifth of the cities and counties report using minicomputers (22%), and 19% use a file-server. Forty percent of the jurisdictions use computer networks in their budget processes. A small percentage (13%) of jurisdictions now use laptops for budget purposes.

SOFTWARE USE

The software products most commonly used in the budget process are spreadsheet programs, used by 81%, and word processing programs, used by 72%. Approximately 47% of local governments use commercial accounting software to help develop their budgets, and almost 30% use database software (Table 5/4). Twenty-

seven percent use commercially developed budgeting software, and slightly over 40% use custom-designed budgeting software. A small percentage of jurisdictions (9%) use statistical forecasting software in developing their budgets.

Interestingly, only 78% of the jurisdictions that have line-item budgets use spreadsheet programs to help develop them, but 43% of those jurisdictions use custom-designed budget software, and 47% use accounting software for budget development. All these are good alternative methods to easily develop line-item budgets using computerized data.

Most of the governments that have performance budgets use spreadsheet programs (93%) and word processing programs (90%), and many use accounting software (49%) and custom-designed budget software (43%). Similar percentages of the governments that develop program-budget presentations use spreadsheets (93%), word processing (90%), accounting (49%) and custom budget software (44%).

BUDGET SUBMISSIONS

Preparation of the budget request is the first phase of the budget cycle. The requests identify

Table 5/4 SOFTWARE USED IN BUDGET DEVELOPMENT AND PRESENTATION

Classification	No. using computers (A)	Word processing % of (A)	Spreadsheet % of (A)	Database % of (A)	Statistical forecasting % of (A)	Accounting % of (A)	Budget software source Commercial % of (A)	Custom % of (A)
Total	1,328	71.5	81.1	28.5	8.7	46.5	27.2	42.3
Population group								
Over 1,000,000	21	90.5	100.0	52.4	19.0	33.3	19.0	47.6
500,000–1,000,000	41	82.9	92.7	51.2	24.4	51.2	12.2	61.0
250,000–499,999	61	83.6	95.1	45.9	19.7	34.4	18.0	36.1
100,000–249,999	178	77.5	86.5	37.1	16.3	41.6	25.3	47.2
50,000–99,999	312	73.7	80.8	26.0	5.8	44.2	28.2	48.7
25,000–49,999	420	69.3	79.5	28.6	7.4	47.1	29.8	36.4
10,000–24,999	108	68.5	82.4	20.4	2.8	50.0	25.9	35.2
5,000–9,999	102	62.7	72.5	13.7	6.9	52.0	26.5	39.2
2,500–4,999	85	57.6	67.1	17.6	2.4	61.2	32.9	44.7
Geographic division								
New England	76	78.9	86.8	25.0	7.9	50.0	26.3	38.2
Mid-Atlantic	124	62.9	76.6	25.8	8.1	46.8	25.8	40.3
East North Central	208	61.1	76.0	26.9	5.8	41.8	35.6	38.9
West North Central	160	64.4	72.5	28.8	10.0	47.5	24.4	42.5
South Atlantic	219	79.9	83.1	31.1	11.4	45.7	35.6	45.7
East South Central	68	60.3	75.0	26.5	7.4	52.9	16.2	41.2
West South Central	175	65.7	77.7	24.6	9.1	47.4	24.0	39.4
Mountain	101	73.3	90.1	30.7	8.9	44.6	21.8	41.6
Pacific Coast	197	89.8	92.4	33.0	8.6	48.2	21.8	48.2
Metro status								
Central City	363	83.2	89.3	39.9	15.2	39.9	23.1	45.2
Suburban	471	73.9	85.8	25.3	7.9	48.4	28.5	38.9
Independent	494	60.7	70.6	23.1	4.9	49.6	28.9	43.5
Type								
Municipalities	739	47.2	86.9	27.2	8.0	44.8	27.9	36.9
Counties	599	24.2	72.6	29.5	9.5	47.9	25.9	48.2
Budget format								
Line-item	1,058	67.7	78.4	27.1	7.1	46.8	27.1	42.6
Performance	252	89.7	92.9	37.3	17.1	48.8	24.5	43.3
Program	478	90.0	92.7	38.1	12.3	49.4	26.4	43.7
Zero-base	89	82.0	84.3	36.0	18.0	46.1	23.6	49.4
Target-base	232	75.0	81.5	42.7	14.2	53.9	25.9	52.6
Other	74	73.0	87.8	32.4	9.5	41.9	27.0	37.8

the funds that departments want for the next fiscal year. The availability of both computers and telecommunications networks makes possible budget request submissions in forms other than the traditional printed page. As Table 5/5 shows, budget requests are submitted on paper to the office or individual responsible for budget preparation in 86% of the responding local governments. About 20% of the governments allow or require budget requests to be submitted on computer disks, and 18% make on-line computer submissions through a mainframe, network, or file-server. Only about 3% use electronic mail (e-mail) for budget request submissions, which is understandable, because so many of the governments have networks or file-server capacity, which allow submissions to be made directly into on-line forms much more easily than could be done on most e-mail systems.

When the method of submitting the budget request is examined by the type of format used, some variations are noticeable. Budget requests are submitted on paper in 89% of the governments that use line-item budgets. Line-item submissions are made on disk and on-line in only 14% and 15% of the governments, respectively. Jurisdictions that prepare program and performance budgets are a little less likely to have their budget requests submitted on paper; 77% of the performance and 82% of the program budget requests are submitted on paper. On the other hand, both program and performance budget requests are submitted on disk in 38% of the jurisdictions, and about 31% of these budget requests are submitted on line. These results are logical, since a higher percentage of the governments that use program and performance budgets also use mainframe computers,

networked PCs, and file-servers than do governments that prepare line-item budgets. On-line budget submissions can be made using all three of these hardware combinations. Governments that use PCs are more likely to want submissions on disk if they are not submitted on-line through a network, because having information on disk can save time and effort for the budget preparers.

IMPACT OF COMPUTERS

When asked whether using computers or particular software had changed the way they develop or present their budgets, approximately 80% report that computers or software have changed some aspect of the budget process (Table 5/6). Of those indicating a change as a result of computers, the format in which the budget is presented is the most frequently changed aspect of the process (86.6%). Slightly over two-thirds (67.7%) changed the information they include in the budget, and slightly under one-half (47.4%) changed the type of analysis they conduct in the budget process.

Computers have the greatest impact in local governments that prepare performance budgets (92%). Of these, 87% changed their presentation format, 74% changed the information included in the budget, and 58% changed the analysis performed. The type of analysis conducted is the element least often changed by all governments, regardless of the budget format used. This pattern is consistent among reporting jurisdictions regardless of the budget format used. Presentation format, then information included, and finally the analysis were affected.

CAPITAL BUDGETING

The survey also asked about preparation of capital budgets. In over half (58%) of the jurisdictions that responded, the capital and operating budgets are prepared in combination (Table 5/7). In 38% of the jurisdictions, capital budgets are prepared separately. Operating and capital budget processes are more likely to be combined in local governments under 250,000 population and in the jurisdictions over one million in population. Combined processes are also more common in counties (64%) than in municipalities (53%), and are more often used in suburban (55%) and independent (67%) jurisdictions than in central cities (48%). Line-item operating budgets are more likely to be combined with the capital budget than are other operating budget formats.

Regardless of whether capital- and operating-budget development is combined, about 62% of the jurisdictions report that development of their capital budgets is based upon a capital-improvement plan (CIP). Most of the governments 250,000 and over in population base their capital budgets on a capital-improvement plan. Central jurisdictions also use CIPs more often (77%) than other types of jurisdictions. Nearly three-quarters (73%) of the responding municipalities use a CIP as the basis of their capital budget, while less than half (49%) of the responding counties do. Because county powers are limited in many states, some municipalities are responsible for a wider range of activities requiring capital investments and might be more likely to use capital-improvement plans to facilitate capital planning and decision making.

Table 5/7 also shows the criteria used by the survey respondents to develop the capital budget. The most frequently used criterion is a capital-projects needs assessment, used by 73% of the jurisdictions. Two-thirds of the counties (66%) and 79% of the municipalities perform needs assessments for capital projects and use them for capital budgeting. Not surprisingly, the next most commonly cited criteria are cost (53%) and cost-benefit analysis (36%). Some jurisdictions also use citizen surveys (15%), performance measures (9.5%), and other criteria (11%) in developing their capital budgets. From the responses, it appears that an evaluation of the need rather than the cost of a capital project is more likely to influence whether it is included

Table 5/5 SUBMISSION OF BUDGET REQUEST TO STAFF PREPARING BUDGET

	No. reporting (A)	Paper % of (A)	Disk % of (A)	On-line % of (A)	E-mail % of (A)	Other % of (A)
Total	1,396	86.2	19.6	18.1	2.7	2.4
Budget format						
Line-item	1,109	89.4	14.3	15.0	1.7	1.6
Performance	256	76.6	37.5	31.3	6.3	3.5
Program	492	81.7	37.6	30.5	6.1	3.0
Zero-base	90	80.0	24.4	21.1	2.2	2.2
Target-base	243	86.8	21.0	15.2	4.5	3.7
Other	77	77.9	29.9	26.0	6.5	3.9

Table 5/6 IMPACT OF COMPUTERS

	No. reporting (A)	Change in process No. reporting (B)	% of (A)	Format No.	Format % of (B)	Information included No.	Information included % of (B)	Analysis No.	Analysis % of (B)	Other No.	Other % of (B)
Total	1,328	1,078	81.2	934	86.6	730	67.7	511	47.4	67	6.2
Budget format											
Line-item	1,058	847	80.1	728	85.9	569	67.1	381	44.9	47	5.5
Performance	252	231	91.7	201	87.0	170	73.5	133	57.5	20	8.6
Program	478	415	86.8	370	89.1	298	71.8	232	55.9	30	7.2
Zero-base	89	80	89.9	68	85.0	58	72.5	51	63.7	11	13.7
Target-base	232	202	87.1	177	87.6	137	67.8	105	51.9	12	5.9
Other	74	62	83.8	58	93.5	49	79.0	32	51.6	7	11.2

in the budget. Cost is not unimportant, but capital projects are by nature large and expensive, and often are financed by debt rather than current tax revenues.

INFORMATION USE

Regardless of the size and organization of the budget office, its main function is to collect, analyze, and report information in a way that the government's decision makers, both elected and appointed, can use. In jurisdictions with combined capital and operating budgets, information tends to be collected simultaneously for both, although it may be analyzed separately. Even if the two types of budgets are prepared separately, staff in most jurisdictions tend to share information. In small jurisdictions, one person may prepare both types of budgets, but in large municipalities and counties, budget staffs may be large and, often, organized by functional area.

Once budget information has been collected, it is distributed to various users. The type of information most often used is the change in the budget from the prior year's expenditures (Table 5/8). Budget-change information is provided to the legislative body in 80% of the responding jurisdictions, to the city or county manager or chief administrative officer (CAO) in 71%, and is included in 65% of budget documents. The second most frequently used information is line-item expenditure detail, which is presented to the manager or CAO in 78% of local governments, to the legislative body in 77%, and to the public in the budget document in 63%. Budget change and expenditure line-item-detail information are most likely to be helpful to decision makers in a stable expenditure and revenue environment, or one that is characterized by incremental changes in the budget from one year to the next. Since most local governments experience a relatively stable budget environment, occasional severe revenue shortages or expenditure emergencies notwithstanding, information that supports incremental budgetary decision making is likely to be widely used.

After budget change and line-item detail, the information used most often for local budgeting is salary and staff-level data. Staff levels are presented to the legislative bodies of 73% of the responding governments, to the manager or CAO of 69%, and in the budget document in 58%. Salary information goes to the manager or CAO in the budget process in 72% of the jurisdictions, to the legislative body in 71%, and to the public in the budget in 53%. Personnel-cost information, including salaries and benefits, is particularly important because these expenditures represent a significant part of most local government budgets. The survey results confirm expectations about the predominant recipients and users of staff and salary data. Administrative officials and legislators are more likely to use this type of data themselves than to provide it to the public in a budget document.

The budget process provides program descriptions, analyses and explanations, and narrative justifications to both the manager, or CAO, and the legislative body in about 50% to 57% of the responding governments. Program descriptions, explanations, and justifications are usually included in program, performance, and zero-base budget requests. Some line-item budgets also include program descriptions. This level of detail is less often provided to the public, however. Nearly one-third of the jurisdic-

---

Table 5/7 CAPITAL BUDGET PROCESS AND CRITERIA

	No. reporting (A)	Capital budget process				Capital budget criteria															
		Separate from operating		Combined with operating		Based on CIP[1]		Cost-benefit		Performance measures		Cost		Citizen survey		Needs assessment		Other	
		No.	% of (A)	No.	% of (A)	No.	% of (A)	No.	% of (A)	No.	% of (A)	No.	% of (A)	No.	% of (A)	No.	% of (A)	No.	% of (A)
Total	1,396	535	38.3	808	57.9	862	61.7	505	36.2	133	9.5	738	52.9	210	15.0	1,021	73.1	152	10.9
Population group																			
Over 1,000,000	21	9	42.9	11	52.4	19	90.5	18	85.7	6	28.6	18	85.7	2	9.5	21	100.0	2	9.5
500,000–1,000,000 .	42	29	69.0	16	38.1	37	88.1	24	57.1	5	11.9	30	71.4	6	14.3	35	83.3	13	31.0
250,000–499,999 ...	61	45	73.8	18	29.5	53	86.9	30	49.2	8	13.1	35	57.4	12	19.7	48	78.7	14	23.0
100,000–249,999 ...	180	79	43.9	96	53.3	128	71.1	71	39.4	27	15.0	103	57.2	28	15.6	136	75.6	27	15.0
50,000–99,999	318	133	41.8	185	58.2	209	65.7	128	40.3	34	10.7	170	53.5	55	17.3	233	73.3	40	12.6
25,000–49,999	443	165	37.2	263	59.4	265	59.8	157	35.4	34	7.7	234	52.8	65	14.7	312	70.4	43	9.7
10,000–24,999	116	40	34.5	72	62.1	67	57.8	36	31.0	4	3.4	62	53.4	19	16.4	90	77.6	8	6.9
5,000–9,999	115	24	20.9	71	61.7	49	42.6	26	22.6	8	7.0	49	42.6	14	12.2	82	71.3	1	0.9
2,500–4,999	100	11	11.0	76	76.0	35	35.0	15	15.0	7	7.0	37	37.0	9	9.0	64	64.0	4	4.0
Geographic division																			
New England	80	42	52.5	42	52.5	59	73.8	30	37.5	12	15.0	45	56.3	10	12.5	66	82.5	13	16.3
Mid-Atlantic	129	62	48.1	65	50.4	87	67.4	53	41.1	15	11.6	85	65.9	16	12.4	103	79.8	7	5.4
East North Central ...	225	79	35.1	129	57.3	123	54.7	74	32.9	21	9.3	127	56.4	30	13.3	166	73.8	13	5.8
West North Central ..	171	65	38.0	97	56.7	97	56.7	56	32.7	13	7.6	78	45.6	20	11.7	112	65.5	12	7.0
South Atlantic	228	97	42.5	126	55.3	160	70.2	86	37.7	30	13.2	124	54.4	36	15.8	165	72.4	33	14.5
East South Central ..	72	17	23.6	50	69.4	22	30.6	19	26.4	4	5.6	28	38.9	9	12.5	47	65.3	4	5.6
West South Central ..	186	44	23.7	113	60.8	78	41.9	50	26.9	14	7.5	70	37.6	25	13.4	123	66.1	16	8.6
Mountain	106	42	39.6	64	60.4	73	68.9	40	37.7	10	9.4	46	43.4	21	19.8	83	78.3	14	13.2
Pacific Coast	199	87	43.7	122	61.3	163	81.9	97	48.7	14	7.0	135	67.8	43	21.6	156	78.4	40	20.1
Metro status																			
Central	365	201	55.1	176	48.2	280	76.7	168	46.0	52	14.2	212	58.1	62	17.0	282	77.3	68	18.6
Suburban	490	207	42.2	268	54.7	333	68.0	191	39.0	44	9.0	280	57.1	81	16.5	369	75.3	51	10.4
Independent	541	127	23.5	364	67.3	249	46.0	146	27.0	37	6.8	246	45.5	67	12.4	370	68.4	33	6.1
Type																			
Municipalities	764	357	46.7	406	53.1	554	72.5	304	39.8	85	11.1	444	58.1	159	20.8	603	78.9	101	13.2
Counties	632	178	28.2	402	63.6	308	48.7	201	31.8	48	7.6	294	46.5	51	8.1	418	66.1	51	8.1
Budget format																			
Line-item	1,109	369	33.3	682	61.5	629	56.7	363	32.7	97	8.7	566	51.0	146	13.2	803	72.4	96	8.7
Performance	256	149	58.2	113	44.1	221	86.3	130	50.8	50	19.5	160	62.5	74	28.9	206	80.5	49	19.1
Program	492	270	54.9	239	48.6	414	84.1	249	50.6	78	15.9	304	61.8	123	25.0	386	78.5	79	16.1
Zero-base	90	50	55.6	44	48.9	70	77.8	42	46.7	19	21.1	48	53.3	27	30.0	76	84.4	11	12.2
Target base	243	98	40.3	139	57.2	163	67.1	110	45.3	37	15.2	140	57.6	54	22.2	187	77.0	28	11.5
Other	77	33	42.9	46	59.7	59	76.6	39	50.6	6	7.8	45	58.4	15	19.5	60	77.9	15	19.5

Note: The data in this table were gathered in three separate questions that are not dependent on one another.
[1] CIP refers to capital improvement plan.

tions include analyses and explanations (31%) and narrative justifications (32%) in the budget document that goes to the public, and 42% include program descriptions.

Statements of program goals and requests for program changes are provided to the manager or CAO by 46% of the responding governments, and to legislative bodies in 46% and 44% of the governments, respectively. Only 36% of the governments include program goals in their public budget documents, and even fewer (25%) publish program change requests. The budget formats used for the internal and external budget documentation influence the types of information provided in them, as does the size of the jurisdiction and the availability of staff to prepare budget requests and documentation.

Other types of information in internal budget requests and published budget documents include expenditure and revenue forecasts, information about the service-delivery levels that can be supported by the proposed budget, and general economic forecasts. Over 40% of the jurisdictions give expenditure and revenue forecasts to the manager or CAO and the legislative body, but only about 28% include these in their budget documents. In 29% of the responding local governments, managers are provided with service-delivery-level information, and 27% provide that detail to legislators. Only about 21% of the responding governments publish service-delivery information in their budgets. Similarly, general economic forecasts are provided to managers by 19% and legislators by 18% of the jurisdictions, but only 11% give that information to the public in their budget documents. All these data indicate that local governments use some information internally, but do not feel it is necessary or cost effective to give the same information to the public. Including more information increases the cost of preparing and printing the budget.

Table 5/8 BUDGET INFORMATION RECIPIENTS

	Presented to		
	Manager/CAO (%)	Legislative body (%)	Public by document (%)
Type of information			
Line-item detail	77.7	76.5	62.5
Program/unit description	49.7	51.1	42.1
Program goals/objectives	46.3	46.0	35.9
Staffing levels	68.6	72.9	58.2
Salary information	71.5	71.3	52.7
Service provision levels	28.6	27.2	20.8
Multi-year revenue forecasts	40.3	43.4	28.9
Multi-year expenditure forecasts	40.4	42.1	28.0
Multi-year economic forecasts	18.8	18.0	10.5
Changes from prior year	70.8	79.5	64.6
Analysis/explanations	54.7	53.7	31.3
Narrative justifications	57.1	54.2	31.6
Program change proposals	45.7	43.9	25.0
Program measures			
Activity measures	33.3	29.9	23.0
Performance measures	25.4	21.6	17.4
Productivity measures	20.8	17.6	13.0
Effectiveness measures	18.2	14.8	11.0
Goal attainment	21.6	18.5	13.7

Note: Percentages are based on 1,396 jurisdictions reporting.

Table 5/9 DEVELOPMENT OF PROGRAM MEASURES

		Responsibility for developing measures			
	Number using program measures (A)	Budget staff % of (A)	Dept./division staff % of (A)	Separate performance evaluation staff % of (A)	Other % of (A)
Total	592	45.4	87.0	3.4	15.4
Population group					
Over 1,000,000	20	45.0	85.0	15.0	5.0
500,000–1,000,000	31	67.7	90.3	12.9	6.5
250,000–499,999	39	56.4	74.4	0.0	2.6
100,000–249,999	110	46.4	71.8	5.5	7.3
50,000–99,999	143	43.4	74.1	2.1	5.6
25,000–49,999	163	41.1	68.1	1.2	15.3
10,000–24,999	38	36.8	65.8	0.0	26.3
5,000–9,999	26	42.3	61.5	0.0	15.4
2,500–4,999	22	54.5	63.6	4.5	27.3
Geographic division					
New England	34	35.3	73.5	2.9	14.7
Mid-Atlantic	44	40.9	63.6	0.0	15.9
East North Central	83	37.3	62.7	1.2	18.1
West North Central	56	37.5	69.6	3.6	3.6
South Atlantic	123	57.7	76.4	5.7	13.0
East South Central	21	57.1	71.4	0.0	19.0
West South Central	58	62.1	70.7	1.7	5.2
Mountain	53	49.1	77.4	5.7	15.1
Pacific Coast	120	35.0	75.0	3.3	4.2
Metro status					
Central	213	50.7	75.6	5.8	6.8
Suburban	224	42.4	68.3	1.8	11.2
Independent	155	42.6	71.6	1.9	16.8
Type					
Municipalities	361	44.9	70.6	3.0	13.3
Counties	231	46.3	73.6	3.5	7.4

PROGRAM MEASURES

As discussed above, inclusion of program measurement in local governments' budget processes began with the advent of program budgeting. Program, activity, and goal attainment measures were also introduced as part of the PPB and program budgeting movement. Measuring the productivity, efficiency, performance, and outcomes of government programs is often difficult and costly, although the inputs and outputs of some programs like street construction and repair are easier to measure.

Use of Program Measures

As Table 5/8 shows, only a third of the responding governments use activity measurements in their budget processes, and other types of measures are used by even fewer governments. More governments provide performance measurement information to their managers or CAOs than to their legislative bodies, and fewer publish these measurements in their budget documents.

Activity or output measures, which usually are the least costly to develop and collect, are the measures most frequently used in local budgets. Thirty-three percent of the responding jurisdictions provide them to managers and 30%, to legislators. Performance measures are indicators of efficiency and cost effectiveness, and so may require more effort to develop and collect, but about one-quarter of the jurisdictions make the effort for their manager's use, and nearly that many (22%) provide them to their legislators. Measurement of goal attainment is often much more difficult and expensive, since it generally must be preceded by a process of goal definition and adoption by the manager and the legislative body, but slightly over one-fifth (22%) of the responding local governments measure their attainment of goals and provide the information to their managers for budget use. About 19% of the legislators also are given that information.

Productivity has traditionally been measured in capital construction and other infrastructure-related activities, where it is relatively easy to define and measure. It is more difficult to measure productivity for such local government functions as health and human services. Nonetheless, over 20% of the responding jurisdictions develop productivity measures for their manager's use, and about 18% give the same information to their legislative bodies. Program effectiveness, perhaps most difficult and costly to measure and most often requiring formal evaluation processes, is least often used by managers (18%) and legislators (15%). Only large cities or those with strong commitments to program evaluation and the budget to match would be able to afford to measure effectiveness under ordinary circumstances. Fewer than 20% of the governments publish measurement information other than activity data in their budget documents.

Development of Program Measures

Program measures may be developed by departmental staff, by the budget office, by a separate evaluation staff, or by many other staff combinations, depending upon the jurisdiction. In 87% of the responding jurisdictions, program measures are developed by the departmental or divisional staff, and in 45% of the jurisdictions, the budget staff develop the measures (Table 5/9). Separate evaluation staff prepare measures in only 3% of the localities reporting, although 15% of those with populations over one million

and nearly 13% of those in the 500,000 to one million range have evaluation staff who develop measures. (The survey did not ask for the size of this staff.) Approximately 15% of respondents use measures developed by other sources, including outside consultants and other individuals within the local government. Clearly some local governments use more than one staff group to develop measures.

Program measures are likely to be more use-

ful if they are developed by staff members in the departments that are being measured, because they know what information would be most useful to them for managerial as well as budget purposes. If measures are developed with dual uses in mind, productivity tends to be enhanced by eliminating duplicative measurement efforts. Most local governments that participated in this survey have budget constraints that prevent them from engaging in activities

Table 5/10   USE OF PROGRAM MEASURES FOR MANAGEMENT PURPOSES

Program measures	Users of program measure information		
	Manager % of (A)	Legis. body % of (A)	Dept. heads/staff % of (A)
Total reporting use of program measures (A) 522			
Activity/workload	78.4	38.3	77.0
Performance	61.7	31.4	61.3
Productivity	54.2	25.3	53.3
Effectiveness	51.3	26.1	49.2
Goal attainment	60.7	34.3	57.7
Municipalities reporting use of program measures (A) 312			
Activity/workload	83.0	31.7	74.0
Performance	69.2	29.8	62.8
Productivity	59.3	23.4	54.5
Effectiveness	57.1	24.4	50.0
Goal attainment	69.9	34.0	61.9
Counties reporting use of program measures (A) 210			
Activity/workload	71.4	48.1	81.4
Performance	50.5	33.8	59.0
Productivity	46.7	28.1	51.4
Effectiveness	42.9	28.6	48.1
Goal attainment	47.1	34.8	51.4

Note: The number reporting use of program measures (522) is 37% of all survey respondents.

Table 5/11   FACTORS ENHANCING PRODUCTIVITY/EFFICIENCY

Classification	No. reporting (A)	Computers		Performance measurement		Benchmarking		Quality improvement[1]		Improved budget process	
		No. reporting	% of (A)	No. reporting	% of (A)	No. reporting	% of (A)	No. reporting	% of (A)	No. reporting	% of (A)
Total	1,396	1,283	91.9	292	20.9	87	6.2	246	17.6	871	62.4
Population group											
Over 1,000,000	21	21	100.0	9	42.9	4	19.0	10	47.6	13	61.9
500,000–1,000,000	42	40	95.2	17	40.5	7	16.7	13	31.0	26	61.9
250,000–499,999	61	60	98.4	17	27.9	4	6.6	17	27.9	47	77.0
100,000–249,999	180	167	92.8	54	30.0	15	8.3	54	30.0	130	72.2
50,000–99,999	318	297	93.4	75	23.6	23	7.2	57	17.9	202	63.5
25,000–49,999	443	405	91.4	81	18.3	29	6.5	63	14.2	264	59.6
10,000–24,999	116	107	92.2	16	13.8	2	1.7	14	12.1	75	64.7
5,000–9,999	115	99	86.1	14	12.2	2	1.7	11	9.6	64	55.7
2,500–4,999	100	87	87.0	9	9.0	1	1.0	7	7.0	50	50.0
Geographic division											
New England	80	75	93.8	21	26.3	1	1.3	17	21.3	55	68.8
Mid-Atlantic	129	118	91.5	23	17.8	6	4.7	13	10.1	77	59.7
East North Central	225	201	89.3	39	17.3	10	4.4	32	14.2	120	53.3
West North Central	171	152	88.9	33	19.3	3	1.8	23	13.5	107	62.6
South Atlantic	228	215	94.3	65	28.5	23	10.1	57	25.0	162	71.1
East South Central	72	68	94.4	13	18.1	5	6.9	5	6.9	41	56.9
West South Central	186	172	92.5	28	15.1	11	5.9	24	12.9	110	59.1
Mountain	106	98	92.5	25	23.6	14	13.2	21	19.8	68	64.2
Pacific Coast	199	184	92.5	45	22.6	14	7.0	54	27.1	131	65.8
Metro status											
Central	365	348	95.3	106	29.0	35	9.6	104	28.5	238	65.2
Suburban	490	458	93.5	108	22.0	36	7.3	76	15.5	323	65.9
Independent	541	477	88.2	78	14.4	16	3.0	66	12.2	310	57.3
Type											
Municipalities	764	711	93.1	171	22.4	54	7.1	141	18.5	482	63.1
Counties	632	572	90.5	121	19.1	33	5.2	105	16.6	389	61.6

[1]Quality improvement includes "reinventing" and "reengineering" techniques.

that do not have direct relevance to their official mission. Measurements developed by the departmental staff that will use them internally as well as include them in budget requests are more likely to be meaningful. Indeed, they are more likely to be developed and collected, since they will not be seen as ''make-work'' projects of a central budget office but as a means of improving management and productivity.

Users of Program Measures

Are program and performance measures used for management purposes in addition to the budget process? If so, who uses them? Thirty-seven percent of responding local governments use program measures for management as well as budgeting. Measures are used slightly more frequently by the manager or CAO than by the departments (Table 5/10). As might be ex-

pected, fewer legislators use the measures for management, since usually they are less involved in the day-to-day operations of the government. In counties, department heads use the measures more often than managers do; in municipalities, the managers are the primary users.

PRODUCTIVITY

What is the result of these efforts to improve management processes? How much impact does the use of computers have on the budget process? Has performance measurement really improved the quality of management and budget decisions? Although a single survey of budget processes cannot answer these and related questions definitively, some answers can be gleaned from the responses to questions about whether the productivity or efficiency of the respondents local governments has been enhanced by the use of computers, performance measurement, benchmarking, quality improvement processes, and improvements in the budget process.

About 92% of the respondents say that computers have improved their government's efficiency and productivity (Table 5/11). This includes over 90% of all the jurisdictions with populations of 10,000 or more, and over 86% of the smaller governments. Improvements in the budget process also are cited as improving overall productivity and efficiency in 62% of the responding governments, including over 60% of the governments with population of 10,000 or more. Productivity improvements were experienced in about equal percentages in both municipalities and counties from both computers and improved budget processes.

Performance measurement had a lesser impact, but about 21% of the local government respondents say that it had improved productivity or efficiency in their jurisdictions. Improvements in productivity were more frequent in larger jurisdictions: over 40% with populations of 500,000 or more experienced such results from performance measurement. Municipalities were slightly more likely to experience productivity enhancement from performance measurement (22%) than were counties (19%).

Quality improvement processes also improved productivity in about 18% of the jurisdictions. Benchmarking had a lesser impact, but it did improve productivity in 6% of the local governments that responded. Since quality processes and benchmarking were used in only 28% and 11% of the responding jurisdictions respectively, these are fairly significant results.

QUALITY IMPROVEMENT ACTIVITIES AND THE BUDGET

Only 28% (393) of all respondents reported a change in the budget process as a result of quality improvement activities. The most often reported changes are in the information collected (41%) and in the development of the budget (41%) (Figure 5/2). The next most commonly

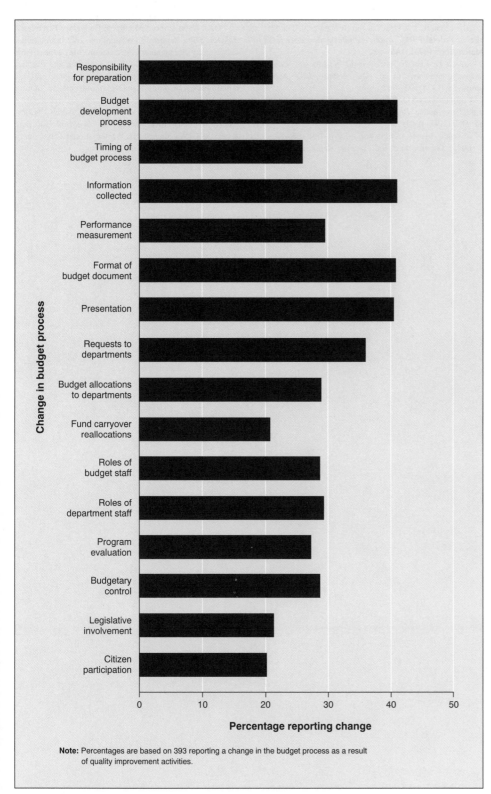

Note: Percentages are based on 393 reporting a change in the budget process as a result of quality improvement activities.

Figure 5/2   *Changes in the budget process as a result of quality improvement activities*

reported changes are in the format of the budget document and in the presentation. At least 20% reported a change in each of the processes listed on the survey instrument.

CONCLUSIONS

Many observers of government have charged that government agencies are inherently inefficient, reluctant to change, and unlikely to be very productive. On the other hand, the quality improvement and government reinvention movements have suggested that these management improvement and productivity enhancement processes can and do improve government management and budgeting. The results of this survey show that governments do indeed change and that productivity and efficiency can improve as a result. The results also show that budget processes have changed to accommodate management improvement processes used by

local governments. Although one survey cannot be definitive, these results indicate that local governments are at the forefront once again in the movement to improve government and make it more productive and responsive to citizen needs.

[1] John L. Mikesell, *Fiscal Administration*, 4th ed. (Belmont, CA: Wadsworth Publishing Company, 1995): 166–70.

[2] Allen Schick, "The Road to PPB: The Stages of Budget Reform," *Public Administration Review* 26 (December 1966): 243–58.

[3] Allen Schick, "A Death in the Bureaucracy: The Demise of Federal PPB," *Public Administration Review* 33 (March/April 1973): 146–56.

[4] Robert D. Lee, Jr., and Ronald W. Johnson, *Public Budgeting Systems*, 5th ed. (Gaithersburg, MD: Aspen Publishers, 1994): 93–95.

[5] Commission on Organization of the Executive Branch of the Government, *Budgeting and Accounting* (Washington, DC: GPO, 1949).

[6] Mikesell, *Fiscal Administration*; 170–73, 186–89.

[7] David Osborne and Ted Gaebler, *Reinventing Government: How the Entrepreneurial Spirit Is Transforming the Public Sector* (Reading, MA: Addison-Wesley, 1992).

[8] Aaron Wildavsky and Arthur Hammond, "Comprehensive Versus Incremental Budgeting in the Department of Agriculture," *Administrative Science Quarterly* 10 (December 1965): 321–46.

[9] Peter A. Pyhrr, *Zero-Base Budgeting* (New York: John Wiley, 1973).

[10] Peter A. Pyhrr, "The Zero-Base Approach to Government Budgeting," *Public Administration Review* 37 (January/February 1977): 1–8.

[11] Thomas W. Wenz and Ann P. Nolan, "Budgeting for the Future: Target Base Budgeting," *Public Budgeting and Finance* 2 (Spring 1982): 88–91.

[12] Glen Hahn Cope, "Municipal Budgetary Practices," *Baseline Data Report* 18 (Washington, DC: International City/County Management Association, May/June 1986): 6; Glen Hahn Cope, "Municipal Budgeting and Productivity," *Baseline Data Report* 21 (Washington, DC: International City/County Management Association, March/April 1989): 2–3.

[13] Kenneth L. Kraemer and Donald F. Norris, "Computers in Local Government," in *The Municipal Year Book 1994* (Washington, DC: International City/County Management Association, 1994): 4.

B The Intergovernmental Dimension

State-Local Relations: Patterns, Problems, and Partnerships

David R. Berman
Department of Political Science
Arizona State University

"Your pressures are no different than ours. We share a common bond. Your taxpayers are our taxpayers.... If there is no state money available for programs initiated by the Legislature, then the implementation of these programs by counties and municipalities should be optional and not mandatory." These remarks by Michael Pappas, president of the New Jersey Association of Counties, in an appearance before the New Jersey state legislature, echo the sentiments of local officials throughout the nation in recent years.[1]

Their basic complaint is that federal and state officials have responded to their own financial problems by passing the costs for programs on to local governments. To add insult to injury, local officials have had to get along with less federal and state financial assistance as a proportion of their total expenditures.

Local officials have not been passive about these developments. On the mandate front, for example, they and organizations representing them have waged extensive lobbying campaigns, put together comprehensive mandate catalogs with assessments of the financial impacts of the mandates, taken their complaints directly to the public through media campaigns, initiated and worked for antimandate ballot measures and brought court suits challenging the validity of mandates and other state controls.[2]

Last year brought continued, though uneven, progress on mandate protection. The situation also improved in regard to state assistance and local revenues, thanks, in large part, to better fiscal conditions in much of the country. Nevertheless, aid to general local governments has had to compete with increased demands for spending in other areas, particularly education, health care, and corrections, and with demands for tax relief. In addition, continued problems and disruptions in state-local relations occur as a result of efforts to reform the funding of education and implement environmental, transportation, and land-use policies on a metropolitan or regional basis.

This article reviews some broad developments affecting the shape of intergovernmental relations, explores state actions affecting local authority and finances, and looks into problems in specific policy areas.

BROAD PATTERNS AND DEVELOPMENTS

Local governments are part of an intergovernmental system in which the actions taken by one level of government have direct and indirect implications for the others. In this complex system, financial and regulatory decisions made by the national government have a forceful impact on state-local relations.

Changes in Federal Policy

Since the late 1970s two basic changes in national policy affecting state-local relations have taken place. One has been a shift in federal grant policy, which has forced state and local governments to become less reliant on federal financial assistance. The other has been a shift toward the use of federal mandates that require state and local governments to pick up more of the costs of government.

Federal aid equaled around 27% of state-local spending in 1978. By 1989 this had fallen to around 17%. Though grants have increased since the mid-1980s, up to around 22% of state-local spending, the increase has done little for local officials. Much of the increase in federal aid has gone to state rather than local governments. The recent increases, moreover, represent a shift away from the type of grants that give state and local officials an opportunity to pursue programs based on their own assessment of needs. The increased aid has been mostly entitlements for individuals. These programs leave little room for discretion because they require state and local officials to provide benefits under federal rules to all who qualify.[3]

Since the mid-1970s, costly federal mandates have occurred in such policy areas as air and water quality, solid waste, hazardous waste, transportation standards, labor management, health care, courts, and corrections. Recent examples of congressional legislation creating unfunded mandates are the Americans with Disabilities Act, the Safe Drinking Water Act, and the National Voter Registration Act.

Local governments, being at the end of the path of "one way federalism"—or what some call "shift and shaft federalism"—end up paying many of these costs.[4] Thus, when Congress decides to increase Medicaid coverage, it forces the states to pay more for their share of the increased costs or risk losing the program. In some places, state governments comply by passing increased costs on to their local governments. In New York, for example, Medicaid costs counties millions of dollars each year because the state pushes on to counties the responsibility for providing a large portion of the matching funds the federal government requires.

Many of the most costly mandates that local governments must deal with are federal mandates regarding such matters as health care or environmental protection that states pass on to them. Local officials sometimes take out their anger about the federal programs on state officials. As the head of the Indiana State Department of Environmental Management has noted: "We have all these environmental mandates coming down, and we have all these cities and counties asking, 'Why are you doing this to us?'"[5]

As the federal government has increased mandated expenditures on the states, the states have increased mandated expenditures on local governments. At the same time, as the federal government has decreased local aid, local governments have sought, with varying degrees of success, to replace these funds with state aid. In addition to this type of shifting, requirements attached to federal grants often directly affect the pattern of state-local relations. One important example is the Intermodal Surface Transportation Efficiency Act of 1991 (ISTEA), which, among other provisions, requires that states give local officials a greater role in transportation decision making.

Local officials have not abandoned the goal of at least a partially restored federal-local partnership and, indeed, many applaud ISTEA as an important step toward improving the status of local governments as partners in the federal system. Local officials probably can expect some relief from Washington on the mandate issue, though Congress failed to take such action in 1994 in spite of a strong lobbying effort by public interest groups.

Local officials, however, probably cannot expect drastic changes in federal aid policies, at least, in the immediate future. Faced with public resistance to increased taxes and a massive debt, it is unlikely that federal officials will find it feasible, either economically or politically, to resume an active role in financing state and local programs. This situation encourages local officials to forge more effective relations with their state governments. The lobbying effort at the state level has always been of great importance to local officials. In this era of "fend for yourself federalism" at the national level, lobbying has become even more important.

Politics and Policy in the States

In the late 1970s local officials began turning to their states for help in making up for lost federal revenues. The initial state response was generally positive, but as economic conditions worsened, state financial aid to local governments in many parts of the country began to diminish. Meanwhile, faced with their own budgetary problems, states shifted more and more of the costs of government to local governments.

Mandates and finances have become the central issues in state-local relations. Along with these have come tussles over local government authority, both generally and in specific policy areas. Over the last few decades, economic, political, and legal pressures have brought about a greater interest by state officials in matters such as education and land use planning, traditionally handled on the local level. Through improvements in staffing, state legislatures have increased their institutional capacity to become involved in these matters. Critics of such centralizing trends see the states doing, at best, a spotty job in helping their localities and, in the long run, the danger of inaction and overload at the state level.

State legislators, governors, and administrators make many of the most important decisions affecting local government. However, the importance of state courts in this respect should not be overlooked. State courts have built up an enormous body of case law on what local governments can and cannot do. They play a major role in determining the extent of home rule or general discretionary authority on the local level. They have had an increasingly important impact on local taxing, spending, and regulatory powers in general and in such policy areas as education, environmental protection, land-use planning, and housing.

On a more political level, state courts in recent years have, in several instances, enhanced the ability of local officials to challenge the authority of the states. State courts have traditionally made it difficult for cities and counties to challenge state governments. Over the past few years, however, they have been more inclined

to regard local governments as "judicial persons," with standing to sue their parent state governments on such matters as failure to meet constitutional funding obligations. In addition, state courts have become more willing to examine basic legal questions such as whether state actions violate state constitutional bans on special or local laws.[6]

Voters in the various states and localities have also become of more direct importance on decisions affecting local authority and operations. Initiative and referendum elections commonly feature measures of vital importance to local officials. Voters have often come down on the side of local officials on the mandate question, for example, in approving measures requiring states to reimburse localities for expenditures mandated by the state. On the negative side, from the local point of view, voters commonly resist proposals to raise revenues, for example, through the adoption of a sales tax—even when reform plans couple this with a property-tax reduction.

One exception to this pattern occurred in Michigan last year, largely because of the way lawmakers framed the question put to the voters. In this case voters were not asked to vote *yes* or *no* on whether they wanted new taxes but to choose, in essence, between an increase in the sales tax or an increase in the income tax. They chose to rely on the sales tax as the principal means of replacing cuts in property taxes. For the previous several years, on a simple yes-or-no vote, Michigan voters had rejected proposals to increase the sales tax as a way of reducing reliance on the property tax.

Voters have also raised havoc in recent years by approving tax-and-spending limitation measures. One type of reform currently being put before voters is that a legislative body can increase taxes or spending only if two-thirds or more of its members agree to do so. Another popular reform idea makes tax increases and spending increases above a certain level dependent on popular approval. Some reform proposals apply to state governments only, while others include both state and local governments. From the local point of view, limiting the states is dangerous because it creates a risk of cuts in local aid and because it encourages state officials to shift more responsibilities to cities, counties, and school districts, bringing either increases in property taxes or reduced services.

A leading example of a proposition adopted by the voters which limits both state and local governments is the Taxpayers Bill of Rights (TABOR) approved by Colorado voters in 1992. TABOR bars tax and spending increases by state and local governments without voter approval. Under the law, voters must also approve increases in spending above a limit set by a formula that takes into account the rate of inflation and population increases.

Thus far, the impact of TABOR has been mixed. Voters, though selective, generally have approved requests for spending above the formula level as long as tax rates did not increase.[7] The courts, too, have eased the impact of the

proposition by rejecting a strict interpretation of the amendment.[8]

The 1994 elections marked a slight retreat from making taxing/spending decisions dependent on voter approval. Such proposals were voted down in Oregon, Missouri, and Montana. Voters in Montana also rejected a proposal requiring a super-majority by state and local legislative bodies in order to raise taxes, fees, or spending levels.

THE STATES AND LOCAL AUTHORITY

State courts have traditionally viewed local governments as the "legal creatures" of their states. Applying Dillion's Rule (after John F. Dillion, a nineteenth-century Iowa jurist and authority on municipal law), they have concluded that local governments have only the powers expressly granted them by the state and that courts must construe these powers narrowly. According to Dillion's Rule, local governments must obtain specific legislative authority for just about everything they wish to do. One result is that lawmakers are kept busy passing local bills.

Home Rule

To circumvent Dillion's Rule, many states have constitutional provisions or statutes that confer "home rule" or broad discretionary authority on local governments, giving them the right to make decisions without specific grants of authority. In some places state law gives local governments exclusive authority to deal with matters that are "municipal" or "local" in nature. In other states, the law authorizes local units to carry out any function or exercise any power not expressly forbidden or preempted by the state.

In practice, the actual scope of local authority in every state is heavily influenced by judicial decisions. How the state courts perform this function varies greatly from state to state, even when essentially the same home rule law is involved. Wyoming's experience is an example. The state patterned its home rule provision after one used in Kansas, in the hope that Wyoming courts would interpret the law in the same liberal manner as Kansas courts. Wyoming courts, however, did not follow the precedent set in Kansas and chose, instead, to keep Dillion's Rule alive in the state.[9]

State courts generally have a tradition of construing narrowly the grants of authority to local governments. There have, however, been numerous exceptions. Last year, for example, the North Carolina Supreme Court rejected the application of Dillion's Rule and instead gave a broad construction of local government authority under a state statute in upholding the right of the City of Charlotte to adopt a system of user fees.[10] A year earlier the Supreme Court of South Carolina gave a liberal construction of the home-rule authority conferred upon municipalities by the state constitution in a decision upholding the right of the town of Hilton Head Island to adopt a real-estate transfer fee.[11]

Many questions concerning local authority

end up in court. State legislatures, however, settled many more of them. Generally, state legislators, regardless of the nature of their constituencies, ideologies, or party identification, have been reluctant to relinquish control over local governments. Attitudes concerning the fundamentals of state-local relations seem to be very much a product of Miles' Law: "Where you stand depends on where you sit."[12] From where they sit, local officials usually see more local autonomy to be a good thing. From where they sit, state legislators often see more local autonomy as something that might bring undesirable results.[13] Businesses and various other groups also worry about the effects of giving local governments more discretion. They find it easier and more comfortable to deal with a single state legislative body than with a multitude of local government authorities.

Nevertheless, over the years the view that local governments should have home rule or greater discretionary authority has gained ground on the creature-of-the-state position. Some degree of home rule is possible for municipalities in 48 states. County governments have such powers in 37 states.[14] Following the lead of the United States Advisory Commission on Intergovernmental Relations, scholars and practitioners generally break down home rule into structural, functional, fiscal, and personnel types.[15] Research suggests that demographic pressures such as changes in urbanization, levels of education, and income may encourage state officials to give more discretion to localities in regard to structure. Changes in discretionary authority about such matters as what functions are to be performed, however, are linked to slower-changing cultural and managerial factors.[16]

In practice, the amount of local discretion varies by region, type of local government unit, and type of authority.[17] The tradition of local self-government is, for example, stronger in New England than in the South. Municipalities, on the whole, enjoy more discretionary authority than do counties and other units of local government. Local governments of all types generally have more discretion on structure and functions than on finances.

The fact that states authorize home rule does not mean that cities or counties will opt for this status or, even if they do, will exercise home rule authority. County and city officials, particularly but not exclusively those in jurisdictions where home rule is a recent development, often appear uncertain about how much authority they have, and thus feel more comfortable receiving specific grants of authority from the legislature. The net result is that home rule changes little in terms of local authority and does next to nothing in reducing the workload of state legislators.

Scope of State Involvement

Because of the inferior legal status of local governments, states have virtually unlimited ability to intervene in local affairs by stipulating rules and requirements, mandating the performance of certain functions, and prohibiting local governments from taking certain types of actions.

The importance of state governments to localities is shown, in part, in the routine passage of legislation affecting local authority, procedures, and finances. On the average, probably around 20% of the hundreds of measures introduced in state legislatures significantly affect local governments.

State laws extend into several areas. They condition the general level of local authority and the types of governmental structures local governments can adopt. State laws also commonly set various regulations on local elections. On matters of finance, state laws often set debt limits, mandate public hearings for adopting budgets, require a referendum for bond issues, and outline the method of assessing property. On personnel matters, most local governments must abide by state laws requiring training of employees and worker's compensation. Open-meeting and open-record requirements are among the most frequent types of regulation affecting the governing process. Other types of basic local-government laws have to do with incorporation, annexation, consolidation, and intergovernmental service agreements. In recent years, new state laws have been particularly common in the areas of financial and personnel management.[18]

State legislators in nearly every session tinker with laws they think will improve local government service delivery. Some state interference and micromanagement represents the desire to make local government more accountable, effective, and efficient. When it comes to mandates, however, a stronger motivation may simply be to shift the costs of programs to local governments. In the case of prohibitions, legislative action often is a matter of acceding to the demand of some private group anxious to avoid local taxes or regulations.

Local officials, not surprisingly, take issue with assumptions that local governments are wasteful and inefficient and that state officials, seeing the big picture, know best when it comes to improving the delivery of local services. From the local point of view, it is state directives rather than locally initiated actions that often lead to misdirected, wasteful, or inefficient services.[19]

Local officials often find state interventions unwarranted or unfair. An example of the former occurred in Florida last year when the legislature decided that municipalities must bid out for private consideration all jobs such as road building and repair that cost $200,000 or more, regardless of their ability to perform such work in-house or of their experience in doing so. In Minnesota, meanwhile, the cry was unfairness as state intervention in local affairs took place as a result of a problem at the state level. Media exposure of ethical lapses by state officials prompted legislation prohibiting gifts to state legislators and other officials at that level. During the process of putting the bill together, however, the legislature impinged upon local authority by extending the prohibition to city and county officials. Adding to the outrage of these officials was the fact that school and township officials were not included in the legislation.

The Mandate Problem

State governments commonly rely on their legislative and regulatory authority to compel local units to assume responsibilities for various programs and services. Individual states impose many more mandates on their local governments than does the federal government, though, as noted above, some of the more expensive mandates are federal requirements that states pass on to localities.[20]

Local officials have little difficulty with the goals of many mandates. Indeed, they sometimes welcome the political "cover" which mandates give them as they try to carry out programs which are unpopular with segments of their communities (for example, low-income housing). While some mandates may be desirable, however, local officials often find them objectionable because they distort local priorities, impair managerial flexibility, and impose costs that have to be picked up out of local revenues. From a range of studies, it appears localities dedicate anywhere from 20% to 90% of their expenditures to implementing federal and state mandates.[21]

Each year local officials have to be on guard against legislation dumping expensive or inefficient state programs on them. Some routine shifts cost relatively little money, though their aggregate effects can be staggering. The big-ticket items are in areas such as health care, education, and environmental protection, and can overwhelm the budgets of local governments.

Local officials and organizations that represent them constantly seek state payments to cover the costs of new mandates. Sometimes they are successful. At other times, legislatures give local governments authority to raise the necessary revenues. This is a less desirable approach because local officials run the risk of incurring the wrath of their taxpayers in order to comply with the mandate.

Other strategies for coping with mandates center on the mandate process. Over 40 states require agencies—in some places, commissions on intergovernmental relations—to estimate the costs imposed on localities by state laws or regulations. These are fiscal note requirements. Several states use fiscal notes in conjunction with a requirement that the state reimburse localities for the expense of undertaking the required activity. In others they are used simply to call attention to the costs local governments will incur.

The usefulness of the fiscal-note process is impaired by problems of securing timely and reliable cost estimates and, more fundamentally, by the disinclination of legislators to pay much attention to them even if they are available and reasonably accurate. Preparation of reliable cost estimates in time to influence legislative decision-making (at least before the full committee has to vote on a proposed mandate) has been frustrated by the lack of staff, time and expertise. Because of these limitations and legislators' lack of enthusiasm for the process, many measures with a potential financial impact on local government may not even be identified.[22]

When employed alone (that is, without a reimbursement requirement), fiscal notes appear to have only a limited effect on legislative behavior. Even if the process makes legislators more aware of the financial burden they are passing along to local governments, this knowledge does not mean that they will refuse to impose the costs. These, after all, are not assumed by the state but by local governments. When used as the sole antimandate strategy, fiscal notes appear to be of value primarily in providing local governments with lobbying ammunition.[23]

Several states have adopted constitutional or statutory limits on their ability to impose mandates on local governments. Some laws call for state reimbursement or partial reimbursement of the costs new mandates impose on local governments. In some places, such as California, the state must either pick up the costs for mandated programs or give localities the authority to raise taxes to finance them. Most laws have a ''safety valve'' allowing the legislature to pass an unfunded mandate through a supermajority (two-thirds or three-fourths) vote.

In practice, the usefulness of reimbursement programs established through the process of constitutional amendment depends greatly on implementing statutes passed by the legislatures that detail the process of reimbursement.[24] Legislatures normally have considerable discretion in interpreting the meaning of the constitutional provisions and, not uncommonly, the devil is in the details of the implementing statutes.

Because of their importance, such details may be difficult to develop. In Florida, the legislature has yet to approve legislation to implement the constitutional amendment regarding mandates that the voters approved in 1990. In 1991, the governor vetoed implementing legislation. Another attempt died in the legislature in 1992. No attempt has been made since. In the absence of implementing legislation, the legislature has relied on guidelines adopted by the House and Senate rules and a memorandum prepared by legislative leaders.

Mandate reimbursement, whether required constitutionally or by statute, appears more effective than simple cost estimation in deterring unfunded mandates. Reimbursement requirements placed in the constitution with the backing of the voters may be more effective in influencing legislative behavior than those created by statute. As time goes by, however, the deterrent effect brought about by the expression of public opinion may diminish. Voters appear more likely to approve such measures when proponents link them to the goals of reducing local property taxes and preserving local control over spending priorities.''[25]

The major effect of reimbursement provisions appears to be in deterring or modifying mandates to make them less expensive rather than in providing extensive funding for mandates.[26] In some places, such as Florida and Maine, antimandate language in state constitutions appears to have helped reduce the total number. Legislatures in some states, however, have simply ignored reimbursement requirements—there is no penalty for doing so—or have gotten around them by earmarking part of the funding already allocated for state aid to localities as mandate reimbursement. Mandate-reimbursement costs are, in effect, deducted from local aid programs.[27]

States have considered or adopted a variety of antimandate measures in addition to fiscal note and reimbursement requirements. These include: requiring an agency such as the state advisory council on intergovernmental relations to compile and update annually a catalog of all mandates, including the fiscal impact of new mandates, as a basic informational base; requiring state agencies to review current mandates on a regular basis to determine if any of them can be relaxed or eliminated; encouraging agencies to implement new mandates on an experimental basis to test out their effectiveness and impacts before spreading them to all localities; and enabling the governor to suspend mandates upon the request of local governments should they be found to impose an unreasonable burden.

Use of sunset legislation to review mandates every five or even ten years to see which ones have outlived their usefulness is strongly recommended in a study that also suggests that local officials may have more success in fending off mandates by challenging the goal or the method of reaching the goal of a mandate rather than focusing on the costs. The study further suggests that fundamentally the mandate problem is linked to the broader problem of increasing the ability of local governments to participate in and influence state level decisions that affect them.[28]

In many states the number of new mandates appears to have decreased because of improved state revenues, the effect of antimandate laws, and the publicity given to the mandate problem. Last year, however, was one of mixed progress. On the plus side, Iowa lawmakers passed an unfunded mandates bill stating that unless the state provides the funding or specifies a proportion of the funding that the state shall provide annually, a local government shall not be required to implement a new service or program. The unfunded mandates law is triggered by any service or program that has a statewide fiscal impact of over $100,000.

In New Jersey, a proposed constitutional amendment requiring the state to pay for any new program it mandates and a proposal to roll back existing mandates were tied up in the legislature. The Maryland legislature also rejected a proposed constitutional amendment prohibiting future unfunded mandates. However, legislation was developed to further sensitize lawmakers to the mandate problem. In response to the efforts of city and county organizations, the legislature required that all bills it considers having a negative fiscal impact on local governments be ''red flagged'' in various ways. Beginning in 1995, the State Department of Legislative Reference must decide which bills impose a mandate on local governments. Those found to do so must have the statement ''this bill imposes a mandate on a local government unit'' included in the bill synopsis prepared by the department and distributed to legislators and their staffs. The law also requires that such language be added to any fiscal note prepared for a bill that imposes a mandate on local governments. In addition, the legislation strengthens the fiscal estimating process by requiring an analysis of the effect of the mandate on local property taxes.

In Ohio, the legislature also strengthened the fiscal-note process, requiring that cost estimates be considered in a timely fashion by legislative committees and before departmental regulations are adopted. In addition, Ohio passed legislation requiring the State and Local Government Commission to create a mandate task force.

Elsewhere, legislatures focused on the elimination of specific mandates found to be unnecessary, outdated, or useless. In several states, legislatures acted upon a series of recommendations made by advisory commissions on intergovernmental relations. The process of identifying and eliminating various mandates enjoyed considerable success in Colorado, Iowa, Utah, and other states.

State Preemption

Local officials have to worry not only about requirements that they do certain things but about mandates of a preemptory or ''thou-shall-not'' nature. Such prohibitions frequently reflect the desire of a particular group to minimize, if not avoid completely, governmental taxation or regulation. Local officials, for example, regularly guard against state legislation that would exempt certain businesses from local sales taxes, or, at the request of businesses, completely preempt local sales tax authority.

In recent years, efforts to avoid local authority have been especially intense on policies concerning controls over guns, billboards, smoking, and pesticides. Thanks in large part to the National Rifle Association, some 30 states prohibit local gun control ordinances. In some states, police chiefs have helped prevent this form of preemption by pointing out that such a prohibition makes it more difficult for them to fight crime. Last year, in Louisiana, a prohibition on both state and local taxes or fees on the purchase of guns and ammunition was proposed and defeated twice.

Tobacco companies have encouraged a move away from local legislation on smoking. Commonly, states have preempted local action through the passage of statewide clean air bills less stringent than the local ordinances they replace. In 1994, California voters rejected a move of this kind by turning down a proposition supported by the tobacco industry calling for statewide standards for indoor smoking and superceding more stringent local ordinances. The Tennessee legislature, on the other hand, prohibited cities and counties from regulating smoking in any building other than city- or county-owned or leased facilities.

Tobacco industry groups have also challenged proposed local bans on cigarette vending machines, arguing that any regulation of this business is reserved for state authority.[29] Local action is clearly preempted in those states where there are state laws specially addressed to the existence or placement of cigarette vending machines. Courts, however, also have voided local regulations on the grounds that state preemption of the field is implied by related state laws. In 1993, for example, the Maryland Court of Appeals rejected the effort of a city to restrict the placement of machines vending cigarettes to locations not accessible to minors, holding that the state, by its adoption of a licensing scheme for cigarette vending machines, had acted with such force that "an intent by the State to occupy the entire field" regarding the sale of cigarettes through vending machines was implied.[30]

Business groups that manufacture pesticides and businesses and agricultural groups that use them have been active in state capitals in an attempt to prevent local regulation of pesticide use. They argue that a multitude of restrictions on pesticide use would do injury to business and agriculture. Proponents of control argue that local regulations are needed to protect the environment and the health and welfare of citizens.[31] Currently, states are free to decide whether localities within their boundaries can regulate pesticide use. About half the states have passed preemption laws. The Wisconsin legislature, in its 1993–94 session, joined the list of states that have preempted municipalities from regulating pesticides.

Two other common types of preemptions took effect last year in Arizona: one restricts the ability of a city or town to regulate billboards and the other prohibits cities or towns from adopting ordinances in conflict with state liquor laws.

Related to the effort to preempt local authority has been a more focused drive to discourage local regulations by requiring localities to compensate property owners financially damaged by them. Currently several state courts are examining cases initiated by property-rights advocates challenging the regulatory authority of state and local governments. U.S. Supreme Court decisions such as *Lucas* v. *South Carolina Coast Council* (1992) and *Dolan* v. *City of Tigard* (1994) have encouraged such litigation.

Property-rights advocates, realtors, and developers have also pushed for legislation requiring compensation for the limitations various types of state and/or local regulations place on the use of private property. In 1994, legislation of this nature passed in Idaho, Mississippi, Tennessee, Utah, and West Virginia. Though most of this legislation is aimed at state regulations, especially those regarding the environment, local officials fear the next step will be to apply such laws to them, and thus make regulatory policies such as zoning more difficult to implement. In 1994, Arizona voters turned down a takings proposal on the state ballot.

THE STATES AND LOCAL REVENUES

State aid to local governments consists of grants and shared taxes. Grants are usually designated for specific programs in such areas as education or transportation, though most states also provide unrestricted grants for general purposes. On shared taxes, states act essentially as tax collectors to avoid a duplication of administration. The state returns all or a portion of the yield from a shared tax either according to an allocation formula or on the basis of origin of collection. As in the case of grants, states earmark much of this shared revenue for specific purposes. For example, states commonly require that localities spend their share of the state gas tax on highway or street improvements. Some shared revenue, however, is unrestricted and can be spent as local officials see fit.

Much of the unrestricted aid comes to local governments as compensation for some state action, such as the granting of a property-tax exemption that reduces local revenues. The aid is usually distributed on a criteria such as place of origin or population rather than on a measurement of local need. Utilization of such criteria results in a more extensive and even allocation of funds among jurisdictions, but it also may aggravate local fiscal disparities.[32]

Although state aid to local governments varies from state to state and fluctuates over time, it usually is a major source of local revenue. Local governments receive about four times as much from state governments as they do from the federal government. State aid accounts for around 30% of all city and county revenue. Differences among the states in regard to the level of local assistance programs are due to factors ranging from per capita income to the percentage of Democrats in the state legislature. The importance of particular factors varies with different types of assistance programs.[33]

Most state aid (62% in 1992) goes to support education, a function usually carried out by independent school districts. City or county governments administer school systems in only a few states, for example, Maryland, North Carolina, and Virginia. As indicated later, some of the more dramatic and controversial changes in the system of state aid over the past two decades have related to elementary and secondary education.

Following education in funding are public welfare (15% of the total), general local government support (around 8%), and highways (4%). Recently, state aid also has appeared in relatively new areas, like corrections, housing, and transit, yet relatively little (only about one out of every eight dollars) goes to cities to support traditional municipal programs.[34] State aid has had a modest equalization effect. It tends to reduce somewhat the revenue gap between poorer and wealthier localities.[35] Only a handful of states, however, have made a conscious effort to target funds on the basis of local need.[36]

During the 1980s, localities turned to their states for financial help because of declines in federal aid, increased mandates, strains on local revenues, and growth in citizen demands for services. The states generally responded with increases in state aid, though, upon inspection, this response was less impressive than it first appeared.

Total state aid to local governments jumped from around $83 billion in 1980 to close to $130 billion in 1986 and $172 billion in 1990. Studies show that the growth of state aid over the 1980s, while substantial, lagged behind the growth in state economies during the period.[37] Moreover, as states experienced trouble balancing their budgets in the late 1980s and early 1990s, the percentage of increase in state aid began to dwindle. From 1985 to 1991, state aid increases lagged behind increases in state and local spending.[38] With good reason, local officials had little confidence in the state's willingness to provide adequate funding for the programs local governments administered.[39] As the economy worsened, examples of state concern with the fiscal problems of local governments became rarer and rarer. During the fiscal crisis of the early 1990s, several legislatures cut direct aid to localities. In many places aid to local governments was the first casualty as state revenues declined.

In the past few years, with a general economic upturn in many parts of the country, the aid picture has been improving. Yet there has been considerable uncertainty as to how much aid, if any, will be forthcoming. As one observer has noted: "Budgeting at the local level has become a nightmare as cities try to anticipate what will happen to state aid when the Legislature convenes."[40]

Last year was a relatively good one for state aid to cities and counties in many states. In New York, the legislature increased state revenue-sharing by 7.6%—the first increase since 1986–87. The Minnesota legislature passed a 2%, or $6.6 million, increase in Local Government Aid (LGA) for 1995, and in New Jersey the state distributed some $32 million through a new municipal block grant fund (though the legislature offset this gain by withholding other funds). While gains were often substantial, legislatures siphoned off much of the increased revenue coming into the states with increases in state aid to education, expenditures for Medicaid and corrections, and by tax cuts for businesses and individuals.[41]

In some states, the provision of aid has taken second place to cutting local costs, for example, by eliminating mandates or by fostering greater efficiency at the local level. Some state lawmakers have also toyed with the idea of encouraging local governments in a given region to share revenues rather than depend on state aid.[42]

In New Jersey last year, Governor Christine Todd Whitman called for eliminating some special state-aid programs and holding others at their current levels. Local officials, faced with rising costs, warned that limits on state aid would force them to increase property taxes in order to balance their budgets. The governor countered that local governments could avoid property tax increases by cutting municipal costs through the privatization of some local services and by the consolidation of others. The governor also offered the services of state efficiency audit teams of management specialists to assist local officials in identifying cost savings. Several local governments—municipalities, counties, and school boards—have taken the governor up on her offer.[43]

Locally Derived Revenues

Since the mid-1980s tax revenues at the local level have generally been increasing and, indeed, at a faster rate than they have at the state level.[44] Locally raised revenues have grown to make up for the loss or slow growth in intergovernmental aid and because of greater costs resulting from unfunded mandates and local service demands.[45]

Among local governments, counties have experienced the largest increases in tax revenues, jumping about 58% between 1985 and 1990. This reflects, in part, increased county expenses because of the growth in demand for health and social-service programs administered by counties and a tendency to shift responsibilities from cities and towns to counties.[46] Counties also have had a greater incentive to raise taxes because the cutback in federal aid hit them especially hard.[47]

The property tax accounts for much of the growth in revenues at the local level. Revenues from local property taxes increased nationally by an astounding 128% between 1980 and 1990. They have continued to increase in the 1990s above the inflation rate. Increased revenues from this source have resulted mostly from increases in assessed values rather than from tax rate increases.[48] The burden has been particularly difficult for homeowners. Indeed, because of the collapse of commercial property values around the nation, much of the burden for paying the tax has shifted from the owners of commercial property to owners of residential property.[49]

As a consequence of this increase in property taxes, it has once again become among the most unpopular taxes in the country.[50] Not surprisingly, state officials have heard demands for property-tax relief in the form of limits, or caps, on increases in assessments or rates. At the same time the usefulness of the property tax in many jurisdictions continues to suffer from exemptions made at the state level, which reduce its base. Counties often find that 60% or more of the property-tax base has been exempted.[51] Figures are nearly as bad for many cities in states like New York. Governments, educational institutions, religious bodies, charitable organizations, and hospitals are the principal owners of tax-exempt property. Major exemptions in regard to residential property are for veterans and the elderly.[52]

Many local governments have sought to move away from reliance on the property tax and toward a more diversified local revenue structure in which they rely on the sales tax, user fees, and local income taxes. Proposals to give municipalities a major alternative revenue source such as a sales tax have been regularly rejected in some states, Mississippi being an example. Generally, however, states in recent years have allowed local governments more discretion in raising revenues. In many places, legislatures have made the adoption of new taxes subject to voter approval.

Counties have had unusual problems securing more revenue authority. In recent years proposals to expand the taxing powers of counties so that they are more comparable to those enjoyed by municipalities have failed in Alabama, Florida, Maryland, and Virginia. In many of these and other states the pressure of increased urbanization and suburbanization has blurred the distinction between the services offered by municipal and county governments. Yet county governments lag behind municipal governments in their ability to raise revenues.

Over the last two decades, user fees have become a particularly popular means of financing a variety of services.[53] Fees are commonly charged to finance services involving public utilities (gas, water, sewage, and garbage), hospitals, and air transportation. The notion that the direct user of a service should pay for it is popular throughout the country. Because of this, user fees are a relatively acceptable way of raising revenues. They are also attractive to local officials because commonly such fees can be levied without securing permission from state legislatures.

Localities also have considerable discretion imposing impact fees on developers to offset the costs of building or expanding facilities such as roads, sewers, and parks and to serve the growth engendered by projects. Several states, however, have acted in recent years to prevent abuses, that is, to ensure that fees are reasonable and related to reliable estimates of the impact of particular developments. Some courts have also declared user fees, such as transportation utility fees, to be disguised taxes and, thus invalid in the absence of specific state authorization.[54]

Local finances have been improved in several places by the legalization of various types of gambling. Local governments in Louisiana, for example, receive 25% of the state taxes and fees on poker devices in bars, restaurants, and truck stops. In addition, municipalities and parishes receive $2.50 per person entry fee to 15 casino-type riverboats located in major metropolitan areas. A land-based casino authorized for the city of New Orleans provides an additional source of revenue.

State Assumption and Cost Reimbursement

Simply looking at the level of state aid gives an incomplete and somewhat misleading measure of the extent to which state governments are easing the fiscal pressures on local governments. A state ranking low in regard to aid to local governments, for example, may actually be doing more than many or most other states to help local governments in financial terms if it has directly assumed the cost of expensive functions borne in other states by local governments.[55]

State legislatures throughout most of the country could help local governments by assuming more responsibility for programs now financed out of local revenues. This often has been done in recent years in the areas of courts and corrections, indigent health care, and cash welfare assistance. Shifting total responsibility for a program to the state provides financial re-

lief to local governments. This comes at the price of a loss of local control, however, and, perhaps, service quality. Some observers have suggested, for example, that a state financed and administered court system might not be as good as a decentralized one that responds to the diverse values among communities within the state. Rather than assume full financial and administrative responsibility for courts, states could provide relief through grants in aid and cost-reimbursement plans and continue to give local governments some control over the administration of the system.[56]

It may, of course, be difficult to get the states either to assume responsibilities or share costs. Bills calling for shifting functions to the state regularly fail. Counties in New York have called for the state to take over the Medicaid program so that counties can deliver some much needed property-tax relief to their citizens. Thus far, the state has responded with a small amount of money for a partial takeover.

Programs for Distressed Local Governments

Since the 1970s, more and more states have adopted policies regarding the problems of financially distressed local governments. The well-publicized economic problems of large cities such as New York, Cleveland, and Philadelphia helped focus attention on state distress policies. Pressure to do something to help distressed local governments grew with the economic difficulties that set in during the 1980s. Some cities, such as Bridgeport, Connecticut, threatened to go into bankruptcy.

Many states have responded to such situations with financial and technical assistance for specific local governments. Several now have more formal and comprehensive programs regarding fiscally distressed sub-state entities. These programs measure distress, monitor it, and, as certain criteria are met, provide various types of assistance and/or impose various types of regulations to execute a fiscal recovery plan.[57]

Critics charge, however, that most distress assistance programs are essentially reactive, providing relief only after considerable damage has already been done, rather than being proactive and heading off problems. The programs also fail to address the root causes of economic distress. They place emphasis on improving the management practices of local governments. While management improvements and greater internal efficiencies are desirable in their own right, the cause of fiscal distress for localities more often stems from economic conditions largely beyond their control, such as demographic shifts and structural changes in the economic base.[58]

Concern over the fiscal problems of distressed central cities—by one measure around 40% of the country's 522 central cities are programmed to fail—and many smaller communities has prompted a search for more fundamental reforms regarding the allocation of responsibilities and the pattern of local government.[59] The financial strain on central cities and hard-pressed smaller communities could be relieved by burden shifting, for example, moving functions from the municipal to the county or state levels. Various steps could also be taken to improve upon the sharing of burdens and revenues among governments in metropolitan areas, though many of these steps are likely to be unpopular in suburban areas.

Reform measures to head off problems include changing state laws to make it more difficult to form (incorporate) new municipal governments in urbanizing areas; make it easier for cities to expand their boundaries through annexation procedures; and make it easier to consolidate local governments.

Some states already give cities considerable power to annex contiguous land. In North Carolina, for example, this can be done without the owner's consent. North Carolina and about a dozen other states also give cities the power to veto the incorporation of new municipalities forming outside their boundaries. Consolidation of local governments has been difficult to accomplish because of opposition by voters in suburban areas. Many states required that voters in each affected jurisdiction approve consolidation. Yet it is also possible to have state-directed consolidations, such as was done in Marion County–Indianapolis, Indiana, that do not require voter approval in the affected jurisdictions.

While the likelihood of more state-directed consolidations is remote, states have shown increased interest in plans calling for local governments in metropolitan areas or regions to share burdens and revenues. In regard to shared burdens, for example, some state legislatures and courts require each municipality to assume its share of responsibility for providing low-income housing. An example of neighboring governments pooling resources is the Minneapolis–Saint Paul's Regional Tax Base Sharing Program, in which each jurisdiction in the area can draw upon a portion of increases in the areas' industrial tax base for revenues.

PROBLEMS AND POLICY AREAS

Among the policy areas in which state actions have become increasingly important to local governments have been education, environmental protection, land use, and transportation planning.

Education: Problems of Equity and Finance
Traditionally, local governments have provided the bulk of support for elementary and secondary education out of local property taxes. In some parts of the country, much of the responsibility for financing growing costs of education continues to rest with local governments, principally independent school districts, and the local property tax. The share borne by state governments, however, has increased over the last several years, and now slightly surpasses the amount supplied by local taxes. As states move toward picking up a larger share of the education expenditure, city and county officials who do not have responsibilities in this area

have had reason to worry about the security of their revenues coming from the states.

The growth of state financial aid has brought increases in state regulations intended to improve the quality of education and caps on local educational expenditures. Shifting education funding responsibilities to the state has meant an undercutting of the decision-making power and control of local school districts.[60] The shift to the state also makes financial support of education less stable. Education financing is tied to ups and downs in the fiscal health of the state, less dependable tax sources, and how effectively education competes with a host of other demands on state funds. Research suggests that shifting to the state level has been most pronounced in states where property-tax pressures have been the greatest and where the degree of "localism" in the culture and history of the state, and thus the resistance to state control, is the weakest.[61]

State aid to education has increased for two primary reasons: to reduce reliance on local property taxes and to equalize expenditures among school districts. Courts in about half the states have added to the pressure by questioning the validity of spending disparities between rich and poor school districts. Last year property-tax-based school financing systems were declared invalid in Arizona and New Jersey (the latter for the third time). Equalization plans in Texas, Kansas, and other states have encountered the wrath of wealthier counties and have become the subject of court suits.

Among the most dramatic developments in state-local financial relations in recent years was the July 1993 decision of the Michigan legislature to eliminate property taxes for elementary and secondary education. This step, which surprised everyone, including the Michigan legislators, was taken even though lawmakers lacked a plan to replace the revenues. The state gave itself about nine months to come up with plans to reform the school system and to determine how to replace approximately $7 billion that would be lost in property-tax revenues.

The legislative action followed several years of trying to devise a way to reform the property-tax system. Michigan had financed education largely out of local property taxes. As a result, its property taxes were among the highest in the nation. A growing property-tax burden eventually led voters to reject proposed increases for increased school costs. In June 1993, voters rejected a proposal that would have increased the state sales tax by 50% in exchange for a cap on local property taxes and a guaranteed minimum of $4,800 spending for every pupil in school.

In the summer of 1993, the Republican governor, John Engler, proposed to cut school property taxes 20%. Democrats attempted to one-up the governor with legislation eliminating all property taxes for operating schools. As it turned out, no one in the legislature dared to oppose a tax cut, and the governor signed the "scorched earth" measure into law.[62] Later in 1993, the legislature approved two alternative school-finance proposals. It submitted one for voter approval on 15, March 1994, with the un-

derstanding that if it was rejected, the other would go into effect. Voters were put in a position of having to choose between a plan which featured a 50% increase in the sales tax—the one on the ballot–and one which called for a 30% increase in the state income tax. At the time, Michigan had a relatively low sales tax and a relatively high income tax. Not surprisingly, 70% of the voters chose the sales-tax alternative. This plan also added a statewide property tax and increased or added a mixture of other taxes and a new lottery game to make up for the lost property-tax revenue.

The result in Michigan was not tax relief but a modest shift in taxation. Property taxes were retained, but in reduced amounts, and the financing of education became more dependent on sales and user taxes. More important, the plan shifted much of the control over financing schools from local governments to the state government.

Following the Michigan vote, several other states gave serious consideration to cutting school-based property taxes. Wisconsin took the most decisive action by eliminating the use of the property tax to finance education and creating a commission to explore how to replace the lost revenues. In Vermont, Idaho, South Carolina, and Minnesota serious efforts to roll back property taxes for education fell short.

Pressures to increase the funding of schools prompted California lawmakers in 1993 to transfer $2.6 billion in property-tax revenues to the state, where they were earmarked for education. Last year Governor Pete Wilson vetoed a one-time county bail-out measure that would have shifted to eight counties some $14 million in property-tax revenues earmarked for schools. Changes in the pattern of state-local financial relations in Oregon have also been underway since the adoption of a severe property-tax-limitation measure—Initiative No. 5—by the voters in November 1990. The measure shifted funding for education from local property taxes to the state over a five-year phase-in period. The unanswered question is, Where will the state find the revenue to meet its new responsibilities in education? Some have called for more fundamental tax reform, including the often rejected sales tax.[63]

**Environmental Protection:
The Solid Waste Problem**
Much of the discontent found on the local level in recent years has been directed at the effects, though not necessarily the broader goals, of environmental mandates. Thus, while local officials are not opposed to clean drinking water, some have contended that many of the testing requirements under the Safe Drinking Water Act are unnecessary as well as costly.

To help finance this particular program, several legislatures have authorized state agencies to collect fees from public water systems. Water-user fees have met considerable resistance in some places. In what one observer has described as "a rare case of open municipal civil disobedience," about a third of the water systems subject to the tax in Vermont simply refused to pay.[64]

Under federal and state mandates local officials have to come up with revenues to comply with federal regulations regarding not only the safety of drinking water but such matters as waste-water treatment projects, underground storage tanks, and the disposal of solid wastes. Since the late 1980s states have been using revolving loan funds, seeded mostly with federal money, which provide loans to localities for waste-water treatment projects. Loans are paid back by locally collected user fees. The system is intended to be self-perpetuating as the loans are repaid. The success of this program has prompted a general movement to utilize revolving loan funds to finance other environmental infrastructure and transportation projects.

Since the mid-1980s, several industrial states—California, Florida, New York, and Pennsylvania—have adopted stringent and costly environmental standards for landfills. These regulations affect about 20% of the landfills now in operation.[65] Implementation of state mandates of this nature invite state-local conflict, especially if they are unfunded. Conflict, however, is not inevitable: state and local officials in some places, at least, have been able to blend their efforts in a problem-solving approach.[66]

Under the federal Resource and Recovery Act, landfills throughout the nation are to be upgraded by standards worked out by the Environmental Protection Agency. These standards affect the location, design, operation, and closing of landfills. State governments may apply their own regulations as long as they meet federal standards and are approved by the EPA. State agencies will develop programs for assessing whether landfills comply with environmental standards before they issue permits for waste disposal. Ultimately, implementation of the regulations will require some localities to close down existing dumps. Others will have to come up with the funds to upgrade their landfills. Because of the expense, many localities are expected to jointly create new regional landfills that meet the standards.

Faced with difficulties regarding landfills, a growing number of states are giving attention to the recovery of solid wastes for reuse or conversion into fuel. Several states have also adopted mandatory recycling laws that require the formulation of waste-management plans, local source separation and recycling programs, and specific statewide reductions in solid waste by a certain year. Under the landmark California Integrated Waste Management Act of 1989, local officials must plan and coordinate their efforts toward the goals of diverting 25% of the waste stream from landfills by 1995 and 50% by the year 2000.

Problems in implementing recycling programs have largely centered on the economic feasibility of recovery programs. Recycling is expensive for some local governments, particularly smaller ones in rural areas that have relied almost entirely on landfills. For others, the problem is not so much the cost of financing a recovery system but of finding a market for the recovered material or energy. Achievement of waste-reduction goals in California and elsewhere requires supportive action on the state level. In this policy area, supportive action includes not only technical assistance but help in developing markets for recycled materials.[67] Some states, however, may have established unrealistic goals.

Land Use and Transportation Planning

Another area of increased state activity has been encouraging local governments to draw up comprehensive land-use plans.[68] Several states require municipalities and counties to develop growth-management plans that are consistent with state comprehensive plans. Such plans focus on the interrelated goals of controlling growth, combating environmental problems such as air and water pollution, and providing an adequate infrastructure. Several states, including Florida, New Jersey, and Washington, have laws that limit new development to places where an adequate infrastructure is already in place or will be in place concurrent with the development. As one analyst has noted: "The old assumption that growth will pay for itself is no longer treated as revealed truth."[69]

Some observers label the approach taken by the states to land-use planning "top down" regionalism, as opposed to "bottoms up" regionalism, and worry about the adverse impact on local authority.[70] For local officials, new growth-management responsibilities present difficult problems of resolving conflicts among groups and individuals with divergent interests.[71] Another problem with state-imposed comprehensive planning is that it sometimes ignores the limitations on the capacity of local governments to do the job. The capacity to plan land use and to implement plans requires a level of professionalism, organization, and management expertise that is very often lacking in local governmental units, especially smaller ones in nonmetropolitan areas.[72] Several states now make an effort to assist rural governments meet their new land-use-management responsibilities. The governor's office in Utah, for example, recently initiated the Local Government Comprehensive Planning Project, which provides consultants and research support for rural counties with little experience in planning and zoning.

Comprehensive planning in approaching transportation, air quality, and growth-management problems is further required by the federal Intermodal Surface Transportation Efficiency Act (ISTEA), which also offers local officials a greater role in the development and implementation of state transportation plans. The extent to which cities and counties have been able to forge effective partnerships with state agencies in planning and project selection as required by the law varies around the country. Local governments in rural areas appear to have had more difficulty than those in metropolitan areas in forging acceptable relationships with state transportation departments.[73] Local officials in some states have discovered that state agencies want to proceed as they have always done, and exclude them from meaningful participation. In other states, such as Ohio, ISTEA appears to have added to the ability of local governments and the state to continue a history of cooperation, i.e., to make a good system even better from the local point of view. South Carolina's Department of Transportation has also been very receptive to recommendations made by Metropolitan Planning Organization (MPOs). An increase in the effectiveness of local officials has also taken place in Montana.

PARTNERSHIPS AND RESPONSIBILITIES

Historically, local officials, working individually or through associations, have had considerable influence on the development of state and federal policies affecting them, the distribution of state and federal funds, and the extent to which state and federal policies are implemented.[74]

From the local point of view, however, the last several years are best described as "combat federalism." They have had to struggle to exert influence over the framing of policies and the implementation of programs affecting them. Part of the problem has been the economic downturn. One law of intergovernmental relations is that in periods of economic stress, local officials can expect less intergovernmental aid and more of the costs of government to be shifted their way. Recent years also lead to the prediction that in times of economic stress, relief coming to localities from the states is particularly likely to take the form of authorizing increased local taxing authority, so that local government officials take the heat for raising taxes.

Local officials throughout the country have expressed concern about the quality of state-local relations. Late in 1993, 28% of the municipal officials who responded to a survey by the National League of Cities felt that relationships with the federal government had worsened since 1990. Even more, some 30% felt that relations with their state government had deteriorated or worsened during this period.[75] Local officials—county as well as city, appointed as well as elected—have been critical of the loss of local government authority, the lack of sufficient discretion to generate revenues, the lack of state financial aid and technical assistance, the lack of support of state agencies and, most of all, the growth of unfunded mandates.[76]

Although considerable progress has been made over the years in regard to local home rule, grants of discretionary authority have been offset by increased mandates and preemptions of local authority. In Indiana, where the legislature has whittled down the value of municipal home rule, municipal officials have called for the preparation of local government impact statements to accompany any legislative or administrative action that would affect local government. More generally, the U.S. Advisory Commission on Intergovernmental Relations has called upon the states to both enhance and clarify local home authority.[77]

Tensions and uncertainties of dealing with federal and state governments have encouraged local officials to look to each other for support and to come together to resolve common problems. Thus, while evidence suggests that relations have soured between local officials and state and federal officials, relations between local officials in the same geographical area seem to have improved.[78]

Local officials have increasingly entered service agreements to jointly plan, finance, or deliver services. Also popular are interlocal contracts through which one unit of local government purchases services such as police or fire protection from another. Such cooperation has been driven principally by cost considerationsas a way of making up for declining revenues.[79] However, local governments, acting voluntarily, can also combat areawide problems through cooperative approaches of an informal and formal nature. Throughout the nation we find patterns of interlocal cooperation, or "interlocal self-governance," that deliver services in an efficient manner.[80]

Metropolitan or regional cooperation seems to be the wave of the future, not only because of the voluntary actions of local officials, but because the federal government and various state governments have encouraged this approach to problems requiring comprehensive areawide planning. Programs of this nature could be enhanced, however, by bringing local officials more directly into the state policy-making process, thereby reducing top-down management, and by giving local governments more discretion in achieving broad state or regional goals.

In many states, there are agencies that function to stimulate greater cooperation activity among local governments and, through this, more effective problem-solving. An example of a relatively new agency of this nature is the Board of Government Innovation and Cooperation, created by the Minnesota legislature in 1993. The major goals of the Board are to increase local government innovation, cooperation, and efficiency. It can help local governments by: (1) giving temporary waivers or exemptions from state rules or regulations that get in the way of innovative and cooperative efforts to improve the delivery of services; (2) providing grants to local governments to encourage and facilitate cooperative efforts among communities; and (3) recommending to the legislature what state restrictions should be eliminated to improve the local delivery of services. Sitting on the board is the state auditor, the commissioners of finance and administration, two administrative law judges, and, as nonvoting members, six members of the legislature (three from each house).

Under economic stress, as they seemingly are most of the time, local officials think in terms of partnerships with just about everyone—people in the federal government, state governments, other local governments, and the private sector. Working individually in their communi-

ties or through state and national associations local officials have been prime partnership builders. In recent years, an obstacle on the state and national levels has been the tendency of lawmakers to view local officials as special pleaders in quest of scarce dollars rather than as legitimate partners or cogovernors in the intergovernmental system.

State governments could do much to help financially strapped local governments. Courses of action include: eliminating unnecessary mandates, increasing financial aid (and targeting it to the places where it is most needed), helping to improve local governmental management practices, encouraging the consolidation of services, encouraging regional burden and tax sharing, assuming the costs of programs financed out of local revenues, and allowing local governments greater discretion in raising revenues.

The recurring disputes between the two levels of government over the proper amount of state assistance and the relative merits of centralization and decentralization are not likely to abate in the immediate future. Fortunately, a number of states have, in recent years, established state-local panels, or commissions, as forums for the discussion of such problems. Perhaps the most basic first step is to reexamine the allocation of responsibilities between state and local governments. In any given state, problems of considerable importance to the state as a whole are being addressed by local officials who lack the perspectives and resources to cope with them. At the same time, in any given state, decisions are being made at the state level that should be made locally in the light of the needs and desires of particular communities.

---

[1]Quoted by Charles Young, "How State's Mandates Make Local Taxes Go Up", *The Sunday Record* (June 19, 1994): NJ-1, NJ-2, 2.

[2]See David R. Berman, "State-Local Relations: Patterns, Politics, and Problems," *The Municipal Year Book 1994* (Washington, DC: International City/County Management Association, 1994): 59–67.

[3]See Brenda Avoletta and Phillip M. Dearborn, "Federal Grants-in-Aid Soar in the 1990s, but Not for Locals or General Purposes," *Intergovernmental Perspective* (Summer 1993): 32–33; and Frank Shafroth, "Overbearing and Unfunded: Entitlements and Federal Mandates Chip Away Local Control," *Nation's Cities Weekly* (August 30, 1993): 12.

[4]On "shift and shaft federalism," see Stephen D. Gold and Sarah Ritchie, "State Policies Affecting Cities and Counties in 1991: Shifting Federalism," *Public Budgeting and Finance* (Spring 1992): 23–46.

[5]Kathy Prosser, director of the Indiana Department of Environmental Management, quoted in Jonathan Walters, "Reinventing the Federal System," *Governing* (January 1994): 49–53.

[6]U.S. Advisory Commission on Intergovernmental Relations, *Local Government Autonomy: Needs for State Constitutional Statutory and Judicial Clarification* (Washington, DC: GPO, October 1993).

[7]Daniel Sloan, "Colorado," in Carl Mott, Daniel Sloan, and Robert Huefner, comps., *State/Local Budgeting: Politics and Trends in the Western States* (Center for Public Policy and Administration, University of Utah, October 1994): 23–27, at 25–26.

[8]In a case involving the Boulder Valley school district, the Colorado Supreme Court rejected the argument that the amendment requires separate votes on new debt and

tax increases. See Mark Walsh, "Educators Claim Victory as Colo. Court Rejects Tax-Limit Interpretation," *Education Week* (September 21, 1994): 15.

[9]Kathy Hunt, *Wyoming Home Rule: A Current Status Report* (Cheyenne, WY: Wyoming Association of Municipalities, 1994).

[10]Homebuilders Association of Charlotte, Inc., v. City of Charlotte N.C. (No. 133PA93—Mecklenburg, April 8, 1994).

[11]See Berman, *The Municipal Year Book 1994*.

[12]Rufus E. Miles, "The Origin and Meaning of Miles' Law," *Public Administration Review* (September/October 1978): 399–403.

[13]David R. Berman, Lawrence L. Martin, and Laura Kajfez, "County Home Rule: Does Where You Stand Depend on Where You Sit?" *State and Local Review* (Spring 1985): 232–34.

[14]See U.S. Advisory Commission on Intergovernmental Relations, *Local Government Autonomy*.

[15]See U.S. Advisory Commission on Intergovernmental Relations, *State Laws Governing Local Government Structure and Administration* (Washington, DC: GPO, March 1993).

[16]David R. Berman and Lawrence L. Martin, "State-Local Relations: An Examination of Local Discretion," *Public Administration Review* (March/April, 1988): 637–41.

[17]Joseph F. Zimmerman, *State-Local Relations: A Partnership Approach* (New York: Praeger, 1983).

[18]U.S. Advisory Commission on Intergovernmental Relations, *State Laws Governing Local Government Structure and Administration*. This report shows the extent of involvement and recent trends.

[19]See, for example, the discussion by Gary Carlson, "Legislative Preview," *Minnesota Cities* (February 1994): 6–9.

[20]According to a survey by the National Association of Counties, large urban counties appear to be more concerned about the fiscal impact of state mandates than the fiscal impact of federal mandates; see *1994 Fiscal Survey: Large Urban Counties* (Washington, DC: National Association of Counties, March 1994).

[21]Estimates of the amount spent by state and local governments on federal mandates or the amount spent by local governments on state mandates vary widely. Part of this variation is due to differences in how researchers define mandate; another problem is coming up with reliable estimates of the costs imposed. Mandates generally refer to directives that state or local governments undertake certain functions or follow certain procedures. Sometimes listed in the category of mandates, however, are laws that prohibit state or local officials from becoming involved in particular policy areas or from taking actions such as raising revenues. Research suggests that prohibitions on revenue raising can have just as devastating an impact on local finances as mandates that local governments spend funds for specific activities. On this point, see Paul Flowers and John T. Torbert, *Mandate Costs: A Kansas Case Study* (Topeka, KS: Kansas Association of Counties, 1993). On the definition of mandates and the different forms they may take, see Janet M. Kelly, *State Mandates: Fiscal Notes, Reimbursement, and Anti-Mandate Strategies* (Washington, DC: National League of Cities, 1992); Janet M. Kelly, "Unfunded Mandates: The View from the States," *Public Administration Review* (July/August 1994): 405–08; Max Neiman and Catherine Lovell, "Federal and State Mandating: A First Look at the Mandate Terrain," *Administration and Society* (November 1982): 343–72; Max Neiman and Catherine Lovell, "Mandating as a Policy Issue—The Definitional Problem," *Policy Studies Journal* (Spring 1981): 667–80; Advisory Commission on Intergovernmental Relations, *State Mandating of Local Expenditures*, (Washington, DC: GPO, 1978; *Calculating the Cost of State and Federal Mandates: Getting Started* (Atlanta, GA: Georgia Municipal Association, March 1993); and Joseph F. Zimmerman, "Some Remedies Suggested for State Mandated Expenditures Distortions," *Current Municipal Problems*, vol. 21, no. 1 (1994): 93–110.

[22]One approach to improving the quality of cost esti-

mates is to include local officials in the process through local cost-estimation networks. This practice is now being employed with considerable success in Connecticut and Nevada and is under consideration in other states. See Janet M. Kelly, "A New Approach to an Old Problem: State Mandates," *Government Finance Review* (December 1993): 27–29.

23. See generally Ann Calvares Barr, "Cost Estimations as an Anti-Mandate Strategy," in Michael Fix and Daphne Kenyon, eds., *Coping with Mandates: What Are the Alternatives?* (Washington, DC: The Urban Institute Press, 1990): 57–61. See also *Legislative Mandates: State Experiences Offer Insights for Federal Action* (Washington, DC: General Accounting Office, 1988) and Kelly, *State Mandates*, 42.

[24]Kelly, ibid.

[25]Susan A. McManus, "Mad About Mandates: The Issue of Who Should Pay for What Resurfaces in the 1990's," *Publius* (Summer 1991): 59–75.

[26]Joint Legislative Audit and Review Commission, *Intergovernmental Mandates and Financial Aid to Local Governments* (Richmond, VA: Commonwealth of Virginia, 1992, House Document No. 56).

[27]See Richard H. Horte, "State Expenditures With Mandate Reimbursement," in Fix and Kenyon, eds., *Coping with Mandates*, and Kelly, *State Mandates*.

[28]Kelly, Ibid.

[29]See overview by Patricia S. Biswanger, "Preserving Democracy in the Face of Special Interest Might: Local Initiatives to Ban Cigarette Vending Machines," *Current Municipal Problems*, vol. 21, no. 1 (1994): 67–92. This is an expanded version of an article published in the November/December 1993 issue of the *Municipal Attorney*.

[30]Allied Vending, Inc. v. City of Bowie, 332 Md. 279, 631 A2d 77 (1993).

[31]Carla Smallwood, "A Struggle for Control," *American City & County* (January, 1993): 60–71.

[32]United States Advisory Commission on Intergovernmental Relations, *State Aid to Local Government* (Washington, DC: GPO, 1969). See also David Kellerman, "State Aid to Local Governments, Fiscal 1990," *Book of the States, 1992–93* (Lexington, KY: Council of State Governments, 1993): 632–35.

[33]Keith J. Mueller, "Explaining Variation in State Assistance Programs to Local Communities: What to Expect and Why," *State and Local Review* (Fall 1987): 101–07. Compare this with David R. Morgan and Robert E. England, "State Aid to Cities: A Causal Inquiry," *Publius* (Spring 1984): 67–82.

[34]Randy Arndt, "NLC Study Shows Lag on City Aid," *Nation's Cities Weekly* 12 (September 1988): 1, 9.

[35]See Thomas R. Dye and Thomas L. Hurley, "The Responsiveness of Federal and State Governments to Urban Problems," *Journal of Politics* 40 (February 1978): 196–207; and John P. Pelissero, "State Aid and City Needs: An Examination of Residual State Aid to Large Cities," *Journal of Politics* 46 (August 1984): 916–35. For a more pessimistic view, see Robert M. Stein and Keith E. Hamm, "A Comparative Analysis of the Targeting Capacity of State and Federal Intergovernmental Aid Allocations: 1977, 1982," *Social Science Quarterly* 68 (September 1987): 447–77; and David R. Morgan and Mei-Chiang Shih, "Targeting State and Federal Aid to City Needs," *State and Local Government Review* (Spring, 1991): 60–67.

[36]See, for example, Robert M. Stein, "The Targeting of State Aid: A Comparison of Grant Delivery Mechanisms," *Urban Interest*, vol. 2, (1981): 47–60; Robert M. Stein, "The Allocation of State Aid to Local Governments: An Examination of Interstate Variation," in U.S. Advisory Commission on Intergovernmental Relations, *State and Local Roles in the Federal System* (Washington, DC: GPO, 1982): 203–26; Theda Skocpol, "Targeting within Universalism," in Christopher Jencks and Paul Peterson, eds., *The Urban Underclass* (Washington, DC: Brookings Institution, 1991): 411–35; Robert M. Stein and Keith E. Hamm, "Explaining State Aid Allocations: Targeting within Universalism," *Social Science Quarterly* (September 1994): 524–40.

[37]Helen F. Ladd, "The State Aid Decision: Changes in

State Aid to Local Governments, 1982–1987," *National Tax Journal* (December 1991): 477–96. For earlier assessments of the performance of the states, see Helen F. Ladd and John Yinger, *America's Ailing Cities* (Baltimore: Johns Hopkins University Press, 1989) and Steven D. Gold, "A Better Scoreboard: States Are Helping Local Governments," *State Legislatures* (April 1990): 27–28.

[38]Steven D. Gold, "Local Taxes Outpace State Taxes," *PA Times* (July 1993): 15, 17.

[39]See, for example, William L. Waugh, Jr., "States, Counties, and the Questions of Trust and Capacity," *Publius*, vol 18, (1988): 189–98.

[40]Carlson, Legislative Preview, 5.

[41]See reviews by Drew Linsay, "State Revenues Up, But School Hikes Uncertain," *Education Week* (September 21, 1994): 14; and Cornia Eckl, "Healthier State Finances," *State Legislatures* (October 1994): 26–31.

[42]Allan D. Wallis, "Governance and the Civic Infrastructure of Metropolitan Regions," *National Civic Review* (Spring 1993): 125–39.

[43]Joseph Sullivan, "Towns Taking Up Whitman, On Offer of Fiscal Review," *New York Times* (August 18, 1994): 7.

[44]For analysis of this growth, see Steven D. Gold, "Local Taxes Outpace State Taxes," *PA Times* (July 1993): 15, 17; and, "Passing the Buck," *State Legislatures* (January 1993): 36–38.

[45]One authority has noted that the slow growth of local aid is one of the primary reasons why local taxes have been increasing faster than state taxes. Steven D. Gold, "State Aid to Localities Fares Poorly in 1990s," *State Fiscal Brief* (New York, NY: Center for the Study of the States, Rockefeller Institute of Government, June 1994): 1–5.

[46]Gold, "Local Taxes Outpace State Taxes."

[47]Steven D. Gold, "The State of State-Local Relations," *State Legislatures* (August 1988): 17–20.

[48]Phillip M. Dearborn, "Local Property Taxes: Emerging Trends," *Intergovernmental Perspective* (Summer 1993): 10–12.

[49]Item in *Governing* (August 1993): 13, citing report by Urban Land Institute: "The Effect of the Collapse of Commercial Property Values on Local Government Revenues and Tax Burdens."

[50]U. S. Advisory Commission on Intergovernmental Relations, *Changing Public Attitudes on Government and Taxes* (Washington, DC: GPO, 1990, 1991, 1992).

[51]John P. Thomas, "Financing County Government: An Overview," *Intergovernmental Perspectives* (Winter 1991): 10–13, 12.

[52]See *Government Finance Review* (June 1991): 4.

[53]See generally Donald Levitan and Adam D. Silverman, "User Fees: Current Practice," *Management Information Report*, vol. 24, no. 12 (December 1992), published by the International City/County Management Association, Washington, DC.

[54]Reid Ewing, "Transportation Utility Fees," *Government Finance Review* (June 1994): 13–17.

[55]See Steven D. Gold, "State Aid to Localities Fares Poorly in 1990s," *State Fiscal Brief* (New York, NY: Center for the Study of the States, Rockefeller Institute of Government, June 1994): 1–5. 56. Barbara Todd, "Counties in the Federal System: The State Connection," *Intergovernmental Perspective* (Winter 1991): 21–25.

[57]See generally Anthony G. Cahill, Joseph A. James, Jean E. Lavigne, Ann Stacey, "State Government Responses to Municipal Fiscal Distress: A Brave New World for State-Local Intergovernmental Relations," *Public Productivity and Management Review* (Spring 1994): 253–64; Anthony G. Cahill and Joseph A. James, "Responding to Municipal Fiscal Distress: An Emerging Issue for State Governments in the 1990s," *Public Administration Review* (January/February, 1992): 88–94; and Scott R. Mackey, *State Programs to Assist Distressed Local Governments* (Denver, Colo.: National Conference of State Legislators, March 1993).

[58]See, for example, Ladd and Yinger, *America's Ailing Cities*.

[59]See, for example, the overview by David Rusk, "Bend or Die: Inflexible State Laws and Policies Are

Dooming Some of the Country's Central Cities," *State Government News* (February 1994): 6–10.

[60]See, for example, Carol S. Weissert, "Property Tax Relief, School Finance Reform and Local Decisionmaking," paper prepared for Annual Meeting of the American Society for Public Administration, 1994.

[61]Kenneth K. Wong, "Fiscal Support for Education in the American States: The Parity to Dominance View Examined," *American Journal of Education* (August 1989): 329–57.

[62]See account in Peter Overby, "The Michigan Experiment," *Common Cause Magazine*, (Spring 1994): 11–16.

[63]Donald J. Stabrowski, "Oregon and Measure Five: One Year Later," *Comparative State Politics* (October 1992): 33–38.

[64]Jeff Wennberg, Mayor of Rutland City, Vermont, "Cooperation, Not Coercion, Will Solve Drinking Water Crisis," *Nation's Cities Weekly* (April 18, 1994): 2.

[65]Tom Arrandale, "The Changing World of Landfills," *Governing* (August 1993): 59–71.

[66]See Stephen Jenks, "County Compliance with North Carolina's Solid-Waste Mandate: A Conflict-Based Model," *Publius* (Spring 1994): 17–36.

[67]Linda Morse, "CaliforniaHow Can We Get to 50 Percent?" *PM* (October 1991): 4–10.

[68]Recent studies on state programs include: Scott A. Bollens, "State Growth Management: Intergovernmental Frameworks and Policy Objectives," *Journal of the American Planning Association* (Autumn 1992): 454–66; Forster Ndubisi and Mary Dyer, "The Role of Regional Entities in Formulating and Implementing Statewide Growth Policies," *State and Local Government Review* (Fall 1992): 117–27; Dennis E. Gale, "Eight State-Sponsored Growth Management Programs: A Comparative Analysis," *Journal of the American Planning Association* (Autumn 1992): 425–39; Raymond J. Burby and Linda C. Dalton, "Plans Can Matter! The Role of Land Use Plans and State Planning Mandates in Limiting the Development of Hazardous Areas," *Public Administration Review* (May/June 1994): 229–38; and K. T. Liou and Todd J. Dicker, "The Effect of the Growth Management Act on Local Comprehensive Planning Expenditures: The South Florida Experience," *Public Administration Review* (May/June 1994): 239–44.

[69]Allan D. Wallis, "Governance and the Civic Infrastructure of Metropolitan Regions," *National Civic Review* (Spring 1993): 125–39.

[70]See, for example, Eileen Shanahan, "Going It Jointly: Regional Solutions for Local Problems," *Governing* (August 1991): 70–75.

[71]See, for example, Barbara Sheen Todd and Robert M. Jones, "Building Consensus on Development Issues," *Intergovernmental Perspective* (Winter 1992): 19–22, 38.

[72]See generally Jane Elizabeth Decker, "Management and Organizational Capacities for Responding to Growth in Florida's Nonmetropolitan Counties," *Journal of Urban Affairs* (1987): 47–61; and Robyne S. Turner, "Intergovernmental Growth Management: A Partnership Framework for State-Local Relations," *Publius* (Summer, 1990): 79–85.

[73]Robert Fogel, "County Experience with ISTEA Inconsistent," *County News* (October 25, 1993).

[74]Michael J. Rich, "Distributive Politics and the Allocation of Federal Grants," *American Political Science Review* 83 (March 1989): 198–213: Richard P. Nathan, "State and Local Governments under Federal Grants: Toward a Predictive Theory," *Political Science Quarterly* 98 (Spring 1983): 47–57; Christopher Hamilton and Donald T. Wells, *Federalism, Power, and Political Economy: A New Theory of Federalism's Impact on American Life* (Englewood Cliffs, NJ: Prentice-Hall, 1990).

[75]See "Unfunded Mandates Rank as Highest Priority Concern of Local Officials," *Nation's Cities Weekly* (January 10, 1994): 8.

[76]Victor S. DeSantis, *State, Local, and Council Relations: Managers' Perceptions*, Baseline Data Report, vol. 23, no. 2 (Washington, DC: International City/County Management Association, 1991). Relevant survey data is also found in William L. Waugh and Gregory Strieb,

"County Capacity and Intergovernmental Relations," and Tanis J. Salant, "Shifting Roles in County-State Relations," which appear as chapters in David R. Berman, ed., *County Government in an Era of Change* (Westport, CT: Greenwood Press, 1993).

[77]U.S. Advisory Commission on Intergovernmental Relations, *Local Government Autonomy*.

[78]See "Unfunded Mandates Rank as Highest Priority Concern of Local Officials," *Nation's Cities Weekly* (January 10, 1994): 8.

[79]David R. Morgan and Michael W. Hirlinger, "Intergovernmental Service Contracts: A Multivariate Explanation," *Urban Affairs Quarterly* (September 1991): 128–44.

[80]See, for example, Advisory Commission on Intergovernmental Relations, *Metropolitan Organization: The Allegheny County Case*, (Washington, DC: GPO, February 1992); Ronald J. Oakerson and Roger B. Parks, "Metropolitan Organization: St. Louis and Allegheny County," *Intergovernmental Perspective* (Summer 1991): 27–30, 34; and Roger B. Parks, "Counties in the Federal System: The Interlocal Connection," *Intergovernmental Perspective* (Winter 1991): 29–32.

THE YEARBOOK
STATE CORRESPONDENTS

Alabama
Perry Roquemore
Alabama League of Municipalities
O.H. Sharpless
Association of County Commissioners of Alabama
Arizona
Kent Fairbairn
League of Arizona Cities and Towns
P. Jerry Orrick
County Supervisors of Arizona
Arkansas
Don Zimmerman
Arkansas Municipal League
Jeff Sikes
Association of Arkansas Counties
Colorado
Peter King
Colorado Counties, Inc.
Samuel D. Mamet
Colorado Municipal League
Geoff Withers
Advisory Commission on Intergovernmental Relations
Connecticut
Gain Carl Casa
Connecticut Conference of Municipalities
Brian E. West
Connecticut Advisory Commission on Intergovernmental Relations
Florida
Kelvin J. Robinson
Florida League of Cities
Vivian Zaricki
Florida Association of Counties
Illinois
LeRoy Whiting
Commission on Intergovernmental Relations
Indiana
Tonya Griffith
Indiana Association of Cities and Towns

Iowa
Paul Coates
Iowa Association of Counties
Louisiana
Susan Gordon
Louisiana Municipal Association
Marvin L. Lyons
Police Jury Association of Louisiana
Maine
Richard G.
Maine Municipal Association
Maryland
Stephen R. McHenry
Maryland Municipal League
Minnesota
Joel J. Jamnik
League of Minnesota Cities
Mississippi
Hollidae Morrison
Mississippi Municipal Association
Missouri
Gary Markenson
Missouri Municipal League
Montana
Alec Hansen
Montana League of Cities and Towns
Sandra S. Oltzinger
Montana Association of Counties
Nevada
Thomas J. Grady
Nevada League of Cities
Robert Hadfield
Nevada Association of Counties
New Jersey
Celeste Carpiano
New Jersey Association of Counties
Michael J. Darcy
New Jersey State League of Municipalities

New Mexico
Pat Romero
New Mexico Association of Counties
New York
Peter A. Baynes
New York Conference of Mayors and Municipal Officials
North Carolina
Andrew Romanet, Jr.
North Carolina League of Municipalities
Ohio
Susan J. Cave
Ohio Municipal League
South Carolina
J. Milton Pope
Municipal Association of South Carolina
Kathleen K. Williams
South Carolina Association of Counties
Tennessee
Robert Wormsley
Tennessee County Services Association
Utah
Wayne Parker
Utah Advisory Council on Intergovernmental Relations
Vermont
Steven E. Jeffrey
Vermont League of Cities and Towns
Virginia
C. Flippo Hicks
Virginia Association of Counties
West Virginia
Lisa Dooley
West Virginia Municipal League
Wisconsin
Kathy L. Bull
League of Wisconsin Municipalities
Wyoming
Carl Classen
Wyoming Association of Municipalities

2

Recent Supreme Court Cases Affecting Local Governments

Rosemary O'Leary
Charles Wise
Indiana University, Bloomington

In the 1993–1994 term, the U.S. Supreme Court decided over 100 cases, 26 of which significantly affect local governments. This article reviews the major holdings of these cases in the important areas of property rights, environmental law, sexual harassment, taxes and user fees, public schools, voting rights, free speech, criminal law, and Medicare reimbursement.

PROPERTY

Two important property cases were decided by the Supreme Court this term. In the first, the Court continued to develop the area of regulatory takings in a local government planning and zoning case that will have profound effects for local government as well as other levels of government. The regulatory takings doctrine has been developed by the Court based on the Fifth Amendment's provision that property not be taken for public use without just compensation. In *Dolan* v. *Tigard* [114 S.Ct. 2309 (1994)], the owner of a plumbing and electrical supply store applied to the city of Tigard, Oregon, for a permit to redevelop the site to expand the size of the store and to pave the parking lot. The city, pursuant to a state-required land-use program, had adopted a comprehensive plan, a plan for pedestrian/bicycle pathways, and a master drainage plan. The city planning commission conditioned the granting of the permit with the requirements that the owner dedicate (convey title to) the portion of her property lying within a 100-year floodplain for improvement of a storm drainage system and that she dedicate an additional 15-foot strip adjacent to the floodplain as a pedestrian/bicycle pathway. The planning commission declared that the required floodplain dedication would be reasonably related to the owner's request to intensify use of the site, given the impervious surface. Creation of a pedestrian/bicycle pathway system as an alternative means of transportation could offset some of the traffic demand on nearby streets and lessen the increase in traffic congestion.

In *Nollan* v. *California Coastal Commission* [483 U.S. 825 (1987)] the Court had laid down a requirement that an agency must be prepared to prove in court that a "legitimate state interest" is "substantially advanced" by the regulation as it is applied to a particular property, and that an "essential nexus" exists between the "end advanced" (the enunciated purpose of the regulation) and the "condition imposed" by the application of the regulation. The Court had not answered the question of how agencies were to supply the requisite proof and what the Court would demand as proof. After reviewing various doctrines that state courts had used to guide such analyses, the Court enunciated its own test of "rough proportionality" and stated: "No precise mathematical calculation is required, but the city must make some sort of individualized determination that the required dedication is related both in nature and extent to the impact of the proposed development."

The Court decided in *Dolan* that the city had not made any individualized determination to support its requirement that a portion of the land be transferred to the city and concluded that the city's findings did not show the required reasonable relationship between the floodplain easement and the owner's proposed new building. With respect to the issue of requisite proof or "rough proportionality," the Court decided that the city had not met its burden of demonstrating that any additional vehicle and bicycle trips generated by the store expansion reasonably related to the city's requirement for a dedication of the pedestrian/bicycle pathway easement. The Court said that the city must make some effort to quantify its findings in support of the dedication for the pedestrian/bicycle pathway beyond the conclusionary statement that it could offset some of the demand generated.

The implications of the Court's doctrine stated in this case are widespread for local government. The facts are hardly unique—they represent everyday zoning decisions that local governments often make. The Court's conclusions apply to the full range of local government regulatory activities. In addition, the decision means that the federal courts can become even more involved in reviewing and judging the adequacy (the dissent in *Dolan* said "micromanaging") local regulatory decisions. Local governments will have to do more individualized analysis of the expected impacts of land-use changes and the regulations they seek to apply. The costs involved could have a chilling effect on regulatory activity. Finally, no one knows exactly what is necessary to demonstrate "rough proportionality," so local regulators should expect continuing litigation, with lower and appellate courts hammering out what demonstrates rough proportionality.

In the second property case, the Supreme Court again applied and interpreted the Fifth Amendment to constrain government action. Even though the decision in *U.S.* v. *James Daniel Good Real Property* [114 S.Ct. 492 (1993)] involved seizure of a convicted drug dealer's house pursuant to a federal forfeiture statute, the principles enunciated by the Court apply also to local law enforcement officials acting pursuant to state forfeiture laws. The Supreme Court took the case to resolve a conflict among the circuit courts.

In this case, the United States filed an action in federal court seeking to seize a house and the four-acre parcel on which it was situated on the grounds that the property had been used to commit or facilitate the commission of a federal drug offense. The court authorized the seizure of the property based on an affidavit recounting the dealer's conviction and the evidence of drugs found in the search of the house. The government had contended that the Fourth rather than the Fifth Amendment should be applied. The Supreme Court disagreed and applied the Fifth Amendment. The Court observed that its general rule is that notice of impending seizure and a hearing afforded the owner is normally required, but that it tolerates some exceptions in "extraordinary situations." Using its usual due-process analysis laid down in *Mathews* v. *Eldridge* [424 U.S. 319 (1976)], the Court found that the private interests at stake in the seizure of real property were significant. Further, the Court found the practice of seizure without a predeprivation hearing creates an unacceptable risk of error, affording little or no protection for an innocent owner. With respect to the government's interest, in contrast to an earlier case in which the Court permitted the seizure of a yacht [*Calero-Toledo* v. *Pearson Yacht Leasing Co.* 416 U.S. 479 (1974)], the Court found no pressing governmental need for an immediate seizure. Real property, unlike a yacht, cannot be moved, and if there is evidence that an owner is likely to destroy it, the Court reasoned the government has other appropriate relief at its disposal. The Court made it clear that the principles enunciated in this case apply to real property in general and not simply to residences.

In conclusion, the Court held that unless exigent circumstances are present, the Due Process Clause requires the government to afford notice and a meaningful opportunity to be heard before seizing real property subject to civil forfeiture. Further, to establish exigent circumstances, the government must show that less restrictive measures would not suffice to protect the government's interests in preventing the sale, destruction, or continued unlawful use of the property.

SOLID WASTE

The Court decided two cases concerning the disposal of solid waste and a third concerning the incineration of solid waste. All three cases have major implications for local governments.

In the first decision, *Oregon Waste Systems, Inc., et al.* v. *Department of Environmental Quality of the State of Oregon et al.* [114 S.Ct. 1345 (1994)], the Supreme Court again struck down a state statute aimed at out-of-state waste. An Oregon statute imposed a $2.25 per ton surcharge on the disposal of solid waste from outside the state, but only an $0.85 per ton charge on the disposal of solid waste from inside the state. The drafters of the Oregon statute had been inspired by a 1992 Supreme Court case, *Chemical Waste Management Inc.* v. *Hunt* [112 S.Ct. 2009 (1992)], where the Court invalidated an Alabama statute that called for different charges for solid waste from different in-state or out-of-state sources. But, in that decision, the Court indicated that if the statute incorporated a cost-based fee differential, it might have been upheld. In fact, the Oregon supreme court upheld the Oregon statute precisely for that reason.

In a 7 to 2 decision, however, Justice Clarence Thomas wrote that the difference in fees was clearly discriminatory on its face. At the heart of the problem was the fact that Oregon never maintained that it is more expensive to dispose of waste from other states. Nor did Oregon offer health or safety reasons to support its different treatment for in-state and out-of-state wastes.

Chief Justice Rehnquist, who in past cases has expressed empathy for state and local governments that must deal with these waste problems, dissented along with Justice Blackmun. "Once again," Rehnquist wrote, the Court has tied " . . . the hands of the States in addressing the vexing national problem of solid waste dis-posal." The Court's majority continues to "stubbornly refuse" to recognize that a healthy environment, not solid waste, is the commodity at issue in this case, he lamented. The chief justice concluded that the Court's decision gives out-of-state producers of solid waste a competitive advantage over in-state producers because they do not have to deal with state taxes, landfill capacity issues, or the cleanup of leaking landfills. Further, Oregon did offer rational health and safety reasons for its differential treatment based on source of the solid waste: "The availability of environmentally sound landfill space and the proper disposal of solid waste strike me as justifiable 'safety and health' rationales for the fee," Rehnquist wrote.

As is evidenced by the *Oregon* case, for years one of the biggest controversies in environmental management has been whether state and local governments may keep trash out of their districts. In 1994, however, the Supreme Court decided a case that reflects a new cutting-edge issue in environmental management: keeping trash *in* a specific state or local government boundary and not allowing it to be shipped out for economic reasons. In the case of *C & A Carbone, Inc., et al.* v. *Clarkstown, New York* [114 S.Ct. 1677 (1994)] the town of Clarkstown agreed to allow a private contractor to construct a solid waste transfer station within the town limits and to operate the facility for five years. At the end of the five years, the town planned to buy the facility for one dollar. To finance the transfer station's cost, the town guaranteed a minimum waste-flow to the facility, for which the contractor charged a tipping fee. In order to meet the waste flow guarantee, the town adopted a flow-control ordinance requiring all nonhazardous solid waste within the town to be deposited at the transfer station. Shipping non-recyclable waste out of the city limits to locations that might charge a lesser tipping fee was forbidden.

After discovering that the Carbone company and other haulers were shipping their wastes to out-of-state locations, Clarkstown filed suit in state court seeking an injunction requiring that the waste be shipped to the town's transfer station. The lower court granted summary judgment to the town and the appellate court affirmed. Carbone and other haulers appealed to the U.S. Supreme Court, arguing, among other things, that the flow-control ordinance violated the Commerce Clause of the U.S. Constitution.

In a 6 to 3 decision, the Supreme Court reversed the lower courts and held that the ordinance did indeed violate the Commerce Clause. The Court reasoned that while the ordinance was local, its economic effects were interstate in nature. Second, the Court reasoned that the article of commerce here was not so much the waste itself, but the service of processing and disposing of it. Third, the Court pointed out that the ordinance favored certain operators, disfavored others, and squelched competition. Finally, the Court maintained that the town had other avenues through which it could address its local interests. For example, health and safety regulations could be promulgated to ad-dress environmental safety concerns, while taxes or municipal bonds could be utilized to subsidize the costs of the facility.

The implications of this case for local administrators are great. Hundreds of local governments have entered into similar arrangements not only for transfer stations, but also for landfills and incinerators. In exchange for providing trash collection in a locality, haulers agree to dispose of the waste in the local landfill, incinerator, or transfer station, thus guaranteeing a minimum level of business. In many instances, hauling the trash to another site, often out of state, would mean a reduction in tipping fees, sometimes by 50%. In Onondaga County, New York, for example, the county has spent $178 million to build a trash incinerator, based on agreements with local governments that they will dispose of their trash at that site. The Supreme Court case now jeopardizes the future of that incinerator and others around the country. (More than $10 billion of bonds have been issued to finance trash-burning plants around the country, and over half the states have enacted laws allowing flow-control ordinances.) Many haulers are using the Court's decision as ammunition in attempts to obtain releases from prior agreements. While most county officials point out that their agreements are contract-based, not ordinance-based, local haulers maintain that the contracts were coercive and the end result—a violation of the Commerce Clause—is the same. Congress currently is being lobbied heavily to overturn the Supreme Court decision.

In a third case, *City of Chicago* v. *Environmental Defense Fund* [114 S.Ct. 1588 (1994)], the Court held that the ash resulting from the incineration of municipal solid waste must be treated as hazardous waste. In doing so, the Court overruled an EPA interpretation of the Resource Conservation and Recovery Act (RCRA) that was beneficial to local governments.

In 1980, EPA excluded household wastes from the definition of hazardous waste, even if those wastes contained toxics such as batteries. An amendment to RCRA in 1984 further convinced EPA that Congress intended household waste to be exempt from hazardous waste regulations. One outcome was less stringent requirements for those local governments that provide trash disposal service to their residents.

The Environmental Defense Fund (EDF) sued, arguing in part that the clear language of the statute demonstrates Congress's intention to exclude a resource recovery facility's management activities but not its *generation* of toxic ash from the burning of household wastes. In defending itself, the city of Chicago pointed to a Senate report stating that solid waste incineration would not be considered generation, transportation, treatment, storage, or disposal of hazardous waste if it burns only household waste and nonhazardous waste. Further, the city argued that it would be an economic hardship if it had to comply with hazardous waste regulations every time it burned solid waste.

The Supreme Court agreed with EDF's arguments. In a 7 to 2 decision, the Court held that although a resource-recovery facility's management activities are excluded from Subtitle C regulation, its generation of toxic ash is not. The implications of this decision are potentially quite dramatic. Whenever the ash from burned solid waste is tested and found to be hazardous, more stringent and costly hazardous waste regulations must be followed. Local governments as well as private parties will incur substantial expense to comply with the ruling. Household waste to be burned will either have to be separated into hazardous and nonhazardous, or its ash treated as hazardous. Incinerators will have to be retrofitted in order to allow the separation of hazardous bottom ash and less hazardous fly ash.

CLEAN WATER

The city of Tacoma and the county of Jefferson want to build a hydroelectric plant on the Dosewallips River in Washington State. Among the legal requirements the city and county must meet is the acquisition of a permit from the state under the Clean Water Act (CWA). The permit issued by the state required specific minimum stream flows to protect salmon and steelhead runs. The city and county objected to this condition, maintaining, among other things, that it exceeds the state's authority under the CWA. Essentially they argued that the CWA concerns water quality, not water quantity. Further, the plaintiffs argued that it is the Federal Energy Regulatory Commission that has the power to consider stream-flow requirements for fish and wildlife. Hence, in the case of *Jefferson County* v. *Washington Department of Ecology* [114 S.Ct. 1900 (1994)] the pivotal question was whether a state may impose minimum streamflow requirements as a condition for a permit for a federally licensed hydroelectric power project under section 401 of the CWA.

In a 7 to 2 decision, the Supreme Court supported the state's position that it did indeed have authority under the CWA to impose such a condition. Reasoning that states may impose limitations on activities—not just discharges—that affect state water quality, Justice O'Connor wrote that separating quantity from quality is an artificial distinction. A sufficient lowering of quantity could destroy all a river's designated uses, and the CWA recognizes that reduced stream flow can constitute water pollution. The decision will make it more difficult to obtain permits for hydropower projects in the future.

SEXUAL HARASSMENT

Among the most pathbreaking decisions of the Court in this last session was one concerning sexual harassment, *Teresa Harris* v. *Forklift Systems, Inc.* [114 S.Ct. 367 (1993)]. It is now easier to prove sexual harassment in court because of this decision. The Court ruled that all that is needed is evidence that a reasonable person would view the work environment as abusive or hostile and that the employee com-

plaining of sexual harassment perceived the work environment as abusive or hostile.

Teresa Harris sued her former employer, Forklift Systems, Inc., claiming that the conduct of the president of the company toward her constituted "abusive work environment" harassment because of her gender, in violation of Title VII of the Civil Rights Act of 1964. To support her case, Harris offered proof that the president often insulted her because of her gender and often made her the target of unwanted sexual innuendos. Examples include saying to her on several occasions in front of other employees, "You're a woman, what do you know?" "We need a man as the rental manager," and calling her "a dumb-ass woman." Again in front of others he suggested that they "go to the Holiday Inn to negotiate [her] raise." When she successfully negotiated a deal with a customer, the president asked Harris, again in front of other employees, "What did you do, promise the guy ... some [sex] Saturday night?" After repeatedly asking the president to stop, Harris collected her paycheck and quit.

The lower courts concluded that the president's comments did not constitute an abusive environment under Title VII because the employer's conduct, although offensive, was not "so severe as to be expected to seriously affect her psychological wellbeing." The Supreme Court disagreed. In a unanimous opinion, the Court held that to be actionable, as "abusive work environment" harassment, conduct need not "seriously affect [an employee's] psychological wellbeing" or lead the plaintiff to "suffer injury." Writing for the Court, Justice Sandra Day O'Connor said that all that is needed is evidence that a reasonable person would view the work environment as abusive or hostile and that the employee complaining of sexual harassment perceived the work environment as abusive or hostile. Each situation must be decided on a case-by-case basis, looking at the aggregate factors. The court reversed and remanded, ordering the lower court to apply the correct legal standard.

Another private-sector case that has implications for municipal employment involved Title VII of the Civil Rights Act [42 U.S.C.A. section 1981 a(a)]. In *Landgraf* v. *U.S.I. Film Products* [114 S.Ct. 1483 (1994)], a woman brought action against her former employer, alleging sexual harassment and retaliation in violation of Title VII. The district court found that she had been sexually harassed by a coworker at the firm, but that the harassment was not so severe as to justify her decision to resign her position. Because the court found that her employment was not terminated in violation of Title VII, she was not entitled to equitable relief, and because Title VII did not at that time authorize any other form of relief, the court dismissed her complaint. While her appeal was pending, the Civil Rights Act of 1991 became law, and section 102 includes provisions that create a right to recover compensatory and punitive damages for intentional discrimination. The new law also authorizes any party to demand a jury trial if such damages are claimed.

The plaintiff asked the Supreme Court to rule that section 102 has retroactive effect and should apply in her case. The Court declined to do that, and held that section 102 does not apply to a Title VII case that was pending on appeal when the 1991 law was enacted. The holding would also apply in similar cases involving current or former municipal employees.

TAXES AND USER FEES

Three tax cases and one user-fee case decided by the Supreme Court in 1993–1994 have important implications for local governments. In the first decision, *Associated Industries of Missouri et al.* v. *Janette M. Lohman, Director of Revenue of Missouri, et al.* [114 S.Ct. 1815 (1994)], the Supreme Court struck down one of Missouri's sales tax schemes, largely because of the different sales tax rates imposed by Missouri's local governments. The state of Missouri imposes a statewide sales tax of 4.225% on the sale of goods within the state and a statewide use tax of 4.225% on goods brought into the state after being purchased elsewhere. Since most local governments in Missouri also impose some sort of additional sales tax (ranging from 0% to 3.5%) on goods purchased in their jurisdictions, the state added a 1.5% tax to the use tax, raising the total use tax rate to 5.725. A trade association and a manufacturer that pays the Missouri use tax sued, arguing that the tax scheme impermissibly discriminates against interstate commerce in violation of the Commerce Clause.

The Supreme Court unanimously agreed with the plaintiffs and found the state's additional use tax unconstitutional. The Court's primary rationale was that the additional use tax exceeded some local governments' rates, hence imposing a discriminatory burden on interstate commerce in those localities. "Whether the 1.5% use tax is equal to (or lower than) the local sales tax is a matter of fortuity, depending entirely upon the locality in which the Missouri purchaser happens to reside," Justice Thomas wrote. "Where the use tax exceeds the sales tax, the discrepancy imposes a discriminatory burden on interstate commerce." The Court, however, did not order a tax refund. It remanded the case to the Missouri courts to determine the appropriate relief.

Whether railroads were discriminated against by an Oregon personal property tax scheme was the issue decided by the Supreme Court in a second tax decision, *Department of Revenue of Oregon* v. *ACF Industries, Inc., et al.* [114 S.Ct. 843 (1994)]. In that case, the state imposed a tax on all personal property in the state, including railroad property, but exempted some other classes of business personal property. ACF industries, a company that owns railroad cars, sued, alleging that the tax scheme violates the 1976 Railroad Revitalization and Regulatory Reform Act (the "4-R act"). The 4-R act prohibits ad valorem taxation of railroad property at a higher assessment ratio or rate than other commercial and industrial property. The act also prohibits states from imposing "another tax that discriminates against a rail carrier."

In an 8 to 1 ruling, the Supreme Court upheld the legality of the Oregon tax scheme. Reasoning that the 4-R act does not limit a state's discretion to exempt some, but not all, business property from generally applicable ad valorem property taxes, the Court found no illegal discrimination against the railroad property. Writing for the Court, Justice Kennedy concluded that "a State may grant exemptions from a generally applicable ad valorem property tax without exposing the taxation of railroad property to invalidation under . . . [the act]."

The taxation of goods sold on Native American lands was the subject of a third case decided by the Court [*Department of Taxation and Finance of New York et al.* v. *Milhelm Attea and Brothers, Inc., et al.*, 114 S.Ct. 2028 (1994)]. For years, goods sold on Native American lands have been particularly attractive to both Native Americans and non-Native Americans because often no sales tax is charged. For example, in New York State, cigarette smokers flocked to stores on Native American reservations to avoid the state's cigarette tax of 56¢ per pack. Earlier Supreme Court cases had concluded that states were without power to collect taxes for cigarettes sold to tribal members for their own consumption on Native American lands. (See, for example, *Moe v. Confederated Salish and Kootenai Tribes of Flathead Reservation,* 425 U.S. 463 [(1976)] and *Warren Trading Post* v. *Arizona Tax Commissioner,* 380 U.S. 685 [(1965)].) An audit by New York State suggested that either cigarettes in reservation stores were also being sold to non-Native Americans or the Native Americans were consuming 32 times the cigarettes of the average New Yorker.

Based on the audit information, New York State enacted regulations imposing record-keeping requirements and quantity limitations on cigarette wholesalers selling untaxed cigarettes to reservation Indians. Wholesalers (1) must ensure that a buyer holds a valid state tax exemption certificate, (2) keep records of their tax-exempt sales, (3) make monthly reports to the state, and (4) precollect taxes on nonexempt sales. A group of cigarette wholesalers licensed by the Bureau of Indian Affairs sued, alleging that the regulations were preempted by the federal Indian Trader Statutes, as interpreted by case law.

In a unanimous decision, the Supreme Court upheld the New York State regulations. Reasoning that the special status of Indian Traders cannot be used to avoid lawfully imposed state taxes, the Court did not find the New York regulations to be inconsistent with the Indian Trader Statutes. Justice Stevens, writing for the Court, said that states have a valid interest in ensuring that cigarette taxes are not easily evaded through purchases of tax-exempt cigarettes on reservations.

In a fourth case, a county airport authority successfully defended its user fees. In the case of *Northwest Airlines, Inc., et al.* v. *County of Kent, Michigan* [114 S.Ct. 855 (1994)], seven commercial airlines sued Kent County, asserting that certain airport user fees charged to them are unreasonable and discriminatory, in violation of the federal Anti-Head Tax Act (AHTA). The AHTA, in part, prohibits airports from charging a "head tax" on passengers boarding flights because such a tax might inhibit the flow of interstate commerce and the right to travel.

In the Kent County case, the airlines specifically protested the fact that the airport's three major groups of clients—commercial airlines, general aviation (corporate and privately owned aircraft not used for commercial, passenger, cargo, or military service), and nonaeronautical concessionaires (such as car-rental agencies, restaurants, and gift shops)—were each assessed different user fees. Especially aggravating to the airlines was the fact that the airport charged commercial airlines 100% of the costs allocated to them but charged general aviation only 20% of their allocated costs. (While undercharging general aviation, the airport overcharged the concessionaires.)

In a 7 to 1 decision, the Supreme Court held in an opinion written by Justice Ginsburg that the airport's fees have not been shown to be unreasonable under the AHTA for several reasons. First, the AHTA sets no standards for determining a fee's reasonableness. Second, examining the fees through the lens provided by previous case law [*Evansville-Vanderburgh Airport Authority District* v. *Delta Air Lines, Inc.,* 405 U.S. 707 (1972)], the Court found that the airport's methodology was not unlawful. The Court also indicated that given the U.S. Department of Transportation's regulatory authority regarding the federal aviation laws, there is no cause for courts to offer a substitute. Finally, the Court said that there was no proof to support the airlines' contention that the lower general aviation fees discriminate against interstate commerce and travel.

PUBLIC SCHOOLS

Two cases concerning education were decided by the Supreme Court in its last term. The pivotal question in the case of *Board of Education of Kiryas Joel Village School District* v. *Louis Grumet et al., Board of Education of Monroe-Woodbury Central School District* [114 S.Ct. 2481 (1994)] was whether a New York statute that set up a special school district in a village consisting entirely of members of a strict Jewish sect—Satmar Hasidim—was an unconstitutional merger of church and state. In a 6 to 3 decision the Court upheld an appellate court decision that concluded that the law's primary effect—to advance religion—was impermissible. The law was thus struck down as unconstitutional.

A special state statute enacted in 1989 carved out a school district following village lines to serve the distinctive population. Prior to 1989, the children of the village attended private religious schools. The special school district was created primarily because the religious schools do not provide special education services for disabled children and the parents of the disabled children refused to allow them to attend schools outside their own community surrounded by people "whose ways were so different."

The New York State School Boards Association and two of its officers challenged the law as an unconstitutional establishment of religion. Justice Souter, writing for the Court, said that the statute violated the constitutional command of neutrality toward religion. The statute "singles out a particular religious sect for special treatment," Souter wrote, "and whatever the limits of permissible legislative accommodations [to religious groups] may be, . . . it is clear that neutrality as among religions must be honored."

The Court also decided a second public school case involving a nonconstitutional issue. The pivotal issue in *Florence County School District Four et al.* v. *Shannon Carter,* [114 S.Ct. 361 (1993)], was whether a court may order reimbursement for parents who unilaterally withdraw their child from a public school that provides an inappropriate education under the Individuals with Disabilities Education Act (IDEA) and put the child in a private school that provides an education that is otherwise proper under IDEA but does not meet all the requirements of the act. In a unanimous decision, the Court held that a court may properly order such reimbursement.

Shannon Carter was classified as learning disabled in 1985 as a ninth-grade student in the Florence County School in South Carolina. As required by IDEA, school officials met with Shannon's parents to formulate an individualized education program (IEP) for her. Shannon's parents challenged the IEP as inappropriate for their child but lost in an administrative hearing on the matter. In the meantime, they enrolled her in the Trident Academy, a private school specializing in educating children with disabilities.

In July 1986, Shannon's parents sued the school district, alleging that it had breached its duty under IDEA to provide their daughter with a "free appropriate public education." They sought reimbursement for tuition and other costs incurred at Trident. They won in the lower court and in the appellate court.

The Supreme Court affirmed, reasoning that under the intent of the act, courts may "order school authorities to reimburse parents for their expenditures on private special education for a child if the court ultimately determines that such placement, rather than a proposed IEP, is proper under the Act." Justice O'Connor, writing for the Court, was not convinced by arguments that the Trident School did not comply with IDEA because it employed two teachers who weren't state certified and did not develop IEPs. It is "somewhat ironic," she wrote, for the state to express concern about state standards not being met when it was the public school's failure to meet Shannon's needs that necessitated the school transfer in the first place. The case presumably will make it easier for parents of learning disabled children to be reimbursed for expenditures tied with their special educational needs.

VOTING RIGHTS

The Supreme Court decided two cases concerning voting rights in this term. In the case of *Jackie Holder, et al.* v. *E.K. Hall, Sr., et al.* [114, S.Ct. 2581 (1994)], the Georgia Legislature authorized Bleckley County in 1985 to change from a single-commissioner form of government to a multimember commission consisting of five commissioners elected from single-member districts. When a referendum on the issue was held in 1986, however, the electorate did not adopt the change. Six African American voters and the Cochran/Bleckley chapter of the National Association for the Advancement of Colored People (NAACP) sued the incumbent county commissioner and the superintendent of elections, alleging that the county's single-member commission was enacted or maintained with an intent to exclude or to limit the political influence of the county's African American community in violation of the Fourteenth and Fifteenth Amendments of the Constitution. The plaintiffs also alleged that such action violated Section 2 of the Voting Rights Act because under that law, Bleckley County must have a county commission of sufficient size that, with single-member election districts, the county's African American citizens would constitute a majority in one of the single-member districts. The plaintiffs lost both the constitutional and the statutory challenges in the lower court. The court of appeals, however, found for the plaintiffs on the statutory claim, but did not rule on the constitutional claim. The U.S. Supreme Court then agreed to review the statutory question. The issue before it, was whether the size of a governing authority is subject to a vote dilution challenge under Section 2 of the Voting Rights Act of 1965, 42 U.S.C. section 1973.

In a 5 to 4 decision, the Court ruled that the size of a governmental authority cannot be the basis for a vote dilution challenge under Section 2 of the Voting Rights Act. Writing for the Court's majority, Justice Kennedy pointed out that the law requires more. First, under the precedent established by the case of *Thornburg* v. *Gingles* [478 U.S. 30 (1986)], it must be shown that the minority group is sufficiently numerous and geographically compact to constitute a majority in a single-member district carved out of the larger district; it must be politically cohesive; and the white majority must vote as a block in most cases, triggering a defeat of the minority-backed candidate. Second, Section 2 of the act requires an examination of the "totality of the circumstances." Third, there must be a "reasonable alternative practice as a benchmark against which to measure the existing voting practices." It was this third factor that was especially lacking, according to the Court: such an alternative was not presented in this case, Kennedy wrote. While the plaintiffs lost their statutory claim, the Court remanded the case to the court of appeals for consideration of the constitutional issues involved.

The second Voting Rights Act case decided by the Court this session was *Bolley Johnson, Speaker of the Florida House of Representatives et al.* v. *Miguel de Grandy, et al.* [114 S.Ct. 2647 (1994)]. In this group of consolidated cases, Hispanic voters, African American voters, and the federal government sued the state of Florida, alleging that Florida's reapportionment plan for the state's single-member Senate and House districts unlawfully dilutes the voting strength of Hispanics and African Americans in the Dade County area. The State Supreme Court reviewed the plan, as mandated by the State Constitution, and found it valid, while admitting to time constraints that precluded full review. When the plaintiffs pursued their case in federal court, a district court ruled that the plan's provisions for the state House districts was in violation of the Voting Rights Act but its provisions for the state Senate districts were not.

The Supreme Court decided three issues in the case. The first was whether the District Court erred by not deferring to the decision of the state supreme court. Justice Souter, writing for the majority in this 7 to 2 decision, concluded that the district court did not err. The state supreme court itself admitted that its review was quite limited. Further, in its decision, the state supreme court wrote that its holding was "without prejudice to the right of any protestor to question the validity of the plan by filing a petition in this Court alleging how the plan violates the Voting Rights Act." That the plaintiffs filed in federal rather than state court was not a problem, Souter maintained, since the plaintiffs "are free to litigate in any court with jurisdiction" and are entitled to "full and fair opportunity to litigate."

The second issue decided by the Supreme Court was whether the Florida plan violated the Voting Rights Act. The Court held that it did not for several reasons. Maintaining that it must look at the totality of circumstances when determining whether minority voters have less opportunity than other members of the electorate to participate in the political process and to elect representatives of their choice, the Court wrote that "in spite of continuing discrimination and racial block voting, minority voters form effective voting majorities" in a number of Florida districts. While not dispositive, this is a relevant and important fact that was pivotal to the Court's decision.

The third issue decided by the Supreme Court was whether the district court's decision to leave undisturbed the state's plan for Senate districts was correct. The Court upheld this decision, although for reasons different than those of the district court. The Court ruled that the totality of the circumstances did not appear to support a finding of dilution in this instance. The message this decision sends to states is that they need not maximize the number of "majority-minority" districts in order to avoid a vote dilution violation of the Voting Rights Act.

FREE SPEECH

Four free speech cases were decided by the Supreme Court in the last term. First, the Court decided a First Amendment case in the context of public-sector employment that has implications for all public-sector employers including local governments. In a previous case, *Connick* v. *Meyers* [461 U.S. 138 (1983)], the Court had set forth a test for determining whether speech by a government employee may, consistent with the First Amendment, serve as a basis for disciplining or discharging that employee. In *Waters* v. *Churchill* [114 S.Ct. 1878 (1994)], the Court decided whether the *Connick* test should be applied to what the government employer thought was said or to what a court reviewing the decision determines to have been said.

Under the *Connick* test, to be protected, the speech must be on a matter of public concern, and the employee's interest in expressing himself or herself must not be outweighed by any injury the speech could cause to the interest of the state, as employer, in promoting the efficiency of the public services it performs through its employees. The Court held that government employees' speech must be treated differently with regard to substantive and procedural requirements. The government's actions are treated differently in the public-employment context than when it is dealing with members of the public. The government's role as an employer gives it a freer hand in regulating the speech of its employees than it has in regulating the speech of the public at large. The Court said that when an employee counsels coworkers to do their job in a way with which the public employer disagrees, managers may tell the employee to stop.

Government employee speech must be treated differently with regard to procedural requirements as well. The Court of Appeals had held that reviewing courts should make their determination based on what the speech actually was and not on what the employer thought it was. The Supreme Court rejected this and said the problem with this procedure is that it would force the government employer to come to its factual conclusions through procedures that substantially mirror the evidentiary rules used in court. The Court saw this as unworkable, and concluded that government employers should be allowed to use personnel procedures that differ from the evidentiary rules used by courts (such as relying on hearsay) without fear that these differences will lead to liability.

With regard to the standard employers should meet in connection with free speech, the Court stated that if an employment action is based on what an employee supposedly said, and a reasonable manager would recognize that there is a substantial likelihood that what was actually said was protected, the manager must tread with a certain amount of care. This should be the care that a reasonable manager would use before making an employment decision—discharge, suspension, reprimand, or whatever else. The Court observed that there will often be situations in which reasonable employers would disagree about who is to be believed, how much investigation needs to be done, or how much evidence is needed to come to a particular conclusion. In those situations many different courses of action will necessarily be reasonable. Thus, the Court directed that only procedures outside the range of what a reasonable manager would use may be condemned as unreasonable and result in liability.

This case implies that government managers will have a freer hand in disciplining employees that engage in speech that disrupts public-sector operations, but that discretion is not unbound. The courts are directed to assess whether the action taken is in the range of behaviors a "reasonable manager" would take in dealing with unprotected speech. The Court made it clear, however, that reviewing courts can inquire whether the action was clearly based on unprotected disruptive speech or whether the employer was basing the action on protected speech and advancing the unprotected speech as a pretext for the action taken. Courts will still be able to review actions on a case-by-case basis.

In another First Amendment case, a resident challenged a city ordinance that banned all residential signs except those falling within one of ten exceptions. (The ban was principally for the purpose of minimizing visual clutter associated with such signs.) In *City of Ladue* v. *Gilleo* [114 S.Ct. 2038 (1994)], a homeowner placed on her front lawn a 24 by 16-inch sign printed with the words, "Say No to War in the Persian Gulf, Call Congress Now." The city council denied her petition for a variance and she sued the city, the mayor, and the city council under the federal Civil Rights Act [42 U.S.C. section 1983], alleging that the ordinance violated her First Amendment right of free speech.

The Court acknowledged that while signs are a form of expression protected by the Free Speech Clause, they pose distinctive problems that are subject to municipalities' police powers. The issue is, Under what circumstances do the city's police powers have to give way to free speech rights? The Court set out a framework for addressing this issue by identifying two analytically distinct grounds for challenging the constitutionality of a municipal ordinance regulating the display of signs. One ground is that a measure in effect restricts too little speech because its exemptions discriminate on the basis of the signs' messages. Such measures are content-based, allowing one message to be favored over another according to an official's view of the content. This ground was the basis of the circuit court's rejection of the city's ordinance, because the ordinance contained exceptions.

The other ground is that a measure simply prohibits too much protected speech. This is the ground the Supreme Court chose to use to reject the city's ordinance. This framework extends to city policies far beyond the context of sign regulations. The Court observed that although prohibitions foreclosing entire media may be completely free of content or viewpoint discrimination, the danger they pose is that by eliminating a common means of speaking, such measures can suppress too much speech.

With respect to the particular ordinance under challenge, the Court was not persuaded by the city that adequate substitutes existed for yard signs and stated that residential signs are an unusually cheap and convenient form of communication, especially for persons of modest means or limited mobility. The Court further added that a person who puts up a sign at his or her residence often intends to reach neighbors, an audience that could not be reached nearly as well by other means.

The Court did not foreclose any city regulation of residential signs, but indicated it was confident the city could find "more temperate measures to satisfy the city's regulatory needs." In a footnote, the Court made it clear that it was not saying that every kind of sign must be permitted in residential areas, nor was it addressing regulations short of a ban.

The implications of this decision extend beyond the context of sign regulation to regulation of other types of communication as well. Municipalities have been put on notice that policies can be challenged on First Amendment grounds for being overinclusive as well as underinclusive.

Yet another free speech case involved the regulation of cable television and the "must carry" rules whereby local programming must be carried on cable television. This is of long-standing interest to municipalities, given their involvement in cable TV regulation under the federal law and their interests in local broadcasting, including the effect of municipally owned stations.

In *Turner Broadcasting System, Inc.* v. *FCC* [114 S.Ct. 2445 (1994)], the Court considered a challenge from cable-system operators and programmers challenging the constitutionality of "must carry" provisions of the Cable Television Consumer Protection and Competition Act of 1992. A three-judge district court panel had granted summary judgment in favor of the FCC. The cable operators had asked the Court to apply the highest level of scrutiny—strict scrutiny—under the First Amendment framework. As the Court discussed, strict scrutiny applies to regulations that suppress, disadvantage, or impose differential burdens upon speech because of its content, while an intermediate level of scrutiny is applied to regulations that are unrelated to the content of speech. The Court decided that the FCC's rules were not content-based and thus an intermediate level of scrutiny should apply.

The Court proceeded to analyze the statute according to the intermediate level of scrutiny and said a regulation could be sustained if "it furthers an important or substantial governmental interest, if the governmental interest is unrelated to the suppression of free expression, and if the incidental restriction on alleged First Amendment freedoms is no greater than essential to the furtherance of that interest." The Court went on to analyze the "must carry" provisions and found that Congress's enunciated interests furthered important governmental purposes and were unrelated to the suppression of free expression. However, the Court said it was insufficient for the government to assert only that the "must carry" rules were necessary to actually fulfill Congress's stated purposes. Rather, the government must demonstrate with evidence that the economic health of local broadcasting is in jeopardy without the rules. Further, the Court required that there be evidence of the actual effects of "must carry" provisions on the speech of cable operators and cable programmers. Examples include the extent to which cable operators will, in fact, be forced to make changes in their current or anticipated programming selections, the degree to which cable programmers will be dropped from cable systems to make room for local broadcasters, and the extent to which cable operators can satisfy their "must carry" obligations by devoting previously unused channel capacity to the carriage of local broadcasters. Without this evidence, the Court said it would not be in a position to say whether the "must carry" provisions suppressed substantially more speech than necessary to ensure the viability of broadcast television. Thus, for purposes of obtaining this information, the Court remanded the case back to the district court for further proceedings to make these determinations.

The Court addressed issues involved in a state court injunction against antiabortion protesters in another First Amendment case. This case has implications for the types and circumstances under which groups may seek injunctions against abortion controversy activities that they feel pose a public safety threat. The case also has implications for those seeking injunctions in other areas affecting public safety and the First Amendment.

In *Madsen* v. *Women's Health Center, Inc.* [114 S.Ct. 2516 (1994)], antiabortion protesters challenged a state court injunction that restricted their protest activity around a Florida women's health center in which abortions were performed. They asked the Supreme Court to strike down the injunction as content-based and thus subject to the Court's standard of "strict scrutiny." The Supreme Court declined to do that and said, first, that the injunction was not directed at the actions of a specific group and therefore was not content-based. Accordingly, the injunction did not demand the application of the strict scrutiny standard. Nonetheless, the Court noted differences between ordinances and injunctions and enunciated a new standard to apply to content-neutral injunctions. This standard directs courts to assess whether the challenged provisions of the injunction burden no more speech than necessary to serve a significant government interest.

In assessing the provisions of the injunction of the state court, the Supreme Court held that: (1) provisions establishing a 36-foot buffer zone around clinic entrances and driveways and imposing limited noise restrictions did not violate the First Amendment and (2) provisions establishing 36-foot buffer zone on private property, banning images put up that were observable from the clinic, and establishing 300-foot buffer zone around residences of the clinic staff burdened more speech than necessary to serve governmental interests.

In striking down these provisions the Court engaged in provision-by-provision analysis, weighing (1) how much each provision contributed to specifically articulated governmental purposes, (2) whether the provisions were necessary to accomplish those purposes, and (3) how much speech activity was limited by the provision. For example, with respect to the 300-foot buffer zone around residences, the court did not find sufficient justification in the record for this broad a ban. The Court observed that it appeared that a limitation on the time and duration of picketing and on the number of picketers outside a smaller zone could have accomplished the desired result.

CRIMINAL LAW

Of the many criminal-law cases decided by the Supreme Court in the 1993–1994 term, four stand out as substantially affecting local governments. The first criminal-law case spoke to the condition under which a suspect must be considered "in custody" and thus must be given the Miranda warning before being interrogated by police officers. In *Stansbury* v. *California* [114 S.Ct 1526 (1994)], police officers asked a man to come to the police station voluntarily as a possible witness in a rape and murder investigation, and he agreed. They did not advise him of his right to counsel because they did not consider him a suspect. In the course of the questioning, the investigating officer, based on the man's answers, realized the man may have committed the crime in question. The officer ceased the questioning and gave the man the Miranda warning. On appeal following the conviction, the man challenged the evidence gathered before the warning. The lower court had found that the man was not in custody prior to mentioning some information indicating possible involvement. Because the man was not a suspect while being questioned, he was not entitled to the Miranda warning.

The Supreme Court stated that whether the officer had considered the man a suspect was irrelevant for purposes of the Miranda warning. The Court observed, "Our decisions make clear that the initial determination of custody depends on the objective circumstances of the interrogation, not the subjective views harbored by either the interrogating officers or the person being questioned." The Court said the only relevant inquiry is how a reasonable person in the suspect's shoes would have understood the situation and that Miranda warnings are required only where there has been such restriction on a person's freedom as to render that person "in custody." The Court remanded the case back to the lower court to determine whether the objective circumstances demonstrated the man was in custody. The implication of this case is that police officers cannot simply claim the fact that they did not consider someone they are interviewing to be a suspect as a reason for not giving the Miranda warning. Rather, they will have to be prepared to show that a reasonable person would not have thought themselves to be in custody during the interview.

In another criminal case, the Court decided what the government must prove in a case involving illegal firearms—machine guns covered under the National Firearms Act [26 U.S.C. sections 5801 to 5872]. In *Staples* v. *U.S.* [114 S.Ct. 1793 (1994)], local police and agents of the Bureau of Alcohol, Tobacco, and Firearms recovered an AR-15 assault rifle. Such a rifle can be modified to fire automatically. Upon testing the rifle, it was discovered that it did fire automatically, and Staples was indicted for unlawful possession of an unregistered machine gun. Staples testified that the rifle had never fired automatically when it was in his possession and that his ignorance of any automatic firing capability should have shielded him from criminal liability for his failure to register the weapon.

The Court took the case to settle a dispute among the circuits about whether the statute contained a *mens rea* requirement, i.e. whether it requires proof that the defendant knew of the characteristics of the weapon that made it an illegal firearm. The Court observed that the statute was silent on the *mens rea* requirement and that it had to construe the statute in light of background rules of common law. According to those rules, the Court stated that the requirement for some *mens rea* was the rule rather than the exception. Accordingly, the Court found that the usual presumption that a defendant must know the facts that make his conduct illegal should apply in this case. Thus, to obtain a conviction, the government should have been required to prove the defendant knew of the features of the AR-15 that made it illegal.

Local law enforcement agencies often work in conjunction with federal law enforcement agencies in cases where illegal firearms are likely to be involved. There has been increased activity in this area as law enforcement has tried to suppress the rapid growth of automatic weapons in urban areas. Under the Court's interpretation in this case, it will not be enough to seize the weapon and show that it possesses illegal characteristics. The officers must also be able to prove that the owner knew it possessed illegal characteristics and did not register it.

In another firearms case, the Court addressed the question of whether a defendant may attack prior state convictions during a federal sentencing hearing under the Armed Career Criminal Act. Congress passed this law to provide for stronger sentences within the federal system for particularly dangerous criminals. The act [18 U.S.C.A. sections 922 (g)(1), 924 (e)] provides that a sentence can be increased for a defendant unlawfully possessing firearms who had three previous convictions for violent felony or serious drug offenses.

Baltimore city police arrested the defendant, and a federal grand jury indicted him on several counts, including possession of a firearm by a convicted felon. He had three prior felony convictions in Maryland and Pennsylvania. The defendant wanted to challenge the use of the two Maryland convictions on grounds of claimed ineffective assistance of counsel. The court of appeals had dismissed the defendant's challenges to his prior convictions as the "fact intensive" type that pose a risk of unduly delaying and protracting the entire sentencing process. The Supreme Court in interpreting the Armed Career Criminal Act found that the statute focuses on the fact of the conviction and nothing suggests that the prior final conviction may be subjected to collateral attack for potential constitutional errors before it can be counted for enhanced sentencing purposes. Thus the Court held that the act does not permit defendants to use the federal sentencing forum to gain review of state convictions.

The case is significant in that it preserves the incentive for prosecutors to seek enhanced sentences of armed career criminals who have three prior felony convictions. If the Court had permitted such challenges, there could have been a chilling effect on the willingness to seek such enhanced penalties because prosecutors would have had to consider the extended litigation resources that could have been involved.

In a case with implications for the operation of local jails, the Court addressed the issue of under what circumstances a prison official will be held accountable for threats to a prisoner's safety. The Court previously had held that a prison official's "deliberate indifference" to a substantial risk of serious harm to an inmate violates the Eighth Amendment [*Helling* v. *McKinney* 113 S.Ct. 2475 (1993)]. In this case, the Court set out to define the term "deliberate indifference." In *Farmer* v. *Brennan* [114 S.Ct. 1970 (1994)], a prisoner alleged that federal prison officials violated the Eighth Amendment by their deliberate indifference to his safety. The prisoner alleged that he was transferred from a higher security prison to a lower security one and placed in its general population despite knowledge that as a transsexual who "projects feminine characteristics" he would be particularly vulnerable to sexual attack. According to the prisoner's allegations, within two weeks he was beaten and raped by another inmate in his cell. The prisoner sought compensatory and punitive damages from prison officials for deliberate indifference. The Court held that a prison official cannot be found liable under the Eighth Amendment for denying an inmate humane conditions of confinement unless the official knows of and disregards an excessive risk to inmate health and safety: The official must both be aware of the facts from which the inference could be drawn that a substantial risk of serious harm exists and must draw the inference. Whether a prison official had the requisite knowledge of a substantial risk is a question of fact for the trial court to determine, including the use of inference from circumstantial evidence. The Court did say that prison officials who actually knew of a substantial risk to inmate health and safety may be found free from liability if they responded reasonably to the risk, even if the harm ultimately was not averted.

MEDICARE REIMBURSEMENT

For those cities that operate hospitals in conjunction with university teaching programs, the Supreme Court handed down a case affecting cost reimbursement under Medicare. In *Thomas Jefferson University* v. *Shalala* [114 S.Ct. 2381 (1994)], the Court considered a challenge to the Secretary of Health and Human Services' ruling disallowing reimbursement costs for certain educational-based activities. Medicare reimburses provider hospitals for the costs of certain educational activities, including the cost of graduate medical education services furnished by the hospital or its affiliated medical school. However, reimbursement is limited by (1) an "anti-redistribution" principle providing that the Medicare program's intent is to support activities that are "customary or traditionally carried on by providers in conjunction with their operations, but that the program should not participate in increased costs resulting from redistribution of costs from educational institutions to patient care institutions, and (2) a "community support" principle providing that Medicare will not assume the cost for educational activities previously borne by the community. In this case, the fiscal intermediary disallowed the hospital's claim for reimbursement for such costs, but the Provider Reimbursement Review Board allowed reimbursement. Then the secretary reinstated the first ruling disallowing reimbursement according to both the limiting principles.

The hospital challenged the secretary's interpretation under the Administrative Procedure Act, which holds unlawful those actions that are arbitrary, capricious, an abuse of discretion, or otherwise not in accordance with law. The Court upheld the secretary's action and held that her construction of the reimbursement principle was faithful to the plain language of the statute.

SUMMARY

This chapter has presented the highlights of 26 Supreme Court cases decided in the 1993–1994 term. The rulings discussed here touch many aspects of local government management: regulation, taxation, finance, protection of the environment, zoning, personnel practices, voting, free speech, schools, police authority, and medical services. While case summaries are presented to inform local government managers and other interested readers about the most significant aspects of these cases, they do not constitute legal advice. Local government managers who find themselves in situations similar to those described are urged to seek the advice of an attorney.

Congressional Actions Affecting Local Governments

Eugene P. Boyd
Congressional Research Service
U.S. Library of Congress

The 103d Congress adjourned on 1 December 1994 after overwhelming passage of the General Agreement on Tariffs and Trade (GATT) and following congressional elections that resulted in the historic change to Republican control of the House and the Senate during the 104th Congress. During the fall election campaign, House Republicans pledged to consider within the first 100 days of the 104th Congress elements of the party's *Contract with America*, its legislative blueprint. Several items on the House Republican agenda—crime and welfare reform, unfunded federal mandates, and a balanced budget amendment—have been of particular concern to the Clinton administration and local governments. Measures designed to address these issues were considered but failed to pass during the 103d Congress. Other elements of the *Contract with America*, such as term limits, capital gains tax reduction, and tax relief for middle-class Americans were not addressed during the final session of the 103d Congress, but will likely be fast-track items in the House of Representatives during the 104th Congress.

The second session of the 103d Congress can be characterized as one that started full of promise for local governments, but ultimately fell short. Important legislation affecting local governments, such as welfare reform, housing and community development reauthorization, unfunded mandates, and environmental legislation, was tabled, stalled, or sidetracked by arguments over the nature and structure of health care and crime legislation and by mid-term electoral politics. Though Congress failed to complete action on several major pieces of legislation affecting local governments, the most notable being health care, it did pass several key measures.

During its second session, the 103d Congress completed action on a package of four education-related initiatives supported by the Clinton administration. These legislative initiatives enjoyed broad bipartisan support:

1. Goals 2000: Educate America Act (P.L. 103-227), which authorizes overall funding of $491 million for FY94 and such sums as may be necessary for FY95-FY98 to establish voluntary national or state standards for schools and students
2. The School-to-Work Opportunities Act (P.L. 103-239), which authorizes $300 million for job training and apprenticeship opportunities for non-college bound students, to ease their transition into the workplace
3. The Human Services Amendments of 1994 (P.L. 103-252), which extends the Head Start program and authorizes an unspecified appropriation for educational and other support services for preschoolers from low-income households
4. The Improving America's Schools Act (P.L. 103-382), which provides $12.7 billion in assistance to the nation's public schools, targeting a significant portion of funds to poor and educationally disadvantaged students.

Taken as a package, the four legislative initiatives continue a dual trend of devolving greater responsibility to lower levels of government, providing states and local governments with greater flexibility to fashion their own strategies to achieve national objectives, and limiting the number of unfunded federal mandates.

In addition, the 103d Congress passed the massive Violent Crime Control Act, (P.L. 103-322). The act passed during the waning days of August despite strong Republican opposition in the House and Senate to the ban on assault weapons and crime prevention programs and after members of the Congressional Black Caucus relented in their opposition to the withdrawal of a provision concerning racial bias in sentencing. The act includes provisions that will promote community policing, crime prevention programs, and prison construction. In addition, the act includes a ''three-strikes-and-you're out'' provision for repeat violent felons, revives capital punishment as a federal sentencing option, and bans 19 types of semiautomatic assault weapons. A significant portion of the act's crime prevention programs might be repealed during the 104th Congress by the new Republican majority in the House.

Other noteworthy accomplishments of the second session of the 103d Congress include passage of the Reigle Community Development and Regulatory Improvement Act of 1994 (P.L. 103-325) and the HUD Multifamily Property Disposition and Reform Act of 1994 (P.L. 103-233). The Reigle Community Development and Regulatory Improvement Act fulfills one of President's Clinton's campaign promises to improve poor neighborhoods by providing low-income persons with greater access to capital through matching grants to alternative lenders such as credit unions and community development banks. The HUD Multifamily Housing Property Disposition and Reform Act revises several programs administered by HUD, including the disposition of its inventory of defaulted multifamily properties, the HOME program, and the Section 108 loan guarantee program through the establishment of economic development grants that can be used in tandem with loan guarantees.

Though these accomplishments are substantial, they fall short of addressing some of the key issues facing local governments, including unfunded federal mandate reform. Both House and Senate considered legislation that would require the Congressional Budget Office to gauge the fiscal impact of all federal legislation on state and local governments and to require congressional committees to identify federal funds that could be used to cover the cost of any mandate that would cost more than $50 million. The legislation failed to win passage in either the House or the Senate. The Republican leadership of the 104th Congress has pledge to address the unfunded federal mandate issue as part of an overall evaluation and rethinking of the roles of government. Though Congress failed to pass unfunded federal mandate legislation, supporters of such measures, including local governments, won an important moral victory by

Significant segments of this article are based on research performed by the author's colleagues at the Congressional Research Service, including Wayne Riddle, James Stedman, David Teasley, and Keith Bea.

heightening congressional awareness of the fiscal impact of federal laws on local and state governments. Several of the laws passed by Congress during the second session, including the Goals 2000 Act and the Improving America's Schools Act, include provisions prohibiting the institution of unfunded mandates, encouraging waivers of federal requirements, and promoting flexibility in meeting national objectives. Despite this trend, Congress imposed several new mandates and preemptions of state authority according to the National Conference of State Legislatures. These include mandating interstate banking by 1995 and interstate branches by 1 June 1997. Bans on assault weapons preempt state authority under the Violent Crime Control Act, and provisions under the Full Faith and Credit Child Support Orders Act prevent a state court from modifying a child support order of another state court.

DISASTER RELIEF

In February 1994, the 103d Congress passed legislation providing $11 billion in disaster relief, including $7.8 billion to individuals and communities that were victims of the earthquake that hit southern California in January. The disaster relief also covered other needs, including continued support for victims of the Midwest floods of 1993. The $11 billion supplemental appropriation was financed in part by $3.3 billion in spending cuts, as a budget-conscious Congress sought to balance humanitarian assistance against the desire to reduce the deficit. The supplemental appropriation, which was signed by President Bill Clinton on 12 February 1994 as P.L. 103-211, also provides $1.2 billion to continue U.S. peacekeeping missions in Haiti, Bosnia, Iraq, and Somalia. During the summer of 1994 Congress passed a second FY94 supplemental appropriation providing additional assistance to victims of the southern California earthquake of 1994.

EDUCATION

In the second session of the 103d Congress, Congress passed four major reform-minded leg-islative initiatives affecting education and job training. Just days before an 1 April 1994 deadline, Congress passed the Goals 2000: Educate America Act (P.L. 103-227), authorizing $491 million in the first year to be used (1) to establish voluntary national educational standards and goals for the nation's public schools and students and (2) to fund local initiatives in support of such goals and other ancillary activities. By mid-May 1994, the Congress had passed two other elements of President Clinton's human investment initiative: the School-to-Work Opportunities Act (P.L. 103-239), which was signed into law 4 May 1994, and the Human Services Amendments of 1994 (P.L. 103-252), which was signed by the president on 18 May 1994. Title I of P.L. 103-252 reauthorizes and amends the Head Start program. A favorite of President Clinton's, Head Start enjoys strong bipartisan support. It provides education, nutrition, health, and social services to low-income preschoolers and their families. The School-to-Work Opportunities Act authorizes $300 million in grants to states to provide job training and apprenticeships to help the 75% of graduating high-school students who do not go on to college make a smooth transition from high school to the labor force. Days prior to adjournment of the second session, the 103d Congress passed the Improving America's Schools Act (IASA) (P.L. 103-382), which reauthorizes and amends the $12.7 billion Elementary and Secondary Education Act of 1965. This is the federal government's largest source of educational assistance to state and local governments.

Though these four legislative initiatives enjoyed overwhelming bipartisan support, they were not without controversy. The Goals 2000: Educate America Act faced a filibuster by a conservative Republican over a provision concerning school prayer. The Senate closed debate and passed the bill just days before a $125 million appropriation would have expired on 1 April 1994. A similar school prayer controversy surfaced during conference committee consideration of the IASA, as a House Republican member of the conference committee unsuccessfully sought to include a school prayer amendment identical in language to that offered during Senate consideration of the Goals 2000:

Educate America Act. The amendment would have denied federal funds to any school district that denied any student the constitutional right to engage in voluntary school prayer. In addition, the Clinton administration's effort to more directly target elementary and secondary education funds to poor and disadvantaged students was rebuffed, although a more modest formula compromise was approved. Though opponents of the School-to-Work Opportunities Act were few, the initiative was questioned by at least one senator, who noted that the federal government currently runs over 150 job-training programs costing an estimated $25 billion annually. The Head Start program came under some scrutiny concerning its long-term impact on the educational success of participating children and quality control issues related to the program's rapid expansion.

Taken together, the four legislative initiatives are the cornerstones of an educational reform package that tries to address the needs of a population ranging from preschoolers to high-school students entering the labor force upon graduation.[1] The four measures encourage flexibility and innovation and target additional assistance to low-income, educationally disadvantaged, and non-college bound students. In addition, the measures attempt to establish flexible national standards but devolve responsibility for implementation to lower levels of government. Further, the package of legislation contains few if any unfunded federal mandates, a reflection of increased congressional sensitivity to the fiscal impacts such mandates have on state and local governments.

Goals 2000: Educate America Act

On 31 March 1994, President Clinton signed into law the Goals 2000: Educate America Act (P.L. 103-227) the first of four education-related initiatives to be approved during the second session of the 103d Congress. The act identifies eight broad national educational goals for the year 2000 and beyond and establishes the framework for gauging the progress of states in meeting voluntary subject content and student performance standards (see sidebar). The act also give states the option of substituting their own standards of equal or higher quality. In addition, the act calls for the National Education Standards and Improvement Council (NESIC) to develop "opportunity to learn standards" that outline what schools should provide in order to ensure that students meet subject content and student performance standards.

The act establishes the National Education Goals Panel (NEGP), an 18-member body comprising two presidential appointees, eight governors, four members of Congress, and four state legislators. NEGP is charged with monitoring and reporting (1) on national and state progress in meeting the eight national goals, (2) on state implementation of Opportunity to Learn (OTL) standards, and (3) on state curriculum and subject content and performance standards. In addition, the NEGP, is responsible for submitting nominations to the president for appointments to the National Education Standards

---

National educational goals for the year 2000 and beyond

1. *To ensure that all students will start school ready to learn*
2. *To attain a high-school graduation rate of at least 90%*
3. *To ensure that students demonstrate competence in a array of subjects, including math, English, civics and government, geography, history, science, and a foreign language*
4. *To support continued education and training for the nation's teachers*
5. *To improve the ranking of U.S. students in math and science achievement*
6. *To promote literacy for all adults*
7. *To ensure school environments free of guns, drugs, and alcohol*
8. *To increase parental involvement in promoting the social, emotional, and intellectual growth of children*

and Improvement Council (NESIC) and with reviewing certification criteria and standards the latter develops.

The NESIC is a 19-member panel comprising professional educators and representatives of business, labor, and the public. In addition to its responsibility to develop OTL standards, it is charged with developing voluntary national curriculum content and student performance standards for state use. These standards identify what students at specific grade levels should know. The NESIC is also charged with developing voluntary national standards. At least one-third of its members must have expertise in the educational needs of disabled, low-income, and minority children and children with limited proficiency in English.

The act requires that OTL standards address such areas as the capacity of teachers to address the diverse needs of students; the quality and availability of instructional materials and technology; the quality of schools' physical facilities; teacher access to professional development activities; and concerns surrounding gender discrimination. In addition to these duties, the NESIC is charged with certifying state adherence to national voluntary standards developed by the state. The NESIC may certify standards developed and voluntarily adopted by a state as long as the state standards meet the same criteria used to certify national standards developed by NESIC. Neither NESIC certifications of state standards nor its assessments may be used as a prerequisite for participating in any educational program authorized by the Goals 2000: Educate America Act or any other federal law.

Title III of the act authorizes a $400 million formula grant program to support state and local educational reform efforts. Funds are to be allocated to State Education Agencies (SEAs) for use in developing Education Improvement Plans (EIPs) and supporting local education reform efforts. In order to receive funds, states must develop content, performance, and OTL standards and assessment instruments. Of the amount appropriated during each of the fiscal years from 1994 to 1998, at least 94% of the funds are to be allocated to SEAs; 1% is to be set aside for Alaskan Native students, Bureau of Indian Affairs schools, and outlying areas; and up to 5% of the annual appropriation is be used to cover the cost of peer review of state EIPs and the evaluation of NEGP and NESIC activities. Funds to SEAs are be allocated based on each state's share of funds allocated in the previous fiscal year under Title I, Chapter 1 and Chapter 2, Part A, of the Elementary and Secondary Education Act (ESEA). Chapter 1 of the ESEA allocates funds based on the number of school-age children living in poverty. Funds are used to support compensatory education for educationally disadvantaged students. Chapter 2, Part A, is an educational block grant that is allocated to states based on school-age population. Funds are used to support a variety of activities.

In applying for Title III funds, a state's first-year application must describe how the SEA will develop its state EIP and how it will use its funds, including awarding subgrants to local school districts and for professional development. A state's second-year application must include the state EIP, which covers activities to be undertaken from the second through the fifth year of participation. The EIP must address a broad range of educational concerns and issues, including development and implementation of strategies that

1. are designed to meet the eight national education goals;
2. are designed to meet OTL standards;
3. improve efforts to recruit and retain teachers and enhance their professional development;
4. involve parents and community representatives in the preparation and implementation of the state plan;
5. give all students in the state an opportunity to achieve content and performance standards established by the state, including ensuring that all school districts in the state have equal access to all curriculum materials and educational technology;
6. foster systemic reform that empowers local communities, school districts, and schools —including waiving state regulations that impede local school districts' and schools' efforts to achieve state goals;
7. assist school districts and schools to meet the educational needs of school dropouts;
8. incorporate school-to-work programs funded by the federal government;
9. include benchmarks and time lines for student performance improvements;
10. coordinate the integration of academic and vocational educational instruction;
11. describe how the state will monitor progress in implementing state and local improvement plans; and
12. provide for the periodic review and updating of state content and performance standards, OTL standards, and assessments.

The plan is to be developed by a state panel comprising the governor, the chief state school officer, chairs of the state board of education and relevant state legislative committees, education measurement experts, educators, parents, and representatives of other segments of the population. The panel should reflect the racial, economic, and geographic diversity of the state and should provide the public with an opportunity to comment on the state's improvement plan.

Sixty percent of an SEA's initial year of funding under Title III may be used to fund local reform and professional development efforts if the total Title III appropriation exceeds $50 million. The remaining funds are to be used to fund the development and implementation of state improvement plans. Eligible activities include the development of subject content, performance, and OTL standards; implementation of management improvement strategies; providing educational outreach and training to parents and others; promotion of public-school choice; support of planning and evaluating private management of public-school reform; school-based violence reduction programs; mentoring programs; and efforts to increase the reform capacity of school districts and schools.

A state may use a portion of its annual allocation to fund competitively selected local-education reform efforts, including implementation of a school district's EIP. The improvement plan is to be developed by a racially and economically diverse panel of parents, teachers, and business leaders. The local plan should outline how it will address the needs of students, improve the flexibility of schools in meeting their educational needs, and identify federal and state requirements that impede educational reform and should be waived.

During the first year that a local education agency receives a subgrant, not more than 25% of the funds may be expended to develop a local improvement plan or related activities and not less than 75% may be used to support individual school initiatives designed to provide all students in the school with the opportunity to meet state content and performance standards. At least 85% of local improvement subgrant funds awarded after the first year are to be used by individual schools to develop and implement comprehensive school improvement plans. At least 50% of the funds made available for local improvement programs shall be awarded to individual schools with a large number of students who are members of low-income families or who have low student achievement records. Special consideration is to be given to awarding subgrants to a consortium of local education agencies and to a Local Education Agency (LEA) that will channel funds to a consortium of schools that will develop a plan for school improvement.

In addition, Title III authorizes SEAs to make subgrants to LEAs or a consortium of LEAs that, in cooperation with colleges, universities, or nonprofit organizations, have developed a plan to support continuing professional education, training, and development of teachers and school administrators. Subgrants may also be used to improve preservice teacher education programs. Priority in awarding of preservice teacher education and professional development subgrants is to be given to LEAs or a consortium of LEAs that (1) serves a higher percentage of disadvantaged students than the state average, or (2) enters into partnerships with college educators to establish professional development sites, or (3) seeks to improve teacher subject-area knowledge, or (4) targets continued professional development to teachers of students with limited English proficiency or with disabilities. The act allows funds to be used to provide training to teachers and administrators of private schools.

In order to foster flexibility and remove any impediments to the ability of SEAs, LEAs, or schools to carry out improvement plans, the act allows the secretary of education to waive any statutory or regulatory provisions governing the following selected educational programs: compensatory education grants for disadvantaged students authorized under Chapter I, Title I of ESEA; block grant assistance authorized by Part A, Chapter 2, Title 1 of ESEA; the Mathematics and Science Education Act; the Drug-Free Schools and Communities Act; and the Perkins Vocational and Applied Technology Education Act. The act prohibits the Department of Education (ED) from waiving any provision relating to maintenance of effort, comparability of services, equitable participation of students and professional staff in private schools, parental participation, or distribution of funds to SEAs or LEAs. Under the Education Flexibility Partnership Demonstration Act, also authorized under Title III, the ED may grant waiver authority of statutory and regulatory requirements under the five selected programs to six eligible states for a period of up to five years. To be eligible as one of the six, Ed-Flex Partnership States must have developed a state improvement plan and must have waived state statutes and regulations affecting LEAs and individual schools while holding them accountable for student performance.

Title III reaffirms that state and local governments are primarily responsible for the control of education and that no action authorized by the act will directly or indirectly change or adversely affect the primacy of state and local control of education. The act also includes a provision that prohibits the federal government from mandating or controlling a state, LEA, or school curriculum or instructional program or the allocation of state or local education funds and from imposing unfunded federal mandates.

Title IV of the act authorizes the ED to award Parental Assistance grants to nonprofit organizations working in partnership with LEAs for the purpose of establishing parental information and resource centers. These centers are intended to help parents become more effective advocates in the education of their children, including helping them understand their children's educational needs, participate in educational decision making, and train other parents. By year 1998 each state should have established at least one parental information and resource center. At least 50% of a grantee's parental assistance funds must be used to assist parents who are economically or educationally disadvantaged.

Title V of the act authorizes the creation of the 28-member National Skills Standards Board (NSSB) that is charged with facilitating the development of voluntary occupational standards and certifications for clusters of occupations. The standards are to be developed with the participation of various groups, including representatives of business, labor, educational institutions, states, and local governments.

In addition, the act authorizes a number of other grant programs and activities, including the International Education Program supporting comparative analysis of foreign education systems; the Safe Schools program grants to LEAs to develop strategies that reduce the incidence of school violence; the creation of the Office of Educational Technology in ED, including the establishment of a national long-range technology plan for education, grants for research and development of educational technology, and support for states to develop plans that would increase the use of technologies in elementary and secondary education; grants to SEAs and other entities to provide technical assistance to states in achieving greater equity in school finances; grants for midnight basketball leagues targeted to residents of public housing; and the establishment of nonsmoking requirements in federally funded facilities. The act also contains provisions prohibiting states and local school districts from adopting policies preventing voluntary prayer and meditation.

School-to-Work Opportunities Act
By the spring of 1994, the 103d Congress had completed action on two other components of a comprehensive education reform effort. On 4 May 1994 the president signed the School-to-Work Opportunities Act (P.L. 103-239). Two weeks later, he signed the Human Services Amendments of 1994 (P.L. 103-252), which reauthorized the Head Start Program. In passing these legislative initiatives, Congress affirmed its support of education as a national concern; it fashioned the legislation in such a manner as to increase state and local government flexibility in program design and implementation and kept the initiatives free of prescriptive and unfunded federal mandates.

The School-to-Work Opportunities Act is intended to provide valuable work experience to the 75% of graduating high-school seniors who do not go on to college. The act provides job training and career counseling, apprenticeships, and career development opportunities through integrated school- and work-based learning. Congressional supporters of the program, which included Democrats and Republicans, argued that the program would further support the national education goals and the objectives of the National Skills Standards Board established by the Goals 2000: Educate America Act. Opponents argued that the federal government presently operates 154 job-training programs at an annual cost of $25 billion.

The act, which is authorized through fiscal year 1999, provides development and implementation grants to states. State applications must be jointly approved by the secretaries of education and labor. Development grants awarded to a state may not exceed $1 million for any fiscal year.

The act allows states seeking assistance under the School-to-Work Program and the Goals 2000: Educate America Act to submit a single application.

Implementation grants are to be awarded to the states for a period not to exceed five years. Applications for assistance must be submitted by the governor and should include the following information: (1) how the state will allocate funds to local partnerships, (2) identification of any waivers that may be requested, (3) a description of how the plan was developed, and (4) a detailed implementation plan. States that receive implementation grants must award a substantial majority of their funds to local partnerships for use in carrying out eligible activities. In the absence of state implementation plans, the act allows local partnerships to apply directly to the federal government for such assistance. Priority for such assistance is to be given to local partnerships with a proven track record and those located in high poverty areas of the state.

The act also authorizes a small number of additional grants, including grants to develop performance and evaluation measures, for training and technical assistance, and for capacity building and information dissemination. In addition, the act requires that an annual report be submitted to Congress on the progress being made in its implementation by state and local partnerships.

Head Start
Two weeks after signing school-to-work legislation, President Clinton, on 18 May 1994, signed legislation reauthorizing and amending the Head Start Program. The program, which provides comprehensive educational, health, nutrition, and social services to economically disadvantaged preschool children and their

---

Applications for development grants under the School-to-Work Opportunities Act are to be submitted by the governor of the state and must include

1. *a description of how officials, including the governor, the state education agency, state officials responsible for economic development, job training, employment vocational education and rehabilitation, representatives of the private sector, and others will collaborate in the development of a comprehensive statewide School-to-Work Opportunities system;*
2. *a timetable and estimate of the amount of funds needed to complete the planning and development of a comprehensive statewide School-to-Work Opportunities system;*
3. *a description of how the state will provide opportunities for special student populations to participate in the School-to-Work program, including students from low-income families, low-achieving students, students with limited English proficiency, students with disabilities, students living in rural communities, academically talented students, and school dropouts.*

families, was reauthorized through fiscal year 1998 as Title I of the Human Services Amendments of 1994 (P.L. 103-252). The act also reauthorizes and amends two other antipoverty programs—Community Services Block Grants and the Low Income Home Energy Assistance Program—and creates the Community-Based Family Resource Program that will fund efforts to reduce the incidence of child abuse.

The Head Start program, which is administered at the federal level by the Department of Health and Human Services (HHS), is considered one of the federal government's more effective and successful antipoverty intervention programs, despite recent concerns about its long-term impacts. The act includes several reforms recommended by an advisory panel, including continuing the practice of setting aside 25% of program funds to support improvements in local programs. Funds, which are awarded to over 1,400 providers including nonprofits and local governments, may also be awarded to states to coordinate Head Start program with other social services. In addition, HHS is required to develop performance standards for the Head Start program and to develop procedures for measuring and evaluating the quality and effectiveness of Head Start programs. The act gives HHS the authority to expand the program to include infants and toddlers younger than three years of age and to expand into full-day and year-round programs. Further, recipients of Head Start funds are encouraged to develop procedures that enhance parental involvement and coordination and cooperation with public schools attended by former Head Start students. The act requires that at least one teacher in each Head Start class room must have completed appropriate training in child development. The requirement may be satisfied in a variety of ways, including earning a state-awarded certificate for preschool teachers, an associate, baccalaureate, or advanced degree in early childhood education, or a degree in any field related to early childhood education.

Improving America's Schools Act

The final element of educational reform was passed by Congress and signed by the president during the last weeks of the 103d Congress. The Improving America's Schools Act (IASA) (P.L. 103-382), reauthorizes and amends the Elementary and Secondary Education Act (ESEA) of 1965. Though the act enjoyed significant bipartisan support, it became a target of conservative House and Senate Republicans, who sought to insert a provision that would bar the awarding of funds to schools that prohibit "constitutionally protected prayer." Members of the conference committee on the bill (H.R. 6) did approve a compromise amendment that denies funding to school districts found guilty by a court of willfully violating a court order to allow constitutionally protected prayer.

School prayer was but one of several issues that the act addresses. Other issues are the allocation or targeting of greater assistance to educationally disadvantaged students, technology integration, improving student performance,

school financing, and teacher development. The IASA authorizes $12.7 billion in financial assistance to the nation's public schools for fiscal year 1995 and such sums as appropriated for each of the remaining four years of authorization through fiscal year 1999. Title I of the act provides grant funds to local education agencies or school districts for the education of disadvantaged prekindergarten through twelfth grade students. It also modifies the formula for allocating funds to local school districts. All funds appropriated up to the FY95 appropriation level of $6.7 billion are to be allocated based upon the existing formula, which uses the number of children from poor families and a state expenditure factor. The act modifies the formula by requiring that appropriations above the FY95 funding level of $6.7 billion be allocated based on one of two formulas. These education finance incentive grants award additional or supplemental funds to states that allocate additional funds based on equity and effort factors. One formula allocates funds to areas with high concentrations of school age children from poor families, and the second formula awards additional funds to states that move to equalize financing inequities among school districts or to states with high levels of educational spending relative to per capita income.

In keeping with the Goals 2000: Educate America Act, Title II of the IASA allocates funds for ongoing professional development and training of teachers. Title III provides grants to support state and local efforts to integrate technology into the nation's schools. In addition, it reauthorizes the Star Schools program, which facilitates distance learning through the use of telecommunications, and creates a new library media resources program grant.

Title IV of the act incorporates violence prevention as an objective of the Drug-Free Schools Act and renames the act the Safe and Drug-Free Schools and Communities Act. The method of allocating funds is modified to give greater assistance to local school districts with the greatest need, as measured by the number of school-age children and a state's share of Title I grants. Twenty percent of the funds are to be controlled by the governor of each state and are to be used to support state Drug Abuse Resistance Education (DARE) and other before- and after-school programs. Eighty percent of the funds are to be used by SEAs and local school districts to support drug and violence prevention programs. The act requires states to enact laws that mandate a one-year suspension for students caught with a firearm on school property.

Title V reauthorizes and expands the magnet school program, which provides competitive grants to local school districts implementing school desegregation plans. The act sets aside up to 5% of its annual allocation for innovative nonmagnet education programs, increases the magnet school award period from two to three years, and gives funding priority to school districts that use "blind selection" of students to participate in magnet school programs. Title V also supports school choice by awarding discretionary grants to support "charter schools."

These are schools operated without direct state or local control. In addition, Title I grants may be used to develop and support public-school choice programs for disadvantaged children with the caveats that (1) only Title I schools participate in the program, (2) participating schools agree to allow children to transfer between schools, and (3) grant funds will not be used to cover the costs of transporting students.

The focus of Title VI of the IASA is the development of innovative education program strategies. The title authorizes an educational block grant formerly authorized under Title I, Chapter 2, of the Elementary and Secondary Education Act. The new title for this education block grant places greater emphasis on the promotion of education reform and innovation, Goals 2000 activities, and at-risk and high-cost students. Funds will continue to be allocated to states based on school-age population; however, each state may use only 15% of its allocation for administrative costs (down from 20%). Eighty-five percent of each state's allocation is to be distributed to local school districts, with additional funds awarded based on the number of high-cost students. The act also revamps bilingual education assistance to states and local school districts. Local school districts may receive funds for bilingual program development and implementation, bilingual enhancement grants, and comprehensive school-wide and system-wide improvement grants. Funds are also awarded to states and may be used to fund personnel training programs.

Title VIII of the act amends the Impact Aid program, which makes funds available to communities as compensation for tax revenues lost because of federal ownership of land and for the cost incurred in educating children whose parents live and work on federal property. The amendments will allocate Impact Aid to local school districts that enroll at least 2,000 qualifying children of civilian parents who live or work on federal property if such children represent at least 15% of the school district's total student population.

In addition, the act provides grant funds to states to develop public charter schools that are to be privately run by parents, teachers, and nonprofit organizations and are exempt from significant federal, state, and local rules. In exchange, a public charter school must develop educational objectives and the means to measure progress in meeting the objectives. The act also provides 80% of the funds for cultural partnerships for at-risk children demonstration grants; funds for research, training, and demonstration project grants for gifted and talented students; grants for school repair, renovation, alteration, and construction activities, with funds made available to local school districts that demonstrate an urgent need for repair of schools; grants that demonstrate innovative practices in the education of disadvantaged children, including former Head Start participants; demonstration grants for charter education; assistance to urban and rural education systems; and grants for service coordination for disadvantaged students.

HOUSING AND COMMUNITY DEVELOPMENT

Though Congress failed to pass legislation reauthorizing major housing and community development programs administered by the Department of Housing and Urban Development (HUD), including public housing, Section 8, HOME, and the Community Development Block Grant programs, it did pass legislation, supported by the president, that modified several HUD programs. The Multifamily Housing Property Disposition Reform Act (P.L. 103-233) addresses a number of urgent concerns facing HUD, including the growing inventory of HUD-held multifamily properties, impediments to the implementation of the HOME program, and the establishment of a community economic development initiative under the Section 108 loan guarantee provisions of the Community Development Block Grant (CDBG) program. In addition, Congress passed legislation that funds community development banks and reorganizes the Department of Agriculture (USDA).

HUD Multifamily Housing Property Disposition Reform Act

On 11 April 1994, fully one year after the Senate Banking Committee and its Subcommittee on Housing and Urban Affairs began a series of hearings on HUD programs, President Clinton signed the Multifamily Housing Property Disposition Reform Act (MHPDRA) of 1994 (P.L. 103-233). At the request of the administration, S. 1299 was introduced in the Senate on 27 July 1993 to address HUD management reform issues. A similar measure, H.R. 4067, was introduced in the House on 17 March 1994. The final bill, which was signed by the president as P.L. 103-233, amends the HOME and Community Development Block Grant programs and Section 203 of the Housing and Community Development Act of 1978, which governs the disposition of defaulted multifamily properties insured or owned by HUD.

Title I of the MHPDRA allows for greater flexibility in the disposition of HUD-held or insured properties while attempting to preserve the stock of low income housing. Title I addresses a growing problem facing HUD—the rise in the number of multifamily housing units held by the department as a result of mortgage defaults, which have quadrupled since 1989. In early 1994 HUD estimated that by the end of 1994 its multifamily housing default inventory would total 69,000 units. In addition, more than half the 2,400 multifamily mortgages held by HUD (accounting for 219,000 units) were delinquent and perilously close to default. Prior to the 1994 amendments to Section 203, HUD's ability to significantly reduce its inventory of multifamily housing was hampered by a statutory provision requiring HUD to provide subsidies to all units occupied by families meeting the definition of low- or very low-income households, including units occupied by households that had not received rental assistance before. The net effect of the provision was to increase the costs of liquidating the defaulted property.

Title I amends Section 203 by revising the subsidy requirement. Under the new provisions only low- and very low-income households that had received rental assistance prior to the default would continue to receive such assistance after HUD transfers ownership of the property. Title I revises the process to be followed in the sale of multifamily housing projects owned by HUD, including the requirement that HUD develop a disposition plan for each project to be sold. The disposition plan must include (1) the minimum terms and conditions for the transfer of the property, (2) the sales price for the property, (3) a description of assistance that HUD will make available to the purchaser in order to preserve the stock of affordable housing, (4) procedures intended to facilitate local government, public, and tenant input into the disposition plan and facilitate the sale of property to tenant organizations when possible. The act allows HUD to enter into contracts with for-profit, nonprofit, and public agencies to manage HUD-owned properties or properties on which HUD holds the mortgage. Further, it allows HUD to exercise a number of options in disposing of and providing assistance to purchasers of HUD-held properties, including (1) allowing the use of project-based and tenant-based Section 8 contracts, (2) reducing the sales price of the property, (3) restricting the use of certain units to very low-income persons, (4) providing short-term loans or up-front grants to cover the costs of rehabilitation and related development costs, (5) allowing a portion of disposed properties to be used for purposes other than rental, (6) allowing the transfer of multifamily housing property to a public housing agency for conversion to public housing or to an eligible nonprofit entity for conversion to elderly and handicapped housing. Funds may also be used to rebuild a development provided it has the financial support of the local government.

The act provides some rent protection for unsubsidized very low-income families living in projects sold by HUD. Title I prohibits purchasers of defaulted multifamily properties from increasing the rent of very low-income families who were tenants prior to the acquisition of the property. The act gives state and local governments the right of first refusal in the purchase of multifamily housing being disposed of by HUD. It provides for relocation assistance for persons displaced when multifamily housing is sold.

According to administration budget documents for FY95, the HOME Investment Partnership (HOME) program ranks as the third largest source of federal housing assistance to states and local governments; it is exceeded only by public and assisted housing. Title II of the MHPDRA makes significant changes in the HOME program. It eliminates the bias against new construction by reducing the new construction match requirement to 25%, consistent with the match requirement for other eligible activities.[2] Bond or debt financing may be used to meet up to 25% of a participating jurisdiction's overall matching fund requirement. Title II expands the definition of state for the purpose of participating and administering HOME funds to include any instrumentality or agency established to act on behalf of the state in carrying out the HOME program. It simplifies the program-wide income targeting provisions governing rental assistance. The new provisions require that 90% of the families receiving assistance have incomes that do not exceed 60% of the median income of the jurisdiction and that 90% of the rental units assisted are occupied by such families. Furthermore, up to 10% of the families receiving assistance may have incomes that fall between 60% and 80% of the median income of the jurisdiction and no more than 10% of the units assisted may be occupied by such families. Title II deletes a HOME provision that limits home-ownership assistance to first-time home buyers; reduces the matching-fund requirement for new construction to 25%; deletes a provision requiring an annual audit of the HOME Investment Trust Fund by an independent accounting firm; includes insular areas and Indian tribes among the entities that may assume environmental review responsibilities; and includes HOME administrative costs as an eligible CDBG activity.

The HOME program, which was first authorized under Title II of the National Affordable Housing Act of 1990, P.L. 101-625 (NAHA), has as its primary objective to increase the supply of housing affordable to low- and very low-income families. Under the HOME program very low-income families are defined as families whose incomes do not exceed 50% of the median income of the jurisdiction participating in the HOME program; low-income families are those whose income is not more than 80% of the jurisdiction's median income. Participating jurisdictions must submit for approval by HUD an annual housing program description. The annual program description, in the case of submission by a local government, must document the jurisdiction's housing needs and strategies it employs to address those needs. States must identify the method they will use to distribute funds. The program distributes funds by formula to 382 states and eligible local governments, including metropolitan cities, urban counties, and consortia; the last are contiguous units of local government that may participate in the program as a single entity.

HOME funds may support such activities as housing rehabilitation, tenant-based assistance, construction of new housing, property acquisition and demolition, site improvements, relocation expenses, and condominium or cooperative housing conversions. Funds also are used to support nonprofit Community Housing Development Organizations (CHDO). Fifteen percent of each grantee's annual allocation must be made available for 24 months for housing activities sponsored by CHDOs.

Authorizing language creating the Economic Development Grants program, one of several HUD community economic development initiatives introduced during the second session of the 103d Congress, was included in Title III of the Multifamily Housing Property Disposition Act of 1994. Title III of the act authorizes the transfer of $100 million in recaptured Urban Development Action Grant (UDAG) funds to be used as grants in conjunction with Section 108 loan guarantees. Further, the act allows communities with unexpended UDAG funds to retain a portion of such funds if they are used to support CDBG-eligible activities. Title III of the act includes a provision governing the UDAG retention program, which prohibits HUD from recapturing unexpended UDAG funds and requires the agency to provide technical assistance to UDAG communities to assist them in developing viable projects. These grants are expected to provide communities with greater flexibility in utilizing Section 108 guarantees for economic development activities.

Community Development Banks

During the 1992 presidential campaign, President Clinton proposed the creation of 100 community development banks to target financial capital to distressed communities underserved by traditional lending institutions. On 15 July 1993, the administration released details of its community development lending initiative. The initiative, introduced in the House as H.R. 2666 and in the Senate as S. 1275, provided funding for existing institutions, principally community development banks; community development credit unions; revolving loan funds; microloan funds; minority-owned banks; depository institutions; and community development institutions that have as their primary mission the provision of capital, credit, and development services to economically distressed areas or low-income and disadvantaged persons. For each dollar committed to CDBs by the federal government, the Clinton proposal required a match of two dollars to be raised from private sources. For FY95 the administration requested $144 million. The VA-HUD-Independent Agencies Appropriations Act for FY95 (P.L. 103-327), allocates $125 million for community development banking activities.

During early August of 1994 the House and Senate completed action on a conference bill creating community development banks. The bill, H.R. 3474, was joined with H.R. 3841, a bill governing interstate banking, during a House-Senate conference, but was later uncoupled by conferees, who were concerned that the joint measure would face opposition and possible defeat in the Senate because of interstate banking related provisions. The community development banking bill, approved by the House on 4 August 1994 and the Senate on 9 August 1994, was signed by the president on 23 September 1994 as P.L. 103-325. The act creates the Community Development Financial Institutions (CDFI) Fund, which is to be managed by an administrative officer selected by the president with the advice and consent of the Senate and overseen by a 15-member panel made up of cabinet officials, CDFI experts, and bank officials. This new government entity, which may not become operational until late 1995, will provide financial and technical assis-

tance to institutions whose primary mission is to provide lending and other services in areas underserved by traditional banking institutions. The act requires that a CDFI grantee match the federal assistance on a dollar-for-dollar basis, although institutions facing financial constraints may be allowed to meet a lower standard of $2 to $1 CDFI/private match. In addition, no CDFI grantee may receive more than $5 million over a three-year period. The act sets aside a third of the amount appropriated to be used by commercial banks and thrifts to subsidize the establishment of lifeline banking services or to make loans in distressed neighborhoods. The provision is intended to fund the Bank Enterprise Act, which was included in the Federal Deposit Insurance Improvement Act of 1991 (P.L. 102-242).

Community Development Corporations

The National Community Economic Development Partnership Act of 1994 (NCEDPA) is one of several crime prevention provisions in Title III of the Violent Crime Control and Law Enforcement Act of 1994 (P.L. 103-322). It was signed by the president on 13 September 1994 and is due to be implemented in FY96. The act is intended to promote community-based economic development, community revitalization, and job creation and retention efforts in low-income rural and urban communities by awarding technical and financial assistance to existing and emerging Community Development Corporations (CDCs). CDCs are private nonprofit entities whose principal purpose is the provision of low-income housing and social and economic development projects that benefit low-income persons or communities.

The NCEDPA establishes three forms of assistance that may be awarded by the Department of Health and Human Services (HHS) to eligible CDCs. Existing and emerging CDCs may receive a line of credit to be used to establish a revolving loan fund. In addition, eligible CDCs may receive skill-enhancement grants or operating grant funds. All assistance is be awarded on a competitive basis. Provisions supporting CDCs are included in the Human Services Amendments of 1994 (P.L. 103-252). Title II of P.L. 103-252 authorizes the awarding of competitive grants under the discretionary portion of the Community Service Block Grant (CSBG) program to CDCs engaged in housing and economic development activities. The provision is a relatively modest attempt to support the growing number of CDCs. It authorizes HHS to use up to 1% of CSBG discretionary funds for such activities.

USDA Reorganization

Congress completed action on the reorganization of the Department of Agriculture (USDA), which will affect not only the administration of farm support programs but also rural community development efforts. At the headquarters level, USDA functions will be organized around six missions, one of which—rural development—would be headed by an Undersecretary for Rural Economic and Community Develop-

ment. Three new organizations will report to the undersecretary: a Rural Utilities Service, which combines the telephone and electric programs of the Rural Electric Administration (REA) with the water and sewer programs of the Rural Development Administration (RDA); the Rural Community Development Service, which will include FmHA rural housing programs and REA and RDA rural community-loan programs; and the Rural Business and Cooperative Development Service, which would include the RDA and REA business development programs, the Agricultural Cooperative Development Service, and the Alternative Agricultural Research and Commercialization Center.

On 29 September 1993, House Agriculture Committee Chairman de la Garza introduced the Department of Agriculture Reorganization Act of 1993 (H.R. 3171; S. 1970), the administration's reorganization plan. The Senate Agriculture Committee reported out an original bill (the rural development structure is identical to that proposed in H.R. 3171), and the Senate passed it on April 23. The House Agriculture Committee reported an amended bill on June 16. During Senate consideration of crop insurance legislation (H.R. 4217; S. 2095), the text of the reorganization bill was attached, and the amended bill passed the Senate on 25 August 1994. On 3 October 1994 the amended bill passed the House. The president signed P.L. 103-354, which included crop insurance and the USDA reorganization plan, on 13 October 1994.

PUBLIC SAFETY AND CRIME

Congress passed a major crime bill during the 103d session as well as a bill aimed at preventing violence at abortion clinics.

Clinic Access Act

In early spring Congress completed action on legislation affecting access to abortion clinics. This action was prompted by concern over the growing violence, including the slaying of a doctor and his security escort in Pensacola, Florida, and the threat of violence surrounding pro-life tactics of blocking access to clinics that include abortions among the reproductive health services they provide. The bill, H.R. 796, was signed by the president on 26 May 1994 as the Freedom of Access to Clinic Entrances Act of 1994 (P.L. 103-259). Supporters of the legislation cast the issue as one of public safety, not an abortion-rights issue; opponents argued the law would impinge on the First Amendment right of free speech. The legislation as signed by the president prohibits the threat or the use of force against persons seeking to enter an abortion clinic and provides for civil and criminal penalties—including fines, prison terms, the payment of compensatory and punitive damages, and injunctive relief—against persons who violate the law. The act, as an acknowledgment of concern surrounding federal mandates and usurpation of state and local authority, explicitly states that the none of its provisions are to be construed as preempting local or state laws governing criminal penalties and civil remedies against persons convicted of blocking clinic entrances or interfering "with enforcement to state or local laws regulating the performance of abortions or other reproductive health services."

Anti-Crime Act

In the spring of 1994, the House resumed action on the second most contentious piece of legislation to confront the second session of the 103d Congress—crime. The administration and the 103d Congress were already engaged in a battle over health care legislation, which was to consume much of its energy and time during the last months of the session. Health care and, to a lesser although significant extent, crime legislation consumed valuable time, stalling possible consideration and passage of other important legislation before the October adjournment for midterm elections. Though Congress tabled health care legislation, it passed a crime bill. The Violent Crime Control and Law Enforcement Act of 1994 (P.L. 103-322), was signed by the president on 13 September 1994. The law's path to enactment was contested by conservatives who argued against crime prevention programs authorized by the act and by the National Rifle Association, which opposed the ban on assault weapons. The Congressional Black Caucus also opposed the measure at one point during the legislative process, threatening to withdraw its support if a racial justice provision regarding alleged racial bias in death penalty sentencing was removed during House and Senate conference committee negotiations.

The Senate completed action on its $22 billion crime package in November 1993. The House leadership, which during the first session of the 103d Congress considered a series of small anti-crime related bills, regrouped and fashioned an omnibus crime bill with a price tag of $28 billion during the spring of 1994.

With fear of crime registering as an important issue in several national polls tracking midterm election year issues, Congress engaged in extended debate over the elements of an anti-crime bill. Central issues confronting the Congress and the administration included the mix between crime control and crime prevention programs, the costs of anti-crime legislation, a ban on assault weapons, sentencing reform, domestic violence, and capital punishment appeals.

After working feverishly during the summer, the Democratic leadership in the House and Senate and the Clinton administration moved to push the bill through to final passage, before the midterm election in November. Floor consideration of the conference report was delayed three times by parliamentary maneuvers in both the House and the Senate. On 11 August 1994 anti-gun control Democrats and Republicans blocked full House consideration of the conference report. Eleven days later, a modestly revised conference report passed the House with the backing of the Democratic leadership and the administration.

Republicans in the Senate also sought to scuttle the compromise legislation, arguing that the bill, with a price tag of $30 billion, was a do-nothing budget buster. The Republican-led effort to send the bill back to a conference committee was twice defeated on close procedural votes. On 25 August 1994 the Senate voted 61 to 39 to waive a budgetary point of order. After three days of debate, Senate Democrats successfully sought to end debate on the measure. A motion to invoke cloture to limit the debate passed by a vote of 61 to 38. The Senate approved the bill by a vote of 61 to 38 on 25 August 1994, giving President Clinton a needed legislative victory. On 13 September 1994, the president signed into law the Violent Crime Control and Law Enforcement Act of 1994 (P.L. 103-322).

The act authorizes $30 billion in spending over the next six fiscal years (1995 to 2000), including $9 billion to support state and local law enforcement efforts, $8 billion for prison construction and expansion, nearly $2 billion to states for housing undocumented criminal aliens; and $5.4 billion in crime prevention programs. The act authorizes the following programs and activities:

1. *COPS on the Beat* grants to states, local governments, regional consortia, and other public and private organizations. The grants support community policing and other efforts to increase the number of officers on the streets. Preference is given to applicants who exceed the 25% match requirement.
2. *Police Recruitment* grants totaling $24 million over five years (1996 to 2000) to assist in recruitment and retention of police applicants from underrepresented neighborhoods and groups.
3. *Police Corps* grants that provide scholarship assistance to persons who agree to work in state or local law enforcement for four years after graduation from a baccalaureate program. The act also authorizes scholarship assistance for in-service personnel.
4. *Family Support* grants to be awarded to states, local governments, and police organizations to provide family counseling, child care, stress reduction, and other family support services to police officers and family members. Annual grant amount cannot exceed $100,000 or $250,000 over a five-year period.
5. *Byrne* grants authorized at $1 billion over five years, to fund gang prevention and anti-gang related activities.
6. *Training and Technical Automation* grants, which authorize $100 million for the period FY96 to 2000 to assist state and local police improve agency efficiency through technology integration.
7. *Truth in Sentencing* grants awarded to states and multistate compacts that mandate that violent offenders serve 85% of their sentence.
8. *Violent Offender* grants awarded on a formula basis, with each state receiving 0.25% of the total; the remaining amount is awarded on the basis of the number of violent offenses reported in 1993. Fifteen percent of the total amount appropriated is to be distributed at the Attorney General's discretion.
9. *Alternative Sentencing for Young Offenders* grants, which are awarded to states and local governments. Two-thirds of a state's formula allocation is to be distributed to local governments. Funds may be used to fund boot camps and other alternative sentencing strategies.
10. *Alien Incarceration* grants, which are awarded to states and local governments to cover the costs associated with the incarceration of undocumented criminal aliens; $1.8 billion over six years (1995 to 2000).

In addition, the act authorizes over $5 billion in prevention programs including:

1. *Local Crime Prevention Block* grants are awarded to local governments to carry out an array of activities, including anti-gang and gang prevention activities and sports and recreation programs, including midnight basketball, family outreach, and anti-crime councils in middle and high schools. Funds total $625 million over five years (1996 to 2000).
2. *Community Schools Youth Services and Supervision* grants are awarded to community-based organizations to support supervised after-school activities, including sports, academic, and extracurricular activities in schools located in areas with significant poverty and juvenile delinquency. Each state receives a 0.25% share of the appropriated amount, with the remaining share allocated based on the state's share of the total number of volent crimes committed. Each state then allocates funds to local governments based on the ratio of each jurisdiction's share of the number of violent crimes committed in the state.
3. *Family and Community Endeavor Schools* grants are awarded to local school districts and community-based organizations to provide mentoring and other after-school programs for at-risk children and their families. The act authorizes an appropriation of $810 million over six years (1995 to 2000).
4. Assistance for At-Risk Youth allows the Attorney General to award $36 million in grants to nonprofit agencies providing residential services to teenage dropouts or delinquents.
5. *Local Partnership Act* grants awarded by HUD to local governments to carry out education, drug treatment, and job training activities intended to reduce or prevent the incidence of crime. Authorizes $1.6 billion over five years (1996 to 2000) in fiscal assistance payments to states for distribution to local governments.
6. *National Community Economic Partnership*

Act grants awarded to community development corporations engaged in community-based economic development, neighborhood revitalization, and job creation and retention efforts in low-income urban and rural communities. Authorizes a five-year (1996 to 2000) funding level of $270 billion.

7. *Urban Recreation* grants awarded by the Department of Interior to local governments to fund improvements and expansion of recreation facilities in urban areas with high crime rates.

8. *Violence Against Women and Children* grants designed to address violence against women and children, including grants to fund domestic violence hotlines, to develop more effective police and prosecutorial protocols when dealing with violent crimes against women, to fund shelters for battered women, to fund programs implementing anti-stalker legislation, and grants to train law officers, teachers, and others to identify victims of child abuse. These grants are awarded to nonprofit organizations, judges, court personnel, and state, local, and tribal governments.

The act also (1) bans the ownership of 19 types of semiautomatic assault weapons; (2) extends the death penalty to 60 federal offenses, including obstruction of justice charges against drug kingpins, the use of a firearm in the commission of a crime, letter bombing, murder of a federal law enforcement officer, and murder resulting from a carjacking; (3) institutes a mandatory ''three strikes you're out'' sentencing requirement for persons convicted of a third violent felony; and (4) institutes penalties against telemarketing fraud, theft, and financial crimes. Further, the act establishes the Violent Crime Reduction Trust Fund to fund the programmatic activities. The trust fund is to be capitalized from savings derived by the elimination of 250,000 federal employees. Total appropriation for the trust fund is not to exceed $30 billion over the six-year period from fiscal years 1995 to 2000.

GATT

The 103d Congress reconvened in late November 1994, with the sole purpose of considering the General Agreement on Tariffs and Trade (GATT), which the president described as the biggest job creation program in the country's history. GATT reduces or eliminates trade barriers among member countries, moving the world closer to an integrated global economy. GATT passage was not assured because opponents sought to portray the agreement as contributing to economic dislocation and job loss particularly among less-skilled workers in such industries as textiles. As was the case with NAFTA, the GATT passed with strong Republican support.

[1]The four initiatives coupled with the National Service Act, which passed during the 1st session of the 103d Congress and which provides financial assistance for vocational education and college-related expenses in exchange for a period of community service, extends Federal support from preschool through college or vocational training.

[2]As originally authorized by the National Affordable Housing Act, the program included a three-tiered matching fund provision that required states and local governments to provide, from non-federal sources, a 50% match for new construction, 33% match for substantial rehabilitation, and 25% for moderate rehabilitation and tenant-based assistance.

C Staffing and Compensation

Salaries of Municipal Officials, 1994

Evelina R. Moulder
International City/County Management Association

Salaries of local government management personnel are determined by a number of factors. Services delivered, size of budget, number of employees, economic growth, population size, and geographic location are but a few of these, and some are interrelated. For example, municipalities with high levels of service delivery and large populations tend to have larger budgets. A city that wants to launch a major economic development initiative may significantly increase the hiring salary for the position of director of economic development. Cities with numerous locally owned and operated parks and a high demand for recreation programs will probably pay the director of parks and recreation a higher salary than the city with parks owned and operated by the county and a moderate demand for recreation activities. This article describes the results of ICMA's annual survey of municipal officials' salaries, focusing in particular on the effect of population size and geographic location on salaries.

METHODOLOGY

The data presented in this article were gathered in ICMA's annual survey, which was mailed in the summer of 1994 to all cities with populations of 2,500 and over and to all ICMA-recognized cities with populations under 2,500.[1] Of the 7,217 cities that received surveys, 4,339 responded, for a survey response rate of 60.1% (Table 1/1).

SALARY TRENDS

Table 1/2 shows the average annual salary for each of 19 municipal positions, as well as the percentage of increase over the course of six years. (Only municipalities that responded to each survey conducted in the six years from 1989 to 1994 are included in this table.) From 1989 to 1990, the overall percentage of increase was approximately 6%. Since that time, the percentage of increase has been noticeably less for all positions. The period from 1993 to 1994 is

the first in this six-year period that shows increases below 5% for every position shown.

Three positions show increases that have dropped by four percentage points since 1989. The percentage of increase for ten positions has dropped by three percentage points over the same period, and six positions show a two percentage point drop.

Table 1/1   SURVEY RESPONSE

	No. cities[1] surveyed (A)	No. cities responding No.	No. cities responding % of (A)
Total	7,217	4,339	60.1
Population group			
Over 1,000,000	8	6	75.0
500,000–1,000,000 ..	17	11	64.7
250,000–499,999	39	24	61.5
100,000–249,999	131	94	71.8
50,000–99,999	338	242	71.6
25,000–49,999	680	475	69.9
10,000–24,999	1,599	1,039	65.0
5,000–9,999	1,805	1,056	58.5
2,500–4,999	2,000	1,075	53.8
Under 2,500	600	317	52.8
Geographic region[2]			
Northeast	1,985	1,007	50.7
North Central	2,096	1,370	65.4
South	2,103	1,261	60.0
West	1,033	701	67.9
Geographic division[3]			
New England	798	429	53.8
Mid-Atlantic	1,187	578	48.7
East North Central ...	1,363	868	63.7
West North Central ..	733	502	68.5
South Atlantic	887	598	67.4
East South Central ...	470	237	50.4
West South Central ..	746	426	57.1
Mountain	373	232	62.2
Pacific Coast	675	469	69.5
Metro status[4]			
Central	516	355	68.8
Suburban	3,860	2,341	60.6
Independent	2,826	1,643	58.1
Form of government[5]			
Mayor-council	3,557	1,854	52.1
Council-manager	3,012	2,159	71.7
Commission	164	88	53.7
Town meeting	412	202	49.0
Rep. town meeting ...	72	36	50.0

From 1993 to 1994, only three positions—planning director, director of parks and recreation, and purchasing director—show a percentage of increase higher than that shown for the previous period (1992–1993).

The Consumer Price Index for All Urban Consumers (CPI-U) rose 2.8% for the 12-month period ending July 1994. Although the CPI-U is a price index, not a cost-of-living index, it is

[1] The term *cities* is used in this and the following tables to refer to cities, villages, towns, townships, and boroughs.

[2] *Geographic regions: Northeast*—the New England and Mid-Atlantic Divisions, which include the states of Connecticut, Maine, Massachusetts, New Hampshire, New Jersey, New York, Pennsylvania, Rhode Island, and Vermont; *North Central*—the East and West North Central Divisions, which include the states of Illinois, Indiana, Iowa, Kansas, Michigan, Minnesota, Missouri, Nebraska, North Dakota, Ohio, South Dakota, and Wisconsin; *South*—the South Atlantic and the East and West South Central Divisions, which include the states of Alabama, Arkansas, Delaware, Florida, Georgia, Kentucky, Louisiana, Maryland, Mississippi, North Carolina, Oklahoma, South Carolina, Tennessee, Texas, Virginia, and West Virginia, plus the District of Columbia; *West*—the Mountain and Pacific Coast Divisions, which include the states of Alaska, Arizona, California, Colorado, Hawaii, Idaho, Montana, Nevada, New Mexico, Oregon, Utah, Washington, and Wyoming.

[3] *Geographic divisions: New England*—the states of Connecticut, Maine, Massachusetts, New Hampshire, Rhode Island, and Vermont; *Mid-Atlantic*—the states of New Jersey, New York, and Pennsylvania; *East North Central*—the states of Illinois, Indiana, Michigan, Ohio, and Wisconsin; *West North Central*—the states of Iowa, Kansas, Minnesota, Missouri, Nebraska, North Dakota, and South Dakota; *South Atlantic*—the states of Delaware, Florida, Georgia, Maryland, North Carolina, South Carolina, Virginia, and West Virginia, plus the District of Columbia; *East South Central*—the states of Alabama, Kentucky, Mississippi, and Tennessee; *West South Central*—the states of Arkansas, Louisiana, Oklahoma, and Texas; *Mountain*—the states of Arizona, Colorado, Idaho, Montana, Nevada, New Mexico, Utah, and Wyoming; *Pacific Coast*—the states of Alaska, California, Hawaii, Oregon, and Washington.

[4] *Metro status: Central*—the city(ies) appearing in the metropolitan statistical area (MSA) title; *Suburban*—the city(ies) located with an MSA; *Independent*—the city(ies) not located within an MSA.

[5] *Form of government: Mayor-council*—an elected council serves as the legislative body with a separately elected head of government; *Council-manager*—the mayor and council make policy and an appointed administrator is responsible for the administration of the city; *Commission*—a board of elected commissioners serves as the legislative body and each commissioner is responsible for administration of one or more departments; *Town meeting*—qualified voters meet to make basic policy and choose a board of selectmen to carry out the policy; *Representative town meeting*—representatives selected by citizens vote at meetings, which may be attended by all town citizens.

Table 1/2 AVERAGE SALARIES OF MUNICIPAL OFFICIALS

Title	No. of cities included[1]	1989 ($)	1990 ($)	Increase from 1989 (%)	1991 ($)	Increase from 1990 (%)	1992 ($)	Increase from 1991 (%)	1993 ($)	Increase from 1992 (%)	1994 ($)	Increase from 1993 (%)
Mayor	1,125	8,472	8,964	6	9,209	3	9,619	4	9,963	4	10,191	2
City manager	851	54,666	57,992	6	60,803	5	63,188	4	65,221	3	67,274	3
Chief apptd. administrator/CAO	386	44,054	46,726	6	49,467	6	51,507	4	53,999	5	56,074	4
Asst. city mgr./asst. CAO	263	46,057	48,965	6	51,945	6	54,077	4	56,285	4	58,216	3
City clerk	1,002	29,733	31,416	6	32,799	4	34,030	4	35,305	4	36,366	3
Chief financial officer	568	44,950	47,742	6	50,136	5	52,099	4	54,050	4	55,946	4
Treasurer	107	31,617	32,944	4	34,851	6	36,229	4	38,122	5	38,236	0
Director of public works	862	41,268	43,631	6	45,919	5	47,983	4	49,689	4	51,274	3
Engineer	265	45,767	48,683	6	51,278	5	53,326	4	55,006	3	56,798	3
Police chief	1,135	40,129	42,544	6	44,563	5	46,680	5	48,412	4	50,104	3
Fire chief	585	40,855	43,321	6	45,406	5	47,593	5	49,263	4	50,820	3
Planning director	332	43,549	46,205	6	48,948	6	50,868	4	52,476	3	54,501	4
Personnel director	318	40,911	43,610	7	46,310	6	48,290	4	50,276	4	52,183	4
Director of parks/recreation	345	41,167	43,687	6	45,948	5	48,167	5	49,650	3	51,453	4
Superintendent of parks	162	33,747	35,590	5	37,743	6	39,052	3	40,707	4	42,042	3
Director of recreation	100	32,300	34,683	7	36,627	6	37,900	3	39,432	4	40,975	4
Librarian	319	32,632	34,672	6	36,297	5	37,641	4	39,376	5	40,889	4
Director of info. services/data proc.	121	43,266	46,199	7	48,495	5	50,729	5	52,262	3	54,088	3
Purchasing director	191	33,767	36,036	7	37,562	4	39,522	5	40,670	3	42,367	4

[1]This table is based on salary data for each of the six years 1989 to 1994. Number of cities included are those that have consistently reported data for the position indicated for each of the six years.

Table 1/3 SALARIES BY POPULATION GROUP

	City manager	CAO	Assistant manager	Chief financial officer	Pesonnel director	Director of economic development	Treasurer	Director of public works	Engineer	Police chief
	Average salary ($)	Average salary ($)	Average salary ($)	Average salary ($)	Average salary ($)	Average salary ($)	Average salary ($)	Average salary ($)	Average salary ($)	Average salary ($)
Total	65,745	50,594	52,083	50,074	46,550	49,406	34,921	47,846	52,317	48,661
Population group										
Over 1,000,000	138,439	113,610	106,940	93,337	89,198	87,331	79,337	99,152	92,673	110,731
500,000–1,000,000	126,423	90,400	98,902	85,601	78,289	75,813	75,404	87,124	75,850	91,710
250,000–499,999	118,459	88,324	85,866	81,216	72,711	70,608	59,515	84,410	72,492	84,123
100,000–249,999	110,152	70,945	83,333	76,621	67,958	69,918	57,906	76,402	69,675	80,640
50,000–99,999	92,957	63,617	73,463	66,833	57,316	62,072	47,733	67,215	59,437	70,847
25,000–49,999	82,390	64,231	59,985	59,675	48,013	53,770	41,712	61,335	53,856	62,364
10,000–24,999	68,540	58,542	47,406	48,629	38,515	44,747	33,217	50,661	47,936	52,894
5,000–9,999	55,722	50,278	38,307	38,833	30,641	35,713	28,765	41,493	42,019	43,598
2,500–4,999	46,429	39,705	32,483	32,667	27,976	31,515	24,048	34,736	40,637	34,601
Under 2,500	38,838	36,883	25,726	31,228	26,458	28,905	22,674	31,702	40,432	33,164

Table 1/3 SALARIES BY POPULATION GROUP (*Continued*)

	Fire chief	Planning director	Risk manager	Director of parks & rec.	Superintendent of parks	Director of recreation	Librarian	Director of information services	Purchasing director
	Average salary ($)	Average salary ($)	Average salary ($)	Average salary ($)	Average salary ($)	Average salary ($)	Average salary ($)	Average salary ($)	Average salary ($)
Total	48,433	50,089	44,763	44,248	38,858	38,306	39,049	48,749	40,140
Population group									
Over 1,000,000	108,720	101,697	67,240	97,478	. . .	. . .	89,701	96,667	76,843
500,000–1,000,000	87,075	76,935	53,723	80,623	62,612	60,073	80,703	84,163	69,296
250,000–499,999	79,229	70,781	57,781	77,288	60,785	59,104	74,817	70,307	59,433
100,000–249,999	75,147	72,520	51,730	71,479	54,581	59,022	67,171	66,827	54,775
50,000–99,999	65,898	59,814	47,379	59,745	46,597	48,652	56,441	54,516	46,776
25,000–49,999	56,765	55,185	43,785	51,870	41,963	41,708	48,991	47,224	40,224
10,000–24,999	46,715	45,279	37,399	41,649	36,056	33,720	39,569	37,842	32,325
5,000–9,999	35,503	38,653	33,492	31,250	28,885	27,096	28,552	31,570	27,126
2,500–4,999	30,245	36,667	31,466	27,876	26,324	20,633	21,132	24,185	26,603
Under 2,500	32,786	38,945	. . .	24,241	28,303	24,422	18,639	20,263	24,228

useful because it is an indicator of inflation. With the exception of the average salary for mayor (2.2% increase) and treasurer (0.2% increase), the percentage of increase for all other positions in Table 1/2 exceeds the CPI-U of 2.8%. (All calculations in Table 1/3 have been rounded. The unrounded calculations are not shown.) The percentage of increase for these remaining positions equals or exceeds 3.0%.

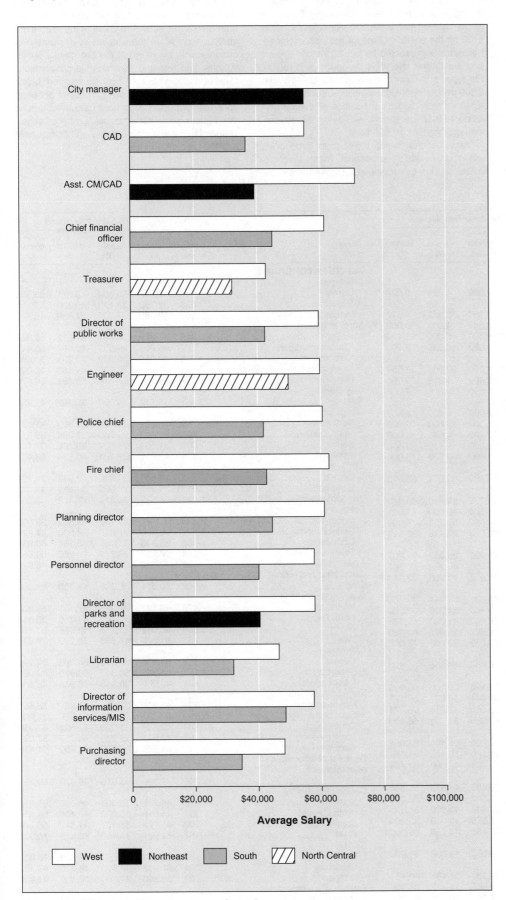

Figure 1/1 *Highest and lowest average salaries by region*

POPULATION SIZE

Population size is clearly a factor influencing average salaries of local government managers and department heads across the United States. For each position shown in Table 1/3, there is a consistent decrease in salary from the largest to the smallest population group. In most instances, the average salary for the jurisdictions with populations over one million is three times the average salary shown for jurisdictions with populations under 2,500. For the positions of librarian and director of information technology, the average salary in the largest cities is 4.8 times the average for these positions in the smallest cities.

GEOGRAPHIC REGION

As has been the case in previous years, the average salary for each position is highest in the West region. Although the CPI-U for the 12-month period ending July 1994 is lowest in the West (2.4%) and may affect the percentage of increase to a certain extent, in a region that has a history of average salaries that far surpass the average salaries in other parts of the country any influence the CPI-U exerts is comparatively negligible.

Figure 1/1 shows the highest and lowest average salary by region for fifteen of the positions covered in the salary survey. With few exceptions, the lowest average salaries are in the South region.

METRO STATUS

When compared with the average salaries of suburban and independent jurisdictions, central cities are typically the highest. Central cities are the core cities of Metropolitan Statistical Areas (MSAs) and must have a population of at least 25,000 and must employ 50% of the residents. In central cities there must be at least 75 jobs per 100 residents, so central cities can be expected to provide extensive services to residential and commercial customers.

SUMMARY

In general, the percentage gains in local appointed officials' salaries have decreased over the last several years. As the economy continues to improve, salaries of local officials should reflect improved economic conditions.

Table 1/4 SALARIES OF MUNICIPAL OFFICIALS: 1 JULY 1994

Salary data for the 21 municipal positions in this table are based on information reported by municipal officials as of 1 July 1994. Data are reported by position title only. Although job responsibilities are generally similar, the titles do not necessarily indicate identical duties and responsibilities.

For the position of city manager, data are shown for only those municipalities recognized by ICMA as having the council-manager form of government. For the position of chief administrative officer (CAO), data are shown for all other reporting municipalities.

Except for the position of mayor, which does include part-time salaries, this table excludes (1) salaries of part-time officials, (2) salaries for vacant positions, (3) salaries of acting officials, (4) those paid in whole or in part by fees, and (5) all salaries below $8,000. All salaries below $100 for the position of mayor are also excluded. Salaries are presented by ten population groups and are further classified by geographic region, city type, and form of government. Cities under 2,500 population include only cities recognized by ICMA as providing for a position of overall professional management or as having the council-manager form of government.

Classifications having fewer than three cities reporting are excluded because meaningful statistics cannot be computed. Consequently the number reporting in some subcategories does not always equal the total reporting. Quartiles are not shown when only three cities reported. The median represents either the value of the middle observation or, when there is an even number of observations, the mean of the two middle observations. The first and third quartile observations represent the value of the observation below which 25% and 75% of the number of observations fall, respectively, and are calculated around the median, such that an equal number of observations fall between the median and first quartile and the median and the third quartile.

Title of official	No. cities reporting	Mean ($)	First quartile ($)	Median ($)	Third quartile ($)
All cities					
Mayor					
Total	3,673	10,646	2,000	4,320	9,024
Geographic region					
Northeast	852	11,097	1,500	2,950	7,572
North Central	1,260	10,515	2,344	4,800	9,000
South	999	11,188	2,400	5,000	11,410
West	562	9,289	3,000	4,800	8,400
City type					
Central	322	34,351	7,200	23,000	56,056
Suburban	1,948	8,996	2,400	4,315	8,000
Independent	1,403	7,496	1,500	3,600	7,200
Form of government					
Mayor-council	1,718	16,088	3,000	6,000	18,802
Council-manager	1,667	5,108	1,500	3,600	6,000
Commission	79	12,456	2,700	4,800	13,000
Town meeting	178	9,875	1,000	1,745	4,500
Rep. town meeting	31	6,614	1,400	2,000	3,000
City manager					
Total	1,924	65,745	48,400	63,014	80,000
Geographic region					
Northeast	343	56,264	40,775	55,000	69,870
North Central	466	62,529	48,104	60,000	74,311
South	661	61,874	47,000	59,298	75,000
West	454	81,846	63,000	80,436	96,993
City type					
Central	196	88,557	74,200	86,032	102,291
Suburban	1,014	71,077	55,000	69,334	84,906
Independent	714	51,911	41,918	50,800	62,244
Form of government					
Mayor-council	92	59,346	46,000	56,944	70,360
Council-manager	1,757	66,783	49,668	64,000	81,000
Commission	9	49,367	38,000	41,000	52,996
Town meeting	60	47,343	31,622	44,082	62,680
Rep. town meeting	6	68,501	66,843	69,666	75,000
Chief appointed administrator					
Total	1,374	50,594	38,000	48,505	61,808
Geographic region					
Northeast	417	51,870	37,128	50,100	65,000
North Central	492	49,922	38,964	48,327	59,577
South	313	47,021	35,000	43,814	56,271
West	152	56,627	42,996	55,754	66,500
City type					
Central	93	69,408	52,000	66,504	84,059
Suburban	810	52,726	40,000	50,688	64,464
Independent	471	43,212	33,705	42,000	51,704
Form of government					
Mayor-council	941	50,213	37,485	47,973	61,808
Council-manager	292	53,273	40,342	51,451	63,300
Commission	33	48,913	38,500	43,000	51,833
Town meeting	87	46,725	35,875	45,000	55,000
Rep. town meeting	21	49,082	36,483	44,760	63,000
Asst. city mgr./asst. CAO					
Total	1,053	52,083	36,000	48,308	64,800
Geographic region					
Northeast	197	39,065	27,750	37,484	46,431
North Central	296	47,224	35,541	46,813	57,999
South	303	48,956	34,000	46,775	62,254
West	257	71,346	54,000	69,858	88,092

Title of official	No. cities reporting	Mean ($)	First quartile ($)	Median ($)	Third quartile ($)
All cities continued					
City type					
Central	155	72,148	58,304	70,071	85,356
Suburban	638	52,752	37,119	49,336	63,706
Independent	260	38,480	27,700	37,736	46,785
Form of government					
Mayor-council	219	41,223	25,867	37,817	52,584
Council-manager	789	56,025	39,537	52,500	68,447
Commission	8	39,316	26,000	33,235	51,583
Town meeting	33	32,165	20,908	33,260	42,000
Rep. town meeting	4	59,035	52,312	54,391	56,470
City clerk					
Total	3,161	34,192	25,000	32,000	41,460
Geographic region					
Northeast	719	33,802	24,174	32,500	41,937
North Central	923	32,602	25,000	31,000	39,678
South	1,001	31,569	23,597	29,400	37,146
West	518	42,636	30,304	40,934	53,404
City type					
Central	319	45,503	34,626	42,848	54,704
Suburban	1,618	36,213	27,000	34,888	44,472
Independent	1,224	28,573	21,814	27,479	33,500
Form of government					
Mayor-council	1,336	31,911	23,192	29,969	39,000
Council-manager	1,567	36,780	27,040	34,500	44,826
Commission	66	33,346	24,461	32,161	40,851
Town meeting	164	27,901	20,343	28,266	33,560
Rep. town meeting	28	37,020	30,830	37,103	46,670
Chief financial officer					
Total	2,062	50,074	36,800	48,738	62,000
Geographic region					
Northeast	470	47,191	33,963	47,181	59,908
North Central	532	48,115	37,107	47,366	59,585
South	625	46,049	33,238	43,638	57,457
West	435	61,370	46,633	60,213	74,865
City type					
Central	304	64,455	53,546	64,208	74,175
Suburban	1,177	51,333	38,397	50,956	62,962
Independent	581	40,000	30,345	38,958	48,587
Form of government					
Mayor-council	677	45,521	32,150	43,851	56,851
Council-manager	1,252	53,362	40,000	52,059	65,000
Commission	34	42,589	25,000	42,608	57,330
Town meeting	82	40,241	28,200	40,757	52,691
Rep. town meeting	17	51,688	35,922	53,869	61,478
Director of economic development					
Total	746	49,406	35,915	46,579	60,759
Geographic region					
Northeast	137	46,775	35,000	46,000	55,519
North Central	252	44,518	33,000	42,466	56,616
South	200	46,773	35,307	44,347	56,179
West	157	62,901	46,440	63,816	78,909
City type					
Central	182	58,585	45,863	57,529	70,000
Suburban	364	51,822	38,400	49,220	63,492
Independent	200	36,656	27,780	36,000	44,025
Form of government					
Mayor-council	285	44,148	32,025	42,300	53,565
Council-manager	433	53,423	38,790	51,967	66,000

Table 1/4   SALARIES OF MUNICIPAL OFFICIALS: 1 JULY 1994
continued

Left

Title of official	No. cities reporting	Mean ($)	First quartile ($)	Median ($)	Third quartile ($)
All cities continued					
Commission	10	42,415	32,989	37,817	60,271
Town meeting	14	35,939	31,000	33,111	43,400
Rep. town meeting	4	53,790	47,000	53,481	59,962
Treasurer					
Total	930	34,921	22,464	32,330	45,344
Geographic region					
Northeast	312	32,786	20,662	31,286	43,049
North Central	297	32,268	22,318	30,560	41,791
South	182	36,760	24,146	35,957	46,718
West	139	42,976	23,856	38,000	58,392
City type					
Central	157	51,545	41,527	49,837	63,169
Suburban	455	34,622	23,000	32,908	44,784
Independent	318	27,143	20,246	26,358	33,000
Form of government					
Mayor-council	368	32,827	20,268	29,997	42,532
Council-manager	444	37,264	25,000	34,042	46,800
Commission	20	33,008	21,500	28,975	46,292
Town meeting	81	30,033	19,675	31,000	38,500
Rep. town meeting	17	44,626	38,041	46,670	50,737
Director of public works					
Total	2,815	47,846	34,497	45,000	58,431
Geographic region					
Northeast	625	48,666	37,373	47,518	58,448
North Central	758	46,732	35,859	45,000	56,377
South	937	41,966	30,000	38,856	51,459
West	495	59,644	42,160	57,600	74,280
City type					
Central	296	64,827	53,003	64,175	75,354
Suburban	1,515	50,473	37,500	48,412	61,000
Independent	1,004	38,874	29,772	37,070	46,590
Form of government					
Mayor-council	1,110	43,862	31,985	41,455	53,163
Council-manager	1,544	50,738	36,538	48,002	62,136
Commission	39	47,686	37,440	46,308	58,806
Town meeting	102	45,036	36,654	44,255	54,176
Rep. town meeting	20	60,311	52,369	62,916	68,064
Engineer					
Total	1,054	52,317	43,493	51,836	60,654
Geographic region					
Northeast	205	51,069	40,604	52,829	63,000
North Central	300	50,197	43,700	50,593	57,500
South	334	50,224	42,000	49,973	57,512
West	215	59,714	47,640	57,288	71,167
City type					
Central	269	57,508	47,999	56,359	65,201
Suburban	500	53,425	44,876	52,999	63,276
Independent	285	45,472	39,501	45,676	52,484
Form of government					
Mayor-council	368	48,477	40,604	47,850	56,638
Council-manager	625	54,714	45,145	53,848	63,230
Commission	20	50,299	44,520	51,570	58,303
Town meeting	25	49,061	45,074	52,018	56,075
Rep. town meeting	16	54,609	51,308	55,319	58,295
Police chief					
Total	3,197	48,661	35,000	45,439	59,524
Geographic region					
Northeast	650	54,787	41,202	53,374	68,000
North Central	961	45,849	34,920	44,025	55,385
South	1,093	42,332	30,450	39,416	50,669
West	493	60,100	42,700	55,320	74,423
City type					
Central	325	66,469	53,269	64,155	76,044
Suburban	1,619	53,363	40,422	51,000	64,062
Independent	1,253	37,968	29,949	36,177	44,032
Form of government					
Mayor-council	1,334	44,411	31,456	40,802	54,171
Council-manager	1,695	51,661	38,304	48,412	62,360
Commission	48	46,524	34,857	41,893	53,000
Town meeting	97	52,496	43,260	53,000	61,459
Rep. town meeting	23	62,444	53,016	64,353	74,490
Fire chief					
Total	1,783	48,433	35,196	46,286	59,257
Geographic region					
Northeast	293	51,782	39,998	50,465	62,329
North Central	500	46,489	36,288	46,772	56,752
South	694	42,365	31,191	39,691	50,669
West	296	62,629	46,251	60,462	76,991

Right

Title of official	No. cities reporting	Mean ($)	First quartile ($)	Median ($)	Third quartile ($)
All cities continued					
City type					
Central	327	63,113	49,859	61,368	73,159
Suburban	831	50,965	38,000	49,860	61,500
Independent	625	37,387	30,000	36,534	44,796
Form of government					
Mayor-council	665	44,748	32,000	42,412	54,953
Council-manager	1,003	50,681	36,910	48,192	62,374
Commission	30	48,262	39,136	45,647	61,977
Town meeting	65	48,128	40,604	51,686	59,995
Rep. town meeting	20	59,504	51,688	64,276	72,227
Planning director					
Total	1,248	50,089	36,930	47,467	60,091
Geographic region					
Northeast	226	46,334	36,750	44,199	54,196
North Central	266	47,797	36,930	46,991	58,233
South	428	45,156	33,928	43,680	53,736
West	328	60,972	45,516	59,946	74,592
City type					
Central	262	59,565	47,175	57,847	70,100
Suburban	657	51,351	37,792	48,547	61,595
Independent	329	40,023	31,500	39,000	46,196
Form of government					
Mayor-council	360	46,265	34,004	44,599	55,000
Council-manager	816	52,300	38,938	49,764	63,336
Commission	17	52,879	43,659	56,786	62,534
Town meeting	40	38,769	33,852	38,520	43,508
Rep. town meeting	15	48,590	43,034	48,973	53,866
Personnel director					
Total	1,043	46,550	33,280	44,829	57,334
Geographic region					
Northeast	128	45,174	35,000	44,192	53,563
North Central	228	47,444	38,314	47,629	56,100
South	460	40,625	28,000	38,363	51,077
West	227	58,437	44,052	57,984	72,420
City type					
Central	297	55,561	43,603	54,496	66,448
Suburban	465	47,584	34,340	45,312	58,764
Independent	281	35,316	25,730	34,356	43,854
Form of government					
Mayor-council	329	42,843	29,365	40,128	53,256
Council-manager	675	48,488	35,381	47,236	60,408
Commission	21	43,537	28,625	42,748	56,500
Town meeting	9	43,174	36,429	44,378	46,208
Rep. town meeting	9	47,152	46,670	52,535	53,800
Risk manager					
Total	369	44,763	35,022	43,984	54,372
Geographic region					
Northeast	24	45,792	38,228	44,071	56,238
North Central	69	42,861	37,500	43,992	48,828
South	168	40,506	31,368	39,599	49,300
West	108	52,370	41,784	53,106	61,956
City type					
Central	168	47,655	39,000	46,791	57,401
Suburban	127	46,330	37,575	45,312	55,665
Independent	74	35,506	27,075	33,898	43,160
Form of government					
Mayor-council	89	41,975	32,220	39,959	51,965
Council-manager	271	45,789	35,520	44,933	55,356
Commission	8	41,823	36,200	44,419	46,908
Director of parks and recreation					
Total	1,427	44,248	30,834	41,534	54,761
Geographic region					
Northeast	243	40,251	29,966	39,415	50,014
North Central	368	42,504	31,496	41,456	52,062
South	545	40,292	28,400	37,584	49,999
West	271	58,155	41,832	57,382	72,024
City type					
Central	248	58,789	47,330	57,258	70,595
Suburban	716	45,477	33,000	42,926	55,335
Independent	463	34,559	26,000	33,197	41,913
Form of government					
Mayor-council	495	39,988	28,475	36,804	49,662
Council-manager	868	47,205	34,000	44,834	57,969
Commission	24	41,332	30,534	37,996	52,500
Town meeting	29	31,527	19,375	33,380	39,801
Rep. town meeting	11	42,499	34,034	40,953	52,566
Superintendent of parks					
Total	832	38,858	29,864	36,951	46,852

Table 1/4
continued

SALARIES OF MUNICIPAL OFFICIALS: 1 JULY 1994

Title of official	No. cities reporting	Distribution of 1994 salaries Mean ($)	First quartile ($)	Median ($)	Third quartile ($)
All cities continued					
Geographic region					
Northeast	105	42,546	34,102	41,776	50,317
North Central	244	38,515	30,883	37,031	45,354
South	285	33,332	25,187	32,194	38,740
West	198	45,280	35,238	42,974	56,155
City type					
Central	190	45,557	36,158	44,690	54,000
Suburban	380	41,065	31,937	39,154	48,901
Independent	262	30,800	24,071	30,702	36,565
Form of government					
Mayor-council	261	37,061	28,850	34,820	42,723
Council-manager	536	39,556	30,329	37,651	47,400
Commission	15	39,585	28,223	38,390	48,308
Town meeting	13	42,154	32,023	42,426	53,673
Rep. town meeting	7	44,788	34,787	45,098	52,566
Director of recreation					
Total	639	38,306	27,320	36,382	47,604
Geographic region					
Northeast	160	34,864	26,000	34,303	43,956
North Central	181	37,381	27,770	36,723	46,590
South	159	35,970	26,010	33,735	44,554
West	139	46,143	30,060	44,328	59,914
City type					
Central	148	47,432	38,636	46,196	55,984
Suburban	299	39,440	28,124	39,208	50,000
Independent	192	29,503	23,212	29,279	34,570
Form of government					
Mayor-council	223	36,235	25,026	34,505	46,000
Council-manager	362	40,550	29,224	38,982	50,429
Commission	17	35,995	28,223	31,142	44,096
Town meeting	27	26,551	17,078	28,325	34,074
Rep. town meeting	10	38,904	36,382	39,771	42,888
Librarian					
Total	1,075	39,049	26,020	36,600	49,352
Geographic region					
Northeast	294	42,281	31,547	41,226	50,052
North Central	267	36,154	25,509	35,124	45,432
South	310	32,916	19,656	29,206	42,993
West	204	47,499	29,295	45,569	60,912
City type					
Central	157	57,014	46,176	54,080	69,624
Suburban	517	41,716	29,971	40,000	51,170
Independent	401	28,576	20,280	27,823	35,978
Form of government					
Mayor-council	385	36,387	23,000	33,418	46,215
Council-manager	579	41,090	27,000	38,953	51,896
Commission	23	35,803	24,315	30,000	52,457
Town meeting	68	36,102	30,300	35,370	43,798
Rep. town meeting	20	44,951	38,500	42,418	50,158
Director of information services					
Total	628	48,749	37,437	47,675	58,392
Geographic region					
Northeast	107	48,020	37,437	45,298	57,950
North Central	137	48,067	40,508	47,529	55,057
South	256	44,612	31,805	43,107	54,808
West	128	58,363	47,008	57,624	67,452
City type					
Central	236	56,346	45,000	54,637	66,150
Suburban	251	48,174	37,437	48,996	58,220
Independent	141	37,058	29,424	37,344	44,283
Form of government					
Mayor-council	188	49,076	37,344	46,845	57,957
Council-manager	410	48,925	38,016	48,858	58,842
Commission	10	49,203	34,670	51,350	58,565
Town meeting	12	34,770	31,239	37,817	43,447
Rep. town meeting	8	52,431	52,535	57,315	57,950
Purchasing director					
Total	681	40,140	29,661	38,875	48,588
Geographic region					
Northeast	125	41,261	31,939	41,443	49,513
North Central	118	42,989	37,000	43,770	49,625
South	323	35,788	25,376	34,070	42,511
West	115	48,222	36,034	45,504	60,120
City type					
Central	234	47,539	37,600	45,378	56,388
Suburban	268	39,999	30,000	39,398	48,187
Independent	179	30,678	23,858	28,516	37,128
Form of government					
Mayor-council	230	39,220	27,729	36,963	48,187

Title of official	No. cities reporting	Distribution of 1994 salaries Mean ($)	First quartile ($)	Median ($)	Third quartile ($)
All cities continued					
Council-manager	434	40,708	30,540	39,714	49,000
Commission	9	38,377	27,205	32,468	55,577
Town meeting	3	31,123	...	30,000	...
Rep. town meeting	5	41,700	31,207	44,473	46,450
Over 1,000,000					
Mayor					
Total	5	112,417	110,000	123,778	130,000
City type					
Central	5	112,417	110,000	123,778	130,000
Form of government					
Mayor-council	4	124,196	123,778	126,889	130,000
Chief appointed administrator					
Total	4	113,610	95,000	97,950	100,900
City type					
Central	4	113,610	95,000	97,950	100,900
Form of government					
Mayor-council	4	113,610	95,000	97,950	100,900
Asst. city mgr./asst. CAO					
Total	4	106,940	101,938	106,427	110,915
City type					
Central	4	106,940	101,938	106,427	110,915
City clerk					
Total	5	79,896	73,639	74,521	76,648
City type					
Central	5	79,896	73,639	74,521	76,648
Form of government					
Mayor-council	3	83,065	...	74,521	...
Chief financial officer					
Total	5	93,337	86,590	90,000	100,900
City type					
Central	5	93,337	86,590	90,000	100,900
Form of government					
Mayor-council	3	98,545	...	100,900	...
Director of economic development					
Total	3	87,331	...	90,000	...
City type					
Central	3	87,331	...	90,000	...
Treasurer					
Total	4	79,337	70,000	74,094	78,187
City type					
Central	4	79,337	70,000	74,094	78,187
Form of government					
Mayor-council	3	79,721	...	70,000	...
Director of public works					
Total	4	99,152	97,117	99,009	100,900
City type					
Central	4	99,152	97,117	99,009	100,900
Engineer					
Total	4	92,673	75,171	84,609	94,046
City type					
Central	4	92,673	75,171	84,609	94,046
Form of government					
Mayor-council	3	98,507	...	94,046	...
Police chief					
Total	6	110,731	99,054	105,165	110,000
City type					
Central	6	110,731	99,054	105,165	110,000
Form of government					
Mayor-council	4	113,975	100,900	105,450	110,000
Fire chief					
Total	6	108,720	85,000	103,464	110,000
City type					
Central	6	108,720	85,000	103,464	110,000
Form of government					
Mayor-council	4	111,348	85,000	97,500	110,000
Planning director					
Total	6	101,697	85,000	98,293	100,900
City type					
Central	6	101,697	85,000	98,293	100,900
Form of government					
Mayor-council	4	107,177	97,806	99,353	100,900
Personnel director					
Total	6	89,198	77,150	83,300	96,429
City type					
Central	6	89,198	77,150	83,300	96,429
Form of government					
Mayor-council	4	90,402	82,600	83,300	84,000

Table 1/4   SALARIES OF MUNICIPAL OFFICIALS: 1 JULY 1994
continued

Title of official	No. cities reporting	Mean ($)	First quartile ($)	Median ($)	Third quartile ($)
Over 1,000,000 continued					
Risk manager					
Total	4	67,240	67,548	69,886	72,224
City type					
Central	4	67,240	67,548	69,886	72,224
Director of parks and recreation					
Total	5	97,478	86,590	93,680	95,000
City type					
Central	5	97,478	86,590	93,680	95,000
Form of government					
Mayor-council	3	102,373	...	95,000	...
Librarian					
Total	6	89,701	82,014	85,410	93,450
City type					
Central	6	89,701	82,014	85,410	93,450
Form of government					
Mayor-council	4	94,736	86,720	90,085	93,450
Director of information services					
Total	5	96,667	77,700	85,163	109,265
City type					
Central	5	96,667	77,700	85,163	109,265
Form of government					
Mayor-council	4	99,543	77,700	93,483	109,265
Purchasing director					
Total	6	76,843	68,300	69,528	70,924
City type					
Central	6	76,843	68,300	69,528	70,924
Form of government					
Mayor-council	4	84,482	70,000	70,462	70,924
500,000–1,000,000					
Mayor					
Total	10	82,693	60,000	92,155	100,000
Geographic region					
North Central	3	95,347	...	93,600	...
South	4	65,641	60,000	67,500	75,000
West	3	92,775	...	100,000	...
City type					
Central	10	82,693	60,000	92,155	100,000
Form of government					
Mayor-council	9	87,475	75,000	93,600	100,000
Chief appointed administrator					
Total	7	90,400	79,500	85,500	94,497
Geographic region					
North Central	3	77,672	...	79,500	...
South	3	87,422	...	85,500	...
City type					
Central	7	90,400	79,500	85,500	94,497
Form of government					
Mayor-council	7	90,400	79,500	85,500	94,497
City clerk					
Total	8	70,692	53,957	73,638	75,712
Geographic region					
South	3	57,408	...	53,957	...
West	3	92,312	...	93,677	...
City type					
Central	8	70,692	53,957	73,638	75,712
Form of government					
Mayor-council	6	66,025	42,555	63,198	74,836
Chief financial officer					
Total	11	85,601	70,000	77,662	106,101
Geographic region					
North Central	3	78,453	...	73,000	...
South	5	78,794	68,049	77,662	83,953
West	3	104,093	...	106,101	...
City type					
Central	11	85,601	70,000	77,662	106,101
Form of government					
Mayor-council	9	83,506	70,000	76,095	92,360
Director of economic development					
Total	8	75,813	70,000	73,385	86,202
Geographic region					
North Central	3	77,067	...	75,000	...
South	4	69,432	65,099	68,435	71,770
City type					
Central	8	75,813	70,000	73,385	86,202
Form of government					
Mayor-council	6	70,333	65,099	70,885	75,000

Title of official	No. cities reporting	Mean ($)	First quartile ($)	Median ($)	Third quartile ($)
500,000–1,000,000 continued					
Treasurer					
Total	9	75,404	59,038	71,770	84,400
Geographic region					
South	5	66,038	53,957	66,737	71,770
City type					
Central	9	75,404	59,038	71,770	84,400
Form of government					
Mayor-council	7	77,739	59,038	71,770	92,360
Director of public works					
Total	10	87,124	73,913	76,925	94,100
Geographic region					
North Central	3	77,398	...	73,095	...
South	4	79,586	75,000	76,377	77,754
West	3	106,901	...	110,453	...
City type					
Central	10	87,124	73,913	76,925	94,100
Form of government					
Mayor-council	8	83,639	73,913	75,548	77,754
Engineer					
Total	8	75,850	69,789	70,784	85,575
Geographic region					
North Central	3	62,526	...	65,000	...
South	3	70,452	...	69,798	...
City type					
Central	8	75,850	69,789	70,784	85,575
Form of government					
Mayor-council	6	73,983	65,000	70,780	85,575
Police chief					
Total	10	91,710	76,095	86,991	106,000
Geographic region					
North Central	3	81,880	...	76,960	...
South	4	88,251	76,591	86,807	97,022
West	3	106,154	...	118,156	...
City type					
Central	10	91,710	76,095	86,991	106,000
Form of government					
Mayor-council	8	87,741	76,095	76,776	101,730
Fire chief					
Total	11	87,075	73,159	76,680	101,730
Geographic region					
North Central	3	80,613	...	73,159	...
South	5	80,477	76,591	76,680	85,266
West	3	104,534	...	113,296	...
City type					
Central	11	87,075	73,159	76,680	101,730
Form of government					
Mayor-council	9	84,362	73,159	76,591	95,000
Planning director					
Total	10	76,935	65,495	75,781	80,871
Geographic region					
North Central	3	68,781	...	67,473	...
South	4	68,693	65,495	70,481	75,467
West	3	96,077	...	93,982	...
City type					
Central	10	76,935	65,495	75,781	80,871
Form of government					
Mayor-council	8	76,234	67,473	75,781	76,800
Personnel director					
Total	11	78,289	59,690	77,662	88,954
Geographic region					
North Central	3	65,548	...	59,690	...
South	5	76,251	73,883	77,662	83,953
West	3	94,425	...	102,624	...
City type					
Central	11	78,289	59,690	77,662	88,954
Form of government					
Mayor-council	9	74,955	59,690	76,095	87,200
Risk manager					
Total	7	53,723	41,600	57,064	61,850
Geographic region					
North Central	3	46,160	...	41,600	...
South	3	57,374	...	60,466	...
City type					
Central	7	53,723	41,600	57,064	61,850
Form of government					
Mayor-council	5	50,027	41,600	49,807	57,064
Director of parks and recreation					
Total	10	80,623	71,770	74,392	84,552

Table 1/4   SALARIES OF MUNICIPAL OFFICIALS: 1 JULY 1994
continued

Title of official	No. cities reporting	Mean ($)	First quartile ($)	Median ($)	Third quartile ($)
500,000–1,000,000 continued					
Geographic region					
South	5	74,526	71,770	72,500	73,883
West	3	97,901	...	107,167	...
City type					
Central	10	80,623	71,770	74,392	84,552
Form of government					
Mayor-council	8	76,405	71,770	73,192	74,900
Superintendent of parks					
Total	5	62,612	56,000	62,492	65,900
Geographic region					
South	3	56,464	...	62,492	...
City type					
Central	5	62,612	56,000	62,492	65,900
Form of government					
Mayor-council	4	62,643	56,000	60,950	65,900
Director of recreation					
Total	5	60,073	48,195	62,492	62,700
Geographic region					
South	3	54,833	...	62,492	...
City type					
Central	5	60,073	48,195	62,492	62,700
Form of government					
Mayor-council	4	59,468	48,195	55,448	62,700
Librarian					
Total	7	80,703	71,938	79,340	88,700
Geographic region					
South	3	78,926	...	76,140	...
West	3	82,935	...	88,220	...
City type					
Central	7	80,703	71,938	79,340	88,700
Form of government					
Mayor-council	5	80,112	71,938	79,340	88,700
Director of information services					
Total	8	84,163	75,467	80,987	86,707
Geographic region					
South	4	80,454	75,467	80,673	85,878
City type					
Central	8	84,163	75,467	80,987	86,707
Form of government					
Mayor-council	7	83,918	71,770	76,095	88,700
Purchasing director					
Total	9	69,296	58,000	62,150	75,886
Geographic region					
North Central	3	56,049	...	55,226	...
South	4	69,395	60,872	66,541	72,209
City type					
Central	9	69,296	58,000	62,150	75,886
Form of government					
Mayor-council	7	67,939	55,226	60,872	86,500
250,000–499,999					
Mayor					
Total	23	54,677	19,200	57,270	75,000
Geographic region					
Northeast	3	86,376	...	79,380	...
North Central	6	61,119	53,029	63,952	75,000
South	8	51,075	14,800	52,503	73,411
West	6	37,189	19,200	33,993	57,270
City type					
Central	23	54,677	19,200	57,270	75,000
Form of government					
Mayor-council	11	78,270	70,000	74,313	97,266
Council-manager	11	29,237	11,100	24,000	53,029
City manager					
Total	13	118,459	110,293	118,560	125,000
Geographic region					
North Central	3	123,868	...	127,104	...
South	4	117,680	115,680	120,340	125,000
West	6	116,274	110,293	118,495	120,000
City type					
Central	13	118,459	110,293	118,560	125,000
Form of government					
Council-manager	12	118,052	110,293	118,495	125,000
Chief appointed administrator					
Total	9	88,324	77,040	92,497	96,678
Geographic region					
North Central	3	86,251	...	92,497	...
South	4	88,278	79,890	88,284	96,678

Title of official	No. cities reporting	Mean ($)	First quartile ($)	Median ($)	Third quartile ($)
250,000–499,999 continued					
City type					
Central	9	88,324	77,040	92,497	96,678
Form of government					
Mayor-council	8	90,615	79,890	94,377	96,678
Asst. city mgr./asst. CAO					
Total	15	85,866	79,582	87,800	97,760
Geographic region					
North Central	4	80,194	79,582	80,274	80,965
South	5	83,856	79,890	87,800	97,760
West	5	93,997	90,000	90,000	94,883
City type					
Central	15	85,866	79,582	87,800	97,760
Form of government					
Mayor-council	5	79,866	77,949	79,890	80,965
Council-manager	9	92,074	87,800	90,000	97,760
City clerk					
Total	20	59,862	51,350	60,111	65,374
Geographic region					
North Central	5	56,482	59,568	61,800	63,736
South	6	59,012	56,472	59,777	65,374
West	7	59,735	46,010	58,300	70,086
City type					
Central	20	59,862	51,350	60,111	65,374
Form of government					
Mayor-council	7	62,651	47,848	60,653	74,188
Council-manager	12	57,849	56,472	59,234	65,374
Chief financial officer					
Total	21	81,216	73,602	85,214	87,681
Geographic region					
North Central	6	81,594	73,602	80,106	88,536
South	6	82,750	65,600	87,193	93,654
West	7	79,704	72,000	85,214	86,390
City type					
Central	21	81,216	73,602	85,214	87,681
Form of government					
Mayor-council	8	78,150	73,602	79,769	85,712
Council-manager	12	83,820	77,266	85,802	88,536
Director of economic development					
Total	16	70,608	68,504	70,557	73,653
Geographic region					
Northeast	3	68,733	...	65,690	...
North Central	3	78,196	...	70,000	...
South	6	66,271	56,035	69,901	73,653
West	4	72,830	71,114	71,619	72,124
City type					
Central	16	70,608	68,504	70,557	73,653
Form of government					
Mayor-council	8	68,577	65,690	70,314	73,653
Council-manager	7	73,016	69,096	71,114	78,984
Treasurer					
Total	18	59,515	49,497	60,990	66,659
Geographic region					
North Central	6	59,216	55,596	58,353	61,335
South	6	55,890	46,296	56,038	64,147
West	5	67,215	61,099	67,330	67,680
City type					
Central	18	59,515	49,497	60,990	66,659
Form of government					
Mayor-council	6	54,126	46,296	52,619	61,335
Council-manager	11	62,865	55,596	62,662	67,680
Director of public works					
Total	18	84,410	72,704	84,347	93,059
Geographic region					
North Central	6	83,972	72,704	83,250	94,430
South	4	92,740	85,259	89,159	93,059
West	6	84,744	77,869	86,718	91,151
City type					
Central	18	84,410	72,704	84,347	93,059
Form of government					
Mayor-council	9	83,019	71,944	72,852	94,250
Council-manager	8	87,489	83,435	89,357	91,151
Engineer					
Total	16	72,492	69,746	72,492	79,884
Geographic region					
North Central	3	79,958	...	83,015	...

Table 1/4 SALARIES OF MUNICIPAL OFFICIALS: 1 JULY 1994
continued

Title of official	No. cities reporting	Mean ($)	First quartile ($)	Median ($)	Third quartile ($)
250,000–499,999 continued					
South	6	74,780	70,990	75,348	80,540
West	5	68,858	63,896	70,200	72,132
City type					
Central	16	72,492	69,746	72,492	79,884
Form of government					
Mayor-council	6	68,347	57,220	65,515	80,540
Council-manager	10	74,979	70,200	73,116	79,884
Police chief					
Total	21	84,123	73,095	82,904	95,516
Geographic region					
Northeast	3	81,606	. . .	81,971	. . .
North Central	6	80,396	72,796	77,068	89,000
South	8	82,606	73,937	83,957	91,000
West	4	94,638	92,000	96,371	100,741
City type					
Central	21	84,123	73,095	82,904	95,516
Form of government					
Mayor-council	9	77,915	67,769	81,040	82,904
Council-manager	11	90,487	80,881	92,000	97,614
Fire chief					
Total	24	79,229	70,000	78,063	87,681
Geographic region					
Northeast	3	77,674	. . .	78,008	. . .
North Central	6	76,740	70,000	75,834	80,520
South	8	79,300	71,600	79,370	85,259
West	7	81,949	68,692	78,280	94,008
City type					
Central	24	79,229	70,000	78,063	87,681
Form of government					
Mayor-council	11	74,926	68,515	73,551	81,512
Council-manager	12	83,943	77,227	84,760	90,582
Planning director					
Total	20	70,781	59,202	69,844	79,295
Geographic region					
Northeast	3	57,408	. . .	55,638	. . .
North Central	5	67,111	60,697	69,588	71,595
South	6	73,975	59,202	70,129	92,507
West	6	77,332	66,539	79,788	82,108
City type					
Central	20	70,781	59,202	69,844	79,295
Form of government					
Mayor-council	8	62,480	56,472	59,438	67,332
Council-manager	11	78,207	69,588	78,177	92,507
Personnel director					
Total	21	72,711	64,281	72,628	81,700
Geographic region					
Northeast	3	60,834	. . .	64,281	. . .
North Central	5	74,415	62,828	80,621	83,912
South	7	74,512	66,372	72,628	81,700
West	6	75,128	68,182	74,728	85,184
City type					
Central	21	72,711	64,281	72,628	81,700
Form of government					
Mayor-council	10	70,208	64,281	67,716	80,621
Council-manager	10	76,835	68,182	78,058	85,184
Risk manager					
Total	17	57,781	53,669	59,220	62,629
Geographic region					
North Central	4	56,262	53,006	56,936	60,865
South	6	60,048	53,669	61,337	63,386
West	5	60,071	58,341	59,220	62,160
City type					
Central	17	57,781	53,669	59,220	62,629
Form of government					
Mayor-council	6	58,635	57,139	60,455	64,147
Council-manager	10	58,517	53,669	58,781	62,629
Director of parks and recreation					
Total	17	77,288	70,000	81,982	85,259
Geographic region					
North Central	4	75,276	71,754	72,123	72,491
South	6	79,160	74,003	82,337	85,259
West	5	82,146	83,280	84,752	85,670
City type					
Central	17	77,288	70,000	81,982	85,259
Form of government					
Mayor-council	7	75,211	67,332	74,003	85,259

Title of official	No. cities reporting	Mean ($)	First quartile ($)	Median ($)	Third quartile ($)
250,000–499,999 continued					
Council-manager	9	79,936	72,491	83,280	87,027
Superintendent of parks					
Total	16	60,785	54,244	55,620	63,240
Geographic region					
North Central	5	71,436	57,384	69,274	86,052
South	4	57,163	54,244	54,922	55,600
West	5	55,938	55,307	55,432	56,212
City type					
Central	16	60,785	54,244	55,620	63,240
Form of government					
Mayor-council	8	61,602	55,432	55,926	69,274
Council-manager	8	59,968	54,244	55,454	57,384
Director of recreation					
Total	16	59,104	52,042	57,842	64,932
Geographic region					
North Central	6	66,626	55,600	65,493	70,548
South	4	55,596	51,300	55,671	60,041
West	4	55,766	56,152	56,182	56,212
City type					
Central	16	59,104	52,042	57,842	64,932
Form of government					
Mayor-council	8	58,044	56,212	60,931	66,054
Council-manager	7	60,815	51,300	56,152	64,932
Librarian					
Total	10	74,817	72,145	75,613	85,184
Geographic region					
South	5	69,286	58,200	72,197	78,383
West	3	81,000	. . .	85,184	. . .
City type					
Central	10	74,817	72,145	75,613	85,184
Form of government					
Mayor-council	4	77,306	80,472	83,071	85,670
Council-manager	6	73,159	72,145	72,520	78,383
Director of information services					
Total	20	70,307	62,280	70,496	81,224
Geographic region					
North Central	6	66,391	55,000	68,212	79,808
South	6	73,856	63,063	75,362	84,563
West	6	74,344	62,280	75,337	85,184
City type					
Central	20	70,307	62,280	70,496	81,224
Form of government					
Mayor-council	10	71,502	63,063	74,070	82,000
Council-manager	9	70,680	62,280	69,500	79,808
Purchasing director					
Total	21	59,433	51,550	59,298	65,746
Geographic region					
Northeast	3	52,664	. . .	54,650	. . .
North Central	6	58,989	50,004	58,649	65,746
South	6	58,997	46,259	63,114	71,531
West	6	63,696	59,111	63,604	64,667
City type					
Central	21	59,433	51,550	59,298	65,746
Form of government					
Mayor-council	9	57,306	54,650	59,298	64,147
Council-manager	11	61,302	50,004	63,060	72,030
100,000–249,999					
Mayor					
Total	87	37,368	11,003	21,755	67,500
Geographic region					
Northeast	11	66,664	48,000	67,650	90,000
North Central	20	49,532	22,000	58,385	69,740
South	26	35,962	12,000	17,593	71,980
West	30	19,736	7,920	12,158	21,000
City type					
Central	62	45,444	15,000	47,596	70,309
Suburban	25	17,339	7,560	9,600	14,893
Form of government					
Mayor-council	34	68,329	57,309	70,025	84,000
Council-manager	50	14,483	7,800	12,158	18,000
Commission	3	67,897	. . .	56,500	. . .
City manager					
Total	58	110,152	99,782	110,308	121,032
Geographic region					
North Central	9	97,291	92,913	97,050	103,168
South	19	107,995	99,782	106,922	117,477

Table 1/4 SALARIES OF MUNICIPAL OFFICIALS: 1 JULY 1994
continued

Title of official	No. cities reporting	Distribution of 1994 salaries			
		Mean ($)	First quartile ($)	Median ($)	Third quartile ($)
100,000–249,999 continued					
West	29	118,279	111,407	120,000	127,656
City type					
Central	33	103,035	95,390	106,056	111,407
Suburban	25	119,547	111,715	120,900	128,927
Form of government					
Council-manager	56	110,226	100,284	110,308	121,032
Chief appointed administrator					
Total	23	70,945	54,349	66,504	84,000
Geographic region					
Northeast	6	63,976	54,349	61,760	77,188
North Central	6	57,486	52,584	59,572	66,300
South	7	83,412	73,236	83,740	97,000
West	4	79,767	66,504	76,752	87,000
City type					
Central	23	70,945	54,349	66,504	84,000
Form of government					
Mayor-council	22	69,760	54,349	66,402	83,740
Asst. city mgr./asst. CAO					
Total	62	83,333	68,527	85,096	95,861
Geographic region					
Northeast	6	59,651	51,242	55,443	68,527
North Central	10	65,299	53,196	66,301	80,790
South	19	85,889	78,360	87,495	92,674
West	27	93,478	80,000	95,856	108,461
City type					
Central	40	77,807	67,944	81,122	90,542
Suburban	22	93,382	79,869	97,510	108,658
Form of government					
Mayor-council	12	65,250	52,584	59,698	80,000
Council-manager	50	87,673	77,628	88,810	97,944
City clerk					
Total	85	54,764	45,423	55,972	64,266
Geographic region					
Northeast	11	51,050	40,000	55,972	61,188
North Central	20	50,437	44,039	48,632	61,500
South	27	51,675	42,338	50,856	61,298
West	27	62,572	56,386	62,379	69,312
City type					
Central	62	52,097	42,338	51,747	62,379
Suburban	23	61,954	57,032	61,344	68,280
Form of government					
Mayor-council	30	51,762	41,832	50,544	61,500
Council-manager	52	56,915	50,856	58,931	66,057
Commission	3	47,502	. . .	44,944	. . .
Chief financial officer					
Total	83	76,621	69,147	77,124	83,471
Geographic region					
Northeast	9	67,132	56,000	64,514	77,500
North Central	21	69,009	62,250	70,595	74,175
South	25	77,325	70,620	76,972	83,329
West	28	84,750	79,044	81,577	93,371
City type					
Central	60	73,913	67,095	74,088	80,780
Suburban	23	83,683	72,600	82,855	94,524
Form of government					
Mayor-council	30	69,173	57,179	69,408	77,500
Council-manager	50	81,347	72,101	79,735	91,581
Commission	3	72,324	. . .	73,237	. . .
Director of economic development					
Total	64	69,918	59,008	69,492	78,909
Geographic region					
Northeast	9	58,343	51,000	59,249	65,000
North Central	14	64,679	58,870	66,114	70,471
South	20	65,465	54,392	66,102	75,396
West	21	82,613	77,625	82,100	93,324
City type					
Central	48	66,034	54,392	65,219	73,757
Suburban	16	81,571	75,396	78,906	86,362
Form of government					
Mayor-council	28	63,420	51,012	60,004	71,115
Council-manager	35	75,279	66,851	75,396	83,866
Treasurer					
Total	53	57,906	49,795	60,042	66,005
Geographic region					
Northeast	8	56,760	50,745	62,016	64,514
North Central	13	56,167	49,795	57,641	60,441
South	16	57,533	49,816	55,626	64,583
West	16	60,266	58,200	65,156	69,480

Title of official	No. cities reporting	Distribution of 1994 salaries			
		Mean ($)	First quartile ($)	Median ($)	Third quartile ($)
100,000–249,999 continued					
City type					
Central	43	57,846	49,260	58,200	67,207
Suburban	10	58,167	52,500	60,300	65,187
Form of government					
Mayor-council	21	55,461	46,917	58,200	65,810
Council-manager	30	60,060	49,816	60,441	69,480
Director of public works					
Total	75	76,402	66,109	76,735	89,184
Geographic region					
Northeast	8	59,573	48,129	53,098	69,274
North Central	18	67,327	63,105	68,744	72,800
South	24	72,789	68,000	76,099	83,554
West	25	91,790	84,000	91,581	97,770
City type					
Central	57	72,287	63,203	74,580	83,554
Suburban	18	89,431	82,308	92,842	98,040
Form of government					
Mayor-council	29	67,625	55,196	68,000	77,500
Council-manager	44	82,567	75,372	83,220	94,416
Engineer					
Total	75	69,675	60,369	68,435	75,828
Geographic region					
Northeast	8	65,041	56,861	64,547	72,868
North Central	18	65,863	58,710	64,988	73,528
South	28	66,775	58,344	64,425	75,000
West	21	78,574	72,592	75,828	84,540
City type					
Central	57	66,469	58,212	65,000	74,376
Suburban	18	79,827	71,633	80,364	86,736
Form of government					
Mayor-council	28	64,467	57,957	63,700	68,994
Council-manager	44	73,027	63,849	74,271	82,399
Commission	3	69,118	. . .	73,528	. . .
Police chief					
Total	79	80,640	70,000	80,000	92,220
Geographic region					
Northeast	9	77,035	68,268	80,000	83,471
North Central	19	67,686	65,134	70,000	73,300
South	26	79,236	71,000	79,530	88,000
West	25	93,242	86,266	93,000	100,487
City type					
Central	60	76,904	69,720	77,010	88,000
Suburban	19	92,438	80,000	94,103	104,686
Form of government					
Mayor-council	30	72,240	65,208	72,404	80,434
Council-manager	46	86,653	75,002	86,198	98,000
Commission	3	72,430	. . .	65,134	. . .
Fire chief					
Total	79	75,147	65,520	74,439	85,008
Geographic region					
Northeast	9	76,418	70,180	75,000	83,471
North Central	19	64,314	60,936	65,134	71,508
South	29	72,064	65,898	71,584	79,360
West	22	88,047	80,211	89,010	98,100
City type					
Central	63	72,369	65,134	71,584	81,200
Suburban	16	86,087	79,653	89,038	94,212
Form of government					
Mayor-council	30	68,242	59,400	68,999	75,000
Council-manager	46	79,997	70,702	79,927	88,452
Commission	3	69,830	. . .	65,134	. . .
Planning director					
Total	69	72,520	62,880	72,800	82,351
Geographic region					
Northeast	7	69,237	57,000	69,274	77,855
North Central	16	63,194	58,906	64,920	67,352
South	25	69,948	62,000	71,241	79,360
West	21	83,782	77,628	82,627	90,612
City type					
Central	50	68,682	59,000	70,894	77,855
Suburban	19	82,620	66,893	86,397	94,103
Form of government					
Mayor-council	21	66,639	57,470	67,620	72,868
Council-manager	45	75,538	63,413	77,628	83,054
Commission	3	68,425	. . .	69,894	. . .
Personnel director					
Total	82	67,958	57,470	68,265	78,132
Geographic region					
Northeast	8	57,093	44,309	51,377	68,577

Table 1/4   SALARIES OF MUNICIPAL OFFICIALS: 1 JULY 1994
continued

Title of official	No. cities reporting	Mean ($)	First quartile ($)	Median ($)	Third quartile ($)
100,000–249,999 continued					
North Central	20	58,869	53,800	59,597	65,208
South	28	66,310	59,842	67,418	72,747
West	26	80,068	71,272	80,554	87,650
City type					
Central	61	63,955	54,939	65,541	72,260
Suburban	21	79,587	71,476	82,919	88,952
Form of government					
Mayor-council	28	60,333	50,524	58,591	68,577
Council-manager	51	72,353	64,510	71,272	81,288
Commission	3	64,412	...	63,156	...
Risk manager					
Total	48	51,730	43,538	52,113	59,338
Geographic region					
Northeast	3	45,358	...	40,951	...
North Central	13	44,815	40,622	43,992	51,771
South	16	48,485	40,456	50,132	56,000
West	16	61,787	58,440	60,647	66,408
City type					
Central	36	50,076	40,951	51,504	58,780
Suburban	12	56,690	52,117	57,981	64,476
Form of government					
Mayor-council	14	44,376	33,142	40,704	52,000
Council-manager	32	55,354	51,236	57,126	60,789
Director of parks and recreation					
Total	61	71,479	62,047	71,136	79,950
Geographic region					
Northeast	6	66,009	51,000	63,598	83,471
North Central	14	63,535	57,685	63,753	70,880
South	26	70,677	66,768	70,442	78,715
West	15	82,472	77,628	84,996	90,852
City type					
Central	47	68,197	58,000	69,792	74,166
Suburban	14	82,499	78,715	83,812	90,852
Form of government					
Mayor-council	20	66,192	57,685	67,449	73,470
Council-manager	38	74,781	69,758	73,299	84,996
Commission	3	64,909	...	63,156	...
Superintendent of parks					
Total	50	54,581	48,308	55,585	61,380
Geographic region					
Northeast	4	44,942	43,968	46,555	49,142
North Central	11	52,371	43,992	50,690	61,339
South	20	51,814	46,171	52,922	57,552
West	15	62,460	58,464	61,618	66,960
City type					
Central	36	51,973	46,171	51,745	58,464
Suburban	14	61,287	57,552	61,390	67,716
Form of government					
Mayor-council	13	51,518	48,399	51,355	58,464
Council-manager	34	55,676	48,305	56,241	63,900
Commission	3	55,437	...	58,097	...
Director of recreation					
Total	43	59,022	50,901	56,436	67,716
Geographic region					
Northeast	7	47,584	41,959	44,964	51,127
North Central	7	54,763	50,901	55,984	57,334
South	14	55,171	46,468	55,015	57,740
West	15	69,942	61,344	68,170	72,766
City type					
Central	32	56,199	46,791	55,509	61,380
Suburban	11	67,235	57,459	67,716	72,766
Form of government					
Mayor-council	14	52,519	45,866	52,937	56,436
Council-manager	27	62,604	54,470	61,416	70,490
Librarian					
Total	50	67,171	58,934	65,292	76,755
Geographic region					
Northeast	5	68,745	52,020	76,045	83,471
North Central	10	61,485	59,906	60,398	67,800
South	17	61,835	54,080	61,104	65,244
West	18	74,933	67,450	76,478	82,894
City type					
Central	34	63,367	56,199	62,387	71,364
Suburban	16	75,256	67,450	78,642	85,357
Form of government					
Mayor-council	16	64,219	60,029	62,387	67,800
Council-manager	31	69,418	57,847	69,814	81,768
Commission	3	59,704	...	59,906	...

Title of official	No. cities reporting	Mean ($)	First quartile ($)	Median ($)	Third quartile ($)
100,000–249,999 continued					
Director of information services					
Total	63	66,827	59,802	66,150	75,219
Geographic region					
Northeast	7	58,530	43,956	54,465	76,188
North Central	12	61,078	56,487	60,853	62,306
South	26	67,663	61,632	69,398	75,581
West	18	72,681	64,200	72,960	81,900
City type					
Central	48	65,080	56,487	64,773	74,861
Suburban	15	72,418	63,500	71,476	78,970
Form of government					
Mayor-council	24	62,255	53,400	61,969	73,200
Council-manager	38	69,495	61,965	68,383	75,581
Purchasing director					
Total	66	54,775	46,470	56,187	60,907
Geographic region					
Northeast	7	50,826	37,416	50,000	66,530
North Central	14	50,171	43,884	49,064	53,500
South	26	53,101	45,365	54,469	59,518
West	19	61,912	57,340	60,840	63,147
City type					
Central	50	53,068	45,302	52,893	60,120
Suburban	16	60,108	56,904	60,309	62,912
Form of government					
Mayor-council	24	53,142	44,853	52,261	60,120
Council-manager	41	55,615	48,502	56,904	61,300
50,000–99,999					
Mayor					
Total	215	24,377	7,000	10,800	47,500
Geographic region					
Northeast	40	43,523	30,000	48,500	62,500
North Central	60	26,166	7,000	10,200	50,187
South	46	21,926	6,300	10,100	42,000
West	69	13,358	6,000	7,632	13,284
City type					
Central	103	28,022	7,000	15,000	51,168
Suburban	109	21,043	7,000	10,000	26,163
Independent	3	20,394	...	4,500	...
Form of government					
Mayor-council	72	50,127	44,238	54,000	65,000
Council-manager	140	10,467	6,000	7,801	12,000
City manager					
Total	160	92,957	82,085	91,377	102,996
Geographic region					
Northeast	12	84,455	65,526	87,310	93,115
North Central	38	86,012	78,372	86,476	91,713
South	42	86,111	75,000	85,378	96,000
West	68	102,567	92,004	101,910	112,520
City type					
Central	70	87,750	77,569	87,855	93,000
Suburban	88	97,193	86,735	96,105	110,000
Form of government					
Mayor-council	8	81,075	72,800	77,514	87,884
Council-manager	151	93,586	82,618	91,713	104,260
Chief appointed administrator					
Total	45	63,617	47,823	63,045	78,773
Geographic region					
Northeast	25	60,122	43,200	59,670	72,800
North Central	11	68,256	58,261	67,308	84,000
South	7	66,077	49,200	63,045	96,304
City type					
Central	26	63,092	48,944	62,523	72,800
Suburban	19	64,336	47,250	66,314	84,000
Form of government					
Mayor-council	38	59,564	47,250	61,393	72,000
Council-manager	5	86,052	72,500	84,059	104,533
Asst. city mgr./asst. CAO					
Total	132	73,463	61,464	72,525	86,136
Geographic region					
Northeast	13	57,424	38,923	58,229	62,000
North Central	34	65,332	59,382	66,723	72,161
South	27	70,554	60,253	67,834	80,476
West	58	83,178	71,434	85,756	96,559
City type					
Central	56	71,393	62,000	70,530	80,476
Suburban	74	75,262	61,464	75,000	90,756
Form of government					
Mayor-council	16	56,309	38,923	58,341	63,172

Table 1/4 continued **SALARIES OF MUNICIPAL OFFICIALS: 1 JULY 1994**

Title of official	No. cities reporting	Mean ($)	First quartile ($)	Median ($)	Third quartile ($)
50,000–99,999 continued					
Council-manager	116	75,829	64,375	74,489	87,537
City clerk					
Total	213	48,366	38,168	47,278	58,308
Geographic region					
Northeast	37	50,545	43,063	48,300	62,166
North Central	59	44,624	38,168	45,364	50,919
South	56	42,117	32,184	39,628	49,225
West	61	56,400	46,363	57,516	66,843
City type					
Central	107	43,822	34,100	42,330	50,328
Suburban	104	53,014	43,377	53,624	63,911
Form of government					
Mayor-council	61	45,061	36,870	43,445	54,000
Council-manager	149	49,737	38,923	49,225	59,844
Chief financial officer					
Total	213	66,833	58,242	66,300	76,590
Geographic region					
Northeast	37	62,959	53,674	62,457	71,606
North Central	59	63,210	57,710	64,522	70,658
South	54	61,336	54,662	60,196	67,424
West	63	77,213	68,004	78,630	87,001
City type					
Central	108	62,524	55,068	63,244	69,000
Suburban	102	71,297	60,000	70,579	82,972
Independent	3	70,141	...	73,464	...
Form of government					
Mayor-council	62	58,901	49,867	58,466	67,015
Council-manager	148	69,878	60,476	68,107	79,188
Director of economic development					
Total	112	62,072	50,440	60,986	73,848
Geographic region					
Northeast	23	55,849	46,899	53,180	60,000
North Central	31	58,461	49,816	58,760	65,246
South	24	52,577	42,000	53,071	62,124
West	34	76,277	64,416	79,658	85,127
City type					
Central	53	55,210	45,863	56,468	62,642
Suburban	58	68,317	53,561	65,604	83,472
Form of government					
Mayor-council	39	51,588	45,384	51,862	57,710
Council-manager	71	67,886	59,674	66,163	82,296
Treasurer					
Total	77	47,733	41,527	49,656	56,347
Geographic region					
Northeast	18	41,219	27,100	47,301	50,204
North Central	24	47,164	44,720	49,041	52,051
South	16	46,218	37,206	46,615	52,027
West	19	55,901	50,715	57,516	73,608
City type					
Central	41	46,125	39,033	49,398	53,725
Suburban	36	49,565	42,577	50,311	58,184
Form of government					
Mayor-council	28	43,205	35,360	48,722	52,500
Council-manager	47	50,337	42,000	50,357	58,656
Director of public works					
Total	192	69,215	58,524	68,484	79,152
Geographic region					
Northeast	37	62,787	52,000	62,056	76,000
North Central	54	66,137	58,968	67,078	72,946
South	47	62,142	55,884	63,625	69,914
West	54	82,854	73,800	84,048	93,870
City type					
Central	96	64,589	57,207	65,614	73,550
Suburban	94	73,849	62,775	74,468	86,484
Form of government					
Mayor-council	56	61,081	52,000	59,374	68,042
Council-manager	132	72,526	62,899	72,384	82,307
Engineer					
Total	163	59,437	50,684	58,280	66,756
Geographic region					
Northeast	26	58,234	50,085	53,990	67,466
North Central	51	57,697	51,140	57,364	65,146
South	50	54,409	46,966	56,218	61,200
West	36	69,753	57,816	70,512	78,780
City type					
Central	95	54,555	48,178	55,328	61,200
Suburban	65	66,307	56,739	65,520	73,520
Independent	3	65,179	...	71,167	...

Title of official	No. cities reporting	Mean ($)	First quartile ($)	Median ($)	Third quartile ($)
50,000–99,999 continued					
Form of government					
Mayor-council	48	54,254	45,400	51,430	63,972
Council-manager	112	61,617	55,200	60,086	67,642
Police chief					
Total	201	70,847	60,900	67,746	80,002
Geographic region					
Northeast	36	69,997	60,807	68,060	79,846
North Central	62	65,974	60,779	64,402	72,413
South	52	63,722	57,000	63,728	68,846
West	51	84,637	72,888	86,486	96,444
City type					
Central	106	65,134	58,516	63,728	70,930
Suburban	93	77,398	65,545	75,000	87,634
Form of government					
Mayor-council	60	63,904	57,383	62,928	70,320
Council-manager	137	73,681	62,770	70,241	84,552
Fire chief					
Total	185	65,898	55,986	63,760	74,471
Geographic region					
Northeast	32	66,157	55,708	67,154	77,291
North Central	56	61,936	57,991	62,015	66,622
South	54	58,170	49,770	57,377	63,937
West	43	80,573	70,300	82,176	93,468
City type					
Central	105	60,457	52,416	60,000	66,622
Suburban	78	73,319	62,472	71,765	84,996
Form of government					
Mayor-council	57	59,955	51,361	60,109	67,366
Council-manager	124	68,350	57,844	65,358	77,497
Planning director					
Total	156	59,814	49,032	58,766	69,588
Geographic region					
Northeast	25	53,308	44,000	51,889	62,830
North Central	46	55,536	47,510	55,947	61,963
South	44	55,150	48,297	54,043	63,173
West	41	73,584	65,000	73,367	80,352
City type					
Central	86	56,140	45,597	55,524	64,626
Suburban	68	64,525	54,480	62,738	73,367
Form of government					
Mayor-council	43	51,472	40,863	50,000	58,318
Council-manager	109	63,109	52,980	62,500	72,405
Personnel director					
Total	178	57,316	48,696	56,689	64,418
Geographic region					
Northeast	26	52,828	43,607	49,472	62,507
North Central	52	56,032	51,260	56,786	61,404
South	53	51,842	44,772	52,200	60,153
West	47	67,392	57,100	65,383	76,272
City type					
Central	99	54,152	47,693	54,005	60,900
Suburban	77	61,323	51,043	61,404	69,408
Form of government					
Mayor-council	50	50,127	43,389	51,149	57,710
Council-manager	124	60,133	51,740	59,632	66,576
Risk manager					
Total	102	47,379	39,000	45,793	55,356
Geographic region					
Northeast	9	49,445	40,000	54,314	57,030
North Central	25	43,280	38,510	44,207	47,278
South	39	44,388	37,575	42,432	52,728
West	29	54,295	46,600	55,308	63,094
City type					
Central	66	44,748	37,910	43,784	52,166
Suburban	35	52,149	40,955	54,314	61,200
Form of government					
Mayor-council	20	42,766	37,640	39,703	43,012
Council-manager	80	48,381	39,707	47,072	56,040
Director of parks and recreation					
Total	158	59,745	49,426	57,703	70,740
Geographic region					
Northeast	26	50,036	40,000	48,032	55,724
North Central	40	57,978	50,659	57,732	65,588
South	46	52,899	47,330	52,551	60,008
West	46	73,616	62,987	75,921	84,059
City type					
Central	87	55,632	48,568	54,600	62,400
Suburban	69	64,756	52,478	67,464	76,644

Table 1/4   SALARIES OF MUNICIPAL OFFICIALS: 1 JULY 1994
continued

Title of official	No. cities reporting	Distribution of 1994 salaries			
		Mean ($)	First quartile ($)	Median ($)	Third quartile ($)
50,000–99,999 continued					
Form of government					
Mayor-council	46	50,277	42,000	49,397	57,264
Council-manager	110	63,784	53,518	62,212	73,520
Superintendent of parks					
Total	122	46,597	37,560	45,200	54,372
Geographic region					
Northeast	19	42,200	33,000	40,863	52,957
North Central	36	46,931	41,932	46,081	51,626
South	34	38,724	33,551	37,334	45,986
West	33	56,874	48,960	58,007	64,205
City type					
Central	71	43,358	35,932	41,932	49,129
Suburban	49	51,419	42,723	52,620	59,840
Form of government					
Mayor-council	32	42,590	36,344	40,944	47,168
Council-manager	87	48,183	37,908	47,250	56,745
Director of recreation					
Total	87	48,652	40,269	46,738	55,458
Geographic region					
Northeast	15	46,052	38,826	46,000	55,298
North Central	29	47,640	42,669	46,808	51,675
South	22	41,192	36,240	42,332	45,986
West	21	59,720	52,620	59,096	65,988
City type					
Central	53	45,384	38,690	44,096	51,196
Suburban	32	54,372	46,518	52,310	58,906
Form of government					
Mayor-council	23	46,332	37,268	45,384	47,500
Council-manager	60	49,398	42,367	49,446	55,458
Librarian					
Total	96	56,441	48,565	54,953	61,532
Geographic region					
Northeast	27	55,507	48,520	54,577	63,454
North Central	25	56,703	53,045	55,952	60,740
South	23	48,237	45,675	49,192	53,749
West	21	66,317	55,716	64,619	80,540
City type					
Central	55	53,255	47,314	53,534	58,011
Suburban	40	61,066	52,872	57,801	68,052
Form of government					
Mayor-council	32	52,803	47,314	53,539	58,000
Council-manager	61	58,339	49,192	56,014	64,619
Director of information services					
Total	146	54,516	47,288	54,153	60,420
Geographic region					
Northeast	26	54,866	45,000	53,791	62,423
North Central	38	51,547	47,257	51,775	55,806
South	45	50,829	45,012	51,890	56,299
West	37	61,804	55,008	60,144	68,808
City type					
Central	86	53,172	47,288	53,133	58,407
Suburban	57	56,414	47,400	55,057	63,336
Independent	3	56,975	...	61,128	...
Form of government					
Mayor-council	42	50,411	45,107	49,643	55,806
Council-manager	100	56,055	50,700	55,228	62,540
Purchasing director					
Total	134	46,776	39,598	47,066	53,065
Geographic region					
Northeast	29	47,324	37,456	48,187	56,500
North Central	35	46,129	42,744	47,569	51,605
South	43	43,542	36,672	44,061	51,948
West	27	52,178	45,504	49,694	60,144
City type					
Central	82	45,000	37,600	45,239	52,010
Suburban	50	49,796	45,318	48,469	56,500
Form of government					
Mayor-council	41	42,555	33,570	44,704	49,120
Council-manager	90	48,519	42,744	47,619	54,060
25,000–49,999					
Mayor					
Total	423	16,271	4,200	7,500	15,000
Geographic region					
Northeast	97	19,814	3,500	8,000	38,000
North Central	122	18,667	5,400	8,800	38,781
South	102	15,621	4,800	8,920	15,000
West	102	10,688	3,600	4,800	9,600

Title of official	No. cities reporting	Distribution of 1994 salaries			
		Mean ($)	First quartile ($)	Median ($)	Third quartile ($)
25,000–49,999 continued					
City type					
Central	104	23,526	6,000	12,000	45,000
Suburban	245	13,345	4,000	6,240	12,000
Independent	74	15,764	4,800	8,250	14,030
Form of government					
Mayor-council	143	35,325	12,000	41,270	52,300
Council-manager	261	6,570	3,600	5,197	8,400
Commission	7	12,265	4,000	7,406	14,000
Town meeting	5	2,900	2,000	2,000	3,000
Rep. town meeting	7	2,326	1,100	1,535	2,000
City manager					
Total	289	82,390	72,500	81,245	90,000
Geographic region					
Northeast	48	76,858	69,870	77,700	82,612
North Central	66	78,270	69,865	79,022	87,100
South	84	77,974	69,566	79,843	84,000
West	91	92,373	81,516	89,976	100,000
City type					
Central	66	77,075	70,000	78,503	83,232
Suburban	166	87,570	78,000	87,003	94,100
Independent	57	73,461	66,310	72,987	81,370
Form of government					
Mayor-council	8	77,185	72,500	76,417	78,270
Council-manager	273	82,813	72,987	81,510	90,588
Town meeting	5	72,493	69,332	72,417	75,500
Chief appointed administrator					
Total	102	64,231	50,676	66,700	78,123
Geographic region					
Northeast	43	64,209	48,000	68,250	78,123
North Central	36	60,444	47,632	64,358	70,428
South	14	67,542	58,489	66,885	79,000
West	9	74,333	67,980	78,384	82,164
City type					
Central	21	55,454	40,069	50,000	70,344
Suburban	70	67,413	59,000	68,196	80,000
Independent	11	60,740	45,000	62,525	74,000
Form of government					
Mayor-council	74	61,455	45,502	62,702	76,938
Council-manager	20	72,542	65,900	71,047	80,000
Commission	3	69,541	...	76,498	...
Rep. town meeting	5	68,881	72,280	76,000	78,123
Asst. city mgr./asst. CAO					
Total	197	59,985	48,172	57,999	69,858
Geographic region					
Northeast	34	46,885	38,775	46,216	55,442
North Central	56	53,869	47,843	54,287	59,796
South	45	58,045	49,633	58,032	65,000
West	62	74,103	61,650	72,176	83,244
City type					
Central	36	57,746	49,633	58,496	65,166
Suburban	127	62,307	50,000	58,427	72,806
Independent	34	53,687	45,295	51,462	63,190
Form of government					
Mayor-council	21	54,035	45,445	53,310	58,427
Council-manager	170	61,076	49,500	58,807	71,094
Rep. town meeting	3	67,816	...	56,470	...
City clerk					
Total	385	42,545	33,680	42,500	50,496
Geographic region					
Northeast	89	44,922	37,488	44,826	51,000
North Central	100	37,655	29,646	36,998	46,036
South	100	39,443	30,472	39,163	45,994
West	96	48,663	39,915	49,165	56,172
City type					
Central	102	38,684	31,154	37,955	45,000
Suburban	211	46,296	38,748	46,712	53,507
Independent	72	37,019	30,015	35,080	44,820
Form of government					
Mayor-council	115	39,285	29,700	39,156	47,000
Council-manager	251	43,909	34,830	44,179	51,444
Commission	7	40,299	27,664	43,659	55,855
Town meeting	5	48,704	46,870	49,360	49,846
Rep. town meeting	7	45,002	38,885	46,670	51,500
Chief financial officer					
Total	383	59,675	51,012	59,592	68,380
Geographic region					
Northeast	96	59,082	53,546	58,000	65,873

Table 1/4 **SALARIES OF MUNICIPAL OFFICIALS: 1 JULY 1994**
continued

Title of official	No. cities reporting	Distribution of 1994 salaries Mean ($)	First quartile ($)	Median ($)	Third quartile ($)
25,000–49,999 continued					
North Central	99	53,981	45,323	55,286	62,400
South	97	56,386	48,510	56,582	64,837
West	91	70,002	61,820	69,408	75,360
City type					
Central	88	54,922	45,368	54,853	62,000
Suburban	225	63,441	55,519	62,776	70,847
Independent	70	53,548	47,153	52,183	60,522
Form of government					
Mayor-council	107	53,824	42,029	53,928	62,680
Council-manager	261	62,307	53,823	61,627	69,867
Commission	4	49,643	55,860	56,595	57,330
Town meeting	5	56,900	52,045	55,138	58,600
Rep. town meeting	6	58,552	54,999	58,385	61,478
Director of economic development					
Total	142	53,770	43,416	53,585	62,680
Geographic region					
Northeast	34	53,492	46,000	55,025	60,669
North Central	43	51,517	42,179	52,250	58,049
South	39	46,812	39,711	44,115	54,954
West	26	68,299	55,949	69,690	77,856
City type					
Central	45	49,617	40,524	47,221	55,000
Suburban	78	57,116	47,100	56,308	65,948
Independent	19	49,870	40,500	52,208	55,855
Form of government					
Mayor-council	44	47,048	40,069	46,257	55,000
Council-manager	97	56,705	46,332	55,855	66,728
Treasurer					
Total	124	41,712	33,500	42,975	49,419
Geographic region					
Northeast	50	42,377	38,733	44,245	49,749
North Central	32	36,493	30,472	36,604	45,931
South	16	42,119	36,952	40,534	47,507
West	26	46,605	33,500	44,710	54,791
City type					
Central	37	40,542	36,000	40,932	46,323
Suburban	64	42,898	30,909	45,893	51,060
Independent	23	40,291	33,093	42,874	46,790
Form of government					
Mayor-council	46	39,397	33,120	41,098	49,419
Council-manager	67	42,195	30,909	42,874	49,416
Rep. town meeting	8	48,930	46,670	49,379	50,737
Director of public works					
Total	381	61,335	52,531	61,176	69,156
Geographic region					
Northeast	94	60,850	52,742	60,114	66,600
North Central	98	58,060	49,421	59,612	64,548
South	104	55,125	47,548	53,546	63,166
West	85	73,247	64,789	71,909	78,816
City type					
Central	96	55,980	47,637	55,648	63,166
Suburban	213	64,910	54,747	64,369	72,787
Independent	72	57,901	51,000	58,903	64,198
Form of government					
Mayor-council	111	57,290	47,548	55,850	64,344
Council-manager	251	62,976	53,429	62,923	71,784
Commission	7	57,606	43,659	58,806	72,830
Town meeting	4	63,781	61,431	63,216	65,000
Rep. town meeting	8	68,016	64,198	64,379	68,064
Engineer					
Total	250	53,856	46,800	53,478	60,744
Geographic region					
Northeast	60	51,850	44,894	53,374	61,400
North Central	67	51,790	46,114	52,250	56,638
South	75	52,384	45,676	52,075	57,979
West	48	61,544	54,800	60,518	68,744
City type					
Central	77	50,825	43,354	50,570	57,204
Suburban	115	56,884	50,898	57,352	64,781
Independent	58	51,873	47,008	51,666	55,889
Form of government					
Mayor-council	72	50,386	44,559	49,144	56,200
Council-manager	164	55,856	48,932	55,314	62,808
Commission	5	49,684	53,704	55,889	58,501
Rep. town meeting	7	53,703	49,089	57,137	60,604

Title of official	No. cities reporting	Distribution of 1994 salaries Mean ($)	First quartile ($)	Median ($)	Third quartile ($)
25,000–49,999 continued					
Police chief					
Total	386	62,364	52,333	60,851	69,717
Geographic region					
Northeast	97	66,235	55,440	64,198	75,682
North Central	107	57,098	49,280	57,324	64,369
South	108	56,352	49,088	55,366	64,296
West	74	73,677	62,600	71,104	83,201
City type					
Central	106	56,364	49,280	54,845	63,188
Suburban	203	68,396	58,303	66,996	75,120
Independent	77	54,718	46,453	53,164	61,699
Form of government					
Mayor-council	121	57,648	47,122	55,676	65,220
Council-manager	247	64,326	55,104	63,188	71,067
Commission	6	57,425	50,215	54,345	68,160
Town meeting	4	73,880	68,500	74,020	79,539
Rep. town meeting	8	71,029	64,198	68,320	75,682
Fire chief					
Total	322	56,765	48,053	55,482	64,656
Geographic region					
Northeast	72	58,911	50,109	57,754	66,269
North Central	91	53,841	47,112	53,508	60,840
South	101	51,287	44,063	50,000	57,864
West	58	68,231	61,000	68,148	77,256
City type					
Central	105	53,773	45,475	52,104	60,000
Suburban	147	62,089	54,929	61,235	68,964
Independent	70	50,074	44,600	48,441	55,546
Form of government					
Mayor-council	107	52,479	43,607	49,350	58,851
Council-manager	198	58,681	49,860	57,360	65,991
Commission	5	51,412	47,959	50,465	53,000
Town meeting	4	64,469	62,232	64,656	67,080
Rep. town meeting	8	66,160	64,198	65,311	72,227
Planning director					
Total	295	55,185	44,633	53,789	63,936
Geographic region					
Northeast	63	51,624	43,034	48,664	57,352
North Central	66	50,979	43,667	50,512	59,434
South	86	48,879	42,494	49,085	55,416
West	80	68,239	60,061	68,522	76,044
City type					
Central	81	51,429	42,956	49,816	58,994
Suburban	159	59,353	48,567	57,352	69,672
Independent	55	48,668	41,173	46,488	56,404
Form of government					
Mayor-council	76	50,388	42,977	48,386	59,160
Council-manager	205	57,341	46,488	55,831	67,488
Commission	4	56,336	47,922	53,078	58,233
Rep. town meeting	8	46,767	46,964	48,111	49,089
Personnel director					
Total	266	48,013	39,861	47,257	54,736
Geographic region					
Northeast	50	44,407	35,734	43,890	52,566
North Central	59	46,326	40,128	46,908	53,300
South	97	45,156	37,939	44,829	52,104
West	60	57,295	49,625	57,048	65,844
City type					
Central	88	45,086	36,560	43,698	53,215
Suburban	121	51,551	42,642	51,235	58,764
Independent	57	45,020	39,515	45,340	50,783
Form of government					
Mayor-council	79	43,847	36,560	43,472	50,960
Council-manager	176	50,178	42,069	49,874	56,748
Commission	4	45,613	42,748	46,691	50,634
Rep. town meeting	5	43,300	46,670	52,535	52,566
Risk manager					
Total	92	43,785	33,966	43,126	51,734
Geographic region					
Northeast	7	48,638	39,891	49,419	55,000
North Central	12	42,263	37,500	45,809	51,734
South	44	38,115	30,185	37,128	43,092
West	29	51,848	44,544	50,724	59,760
City type					
Central	35	42,925	29,043	39,536	50,724
Suburban	37	46,052	38,000	45,129	53,051

Table 1/4   SALARIES OF MUNICIPAL OFFICIALS: 1 JULY 1994
continued

Title of official	No. cities reporting	Distribution of 1994 salaries Mean ($)	First quartile ($)	Median ($)	Third quartile ($)
25,000–49,999 continued					
Independent	20	41,099	32,856	38,613	45,943
Form of government					
Mayor-council	26	41,437	29,009	44,547	51,965
Council-manager	65	44,923	35,520	43,092	51,734
Director of parks and recreation					
Total	275	51,870	42,848	50,014	59,434
Geographic region					
Northeast	51	47,547	37,411	45,445	53,105
North Central	71	48,489	41,913	48,349	56,645
South	85	48,215	41,641	47,250	54,309
West	68	63,209	54,084	61,942	70,878
City type					
Central	71	48,874	40,172	48,349	55,689
Suburban	151	54,798	45,045	52,980	63,787
Independent	53	47,539	41,267	47,008	54,600
Form of government					
Mayor-council	82	48,263	38,882	46,710	55,700
Council-manager	184	53,816	44,556	52,081	62,064
Commission	6	43,363	35,740	44,580	50,227
Rep. town meeting	3	48,073	...	52,566	...
Superintendent of parks					
Total	195	41,963	34,316	40,950	48,432
Geographic region					
Northeast	38	45,453	39,456	44,006	52,566
North Central	48	41,016	35,883	40,596	45,511
South	63	35,476	30,461	34,198	40,912
West	46	48,953	40,800	46,590	56,108
City type					
Central	53	39,294	33,953	37,894	45,987
Suburban	99	45,484	37,645	43,794	52,566
Independent	43	37,145	31,350	36,650	41,046
Form of government					
Mayor-council	53	40,321	34,181	37,839	42,632
Council-manager	132	42,504	34,406	41,881	48,432
Commission	3	34,770	...	38,070	...
Rep. town meeting	5	49,746	45,098	49,089	52,566
Director of recreation					
Total	143	41,708	32,000	41,477	48,360
Geographic region					
Northeast	39	42,399	34,181	41,937	50,680
North Central	37	37,691	31,326	37,894	44,028
South	36	36,218	29,185	37,243	42,552
West	31	52,012	41,300	49,416	66,408
City type					
Central	37	36,754	30,616	36,244	42,552
Suburban	79	45,414	33,948	43,572	54,226
Independent	27	37,656	30,977	38,892	44,678
Form of government					
Mayor-council	44	38,391	31,716	36,686	44,606
Council-manager	92	43,743	33,948	42,546	50,429
Rep. town meeting	4	40,585	40,715	41,534	42,353
Librarian					
Total	167	48,991	40,000	46,827	54,739
Geographic region					
Northeast	56	51,014	42,062	49,237	58,462
North Central	35	45,113	40,000	45,000	50,412
South	40	41,303	35,748	39,795	46,827
West	36	58,157	46,020	53,864	66,414
City type					
Central	41	45,829	38,781	45,000	50,539
Suburban	85	52,846	42,592	50,000	59,273
Independent	41	44,161	39,200	43,599	50,412
Form of government					
Mayor-council	41	46,884	39,600	42,956	51,684
Council-manager	112	49,930	40,255	48,895	55,628
Commission	4	51,700	46,719	50,540	54,360
Town meeting	3	40,281	...	42,513	...
Rep. town meeting	7	48,503	41,269	50,158	54,739
Director of information services					
Total	188	47,224	39,230	47,113	54,486
Geographic region					
Northeast	40	46,111	37,437	44,376	54,486
North Central	45	45,807	41,627	45,706	52,080
South	64	45,056	38,397	44,737	50,726
West	39	53,558	47,008	54,241	58,994

Title of official	No. cities reporting	Distribution of 1994 salaries Mean ($)	First quartile ($)	Median ($)	Third quartile ($)
25,000–49,999 continued					
City type					
Central	62	45,359	39,446	44,023	48,893
Suburban	81	50,930	44,574	52,500	58,220
Independent	45	43,122	36,000	43,536	50,726
Form of government					
Mayor-council	51	44,221	37,300	43,750	51,018
Council-manager	129	48,202	40,183	48,543	55,244
Rep. town meeting	4	55,193	52,535	55,083	57,630
Purchasing director					
Total	169	40,244	34,181	39,622	45,252
Geographic region					
Northeast	47	41,989	35,732	41,443	49,080
North Central	27	40,311	36,036	39,957	42,291
South	69	38,219	31,938	38,522	42,660
West	26	42,396	34,512	43,020	45,408
City type					
Central	59	37,676	32,867	38,580	42,308
Suburban	70	43,074	36,982	42,031	47,532
Independent	40	39,080	31,938	38,254	45,252
Form of government					
Mayor-council	51	38,143	30,638	37,128	42,597
Council-manager	113	41,511	35,990	41,158	45,408
Commission	3	29,278	...	28,160	...
10,000–24,999					
Mayor					
Total	884	11,369	2,880	5,420	11,148
Geographic region					
Northeast	231	9,689	2,000	3,300	7,200
North Central	307	13,044	3,700	6,534	15,000
South	227	12,944	3,600	6,500	14,700
West	119	7,301	3,600	4,320	7,200
City type					
Central	15	17,604	4,900	7,200	35,000
Suburban	597	10,538	2,735	5,000	8,963
Independent	272	12,849	3,000	6,641	18,000
Form of government					
Mayor-council	356	19,804	6,000	12,000	35,555
Council-manager	450	4,608	2,200	3,670	6,000
Commission	28	10,901	2,600	4,900	15,000
Town meeting	43	12,633	1,200	1,800	5,500
Rep. town meeting	7	11,105	1,340	1,500	5,000
City manager					
Total	524	68,540	58,848	67,361	75,687
Geographic region					
Northeast	103	67,330	57,500	64,978	75,288
North Central	135	65,537	57,330	65,881	72,450
South	185	66,710	57,783	65,454	74,464
West	101	77,140	66,000	74,796	86,652
City type					
Central	10	65,788	60,000	65,501	71,796
Suburban	346	71,401	62,000	70,000	79,000
Independent	168	62,812	55,000	62,364	69,498
Form of government					
Mayor-council	19	65,495	54,736	62,675	76,795
Council-manager	485	68,849	59,071	67,500	76,000
Town meeting	14	66,326	61,850	65,795	71,000
Rep. town meeting	4	64,044	66,843	67,922	69,000
Chief appointed administrator					
Total	314	58,542	48,400	58,351	68,910
Geographic region					
Northeast	127	59,345	46,000	58,422	74,022
North Central	106	60,079	50,923	59,727	69,503
South	57	51,667	42,246	53,144	62,273
West	24	63,831	56,220	63,742	70,752
City type					
Central	3	45,361	...	52,000	...
Suburban	236	60,684	49,912	61,275	72,028
Independent	75	52,329	41,330	55,100	61,808
Form of government					
Mayor-council	206	58,086	46,823	58,036	68,160
Council-manager	61	64,235	56,220	63,419	73,552
Commission	15	45,460	38,563	43,000	50,000
Town meeting	29	56,826	49,500	54,850	67,276
Rep. town meeting	3	56,076	...	53,096	...
Asst. city mgr./asst. CAO					
Total	310	47,406	37,559	45,891	55,515

Table 1/4 **SALARIES OF MUNICIPAL OFFICIALS: 1 JULY 1994**
continued

Title of official	No. cities reporting	Distribution of 1994 salaries			
		Mean ($)	First quartile ($)	Median ($)	Third quartile ($)
10,000–24,999 continued					
Geographic region					
Northeast	68	40,912	35,000	39,000	45,820
North Central	103	45,626	38,000	45,890	51,208
South	96	46,509	37,559	45,996	56,266
West	43	63,946	53,952	62,292	70,752
City type					
Suburban	238	48,665	38,384	46,942	57,000
Independent	70	43,335	36,000	42,257	51,771
Form of government					
Mayor-council	56	43,361	35,988	41,665	47,856
Council-manager	237	48,807	38,384	47,000	56,650
Commission	3	39,492	...	26,000	...
Town meeting	13	42,248	36,000	42,000	51,771
City clerk					
Total	737	36,020	28,901	35,250	42,972
Geographic region					
Northeast	205	35,746	28,532	35,267	42,226
North Central	203	34,908	28,392	34,940	42,583
South	234	34,866	28,136	33,847	40,152
West	95	41,827	34,068	41,477	49,344
City type					
Central	15	32,574	20,000	31,323	36,050
Suburban	495	37,073	30,144	36,355	44,290
Independent	227	33,950	26,811	32,000	40,152
Form of government					
Mayor-council	253	34,746	28,136	34,600	40,896
Council-manager	411	37,156	29,800	36,283	44,408
Commission	18	35,215	24,461	36,888	43,084
Town meeting	47	32,859	28,532	32,496	38,185
Rep. town meeting	8	38,274	34,346	39,653	44,867
Chief financial officer					
Total	636	48,629	40,000	47,992	56,744
Geographic region					
Northeast	171	47,807	38,335	47,041	57,820
North Central	174	47,835	40,700	47,992	56,118
South	195	45,613	37,465	44,580	53,221
West	96	57,661	49,520	55,464	62,760
City type					
Central	11	41,806	38,352	43,284	50,784
Suburban	445	50,493	41,050	50,318	59,600
Independent	180	44,437	38,000	44,458	50,894
Form of government					
Mayor-council	204	45,013	36,101	45,384	54,080
Council-manager	382	50,807	42,182	49,699	58,636
Commission	13	36,595	29,691	43,815	45,732
Town meeting	31	49,671	41,200	50,000	61,015
Rep. town meeting	6	53,631	38,955	46,974	63,220
Director of economic development					
Total	205	44,747	36,056	44,000	52,053
Geographic region					
Northeast	37	40,326	35,681	42,230	46,206
North Central	68	42,823	36,757	43,551	48,480
South	63	43,446	33,291	40,465	53,843
West	37	54,921	45,398	53,160	66,744
City type					
Central	9	37,296	33,154	35,307	40,000
Suburban	136	46,775	38,000	45,280	55,160
Independent	60	41,268	35,849	40,736	46,486
Form of government					
Mayor-council	63	40,526	33,250	40,100	47,004
Council-manager	131	47,349	38,146	45,500	56,090
Commission	4	35,177	37,196	37,817	38,438
Town meeting	6	38,875	31,000	39,200	45,608
Treasurer					
Total	230	33,217	24,648	33,500	42,726
Geographic region					
Northeast	97	33,523	22,660	33,000	43,792
North Central	67	31,837	26,587	33,549	39,060
South	42	37,272	28,166	38,778	43,908
West	24	28,731	20,232	26,694	34,300
City type					
Central	5	29,341	25,378	27,040	27,517
Suburban	154	33,805	22,660	34,896	43,792
Independent	71	32,212	26,500	31,880	39,000
Form of government					
Mayor-council	83	29,756	19,845	32,333	37,544

Title of official	No. cities reporting	Distribution of 1994 salaries			
		Mean ($)	First quartile ($)	Median ($)	Third quartile ($)
10,000–24,999 continued					
Council-manager	98	34,907	25,445	34,314	43,792
Commission	11	29,136	19,500	27,830	36,305
Town meeting	33	36,549	30,613	38,220	46,500
Rep. town meeting	5	44,499	38,041	40,840	52,821
Director of public works					
Total	714	50,661	42,000	50,318	57,786
Geographic region					
Northeast	185	52,369	43,900	52,369	60,399
North Central	192	50,522	44,764	50,390	56,800
South	240	45,740	37,000	44,791	53,685
West	97	59,854	49,140	56,724	67,152
City type					
Central	15	47,109	39,750	44,172	55,348
Suburban	484	52,699	44,456	51,962	60,216
Independent	215	46,321	38,480	46,590	54,000
Form of government					
Mayor-council	233	48,268	39,672	48,231	56,243
Council-manager	427	51,639	42,854	50,508	59,319
Commission	12	48,095	40,456	49,378	53,954
Town meeting	36	53,689	47,875	54,451	60,483
Rep. town meeting	6	60,957	52,369	60,765	70,284
Engineer					
Total	353	47,936	41,109	48,510	54,101
Geographic region					
Northeast	81	49,965	39,947	51,358	60,065
North Central	105	46,995	43,906	48,664	53,840
South	114	45,605	39,832	45,050	51,123
West	53	51,708	43,967	50,052	57,288
City type					
Central	12	37,284	30,388	39,878	44,686
Suburban	211	50,275	43,363	50,404	56,343
Independent	130	45,122	40,000	45,182	51,500
Form of government					
Mayor-council	120	45,170	40,000	45,176	52,353
Council-manager	198	49,231	41,400	49,473	55,227
Commission	9	47,115	44,520	46,000	50,640
Town meeting	20	50,427	47,231	51,688	56,075
Rep. town meeting	6	53,416	49,627	55,319	57,366
Police chief					
Total	792	52,894	43,815	51,282	60,513
Geographic region					
Northeast	192	59,433	49,174	57,900	70,019
North Central	236	51,285	45,439	51,105	57,449
South	266	46,941	39,416	45,282	53,568
West	98	60,119	50,268	55,110	68,000
City type					
Central	16	47,571	44,000	45,110	52,528
Suburban	515	56,509	47,989	54,968	63,590
Independent	261	46,088	39,464	44,800	51,348
Form of government					
Mayor-council	278	50,419	40,019	49,513	57,097
Council-manager	451	53,754	45,000	51,780	60,660
Commission	16	44,789	40,123	42,914	47,000
Town meeting	39	60,952	52,499	61,267	66,972
Rep. town meeting	8	67,413	56,360	72,277	74,418
Fire chief					
Total	569	46,715	38,500	45,576	53,588
Geographic region					
Northeast	105	50,391	42,000	49,193	57,000
North Central	172	46,490	39,928	46,536	53,400
South	219	41,954	35,129	40,500	47,347
West	73	56,245	46,116	53,588	65,952
City type					
Central	13	44,067	39,998	43,973	45,156
Suburban	329	50,360	42,016	50,000	56,616
Independent	227	41,585	35,700	40,250	46,714
Form of government					
Mayor-council	202	44,076	36,534	42,517	51,378
Council-manager	320	47,290	38,831	46,014	53,088
Commission	10	43,316	38,438	41,465	47,000
Town meeting	31	55,966	51,686	56,561	60,525
Rep. town meeting	6	62,787	52,025	60,493	75,000
Planning director					
Total	381	45,279	35,630	43,680	52,208
Geographic region					
Northeast	79	43,756	35,020	43,095	50,725

Table 1/4   **SALARIES OF MUNICIPAL OFFICIALS: 1 JULY 1994**
continued

Title of official	No. cities reporting	Mean ($)	First quartile ($)	Median ($)	Third quartile ($)
10,000–24,999 continued					
North Central	83	43,015	35,000	42,383	48,900
South	149	41,747	34,284	40,000	48,100
West	70	57,200	45,672	54,113	63,300
City type					
Central	9	42,554	38,993	42,296	46,089
Suburban	240	47,602	36,930	46,434	54,123
Independent	132	41,240	34,284	39,958	46,828
Form of government					
Mayor-council	104	41,041	33,105	41,417	47,250
Council-manager	247	47,450	37,258	45,054	54,696
Commission	5	45,211	31,289	49,830	60,000
Town meeting	21	39,590	33,852	38,627	44,278
Rep. town meeting	4	51,322	48,400	51,133	53,866
Personnel director					
Total	321	38,515	30,389	37,648	45,180
Geographic region					
Northeast	36	38,844	31,177	38,164	45,603
North Central	71	39,264	32,500	38,944	46,100
South	165	35,476	27,500	34,623	41,479
West	49	47,423	37,504	44,052	54,720
City type					
Central	11	31,670	27,384	31,138	38,013
Suburban	180	40,812	32,000	39,003	46,645
Independent	130	35,914	27,700	35,259	41,787
Form of government					
Mayor-council	93	34,310	26,000	34,000	41,308
Council-manager	213	40,161	32,000	38,792	45,820
Commission	7	34,559	25,730	30,244	43,500
Town meeting	6	46,876	41,828	44,991	46,208
Risk manager					
Total	64	37,399	28,837	35,857	44,922
Geographic region					
North Central	6	35,359	24,821	37,225	48,266
South	45	35,470	28,825	34,495	41,068
West	11	46,764	37,670	41,028	55,491
City type					
Central	3	40,096	. . .	41,068	. . .
Suburban	30	39,917	30,243	39,238	47,022
Independent	31	34,702	26,836	33,830	40,728
Form of government					
Mayor-council	6	26,817	21,611	26,695	31,368
Council-manager	55	38,789	29,440	39,372	47,022
Director of parks and recreation					
Total	468	41,649	33,097	40,492	50,000
Geographic region					
Northeast	97	39,600	31,700	39,300	47,795
North Central	124	41,996	35,988	41,904	49,764
South	188	38,616	31,619	37,610	43,799
West	59	53,952	45,250	54,849	61,264
City type					
Central	11	41,534	33,132	40,664	43,583
Suburban	298	42,855	33,756	41,135	50,900
Independent	159	39,396	31,500	39,211	45,927
Form of government					
Mayor-council	154	38,399	30,659	37,213	44,293
Council-manager	291	43,461	35,464	42,273	51,001
Commission	7	36,888	31,449	35,000	41,378
Town meeting	12	40,463	39,067	41,911	48,000
Rep. town meeting	4	46,791	40,953	43,965	46,976
Superintendent of parks					
Total	240	36,056	30,000	34,344	42,040
Geographic region					
Northeast	30	41,346	34,102	41,428	46,930
North Central	76	36,443	31,261	35,322	42,494
South	85	31,177	25,185	31,618	33,720
West	49	40,680	34,284	38,016	45,432
City type					
Central	7	30,321	26,000	30,743	34,102
Suburban	140	38,381	31,836	36,369	45,432
Independent	93	32,988	27,745	32,952	37,627
Form of government					
Mayor-council	71	35,903	30,394	34,284	41,837
Council-manager	156	35,761	29,494	34,272	41,060
Commission	6	33,806	28,223	34,424	40,456
Town meeting	7	46,108	33,627	45,825	54,605

Title of official	No. cities reporting	Mean ($)	First quartile ($)	Median ($)	Third quartile ($)
10,000–24,999 continued					
Director of recreation					
Total	201	33,720	25,464	33,129	40,580
Geographic region					
Northeast	55	32,842	17,856	33,289	40,991
North Central	70	33,802	25,602	33,482	41,603
South	45	31,243	24,936	30,027	36,135
West	31	38,690	29,224	37,282	45,480
City type					
Central	3	29,763	. . .	29,437	. . .
Suburban	115	35,794	25,464	35,422	44,580
Independent	83	30,991	25,105	30,472	36,337
Form of government					
Mayor-council	71	33,339	24,832	31,962	41,464
Council-manager	102	35,300	27,726	34,370	40,580
Commission	7	31,190	28,223	29,300	33,134
Town meeting	18	27,745	14,398	30,786	40,176
Rep. town meeting	3	30,826	. . .	31,796	. . .
Librarian					
Total	311	39,569	31,735	38,220	45,781
Geographic region					
Northeast	111	43,019	34,780	42,215	49,452
North Central	74	37,691	31,500	37,000	42,616
South	82	34,070	28,000	32,974	39,806
West	44	44,273	32,884	44,053	48,276
City type					
Central	4	34,358	35,672	35,824	35,976
Suburban	201	41,960	33,860	40,835	48,464
Independent	106	35,232	29,496	33,563	41,796
Form of government					
Mayor-council	95	39,614	31,122	37,985	45,781
Council-manager	171	39,288	30,888	38,038	45,816
Commission	7	31,768	28,635	31,357	35,080
Town meeting	30	41,642	35,787	43,679	47,937
Rep. town meeting	8	44,092	38,726	41,060	42,883
Director of information services					
Total	142	37,842	29,991	38,120	43,908
Geographic region					
Northeast	27	40,836	31,239	39,901	51,241
North Central	27	38,652	33,980	37,600	44,907
South	75	35,845	28,236	35,984	42,361
West	13	41,457	39,600	41,912	43,600
City type					
Central	7	32,273	28,798	31,805	35,460
Suburban	78	38,966	29,598	38,631	45,298
Independent	57	36,986	30,930	38,480	42,516
Form of government					
Mayor-council	32	37,876	30,595	38,214	42,000
Council-manager	96	38,138	30,284	38,120	44,000
Commission	4	34,235	29,484	32,077	34,670
Town meeting	8	34,944	31,239	39,364	43,447
Purchasing director					
Total	166	32,325	25,147	31,195	37,500
Geographic region					
Northeast	30	32,928	25,024	31,573	42,610
North Central	21	37,863	30,912	37,224	45,408
South	102	30,266	23,845	29,302	35,700
West	13	38,140	32,124	36,034	44,138
City type					
Central	7	32,162	28,163	31,996	36,357
Suburban	86	33,995	24,975	31,967	41,600
Independent	73	30,373	25,104	29,683	36,034
Form of government					
Mayor-council	53	32,266	25,248	30,368	37,335
Council-manager	107	32,469	25,147	31,966	37,559
5,000–9,999					
Mayor					
Total	885	7,243	2,000	4,000	7,200
Geographic region					
Northeast	225	6,739	1,500	2,400	5,000
North Central	305	7,145	2,400	4,800	7,500
South	241	8,959	2,700	4,800	9,600
West	114	4,873	2,400	3,600	6,000
City type					
Suburban	505	6,447	2,000	3,600	6,180
Independent	380	8,301	2,100	4,200	8,400

Table 1/4 continued   SALARIES OF MUNICIPAL OFFICIALS: 1 JULY 1994

Title of official	No. cities reporting	Distribution of 1994 salaries Mean ($)	First quartile ($)	Median ($)	Third quartile ($)
5,000–9,999 continued					
Form of government					
Mayor-council	437	9,676	3,600	6,000	10,800
Council-manager	365	3,425	1,200	2,400	4,130
Commission	18	8,044	3,600	5,350	6,500
Town meeting	56	13,622	1,400	2,278	31,500
Rep. town meeting	9	2,671	2,500	2,600	3,000
City manager					
Total	429	55,722	46,358	53,000	62,148
Geographic region					
Northeast	91	49,460	42,361	46,288	55,837
North Central	101	55,947	48,150	55,174	61,326
South	154	54,175	46,322	52,000	59,940
West	83	65,181	53,180	62,400	75,017
City type					
Suburban	230	59,235	48,150	57,267	67,740
Independent	199	51,660	44,940	50,800	57,000
Form of government					
Mayor-council	27	54,583	48,000	55,000	59,425
Council-manager	392	55,942	46,573	53,013	62,332
Town meeting	9	51,378	44,000	47,595	51,300
Chief appointed administrator					
Total	372	50,278	41,000	49,937	58,957
Geographic region					
Northeast	115	50,530	40,000	49,665	60,000
North Central	129	50,407	43,200	50,000	56,589
South	82	46,474	37,400	44,750	54,840
West	46	56,067	48,624	56,058	63,396
City type					
Suburban	249	51,993	41,858	51,000	61,440
Independent	123	46,806	39,998	46,368	54,147
Form of government					
Mayor-council	251	50,009	40,117	49,452	59,016
Council-manager	80	53,643	44,991	54,096	59,500
Commission	6	38,837	37,960	41,250	48,730
Town meeting	29	47,084	40,000	45,000	55,000
Rep. town meeting	6	43,536	36,500	42,277	51,754
Asst. city mgr./asst. CAO					
Total	184	38,307	29,365	37,086	45,000
Geographic region					
Northeast	42	31,470	26,000	31,240	37,564
North Central	48	37,887	30,500	35,928	45,775
South	64	37,654	28,687	37,494	43,547
West	30	49,946	38,220	45,311	58,474
City type					
Suburban	113	39,564	29,562	37,850	48,000
Independent	71	36,307	28,634	36,878	43,412
Form of government					
Mayor-council	48	33,638	26,429	28,817	40,132
Council-manager	126	40,534	32,003	38,480	46,866
Town meeting	10	32,662	23,500	33,805	39,709
City clerk					
Total	733	31,084	24,800	30,160	36,582
Geographic region					
Northeast	190	31,327	24,311	30,776	37,200
North Central	210	31,497	25,890	30,802	36,854
South	233	28,762	23,515	28,059	34,011
West	100	35,163	28,195	34,220	40,819
City type					
Suburban	402	32,483	25,771	31,860	38,620
Independent	331	29,384	24,100	28,670	34,011
Form of government					
Mayor-council	331	31,518	24,645	30,000	37,500
Council-manager	322	31,220	24,996	30,526	36,582
Commission	17	32,278	27,040	32,884	35,008
Town meeting	56	27,117	23,660	27,824	32,640
Rep. town meeting	7	33,091	30,621	33,270	36,480
Chief financial officer					
Total	429	38,833	31,200	37,616	45,584
Geographic region					
Northeast	105	36,380	26,648	34,975	45,100
North Central	100	38,706	33,009	38,449	44,511
South	143	36,651	30,000	35,280	41,995
West	81	46,020	37,964	45,150	51,852
City type					
Suburban	261	39,869	32,023	39,000	47,724
Independent	168	37,223	30,345	36,378	43,638

Title of official	No. cities reporting	Distribution of 1994 salaries Mean ($)	First quartile ($)	Median ($)	Third quartile ($)
5,000–9,999 continued					
Form of government					
Mayor-council	144	37,294	28,955	36,695	45,000
Council-manager	249	40,127	32,500	39,000	47,023
Commission	7	33,814	22,800	33,800	41,400
Town meeting	26	37,033	28,200	36,000	43,311
Rep. town meeting	3	32,557	. . .	35,334	. . .
Director of economic development					
Total	115	35,713	29,000	35,485	42,014
Geographic region					
Northeast	20	34,479	28,500	32,150	35,880
North Central	42	34,457	27,600	35,406	41,038
South	32	36,642	29,740	35,620	44,000
West	21	37,984	32,394	37,964	43,680
City type					
Suburban	48	37,740	32,000	37,139	44,000
Independent	67	34,261	28,000	33,000	39,804
Form of government					
Mayor-council	48	34,404	27,600	32,361	41,459
Council-manager	59	36,744	29,740	36,400	42,474
Town meeting	5	34,301	31,800	32,827	33,000
Treasurer					
Total	200	28,765	21,900	28,673	35,520
Geographic region					
Northeast	79	28,450	21,000	28,686	34,000
North Central	62	28,747	22,318	28,861	36,230
South	42	29,010	21,755	28,867	36,503
West	17	29,683	22,128	23,631	37,397
City type					
Suburban	113	30,881	23,475	31,000	38,000
Independent	87	26,016	20,721	26,000	32,635
Form of government					
Mayor-council	80	27,433	21,000	25,493	34,000
Council-manager	87	30,500	22,318	29,352	36,982
Town meeting	28	27,160	18,759	28,973	34,000
Rep. town meeting	3	32,286	. . .	32,650	. . .
Director of public works					
Total	667	41,493	33,685	40,294	48,000
Geographic region					
Northeast	177	43,129	35,571	42,390	49,319
North Central	165	41,608	36,282	40,700	46,425
South	223	37,395	30,264	35,863	43,638
West	102	47,426	39,500	46,763	53,892
City type					
Suburban	395	43,515	35,571	42,850	50,315
Independent	272	38,557	32,344	37,821	43,494
Form of government					
Mayor-council	278	40,694	32,761	39,854	48,000
Council-manager	344	42,067	34,549	40,957	48,000
Commission	8	40,949	39,102	40,729	46,308
Town meeting	33	42,846	38,700	42,786	47,576
Rep. town meeting	4	37,548	37,373	38,353	39,332
Engineer					
Total	137	42,019	34,917	42,920	50,172
Geographic region					
Northeast	19	50,036	33,624	54,561	65,000
North Central	48	39,460	33,495	40,905	47,946
South	46	40,869	35,516	41,530	48,027
West	24	42,993	39,000	43,600	48,105
City type					
Suburban	72	43,554	33,495	44,091	52,785
Independent	65	40,318	35,516	40,501	46,296
Form of government					
Mayor-council	57	38,321	26,420	39,948	45,996
Council-manager	74	44,393	37,800	43,951	50,594
Town meeting	3	55,516	. . .	54,561	. . .
Police chief					
Total	783	43,598	35,070	41,599	49,408
Geographic region					
Northeast	180	50,234	38,517	46,345	60,000
North Central	226	41,922	36,010	41,427	47,112
South	263	38,213	31,548	37,000	42,660
West	114	48,867	41,484	46,052	55,872
City type					
Suburban	433	47,937	39,500	45,979	54,679
Independent	350	38,230	32,560	37,180	42,827

Table 1/4   SALARIES OF MUNICIPAL OFFICIALS: 1 JULY 1994
continued

Title of official	No. cities reporting	Distribution of 1994 salaries			
		Mean ($)	First quartile ($)	Median ($)	Third quartile ($)
5,000–9,999 continued					
Form of government					
Mayor-council	335	42,815	33,020	40,500	48,500
Council-manager	406	43,705	36,717	41,808	49,148
Commission	9	43,644	34,857	38,616	45,741
Town meeting	29	51,730	43,356	51,843	57,915
Rep. town meeting	4	39,269	33,280	35,390	37,500
Fire chief					
Total	387	35,503	29,445	35,000	41,600
Geographic region					
Northeast	55	37,125	32,000	37,000	42,813
North Central	113	33,436	27,700	35,000	41,033
South	168	33,551	28,579	32,035	37,606
West	51	44,767	36,909	43,243	53,784
City type					
Suburban	177	38,109	31,082	38,186	45,640
Independent	210	33,308	28,652	33,444	37,589
Form of government					
Mayor-council	152	33,758	27,693	33,474	38,628
Council-manager	203	36,312	30,726	35,501	41,600
Commission	8	36,145	28,000	39,997	44,568
Town meeting	21	39,797	38,000	41,500	45,986
Rep. town meeting	3	37,491	. . .	35,050	. . .
Planning director					
Total	202	38,653	29,611	36,575	45,341
Geographic region					
Northeast	37	37,046	31,500	37,900	42,120
North Central	31	34,859	25,175	33,717	44,310
South	75	34,879	28,000	32,804	40,893
West	59	46,453	35,100	45,427	55,640
City type					
Suburban	117	41,168	30,450	38,938	49,000
Independent	85	35,192	29,611	34,207	40,081
Form of government					
Mayor-council	55	35,773	26,210	31,200	45,130
Council-manager	132	39,998	31,233	37,000	46,911
Town meeting	12	38,605	38,000	40,493	42,523
Personnel director					
Total	115	30,641	22,672	28,200	35,238
Geographic region					
North Central	13	32,471	24,735	30,849	35,381
South	80	28,229	21,154	26,527	30,638
West	21	39,586	34,000	36,296	46,592
City type					
Suburban	49	32,774	23,192	30,014	36,296
Independent	66	29,058	21,860	27,830	34,356
Form of government					
Mayor-council	37	26,501	19,259	25,050	30,214
Council-manager	75	32,769	24,458	30,190	37,390
Commission	3	28,524	. . .	26,500	. . .
Risk manager					
Total	25	33,492	25,750	32,000	41,475
Geographic region					
North Central	5	31,789	26,852	33,641	36,000
South	9	35,015	21,460	36,400	48,335
West	10	35,322	28,460	30,695	41,784
City type					
Suburban	10	37,910	29,390	41,392	51,333
Independent	15	30,546	23,979	29,000	36,400
Form of government					
Mayor-council	7	25,631	19,032	23,979	36,000
Council-manager	18	36,549	28,460	35,021	48,335
Director of parks and recreation					
Total	293	31,250	25,000	30,576	36,804
Geographic region					
Northeast	48	28,218	19,375	28,423	35,152
North Central	75	31,313	26,162	32,000	37,000
South	126	30,186	24,586	28,375	34,820
West	44	37,494	30,588	35,783	42,000
City type					
Suburban	132	33,192	26,019	33,275	40,000
Independent	161	29,657	24,700	29,400	34,322
Form of government					
Mayor-council	111	29,278	23,868	29,381	35,068
Council-manager	161	33,174	26,312	32,000	39,000
Commission	5	26,767	22,714	25,000	26,162
Town meeting	14	26,004	13,371	28,683	33,837
5,000–9,999 continued					
Superintendent of parks					
Total	127	28,885	24,000	29,064	33,000
Geographic region					
Northeast	10	30,412	26,000	30,453	31,139
North Central	41	30,249	26,312	31,145	33,592
South	50	25,711	18,366	25,841	30,200
West	26	32,250	27,500	31,639	37,366
City type					
Suburban	55	29,948	25,292	30,059	34,917
Independent	72	28,072	23,355	27,741	32,156
Form of government					
Mayor-council	44	27,320	24,000	27,650	31,600
Council-manager	78	29,489	23,701	29,038	34,964
Town meeting	3	37,018	. . .	32,760	. . .
Director of recreation					
Total	98	27,096	20,500	26,477	33,096
Geographic region					
Northeast	31	23,120	13,300	24,532	31,250
North Central	22	26,749	18,556	27,546	33,390
South	24	29,206	21,982	29,853	33,821
West	21	30,920	24,985	29,500	34,505
City type					
Suburban	44	28,339	19,500	29,950	34,941
Independent	54	26,084	20,845	25,722	31,682
Form of government					
Mayor-council	38	26,408	18,556	25,097	32,834
Council-manager	52	27,884	21,982	28,834	33,121
Town meeting	5	25,850	23,619	26,000	30,873
Librarian					
Total	255	28,552	22,009	28,000	33,696
Geographic region					
Northeast	69	31,864	26,577	30,899	37,748
North Central	67	28,691	24,000	28,668	32,926
South	75	24,051	17,511	22,593	28,000
West	44	30,820	23,010	29,102	35,844
City type					
Suburban	121	30,994	23,500	31,039	37,232
Independent	134	26,347	21,528	26,000	29,867
Form of government					
Mayor-council	97	28,579	21,703	28,732	35,000
Council-manager	126	28,094	22,009	26,010	32,070
Commission	5	23,023	18,700	24,315	27,000
Town meeting	24	31,849	29,000	31,383	35,250
Rep. town meeting	3	29,736	. . .	33,202	. . .
Director of information services					
Total	39	31,570	23,000	28,604	37,627
Geographic region					
Northeast	4	25,316	20,022	23,694	27,366
North Central	4	29,925	30,565	31,399	32,232
South	21	27,840	23,000	25,000	32,900
West	10	42,563	33,228	40,761	50,414
City type					
Suburban	17	32,756	23,268	27,366	37,380
Independent	22	30,653	21,216	29,623	37,627
Form of government					
Mayor-council	10	26,761	23,000	26,103	28,604
Council-manager	27	33,580	23,268	32,232	42,974
Purchasing director					
Total	72	27,126	20,148	25,234	32,000
Geographic region					
Northeast	8	30,012	21,057	27,500	36,925
North Central	6	26,439	25,563	26,105	26,730
South	45	25,919	20,072	23,878	28,210
West	13	29,845	25,092	32,000	34,403
City type					
Suburban	32	29,532	21,923	28,605	35,730
Independent	40	25,201	19,781	24,347	27,040
Form of government					
Mayor-council	23	25,478	19,656	25,376	27,759
Council-manager	48	27,931	20,148	24,347	33,203
2,500–4,999					
Mayor					
Total	909	4,492	1,400	2,700	4,944
Geographic region					
Northeast	194	4,471	1,000	1,500	3,750

Table 1/4 SALARIES OF MUNICIPAL OFFICIALS: 1 JULY 1994
continued

Title of official	No. cities reporting	Distribution of 1994 salaries Mean ($)	First quartile ($)	Median ($)	Third quartile ($)
2,500–4,999 continued					
North Central	347	3,664	1,500	3,000	4,650
South	277	5,490	1,500	3,472	6,490
West	91	4,658	1,800	3,600	6,000
City type					
Suburban	397	4,520	1,500	3,000	4,800
Independent	512	4,471	1,200	2,570	5,000
Form of government					
Mayor-council	549	5,295	2,000	3,600	6,000
Council-manager	280	2,395	1,200	1,975	3,420
Commission	17	4,206	2,080	3,600	4,700
Town meeting	57	7,416	1,000	1,500	4,100
Rep. town meeting	6	1,950	1,500	2,100	2,500
City manager					
Total	286	46,429	38,200	45,259	51,132
Geographic region					
Northeast	48	39,402	31,500	37,120	43,187
North Central	78	45,482	39,710	45,401	49,962
South	114	44,721	39,000	45,000	50,000
West	46	59,603	48,000	55,566	66,980
City type					
Suburban	114	49,939	40,419	48,000	55,167
Independent	172	44,103	37,400	43,550	48,760
Form of government					
Mayor-council	16	46,029	37,050	46,306	49,700
Council-manager	251	47,097	39,395	45,786	52,000
Town meeting	17	37,465	30,537	36,000	42,432
Chief appointed administrator					
Total	402	39,705	32,000	39,656	47,514
Geographic region					
Northeast	83	34,481	23,835	34,611	45,423
North Central	148	41,371	35,600	41,000	47,632
South	118	38,207	30,000	38,000	45,240
West	53	46,571	37,152	42,120	56,000
City type					
Suburban	197	40,778	33,555	41,000	48,290
Independent	205	38,675	31,312	37,591	45,000
Form of government					
Mayor-council	268	38,638	30,300	39,000	46,300
Council-manager	99	44,153	36,067	42,452	50,436
Commission	5	36,995	35,000	36,200	41,000
Town meeting	25	36,451	29,000	35,663	42,000
Rep. town meeting	5	27,863	23,835	27,997	36,483
Asst. city mgr./asst. CAO					
Total	107	32,483	24,000	30,000	40,950
Geographic region					
Northeast	19	25,835	20,189	24,000	31,710
North Central	33	30,073	23,296	28,392	37,119
South	33	28,977	23,700	26,624	32,688
West	22	47,096	39,360	45,714	54,638
City type					
Suburban	53	33,343	24,000	30,435	42,492
Independent	54	31,638	24,000	28,395	39,731
Form of government					
Mayor-council	48	26,709	21,000	24,900	30,660
Council-manager	54	38,755	29,078	37,647	45,427
Town meeting	4	20,715	17,241	20,621	24,000
City clerk					
Total	767	26,270	19,884	25,759	31,000
Geographic region					
Northeast	150	24,764	17,580	24,001	30,000
North Central	260	26,874	21,153	26,773	31,500
South	266	24,906	19,692	24,629	29,000
West	91	31,010	23,064	29,270	36,168
City type					
Suburban	315	27,644	21,000	26,625	32,982
Independent	452	25,312	19,401	25,000	29,931
Form of government					
Mayor-council	446	25,905	19,593	24,934	31,000
Council-manager	258	27,496	21,500	27,383	31,401
Commission	15	26,496	17,620	26,603	31,690
Town meeting	44	23,266	18,200	23,443	28,777
Rep. town meeting	4	20,050	16,380	17,810	19,240
Chief financial officer					
Total	227	32,667	23,774	30,250	39,674
Geographic region					
Northeast	42	27,464	20,000	26,190	34,240
North Central	61	30,068	22,547	27,460	38,480

Title of official	No. cities reporting	Distribution of 1994 salaries Mean ($)	First quartile ($)	Median ($)	Third quartile ($)
2,500–4,999 continued					
South	73	29,874	23,500	27,500	35,637
West	51	44,060	31,403	41,495	53,531
City type					
Suburban	103	34,075	25,000	31,460	41,148
Independent	124	31,498	23,350	29,247	37,565
Form of government					
Mayor-council	97	28,360	22,150	27,300	33,611
Council-manager	110	37,806	26,500	35,713	43,905
Commission	3	25,487	...	24,900	...
Town meeting	16	25,816	21,000	24,500	29,712
Director of economic development					
Total	67	31,515	25,000	29,316	36,000
Geographic region					
Northeast	9	31,171	28,500	30,650	33,222
North Central	39	29,337	25,000	28,970	33,780
South	10	30,480	19,830	27,376	42,598
West	9	42,447	30,212	38,724	55,224
City type					
Suburban	24	34,471	28,970	32,086	36,909
Independent	43	29,865	25,000	28,000	34,500
Form of government					
Mayor-council	40	29,464	25,000	28,985	33,000
Council-manager	24	34,773	26,700	30,247	38,845
Town meeting	3	32,797	...	33,222	...
Treasurer					
Total	164	24,048	18,200	23,088	29,349
Geographic region					
Northeast	46	21,972	16,000	20,672	27,087
North Central	62	23,841	18,750	24,820	28,995
South	34	23,205	17,702	22,348	28,200
West	22	30,273	21,236	27,010	35,448
City type					
Suburban	64	25,408	19,500	25,850	30,117
Independent	100	23,177	17,763	21,941	27,300
Form of government					
Mayor-council	73	22,427	17,702	21,174	27,087
Council-manager	74	26,577	21,000	26,170	30,720
Town meeting	15	20,206	14,940	20,343	24,000
Director of public works					
Total	580	34,735	27,820	32,994	40,083
Geographic region					
Northeast	100	37,254	29,869	34,796	43,323
North Central	165	35,376	29,745	35,089	40,753
South	228	30,621	25,532	29,696	34,736
West	87	41,403	32,640	37,908	48,352
City type					
Suburban	248	37,338	30,000	35,190	43,044
Independent	332	32,790	26,784	31,626	37,521
Form of government					
Mayor-council	317	33,685	27,300	32,000	39,552
Council-manager	230	36,458	30,000	34,294	40,685
Commission	6	28,117	20,800	27,300	37,440
Town meeting	27	33,844	26,520	31,000	43,044
Engineer					
Total	39	40,637	30,000	42,120	54,845
Geographic region					
Northeast	7	24,316	10,000	19,500	46,027
North Central	3	34,789	...	35,000	...
South	10	40,212	32,500	38,000	51,070
West	19	47,798	36,000	50,000	57,179
City type					
Suburban	15	36,536	19,500	35,000	56,000
Independent	24	43,200	34,029	42,660	50,710
Form of government					
Mayor-council	24	38,043	30,000	38,500	50,087
Council-manager	15	44,788	32,500	46,405	57,179
Police chief					
Total	718	34,601	27,600	33,000	39,354
Geographic region					
Northeast	107	39,743	31,388	36,261	46,082
North Central	235	34,498	29,354	34,150	38,854
South	288	30,379	25,280	29,416	34,080
West	88	42,446	34,236	40,058	47,500
City type					
Suburban	285	38,749	31,392	36,712	44,500

Table 1/4   SALARIES OF MUNICIPAL OFFICIALS: 1 JULY 1994
continued

Title of official	No. cities reporting	Mean ($)	First quartile ($)	Median ($)	Third quartile ($)
2,500–4,999 continued					
Independent	433	31,871	26,675	30,868	36,000
Form of government					
Mayor-council	406	33,128	26,600	31,568	37,286
Council-manager	280	36,662	30,000	35,372	40,830
Commission	10	29,566	24,088	27,438	32,000
Town meeting	21	38,217	31,388	36,000	44,402
Fire chief					
Total	173	30,245	23,182	28,682	34,800
Geographic region					
Northeast	14	28,635	15,500	29,175	36,045
North Central	32	27,688	23,182	28,824	33,396
South	96	26,817	21,049	27,447	31,247
West	31	44,225	32,952	40,089	53,518
City type					
Suburban	71	33,008	23,644	32,000	39,000
Independent	102	28,321	22,984	27,550	32,026
Form of government					
Mayor-council	83	28,314	20,740	27,185	33,471
Council-manager	80	32,038	24,700	29,944	35,693
Town meeting	8	32,119	26,000	32,316	42,918
Planning director					
Total	89	36,667	28,392	33,600	40,000
Geographic region					
Northeast	10	28,541	28,800	30,360	33,600
North Central	14	31,524	27,775	31,433	35,000
South	28	32,860	27,084	31,203	39,528
West	37	43,690	29,844	39,984	52,000
City type					
Suburban	47	37,927	29,619	35,000	39,986
Independent	42	35,256	27,084	31,907	40,862
Form of government					
Mayor-council	37	35,174	28,870	33,765	38,556
Council-manager	47	38,330	25,611	35,000	43,908
Town meeting	5	32,079	30,000	30,719	33,600
Personnel director					
Total	38	27,976	20,856	24,321	32,236
Geographic region					
Northeast	3	22,896	. . .	23,564	. . .
North Central	4	32,933	23,732	25,866	28,000
South	20	23,601	18,360	22,829	26,000
West	11	35,514	26,894	32,236	49,192
City type					
Suburban	16	32,860	20,979	31,118	34,340
Independent	22	24,424	19,806	23,126	26,894
Form of government					
Mayor-council	18	28,404	18,360	24,782	33,349
Council-manager	18	27,435	22,651	23,437	32,236
Risk manager					
Total	8	31,466	26,874	28,113	32,220
Geographic region					
South	4	22,916	21,903	24,389	26,874
West	4	40,016	32,220	37,956	43,692
City type					
Suburban	3	32,605	. . .	32,220	. . .
Independent	5	30,782	26,874	27,075	29,150
Form of government					
Mayor-council	3	38,790	. . .	32,220	. . .
Council-manager	5	27,071	21,903	26,874	27,075
Director of parks and recreation					
Total	118	27,876	22,368	26,000	31,191
Geographic region					
Northeast	8	28,541	24,916	27,449	30,022
North Central	35	25,058	20,993	25,220	27,250
South	51	25,434	22,000	25,200	28,689
West	24	36,953	28,684	33,122	42,372
City type					
Suburban	49	29,264	24,000	27,478	32,000
Independent	69	26,890	20,475	25,338	30,000
Form of government					
Mayor-council	55	25,287	20,475	24,380	28,500
Council-manager	60	30,588	25,000	27,710	34,500
Superintendent of parks					
Total	62	26,324	21,798	25,542	30,800
Geographic region					
North Central	22	27,354	22,500	28,266	30,883
South	21	21,607	18,900	22,100	25,584

Title of official	No. cities reporting	Mean ($)	First quartile ($)	Median ($)	Third quartile ($)
2,500–4,999 continued					
West	18	30,253	23,000	29,710	37,608
City type					
Suburban	19	29,838	26,633	28,989	35,107
Independent	43	24,772	20,946	23,568	28,800
Form of government					
Mayor-council	30	26,319	22,100	25,935	30,800
Council-manager	31	26,146	21,009	25,500	28,989
Director of recreation					
Total	35	20,633	15,413	21,324	25,200
Geographic region					
Northeast	7	22,537	11,674	21,571	32,110
North Central	8	19,109	17,021	20,089	21,324
South	10	22,344	20,997	23,802	26,000
West	10	18,810	13,901	18,240	22,500
City type					
Suburban	15	20,363	11,674	21,571	26,000
Independent	20	20,836	17,021	20,235	23,836
Form of government					
Mayor-council	17	21,390	18,480	23,000	25,200
Council-manager	15	20,142	15,032	19,177	26,731
Librarian					
Total	143	21,132	14,691	19,405	26,000
Geographic region					
Northeast	23	26,162	20,808	27,033	31,667
North Central	45	19,986	16,000	18,266	23,795
South	52	16,901	13,229	16,825	19,489
West	23	27,911	17,680	24,996	38,475
City type					
Suburban	50	23,390	17,696	21,970	30,000
Independent	93	19,918	13,229	18,000	23,700
Form of government					
Mayor-council	79	19,618	12,600	18,500	24,460
Council-manager	52	22,099	15,558	19,069	25,469
Town meeting	10	28,789	23,700	30,297	33,191
Director of information services					
Total	14	24,185	19,490	22,414	25,626
Geographic region					
South	11	22,287	19,310	22,000	24,318
City type					
Suburban	3	22,758	. . .	23,157	. . .
Independent	11	24,574	19,310	22,027	27,000
Form of government					
Mayor-council	7	23,539	19,310	23,157	25,626
Council-manager	7	24,831	19,490	22,000	27,000
Purchasing director					
Total	33	26,603	19,635	25,164	35,880
Geographic region					
North Central	3	23,847	. . .	21,840	. . .
South	23	25,652	19,635	25,000	30,841
West	7	30,912	18,304	35,880	37,275
City type					
Suburban	12	29,128	24,000	30,168	36,606
Independent	21	25,161	18,990	22,000	35,399
Form of government					
Mayor-council	15	23,821	18,000	22,000	25,880
Council-manager	18	28,922	20,618	30,168	36,606
Under 2,500					
Mayor					
Total	232	2,313	720	1,500	2,800
Geographic region					
Northeast	50	1,352	500	800	1,500
North Central	89	1,947	900	1,215	2,460
South	67	3,252	1,200	2,100	3,600
West	26	2,990	840	2,400	4,800
City type					
Suburban	70	2,650	900	1,700	3,000
Independent	162	2,167	600	1,200	2,400
Form of government					
Mayor-council	103	3,157	1,200	2,400	3,600
Council-manager	108	1,761	600	1,200	2,069
Commission	3	1,333	. . .	1,200	. . .
Town meeting	17	852	500	700	1,200
City manager					
Total	161	38,838	29,796	37,000	45,000

Table 1/4   **SALARIES OF MUNICIPAL OFFICIALS: 1 JULY 1994**
continued

Title of official	No. cities reporting	Distribution of 1994 salaries			
		Mean ($)	First quartile ($)	Median ($)	Third quartile ($)
Under 2,500 continued					
Geographic region					
Northeast	40	30,936	25,000	30,212	38,850
North Central	36	39,200	31,850	36,500	43,973
South	57	37,991	26,691	37,142	45,155
West	28	51,387	39,708	46,559	64,878
City type					
Suburban	45	43,830	30,617	39,246	59,344
Independent	116	36,902	29,000	36,000	43,000
Form of government					
Mayor-council	11	36,335	27,251	29,410	37,142
Council-manager	133	40,128	30,000	37,960	45,874
Town meeting	15	30,018	17,500	30,900	39,600
Chief appointed administrator					
Total	96	36,883	30,500	36,085	42,308
Geographic region					
Northeast	16	35,243	25,000	33,110	41,000
North Central	49	34,765	30,500	35,650	39,000
South	20	37,695	30,481	37,371	43,653
West	11	47,228	37,080	47,000	51,700
City type					
Suburban	39	37,595	30,530	36,900	42,382
Independent	57	36,397	29,925	36,000	42,308
Form of government					
Mayor-council	63	35,232	28,655	34,720	41,000
Council-manager	27	40,509	36,741	38,110	45,383
Town meeting	4	35,090	31,200	31,350	31,500
Asst. city mgr./asst. CAO					
Total	40	25,726	18,886	23,686	28,704
Geographic region					
Northeast	14	23,202	20,000	21,605	25,000
North Central	7	22,157	14,560	21,840	29,500
South	13	25,596	17,500	23,609	28,114
West	6	36,061	24,876	32,352	47,000
City type					
Suburban	11	27,184	21,840	24,121	31,200
Independent	29	25,173	17,500	21,210	28,704
Form of government					
Mayor-council	10	20,666	16,300	18,903	23,762
Council-manager	24	29,063	21,840	25,663	29,500
Town meeting	5	18,679	16,000	18,886	20,908
City clerk					
Total	208	24,531	19,204	23,570	28,932
Geographic region					
Northeast	35	21,052	14,500	18,545	27,469
North Central	63	24,404	21,000	23,795	27,241
South	74	23,545	19,539	22,830	27,475
West	36	30,161	22,090	28,839	37,372
City type					
Suburban	68	25,997	21,000	25,213	28,953
Independent	140	23,819	18,000	22,013	28,500
Form of government					
Mayor-council	84	23,251	17,171	22,000	27,009
Council-manager	108	26,028	20,470	24,615	30,304
Commission	4	23,185	22,138	24,550	26,962
Town meeting	12	20,468	16,689	18,023	25,000
Chief financial officer					
Total	54	31,228	21,312	29,558	36,800
Geographic region					
Northeast	7	24,914	20,093	20,660	37,847
North Central	8	27,557	22,200	24,731	27,550
South	26	29,791	21,639	28,792	34,058
West	13	39,760	30,000	35,532	46,633
City type					
Suburban	18	31,281	21,639	26,308	37,711
Independent	36	31,201	21,312	30,038	36,716
Form of government					
Mayor-council	13	27,289	19,580	21,298	30,000
Council-manager	36	33,693	26,062	32,200	37,711
Town meeting	4	24,898	20,340	20,826	21,312
Director of economic development					
Total	14	28,905	19,760	29,500	35,915
Geographic region					
North Central	8	26,940	19,760	25,500	32,468
West	3	33,247	. . .	39,140	. . .
City type					
Suburban	4	35,095	35,700	35,808	35,915

Title of official	No. cities reporting	Distribution of 1994 salaries			
		Mean ($)	First quartile ($)	Median ($)	Third quartile ($)
Under 2,500 continued					
Independent	10	26,429	18,000	22,750	32,468
Form of government					
Mayor-council	7	25,676	16,824	27,000	35,700
Council-manager	6	34,197	24,000	33,958	41,766
Treasurer					
Total	51	22,674	18,000	23,000	27,000
Geographic region					
Northeast	12	24,161	20,000	23,600	27,000
North Central	28	21,014	16,500	20,775	24,287
South	5	23,596	20,717	22,306	27,502
West	6	26,681	24,000	25,143	30,000
City type					
Suburban	14	22,845	17,082	23,155	28,500
Independent	37	22,610	19,000	23,000	25,285
Form of government					
Mayor-council	21	23,052	17,909	24,000	26,618
Council-manager	27	22,408	20,000	23,000	27,000
Town meeting	3	22,424	. . .	19,000	. . .
Director of public works					
Total	174	31,702	25,938	29,687	35,844
Geographic region					
Northeast	22	32,416	23,100	28,530	34,760
North Central	56	30,535	26,820	30,181	34,000
South	61	28,282	24,619	27,092	31,487
West	35	39,078	29,806	36,000	48,193
City type					
Suburban	63	33,893	28,000	31,487	36,873
Independent	111	30,458	24,600	28,800	33,750
Form of government					
Mayor-council	67	31,026	24,336	29,806	34,750
Council-manager	104	32,056	26,766	29,464	36,000
Engineer					
Total	9	40,432	20,592	46,679	56,522
Geographic region					
West	5	53,587	55,213	56,522	57,330
City type					
Suburban	4	32,970	16,000	31,340	46,679
Independent	5	46,401	41,000	55,213	57,330
Form of government					
Mayor-council	4	33,791	20,592	33,636	46,679
Council-manager	5	45,744	41,000	56,522	57,330
Police chief					
Total	201	33,164	25,800	30,930	36,048
Geographic region					
Northeast	25	37,527	25,000	30,500	39,525
North Central	66	31,232	26,128	30,428	34,400
South	76	30,280	24,600	29,440	34,956
West	34	40,153	31,000	36,861	51,598
City type					
Suburban	71	37,365	27,768	33,800	40,995
Independent	130	30,870	24,600	29,200	34,500
Form of government					
Mayor-council	83	31,313	24,000	28,225	33,473
Council-manager	113	34,730	27,539	33,134	39,500
Town meeting	4	29,193	24,000	27,250	30,500
Fire chief					
Total	27	32,786	22,969	29,500	42,845
Geographic region					
North Central	7	29,870	21,000	29,500	37,230
South	12	28,828	24,274	26,902	30,028
West	6	42,693	19,911	52,272	59,166
City type					
Suburban	13	36,228	28,312	34,296	41,577
Independent	14	29,590	19,924	24,234	42,845
Form of government					
Mayor-council	10	26,370	19,924	26,902	29,500
Council-manager	16	36,167	25,499	34,398	44,209
Planning director					
Total	20	38,945	31,844	39,300	46,800
Geographic region					
South	9	32,502	25,354	34,000	34,554
West	9	45,110	39,600	45,000	50,965
City type					
Suburban	7	45,587	39,600	46,800	50,965
Independent	13	35,368	28,930	34,000	40,000

Table 1/4   SALARIES OF MUNICIPAL OFFICIALS: 1 JULY 1994
continued

Title of official	No. cities reporting	Distribution of 1994 salaries			
		Mean ($)	First quartile ($)	Median ($)	Third quartile ($)
Under 2,500 continued					
Form of government					
Mayor-council	4	34,397	25,354	32,477	39,600
Council-manager	16	40,082	34,000	39,500	46,800
Personnel director					
Total	5	26,458	17,888	22,381	27,700
Geographic region					
South	3	18,380	. . .	17,888	. . .
City type					
Independent	4	28,601	22,381	25,041	27,700
Form of government					
Council-manager	4	29,355	22,381	25,041	27,700
Director of parks and recreation					
Total	22	24,241	15,000	21,420	29,700
Geographic region					
Northeast	5	21,622	19,981	21,840	23,400
South	10	19,352	13,020	16,000	29,700
West	5	39,633	26,500	46,195	47,138
City type					
Suburban	3	25,983	. . .	23,524	. . .
Independent	19	23,966	14,000	19,981	29,700
Form of government					
Mayor-council	9	22,320	14,000	21,000	23,524
Council-manager	11	26,915	15,000	23,400	31,025
Superintendent of parks					
Total	13	28,303	22,391	26,062	36,399
Geographic region					
North Central	3	29,137	. . .	26,062	. . .
South	5	24,867	22,391	22,660	23,580
West	5	31,239	28,029	28,082	36,399
City type					
Suburban	4	34,164	23,580	34,290	45,000
Independent	9	25,698	18,000	26,062	28,082
Form of government					
Mayor-council	4	23,275	22,660	24,361	26,062

Title of official	No. cities reporting	Distribution of 1994 salaries			
		Mean ($)	First quartile ($)	Median ($)	Third quartile ($)
Under 2,500 continued					
Council-manager	9	30,538	22,391	28,082	37,858
Director of recreation					
Total	9	24,422	18,870	20,000	27,322
Geographic region					
Northeast	3	16,529	. . .	13,965	. . .
West	5	30,132	20,000	24,000	38,400
City type					
Suburban	3	18,945	. . .	18,870	. . .
Independent	6	27,161	19,552	23,661	38,400
Form of government					
Council-manager	6	26,607	19,552	22,000	38,400
Librarian					
Total	30	18,639	12,500	14,850	26,728
Geographic region					
North Central	7	15,553	9,432	12,500	24,500
South	11	15,241	12,250	13,298	19,062
West	10	22,011	12,919	25,714	27,500
City type					
Suburban	4	18,751	18,162	18,612	19,062
Independent	26	18,622	12,500	14,350	26,728
Form of government					
Mayor-council	12	16,290	12,500	13,109	19,062
Council-manager	16	19,909	12,580	19,881	24,700
Director of information services					
Total	3	20,263	. . .	16,750	. . .
City type					
Independent	3	20,263	. . .	16,750	. . .
Purchasing director					
Total	5	24,228	19,460	20,800	32,290
Geographic region					
South	3	23,131	. . .	20,800	. . .
City type					
Independent	3	28,761	. . .	32,290	. . .
Form of government					
Mayor-council	3	24,183	. . .	20,800	. . .

C **2**

Salaries of County Officials, 1994

Gwen Hall
International City/County Management Association

Despite an economy on the mend, average salaries for top-level county employees remain relatively stagnant, with most positions showing little or no increase in 1994. This seems especially true in the largest and smallest counties. Local officials' salaries may continue to suffer as counties try to balance dwindling revenues with citizen demands for improved government services at lower costs, unfunded federal and state mandates, and local government modernization expenses.

METHODOLOGY

The data in this article are based on the results of ICMA's annual salary survey, which was mailed in the summer of 1994 to all counties with populations of 2,500 and over and to all ICMA-recognized counties with populations under 2,500[1]. Of the 3,107 counties that received surveys, 1,506 responded, for a survey response of 48.5% (Table 2/1).

SALARY TRENDS

Table 2/2 shows the percentage of increase in average salary for twelve county positions over a six-year period. In order to be included in this table, a jurisdiction must have responded to the

salary survey for each of the six years covered in the survey (1989 through 1994). From 1993 to 1994 the percentage of increase for most positions either remained what it had been the previous year or dropped. For the three positions that show increases in average salaries from 1993 to 1994—county administrator, county health officer, and planning director—the increase is only one percentage point.

Over the six-year period, the position of county health officer shows the highest percentage of increase (26%), followed by the positions of chief financial officer (25%) and personnel director (25%). Over that same period, the lowest percentage of increase is for the position of director of welfare/human services (20%).

POPULATION

Population size of a county is an influential factor in salary. Size of a local government often affects the range of services provided and the complexity of management. Table 2/3 shows by population group the average salary for each county position covered in the survey. A downward trend in average salary is apparent as the population groups decrease in size. In general, jurisdictions with populations from 50,000 and

Table 2/1   SURVEY RESPONSE

Classification	No. counties surveyed (A)	No. counties responding No.	No. counties responding % of (A)
Total, all counties	3,107	1,506	48.5
Population group			
Over 1,000,000	27	12	44.4
500,000–1,000,000 ...	63	41	65.1
250,000–499,999	99	56	56.6
100,000–249,999	255	155	60.8
50,000–99,999	381	221	58.0
25,000–49,999	619	284	45.9
10,000–24,999	921	413	44.8
5,000–9,999	449	193	43.0
2,500–4,999	178	81	45.5
Under 2,500	115	50	43.5
Geographic region			
Northeast	200	103	51.5
North Central	1,055	555	52.6
South	1,423	597	42.0
West	429	251	58.5
Geographic division			
New England	54	17	31.5
Mid-Atlantic	146	86	58.9
East North Central	437	230	52.6
West North Central ...	618	325	52.6
South Atlantic	589	328	55.7
East South Central	364	93	25.5
West South Central ...	470	176	37.4
Mountain	280	155	55.4
Pacific Coast	149	96	64.4
Metro status			
Metro	725	404	55.7
Nonmetro	2,382	1,102	46.3

Table 2/2   AVERAGE SALARIES OF COUNTY OFFICIALS

Title	No. counties included	1989 ($)	1990 ($)	Increase from 1989 (%)	1991 ($)	Increase from 1990 (%)	1992 ($)	Increase from 1991 (%)	1993 ($)	Increase from 1992 (%)	1994 ($)	Increase from 1993 (%)
Governing board chair/president/county judge	456	16,512	17,266	5	18,016	4	19,032	6	19,741	4	19,947	1
County manager	91	62,388	66,232	6	68,742	4	70,721	3	73,712	4	76,183	3
County administrator	102	47,413	50,127	6	51,804	3	53,714	4	55,890	4	58,539	5
Clerk to the governing board	344	27,174	28,556	5	29,956	5	30,989	3	32,027	3	32,976	3
Chief financial officer	251	36,602	38,573	5	40,269	4	43,072	7	44,357	3	45,815	3
County health officer	132	46,036	48,265	5	50,514	5	53,333	6	55,100	3	58,037	5
Planning director	174	39,635	42,204	6	44,229	5	46,167	4	47,140	2	49,064	4
County engineer	60	49,268	51,974	5	54,182	4	56,470	4	57,764	2	59,581	3
Director of welfare/human services ...	164	44,178	46,894	6	48,700	4	49,804	2	51,271	3	52,931	3
Chief law enforcement official	401	37,904	39,526	4	41,257	4	42,957	4	44,179	3	45,72?	3
Purchasing director	96	38,091	40,607	7	42,226	4	43,066	2	44,870	4	46,3?.5	3
Personnel director	125	42,986	46,030	7	47,976	4	50,321	5	51,932	3	53,?.8	4

Note: Only those counties that have reported for each of the six years from 1989 through 1994 are included.

Table 2/3 SALARIES BY POPULATION GROUP

	Position											
	Governing board chair/president		County manager		County administrator		Clerk		Chief financial officer		Health officer	
Classification	No. reporting	Avg. salary ($)	No. reporting	Avg. salary ($)	No. reporting	Avg. salary ($)	No. reporting	Avg. salary ($)	No. reporting	Avg. salary ($)	No. reporting	Avg. salary ($)
Total, all counties	1,425	21,614	232	75,113	458	49,066	1,179	32,501	959	41,396	609	48,914
Population group												
Over 1,000,000	11	78,449	4	132,479	6	78,944	7	64,716	10	89,891	8	103,480
500,000–1,000,000	38	53,909	17	120,206	13	84,477	32	61,036	35	80,820	27	97,637
250,000–499,999 ..	54	43,428	23	95,075	19	77,961	45	50,156	53	66,450	33	77,202
100,000–249,999 ..	146	32,132	50	81,017	63	64,101	122	43,207	138	53,132	87	63,148
50,000–99,999	209	24,540	63	70,304	82	50,135	181	34,494	181	46,313	118	50,633
25,000–49,999	264	18,809	44	59,319	102	45,212	209	32,384	180	37,349	133	43,202
10,000–24,999	395	17,067	28	50,030	127	40,582	320	28,618	221	30,671	136	34,550
5,000–9,999	183	14,446	3	58,380	31	34,360	151	24,943	83	23,954	41	30,622
2,500–4,999	78	11,319	...	...	8	34,417	68	22,535	37	22,169	16	25,968
Under 2,500	47	10,404	...	...	7	23,401	44	20,812	21	20,240	10	19,274

	Position											
	Planning director		Engineer		Director welfare/ human services		Chief law enforcement official		Purchasing director		Personnel director	
Classification	No. reporting	Avg. salary ($)	No. reporting	Avg. salary ($)	No. reporting	Avg. salary ($)	No. reporting	Avg. salary ($)	No. reporting	Avg. salary ($)	No. reporting	Avg. salary ($)
Total, all counties	681	43,593	692	50,938	593	48,126	1,434	41,744	423	38,915	486	45,102
Population group												
Over 1,000,000	11	78,449	17	90,134	10	85,766	10	90,837	11	74,511	11	79,634
500,000–1,000,000	35	74,815	34	79,400	30	77,194	40	80,337	35	63,572	36	72,664
250,000–499,999	42	62,239	44	69,149	36	69,151	53	69,274	47	48,803	46	61,212
100,000–249,999	117	52,646	113	60,223	86	56,121	147	55,385	95	42,399	110	50,175
50,000–99,999	155	43,616	124	51,169	113	49,790	213	48,012	111	33,772	136	40,163
25,000–49,999	136	36,945	125	47,756	101	46,975	270	40,168	59	28,326	79	35,030
10,000–24,999	138	32,375	157	45,034	140	38,008	396	35,939	54	26,153	49	27,770
5,000–9,999	32	28,097	59	32,548	52	30,785	179	30,382	8	26,969	15	26,483
2,500–4,999	15	26,061	22	26,981	18	30,624	77	25,989	3	15,553	4	26,262
Under 2,500	3	19,385	7	24,564	7	29,353	49	24,136	...	...	...	...

above show average salaries that are slightly above the national average. Counties with populations under 50,000 show average salaries that are below the national average. Also, jurisdictions with populations over one million show declines in average salaries for ten of the twelve positions surveyed and counties with populations under 2,500 show declines in eight.

GEOGRAPHIC REGION

Geographic region seems to also play a part in the fluctuations among average salaries. An indication of the differences in salary levels for the varying regions can be gained from Figure 2/1 which shows the average 1994 salary of county managers and the percentage of change from the previous year. The highest average salary for county managers was in the West region ($83,333), while the lowest average salary was found in the Northeast region ($67,856). From 1993 to 1994 average salary for the county manager declined in the West (3.6%) and Northeast (11.2%) regions from 1993 to 1994, while the North Central and South regions showed small increases, 3.2% and 1.8% respectively.

For nine of the twelve positions surveyed, the average salary is highest in the Western region (not shown). The average salary for the remaining three positions is highest in the Northeast region. With the exception of four positions (county administrator, county manager, purchasing director, and personnel director), the lowest average salary is in the North Central region.

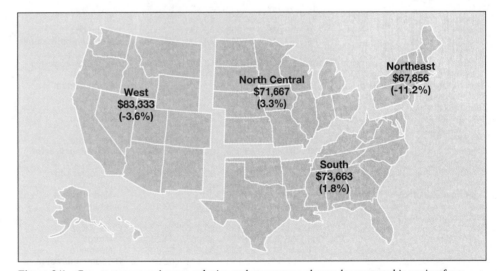

Figure 2/1 *County managers' mean salaries and percentage change by geographic region from 1993 to 1994*

METRO STATUS

Metro counties, those located within a metropolitan statistical area, have higher average salaries than nonmetro counties. Metropolitan statistical areas (MSAs) have at least one central county and may include outlying counties with economic and social ties to the central cities and the central county in the MSA. Because population is a factor in defining an MSA, it is not surprising that the average salaries in metro counties would be higher.

SALARIES BY POSITION

Table 2/4 presents the average salaries for the twelve positions covered in the survey. The data are arrayed by population group, geographic region, and metro status.

[1]Governments recognized by ICMA have the council-manager form of government or provide for a general management position.

Table 2/4   **SALARIES OF COUNTY OFFICIALS: 1 JULY 1994**

Salary data for the 12 selected county officials in this table are based on information reported by county officials as of 1 July 1994. Data are reported by position titles only, which while representing similar job responsibilities, do not purport to represent identical duties and responsibilities.

For the position of county manager, data are shown for only those counties recognized by ICMA as either having a council-manager form of government or providing for a position of overall general management. For the position of county administrator, data are shown for all other reporting counties.

Except for the position of governing board chairman/president/county judge which includes part-time salaries, this table excludes: (1) salaries of part-time officials, (2) salaries for vacant positions, (3) salaries of acting officials, (4) salaries of those paid in whole or in part by fees, and (5) all salaries below $8,000. Salaries are presented for ten population groups and are further classified by geographic region and county type.

Classifications having less than three counties reporting are excluded because meaningful statistics cannot be computed. Consequently the number reporting in some of the subcategories does not always equal the total reporting. Quartiles are not shown when only three counties reported.

Title of official	No. counties reporting	Distribution of 1994 salaries			
		Mean ($)	First quartile ($)	Median ($)	Third quartile ($)
All counties					
Governing board chair/ president/county judge					
Total	1,425	21,614	7,500	16,110	31,000
Geographic region					
Northeast	97	30,259	15,000	24,014	37,800
North Central	519	13,810	6,240	10,700	16,600
South	571	24,317	7,200	22,046	36,412
West	238	28,621	15,000	25,782	40,100
County type					
Metro	378	33,561	15,000	30,000	47,123
Nonmetro	1,047	17,300	6,720	13,451	25,212
County manager					
Total	232	75,113	57,000	71,491	88,395
Geographic region					
Northeast	14	67,856	56,346	64,730	75,470
North Central	33	71,667	51,825	70,988	89,175
South	135	73,663	54,825	67,236	89,250
West	50	83,333	67,156	79,232	91,312
County type					
Metro	117	88,001	66,783	86,560	105,000
Nonmetro	115	62,000	50,000	62,000	72,108
County administrator					
Total	458	49,066	33,439	47,465	60,000
Geographic region					
Northeast	42	49,147	32,000	47,428	59,862
North Central	101	48,426	36,705	48,800	56,820
South	230	48,058	31,008	46,636	60,000
West	85	52,516	35,000	49,500	69,708
County type					
Metro	158	61,880	48,383	58,819	75,532
Nonmetro	300	42,318	29,700	41,781	53,285
Clerk to the governing board					
Total	1,179	32,501	23,728	29,000	37,549
Geographic region					
Northeast	62	33,933	26,457	29,954	37,423
North Central	466	30,341	23,241	28,417	34,728
South	428	33,659	23,000	28,481	38,933
West	223	34,391	25,800	31,068	40,752
County type					
Metro	306	43,007	31,304	39,597	50,463
Nonmetro	873	28,818	22,700	27,000	33,000
Chief financial officer					
Total	959	41,396	26,009	37,800	52,386
Geographic region					
Northeast	82	45,220	33,100	40,276	55,733
North Central	303	36,381	24,277	32,065	44,200
South	411	41,547	25,830	38,874	51,896
West	163	48,415	32,713	46,424	62,016
County type					
Metro	330	56,406	42,576	54,189	69,451
Nonmetro	629	33,522	23,500	31,250	40,730
County health officer					
Total	609	48,914	30,384	42,783	61,752
Geographic region					
Northeast	41	62,357	50,860	57,602	68,778
North Central	284	39,427	27,466	35,000	48,984
South	168	58,815	38,000	51,890	83,459
West	116	53,051	28,663	47,341	69,612
County type					
Metro	209	65,920	46,945	61,752	85,467
Nonmetro	400	40,028	27,529	36,139	48,156
Planning director					
Total	681	43,593	31,020	41,400	53,628
Geographic region					
Northeast	80	44,378	33,201	42,092	54,585

Title of official	No. counties reporting	Distribution of 1994 salaries			
		Mean ($)	First quartile ($)	Median ($)	Third quartile ($)
All counties continued					
North Central	182	36,137	25,089	33,968	45,216
South	252	45,861	33,756	43,202	55,048
West	167	47,919	34,000	46,980	56,856
County type					
Metro	286	53,474	38,760	51,001	65,965
Nonmetro	395	36,439	26,522	35,020	45,469
County engineer					
Total	692	50,938	40,227	50,000	60,714
Geographic region					
Northeast	39	58,417	44,774	59,400	70,000
North Central	332	46,719	37,500	47,807	55,859
South	208	52,289	40,227	50,878	62,812
West	113	58,263	44,952	55,992	67,092
County type					
Metro	264	62,104	50,000	61,046	72,498
Nonmetro	428	44,050	33,020	45,529	53,300
Director of welfare/human services					
Total	593	48,126	36,000	46,548	57,936
Geographic region					
Northeast	68	49,726	38,946	48,201	60,800
North Central	189	45,580	35,000	46,571	55,400
South	223	47,098	35,636	44,698	55,271
West	113	53,450	37,248	51,000	65,832
County type					
Metro	217	60,469	47,500	60,228	71,628
Nonmetro	376	41,002	33,000	41,383	50,292
Chief law enforcement official					
Total	1,434	41,744	30,000	38,000	49,557
Geographic region					
Northeast	94	42,491	31,923	37,951	51,200
North Central	542	36,916	28,000	34,708	43,391
South	556	44,688	32,086	42,479	52,008
West	242	45,505	30,600	41,188	54,400
County type					
Metro	383	57,012	43,572	53,926	68,369
Nonmetro	1,051	36,181	27,932	35,000	42,828
Purchasing director					
Total	423	38,915	25,656	36,072	49,454
Geographic region					
Northeast	55	37,680	25,343	33,933	44,750
North Central	59	39,917	29,000	38,500	50,684
South	243	36,542	23,840	32,551	45,500
West	66	47,785	32,942	47,063	58,573
County type					
Metro	247	45,204	31,699	43,825	56,290
Nonmetro	176	30,088	20,758	27,362	36,072
Personnel director					
Total	486	45,102	30,784	43,129	58,054
Geographic region					
Northeast	61	43,649	31,982	39,812	56,756
North Central	110	44,945	33,153	42,390	55,598
South	213	43,392	28,184	40,941	57,088
West	102	49,711	38,000	50,319	60,000
County type					
Metro	256	53,682	39,811	53,171	66,624
Nonmetro	230	35,552	23,691	34,195	45,384
Over 1,000,000					
Governing board chair/ president/county judge					
Total	11	78,449	62,001	82,056	100,716
Geographic region					
South	5	83,821	74,676	90,740	90,972

Table 2/4   SALARIES OF COUNTY OFFICIALS: 1 JULY 1994
continued

Left column — 1,000,000 continued

Title of official	No. counties reporting	Mean ($)	First quartile ($)	Median ($)	Third quartile ($)
1,000,000 continued					
West	3	69,174	...	75,911	...
County type					
Metro	11	78,449	62,001	82,056	100,716
County manager					
Total	4	132,479	134,930	135,221	135,512
Geographic region					
West	3	137,023	...	135,512	...
County type					
Metro	4	132,479	134,930	135,221	135,512
County administrator					
Total	6	78,944	59,638	75,828	94,152
Geographic region					
South	4	76,149	73,632	75,828	78,024
County type					
Metro	6	78,944	59,638	75,828	94,152
Clerk to the governing board					
Total	7	64,716	52,344	63,731	79,356
Geographic region					
West	3	64,507	...	63,731	...
County type					
Metro	7	64,716	52,344	63,731	79,356
Chief financial officer					
Total	10	89,891	84,212	87,999	100,568
Geographic region					
South	4	86,871	78,984	84,372	89,760
West	3	96,980	...	100,568	...
County type					
Metro	10	89,891	84,212	87,999	100,568
County health officer					
Total	8	103,480	98,475	105,148	112,008
Geographic region					
West	3	114,821	...	112,008	...
County type					
Metro	8	103,480	98,475	105,148	112,008
Planning director					
Total	8	86,708	80,750	90,360	93,060
Geographic region					
West	3	95,937	...	93,060	...
County type					
Metro	8	86,708	80,750	90,360	93,060
County engineer					
Total	7	90,134	78,085	99,652	100,441
Geographic region					
South	3	83,604	...	99,852	...
County type					
Metro	7	90,134	78,085	99,652	100,441
Director of welfare/human services					
Total	10	85,766	64,956	89,625	102,377
Geographic region					
South	4	66,038	55,680	60,318	64,956
West	3	108,585	...	110,926	...
County type					
Metro	10	85,766	64,956	89,625	102,377
Chief law enforcement official					
Total	10	90,837	81,498	87,198	94,351
Geographic region					
South	4	79,428	77,892	80,358	82,824
West	3	110,684	...	111,238	...
County type					
Metro	10	90,837	81,498	87,198	94,351
Purchasing director					
Total	11	74,511	62,712	70,096	87,618
Geographic region					
South	5	69,653	58,200	62,712	77,916
West	3	83,888	...	77,792	...
County type					
Metro	11	74,511	62,712	70,096	87,618
Personnel director					
Total	11	79,634	63,972	78,085	96,335
Geographic region					
South	5	68,263	60,000	63,972	71,004
West	3	96,748	...	99,091	...
County type					
Metro	11	79,634	63,972	78,085	96,335

Right column — 500,000–1,000,000

Title of official	No. counties reporting	Mean ($)	First quartile ($)	Median ($)	Third quartile ($)
500,000–1,000,000					
Governing board chair/president/county judge					
Total	38	53,909	44,720	54,882	64,543
Geographic region					
Northeast	8	41,646	24,014	37,201	50,950
North Central	7	62,045	51,000	60,299	73,000
South	14	57,574	45,000	57,671	80,000
West	9	52,781	45,000	54,638	60,346
County type					
Metro	38	53,909	44,720	54,882	64,543
County manager					
Total	17	120,206	112,855	118,717	132,105
Geographic region					
South	9	118,991	102,971	118,456	137,509
West	5	123,281	118,717	121,000	123,630
County type					
Metro	17	120,206	112,855	118,717	132,105
County administrator					
Total	13	84,477	68,562	85,500	95,000
Geographic region					
Northeast	4	72,482	64,480	73,740	83,000
North Central	3	74,507	...	68,562	...
South	4	92,783	85,500	85,878	86,256
County type					
Metro	13	84,477	68,562	85,500	95,000
Clerk to the governing board					
Total	32	61,036	45,990	62,253	69,642
Geographic region					
Northeast	6	49,012	37,241	44,995	65,000
North Central	7	49,455	37,518	48,674	62,564
South	11	71,588	50,430	69,642	90,948
West	8	65,678	60,000	65,144	71,393
County type					
Metro	32	61,036	45,990	62,253	69,642
Chief financial officer					
Total	35	80,820	68,900	81,788	92,612
Geographic region					
Northeast	7	70,718	55,000	68,900	72,478
North Central	7	76,029	65,112	81,788	86,400
South	12	84,473	76,407	85,159	95,472
West	9	87,531	80,000	87,669	97,370
County type					
Metro	35	80,820	68,900	81,788	92,612
County health officer					
Total	27	97,637	88,024	95,514	104,998
Geographic region					
Northeast	5	84,122	76,913	77,677	94,411
North Central	6	89,211	85,467	91,331	95,000
South	10	101,148	90,000	100,520	115,797
West	6	111,475	95,514	104,018	125,216
County type					
Metro	27	97,637	88,024	95,514	104,998
Planning director					
Total	35	74,815	65,166	75,528	84,926
Geographic region					
Northeast	7	64,020	59,488	65,166	73,453
North Central	5	73,865	65,965	74,189	82,743
South	15	75,844	71,705	76,800	87,526
West	8	82,925	76,895	84,313	89,724
County type					
Metro	35	74,815	65,166	75,528	84,926
County engineer					
Total	34	79,400	71,040	77,593	90,482
Geographic region					
Northeast	8	69,215	50,000	62,855	86,790
North Central	6	79,140	72,993	74,272	90,400
South	13	80,060	66,997	78,021	93,722
West	7	90,040	76,895	87,000	102,700
County type					
Metro	34	79,400	71,040	77,593	90,482
Director of welfare/human services					
Total	30	77,194	64,480	74,650	86,174
Geographic region					
Northeast	5	69,275	62,448	63,150	73,772

Table 2/4   **SALARIES OF COUNTY OFFICIALS: 1 JULY 1994**
continued

Title of official	No. counties reporting	Distribution of 1994 salaries			
		Mean ($)	First quartile ($)	Median ($)	Third quartile ($)
500,000–1,000,000 continued					
North Central	5	79,304	64,480	72,421	94,004
South	13	72,208	66,830	71,628	80,000
West	7	90,605	83,356	84,366	94,260
County type					
Metro	30	77,194	64,480	74,650	86,174
Chief law enforcement official					
Total	40	80,337	70,000	82,168	95,103
Geographic region					
Northeast	8	66,166	57,000	69,800	76,437
North Central	7	67,974	53,926	74,210	81,500
South	16	87,804	75,662	92,535	98,178
West	9	89,274	83,700	86,879	95,732
County type					
Metro	40	80,337	70,000	82,168	95,103
Purchasing director					
Total	35	63,572	54,000	60,994	71,196
Geographic region					
Northeast	8	55,382	43,545	49,419	67,600
North Central	6	55,323	49,691	54,700	59,433
South	16	67,705	60,872	68,471	71,196
West	5	73,351	57,308	64,591	97,695
County type					
Metro	35	63,572	54,000	60,994	71,196
Personnel director					
Total	36	72,664	68,390	72,665	78,721
Geographic region					
Northeast	6	66,159	66,842	71,509	72,512
North Central	7	71,389	58,942	71,721	87,880
South	17	72,798	68,390	73,883	78,721
West	6	80,278	72,818	81,057	89,724
County type					
Metro	36	72,664	68,390	72,665	78,721
250,000–499,999					
Governing board chair/ president/county judge					
Total	54	43,428	28,650	45,203	54,653
Geographic region					
Northeast	9	45,385	22,105	45,106	55,713
North Central	14	42,008	27,996	39,948	56,636
South	19	40,459	16,944	45,300	50,572
West	12	48,316	41,995	49,128	51,432
County type					
Metro	54	43,428	28,650	45,203	54,653
County manager					
Total	23	95,075	86,560	96,813	105,441
Geographic region					
North Central	4	99,104	96,813	99,788	102,762
South	13	95,559	86,560	97,573	106,210
West	6	91,339	84,323	87,698	99,736
County type					
Metro	23	95,075	86,560	96,813	105,441
County administrator					
Total	19	77,961	63,000	79,250	92,508
Geographic region					
Northeast	6	76,272	63,000	80,410	88,886
North Central	5	77,212	66,837	79,250	88,870
South	5	74,016	49,208	66,000	94,952
West	3	89,166	. . .	90,527	. . .
County type					
Metro	19	77,961	63,000	79,250	92,508
Clerk to the governing board					
Total	45	50,156	37,871	47,606	59,614
Geographic region					
Northeast	6	47,102	37,317	46,307	52,302
North Central	13	51,638	43,606	51,996	59,000
South	17	53,402	35,172	44,023	70,787
West	9	43,921	37,871	42,072	49,181
County type					
Metro	45	50,156	37,871	47,606	59,614
Chief financial officer					
Total	53	66,450	60,280	66,355	74,440
Geographic region					
Northeast	10	63,280	50,741	64,830	72,120
North Central	13	66,578	59,012	69,482	72,514

Title of official	No. counties reporting	Distribution of 1994 salaries			
		Mean ($)	First quartile ($)	Median ($)	Third quartile ($)
250,000–499,999 continued					
South	19	67,063	61,200	64,634	76,500
West	11	68,120	63,211	70,345	79,860
County type					
Metro	53	66,450	60,280	66,355	74,440
County health officer					
Total	33	77,202	63,169	82,908	92,711
Geographic region					
Northeast	4	76,532	70,641	78,187	85,732
North Central	11	67,216	55,404	66,743	76,414
South	11	83,452	70,000	90,588	95,000
West	7	83,458	63,169	92,929	95,028
County type					
Metro	33	77,202	63,169	82,908	92,711
Planning director					
Total	42	62,239	55,933	64,095	70,200
Geographic region					
Northeast	6	68,802	64,970	69,549	74,172
North Central	10	57,865	56,880	60,518	64,771
South	17	60,713	55,328	62,868	66,759
West	9	65,605	54,325	68,319	76,491
County type					
Metro	42	62,239	55,933	64,095	70,200
County engineer					
Total	44	69,149	61,610	68,535	76,515
Geographic region					
Northeast	7	69,681	59,400	70,000	78,100
North Central	12	72,340	67,900	73,497	77,400
South	16	66,238	61,610	66,596	74,547
West	9	69,654	59,176	63,211	83,964
County type					
Metro	44	69,149	61,610	68,535	76,515
Director of welfare/human services					
Total	36	69,151	60,228	68,150	78,562
Geographic region					
Northeast	7	64,219	56,513	64,970	70,000
North Central	8	78,013	71,890	80,513	83,900
South	13	61,281	49,900	57,482	76,452
West	8	77,392	67,038	73,772	83,137
County type					
Metro	36	69,151	60,228	68,150	78,562
Chief law enforcement official					
Total	53	69,274	56,580	72,096	81,370
Geographic region					
Northeast	10	58,000	46,760	59,638	73,052
North Central	13	64,928	56,580	61,526	73,551
South	18	75,647	68,369	80,673	86,344
West	12	73,818	65,644	73,450	82,530
County type					
Metro	53	69,274	56,580	72,096	81,370
Purchasing director					
Total	47	48,803	42,298	47,940	56,290
Geographic region					
Northeast	7	46,608	28,389	44,452	59,640
North Central	12	49,860	46,827	50,332	58,526
South	19	48,338	42,298	47,445	52,700
West	9	50,081	45,011	47,076	54,319
County type					
Metro	47	48,803	42,298	47,940	56,290
Personnel director					
Total	46	61,212	52,645	62,409	71,347
Geographic region					
Northeast	7	57,962	50,808	58,051	62,377
North Central	13	64,283	58,354	67,166	76,620
South	16	57,189	52,645	60,271	64,104
West	10	65,933	57,990	68,827	75,948
County type					
Metro	46	61,212	52,645	62,409	71,347
100,000–249,999					
Governing board chair/ president/county judge					
Total	146	32,132	14,560	33,266	43,700
Geographic region					
Northeast	20	31,770	12,000	34,118	42,000

Table 2/4 SALARIES OF COUNTY OFFICIALS: 1 JULY 1994
continued

Title of official	No. counties reporting	Mean ($)	First quartile ($)	Median ($)	Third quartile ($)
100,000–249,999 continued					
North Central	45	23,598	9,500	20,157	41,113
South	56	34,599	15,790	32,831	48,155
West	25	42,255	36,000	43,700	50,004
County type					
Metro	124	32,307	15,000	32,977	43,960
Nonmetro	22	31,144	14,000	35,516	42,205
County manager					
Total	50	81,017	67,115	78,171	90,747
Geographic region					
North Central	13	76,324	63,756	77,936	87,634
South	26	83,055	67,115	77,428	103,166
West	9	85,820	78,144	82,800	91,312
County type					
Metro	38	81,708	67,496	78,908	90,747
Nonmetro	12	78,828	64,100	76,572	82,964
County administrator					
Total	63	64,101	49,900	60,670	74,431
Geographic region					
Northeast	11	51,380	42,225	50,192	57,457
North Central	20	54,660	48,565	54,115	60,000
South	21	73,294	55,502	72,427	80,398
West	11	76,435	66,518	73,899	79,260
County type					
Metro	55	63,476	49,878	57,457	73,964
Nonmetro	8	68,395	62,000	71,804	79,000
Clerk to the governing board					
Total	122	43,207	33,902	42,243	50,004
Geographic region					
Northeast	11	32,368	29,504	31,669	39,000
North Central	41	41,431	37,250	42,645	46,309
South	49	45,501	33,981	42,000	55,602
West	21	46,998	36,400	50,000	52,604
County type					
Metro	105	43,228	35,351	42,500	50,000
Nonmetro	17	43,072	26,398	36,400	58,573
Chief financial officer					
Total	138	53,132	43,500	51,995	62,016
Geographic region					
Northeast	20	41,241	34,955	39,696	49,654
North Central	42	49,745	42,248	49,554	56,756
South	56	56,240	45,120	54,903	66,215
West	20	63,436	59,082	62,364	67,846
County type					
Metro	115	52,642	42,576	50,777	61,543
Nonmetro	23	55,584	49,654	55,733	66,384
County health officer					
Total	87	63,148	51,000	60,010	76,639
Geographic region					
Northeast	8	59,553	56,000	61,700	63,083
North Central	35	55,475	47,174	56,270	60,010
South	27	66,232	45,500	62,936	84,714
West	17	75,739	62,092	73,736	83,160
County type					
Metro	74	62,330	51,000	59,934	75,000
Nonmetro	13	67,806	51,320	62,599	77,064
Planning director					
Total	117	52,646	43,185	50,161	60,870
Geographic region					
Northeast	15	47,164	42,133	47,834	50,976
North Central	33	44,563	40,000	43,743	50,648
South	44	55,898	44,791	57,527	63,582
West	25	60,880	51,150	57,960	66,518
County type					
Metro	95	52,350	43,185	49,712	61,470
Nonmetro	22	53,920	43,000	52,025	60,870
County engineer					
Total	113	60,223	49,899	58,760	68,560
Geographic region					
Northeast	10	47,561	39,976	46,189	51,455
North Central	35	59,914	50,000	57,658	67,084
South	46	61,112	52,038	58,812	69,016
West	22	64,610	54,355	66,738	73,320
County type					
Metro	95	59,692	49,494	58,548	68,004
Nonmetro	18	63,022	54,355	61,352	69,156

Title of official	No. counties reporting	Mean ($)	First quartile ($)	Median ($)	Third quartile ($)
100,000–249,999 continued					
Director of welfare/ human services					
Total	86	56,121	44,388	53,443	65,905
Geographic region					
Northeast	17	45,620	37,850	47,415	54,999
North Central	21	55,644	45,989	54,849	64,480
South	31	56,081	37,256	52,212	75,546
West	17	67,285	61,086	66,518	69,950
County type					
Metro	68	55,712	42,500	53,081	65,905
Nonmetro	18	57,668	47,415	56,100	64,020
Chief law enforcement official					
Total	147	55,385	45,899	53,431	62,936
Geographic region					
Northeast	20	40,357	35,828	37,404	42,210
North Central	48	53,275	47,278	52,738	59,503
South	54	59,817	49,514	55,000	78,513
West	25	61,884	52,000	59,892	67,561
County type					
Metro	126	55,356	45,899	53,466	61,750
Nonmetro	21	55,558	47,280	53,378	69,972
Purchasing director					
Total	95	42,399	32,942	40,057	51,592
Geographic region					
Northeast	14	31,559	24,069	30,982	36,231
North Central	17	38,412	33,501	38,500	43,263
South	48	44,404	36,156	42,680	52,260
West	16	50,105	37,500	48,930	62,376
County type					
Metro	82	42,192	32,124	39,976	51,592
Nonmetro	13	43,705	34,944	42,500	49,396
Personnel director					
Total	110	50,175	39,427	49,388	59,263
Geographic region					
Northeast	14	40,479	34,705	37,696	42,000
North Central	27	48,975	40,560	48,915	58,387
South	51	50,419	38,000	49,335	60,570
West	18	58,824	49,600	55,390	66,384
County type					
Metro	90	49,523	39,195	46,993	59,263
Nonmetro	20	53,109	49,081	52,997	59,000
50,000–99,999					
Governing board chair/ president/county judge					
Total	209	24,540	8,500	22,000	36,498
Geographic region					
Northeast	27	26,973	12,000	20,788	36,498
North Central	54	16,982	6,000	13,900	30,082
South	96	23,402	8,100	20,084	36,400
West	32	38,658	30,189	39,658	47,832
County type					
Metro	85	26,162	12,500	24,498	36,000
Nonmetro	124	23,429	7,000	19,994	37,500
County manager					
Total	63	70,304	60,382	68,328	79,043
Geographic region					
Northeast	8	70,628	65,085	71,001	75,470
North Central	5	57,165	51,825	60,000	60,382
South	42	71,602	61,958	67,782	79,723
West	8	71,380	68,308	71,817	76,458
County type					
Metro	23	74,915	62,000	65,085	90,189
Nonmetro	40	67,653	59,160	68,604	75,470
County administrator					
Total	82	50,135	35,500	50,316	62,195
Geographic region					
Northeast	10	38,377	26,516	36,997	49,431
North Central	25	46,570	35,500	47,054	60,000
South	33	53,694	36,000	52,500	66,372
West	14	56,511	47,262	59,094	68,510
County type					
Metro	34	48,481	30,000	50,657	60,000
Nonmetro	48	51,307	37,933	50,117	62,784
Clerk to the governing board					
Total	181	34,494	28,356	33,610	38,690

Table 2/4 continued   SALARIES OF COUNTY OFFICIALS: 1 JULY 1994

Title of official	No. counties reporting	Mean ($)	First quartile ($)	Median ($)	Third quartile ($)
50,000–99,999 continued					
Geographic region					
Northeast	19	32,944	28,500	30,786	34,337
North Central	51	32,860	30,171	33,841	38,298
South	83	35,649	25,000	33,475	40,360
West	28	35,097	29,976	35,190	39,707
County type					
Metro	70	34,080	27,322	32,871	39,033
Nonmetro	111	34,755	28,357	33,921	38,298
Chief financial officer					
Total	181	46,313	37,800	45,236	54,000
Geographic region					
Northeast	22	43,818	34,252	41,276	52,000
North Central	45	42,800	36,000	42,771	51,137
South	86	47,598	38,646	47,148	54,340
West	28	49,975	39,420	52,692	57,953
County type					
Metro	70	48,345	39,273	47,148	56,555
Nonmetro	111	45,033	37,472	44,040	52,853
County health officer					
Total	118	50,633	40,800	49,565	59,388
Geographic region					
Northeast	16	54,134	50,698	53,419	56,200
North Central	43	42,398	34,009	43,181	50,201
South	38	55,918	43,531	52,416	74,021
West	21	55,264	46,000	56,784	69,612
County type					
Metro	42	47,543	34,009	47,754	59,916
Nonmetro	76	52,340	43,036	50,734	59,183
Planning director					
Total	155	43,616	36,254	43,590	49,546
Geographic region					
Northeast	26	41,854	35,157	40,975	44,623
North Central	32	40,402	34,650	38,741	47,771
South	70	44,121	36,929	42,848	49,210
West	27	47,815	43,590	47,544	54,590
County type					
Metro	61	44,515	36,090	42,619	51,370
Nonmetro	94	43,033	36,504	44,029	48,000
County engineer					
Total	124	51,169	42,590	50,766	61,380
Geographic region					
Northeast	12	53,985	37,075	61,120	68,016
North Central	36	51,026	42,848	50,983	62,650
South	53	49,287	40,227	48,187	56,716
West	23	54,261	46,315	55,920	61,380
County type					
Metro	53	53,026	44,407	54,107	62,538
Nonmetro	71	49,783	40,227	48,652	59,406
Director of welfare/human services					
Total	113	49,790	42,827	52,000	58,600
Geographic region					
Northeast	21	48,162	42,490	48,401	54,534
North Central	27	54,820	49,600	54,893	61,256
South	50	47,089	37,579	48,559	56,223
West	15	52,016	47,759	58,697	60,369
County type					
Metro	44	51,307	42,458	53,368	63,252
Nonmetro	69	48,822	43,728	51,326	56,524
Chief law enforcement official					
Total	213	48,012	40,241	46,800	54,823
Geographic region					
Northeast	26	41,594	33,054	39,890	51,524
North Central	57	45,563	38,413	44,982	51,801
South	98	50,438	43,200	49,825	56,554
West	32	50,161	44,074	51,468	55,718
County type					
Metro	87	47,494	38,414	46,800	55,108
Nonmetro	126	48,370	40,983	46,810	54,659
Purchasing director					
Total	111	33,772	25,128	31,553	41,301
Geographic region					
Northeast	19	31,844	24,424	28,347	40,650
North Central	13	35,448	26,265	34,060	41,050
South	64	32,486	25,100	30,837	39,249

Title of official	No. counties reporting	Mean ($)	First quartile ($)	Median ($)	Third quartile ($)
50,000–99,999 continued					
West	15	40,251	31,805	39,915	52,384
County type					
Metro	50	33,335	24,000	31,491	42,894
Nonmetro	61	34,131	26,244	31,805	40,063
Personnel director					
Total	136	40,163	29,959	40,793	50,555
Geographic region					
Northeast	22	38,997	28,275	38,276	51,550
North Central	25	40,107	34,060	40,789	50,555
South	63	38,348	29,124	36,447	46,468
West	26	45,602	38,940	45,310	54,348
County type					
Metro	56	41,348	29,419	40,395	53,456
Nonmetro	80	39,333	30,784	40,869	47,382
25,000–49,999					
Governing board chair/president/county judge					
Total	264	18,809	7,200	15,550	27,483
Geographic region					
Northeast	23	21,443	11,000	25,726	29,000
North Central	97	12,549	5,000	12,996	17,186
South	114	21,779	7,000	22,089	33,520
West	30	25,742	15,600	26,114	34,000
County type					
Metro	43	19,709	6,800	16,363	26,113
Nonmetro	221	18,634	7,200	15,459	27,514
County manager					
Total	44	59,319	49,980	54,972	67,014
Geographic region					
North Central	7	53,504	46,000	48,000	64,000
South	26	57,658	51,356	54,708	61,100
West	9	70,542	66,193	71,520	79,300
County type					
Metro	11	58,640	46,813	53,900	70,338
Nonmetro	33	59,546	51,356	55,119	67,014
County administrator					
Total	102	45,212	32,682	46,467	54,320
Geographic region					
Northeast	9	31,504	22,316	32,000	33,439
North Central	27	45,548	41,500	47,134	54,320
South	55	44,515	26,208	46,934	53,448
West	11	59,088	42,973	56,631	75,280
County type					
Metro	17	47,478	33,000	48,479	55,785
Nonmetro	85	44,759	32,682	46,000	53,976
Clerk to the governing board					
Total	209	32,384	26,400	30,500	36,697
Geographic region					
Northeast	13	25,412	24,334	26,774	27,672
North Central	89	32,633	28,700	32,000	35,618
South	78	31,515	24,000	27,691	37,560
West	29	37,085	28,242	36,602	44,512
County type					
Metro	27	35,951	28,183	33,335	38,896
Nonmetro	182	31,855	26,000	29,987	35,900
Chief financial officer					
Total	180	37,349	29,059	36,050	42,279
Geographic region					
Northeast	14	30,838	26,000	32,230	36,601
North Central	68	34,750	29,565	33,792	39,204
South	74	37,303	27,818	36,411	44,125
West	24	48,657	38,000	50,404	54,017
County type					
Metro	33	41,473	31,253	41,361	49,606
Nonmetro	147	36,424	28,700	35,504	40,800
County health officer					
Total	133	43,202	30,384	40,764	50,882
Geographic region					
Northeast	5	48,298	42,500	50,374	50,860
North Central	69	37,719	27,500	37,636	43,925
South	40	54,116	39,790	45,314	75,000
West	19	38,800	16,295	38,812	56,301
County type					
Metro	21	43,195	35,000	41,719	46,945

Table 2/4 SALARIES OF COUNTY OFFICIALS: 1 JULY 1994
continued

Title of official	No. counties reporting	Mean ($)	First quartile ($)	Median ($)	Third quartile ($)
25,000–49,999 continued					
Nonmetro	112	43,204	29,610	40,747	50,882
Planning director					
Total	136	36,945	29,019	34,632	45,000
Geographic region					
Northeast	17	31,945	24,415	32,085	38,238
North Central	42	31,185	24,000	30,534	37,034
South	52	37,372	31,590	34,880	42,000
West	25	49,132	39,960	48,864	56,808
County type					
Metro	32	36,791	29,741	34,780	47,593
Nonmetro	104	36,992	29,019	34,420	44,880
County engineer					
Total	125	47,756	41,000	50,000	56,596
Geographic region					
North Central	71	48,332	42,000	50,533	56,596
South	34	42,333	32,791	42,185	51,140
West	19	56,464	48,147	56,112	64,141
County type					
Metro	20	51,634	47,786	52,140	59,164
Nonmetro	105	47,017	40,437	48,370	56,520
Director of welfare/human services					
Total	101	46,975	42,336	47,881	53,580
Geographic region					
Northeast	11	41,213	32,000	41,365	45,799
North Central	43	47,847	43,534	50,292	55,120
South	35	45,786	42,343	46,291	50,396
West	12	52,599	48,245	53,906	55,320
County type					
Metro	23	49,138	43,771	49,896	55,120
Nonmetro	78	46,338	40,706	47,455	53,560
Chief law enforcement official					
Total	270	40,168	33,050	39,599	46,045
Geographic region					
Northeast	21	30,995	25,356	30,274	34,012
North Central	106	38,547	33,243	38,225	42,959
South	112	41,834	33,693	42,740	47,662
West	31	45,904	38,161	45,780	55,247
County type					
Metro	44	44,493	38,325	44,020	50,425
Nonmetro	226	39,326	32,725	38,950	45,060
Purchasing director					
Total	59	28,326	20,232	26,871	33,425
Geographic region					
Northeast	3	23,233	. . .	16,688	. . .
North Central	4	25,649	25,402	25,701	26,000
South	43	25,674	19,998	22,440	31,350
West	9	43,885	28,569	49,272	51,958
County type					
Metro	15	32,397	26,871	31,350	39,153
Nonmetro	44	26,938	19,998	22,220	28,569
Personnel director					
Total	79	35,030	27,000	34,132	42,680
Geographic region					
Northeast	7	28,189	20,000	29,716	35,500
North Central	26	36,083	31,000	35,503	42,000
South	31	30,473	21,400	27,673	36,099
West	15	45,817	32,830	49,068	56,006
County type					
Metro	14	37,707	29,520	36,887	42,680
Nonmetro	65	34,454	26,566	32,830	42,436
10,000–24,999					
Governing board chair/ president/county judge					
Total	395	17,067	6,750	14,040	24,660
Geographic region					
Northeast	4	14,535	12,000	15,863	19,725
North Central	154	11,326	7,500	11,255	15,540
South	179	20,201	5,191	19,600	31,000
West	58	22,815	13,797	23,800	33,000
County type					
Metro	22	15,923	5,000	8,450	23,085
Nonmetro	373	17,135	7,000	14,177	24,660
County manager					
Total	28	50,030	40,525	48,946	55,536

Title of official	No. counties reporting	Mean ($)	First quartile ($)	Median ($)	Third quartile ($)
25,000–49,999 continued					
Geographic region					
South	16	46,165	40,525	47,836	50,000
West	9	60,636	52,212	64,500	72,108
County type					
Nonmetro	27	49,549	40,000	48,264	55,536
County administrator					
Total	127	40,582	30,000	37,500	49,889
Geographic region					
North Central	16	35,363	27,000	34,612	39,500
South	86	40,263	29,940	37,464	49,889
West	24	45,873	35,700	43,498	57,384
County type					
Metro	14	55,516	43,470	53,854	65,500
Nonmetro	113	38,732	29,940	36,254	46,372
Clerk to the governing board					
Total	320	28,618	23,958	27,754	32,100
Geographic region					
Northeast	3	22,486	. . .	22,000	. . .
North Central	138	28,346	25,309	27,950	30,857
South	126	27,698	21,840	25,606	32,000
West	53	31,860	28,000	31,185	35,112
County type					
Metro	20	30,091	25,290	28,243	35,902
Nonmetro	300	28,519	23,958	27,720	32,000
Chief financial officer					
Total	221	30,671	23,747	28,272	35,982
Geographic region					
Northeast	4	26,514	20,332	26,666	33,000
North Central	69	27,153	23,690	26,658	30,238
South	111	30,639	22,888	27,750	37,549
West	37	37,779	31,500	35,000	42,948
County type					
Metro	14	39,849	28,074	39,775	46,799
Nonmetro	207	30,051	23,500	28,000	35,000
County health officer					
Total	136	34,550	27,515	32,560	38,652
Geographic region					
North Central	81	30,704	26,050	31,100	34,917
South	31	44,076	31,536	36,756	48,000
West	24	35,223	27,758	34,426	41,652
County type					
Metro	4	62,322	37,000	56,578	76,156
Nonmetro	132	33,708	27,515	32,429	38,000
Planning director					
Total	138	32,375	23,375	30,316	40,019
Geographic region					
Northeast	4	26,533	24,502	25,251	26,000
North Central	45	26,294	20,012	26,652	30,325
South	45	34,442	25,290	32,720	43,938
West	44	37,011	27,600	36,849	46,835
County type					
Metro	13	38,554	29,358	34,122	44,375
Nonmetro	125	31,732	23,080	30,298	40,000
County engineer					
Total	157	45,034	40,031	46,500	51,907
Geographic region					
North Central	103	45,878	43,092	47,000	52,000
South	36	41,755	31,410	41,101	50,700
West	18	46,765	40,031	48,186	53,854
County type					
Metro	11	46,223	39,708	50,000	50,879
Nonmetro	146	44,945	40,031	46,452	52,000
Director of welfare/human services					
Total	140	38,008	31,491	39,696	45,411
Geographic region					
Northeast	3	33,354	. . .	35,350	. . .
North Central	59	35,930	23,965	38,914	47,689
South	52	38,880	35,000	38,606	41,715
West	26	41,519	40,000	42,399	51,000
County type					
Metro	6	47,142	39,408	41,074	47,689
Nonmetro	134	37,599	31,000	39,494	45,411
Chief law enforcement official					
Total	396	35,939	30,385	35,000	41,138

Table 2/4 SALARIES OF COUNTY OFFICIALS: 1 JULY 1994
continued

Title of official	No. counties reporting	Mean ($)	First quartile ($)	Median ($)	Third quartile ($)
10,000–24,999 continued					
Geographic region					
Northeast	4	30,785	24,416	30,708	37,000
North Central	163	33,445	30,194	33,766	36,773
South	173	37,440	29,220	37,308	44,048
West	56	38,932	32,923	37,800	43,380
County type					
Metro	23	42,506	36,598	41,304	49,551
Nonmetro	373	35,535	29,768	35,000	40,036
Purchasing director					
Total	54	26,153	17,742	24,122	31,018
Geographic region					
North Central	6	23,805	18,096	22,901	29,000
South	38	25,588	17,742	24,122	31,018
West	8	33,083	26,000	28,711	32,110
County type					
Metro	7	30,667	19,822	31,018	44,000
Nonmetro	47	25,481	17,556	23,843	30,693
Personnel director					
Total	49	27,770	18,241	24,144	33,197
Geographic region					
North Central	9	23,385	15,946	23,338	30,851
South	25	26,891	18,241	23,896	28,158
West	14	32,228	19,908	28,407	44,221
County type					
Metro	3	44,789	...	48,000	...
Nonmetro	46	26,661	17,676	24,020	31,266
5,000–9,999					
Governing board chair/president/county judge					
Total	183	14,446	6,295	11,275	21,708
Geographic region					
Northeast	3	14,275	...	19,625	...
North Central	83	9,035	6,000	8,975	11,750
South	61	18,461	4,200	19,560	27,005
West	36	20,133	11,800	22,105	23,981
County type					
Nonmetro	182	14,515	6,322	11,335	21,708
County manager					
Total	3	58,380	...	62,000	...
County type					
Nonmetro	3	58,380	...	62,000	...
County administrator					
Total	31	34,360	21,000	35,000	44,000
Geographic region					
South	18	34,906	18,800	35,122	44,000
West	11	34,445	24,000	27,000	49,500
County type					
Nonmetro	31	34,360	21,000	35,000	44,000
Clerk to the governing board					
Total	151	24,943	21,289	23,946	26,743
Geographic region					
North Central	73	23,726	21,489	23,500	25,033
South	39	25,261	18,492	22,000	28,000
West	37	26,996	23,646	25,950	29,040
County type					
Nonmetro	151	24,943	21,289	23,946	26,743
Chief financial officer					
Total	83	23,954	20,500	22,952	25,912
Geographic region					
North Central	32	23,475	21,500	23,197	24,277
South	33	21,894	17,000	20,500	25,608
West	16	28,695	23,205	25,497	35,535
County type					
Nonmetro	83	23,954	20,500	22,952	25,912
County health officer					
Total	41	30,622	25,355	28,500	33,108
Geographic region					
North Central	22	28,782	25,355	28,576	32,245
South	8	35,455	25,608	31,739	36,524
West	10	29,191	23,984	26,942	29,880
County type					
Nonmetro	41	30,622	25,355	28,500	33,108
Planning director					
Total	32	28,097	22,572	27,122	34,416

Title of official	No. counties reporting	Mean ($)	First quartile ($)	Median ($)	Third quartile ($)
5,000–9,999 continued					
Geographic region					
North Central	8	18,595	9,305	20,783	25,089
South	5	27,369	19,836	30,450	37,661
West	17	33,070	24,900	31,470	40,608
County type					
Nonmetro	32	28,097	22,572	27,122	34,416
County engineer					
Total	59	32,548	23,352	29,355	41,475
Geographic region					
North Central	47	31,070	23,040	27,734	41,475
South	4	26,291	25,000	26,500	28,000
West	8	44,357	38,403	40,569	44,952
County type					
Nonmetro	59	32,548	23,352	29,355	41,475
Director of welfare/human services					
Total	52	30,785	22,575	31,729	38,436
Geographic region					
North Central	15	27,505	16,128	27,900	40,296
South	21	31,939	29,000	31,887	38,000
West	14	32,567	22,880	32,800	38,821
County type					
Nonmetro	52	30,785	22,575	31,729	38,436
Chief law enforcement official					
Total	179	30,382	25,099	28,980	34,230
Geographic region					
Northeast	3	35,413	...	35,646	...
North Central	85	27,878	24,900	28,000	30,268
South	55	31,964	25,000	30,000	38,000
West	36	33,461	28,000	30,390	37,800
County type					
Nonmetro	179	30,382	25,099	28,980	34,230
Purchasing director					
Total	8	26,969	19,552	23,370	23,840
Geographic region					
South	7	28,029	18,530	23,760	36,000
County type					
Nonmetro	8	26,969	19,552	23,370	23,840
Personnel director					
Total	15	26,483	16,640	21,100	29,952
Geographic region					
South	4	30,577	16,500	24,475	32,449
West	9	26,352	18,024	21,100	29,760
County type					
Nonmetro	15	26,483	16,640	21,100	29,952
2,500–4,999					
Governing board chair/president/county judge					
Total	78	11,319	5,700	9,041	17,223
Geographic region					
North Central	44	7,287	5,400	7,208	9,186
South	17	18,418	15,415	18,095	24,600
West	16	14,198	7,000	14,445	18,000
County type					
Nonmetro	78	11,319	5,700	9,041	17,223
County administrator					
Total	8	34,417	29,000	35,280	39,000
Geographic region					
South	3	42,718	...	52,000	...
West	4	27,045	29,000	31,402	33,804
County type					
Nonmetro	8	34,417	29,000	35,280	39,000
Clerk to the governing board					
Total	68	22,535	19,022	21,804	24,635
Geographic region					
North Central	37	22,512	20,758	21,730	22,420
South	14	20,512	17,463	18,313	24,873
West	16	24,735	21,890	25,230	25,800
County type					
Nonmetro	68	22,535	19,022	21,804	24,635
Chief financial officer					
Total	37	22,169	19,100	21,889	22,894
Geographic region					
North Central	16	21,326	21,309	21,851	22,100

Table 2/4   **SALARIES OF COUNTY OFFICIALS: 1 JULY 1994**
continued

Title of official	No. counties reporting	Mean ($)	First quartile ($)	Median ($)	Third quartile ($)
2,500–4,999 continued					
South	11	19,306	15,415	18,095	22,894
West	9	27,190	21,929	25,800	29,424
County type					
Nonmetro	37	22,169	19,100	21,889	22,894
County health officer					
Total	16	25,968	19,872	24,000	31,423
Geographic region					
North Central	12	24,217	19,872	23,388	25,000
West	3	38,424	. . .	36,000	. . .
County type					
Nonmetro	16	25,968	19,872	24,000	31,423
Planning director					
Total	15	26,061	18,360	24,173	31,364
Geographic region					
North Central	5	25,066	16,800	18,360	22,000
West	7	27,293	24,173	28,082	34,424
County type					
Nonmetro	15	26,061	18,360	24,173	31,364
County engineer					
Total	22	26,981	22,000	24,800	29,000
Geographic region					
North Central	17	26,384	22,663	25,000	27,500
South	3	17,883	. . .	18,378	. . .
County type					
Nonmetro	22	26,981	22,000	24,800	29,000
Director of welfare/human services					
Total	18	30,624	25,212	34,872	36,000
Geographic region					
North Central	9	26,748	11,206	25,212	40,000
South	3	32,461	. . .	35,223	. . .
West	6	35,519	34,620	35,175	36,000
County type					
Nonmetro	18	30,624	25,212	34,872	36,000
Chief law enforcement official					
Total	77	25,989	21,653	24,600	28,000
Geographic region					
North Central	41	24,948	21,804	24,000	27,384
South	17	25,742	18,126	23,525	31,815
West	18	28,834	24,900	28,400	30,744
County type					
Nonmetro	77	25,989	21,653	24,600	28,000
Purchasing director					
Total	3	15,553	. . .	15,160	. . .
Geographic region					
South	3	15,553	. . .	15,160	. . .
County type					
Nonmetro	3	15,553	. . .	15,160	. . .
Personnel director					
Total	4	26,262	21,998	22,845	23,691
County type					
Nonmetro	4	26,262	21,998	22,845	23,691
Under 2,500					
Governing board chair/ president/county judge					
Total	47	10,404	5,280	6,891	16,865
Geographic region					
North Central	20	5,575	4,800	6,000	6,768

Title of official	No. counties reporting	Mean ($)	First quartile ($)	Median ($)	Third quartile ($)
2,500–4,999 continued					
South	10	16,900	7,200	17,691	26,600
West	17	12,264	6,153	8,000	18,000
County type					
Nonmetro	47	10,404	5,280	6,891	16,865
County administrator					
Total	7	23,401	19,896	24,000	27,030
Geographic region					
West	5	22,561	19,896	24,000	24,470
County type					
Nonmetro	7	23,401	19,896	24,000	27,030
Clerk to the governing board					
Total	44	20,812	18,200	19,875	22,905
Geographic region					
North Central	16	19,927	18,600	19,875	21,313
South	9	18,929	14,520	17,000	18,000
West	19	22,449	18,807	22,176	25,800
County type					
Nonmetro	44	20,812	18,200	19,875	22,905
Chief financial officer					
Total	21	20,240	17,653	19,150	22,800
Geographic region					
North Central	10	19,742	18,600	19,775	21,521
South	5	20,284	12,840	17,653	25,200
West	6	21,033	18,419	20,838	24,048
County type					
Nonmetro	21	20,240	17,653	19,150	22,800
County health officer					
Total	10	19,274	14,400	20,632	24,660
Geographic region					
North Central	4	18,555	14,400	18,432	22,464
West	6	19,754	15,600	20,632	24,660
County type					
Nonmetro	10	19,274	14,400	20,632	24,660
Planning director					
Total	3	19,385	. . .	20,354	. . .
County type					
Nonmetro	3	19,385	. . .	20,354	. . .
County engineer					
Total	7	24,564	20,700	24,000	29,536
Geographic region					
North Central	4	22,530	20,700	22,350	24,000
West	3	27,276	. . .	29,536	. . .
County type					
Nonmetro	7	24,564	20,700	24,000	29,536
Director of welfare/human services					
Total	7	29,353	27,000	30,000	35,800
Geographic region					
West	5	31,376	27,600	30,000	35,800
County type					
Nonmetro	7	29,353	27,000	30,000	35,800
Chief law enforcement official					
Total	49	24,136	20,243	23,446	27,300
Geographic region					
North Central	20	21,983	19,000	20,879	25,440
South	9	25,693	20,100	25,451	31,305
West	20	25,589	22,176	26,065	28,800
County type					
Nonmetro	49	24,136	20,243	23,446	27,300

Police and Fire Department Personnel and Expenditures, 1994

Tari Renner
Illinois Wesleyan University

The public safety expenditure patterns and personnel practices of U.S. local governments are likely to experience some substantial shifts as we approach the millennium. This is especially probable for police departments because the issue of crime has moved to the forefront of public concern. The national and state movements toward tougher sentencing, more police officers, and prison construction are likely to affect the fiscal and administrative decisions of local governments.

In the summer of 1994, Congress passed President Clinton's omnibus anti-crime bill, which was designed to both address the causes of crime and seek prevention through punitive measures. It includes provisions for intergovernmental grants for the hiring of up to 100,000 new police officers, drug treatment for inmates, and prison construction. It also adds to the list of crimes that are punishable by death, includes tougher sentencing policies, and bans certain assault weapons. The programs are to be financed by a unique payment scheme—a special crime trust fund is created by savings from planned reductions in the federal workforce.

Future policy analyses of the impact of the Clinton crime bill may use 1994 as a baseline. Assuming that they are not terminated by the Republican majorities in both houses of Congress, these programs will be implemented over the next five fiscal years. The 1994 data presented in this report are, therefore, the last data available before implementation of the bill.

It will be complicated to sort out the independent effects of this legislation. There are a variety of factors, other than the Clinton crime bill, which will inevitably influence the administrative and fiscal actions of local governments on the front lines of law enforcement. Public officials at all levels of government are experiencing public pressures. Consequently, not all of the possible shifts in personnel and expenditures will be attributable to the crime bill.

It is often difficult for researchers to evaluate the fiscal effects of intergovernmental grant programs. On one hand, there might be a *substitutive* effect where the grants have not been accompanied by any additional commitment of public resources to the problem. The recipient government merely substitutes the funds received for those they would have spent on the function in the absence of the program. On the other hand, the fiscal impact might be *stimulative* where the recipient government actually spends more of its own resources than it would have without the incentive of the program. This results in a substantially increased commitment of public resources to the problem since the fiscal impact includes the dollar amount of the grant plus the additional funds the recipient government has been stimulated to contribute. It is also possible for a grant to have *additive* effects. In this scenario, the recipient government's spending is neither higher nor lower than it would have been in the absence of the program. The overall commitment of public resources, however, is increased because the total spending is equal to the recipient government's unaffected contribution plus the amount of the intergovernmental grant.

Regardless of the community need or the desires of public officials, there are possible countervailing fiscal pressures that may actually constrain the ability of local governments to respond to the grant incentives and mandates of other levels of government. Shortly after the passage of the federal crime bill last year, for example, New York City was faced with having to *reduce* the number of police officers in light of a possible billion dollar budget deficit. Their workforce reduction decisions were further complicated by the minimum staffing requirements of a state fiscal assistance program.

The purpose of this research project, however, is to examine the current cross-sectional patterns and longitudinal trends in American municipalities' public safety personnel, salaries, and expenditures. As discussed above, the 1994 data are likely to become an important baseline for future policy research.

METHODOLOGY

The data in this research are based upon responses to ICMA's annual *Police and Fire Per-* *sonnel, Salaries, and Expenditure Survey.* The questionnaire was mailed to all 2,812 municipalities with a population of 10,000 or more. A total of 1,470 jurisdictions returned the surveys for an overall response rate of 52.3%. The survey response patterns are presented in Table 3/1 by population group, geographic division, and

Table 3/1   SURVEY RESPONSE

	No. cities surveyed (A)	No. cities responding	% of (A)
Total[1]	2,812	1,470	52.3
Population group			
Over 1,000,000	8	5	62.5
500,000–1,000,000 ..	17	6	35.3
250,000–499,999	39	23	59.0
100,000–249,999	131	87	66.4
50,000–99,999	338	196	58.0
25,000–49,999	680	368	54.1
10,000–24,999	1,599	785	49.1
Geographic division[2]			
New England	327	127	38.8
Mid-Atlantic	452	150	33.2
East North Central ...	558	283	50.7
West North Central ..	224	131	58.5
South Atlantic	314	219	69.7
East South Central ...	149	65	43.6
West South Central ..	265	146	55.1
Mountain	129	83	64.3
Pacific Coast	394	266	67.5
Metro status[3]			
Central	514	297	57.8
Suburban	1,702	855	50.2
Independent	594	318	53.5

[1]The term *cities* refers also to towns, villages, boroughs, and townships.
[2]*Divisions: New England*—the states of Connecticut, Maine, Massachusetts, New Hampshire, Rhode Island, and Vermont; *Mid-Atlantic*—the states of New Jersey, New York, and Pennsylvania; *East North Central*—the states of Illinois, Indiana, Michigan, Ohio, and Wisconsin; *West North Central*—the states of Iowa, Kansas, Minnesota, Missouri, Nebraska, North Dakota, and South Dakota; *South Atlantic*—the states of Delaware, Florida, Georgia, Maryland, North Carolina, South Carolina, Virginia, and West Virginia, plus the District of Columbia; *East South Central*—the states of Alabama, Kentucky, Mississippi, and Tennessee; *West South Central*—the states of Arkansas, Louisiana, Oklahoma, and Texas; *Mountain*—the states of Arizona, Colorado, Idaho, Montana, Nevada, New Mexico, Utah, and Wyoming; *Pacific Coast*—the states of Alaska, California, Hawaii, Oregon, and Washington.
[3]*Metro status: Central*—core city of an MSA; *Suburban*—incorporated city located within an MSA; *Independent*—city located outside of an MSA.

metropolitan status. The responses do not vary consistently by population group and the differences by metropolitan status are comparatively small. The response rates by geographic division, however, indicate that New England and Mid-Atlantic cities are underrepresented and South Atlantic and Pacific Coast jurisdictions are overrepresented.

PERSONNEL

The results on the overall size of the workforce for each of the services are presented in Table 3/2. The data include both uniformed and civilian, or nonuniformed, personnel. The average number of total police department employees is 133, and the average per 1,000 people is 2.59. The average number of total fire department employees is 92, with 1.56 employees per 1,000 residents. For both services, these figures represent a slight increase in average number of total employees since last year's survey and a slight decrease in the number of employees per capita. In the 1993 survey, the average total number of police department employees was 127 with 2.68 per 1,000 people and the average total number of fire department employees was 90 with 1.64 per 1,000 people. Figure 3/1 displays time series data for the per capita statistics over the past decade. The patterns have been remarkably stable for both services.

The overall increase in the average number of employees in both police and fire departments from 1993 to 1994 is primarily a result of the greater statistical skew produced by the over one million jurisdictions in 1994. The police averages for the largest cities went up from 5,813 in 1993 to 7,176 in 1994. The fire averages went up from 2,310 in 1993 to 2,834 in 1994. In addition, five cities responded in this category in 1994 compared to four in 1993. This produces a slightly higher overall average in 1994. The per capita data is less likely to be affected by this pattern. For example, the average number of police employees for the cities with populations over one million (7,176) is almost two hundred times the average (38) of cities in the 10,000 to 24,999 population range. The per capita figures of the largest cities (3.58), however, are only about one and one-half times the size of the smallest group (2.36).

The cross-sectional patterns in the 1994 data indicate that although police departments in central cities tend to have more employees per thousand people served than smaller suburban and independent cities do, the same can not be said of fire departments. In fact, the largest jurisdictions appear to have the lowest ratio of fire employees to population served among the population categories and independent cities have a higher ratio than either central or suburban cities.

Table 3/3 presents the average number of civilian, or nonuniformed, personnel in police and fire departments in 1994. The police civilian personnel average was 36 per department, up from 33 in 1993 and 30 in 1992. Fire departments, on the other hand, had an average of

9 civilian employees in 1994. This represents a decrease from the 13 and 11 reported in 1993 and 1992, respectively. The average number declines consistently with the population size of cities for both services. In addition, the averages are highest in central cities followed by suburban and independent cities for both police and fire. The regional patterns, however, are quite different between the services. The largest average number of civilian employees in police de-

Table 3/2   FULL-TIME PAID PERSONNEL, 1994[1]

	Police department			Fire department		
	No. cities reporting	Mean	Per 1,000 population	No. cities reporting	Mean	Per 1,000 population
Total	1,324	133	2.59	1,054	92	1.56
Population group						
Over 1,000,000	5	7,176	3.58	5	2,834	1.41
500,000–1,000,000	5	2,346	3.26	5	1,221	1.69
250,000–499,999	22	835	2.43	23	522	1.54
100,000–249,999	82	362	2.45	78	235	1.57
50,000–99,999	176	157	2.32	165	106	1.55
25,000–49,999	321	80	2.31	269	59	1.68
10,000–24,999	713	38	2.36	509	26	1.59
Geographic division						
New England	124	53	2.12	95	50	1.89
Mid-Atlantic	141	81	2.52	54	101	2.02
East North Central	268	132	2.79	225	85	1.61
West North Central	119	91	2.11	92	70	1.40
South Atlantic	198	143	3.14	176	94	1.95
East South Central	61	129	2.65	58	108	2.15
West South Central	145	189	2.82	127	127	1.73
Mountain	73	158	2.48	58	101	1.33
Pacific Coast	195	187	2.28	169	99	1.09
Metro status						
Central	285	408	2.83	277	238	1.61
Suburban	740	61	2.16	509	42	1.35
Independent	299	49	2.49	268	36	1.81

[1]Includes uniformed and civilian/nonuniformed personnel.

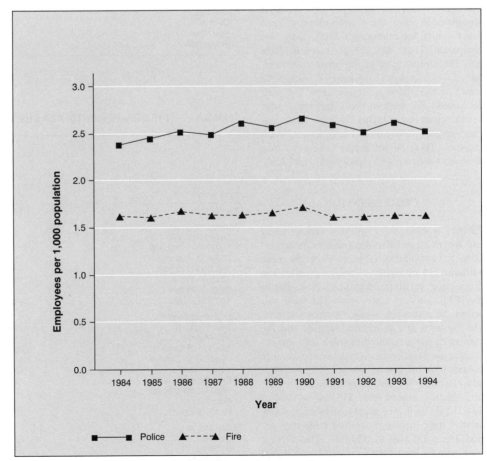

Figure 3/1   *Police and fire trends in employees per 1,000 population*

partments is in communities in the Pacific Coast division. The largest average number of civilian employees in fire departments is found in the East South Central division.

Table 3/4 shows data collected on minimum staffing requirements per shift in fire departments. According to the survey results, nearly three-quarters of responding jurisdictions have minimum staffing requirements in their fire departments (73.9%). Although the pattern is not totally consistent, mid-size cities are more likely than others to report having these requirements. However, a majority of cities in all population categories report having minimum staffing requirements in their fire departments. This is also true of each of the geographic divisions except for the Mid-Atlantic. Central cities are more likely to report minimum staffing requirements per shift (82.5%) than either suburban (68.1%) or independent cities (78.9%).

Survey respondents were asked whether they require a minimum number of crew members per fire apparatus. A narrow majority of responding jurisdictions (54.6%) indicate that they have minimum staffing requirements per apparatus (not shown). As with the minimum per shift patterns discussed above, larger central cities are generally more likely to report that they have requirements than smaller suburban and independent cities. Pacific Coast and Mountain jurisdictions are the most likely to have minimum per apparatus requirements while New England and Mid-Atlantic communities are the least likely to report them.

The respondents indicating that they had minimum crew requirements per apparatus were also asked to report the specific values of these lower limits for pumpers, ladders, and other equipment. These data are presented in Table 3/5. The highest average minimum crew is reported for pumpers (3.0); ladders average 2.8 crew; and 2.3 is the average crew for other equipment. For each of these, however, larger central cities have higher average minimums than smaller suburban and independent communities. There do not appear to be any strong consistent differences by geographic division.

COMPENSATION

Tables 3/6 through 3/14 present various salary and longevity pay data for full-time police officers and firefighters. Table 3/6 shows the mean entrance and maximum salaries for police and fire services for all municipalities responding to the ICMA surveys since 1984. The table also shows the percentage spread between the average entrance and maximum salaries and the number of years required to reach the latter.

Over the past decade, average police entrance salaries have increased from $17,115 in 1984 to $25,770 in 1994. The comparable figures for firefighters increased from $16,436 in 1984 to $24,212 in 1994. The average maximum police salaries have increased over the same time period from $21,681 to $34,680. The average maximum for firefighters increased from $20,500 to $32,219. The percentage spread has also in-

creased during the last ten years for both services. This latter pattern indicates that maximum salaries have risen at a greater rate than minimum salaries. In addition, the average number of years of service required to reach the maximum annual base salary has increased from 5.0 to 6.0 for both police and fire.

Tables 3/7 and 3/8 present average entrance salaries and hourly wages from responding cities of 500,000 and more population for police officers and firefighters, respectively. This group has been consistently selected in ICMA analyses for closer examination because large urban jurisdictions often set benchmark salaries for smaller suburban cities in the surrounding metropolitan area. Complete data are available for only those cities that responded in both 1993 and 1994.

Tables 3/9 and 3/10 show detailed entrance and maximum salary information as well as the average number of years required to reach the maximum for police officers and firefighters, re-

---

Table 3/3   CIVILIAN/NONUNIFORMED PERSONNEL, 1994

	Police department		Fire department	
	No. cities reporting	Mean personnel	No. cities reporting	Mean personnel
Total	1,236	36	760	9
Population group				
Over 1,000,000	5	2,040	5	241
500,000–1,000,000	5	631	5	116
250,000–499,999	22	231	23	34
100,000–249,999	82	92	78	20
50,000–99,999	170	39	156	7
25,000–49,999	309	19	227	4
10,000–24,999	643	9	266	2
Geographic division				
New England	109	8	67	5
Mid-Atlantic	117	15	31	5
East North Central	248	37	140	7
West North Central	115	27	54	4
South Atlantic	192	37	138	8
East South Central	58	37	37	25
West South Central	139	48	102	9
Mountain	71	47	48	14
Pacific Coast	187	54	143	11
Metro status				
Central	278	109	257	19
Suburban	685	16	353	4
Independent	273	12	150	3

Table 3/4   FIRE DEPARTMENTS' PER SHIFT MINIMUM STAFFING REQUIREMENT

		Minimum staffing requirement per shift			
		Yes		No	
Classification	No. reporting (A)	No.	% of (A)	No.	% of (A)
Total	1,262	933	73.9	329	26.1
Population group					
Over 1,000,000	5	4	80.0	1	20.0
500,000–1,000,000	5	3	60.0	2	40.0
250,000–499,999	24	20	83.3	4	16.7
100,000–249,999	81	71	87.7	10	12.3
50,000–99,999	174	147	84.5	27	15.5
25,000–49,999	303	238	78.5	65	21.5
10,000–24,999	670	450	67.2	220	32.8
Geographic division					
New England	119	72	60.5	47	39.5
Mid-Atlantic	119	45	37.8	74	62.2
East North Central	252	203	80.6	49	19.4
West North Central	116	78	67.2	38	32.8
South Atlantic	195	163	83.6	32	16.4
East South Central	62	54	87.1	8	12.9
West South Central	137	101	73.7	36	26.3
Mountain	73	59	80.8	14	19.2
Pacific Coast	189	158	83.6	31	16.4
Metro status					
Central	291	240	82.5	51	17.5
Suburban	673	458	68.1	215	31.9
Independent	298	235	78.9	63	21.1

Table 3/5   MINIMUM NUMBER OF CREW PER APPARATUS

	Pumpers		Ladders		Other	
Classification	No. reporting	Average minimum crew	No. reporting	Average minimum crew	No. reporting	Average minimum crew
Total	613	3.0	540	2.8	269	2.3
Population group						
Over 1,000,000	4	4.3	3	4.3	0	...
500,000–1,000,000	3	3.7	3	4.0	2	3.5
250,000–499,999	17	3.7	17	3.5	9	3.2
100,000–249,999	55	3.3	55	3.3	26	2.5
50,000–99,999	116	3.0	112	2.8	60	2.3
25,000–49,999	170	2.9	147	2.5	77	2.1
10,000–24,999	248	3.0	203	2.7	95	2.4
Geographic division						
New England	32	2.8	29	2.5	18	2.3
Mid-Atlantic	37	3.6	34	3.2	12	3.1
East North Central	118	3.0	112	2.7	61	2.5
West North Central	50	3.2	45	2.7	15	2.5
South Atlantic	112	3.0	101	2.7	50	2.3
East South Central	35	3.2	28	2.7	16	2.4
West South Central	57	3.0	50	2.6	20	2.1
Mountain	46	3.2	36	3.0	20	2.1
Pacific Coast	126	2.9	105	3.0	57	2.1
Metro status						
Central	184	3.2	181	2.9	83	2.5
Suburban	302	3.1	252	2.8	149	2.3
Independent	127	2.8	107	2.4	37	2.1

Table 3/6   COMPARISON OF MEAN ENTRANCE AND MAXIMUM SALARIES, 1984 to 1994

	Mean entrance salary ($)	Mean maximum salary ($)	Spread (%)	No. of years to maximum
Police				
1984	17,115	21,681	26.7	5
1985	18,112	22,891	26.4	5
1986	18,897	24,204	28.1	5[1]
1987	19,825	25,484	28.5	5
1988	20,636	26,734	29.6	5
1989	21,356	27,850	30.4	5[1]
1990	22,350	29,139	30.4	6[1]
1991	23,474	30,881	31.6	6[1]
1992	23,921	31,891	33.3	6[1]
1993	25,126	33,880	34.8	6[1]
1994	25,770	34,680	34.6	6[1]
Fire				
1984	16,436	20,500	24.7	5
1985	17,487	21,734	24.3	5
1986	18,054	22,776	26.2	5
1987	18,942	23,965	26.5	5
1988	19,713	25,010	26.9	5
1989	20,406	26,058	27.7	5
1990	21,062	27,076	28.6	6
1991	22,237	28,861	29.8	6
1992	22,559	29,601	31.2	6[1]
1993	23,753	31,615	33.1	6[1]
1994	24,212	32,219	33.1	6

[1]Cities 100,000 and over in population average six or more
years to reach maximum.

Table 3/7   POLICE DEPARTMENT ENTRANCE SALARIES FOR BENCHMARK CITIES[1]

	Hourly rate[2] 1994 ($)	January 1993 entrance salary mean ($)[3]	January 1994 entrance salary mean ($)	1993–94 change (%)
Total	13.70	27,814	28,774	3.5
Chicago[4]	15.97	...	34,884	...
Dallas	12.06	...	25,093	...
Honolulu	13.10	27,240	27,240	0.0
Houston	13.05	27,259	27,154	−0.4
Jacksonville	14.12	28,590	29,364	2.7
Los Angeles	15.94	33,157	33,157	0.0
Milwaukee	12.96	26,954	26,954	0.0
Nashville/Davidson[4]	11.56	21,012	25,247	20.2
Phoenix	13.00	27,789	27,040	−2.7
San Diego	15.20	31,026	31,609	1.9

[1]Cities 500,000 and over in population reporting in 1993 and 1994.
[2]Rates were calculated based on a 40-hour work times 52 weeks unless otherwise noted.
[3]Only cities responding in both 1993 and 1994 are included.
[4]Chicago and Nashville/Davidson County have a 42-hour work week.

spectively. In addition to the measures of central tendency for the data, such as the mean and the median and the first and third quartiles are included in order to understand the degree of dispersion.

The annual base salaries are the entrance salaries paid during the first 12 months with the department as a sworn police officer or firefighter. The amount excludes uniform allowances, holiday pay, hazardous duty pay, or any other additional compensation. The maximum is the highest annual base salary paid to uniformed personnel who do not hold any promotional rank.

The survey results for average entrance and maximum salaries indicate that they are positively skewed for both services. This means that some unusually high scores are pulling the average above the fiftieth percentile (the median). The median is lower than the mean for entrance and maximum salaries in both police and fire. The gap between the mean and the median, however, appears to be slightly greater for maximum than for entrance salaries.

The median entrance salary for police is $25,500 and the mean is $25,770. The median maximum is $34,118 and the mean is $34,680. For firefighters, on the other hand, the entrance salary median and mean are $24,010 and $24,212, respectively. The maximum fire salary median and mean are $31,325 and $32,219, respectively.

Predictably, the highest salaries are paid in the largest cities for both police and fire. Suburban jurisdictions, on the other hand, pay more than either central or independent cities. Among the geographic divisions, the East South Central division consistently shows the lowest average salaries for both services, while the Pacific Coast division shows the highest average salaries.

Salary Trends

Longitudinal salary data are presented in Table 3/11, which shows the changes in entrance and maximum base salaries for both police officers and firefighters from 1989 to 1994. Police entrance salaries increased 18% over this period and maximum salaries increased 23%. The comparable figures for firefighters are almost identical. Their minimum salaries increased 19% and their maximum salaries rose 23%. The increases from 1993 to 1994 for both services were 2% and 3%, respectively, for entrance and maximum salaries.

Longevity Pay

Longevity pay is compensation beyond the regular maximum salary based upon number of years of service; it is often used as an incentive to reduce employee turnover and to reward those who have already reached the maximum salary and have limited opportunities for promotion. Longevity pay can be administered in several ways. It may come as a flat dollar amount, a percentage of the base salary, a percentage of the maximum pay or a step increase in the basic salary plan.

Tables 3/12 and 3/13 present a variety of longevity pay data for police officers and firefighters: whether personnel can receive longevity pay, the maximum salary including longevity pay that personnel can receive (without promotion), and the average number of years of service required to receive longevity pay.

Table 3/12 indicates that nearly two-thirds of responding jurisdictions have some form of longevity pay for their police officers (63.8%). It appears most likely to be found in cities with populations of 250,000 and above and in those with less than 50,000 population. The population groups from 50,000 to 99,999 and from 100,000 to 249,999 are the least likely to report having longevity pay. Mid-Atlantic cities almost unanimously (95.7%) indicate the use of police longevity pay as do a solid majority of New England (81.1%) and West South Central cities (84.7%). In the Mountain and Pacific Coast divisions, on the other hand, a small minority of jurisdictions report longevity pay (33.3% and 26.0%, respectively). Longevity pay is also more likely to be found in suburban and central cities than in independent cities.

Those communities reporting longevity pay were asked to indicate the maximum salary including longevity. The average police department maximum of the responding jurisdictions is $36,563 and median is $36,036 (Table 3/12). As with the base salary data in Tables 3/9 and 3/10, this indicates a slight positive skew. The first quartile value is $31,152 and the third quartile value is $41,878. Surprisingly, the maximum salary variation by population size is very small compared to that among the geographic divisions and the metro status of cities. The maximums are the highest in Mid-Atlantic and

Pacific Coast communities. Suburban jurisdictions report higher maximum salaries than either central or independent cities.

It takes an average of five years to reach the maximum salary with longevity pay in police departments. This ranges from a high of eleven years for the over one million population group to a low of five for the cities with populations from 50,000 to 99,999 and 10,000 to 24,999. The number of years is the highest in Pacific coast cities and the lowest among respondents from the West South Central division. Central cities report a slightly higher average number of years than either suburban or independent jurisdictions.

Table 3/13 indicates that nearly three-fifths of responding jurisdictions (59.4%) have longevity pay for firefighters. Longevity pay is most likely to be found in the largest cities and in the West South Central division. The responses by metropolitan status indicate a slightly different pattern for firefighters than for police officers. Central cities are the most likely to have some form of longevity pay (64.7%) followed by suburban (60.2%) and independent cities (52.6%). In fact, central cities are the only category showing virtually the same percentages for both services. Suburban and independent respondents are less likely to have longevity pay for firefighters than for police officers.

Table 3/8   FIRE DEPARTMENT ENTRANCE SALARIES FOR BENCHMARK CITIES[1]

	Hourly rate[2] 1994 ($)	January 1993 entrance salary mean ($)[3]	January 1994 entrance salary mean ($)	1993–94 change (%)
Total	9.41	26,767	26,403	−1.4
Chicago	12.89	. . .	29,496	. . .
Dallas	8.51	. . .	23,901	. . .
Honolulu	8.65	24,192	25,184	4.1
Houston	11.35	27,259	27,154	−0.4
Jacksonville	9.00	24,732	26,196	5.9
Los Angeles	10.83	34,659	31,529	−9.0
Milwaukee	8.42	21,447	21,447	. . .
Nashville/Davidson	8.72	20.622	24,021	16.5
Phoenix	9.25	27,664	29,936	−2.6
San Diego	8.41	30,927	32,790	6.0

[1]Cities 500,000 and over in population reporting in 1993 and 1994.
[2]Hourly work weeks vary among fire departments. Hourly rates are based on the actual work week in each city times 52 weeks.
[3]Only cities responding in both 1993 and 1994 are included.

Table 3/9   POLICE OFFICERS' ANNUAL BASE SALARIES, 1 JANUARY 1994

	Entrance salary[1]				Maximum salary[2]					No. of years to reach maximum	
	No. of cities reporting	Mean ($)	First quartile ($)	Median ($)	Third quartile ($)	No. of cities reporting	Mean ($)	First quartile ($)	Median ($)	Third quartile ($)	No. of cities reporting	Mean ($)
Total	1,324	25,770	21,016	25,500	29,148	1,279	34,680	29,148	34,118	39,835	1,014	6
Population group												
Over 1,000,000	5	30,379	25,093	31,609	33,157	5	42,005	32,025	44,922	47,001	4	12
500,000–1,000,000	5	27,169	25,247	27,040	27,240	5	38,796	32,745	40,608	40,893	5	13
250,000–499,999	22	27,816	23,270	27,875	30,278	22	38,218	33,322	38,552	43,065	20	9
100,000–249,999	82	28,254	23,376	27,456	33,036	81	38,712	32,995	39,157	43,896	71	6
50,000–99,999	176	28,322	23,424	27,835	31,949	171	37,973	32,601	38,157	42,540	144	6
25,000–49,999	321	26,496	21,840	26,448	30,184	311	35,651	29,872	35,556	40,737	243	6
10,000–24,999	713	24,421	20,214	24,360	28,059	684	32,740	27,562	31,763	37,485	527	6
Geographic division												
New England	123	26,579	23,515	26,375	29,533	120	32,571	28,829	31,399	36,373	108	4
Mid-Atlantic	138	28,372	25,378	27,643	30,930	136	41,475	36,125	40,788	46,894	122	5
East North Central	268	26,703	24,419	26,874	29,146	259	35,393	31,156	36,061	39,331	232	5
West North Central	121	23,825	20,433	23,886	26,448	118	31,910	27,103	32,011	36,085	86	6
South Atlantic	199	21,753	19,033	21,000	23,270	195	31,852	27,461	30,421	34,918	100	10
East South Central	61	19,266	17,722	19,325	20,467	57	26,474	22,484	26,526	29,216	45	9
West South Central	144	21,317	18,574	20,700	23,665	129	28,113	23,628	27,812	32,666	96	6
Mountain	74	23,794	20,598	23,462	27,684	71	33,681	29,820	34,340	38,268	49	9
Pacific Coast	196	33,473	29,004	34,008	37,776	194	41,939	36,276	42,288	46,812	176	4
Metro status												
Central	285	25,594	21,008	25,072	28,802	277	34,746	29,731	33,897	39,500	219	7
Suburban	742	27,464	23,332	27,206	30,428	719	37,059	31,737	37,045	41,725	586	5
Independent	297	21,705	18,852	20,758	24,624	283	28,572	25,477	28,413	31,164	209	7

[1]Entrance salary is defined as the base salary paid during the first 12 months with the department as a sworn police officer (excludes uniform allowance, holiday pay, or additional compensation).

[2]Maximum salary is the maximum amount paid to personnel who do not hold any promotional rank (excluding uniform allowance, holiday pay, hazard pay, or any additional compensation).

Table 3/10 FIREFIGHTERS' ANNUAL BASE SALARIES, 1 JANUARY 1994

	Entrance salary[1]					Maximum salary[2]					No. of years to reach maximum	
	No. of cities reporting	Mean ($)	First quartile ($)	Median ($)	Third quartile ($)	No. of cities reporting	Mean ($)	First quartile ($)	Median ($)	Third quartile ($)	No. of cities reporting	Mean ($)
Total	1,038	24,212	19,969	24,010	28,416	994	32,219	27,118	31,325	37,000	776	6
Population group												
Over 1,000,000	5	27,312	23,901	27,154	29,496	5	40,412	32,025	41,616	45,366	4	12
500,000–1,000,000	5	24,757	21,447	25,184	26,196	5	35,399	32,745	35,724	36,500	4	12
250,000–499,999	23	26,378	22,281	26,688	28,609	23	37,035	33,259	36,660	41,262	21	8
100,000–249,999	77	26,570	22,126	26,295	30,480	75	36,066	30,804	36,267	41,577	66	6
50,000–99,999	165	26,790	22,222	26,255	31,262	158	35,534	30,512	35,631	40,000	135	6
25,000–49,999	263	24,802	20,232	24,348	27,996	254	32,716	28,069	32,070	36,548	197	6
10,000–24,999	500	22,551	18,840	21,750	25,920	474	29,886	25,525	28,929	33,819	349	6
Geographic division												
New England	94	25,115	21,975	24,381	27,167	91	30,684	27,118	29,934	33,114	86	4
Mid-Atlantic	50	26,908	23,551	26,255	29,575	46	36,265	31,380	35,071	42,750	39	5
East North Central	216	25,847	23,512	26,034	28,263	210	34,044	30,052	34,857	38,337	190	5
West North Central	90	22,207	18,945	22,015	24,694	90	29,138	25,632	28,882	32,090	64	6
South Atlantic	177	20,092	17,992	19,591	21,519	172	29,444	25,636	28,647	31,793	80	9
East South Central	58	18,552	17,006	18,408	19,787	52	25,772	22,613	25,546	28,380	42	9
West South Central	127	20,590	17,914	19,947	23,025	111	27,137	22,875	26,270	30,960	82	5
Mountain	59	23,041	19,900	22,848	26,279	58	32,183	28,492	32,070	36,250	42	8
Pacific Coast	167	31,362	27,492	31,788	34,614	164	39,699	35,748	40,248	43,956	151	4
Metro status												
Central	276	24,449	20,500	23,630	27,633	266	33,021	28,111	32,000	37,078	212	6
Suburban	498	26,000	21,414	25,950	29,858	477	34,469	29,615	34,476	39,384	389	5
Independent	264	20,591	17,992	19,987	23,462	251	27,095	24,000	26,978	29,931	175	6

[1]Entrance salary is defined as the base salary paid during the first 12 months with the department as a sworn fire fighter (excludes uniform allowance, holiday pay, or additional compensation).

[2]Maximum salary is the maximum amount paid to personnel who do not hold any promotional rank (excluding uniform allowance, holiday pay, hazard pay, or any additional compensation).

Table 3/11 TRENDS IN POLICE AND FIRE ENTRANCE AND MAXIMUM AVERAGE SALARIES

	No. of cities included[1]	1 Jan 1989 ($)	1 Jan. 1990 ($)	Change from 1989 (%)	1 Jan. 1991 ($)	Change from 1990 (%)	1 Jan. 1992 ($)	Change from 1991 (%)	1 Jan. 1993 ($)	Change from 1992 (%)	1 Jan. 1994 ($)	Change from 1993 (%)	Change from 1989 (%)
Fire													
Entrance salary	355	19,914	20,812	5	21,693	4	22,402	3	23,158	3	23,556	2	18
Maximum salary	320	26,170	27,628	6	28,994	5	30,147	4	31,457	4	32,318	3	23
Police													
Entrance salary	448	21,154	22,154	5	23,117	4	23,841	3	24,660	3	25,275	2	19
Maximum salary	409	27,810	29,293	5	30,762	5	31,977	4	33,373	4	34,252	3	23

[1]Cities included in this table must have reported data on salaries and wages for each of the six years.

Table 3/12 LONGEVITY PAY FOR POLICE OFFICERS, 1 JANUARY 1994

	Personnel can receive longevity pay					Maximum salary including longevity					No. of years of service to receive longevity pay	
	No. of cities reporting	Yes No.	Yes % of (A)	No No.	No % of (A)	No. of cities reporting	Mean ($)	First quartile ($)	Median ($)	Third quartile ($)	No. of cities reporting	Mean
Total	1,297	828	63.8	469	36.1	656	36,563	31,152	36,036	41,878	746	5
Population group												
Over 1,000,000	5	4	80.0	1	20.0	3	40,349	33,225	36,832	36,832	4	11
500,000–1,000,000	5	4	80.0	1	20.0	4	39,536	33,595	37,250	41,661	4	7
250,000–499,999	22	16	72.7	6	27.2	16	38,788	33,417	38,899	41,681	15	7
100,000–249,999	81	47	58.0	34	41.9	42	38,775	34,176	38,777	42,780	47	6
50,000–99,999	172	102	59.3	70	40.6	82	38,266	33,427	36,499	43,262	95	5
25,000–49,999	315	195	61.9	120	38.0	166	37,557	31,615	36,573	43,121	178	6
10,000–24,999	697	460	65.9	237	34.0	343	35,232	29,390	34,426	40,569	403	5
Geographic division												
New England	122	99	81.1	23	18.8	81	33,929	29,761	33,568	37,401	90	6
Mid-Atlantic	140	134	95.7	6	4.2	112	44,404	37,783	43,967	49,645	118	5
East North Central	269	203	75.4	66	24.5	167	36,554	32,442	37,022	40,569	184	6
West North Central	115	71	61.7	44	38.2	58	34,656	30,025	33,753	42,334	65	6
South Atlantic	191	98	51.3	93	48.6	67	33,930	29,821	33,583	39,122	85	6
East South Central	60	29	48.3	31	51.6	15	26,418	22,104	25,131	29,306	26	5
West South Central	144	122	84.7	22	15.2	88	30,188	25,314	30,457	34,078	110	2
Mountain	72	24	33.3	48	66.6	21	36,780	31,836	35,122	40,899	22	6
Pacific Coast	184	48	26.0	136	73.9	47	43,633	37,853	43,040	47,952	46	8
Metro status												
Central	280	183	65.3	97	34.6	152	35,958	31,716	35,388	39,778	172	6
Suburban	724	484	66.8	240	33.1	382	39,008	33,766	38,534	43,703	433	5
Independent	293	161	54.9	132	45.0	122	29,663	25,540	30,025	32,359	141	5

Table 3/13 LONGEVITY PAY FOR FIREFIGHTERS, 1 JANUARY 1994

	No. of cities reporting	Personnel can receive longevity pay				Maximum salary including logevity					No. of years of service to receive longevity pay	
		Yes		No		No. of cities reporting	Mean ($)	First quartile ($)	Median ($)	Third quartile ($)	No. of cities reporting	Mean
		No.	% of (A)	No.	% of (A)							
Total	1,046	622	59.4	424	40.5	482	33,599	28,437	33,007	38,200	555	5
Population group												
Over 1,000,000	5	4	80.0	1	20.0	3	40,114	32,125	36,832	36,832	4	11
500,000–1,000,000	5	4	80.0	1	20.0	4	36,924	33,595	35,772	38,124	4	7
250,000–499,999	23	16	69.5	7	30.4	15	37,386	32,059	37,035	40,142	16	6
100,000–249,999	77	44	57.1	33	42.8	40	36,179	30,626	35,882	40,307	44	7
50,000–99,999	159	97	61.0	62	38.9	81	35,739	30,600	35,531	40,946	89	5
25,000–49,999	266	153	57.5	113	42.4	123	34,232	30,070	33,982	37,580	138	6
10,000–24,999	511	304	59.4	207	40.5	216	31,543	26,590	30,729	35,883	260	5
Geographic division												
New England	96	77	80.2	19	19.7	62	32,134	28,135	31,296	35,842	69	6
Mid-Atlantic	57	47	82.4	10	17.5	41	39,673	33,280	38,278	45,859	40	6
East North Central	228	168	73.6	60	26.3	132	35,309	31,068	35,754	39,575	149	6
West North Central	90	51	56.6	39	43.3	40	31,673	27,264	31,407	34,320	46	6
South Atlantic	171	83	48.5	88	51.4	60	31,358	26,681	30,858	35,196	73	6
East South Central	57	27	47.3	30	52.6	15	25,722	22,002	26,020	28,547	25	5
West South Central	126	107	84.9	19	15.0	76	28,276	23,547	27,470	32,125	95	2
Mountain	60	24	40.0	36	60.0	21	36,491	31,500	34,927	40,226	22	5
Pacific Coast	161	38	23.6	123	76.3	35	41,871	35,865	40,946	45,078	36	8
Metro status												
Central	272	176	64.7	96	35.2	148	34,157	29,600	33,467	38,277	163	6
Suburban	508	306	60.2	202	39.7	228	35,818	30,989	35,760	40,783	270	5
Independent	266	140	52.6	126	47.3	106	28,047	24,300	27,911	31,310	122	5

The median and average maximum fire salaries including longevity are $33,007 and $33,599, respectively. As with the police salary figures, this indicates a positive skew. Although the pattern is not consistent, larger communities generally report higher average and median maximum salaries than smaller communities. Pacific Coast respondents have the highest average and median maximum salaries while East South Central cities have the lowest. As with the police officer maximum figures reported above, suburban jurisdictions have higher salaries than either central or independent cities.

The average number of years for firefighters to obtain the maximum salary including longevity pay is five. This figure and its patterns by population group, geographic division, and metropolitan status are virtually identical to those for police officers reported above.

EXPENDITURES

Questionnaire respondents were asked to provide expenditure (not budget) figures for the department's most recently completed fiscal year. The items include salaries and wages for all departmental personnel, contributions for employee benefits, capital outlays, and all other department expenditures. These data are presented in Tables 3/14 through 3/21.

Salaries and Wages
Table 3/14 presents salary and wage expenditures for all departmental personnel—permanent and temporary, full- and part-time. The average police expenditures are $4,574,000, which translates into a per capita average of $95.28. This represents a slight decrease in both figures from the 1993 survey results, which were $5,117,000 and $99.75 for the mean and per capita police expenditures, respectively.

There is a consistent increase in both statistics as population size of the jurisdiction increases. Geographically, the highest average per capita police personnel expenditures are in Mid-Atlantic and Pacific Coast jurisdictions. Central cities have higher per capita spending ($99.16) than either suburban ($96.01) or independent ($69.76) cities. The differences by metropolitan

Table 3/14 EXPENDITURES FOR SALARIES AND WAGES (CIVILIAN AND UNIFORMED)

	Police			Fire		
	No. of cities reporting	Mean ($000)	Per capita ($)	No. of cities reporting	Mean ($000)	Per capita ($)
Total	889	4,574	95.28	652	3,436	61.75
Population group						
Over 1,000,000	2	164,819	120.25	2	83,355	60.18
500,000–1,000,000	4	86,727	116.97	4	46,056	62.11
250,000–499,999	16	34,664	103.08	16	22,735	66.98
100,000–249,999	57	14,257	96.37	51	9,732	64.23
50,000–99,999	112	6,234	91.60	88	4,500	65.05
25,000–49,999	223	3,107	88.36	168	2,132	59.43
10,000–24,999	475	1,329	82.08	323	851	51.92
Geographic division						
New England	53	2,002	85.93	44	1,465	65.53
Mid-Atlantic	86	3,879	115.89	30	4,550	88.35
East North Central	163	2,872	83.57	102	2,625	62.06
West North Central	98	3,441	75.22	72	2,661	54.22
South Atlantic	151	4,374	100.81	128	2,943	62.64
East South Central	42	4,427	81.68	41	3,631	65.96
West South Central	121	5,411	87.63	103	4,005	58.81
Mountain	52	5,966	94.11	35	3,815	53.42
Pacific Coast	123	8,208	113.70	97	5,240	62.62
Metro status						
Central	203	12,237	99.16	176	8,652	64.60
Suburban	476	2,709	96.01	307	1,744	57.83
Independent	210	1,392	69.76	169	1,077	52.81

Table 3/15   TOTAL MUNICIPAL CONTRIBUTIONS[1] TO SOCIAL SECURITY AND STATE/CITY ADMINISTERED EMPLOYEE RETIREMENT SYSTEMS[2]

	Police			Fire		
	No. of cities reporting	Mean ($000)	Per capita ($)	No. of cities reporting	Mean ($000)	Per capita ($)
Total	889	645	13.44	652	463	8.33
Population group						
Over 1,000,000	2	21,871	15.95	2	11,198	8.17
500,000–1,000,000	4	11,727	15.81	4	6,154	8.30
250,000–499,999	16	4,487	13.34	16	2,769	8.16
100,000–249,999	57	2,072	14.01	51	1,369	9.03
50,000–99,999	112	965	14.18	88	618	8.94
25,000–49,999	223	439	12.49	168	297	8.28
10,000–24,999	475	183	11.30	323	113	6.92
Geographic division						
New England	53	241	10.37	44	174	7.79
Mid-Atlantic	86	484	14.48	30	561	10.90
East North Central	163	417	12.14	102	349	8.26
West North Central	98	493	10.78	72	379	7.73
South Atlantic	151	617	14.21	128	407	8.67
East South Central	42	691	12.75	41	552	10.04
West South Central	121	694	11.25	103	511	7.51
Mountain	52	679	10.71	35	402	5.64
Pacific Coast	123	1,310	18.15	97	753	9.00
Metro status						
Central	203	1,698	13.76	176	1,143	8.53
Suburban	475	393	1.934	307	250	8.30
Independent	210	198	9.92	169	143	7.01

[1]The expenditures are the municipal contributions.
[2]For civilian and uniformed employees.

Table 3/16   TOTAL MUNICIPAL CONTRIBUTIONS FOR HEALTH, HOSPITALIZATION, DISABILITY, AND LIFE INSURANCE PROGRAMS[1]

	Police			Fire		
	No. of cities reporting	Mean ($000)	Per capita ($)	No. of cities reporting	Mean ($000)	Per capita ($)
Total	889	453	9.45	652	329	5.92
Population group						
Over 1,000,000	2	12,381	9.03	2	6,741	4.91
500,000–1,000,000	4	7,293	9.83	4	4,058	5.47
250,000–499,999	16	2,824	8.40	16	1,755	5.17
100,000–249,999	57	1,426	9.64	51	938	6.19
50,000–99,999	112	656	9.64	88	463	6.69
25,000–49,999	223	348	9.91	168	227	6.34
10,000–24,999	475	151	9.34	323	93	5.70
Geographic division						
New England	53	261	11.19	44	209	9.35
Mid-Atlantic	86	481	14.38	30	523	10.16
East North Central	163	345	10.04	102	303	7.16
West North Central	98	315	6.89	72	245	4.99
South Atlantic	151	353	8.13	128	234	4.98
East South Central	42	410	7.56	41	348	6.33
West South Central	121	443	7.18	103	335	4.92
Mountain	52	626	9.87	35	405	5.67
Pacific Coast	123	848	11.75	97	498	5.95
Metro status						
Central	203	1,108	8.98	176	790	5.90
Suburban	476	308	10.94	307	183	6.06
Independent	210	150	7.52	169	116	5.69

[1]For civilian and uniformed employees.

patterns, the range of per capita salary and wage expenditures is greater for police than for fire departments. The average per capita police figures range from a low of $82.08 for cities with populations from 10,000 to 24,999, to a high of $120.25 for jurisdictions with over one million people. The latter is almost 50% greater than the former. The per capita fire expenditures range from a low of $51.92 for cities with populations from 10,000 to 24,999, to a high of $66.98 for cities with populations from 250,000 to 499,999.

Employee Benefits

The data for total municipal contributions for federal social security and other employee retirement programs are reported in Table 3/15. This, of course, includes both uniformed and civilian personnel. The questionnaire instructed respondents to exclude employee contributions.

The mean total social security and retirement expenditures for police departments is $645,000 and the per capita mean is $13.44. These figures show fairly consistent increases as population size of the responding jurisdictions increase. The per capita statistics range from $11.30 for cities with populations from 10,000 to 24,999, to $15.95 for those with populations with over one million. The highest average expenditures are in the Pacific Coast division ($18.15), and the lowest are found in the New England division ($10.37). Suburban jurisdictions have a slightly higher per capita figure ($13.93) than central cities ($13,76), and the lowest is in independent cities ($9.92).

The mean total social security and retirement expenditures for fire departments is $463,000 and the per capita mean is $8.33. These statistics do not vary as consistently with population size of the responding communities as the patterns for the police data discussed above. The lowest value ($6.92) is found in the smallest population group (10,000 to 24,999), but the $8.17 figure reported by cities with over one million in population is the second lowest of the remaining population groups. The highest fire department per capita social security and retirement expenditures are found in the 100,000 to 249,999 population group. The geographic division patterns are also different from the corresponding police figures discussed above. The Mid-Atlantic division shows the highest per capita expenditures ($10.90) and the Mountain division shows the lowest ($5.64). Central cities have the highest ($8.53) among metro types, followed by suburban ($8.30) and independent cities ($7.01).

Table 3/16 shows data for total municipal contributions for health, hospitalization, disability, and life insurance programs. The average expenditures are $453,000 for police and $329,000 for fire. The mean per capita statistics are $9.45 for police and $5.92 for fire. There is surprisingly little variation in the per capita data for both services by population size of the responding jurisdictions. Mid-Atlantic and suburban cities have the highest values for both services.

status, however, are substantially smaller than those reported in the 1993 survey results, which showed central cities with per capita police personnel expenditures of $109.85, compared to only $88.41 for suburban communities and $63.50 in independent jurisdictions.

The average fire department personnel expen-

ditures are $3,436,000 and the per capita figure is $61.75. As with the police department results, these figures represent a slight decline from the 1993 survey results, which show that the fire department average was $3,663,000 and the per capita expenditure was $63.28.

It appears that, consistent with the 1993 data

Total Personnel Expenditures

Table 3/17 presents the total personnel expenditures for civilian and uniformed employees for both services. These data represent the total salaries and wages; contributions to federal social security and other retirement systems; and contributions to health, hospital, disability, and life insurance programs. Average total personnel expenditures are $5,673,000 for police and $4,229,000 for fire departments. The corresponding per capita figures are $118.18 and $76.01 for police and fire, respectively. The data show that there is a strong positive correlation between per capita personnel expenditures and population size of the community served for police but not for fire departments. The figures for the former service consistently increase from a low of $102.73 for cities with populations from 10,000 to 24,999, to $145.24 for the over one million group. For fire departments, however, the over one million cities report the second *lowest* per capita average among the population categories. Mid-Atlantic communities and central cities have the highest figures for both services among the geographic divisions and metropolitan status groups, respectively.

Capital Outlays

Table 3/18 presents the survey responses for departmental expenditures for capital outlays. These include the purchase and replacement of equipment, purchase of land and existing structures and construction. The reported figures include capital expenditures within individual departmental budgets as well as those expenditures included in a citywide capital budget but designated for departmental programs or equipment. Total capital outlay expenditures may fluctuate dramatically from one year to the next for both police and fire.

The latter point is clear from an comparison of the current survey results with those from the previous year (1993). The 1994 average totals are $1,065,000 and $1,471,000 and the per capita figures are $21.97 and $25.83 for police and fire, respectively. The 1993 data are, however, substantially lower. The mean total expenditures were $172,000 and $155,000 and the per capita statistics were $3.24 and $2.63 for police and fire, respectively. Previous ICMA *Municipal Year Book* articles examining the survey data have continuously noted this important pattern.

Other Expenditures

Table 3/19 presents the data for all other departmental expenditures not included in the above tables. These include such additional expenditures as ongoing maintenance, utilities, fuel, supplies and other miscellaneous items.

Table 3/17   TOTAL PERSONNEL[1] EXPENDITURES[2]

	Police			Fire		
	No. of cities reporting	Mean ($000)	Per capita ($)	No. of cities reporting	Mean ($000)	Per capita ($)
Total	889	5,673	118.18	652	4,229	76.01
Population group						
Over 1,000,000	2	199,071	145.24	2	101,295	73.90
500,000–1,000,000	4	105,748	142.63	4	56,270	75.89
250,000–499,999	16	41,976	124.83	16	27,260	80.31
100,000–249,999	57	17,756	120.03	51	12,040	79.46
50,000–99,999	112	7,856	115.43	88	5,582	80.69
25,000–49,999	223	3,895	110.77	168	2,657	74.06
10,000–24,999	475	1,663	102.73	323	1,059	64.55
Geographic division						
New England	53	2,505	107.50	44	1,849	82.68
Mid-Atlantic	86	4,845	144.75	30	5,636	109.41
East North Central	163	3,634	105.76	102	3,277	77.48
West North Central	98	4,250	92.89	72	3,286	66.96
South Atlantic	151	5,345	123.17	128	3,585	76.31
East South Central	42	5,528	102.00	41	4,533	82.34
West South Central	121	6,549	106.07	103	4,852	71.26
Mountain	52	7,272	114.70	35	4,623	64.73
Pacific Coast	123	10,368	143.62	97	6,493	77.59
Metro status						
Central	203	15,045	121.91	176	10,585	79.04
Suburban	476	3,411	120.89	307	2,178	72.19
Independent	210	1,740	87.22	169	1,337	65.53

[1]Personnel refers to civilian and uniformed employees.
[2]Total personnel expenditures comprise salaries and wages (Table 3/14), contributions for Social Security and employee retirement programs (Table 3/15), and contributions for health and life insurance programs (Table 3/16).

Table 3/18   MUNICIPAL EXPENDITURES FOR CAPITAL OUTLAY[1]

	Police			Fire		
	No. of cities reporting	Mean ($000)	Per capita ($)	No. of cities reporting	Mean ($000)	Per capita ($)
Total	853	1,065	21.97	607	1,471	25.83
Population group						
Over 1,000,000	2	104,065	75.92	2	102,944	75.11
500,000–1,000,000	4	49,281	66.46	4	72,892	98.31
250,000–499,999	15	1,450	4.31	15	6,849	20.15
100,000–249,999	57	1,064	7.19	50	940	6.22
50,000–99,999	106	1,113	16.34	82	859	12.51
25,000–49,999	216	561	15.99	160	647	17.99
10,000–24,999	453	401	24.69	294	244	14.88
Geographic division						
New England	50	351	15.22	34	145	6.36
Mid-Atlantic	78	724	20.69	25	445	7.74
East North Central	154	567	16.42	96	619	15.64
West North Central	95	302	703	68	1,726	33.95
South Atlantic	147	2,011	45.88	123	2,783	59.41
East South Central	42	355	6.55	39	835	14.60
West South Central	117	675	10.80	98	689	9.84
Mountain	51	643	9.99	33	487	6.50
Pacific Coast	119	2,482	33.96	91	2,655	31.10
Metro status						
Central	194	2,999	23.96	165	4,400	32.11
Suburban	454	574	20.15	282	422	13.76
Independent	205	321	16.01	160	298	14.48

[1]The capital outlay expenditures include purchase and/or replacement of equipment, land, existing structures, and/or new construction.

Table 3/19   ALL OTHER DEPARTMENT EXPENDITURES[1]

	Police			Fire		
	No. of cities reporting	Mean ($000)	Per capita ($)	No. of cities reporting	Mean ($000)	Per capita ($)
Total	889	1,046	21.80	652	597	10.73
Population group						
Over 1,000,000	2	26,198	19.11	2	11,528	8.41
500,000–1,000,000	4	22,187	29.92	4	8,404	11.33
250,000–499,999	16	7,120	21.17	16	3,252	9.58
100,000–249,999	57	2,986	20.19	51	1,257	8.29
50,000–99,999	112	1,453	21.36	88	931	13.46
25,000–49,999	223	761	21.64	168	415	11.58
10,000–24,999	475	363	22.45	323	200	12.23
Geographic division						
New England	53	237	10.17	44	247	11.06
Mid-Atlantic	86	569	17.02	30	610	11.84
East North Central	163	649	18.89	102	494	11.67
West North Central	98	803	17.56	72	357	7.29
South Atlantic	151	1,203	27.72	128	586	12.49
East South Central	42	1,015	18.72	41	432	7.85
West South Central	121	1,030	16.69	103	678	9.95
Mountain	52	1,364	21.52	35	749	10.49
Pacific Coast	123	2,150	29.78	97	981	11.72
Metro status						
Central	203	2,645	21.43	176	1,359	10.14
Suburban	476	622	22.07	307	376	12.48
Independent	210	461	23.14	169	204	10.02

[1]Includes fuel, utilities, supplies, and other expenditures not
  covered in Tables 3/17 and 3/18.

Table 3/20   TOTAL EXPENDITURES[1]

	Police			Fire		
	No. of cities reporting	Mean ($000)	Per capita ($)	No. of cities reporting	Mean ($000)	Per capita ($)
Total	889	6,720	139.99	652	4,826	86.74
Population group						
Over 1,000,000	2	225,269	164.36	2	112,823	82.31
500,000–1,000,000	4	127,935	172.55	4	64,674	87.23
250,000–499,999	16	49,097	146.01	16	30,512	89.90
100,000–249,999	57	20,743	140.22	51	13,298	87.76
50,000–99,999	112	9,310	136.79	88	6,514	94.16
25,000–49,999	223	4,656	132.42	168	3,072	85.64
10,000–24,999	475	2,027	125.18	323	1,259	76.78
Geographic division						
New England	53	2,742	117.68	44	2,096	93.75
Mid-Atlantic	86	5,415	161.78	30	6,246	121.26
East North Central	163	4,283	124.65	102	3,771	89.16
West North Central	98	5,053	110.46	72	3,644	74.25
South Atlantic	151	6,548	150.89	128	4,172	88.80
East South Central	42	6,543	120.73	41	4,965	90.20
West South Central	121	7,579	122.76	103	5,530	81.21
Mountain	52	8,637	136.23	35	5,373	75.23
Pacific Coast	123	12,518	173.40	97	7,474	89.32
Metro status						
Central	203	17,691	143.35	175	11,945	89.19
Suburban	476	4,034	142.97	307	2,554	84.68
Independent	210	2,202	110.36	169	1,541	75.55

[1]Includes expenditures in Tables 3/17 through 3/19.

Although these figures have generally risen in recent years, the current survey data compared with 1993 indicates that there has been a slight increase for fire departments but a slight decline for police departments. In 1994, the average other departmental expenditures for police is $1,046,000 and the per capita figure is $21.80. This compares to $1,283,000 and $25.02 per capita in the 1993 data. Fire departments, on the other hand, demonstrate a small increase in both statistics. The average totals increased from $581,000 to $597,000 and the corresponding per capita figures increased from $10.05 to $10.73 between 1993 and 1994.

TOTAL EXPENDITURES

Table 3/20 presents the survey results for total personnel, capital outlay, and all other departmental expenditures combined. The average overall total expenditures totals are $6,720,000 for police and $4,826,000 for fire. The corresponding per capita figures are $139.99 and $86.74 for police and fire, respectively. Compared with the responses from the previous survey, these data indicate that the average total and per capita department expenditures declined from 1993 to 1994 for both services. The 1993 survey results showed the average totals to be $7,965,000 and $5,375,000 for police and fire, respectively. The corresponding per capita figures in the last survey were $155.26 and $92.85. The decline for both, however, is primarily a result of the fact that twice as many of the largest cities (over one million population) responded in 1993 as did in 1994.

Table 3/21 presents five-year longitudinal data for those cities who responded to each of the surveys over the last five years (1989 to 1994). As is expected in any panel study of this variety, the number of cities that responded to the survey in every year is smaller than the number who respond to any individual year.

The salary data for both services demonstrates that small incremental increases occurred in each year. Over the entire five year period, however, the increases average around 20% for base and maximum base salaries. The total salary and wage expenditures rose by 27% for police departments and 41% for fire departments over the 1989 to 1994 reporting period. This general pattern of comparatively small incremental shifts for any given year but substantial changes over the entire five years, is also apparent for most of the expenditure data. The major exception to this, of course, is capital outlays which are more likely to fluctuate from year to year. Over the combined five years, however, the capital expenditure figures show a clear increase. The overall increases during this period

Table 3/21   TRENDS IN AVERAGE EXPENDITURES FOR POLICE AND FIRE DEPARTMENTS

	No. of cities[1] included	Mean annual expense 1989	Mean annual expense 1990	Change from 1989 (%)	Mean annual expense 1991	Change from (%) 1989	Change from (%) 1990	Mean annual expense 1992	Change from (%) 1989	Change from (%) 1991	Mean annual expense 1993	Change from (%) 1989	Change from (%) 1992	Mean annual expense 1994	Change from (%) 1993	Change from (%) 1989
Police																
Base salary, first year	448	21,154	22,154	5	23,117	9	4	23,851	13	3	24,660	17	3	25,275	2	19
Maximum base salary	409	27,810	29,293	5	30,762	11	5	31,977	15	4	33,373	20	4	34,252	3	23
Total salaries and wages	310	3,257,000	3,493,000	7	3,727,000	14	7	4,017,000	23	8	4,078,000	25	2	4,603,000	13	41
Capital outlay	266	229,000	240,000	5	194,000	−15	−19	192,000	−16	−1	156,000	−32	−19	211,000	35	−8
Total employee benefits	310	789,000	842,000	7	937,000	19	11	996,000	26	6	1,192,000	51	20	1,035,000	−13	31
All other expenditures	310	681,000	710,000	4	764,000	12	8	996,000	46	30	803,000	18	−19	1,069,000	35	57
Total	310	4,913,000	5,237,000	7	5,587,000	14	7	6,160,000	25	10	6,200,000	26	1	6,876,000	11	40
Fire																
Base salary, first year	355	19,914	20,812	5	21,693	9	4	22,402	12	3	23,158	16	3	23,556	2	18
Maximum base salary	320	26,170	27,628	6	28,994	11	5	30,147	15	4	31,457	20	4	32,318	3	23
Total salaries and wages	236	2,672,000	2,779,000	4	2,961,000	11	7	3,168,000	19	7	3,242,000	21	2	3,389,000	5	27
Capital outlay	189	167,000	153,000	−8	192,000	15	25	153,000	−8	−20	167,000	0	9	269,000	61	61
Total employee benefits	236	666,000	672,000	1	731,000	10	9	758,000	14	4	859,000	29	13	724,000	−16	9
All other expenditures	236	425,000	453,000	7	479,000	13	6	580,000	36	21	629,000	48	8	594,000	−6	40
Total	236	3,923,000	4,031,000	3	4,324,000	10	7	4,616,000	18	7	4,858,000	24	5	5,284,000	9	35

[1]Cities included in this table must have reported data on salaries and wages, capital outlays, contributions to retirement systems, insurance programs, and "all other expenditures" categories on the survey for each of the six years.

are 61% and 31% for police and fire departments, respectively.

CONCLUSION

This report has examined the cross-sectional patterns and mostly incremental longitudinal trends in police and fire employment and expenditures. For the reasons discussed in the introduction, 1994 may become an important baseline in analyzing the local impact of national intergovernmental grants. Consequently, the future personnel and expenditure patterns may demonstrate more substantial shifts in the years ahead than were discovered in the current survey.

Table 3/22   POLICE AND FIRE DEPARTMENT PERSONNEL, SALARIES, AND EXPENDITURES FOR CITIES 10,000 AND OVER: 1994

This table comprises 1,470 cities 10,000 and over in population (based on U.S. Bureau of the Census 1990 population figures. Data were collected in the spring of 19943. All personnel and salary figures are as of 1 January 1994. Expenditure figures are for the fiscal year from 1 January 1993 to 1 January 1994. Leaders (. . . or . .) indicate data not reported or not applicable.

City: letter identifies municipal designation: "b," borough; "t," town; "tp," township; "v," village.

Service provision: The 1993 survey gathered data on service provision. The numbers that appear in parentheses following the jurisdiction name indicate the following: left, reflects information on the police department; right, reflects fire department. If there are no parentheses, the respondent did not answer this section. See key for detail.

Department: Letter identifies department to which the line of data pertains: "P," police department; "F," fire department.

Total personnel, no. uniformed, duty hours per week: Left, total actual (not authorized) number of full-time paid employees; middle, number of uniformed or sworn (not including civilian or nonuniformed) employees: regular workweek (in hours) for each department.

Entrance, maximum salary ($): Left, annual base salary of a full-time employee (patrol personnel, firefighter) during the first 12 months on the force; right, maximum annual base salary paid to a full-time employee not holding any promotional rank.

Longevity pay, maximum ($), no. years of service to receive longevity pay: Left, indicates whether municipality has longevity pay—extra compensation over the regular maximum salary based on the number of years of service—("Y" yes); center, maximum salary with longevity; right, the number of years of service required to receive longevity pay.

Total expenditures (A) ($): Sum of the other total figures (columns **B, E, F**). (This sum represents the total amount of department expenditures *reported* and may not, in all cases, be the complete expenditure figure for the department. Omissions can be found by examining the individual figures for each city.)

Total personnel expenditures (B) ($), % of (A): Left, sum of columns C and D; right, total personnel expenditures as a percentage of the total reported expenditures (B ÷ A).

Salaries and wages (C) ($): Amount of salaries and wages for all department personnel—regular, temporary, full-time, and part-time. (The gross amount is reported, including longevity pay, hazard pay, holiday pay, etc., without deduction of withholding for income tax or employee contributions for social security or retirement.)

City contributions to employee retirement, [to employee] insurance (D) ($): Left, amount the municipality contributes to federal social security, to a state-administered employee retirement system, and/or to a city-administered employee retirement system for civilian and uniformed personnel; right, amount the municipality contributes to health, hospital, or disability, and to life insurance programs for civilian and uniformed personnel.

Capital outlay (E) ($): Figure includes purchase and replacement of equipment, purchase of land and existing structures, and construction.

All other (F) ($): All other expenditures not reported in the above categories.

KEY

Numbers in parentheses after city names indicate how the service is provided.

Police and Fire (left and right numbers respectively)
1 full-time department
2 volunteer department
3 combined full-time paid and volunteer department
4 public safety department (consolidated police and fire)
5 special district provides service
6 regional service (multijurisdictional)
7 county provides service
8 contract with private company
9 other

(-) indicates data not reported or not available. In some instances the respondent indicated that a service was provided but did not indicate how. This is reflected as (-,-).

City (Service provision)	Depart-ment	Total personnel, no. uniformed, duty hours per week	Entrance, maximum salary ($)	Longevity pay, maximum ($), no. years to receive longevity pay	Total expenditures (A) ($)	Total personnel expenditures (B) ($), % of (A)	Salaries and wages (C) ($)	City contrib. to employee retirement, insurance (D) ($)	Capital outlay (E) ($)	All other (F) ($)
Over 1,000,000										
Chicago, Ill. (1,1)	P	13,067-8,649-42	34,884-50,544	Y-...-30	...	...-..	...	...-...	14,616	...
	F	4,931-4,576-44	29,496-45,366	Y-...-30	...	...-..	...	...-...	10,361	...
Dallas, Tex. (1,1)	P	3,490-2,774-40	25,093-32,025	Y-33,225-1	...	...-..	...	...-...	128,760	...
	F	1,664-1,562-54	23,901-32,025	Y-32,125-1	...	...-..	...	...-...	130,349	...
Houston, Tex. (1,1)	P	6,778-4,763-40	27,154-35,532	Y-36,832-1	291,312	259,602-89	216,210	26,821-16,571	1,742	29,968
	F	3,262-2,936-46	27,154-35,532	Y-36,832-1	163,665	147,039-89	118,813	17,968-10,258	301	16,325
Los Angeles, Calif. (1,1)	P	10,070-7,640-40	33,157-47,001	Y-50,989-10	...	...-..	...	...-...	5,722	...
	F	3,365-3,059-56	31,529-47,522	Y-51,385-10	...	...-..	...	...-...	6,068	...
San Diego, Calif. (1,1)	P	2,476-1,857-40	31,609-44,922	NONE	367,357	138,541-37	113,428	16,922-8,191	206,388	22,428
	F	951-836-56	32,790-41,616	NONE	267,869	55,551-20	47,898	4,428-3,225	205,587	6,731
500,000–1,000,000										
Columbus, Ohio (4,4)	P	...-..-..	...-...	..-...-..	...	...-..	...	...-...	...	...
	F	...-..-..	...-...	..-...-..	...	...-..	...	...-...	...	...
Honolulu, Hawaii (1,1)	P	2,329-1,888-40	27,240-40,608	NONE	160,466	125,215-78	99,737	20,539-4,939	18,934	16,317
	F	1,031-999-56	25,184-33,120	Y-35,772-10	57,888	51,222-88	41,269	7,600-2,353	3,027	3,639
Jacksonville, Fla. (1,1)	P	2,303-1,283-40	29,364-43,236	Y-45,636-5	317,349	102,881-32	90,666	6,347-5,868	174,713	39,755
	F	980-952-56	26,196-35,724	Y-38,124-5	324,817	52,790-16	47,000	3,290-2,500	260,000	12,027
Milwaukee, Wis. (1,1)	P	2,545-2,067-40	26,954-36,500	Y-37,250-10	...	...-..	...	...-...	...	...
	F	1,631-1,574-49	21,447-36,500	NONE	...	...-..	...	...-...	...	...
Nashville-Davidson, Tenn. (1,1)	P	1,480-1,093-42	25,247-32,745	Y-33,595-5	68,550	59,135-86	44,562	9,413-5,160	975	8,440
	F	1,089-827-53	24,021-32,745	Y-33,595-5	77,973	48,800-62	36,900	7,600-4,300	25,473	3,700
Phoenix, Ariz. (1,1)	P	3,073-2,243-40	27,040-40,893	Y-41,661-8	162,501	135,761-83	111,944	10,611-13,206	2,504	24,236
	F	1,375-1,175-56	26,936-38,904	Y-40,206-7	89,591	72,268-80	59,057	6,129-7,082	3,070	14,253
250,000–499,999										
Albuquerque, N.M. (1,1)	P	769-485-40	16,640-33,322	Y-35,122-10	...	...-..	...	...-...	8,005	...
	F	496-454-56	16,647-31,683	Y-34,803-8	...	...-..	...	...-...	2,496	...
Anaheim, Calif. (1,1)	P	527-376-40	34,736-46,550	NONE	49,503	34,854-70	29,496	2,765-2,593	553	14,096
	F	243-219-56	29,906-44,204	NONE	29,518	19,293-65	16,305	1,763-1,225	77	10,148

Table 3/22 continued

POLICE AND FIRE DEPARTMENT PERSONNEL, SALARIES, AND EXPENDITURES FOR CITIES 10,000 AND OVER: 1994

City (Service provision)	Department	Total personnel, no. uniformed, duty hours per week	Entrance, maximum salary ($)	Longevity pay, maximum ($), no. years to receive longevity pay	Reported expenditures (in thousands)					
					Total expenditures (A) ($)	Total personnel expenditures (B) ($), % of (A)	Salaries and wages (C) ($)	City contrib. to employee retirement, insurance (D) ($)	Capital outlay (E) ($)	All other (F) ($)
250,000–499,999 continued										
Arlington, Tex. (1,1)	P	393-275-40	28,632-35,640	Y-38,448-..	25,524	21,303-83	16,870	1,965-2,468	162	4,059
	F	284-254-56	26,688-34,056	Y-36,725-1	16,752	14,447-86	11,459	1,319-1,669	72	2,233
Austin, Tex. (1,1)	P	1,270-932-40	24,086-44,633	Y-48,000-1	75,459	66,152-87	55,483	7,621-3,048	2,073	7,234
	F	850-799-53	22,266-43,347	Y-...-1	50,055	45,959-91	39,566	4,374-2,019	776	3,320
Buffalo, N.Y. (1,1)	P	1,080-937-40	28,814-38,956	Y-40,156-5	...	...-..	...	...-...	2,795	...
	F	885-860-40	27,427-37,078	Y-38,278-5	...	...	...	...-...	2,355	...
Cincinnati, Ohio (1,1)	P	986-763-40	34,625-38,552	Y-39,027-8	...	...-..	...	...-...	...	...
	F	751-718-48	32,835-36,560	Y-37,035-8	...	...-..	...	...-...	...	...
Corpus Christi, Tex. (1,1)	P	554-394-40	23,076-32,736	Y-34,176-1	26,284	23,791-90	18,688	3,375-1,728	144	2,349
	F	325-316-54	22,236-29,592	Y-31,152-1	15,356	13,955-90	10,813	2,125-1,017	428	973
Fort Worth, Tex. (3,1)	P	1,374-1,064-40	26,760-32,217	Y-33,417-1	64,667	50,707-78	45,147	3,660-1,900	7,486	6,474
	F	681-656-56	25,632-30,859	Y-32,059-1	37,201	28,399-76	25,368	2,082-949	5,042	3,760
Fresno, Calif. (1,1)	P	455-205-40	41,520-49,656	NONE	...	...-..	...	...-...	209	...
	F	247-216-56	39,438-46,692	NONE	28,909	26,841-92	24,916	1,004-921	495	1,573
Las Vegas, Nev. (9,1)	P	...-..-..	...-...	..-...-..	...	...-..	...	...-...	...	...
	F	376-220-56	29,328-42,172	Y-48,498-6	...	...-..	...	...-...	699	...
Louisville, Ky. (1,1)	P	235-53-40	19,781-25,334	Y-29,306-5	43,740	32,061-73	25,496	4,644-1,921	3,561	8,118
	F	541-466-56	21,569-24,762	Y-28,547-5	25,034	21,861-87	17,226	3,243-1,392	696	2,477
Mesa, Ariz. (1,1)	P	708-467-40	28,470-40,443	Y-44,487-5	...	...-..	...	...-...	4,220	...
	F	301-266-56	24,479-36,569	Y-40,226-5	...	...-..	...	...-...	841	...
Minneapolis, Minn. (1,1)	P	1,034-160-40	27,875-43,065	Y-44,683-7	63,214	49,583-78	41,191	5,438-2,954	849	12,782
	F	477-457-54	26,728-41,262	Y-41,964-8	32,275	25,894-80	21,702	2,779-1,413	2,090	4,291
Norfolk, Va. (1,1)	P	772-678-40	23,270-38,841	NONE	35,402	28,453-80	24,496	2,707-1,250	874	6,075
	F	479-471-52	22,162-36,991	NONE	20,377	18,923-92	16,331	1,812-780	264	1,190
Oklahoma City, Okla. (1,-)	P	1,214-979-40	26,851-30,004	Y-31,379-3	...	...-..	...	...-...	...	...
	F	994-960-40	24,211-33,259	Y-34,516-3	...	...-..	...	...-...	...	...
Omaha, Nebr. (1,1)	P	761-621-37	30,217-39,525	Y-40,605-7	42,268	38,130-90	31,851	4,112-2,167	...	4,138
	F	538-528-56	28,609-37,190	Y-38,210-7	117,089	28,190-24	23,455	3,146-1,589	87,576	1,323
Pittsburgh, Pa. (1,1)	P	1,365-1,268-40	26,645-38,065	Y-41,681-4	76,584	64,152-83	53,387	3,713-7,052	2,395	10,037
	F	904-896-42	22,647-36,660	Y-40,142-4	55,899	45,501-81	37,613	3,138-4,750	2,900	7,498
Sacramento, Calif. (1,1)	P	930-584-40	32,463-49,435	Y-49,635-20	86,565	77,130-89	63,955	8,091-5,084	179	9,256
	F	468-437-56	31,615-46,627	Y-46,827-20	52,078	47,348-90	38,757	5,723-2,868	6	4,724
St. Paul, Minn. (1,1)	P	719-524-40	32,745-43,124	NONE	43,369	37,271-85	31,129	4,936-1,206	500	5,598
	F	441-381-56	32,745-43,124	NONE	31,658	27,438-86	23,975	2,673-790	1,133	3,087
Toledo, Ohio (1,1)	P	710-656-40	30,278-38,606	Y-38,899-26	48,400	44,000-90	32,000	6,500-5,500	500	3,900
	F	534-525-48	26,822-38,611	NONE	34,862	32,994-94	23,664	5,143-4,187	...	1,868
Tucson, Ariz. (1,1)	P	1,010-756-40	28,548-38,268	NONE	56,003	44,400-79	36,793	3,724-3,883	1,547	10,056
	F	461-433-56	27,192-36,444	NONE	26,151	23,222-88	19,466	1,882-1,874	1,174	1,755
Virginia Beach, Va. (1,3)	P	865-638-40	23,237-33,693	NONE	41,594	33,846-81	28,760	4,567-519	811	6,937
	F	363-342-56	23,237-33,693	NONE	17,724	15,902-89	13,152	2,110-640	9	1,813
Wichita, Kan. (1,1)	P	657-489-40	22,688-30,140	Y-31,580-6	28,739	25,797-89	19,887	3,989-1,921	119	2,823
	F	381-368-56	22,281-30,371	Y-31,811-6	...	...-..	...	...-...	501	...
100,000–249,999										
Abilene, Tex. (1,1)	P	223-170-40	20,468-28,812	Y-30,012-1	16,341	7,541-46	6,269	842-430	7,598	1,202
	F	171-164-52	18,899-26,480	Y-27,680-1	14,004	5,957-42	5,018	595-344	7,527	520
Alexandria, Va. (1,1)	P	360-260-40	28,695-46,618	NONE	...	...-..	...	...-...	419	...
	F	228-143-56	27,332-...	NONE	...	...-..	...	...-...	219	...
Allentown, Pa. (1,1)	P	229-205-40	24,056-33,425	Y-34,675-4	12,333	11,750-95	8,703	1,422-1,625	12	571
	F	146-144-42	22,987-31,469	Y-33,420-4	...	...-..	...	...-...	10	...
Amarillo, Tex. (1,1)	P	256-178-40	21,564-30,300	Y-31,500-25	12,044	9,774-81	8,212	1,025-537	70	2,200
	F	210-207-56	20,088-28,476	Y-29,676-25	8,157	7,927-97	6,788	681-458	52	178
Anchorage, Alaska (3,3)	P	402-262-40	39,354-57,470	NONE	37,278	32,262-86	26,602	2,956-2,704	800	4,216
	F	256-228-56	32,245-51,397	NONE	27,820	22,830-82	19,063	1,740-2,027	911	4,079
Ann Arbor, Mich. (1,1)	P	218-176-40	27,456-39,208	Y-40,708-5	18,359	11,297-61	9,403	1,050-844	5,756	1,306
	F	111-109-50	29,410-38,420	NONE	12,668	6,254-49	5,241	584-429	5,653	761
Arlington, Va. (1,1)	P	397-320-40	30,724-43,337	NONE	...	...-..	...	...-...	...	...
	F	271-261-56	30,709-40,002	NONE	23,393	21,211-90	16,853	3,296-1,062	...	2,182
Baton Rouge, La. (1,1)	P	730-645-40	18,639-23,978	Y-28,774-10	31,158	26,684-85	21,529	2,631-2,524	319	4,155
	F	571-567-56	14,795-20,703	Y-24,844-10	22,167	20,191-91	16,293	1,861-2,037	695	1,281
Berkeley, Calif. (1,1)	P	316-183-40	40,920-46,896	Y-53,292-19	...	...-..	...	...-...	489	...
	F	149-132-46	42,312-46,548	NONE	...	...-..	...	...-...	552	...
Boise City, Idaho (1,1)	P	214-169-40	22,920-36,060	NONE	10,826	10,117-93	7,917	1,079-1,121	531	178
	F	187-170-54	23,892-32,724	NONE	...	...-..	...	...-...	877	...
Cedar Rapids, Iowa (1,1)	P	210-166-40	25,105-31,730	Y-32,930-5	10,114	8,954-88	6,894	1,108-952	344	816
	F	155-145-53	25,841-30,922	Y-32,122-5	7,934	7,065-89	5,403	901-761	323	546
Columbus-Muscogee, Ga. (1,1)	P	472-370-51	17,097-27,747	NONE	15,309	13,518-88	11,022	1,327-1,169	348	1,443
	F	289-284-56	15,267-24,773	NONE	11,193	10,502-93	8,095	1,571-836	169	522
Dayton, Ohio (1,1)	P	583-484-40	19,386-36,118	Y-36,840-..	42,002	39,316-93	32,293	4,851-2,172	637	2,049
	F	436-326-49	22,339-35,928	Y-36,528-..	32,351	30,613-94	24,501	4,401-1,711	739	999
Des Moines, Iowa (1,1)	P	471-351-40	29,531-33,891	Y-35,791-5	26,899	21,844-81	16,835	2,705-2,304	917	4,138
	F	282-274-56	27,165-30,790	Y-32,637-5	14,522	13,138-90	10,017	1,710-1,411	597	787
Durham, N.C. (1,1)	P	347-294-42	23,784-37,622	Y-39,122-5	17,395	14,814-85	12,528	1,377-909	866	1,715
	F	224-212-56	20,984-32,190	Y-33,690-5	...	...-..	...	...-...	332	...
El Monte, Calif. (1,1)	P	163-123-40	35,656-42,288	Y-42,588-5	...	...-..	...	...-...	1,027	...

Table 3/22 POLICE AND FIRE DEPARTMENT PERSONNEL, SALARIES, AND EXPENDITURES FOR
continued CITIES 10,000 AND OVER: 1994

City (Service provision)	Depart-ment	Total personnel, no. uniformed, duty hours per week	Entrance, maximum salary ($)	Longevity pay, maximum ($), no. years to receive longevity pay	Reported expenditures (in thousands)					
					Total expendi-tures (A) ($)	Total personnel expendi-tures (B) ($), % of (A)	Salaries and wages (C) ($)	City contrib. to employee retirement, insurance (D) ($)	Capital outlay (E) ($)	All other (F) ($)
100,000–249,999 continued										
El Monte, Calif. (1,1) cont.	F	73-63-56	32,556-38,604	Y-38,904-5	...	...-...	...	...-...	347	...
Elizabeth, N.J. (1,1)	P	378-326-40	25,000-44,135	Y-48,548-5	...	...-...	...	...-...	...	...
	F	272-265-42	25,000-44,135	Y-48,548-5	...	...-...	...	...-...	...	...
Erie, Pa. (1,1)	P	188-154-40	25,383-33,021	Y-35,663-4	10,440	8,819-84	7,674	91-1,054	1,023	598
	F	204-200-42	26,295-33,277	Y-35,882-4	9,364	8,153-87	7,100	69-984	828	383
Escondido, Calif. (3,9)	P	210-150-43	33,810-42,096	NONE	13,971	11,843-84	9,336	1,847-660	351	1,777
	F	96-91-56	31,998-40,104	NONE	8,659	6,874-79	5,400	1,105-369	1,341	444
Eugene, Ore. (4,4)	P	...-...-..	...-...	..-...-..	...	...-...	...	...-...	...	...
	F	...-...-..	...-...	..-...-..	...	...-...	...	...-...	...	...
Evansville, Ind. (1,1)	P	275-249-40	26,795-32,511	Y-...-3	12,785	11,065-86	8,714	1,013-1,338	260	1,460
	F	277-270-56	...-...	Y-...-3	12,389	10,697-86	8,327	976-1,394	882	810
Fort Lauderdale, Fla. (1,1)	P	717-456-40	30,098-42,682	Y-48,017-5	43,747	37,761-86	29,179	6,082-2,500	194	5,792
	F	282-265-48	28,629-36,267	Y-40,800-5	17,459	15,318-87	11,875	2,508-935	71	2,070
Fort Wayne, Ind. (1,1)	P	341-281-..	26,038-28,931	Y-29,431-4	...	...-...	...	...-...	2,906	...
	F	243-232-56	23,446-27,437	Y-28,437-25	13,394	7,531-56	7,322	65-144	2,906	2,957
Fremont, Calif. (1,1)	P	261-177-40	44,232-53,724	NONE	21,176	18,750-88	14,565	2,667-1,518	1,330	1,096
	F	142-125-56	37,728-45,840	NONE	12,900	11,133-86	8,655	1,659-819	1,320	456
Fullerton, Calif. (1,1)	P	212-143-40	38,522-49,165	NONE	17,383	13,953-80	11,662	1,334-957	204	3,226
	F	90-82-56	32,577-41,577	NONE	8,104	6,804-83	5,615	762-427	26	1,274
Garden Grove, Calif. (-,-)	P	225-161-40	36,924-44,856	NONE	19,701	16,246-82	11,815	2,167-2,264	94	3,361
	F	96-5-56	30,480-37,080	NONE	9,119	7,695-84	5,558	1,046-1,091	28	1,396
Garland, Tex. (1,1)	P	259-170-40	29,785-36,254	Y-...-1	17,221	14,975-86	12,232	1,754-989	617	1,629
	F	205-201-56	25,480-32,760	Y-...-1	10,959	9,945-90	8,216	1,074-655	199	815
Grand Rapids, Mich. (1,1)	P	373-301-40	28,102-39,772	Y-40,432-5	23,559	18,147-77	15,461	697-1,989	2,339	3,073
	F	263-254-50	27,789-39,290	Y-39,950-5	15,676	12,994-82	11,340	135-1,519	1,169	1,513
Greensboro, N.C. (1,1)	P	540-418-40	22,008-36,072	Y-38,777-5	26,766	23,099-86	19,380	2,309-1,410	753	2,914
	F	370-361-56	19,980-29,628	Y-31,850-5	15,132	14,038-92	11,951	1,183-904	108	986
Hampton, Va. (1,3)	P	315-253-..	21,240-31,860	Y-...-3	14,409	10,715-74	8,549	1,603-563	2,079	1,615
	F	219-205-..	21,240-31,860	Y-...-3	11,203	8,716-77	6,979	1,269-468	1,586	901
Hollywood, Fla. (-,-)	P	450-302-42	29,827-41,000	Y-44,000-10	...	...-...	...	...-...	...	...
	F	210-198-48	27,676-37,000	Y-41,000-10	...	...-...	...	...-...	...	...
Huntington Beach, Calif. (1,1)	P	376-269-40	40,104-49,692	NONE	32,368	28,331-87	21,891	3,220-3,220	859	3,178
	F	177-151-56	36,504-45,204	NONE	...	...-...	...	...-...	425	...
Huntsville, Ala. (1,1)	P	454-337-40	22,464-31,637	Y-32,207-5	24,172	21,541-89	18,034	1,986-1,521	385	2,246
	F	321-297-48	21,445-30,056	Y-30,626-5	16,549	15,468-93	12,917	1,457-1,094	1	1,080
Inglewood, Calif. (3,3)	P	278-200-40	37,814-46,140	Y-48,978-10	24,906	22,335-89	16,403	3,281-2,651	203	2,368
	F	87-85-56	30,078-51,991	Y-55,190-10	8,829	8,073-91	5,893	1,228-952	74	682
Irvine, Calif. (1,7)	P	166-119-40	38,614-52,129	NONE	36,936	28,882-78	22,540	4,147-2,195	7	8,047
	F	...-...-..	...-...	..-...-..	...	...-...	...	...-...	...	...
Jackson, Miss. (1,1)	P	661-414-40	20,904-28,224	NONE	27,090	18,521-68	16,383	1,394-744	475	8,094
	F	402-5-56	20,240-30,396	NONE	15,638	13,673-87	12,367	716-590	535	1,430
Kansas City, Kan. (1,1)	P	484-347-40	25,104-41,134	Y-42,334-5	29,385	20,026-68	15,400	2,343-2,283	5,334	4,025
	F	392-385-56	24,279-37,445	Y-38,645-5	22,244	19,739-88	15,311	2,415-2,013	707	1,798
Lakewood, Colo. (1,5)	P	316-213-40	27,913-42,619	NONE	16,742	14,871-88	12,483	1,149-1,239	90	1,781
	F	...-...-..	...-...	..-...-..	...	...-...	...	...-...	...	...
Lansing, Mich. (1,1)	P	335-251-40	26,325-37,782	Y-39,382-5	...	...-...	...	...-...	174	...
	F	237-223-54	26,191-38,055	Y-39,575-5	...	...-...	...	...-...	767	...
Lexington-Fayette, Ky. (1,1)	P	533-404-40	19,404-27,333	Y-...-4	21,448	19,732-91	16,217	2,488-1,027	852	864
	F	437-405-56	19,404-27,333	Y-...-4	18,969	16,768-88	13,625	2,258-885	84	2,117
Lincoln, Nebr. (1,1)	P	350-265-40	23,554-32,995	Y-34,176-5	...	...-...	...	...-...	9	...
	F	251-246-56	23,905-30,183	Y-31,383-5	...	...-...	...	...-...	236	...
Little Rock, Ark. (1,1)	P	509-423-40	20,202-29,707	Y-30,457-1	21,441	17,810-83	15,541	976-1,293	681	2,950
	F	349-346-56	19,947-29,387	Y-30,107-1	16,834	13,723-81	12,014	723-986	857	2,254
Livonia, Mich. (1,1)	P	178-160-40	29,141-40,830	Y-42,780-21	...	...-...	...	...-...	189	...
	F	93-91-56	27,456-38,833	Y-40,783-21	...	...-...	...	...-...	310	...
Lubbock, Tex. (1,1)	P	353-306-40	22,567-...	..-...-3	18,302	15,152-82	11,755	2,054-1,343	608	2,542
	F	258-247-56	22,567-...	..-...-3	12,678	11,322-89	9,097	1,361-864	155	1,201
Macon, Ga. (1,1)	P	356-293-40	18,428-24,648	NONE	...	...-...	...	...-...	...	...
	F	351-339-60	18,428-24,648	NONE	...	...-...	...	...-...	...	...
Madison, Wis. (1,1)	P	375-304-37	28,370-32,474	Y-36,036-4	...	...-...	...	...-...	16,196	...
	F	280-264-48	28,159-32,374	Y-35,932-4	...	...-...	...	...-...	16,457	...
Mesquite, Tex. (1,1)	P	234-169-40	28,416-36,264	Y-37,464-25	13,092	10,657-81	8,328	1,562-767	1,440	995
	F	161-155-56	28,416-36,264	Y-37,464-25	9,587	7,920-82	6,157	1,153-610	1,156	511
Mobile, Ala. (1,1)	P	541-424-40	19,860-30,804	NONE	...	...-...	...	...-...	847	...
	F	419-396-56	19,860-30,804	NONE	...	...-...	...	...-...	212	...
Modesto, Calif. (1,1)	P	288-202-40	34,212-40,570	NONE	22,607	15,471-68	12,057	2,371-1,043	111	7,025
	F	164-151-56	35,868-42,534	NONE	13,313	10,749-80	8,476	1,737-536	876	1,688
Montgomery, Ala. (1,1)	P	571-369-40	15,477-23,517	NONE	...	...-...	...	...-...	181	...
	F	422-402-56	17,295-23,517	NONE	...	...-...	...	...-...	84	...
Newport News, Va. (1,1)	P	414-308-34	21,250-42,350	NONE	...	...-...	...	...-...	12,950	...
	F	309-295-56	21,250-42,350	NONE	...	...-...	...	...-...	2,000	...
Ontario, Calif. (-,-)	P	...-...-..	...-...	..-...-..	...	...-...	...	...-...	...	...
	F	...-...-..	...-...	..-...-..	...	...-...	...	...-...	...	...
Orange, Calif. (1,1)	P	201-133-40	36,180-46,392	NONE	16,252	13,778-84	11,191	1,821-766	188	2,286

Table 3/22 continued   **POLICE AND FIRE DEPARTMENT PERSONNEL, SALARIES, AND EXPENDITURES FOR CITIES 10,000 AND OVER: 1994**

City (Service provision)	Department	Total personnel, no. uniformed, duty hours per week	Entrance, maximum salary ($)	Longevity pay, maximum ($) no. years to receive longevity pay	Reported expenditures (in thousands)					
					Total expenditures (A) ($)	Total personnel expenditures (B) ($), % of (A)	Salaries and wages (C) ($)	City contrib. to employee retirement, insurance (D) ($)	Capital outlay (E) ($)	All other (F) ($)
100,000–249,999 continued										
Orange, Calif. (1,1) cont.	F	115-111-56	36,156-43,956	NONE	12,647	10,863-85	8,211	1,875-777	352	1,432
Pasadena, Calif. (1,1)	P	340-223-40	39,756-48,692	NONE	...	...-..	...	...-...	677	...
	F	181-170-56	27,854-48,504	NONE	...	...-..	...	...-...	399	...
Pasadena, Tex. (1,2)	P	261-205-40	28,271-38,498	Y-...-1	...	...-..	...	...-...	1,870	...
	F	...-..-..	...-...	..-...-..	...	...-..	...	...-...	...	...
Peoria, Ill. (1,1)	P	267-49-41	27,485-42,867	Y-46,296-5	...	...-..	...	...-...	3,481	...
	F	197-188-53	25,822-36,561	Y-39,486-5	...	...-..	...	...-...	436	...
Plano, Tex. (1,1)	P	262-194-40	31,564-37,168	Y-38,128-1	16,805	12,307-73	10,226	1,173-908	2,652	1,846
	F	183-168-56	30,009-34,726	Y-34,870-1	13,442	8,971-66	7,553	725-693	3,153	1,318
Pomona, Calif. (3,3)	P	289-173-..	34,956-42,660	NONE	...	...-..	...	...-...	598	...
	F	120-101-..	34,956-42,660	NONE	...	...-..	...	...-...	21	...
Raleigh, N.C. (1,1)	P	507-457-42	23,436-34,625	Y-36,183-5	...	...-..	...	...-...	...	...
	F	353-347-56	21,257-31,406	Y-32,819-5	...	...-..	...	...-...	...	...
Rancho Cucamonga, Calif. (-,1)	P	...-..-..	...-...	..-...-..	...	...-..	...	...-...	...	...
	F	76-63-56	35,106-41,631	NONE	8,093	6,806-84	5,250	899-657	157	1,130
Reno, Nev. (1,1)	P	414-287-40	27,999-38,368	Y-39,928-5	30,675	23,309-75	17,557	4,010-1,742	731	6,635
	F	208-199-56	28,376-38,514	Y-42,365-5	...	...-..	...	...-...	107	...
Richmond, Va. (1,1)	P	739-642-40	26,572-46,904	NONE	...	...-..	...	...-...	205	...
	F	480-470-56	26,572-46,904	NONE	...	...-..	...	...-...	1,350	...
Riverside, Calif. (3,-)	P	534-338-40	33,036-44,268	NONE	37,931	28,685-75	22,422	4,311-1,952	2,334	6,912
	F	201-180-56	31,668-42,432	NONE	16,799	14,114-84	11,224	2,220-670	470	2,215
Rochester, N.Y. (1,1)	P	820-683-40	27,410-39,157	Y-40,307-3	50,760	44,846-88	35,738	6,436-2,672	816	5,098
	F	534-512-40	27,410-39,157	Y-40,307-3	34,132	32,258-94	25,389	4,797-2,072	681	1,193
St. Petersburg, Fla. (1,1)	P	709-508-40	25,072-36,160	NONE	...	...-..	...	...-...	96	...
	F	336-314-52	22,179-31,779	NONE	...	...-..	...	...-...	135	...
Salem, Ore. (1,1)	P	241-164-40	30,792-43,176	NONE	...	...-..	...	...-...	238	...
	F	142-132-56	24,636-34,884	NONE	...	...-..	...	...-...	87	...
Salinas, Calif. (1,1)	P	166-129-40	36,108-43,896	NONE	15,691	12,142-77	9,603	1,767-772	420	3,129
	F	86-84-53	31,800-38,688	NONE	7,758	6,779-87	5,566	794-419	613	366
San Bernardino, Calif. (1,1)	P	390-252-40	37,158-45,840	NONE	...	...-..	...	...-...	2,883	...
	F	174-154-56	34,614-42,588	NONE	...	...-..	...	...-...	1,789	...
Santa Rosa, Calif. (1,1)	P	204-136-40	38,556-46,860	NONE	19,885	14,059-70	10,744	1,892-1,423	4,165	1,661
	F	112-107-56	36,828-44,184	NONE	12,381	7,537-60	5,580	1,206-751	3,933	911
Savannah, Ga. (1,1)	P	477-387-40	19,033-26,135	Y-27,080-10	20,867	16,470-78	13,174	1,453-1,843	382	4,015
	F	206-195-56	19,033-24,291	Y-25,236-10	9,756	7,325-75	5,997	508-820	331	2,100
Scottsdale, Ariz. (1,8)	P	337-224-40	29,910-42,453	NONE	20,782	16,470-79	16,229	151-90	236	4,076
	F	...-..-..	...-...	..-...-..	...	...-..	...	...-...	...	...
Simi Valley, Calif. (1,5)	P	162-109-40	35,550-46,477	NONE	9,091	8,097-89	6,073	1,255-769	137	857
	F	...-..-..	...-...	..-...-..	...	...-..	...	...-...	...	...
Sioux Falls, S.D. (1,1)	P	172-148-40	26,173-35,409	NONE	8,672	7,291-84	5,907	800-584	560	821
	F	157-148-53	22,880-31,118	NONE	9,222	8,070-87	6,111	1,249-710	545	607
Spokane, Wash. (1,1)	P	352-256-40	26,058-40,528	Y-43,785-5	27,657	19,042-68	16,280	1,408-1,354	2,636	5,979
	F	336-322-47	25,682-39,254	Y-42,345-5	21,108	17,729-83	15,478	853-1,398	166	3,213
Springfield, Ill. (1,1)	P	278-229-42	26,613-35,484	Y-39,387-5	16,061	12,915-80	10,471	1,527-917	2,266	880
	F	223-203-51	26,613-35,484	Y-39,033-5	12,831	11,144-86	8,833	1,575-736	1,200	487
Springfield, Mo. (1,1)	P	257-200-40	23,234-28,579	Y-29,779-5	11,699	9,941-84	8,196	1,186-559	366	1,392
	F	201-197-56	22,214-28,163	Y-29,363-5	8,157	7,405-90	6,039	875-491	313	439
Sterling Heights, Mich. (1,1)	P	223-166-40	27,662-44,823	Y-48,823-5	15,389	14,468-94	10,646	2,314-1,508	305	616
	F	106-101-56	26,712-42,748	Y-45,548-5	8,434	7,857-93	5,762	1,288-807	57	520
Stockton, Calif. (1,1)	P	509-343-40	33,468-42,960	Y-48,908-6	37,298	29,969-80	21,050	4,249-4,670	1,646	5,683
	F	254-230-56	31,860-38,916	Y-41,910-4	21,749	18,981-87	13,039	2,947-2,995	37	2,731
Sunnyvale, Calif. (4,4)	P	...-..-..	...-...	..-...-..	...	...-..	...	...-...	...	...
	F	...-..-..	...-...	..-...-..	...	...-..	...	...-...	...	...
Tacoma, Wash. (1,1)	P	392-347-40	32,301-44,641	Y-48,212-5	31,523	21,940-69	18,600	1,190-2,150	118	9,465
	F	379-359-40	33,930-44,641	Y-48,212-5	23,292	21,748-93	18,446	1,027-2,275	65	1,479
Tallahassee, Fla. (1,1)	P	441-308-40	24,695-34,900	NONE	22,293	17,097-76	14,531	1,698-868	37	5,159
	F	247-240-53	22,599-31,900	NONE	11,623	8,817-75	7,711	695-411	2	2,804
Tempe, Ariz. (1,1)	P	369-254-40	29,733-40,136	NONE	19,809	17,008-85	13,857	1,857-1,294	563	2,238
	F	146-132-56	28,294-38,200	NONE	10,132	7,288-71	6,246	487-555	2,246	598
Thousand Oaks, Calif. (-,-)	P	...-..-..	...-...	..-...-..	...	...-..	...	...-...	...	...
	F	...-..-..	...-...	..-...-..	...	...-..	...	...-...	...	...
Topeka, Kan. (1,1)	P	325-201-40	24,528-33,408	Y-34,864-20	16,753	14,258-85	11,963	1,813-482	450	2,045
	F	236-232-53	22,126-25,759	Y-27,217-20	11,502	10,922-94	9,129	1,479-314	97	483
Vallejo, Calif. (1,1)	P	189-128-40	44,307-53,856	NONE	...	...-..	...	...-...	747	...
	F	100-91-56	40,620-49,374	NONE	...	...-..	...	...-...	747	...
Waco, Tex. (1,1)	P	258-185-40	23,376-30,960	Y-32,160-1	11,092	9,720-87	7,987	1,462-271	33	1,339
	F	182-179-56	23,376-30,960	Y-32,160-1	8,163	7,300-89	6,080	1,030-190	423	440
Winston-Salem, N.C. (1,1)	P	540-418-40	22,609-37,003	Y-39,778-5	26,350	21,733-82	16,412	3,471-1,850	1,139	3,478
	F	267-251-56	18,258-28,477	Y-30,613-5	10,783	9,145-84	7,242	1,087-816	595	1,043
50,000–99,999										
Alameda, Calif. (1,1)	P	...-..-..	...-...	..-...-..	...	...-..	...	...-...	210	...
	F	92-89-56	32,028-46,584	NONE	...	...-..	...	...-...	54	...
Albany, Ga. (1,1)	P	238-213-40	17,950-29,453	NONE	7,959	6,561-82	5,104	844-613	181	1,217
	F	166-160-56	16,482-26,412	NONE	5,522	5,015-90	3,874	641-500	122	385

Table 3/22 continued POLICE AND FIRE DEPARTMENT PERSONNEL, SALARIES, AND EXPENDITURES FOR CITIES 10,000 AND OVER: 1994

City (Service provision)	Department	Total personnel, no. uniformed, duty hours per week	Entrance, maximum salary ($)	Longevity pay, maximum ($) no. years to receive longevity pay	Total expenditures (A) ($)	Total personnel expenditures (B) ($), % of (A)	Salaries and wages (C) ($)	City contrib. to employee retirement, insurance (D) ($)	Capital outlay (E) ($)	All other (F) ($)
50,000–99,999 continued										
Alhambra, Calif. (3,1) ....P	P	167-86-40	34,044-41,376	NONE	...	...-...	...	...-...	6,013	...
	F	86-77-53	32,712-39,756	NONE	...	...-...	...	...-...	1,381	...
Antioch, Calif. (1,6) ....P	P	118-83-40	38,688-47,028	NONE	...	...-...	...	...-...	44	...
	F	...-...-..	...-...	..-...-..	...	...-...	...	...-...	...	...
Arlington Heights v, Ill. (1,1) ....P	P	136-105-40	28,198-43,745	Y-44,495-5	...	...-...	...	...-...	212	...
	F	94-92-49	27,379-40,451	Y-41,201-5	...	...-...	...	...-...	401	...
Asheville, N.C. (1,1) ....P	P	184-144-44	18,720-32,219	Y-32,619-5	8,563	6,777-79	5,180	1,115-482	357	1,429
	F	175-169-56	18,720-30,659	Y-31,049-5	8,603	7,081-82	5,550	1,012-519	779	743
Baldwin Park, Calif. (1,-) ....P	P	69-48-40	35,412-43,043	NONE	6,787	5,507-81	4,043	605-859	553	727
	F	...-...-..	...-...	..-...-..	...	...-...	...	...-...	...	...
Battle Creek, Mich. (1,1) ....P	P	154-116-40	27,295-35,559	Y-36,559-7	9,355	7,882-84	6,027	1,130-725	11	1,462
	F	99-97-53	26,034-34,531	Y-35,531-7	5,853	5,374-91	3,965	860-549	6	473
Baytown, Tex. (1,1) ....P	P	137-110-40	22,992-...	Y-34,920-1	...	...-...	...	...-...	219	...
	F	75-71-52	22,992-33,240	Y-34,440-1	...	...-...	...	...-...	110	...
Beaverton, Ore. (1,1) ....P	P	87-67-40	29,700-39,816	Y-41,806-15	5,386	4,826-89	3,493	752-581	35	525
	F	48-44-56	27,192-38,700	NONE	4,538	3,679-81	2,653	571-455	8	851
Bellevue, Wash. (1,1) ....P	P	222-138-40	31,788-44,052	NONE	15,960	12,570-78	10,265	1,269-1,036	622	2,768
	F	171-155-50	34,572-43,980	NONE	12,005	9,972-83	8,193	1,004-775	623	1,410
Bellflower, Calif. (7,7) ....P	P	...-...-..	...-...	..-...-..	...	...-...	...	...-...	...	...
	F	...-...-..	...-...	..-...-..	...	...-...	...	...-...	...	...
Bethlehem, Pa. (1,1) ....P	P	133-133-40	24,788-32,624	Y-33,929-4	6,910	6,502-94	5,440	522-540	142	266
	F	108-108-42	23,787-31,998	Y-33,248-4	...	...-...	...	...-...	10	...
Billings, Mont. (1,1) ....P	P	120-102-40	21,506-31,699	NONE	5,325	4,546-85	3,534	455-557	212	567
	F	131-103-44	24,114-26,519	Y-26,825-1	5,685	4,725-83	3,745	494-486	446	514
Bloomington, Ill. (1,1) ....P	P	96-86-40	28,470-36,426	Y-41,184-..	...	...-...	...	...-...	...	...
	F	78-74-52	28,087-35,778	Y-41,145-..	...	...-...	...	...-...	...	...
Bloomington, Ind. (1,1) ....P	P	81-61-..	22,500-31,560	Y-...-2	3,169	2,724-85	2,289	316-119	4	441
	F	82-81-56	23,838-27,138	Y-28,230-3	2,741	2,541-92	2,186	250-105	5	195
Bloomington, Minn. (1,2) ....P	P	125-96-40	27,768-43,032	NONE	8,766	6,868-78	6,042	543-283	105	1,793
	F	...-...-..	...-...	..-...-..	...	...-...	...	...-...	2,328	...
Boca Raton, Fla. (1,1) ....P	P	205-133-40	29,785-44,137	Y-44,637-5	11,461	9,348-81	7,669	1,385-294	608	1,505
	F	153-144-42	24,182-41,278	Y-41,878-5	10,793	8,090-74	6,636	1,215-239	1,192	1,511
Bristol, Conn. (1,1) ....P	P	105-100-38	31,090-38,241	NONE	...	...-...	...	...-...	134	...
	F	91-90-42	31,262-37,236	NONE	6,270	6,054-96	4,330	743-981	68	148
Bristol tp, Pa. (1,2) ....P	P	60-60-40	24,453-42,053	Y-...-5	...	...-...	...	...-...	...	...
	F	...-...-..	...-...	...-...-..	...	...-...	...	...-...	...	...
Brownsville, Tex. (1,1) ....P	P	229-160-40	20,108-26,410	Y-27,610-1	7,648	6,940-90	5,529	797-614	...	708
	F	116-114-53	19,969-25,521	Y-26,721-1	...	...-...	...	...-...	...	...
Bryan, Tex. (-,1) ....P	P	112-95-40	21,792-33,228	Y-...-1	...	...-...	...	...-...	...	...
	F	74-72-56	20,844-28,188	Y-...-1	...	...-...	...	...-...	...	...
Burbank, Calif. (1,1) ....P	P	228-149-40	39,660-48,324	NONE	...	...-...	...	...-...	1,106	...
	F	121-115-56	39,108-47,652	NONE	...	...-...	...	...-...	22	...
Burnsville, Minn. (1,1) ....P	P	76-57-40	28,416-40,572	NONE	4,580	4,009-87	3,389	398-222	131	440
	F	35-35-53	27,768-39,672	NONE	3,261	2,611-80	2,211	256-144	274	376
Camden, N.J. (1,1) ....P	P	460-327-35	29,989-42,212	Y-45,491-..	27,210	25,316-93	20,651	1,988-2,677	614	1,280
	F	265-255-42	29,989-42,212	Y-45,491-..	19,414	17,744-91	15,162	1,040-1,542	585	1,085
Cape Coral, Fla. (1,1) ....P	P	155-111-40	21,964-34,112	Y-36,499-10	...	...-...	...	...-...	337	...
	F	129-123-52	21,307-25,904	Y-26,681-10	...	...-...	...	...-...	14	...
Carlsbad, Calif. (1,1) ....P	P	101-82-40	34,381-41,801	NONE	...	...-...	...	...-...	116	...
	F	75-69-56	31,954-38,766	NONE	...	...-...	...	...-...	3	...
Carrollton, Tex. (1,1) ....P	P	179-137-40	29,939-34,676	Y-...-1	9,147	7,027-76	5,940	572-515	234	1,886
	F	116-114-56	29,016-33,598	Y-...-1	6,897	5,675-82	4,752	419-504	63	1,159
Carson, Calif. (7,5) ....P	P	...-...-..	...-...	..-...-..	...	...-...	...	...-...	...	...
	F	...-...-..	...-...	..-...-..	...	...-...	...	...-...	...	...
Cerritos, Calif. (-,-) ....P	P	...-...-..	...-...	..-...-..	...	...-...	...	...-...	...	...
	F	...-...-..	...-...	..-...-..	...	...-...	...	...-...	...	...
Champaign, Ill. (1,1) ....P	P	129-108-40	29,037-34,191	Y-40,277-5	...	...-...	...	...-...	236	...
	F	89-79-54	28,020-32,379	NONE	...	...-...	...	...-...	25	...
Chandler, Ariz. (1,1) ....P	P	166-116-40	28,901-40,461	NONE	...	...-...	...	...-...	217	...
	F	90-85-56	26,279-36,791	NONE	...	...-...	...	...-...	628	...
Charleston, S.C. (1,1) ....P	P	372-270-40	21,741-28,276	NONE	17,590	13,042-74	10,100	1,792-1,150	2,410	2,138
	F	207-...-47	15,575-23,425	NONE	9,102	6,511-71	5,171	750-590	2,237	354
Cleveland Heights, Ohio (1,1) ......P	P	111-97-40	32,523-36,998	Y-38,348-..	...	...-...	...	...-...	228	...
	F	81-80-52	32,260-36,758	Y-38,103-..	...	...-...	...	...-...	262	...
Clovis, Calif. (1,1) ....P	P	100-52-40	37,776-45,912	NONE	...	...-...	...	...-...	17	...
	F	50-47-56	35,448-43,080	NONE	...	...-...	...	...-...	8	...
Columbia, S.C. (1,3) ....P	P	309-268-42	20,983-29,526	Y-29,821-14	12,258	10,114-82	8,224	1,370-520	534	1,610
	F	314-300-53	19,984-28,120	Y-28,401-14	18,143	10,160-55	8,182	1,448-530	311	7,672
Compton, Calif. (1,1) ....P	P	194-125-40	35,688-41,760	NONE	...	...-...	...	...-...	69	...
	F	73-69-56	35,016-40,956	NONE	...	...-...	...	...-...	31	...
Coral Springs, Fla. (1,2) ....P	P	221-144-40	31,339-42,152	Y-...-7	13,098	11,349-86	8,796	1,603-950	414	1,335
	F	...-...-..	...-...	..-...-..	...	...-...	...	...-...	150	...
Corona, Calif. (1,1) ....P	P	176-114-40	34,008-41,340	Y-48,606-5	14,168	11,153-78	8,196	1,780-1,177	715	2,300
	F	81-70-56	33,156-40,296	Y-40,946-5	7,529	6,697-88	4,988	1,114-595	...	832

Table 3/22 continued

POLICE AND FIRE DEPARTMENT PERSONNEL, SALARIES, AND EXPENDITURES FOR CITIES 10,000 AND OVER: 1994

City (Service provision)	Department	Total personnel, no. uniformed, duty hours per week	Entrance, maximum salary ($)	Longevity pay, maximum ($) no. years to receive longevity pay	Reported expenditures (in thousands)					
					Total expenditures (A) ($)	Total personnel expenditures (B) ($), % of (A)	Salaries and wages (C) ($)	City contrib. to employee retirement, insurance (D) ($)	Capital outlay (E) ($)	All other (F) ($)
50,000–99,999 continued										
Costa Mesa, Calif. (1,1)	P	196-138-40	39,804-48,384	NONE	18,125	14,552-80	10,879	2,154-1,519	10	3,563
	F	110-103-56	37,908-46,080	Y-48,120-5	...	...-..	...	...-...	7	...
Daly City, Calif. (1,1)	P	158-125-40	35,802-43,576	NONE	11,297	7,505-66	5,907	1,099-499	1,924	1,868
	F	77-74-56	37,296-45,336	Y-46,476-5	6,050	4,979-82	4,171	518-290	81	990
Danbury, Conn. (3,3)	P	134-128-40	30,597-38,688	NONE	...	...-..	...	...-...	1,118	...
	F	108-105-42	32,387-39,966	Y-40,216-10	...	...-..	...	...-...	1,076	...
Danville, Va. (1,1)	P	133-115-42	19,656-29,474	NONE	4,506	3,702-82	3,107	410-185	...	804
	F	119-118-52	19,656-29,474	NONE	4,669	3,876-83	3,274	391-211	347	446
Daytona Beach, Fla. (4,4)	P	...-.-..	...-...	..-...-..	...	...-..	...	...-...	...	...
	F	...-.-..	...-...	..-...-..	...	...-..	...	...-...	...	...
Denton, Tex. (1,1)	P	128-98-40	23,665-33,897	Y-...-1	7,094	6,283-88	5,238	569-476	7	804
	F	104-83-56	24,223-30,399	Y-...-1	6,475	5,723-88	4,777	601-345	52	700
Des Plaines, Ill. (1,1)	P	112-98-40	31,121-43,572	Y-46,030-10	8,034	5,904-73	5,194	102-608	626	1,504
	F	95-92-56	31,677-42,861	Y-45,409-10	6,923	5,003-72	4,442	29-532	535	1,385
Dothan, Ala. (1,1)	P	159-106-40	19,162-26,884	NONE	6,678	5,398-80	4,495	633-270	260	1,020
	F	122-120-40	19,162-26,884	NONE	4,811	4,049-84	3,358	465-226	565	197
Downey, Calif. (1,1)	P	153-120-40	35,535-44,026	Y-47,724-5	...	...-..	...	...-...	72	...
	F	81-69-56	31,983-39,625	Y-42,954-10	...	...-..	...	...-...	429	...
Dubuque, Iowa (1,1)	P	84-77-40	27,418-29,702	Y-31,187-6	4,571	4,001-87	2,973	484-544	...	570
	F	89-88-56	26,619-29,702	Y-31,781-5	4,587	4,113-89	3,059	500-554	99	375
Duluth, Minn. (1,1)	P	152-131-40	25,848-34,236	NONE	...	...-..	...	...-...	441	...
	F	139-137-56	25,800-34,332	NONE	...	...-..	...	...-...	177	...
East Lansing, Mich. (1,1)	P	85-53-40	26,977-36,212	Y-37,336-5	...	...-..	...	...-...	640	...
	F	55-54-50	25,185-32,347	Y-33,467-5	...	...-..	...	...-...	4	...
Edison tp, N.J. (4,4)	P	...-.-..	...-...	..-...-..	...	...-..	...	...-...	...	...
	F	...-.-..	...-...	..-...-..	...	...-..	...	...-...	...	...
Edmond, Okla. (1,1)	P	94-82-40	18,558-30,149	Y-32,149-4	4,171	3,659-87	2,930	482-247	130	382
	F	82-80-56	15,191-28,335	Y-30,335-4	3,173	2,941-92	2,466	264-211	76	156
El Cajon, Calif. (1,1)	P	187-123-40	30,034-40,386	NONE	...	...-..	...	...-...	42	...
	F	68-62-56	28,092-35,961	NONE	...	...-..	...	...-...	99	...
Elgin, Ill. (1,1)	P	170-127-41	31,008-42,660	NONE	20,223	9,169-45	7,400	599-1,170	10,068	986
	F	106-104-53	30,744-40,980	NONE	16,233	5,797-35	4,600	463-734	10,057	379
Elyria, Ohio (1,1)	P	98-83-40	27,022-29,523	Y-35,428-1	7,138	5,818-81	4,433	824-561	758	562
	F	73-72-52	27,153-29,617	Y-35,541-1	...	...-..	...	...-...	46	...
Encinitas, Calif. (7,5)	P	...-.-..	...-...	..-...-..	...	...-..	...	...-...	...	...
	F	59-49-56	31,900-40,272	NONE	...	...-..	...	...-...	362	...
Euclid, Ohio (1,1)	P	161-97-40	31,060-35,152	Y-37,965-5	...	...-..	...	...-...	218	...
	F	94-90-48	27,641-35,153	Y-37,965-5	...	...-..	...	...-...	278	...
Fairfield, Calif. (3,3)	P	...-.-..	...-...	NONE	...	...-..	...	...-...	...	...
	F	...-.-..	...-...	NONE	...	...-..	...	...-...	...	...
Fargo, N.D. (1,1)	P	113-90-41	24,500-33,300	Y-34,800-30	4,854	4,138-85	3,492	417-229	216	500
	F	84-83-56	24,500-33,300	Y-34,800-30	3,638	3,278-90	2,733	352-193	40	320
Farmington Hills, Mich. (1,3)	P	144-100-40	28,714-41,340	Y-45,474-3	10,656	8,185-76	6,305	1,097-783	1,695	776
	F	21-17-40	25,950-38,917	Y-42,036-3	3,749	1,965-52	1,591	231-143	1,479	305
Fayetteville, N.C. (1,1)	P	298-235-40	20,048-30,060	Y-32,315-5	11,888	9,367-78	7,397	1,309-661	901	1,620
	F	153-149-56	18,184-27,265	Y-29,310-5	6,054	5,073-83	4,171	516-386	40	941
Fountain Valley, Calif. (1,1)	P	65-63-40	38,500-47,232	NONE	...	...-..	...	...-...	10	...
	F	42-38-56	35,376-42,984	NONE	...	...-..	...	...-...	8	...
Gainesville, Fla. (1,1)	P	353-236-40	20,876-30,239	Y-32,053-5	...	...-..	...	...-...	...	...
	F	143-137-56	22,472-29,486	Y-31,255-5	...	...-..	...	...-...	...	...
Galveston, Tex. (1,1)	P	181-165-40	23,987-27,812	Y-...-1	8,773	7,395-84	5,764	759-872	413	965
	F	114-110-56	22,416-27,780	Y-...-1	5,819	4,969-85	3,906	473-590	375	475
Gastonia, N.C. (1,1)	P	156-115-40	20,696-32,604	Y-33,254-5	7,488	6,443-86	5,516	528-399	155	890
	F	129-127-51	16,328-25,636	Y-26,286-5	4,153	3,663-88	3,243	175-245	246	244
Great Falls, Mont. (1,1)	P	94-62-40	24,000-26,400	Y-28,380-1	3,662	2,866-78	2,198	300-368	146	650
	F	64-63-42	27,240-30,000	Y-33,750-1	3,200	2,718-84	2,116	263-339	64	418
Greeley, Colo. (1,1)	P	147-88-40	26,868-38,508	NONE	7,929	5,674-71	4,744	496-434	1,099	1,156
	F	73-71-56	23,807-35,716	NONE	3,635	3,351-92	2,782	292-277	54	230
Green tp, Ohio (1,1)	P	20-19-40	30,051-36,181	NONE	1,359	1,049-77	789	127-133	...	310
	F	23-21-60	30,060-36,190	NONE	2,338	1,788-76	1,367	246-175	...	550
Green Bay, Wis. (1,1)	P	228-175-38	25,736-35,256	Y-35,616-7	15,719	11,702-74	9,186	1,690-826	1,518	2,499
	F	203-194-56	25,736-35,256	Y-35,616-7	14,431	11,597-80	8,692	1,942-963	302	2,532
Greenwich t, Conn. (1,3)	P	177-158-35	33,555-42,323	NONE	...	...-..	...	...-...	...	...
	F	77-75-42	31,462-39,683	NONE	...	...-..	...	...-...	...	...
Gresham, Ore. (3,3)	P	125-97-40	29,844-39,996	NONE	8,894	6,147-69	4,631	1,054-462	86	2,661
	F	85-81-48	28,764-38,652	NONE	6,703	4,836-72	3,688	809-339	70	1,797
Hamden t, Conn. (1,1)	P	103-93-40	30,000-41,000	Y-...-5	...	...-..	...	...-...	4	...
	F	89-86-42	36,000-40,000	Y-41,000-5	...	...-..	...	...-...	...	...
Hammond, Ind. (1,1)	P	236-191-40	23,582-29,986	Y-31,366-3	9,645	8,856-91	7,153	831-872	60	729
	F	179-174-53	21,371-29,106	Y-...-3	7,653	7,093-92	5,617	587-889	...	560
Harrisburg, Pa. (1,3)	P	225-178-40	29,633-32,367	Y-36,251-3	12,250	10,877-88	7,929	1,674-1,274	1,053	320
	F	100-97-42	27,918-...	NONE	...	...-..	...	...-...	310	...
Hawthorne, Calif. (1,1)	P	149-97-40	38,256-47,568	NONE	14,139	8,861-62	7,170	879-812	429	4,849
	F	63-59-56	31,788-45,264	NONE	6,907	4,852-70	3,956	599-297	...	2,055

Table 3/22
continued

POLICE AND FIRE DEPARTMENT PERSONNEL, SALARIES, AND EXPENDITURES FOR CITIES 10,000 AND OVER: 1994

City (Service provision)	Department	Total personnel, no. uniformed, duty hours per week	Entrance, maximum salary ($)	Longevity pay, maximum ($) no. years to receive longevity pay	Reported expenditures (in thousands)					
					Total expenditures (A) ($)	Total personnel expenditures (B) ($), % of (A)	Salaries and wages (C) ($)	City contrib. to employee retirement, insurance (D) ($)	Capital outlay (E) ($)	All other (F) ($)
50,000–99,999 continued										
Henderson, Nev. (1,-)	P	157-98-40	33,530-44,934	NONE	14,740	8,567-58	6,358	1,436-773	5,468	705
	F	104-100-40	32,430-44,288	NONE	...	...-...	...	...-...	85	...
High Point, N.C. (1,1)	P	195-175-42	20,105-31,318	..-...-..	7,808	6,347-81	5,309	598-440	41	1,420
	F	180-177-56	20,105-31,319	..-...-..	6,892	6,032-87	5,225	582-225	45	815
Huntington, W.Va. (1,1)	P	108-98-40	18,514-21,664	Y-...-4	4,110	3,652-88	2,852	326-474	84	374
	F	105-104-72	16,908-20,591	Y-...-3	...	...-..	...	...-...	41	...
Huntington Park, Calif. (1,7)	P	98-63-40	40,908-52,848	NONE	...	...-..	...	...-...	2,791	...
	F	...-..-..	...-...	..-...-..	...	...-..	...	...-...	...	...
Iowa City, Iowa (1,1)	P	78-59-40	24,461-35,464	Y-36,214-5	3,951	3,346-84	2,602	424-320	261	344
	F	52-51-56	25,538-31,537	Y-32,287-5	2,809	2,303-81	1,759	300-244	168	338
Irondequoit t, N.Y. (1,-)	P	66-53-40	32,182-43,813	Y-45,688-..	8,448	4,111-48	3,283	449-379	97	4,240
	F	...-..-..	...-...	..-...-..	...	...-..	...	...-...	...	...
Irvington tp, N.J. (1,1)	P	195-158-..	29,701-44,241	Y-48,665-5	...	...-..	...	...-...	...	...
	F	137-131-..	28,810-42,918	Y-47,210-5	...	...-..	...	...-...	...	...
Janesville, Wis. (1,1)	P	100-87-39	26,776-38,180	Y-...-2	...	...-..	...	...-...	124	...
	F	83-81-56	28,013-36,779	Y-...-2	...	...-..	...	...-...	131	...
Kalamazoo, Mich. (4,4)	P	...-..-..	...-...	..-...-..	...	...-..	...	...-...	...	...
	F	...-..-..	...-...	..-...-..	...	...-..	...	...-...	...	...
Kenosha, Wis. (1,1)	P	180-168-37	29,950-35,088	Y-35,388-5	14,674	12,719-86	9,756	1,914-1,049	286	1,669
	F	133-132-56	29,940-34,968	Y-35,268-5	10,973	9,904-90	7,684	1,419-801	411	658
Kettering, Ohio (1,3)	P	104-79-40	30,805-41,600	NONE	7,498	6,110-81	4,611	938-561	138	1,250
	F	53-48-40	29,390-38,626	NONE	...	...-..	...	...-...	522	...
La Mesa, Calif. (3,1)	P	81-61-40	29,730-40,836	NONE	6,052	4,558-75	3,460	790-308	547	947
	F	53-50-56	26,730-36,720	NONE	...	...-..	...	...-...	96	...
Lafayette, La. (1,3)	P	261-194-40	18,028-...	Y-32,656-1	8,400	6,598-78	5,783	413-402	63	1,739
	F	203-203-48	17,053-...	..-...-..	7,437	5,709-76	4,940	434-335	1,064	664
Lake Charles, La. (1,1)	P	147-146-40	14,165-...	Y-...-1	...	...-..	...	...-...	267	...
	F	126-123-56	13,424-...	Y-...-1	...	...-..	...	...-...	365	...
Lakeland, Fla. (1,1)	P	291-219-42	24,800-34,900	Y-35,400-10	26,304	11,635-44	9,900	1,295-440	13,039	1,630
	F	119-115-56	21,400-30,100	Y-30,600-10	5,705	5,160-90	4,400	540-220	265	280
Lakewood, Calif. (9,5)	P	...-..-..	...-...	..-...-..	...	...-..	...	...-...	...	...
	F	...-..-..	...-...	..-...-..	...	...-..	...	...-...	...	...
Lancaster, Calif. (-,5)	P	...-..-..	...-...	..-...-..	...	...-..	...	...-...	...	...
	F	...-..-..	...-...	..-...-..	...	...-..	...	...-...	...	...
Lancaster, Pa. (1,1)	P	167-137-40	24,864-32,321	Y-34,321-4	...	...-..	...	...-...	200	...
	F	113-105-42	21,720-31,028	Y-32,568-4	...	...-..	...	...-...	100	...
Largo, Fla. (1,1)	P	170-115-40	24,149-37,419	Y-...-5	7,712	6,458-83	5,288	637-533	287	967
	F	128-122-50	21,328-32,261	Y-...-5	5,774	4,924-85	4,052	519-353	68	782
Lawrence, Kan. (1,1)	P	128-103-40	24,960-32,913	Y-33,753-5	5,493	4,704-85	4,295	379-30	186	603
	F	88-85-56	23,296-30,567	Y-31,407-5	4,074	3,355-82	3,086	248-21	467	252
Lawton, Okla. (1,1)	P	190-150-40	19,182-25,693	Y-28,093-4	9,907	6,172-62	5,161	591-420	1,651	2,084
	F	121-119-56	18,858-25,316	Y-27,716-4	7,926	4,947-62	4,192	452-303	1,866	1,113
Livermore, Calif. (1,1)	P	88-60-40	39,576-48,108	NONE	8,682	7,360-84	5,375	1,181-804	341	981
	F	58-47-56	37,944-48,420	NONE	...	...-..	...	...-...	66	...
Lodi, Calif. (-,-)	P	102-102-40	29,000-35,000	NONE	6,934	5,683-81	4,151	861-671	147	1,104
	F	47-47-56	26,000-32,000	NONE	...	...-..	...	...-...	...	...
Longview, Tex. (1,1)	P	180-133-40	22,684-32,666	Y-...-1	7,445	6,511-87	5,242	831-438	178	756
	F	151-146-40	22,684-32,666	Y-...-1	6,206	5,686-91	4,784	475-427	126	394
Lynwood, Calif. (9,1)	P	...-..-..	...-...	..-...-..	...	...-..	...	...-...	...	...
	F	33-33-56	31,454-38,243	Y-40,043-5	...	...-..	...	...-...	371	...
Mc Allen, Tex. (1,1)	P	265-171-42	19,302-26,956	Y-27,956-1	8,663	6,921-79	5,965	898-58	472	1,270
	F	132-123-56	19,510-20,820	Y-22,023-1	4,619	4,041-87	3,446	566-29	81	497
Old Bridge tp, N.J. (1,2)	P	184-127-37	29,048-45,900	Y-47,047-5	...	...-..	...	...-...	150	...
	F	...-..-..	...-...	..-...-..	...	...-..	...	...-...	...	...
Manchester t, Conn. (1,9)	P	133-105-40	34,112-43,867	Y-44,267-10	8,494	7,756-91	5,880	1,237-639	217	521
	F	80-77-42	34,627-38,000	Y-38,200-10	...	...-..	...	...-...	120	...
Mansfield, Ohio (1,1)	P	122-92-40	16,630-30,077	Y-30,577-1	6,531	4,797-73	3,680	662-455	119	1,615
	F	92-88-48	15,500-29,100	Y-29,600-1	5,664	4,650-82	3,424	681-545	147	867
Medford, Mass. (1,1)	P	104-98-41	29,533-33,339	Y-34,339-10	...	...-..	...	...-...	70	...
	F	129-126-42	29,858-33,335	Y-34,235-5	...	...-..	...	...-...	1,048	...
Melbourne, Fla. (1,1)	P	139-139-40	23,279-32,091	Y-...-15	9,565	7,520-78	5,808	1,225-487	855	1,190
	F	96-96-56	22,740-25,732	Y-26,247-..	...	...-..	...	...-...	79	...
Merced, Calif. (3,1)	P	98-83-40	28,003-34,026	NONE	...	...-..	...	...-...	36	...
	F	50-48-56	26,168-31,808	NONE	...	...-..	...	...-...	40	...
Meriden, Conn. (1,1)	P	115-99-40	28,802-39,647	Y-39,997-5	...	...-..	...	...-...	128	...
	F	104-101-42	30,418-36,483	Y-36,883-5	...	...-..	...	...-...	11,032	...
Miami Beach, Fla. (1,1)	P	435-280-40	23,976-39,702	Y-44,069-7	...	...-..	...	...-...	...	...
	F	167-154-48	23,975-39,701	Y-44,068-7	...	...-..	...	...-...	...	...
Middletown tp, N.J. (1,2)	P	119-96-40	27,294-47,979	Y-51,817-5	12,067	7,872-65	6,700	357-815	3,728	467
	F	...-..-..	...-...	..-...-..	...	...-..	...	...-...	3,163	...
Midland, Tex. (1,1)	P	193-148-40	23,400-28,500	Y-...-1	12,236	9,198-75	7,584	1,133-481	1,305	1,733
	F	155-141-56	22,920-...	Y-...-1	...	...-..	...	...-...	...	...
Midwest City, Okla. (1,1)	P	108-93-45	18,240-33,422	NONE	...	...-..	...	...-...	974	...
	F	94-88-48	18,240-32,724	NONE	...	...-..	...	...-...	984	...

Table 3/22 continued   POLICE AND FIRE DEPARTMENT PERSONNEL, SALARIES, AND EXPENDITURES FOR CITIES 10,000 AND OVER: 1994

City (Service provision)	Depart-ment	Total personnel, no. uniformed, duty hours per week	Entrance, maximum salary ($)	Longevity pay, maximum ($), no. years to receive longevity pay	Reported expenditures (in thousands)					
					Total expendi-tures (A) ($)	Total personnel expendi-tures (B) ($), % of (A)	Salaries and wages (C) ($)	City contrib. to employee retirement, insurance (D) ($)	Capital outlay (E) ($)	All other (F) ($)
50,000–99,999 continued										
Milpitas, Calif. (1,1)	P	107-76-40	40,312-48,999	NONE	9,649	8,061-83	6,272	1,265-524	168	1,420
	F	75-69-56	44,494-54,083	NONE	...	...-...	...	...-...	390	...
Mission Viejo, Calif. (-,7)	P	...-...-..	...-...	..-...-..	...	...-..	...	...-...	...	...
	F	...-...-..	...-...	..-...-..	...	...-..	...	...-...	...	...
Monroe, La. (1,1)	P	220-208-40	13,364-36,338	Y-38,438-1	...	...-..	...	...-...	220	...
	F	195-190-56	14,640-...	Y-22,886-..	...	...-..	...	...-...	521	...
Monterey Park, Calif. (1,1)	P	120-79-40	37,872-45,960	NONE	9,094	6,375-70	4,929	1,018-428	806	1,913
	F	56-52-56	31,572-38,352	NONE	4,675	2,919-62	2,277	511-131	713	1,043
Mountain View, Calif. (1,1)	P	109-70-40	41,012-49,856	NONE	8,600	7,692-89	5,983	1,231-478	184	724
	F	90-47-..	36,994-44,951	NONE	7,329	6,594-89	5,059	1,046-489	225	510
Napa, Calif. (1,1)	P	101-65-40	34,956-42,540	NONE	8,491	7,169-84	5,454	1,002-713	29	1,293
	F	59-53-56	32,136-40,788	NONE	4,595	4,083-88	3,009	676-398	46	466
Naperville, Ill. (1,1)	P	198-128-40	30,156-38,157	NONE	12,238	9,206-75	7,806	423-977	1,921	1,111
	F	153-144-52	27,480-44,942	NONE	9,557	6,436-67	5,552	150-734	2,225	896
National City, Calif. (1,1)	P	92-66-40	32,604-41,610	NONE	...	...-..	...	...-...	154	...
	F	35-34-56	31,138-37,849	NONE	...	...-..	...	...-...	4	...
New Britain, Conn. (1,1)	P	161-161-40	35,881-39,103	Y-39,578-10	...	...-..	...	...-...	134	...
	F	147-147-42	35,636-39,210	Y-39,610-10	...	...-..	...	...-...	152	...
New Rochelle, N.Y. (1,1)	P	212-179-38	32,185-46,581	Y-47,581-5	14,414	12,413-86	9,964	1,812-637	927	1,074
	F	157-156-38	26,000-44,600	Y-45,600-5	12,293	10,269-83	8,321	1,450-498	657	1,367
Newport Beach, Calif. (1,1)	P	216-144-45	38,808-49,536	NONE	17,899	15,661-87	12,603	1,399-1,659	394	1,844
	F	105-103-56	36,214-42,945	NONE	9,838	8,327-84	6,920	720-687	357	1,154
Niagara Falls, N.Y. (1,1)	P	180-161-40	33,064-36,798	NONE	9,716	9,381-96	7,477	1,184-720	51	284
	F	162-156-40	29,575-32,915	NONE	8,601	8,344-97	6,599	1,058-687	38	219
Norwalk, Calif. (7,5)	P	...-...-..	...-...	..-...-..	...	...-..	...	...-...	...	...
	F	...-...-..	...-...	..-...-..	...	...-..	...	...-...	...	...
Norwalk, Conn. (1,3)	P	208-179-40	34,508-41,542	Y-42,197-8	14,401	12,163-84	8,785	1,548-1,830	363	1,875
	F	129-121-42	32,251-41,543	Y-42,333-8	12,738	11,091-87	8,364	1,357-1,370	498	1,149
Oak Lawn v, Ill. (1,1)	P	121-106-..	29,592-42,732	NONE	8,153	7,501-92	6,356	572-573	465	187
	F	104-102-48	28,752-41,088	NONE	6,507	5,880-90	4,903	404-573	476	151
Odessa, Tex. (1,1)	P	227-169-40	21,360-34,968	Y-35,068-1	9,873	7,938-80	6,306	1,094-538	563	1,372
	F	167-151-56	23,304-34,968	Y-35,068-1	6,821	6,036-88	4,812	824-400	...	785
Ogden City, Utah (1,1)	P	120-105-40	20,598-35,601	NONE	9,536	5,283-55	4,236	659-388	3,019	1,234
	F	123-107-56	20,702-30,819	NONE	9,510	4,995-52	4,165	481-349	3,005	1,510
Orem, Utah (4,4)	P	...-...-..	...-...	..-...-..	...	...-..	...	...-...	...	...
	F	...-...-..	...-...	..-...-..	...	...-..	...	...-...	...	...
Oshkosh, Wis. (1,1)	P	107-95-40	30,196-35,486	NONE	...	...-..	...	...-...	145	...
	F	96-94-56	26,253-36,069	Y-36,405-20	...	...-..	...	...-...	326	...
Owensboro, Ky. (1,1)	P	125-101-40	20,500-29,216	Y-31,716-5	5,454	4,681-85	3,578	691-412	236	537
	F	100-98-56	20,500-29,216	Y-31,716-5	4,145	3,693-89	2,825	529-339	148	304
Palm Bay, Fla. (1,1)	P	163-100-40	21,000-29,000	Y-...-10	12,146	5,596-46	4,525	586-485	5,584	966
	F	137-110-56	18,062-22,224	Y-...-10	10,828	4,201-38	3,298	488-415	5,584	1,043
Palmdale, Calif. (7,7)	P	...-...-..	...-...	..-...-..	...	...-..	...	...-...	...	...
	F	...-...-..	...-...	..-...-..	...	...-..	...	...-...	...	...
Palo Alto, Calif. (1,1)	P	123-88-40	41,850-50,232	NONE	20,507	12,386-60	9,317	1,905-1,164	4,000	4,121
	F	115-112-..	37,987-47,944	NONE	...	...-..	...	...-...	4,000	...
Pawtucket, R.I. (1,1)	P	181-146-38	27,818-30,512	Y-33,427-5	...	...-..	...	...-...	...	...
	F	146-144-42	27,633-30,512	Y-32,495-5	...	...-..	...	...-...	...	...
Pembroke Pines, Fla. (1,1)	P	200-156-40	27,744-38,728	Y-39,872-10	25,077	8,519-33	6,721	1,122-676	15,234	1,324
	F	153-146-48	22,675-35,232	Y-36,376-10	22,613	6,999-30	5,468	919-612	14,936	678
Pensacola, Fla. (1,1)	P	203-51-40	19,370-31,174	Y-34,294-5	9,096	7,364-80	6,028	911-425	347	1,385
	F	124-119-53	16,683-24,385	Y-26,823-5	...	...-..	...	...-...	770	...
Peoria, Ariz. (1,1)	P	96-67-40	26,949-39,354	..-...-..	5,167	4,110-79	3,372	454-284	155	902
	F	59-55-56	22,102-36,138	..-...-..	3,263	2,811-86	2,475	152-184	22	430
Pico Rivera, Calif. (7,7)	P	...-...-..	...-...	..-...-..	...	...-..	...	...-...	...	...
	F	...-...-..	...-...	..-...-..	...	...-..	...	...-...	...	...
Pine Bluff, Ark. (1,1)	P	141-115-40	18,542-21,559	Y-24,902-1	4,623	3,861-83	3,281	263-317	201	561
	F	95-89-52	17,590-21,559	Y-24,902-1	3,071	2,921-95	2,551	154-216	21	129
Pleasanton, Calif. (1,1)	P	103-71-40	44,136-53,772	NONE	8,924	7,819-87	5,879	1,158-782	263	842
	F	56-51-56	41,388-50,304	NONE	5,604	5,215-93	4,039	743-433	200	189
Pompano Beach, Fla. (1,1)	P	347-245-40	28,747-40,449	Y-44,681-14	24,068	15,096-62	12,687	2,315-94	1,635	7,337
	F	145-142-48	27,713-38,996	Y-43,076-14	9,805	6,897-70	5,739	1,115-43	575	2,333
Pontiac, Mich. (1,1)	P	184-140-40	27,810-34,932	Y-38,425-5	...	...-..	...	...-...	407	...
	F	123-122-50	27,283-32,504	Y-35,754-5	9,409	8,818-93	7,554	40-1,224	173	418
Port St. Lucie, Fla. (1,5)	P	146-99-40	22,084-32,601	NONE	...	...-..	...	...-...	134	...
	F	...-...-..	...-...	..-...-..	...	...-..	...	...-...	...	...
Portland, Me. (1,-)	P	170-139-40	20,984-30,180	NONE	8,341	7,965-95	6,212	1,010-743	116	260
	F	239-196-42	19,618-27,696	NONE	10,676	9,756-91	7,541	1,251-964	248	672
Pueblo, Colo. (1,1)	P	222-179-40	23,424-31,176	Y-31,836-5	9,439	8,167-86	6,897	583-687	323	949
	F	142-140-56	22,848-28,740	Y-29,400-5	4,857	4,344-89	3,977	12-355	20	493
Quincy, Mass. (1,1)	P	215-186-40	25,305-32,068	Y-33,568-5	...	...-..	...	...-...	8,290	...
	F	209-200-42	25,305-32,068	Y-33,568-5	...	...-..	...	...-...	8,481	...
Redding, Calif. (1,1)	P	147-88-40	29,307-39,146	NONE	11,035	8,830-80	6,288	1,207-1,335	347	1,858
	F	68-66-56	26,150-31,945	NONE	5,813	4,852-83	3,506	706-640	180	781

Table 3/22 continued   POLICE AND FIRE DEPARTMENT PERSONNEL, SALARIES, AND EXPENDITURES FOR CITIES 10,000 AND OVER: 1994

City (Service provision)	Department	Total personnel, no. uniformed, duty hours per week	Entrance, maximum salary ($)	Longevity pay, maximum ($), no. years to receive longevity pay	Reported expenditures (in thousands)					
					Total expenditures (A) ($)	Total personnel expenditures (B) ($), % of (A)	Salaries and wages (C) ($)	City contrib. to employee retirement, insurance (D) ($)	Capital outlay (E) ($)	All other (F) ($)
50,000–99,999 continued										
Redlands, Calif. (1,-)	P	93-69-40	30,300-36,852	NONE	...	...-..	...	...-...	20	...
	F	56-54-56	28,500-34,632	NONE	...	...-..	...	...-...	33	...
Redondo Beach, Calif. (1,1)	P	176-101-36	36,456-51,300	NONE	...	...-..	...	...-...	715	...
	F	67-62-56	35,267-46,003	Y-...-10	...	...-..	...	...-...	27	...
Richardson, Tex. (1,1)	P	228-154-40	28,344-35,568	Y-36,768-1	...	...-..	...	...-...	...	...
	F	133-130-56	28,464-33,792	Y-34,992-1	...	...-..	...	...-...	...	...
Roanoke, Va. (1,1)	P	297-262-40	22,222-...	NONE	...	...-..	...	...-...	...	...
	F	241-238-56	22,222-...	NONE	...	...-..	...	...-...	...	...
Rochester, Minn. (1,1)	P	123-98-42	30,945-41,241	NONE	8,668	7,544-87	5,761	1,310-473	621	503
	F	93-90-56	30,945-41,241	NONE	...	...-..	...	...-...	466	...
Rosemead, Calif. (9,5)	P	...-..-..	...-...	..-...-..	...	...-..	...	...-...	...	...
	F	...-..-..	...-...	..-...-..	...	...-..	...	...-...	...	...
Roseville, Mich. (1,1)	P	96-83-40	25,994-40,842	Y-44,926-25	6,941	6,108-87	4,692	845-571	104	729
	F	40-39-56	24,380-37,220	Y-40,942-25	3,000	2,611-87	2,015	356-240	20	369
Royal Oak, Mich. (1,1)	P	106-88-40	28,703-39,790	Y-43,769-5	7,438	6,888-92	5,175	976-737	21	529
	F	69-69-53	28,361-39,790	Y-43,769-5	4,719	4,578-97	3,357	675-546	16	125
St. Joseph, Mo. (1,1)	P	138-105-..	22,443-29,078	Y-...-4	...	...-..	...	...-...	1,950	...
	F	133-131-..	22,015-27,810	Y-...-4	...	...-..	...	...-...	110	...
San Leandro, Calif. (1,1)	P	122-83-40	39,024-49,764	..-...-..	...	...-..	...	...-...	53	...
	F	91-87-56	34,212-45,888	..-...-..	...	...-..	...	...-...	84	...
San Mateo, Calif. (1,1)	P	145-104-40	39,041-46,550	NONE	13,759	12,126-88	10,066	1,351-709	151	1,482
	F	93-89-56	35,206-41,961	NONE	8,873	8,353-94	6,881	840-632	25	495
Sandy City, Utah (1,3)	P	94-75-40	19,438-30,807	NONE	...	...-..	...	...-...	372	...
	F	50-48-..	18,275-30,904	NONE	...	...-..	...	...-...	526	...
Santa Barbara, Calif. (1,1)	P	214-136-40	34,741-42,228	NONE	15,691	12,354-78	9,723	1,744-887	...	3,337
	F	114-108-53	34,921-42,447	NONE	9,447	8,403-88	6,515	1,426-462	...	1,044
Santa Clara, Calif. (1,1)	P	179-140-40	52,293-63,563	Y-66,743-..	...	...-..	...	...-...	61	...
	F	169-162-56	50,664-61,608	Y-64,644-..	...	...-..	...	...-...	102	...
Santa Maria, Calif. (1,1)	P	99-75-40	38,505-47,008	NONE	7,960	6,993-87	4,950	1,106-937	108	859
	F	33-30-55	35,199-...	NONE	2,585	2,424-93	1,712	352-360	23	138
Santa Monica, Calif. (1,1)	P	327-184-40	40,680-50,220	Y-54,288-5	28,879	25,231-87	21,078	1,863-2,290	635	3,013
	F	109-97-56	38,976-45,708	NONE	11,592	10,554-91	8,901	936-717	488	550
Santee, Calif. (7,1)	P	...-..-..	...-...	..-...-..	...	...-..	...	...-...	...	...
	F	52-49-56	23,248-35,925	NONE	...	...-..	...	...-...	174	...
Schenectady, N.Y. (1,1)	P	151-136-40	24,047-35,126	Y-36,726-5	9,581	8,909-92	6,738	1,400-771	294	378
	F	147-146-48	26,255-36,777	Y-38,277-5	...	...-..	...	...-...	512	...
Sioux City, Iowa (1,1)	P	139-112-40	25,286-33,385	Y-36,073-5	7,328	5,958-81	4,491	780-687	1	1,369
	F	120-116-56	24,389-33,326	Y-36,350-5	6,192	5,534-89	4,170	738-626	74	584
Southfield, Mich. (1,1)	P	142-142-40	27,674-40,004	Y-43,204-3	...	...-..	...	...-...	14	...
	F	101-101-54	28,990-41,907	Y-45,260-3	...	...-..	...	...-...	19	...
Sparks, Nev. (1,1)	P	110-71-40	26,223-33,629	Y-36,991-..	...	...-..	...	...-...	513	...
	F	64-61-56	28,366-33,745	Y-37,119-..	...	...-..	...	...-...	14	...
Springfield, Ohio (3,1)	P	155-119-40	24,876-33,030	Y-...-5	8,117	6,950-85	5,221	1,064-665	207	960
	F	130-124-53	26,229-33,124	Y-...-5	...	...-..	...	...-...	211	...
Suffolk, Va. (1,3)	P	119-95-43	21,540-31,233	..-...-..	5,419	4,265-78	3,400	602-263	207	947
	F	...-..-50	21,540-31,233	..-...-..	2,822	2,363-83	1,871	327-165	16	443
Troy, Mich. (1,3)	P	178-128-40	24,721-40,403	Y-43,043-4	...	...-..	...	...-...	7,945	...
	F	10-9-40	...-...	..-...-..	...	...-..	...	...-...	8,523	...
Troy, N.Y. (1,1)	P	126-109-40	24,290-34,662	Y-36,362-5	9,584	8,574-89	6,812	1,121-641	12	998
	F	167-158-40	21,880-33,846	Y-35,546-5	9,891	9,202-93	7,194	1,246-762	6	683
Tustin, Calif. (1,7)	P	119-86-72	39,044-47,458	NONE	8,907	7,630-85	5,951	1,151-528	377	900
	F	...-..-..	...-...	..-...-..	...	...-..	...	...-...	...	...
Tyler, Tex. (3,1)	P	186-136-40	24,018-28,152	Y-31,752-1	8,904	7,096-79	5,699	911-486	60	1,748
	F	122-115-56	22,440-27,504	Y-28,704-1	5,154	4,286-83	3,515	433-338	56	812
Upper Darby tp, Pa. (1,3)	P	113-104-40	30,365-37,365	Y-42,970-5	...	...-..	...	...-...	189	...
	F	35-32-40	30,365-37,365	Y-42,970-5	2,231	1,739-77	1,354	96-289	30	462
Victoria, Tex. (1,1)	P	135-106-40	21,424-31,070	Y-32,270-1	5,313	4,320-81	3,355	632-333	27	966
	F	79-77-48	17,914-25,389	Y-26,589-1	2,912	2,495-85	1,969	362-164	28	389
Walnut Creek, Calif. (1,5)	P	104-76-40	42,072-51,096	NONE	...	...-..	...	...-...	583	...
	F	...-..-..	...-...	..-...-..	...	...-..	...	...-...	...	...
Warren, Ohio (1,1)	P	96-73-40	20,842-29,744	Y-...-5	5,264	4,301-81	3,194	633-474	144	819
	F	77-75-52	21,199-30,285	Y-...-5	...	...-..	...	...-...	14	...
Waterloo, Iowa (1,1)	P	127-108-40	24,253-32,011	Y-33,571-..	7,094	6,321-89	4,662	766-893	129	644
	F	120-110-56	22,296-29,048	Y-30,608-..	6,468	5,848-90	4,267	714-867	310	310
Waukegan, Ill. (1,1)	P	180-131-40	27,540-42,910	NONE	26,655	7,668-28	6,397	709-562	7,202	11,785
	F	95-92-50	26,268-39,275	NONE	23,804	5,020-21	3,842	775-403	6,999	11,785
Waukesha, Wis. (1,1)	P	128-96-40	31,181-38,735	Y-...-5	...	...-..	...	...-...	69	...
	F	97-95-52	23,908-38,438	Y-38,918-5	...	...-..	...	...-...	1,028	...
West Allis, Wis. (1,1)	P	154-113-38	25,654-39,106	NONE	...	...-..	...	...-...	25	...
	F	122-116-52	25,654-39,106	Y-41,681-5	...	...-..	...	...-...	211	...
West Covina, Calif. (-,1)	P	150-108-37	37,392-44,352	NONE	13,259	10,739-80	8,411	1,524-804	377	2,143
	F	77-73-56	34,134-40,488	NONE	8,768	5,912-67	4,639	873-400	1,904	952
West Haven, Conn. (1,5)	P	130-115-40	31,949-38,732	Y-39,382-5	...	...-..	...	...-...	596	...
	F	...-..-..	...-...	..-...-..	...	...-..	...	...-...	...	...

Table 3/22 continued   **POLICE AND FIRE DEPARTMENT PERSONNEL, SALARIES, AND EXPENDITURES FOR CITIES 10,000 AND OVER: 1994**

City (Service provision)	Department	Total personnel, no. uniformed, duty hours per week	Entrance, maximum salary ($)	Longevity pay, maximum ($) no. years to receive longevity pay	Reported expenditures (in thousands)					
					Total expenditures (A) ($)	Total personnel expenditures (B) ($), % of (A)	Salaries and wages (C) ($)	City contrib. to employee retirement, insurance (D) ($)	Capital outlay (E) ($)	All other (F) ($)
50,000–99,999 continued										
Westminster, Calif. (1,1)	P	152-106-40	39,708-47,412	Y-49,212-10	22,544	10,203-45	8,685	905-613	7,225	5,116
	F	68-61-53	37,584-44,820	..-...-..	8,332	5,884-70	5,249	418-217	14	2,434
Westminster, Colo. (1,3)	P	170-112-45	27,835-39,330	Y-43,262-3	...	...-..	...	...-...	320	...
	F	83-80-56	25,847-35,631	Y-39,194-3	...	...-..	...	...-...	238	...
Wheaton, Ill. (1,3)	P	91-33-40	26,740-40,149	NONE	4,851	3,800-78	3,138	202-460	...	1,051
	F	28-27-53	28,719-38,058	NONE	3,077	1,403-45	1,182	53-168	482	1,192
Whittier, Calif. (3,7)	P	133-95-40	35,136-46,164	NONE	...	...-..	...	...-...	3,445	...
	F	...-..-..	...-...	..-...-..	...	...-..	...	...-...	...	...
Wichita Falls, Tex. (1,1)	P	252-181-40	27,342-...	Y-30,414-1	9,241	8,335-90	6,753	1,037-545	2	904
	F	157-152-54	20,994-24,301	Y-26,702-1	5,822	5,303-91	4,318	635-350	1	518
Wilmington, Del. (1,1)	P	321-264-40	27,652-37,314	NONE	26,078	19,032-72	14,119	3,035-1,878	3,712	3,334
	F	182-178-48	22,260-35,660	NONE	15,097	9,555-63	8,112	343-1,100	3,692	1,850
Wilmington, N.C. (1,1)	P	184-154-42	20,079-29,530	..-...-..	7,211	6,137-85	5,052	717-368	136	938
	F	132-127-57	18,189-28,111	..-...-..	4,759	4,042-84	3,442	329-271	13	704
Wyoming, Mich. (1,3)	P	106-78-40	29,411-35,339	Y-36,139-5	...	...-..	...	...-...	65	...
	F	28-27-42	25,370-31,217	Y-32,017-5	...	...-..	...	...-...	12	...
Yorba Linda, Calif. (9,7)	P	...-..-..	...-...	..-...-..	...	...-..	...	...-...	...	...
	F	...-..-..	...-...	..-...-..	...	...-..	...	...-...	...	...
25,000–49,999										
Addison v, Ill. (1,5)	P	80-61-40	32,428-44,348	NONE	4,793	4,514-94	3,400	672-442	135	144
	F	...-..-..	...-...	..-...-..	...	...-..	...	...-...	...	...
Agawam t, Mass. (1,1)	P	53-45-37	26,029-30,060	Y-30,660-5	...	...-..	...	...-...	...	...
	F	52-51-42	25,668-29,651	Y-30,251-5	...	...-..	...	...-...	695	...
Alamogordo, N.M. (4,4)	P	...-..-..	...-...	..-...-..	...	...-..	...	...-...	...	...
	F	...-..-..	...-...	..-...-..	...	...-..	...	...-...	...	...
Albany, Ore. (1,1)	P	61-48-40	28,248-35,556	NONE	3,428	2,808-81	2,057	426-325	186	434
	F	52-49-56	27,852-35,196	NONE	3,567	2,770-77	2,027	421-322	90	707
Altamonte Springs, Fla. (1,1)	P	119-85-40	21,011-29,415	Y-31,180-..	...	...-..	...	...-...	...	...
	F	69-56-56	21,011-29,415	Y-31,180-..	...	...-..	...	...-...	...	...
Alton, Ill. (1,1)	P	77-65-40	27,167-27,886	Y-...-2	3,826	3,360-87	2,866	370-124	163	303
	F	68-67-56	27,167-27,886	Y-...-2	3,616	3,168-87	2,585	447-136	239	209
Ames, Iowa (1,1)	P	66-49-40	26,502-32,038	Y-32,588-5	3,610	2,992-82	2,369	367-256	52	566
	F	54-44-48	25,219-29,979	Y-30,579-5	2,710	2,262-83	1,785	291-186	166	282
Andover t, Mass. (1,1)	P	60-46-38	...-...	Y-...-5	...	...-..	...	...-...	123	...
	F	68-67-42	...-...	Y-...-5	...	...-..	...	...-...	97	...
Annapolis, Md. (1,3)	P	156-115-40	24,268-39,531	Y-45,460-7	...	...-..	...	...-...	133	...
	F	95-92-56	23,113-39,531	Y-45,460-7	...	...-..	...	...-...	56	...
Anniston, Ala. (1,1)	P	120-88-40	19,032-21,798	Y-22,038-3	3,373	2,551-75	2,203	246-102	193	629
	F	80-79-56	19,016-21,762	Y-22,002-3	2,406	2,075-86	1,807	190-78	38	293
Arcadia, Calif. (1,1)	P	90-76-40	41,340-52,740	..-...-..	...	...-..	...	...-...	192	...
	F	78-61-56	36,168-46,164	..-...-..	6,622	5,585-84	4,256	901-428	449	588
Arlington t, Mass. (1,1)	P	67-61-38	29,090-31,399	Y-32,969-..	...	...-..	...	...-...	105	...
	F	77-62-42	27,641-30,402	Y-30,570-..	...	...-..	...	...-...	412	...
Athens, Ga. (1,1)	P	243-195-..	18,886-30,181	NONE	...	...-..	...	...-...	...	...
	F	153-151-..	18,886-30,181	NONE	...	...-..	...	...-...	...	...
Auburn, Ala. (4,4)	P	...-..-..	...-...	..-...-..	...	...-..	...	...-...	...	...
	F	...-..-..	...-...	..-...-..	...	...-..	...	...-...	...	...
Auburn, Wash. (1,1)	P	90-66-40	33,727-42,649	Y-46,060-5	...	...-..	...	...-...	5,457	...
	F	66-63-47	33,082-42,313	Y-48,698-4	...	...-..	...	...-...	55	...
Augusta, Ga. (1,1)	P	205-167-42	17,288-24,978	Y-...-10	...	...-..	...	...-...	419	...
	F	134-134-40	17,980-23,764	NONE	...	...-..	...	...-...	213	...
Bangor, Me. (1,1)	P	75-64-40	18,886-26,185	NONE	...	...-..	...	...-...	...	...
	F	95-...-42	19,379-25,812	NONE	...	...-..	...	...-...	...	...
Bartlesville, Okla. (1,1)	P	79-51-41	20,238-27,123	Y-28,095-5	3,334	2,522-75	2,008	302-212	434	378
	F	59-58-56	18,345-24,111	Y-25,083-5	2,840	2,060-72	1,700	198-162	471	309
Bartlett t, Tenn. (3,3)	P	67-45-43	19,839-27,285	Y-27,830-10	4,090	3,233-79	2,600	338-295	511	346
	F	48-47-56	19,198-26,285	Y-26,810-10	3,098	2,422-78	1,950	255-217	499	177
Beavercreek, Ohio (1,-)	P	49-39-40	26,874-37,544	Y-37,944-..	3,216	2,012-62	1,557	257-198	24	1,180
	F	...-..-..	...-...	..-...-..	...	...-..	...	...-...	...	...
Belleville tp, N.J. (1,1)	P	92-88-40	29,361-42,750	Y-47,025-4	...	...-..	...	...-...	...	...
	F	66-65-42	29,361-42,750	Y-47,025-4	...	...-..	...	...-...	...	...
Beloit, Wis. (1,1)	P	92-74-40	24,544-34,424	NONE	...	...-..	...	...-...	15	...
	F	65-63-53	24,274-33,984	NONE	...	...-..	...	...-...	28	...
Bettendorf, Iowa (1,3)	P	47-36-40	24,896-37,305	NONE	7,029	2,132-30	1,690	255-187	4,518	379
	F	14-14-56	23,415-32,254	NONE	5,393	573-10	444	70-59	4,588	232
Beverly Hills, Calif. (1,1)	P	180-127-40	39,803-45,585	NONE	18,413	14,977-81	10,724	2,247-2,006	277	3,159
	F	79-75-56	37,469-46,551	NONE	10,434	8,751-83	6,593	1,489-669	51	1,632
Biloxi, Miss. (1,1)	P	94-58-40	18,907-25,947	NONE	3,086	2,622-84	2,204	225-193	134	330
	F	88-80-51	18,907-25,947	NONE	2,899	2,376-81	2,033	152-191	142	381
Bismarck, N.D. (1,1)	P	95-71-48	22,600-34,000	NONE	3,913	3,450-88	2,832	337-281	149	314
	F	54-53-53	22,600-34,000	NONE	2,682	2,228-83	1,770	266-192	214	240
Blacksburg t, Va. (1,2)	P	58-46-40	19,036-27,049	NONE	2,593	2,121-81	1,678	265-178	83	389
	F	...-..-..	...-...	..-...-..	...	...-..	...	...-...	13	...
Blue Springs, Mo. (1,5)	P	75-55-40	22,224-31,704	NONE	3,668	3,091-84	2,442	337-312	145	432

Table 3/22 continued POLICE AND FIRE DEPARTMENT PERSONNEL, SALARIES, AND EXPENDITURES FOR CITIES 10,000 AND OVER: 1994

City (Service provision)	Department	Total personnel, no. uniformed, duty hours per week	Entrance, maximum salary ($)	Longevity pay, maximum ($) no. years to receive longevity pay	Total expenditures (A) ($)	Total personnel expenditures (B) ($), % of (A)	Salaries and wages (C) ($)	City contrib. to employee retirement, insurance (D) ($)	Capital outlay (E) ($)	All other (F) ($)
25,000–49,999 continued										
Blue Springs, Mo. (1,5) cont.	F	...-...-..	...-...	..-...-..	...	...-..	...	...-...	...	...
Bolingbrook v, Ill. (3,3)	P	94-67-40	30,489-43,556	Y-44,956-8	5,342	4,710-88	3,747	572-391	98	534
	F	55-53-53	30,545-40,773	Y-42,173-8	3,863	3,197-82	2,641	286-270	139	527
Bountiful, Utah (1,1)	P	39-30-40	21,985-35,818	NONE	2,354	1,926-81	1,463	314-149	117	311
	F	14-13-57	20,700-32,070	NONE	1,020	733-71	627	84-22	54	233
Bowie, Md. (7,7)	P	...-...-..	...-...	..-...-..	...	...-..	...	...-...	...	...
	F	...-...-..	...-...	..-...-..	...	...-..	...	...-...	...	...
Bowling Green, Ohio (1,1)	P	42-32-40	22,505-31,906	Y-33,501-5	2,447	2,069-84	1,508	280-281	112	266
	F	28-27-52	23,630-31,128	NONE	...	...-..	...	...-...	64	...
Boynton Beach, Fla. (1,1)	P	150-126-40	29,556-35,942	Y-45,905-5	8,451	7,763-91	6,320	1,037-406	48	640
	F	96-90-48	23,420-28,412	Y-36,275-5	5,948	5,450-91	4,379	810-261	170	328
Braintree t, Mass. (1,1)	P	84-77-37	30,184-34,060	Y-36,060-10	...	...-..	...	...-...	...	...
	F	92-89-42	30,184-34,060	Y-36,060-10	...	...-..	...	...-...	91	...
Brea, Calif. (1,1)	P	125-101-40	38,362-51,688	NONE	11,193	9,428-84	7,042	1,405-981	238	1,527
	F	53-46-56	34,125-43,789	NONE	4,697	4,045-86	3,042	639-364	56	596
Bridgewater tp, N.J	P	60-55-40	28,848-47,254	Y-51,117-5	5,418	4,083-75	3,285	536-262	1,105	230
	F	...-...-..	...-...	..-...-..	...	...-..	...	...-...	...	...
Brookfield, Wis. (1,1)	P	84-63-39	27,456-38,414	NONE	...	...-..	...	...-...	1,458	...
	F	55-54-56	32,928-38,148	NONE	...	...-..	...	...-...	1,431	...
Brunswick, Ohio (1,9)	P	36-28-40	27,860-34,674	Y-35,747-4	...	...-..	...	...-...	1,604	...
	F	...-...-..	...-...	..-...-..	...	...-..	...	...-...	45	...
Buffalo Grove v, Ill. (1,1)	P	75-61-40	29,985-40,416	Y-40,916-5	...	...-..	...	...-...	132	...
	F	58-53-56	29,985-40,416	Y-40,916-5	...	...-..	...	...-...	1,184	...
Burlingame, Calif. (1,1)	P	65-46-40	37,871-46,004	NONE	5,283	4,457-84	3,400	643-414	148	678
	F	51-50-56	37,440-45,624	NONE	4,923	4,281-86	3,477	397-407	424	218
Burlington, N.C. (1,1)	P	121-97-40	19,596-28,536	Y-30,248-..	...	...-..	...	...-...	...	...
	F	72-71-56	19,176-27,312	Y-28,951-..	...	...-..	...	...-...	...	...
Campbell, Calif. (1,1)	P	56-49-40	42,012-51,060	NONE	6,458	3,840-59	3,217	406-217	699	1,919
	F	...-...-..	...-...	..-...-..	...	...-..	...	...-...	...	...
Cape Girardeau, Mo. (1,1)	P	81-61-40	19,000-26,441	NONE	3,150	2,530-80	2,002	282-246	69	551
	F	56-55-56	18,516-25,804	NONE	2,407	2,009-83	1,490	319-200	189	209
Carol Stream v, Ill. (1,5)	P	70-49-40	28,341-40,294	NONE	3,521	2,845-80	2,320	342-183	55	621
	F	...-...-..	...-...	..-...-..	...	...-..	...	...-...	...	...
Carson City-Ormsby, Nev. (3,3)	P	100-75-40	25,408-35,902	NONE	...	...-..	...	...-...	...	...
	F	56-52-56	25,655-36,250	NONE	...	...-..	...	...-...	58	...
Cary t, N.C. (1,1)	P	82-63-40	21,902-35,651	NONE	3,525	2,892-82	2,342	390-160	114	519
	F	89-86-53	19,843-27,913	NONE	3,832	2,713-70	2,188	376-149	756	363
Casper, Wyo. (4,4)	P	...-...-..	...-...	..-...-..	...	...-..	...	...-...	...	...
	F	...-...-..	...-...	..-...-..	...	...-..	...	...-...	...	...
Cathedral City, Calif. (1,1)	P	61-42-40	36,744-...	Y-54,024-6	...	...-..	...	...-...	...	...
	F	32-32-57	33,276-...	Y-43,524-6	...	...-..	...	...-...	...	...
Cedar Falls, Iowa (4,4)	P	...-...-..	...-...	..-...-..	...	...-..	...	...-...	...	...
	F	...-...-..	...-...	..-...-..	...	...-..	...	...-...	...	...
Ceres, Calif. (4,4)	P	...-...-..	...-...	..-...-..	...	...-..	...	...-...	...	...
	F	...-...-..	...-...	..-...-..	...	...-..	...	...-...	...	...
Cheltenham tp, Pa. (1,2)	P	86-76-40	34,410-38,234	Y-38,534-5	4,860	4,515-92	3,552	363-600	...	345
	F	...-...-..	...-...	..-...-..	...	...-..	...	...-...	...	...
Chesterfield, Mo. (3,5)	P	62-57-40	26,905-36,321	NONE	4,866	2,720-55	2,239	254-227	1,698	448
	F	...-...-..	...-...	..-...-..	...	...-..	...	...-...	...	...
Chico, Calif. (3,3)	P	...-..-40	27,830-35,506	NONE	...	...-..	...	...-...	373	...
	F	49-47-56	24,752-30,110	NONE	...	...-..	...	...-...	99	...
Claremont, Calif. (3,7)	P	56-36-42	38,040-51,048	NONE	...	...-..	...	...-...	2,408	...
	F	...-...-..	...-...	..-...-..	...	...-..	...	...-...	...	...
Cleveland, Tenn. (1,1)	P	79-64-40	19,801-26,665	Y-...-..	2,809	2,254-80	1,850	220-184	121	434
	F	63-63-66	19,801-26,665	Y-...-..	2,414	1,997-82	1,640	202-155	136	281
Clinton, Iowa (3,1)	P	50-42-40	22,778-32,468	NONE	2,738	2,132-77	1,646	260-226	212	394
	F	45-45-52	20,714-30,797	NONE	2,222	1,991-89	1,520	255-216	79	152
Clovis, N.M. (1,1)	P	76-58-40	19,156-28,953	NONE	...	...-..	...	...-...	...	...
	F	65-63-52	17,056-24,000	NONE	...	...-..	...	...-...	...	...
Colton, Calif. (1,1)	P	88-64-40	34,164-41,508	Y-42,338-5	...	...-..	...	...-...	65	...
	F	58-52-56	29,532-35,892	Y-36,610-5	...	...-..	...	...-...	43	...
Concord, N.H. (1,1)	P	78-64-40	24,772-33,924	NONE	4,210	3,476-82	2,842	126-508	85	649
	F	93-86-42	22,953-29,680	NONE	4,623	3,919-84	3,085	229-605	65	639
Concord, N.C. (1,1)	P	89-71-42	21,778-33,134	Y-34,790-3	16,605	2,896-17	2,417	375-104	13,286	423
	F	101-101-56	19,739-30,014	Y-31,514-3	16,966	3,224-19	2,761	341-132	13,284	458
Conroe, Tex. (1,3)	P	76-60-40	22,505-30,035	Y-31,235-1	3,333	2,722-81	2,153	364-205	168	443
	F	48-46-53	22,500-30,040	Y-31,240-1	2,328	1,977-84	1,569	276-132	57	294
Conway, Ark. (1,1)	P	70-64-40	17,872-...	NONE	...	...-..	...	...-...	77	...
	F	40-39-48	17,872-...	NONE	...	...-..	...	...-...	71	...
Culver City, Calif. (1,1)	P	160-116-40	37,080-48,552	NONE	...	...-..	...	...-...	2	...
	F	94-66-56	32,808-46,525	NONE	9,447	7,306-77	5,355	1,194-757	22	2,119
Cupertino, Calif. (-,5)	P	...-...-..	...-...	..-...-..	...	...-..	...	...-...	...	...
	F	...-...-..	...-...	..-...-..	...	...-..	...	...-...	...	...
Cypress, Calif. (1,7)	P	80-53-40	37,224-45,252	NONE	91,283	71,983-78	57,564	7,906-6,513	5,501	13,799
	F	...-...-..	...-...	..-...-..	...	...-..	...	...-...	...	...

Table 3/22 continued **POLICE AND FIRE DEPARTMENT PERSONNEL, SALARIES, AND EXPENDITURES FOR CITIES 10,000 AND OVER: 1994**

City (Service provision)	Depart-ment	Total personnel, no. uniformed, duty hours per week	Entrance, maximum salary ($)	Longevity pay, maximum ($) no. years to receive longevity pay	Reported expenditures (in thousands)					
					Total expendi-tures (A) ($)	Total personnel expendi-tures (B) ($), % of (A)	Salaries and wages (C) ($)	City contrib. to employee retirement, insurance (D) ($)	Capital outlay (E) ($)	All other (F) ($)
25,000–49,999 continued										
Dana Point, Calif. (-,7)	P	...-..-..	...-...	..-...-..	...	...-..	...	...-...	...	...
	F	...-..-..	...-...	..-...-..	...	...-..	...	...-...	...	...
Danville, Ill. (1,1)	P	77-61-41	26,872-31,065	Y-34,482-4	4,571	3,002-65	2,254	474-274	337	1,232
	F	61-59-48	23,898-29,872	Y-33,158-4	...	...-..	...	...-...	297	...
Dartmouth t, Mass. (1,-)	P	65-65-40	18,939-28,784	Y-29,084-15	...	...-..	...	...-...	58	...
	F	...-..-..	...-...	..-...-..	...	...-..	...	...-...	...	...
Davis, Calif. (3,3)	P	69-49-40	30,326-36,858	..-...-..	5,284	3,436-65	2,528	472-436	96	1,752
	F	40-39-56	30,662-37,268	..-...-..	2,888	2,042-70	1,540	296-206	53	793
De Soto, Tex. (1,1)	P	64-46-40	24,852-33,792	Y-34,992-1	2,871	2,569-89	2,059	283-227	24	278
	F	49-48-53	24,348-33,096	Y-34,296-1	2,280	2,029-88	1,619	226-184	115	136
Deer Park, Tex. (1,2)	P	56-44-40	30,658-41,974	Y-42,502-1	3,026	2,870-94	2,205	430-235	108	48
	F	...-..-..	...-...	..-...-..	...	...-..	...	...-...	83	...
Deerfield Beach, Fla. (7,-)	P	...-..-..	...-...	..-...-..	...	...-..	...	...-...	...	...
	F	106-95-48	24,174-34,518	Y-37,279-5	5,707	5,237-91	4,132	855-250	270	200
Delray Beach, Fla. (1,1)	P	202-132-40	26,686-40,693	NONE	11,101	9,255-83	7,551	1,225-479	47	1,799
	F	134-126-48	24,578-35,285	NONE	9,080	5,773-63	4,705	801-267	2,291	1,016
Dover, N.H. (1,1)	P	61-46-41	26,169-35,393	Y-36,117-20	3,507	2,780-79	2,293	126-361	369	358
	F	46-44-42	22,058-25,575	Y-26,598-20	2,499	1,945-77	1,540	123-282	310	244
Downers Grove v, Ill. (1,1)	P	96-70-40	31,096-41,672	NONE	5,158	4,031-78	3,515	126-390	45	1,082
	F	88-79-56	26,750-37,875	NONE	4,419	3,670-83	3,091	161-418	292	457
Duncanville, Tex. (1,1)	P	76-51-40	26,232-32,964	Y-34,164-1	6,858	3,318-48	2,618	469-231	111	3,429
	F	53-52-56	25,020-31,380	Y-32,580-1	4,864	2,427-49	1,916	344-167	5	2,432
Dunedin, Fla. (1,1)	P	70-54-40	22,779-32,327	NONE	4,345	3,163-72	2,498	453-212	216	966
	F	38-37-56	20,832-31,457	NONE	2,414	1,752-72	1,346	279-127	206	456
East Brunswick tp, N.J. (1,2)	P	118-91-40	30,000-51,835	Y-59,092-5	12,667	8,392-66	6,378	1,087-927	3,482	793
	F	...-..-..	...-...	..-...-..	...	...-..	...	...-...	...	...
East Cleveland, Ohio (3,3)	P	87-72-40	18,387-...	Y-19,687-5	...	...-..	...	...-...	356	...
	F	53-52-48	16,911-30,112	Y-31,212-5	...	...-..	...	...-...	55	...
East Point, Ga. (1,1)	P	114-94-40	19,715-27,603	NONE	...	...-..	...	...-...	1,584	...
	F	71-70-40	19,715-27,603	NONE	...	...-..	...	...-...	1,415	...
Edina, Minn. (1,3)	P	58-48-40	31,504-40,772	Y-44,441-4	6,651	3,375-50	2,704	524-147	121	3,155
	F	29-28-55	...-...	Y-...-5	3,952	2,010-50	1,622	300-88	34	1,908
Edinburg, Tex. (1,2)	P	63-44-40	17,784-...	Y-21,564-1	...	...-..	...	...-...	62	...
	F	..-..-..	...-...	..-...-..	...	...-..	...	...-...	46	...
El Centro, Calif. (1,1)	P	74-48-40	30,300-36,840	NONE	...	...-..	...	...-...	304	...
	F	41-37-56	27,492-35,184	NONE	...	...-..	...	...-...	91	...
Elk Grove Village v, Ill. (1,1)	P	112-99-40	30,225-42,475	NONE	6,371	5,532-86	4,977	118-437	248	591
	F	103-94-56	27,965-40,710	NONE	5,455	4,983-91	4,470	58-455	165	307
Emporia, Kan. (1,1)	P	59-44-40	20,433-29,613	NONE	2,296	1,930-84	1,643	178-109	48	318
	F	48-47-53	18,218-30,337	NONE	1,999	1,666-83	1,417	158-91	63	270
Englewood, Colo. (4,4)	P	...-..-..	...-...	..-...-..	...	...-..	...	...-...	...	...
	F	...-..-..	...-...	..-...-..	...	...-..	...	...-...	...	...
Euless, Tex. (1,1)	P	91-61-37	25,080-32,100	Y-...-1	3,570	3,269-91	2,698	297-274	38	263
	F	48-47-72	24,144-30,900	Y-...-1	2,393	2,226-93	1,855	206-165	14	153
Ewing tp, N.J. (1,3)	P	83-73-40	35,585-52,536	Y-54,061-..	...	...-..	...	...-...	106	...
	F	3-3-40	33,306-...	Y-34,346-..	...	...-..	...	...-...	35	...
Fairborn, Ohio (3,1)	P	52-40-40	27,830-36,296	Y-37,022-5	3,299	2,690-81	2,100	357-233	89	520
	F	47-46-56	27,287-35,758	Y-36,473-5	2,988	2,571-86	1,934	421-216	124	293
Fairfield, Ohio (1,9)	P	62-48-40	25,355-32,760	Y-35,381-5	...	...-..	...	...-...	914	...
	F	6-4-40	26,468-...	Y-...-1	...	...-..	...	...-...	43	...
Falls tp, Pa. (1,2)	P	57-49-40	25,441-42,402	Y-43,967-5	4,436	3,353-75	2,628	203-522	462	621
	F	...-..-..	...-...	..-...-..	...	...-..	...	...-...	...	...
Falmouth t, Mass. (1,1)	P	63-55-40	24,044-27,414	Y-28,014-5	...	...-..	...	...-...	109	...
	F	64-58-42	25,006-29,724	Y-30,324-5	...	...-..	...	...-...	80	...
Farmington, N.M. (1,1)	P	140-90-40	21,769-29,820	Y-32,795-5	5,474	4,595-83	3,768	632-195	131	748
	F	62-57-56	19,900-27,259	Y-29,984-5	3,515	2,474-70	1,925	392-157	236	805
Findlay, Ohio (1,1)	P	72-56-40	22,942-33,426	Y-34,986-10	4,926	3,261-66	2,463	454-344	803	862
	F	57-56-52	22,986-33,390	Y-33,982-10	...	...-..	...	...-...	732	...
Florence, Ala. (1,1)	P	112-86-41	17,946-25,546	NONE	...	...-..	...	...-...	805	...
	F	83-81-56	17,945-25,546	NONE	...	...-..	...	...-...	361	...
Florence, S.C. (1,1)	P	91-91-40	16,572-27,744	NONE	2,979	2,613-87	2,053	361-199	103	263
	F	65-65-..	17,056-22,889	NONE	2,196	2,024-92	1,554	279-191	27	145
Folsom, Calif. (3,3)	P	35-33-..	27,516-33,444	..-35,948-10	...	...-..	...	...-...	92	...
	F	44-43-..	26,064-32,652	..-35,100-10	...	...-..	...	...-...	69	...
Fort Dodge, Iowa (1,1)	P	47-44-40	20,113-21,091	Y-25,500-2	2,052	1,815-88	1,300	255-260	62	175
	F	36-36-56	18,990-19,947	Y-24,232-2	1,365	1,291-94	913	179-199	8	66
Foster City, Calif. (3,3)	P	54-41-40	41,568-50,532	NONE	...	...-..	...	...-...	11	...
	F	37-36-56	40,752-49,536	NONE	...	...-..	...	...-...	27	...
Frankfort, Ky. (1,1)	P	58-53-40	19,325-28,380	Y-...-5	...	...-..	...	...-...	...	...
	F	64-62-40	19,325-28,380	Y-...-5	...	...-..	...	...-...	...	...
Frederick, Md. (1,7)	P	100-84-40	24,757-34,918	NONE	...	...-..	...	...-...	155	...
	F	...-..-..	...-...	..-...-..	...	...-..	...	...-...	...	...
Fridley, Minn. (1,3)	P	46-36-..	27,227-40,269	Y-43,893-4	2,590	2,279-87	1,916	191-172	78	233

Table 3/22 continued   POLICE AND FIRE DEPARTMENT PERSONNEL, SALARIES, AND EXPENDITURES FOR CITIES 10,000 AND OVER: 1994

City (Service provision)	Department	Total personnel, no. uniformed, duty hours per week	Entrance, maximum salary ($)	Longevity pay, maximum ($) no. years to receive longevity pay	Reported expenditures (in thousands)					
					Total expenditures (A) ($)	Total personnel expenditures (B) ($), % of (A)	Salaries and wages (C) ($)	City contrib. to employee retirement, insurance (D) ($)	Capital outlay (E) ($)	All other (F) ($)
25,000–49,999 continued										
Fridley, Minn. (1,3) cont.	F	6-5-50	23,600-31,694	Y-...-5	584	443-75	377	20-46	58	83
Gadsden, Ala. (1,1)	.P	117-92-40	20,467-...	Y-22,104-10	5,436	4,662-85	3,272	682-708	220	554
	F	111-109-56	17,006-...	Y-18,366-10	4,998	4,537-90	3,242	685-610	52	409
Gahanna, Ohio (1,-)	.P	43-38-40	17,462-37,502	Y-38,002-5	2,643	2,382-90	1,694	328-360	113	148
	F	...-...-...	...-...	..-...-..	...	...-..	...	...-...	...	...
Gaithersburg, Md. (9,7)	.P	29-27-40	26,731-45,954	NONE	2,050	1,164-56	903	163-98	745	141
	F	...-...-...	...-...	..-...-..	...	...-..	...	...-...	...	...
Garden City, Mich. (1,1)	.P	51-40-40	24,270-38,570	Y-38,710-1	3,172	2,747-86	2,173	165-409	95	330
	F	21-21-53	24,833-37,652	NONE	1,465	1,382-94	1,104	82-196	19	64
Gardena, Calif. (1,1)	.P	110-88-40	39,276-47,736	NONE	12,231	8,637-70	6,716	1,390-531	1,656	1,938
	F	52-48-56	39,564-48,084	NONE	6,946	4,721-67	3,681	789-251	1,541	684
Germantown, Tenn. (1,1)	.P	61-50-43	21,303-30,759	NONE	3,181	2,314-72	1,873	240-201	465	402
	F	60-54-56	18,744-23,004	NONE	2,445	2,205-90	1,890	126-189	1	239
Gilbert t, Ariz. (1,1)	.P	50-26-40	28,309-39,042	NONE	2,204	1,830-83	1,475	223-132	84	290
	F	22-21-68	26,957-37,170	NONE	...	...-..	...	...-...	77	...
Gilroy, Calif. (1,1)	.P	74-51-40	38,520-46,812	NONE	6,519	4,306-66	3,419	545-342	78	2,135
	F	30-24-56	36,612-44,508	NONE	2,816	1,922-68	1,441	319-162	16	878
Gladstone, Mo. (4,4)	.P	...-...-...	...-...	..-...-..	...	...-..	...	...-...	...	...
	F	...-...-...	...-...	..-...-..	...	...-..	...	...-...	...	...
Glastonbury t, Conn. (1,2)	.P	69-51-40	32,376-40,919	Y-...-5	4,788	4,373-91	3,181	706-486	103	312
	F	...-...-37	...-...	..-...-..	...	...-..	...	...-...	...	...
Glendale Heights v, Ill. (1,-)	.P	...-...-40	...-...	..-...-..	...	...-..	...	...-...	...	...
	F	...-...-...	...-...	..-...-..	...	...-..	...	...-...	...	...
Glenview v, Ill. (1,-)	.P	102-82-40	34,655-...	Y-47,191-7	6,264	4,398-70	4,137	216-45	1,299	567
	F	89-84-53	32,884-...	Y-...-7	6,918	4,721-68	4,651	30-40	1,317	880
Goldsboro, N.C. (1,1)	.P	110-89-40	20,613-29,744	Y-30,933-5	3,795	3,175-83	2,560	408-207	72	548
	F	77-76-56	18,678-26,978	Y-28,057-5	2,820	2,539-90	2,113	267-159	37	244
Grand Island, Nebr. (1,1)	.P	64-64-40	21,876-30,768	NONE	2,535	2,358-93	1,908	256-194	5	172
	F	54-54-54	20,808-29,280	NONE	2,496	2,141-85	1,761	207-173	127	228
Grand Junction, Colo. (1,1)	.P	99-69-40	29,580-35,868	NONE	5,792	4,265-73	3,455	449-361	317	1,210
	F	65-62-56	26,652-33,312	NONE	4,269	3,580-83	2,595	555-430	178	511
Grapevine, Tex. (1,1)	.P	78-53-40	27,225-33,093	Y-33,285-1	...	...-..	...	...-...	...	...
	F	50-49-56	23,147-29,329	Y-29,521-1	...	...-..	...	...-...	...	...
Greenfield, Wis. (1,1)	.P	...-...-..	...-...	Y-...-..	...	...-..	...	...-...	...	...
	F	...-...-..	...-...	Y-...-..	...	...-..	...	...-...	...	...
Greenville, N.C. (1,3)	.P	107-77-40	21,840-32,406	Y-33,864-5	7,474	4,631-61	3,702	579-350	2,177	666
	F	117-114-56	19,781-32,406	Y-33,864-5	6,992	3,727-53	2,931	357-439	3,027	238
Greenwood, Ind. (1,3)	.P	60-43-40	23,500-...	Y-...-..	2,625	2,213-84	1,793	258-162	153	259
	F	7-6-40	...-...	Y-...-..	801	253-31	199	36-18	311	237
Groton t, Conn. (1,5)	.P	69-63-40	30,680-37,336	Y-38,536-5	4,338	4,007-92	3,567	130-310	80	251
	F	...-...-..	...-...	..-...-..	...	...-..	...	...-...	...	...
Hagerstown, Md. (1,3)	.P	111-98-40	20,236-28,542	Y-28,685-12	5,209	4,440-85	3,596	558-286	128	641
	F	54-53-48	19,774-28,069	Y-28,209-12	3,196	2,078-65	1,683	238-157	772	346
Hallandale, Fla. (1,1)	.P	112-79-40	28,064-41,814	Y-45,414-7	7,272	6,156-84	5,164	619-373	423	693
	F	63-61-48	29,780-36,548	Y-42,548-7	4,596	4,024-87	3,388	397-239	47	525
Hanford, Calif. (3,3)	.P	54-39-40	27,830-33,509	NONE	3,226	2,331-72	1,840	308-142	98	797
	F	25-24-56	24,898-29,964	NONE	1,404	1,185-84	894	174-117	13	206
Hanover Park v, Ill	.P	62-43-40	28,704-39,520	NONE	4,003	2,870-71	2,322	228-320	633	500
	F	...-...-..	...-...	..-...-..	...	...-..	...	...-...	...	...
Harrisonburg, Va. (1,1)	.P	62-50-40	20,446-27,373	NONE	2,317	1,816-78	1,406	268-142	99	402
	F	56-55-53	20,446-27,373	NONE	2,194	1,556-70	1,219	233-104	88	550
Hattiesburg, Miss. (1,1)	.P	134-76-40	15,000-26,228	NONE	3,916	3,318-84	2,800	288-230	216	382
	F	109-106-52	15,000-26,228	NONE	2,962	2,499-84	2,219	110-170	254	209
Haverford tp, Pa. (1,3)	.P	75-63-40	34,707-38,397	Y-42,147-5	5,002	4,105-82	3,546	68-491	365	532
	F	...-...-..	...-...	..-...-..	654	48-7	39	2-7	228	378
Hickory, N.C. (1,3)	.P	105-85-43	19,934-31,032	Y-...-5	...	...-..	...	...-...	318	...
	F	103-100-48	17,220-26,806	Y-...-5	3,726	2,864-76	2,421	302-141	16	846
Highland, Calif. (9,7)	.P	...-...-..	...-...	..-...-..	...	...-..	...	...-...	...	...
	F	...-...-..	...-...	..-...-..	...	...-..	...	...-...	...	...
Hilo, Hawaii (1,3)	.P	472-343-40	27,240-40,608	NONE	...	...-..	...	...-...	339	...
	F	300-278-56	25,164-33,120	Y-35,772-..	...	...-..	...	...-...	203	...
Hoffman Estates v, Ill. (1,1)	.P	113-88-40	27,500-43,135	NONE	5,903	5,447-92	4,442	572-433	174	282
	F	89-84-56	27,000-40,555	NONE	5,888	4,527-76	3,760	455-312	1,179	182
Hoover t, Ala. (1,1)	.P	104-83-40	26,892-34,321	..-...-..	5,204	4,301-82	3,565	550-186	299	604
	F	115-114-53	26,892-34,321	..-...-..	5,713	5,317-93	4,399	531-387	40	356
Hot Springs, Ark. (1,1)	.P	95-77-40	17,523-21,236	Y-21,836-1	3,538	2,557-72	2,172	202-183	125	856
	F	77-75-53	16,226-19,680	Y-20,280-1	2,816	2,318-82	1,810	353-155	236	262
Huber Heights, Ohio (1,1)	.P	57-44-40	25,254-35,856	NONE	3,269	3,052-93	2,173	424-455	...	217
	F	45-44-52	24,995-36,325	NONE	...	...-..	...	...-...	...	...
Huntsville, Tex. (1,3)	.P	43-33-40	22,944-30,864	Y-31,152-1	2,005	1,479-73	1,289	105-85	253	273
	F	3-3-40	22,944-30,864	Y-31,152-1	478	180-37	153	22-5	194	104
Hurst, Tex. (1,1)	.P	88-58-40	31,752-34,728	Y-35,928-1	4,597	3,957-86	2,979	605-373	13	627
	F	39-37-53	31,476-34,380	Y-35,580-1	2,333	2,079-89	1,568	315-196	30	224
Idaho Falls, Idaho (3,1)	.P	111-79-40	23,462-34,340	Y-34,968-3	...	...-..	...	...-...	250	...

Table 3/22 continued   POLICE AND FIRE DEPARTMENT PERSONNEL, SALARIES, AND EXPENDITURES FOR CITIES 10,000 AND OVER: 1994

City (Service provision)	Department	Total personnel, no. uniformed, duty hours per week	Entrance, maximum salary ($)	Longevity pay, maximum ($) no. years to receive longevity pay	Reported expenditures (in thousands) Total expenditures (A) ($)	Total personnel expenditures (B) ($), % of (A)	Salaries and wages (C) ($)	City contrib. to employee retirement, insurance (D) ($)	Capital outlay (E) ($)	All other (F) ($)
25,000–49,999 continued										
Idaho Falls, Idaho (3,1) cont.	F	89-87-56	23,468-33,779	Y-34,927-3	...	...-..	...	...-...	225	...
Imperial Beach, Calif. (7,1)	P	...-..-..	...-...	..-..-..	...	...-..	...	...-...	...	...
	F	12-12-56	28,032-35,784	NONE	...	...-..	...	...-...	51	...
Indio, Calif. (1,1)	P	60-41-40	31,678-38,480	Y-41,366-10	4,253	3,532-83	2,817	389-326	7	714
	F	49-49-56	27,456-33,363	Y-35,865-10	...	...-..	...	...-...	5	...
Inkster, Mich. (1,1)	P	73-53-40	20,000-33,755	NONE	...	...-..	...	...-...	...	...
	F	19-18-53	28,065-33,638	NONE	...	...-..	...	...-...	...	...
Jackson tp, N.J. (1,2)	P	55-35-40	28,805-52,373	Y-57,610-6	...	...-..	...	...-...	...	...
	F	...-..-..	...-...	..-...-..	...	...-..	...	...-...	...	...
Jackson, Tenn. (1,1)	P	215-160-40	20,883-29,785	Y-...-5	8,979	6,420-71	5,223	724-473	1,542	1,017
	F	174-153-56	20,858-23,457	Y-...-5	6,419	5,716-89	4,661	633-422	343	360
Jacksonville, Ark. (1,1)	P	73-56-40	17,000-22,300	NONE	16,807	1,921-11	1,512	232-177	14,461	425
	F	56-51-53	17,000-22,300	NONE	29,014	1,784-6	1,473	165-146	27,034	196
Jacksonville, N.C. (1,1)	P	118-97-40	17,160-24,128	..-...-..	4,171	3,169-75	2,607	414-148	349	653
	F	66-66-56	16,504-23,211	..-...-..	2,299	1,981-86	1,681	207-93	33	285
Johnson City, Tenn. (4,4)	P	...-..-..	...-...	..-...-..	...	...-..	...	...-...	...	...
	F	...-..-..	...-...	..-...-..	...	...-..	...	...-...	...	...
Jonesboro, Ark. (1,1)	P	68-60-40	18,574-23,088	NONE	2,657	1,881-70	1,638	119-124	155	621
	F	70-69-53	18,574-23,088	NONE	2,604	1,947-74	1,693	118-136	426	231
Joplin, Mo. (1,1)	P	79-60-40	22,038-29,638	Y-31,438-5	3,533	2,680-75	2,164	337-179	243	610
	F	66-66-56	20,976-28,210	Y-30,010-5	2,664	2,234-83	1,775	290-169	286	144
Kannapolis, N.C. (1,3)	P	74-66-42	20,279-31,457	Y-35,231-2	3,251	2,592-79	2,209	220-163	203	456
	F	4-4-40	20,279-31,457	Y-35,231-2	282	134-47	107	13-14	22	126
Kennewick, Wash. (1,1)	P	76-60-40	29,592-40,128	Y-41,448-10	5,212	3,871-74	3,056	395-420	93	1,248
	F	60-59-50	30,900-40,524	Y-41,484-15	4,447	2,711-60	2,284	130-297	1,361	375
Kent, Ohio (1,1)	P	53-49-40	26,874-36,213	Y-36,693-10	...	...-..	...	...-...	24	...
	F	30-29-51	26,114-35,128	Y-35,788-10	...	...-..	...	...-...	24	...
Kentwood, Mich. (1,3)	P	54-48-40	26,550-37,504	Y-39,504-4	3,649	2,897-79	2,178	461-258	170	582
	F	25-24-53	25,582-38,085	Y-40,085-4	3,401	1,278-37	1,056	168-54	1,816	307
Kinston, N.C. (1,1)	P	89-78-42	18,129-24,295	Y-24,888-5	3,401	2,866-84	2,347	373-146	123	412
	F	71-67-53	17,266-23,138	Y-23,716-5	2,302	1,797-78	1,502	187-108	238	267
Kirkland, Wash. (1,3)	P	74-55-48	35,292-46,044	Y-47,844-6	...	...-..	...	...-...	100	...
	F	66-57-50	37,632-44,832	NONE	4,740	3,563-75	3,051	145-367	247	930
Kissimmee, Fla. (1,1)	P	128-93-40	22,731-31,984	Y-33,583-9	8,964	5,035-56	4,139	595-301	3,342	587
	F	68-65-56	21,212-29,848	Y-31,340-9	3,386	3,012-88	2,383	470-159	65	309
Kokomo, Ind. (1,1)	P	135-100-40	28,109-29,309	Y-...-1	...	...-..	...	...-...	815	...
	F	114-113-56	26,670-27,970	Y-30,070-4	...	...-..	...	...-...	805	...
La Grange, Ga. (1,1)	P	84-72-40	18,900-29,300	NONE	3,295	2,736-83	2,151	280-305	80	479
	F	62-61-48	17,900-28,800	NONE	2,409	1,954-81	1,553	202-199	160	295
La Mirada, Calif. (7,5)	P	...-..-..	...-...	..-...-..	...	...-..	...	...-...	...	...
	F	...-..-..	...-...	..-...-..	...	...-..	...	...-...	...	...
La Puente, Calif. (-,5)	P	...-..-..	...-...	..-...-..	...	...-..	...	...-...	...	...
	F	...-..-..	...-...	..-...-..	...	...-..	...	...-...	...	...
La Verne, Calif. (1,1)	P	56-38-40	37,632-45,756	NONE	5,712	5,018-87	3,851	362-805	71	623
	F	27-27-56	35,100-42,660	NONE	3,110	2,909-93	2,214	209-486	48	153
Laguna Niguel, Calif. (7,7)	P	...-..-..	...-...	..-...-..	...	...-..	...	...-...	...	...
	F	...-..-..	...-...	..-...-..	...	...-..	...	...-...	...	...
Lauderhill, Fla. (9,1)	P	...-..-..	...-...	..-...-..	...	...-..	...	...-...	...	...
	F	67-66-48	25,456-35,641	NONE	3,856	3,375-87	2,647	492-236	123	358
Lawndale, Calif. (7,5)	P	...-..-..	...-...	..-...-..	...	...-..	...	...-...	...	...
	F	...-..-..	...-...	..-...-..	...	...-..	...	...-...	...	...
Lawrence tp, N.J. (1,3)	P	67-57-40	26,000-53,632	Y-57,932-28	8,349	4,058-48	3,468	190-400	4,231	60
	F	4-4-40	25,720-35,706	Y-37,706-20	239	167-69	131	11-25	...	72
Leavenworth, Kan. (1,1)	P	71-53-43	22,087-33,131	Y-33,731-5	2,763	2,093-75	1,782	155-156	234	436
	F	46-46-54	20,590-30,886	Y-31,486-5	1,860	1,579-84	1,364	106-109	153	128
Lewiston, Idaho (1,1)	P	59-41-40	26,079-31,151	NONE	2,622	2,128-81	1,747	132-249	119	375
	F	44-44-56	23,854-28,492	Y-28,732-5	...	...-..	...	...-...	161	...
Lewisville, Tex. (1,1)	P	117-81-40	26,500-32,878	Y-34,078-1	5,473	4,131-75	3,399	363-369	134	1,208
	F	81-79-56	25,091-31,469	Y-32,669-1	4,100	3,352-81	2,743	322-287	8	740
Lincoln Park, Mich. (1,1)	P	61-61-40	27,282-34,750	Y-36,488-2	5,748	4,965-86	3,591	791-583	287	496
	F	36-36-50	30,332-38,102	Y-40,388-1	2,933	2,826-96	2,047	421-358	7	100
Lindenhurst v, N.Y	P	...-..-..	...-...	..-...-..	...	...-..	...	...-...	...	...
	F	...-..-..	...-...	..-...-..	...	...-..	...	...-...	...	...
Littleton, Colo. (1,1)	P	71-55-40	28,000-42,000	NONE	3,964	3,356-84	2,850	277-229	163	445
	F	101-98-56	25,000-37,000	NONE	6,418	5,386-83	4,567	442-377	304	728
Logan, Utah (1,1)	P	43-32-40	19,801-35,850	NONE	5,342	1,714-32	1,293	257-164	3,320	308
	F	28-26-53	19,801-32,505	NONE	1,775	1,433-80	1,107	239-87	69	273
Lombard v, Ill. (1,1)	P	81-64-..	30,427-42,463	NONE	5,161	4,240-82	3,424	511-305	238	683
	F	48-48-..	28,415-39,292	NONE	4,008	3,394-84	2,749	415-230	87	527
Lompoc, Calif. (1,1)	P	56-41-40	34,596-42,048	NONE	3,178	2,872-90	2,531	38-303	36	270
	F	24-23-56	33,894-41,196	NONE	1,875	1,774-94	1,316	297-161	...	101
Longview, Wash. (1,1)	P	58-55-..	33,792-41,532	Y-42,372-10	4,269	2,876-67	2,332	303-241	91	1,302
	F	39-38-..	32,160-37,848	Y-38,688-5	2,188	1,903-86	1,714	93-96	22	263
Los Gatos t, Calif. (3,5)	P	58-39-41	38,605-46,925	Y-49,296-15	7,928	4,233-53	3,093	564-576	3,192	503

Table 3/22
continued

POLICE AND FIRE DEPARTMENT PERSONNEL, SALARIES, AND EXPENDITURES FOR CITIES 10,000 AND OVER: 1994

City (Service provision)	Depart-ment	Total personnel, no. uniformed, duty hours per week	Entrance, maximum salary ($)	Longevity pay, maximum ($) no. years to receive longevity pay	Reported expenditures (in thousands) Total expendi-tures (A) ($)	Total personnel expendi-tures (B) ($), % of (A)	Salaries and wages (C) ($)	City contrib. to employee retirement, insurance (D) ($)	Capital outlay (E) ($)	All other (F) ($)
25,000–49,999 continued										
Los Gatos t, Calif. (3,5) cont.	F	...-..-..	...-...	..-..-..	...	...-..	...	...-...	...	...
Loveland, Colo. (1,3) ....P		82-59-40	30,636-41,136	NONE	4,263	3,475-81	2,970	303-202	52	736
	F	27-23-72	31,356-42,336	NONE	2,234	1,418-63	1,244	115-59	560	256
Lower Makefield tp, Pa. (1,2) ....P		25-22-40	22,678-41,235	Y-42,335-5	1,840	1,632-88	1,348	103-181	41	167
	F	...-..-..	...-...	..-..-..	...	...-..	...	...-...	...	...
Lufkin, Tex. (1,1) ....P		79-61-40	20,700-...	Y-...-1	3,388	2,766-81	2,137	310-319	117	505
	F	64-60-56	21,296-...	Y-...-1	5,142	2,264-44	1,809	208-247	69	2,809
Lynnwood, Wash. (1,1) ....P		57-49-40	35,987-42,357	Y-43,377-4	4,170	3,388-81	2,666	355-367	68	714
	F	34-33-48	34,884-41,227	Y-44,575-4	3,187	2,164-67	1,747	143-274	296	727
Mc Candless t, Pa. (1,2) ....P		34-28-40	31,051-40,037	..-..-..	2,230	1,630-73	1,348	104-178	307	293
	F	...-..-..	...-...	..-..-..	...	...-..	...	...-...	...	...
Madison Heights, Mich. (1,1) ....P		78-61-40	27,667-40,210	Y-43,427-5	...	...-..	...	...-...	131	...
	F	44-43-54	27,667-39,903	Y-43,095-5	...	...-..	...	...-...	19	...
Manalapan tp, N.J. (1,2) ....P		44-44-40	34,230-47,477	Y-51,276-5	...	...-..	...	...-...	57	...
	F	...-..-..	...-...	..-..-..	...	...-..	...	...-...	...	...
Manassas, Va. (3,3) ....P		80-63-40	27,779-45,250	NONE	4,662	3,911-83	3,138	487-286	4	747
	F	7-..-50	31,512-51,298	NONE	520	333-64	267	44-22	85	102
Manhattan, Kan. (7,1) ....P		...-..-..	...-...	..-..-..	...	...-..	...	...-...	...	...
	F	49-47-56	18,520-22,102	NONE	14,091	1,759-12	1,398	190-171	12,219	113
Manhattan Beach, Calif. (1,1) ....P		86-56-40	36,840-46,128	NONE	8,418	5,144-61	4,089	757-298	73	3,201
	F	30-29-56	37,524-45,612	NONE	3,701	2,519-68	1,955	414-150	15	1,167
Manheim tp, Pa. (1,2) ....P		58-44-40	22,190-36,623	Y-38,373-5	3,217	2,284-70	1,952	172-160	95	838
	F	...-..-..	...-...	..-..-..	...	...-..	...	...-...	...	...
Manitowoc, Wis. (1,1) ....P		72-61-37	26,088-31,164	Y-31,644-6	...	...-..	...	...-...	54	...
	F	46-45-52	24,516-31,032	Y-31,512-5	...	...-..	...	...-...	16	...
Mankato, Minn. (4,4) ....P		...-..-..	...-...	..-..-..	...	...-..	...	...-...	...	...
	F	...-..-..	...-...	..-..-..	...	...-..	...	...-...	...	...
Maple Heights, Ohio (1,1) ....P		60-42-40	29,745-34,994	Y-36,074-5	3,298	2,822-85	2,197	396-229	74	402
	F	40-40-51	26,457-35,027	Y-36,107-5	...	...-..	...	...-...	37	...
Maplewood, Minn. (3,2) ....P		57-47-40	26,121-...	..-..-..	3,635	2,931-80	2,311	376-244	148	556
	F	...-..-..	...-...	..-..-..	...	...-..	...	...-...	...	...
Margate, Fla. (1,1) ....P		156-105-40	22,343-37,237	Y-...-5	...	...-..	...	...-...	197	...
	F	54-52-56	23,556-33,450	Y-...-7	...	...-..	...	...-...	86	...
Marietta, Ga. (1,1) ....P		138-114-40	21,819-31,595	Y-...-5	6,909	5,874-85	4,343	810-721	327	708
	F	120-117-56	21,782-31,624	Y-...-5	6,286	5,638-89	4,190	790-658	171	477
Marion, Ind. (1,1) ....P		79-69-40	19,165-32,957	NONE	...	...-..	...	...-...	467	...
	F	79-76-56	21,561-23,957	NONE	...	...-..	...	...-...	37	...
Marion, Ohio (1,1) ....P		61-51-40	25,459-31,470	Y-32,344-5	...	...-..	...	...-...	1,521	...
	F	63-63-48	23,512-31,125	Y-32,074-5	...	...-..	...	...-...	6	...
Marshalltown, Iowa (1,1) ....P		53-39-41	21,214-31,596	NONE	2,265	2,096-92	1,632	268-196	11	158
	F	32-31-49	21,799-30,456	Y-31,822-10	1,408	1,353-96	1,026	180-147	7	48
Martinez, Calif. (1,7) ....P		54-42-40	36,816-43,644	Y-46,740-15	5,613	3,834-68	2,922	652-260	84	1,695
	F	...-..-..	...-...	..-..-..	...	...-..	...	...-...	...	...
Maryland Heights, Mo. (1,5) ....P		70-56-40	27,703-36,077	Y-...-4	3,249	2,892-89	2,335	317-240	86	271
	F	...-..-..	...-...	..-..-..	...	...-..	...	...-...	...	...
Massillon, Ohio (1,1) ....P		46-44-40	26,000-32,200	Y-...-5	2,562	2,396-93	1,970	238-188	57	109
	F	42-42-50	25,592-34,019	Y-...-5	2,347	2,061-87	1,630	281-150	151	135
Maywood, Calif. (1,7) ....P		31-23-40	39,936-44,040	Y-44,921-5	...	...-..	...	...-...	...	...
	F	...-..-..	...-...	..-..-..	...	...-..	...	...-...	...	...
Medford, Ore. (1,1) ....P		102-84-40	28,164-35,964	NONE	...	...-..	...	...-...	229	...
	F	67-66-56	29,028-36,300	NONE	...	...-..	...	...-...	69	...
Menlo Park, Calif. (1,5) ....P		63-45-40	40,331-48,982	NONE	5,484	4,724-86	3,796	700-228	102	658
	F	...-..-..	...-...	..-..-..	...	...-..	...	...-...	...	...
Menomonee Falls v, Wis. (1,3) .....P		68-53-40	31,446-37,812	NONE	...	...-..	...	...-...	268	...
	F	6-5-50	26,978-31,762	NONE	661	443-67	337	75-31	35	183
Mentor, Ohio (1,1) ....P		92-64-40	30,859-38,948	Y-40,448-5	9,145	4,481-48	3,510	533-438	4,137	527
	F	64-60-53	30,859-38,948	Y-40,448-5	9,408	4,506-47	3,468	715-323	4,112	790
Meridian, Miss. (1,1) ....P		125-97-43	17,014-25,251	NONE	3,690	2,902-78	2,341	334-227	170	618
	F	111-107-56	16,203-24,045	NONE	3,339	2,858-85	2,378	278-202	159	322
Merrillville, Ind. (1,2) ....P		46-46-40	21,934-27,895	Y-28,895-5	...	...-..	...	...-...	...	...
	F	...-..-..	...-...	..-..-..	...	...-..	...	...-...	...	...
Methuen t, Mass. (1,1) ....P		79-67-40	24,551-27,554	Y-28,079-5	3,367	3,164-93	2,807	13-344	100	103
	F	91-90-42	25,468-28,677	Y-...-1	4,297	4,157-96	3,677	7-473	37	103
Middletown, Ohio (1,1) ....P		116-82-40	28,661-36,061	Y-37,143-10	6,352	5,346-84	4,141	820-385	71	935
	F	81-80-52	18,000-35,719	Y-36,791-10	...	...-..	...	...-...	84	...
Midland, Mich. (1,1) ....P		50-46-42	26,000-39,500	Y-42,524-20	...	...-..	...	...-...	249	...
	F	47-46-56	22,000-34,800	Y-37,580-20	...	...-..	...	...-...	38	...
Milford t, Mass. (1,1) ....P		42-42-40	28,788-31,723	Y-33,626-10	...	...-..	...	...-...	111	...
	F	38-38-42	25,432-31,264	Y-32,355-5	...	...-..	...	...-...	185	...
Minot, N.D. (1,1) ....P		70-54-40	18,852-28,284	NONE	11,583	2,163-18	1,925	127-111	983	8,437
	F	46-44-56	18,852-28,284	NONE	...	...-..	...	...-...	68	...
Miramar, Fla. (1,1) ....P		100-83-40	27,258-46,612	NONE	6,964	5,858-84	4,664	803-391	158	948
	F	61-54-48	25,500-40,500	NONE	3,980	3,298-82	2,596	468-234	80	602
Mishawaka, Ind. (1,1) ....P		91-80-48	23,275-27,379	..-..-..	3,276	3,052-93	2,631	25-396	170	54

Table 3/22 continued **POLICE AND FIRE DEPARTMENT PERSONNEL, SALARIES, AND EXPENDITURES FOR CITIES 10,000 AND OVER: 1994**

City (Service provision)	Depart-ment	Total personnel, no. uniformed, duty hours per week	Entrance, maximum salary ($)	Longevity pay, maximum ($) no. years to receive longevity pay	Reported expenditures (in thousands)					
					Total expendi-tures (A) ($)	Total personnel expendi-tures (B) ($), % of (A)	Salaries and wages (C) ($)	City contrib. to employee retirement, insurance (D) ($)	Capital outlay (E) ($)	All other (F) ($)
25,000–49,999 continued										
Mishawaka, Ind. (1,1) cont.	F	92-91-56	23,275-27,379	..-...-..	3,321	3,130-94	2,717	13-400	99	92
Moline, Ill. (1,1)	P	96-73-40	27,947-36,428	Y-38,086-9	4,499	4,171-92	3,560	296-315	17	311
	F	67-67-56	27,067-35,035	Y-38,194-9	3,411	3,181-93	2,690	216-275	6	224
Monrovia, Calif. (1,1)	P	77-57-40	33,480-42,744	NONE	5,524	4,425-80	3,353	755-317	3	1,096
	F	38-37-56	32,268-41,172	NONE	3,164	2,526-79	1,957	417-152	10	628
Montclair, Calif. (3,3)	P	73-51-40	37,836-45,996	NONE	...	...-...	...	...-...	213	...
	F	45-38-56	33,420-40,632	NONE	...	...-...	...	...-...	66	...
Moorhead, Minn. (1,1)	P	55-41-45	28,152-33,300	NONE	3,024	2,092-69	1,738	216-138	53	879
	F	29-28-56	25,788-29,676	NONE	1,636	1,274-77	1,045	128-101	14	348
Moorpark, Calif. (9,5)	P	...-..-..	...-...	..-...-..	...	...-...	...	...-...	...	...
	F									
Mount Laurel tp, N.J. (1,5)	P	63-48-40	30,966-40,852	Y-43,352-10	...	...-...	...	...-...	25	...
	F	...-..-..	...-...	..-...-..	...	...-...	...	...-...	...	...
Mt. Lebanon, Pa. (1,3)	P	54-41-40	31,223-42,484	Y-43,121-4	...	...-...	...	...-...	147	...
	F	16-15-42	36,088-42,822	Y-43,512-4	...	...-...	...	...-...	76	...
Mount Pleasant t, S.C. (1,3)	P	87-61-40	19,323-28,412	NONE	2,991	2,300-76	1,743	304-253	242	449
	F	62-61-68	17,451-25,672	NONE	2,352	1,544-65	1,202	176-166	510	298
Murfreesboro, Tenn. (1,1)	P	122-96-37	18,943-21,905	Y-...-1	...	...-...	...	...-...	257	...
	F	139-136-52	17,955-21,656	Y-...-1	...	...-...	...	...-...	31	...
Murray, Utah (3,3)	P	64-54-40	22,008-36,372	NONE	3,718	2,955-79	2,262	380-313	173	590
	F	37-35-56	22,008-36,372	NONE	2,345	1,851-78	1,439	243-169	204	290
Muskegon, Mich. (1,1)	P	87-77-40	23,227-34,790	Y-35,290-..	4,734	4,041-85	2,834	647-560	12	681
	F	39-38-54	21,000-31,580	Y-32,080-..	2,076	1,898-91	1,328	305-265	15	163
Muskogee, Okla. (1,1)	P	113-87-40	15,017-23,275	NONE	...	...-...	...	...-...	...	...
	F	...-..-..	...-...	..-...-..	...	...-...	...	...-...	...	...
Nacogdoches, Tex. (1,1)	P	63-50-40	22,644-26,764	Y-27,964-..	2,296	1,918-83	1,557	258-103	72	306
	F	53-51-53	20,040-23,800	Y-25,000-..	2,201	1,915-87	1,562	263-90	46	240
Neptune tp, N.J. (1,5)	P	82-65-40	23,000-51,905	Y-53,805-5	...	...-...	...	...-...	...	...
	F	...-..-..	...-...	..-...-..	...	...-...	...	...-...	...	...
New Braunfels, Tex. (1,3)	P	62-45-40	18,970-25,368	Y-27,318-1	...	...-...	...	...-...	143	...
	F	45-44-52	18,970-22,984	Y-24,934-1	1,532	1,374-89	1,134	170-70	5	153
New London, Conn. (1,1)	P	77-65-40	34,768-38,480	Y-39,030-5	4,815	4,509-93	3,544	444-521	20	286
	F	65-63-42	33,242-35,192	Y-35,842-5	3,615	3,370-93	2,664	185-521	...	245
Newark, Del. (1,2)	P	65-51-40	25,378-33,048	Y-34,048-7	3,859	3,169-82	2,382	314-473	348	342
	F	...-..-..	...-...	..-...-..	...	...-...	...	...-...	...	...
Newark, Ohio (1,1)	P	67-57-40	19,635-28,974	Y-29,679-5	3,875	2,459-63	1,822	354-283	377	1,039
	F	79-66-42	18,803-29,328	Y-30,033-5	...	...-...	...	...-...	340	...
Newburgh, N.Y. (1,1)	P	87-70-40	26,157-38,237	Y-39,587-7	5,464	4,890-89	3,661	594-635	20	554
	F	65-61-40	25,481-34,706	Y-35,956-7	3,912	3,728-95	2,707	462-559	6	178
Newington t, Conn. (1,2)	P	50-47-40	34,190-43,680	Y-44,680-10	4,089	3,754-91	2,852	580-322	81	254
	F	...-..-..	...-...	..-...-..	...	...-...	...	...-...	88	...
Newport, R.I. (1,1)	P	114-91-40	25,274-31,515	Y-36,242-3	...	...-...	...	...-...	...	...
	F	98-98-42	23,100-32,889	Y-37,658-7	...	...-...	...	...-...	...	...
Niles v, Ill. (1,1)	P	62-50-40	32,818-43,979	Y-45,671-8	3,643	736-20	646	82-8	112	2,795
	F	49-48-53	32,818-43,979	Y-45,671-8	...	...-...	...	...-...	25	...
Normal t, Ill. (1,1)	P	62-47-40	23,430-39,050	NONE	2,697	2,379-88	2,119	136-124	47	271
	F	40-40-54	26,505-...	NONE	2,470	1,889-76	1,505	292-92	149	432
North Chicago, Ill. (1,1)	P	71-50-40	25,139-41,129	NONE	2,323	2,066-88	1,835	35-196	205	52
	F	27-26-50	21,782-34,857	NONE	1,006	941-93	863	1-77	37	28
North Las Vegas, Nev. (1,1)	P	164-113-40	30,868-42,655	Y-46,921-7	...	...-...	...	...-...	1,138	...
	F	68-64-56	29,330-42,184	Y-46,402-7	...	...-...	...	...-...	338	...
North Lauderdale, Fla. (4,4)	P	...-..-..	...-...	..-...-..	...	...-...	...	...-...	...	...
	F	...-..-..	...-...	..-...-..	...	...-...	...	...-...	...	...
North Miami, Fla. (1,7)	P	148-111-40	30,700-39,353	Y-...-..	...	...-...	...	...-...	406	...
	F	...-..-..	...-...	..-...-..	...	...-...	...	...-...	...	...
North Richland Hills, Tex. (1,1)	P	116-88-40	26,616-35,880	Y-36,360-1	4,642	3,910-84	3,312	329-269	140	592
	F	67-65-56	26,616-38,870	Y-...-1	3,378	3,057-90	2,433	243-381	31	290
Northglenn, Colo. (1,5)	P	60-44-40	27,970-40,419	Y-40,899-7	...	...-...	...	...-...	19	...
	F	...-..-..	...-...	..-...-..	...	...-...	...	...-...	...	...
Norwich, Conn. (1,1)	P	101-86-40	29,544-35,860	NONE	5,316	4,563-85	3,780	433-350	177	576
	F	62-60-42	25,684-32,772	NONE	3,936	3,288-83	2,646	287-355	...	648
Oakland Park, Fla. (1,1)	P	103-73-40	26,736-37,778	Y-...-6	6,124	5,467-89	4,371	736-360	5	652
	F	53-52-48	26,057-35,045	Y-...-6	2,719	2,267-83	1,787	320-160	...	452
Orland Park v, Ill. (1,-)	P	85-66-..	32,327-43,137	Y-44,437-5	...	...-...	...	...-...	937	...
	F	...-..-..	...-...	..-...-..	...	...-...	...	...-...	...	...
Pacifica, Calif. (3,3)	P	50-37-40	30,432-45,672	NONE	3,777	3,003-79	2,343	436-224	11	763
	F	24-23-56	22,632-41,268	NONE	1,950	1,673-85	1,296	264-113	...	277
Paducah, Ky. (1,1)	P	74-68-40	21,600-28,584	NONE	3,206	2,921-91	2,117	409-395	127	158
	F	90-85-56	21,565-25,060	NONE	4,208	3,834-91	2,698	586-550	217	157
Palm Springs, Calif. (1,1)	P	125-80-40	34,452-46,341	NONE	...	...-...	...	...-...	529	...
	F	63-58-56	32,148-42,150	NONE	5,151	4,356-84	3,016	683-657	16	779
Panama City, Fla. (1,1)	P	115-35-41	18,200-27,872	NONE	4,557	3,653-80	2,804	430-419	191	713
	F	91-3-56	17,680-26,520	NONE	3,723	3,349-89	2,569	393-387	71	303
Paramount, Calif. (9,5)	P	...-..-..	...-...	..-...-..	...	...-...	...	...-...	...	...

Table 3/22
continued

POLICE AND FIRE DEPARTMENT PERSONNEL, SALARIES, AND EXPENDITURES FOR CITIES 10,000 AND OVER: 1994

City (Service provision)	Depart-ment	Total personnel, no. uniformed, duty hours per week	Entrance, maximum salary ($)	Longevity pay, maximum ($), no. years to receive longevity pay	Reported expenditures (in thousands)					
					Total expendi-tures (A) ($)	Total personnel expendi-tures (B) ($), % of (A)	Salaries and wages (C) ($)	City contrib. to employee retirement, insurance (D) ($)	Capital outlay (E) ($)	All other (F) ($)
25,000–49,999 continued										
Paramount, Calif. (9,5) cont.	F	...-.-..	...-...	..-...-...	...	...-..	...	...-...	...	...
Park Ridge, Ill. (4,4)	P	...-.-..	...-...	..-...-...	...	...-..	...	...-...	...	...
	F	...-.-..	...-...	..-...-...	...	...-..	...	...-...	...	...
Pascagoula, Miss. (1,1)	P	83-54-40	17,954-26,526	NONE	2,981	2,508-84	1,976	261-271	195	278
	F	59-58-50	17,954-26,526	NONE	2,021	1,800-89	1,465	132-203	151	70
Pemberton tp, N.J. (1,2)	P	53-47-40	28,500-39,908	Y-42,902-5	3,194	3,005-94	2,522	279-204	...	189
	F	...-.-..	...-...	..-...-...	...	...-..	...	...-...	293	...
Perth Amboy, N.J. (-,3)	P	149-121-40	27,893-47,887	Y-54,711-5	13,853	8,229-59	6,802	914-513	152	5,472
	F	46-45-42	31,112-47,687	Y-54,482-5	5,303	2,758-52	2,296	304-158	38	2,507
Petaluma, Calif. (1,1)	P	78-54-40	...-...	NONE	6,085	5,262-86	4,038	807-417	63	760
	F	55-54-56	...-...	NONE	...	...-..	...	...-...	22	...
Petersburg, Va. (3,1)	P	129-96-40	20,323-32,602	NONE	...	...-..	...	...-...	...	...
	F	77-73-56	19,377-28,961	NONE	...	...-..	...	...-...	...	...
Pinellas Park, Fla. (1,1)	P	106-70-40	24,170-35,818	NONE	5,825	4,615-79	3,714	604-297	230	980
	F	78-71-56	23,908-33,837	NONE	5,226	3,664-70	2,927	509-228	923	639
Placentia, Calif. (1,7)	P	66-50-40	37,596-46,404	NONE	...	...-..	...	...-...	1,189	...
	F	...-.-..	...-...	..-...-...	...	...-..	...	...-...	...	...
Pleasant Hill, Calif. (1,5)	P	40-20-40	37,056-47,856	..-...-..	4,553	3,736-82	3,006	331-399	58	759
	F	...-.-..	...-...	..-...-...	...	...-..	...	...-...	...	...
Plymouth t, Mass. (1,1)	P	92-80-40	26,613-30,290	Y-30,540-5	5,937	5,557-93	4,402	244-911	154	226
	F	114-109-42	23,828-28,511	Y-28,761-5	...	...-..	...	...-...	170	...
Pocatello, Idaho (1,1)	P	96-75-40	24,731-27,476	Y-30,779-5	...	...-..	...	...-...	2	...
	F	71-68-56	23,762-30,284	Y-33,586-5	...	...-..	...	...-...	122	...
Ponca City, Okla. (1,1)	P	78-63-40	20,043-24,220	Y-24,700-3	2,696	2,184-81	1,749	180-255	140	372
	F	69-68-50	18,246-22,875	Y-23,355-3	2,623	2,473-94	2,000	190-283	79	71
Port Huron, Mich. (1,1)	P	70-53-40	32,300-37,028	Y-40,731-..	4,237	3,608-85	2,934	295-379	11	618
	F	56-54-56	31,014-35,924	Y-39,516-..	2,934	2,605-88	2,241	76-288	22	307
Port Orange, Fla. (3,1)	P	77-62-43	22,503-33,308	Y-...-..	3,340	2,561-76	2,121	229-211	18	761
	F	51-48-53	19,522-28,893	Y-...-..	2,536	2,040-80	1,673	214-153	11	485
Portage, Ind. (1,1)	P	52-38-40	22,308-28,496	Y-29,096-3	...	...-..	...	...-...	56	...
	F	40-39-48	22,308-28,912	Y-29,512-3	...	...-..	...	...-...	20	...
Portage, Mich. (1,3)	P	67-53-35	27,138-40,805	Y-43,865-5	...	...-..	...	...-...	204	...
	F	34-33-72	25,415-36,744	Y-...-5	...	...-..	...	...-...	142	...
Portsmouth, N.H. (1,1)	P	84-63-40	26,956-31,952	Y-...-5	4,496	3,773-83	3,111	154-508	200	523
	F	70-70-40	23,413-27,914	Y-...-5	3,716	2,775-74	2,234	166-375	600	341
Poway, Calif. (-,3)	P	...-.-..	...-...	..-...-...	...	...-..	...	...-...	...	...
	F	28-28-56	33,384-40,764	NONE	3,185	2,619-82	1,912	306-401	37	529
Prescott, Ariz. (1,1)	P	75-52-40	25,806-37,122	NONE	3,705	3,353-90	2,758	433-162	17	335
	F	52-49-56	24,290-33,623	NONE	2,645	1,799-68	1,631	57-111	209	637
Quincy, Ill. (1,1)	P	81-71-..	23,756-31,156	NONE	3,256	2,861-87	2,241	437-183	26	369
	F	61-57-..	23,756-32,256	NONE	...	...-..	...	...-...	74	...
Radnor tp, Pa. (1,2)	P	45-45-40	35,423-40,737	Y-...-..	...	...-..	...	...-...	553	...
	F	...-.-..	...-...	NONE	...	...-..	...	...-...	42	...
Rancho Palos Verdes, Calif	P	...-.-..	...-...	..-...-...	...	...-..	...	...-...	...	...
	F	...-.-..	...-...	..-...-...	...	...-..	...	...-...	...	...
Revere, Mass. (1,1)	P	86-75-42	26,375-29,753	Y-29,761-9	...	...-..	...	...-...	37	...
	F	103-103-42	26,375-29,753	Y-29,761-9	...	...-..	...	...-...	...	...
Reynoldsburg, Ohio (1,9)	P	55-42-40	22,146-35,115	Y-35,665-4	2,871	2,497-86	1,791	335-371	75	299
	F	...-.-..	...-...	..-...-...	...	...-..	...	...-...	...	...
Richland, Wash. (1,1)	P	51-44-40	34,272-38,832	Y-39,072-10	3,658	2,702-73	2,322	155-225	28	928
	F	52-50-51	31,536-40,980	Y-45,078-20	3,637	3,167-87	2,752	161-254	75	395
Richmond, Ind. (1,1)	P	101-77-40	22,747-23,472	Y-26,440-1	3,822	3,295-86	2,673	347-275	209	318
	F	82-81-56	22,190-24,182	Y-26,182-2	3,863	2,978-77	2,478	282-218	227	658
Ridley tp, Pa. (1,2)	P	34-34-40	28,000-36,000	Y-43,200-6	...	...-..	...	...-...	425	...
	F	...-.-..	...-...	..-...-...	...	...-..	...	...-...	136	...
Rio Rancho, N.M. (4,4)	P	...-.-..	...-...	..-...-...	...	...-..	...	...-...	...	...
	F	...-.-..	...-...	..-...-...	...	...-..	...	...-...	...	...
Rochester, N.H. (1,3)	P	48-38-40	21,008-27,880	Y-28,480-3	2,149	1,775-82	1,466	79-230	86	288
	F	29-28-42	21,612-27,579	Y-28,179-3	1,819	1,111-61	890	71-150	364	344
Rock Hill, S.C. (1,1)	P	107-98-41	21,445-30,181	NONE	3,969	3,284-82	2,762	506-16	157	528
	F	69-68-53	19,344-27,227	NONE	2,301	2,133-92	1,794	329-10	27	141
Rock Island, Ill. (1,1)	P	111-81-40	22,258-29,872	Y-32,872-5	4,988	4,039-80	3,229	549-261	...	949
	F	63-62-56	21,403-33,204	Y-36,704-5	3,239	2,803-86	2,233	374-196	2	434
Rockville, Md. (1,7)	P	49-34-40	28,339-49,572	NONE	3,824	3,549-92	3,152	297-100	124	151
	F	...-.-..	...-...	..-...-...	...	...-..	...	...-...	...	...
Rocky Mount, N.C. (1,1)	P	158-127-40	20,342-28,480	Y-30,331-5	5,795	5,070-87	3,949	855-266	317	408
	F	126-123-56	18,459-25,845	Y-27,525-5	4,949	4,232-85	3,365	652-215	506	211
Rohnert Park, Calif. (4,4)	P	...-.-..	...-...	..-...-...	...	...-..	...	...-...	...	...
	F	...-.-..	...-...	..-...-...	...	...-..	...	...-...	...	...
Rome, Ga. (3,1)	P	77-55-40	17,356-27,919	NONE	3,649	2,868-78	2,247	353-268	186	595
	F	150-147-48	17,356-27,919	NONE	5,870	4,865-82	4,008	355-502	61	944
Roseville, Calif. (3,1)	P	109-69-40	29,910-39,065	Y-41,018-10	7,237	5,656-78	4,115	803-738	236	1,345
	F	67-63-56	30,070-36,550	Y-36,800-15	5,429	4,134-76	2,876	660-598	489	806
Roseville, Minn. (1,2)	P	52-38-40	25,680-39,504	Y-42,803-..	3,380	2,500-73	2,094	258-148	96	784

Table 3/22 continued

POLICE AND FIRE DEPARTMENT PERSONNEL, SALARIES, AND EXPENDITURES FOR CITIES 10,000 AND OVER: 1994

City (Service provision)	Department	Total personnel, no. uniformed, duty hours per week	Entrance, maximum salary ($)	Longevity pay, maximum ($), no. years to receive longevity pay	Reported expenditures (in thousands)					
					Total expenditures (A) ($)	Total personnel expenditures (B) ($), % of (A)	Salaries and wages (C) ($)	City contrib. to employee retirement, insurance (D) ($)	Capital outlay (E) ($)	All other (F) ($)
25,000–49,999 continued										
Roseville, Minn. (1,2) cont.	F	...-..-..	...-...	..-...-..	...	...-..	...	...-...	57	...
Roswell, Ga. (1,2)	P	...-..-40	21,237-27,165	Y-29,994-10	9,442	4,199-44	3,245	494-460	3,753	1,490
	F	...-..-..	...-...	..-...-..	...	...-..	...	...-...	...	...
Round Rock, Tex. (1,1)	P	69-51-40	22,610-26,872	Y-...-1	2,858	2,047-71	1,671	216-160	521	290
	F	44-43-56	20,509-21,024	Y-...-1	1,691	1,420-83	1,178	153-89	85	186
Saginaw tp, Mich. (1,3)	P	42-39-40	23,795-37,056	NONE	2,808	2,226-79	1,656	305-265	59	523
	F	5-4-..	...-...	NONE	...	...-..	...	...-...	298	...
St. Cloud, Minn. (1,1)	P	83-68-40	28,800-35,196	Y-36,396-5	...	...-..	...	...-...	165	...
	F	56-55-56	30,288-34,884	Y-36,084-5	...	...-..	...	...-...	56	...
St. Louis Park, Minn. (1,1)	P	72-50-40	28,861-40,095	Y-43,703-4	4,315	3,561-82	2,985	366-210	44	710
	F	29-27-56	32,961-40,075	Y-43,681-5	...	...-..	...	...-...	9	...
Salem, Mass. (1,1)	P	101-91-40	25,807-27,517	Y-28,417-10	5,354	4,966-92	3,992	685-289	130	258
	F	90-88-42	23,128-25,931	Y-26,600-5	4,643	4,001-86	3,295	458-248	...	642
Salem t, N.H. (1,1)	P	63-48-40	24,774-30,966	Y-...-5	...	...-..	...	...-...	124	...
	F	63-58-42	25,537-30,645	Y-...-5	...	...-..	...	...-...	...	...
Salina, Kan. (1,1)	P	72-13-40	20,758-27,102	Y-...-5	3,168	2,624-82	2,041	299-284	118	426
	F	86-82-56	19,772-25,771	Y-...-5	3,695	3,258-88	2,606	330-322	125	312
San Bruno, Calif. (1,1)	P	55-46-40	38,784-47,604	NONE	4,954	4,244-85	3,423	456-365	75	635
	F	34-34-56	35,268-43,272	NONE	...	...-..	...	...-...	25	...
San Clemente, Calif. (1,1)	P	...-..-..	...-...	...-...-..	...	...-..	...	...-...	...	...
	F	42-30-56	28,368-39,828	NONE	...	...-..	...	...-...	...	...
San Dimas, Calif. (9,5)	P	...-..-..	...-...	..-...-..	...	...-..	...	...-...	...	...
	F	...-..-..	...-...	..-...-..	...	...-..	...	...-...	...	...
San Gabriel, Calif. (1,1)	P	65-52-36	36,372-44,208	NONE	...	...-..	...	...-...	100	...
	F	35-34-56	32,808-39,876	NONE	...	...-..	...	...-...	30	...
San Luis Obispo, Calif. (1,1)	P	78-54-40	33,300-45,300	NONE	6,158	5,151-83	4,045	739-367	208	799
	F	48-41-56	33,500-41,200	NONE	6,684	3,813-57	2,998	581-234	2,462	409
San Marcos, Calif. (7,3)	P	...-..-..	...-...	..-...-..	...	...-..	...	...-...	...	...
	F	34-33-56	30,708-37,320	NONE	...	...-..	...	...-...	670	...
San Rafael, Calif. (1,1)	P	93-67-40	33,319-40,040	NONE	8,102	5,932-73	4,514	1,006-412	881	1,289
	F	89-85-56	31,973-38,418	NONE	7,922	6,271-79	4,756	1,047-468	882	769
Sandusky, Ohio (1,1)	P	47-47-40	20,856-22,848	Y-...-3	2,765	2,483-89	1,834	383-266	60	222
	F	56-56-52	25,056-30,072	Y-...-3	...	...-..	...	...-...	181	...
Sanford, Fla. (1,1)	P	101-83-40	20,232-30,421	NONE	7,030	3,768-53	3,033	534-201	2,782	480
	F	55-54-53	20,232-30,421	NONE	5,253	2,264-43	1,837	310-117	2,751	238
Santa Cruz, Calif. (1,1)	P	111-83-40	32,634-42,660	NONE	8,290	5,828-70	4,717	647-464	1,078	1,384
	F	46-45-56	30,366-41,820	NONE	3,148	2,700-85	2,202	321-177	49	399
Santa Paula, Calif. (1,3)	P	34-28-40	30,428-36,985	NONE	...	...-..	...	...-...	385	...
	F	3-3-40	...-...	NONE	357	279-78	245	25-9	1	77
Saratoga, Calif. (7,5)	P	...-..-..	...-...	..-...-..	...	...-..	...	...-...	...	...
	F	...-..-..	...-...	..-...-..	...	...-..	...	...-...	...	...
Saratoga Springs, N.Y. (1,1)	P	63-63-40	25,745-36,125	Y-37,325-5	3,752	3,366-89	2,577	377-412	178	208
	F	49-49-40	28,386-35,071	Y-36,271-5	2,667	2,534-95	1,941	283-310	8	125
Saugus t, Mass. (1,1)	P	65-63-40	25,616-29,771	Y-30,664-5	...	...-..	...	...-...	73	...
	F	50-47-42	26,034-30,261	Y-31,169-5	...	...-..	...	...-...	69	...
Seal Beach, Calif. (1,7)	P	42-32-40	34,512-41,964	Y-46,164-10	4,319	3,207-74	2,521	421-265	299	813
	F	...-..-..	...-...	..-...-..	...	...-..	...	...-...	...	...
Seaside, Calif. (3,3)	P	48-39-..	33,720-41,040	Y-43,040-..	...	...-..	...	...-...	204	...
	F	24-23-..	29,520-35,760	Y-39,396-..	...	...-..	...	...-...	30	...
Shaker Heights, Ohio (1,1)	P	69-37-40	26,370-39,037	Y-40,906-7	6,758	5,631-83	4,219	692-720	118	1,009
	F	72-67-..	26,370-39,037	Y-40,837-7	...	...-..	...	...-...	304	...
Shawnee, Kan. (1,3)	P	74-61-40	25,064-37,045	NONE	3,974	3,261-82	2,569	360-332	115	598
	F	33-32-56	22,734-33,571	NONE	1,808	1,485-82	1,144	169-172	21	302
Sheboygan, Wis. (1,1)	P	111-85-38	26,634-32,269	Y-33,729-15	...	...-..	...	...-...	246	...
	F	79-77-56	25,958-31,387	Y-32,802-15	...	...-..	...	...-...	587	...
Sherman, Tex. (1,1)	P	55-55-40	22,680-31,272	Y-32,772-1	...	...-..	...	...-...	...	...
	F	69-69-56	19,884-25,260	Y-26,760-1	...	...-..	...	...-...	...	...
Sierra Vista, Ariz. (4,4)	P	...-..-..	...-...	..-...-..	...	...-..	...	...-...	...	...
	F	...-..-..	...-...	..-...-..	...	...-..	...	...-...	...	...
South Brunswick tp, N.J. (1,5)	P	85-62-40	32,171-46,991	Y-51,991-5	5,321	5,306-99	4,163	723-420	5	10
	F	...-..-..	...-...	..-...-..	...	...-..	...	...-...	...	...
Southington t, Conn. (3,3)	P	63-56-40	28,645-36,373	Y-36,573-5	4,268	3,410-79	2,594	433-383	206	652
	F	25-24-42	30,689-35,641	Y-36,041-5	...	...-..	...	...-...	625	...
Springdale, Ark. (1,3)	P	72-66-..	19,608-25,020	NONE	2,656	1,929-72	1,661	150-118	289	438
	F	66-65-..	19,608-25,020	NONE	...	...-..	...	...-...	...	...
Stanton, Calif. (7,7)	P	...-..-..	...-...	..-...-..	...	...-..	...	...-...	...	...
	F	...-..-..	...-...	..-...-..	...	...-..	...	...-...	...	...
State College b, Pa. (1,2)	P	69-53-40	29,162-34,778	Y-36,525-5	3,339	2,796-83	2,233	190-373	107	436
	F	...-..-..	...-...	..-...-..	...	...-..	...	...-...	...	...
Stillwater, Okla. (1,1)	P	86-60-40	19,469-28,787	NONE	6,767	2,850-42	2,344	251-255	3,636	281
	F	70-68-56	18,636-27,577	NONE	2,714	2,496-91	2,068	224-204	86	132
Sumter, S.C. (3,1)	P	82-71-40	17,836-24,270	NONE	3,411	2,639-77	2,060	340-239	34	738
	F	71-71-60	16,395-22,953	NONE	2,090	1,806-86	1,402	245-159	93	191
Tamarac, Fla. (7,1)	P	...-..-..	...-...	..-...-..	...	...-..	...	...-...	...	...

Table 3/22 continued POLICE AND FIRE DEPARTMENT PERSONNEL, SALARIES, AND EXPENDITURES FOR CITIES 10,000 AND OVER: 1994

City (Service provision)	Department	Total personnel, no. uniformed, duty hours per week	Entrance, maximum salary ($)	Longevity pay, maximum ($) no. years to receive longevity pay	Reported expenditures (in thousands)					
					Total expenditures (A) ($)	Total personnel expenditures (B) ($), % of (A)	Salaries and wages (C) ($)	City contrib. to employee retirement, insurance (D) ($)	Capital outlay (E) ($)	All other (F) ($)
25,000–49,999 continued										
Tamarac, Fla. (7,1) cont.	F	43-41-48	23,780-...	NONE	4,260	2,460-57	1,903	435-122	1,639	161
Temple, Tex. (1,1)	P	114-99-40	20,709-29,731	NONE	4,999	4,362-87	3,647	427-288	28	609
	F	94-92-56	19,573-25,605	NONE	3,799	3,491-91	2,929	345-217	16	292
Temple City, Calif. (7,5)	P	...-...-..	...-...	..-...-..	...	...-..	...	...-...	...	...
	F	...-...-..	...-...	..-...-..	...	...-..	...	...-...	...	...
Tewksbury t, Mass. (1,1)	P	49-47-40	26,007-31,834	Y-38,042-5	...	...-..	...	...-...	69	...
	F	47-42-42	20,949-31,828	Y-36,960-5	...	...-..	...	...-...	6	...
Texarkana, Tex. (1,1)	P	80-75-43	20,883-25,409	Y-26,609-1	3,751	2,826-75	2,339	275-212	79	846
	F	70-69-56	19,890-24,192	Y-25,392-1	2,603	2,372-91	2,002	197-173	63	168
Tigard, Ore. (1,5)	P	51-44-40	28,140-34,560	Y-38,016-5	...	...-..	...	...-...	2,072	...
	F	...-...-..	...-...	..-...-..	...	...-..	...	...-...	...	...
Titusville, Fla. (1,1)	P	79-52-40	21,112-29,598	Y-...-14	4,727	3,945-83	2,918	509-518	179	603
	F	57-55-56	21,025-28,305	Y-...-10	2,979	2,446-82	1,781	317-348	217	316
Tulare, Calif. (1,1)	P	63-45-40	26,587-32,000	NONE	3,662	2,902-79	2,121	304-477	50	710
	F	30-28-56	22,244-27,000	NONE	1,571	1,330-84	989	150-191	13	228
Turlock, Calif. (1,3)	P	74-60-40	28,044-41,040	NONE	4,986	4,028-80	2,929	646-453	...	958
	F	32-30-56	20,928-34,164	NONE	...	...-..	...	...-...	301	...
Union tp, Ohio (1,3)	P	49-38-40	26,340-32,655	Y-...-5	2,605	2,204-84	1,729	260-215	...	401
	F	14-...-43	25,459-35,139	Y-...-5	2,187	1,419-64	1,137	196-86	496	272
University City, Mo. (1,1)	P	75-56-40	26,448-34,296	Y-35,268-5	4,464	3,540-79	3,110	252-178	65	859
	F	49-48-56	28,236-32,292	Y-35,099-5	2,169	1,780-82	1,573	110-97	49	340
Upper Arlington, Ohio (1,1)	P	62-53-40	24,542-38,673	Y-41,173-4	3,920	3,660-93	2,706	545-409	115	145
	F	65-60-56	22,983-36,243	Y-38,743-4	...	...-..	...	...-...	133	...
Upper Merion tp, Pa. (1,3)	P	71-53-35	30,091-41,506	Y-44,006-5	...	...-..	...	...-...	2,605	...
	F	...-...-..	...-...	NONE	...	...-..	...	...-...	303	...
Upper Moreland tp, Pa. (1,3)	P	48-40-40	31,242-39,336	Y-42,368-..	2,792	2,507-89	1,950	362-195	96	189
	F	3-3-40	27,664-32,580	Y-33,280-..	330	134-40	96	17-21	1	195
Urbana, Ill. (1,1)	P	57-45-40	30,903-32,103	Y-36,597-2	3,815	2,505-65	2,025	397-83	596	714
	F	42-41-56	27,652-30,052	Y-33,057-2	2,859	1,933-67	1,524	343-66	557	369
Valdosta, Ga. (1,1)	P	100-88-40	18,351-26,792	Y-31,615-..	3,638	2,778-76	2,269	339-170	12	848
	F	86-85-56	18,351-26,792	Y-31,615-..	2,999	2,794-93	2,295	340-159	14	191
Vancouver, Wash. (1,1)	P	114-94-40	33,468-40,320	NONE	6,747	6,018-89	5,246	332-440	62	667
	F	78-75-49	30,900-40,956	NONE	4,743	4,012-84	3,526	192-294	429	302
Victorville, Calif. (7,1)	P	...-...-..	...-...	..-...-..	...	...-..	...	...-...	...	...
	F	58-34-53	27,660-33,696	Y-35,100-5	...	...-..	...	...-...	...	...
Walnut, Calif. (7,7)	P	...-...-..	...-...	..-...-..	...	...-..	...	...-...	...	...
	F	...-...-..	...-...	..-...-..	...	...-..	...	...-...	...	...
Warner Robins, Ga. (1,1)	P	97-83-..	20,328-26,426	NONE	3,621	3,244-89	2,396	379-469	37	340
	F	83-81-..	18,313-23,807	NONE	...	...-..	...	...-...	56	...
Washington (Glcstr) tp, N.J. (1,5)	P	70-65-36	30,030-...	Y-...-5	18,000	9,188-51	7,051	663-1,474	6,449	2,363
	F	...-...-..	...-...	..-...-..	...	...-..	...	...-...	...	...
Wausau, Wis. (1,1)	P	67-55-41	25,163-30,900	Y-31,380-5	...	...-..	...	...-...	60	...
	F	60-59-56	25,555-30,065	Y-30,545-5	...	...-..	...	...-...	121	...
West Hollywood, Calif. (-,-)	P	...-...-..	...-...	..-...-..	...	...-..	...	...-...	...	...
	F	...-...-..	...-...	..-...-..	...	...-..	...	...-...	...	...
West Lafayette, Ind. (1,1)	P	38-27-40	27,119-30,298	NONE	...	...-..	...	...-...	33	...
	F	32-32-52	27,119-30,298	NONE	...	...-..	...	...-...	6	...
West Memphis, Ark. (1,1)	P	89-83-40	18,648-24,144	NONE	2,654	2,178-82	1,794	255-129	115	361
	F	69-64-56	18,648-24,144	NONE	2,239	1,965-87	1,690	164-111	20	254
West Milford tp, N.J. (1,2)	P	52-43-40	35,746-48,088	Y-52,899-4	5,365	3,114-58	2,816	273-25	2,094	157
	F	...-...-..	...-...	..-...-..	...	...-..	...	...-...	...	...
West Orange tp, N.J. (1,1)	P	98-50-40	26,465-43,929	Y-48,322-5	6,721	6,206-92	5,579	88-539	355	160
	F	87-85-42	26,350-44,087	Y-48,495-5	5,306	4,740-89	4,196	66-478	440	126
West Sacramento, Calif. (1,1)	P	78-56-40	29,256-35,712	NONE	6,687	4,832-72	3,410	769-653	379	1,476
	F	53-48-56	29,088-36,276	NONE	...	...-..	...	...-...	748	...
West Springfield t, Mass. (1,1)	P	75-67-..	23,307-27,017	Y-27,467-5	...	...-..	...	...-...	67	...
	F	67-66-42	22,823-26,542	Y-26,992-5	...	...-..	...	...-...	17	...
Westerville, Ohio (1,9)	P	68-54-40	26,416-37,897	Y-38,797-5	4,205	3,716-88	2,795	513-408	121	368
	F	54-50-56	26,686-36,316	Y-37,216-5	...	...-..	...	...-...	19	...
Wethersfield t, Conn. (1,2)	P	52-41-40	29,816-40,160	Y-40,560-5	3,423	3,230-94	2,564	236-430	13	180
	F	...-...-..	...-...	..-...-..	...	...-..	...	...-...	382	...
Wheat Ridge, Colo. (1,5)	P	84-60-40	27,684-40,188	NONE	4,510	3,724-82	3,147	312-265	523	263
	F	...-...-..	...-...	..-...-..	...	...-..	...	...-...	...	...
Wheeling v, Ill. (1,1)	P	77-25-40	32,491-43,795	Y-44,395-12	4,306	3,434-79	2,964	170-300	151	721
	F	43-2-53	28,975-40,939	Y-41,539-12	2,786	2,082-74	1,874	6-202	326	378
Wheeling, W.Va. (1,1)	P	81-79-40	19,839-20,972	Y-21,692-3	3,540	2,661-75	2,079	277-305	763	116
	F	97-94-56	19,839-20,972	Y-21,692-3	3,466	3,070-88	2,443	259-368	29	367
White Plains, N.Y. (4,4)	P	...-...-..	...-...	..-...-..	...	...-..	...	...-...	...	...
	F	...-...-..	...-...	..-...-..	...	...-..	...	...-...	...	...
Wilkes-Barre, Pa. (1,1)	P	106-91-40	27,873-29,368	Y-33,773-2	...	...-..	...	...-...	...	...
	F	100-94-42	26,760-28,930	Y-33,268-2	...	...-..	...	...-...	...	...
Williamsport, Pa. (1,1)	P	55-52-35	27,560-30,247	NONE	...	...-..	...	...-...	105	...
	F	49-49-42	21,423-32,908	Y-...-..	...	...-..	...	...-...	...	...
Wilmette v, Ill. (1,1)	P	57-40-40	33,680-41,399	Y-45,311-5	...	...-..	...	...-...	86	...

Table 3/22 continued   POLICE AND FIRE DEPARTMENT PERSONNEL, SALARIES, AND EXPENDITURES FOR CITIES 10,000 AND OVER: 1994

City (Service provision)	Depart-ment	Total personnel, no. uniformed, duty hours per week	Entrance, maximum salary ($)	Longevity pay, maximum ($) no. years to receive longevity pay	Total expendi-tures (A) ($)	Total personnel expendi-tures (B) ($), % of (A)	Salaries and wages (C) ($)	City contrib. to employee retirement, insurance (D) ($)	Capital outlay (E) ($)	All other (F) ($)
25,000–49,999 continued										
Wilmette v, Ill. (1,1) cont.	F	45-44-54	32,168-40,472	Y-44,297-5	...	...-...	...	...-...	18	...
Wilson, N.C. (1,1)	P	94-78-40	20,109-29,389	Y-30,858-5	4,419	3,348-75	2,680	452-216	186	885
	F	87-85-56	20,109-29,389	Y-30,858-5	2,898	2,364-81	1,792	386-186	147	387
Windsor t, Conn. (1,2)	P	61-51-40	33,445-43,715	Y-44,265-6	...	...-...	...	...-...	...	...
	F	...-...-...	...-...	..-...-..	...	...-..	...	...-...	...	...
Winona, Minn. (1,3)	P	39-35-40	29,148-34,380	Y-35,755-5	...	...-...	...	...-...	25	...
	F	22-21-56	27,996-33,001	Y-34,320-5	...	...-...	...	...-...	120	...
Woodland, Calif. (1,3)	P	65-48-40	31,008-37,728	Y-37,853-10	5,498	4,052-73	3,039	527-486	...	1,446
	F	40-38-40	28,284-34,416	Y-34,541-10	3,134	2,545-81	1,909	331-305	...	589
Woonsocket, R.I. (1,1)	P	120-105-37	21,215-29,015	Y-31,047-5	...	...-...	...	...-...	62	...
	F	138-137-42	20,756-29,934	Y-32,029-5	...	...-...	...	...-...	84	...
Wyandotte, Mich. (1,1)	P	47-37-40	26,706-37,409	Y-38,309-6	3,098	2,760-89	2,391	40-329	100	238
	F	35-34-50	26,024-37,833	Y-38,733-6	2,045	1,721-84	1,513	9-199	100	224
Yucaipa, Calif. (7,5)	P	...-...-...	...-...	..-...-..	...	...-...	...	...-...	...	...
	F	...-...-...	...-...	..-...-..	...	...-...	...	...-...	...	...
10,000–24,999										
Abbeville t, La. (1,1)	P	37-36-42	10,692-...	Y-...-3	1,087	780-71	639	60-81	39	268
	F	36-36-42	11,730-...	Y-...-3	971	827-85	645	101-81	18	126
Aberdeen t, Md. (3,2)	P	46-37-40	19,671-35,207	Y-...-..	2,050	1,680-81	1,368	133-179	171	199
	F	...-...-...	...-...	..-...-..	...	...-...	...	...-...	37	...
Aberdeen, S.D. (1,1)	P	46-38-40	20,327-23,459	Y-...-..	...	...-...	...	...-...	...	...
	F	32-32-56	18,945-22,214	Y-...-..	...	...-...	...	...-...	...	...
Acton t, Mass. (1,1)	P	30-26-40	28,337-31,704	NONE	2,041	1,969-96	1,429	233-307	6	66
	F	41-41-42	26,158-30,639	Y-31,639-5	2,330	2,248-96	1,628	266-354	11	71
Ada, Okla. (1,1)	P	45-32-40	18,300-21,156	Y-...-4	1,375	1,226-89	967	174-85	30	119
	F	32-32-56	17,568-21,432	Y-...-4	1,088	964-88	798	84-82	52	72
Adrian, Mich. (3,1)	P	38-32-40	23,633-30,629	Y-31,629-5	2,118	1,536-72	1,356	18-162	384	198
	F	21-21-54	24,314-30,310	Y-31,310-5	1,345	897-66	786	6-105	330	118
Agoura Hills, Calif. (8,5)	P	...-...-...	...-...	..-...-..	...	...-...	...	...-...	...	...
	F	...-...-...	...-...	..-...-..	...	...-...	...	...-...	...	...
Albert Lea, Minn. (1,3)	P	37-29-40	31,200-35,048	NONE	1,955	1,713-87	1,344	164-205	1	241
	F	21-21-53	23,659-32,837	NONE	1,215	1,072-88	774	176-122	23	120
Albertville, Ala. (1,1)	P	40-32-42	13,313-20,670	NONE	1,336	1,000-74	742	89-169	147	189
	F	26-26-53	13,200-24,000	NONE	876	771-88	569	72-130	9	96
Albion, Mich. (4,4)	P	...-...-...	...-...	..-...-..	...	...-...	...	...-...	...	...
	F	...-...-...	...-...	..-...-..	...	...-...	...	...-...	...	...
Allen, Tex. (3,3)	P	40-24-40	24,612-32,004	Y-...-1	2,056	1,782-86	1,517	170-95	8	266
	F	34-33-56	23,568-30,636	Y-...-1	1,579	1,459-92	1,226	135-98	15	105
Allouez v, Wis. (7,3)	P	...-...-...	...-...	..-...-..	...	...-...	...	...-...	...	...
	F	12-12-56	28,527-34,993	Y-35,305-5	...	...-...	...	...-...	99	...
Alpharetta, Ga. (1,3)	P	51-36-43	21,966-30,752	NONE	2,234	1,434-64	1,110	124-200	208	592
	F	30-29-52	21,966-30,752	NONE	1,949	1,159-59	975	88-96	51	739
Alvin, Tex. (1,2)	P	41-33-40	21,366-32,905	Y-...-1	6,979	1,527-21	1,169	185-173	5,162	290
	F	...-...-...	...-...	..-...-..	...	...-...	...	...-...	5,162	...
American Fork, Utah (1,2)	P	22-19-40	19,800-...	NONE	...	...-...	...	...-...	125	...
	F	...-...-...	...-...	..-...-..	...	...-...	...	...-...	25	...
Americus, Ga. (1,1)	P	54-46-43	18,105-24,242	Y-24,992-2	2,056	1,575-76	1,281	162-132	41	440
	F	36-35-..	15,507-22,012	Y-22,762-2	1,183	966-81	810	88-68	47	170
Andrews, Tex. (1,2)	P	14-14-40	19,938-29,844	NONE	792	667-84	514	118-35	16	109
	F	...-...-...	...-...	..-...-..	...	...-...	...	...-...	8	...
Angleton, Tex. (1,2)	P	38-30-40	19,510-26,228	Y-...-1	1,508	1,289-85	1,018	155-116	22	197
	F	...-...-...	...-...	NONE	...	...-...	...	...-...	28	...
Ankeny, Iowa (1,3)	P	33-26-49	22,495-29,356	Y-29,756-5	1,686	1,323-78	961	212-150	66	297
	F	...-...-...	...-...	..-...-..	334	190-56	160	18-12	31	113
Apache Junction, Ariz. (1,5)	P	54-37-40	25,147-37,710	NONE	3,298	2,156-65	1,672	229-255	858	284
	F	...-...-...	...-...	..-...-..	...	...-...	...	...-...	...	...
Apopka, Fla. (1,1)	P	55-47-40	20,167-28,158	NONE	2,577	1,895-73	1,544	177-174	184	498
	F	58-45-56	20,772-29,873	NONE	2,248	1,789-79	1,437	191-161	176	283
Arcata, Calif. (3,5)	P	28-21-40	25,104-30,528	Y-32,054-5	2,944	1,325-45	1,062	157-106	1,168	451
	F	...-...-...	...-...	..-...-..	...	...-...	...	...-...	...	...
Arkansas City, Kan. (1,1)	P	29-22-40	20,158-25,795	Y-...-3	1,279	1,107-86	831	132-144	54	118
	F	24-23-56	18,284-23,396	Y-...-3	843	773-91	567	95-111	19	51
Artesia, N.M. (1,3)	P	35-30-42	21,288-26,100	Y-...-6	1,482	1,168-78	947	140-81	27	287
	F	18-17-56	21,288-26,772	Y-...-6	819	710-86	591	80-39	...	109
Asheboro, N.C. (3,3)	P	49-44-42	18,952-26,032	Y-28,635-3	2,026	1,435-70	1,188	130-117	180	411
	F	39-38-56	18,952-26,032	Y-28,635-3	1,448	1,204-83	1,000	126-78	32	212
Ashland, Ohio (1,1)	P	39-29-40	23,338-28,413	NONE	1,892	1,676-88	1,332	232-112	63	153
	F	37-32-53	24,776-27,367	NONE	1,723	1,594-92	1,221	265-108	43	86
Ashland, Ore. (1,1)	P	34-25-40	24,360-30,948	NONE	2,043	1,514-74	1,141	220-153	33	496
	F	24-1-56	25,536-32,244	NONE	1,510	1,137-75	856	175-106	15	358
Ashtabula, Ohio (3,1)	P	39-33-42	28,799-31,754	Y-...-..	...	...-...	...	...-...	222	...
	F	25-25-56	28,389-29,416	Y-30,916-..	...	...-...	...	...-...	191	...
Aston tp, Pa. (-,2)	P	19-17-40	28,494-37,992	Y-44,071-3	...	...-...	...	...-...	64	...
	F	...-...-...	...-...	..-...-..	...	...-...	...	...-...	...	...

Table 3/22
continued

POLICE AND FIRE DEPARTMENT PERSONNEL, SALARIES, AND EXPENDITURES FOR CITIES 10,000 AND OVER: 1994

City (Service provision)	Depart-ment	Total personnel, no. uniformed, duty hours per week	Entrance, maximum salary ($)	Longevity pay, maximum ($) no. years to receive longevity pay	Total expenditures (A) ($)	Total personnel expenditures (B) ($), % of (A)	Salaries and wages (C) ($)	City contrib. to employee retirement, insurance (D) ($)	Capital outlay (E) ($)	All other (F) ($)
10,000–24,999 continued										
Atascadero, Calif. (1,1)	P	35-28-..	28,958-35,198	NONE	...	...-..	...	...-...	23	...
	F	16-15-56	28,416-34,540	NONE	...	...-..	...	...-...	32	...
Atchison, Kan. (1,1)	P	28-24-40	18,360-22,440	Y-23,190-5	1,463	779-53	604	94-81	448	236
	F	29-29-56	18,360-22,440	Y-23,190-5	1,362	826-60	676	62-88	421	115
Athens, Ala. (1,1)	P	42-32-40	19,656-26,229	NONE	1,535	1,145-74	935	127-83	54	336
	F	36-36-56	17,929-23,836	NONE	1,268	1,175-92	964	131-80	1	92
Athens, Ohio (3,1)	P	29-27-40	21,965-28,891	Y-30,624-5	1,529	1,308-85	967	186-155	74	147
	F	23-23-48	20,651-28,624	Y-30,341-5	...	...-..	...	...-...	3	...
Athol t, Mass. (1,3)	P	28-24-37	24,238-26,700	Y-27,350-5	...	...-..	...	...-...	15	...
	F	23-23-42	21,238-24,315	Y-24,865-5	928	846-91	644	58-144	10	72
Atwater, Calif. (3,3)	P	28-22-40	22,932-29,280	NONE	...	...-..	...	...-...	58	...
	F	8-8-56	19,740-25,188	NONE	...	...-..	...	...-...	46	...
Auburn, Me. (1,1)	P	52-46-40	19,121-24,423	Y-24,923-7	2,248	1,902-84	1,490	199-213	115	231
	F	67-62-42	18,868-22,687	Y-23,187-7	2,948	2,468-83	1,919	246-303	268	212
Auburn t, Mass. (1,3)	P	29-24-37	24,085-30,797	NONE	1,356	1,214-89	1,117	5-92	25	117
	F	5-4-50	29,440-35,287	NONE	...	...-..	...	...-...	55	...
Augusta, Me. (1,1)	P	49-37-42	20,540-30,836	NONE	...	...-..	...	...-...	64	...
	F	41-39-48	20,644-27,118	Y-27,868-5	...	...-..	...	...-...	44	...
Avondale, Ariz. (3,3)	P	39-31-40	22,547-30,222	NONE	1,386	1,231-88	969	129-133	111	44
	F	15-15-56	22,539-30,227	NONE	667	399-59	342	14-43	209	59
Bainbridge, Ga. (4,4)	P	...-..-..	...-...	..-...-..	...	...-..	...	...-...	...	...
	F	...-..-..	...-...	..-...-..	...	...-..	...	...-...	...	...
Balch Springs, Tex. (3,3)	P	37-25-40	20,913-...	Y-...-1	...	...-..	...	...-...	...	...
	F	19-18-54	20,913-...	Y-...-1	...	...-..	...	...-...	...	...
Baldwin b, Pa. (1,2)	P	22-22-40	27,190-37,247	Y-39,110-5	...	...-..		...-...	332	...
	F	...-..-..	...-...	..-...-..	...	...-..	...	...-...	...	...
Ballwin, Mo. (1,5)	P	51-42-38	22,000-36,085	NONE	2,480	1,996-80	1,623	243-130	97	387
	F	...-..-..	...-...	..-...-..	...	...-..	...	...-...	...	...
Banning, Calif. (1,1)	P	42-28-40	29,229-35,528	NONE	...	...-..	...	...-...	47	...
	F	22-20-56	27,149-33,000	Y-33,600-5	...	...-..	...	...-...	4	...
Barstow, Calif. (1,5)	P	54-50-40	35,220-42,180	NONE	3,522	2,691-76	2,242	151-298	57	774
	F	...-..-..	...-...	..-...-..	...	...-..	...	...-...	...	...
Beaver Falls, Pa. (1,3)	P	17-17-40	24,488-27,652	Y-27,789-5	...	...-..	...	...-...	16	...
	F	8-8-53	25,845-26,931	Y-27,068-5	...	...-..	...	...-...	...	...
Bedford t, Mass. (1,1)	P	24-23-37	28,532-31,847	Y-34,398-5	1,542	1,427-92	1,297	77-53	29	86
	F	23-22-42	31,132-34,448	Y-36,998-5	1,243	1,148-92	1,031	61-56	5	90
Bedford t, N.H. (1,3)	P	30-21-40	26,353-37,689	NONE	1,410	1,314-93	1,125	44-145	1	95
	F	10-10-42	20,600-27,500	NONE	662	565-85	472	31-62	17	80
Bedford, Ohio (1,1)	P	35-29-40	28,214-37,485	Y-...-5	3,788	1,994-52	1,531	239-224	1,499	295
	F	20-20-48	28,508-34,508	Y-...-5	2,721	1,147-42	825	188-134	1,478	96
Bellaire, Tex. (1,3)	P	49-13-..	28,600-37,180	Y-38,380-..	...	...-..	...	...-...	84	...
	F	21-20-..	26,832-34,892	Y-36,092-..	1,050	881-83	732	83-66	26	143
Belle Glade, Fla. (1,3)	P	51-39-40	22,193-...	NONE	...	...-..	...	...-...	68	...
	F	17-16-52	19,160-...	NONE	975	646-66	520	54-72	233	96
Bellefontaine, Ohio (1,1)	P	29-22-40	23,234-30,368	NONE	1,365	1,172-85	896	139-137	21	172
	F	15-15-56	23,325-30,372	NONE	...	...-..	...	...-...	16	...
Belmont, Calif. (1,5)	P	44-31-..	38,928-47,328	..-...-..	3,375	2,616-77	2,146	230-240	389	370
	F	...-..-..	...-...	..-...-..	...	...-..	...	...-...	...	...
Belton, Mo. (1,1)	P	34-25-42	22,485-30,132	Y-...-6	2,172	1,316-60	1,067	139-110	207	649
	F	21-20-53	21,414-28,697	Y-...-6	1,493	1,050-70	840	139-71	239	204
Belton, Tex. (1,3)	P	28-19-40	16,536-25,750	Y-...-1	1,218	701-57	570	82-49	378	139
	F	16-15-56	16,482-25,750	Y-...-1	1,031	446-43	365	52-29	471	114
Belvidere, Ill. (1,1)	P	25-24-42	24,419-30,678	Y-32,442-2	1,322	1,153-87	899	129-125	60	109
	F	17-17-56	24,419-30,678	Y-32,442-2	...	...-..	...	...-...	61	...
Bemidji, Minn. (4,4)	P	...-..-..	...-...	..-...-..	...	...-..	...	...-...	...	...
	F	...-..-..	...-...	..-...-..	...	...-..	...	...-...	...	...
Benbrook, Tex. (1,3)	P	40-40-40	28,165-32,997	Y-33,657-1	1,988	1,799-90	1,433	220-146	11	178
	F	4-3-40	32,373-37,927	Y-38,686-1	605	384-63	325	42-17	4	217
Benicia, Calif. (1,1)	P	47-35-40	36,024-43,800	NONE	3,346	3,122-93	2,378	524-220	40	184
	F	36-35-56	32,760-39,828	NONE	2,607	2,376-91	1,930	264-182	58	173
Benton Harbor, Mich. (1,1)	P	20-4-..	20,790-26,790	Y-...-..	1,223	959-78	789	86-84	...	264
	F	12-12-..	23,220-28,181	Y-...-..	820	693-84	584	58-51	...	127
Bentonville, Ark. (1,1)	P	33-24-40	18,560-26,744	NONE	1,443	998-69	808	105-85	284	161
	F	25-24-56	14,351-26,744	NONE	1,176	829-70	704	57-68	148	199
Berea, Ohio (1,1)	P	38-30-40	29,516-39,331	Y-...-5	...	...-..	...	...-...	...	...
	F	23-23-51	29,510-39,378	Y-...-5	...	...-..	...	...-...	...	...
Berkeley Heights tp, N.J. (-,2)	P	27-23-40	34,281-43,185	Y-50,138-5	2,192	2,042-93	1,466	278-298	...	150
	F	...-..-..	...-...	..-...-..	...	...-..	...	...-...	...	...
Berkley, Mich. (4,4)	P	...-..-..	...-...	..-...-..	...	...-..	...	...-...	...	...
	F	...-..-..	...-...	..-...-..	...	...-..	...	...-...	...	...
Berlin t, Conn. (1,2)	P	45-37-40	31,237-38,000	Y-38,500-5	3,814	2,670-70	2,117	253-300	936	208
	F	...-..-..	...-...	..-...-..	...	...-..	...	...-...	876	...
Berlin, N.H. (1,3)	P	23-21-40	27,830-28,829	NONE	1,162	1,039-89	828	50-161	7	116
	F	23-21-42	25,050-25,990	Y-26,590-5	1,082	1,036-95	819	59-158	1	45

Table 3/22 continued POLICE AND FIRE DEPARTMENT PERSONNEL, SALARIES, AND EXPENDITURES FOR CITIES 10,000 AND OVER: 1994

City (Service provision)	Department	Total personnel, no. uniformed, duty hours per week	Entrance, maximum salary ($)	Longevity pay, maximum ($) no. years to receive longevity pay	Reported expenditures (in thousands)					
					Total expenditures (A) ($)	Total personnel expenditures (B) ($), % of (A)	Salaries and wages (C) ($)	City contrib. to employee retirement, insurance (D) ($)	Capital outlay (E) ($)	All other (F) ($)
10,000–24,999 continued										
Bethany, Okla. (1,1)	P	33-23-41	20,214-30,360	Y-...-5	1,276	1,143-89	849	141-153	28	105
	F	26-25-56	19,170-23,700	Y-...-5	1,192	888-74	685	79-124	249	55
Beverly Hills v, Mich. (4,4)	P	...-..-..	...-...	..-...-..	...	...-..	...	...-...	...	...
	F	...-..-..	...-...	..-...-..	...	...-..	...	...-...	...	...
Big Rapids, Mich. (1,3)	P	13-13-40	25,520-29,335	Y-30,055-5	...	...-..	...	...-...	12	...
	F	9-9-56	23,733-27,318	Y-28,018-5	...	...-..	...	...-...	83	...
Bloomingdale v, Ill. (1,5)	P	58-41-40	29,973-43,701	NONE	6,034	2,893-47	2,364	331-198	39	3,102
	F	...-..-..	...-...	..-...-..	...	...-..	...	...-...	...	...
Blue Ash, Ohio (1,1)	P	42-35-34	34,174-39,582	Y-...-3	...	...-..	...	...-...	4,339	...
	F	20-20-48	31,006-39,572	Y-...-3	...	...-..	...	...-...	4,525	...
Bogalusa, La. (1,1)	P	44-44-40	13,168-15,790	NONE	1,441	1,337-92	1,044	187-106	15	89
	F	36-36-55	13,168-15,790	NONE	...	...-..	...	...-...	8	...
Boone, Iowa (1,1)	P	14-14-42	22,626-28,667	Y-31,706-..	816	749-91	597	87-65	14	53
	F	13-13-53	22,045-27,943	Y-28,773-..	596	550-92	409	73-68	14	32
Boone t, N.C. (1,3)	P	31-31-42	19,828-28,013	NONE	1,220	949-77	779	115-55	64	207
	F	4-3-40	...-...	NONE	470	166-35	138	20-8	125	179
Borger, Tex. (1,1)	P	28-20-40	20,112-25,752	Y-...-1	1,239	931-75	750	107-74	113	195
	F	20-20-56	19,152-24,516	Y-...-1	770	695-90	564	77-54	...	75
Bothell, Wash. (1,3)	P	46-32-40	31,344-41,016	..-...-..	2,678	1,882-70	1,604	257-21	152	644
	F	35-32-40	29,328-41,916	Y-43,174-5	2,124	1,797-84	1,471	130-196	40	287
Boulder City, Nev. (9,9)	P	27-22-40	28,041-36,608	Y-40,269-6	1,832	1,619-88	1,202	274-143	42	171
	F	15-14-56	28,098-37,161	Y-40,877-6	...	...-..	...	...-...	26	...
Bourne t, Mass. (1,3)	P	35-32-37	21,276-28,891	Y-29,366-10	...	...-..	...	...-...	139	...
	F	26-25-42	21,270-29,365	NONE	...	...-..	...	...-...	...	...
Bozeman, Mont. (1,1)	P	30-27-40	19,308-27,696	Y-29,856-1	...	...-..	...	...-...	581	...
	F	25-24-48	19,290-28,260	Y-31,500-1	...	...-..	...	...-...	608	...
Brainerd, Minn. (1,3)	P	23-19-40	28,544-32,035	Y-33,079-10	1,287	1,005-78	753	163-89	34	248
	F	8-7-56	28,544-32,035	Y-33,079-10	...	...-..	...	...-...	488	...
Brentwood, Tenn. (1,1)	P	46-37-40	17,576-30,160	Y-...-5	1,938	1,578-81	1,319	211-48	96	264
	F	40-39-..	17,576-26,416	Y-...-5	2,032	1,291-63	1,072	182-37	268	473
Bridge View v, Ill. (1,3)	P	46-38-41	26,599-35,882	NONE	2,636	2,246-85	1,729	287-230	242	148
	F	35-34-48	26,120-41,046	NONE	2,362	2,136-90	1,718	243-175	100	126
Bridgeton, Mo. (1,5)	P	67-56-40	27,726-34,861	NONE	3,500	3,105-88	2,498	324-283	104	291
	F	...-..-..	...-...	..-...-..	...	...-..	...	...-...	...	...
Brigham City, Utah (1,2)	P	27-22-40	23,044-30,882	Y-...-1	...	...-..	...	...-...	64	...
	F	...-..-..	...-...	NONE	...	...-..	...	...-...	43	...
Brighton, Colo. (1,9)	P	38-28-44	23,940-35,370	NONE	11,668	4,276-36	3,614	250-412	3,570	3,822
	F	...-..-..	...-...	..-...-..	...	...-..	...	...-...	...	...
Bristol t, R.I. (1,3)	P	35-35-40	27,344-30,908	Y-32,917-5	...	...-..	...	...-...	75	...
	F	...-..-40	...-...	..-...-..	235	43-18	34	4-5	8	184
Brook Park, Ohio (1,1)	P	48-38-38	31,362-...	Y-...-5	2,917	2,499-85	1,870	321-308	191	227
	F	36-35-35	...-...	Y-...-5	2,670	2,489-93	1,836	402-251	59	122
Brownwood, Tex. (1,1)	P	41-29-40	19,320-21,312	Y-22,512-1	2,171	1,158-53	942	154-62	822	191
	F	30-30-56	18,828-20,700	Y-21,900-1	1,868	866-46	708	113-45	885	117
Brunswick, Ga. (1,1)	P	86-73-43	16,536-26,957	NONE	3,195	2,256-70	2,012	157-87	49	890
	F	43-42-53	16,536-26,957	NONE	1,724	1,360-78	1,224	93-43	23	341
Burleson, Tex. (1,2)	P	44-33-40	22,694-31,763	Y-32,963-1	1,624	1,342-82	1,102	135-105	18	264
	F	...-..-..	...-...	Y-...-1	...	...-..	...	...-...	8	...
Cadillac, Mich. (1,1)	P	20-16-42	26,103-29,148	Y-29,698-3	...	...-..	...	...-...	31	...
	F	11-11-56	24,450-27,136	Y-27,911-3	...	...-..	...	...-...	10	...
Cahokia v, Ill	P	35-26-40	25,235-28,524	Y-31,376-1	2,249	1,972-87	1,481	231-260	84	193
	F	...-..-..	...-...	..-...-..	...	...-..	...	...-...	...	...
Callaway, Fla. (1,3)	P	...-..-..	...-...	..-...-..	...	...-..	...	...-...	...	...
	F	11-11-48	15,400-22,564	NONE	389	273-70	222	27-24	61	55
Cambridge, Md. (1,2)	P	51-40-37	20,329-26,600	NONE	2,636	1,729-65	1,385	204-140	584	323
	F	...-..-..	...-...	..-...-..	...	...-..	...	...-...	...	...
Camden, Ark. (1,1)	P	40-29-43	17,110-19,246	NONE	1,987	1,163-58	900	88-175	687	137
	F	29-29-56	16,018-19,962	NONE	1,011	888-87	709	51-128	14	109
Canandaigua, N.Y. (1,3)	P	29-24-38	25,670-30,691	Y-31,391-5	2,435	1,379-56	1,109	165-105	907	149
	F	16-16-40	25,001-31,880	Y-32,630-5	1,825	848-46	670	100-78	868	109
Canyon, Tex. (1,3)	P	17-15-40	19,944-26,820	Y-28,020-1	661	559-84	437	71-51	25	77
	F	4-3-40	18,984-25,536	Y-26,736-1	...	...-..	...	...-...	11	...
Carlisle b, Pa. (1,2)	P	36-30-40	24,732-31,446	Y-...-4	1,760	1,478-83	1,283	93-102	169	113
	F	...-..-..	...-...	NONE	...	...-..	...	...-...	171	...
Carlsbad, N.M. (1,1)	P	70-56-40	18,137-28,038	NONE	...	...-..	...	...-...	207	...
	F	38-38-56	19,600-25,637	NONE	2,291	2,082-90	1,794	278-10	72	137
Carpentersville v, Ill. (1,5)	P	...-..-40	30,924-41,592	Y-42,272-1	3,251	1,586-48	1,189	233-164	77	1,588
	F	...-..-..	...-...	..-...-..	...	...-..	...	...-...	...	...
Carrboro t, N.C. (1,3)	P	27-25-42	22,548-34,147	Y-...-5	1,064	932-87	761	103-68	31	101
	F	13-13-56	19,478-34,147	Y-...-5	558	419-75	353	44-22	61	78
Carrollton, Ga. (1,1)	P	62-51-43	16,936-26,097	NONE	2,923	1,874-64	1,445	190-239	644	405
	F	44-44-53	16,083-24,903	NONE	1,824	1,055-57	782	102-171	663	106
Carteret b, N.J. (1,3)	P	50-41-40	33,401-41,924	Y-46,955-4	4,264	3,759-88	2,845	374-540	265	240
	F	16-15-42	32,640-41,924	Y-46,955-4	1,443	1,295-89	980	129-186	28	120

Table 3/22 continued POLICE AND FIRE DEPARTMENT PERSONNEL, SALARIES, AND EXPENDITURES FOR CITIES 10,000 AND OVER: 1994

City (Service provision)	Department	Total personnel, no. uniformed, duty hours per week	Entrance, maximum salary ($)	Longevity pay, maximum ($) no. years to receive longevity pay	Reported expenditures (in thousands)					
					Total expenditures (A) ($)	Total personnel expenditures (B) ($), % of (A)	Salaries and wages (C) ($)	City contrib. to employee retirement, insurance (D) ($)	Capital outlay (E) ($)	All other (F) ($)
10,000–24,999 continued										
Cartersville, Ga. (4,4)	P	...-...-..	...-...	..-...-..	...	...-..	...	...-...	...	...
	F	...-...-..	...-...	..-...-..	...	...-..	...	...-...	...	...
Casa Grande, Ariz. (1,1)	P	60-42-40	25,992-35,808	NONE	3,044	2,537-83	2,077	283-177	119	388
	F	19-17-56	21,612-35,808	NONE	1,381	985-71	899	40-46	180	216
Casselberry, Fla. (1,1)	P	52-52-40	21,595-31,358	Y-32,926-10	...	...-..	...	...-...	103	...
	F	20-20-56	20,808-30,188	Y-31,697-10	...	...-..	...	...-...	33	...
Cedar City, Utah (1,3)	P	20-17-40	21,300-33,630	NONE	1,068	761-71	544	113-104	46	261
	F	2-2-40	22,512-35,550	NONE	211	172-81	140	19-13	5	34
Centerville, Ohio (1,9)	P	39-31-40	27,830-37,294	Y-37,694-6	...	...-..	...	...-...	...	...
	F	...-...-..	...-...	..-...-..	...	...-..	...	...-...	...	...
Centerville, Utah (1,6)	P	12-10-43	21,672-31,368	NONE	621	536-86	413	69-54	43	42
	F	...-...-..	...-...	...-...	...	...-..	...	...-...	...	...
Centralia, Wash. (3,1)	P	28-24-40	30,036-36,780	Y-37,620-2	...	...-..	...	...-...	...	...
	F	16-16-42	32,436-39,456	NONE	...	...-..	...	...-...	...	...
Chambersburg b, Pa. (1,3)	P	25-25-40	24,398-30,202	NONE	1,613	1,323-82	1,001	215-107	1	289
	F	19-19-56	21,312-28,120	NONE	...	...-..	...	...-...	42	...
Champlin, Minn. (3,9)	P	20-19-40	25,221-38,925	Y-42,428-16	1,484	1,091-73	890	112-89	191	202
	F	...-...-..	...-...	..-...-..	...	...-..	...	...-...	...	...
Charleston, Ill. (1,1)	P	29-29-40	20,700-34,584	Y-...-1	1,558	1,408-90	1,126	174-108	61	89
	F	33-33-53	20,328-33,576	Y-...-1	1,740	1,527-87	1,175	242-110	142	71
Chicago Ridge v, Ill. (1,3)	P	30-27-40	28,326-36,911	Y-42,803-4	3,807	1,861-48	1,542	118-201	30	1,916
	F	15-15-48	28,326-36,911	Y-42,803-4	1,736	806-46	661	50-95	2	928
Chickasha, Okla. (1,1)	P	40-30-40	14,747-21,826	Y-22,330-1	1,098	990-90	827	130-33	66	42
	F	40-39-56	17,156-24,684	Y-25,104-1	1,233	1,206-97	1,038	137-31	4	23
Chillicothe, Ohio (1,1)	P	56-50-40	21,632-27,810	Y-28,610-2	7,884	2,466-31	1,860	330-276	2,555	2,863
	F	50-49-56	20,908-25,422	Y-26,672-5	...	...-..	...	...-...	2,576	...
Christiansburg t, Va. (1,2)	P	36-28-40	19,000-25,000	Y-26,000-14	...	...-..	...	...-...	3	...
	F	...-...-..	...-...	..-...-..	...	...-..	...	...-...	253	...
Circleville, Ohio (1,3)	P	31-22-40	20,560-24,668	Y-...-5	...	...-..	...	...-...	1,422	...
	F	19-19-56	20,820-23,820	Y-...-5	...	...-..	...	...-...	1,730	...
Claremont, N.H. (1,1)	P	25-24-40	23,000-28,000	Y-28,450-..	1,367	905-66	861	38-6	326	136
	F	23-22-42	24,190-25,187	Y-26,137-..	999	778-77	720	53-5	...	221
Clarksdale, Miss. (1,1)	P	49-39-40	18,690-21,855	Y-24,041-3	1,606	1,242-77	1,007	162-73	96	268
	F	54-53-48	16,980-20,063	Y-22,069-3	1,573	1,417-90	1,198	138-81	18	138
Clawson, Mich. (1,3)	P	23-21-40	25,000-41,016	NONE	1,725	1,593-92	1,195	169-229	41	91
	F	...-...-..	...-...	...-...	173	54-31	43	5-6	88	31
Cleburne, Tex. (1,1)	P	52-38-40	23,148-27,456	Y-32,256-1	10,946	2,084-19	1,609	293-182	366	8,496
	F	43-41-56	22,031-25,501	Y-30,301-1	10,946	1,650-15	1,358	131-161	257	9,039
Clinton t, Mass. (1,3)	P	24-23-38	22,395-28,711	Y-29,261-5	...	...-..	...	...-...	...	...
	F	25-25-..	17,640-26,460	Y-27,560-5	...	...-..	...	...-...	...	...
Coatesville, Pa. (1,3)	P	22-19-..	26,895-32,905	Y-34,905-5	1,321	1,069-80	868	61-140	47	205
	F	4-..-..	...-...	..-...-..	...	...-..	...	...-...	9	...
Cocoa, Fla. (1,1)	P	78-50-40	20,571-29,037	NONE	3,297	2,746-83	2,057	457-232	236	315
	F	41-41-50	20,228-28,288	NONE	...	...-..	...	...-...	295	...
Coeur D'Alene, Idaho (1,3)	P	57-46-40	25,128-34,500	NONE	2,696	2,490-92	1,875	317-298	73	133
	F	25-24-56	21,924-31,056	NONE	...	...-..	...	...-...	116	...
Coffeyville, Kan. (1,1)	P	31-20-40	20,696-24,003	NONE	1,746	1,091-62	844	146-101	531	124
	F	19-19-56	20,702-24,615	NONE	1,279	726-56	549	106-71	510	43
Cohoes, N.Y. (1,1)	P	32-29-40	23,264-33,042	Y-33,692-5	...	...-..	...	...-...	40	...
	F	49-42-40	22,354-25,590	Y-26,410-5	...	...-..	...	...-...	...	...
College Park, Ga. (1,1)	P	94-79-42	21,537-32,305	NONE	5,617	3,581-63	2,895	334-352	1,577	459
	F	61-60-53	21,537-32,305	NONE	3,951	2,416-61	1,958	230-228	1,361	174
College Park, Md. (7,2)	P	...-...-..	...-...	..-...-..	...	...-..	...	...-...	...	...
	F	...-...-..	...-...	..-...-..	...	...-..	...	...-...	...	...
Collierville t, Tenn. (3,3)	P	48-34-41	20,268-28,217	NONE	1,881	1,586-84	1,234	162-190	115	180
	F	28-27-56	20,347-27,529	NONE	1,365	1,152-84	896	122-134	74	139
Collingswood b, N.J. (1,3)	P	28-26-54	30,296-38,322	Y-40,238-5	1,603	1,484-92	1,211	123-150	58	61
	F	9-9-54	30,296-37,604	Y-39,484-5	555	496-89	388	54-54	28	31
Collinsville, Ill. (1,1)	P	44-34-40	34,630-34,948	Y-38,102-2	2,377	1,868-78	1,625	63-180	97	412
	F	25-25-42	29,624-34,979	Y-37,786-4	1,473	1,236-83	1,113	3-120	44	193
Colonial Heights, Va. (3,3)	P	49-36-42	...-...	Y-34,720-10	2,154	1,899-88	1,453	276-170	54	201
	F	14-2-40	21,315-29,993	Y-34,720-10	...	...-..	...	...-...	18	...
Columbus, Miss. (1,1)	P	66-57-40	19,703-21,319	Y-...-1	2,364	1,984-83	1,649	241-94	64	316
	F	62-62-56	19,703-21,319	Y-...-1	2,245	2,060-91	1,711	258-91	36	149
Commerce, Calif. (7,7)	P	...-...-..	...-...	..-...-..	...	...-..	...	...-...	...	...
	F	...-...-..	...-...	..-...-..	...	...-..	...	...-...	...	...
Concord t, Mass. (1,1)	P	36-30-40	26,008-34,118	Y-34,718-5	...	...-..	...	...-...	85	...
	F	35-34-42	25,531-32,584	Y-33,184-5	...	...-..	...	...-...	30	...
Connersville, Ind. (1,1)	P	33-32-40	20,786-25,983	Y-27,183-1	1,384	1,302-94	986	111-205	20	62
	F	40-40-56	24,930-25,430	Y-27,210-1	1,599	1,434-89	1,146	67-221	100	65
Cooper City, Fla. (1,1)	P	57-43-40	28,462-40,000	Y-40,750-5	3,716	2,487-66	2,115	272-100	1,076	153
	F	25-24-48	25,574-37,042	Y-37,792-5	1,212	1,081-89	917	108-56	80	51
Coos Bay, Ore. (1,1)	P	28-28-40	24,060-30,708	Y-...-10	2,587	1,434-55	1,076	216-142	1,022	131
	F	18-18-48	22,920-29,256	..-...-..	2,016	799-39	595	121-83	1,070	147

Table 3/22 continued POLICE AND FIRE DEPARTMENT PERSONNEL, SALARIES, AND EXPENDITURES FOR CITIES 10,000 AND OVER: 1994

City (Service provision)	Department	Total personnel, no. uniformed, duty hours per week	Entrance, maximum salary ($)	Longevity pay, maximum ($) no. years to receive longevity pay	Reported expenditures (in thousands)					
					Total expenditures (A) ($)	Total personnel expenditures (B) ($), % of (A)	Salaries and wages (C) ($)	City contrib. to employee retirement, insurance (D) ($)	Capital outlay (E) ($)	All other (F) ($)
10,000–24,999 continued										
Coppell, Tex. (1,1)	P	31-29-40	27,159-32,461	Y-38,790-..	1,528	1,282-83	1,148	67-67	112	134
	F	39-38-..	24,917-29,781	Y-38,790-..	1,626	1,425-87	1,280	74-71	22	179
Copperas Cove, Tex. (1,3)	P	65-48-40	20,552-21,374	Y-21,662-1	1,725	1,447-83	1,214	171-62	20	258
	F	40-40-56	19,236-21,305	Y-21,593-1	1,243	1,031-82	866	123-42	22	190
Coralville, Iowa (1,2)	P	25-22-40	21,886-32,236	NONE	3,595	981-27	751	121-109	2,383	231
	F	..-..-..	...-...	..-..-..	...	...-..	...	...-...	214	...
Corcoran, Calif. (1,7)	P	21-21-40	23,736-29,708	..-..-..	1,173	920-78	674	109-137	...	253
	F	..-..-..	...-...	..-..-..	...	...-..	...	...-...	...	...
Cordele, Ga. (1,1)	P	33-28-42	13,825-21,818	NONE	2,151	884-41	739	88-57	985	282
	F	23-23-58	13,615-21,477	NONE	1,355	487-35	394	50-43	777	91
Corsicana, Tex. (1,-)	P	48-39-40	22,704-23,628	Y-25,540-1	2,575	1,690-65	1,327	206-157	253	632
	F	37-35-36	22,704-23,628	Y-25,540-1	...	...-..	...	...-...	11	...
Cortland, N.Y. (1,3)	P	...-3-40	...-...	NONE	...	...-..	...	...-...	1,919	...
	F	...-1-56	...-...	NONE	...	...-..	...	...-...	1,831	...
Country Club Hills, Ill. (1,5)	P	30-23-40	28,128-38,513	Y-41,305-5	1,682	1,399-83	1,079	191-129	83	200
	F	..-..-..	...-...	..-..-..	...	...-..	...	...-...	...	...
Coventry t, Conn. (1,2)	P	15-10-40	32,406-35,901	Y-37,401-..	962	786-81	592	117-77	150	26
	F	..-..-..	...-...	..-..-..	...	...-..	...	...-...	140	...
Covington, Ga. (1,1)	P	46-38-40	18,470-29,411	NONE	...	...-..	...	...-...	150	...
	F	30-29-56	19,481-31,012	NONE	...	...-..	...	...-...	134	...
Cranberry tp, Pa. (1,2)	P	17-15-40	34,105-37,105	Y-...-4	1,190	899-75	680	106-113	184	107
	F	..-..-..	...-...	..-..-..	...	...-..	...	...-...	238	...
Crawfordsville, Ind. (1,1)	P	42-28-40	21,876-29,697	Y-...-2	1,413	1,258-89	992	130-136	41	114
	F	36-35-56	21,871-...	Y-28,761-1	1,285	1,164-90	888	137-139	23	98
Crest Hill, Ill. (1,-)	P	25-18-40	29,161-37,606	Y-38,386-6	2,723	1,228-45	992	81-155	120	1,375
	F	..-..-..	...-...	..-..-..	...	...-..	...	...-...	...	...
Creve Coeur, Mo	P	48-38-40	32,712-41,856	Y-...-1	...	...-..	...	...-...	...	...
	F	..-..-..	...-...	..-..-..	...	...-..	...	...-...	...	...
Crystal, Minn. (1,9)	P	29-25-40	25,740-39,564	Y-43,124-4	2,139	1,835-85	1,501	181-153	120	184
	F	..-..-..	...-...	..-..-..	...	...-..	...	...-...	75	...
Cudahy, Calif. (9,7)	P	..-..-..	...-...	..-..-..	...	...-..	...	...-...	...	...
	F	..-..-..	...-...	..-..-..	...	...-..	...	...-...	...	...
Cumberland, Md. (1,1)	P	60-55-40	20,873-25,258	NONE	2,320	2,027-87	1,624	140-263	18	275
	F	64-63-40	18,793-25,264	NONE	2,360	2,198-93	1,621	269-308	8	154
Daphne t, Ala. (1,3)	P	35-26-40	19,406-27,581	NONE	1,610	1,199-74	949	110-140	119	292
	F	5-5-40	19,406-27,581	NONE	...	...-..	...	...-...	119	...
Darien, Ill. (1,-)	P	32-4-40	26,000-37,666	Y-41,056-11	3,330	1,640-49	1,490	47-103	493	1,197
	F	..-..-..	...-...	..-..-..	...	...-..	...	...-...	...	...
De Land, Fla. (1,1)	P	79-55-42	18,886-27,643	Y-28,243-8	4,625	2,607-56	2,131	295-181	1,694	324
	F	24-23-56	17,992-26,325	Y-26,925-8	2,680	947-35	745	136-66	1,616	117
De Pere, Wis. (1,3)	P	30-25-38	26,952-36,444	Y-36,924-5	...	...-..	...	...-...	53	...
	F	28-28-56	26,913-35,280	Y-35,760-5	...	...-..	...	...-...	565	...
Decatur, Ga. (1,1)	P	55-42-40	21,195-29,827	NONE	3,212	2,109-65	1,823	127-159	709	394
	F	40-40-56	21,195-29,827	NONE	2,324	1,623-69	1,427	81-115	607	94
Defiance, Ohio (1,3)	P	28-22-40	22,444-30,756	Y-31,956-5	2,189	1,190-54	903	167-120	730	269
	F	18-18-56	22,909-28,933	Y-30,133-5	...	...-..	...	...-...	756	...
Del City, Okla. (1,1)	P	46-34-40	19,926-25,833	Y-26,433-5	1,608	1,470-91	1,113	177-180	35	103
	F	28-28-72	23,025-31,251	NONE	1,202	1,113-92	997	104-12	45	44
Delano, Calif. (1,7)	P	42-26-40	25,812-31,380	Y-32,340-7	2,328	1,981-85	1,651	209-121	1	346
	F	..-..-..	...-...	..-..-..	...	...-..	...	...-...	...	...
Delaware, Ohio (1,1)	P	41-29-40	26,374-32,989	Y-33,489-5	...	...-..	...	...-...	20	...
	F	32-31-50	24,427-30,588	Y-31,788-5	...	...-..	...	...-...	39	...
Dennis t, Mass. (1,1)	P	42-33-40	26,973-29,752	Y-30,097-5	...	...-..	...	...-...	65	...
	F	28-27-40	24,477-28,549	Y-28,799-5	...	...-..	...	...-...	54	...
Depew v, N.Y. (1,2)	P	39-29-40	22,000-38,768	NONE	2,028	1,930-95	1,555	205-170	26	72
	F	..-..-..	...-...	..-..-..	...	...-..	...	...-...	...	...
Derby, Conn. (1,2)	P	29-29-40	40,115-...	Y-...-..	...	...-..	...	...-...	...	...
	F	..-..-..	...-...	..-..-..	...	...-..	...	...-...	...	...
Derby, Kan. (1,2)	P	35-25-40	20,760-...	Y-...-5	...	...-..	...	...-...	...	...
	F	..-..-..	...-...	..-..-..	...	...-..	...	...-...	...	...
Derry tp, Pa. (1,2)	P	37-30-40	25,378-33,837	Y-34,487-5	2,382	1,564-65	1,241	167-156	592	226
	F	..-..-..	...-...	..-..-..	...	...-..	...	...-...	...	...
Des Moines, Wash. (3,7)	P	37-27-40	29,044-41,964	..-..-..	...	...-..	...	...-...	417	...
	F	..-..-..	...-...	..-..-..	...	...-..	...	...-...	...	...
Desert Hot Springs, Calif. (7,7)	P	..-..-..	...-...	..-..-..	...	...-..	...	...-...	...	...
	F	..-..-..	...-...	..-..-..	...	...-..	...	...-...	...	...
Dickinson, N.D. (1,3)	P	34-24-40	20,340-22,440	Y-23,880-5	1,213	1,067-87	786	161-120	32	114
	F	3-3-40	20,340-22,440	Y-23,880-5	...	...-..	...	...-...	3	...
Dixon, Calif. (3,3)	P	19-16-40	29,148-35,436	NONE	...	...-..	...	...-...	22	...
	F	4-4-40	25,992-31,584	NONE	443	229-51	188	26-15	5	209
Dodge City, Kan. (1,1)	P	47-36-42	19,726-27,103	Y-28,103-1	...	...-..	...	...-...	435	...
	F	22-22-56	17,584-27,103	Y-...-1	...	...-..	...	...-...	402	...
Douglas, Ariz. (1,1)	P	48-36-40	21,236-26,751	NONE	1,664	1,488-89	1,181	75-232	2	174
	F	23-22-56	21,236-26,751	NONE	1,051	879-83	688	80-111	96	76

Table 3/22 continued POLICE AND FIRE DEPARTMENT PERSONNEL, SALARIES, AND EXPENDITURES FOR CITIES 10,000 AND OVER: 1994

City (Service provision)	Department	Total personnel, no. uniformed, duty hours per week	Entrance, maximum salary ($)	Longevity pay, maximum ($) no. years to receive longevity pay	Reported expenditures (in thousands)					
					Total expenditures (A) ($)	Total personnel expenditures (B) ($), % of (A)	Salaries and wages (C) ($)	City contrib. to employee retirement, insurance (D) ($)	Capital outlay (E) ($)	All other (F) ($)
10,000–24,999 continued										
Douglas, Ga. (1,3)	P	46-38-43	15,600-19,760	NONE	1,463	1,111-75	887	149-75	116	236
	F	29-29-56	15,080-19,240	NONE	926	824-88	668	106-50	28	74
Dover, Ohio (1,1)	P	19-16-40	27,425-...	Y-28,025-7	1,829	852-46	739	18-95	842	135
	F	13-13-56	21,679-24,431	Y-24,806-5	1,479	612-41	508	47-57	823	44
Doylestown tp, Pa. (1,2)	P	20-17-40	28,145-39,500	Y-...-1	1,402	1,226-87	880	146-200	63	113
	F	...-..-..	...-...	..-...-..	...	...-..	...	...-...	...	...
Duarte, Calif. (7,7)	P	...-..-..	...-...	..-...-..	...	...-..	...	...-...	...	...
	F	...-..-..	...-...	..-...-..	...	...-..	...	...-...	...	...
Dublin, Calif. (9,9)	P	...-..-..	...-...	..-...-..	...	...-..	...	...-...	...	...
	F	...-..-..	...-...	..-...-..	...	...-..	...	...-...	...	...
Dublin, Ohio (1,9)	P	55-41-40	26,971-40,186	Y-41,111-4	5,997	2,731-45	2,079	316-336	3,003	263
	F	...-..-..	...-...	..-...-..	...	...-..	...	...-...	...	...
Dumont b, N.J. (1,2)	P	36-33-40	22,465-49,142	Y-...-4	2,677	2,550-95	2,083	257-210	...	127
	F	...-..-..	...-...	..-...-..	...	...-..	...	...-...	...	...
Duncan, Okla. (1,1)	P	50-43-..	15,995-26,062	NONE	2,056	1,752-85	1,455	217-80	97	207
	F	41-40-..	15,226-24,794	NONE	1,308	1,238-94	1,051	117-70	13	57
Durango, Colo. (1,1)	P	50-32-40	20,696-31,241	NONE	2,031	1,605-79	1,313	127-165	48	378
	F	16-15-56	19,656-29,931	NONE	771	630-81	528	47-55	31	110
Durham t, N.H. (1,1)	P	16-14-40	25,272-29,848	Y-30,448-5	...	...-..	...	...-...	...	...
	F	18-17-42	19,000-24,000	Y-24,600-5	...	...-..	...	...-...	...	...
Dyersburg, Tenn. (1,1)	P	58-47-40	19,645-23,054	NONE	3,374	1,630-48	1,334	151-145	1,401	343
	F	50-49-48	18,018-22,613	NONE	3,111	1,541-49	1,265	139-137	1,354	216
East Goshen tp, Pa. (6,6)	P	...-..-..	...-...	..-...-..	...	...-..	...	...-...	...	...
	F	...-..-..	...-...	..-...-..	...	...-..	...	...-...	...	...
Lake Station, Ind. (1,2)	P	24-19-40	22,165-27,539	Y-27,959-3	1,087	801-73	617	69-115	191	95
	F	...-..-..	...-...	..-...-..	...	...-..	...	...-...	...	...
East Grand Rapids, Mich. (4,4)	P	...-..-..	...-...	..-...-..	...	...-..	...	...-...	...	...
	F	...-..-..	...-...	..-...-..	...	...-..	...	...-...	...	...
East Greenwich t, R.I	P	36-8-37	25,155-29,739	Y-31,077-3	...	...-..	...	...-...	...	...
	F	...-..-..	...-...	..-...-..	...	...-..	...	...-...	...	...
East Liverpool, Ohio (1,1)	P	22-22-40	17,971-28,745	Y-29,405-3	1,217	1,088-89	802	116-170	...	129
	F	32-32-..	21,031-29,371	Y-30,031-3	...	...-..	...	...-...	...	...
East Longmeadow t, Mass. (1,3)	P	23-21-40	27,089-28,794	Y-29,350-5	1,261	1,152-91	992	70-90	29	80
	F	8-8-40	25,564-27,585	Y-28,135-5	704	381-54	327	22-32	284	39
East Norriton tp, Pa. (1,2)	P	21-16-40	34,555-43,513	Y-45,036-5	...	...-..	...	...-...	41	...
	F	...-..-..	...-...	..-...-..	...	...-..	...	...-...	...	...
East Pennsboro tp, Pa. (1,2)	P	15-15-40	26,517-33,782	Y-35,582-1	857	722-84	551	100-71	49	86
	F	...-..-..	...-...	..-...-..	...	...-..	...	...-...	1	...
East Rockaway v, N.Y. (7,2)	P	...-..-..	...-...	..-...-..	...	...-..	...	...-...	...	...
	F	...-..-..	...-...	..-...-..	...	...-..	...	...-...	146	...
East Windsor t, Conn. (1,2)	P	22-17-40	28,273-36,556	Y-37,256-5	1,275	1,023-80	823	78-122	41	211
	F	...-..-..	...-...	..-...-..	...	...-..	...	...-...	...	...
East Windsor tp, N.J. (1,2)	P	69-45-..	29,097-45,833	Y-47,779-5	...	...-..	...	...-...	...	...
	F	...-..-..	...-...	..-...-..	...	...-..	...	...-...	...	...
Easton t, Mass. (1,1)	P	30-29-40	26,053-32,198	Y-...-5	...	...-..	...	...-...	49	...
	F	31-30-40	22,358-29,930	Y-...-5	...	...-..	...	...-...	42	...
Eden, N.C. (1,3)	P	49-44-40	18,469-24,751	Y-25,800-5	1,992	1,448-72	1,151	213-84	198	346
	F	17-17-53	18,469-24,751	Y-25,800-5	683	496-72	401	60-35	12	175
Edgewater, Fla. (3,3)	P	39-29-42	21,063-29,488	NONE	2,153	1,415-65	1,113	195-107	462	276
	F	11-10-42	20,021-28,030	NONE	1,056	420-39	343	45-32	433	203
Edwardsville, Ill. (1,3)	P	32-23-40	30,846-31,470	Y-32,614-5	...	...-..	...	...-...	275	...
	F	19-19-56	26,150-32,381	Y-33,226-5	...	...-..	...	...-...	173	...
Egg Harbor tp, N.J. (1,2)	P	84-65-40	26,999-46,659	Y-48,992-2	...	...-..	...	...-...	3,536	...
	F	...-..-..	...-...	..-...-..	...	...-..	...	...-...	...	...
El Cerrito, Calif. (1,1)	P	42-32-40	39,780-47,172	NONE	...	...-..	...	...-...	56	...
	F	27-26-56	40,674-48,228	NONE	2,295	2,057-89	1,607	343-107	51	187
El Dorado, Ark. (1,1)	P	55-9-40	20,005-25,530	NONE	2,476	1,990-80	1,693	188-109	...	486
	F	50-45-56	22,410-25,525	NONE	2,451	1,953-79	1,677	168-108	...	498
El Dorado, Kan. (4,4)	P	...-..-..	...-...	..-...-..	...	...-..	...	...-...	...	...
	F	...-..-..	...-...	..-...-..	...	...-..	...	...-...	...	...
El Paso De Robles, Calif. (1,3)	P	35-29-40	29,424-36,876	NONE	...	...-..	...	...-...	2,628	...
	F	5-..-56	27,108-34,416	NONE	...	...-..	...	...-...	...	...
El Reno, Okla. (1,1)	P	25-20-40	18,839-20,493	Y-...-3	1,115	836-74	665	107-64	154	125
	F	20-20-53	18,972-19,392	Y-...-3	697	592-84	496	51-45	20	85
El Segundo, Calif. (3,1)	P	86-61-40	37,638-50,832	NONE	7,660	6,272-81	5,092	561-619	152	1,236
	F	65-58-56	37,272-45,312	NONE	5,834	5,175-88	4,302	401-472	22	637
Elizabeth City, N.C. (1,1)	P	44-37-40	19,383-26,526	NONE	1,549	1,226-79	990	162-74	77	246
	F	38-37-56	19,383-26,526	NONE	1,703	1,171-68	935	165-71	234	298
Elizabethton, Tenn. (1,1)	P	33-33-40	17,185-26,137	Y-26,633-..	...	...-..	...	...-...	...	...
	F	26-26-56	17,185-26,137	Y-26,633-..	...	...-..	...	...-...	...	...
Elko, Nev. (1,1)	P	49-33-40	28,236-35,100	Y-47,100-8	...	...-..	...	...-...	100	...
	F	18-18-56	31,368-33,360	Y-45,360-8	...	...-..	...	...-...	48	...
Ellensburg, Wash. (1,1)	P	26-26-40	24,624-35,052	..-...-..	1,324	1,123-84	844	122-157	2	199
	F	19-18-56	23,136-28,920	..-...-..	1,132	951-84	775	59-117	48	133

Table 3/22 continued **POLICE AND FIRE DEPARTMENT PERSONNEL, SALARIES, AND EXPENDITURES FOR CITIES 10,000 AND OVER: 1994**

City (Service provision)	Depart-ment	Total personnel, no. uniformed, duty hours per week	Entrance, maximum salary ($)	Longevity pay, maximum ($) no. years to receive longevity pay	Total expendi-tures (A) ($)	Total personnel expendi-tures (B) ($), % of (A)	Salaries and wages (C) ($)	City contrib. to employee retirement, insurance (D) ($)	Capital outlay (E) ($)	All other (F) ($)
10,000–24,999 continued										
Ellington t, Conn. (6,2)	P	...-..-..	...-...	..-...-..	...	...-...	...	...-...	...	...
	F	...-..-..	...-...	..-...-..	...	...-...	...	...-...	...	...
Elmwood Park v, Ill. (1,1)	P	42-30-40	30,351-38,340	Y-41,407-3	2,224	2,113-95	1,576	353-184	91	20
	F	22-21-53	26,506-38,523	Y-41,605-3	...	...-...	...	...-...	73	...
Englewood, Ohio (1,9)	P	21-16-40	26,707-34,050	NONE	1,281	920-71	741	101-78	2	359
	F	...-..-..	...-...	..-...-..	...	...-...	...	...-...	...	...
Ennis, Tex. (1,1)	P	32-25-40	20,738-25,916	Y-27,632-1	1,363	1,176-86	949	130-97	53	134
	F	27-26-53	18,450-26,425	Y-28,141-1	1,029	944-91	763	103-78	18	67
Erlanger, Ky. (1,2)	P	33-27-40	19,552-26,676	NONE	...	...-...	...	...-...	57	...
	F	...-..-..	...-...	..-...-..	...	...-...	...	...-...	38	...
Escanaba, Mich. (4,4)	P	...-..-..	...-...	..-...-..	...	...-...	...	...-...	...	...
	F	...-..-..	...-...	..-...-..	...	...-...	...	...-...	...	...
Eufaula, Ala. (1,1)	P	38-7-40	14,893-20,238	NONE	...	...-...	...	...-...	...	...
	F	27-26-53	14,607-18,707	NONE	...	...-...	...	...-...	...	...
Eunice, La. (3,3)	P	37-35-42	18,600-21,000	NONE	1,060	786-74	640	106-40	74	200
	F	19-19-51	18,400-22,500	NONE	557	404-72	350	30-24	25	128
Eustis, Fla. (1,3)	P	43-32-42	19,822-29,203	Y-...-..	1,904	1,141-59	966	104-71	638	125
	F	15-14-53	17,992-27,361	Y-30,659-3	648	542-83	448	64-30	42	64
Evergreen Park v, Ill. (1,3)	P	67-50-40	27,436-40,636	Y-40,781-..	3,951	3,698-93	2,807	516-375	88	165
	F	...-..-..	...-...	Y-...-..	1,212	957-78	827	100-30	46	209
Fairfax, Va. (1,3)	P	71-58-40	28,579-44,336	NONE	...	...-...	...	...-...	116	...
	F	57-51-56	27,218-42,225	NONE	...	...-...	...	...-...	65	...
Fairhaven t, Mass. (1,3)	P	28-27-40	23,170-26,565	Y-27,415-10	1,358	1,175-86	1,027	56-92	74	109
	F	19-18-42	24,381-26,168	Y-27,346-10	772	702-90	629	36-37	14	56
Fairmont, Minn. (1,2)	P	18-16-40	25,920-27,368	Y-30,025-25	...	...-...	...	...-...	490	...
	F	...-..-..	...-...	..-...-..	...	...-...	...	...-...	652	...
Fairmont, W.Va. (1,1)	P	37-30-40	18,711-20,838	Y-21,538-..	...	...-...	...	...-...	43	...
	F	39-38-40	17,992-20,037	Y-20,737-..	...	...-...	...	...-...	5	...
Fairview tp, Pa. (1,3)	P	14-13-40	28,520-36,451	Y-38,851-4	...	...-...	...	...-...	99	...
	F	4-4-40	17,680-...	..-...-..	...	...-...	...	...-...	...	...
Fairview Heights, Ill. (1,-)	P	48-37-42	31,219-34,127	Y-39,929-3	2,072	2,005-96	1,796	189-20	56	11
	F	...-..-..	...-...	..-...-..	...	...-...	...	...-...	...	...
Farmers Branch, Tex. (1,1)	P	81-67-40	32,760-35,736	Y-37,236-..	4,292	3,728-86	2,982	306-440	100	464
	F	62-58-56	32,760-35,736	Y-37,236-..	4,887	3,203-65	2,598	272-333	1,110	574
Farmington, Mich. (4,4)	P	...-..-..	...-...	..-...-..	...	...-...	...	...-...	...	...
	F	...-..-..	...-...	..-...-..	...	...-...	...	...-...	...	...
Farragut t, Tenn. (7,9)	P	...-..-..	...-...	..-...-..	...	...-...	...	...-...	...	...
	F	...-..-..	...-...	..-...-..	...	...-...	...	...-...	...	...
Ferguson, Mo. (1,1)	P	58-51-40	27,285-35,471	..-...-..	2,810	2,197-78	1,778	178-241	91	522
	F	25-25-56	24,694-32,090	..-...-..	1,224	1,006-82	827	77-102	...	218
Florence, Ky. (1,3)	P	46-42-40	20,919-33,212	NONE	...	...-...	...	...-...	146	...
	F	21-20-56	19,019-33,212	NONE	...	...-...	...	...-...	664	...
Flower Mound t, Tex. (1,3)	P	41-32-40	24,097-35,772	Y-...-1	...	...-...	...	...-...	159	...
	F	26-25-53	24,097-39,480	Y-...-1	...	...-...	...	...-...	187	...
Forest Grove, Ore. (1,3)	P	22-22-40	28,356-35,448	NONE	1,156	901-77	711	130-60	5	250
	F	13-12-56	28,596-35,748	..-...-..	879	624-70	488	89-47	27	228
Forest Hill, Tex. (1,1)	P	26-16-..	22,200-36,000	Y-51,876-..	2,029	1,272-62	963	130-179	253	504
	F	15-13-..	22,200-36,000	Y-51,876-..	1,289	597-46	452	61-84	188	504
Forest Park, Ga. (4,4)	P	...-..-..	...-...	..-...-..	...	...-...	...	...-...	...	...
	F	...-..-..	...-...	..-...-..	...	...-...	...	...-...	...	...
Forest Park v, Ill. (1,1)	P	50-34-40	28,445-41,643	NONE	...	...-...	...	...-...	...	...
	F	23-23-..	24,297-40,297	NONE	...	...-...	...	...-...	...	...
Fort Atkinson, Wis. (1,3)	P	23-18-40	29,100-32,844	Y-33,344-2	...	...-...	...	...-...	148	...
	F	4-4-55	28,116-31,008	Y-31,508-2	...	...-...	...	...-...	64	...
Fort Madison, Iowa (1,1)	P	27-22-40	18,075-24,502	Y-25,522-5	954	867-90	739	62-66	...	87
	F	20-20-56	17,216-24,020	Y-24,740-5	718	661-92	568	45-48	...	57
Fostoria, Ohio (1,1)	P	29-24-40	25,084-34,153	Y-36,885-5	1,596	1,427-89	1,159	163-105	14	155
	F	17-17-52	21,153-30,180	Y-32,595-5	894	783-87	631	100-52	24	87
Fountain Hills t, Ariz. (7,8)	P	...-..-..	...-...	..-...-..	...	...-...	...	...-...	...	...
	F	...-..-..	...-...	..-...-..	...	...-...	...	...-...	...	...
Frankfort, Ind. (1,1)	P	39-26-40	24,659-...	NONE	1,563	1,137-72	899	65-173	125	301
	F	33-28-36	24,659-...	NONE	1,286	1,112-86	938	49-125	15	159
Franklin, Ind. (1,1)	P	28-22-40	25,176-...	NONE	1,441	1,077-74	798	111-168	231	133
	F	34-34-..	24,176-25,176	NONE	1,545	1,300-84	971	113-216	86	159
Franklin t, Mass. (1,3)	P	37-31-40	28,451-31,339	Y-31,589-5	2,000	1,782-89	1,374	198-210	64	154
	F	28-23-40	26,133-29,492	Y-29,842-5	1,543	1,269-82	1,010	158-101	154	120
Murrysville, Pa. (1,2)	P	17-17-40	...-...	..-...-..	...	...-...	...	...-...	60	...
	F	...-..-..	...-...	..-...-..	...	...-...	...	...-...	43	...
Franklin, Wis. (1,1)	P	45-35-38	30,227-37,982	Y-38,282-5	...	...-...	...	...-...	136	...
	F	21-21-56	26,569-37,363	Y-38,167-5	...	...-...	...	...-...	112	...
Franklin Park v, Ill. (1,1)	P	70-50-40	30,376-42,000	NONE	...	...-...	...	...-...	...	...
	F	50-49-50	29,140-40,212	NONE	...	...-...	...	...-...	...	...
Fraser, Mich. (4,4)	P	...-..-..	...-...	..-...-..	...	...-...	...	...-...	...	...
	F	...-..-..	...-...	..-...-..	...	...-...	...	...-...	...	...

Table 3/22 continued
POLICE AND FIRE DEPARTMENT PERSONNEL, SALARIES, AND EXPENDITURES FOR CITIES 10,000 AND OVER: 1994

City (Service provision)	Department	Total personnel, no. uniformed, duty hours per week	Entrance, maximum salary ($)	Longevity pay, maximum ($), no. years to receive longevity pay	Total expenditures (A) ($)	Total personnel expenditures (B) ($), % of (A)	Salaries and wages (C) ($)	City contrib. to employee retirement, insurance (D) ($)	Capital outlay (E) ($)	All other (F) ($)
10,000–24,999 continued										
Fredericksburg, Va. (3,3)	P	74-50-..	22,887-33,818	Y-...-11	3,023	2,542-84	1,992	328-222	56	425
	F	30-25-..	22,887-33,818	Y-...-11	1,889	1,620-85	1,255	216-149	103	166
Fredonia v, N.Y. (1,3)	P	16-16-40	25,062-34,901	Y-35,354-..	940	873-92	655	147-71	9	58
	F	6-6-44	23,551-29,092	NONE	631	284-45	217	36-31	258	89
Freehold b, N.J. (1,2)	P	24-16-40	28,000-47,755	Y-50,255-3	1,822	1,724-94	1,460	167-97	...	98
	F	...-..-..	...-...	...-...-..	...	...-..	...	...-...	...	...
Freeport, Tex. (1,3)	P	29-23-40	21,500-22,300	Y-23,600-1	1,133	932-82	788	98-46	46	155
	F	3-2-50	19,300-21,200	Y-21,800-1	194	128-65	106	13-9	...	66
Fremont, Nebr. (1,1)	P	39-29-40	18,720-26,386	NONE	1,436	1,315-91	1,040	131-144	73	48
	F	30-29-56	17,820-25,080	NONE	...	...-..	...	...-...	86	...
Fremont, Ohio (1,1)	P	37-32-40	23,379-30,430	NONE	2,037	1,746-85	1,263	251-232	25	266
	F	25-25-50	25,071-28,927	NONE	...	...-..	...	...-...	...	...
Front Royal t, Va. (3,3)	P	38-29-40	22,522-31,504	NONE	2,683	1,693-63	1,349	215-129	838	152
	F	...-..-..	...-...	..-...-..	...	...-..	...	...-...	...	...
Fulton, Mo. (3,3)	P	28-23-40	16,500-24,500	NONE	669	503-75	399	39-65	22	144
	F	18-18-42	14,100-16,200	NONE	533	451-84	349	49-53	52	30
Gaffney, S.C. (1,3)	P	31-23-56	18,921-19,489	NONE	...	...-..	...	...-...	...	...
	F	20-20-53	17,217-...	NONE	...	...-..	...	...-...	...	...
Gainesville, Ga. (1,1)	P	90-74-42	18,865-28,038	Y-28,698-1	3,940	2,590-65	2,264	167-159	84	1,266
	F	65-65-56	18,878-31,769	Y-32,504-1	2,763	1,984-71	1,741	129-114	593	186
Gallatin, Tenn. (1,1)	P	43-23-40	19,198-22,235	Y-23,135-5	1,959	1,603-81	1,341	155-107	86	270
	F	36-33-56	18,283-21,195	Y-22,095-5	1,306	1,123-85	925	117-81	58	125
Gallup t, N.M. (1,1)	P	109-51-42	17,657-27,977	NONE	2,652	2,181-82	1,829	263-89	94	377
	F	43-42-53	16,192-26,688	NONE	1,793	1,606-89	1,322	200-84	24	163
Garden City, Kan. (1,3)	P	75-48-40	21,016-28,028	NONE	2,886	2,438-84	1,887	176-375	108	340
	F	8-8-53	16,536-21,146	NONE	343	264-76	217	19-28	28	51
Garden City v, N.Y. (1,3)	P	63-50-40	33,355-55,505	Y-58,130-6	5,298	4,895-92	3,662	653-580	136	267
	F	34-34-42	32,935-44,459	Y-45,859-8	3,248	2,693-82	1,945	346-402	74	481
Gardner, Mass. (1,3)	P	34-31-37	20,069-26,556	Y-...-5	...	...-..	...	...-...	47	...
	F	55-52-42	20,061-26,317	Y-...-5	...	...-..	...	...-...	38	...
Gatesville, Tex. (1,2)	P	16-11-40	14,435-19,947	NONE	...	...-..	...	...-...	295	...
	F	...-..-..	...-...	...-...-..	...	...-..	...	...-...	286	...
Georgetown, Tex. (-,1)	P	40-27-40	21,528-32,302	Y-35,662-1	1,678	1,218-72	1,008	134-76	64	396
	F	19-16-53	19,531-29,307	Y-32,667-1	916	509-55	425	57-27	57	350
Germantown v, Wis. (1,3)	P	33-24-40	30,416-36,257	NONE	...	...-..	...	...-...	99	...
	F	...-..-..	...-...	NONE	699	239-34	201	28-10	10	450
Gillette, Wyo. (1,-)	P	51-38-45	22,392-...	..-...-..	2,481	2,006-80	1,571	296-139	104	371
	F	...-..-..	...-...	...-...-..	...	...-..	...	...-...	...	...
Gladstone, Ore. (3,2)	P	12-12-40	29,004-33,576	NONE	...	...-..	...	...-...	744	...
	F	...-..-40	...-...	NONE	...	...-..	...	...-...	51	...
Glen Cove, N.Y. (1,2)	P	48-48-40	30,500-54,124	Y-57,274-6	...	...-..	...	...-...	76	...
	F	...-..-..	...-...	...-...-..	...	...-..	...	...-...	...	...
Glen Ellyn v, Ill. (3,2)	P	41-29-40	29,141-40,810	NONE	...	...-..	...	...-...	7,759	...
	F	...-..-..	...-...	NONE	...	...-..	...	...-...	626	...
Goffstown t, N.H. (1,3)	P	25-22-40	26,437-35,464	Y-37,284-8	...	...-..	...	...-...	51	...
	F	11-11-45	23,189-33,509	Y-35,329-8	...	...-..	...	...-...	73	...
Golden, Colo. (1,2)	P	36-26-40	28,114-37,954	NONE	1,924	1,503-78	1,244	138-121	34	387
	F	...-..-..	...-...	..-...-..	...	...-..	...	...-...	342	...
Golden Valley, Minn. (3,2)	P	37-29-40	25,488-39,192	Y-42,720-4	2,284	1,866-81	1,513	187-166	131	287
	F	...-..-..	...-...	..-...-..	...	...-..	...	...-...	479	...
Goodlettsville, Tenn. (1,3)	P	41-30-43	17,326-22,131	Y-25,131-1	1,692	1,317-77	1,061	109-147	39	336
	F	11-11-56	15,704-20,072	Y-23,072-1	467	335-71	264	27-44	...	132
Goose Creek, S.C. (1,1)	P	42-33-41	17,763-24,868	NONE	1,430	1,106-77	942	119-45	151	173
	F	23-23-40	17,763-20,589	NONE	680	576-84	497	52-27	5	99
Gorham t, Me. (1,3)	P	21-15-40	25,381-28,362	NONE	874	775-88	641	70-64	...	99
	F	6-5-42	21,783-...	NONE	423	195-46	153	20-22	...	228
Goshen, Ind. (1,1)	P	39-34-40	23,065-24,407	Y-26,407-..	1,937	1,756-90	1,409	190-157	28	153
	F	40-39-56	23,562-24,792	Y-26,792-..	1,844	1,510-81	1,212	137-161	226	108
Graham, N.C. (3,3)	P	23-21-43	19,452-28,739	Y-...-2	848	686-80	558	78-50	30	132
	F	9-9-53	19,452-28,739	Y-...-2	306	254-83	196	40-18	...	52
Grand Terrace, Calif	P	...-..-..	...-...	...-...-..	...	...-..	...	...-...	...	...
	F	...-..-..	...-...	...-...-..	...	...-..	...	...-...	...	...
Grandview, Mo. (1,1)	P	58-47-40	21,600-30,240	Y-31,104-3	2,892	2,389-82	1,929	248-212	228	275
	F	38-37-56	18,840-26,400	Y-27,264-3	2,195	1,701-77	1,327	229-145	330	164
Grandville, Mich. (1,3)	P	21-18-40	26,515-35,765	Y-36,365-5	...	...-..	...	...-...	20	...
	F	...-..-..	...-...	...-...-..	399	195-48	161	11-23	109	95
Grants Pass, Ore. (4,4)	P	...-..-..	...-...	...-...-..	...	...-..	...	...-...	...	...
	F	...-..-..	...-...	...-...-..	...	...-..	...	...-...	...	...
Great Bend, Kan. (1,3)	P	40-29-42	17,514-19,282	..-...-..	1,471	1,191-80	991	119-81	80	200
	F	29-25-56	17,502-19,273	..-...-..	1,155	918-79	755	90-73	80	157
Greenacres City, Fla. (4,4)	P	...-..-..	...-...	...-...-..	...	...-..	...	...-...	...	...
	F	...-..-..	...-...	...-...-..	...	...-..	...	...-...	...	...
Greenbelt, Md. (1,9)	P	59-45-40	26,229-28,350	NONE	...	...-..	...	...-...	224	...
	F	...-..-..	...-...	...-...-..	...	...-..	...	...-...	...	...

Table 3/22 continued

POLICE AND FIRE DEPARTMENT PERSONNEL, SALARIES, AND EXPENDITURES FOR CITIES 10,000 AND OVER: 1994

City (Service provision)	Department	Total personnel, no. uniformed, duty hours per week	Entrance, maximum salary ($)	Longevity pay, maximum ($) no. years to receive longevity pay	Reported expenditures (in thousands)					
					Total expenditures (A) ($)	Total personnel expenditures (B) ($), % of (A)	Salaries and wages (C) ($)	City contrib. to employee retirement, insurance (D) ($)	Capital outlay (E) ($)	All other (F) ($)
10,000–24,999 continued										
Greendale v, Wis. (1,1)	P	33-28-39	26,150-37,016	NONE	...	...-..	...	...-...	68	...
	F	19-19-56	25,140-36,650	Y-36,950-..	...	...-..	...	...-...	72	...
Greenfield t, Mass. (1,3)	P	38-34-40	20,672-25,620	NONE	...	...-..	...	...-...	155	...
	F	27-26-42	21,174-25,296	NONE	...	...-..	...	...-...	185	...
Greenville, Ohio (1,1)	P	29-22-40	21,299-29,972	NONE	...	...-..	...	...-...	27	...
	F	21-20-53	19,281-29,120	NONE	1,654	851-51	661	118-72	24	779
Greer, S.C. (3,3)	P	42-32-43	18,032-25,245	NONE	...	...-..	...	...-...	36	...
	F	23-23-53	16,621-23,269	NONE	...	...-..	...	...-...	15	...
Griffith t, Ind. (1,2)	P	35-26-38	26,560-32,135	Y-...-3	1,624	1,349-83	1,149	135-65	48	227
	F	...-..-..	...-...	..-...-..	...	...-..	...	...-...	17	...
Griswold t, Conn. (-,2)	P	...-..-..	...-...	..-...-..	...	...-..	...	...-...	...	...
	F	...-..-..	...-...	..-...-..	...	...-..	...	...-...	...	...
Grove City, Ohio (1,-)	P	48-36-40	24,024-38,438	Y-39,188-5	4,757	2,460-51	1,906	272-282	1,976	321
	F	...-..-..	...-...	..-...-..	...	...-..	...	...-...	...	...
Grover Beach, Calif. (1,3)	P	22-15-40	26,040-30,480	Y-32,004-..	1,405	1,163-82	847	162-154	31	211
	F	...-..-40	...-...	NONE	262	151-57	120	18-13	53	58
Groves, Tex. (1,3)	P	16-15-40	19,011-28,267	Y-29,467-1	897	694-77	528	98-68	25	178
	F	9-9-56	19,006-28,277	Y-29,477-1	491	421-85	317	64-40	13	57
Gulfport, Fla. (1,2)	P	34-27-40	21,500-30,020	NONE	1,976	1,480-74	1,108	209-163	31	465
	F	...-..-..	...-...	..-...-..	...	...-..	...	...-...	68	...
Gurnee v, Ill. (1,3)	P	39-36-42	29,965-44,271	Y-45,271-10	2,520	1,899-75	1,568	204-127	130	491
	F	23-22-56	29,965-44,271	Y-45,271-10	1,777	1,119-62	920	130-69	212	446
Haddon tp, N.J. (1,5)	P	23-21-40	28,314-38,776	Y-41,878-5	2,921	1,476-50	1,172	153-151	1,291	154
	F	...-..-..	...-...	..-...-..	...	...-..	...	...-...	...	...
Haddonfield b, N.J. (1,3)	P	21-16-48	25,000-40,788	Y-44,824-24	2,057	1,497-72	1,151	218-128	405	155
	F	5-5-40	33,276-37,886	Y-41,674-25	743	354-47	279	45-30	358	31
Haines City, Fla. (1,1)	P	49-36-40	20,011-22,346	Y-...-..	1,827	1,359-74	1,139	116-104	41	427
	F	...-..-56	18,870-24,056	Y-...-..	573	509-88	417	57-35	1	63
Hampden tp, Pa. (1,2)	P	15-15-40	18,000-...	Y-...-5	...	...-..	...	...-...	124	...
	F	...-..-..	...-...	..-...-..	...	...-..	...	...-...	...	...
Hamtramck, Mich. (1,1)	P	52-52-40	22,346-31,024	Y-31,724-2	...	...-..	...	...-...	137	...
	F	39-39-50	22,346-31,024	Y-31,724-2	2,025	1,746-86	1,395	51-300	174	105
Hannibal, Mo. (1,1)	P	46-33-40	16,358-19,479	Y-22,596-1	...	...-..	...	...-...	...	...
	F	39-39-53	16,358-19,479	Y-22,596-1	...	...-..	...	...-...	...	...
Hanover t, Mass. (1,3)	P	29-27-40	29,040-33,826	Y-34,826-5	1,217	1,154-94	1,030	55-69	16	47
	F	14-13-42	26,465-30,707	NONE	951	713-74	640	38-35	122	116
Harker Heights, Tex. (3,3)	P	34-25-40	16,937-19,409	Y-...-1	984	752-76	629	60-63	91	141
	F	19-18-53	16,937-19,409	Y-...-1	450	382-84	345	16-21	2	66
Harper Woods, Mich. (1,1)	P	40-34-40	26,580-41,081	Y-44,045-4	...	...-..	...	...-...	16	...
	F	20-19-56	27,190-38,576	Y-40,891-4	...	...-..	...	...-...	73	...
Hastings, Nebr. (1,3)	P	44-36-40	19,494-25,649	NONE	1,511	1,346-89	1,047	139-160	45	120
	F	28-27-56	18,746-24,663	NONE	968	899-92	701	89-109	10	59
Havre, Mont. (1,1)	P	17-17-40	19,484-...	NONE	613	525-85	410	57-58	7	81
	F	17-17-48	17,797-...	NONE	581	539-92	425	52-62	3	39
Hawaiian Gardens, Calif. (9,9)	P	...-..-..	...-...	..-...-..	...	...-..	...	...-...	...	...
	F	...-..-..	...-...	..-...-..	...	...-..	...	...-...	...	...
Hays, Kan. (1,3)	P	38-26-40	21,750-28,128	Y-30,097-5	...	...-..	...	...-...	39	...
	F	17-17-56	21,750-28,128	Y-30,097-5	...	...-..	...	...-...	451	...
Hazelwood, Mo. (1,1)	P	49-38-40	26,044-38,555	NONE	3,069	2,278-74	1,840	265-173	23	768
	F	34-32-56	23,016-37,391	NONE	2,491	1,651-66	1,347	192-112	4	836
Hazlet tp, N.J. (1,5)	P	55-44-..	25,630-46,894	Y-...-5	3,645	3,276-89	2,470	417-389	255	114
	F	...-..-..	...-...	..-...-..	...	...-..	...	...-...	...	...
Helena, Mont. (1,1)	P	45-41-40	18,852-26,184	Y-27,744-2	1,823	1,488-81	1,175	183-130	74	261
	F	34-33-44	20,484-27,576	Y-...-1	1,479	1,278-86	1,036	138-104	99	102
Henderson, N.C. (1,1)	P	61-54-..	17,770-24,649	NONE	1,882	1,432-76	1,215	141-76	126	324
	F	34-33-56	17,770-24,649	NONE	1,129	925-81	780	98-47	60	144
Henderson, Tex. (1,1)	P	28-24-40	18,416-21,510	Y-24,271-1	1,032	878-85	687	99-92	44	110
	F	16-16-48	16,673-...	Y-18,269-1	460	415-90	328	46-41	2	43
Hercules, Calif. (3,5)	P	22-18-40	36,888-44,832	NONE	1,780	1,442-81	1,134	190-118	27	311
	F	...-..-..	...-...	..-...-..	...	...-..	...	...-...	...	...
Hereford, Tex. (1,2)	P	30-23-40	...-...	Y-...-2	1,055	852-80	759	53-40	52	151
	F	...-..-..	...-...	..-...-..	...	...-..	...	...-...	28	...
Hermiston, Ore. (1,3)	P	22-22-40	23,928-27,600	NONE	1,023	824-80	618	124-82	40	159
	F	15-13-52	23,472-28,308	NONE	730	608-83	453	91-64	27	95
Hermosa Beach, Calif. (-,-)	P	...-..-40	36,204-41,904	Y-44,000-21	...	...-..	...	...-...	322	...
	F	...-..-56	32,724-41,772	NONE	...	...-..	...	...-...	40	...
Herndon t, Va. (1,7)	P	41-32-40	27,887-46,408	..-...-..	2,687	2,210-82	1,789	293-128	96	381
	F	...-..-..	...-...	..-...-..	...	...-..	...	...-...	...	...
Hermitage, Pa. (1,3)	P	27-24-40	22,436-33,950	Y-34,969-6	...	...-..	...	...-...	32	...
	F	3-2-40	...-...	Y-...-6	...	...-..	...	...-...	41	...
Hilliard, Ohio (1,9)	P	45-32-40	22,500-35,900	Y-37,400-5	...	...-..	...	...-...	170	...
	F	...-..-..	...-...	..-...-..	...	...-..	...	...-...	...	...
Hilton Head Island t, S.C	P	...-..-..	...-...	..-...-..	...	...-..	...	...-...	...	...
	F	155-155-53	18,592-35,704	NONE	...	...-..	...	...-...	...	...

Table 3/22
continued

POLICE AND FIRE DEPARTMENT PERSONNEL, SALARIES, AND EXPENDITURES FOR CITIES 10,000 AND OVER: 1994

City (Service provision)	Department	Total personnel, no. uniformed, duty hours per week	Entrance, maximum salary ($)	Longevity pay, maximum ($) no. years to receive longevity pay	Reported expenditures (in thousands)					
					Total expenditures (A) ($)	Total personnel expenditures (B) ($), % of (A)	Salaries and wages (C) ($)	City contrib. to employee retirement, insurance (D) ($)	Capital outlay (E) ($)	All other (F) ($)
10,000–24,999 continued										
Hinesville, Ga. (1,1)	P	59-52-40	18,000-27,389	NONE	...	...-...	...	...-...	...	...
	F	17-17-48	18,000-27,389	NONE	...	...-...	...	...-...	...	...
Hingham t, Mass. (1,-)	P	47-43-40	28,399-31,260	Y-31,860-10	2,535	2,175-85	1,964	110-101	167	193
	F	...-...-..	...-...	..-...-..	...	...-...	...	...-...	...	...
Hinsdale v, Ill. (1,1)	P	37-27-40	28,920-41,504	Y-42,004-10	2,055	1,733-84	1,309	258-166	65	257
	F	21-20-53	30,137-42,406	Y-42,906-10	1,401	1,139-81	854	191-94	28	234
Hobart, Ind. (1,1)	P	56-45-40	22,050-27,562	Y-29,062-1	...	...-...	...	...-...	213	...
	F	40-39-72	21,525-29,975	Y-...-1	...	...-...	...	...-...	456	...
Hollister, Calif. (3,3)	P	30-25-40	29,856-36,468	Y-37,118-1	...	...-...	...	...-...	66	...
	F	10-10-60	28,296-36,324	..-...-..	...	...-...	...	...-...	143	...
Holliston t, Mass. (1,2)	P	20-20-40	23,571-35,392	Y-35,892-5	1,303	1,164-89	973	131-60	82	57
	F	...-...-..	...-...	Y-...-..	...	...-...	...	...-...	44	...
Holly Hill, Fla. (1,3)	P	32-23-40	21,690-31,884	..-...-..	...	...-...	...	...-...	162	...
	F	10-10-56	20,657-30,366	..-...-..	...	...-...	...	...-...	317	...
Homewood, Ala. (1,1)	P	80-66-40	24,460-34,424	Y-...-6	...	...-...	...	...-...	...	...
	F	53-52-53	24,460-34,424	Y-...-6	...	...-...	...	...-...	20,570	...
Homewood v, Ill. (1,9)	P	48-37-41	29,726-39,835	Y-40,835-6	3,345	2,784-83	2,249	290-245	226	335
	F	15-13-53	30,334-40,650	Y-41,650-6	1,152	954-82	768	106-80	77	121
Hopewell tp, N.J. (1,2)	P	36-28-..	27,264-49,967	Y-...-10	3,114	2,039-65	1,577	192-270	847	228
	F	...-...-..	...-...	..-...-..	...	...-...	...	...-...	...	...
Hopewell, Va. (1,1)	P	52-42-40	22,003-33,503	Y-36,880-11	...	...-...	...	...-...	...	...
	F	38-37-60	20,993-30,398	Y-...-11	...	...-...	...	...-...	...	...
Hudson t, N.H. (1,1)	P	41-31-40	22,464-31,595	NONE	1,791	1,499-83	1,282	74-143	65	227
	F	26-23-42	21,373-27,295	NONE	1,443	1,181-81	997	77-107	51	211
Hueytown, Ala. (1,1)	P	29-23-40	23,067-30,867	NONE	1,309	1,099-83	876	124-99	30	180
	F	25-25-52	23,067-30,867	NONE	1,152	1,014-88	797	112-105	14	124
Hutchinson, Minn. (1,2)	P	25-19-40	24,627-33,321	..-...-..	...	...-...	...	...-...	13	...
	F	...-...-..	...-...	..-...-..	...	...-...	...	...-...	17	...
Hyattsville, Md. (1,7)	P	41-29-40	25,324-31,146	Y-32,080-1	1,728	1,335-77	1,099	138-98	199	194
	F	...-...-..	...-...	..-...-..	...	...-...	...	...-...	...	...
Indianola, Iowa (1,3)	P	16-14-42	21,568-27,496	Y-27,871-5	1,439	574-39	430	69-75	849	16
	F	2-1-..	...-...	NONE	1,139	116-10	88	15-13	1,009	14
Ipswich t, Mass. (1,3)	P	24-23-37	27,987-31,213	NONE	1,359	1,127-82	978	113-36	34	198
	F	16-16-42	27,167-30,300	NONE	851	732-86	634	75-23	15	104
Ironton, Ohio (1,1)	P	14-14-40	19,839-21,823	Y-...-1	789	558-70	421	82-55	97	134
	F	14-14-56	19,839-21,823	Y-...-1	548	498-90	368	75-55	4	46
Jacksonville, Tex. (1,1)	P	33-24-40	19,200-20,160	Y-21,360-25	1,788	923-51	702	108-113	767	98
	F	24-23-56	16,944-20,532	Y-21,732-25	1,679	817-48	653	85-79	804	58
Jacksonville Beach, Fla. (1,1)	P	73-51-40	25,064-40,227	Y-40,947-5	6,075	3,176-52	2,549	398-229	2,163	736
	F	33-31-56	21,840-23,171	Y-...-5	4,057	1,573-38	1,268	173-132	2,157	327
Jamestown, N.D. (1,3)	P	32-28-40	19,044-25,632	Y-26,657-5	...	...-...	...	...-...	7	...
	F	6-6-40	19,044-25,632	Y-26,657-5	...	...-...	...	...-...	17	...
Jasper, Ala. (1,3)	P	60-39-40	20,638-20,878	Y-...-5	1,772	1,419-80	1,118	149-152	66	287
	F	19-19-48	19,292-...	Y-...-5	693	539-77	434	38-67	...	154
Jeffersontown, Ky. (1,9)	P	48-39-40	21,000-30,000	Y-...-5	...	...-...	...	...-...	...	...
	F	...-...-..	...-...	..-...-..	...	...-...	...	...-...	...	...
Jennings, La. (3,3)	P	36-34-43	13,103-...	Y-...-3	...	...-...	...	...-...	...	...
	F	13-12-53	13,504-...	Y-...-3	...	...-...	...	...-...	...	...
Jennings, Mo. (3,1)	P	...-...-40	23,314-26,631	Y-...-..	...	...-...	...	...-...	...	...
	F	18-18-52	22,311-25,471	Y-...-..	...	...-...	...	...-...	...	...
Junction City, Kan. (1,1)	P	72-48-43	19,240-28,250	NONE	...	...-...	...	...-...	615	...
	F	36-35-56	17,695-25,715	NONE	...	...-...	...	...-...	660	...
Jupiter t, Fla. (1,7)	P	95-75-40	23,982-33,779	Y-34,529-5	4,404	3,894-88	3,051	453-390	28	482
	F	...-...-..	...-...	..-...-..	...	...-...	...	...-...	...	...
Kearney, Nebr. (1,3)	P	48-37-41	20,986-29,530	Y-...-12	1,802	1,436-79	1,213	157-66	92	274
	F	5-4-40	19,987-28,124	Y-...-12	271	117-43	101	9-7	1	153
Keizer, Ore. (3,5)	P	27-23-40	27,936-33,888	NONE	1,837	1,229-66	902	136-191	115	493
	F	...-...-..	...-...	..-...-..	...	...-...	...	...-...	...	...
Kelso, Wash. (1,5)	P	29-25-..	30,324-37,908	Y-40,941-5	2,352	1,579-67	1,258	160-161	421	352
	F	...-...-..	...-...	..-...-..	...	...-...	...	...-...	...	...
Kenmore v, N.Y. (1,3)	P	25-25-40	36,607-41,219	Y-...-1	...	...-...	...	...-...	120	...
	F	4-4-40	23,601-26,905	Y-...-1	...	...-...	...	...-...	15	...
Kernersville t, N.C. (1,1)	P	37-27-40	18,235-26,926	NONE	3,578	1,331-37	1,104	144-83	1,703	544
	F	31-30-50	17,358-25,627	NONE	3,028	853-28	735	56-62	1,807	368
Kewanee, Ill. (1,1)	P	23-18-39	22,063-24,689	NONE	...	...-...	...	...-...	783	...
	F	19-19-56	19,318-24,315	Y-25,575-5	...	...-...	...	...-...	539	...
Key West, Fla. (1,1)	P	107-79-40	30,589-58,439	NONE	21,969	5,506-25	4,316	801-389	1,463	15,000
	F	67-66-56	23,425-34,500	NONE	...	...-...	...	...-...	1	...
Kingman, Ariz. (1,3)	P	50-34-40	24,635-32,026	NONE	2,391	2,008-83	1,586	205-217	74	309
	F	28-26-56	23,462-30,501	NONE	1,521	1,195-78	975	82-138	73	253
Kirksville, Mo. (1,1)	P	28-22-41	17,092-22,347	NONE	1,078	894-82	742	84-68	64	120
	F	22-21-58	14,476-19,400	NONE	766	708-92	553	80-75	...	58
Klamath Falls, Ore. (1,5)	P	32-30-40	28,284-34,728	NONE	7,323	1,723-23	1,324	287-112	5,050	550
	F	...-...-..	...-...	..-...-..	...	...-...	...	...-...	...	...

Table 3/22 continued

POLICE AND FIRE DEPARTMENT PERSONNEL, SALARIES, AND EXPENDITURES FOR CITIES 10,000 AND OVER: 1994

City (Service provision)	Depart-ment	Total personnel, no. uniformed, duty hours per week	Entrance, maximum salary ($)	Longevity pay, maximum ($), no. years to receive longevity pay	Reported expenditures (in thousands)					
					Total expendi-tures (A) ($)	Total personnel expendi-tures (B) ($), % of (A)	Salaries and wages (C) ($)	City contrib. to employee retirement, insurance (D) ($)	Capital outlay (E) ($)	All other (F) ($)
10,000–24,999 continued										
La Canada Flintridge, Calif	P	...-..-..	...-...	..-...-..	...	...-..	...	...-...	...	...
	F	...-..-..	...-...	..-...-..	...	...-..	...	...-...	...	...
La Grande, Ore. (1,3)	P	30-16-40	23,243-28,944	NONE	1,000	980-98	723	155-102	4	16
	F	11-10-56	15,622-19,939	NONE	...	...-..	...	...-...	...	...
La Grange v, Ill. (3,1)	P	35-28-41	28,622-40,862	NONE	1,891	1,708-90	1,439	135-134	64	119
	F	19-18-54	28,798-39,860	NONE	1,289	1,026-79	844	92-90	52	211
La Marque, Tex. (1,1)	P	30-23-40	19,986-26,170	Y-26,362-1	2,804	1,098-39	857	119-122	1,410	296
	F	8-8-53	20,100-26,148	Y-26,388-1	1,677	293-17	226	32-35	1,325	59
La Palma, Calif. (1,7)	P	30-24-36	36,474-47,820	NONE	2,841	2,299-80	1,724	391-184	8	534
	F	...-..-..	...-...	..-...-..	...	...-..	...	...-...	...	...
La Porte, Ind. (1,1)	P	39-34-40	22,076-...	Y-25,166-3	...	...-..	...	...-...	134	...
	F	43-43-..	22,076-...	Y-25,166-3	...	...-..	...	...-...	85	...
La Quinta, Calif. (7,7)	P	...-..-..	...-...	..-...-..	...	...-..	...	...-...	...	...
	F	...-..-..	...-...	..-...-..	...	...-..	...	...-...	...	...
Lackawanna, N.Y. (1,1)	P	42-42-40	25,441-30,241	Y-31,141-10	2,594	2,405-92	1,835	387-183	75	114
	F	52-52-40	22,905-28,996	Y-29,896-10	...	...-..	...	...-...	10	...
Lafayette, Colo. (1,2)	P	29-23-40	26,297-31,274	NONE	1,390	1,177-84	1,013	101-63	68	145
	F	...-..-..	...-...	..-...-..	...	...-..	...	...-...	6	...
Laguna Beach, Calif. (1,1)	P	69-45-40	35,292-47,328	NONE	6,163	4,531-73	3,478	533-520	292	1,340
	F	39-38-56	30,660-41,100	NONE	3,968	2,927-73	2,215	345-367	135	906
Lake City, Fla. (1,3)	P	35-28-40	17,728-25,477	..-...-..	1,151	938-81	820	71-47	73	140
	F	35-32-52	17,433-22,812	NONE	1,015	910-89	739	118-53	7	98
Lake Havasu City, Ariz. (-,-)	P	68-48-40	23,171-38,397	Y-38,897-5	6,609	3,360-50	2,844	241-275	2,484	765
	F	57-50-56	23,171-33,093	Y-33,593-5	3,487	2,964-85	2,518	192-254	81	442
Lamesa, Tex. (1,3)	P	23-16-40	18,732-25,764	Y-26,964-1	1,960	656-33	516	89-51	1,108	196
	F	9-9-56	15,480-18,600	Y-19,800-1	1,700	254-14	199	33-22	1,117	329
Lansdale b, Pa. (1,2)	P	30-22-40	25,784-44,988	Y-49,037-5	1,864	1,633-87	1,359	38-236	11	220
	F	...-..-..	...-...	..-...-..	...	...-..	...	...-...	...	...
Lansdowne b, Pa. (1,2)	P	18-15-42	36,057-...	Y-41,466-..	...	...-..	...	...-...	17	...
	F	...-..-..	...-...	..-...-..	...	...-..	...	...-...	...	...
Larkspur, Calif. (9,1)	P	...-..-..	...-...	..-...-..	...	...-..	...	...-...	...	...
	F	18-18-56	33,576-40,248	NONE	1,625	1,182-72	942	125-115	102	341
Las Vegas, N.M. (1,3)	P	70-42-40	14,472-21,864	NONE	...	...-..	...	...-...	2	...
	F	13-13-..	11,664-14,400	NONE	...	...-..	...	...-...	41	...
Laurinburg, N.C. (1,3)	P	30-25-42	20,016-28,165	NONE	1,418	933-65	775	92-66	261	224
	F	5-5-42	19,063-26,824	NONE	451	172-38	145	16-11	206	73
Leawood, Kan. (1,1)	P	58-41-40	23,171-33,355	NONE	2,666	2,208-82	1,784	260-164	113	345
	F	41-40-53	21,394-28,882	NONE	1,902	1,714-90	1,364	215-135	32	156
Lebanon, Ore. (1,5)	P	24-18-40	25,446-30,828	NONE	1,242	1,104-88	839	160-105	8	130
	F	...-..-..	...-...	..-...-..	...	...-..	...	...-...	...	...
Lebanon, Tenn. (1,1)	P	50-46-40	19,260-22,484	NONE	1,395	1,315-94	1,074	130-111	40	40
	F	34-34-56	17,969-23,770	NONE	1,083	1,054-97	879	92-83	25	4
Ledyard t, Conn. (1,3)	P	16-16-40	28,472-34,344	NONE	920	755-82	626	76-53	25	140
	F	4-4-45	25,054-32,457	Y-33,007-5	384	191-49	153	16-22	88	105
Leesburg, Fla. (1,1)	P	63-51-40	20,904-26,666	NONE	4,251	2,099-49	1,720	235-144	1,662	490
	F	31-30-56	19,947-26,761	NONE	3,064	1,234-40	1,003	146-85	1,628	202
Leesburg t, Va. (1,9)	P	36-33-40	25,559-39,583	NONE	...	...-..	...	...-...	2,547	...
	F	...-..-..	...-...	..-...-..	...	...-..	...	...-...	...	...
Lemon Grove, Calif. (7,1)	P	...-..-..	...-...	..-...-..	...	...-..	...	...-...	...	...
	F	22-21-56	30,881-48,131	NONE	1,567	1,355-86	1,067	208-80	24	188
Lemoore, Calif. (1,2)	P	24-20-..	25,926-32,460	NONE	7,028	1,149-16	970	131-48	311	5,568
	F	...-..-..	...-...	..-...-..	...	...-..	...	...-...	37	...
Lenoir, N.C. (1,1)	P	59-49-..	17,886-26,534	Y-...-..	...	...-..	...	...-...	...	...
	F	56-..-56	17,034-23,272	Y-24,067-..	...	...-..	...	...-...	...	...
Levelland, Tex. (1,3)	P	26-20-40	18,749-23,753	Y-23,803-1	823	671-81	500	104-67	120	32
	F	7-..-56	18,749-23,753	Y-23,803-1	284	224-78	178	29-17	54	6
Lexington, N.C. (1,1)	P	81-65-40	18,400-25,800	Y-...-1	4,837	2,700-55	2,098	398-204	1,745	392
	F	51-51-56	16,700-28,600	Y-...-1	2,170	1,857-85	1,470	258-129	101	212
Liberal, Kan. (1,3)	P	34-27-42	18,343-26,409	NONE	...	...-..	...	...-...	834	...
	F	11-10-53	18,052-26,760	NONE	...	...-..	...	...-...	71	...
Liberty, Mo. (3,3)	P	39-29-40	23,580-31,824	NONE	1,751	1,452-82	1,175	148-129	102	197
	F	27-27-50	23,580-31,824	NONE	1,456	1,192-81	931	143-118	143	121
Lighthouse Point, Fla. (1,1)	P	39-30-40	27,856-39,223	Y-40,048-8	2,127	1,826-85	1,478	253-95	89	212
	F	19-18-51	24,328-35,277	Y-36,102-8	1,022	892-87	721	129-42	42	88
Lincoln t, R.I. (1,3)	P	38-33-37	23,035-34,215	Y-37,123-3	...	...-..	...	...-...	...	...
	F	...-..-..	...-...	..-...-..	...	...-..	...	...-...	...	...
Lincoln Park b, N.J. (1,2)	P	29-26-40	22,709-46,687	Y-...-..	...	...-..	...	...-...	2,514	...
	F	...-..-..	...-...	..-...-..	...	...-..	...	...-...	265	...
Lincolnwood v, Ill	P	46-32-40	29,516-44,538	NONE	...	...-..	...	...-...	...	...
	F	...-..-..	...-...	..-...-..	...	...-..	...	...-...	...	...
Lisle v, Ill. (1,6)	P	48-35-40	28,500-39,750	NONE	2,928	2,336-79	1,793	308-235	110	482
	F	...-..-..	...-...	..-...-..	...	...-..	...	...-...	...	...
Logansport, Ind. (1,1)	P	40-31-..	20,801-21,537	Y-22,637-1	...	...-..	...	...-...	51	...
	F	39-39-..	...-21,537	Y-22,637-1	...	...-..	...	...-...	6	...

Table 3/22 continued

POLICE AND FIRE DEPARTMENT PERSONNEL, SALARIES, AND EXPENDITURES FOR CITIES 10,000 AND OVER: 1994

City (Service provision)	Depart-ment	Total personnel, no. uniformed, duty hours per week	Entrance, maximum salary ($)	Longevity pay, maximum ($), no. years to receive longevity pay	Reported expenditures (in thousands)					
					Total expendi-tures (A) ($)	Total personnel expendi-tures (B) ($), % of (A)	Salaries and wages (C) ($)	City contrib. to employee retirement, insurance (D) ($)	Capital outlay (E) ($)	All other (F) ($)
10,000–24,999 continued										
Loma Linda, Calif. (9,3)	P	...-.-.	...-...	.-...-..	...	...-.	...	...-...	...	...
	F	17-15-56	...-...	NONE	...	...-.	...	...-...	1,429	...
Lomita, Calif. (9,5)	P	...-.-.	...-...	.-...-..	...	...-.	...	...-...	...	...
	F	...-.-.	...-...	.-...-..	...	...-.	...	...-...	...	...
Longmeadow t, Mass. (1,1)	P	30-30-37	24,908-28,496	Y-...-5	...	...-.	...	...-...	76	...
	F	18-18-42	23,296-29,328	Y-...-5	...	...-.	...	...-...	317	...
Los Banos, Calif. (1,3)	P	24-12-40	27,192-32,832	NONE	...	...-.	...	...-...	102	...
	F	3-3-40	27,192-32,832	NONE	...	...-.	...	...-...	140	...
Lower Allen tp, Pa. (1,2)	P	20-17-40	27,582-34,505	Y-36,305-5	...	...-.	...	...-...	258	...
	F	...-.-.	...-...	NONE	...	...-.	...	...-...	232	...
Lower Burrell, Pa. (1,2)	P	14-14-40	26,291-35,532	Y-39,797-30	1,062	737-69	550	81-106	261	64
	F	...-.-.	...-...	...-...	...	...	...	...		
Lower Moreland tp, Pa. (1,2)	P	28-21-40	32,989-40,290	Y-44,319-..	1,580	1,419-89	1,115	121-183	100	61
	F	...-.-.	...-...	.-...-..	...	...-.	...	...-...	...	...
Ludlow t, Mass. (1,1)	P	30-29-40	25,054-28,630	Y-29,030-5	1,338	1,244-92	1,148	73-23	11	83
	F	28-28-42	23,226-26,539	Y-26,939-5	1,238	1,160-93	1,076	61-23	23	55
Lumberton, N.C. (1,1)	P	73-63-42	16,267-17,091	Y-17,131-..	2,616	2,098-80	1,709	278-111	198	320
	F	59-57-51	16,267-17,091	Y-17,131-..	2,662	1,578-59	1,324	166-88	817	267
Lyndhurst tp, N.J. (1,2)	P	48-48-38	51,586-54,553	Y-...-4	4,696	3,686-78	2,800	406-480	870	140
	F	...-.-.	...-...	...-...	...	...	...	...		
Lyndhurst, Ohio (1,1)	P	37-29-40	29,983-38,456	Y-40,379-5	3,415	2,097-61	1,604	289-204	1,056	262
	F	23-23-53	29,885-38,337	Y-40,254-5	...	...-.	...	...-...	59	...
Lynnfield t, Mass. (1,3)	P	25-19-37	25,274-30,239	Y-30,864-5	...	...-.	...	...-...	419	...
	F	7-7-42	24,158-30,233	Y-30,783-5	...	...-.	...	...-...	419	...
Mc Comb, Miss. (4,4)	P	...-.-.	...-...	.-...-..	...	...-.	...	...-...	...	...
	F	...-.-.	...-...	.-...-..	...	...-.	...	...-...	...	...
Mc Henry, Ill. (1,5)	P	40-28-40	24,842-39,013	Y-40,574-6	2,785	2,052-73	1,598	318-136	460	273
	F	...-.-.	...-...	.-...-..	...	...-.	...	...-...	...	...
Mc Kinney, Tex. (1,1)	P	46-34-40	27,184-33,101	Y-34,301-1	...	...-.	...	...-...	19	...
	F	37-36-53	24,398-32,800	Y-...-1	...	...-.	...	...-...	27	...
Mc Minnville, Ore. (3,3)	P	29-25-40	26,808-34,212	Y-36,012-10	4,380	1,439-32	1,032	225-182	2,751	190
	F	12-12-40	26,808-34,212	Y-36,012-10	3,822	763-19	554	126-83	2,646	413
Machesney Park v, Ill. (9,9)	P	...-.-.	...-...	.-...-..	...	...-.	...	...-...	...	...
	F	...-.-.	...-...	.-...-..	...	...-.	...	...-...	...	...
Madison, Ala. (1,3)	P	46-32-43	18,994-30,479	NONE	1,254	1,185-94	948	126-111	12	57
	F	28-27-53	18,994-30,479	NONE	806	799-99	650	81-68	1	6
Mansfield t, Conn. (-,8)	P	4-3-40	31,387-35,880	Y-36,630-6	428	244-57	197	27-20	17	167
	F	...-.-.	...-...	.-...-..	...	...-.	...	...-...	...	...
Mansfield t, Mass. (3,3)	P	32-27-40	25,913-33,162	Y-33,562-5	...	...-.	...	...-...	3	...
	F	28-27-42	24,242-31,952	Y-32,302-5	...	...-.	...	...-...	21	...
Manville b, N.J. (1,2)	P	25-23-40	24,000-47,342	Y-48,617-5	1,829	1,704-93	1,322	169-213	...	125
	F	...-.-.	...-...	.-...-..	...	...-.	...	...-...	...	...
Maple Shade tp, N.J. (1,2)	P	30-23-40	31,834-45,379	Y-...-6	2,491	2,267-91	1,764	183-320	58	166
	F	...-.-.	...-...	.-...-..	...	...-.	...	...-...	25	...
Maplewood tp, N.J. (1,1)	P	69-56-40	36,444-44,496	Y-48,946-5	5,147	4,400-85	3,450	536-414	552	195
	F	39-39-..	36,444-44,496	Y-48,946-5	3,262	2,639-80	2,078	345-216	543	80
Marion, Iowa (1,1)	P	37-30-40	22,627-28,736	Y-29,436-5	1,803	1,476-81	1,142	182-152	83	244
	F	22-22-56	23,056-27,865	Y-28,565-5	1,040	942-90	717	121-104	10	88
Marple tp, Pa. (1,2)	P	36-30-40	27,457-39,224	Y-47,461-4	2,796	1,916-68	1,591	24-301	80	800
	F	...-.-.	...-...	.-...-..	...	...-.	...	...-...	37	...
Marquette, Mich. (1,1)	P	40-40-40	24,170-30,243	Y-30,583-5	1,887	1,558-82	1,250	161-147	68	261
	F	22-22-54	21,356-28,474	Y-...-5	1,253	917-73	727	95-95	8	328
Marshall, Tex. (1,1)	P	57-45-40	20,192-22,339	Y-23,539-1	5,470	1,683-30	1,394	172-117	3,534	253
	F	43-41-56	20,192-22,339	Y-23,547-1	5,035	1,366-27	1,135	143-88	3,552	117
Martinsburg, W.Va. (1,1)	P	50-41-40	19,329-25,411	Y-26,660-5	...	...-.	...	...-...	75	...
	F	25-25-56	18,439-23,048	Y-24,300-5	...	...-.	...	...-...	20	...
Martinsville, Va. (1,1)	P	61-51-40	22,491-31,100	NONE	2,427	2,085-85	1,660	328-97	88	254
	F	26-26-48	18,504-26,867	NONE	1,057	895-84	711	138-46	72	90
Marysville, Wash. (3,6)	P	47-24-48	28,290-35,916	Y-36,936-6	2,266	1,954-86	1,546	210-198	23	289
	F	...-.-.	...-...	.-...-..	...	...-.	...	...-...	...	...
Maryville, Tenn. (3,3)	P	39-33-40	19,489-28,766	NONE	1,534	1,154-75	919	90-145	30	350
	F	31-30-57	16,806-24,856	NONE	1,301	1,122-86	904	88-130	34	145
Massapequa Park v, N.Y. (7,9)	P	...-.-.	...-...	.-...-..	...	...-.	...	...-...	...	...
	F	...-.-.	...-...	.-...-..	...	...-.	...	...-...	...	...
Massena v, N.Y. (1,3)	P	20-20-40	18,500-30,940	Y-31,990-5	...	...-.	...	...-...	37	...
	F	9-9-42	...-...	.-...-..	...	...-.	...	...-...	12	...
Matteson v, Ill. (1,3)	P	45-34-39	30,754-41,264	NONE	...	...-.	...	...-...	82	...
	F	25-24-56	30,754-41,263	NONE	...	...-.	...	...-...	225	...
Mauldin, S.C. (1,3)	P	34-27-40	18,718-26,206	..-...-..	1,189	882-74	705	119-58	66	241
	F	29-28-60	18,718-26,206	..-...-..	948	765-80	601	112-52	15	168
Maumee, Ohio (1,3)	P	51-40-40	25,452-32,383	Y-...-5	2,830	2,354-83	1,851	343-160	51	425
	F	4-...-40	...-...	Y-...-5	429	296-68	234	48-14	27	106
Medford tp, N.J. (1,2)	P	42-33-40	26,865-46,064	Y-48,564-4	3,490	2,714-77	2,091	349-274	526	250
	F	...-.-.	...-...	.-...-..	...	...-.	...	...-...	...	...

Table 3/22 continued

POLICE AND FIRE DEPARTMENT PERSONNEL, SALARIES, AND EXPENDITURES FOR CITIES 10,000 AND OVER: 1994

City (Service provision)	Department	Total personnel, no. uniformed, duty hours per week	Entrance, maximum salary ($)	Longevity pay, maximum ($), no. years to receive longevity pay	Reported expenditures (in thousands)					
					Total expenditures (A) ($)	Total personnel expenditures (B) ($), % of (A)	Salaries and wages (C) ($)	City contrib. to employee retirement, insurance (D) ($)	Capital outlay (E) ($)	All other (F) ($)
10,000–24,999 continued										
Melvindale, Mich. (1,1)	P	27-25-40	27,206-36,296	Y-37,296-1	...	...-..	...	...-..	15	...
	F	16-16-50	26,030-34,740	Y-35,740-1	...	...-..	...	...-..	52	...
Menasha, Wis. (1,1)	P	34-29-40	24,660-31,848	NONE	...	...-..	...	...-..	56	...
	F	29-29-56	28,908-34,476	NONE	...	...-..	...	...-..	224	...
Menomonie, Wis. (1,3)	P	35-26-43	27,756-30,396	Y-31,612-4	...	...-..	...	...-..	342	...
	F	21-20-56	24,348-30,240	Y-31,450-4	...	...-..	...	...-..	343	...
Mequon, Wis. (1,2)	P	39-38-40	33,336-38,676	Y-39,126-25	...	...-..	...	...-..	47	...
	F	...-..	...-...	..-..-..	...	...-..	...	...-..	131	...
Mercedes, Tex. (1,2)	P	31-23-43	14,788-16,536	NONE	841	586-69	479	61-46	133	122
	F	...-..	...-...	..-..-..	...	...-..	...	...-..	45	...
Mercer Island, Wash. (4,4)	P	...-..	...-...	..-..-..	...	...-..	...	...-..	...	...
	F	...-..	...-...	..-..-..	...	...-..	...	...-..	...	...
Merriam, Kan. (1,3)	P	24-21-40	24,022-32,430	NONE	1,516	1,146-75	936	135-75	212	158
	F	16-16-56	22,687-30,628	NONE	992	749-75	590	85-74	184	59
Mexico, Mo. (4,4)	P	...-..	...-...	..-..-..	...	...-..	...	...-..	...	...
	F	...-..	...-...	..-..-..	...	...-..	...	...-..	...	...
Miami Springs, Fla. (1,7)	P	52-42-40	29,944-41,392	Y-42,642-5	2,868	2,501-87	1,959	327-215	3	364
	F	...-..	...-...	..-..-..	...	...-..	...	...-..	...	...
Middleburg Heights, Ohio (1,1)	P	34-28-40	26,790-36,275	Y-37,525-5	...	...-..	...	...-..	1,356	...
	F	20-19-52	26,810-36,271	Y-37,521-5	...	...-..	...	...-..	1,360	...
Middletown tp, Pa. (9,2)	P	...-..	...-...	..-..-..	...	...-..	...	...-..	...	...
	F	...-..	...-...	..-..-..	...	...-..	...	...-..	44	...
Middletown t, R.I. (1,1)	P	40-38-37	24,043-29,415	Y-...-..	...	...-..	...	...-..	372	...
	F	34-33-42	24,247-28,756	Y-...-..	...	...-..	...	...-..	45	...
Midvale, Utah (1,2)	P	25-23-40	19,896-32,868	NONE	...	...-..	...	...-..	344	...
	F	...-..	...-...	NONE	...	...-..	...	...-..	17	...
Milford t, N.H. (1,2)	P	22-20-32	23,332-31,385	Y-...-5	1,100	968-88	775	73-120	30	102
	F	...-..	...-...	..-..-..	...	...-..	...	...-..	129	...
Mill Valley, Calif. (1,1)	P	34-20-40	35,292-42,888	NONE	2,204	1,726-78	1,357	166-203	155	323
	F	29-25-56	33,936-41,256	NONE	2,175	1,633-75	1,305	158-170	267	275
Millbrae, Calif. (1,1)	P	22-22-40	32,400-39,780	NONE	...	...-..	...	...-..	...	...
	F	20-20-56	33,780-41,484	NONE	...	...-..	...	...-..	...	...
Millington, Tenn. (1,1)	P	29-23-40	19,259-25,461	NONE	...	...-..	...	...-..	...	...
	F	18-18-54	17,564-23,189	NONE	...	...-..	...	...-..	...	...
Milwaukie, Ore. (1,1)	P	36-25-40	28,164-36,120	..-..-..	3,299	1,628-49	1,207	256-165	1,514	157
	F	26-25-56	27,156-38,784	..-..-..	3,218	1,467-45	1,106	240-121	1,502	249
Mitchell, S.D. (1,3)	P	30-22-40	18,948-24,462	NONE	1,026	877-85	717	104-56	58	91
	F	16-16-53	18,627-23,474	NONE	556	507-91	402	74-31	13	36
Moberly, Mo. (1,1)	P	38-32-40	15,392-21,382	NONE	1,114	979-87	795	106-78	18	117
	F	23-23-56	12,418-19,864	NONE	608	568-93	449	69-50	6	34
Monroe t, Conn. (1,3)	P	32-25-40	31,997-...	..-..-..	...	...-..	...	...-..	37	...
	F	...-..	...-...	..-..-..	49	44-89	37	3-4	...	5
Monroe, Mich. (1,1)	P	47-43-40	25,246-35,586	Y-35,711-5	3,001	2,629-87	2,234	135-260	55	317
	F	46-46-54	25,295-35,575	Y-35,700-5	2,456	2,306-93	1,951	109-246	32	118
Monroe, N.C. (4,4)	P	...-..	...-...	..-..-..	...	...-..	...	...-..	...	...
	F	...-..	...-...	..-..-..	...	...-..	...	...-..	...	...
Montville tp, N.J. (1,5)	P	34-34-40	27,739-49,868	Y-52,361-5	3,302	2,532-76	2,060	222-250	585	185
	F	...-..	...-...	..-..-..	...	...-..	...	...-..	...	...
Moon tp, Pa. (1,3)	P	31-26-40	27,643-39,478	Y-40,978-5	...	...-..	...	...-..	61	...
	F	...-..	...-...	..-..-..	162	51-31	38	5-8	...	111
Moorestown tp, N.J. (1,5)	P	42-33-40	32,182-44,647	Y-48,219-5	...	...-..	...	...-..	25	...
	F	...-..	...-...	..-..-..	...	...-..	...	...-..	...	...
Moraga t, Calif. (1,5)	P	12-11-40	36,705-44,643	NONE	1,276	931-72	699	115-117	101	244
	F	...-..	...-...	..-..-..	...	...-..	...	...-..	...	...
Morgan City, La. (1,1)	P	57-53-40	15,911-...	Y-16,260-1	1,680	1,299-77	1,120	104-75	...	381
	F	37-36-53	14,700-...	Y-15,048-1	2,034	1,035-50	892	79-64	883	116
Morganton, N.C. (4,4)	P	...-..	...-...	..-..-..	...	...-..	...	...-..	...	...
	F	...-..	...-...	..-..-..	...	...-..	...	...-..	...	...
Morristown, Tenn. (1,1)	P	65-62-40	20,321-29,452	Y-...-5	2,524	2,041-80	1,630	142-269	31	452
	F	51-51-48	18,408-26,665	Y-...-5	2,031	1,839-90	1,440	123-276	24	168
Moscow, Idaho (1,3)	P	35-28-40	23,772-30,672	Y-33,624-25	1,831	1,530-83	1,201	214-115	112	189
	F	...-..	...-...	..-..-..	474	171-36	132	30-9	217	86
Moses Lake, Wash. (3,3)	P	32-22-40	26,709-33,368	NONE	1,721	1,404-81	1,100	142-162	4	313
	F	14-14-52	25,848-32,310	NONE	1,161	872-75	759	43-70	3	286
Moss Point, Miss. (1,1)	P	44-40-48	17,906-...	Y-18,686-1	1,648	1,255-76	1,005	165-85	111	282
	F	40-40-72	17,906-...	Y-18,686-1	1,374	1,122-81	880	143-99	109	143
Mount Clemens, Mich. (1,1)	P	32-26-40	31,262-38,147	Y-...-5	...	...-..	...	...-..	11	...
	F	15-15-56	27,746-36,752	Y-...-5	...	...-..	...	...-..	6	...
Mount Pleasant, Mich. (1,3)	P	25-22-42	...-...	Y-...-5	...	...-..	...	...-..	...	...
	F	11-10-56	24,000-32,277	Y-35,000-5	...	...-..	...	...-..	...	...
Mount Pleasant, Tex. (1,3)	P	27-19-40	20,862-29,494	Y-30,694-1	963	777-80	647	78-52	25	161
	F	14-13-56	19,864-28,059	Y-29,259-1	553	416-75	345	41-30	...	137
Mount Vernon, Ill. (3,3)	P	34-32-40	24,655-29,618	NONE	1,738	1,311-75	1,212	39-60	92	335
	F	26-26-56	24,655-29,618	NONE	1,319	1,031-78	969	15-47	37	251

Table 3/22
continued

POLICE AND FIRE DEPARTMENT PERSONNEL, SALARIES, AND EXPENDITURES FOR CITIES 10,000 AND OVER: 1994

City (Service provision)	Department	Total personnel, no. uniformed, duty hours per week	Entrance, maximum salary ($)	Longevity pay, maximum ($) no. years to receive longevity pay	Total expenditures (A) ($)	Total personnel expenditures (B) ($), % of (A)	Salaries and wages (C) ($)	City contrib. to employee retirement, insurance (D) ($)	Capital outlay (E) ($)	All other (F) ($)
10,000 – 24,999 continued										
Mount Vernon, Ohio (1,1)	P	29-21-40	21,091-25,771	NONE	1,907	1,096-57	804	142-150	550	261
	F	30-22-48	21,103-25,833	NONE	1,911	1,293-67	935	183-175	528	90
Mount Vernon, Wash. (1,3)	P	39-33-40	28,712-35,764	NONE	2,366	1,847-78	1,435	183-229	32	487
	F	30-27-48	28,657-34,792	Y-...-5	1,877	1,276-67	1,053	68-155	254	347
Mundelein v, Ill. (1,9)	P	40-32-40	33,771-42,220	NONE	...	...-..	...	...-...	105	...
	F	16-14-56	33,771-42,220	NONE	1,544	1,135-73	860	194-81	292	117
Munster t, Ind. (1,2)	P	40-31-40	23,691-34,216	Y-34,936-4	1,888	1,663-88	1,309	179-175	46	179
	F	...-..-..	...-...	..-...-..	...	...-..	...	...-...	...	...
Muskego, Wis. (1,2)	P	36-28-40	31,519-38,518	Y-38,698-5	...	...-..	...	...-...	778	...
	F	...-..-..	...-...	...-...	...	...-..	...	...-...	...	...
Mustang, Okla. (1,3)	P	19-19-40	19,477-21,021	Y-...-1	613	535-87	424	59-52	2	76
	F	5-5-43	17,700-19,500	Y-...-1	219	146-66	118	14-14	36	37
Myrtle Beach, S.C. (1,1)	P	129-32-44	18,274-26,466	NONE	4,846	3,973-81	3,229	542-202	123	750
	F	103-101-53	16,151-22,821	NONE	3,017	2,542-84	2,054	356-132	22	453
Naples, Fla. (1,1)	P	120-78-41	24,385-34,761	NONE	4,805	4,057-84	3,496	267-294	263	485
	F	58-53-52	21,601-32,401	NONE	2,271	2,063-90	1,734	133-196	39	169
Narragansett t, R.I. (1,1)	P	46-36-39	24,872-28,858	Y-34,034-3	1,383	1,261-91	943	201-117	...	122
	F	35-34-42	22,077-27,333	Y-31,296-3	1,122	1,042-92	824	131-87	7	73
Neenah, Wis. (1,1)	P	50-41-39	28,884-33,564	Y-33,864-..	...	...-..	...	...-...	...	...
	F	42-42-56	29,856-33,372	Y-33,672-..	...	...-..	...	...-...	...	...
New Bern, N.C. (1,3)	P	87-67-42	20,403-37,212	Y-...-5	2,991	2,538-84	2,055	330-153	41	412
	F	34-33-53	16,009-29,316	Y-...-5	1,759	1,115-63	889	157-69	271	373
New Canaan t, Conn. (1,3)	P	42-38-40	31,620-44,150	Y-44,600-5	...	...-..	...	...-...	49	...
	F	12-12-42	28,948-39,917	Y-40,367-5	...	...-..	...	...-...	25	...
New Castle, Ind. (1,1)	P	36-36-48	19,240-19,890	Y-21,690-3	...	...-..	...	...-...	449	...
	F	32-32-48	19,630-20,202	Y-21,642-3	...	...-..	...	...-...	1	...
New Fairfield t, Conn. (1,2)	P	13-13-40	27,014-38,136	Y-38,594-..	...	...-..	...	...-...	33	...
	F	...-..-..	...-...	..-...-..	...	...-..	...	...-...	122	...
New Philadelphia, Ohio (1,1)	P	23-19-40	23,706-26,561	Y-26,861-5	1,039	852-82	762	1-89	39	148
	F	19-19-56	23,514-26,149	Y-26,449-5	740	679-91	579	26-74	2	59
New Port Richey, Fla. (1,1)	P	39-30-40	20,426-27,461	NONE	1,636	1,395-85	1,056	227-112	57	184
	F	25-24-56	22,978-30,937	NONE	1,593	1,051-65	789	177-85	363	179
Tinton Falls b, N.J. (1,2)	P	38-30-40	31,926-49,042	Y-54,438-4	2,713	2,606-96	2,029	347-230	70	37
	F	...-..-..	...-...	..-...-..	...	...-..	...	...-...	...	...
Newberg, Ore. (3,3)	P	27-19-40	26,532-33,696	Y-37,380-10	...	...-..	...	...-...	35	...
	F	5-5-52	25,920-29,928	Y-33,204-10	...	...-..	...	...-...	27	...
Newberry, S.C. (1,3)	P	25-23-40	18,042-27,345	Y-...-..	...	...-..	...	...-...	...	...
	F	18-18-48	17,341-26,283	Y-...-..	...	...-..	...	...-...	...	...
Newburyport, Mass. (1,1)	P	33-33-40	22,748-29,488	Y-...-5	...	...-..	...	...-...	115	...
	F	34-34-42	25,439-32,976	Y-...-5	...	...-..	...	...-...	450	...
Newnan, Ga. (1,1)	P	41-40-42	18,491-27,310	NONE	1,439	1,172-81	944	140-88	65	202
	F	26-26-..	18,672-27,617	NONE	902	729-80	589	87-53	91	82
Newton, Iowa (1,3)	P	33-26-40	23,952-29,604	Y-30,624-6	1,408	1,253-88	939	145-169	29	126
	F	23-23-56	20,904-29,388	Y-30,288-8	1,253	1,062-84	818	130-114	119	72
Newtown tp, Pa. (1,2)	P	13-13-40	29,326-38,327	Y-42,077-4	909	764-84	586	81-97	48	97
	F	...-..-..	...-...	..-...-..	...	...-..	...	...-...	...	...
Niles, Mich. (3,3)	P	27-25-40	20,293-31,246	Y-34,371-5	1,553	1,035-66	837	82-116	323	195
	F	14-14-54	18,000-31,744	Y-34,918-5	917	567-61	484	22-61	261	89
Norco, Calif. (7,1)	P	...-..-..	...-...	..-...-..	...	...-..	...	...-...	...	...
	F	19-19-56	27,876-35,976	Y-...-5	2,571	1,369-53	1,132	109-128	1,049	153
Norfolk, Nebr. (1,3)	P	51-37-40	20,136-26,604	..-...-..	1,841	1,534-83	1,248	162-124	54	253
	F	29-23-53	19,224-25,368	..-...-..	1,332	1,169-87	900	187-82	29	134
North Adams, Mass. (4,4)	P	...-..-..	...-...	..-...-..	...	...-..	...	...-...	...	...
	F	...-..-..	...-...	..-...-..	...	...-..	...	...-...	...	...
North Augusta, S.C. (4,4)	P	...-..-..	...-...	..-...-..	...	...-..	...	...-...	...	...
	F	...-..-..	...-...	..-...-..	...	...-..	...	...-...	...	...
North Branford t, Conn. (1,2)	P	20-19-40	29,203-37,814	Y-39,049-5	...	...-..	...	...-...	493	...
	F	...-..-..	...-...	..-...-..	...	...-..	...	...-...	...	...
North Haven t, Conn. (1,3)	P	48-41-40	31,096-36,962	Y-37,337-5	...	...-..	...	...-...	67	...
	F	28-27-42	29,969-36,537	Y-37,062-5	...	...-..	...	...-...	14	...
North Mankato, Minn. (3,2)	P	10-9-40	29,250-36,000	Y-37,800-4	604	480-79	380	49-51	38	86
	F	...-..-..	...-...	NONE	...	...-..	...	...-...	21	...
North Palm Beach v, Fla. (4,4)	P	...-..-..	...-...	..-...-..	...	...-..	...	...-...	...	...
	F	...-..-..	...-...	..-...-..	...	...-..	...	...-...	...	...
North Platte, Nebr. (1,3)	P	53-34-40	19,760-26,478	Y-26,658-5	1,725	1,703-98	1,385	179-139	7	15
	F	31-29-56	19,160-26,411	NONE	1,490	1,146-76	966	95-85	94	250
North Port, Fla. (1,1)	P	35-33-40	18,512-...	Y-...-4	...	...-..	...	...-...	7	...
	F	35-29-56	18,007-28,929	Y-...-4	1,931	1,348-69	1,012	193-143	182	401
North Royalton, Ohio (1,1)	P	38-29-40	28,267-34,819	Y-36,319-..	2,046	1,881-91	1,442	265-174	10	155
	F	23-22-51	28,866-34,785	Y-36,285-..	...	...-..	...	...-...	56	...
North St. Paul, Minn. (1,3)	P	17-14-40	25,964-39,945	NONE	949	819-86	682	84-53	28	102
	F	...-..-..	...-...	..-...-..	179	83-46	71	8-4	23	73
Northborough t, Mass. (1,3)	P	16-16-40	28,884-36,528	NONE	...	...-..	...	...-...	32	...
	F	9-9-40	26,731-33,819	Y-34,294-5	...	...-..	...	...-...	10	...

Table 3/22 continued

POLICE AND FIRE DEPARTMENT PERSONNEL, SALARIES, AND EXPENDITURES FOR CITIES 10,000 AND OVER: 1994

City (Service provision)	Department	Total personnel, no. uniformed, duty hours per week	Entrance, maximum salary ($)	Longevity pay, maximum ($) no. years to receive longevity pay	Reported expenditures (in thousands)					
					Total expenditures (A) ($)	Total personnel expenditures (B) ($), % of (A)	Salaries and wages (C) ($)	City contrib. to employee retirement, insurance (D) ($)	Capital outlay (E) ($)	All other (F) ($)
10,000–24,999 continued										
Northlake, Ill. (1,5) ....P		31-13-40	33,416-39,742	NONE	6,567	1,367-20	1,100	125-142	1,200	4,000
	F	...-...-..	...-...-...	..-...-..	...	...-..	...	...-...	...	...
Norton t, Mass. (1,1) ....P		20-18-37	22,432-27,390	Y-29,390-5	885	823-92	765	46-12	8	54
	F	21-20-42	21,552-28,825	Y-29,825-5	924	874-94	813	49-12	4	46
Norton, Ohio (1,3) ....P		18-13-40	26,790-35,048	Y-35,668-5	1,083	957-88	752	130-75	...	126
	F	4-3-40	26,229-31,325	Y-31,945-5	...	...-..	...	...-...	10	...
Norton Shores, Mich. (1,3) ....P		25-23-40	27,523-34,795	Y-38,275-5	1,566	1,220-77	994	76-150	84	262
	F	10-9-48	25,175-30,543	Y-33,597-5	861	629-73	530	41-58	84	148
Oak Creek, Wis. (1,1) ....P		46-40-40	32,060-39,539	Y-39,899-5	...	...-..	...	...-...	498	...
	F	37-36-56	32,688-38,649	Y-38,889-5	...	...-..	...	...-...	439	...
Oak Harbor, Wash. (1,3) ....P		38-24-48	28,152-35,196	NONE	...	...-..	...	...-...	...	...
	F	5-4-53	27,654-32,676	NONE	...	...-..	...	...-...	12	...
Oakdale, Calif. (1,3) ....P		29-21-40	25,500-34,296	NONE	...	...-..	...	...-...	43	...
	F	13-13-..	24,372-29,736	NONE	...	...-..	...	...-...	31	...
Ocean Springs, Miss. (3,3) ....P		37-28-40	16,661-20,676	Y-...-1	1,710	1,110-64	900	150-60	300	300
	F	26-26-48	16,641-20,651	Y-...-1	880	750-85	600	110-40	50	80
Ocoee, Fla. (1,3) ....P		43-35-40	21,519-33,250	Y-36,198-5	7,302	6,481-88	6,083	253-145	59	762
	F	31-30-56	21,519-31,793	Y-34,336-5	1,522	1,323-86	944	175-204	63	136
Oconomowoc, Wis. (1,3) ....P		28-21-40	29,146-35,210	Y-35,270-5	...	...-..	...	...-...	750	...
	F	4-3-40	30,127-...	Y-...-..	...	...-..	...	...-...	97	...
Ogdensburg, N.Y. (1,1) ....P		29-23-40	19,795-30,098	NONE	1,350	1,191-88	912	147-132	61	98
	F	34-34-40	24,689-27,960	Y-29,835-10	1,512	1,422-94	1,083	184-155	27	63
Okmulgee, Okla. (1,1) ....P		32-25-40	15,792-18,792	Y-20,692-..	1,044	862-82	646	108-108	99	83
	F	24-24-60	13,800-16,271	Y-19,831-..	806	712-88	547	60-105	6	88
Oneida, N.Y. (1,1) ....P		23-20-40	23,920-32,614	Y-34,014-10	...	...-..	...	...-...	...	...
	F	23-23-40	18,375-27,445	Y-29,445-5	...	...-..	...	...-...	...	...
Opelousas, La. (1,1) ....P		49-40-40	13,998-...	NONE	2,158	1,447-67	1,145	242-60	37	674
	F	38-37-55	13,477-...	NONE	1,403	1,072-76	952	75-45	130	201
Orange, Tex. (1,1) ....P		51-41-40	20,883-28,724	NONE	2,422	1,863-76	1,403	231-229	...	559
	F	44-43-53	19,016-26,816	NONE	1,993	1,801-90	1,369	216-216	4	188
Oregon, Ohio (1,3) ....P		43-43-40	30,409-37,336	Y-39,950-5	3,434	2,451-71	1,843	354-254	703	280
	F	11-11-..	31,799-39,781	NONE	...	...-..	...	...-...	592	...
Orinda, Calif. (-,5) ....P		...-...-..	...-...-...	..-...-..	...	...-..	...	...-...	...	...
	F	...-...-..	...-...-...	..-...-..	...	...-..	...	...-...	...	...
Orono t, Me. (1,1) ....P		17-13-40	18,480-25,060	..-...-..	...	...-..	...	...-...	...	...
	F	15-14-53	17,940-22,620	..-...-..	722	554-76	459	48-47	...	168
Oroville, Calif. (1,3) ....P		31-21-40	25,808-...	NONE	2,506	2,266-90	1,797	253-216	20	220
	F	21-..-56	25,264-...	NONE	1,307	1,137-86	824	184-129	59	111
Oskaloosa, Iowa (1,1) ....P		20-18-40	19,879-26,451	Y-27,351-6	716	631-88	505	85-41	12	73
	F	18-18-..	19,295-25,058	Y-25,958-6	689	641-93	509	89-43	5	43
Oswego, N.Y. (1,1) ....P		54-49-40	27,040-33,358	Y-37,783-10	2,963	2,868-96	2,152	455-261	...	95
	F	75-74-44	24,331-31,380	Y-34,658-10	4,103	3,893-94	2,864	620-409	...	210
Ottawa, Kan. (1,3) ....P		26-21-40	19,240-...	...-...-..	...	...-..	...	...-...	...	...
	F	17-17-53	16,408-20,657	NONE	677	590-87	470	64-56	15	72
Ottumwa, Iowa (1,1) ....P		39-32-40	20,384-25,376	Y-...-5	1,563	1,352-86	1,063	169-120	71	140
	F	33-33-56	22,224-26,499	Y-...-5	1,442	1,336-92	1,033	154-149	...	106
Overland, Mo. (1,5) ....P		47-47-40	24,852-31,716	Y-...-5	3,456	2,600-75	2,119	162-319	334	522
	F	...-...-..	...-...-...	..-...-..	...	...-..	...	...-...	...	...
Owatonna, Minn. (1,3) ....P		26-24-40	27,684-34,608	Y-35,819-5	1,404	1,239-88	1,002	124-113	71	94
	F	8-8-53	27,924-31,027	Y-31,627-5	560	449-80	375	41-33	51	60
Ozark, Ala. (1,1) ....P		45-39-40	15,628-19,946	Y-20,196-10	...	...-..	...	...-...	55	...
	F	33-32-56	15,310-19,453	Y-19,703-10	...	...-..	...	...-...	19	...
Pacific Grove, Calif. (1,3) ....P		38-27-40	29,844-36,276	NONE	3,483	2,779-79	2,321	280-178	311	393
	F	19-18-56	26,172-31,800	NONE	1,880	1,410-75	1,183	133-94	316	154
Painesville, Ohio (1,1) ....P		36-27-40	30,100-38,415	Y-42,257-10	6,412	2,011-31	1,578	292-141	4,173	228
	F	22-22-50	30,100-38,415	Y-42,257-10	...	...-..	...	...-...	33	...
Palestine, Tex. (3,1) ....P		43-32-40	21,132-24,084	Y-25,884-..	1,503	1,340-89	1,048	144-148	10	153
	F	40-37-53	18,648-20,652	Y-22,452-..	1,270	1,193-93	914	128-151	2	75
Palm Beach Gardens, Fla. (1,1) .....P		109-84-40	26,958-37,210	Y-40,931-4	4,301	3,872-90	3,324	248-300	185	244
	F	50-48-48	21,382-27,790	Y-30,569-4	1,900	1,406-74	1,194	87-125	163	331
Palm Desert, Calif. (7,6) ....P		...-...-..	...-...-...	..-...-..	...	...-..	...	...-...	...	...
	F	...-...-..	...-...-...	..-...-..	...	...-..	...	...-...	...	...
Palos Verdes Estates, Calif. (1,-) .....P		35-23-39	27,552-34,536	Y-46,609-5	5,138	2,100-40	1,610	295-195	2,465	573
	F	...-...-..	...-...-...	..-...-..	...	...-..	...	...-...	...	...
Paragould, Ark. (1,3) ....P		33-28-40	17,480-19,000	Y-20,900-10	1,064	876-82	697	118-61	51	137
	F	19-19-48	18,615-20,234	Y-22,257-10	744	519-69	437	33-49	151	74
Parma Heights, Ohio (1,1) ....P		34-29-40	24,468-33,699	Y-35,199-4	2,522	1,772-70	1,370	267-135	39	711
	F	26-25-52	24,468-33,699	Y-35,199-4	...	...-..	...	...-...	127	...
Peachtree City, Ga. (1,3) ....P		41-31-43	21,294-30,088	NONE	...	...-..	...	...-...	90	...
	F	23-22-48	21,294-30,088	NONE	...	...-..	...	...-...	130	...
Pearland, Tex. (1,2) ....P		55-40-40	28,059-32,802	Y-32,850-1	2,222	1,903-85	1,522	230-151	116	203
	F	...-...-..	...-...-...	..-...-..	...	...-..	...	...-...	55	...
Pecos, Tex. (3,3) ....P		24-17-40	18,684-22,836	Y-23,796-1	799	658-82	517	69-72	45	96
	F	...-...-..	...-...-...	..-...-..	...	...-..	...	...-...	9	...

Table 3/22 continued   POLICE AND FIRE DEPARTMENT PERSONNEL, SALARIES, AND EXPENDITURES FOR CITIES 10,000 AND OVER: 1994

City (Service provision)	Department	Total personnel, no. uniformed, duty hours per week	Entrance, maximum salary ($)	Longevity pay, maximum ($) no. years to receive longevity pay	Reported expenditures (in thousands)					
					Total expenditures (A) ($)	Total personnel expenditures (B) ($), % of (A)	Salaries and wages (C) ($)	City contrib. to employee retirement, insurance (D) ($)	Capital outlay (E) ($)	All other (F) ($)
10,000–24,999 continued										
Pepperell t, Mass. (1,2)	P	17-16-40	27,353-29,858	Y-33,740-..	...	...-..	...	...-...	31	...
	F	..-.-..	..-...	..-...-..	...	...-..	...	...-...		
Perrysburg, Ohio (1,3)	P	28-21-40	25,760-34,880	Y-...-10	1,584	1,320-83	1,007	187-126	112	152
	F	12-12-50	23,998-32,240	Y-...-12	...	...-..	...	...-...	228	...
Pierre, S.D. (1,2)	P	29-20-40	20,240-24,102	Y-...-5	...	...-..	...	...-...	43	...
	F	..-..-..	..-...	..-...-..	...	...-..	...	...-...	142	...
Pinole, Calif. (1,1)	P	42-23-40	37,668-45,792	NONE	2,780	2,473-88	2,101	206-166	12	295
	F	16-16-56	32,796-40,236	NONE	1,119	1,010-90	866	91-53	3	106
Piqua, Ohio (1,1)	P	28-28-40	30,591-38,690	NONE	2,140	1,828-85	1,351	261-216	23	289
	F	26-26-56	31,236-39,014	NONE	...	...-..	...	...-...	189	...
Pittsburg, Kan. (1,1)	P	36-30-40	19,272-27,720	NONE	1,491	1,228-82	1,010	129-89	40	223
	F	31-31-56	19,272-27,720	NONE	1,158	1,041-89	854	112-75	5	112
Plainsboro tp, N.J. (1,5)	P	35-26-40	30,386-49,305	Y-51,605-7	15,188	2,155-14	1,606	288-261	12,888	145
	F	...-..-..	..-...	..-...-..	...	...-..	...	...-...	...	...
Plainville t, Conn. (1,2)	P	37-31-37	30,447-40,115	NONE	2,219	2,005-90	1,550	275-180	125	89
	F	...-..-..	..-...	NONE	...	...-..	...	...-...	118	...
Plant City, Fla. (1,1)	P	56-35-40	23,128-33,767	..-...-..	3,287	2,485-75	2,041	282-162	202	600
	F	31-30-56	20,953-28,873	..-...-..	1,693	1,025-60	843	115-67	384	284
Pleasant Grove, Utah (1,2)	P	15-14-40	18,288-25,560	NONE	...	...-..	...	...-...	30	...
	F	..-..-..	..-...	..-...-..	...	...-..	...	...-...	...	...
Pleasantville, N.J. (1,1)	P	51-43-40	25,523-37,991	Y-41,030-4	3,123	2,666-85	2,145	260-261	309	148
	F	32-32-42	21,710-35,535	Y-38,378-5	2,135	1,683-78	1,328	183-172	425	27
Plymouth tp, Pa. (1,2)	P	39-32-40	33,961-40,531	Y-...-5	...	...-..	...	...-...	97	...
	F	...-..-..	..-...	..-...-..	...	...-..	...	...-...	...	...
Point Pleasant b, N.J. (1,2)	P	34-26-40	27,581-45,968	Y-49,645-3	2,446	2,313-94	1,675	314-324	36	97
	F	...-..-..	..-...	..-...-..	...	...-..	...	...-...	62	...
Pompton Lakes b, N.J. (1,2)	P	27-21-40	26,000-54,000	Y-58,000-3	...	...-..	...	...-...	125	...
	F	...-..-..	..-...	..-...-..	...	...-..	...	...-...	...	...
Poplar Bluff, Mo. (1,1)	P	47-39-40	23,064-26,040	NONE	1,682	1,513-89	1,271	57-185	65	104
	F	33-32-48	21,156-24,516	NONE	1,183	1,103-93	930	31-142	22	58
Poquoson, Va. (1,1)	P	...-..-40	20,120-28,311	NONE	946	822-86	688	85-49	...	124
	F	14-14-..	20,120-28,311	NONE	817	658-80	539	66-53	15	144
Port Neches, Tex. (1,3)	P	20-17-40	27,945-28,413	Y-...-1	1,570	928-59	701	136-91	469	173
	F	13-12-56	27,945-28,413	Y-...-1	750	586-78	441	86-59	37	127
Portales, N.M. (1,1)	P	25-22-40	17,000-20,629	NONE	3,592	727-20	572	94-61	2,675	190
	F	17-16-56	13,500-27,720	NONE	3,367	550-16	427	72-51	2,701	116
Portland, Tex. (1,2)	P	25-17-40	20,800-24,544	Y-...-1	1,876	720-38	579	72-69	941	215
	F	...-..-..	..-...	..-...-..	...	...-..	...	...-...	949	...
Portsmouth, Ohio (1,1)	P	40-37-40	18,096-26,395	NONE	2,142	1,703-79	1,340	202-161	99	340
	F	36-30-53	19,944-24,972	NONE	2,319	1,845-79	1,331	298-216	191	283
Portsmouth t, R.I. (1,1)	P	25-23-37	22,011-28,682	Y-30,403-5	...	...-..	...	...-...	48	...
	F	25-23-42	24,329-27,678	Y-29,338-5	...	...-..	...	...-...	5	...
Potsdam v, N.Y. (1,2)	P	18-18-40	24,320-31,300	Y-32,200-1	...	...-..	...	...-...	28	...
	F	...-..-40	..-...	..-...-..	...	...-..	...	...-...	3	...
Prairie Village, Kan. (1,-)	P	46-37-40	24,000-37,200	..-...-..	2,709	2,011-74	1,637	200-174	78	620
	F	...-..-..	..-...	..-...-..	...	...-..	...	...-...	...	...
Prattville, Ala. (-,-)	P	52-47-40	15,891-28,433	NONE	3,545	1,397-39	1,157	137-103	473	1,675
	F	37-36-56	15,226-28,433	NONE	...	...-..	...	...-...	62	...
Presque Isle, Me. (1,3)	P	22-16-40	19,656-23,441	Y-26,561-7	...	...-..	...	...-...	20	...
	F	16-16-56	19,883-23,770	Y-26,890-7	739	664-89	477	109-78	7	68
Prior Lake, Minn. (1,2)	P	19-16-40	28,500-39,660	Y-43,230-4	1,230	944-76	785	100-59	186	100
	F	...-..-..	..-...	..-...-..	...	...-..	...	...-...	126	...
Prospect Heights, Ill. (1,5)	P	26-22-40	28,632-42,968	NONE	1,814	1,020-56	841	99-80	505	289
	F	...-..-..	..-...	..-...-..	...	...-..	...	...-...	...	...
Punta Gorda, Fla. (1,3)	P	38-27-40	22,455-33,022	NONE	1,756	1,239-70	1,024	81-134	147	370
	F	28-23-42	19,394-28,736	NONE	1,151	922-80	729	97-96	10	219
Ramsey, Minn. (1,2)	P	13-11-40	28,529-39,624	Y-43,202-5	702	601-85	483	58-60	47	54
	F	...-..-..	..-...	..-...-..	...	...-..	...	...-...	2	...
Ramsey b, N.J. (1,2)	P	38-27-40	14,500-51,500	Y-52,600-4	...	...-..	...	...-...	43	...
	F	...-..-..	..-...	..-...-..	...	...-..	...	...-...	...	...
Raritan tp, N.J. (1,2)	P	32-28-40	29,728-41,109	Y-44,398-5	2,279	1,977-86	1,536	251-190	197	105
	F	...-..-..	..-...	..-...-..	...	...-..	...	...-...	27	...
Ravenna, Ohio (1,1)	P	26-26-40	23,878-30,409	Y-31,609-5	1,566	1,355-86	999	202-154	44	167
	F	18-18-56	23,470-29,789	Y-30,989-5	...	...-..	...	...-...	20	...
Reading, Ohio (1,1)	P	23-19-40	29,159-33,941	Y-34,816-2	...	...-..	...	...-...	258	...
	F	14-14-55	30,081-35,217	Y-36,092-2	...	...-..	...	...-...	4	...
Red Bank b, N.J. (1,2)	P	43-40-40	27,409-47,708	Y-51,047-5	2,910	2,762-94	2,260	302-200	...	148
	F	...-..-..	..-...	..-...-..	...	...-..	...	...-...	...	...
Red Bluff, Calif. (4,4)	P	...-..-..	..-...	..-...-..	...	...-..	...	...-...	...	...
	F	...-..-..	..-...	..-...-..	...	...-..	...	...-...	...	...
Red Wing, Minn. (1,3)	P	25-23-40	29,736-35,328	Y-36,288-7	...	...-..	...	...-...	62	...
	F	27-27-56	27,768-34,272	NONE	1,414	1,134-80	917	131-86	47	233
Reedley, Calif. (1,2)	P	31-23-40	27,024-32,844	NONE	...	...-..	...	...-...	83	...
	F	...-..-..	..-...	..-...-..	...	...-..	...	...-...	8	...

Table 3/22 continued **POLICE AND FIRE DEPARTMENT PERSONNEL, SALARIES, AND EXPENDITURES FOR CITIES 10,000 AND OVER: 1994**

City (Service provision)	Department	Total personnel, no. uniformed, duty hours per week	Entrance, maximum salary ($)	Longevity pay, maximum ($) no. years to receive longevity pay	Total expenditures (A) ($)	Total personnel expenditures (B) ($), % of (A)	Salaries and wages (C) ($)	City contrib. to employee retirement, insurance (D) ($)	Capital outlay (E) ($)	All other (F) ($)
10,000–24,999 continued										
Reidsville, N.C. (3,3)	P	51-43-42	20,472-28,806	Y-30,306-2	2,060	1,525-74	1,197	229-99	160	375
	F	22-21-53	19,497-27,434	Y-28,934-2	1,121	673-60	546	84-43	100	348
Rexburg, Idaho (3,3)	P	17-15-40	20,460-28,008	NONE	779	560-71	438	77-45	56	163
	F	3-3-54	18,924-28,008	NONE	...	...-...	...	...-...	19	...
Richmond Heights, Mo. (1,1)	P	33-28-40	25,804-37,053	NONE	1,106	941-85	783	61-97	62	103
	F	22-22-53	25,804-37,053	NONE	...	...-..	...	...-...	10	...
Ridgefield t, Conn. (1,3)	P	41-36-40	29,600-41,312	Y-42,512-5	2,627	2,333-88	1,731	366-236	99	195
	F	25-24-42	26,373-37,581	Y-38,781-5	1,597	1,402-87	1,038	220-144	72	123
Ridgewood v, N.J. (1,1)	P	53-45-72	29,633-48,543	Y-54,854-..	...	...-..	...	...-...	187	...
	F	43-42-40	29,510-52,058	Y-58,826-..	...	...-..	...	...-...	415	...
River Edge b, N.J. (1,2)	P	27-24-40	24,000-54,308	Y-59,738-4	2,192	2,054-93	1,653	217-184	13	125
	F	...-..-..	...-...	...-..-..	...	...-..	...	...-...	19	...
River Falls, Wis. (1,2)	P	21-18-40	29,786-33,946	Y-34,546-1	...	...-..	...	...-...	1,599	...
	F	...-..-..	...-...	...-..-..	...	...-..	...	...-...	1,573	...
River Forest v, Ill. (1,1)	P	31-21-40	29,007-42,851	NONE	...	...-..	...	...-...	207	...
	F	21-21-53	26,172-41,862	NONE	1,508	1,243-82	977	185-81	209	56
Riverton, Utah	P	...-..-..	...-...	..-...-..	...	...	...	...	...	...
	F	...-..-..	...-...	..-...-..	...	...	...	...	...	...
Riverview, Mich. (1,9)	P	32-28-40	23,406-40,069	Y-40,569-5	...	...-..	...	...-...	40	...
	F	3-2-..	...-...	NONE	497	472-94	421	37-14	5	20
Roanoke Rapids, N.C. (1,1)	P	40-40-42	17,403-24,489	Y-...-5	2,174	1,219-56	945	201-73	708	247
	F	27-..-53	15,785-23,323	Y-...-5	1,559	867-55	674	115-78	642	50
Robbinsdale, Minn. (3,2)	P	27-19-40	25,704-39,552	Y-43,112-4	...	...-..	...	...-...	66	...
	F	...-..-..	...-...	..-...-..	...	...-..	...	...-...	22	...
Robinson tp, Pa. (-,2)	P	20-16-40	29,203-41,662	Y-44,533-5	...	...-..	...	...-...	...	...
	F	...-..-..	...-...	..-...-..	...	...-..	...	...-...	...	...
Rock Springs, Wyo. (1,1)	P	58-34-40	26,040-36,654	NONE	2,487	2,206-88	1,735	223-248	111	170
	F	37-36-53	30,785-33,237	Y-37,392-1	2,379	1,898-79	1,451	273-174	297	184
Rockledge, Fla. (3,1)	P	46-36-40	21,000-27,900	NONE	...	...-..	...	...-...	1,757	...
	F	36-35-56	18,999-25,200	NONE	...	...-..	...	...-...	1,505	...
Rocklin, Calif. (3,3)	P	40-14-40	27,756-33,876	Y-35,570-7	2,381	1,787-75	1,389	127-271	65	529
	F	20-16-56	27,072-32,904	Y-34,549-7	1,324	948-71	736	75-137	54	322
Rockville Centre v, N.Y. (1,2)	P	59-49-40	33,258-58,863	Y-...-..	...	...-..	...	...-...	...	...
	F	...-..-..	...-...	..-...-..	...	...-..	...	...-...	...	...
Rockwall, Tex. (1,2)	P	34-22-40	23,856-30,876	Y-...-1	...	...-..	...	...-...	281	...
	F	...-..-..	...-...	..-...-..	...	...-..	...	...-...	3	...
Rocky River, Ohio (1,1)	P	32-32-40	27,908-36,483	Y-38,125-6	...	...-..	...	...-...	116	...
	F	29-29-56	29,035-37,956	Y-39,665-6	...	...-..	...	...-...	20	...
Rogers, Ark. (1,1)	P	61-44-40	15,558-22,963	Y-25,314-7	...	...-..	...	...-...	67	...
	F	48-39-56	23,500-38,340	NONE	...	...-..	...	...-...	699	...
Rolla, Mo. (1,1)	P	35-24-..	16,624-24,448	NONE	...	...-..	...	...-...	71	...
	F	21-20-..	15,042-22,121	NONE	...	...-..	...	...-...	135	...
Romulus, Mich. (1,3)	P	71-58-40	27,983-37,716	NONE	4,259	3,716-87	2,845	501-370	63	480
	F	...-..-..	...-...	..-...-..	537	357-66	292	27-38	60	120
Roseburg, Ore. (1,1)	P	36-32-40	25,128-32,076	NONE	...	...-..	...	...-...	102	...
	F	32-31-56	27,276-33,156	NONE	...	...-..	...	...-...	21	...
Roselle v, Ill. (1,3)	P	36-5-42	29,306-40,254	NONE	...	...-..	...	...-...	298	...
	F	7-4-48	25,919-38,294	NONE	...	...-..	...	...-...	25	...
Rosenberg, Tex. (-,3)	P	58-44-40	23,358-31,304	Y-32,804-1	2,426	1,986-81	1,637	187-162	5	435
	F	23-22-56	22,015-29,615	Y-31,115-1	1,181	869-73	720	89-60	70	242
Rowlett, Tex. (1,1)	P	54-39-40	29,958-...	Y-31,158-..	2,040	1,715-84	1,455	91-169	99	226
	F	43-42-56	25,962-...	Y-27,162-..	1,956	1,497-76	1,295	80-122	280	179
Roy, Utah (1,1)	P	31-31-40	23,293-32,244	Y-33,856-15	1,568	1,330-84	1,040	233-57	170	68
	F	20-20-40	22,184-30,708	NONE	1,125	977-86	779	161-37	60	88
Rutland, Vt. (1,1)	P	44-35-40	20,504-27,791	Y-...-5	1,826	1,781-97	1,437	160-184	6	39
	F	34-34-46	20,880-25,525	Y-...-10	1,527	1,293-84	1,013	122-158	...	234
Rye, N.Y. (1,3)	P	41-36-40	...-...	Y-...-..	...	...-..	...	...-...	...	...
	F	15-15-40	...-...	Y-...-..	...	...-..	...	...-...	...	...
Saddle Brook tp, N.J. (1,2)	P	35-33-37	40,943-56,816	Y-70,000-3	2,743	2,433-88	2,038	170-225	260	50
	F	...-..-..	...-...	..-...-..	...	...-..	...	...-...	310	...
Safety Harbor, Fla. (7,1)	P	...-..-..	...-...	..-...-..	...	...-..	...	...-...	...	...
	F	31-30-53	21,724-47,348	Y-48,348-5	...	...-..	...	...-...	4,690	...
St. Albans, W.Va. (1,3)	P	14-14-40	18,871-20,806	Y-21,806-6	...	...-..	...	...-...	35	...
	F	17-17-..	18,871-20,806	Y-21,806-6	...	...-..	...	...-...	33	...
St. Augustine, Fla. (3,1)	P	46-37-40	21,926-29,600	NONE	2,377	1,670-70	1,269	243-158	540	167
	F	25-25-56	21,282-28,731	NONE	...	...-..	...	...-...	2	...
St. Cloud, Fla. (1,3)	P	45-32-43	21,589-29,277	NONE	1,973	1,624-82	1,209	234-181	94	255
	F	31-30-48	23,183-31,438	NONE	1,775	1,302-73	926	193-183	307	166
St. Matthews, Ky. (1,2)	P	33-27-40	18,318-22,126	Y-...-..	...	...-..	...	...-...	...	...
	F	...-..-..	...-...	..-...-..	...	...-..	...	...-...	...	...
Salem, Ohio (1,1)	P	19-19-40	15,746-25,480	Y-26,632-..	944	853-90	672	104-77	22	69
	F	16-16-54	17,958-25,534	Y-26,704-..	...	...-..	...	...-...	84	...
Salem, Va. (1,1)	P	74-55-40	20,800-30,680	NONE	3,276	2,730-83	2,149	379-202	199	347
	F	49-48-42	19,802-29,245	NONE	2,095	1,885-89	1,484	256-145	8	202

Table 3/22 continued   POLICE AND FIRE DEPARTMENT PERSONNEL, SALARIES, AND EXPENDITURES FOR CITIES 10,000 AND OVER: 1994

City (Service provision)	Department	Total personnel, no. uniformed, duty hours per week	Entrance, maximum salary ($)	Longevity pay, maximum ($) no. years to receive longevity pay	Reported expenditures (in thousands)					
					Total expenditures (A) ($)	Total personnel expenditures (B) ($), % of (A)	Salaries and wages (C) ($)	City contrib. to employee retirement, insurance (D) ($)	Capital outlay (E) ($)	All other (F) ($)
10,000–24,999 continued										
Salisbury, N.C. (1,1)	P	88-68-40	18,165-25,665	NONE	3,196	2,727-85	2,140	384-203	113	356
	F	64-64-56	16,867-24,428	NONE	1,916	1,728-90	1,488	77-163	10	178
San Anselmo, Calif. (1,9)	P	22-16-40	32,160-39,084	..-...-..	...	...-..	...	...-...	53	...
	F	...-..-..	...-...	..-...-..	...	...-..	...	...-...	...	...
San Benito, Tex. (3,3)	P	37-30-40	17,250-18,750	Y-20,670-..	...	...-..	...	...-...	26	...
	F	20-20-53	15,500-18,000	Y-20,100-..	644	510-79	389	41-80	70	64
San Fernando, Calif. (1,9)	P	49-35-40	35,196-43,596	Y-47,952-4	...	...-..	...	...-...	233	...
	F	...-..-..	...-...	..-...-..	...	...-..	...	...-...	...	...
Sand Springs, Okla. (1,1)	P	31-28-40	18,360-20,520	Y-21,408-..	1,164	917-78	724	115-78	64	183
	F	26-25-56	15,636-20,160	Y-22,260-..	1,088	869-79	703	78-88	40	179
Sandwich t, Mass. (1,1)	P	29-28-40	25,027-29,772	Y-30,097-5	...	...-..	...	...-...	80	...
	F	29-29-42	24,010-29,304	Y-29,764-5	...	...-..	...	...-...	27	...
Sanford t, Me. (1,3)	P	47-34-40	20,115-23,993	Y-27,750-..	...	...-..	...	...-...	46	...
	F	42-42-42	21,822-...	Y-27,708-..	1,952	1,274-65	999	96-179	36	642
Sanford, N.C. (1,1)	P	82-67-40	19,297-28,647	Y-...-5	3,085	2,463-79	1,931	306-226	201	421
	F	47-46-40	19,297-28,647	Y-...-5	1,793	1,444-80	1,155	140-149	33	316
Santa Clarita, Calif. (7,7)	P	...-..-..	...-...	..-...-..	...	...-..	...	...-...	...	...
	F	...-..-..	...-...	..-...-..	...	...-..	...	...-...	...	...
Santa Fe Springs, Calif. (9,1)	P	...-..-..	...-...	..-...-..	...	...-..	...	...-...	...	...
	F	71-67-56	34,590-41,880	Y-49,879-22	...	...-..	...	...-...	1,143	...
Sapulpa, Okla. (1,1)	P	46-36-40	16,800-18,264	Y-25,569-1	1,841	1,494-81	1,176	121-197	113	234
	F	37-36-72	13,200-18,024	Y-25,233-1	1,504	1,392-92	1,230	133-29	38	74
Saraland, Ala. (1,1)	P	33-33-40	16,332-25,344	NONE	...	...-..	...	...-...	113	...
	F	17-17-56	16,332-25,344	NONE	857	588-68	443	53-92	167	102
Scarsdale v, N.Y. (1,3)	P	45-40-40	25,000-49,057	Y-49,807-17	5,522	3,304-59	2,440	465-399	2,079	139
	F	43-42-40	20,000-47,988	Y-48,738-17	5,141	2,982-58	2,208	423-351	2,054	105
Scituate t, Mass. (1,1)	P	29-21-38	20,050-31,542	Y-31,993-21	...	...-..	...	...-...	68	...
	F	55-50-..	28,240-...	Y-31,630-..	...	...-..	...	...-...	33	...
Scotch Plains tp, N.J. (1,2)	P	47-42-40	34,546-47,209	Y-51,929-5	3,314	2,717-81	2,154	326-237	418	179
	F	...-..-..	...-...	..-...-..	...	...-..	...	...-...	357	...
Seguin, Tex. (1,3)	P	52-36-40	21,029-27,580	Y-28,780-..	1,900	1,492-78	1,209	189-94	98	310
	F	37-36-53	20,009-26,270	Y-27,470-..	1,402	1,071-76	866	137-68	23	308
Selma, Calif. (1,3)	P	33-22-40	25,064-30,465	NONE	...	...-..	...	...-...	24	...
	F	14-14-56	22,852-27,777	NONE	...	...-..	...	...-...	1	...
Seven Hills, Ohio (1,2)	P	15-15-40	25,961-31,907	Y-33,407-5	1,348	887-65	650	145-92	414	47
	F	...-..-..	...-...	..-...-..	...	...-..	...	...-...	405	...
Shakopee, Minn. (1,2)	P	22-19-40	29,556-39,408	Y-41,747-5	1,208	1,029-85	840	102-87	56	123
	F	...-..-..	...-...	..-...-..	...	...-..	...	...-...	12	...
Sharonville, Ohio (1,3)	P	43-32-40	28,263-37,268	Y-38,572-5	5,931	2,339-39	1,829	329-181	3,059	533
	F	5-4-40	28,263-37,268	Y-38,572-5	3,987	624-15	528	78-18	3,096	267
Shelby, N.C. (3,3)	P	52-38-42	17,472-22,412	Y-22,812-5	2,490	1,904-76	1,586	191-127	97	489
	F	40-38-51	16,692-21,320	Y-21,720-5	1,633	1,379-84	1,154	145-80	5	249
Shelbyville, Tenn. (1,3)	P	34-34-42	18,065-23,216	Y-23,776-3	...	...-..	...	...-...	716	...
	F	32-32-53	18,665-20,739	Y-26,020-3	...	...-..	...	...-...	31	...
Sheridan, Wyo. (1,1)	P	41-27-40	22,394-30,010	Y-33,010-5	1,883	1,468-77	1,138	144-186	113	302
	F	19-1-56	21,328-28,581	Y-31,581-5	...	...-..	...	...-...	35	...
Sherwood, Ark. (1,2)	P	63-45-40	20,315-27,211	NONE	3,484	1,881-53	1,545	206-130	1,296	307
	F	...-..-..	...-...	..-...-..	...	...-..	...	...-...	33	...
Shoreview, Minn. (-,-)	P	...-..-..	...-...	..-...-..	...	...-..	...	...-...	...	...
	F	...-..-..	...-...	..-...-..	...	...-..	...	...-...	...	...
Shrewsbury t, Mass. (1,3)	P	40-32-37	27,764-31,681	Y-...-5	...	...-..	...	...-...	58	...
	F	34-33-42	26,704-30,463	Y-...-5	...	...-..	...	...-...	8	...
Sidney, Ohio (1,1)	P	31-31-40	25,168-32,489	Y-34,113-25	2,644	1,577-59	1,224	239-114	124	943
	F	30-30-54	24,900-32,155	Y-33,762-25	...	...-..	...	...-...	159	...
Sikeston, Mo. (4,4)	P	...-..-..	...-...	..-...-..	...	...-..	...	...-...	...	...
	F	...-..-..	...-...	..-...-..	...	...-..	...	...-...	...	...
Silver City t, N.M. (1,1)	P	31-23-40	13,333-15,476	NONE	...	...-..	...	...-...	70	...
	F	24-24-56	13,333-18,094	NONE	...	...-..	...	...-...	...	...
Simsbury t, Conn. (1,5)	P	38-32-..	35,798-46,729	Y-47,429-4	2,552	2,375-93	1,893	250-232	...	177
	F	...-..-..	...-...	..-...-..	...	...-..	...	...-...	...	...
Slidell, La. (3,5)	P	92-76-40	15,704-29,452	Y-30,352-5	7,435	2,801-37	2,414	372-15	4,191	443
	F	...-..-..	...-...	..-...-..	...	...-..	...	...-...	...	...
Smithfield t, R.I. (1,1)	P	45-36-40	25,195-29,641	NONE	...	...-..	...	...-...	90	...
	F	40-34-40	23,890-26,556	NONE	2,602	2,237-85	1,642	365-230	100	265
Smyrna t, Tenn. (1,3)	P	39-27-40	23,969-25,813	NONE	...	...-..	...	...-...	120	...
	F	4-4-43	18,550-...	NONE	...	...-..	...	...-...	127	...
Snellville, Ga. (4,7)	P	32-26-40	20,675-28,496	NONE	1,302	1,024-78	875	98-51	92	186
	F	...-..-..	...-...	..-...-..	...	...-..	...	...-...	...	...
Solana Beach, Calif. (9,1)	P	...-..-..	...-...	..-...-..	...	...-..	...	...-...	...	...
	F	22-20-56	30,558-37,674	..-...-..	...	...-..	...	...-...	4	...
Solon, Ohio (1,1)	P	53-40-40	32,109-38,391	Y-42,230-5	2,968	2,710-91	2,043	369-298	...	258
	F	43-42-53	26,222-38,391	Y-42,230-5	2,778	2,523-90	1,815	417-291	...	255
Somerset, Ky. (1,1)	P	28-26-40	12,450-...	NONE	...	...-..	...	...-...	...	...
	F	18-18-40	11,846-...	NONE	...	...-..	...	...-...	...	...

Table 3/22 continued

POLICE AND FIRE DEPARTMENT PERSONNEL, SALARIES, AND EXPENDITURES FOR CITIES 10,000 AND OVER: 1994

City (Service provision)	Depart-ment	Total personnel, no. uniformed, duty hours per week	Entrance, maximum salary ($)	Longevity pay, maximum ($) no. years to receive longevity pay	Reported expenditures (in thousands)					
					Total expendi-tures (A) ($)	Total personnel expendi-tures (B) ($), % of (A)	Salaries and wages (C) ($)	City contrib. to employee retirement, insurance (D) ($)	Capital outlay (E) ($)	All other (F) ($)
10,000–24,999 continued										
Somerset t, Mass. (1,3)	P	33-30-40	24,224-30,280	Y-31,580-..	1,653	1,494-90	1,270	75-149	67	92
	F	33-30-42	24,364-30,456	Y-31,756-..	1,434	1,359-94	1,133	77-149	...	75
Somersworth, N.H. (1,3)	P	26-19-40	19,989-24,253	Y-24,877-5	1,083	849-78	728	34-87	16	218
	F	14-13-42	20,399-24,832	Y-25,872-5	652	553-84	469	32-52	...	99
South Burlington, Vt. (1,3)	P	35-28-40	23,515-26,920	Y-...-1	2,194	1,423-64	1,145	129-149	507	264
	F	10-10-56	21,975-25,160	Y-...-1	1,123	467-41	385	42-40	503	153
South Daytona, Fla. (3,3)	P	32-23-40	20,570-30,426	NONE	...	...-..	...	...-...	56	...
	F	12-12-53	19,591-28,977	NONE	...	...-..	...	...-...	8	...
South El Monte, Calif	P	...-..-..	...-...	..-...-..	...	...-..	...	...-...	...	...
	F	...-..-..	...-...	..-...-..	...	...-..	...	...-...	...	...
South Fayette tp, Pa. (1,2)	P	14-14-40	24,000-40,000	Y-...-..	...	...-..	...	...-...	5	...
	F	...-..-..	...-...	..-...-..	...	...-..	...	...-...	14	...
South Lake Tahoe, Calif. (3,3)	P	70-49-40	31,464-38,244	NONE	4,634	3,873-83	2,996	589-288	109	652
	F	39-36-56	29,952-36,408	NONE	2,651	2,372-89	1,815	388-169	11	268
South Miami, Fla. (1,7)	P	59-58-40	27,180-34,689	Y-37,811-10	3,268	2,633-80	2,330	177-126	482	153
	F	...-..-..	...-...	..-...-..	...	...-..	...	...-...	...	...
South Milwaukee, Wis. (1,1)	P	34-32-40	34,477-37,597	Y-...-5	...	...-..	...	...-...	20	...
	F	29-29-56	31,918-36,059	Y-36,359-5	...	...-..	...	...-...	43	...
South Pasadena, Calif. (3,3)	P	48-31-40	34,908-41,388	Y-...-5	...	...-..	...	...-...	34	...
	F	25-25-56	33,210-39,384	Y-...-5	...	...-..	...	...-...	23	...
South St. Paul, Minn. (1,1)	P	23-23-63	32,328-38,388	Y-42,828-..	...	...-..	...	...-...	4	...
	F	18-18-60	32,328-38,388	Y-42,840-..	...	...-..	...	...-...	9	...
South Windsor t, Conn. (1,3)	P	37-32-40	31,250-39,200	Y-39,420-5	2,624	2,381-90	1,836	333-212	95	148
	F	...-..-..	...-...	..-...-..	1,052	62-5	49	8-5	240	750
Southbury t, Conn. (1,2)	P	16-14-40	27,226-36,487	Y-...-5	...	...-..	...	...-...	333	...
	F	...-..-..	...-...	..-...-..	...	...-..	...	...-...	337	...
Spanish Fork, Utah (1,2)	P	17-17-40	24,456-28,992	NONE	...	...-..	...	...-...	3,469	...
	F	...-..-..	...-...	..-...-..	...	...-..	...	...-...	...	...
Speedway t, Ind. (1,1)	P	27-19-40	26,896-28,687	Y-...-1	1,626	1,319-81	1,072	155-92	125	182
	F	33-33-56	26,896-28,687	Y-...-1	1,438	1,323-92	1,041	196-86	26	89
Spencer, Iowa (1,3)	P	26-26-42	23,886-29,015	NONE	893	775-86	698	5-72	33	85
	F	5-5-56	21,674-26,312	Y-27,212-10	...	...-..	...	...-...	20	...
Spring Garden tp, Pa. (1,3)	P	18-17-40	26,486-37,493	Y-...-..	947	845-89	684	78-83	19	83
	F	14-14-52	30,950-...	Y-...-..	757	651-85	492	88-71	26	80
Springfield, Tenn. (1,3)	P	42-31-40	17,722-24,148	NONE	1,493	1,164-77	969	102-93	102	227
	F	20-20-53	16,078-21,882	NONE	828	609-73	528	67-14	17	202
Springville, Utah (1,3)	P	...-26-40	19,946-28,106	Y-...-..	916	805-87	586	115-104	...	111
	F	...-2-40	20,943-29,511	Y-...-..	116	83-71	62	11-10	...	33
Starkville, Miss. (1,1)	P	37-36-43	18,639-...	NONE	1,368	993-72	805	137-51	56	319
	F	39-38-53	12,973-...	NONE	1,373	910-66	736	125-49	232	231
Staunton, Va. (1,1)	P	61-44-40	19,446-27,747	NONE	4,085	2,026-49	1,537	326-163	1,749	310
	F	22-22-48	18,510-26,411	NONE	2,438	715-29	532	120-63	1,665	58
Sterling, Colo. (1,3)	P	21-11-43	19,623-26,870	NONE	1,119	957-85	786	64-107	45	117
	F	8-8-53	19,600-26,843	NONE	392	303-77	256	14-33	25	64
Steubenville, Ohio (1,1)	P	45-45-40	23,254-27,673	Y-...-5	...	...-..	...	...-...	70	...
	F	40-40-40	20,547-27,284	Y-...-5	...	...-..	...	...-...	...	...
Stoneham t, Mass. (1,1)	P	41-36-37	28,117-32,616	Y-33,766-5	...	...-..	...	...-..	...	...
	F	42-41-42	29,000-36,778	Y-...-..	...	...-..	...	...-..	...	...
Struthers, Ohio (1,1)	P	13-13-40	23,482-27,785	Y-28,385-5	650	541-83	402	74-65	26	83
	F	8-8-53	22,561-26,742	Y-27,342-5	442	391-88	287	64-40	...	51
Stuart, Fla. (3,3)	P	56-43-40	22,361-32,731	Y-34,731-3	...	...-..	...	...-...	3,371	...
	F	20-18-53	20,053-33,196	Y-35,196-3	...	...-..	...	...-...	3,371	...
Sturgis, Mich. (1,1)	P	19-16-40	25,064-30,056	Y-30,556-5	1,864	774-41	596	104-74	840	250
	F	14-14-56	23,400-26,557	Y-...-5	...	...-..	...	...-...	790	...
Sudbury t, Mass. (1,1)	P	32-25-37	30,078-32,845	Y-34,159-6	...	...-..	...	...-...	15	...
	F	35-34-42	29,047-33,114	Y-34,439-6	...	...-..	...	...-...	...	...
Suffern v, N.Y. (1,2)	P	31-26-40	30,930-53,582	Y-...-3	...	...-..	...	...-...	...	...
	F	...-..-..	...-...	..-...-..	...	...-..	...	...-...	...	...
Sugar Land, Tex. (1,1)	P	79-58-40	24,834-34,763	Y-...-..	3,360	2,524-75	2,155	139-230	50	786
	F	57-56-48	21,472-33,404	Y-...-..	2,883	2,051-71	1,758	110-183	273	559
Suisun City, Calif. (1,3)	P	28-21-40	29,710-39,814	NONE	...	...-..	...	...-...	39	...
	F	...-..-..	...-...	..-...-..	...	...-..	...	...-...	9	...
Sulphur, La. (1,1)	P	44-44-40	18,927-...	Y-...-3	1,831	1,151-62	975	84-92	347	333
	F	32-31-53	18,927-...	Y-...-..	1,279	999-78	844	83-72	73	207
Summerville t, S.C. (3,3)	P	38-35-40	19,549-30,658	NONE	...	...-..	...	...-..	481	...
	F	33-33-..	15,703-36,225	NONE	...	...-..	...	...-..	554	...
Summit, N.J. (1,3)	P	38-30-40	49,545-51,032	Y-56,125-5	3,732	3,520-94	2,712	308-500	23	189
	F	30-25-42	47,126-48,612	Y-51,839-5	2,546	2,442-95	1,796	246-400	...	104
Sun Prairie, Wis. (1,2)	P	39-27-37	26,562-30,901	Y-...-5	...	...-..	...	...-...	76	...
	F	...-..-..	...-...	NONE	...	...-..	...	...-...	...	...
Sunbury, Pa. (1,2)	P	13-13-40	19,216-29,610	Y-30,910-6	...	...-..	...	...-..	20	...
	F	...-..-..	...-...	..-...-..	...	...-..	...	...-..	...	...
Sunnyside, Wash. (1,3)	P	28-20-48	27,864-32,256	NONE	1,739	1,139-65	882	115-142	28	572
	F	11-10-48	26,280-30,444	NONE	783	508-64	445	24-39	9	266

Table 3/22 continued   POLICE AND FIRE DEPARTMENT PERSONNEL, SALARIES, AND EXPENDITURES FOR CITIES 10,000 AND OVER: 1994

City (Service provision)	Depart-ment	Total personnel, no. uniformed, duty hours per week	Entrance, maximum salary ($)	Longevity pay, maximum ($) no. years to receive longevity pay	Reported expenditures (in thousands)					
					Total expendi-tures (A) ($)	Total personnel expendi-tures (B) ($), % of (A)	Salaries and wages (C) ($)	City contrib. to employee retirement, insurance (D) ($)	Capital outlay (E) ($)	All other (F) ($)
10,000–24,999 continued										
Swatara tp, Pa. (1,2)	P	34-31-40	26,163-31,737	Y-34,426-4	...	...-...	...	...-...	26	...
	F	...-...-..	...-...	..-...-..	...	...-..	...	...-...	205	...
Sweetwater, Fla	P	21-18-40	26,618-35,671	Y-39,373-7	1,380	1,244-90	1,000	128-116	24	112
	F	...-...-..	...-...	..-...-..	...	...-..	...	...-...	...	...
Sweetwater, Tex. (1,1)	P	26-21-40	20,100-22,932	Y-23,652-1	2,128	896-42	674	118-104	996	236
	F	25-24-53	20,100-22,932	Y-23,652-1	...	...-..	...	...-...	998	...
Sylacauga, Ala. (1,1)	P	41-35-40	19,787-20,363	NONE	1,714	1,203-70	1,010	124-69	76	435
	F	19-19-56	19,787-20,363	NONE	673	547-81	459	56-32	7	119
Takoma Park, Md. (1,-)	P	34-24-40	25,876-35,226	NONE	3,123	1,984-63	1,624	161-199	466	673
	F	...-...-..	...-...	..-...-..	...	...-..	...	...-...	...	...
Tallmadge, Ohio (-,-)	P	35-32-40	31,117-42,390	Y-43,590-5	...	...-..	...	...-...	47	...
	F	5-4-56	31,467-35,135	Y-36,335-5	...	...-..	...	...-...	14	...
Tarpon Springs, Fla. (1,1)	P	56-41-40	22,510-31,514	Y-31,829-12	5,550	1,874-33	1,537	221-116	2,956	720
	F	36-34-56	18,748-26,247	NONE	...	...-..	...	...-...	2,896	...
Taylor, Tex. (1,1)	P	22-17-40	21,231-22,859	Y-24,059-1	768	615-80	504	64-47	26	127
	F	16-16-..	20,717-21,717	Y-22,917-1	576	455-78	376	46-33	5	116
Taylorville, Ill. (3,3)	P	23-17-48	23,400-25,667	NONE	...	...-..	...	...-...	...	...
	F	11-11-..	22,356-25,998	NONE	...	...-..	...	...-...	...	...
Temple Terrace, Fla. (1,3)	P	56-39-42	24,526-34,332	NONE	...	...-..	...	...-...	187	...
	F	30-29-54	18,304-25,626	NONE	1,424	1,070-75	853	140-77	32	322
The Dalles, Ore. (1,3)	P	18-16-40	24,456-29,016	NONE	...	...-..	...	...-...	47	...
	F	15-14-56	23,736-29,832	NONE	...	...-..	...	...-...	55	...
Thibodaux, La. (1,2)	P	50-44-40	13,233-25,011	NONE	1,634	1,110-67	912	91-107	135	389
	F	...-...-..	...-...	..-...-..	...	...-..	...	...-...	6	...
Thomasville, N.C. (1,1)	P	59-51-50	16,595-23,938	Y-25,254-1	2,160	1,612-74	1,286	206-120	247	301
	F	50-50-56	16,595-23,938	Y-25,254-1	1,844	1,393-75	1,147	141-105	288	163
Tiffin, Ohio (1,1)	P	40-28-40	23,236-29,417	Y-32,359-4	1,753	1,574-89	1,221	222-131	85	94
	F	27-26-52	22,052-27,935	Y-30,729-4	...	...-..	...	...-...	14	...
Tolland t, Conn. (9,3)	P	2-2-40	22,840-35,927	NONE	...	...-..	...	...-...	16	...
	F	4-4-40	22,840-35,927	NONE	398	186-46	145	19-22	121	91
Tonawanda, N.Y. (1,3)	P	35-31-40	26,965-33,240	Y-34,140-5	3,765	1,873-49	1,443	320-110	343	1,549
	F	30-29-40	27,264-32,926	Y-34,126-5	...	...-..	...	...-...	333	...
Traverse City, Mich. (1,1)	P	33-32-40	27,102-30,826	Y-32,983-..	...	...-..	...	...-...	...	...
	F	22-22-56	21,112-27,751	Y-29,702-..	...	...-..	...	...-...	58	...
Troy, Ohio (1,1)	P	36-35-48	25,690-35,566	Y-...-..	2,191	1,889-86	1,470	267-152	23	279
	F	40-39-48	25,690-35,566	Y-...-..	2,107	1,812-85	1,390	293-129	50	245
Tualatin, Ore. (1,5)	P	27-24-40	29,424-35,748	Y-37,535-6	...	...-..	...	...-...	952	...
	F	...-...-..	...-...	..-...-..	...	...-..	...	...-...	...	...
Tukwila, Wash. (1,1)	P	70-60-40	38,364-45,576	NONE	5,887	4,420-75	3,537	447-436	77	1,390
	F	63-59-51	34,452-43,164	NONE	4,585	3,864-84	3,281	191-392	39	682
University Park, Tex. (1,1)	P	42-34-40	29,112-35,748	Y-36,948-1	2,784	2,217-79	1,727	265-225	209	358
	F	32-32-55	26,724-...	Y-27,924-1	1,977	1,707-86	1,334	218-155	140	130
Upper Dublin tp, Pa. (1,2)	P	40-35-40	33,005-40,232	Y-43,232-5	2,539	2,305-90	1,716	197-392	34	200
	F	...-...-..	...-...	..-...-..	...	...-..	...	...-...	18	...
Upper St. Clair tp, Pa. (1,2)	P	34-27-40	28,288-40,498	Y-42,478-4	2,210	1,871-84	1,375	193-303	158	181
	F	...-...-..	...-...	..-...-..	...	...-..	...	...-...	10	...
Urbandale, Iowa (1,2)	P	40-33-40	25,629-30,758	Y-31,726-5	1,831	1,528-83	1,278	104-146	49	254
	F	...-...-..	...-...	..-...-..	...	...-..	...	...-...	48	...
Uwchlan tp, Pa. (1,2)	P	21-19-40	...-45,736	Y-48,486-..	1,489	1,189-79	982	74-133	46	254
	F	...-...-..	...-...	..-...-..	...	...-..	...	...-...	...	...
Vadnais Heights, Minn	P	...-...-..	...-...	..-...-..	...	...-..	...	...-...	...	...
	F	...-...-..	...-...	..-...-..	...	...-..	...	...-...	...	...
Van Wert, Ohio (1,1)	P	30-22-40	19,600-26,094	Y-27,344-5	1,293	1,055-81	757	147-151	90	148
	F	22-22-56	20,693-25,760	Y-27,010-5	...	...-..	...	...-...	7	...
Vandalia, Ohio (3,3)	P	37-28-39	28,123-37,478	NONE	2,475	2,097-84	1,575	280-242	136	242
	F	5-5-40	28,330-33,862	NONE	739	466-63	368	65-33	140	133
Venice, Fla. (1,1)	P	62-41-40	22,738-34,417	NONE	...	...-..	...	...-...	129	...
	F	35-33-52	18,780-31,300	NONE	...	...-..	...	...-...	9	...
Vermilion, Ohio (1,2)	P	21-16-40	22,896-28,498	Y-28,738-5	2,378	1,080-45	834	121-125	1,086	212
	F	...-...-..	...-...	..-...-..	...	...-..	...	...-...	...	...
Vero Beach, Fla. (1,7)	P	88-61-40	23,150-31,200	Y-...-5	6,669	3,475-52	2,908	246-321	2,662	532
	F	...-...-..	...-...	..-...-..	...	...-..	...	...-...	...	...
Verona tp, N.J. (1,2)	P	30-26-40	33,348-41,848	Y-46,033-5	...	...-..	...	...-...	...	...
	F	...-...-..	...-...	..-...-..	...	...-..	...	...-...	...	...
Vestavia Hills, Ala. (1,1)	P	37-36-40	24,690-33,072	Y-35,883-6	2,091	1,498-71	1,172	170-156	431	162
	F	51-50-52	24,690-33,072	Y-35,883-6	2,861	2,148-75	1,679	245-224	570	143
Vidalia, Ga	P	...-...-..	...-...	..-...-..	...	...-..	...	...-...	...	...
	F	...-...-..	...-...	..-...-..	...	...-..	...	...-...	...	...
Vienna, W.Va. (1,2)	P	19-12-40	21,964-...	Y-32,198-1	823	631-76	522	22-87	49	143
	F	...-...-..	...-...	..-...-..	...	...-..	...	...-...	...	...
Wabash, Ind. (1,1)	P	22-17-..	24,918-...	Y-27,409-1	...	...-..	...	...-...	...	...
	F	31-31-..	24,918-...	Y-27,409-1	...	...-..	...	...-...	...	...
Wakefield t, Mass. (1,1)	P	46-46-39	28,756-30,732	Y-30,882-5	...	...-..	...	...-...	46	...
	F	52-52-42	28,236-30,108	Y-30,258-5	...	...-..	...	...-...	10	...

Table 3/22 continued

POLICE AND FIRE DEPARTMENT PERSONNEL, SALARIES, AND EXPENDITURES FOR CITIES 10,000 AND OVER: 1994

City (Service provision)	Department	Total personnel, no. uniformed, duty hours per week	Entrance, maximum salary ($)	Longevity pay, maximum ($), no. years to receive longevity pay	Total expenditures (A) ($)	Total personnel expenditures (B) ($), % of (A)	Salaries and wages (C) ($)	City contrib. to employee retirement, insurance (D) ($)	Capital outlay (E) ($)	All other (F) ($)
10,000–24,999 continued										
Walker, Mich. (1,2)	P	38-32-40	26,473-38,750	Y-40,250-5	2,241	1,769-78	1,477	172-120	262	210
	F	...-..-..	..-...	..-...-..	...	...-..	...	...-...	1	...
Wall tp, N.J. (1,2)	P	60-49-40	26,979-53,280	Y-58,928-..	...	...-..	...	...-..	...	...
	F	...-..-..	...-...	..-...-..	...	...-..	...	...-...	...	...
Warrenville, Ill. (1,5)	P	22-16-40	26,780-40,100	NONE	2,363	1,210-51	915	172-123	869	284
	F	...-..-..	...-...	..-...-..	...	...-..	...	...-..	...	...
Warsaw, Ind. (1,3)	P	40-32-40	25,650-27,170	Y-32,604-1	...	...-..	...	...-..	...	...
	F	26-26-56	...-27,170	Y-...-1	...	...-..	...	...-..	...	...
Washington, Mo. (1,2)	P	26-5-42	18,346-24,398	NONE	990	791-79	634	84-73	47	152
	F	...-..-..	...-...	..-...-..	...	...-..	...	...-..	35	...
Washington (Morris) tp, N.J. (1,2)	P	29-27-40	28,585-45,341	Y-47,608-5	2,067	1,910-92	1,476	278-156	42	115
	F	...-..-..	...-...	...-...	...	...-..	...	...-..	255	...
Watauga, Tex. (4,4)	P	...-..-..	...-...	..-...-..	...	...-..	...	...-..	...	...
	F	...-..-..	...-...	..-...-..	...	...-..	...	...-..	...	...
Waterford t, Conn. (1,3)	P	48-48-40	29,765-37,856	Y-38,456-5	16,124	3,425-21	2,595	470-360	12,229	470
	F	17-16-50	35,751-47,915	Y-48,515-5	2,743	1,385-50	1,077	186-122	577	781
Watertown, Wis. (1,1)	P	45-33-40	26,247-30,971	Y-31,498-16	...	...-..	...	...-..	48	...
	F	20-20-56	24,920-30,541	Y-31,068-16	...	...-..	...	...-..	9	...
Waterville, Me. (1,3)	P	36-28-42	18,367-25,116	Y-...-6	1,403	1,198-85	1,077	9-112	57	148
	F	23-19-51	22,685-26,677	Y-...-6	998	841-84	774	5-62	30	127
Waxahachie, Tex. (1,1)	P	43-33-40	23,018-24,517	Y-...-1	2,235	1,309-58	1,051	188-70	770	156
	F	34-33-48	23,727-24,762	Y-...-1	2,316	1,233-53	1,002	170-61	926	157
Waycross, Ga. (1,1)	P	64-49-43	15,828-20,941	NONE	2,233	1,823-81	1,506	170-147	69	341
	F	46-45-53	14,026-18,496	NONE	1,374	1,256-91	1,049	117-90	45	73
Waynesboro, Va. (3,3)	P	49-46-40	18,558-28,569	NONE	2,574	1,588-61	1,191	239-158	709	277
	F	23-22-56	15,863-24,420	NONE	1,642	819-49	620	121-78	646	177
Wenatchee, Wash. (1,1)	P	48-36-..	30,540-38,484	Y-41,022-5	3,398	2,344-68	1,902	247-195	37	1,017
	F	40-31-..	31,152-38,940	Y-40,108-5	2,355	2,040-86	1,750	120-170	7	308
West Bend, Wis. (1,3)	P	60-46-56	29,017-32,784	Y-33,444-5	...	...-..	...	...-..	55	...
	F	26-26-40	24,596-29,594	Y-30,254-5	...	...-..	...	...-..	17	...
West Carrollton, Ohio (1,3)	P	32-25-40	28,642-37,024	NONE	1,815	1,592-87	1,285	190-117	68	155
	F	5-5-53	27,643-37,041	NONE	1,153	610-52	498	93-19	439	104
West Linn, Ore. (3,3)	P	23-19-40	25,272-34,632	..-...-..	2,635	1,176-44	899	194-83	42	1,417
	F	13-13-56	26,409-36,132	..-...-..	1,722	714-41	541	117-56	60	948
West Manchester tp, Pa. (1,2)	P	23-21-40	24,956-37,729	Y-41,502-4	1,079	988-91	881	67-40	12	79
	F	...-..-..	...-...	..-...-..	...	...-..	...	...-..	...	...
West St. Paul, Minn. (1,1)	P	27-22-40	25,751-39,603	Y-43,167-4	1,639	1,390-84	1,120	193-77	90	159
	F	20-20-53	28,166-40,216	Y-42,256-5	1,600	990-61	835	100-55	491	119
West University Place, Tex. (1,3)	P	28-21-40	22,308-31,812	Y-33,312-1	1,412	1,163-82	926	145-92	60	189
	F	19-19-53	20,784-29,268	Y-30,768-1	1,076	906-84	722	117-67	84	86
West Whiteland tp, Pa. (1,2)	P	20-18-42	24,000-49,655	Y-...-5	1,716	1,218-70	1,036	97-85	300	198
	F	...-..-..	...-...	..-...-..	...	...-..	...	...-..	65	...
Westborough t, Mass. (1,1)	P	30-30-40	27,993-34,783	NONE	...	...-..	...	...-..	61	...
	F	22-22-42	25,607-34,158	NONE	...	...-..	...	...-..	7	...
Westbrook, Me. (3,3)	P	32-27-40	19,741-25,584	NONE	...	...-..	...	...-..	81	...
	F	25-20-42	18,776-25,237	NONE	...	...-..	...	...-..	23	...
Westbury v, N.Y. (7,5)	P	...-..-..	...-...	..-...-..	...	...-..	...	...-..	...	...
	F	...-..-..	...-...	..-...-..	...	...-..	...	...-..	...	...
Westchester v, Ill. (1,1)	P	35-22-40	26,408-39,287	Y-...-..	...	...-..	...	...-..	114	...
	F	25-25-50	28,191-40,947	NONE	...	...-..	...	...-..	4	...
Westford t, Mass. (1,1)	P	32-25-38	24,632-30,506	Y-31,306-5	...	...-..	...	...-..	61	...
	F	13-13-42	26,862-32,996	Y-34,696-5	...	...-..	...	...-..	85	...
Westminster, Md. (1,2)	P	41-32-43	22,287-30,215	Y-...-9	2,871	1,516-52	1,204	190-122	785	570
	F	...-..-..	...-...	..-...-..	...	...-..	...	...-..	...	...
Westmont v, Ill. (1,9)	P	49-35-40	28,073-43,558	Y-45,736-5	3,206	2,839-88	2,226	209-404	101	266
	F	...-..-..	...-...	..-...-..	...	...-..	...	...-..	54	...
Whitefish Bay v, Wis. (1,1)	P	28-23-40	33,508-39,216	Y-39,396-5	1,741	1,208-69	975	115-118	53	480
	F	19-19-56	26,500-39,800	Y-40,100-5	...	...-..	...	...-..	130	...
Whitehall tp, Pa. (1,2)	P	51-40-40	25,917-36,171	Y-37,491-5	2,594	2,396-92	1,926	241-229	57	141
	F	...-..-..	...-...	NONE	226	31-13	25	1-5	...	195
Whitemarsh tp, Pa. (1,2)	P	31-28-40	28,590-40,876	Y-42,001-5	...	...-..	...	...-..	354	...
	F	...-..-..	...-...	..-...-..	...	...-..	...	...-..	...	...
Whitewater, Wis. (1,2)	P	30-20-39	26,124-30,501	Y-31,501-3	...	...-..	...	...-..	51	...
	F	...-..-..	...-...	..-...-..	...	...-..	...	...-..	23	...
Wilkinsburg b, Pa. (1,1)	P	22-22-40	24,480-32,000	Y-...-4	...	...-..	...	...-..	...	...
	F	25-25-48	23,884-27,704	Y-...-5	...	...-..	...	...-..	...	...
Williamsburg, Va. (1,1)	P	42-29-40	20,414-58,416	NONE	1,814	1,435-79	1,155	189-91	64	315
	F	26-25-56	20,414-58,416	NONE	1,400	1,099-78	886	146-67	115	186
Willoughby, Ohio (1,1)	P	45-36-40	29,744-41,725	NONE	...	...-..	...	...-..	1,082	...
	F	39-36-49	29,729-41,718	NONE	...	...-..	...	...-..	1,117	...
Wilmington, Ohio (1,3)	P	19-17-40	18,013-29,453	NONE	1,001	740-73	566	103-71	42	219
	F	14-14-53	18,013-29,453	NONE	970	732-75	577	107-48	41	197
Wilton Manors, Fla. (1,2)	P	40-30-40	28,623-40,189	Y-...-..	2,994	2,263-75	1,858	241-164	286	445
	F	...-..-..	...-...	..-...-..	...	...-..	...	...-..	257	...

Table 3/22 continued   POLICE AND FIRE DEPARTMENT PERSONNEL, SALARIES, AND EXPENDITURES FOR CITIES 10,000 AND OVER: 1994

City (Service provision)	Department	Total personnel, no. uniformed, duty hours per week	Entrance, maximum salary ($)	Longevity pay, maximum ($) no. years to receive longevity pay	Reported expenditures (in thousands)					
					Total expenditures (A) ($)	Total personnel expenditures (B) ($), % of (A)	Salaries and wages (C) ($)	City contrib. to employee retirement, insurance (D) ($)	Capital outlay (E) ($)	All other (F) ($)
10,000–24,999 continued										
Winchester, Ky. (1,1)	P	39-28-40	17,633-28,660	Y-...-4	...	...-..	...	...-...	441	...
	F	50-50-56	17,633-28,660	Y-...-4	...	...-..	...	...-...	115	...
Windham t, Me. (1,2)	P	18-14-40	17,669-23,088	Y-23,488-10	893	767-85	619	67-81	98	28
	F	...-..-..	...-...	..-..-..	...	...-..	...	...-...	...	...
Windsor Locks t, Conn. (1,2)	P	28-22-37	30,716-36,425	Y-39,567-5	...	...-..	...	...-...	...	...
	F	...-..-..	...-...	..-...-..	...	...-..	...	...-...	...	...
Winnetka v, Ill. (1,1)	P	38-27-40	31,632-44,162	Y-45,266-10	3,075	2,574-83	1,836	411-327	117	384
	F	24-23-56	34,380-44,172	Y-45,276-10	...	...-..	...	...-...	40	...
Winter Park, Fla. (1,1)	P	96-71-42	22,500-35,971	Y-...-5	4,987	3,853-77	3,066	527-260	...	1,134
	F	49-48-56	20,850-33,196	Y-...-5	2,808	2,263-80	1,763	365-135	...	545
Winter Springs, Fla. (1,1)	P	53-37-43	19,471-48,542	NONE	1,676	1,449-86	1,249	97-103	...	227
	F	35-34-56	18,991-47,000	NONE	1,196	954-79	831	64-59	...	242
Wisconsin Rapids, Wis. (1,1)	P	51-39-39	26,986-33,078	NONE	...	...-..	...	...-...	39	...
	F	32-32-56	24,431-32,376	NONE	...	...-..	...	...-...	564	...
Wolcott t, Conn. (1,2)	P	31-23-40	31,720-...	Y-...-5	...	...-..	...	...-...	...	...
	F	...-..-..	...-...	..-..-..	...	...-..	...	...-...	...	...
Woodburn, Ore. (1,5)	P	23-20-40	27,000-32,784	..-...-..	...	...-..	...	...-...	28	...
	F	...-..-..	...-...	..-...-..	...	...-..	...	...-...	...	...
Woodbury, Minn. (1,3)	P	...-2-40	28,560-39,216	Y-42,756-16	1,912	1,463-76	1,198	150-115	151	298
	F	...-..-..	...-...	..-...-..	335	204-60	165	16-23	55	76
Woodward, Okla. (3,3)	P	26-20-40	19,159-20,117	Y-21,317-1	877	792-90	612	138-42	34	51
	F	17-17-56	17,457-21,707	Y-22,907-1	561	524-93	449	46-29	9	28
Worthington, Ohio (1,1)	P	40-32-40	26,737-39,546	Y-40,396-5	6,698	2,165-32	1,662	303-200	4,348	185
	F	39-33-56	21,861-37,511	Y-38,361-5	...	...-..	...	...-...	...	...
Xenia, Ohio (1,1)	P	51-48-40	25,563-35,339	Y-...-..	4,272	2,261-52	1,837	236-188	1,658	353
	F	46-41-53	27,580-33,575	Y-...-..	4,043	2,221-54	1,682	381-158	1,588	234
Yankton, S.D. (1,3)	P	31-22-40	21,405-24,078	Y-24,578-5	1,069	905-84	732	109-64	33	131
	F	...-..-..	...-...	..-...-..	217	79-36	62	10-7	75	63
Ypsilanti, Mich. (1,1)	P	56-45-40	27,131-40,578	NONE	3,452	3,081-89	2,511	320-250	22	349
	F	29-23-54	23,253-37,495	NONE	1,805	1,557-86	1,266	161-130	66	182
Yukon, Okla. (3,3)	P	35-26-40	17,282-26,930	Y-...-5	827	757-91	568	65-124	9	61
	F	26-25-56	16,965-25,635	Y-...-5	...	...-..	...	...-...	...	...

D Directories

The Year Book Directories

The directories in this section of the *Year Book* contain the names of municipal and county officials in the United States as reported in the fall of 1994 along with the names of appointed chief administrative officers in other countries. In addition, this section includes directories for state municipal leagues; provincial associations and unions in Canada; state and territorial agencies for community affairs; provincial and territorial agencies for local affairs in Canada; state and provincial municipal management associations; state associations of counties; and directors of councils of governments recognized by ICMA.

The names of municipal and county managers and other chief appointed management executives for the United States and other countries are shown in directories 1/8, 1/9, and 1/10. Information on recognized places, including legal basis, title of position, form of government, and year of recognition, plus the number of administrators the community has had and information on the current administrator, is presented in the annual ICMA publication *Who's Who in Local Government Management.*

Information in directories 1/1 through 1/8 was obtained from the National League of Cities (1/1), the Federation of Canadian Municipalities (1/2), the Council of State Community Affairs Agencies (1/3), the Ontario Ministry of Municipal Affairs (1/4), ICMA files (1/5, 1/7, and 1/8), and the National Association of Counties (1/6), and is current as of November 1994 unless otherwise indicated. Information for Directory 1/9 was obtained by a *Year Book* mailing to all cities 2,500 and over in population, to recognized council-manager or general management places under 2,500 in July 1994, and to those communities whose populations dropped below 2,500 since the 1986 Census. Information for Directory 1/10 was obtained by a similar mailing to all county-type governments in July 1994.

The phone numbers in directories 1/7, 1/8, 1/9, and 1/10, preceded by the area code, are for the city hall, municipal building, or county building, or for some municipal or county official such as the manager, clerk, or mayor.

State Municipal Leagues
Directory 1/1 shows 49 state leagues of municipalities serving 49 states. (Hawaii does not have a league.) Information includes league address, name of the executive director, phone number, and year organized. State municipal leagues provide a wide range of research, consulting, training, publications, and legislative representation services for their cities.

Provincial and Territorial Associations and Unions in Canada
Directory 1/2 shows the organizations serving the provinces and territories of Canada. The name of the president and a permanent officer are shown along with the address and phone number.

State Agencies for Community Affairs
Directory 1/3 presents the name and address of 50 agencies for community affairs in the United States. It includes the name of the executive director or head of the agency. These agencies of state governments offer a variety of research, financial information, and coordination services for cities and other local governments.

Provincial and Territorial Agencies for Local Affairs in Canada
Directory 1/4 shows agencies for local affairs serving provinces and territories in Canada. The directory lists the name and address of the minister as well as the minister's phone number when available.

United States and International Municipal Management Associations
Directory 1/5 shows the name, president, address, and phone number of municipal management associations serving 48 of the United States, the District of Columbia, Canada, and 5 other countries.[1]

State Associations of Counties
Directory 1/6 shows the name, address, phone number, FAX number, name of executive director, and year organized for 50 county associations serving 47 states. (Two associations serve

the state of Washington; three states do not have associations: Connecticut, Rhode Island, and Vermont.) Like their municipal league counterparts, these associations provide a wide range of research, training, consulting, publications, and legislative representation services.

Directors of Councils of Governments
Directory 1/7 gives the official name of the council of governments, the director, and the telephone number for COGs recognized by ICMA.

International Administrators
Directory 1/8 gives the name of the appointed administrator and phone number, if available, for the chief appointed administrator in communities overseas.

Municipal Officials in U.S. Cities
Directory 1/9 lists, alphabetically by state, all incorporated places in the United States 2,500 and over in population, those places under 2,500 recognized by ICMA. It shows the current form of government; the population (in thousands) according to the 1990 Census of Population estimates; municipal phone number; name of mayor; appointed administrator; city clerk; finance officer; fire chief; police chief; and public works director. Leaders (. .) in the population column mean that the population of the place is under 500.

County Officials in U.S. Counties
Directory 1/10 lists, alphabetically by state, all county-type governments. It shows the 1990 Census of Population estimates; the county telephone number; name of the board chairman, county judge, or president; appointed administrator; clerk to the governing board; chief financial officer; personnel director; and chief law enforcement official.

Other Local Government Directories
The names of municipal officials not reported in the *Year Book* are available in many states through directories published by state municipal leagues, state municipal management associations, and state associations of counties. Names

and addresses of these leagues and associations are shown in directories 1/1, 1/5, and 1/6. In some states the secretary of state, the state agency for community affairs (Directory 1/3), or another state agency publishes a directory that includes municipal and county officials. In addition, several directories with national coverage are published for health officers, welfare workers, housing and urban renewal officials, and other professional groups.

[1]The states of Wyoming, North Dakota, South Dakota, Idaho, and Montana are served by the Great Open Spaces City Management Association. In addition, Idaho is also served by its own association.

Directory 1/1   STATE MUNICIPAL LEAGUES

State	Name of league and headquarters address	Name and title of executive director[1]	Phone number FAX	Year first effort to cooperate[2]	Year first organized[3]
Alabama	Alabama League of Municipalities, P.O. Box 1270, Montgomery 36102	Perry Roquemore, ED	205 262-2566 205 263-0200	1914	1930
Alaska	Alaska Municipal League, 217 Second Street, Suite 200, Juneau 99801	(Vacant)	907 586-1325 907 463-5480	1950	1950
Arizona	League of Arizona Cities and Towns, 1820 West Washington Street, Phoenix 85007	John J. DeBolske, ED	602 258-5786 602 253-3874	1925	1937
Arkansas	Arkansas Municipal League, P.O. Box 38, North Little Rock 72115	Don A. Zimmerman, ED	501 374-3484 501 374-0541	1917	1934
California	League of California Cities, 1400 K Street, Suite 400, Sacramento 95814	Don Benninghoven, ED	916 444-5790 916 444-8671	1898	1898
Colorado	Colorado Municipal League, 1660 Lincoln Street, Suite 2100, Denver 80264	Kenneth G. Bueche, ED	303 831-6411 303 860-8175	1900	1923
Connecticut	Connecticut Conference of Municipalities, 900 Chapel Street, Suite 900, New Haven 06510-2807	Joel Cogen, ED	203 498-3000 203 562-6314	. . .	1966
Delaware	Delaware League of Local Governments, P.O. Box 484, Dover 19903-0484	George C. Wright, ED	302 678-0991 302 678-4777	1965	1965
Florida	Florida League of Cities, P.O. Box 1757, Tallahassee 32302-1757	Raymond C. Sittig, ED	904 222-9684 904 222-3806	1922	1922
Georgia	Georgia Municipal Association, 201 Pryor Street, S.W., Atlanta 30303	James V. Burgess, Jr., ED	404 688-0472 404 577-6663	1916	1934
Idaho	Association of Idaho Cities, 3314 Grace Street, Boise 83703	Scott B. McDonald, ED	208 344-8594 208 344-8677	1918	1941
Illinois	Illinois Municipal League, P.O. Box 3387, Springfield 62708	Thomas G. Fitzsimmons, ED	217 525-1220 217 525-7438	1899	1914
Indiana	Indiana Association of Cities and Towns, 150 West Market Street, Suite 728, Indianapolis 46204-2882	Michael J. Quinn, ED	317 237-6200 317 237-6206	1891	1899
Iowa	League of Iowa Municipalities, 317 Sixth Avenue, Suite 1400, Des Moines 50309	Thomas G. Bredeweg, ED	515 244-7282 515 244-0740	1898	1898
Kansas	League of Kansas Municipalities, 112 West Seventh Street, Topeka 66603	Christopher K. McKenzie, ED	913 354-9565 913 354-4186	1910	1910
Kentucky	Kentucky League of Cities, 2201 Regency Road, Suite 100, Lexington 40503	Sylvia L. Lovely, ED	606 277-2886 606 278-5766	1929	1929
Louisiana	Louisiana Municipal Association, P.O. Box 4327, Baton Rouge 70821	L. Gordon King, ED	504 344-5001 504 344-3057	1935	1937
Maine	Maine Municipal Association, 60 Community Drive, Augusta 04330	Christopher G. Lockwood, ED	207 623-8429 207 626-5947	1936	1936
Maryland	Maryland Municipal League, 1212 West Street, Annapolis 21401	Jon C. Burrell, ED	410 268-5514 410 268-7004	1937	1948
Massachusetts	Massachusetts Municipal Association, 60 Temple Place, Second Floor, Boston 02111	Geoffrey Beckwith, ED	617 426-7272 617 695-1314	1961	1961
Michigan	Michigan Municipal League, P.O. Box 1487, Ann Arbor 48106	George D. Goodman, ED	313 662-3246 313 662-8083	1899	1899
Minnesota	League of Minnesota Cities, 3490 Lexington Avenue North, St. Paul 55126-8044	James F. Miller, ED	612 490-5600 612 490-0072	1903	1913
Mississippi	Mississippi Municipal Association, 600 East Amite Street, Jackson 39302	(Vacant)	601 353-5854 601 353-0435	1918	1936
Missouri	Missouri Municipal League, 1727 Southridge Drive, Jefferson City 65109	Gary Markenson, ED	314 635-9134 314 635-9009	1914	1927
Montana	Montana League of Cities and Towns, P.O. Box 1704, Helena 59624	Alec Hansen, ED	406 442-8768 406 442-9231	1910	1932
Nebraska	League of Nebraska Municipalities, 1335 L Street, Lincoln 68508	Lynn Rex, ED	402 476-2829 402 476-7052	1910	1910
Nevada	Nevada League of Cities, P.O. Box 2307, Carson City 89702	Thomas J. Grady, ED	702 882-2121 702 882-2813	. . .	1950
New Hampshire	New Hampshire Municipal Association, P.O. Box 617, Concord 03302-0617	John B. Andrews, ED	603 224-7447 603 226-2988	1955	1961
New Jersey	New Jersey State League of Municipalities, 407 West State Street, Trenton 08618	John E. Trafford, ED	609 695-3481 609 695-0151	1915	1915
New Mexico	New Mexico Municipal League, P.O. Box 846, Santa Fe 87504	William F. Fulginiti, ED	505 982-5573 505 984-1392	. . .	1958
New York	New York State Conference of Mayors and Municipal Officials, 119 Washington Avenue, Albany 12210	Edward C. Farrell, ED	518 463-1185 518 463-1190	1910	1910

Directory 1/1   STATE MUNICIPAL LEAGUES
continued

State	Name of league and headquarters address	Name and title of executive director[1]	Phone number	Year first effort to cooperate[2]	Year first organized[3]
North Carolina	North Carolina League of Municipalities, P.O. Box 3069, Raleigh 27602	David E. Reynolds	919 715-4000 919 733-9519	1908	1922
North Dakota	North Dakota League of Cities, P.O. Box 2235, Bismarck 58502	Robert E. Johnson, ED	701 223-3518 701 223-5174	1912	1927
Ohio	Ohio Municipal League, 175 South Third Street, Suite 510, Columbus 43215	John P. Coleman, ED	614 221-4349 614 221-4390	1912	1952
Oklahoma	Oklahoma Municipal League, 201 N.E. 23rd Street, Oklahoma City 73105	William A. Moyer, ED	405 528-7515 405 528-7560	1913	1913
Oregon	League of Oregon Cities, P.O. Box 928, Salem 97308	Richard C. Townsend, ED	503 588-6550 503 378-5859	1913	1913
Pennsylvania	Pennsylvania League of Cities and Municipalities, 414 North Second Street, Harrisburg 17101	John A. Garner, Jr., ED	717 236-9469 717 236-6716	1900	1900
Rhode Island	Rhode Island League of Cities and Towns, 1 State Street, Suite 502, Providence 02908	Daniel Beardsley, ED	401 272-3434 401 421-0824	1959	1965
South Carolina	Municipal Association of South Carolina, P.O. Box 12109, Columbia 29211	Howard Duvall, ED	803 799-9574 803 799-9520	1936	1939
South Dakota	South Dakota Municipal League, 214 East Capitol, Pierre 57501	John R. Thune, ED	605 224-8654 605 224-8655	1925	1935
Tennessee	Tennessee Municipal League, 226 Capitol Boulevard, Room 710, Nashville 37219	Joseph A. Sweat, ED	615 255-6416 615 255-4752	1913	1940
Texas	Texas Municipal League, 1821 Rutherford Lane, Suite 400, Austin 78754	Frank Sturzl, ED	512 719-6300 512 719-6390	1913	1913
Utah	Utah League of Cities and Towns, 50 South 600 East, Suite 150, Salt Lake City 84102	Kenneth Bullock, ED	801 328-1601 801 531-1872	1907	1907
Vermont	Vermont League of Cities and Towns, 12$^1/_2$ Main Street, Montpelier 05602	Steven E. Jeffrey, ED	802 229-9111 802 229-2211	1967	1967
Virginia	Virginia Municipal League, P.O. Box 12164, Richmond 23241	R. Michael Amyx, ED	804 649-8471 804 343-3758	1905	1905
Washington	Association of Washington Cities, 1076 South Franklin Street, Olympia 98501	Stan Finkelstein, ED	206 753-4137 206 753-4896	1910	1910
West Virginia	West Virginia Municipal League, 1620 Kanawha Boulevard, Suite 1B, Charleston 25311	Lisa Dooley, ED	304 342-5564 304 342-5586	1917	1935
Wisconsin	League of Wisconsin Municipalities, 202 State Street, Suite 300, Madison 53703-2215	Dan Thompson, ED	608 267-2380 608 267-0645	1898	1898
Wyoming	Wyoming Association of Municipalities, P.O. Box 3110, Cheyenne 82003-3110	Carl Classen, ED	307 632-0398 307 632-1942	. . .	1952

Note: Leaders (. . .) indicate information not available.
[1] Titles abbreviated as follows: AED, Acting Executive Director; ED, Executive Director; D, Director.

[2] The date in this column refers in most instances to the beginning of a loosely knit organization of cities on a cooperative basis for the purpose of presenting municipal problems before the legislature.

[3] This date is the year when an active organization, as now known, was established.

Directory 1/2   PROVINCIAL AND TERRITORIAL ASSOCIATIONS AND UNIONS IN CANADA

Province or territory	Association/union	President[1]	Permanent officer
Alberta	Alberta Association of Municipal Districts and Counties	Roelof Heinen	Larry Goodhope, Executive Director 4504–101 Street Edmonton T6E 5G9 Phone: 403 436-9375 Fax: 403 437-5993
	Alberta Urban Municipalities Association	Mayor Bill Purdy P.O. Box 4607 Station SE Edmonton T6E 5G4	John E. Maddison, Executive Director P.O. Box 4607, Postal Station SE Edmonton T6E 5G4 Phone: 403 433-4431 Fax: 403 433-4454
British Columbia	Union of British Columbia Municipalities	Mayor Bill Trewhella 10551 Shellbridge Way Suite 15 Richmond V6X 2W9 Phone: 604 270-8226 Fax: 604 660-2271	Richard Taylor, Executive Director 10551 Shellbridge Way, Suite 15 Richmond V6X 2W9 Phone: 604 270-8226 Fax: 604 660-2271
Manitoba	Manitoba Association of Urban Municipalities	Mayor Art Dyck Room 200, 611 Corydon Avenue Winnipeg R3L 0P3 Phone: 204 982-6286 Fax: 204 478-1005	Rochelle Zimberg, Executive Director-Room 200 611 Corydon Avenue Winnipeg R3L 0P3 Phone: 204 982-6286 Fax: 204 478-1005

Directory 1/2 **PROVINCIAL AND TERRITORIAL ASSOCIATIONS**
continued **AND UNIONS IN CANADA**

Province or territory	Association/union	President[1]	Permanent officer
	Union of Manitoba Municipalities	Jack Nichol Box 2 Group 40 Rural Route 2 Dugald Manitoba R0E 0K0 Phone: 204 853-2030	Jerome Mauws, Executive Director P.O. Box 397 Portage-la-Prairie R1N 3B7 Phone: 204 857-8666
New Brunswick	Association des Municipalitiés du Nouveau-Brunswick, Inc.	Jacques P. Martin	Léopold Chiasson C.P. 849 Petit-Rocher, NB E0B 2E0 Phone: 506 783-4211 Fax: 506 783-0808
	Cities of New Brunswick Association	Mayor Bruce McIntosh 200 Prospect Street West, Suite 404 Fredericton E3B 2T8 Phone: 506 457-7297 Fax: 506 453-7954	Frederick J. Martin, Executive Director 200 Prospect Street West, Suite 404 Fredericton E3B 2T8 Phone: 506 457-7297 Fax: 506 453-7954
	Towns of New Brunswick Association	Mayor Peter Murphy	Emory Landry, Vice President Emil Olsen, Vice President P.O. Box 1443 Shediac E0A 3G0 Phone: 506 532-4520
	Villages of New Brunswick Association	Mayor Laura Reynolds	Yvonne Gibb, Executive Director 115 Allan-A-dele Lane Rothsay, New Brunswick E2E 1H2 Phone: 506 849-2666 Fax: 506 849-6994
Newfoundland and Labrador	Newfoundland and Labrador Federation of Municipalities	Mayor Tibbo P.O. Box 5756 St. John's A1C 5X3 Phone: 709 753-6820 Fax: 709 738-0071	Patricia Hempstead Chief Administrator St. John's A1C 5X3 Phone: 709 753-6820 Fax: 709 738-0071
Northwest Territories	Northwest Territories Association of Municipalities	Mayor Pat McMahon P.O. Box 580 Yellowknife X1A 2N4 Phone: 403 873-8359 Fax: 403 873-5801	Yvette Bungay, Executive Director 5201 50th Ave-Suite 904 Yellowknife X1A 3S9 Phone: 403 873-8359 Fax: 403 873-5801
Nova Scotia	Union of Nova Scotia Municipalities	Mayor John Coady	Kenneth R. B. Simpson, Executive Director 1809 Barrington Street, Suite 1106 Halifax B3J 3K8 Phone: 902 423-8331 Fax: 902 425-5592
Ontario	Association of Municipalities of Ontario	Bill Mickel	Doug Razen, Executive Director 250 Bloor Street East, Suite 701 Toronto M4W 1E6 Phone: 416 929-7573 Fax: 416 929-7574
	Federation of Canadian Municipalities	Mayor Laurence Mawhinney	James W. Knight, Executive Director 24 Clarence Street, 2nd floor Ottawa K1N 5P3 Phone: 613 241-5221 Fax: 613 241-7440
Prince Edward Island	Federation of Prince Edward Island Municipalities	Councillor Cecil Murl	Lisa Doyle-MacBain, Executive Director P.O. Box 98 Charlottetown C1A 7K2 Phone: 902 566-1493 Fax: 902 566-4701
Québec	Union des Conseils de Comités du Québec	Pierre Maurice Vachon 2954 boul. Laurier, Bureau 560 Ste-Foy G1V 4P2 Phone: 418 651-3343	Michelle Fernet, Directeur-général 2954 boul. Laurier, Bureau 560 Ste-Foy G1V 4P2 Phone: 418 651-3343 Fax: 418 651-1127
	Union des Municipalités du Québec	Ulrick Blacburn	Raymond L'Italien, Directeur-général 680, 680 Sherbrook West Montréal H3A 2M7 Phone: 514 282-7700 Fax: 514 282-7711

Directory 1/2 continued   PROVINCIAL AND TERRITORIAL ASSOCIATIONS AND UNIONS IN CANADA

Province or territory	Association/union	President[1]	Permanent officer
Saskatchewan	Saskatchewan Assocation of Rural Municipalities	Sanclair Harris Box 89 Sachsketwen F0G 3M0 Phone: 306 435-4110	Darryl Chambers, Executive Director 2075 Hamilton Street Regina S4P 2E1 Phone: 306 757-3577 Fax: 306 565-2141
	Saskatchewan Urban Municipalities Association	Councillor Ted Cholod 200, 1819 Cornwall Street Regina S4P 2K4 Phone: 306 525-3727	Keith Schneider, Executive Director 200, 1819 Cornwall Street Regina S4P 2K4 Phone: 306 525-3727 Fax: 306 565-3552
Yukon	Association of Yukon Communities	Pat McMahon	Yvette Bungay, Executive Director 5201 50th Avenue Ste. 904 Yellowknife X1A 3S9 Phone: 403 873-8359 Fax: 403 873-5801

[1]Presidents without an address can be reached at the address of the permanent officer.

Directory 1/3   STATE AGENCIES FOR COMMUNITY AFFAIRS

State or territory	Agency and address	Name and title of executive director
Alabama	Department of Economic and Community Affairs 401 Adams Street, P.O. Box 5690 Montgomery 36103	David Hooks Director
Alaska	Department of Community and Regional Affairs Post Office Box 112100 Juneau 99811	Edgar Blatchford Commissioner
Arizona	Department of Commerce 3800 North Central Street Suite 1400 Phoenix 85012	James E. Marsh Executive Director
Arkansas	Industrial Development Commission 1 State Capitol Mall Little Rock 72201	Bill Young Interim Director Community Development Division
California	Department of Housing and Community Development P.O. Box 952051 Sacramento 94252-2051	Tim Coyle Director
Colorado	Department of Local Affairs 1313 Sherman Street 518 Centennial Building Denver 80203	Larry Kallenberger Executive Director
Connecticut	Department of Housing 505 Hudson Street Hartford 06106	Henry S. Scherer, Jr. Commissioner
Delaware	Delaware State Housing Authority 18 The Green P.O. Box 1401 Dover 19903	Susan Frank Director
Florida	Department of Community Affairs 2740 Centerview Drive Tallahassee 32399-2100	Linda L. Shelley Secretary
Georgia	Department of Community Affairs 1200 Equitable Building 100 Peachtree Street Atlanta 30303	Jim Higdon Commissioner
Hawaii	Department of Planning and Economic Development P.O. Box 2359 Honolulu 96804	Roger A. Ulveling Director
Idaho	Department of Commerce 700 West State Street State House Mail Room 108 Boise 83720-2700	Karl Tueller Deputy Director

State or territory	Agency and address	Name and title of executive director
Illinois	Department of Commerce and Community Affairs 620 East Adams Street Springfield 62701	Jan Grayson Director
Indiana	Department of Commerce One North Capitol, Suite 700 Indianapolis 46204-2243	Curt Wiley Executive Director
Iowa	Department of Economic Development 200 East Grand Avenue Des Moines 50319	Allan T. Thoms Director
Kansas	Department of Commerce and Housing 700 SW Harrison Street, #1300 Topeka 66603-3912	Marty Miller Director of Community Development
Kentucky	Department of Local Government 1024 Capital Center Drive Frankfort 40601	Bruce Ferguson Commissioner
Louisiana	Division of Administration State Planning Office P.O. Box 94095 Baton Rouge 70804	Suzie Elkins Director
Maine	Department of Economic and Community Development 219 Capitol Street State House Station 130 Augusta 04333	Carolyn Manson Director
Maryland	Department of Housing and Community Development 100 Community Place Crownsville 21032-2023	Patricia Payne Deputy Secretary
Massachusetts	Executive Office of Communities and Development 100 Cambridge Street 14th Floor Boston 02202	Mary Padula Deputy Director
Michigan	Office of Federal Grants Department of Commerce 525 West Ottawa, P.O. Box 30225 Lansing 48909	Richard Pastula Director
Minnesota	Department of Trade and Economic Development 121 7th Place East 500 Metro Square St. Paul 55101-2146	Jennifer Engh Deputy Commissioner

Directory 1/3
continued

STATE AGENCIES
FOR COMMUNITY AFFAIRS

State or territory	Agency and address	Name and title of executive director	State or territory	Agency and address	Name and title of executive director
Mississippi	Division of Community Services Department of Economic and Community Development 1200 Walter Sillers Building P.O. Box 849 Jackson 39205	Alice Lusk Director	Oregon	Department of Community Development 808 SE Third Street-P.O. Box 600 Portland 97204	Steve Rudman Director
Missouri	Department of Economic Development 301 West High Street Room 770, P.O. Box 1157 Jefferson City 65102	Joseph L. Driskell Director	Pennsylvania	Department of Community Affairs 317 Forum Building Harrisburg 17120	Karen Miller Secretary
Montana	Department of Commerce 1424 Ninth Avenue P.O. Box 200501 Helena 59620-0501	John Noel Director	Puerto Rico	Municipal Services Administration G.P.O. Box 70167 San Juan 00936	Ms. Luc Delia Oquendo Sub-Administrator
Nebraska	Department of Economic Development Box 94666 301 Centennial Mall South Lincoln 68509	Jenne Rodriguez Director	Rhode Island	Governor's Office of Housing, Energy, and Intergovernmental Relations State House Providence 02903	Scott Wolfe Director
Nevada	Commission on Economic Development Capitol Complex Carson City 89710	James L. Spoo Director	South Carolina	Division of Economic Development 1205 Pendleton Street Suite 418 Columbia 29201	Olney England Director
New Hampshire	Office of State Planning $2^1/_2$ Beacon Street Concord 03301	David Scott Director of Policy Planning	South Dakota	Governor's Office of Economic Development 711 East Wells Avenue Pierre 57501-3369	Dave O'Hara Commissioner
New Jersey	Department of Community Affairs South Broad and Front Street CN 806 Trenton 08625-0806	Stephanie Bush Commissioner	Tennessee	Department of Economic and Community Development 320 Sixth Avenue North, Sixth Floor Nashville 37243-0405	Mike McGuire Assistant Commissioner
New Mexico	Department of Finance and Administration Bataan Memorial Building Room 201 Santa Fe 87501	Teodoro (Ted) Guambana Director	Texas	Community Affairs Division Department of Housing and Community Affairs P.O. Box 13941 Austin 78711-3941	Henry Flores Executive Director
New York	Division of Housing and Community Renewal One Fordham Plaza, Fourth Floor Bronx 10458	Donald M. Halperin Commissioner	Utah	Department of Community and Economic Development 324 South State, Suite 500 Salt Lake City 84111	Carol Nixon Director
North Carolina	Division of Community Assistance Department of Commerce 1307 Glenwood Avenue Suite 250, P.O. Box 12600 Raleigh 27605-2600	Robert Chandler Director	Vermont	Department of Housing and Community Affairs Pavilion Office Building Montpelier 05609	Barbara Grimes Commissioner
North Dakota	Office of Intergovernmental Assistance State Capitol, 14th Floor Bismarck 58505	Shirley R. Dykshoorn Director	Virginia	Department of Housing and Community Development 501 North Second Street Richmond 23219	Neal Barber Director
Ohio	Housing and Community Development Programs Department of Development 77 South High Street P.O. Box 1001 Columbus 43266-0101	Vincent Lombardi Director	Washington	Department of Community Development 906 Columbia Street, GH-51 Olympia 98504-8300	Ms. Gene Liddell Director
Oklahoma	Department of Commerce P.O. Box 26980 Oklahoma City 73126-0980	Sherwood Washington Assistant Director	West Virginia	Community Development Division West Virginia Development Office State Capitol Complex, Building 6, Room 553 Charleston 25305	Fred Cutlip Director
Oregon	Economic Development Department 775 Summer Street, N.E. Salem 97310	Yvonne Addington Director	Wisconsin	Division of Community Development Department of Development 123 West Washington Avenue P.O. Box 7970 Madison 53703	Philip Albert Executive Assistant
			Wyoming	Division of Economic and Community Development Barrett Building Cheyenne 82002	George H. Gault Director

Directory 1/4 PROVINCIAL AND TERRITORIAL AGENCIES FOR LOCAL AFFAIRS IN CANADA

Province or territory	Minister address	Phone number
Alberta	Hon. R. Steve West Minister of Municipal Affairs 425 Legislative Building, Edmonton T5K 2B6	403 427-3744
British Columbia	Hon. Darlene Marzari Municipal Affairs 306 Parliament Building Victoria, V8V 1X4	604 387-3602
Manitoba	Hon. Linda McIntosh Minister of Urban Affairs and Housing Legislative Building, Room 343 450 Broadway Winnipeg R3C 0V8	204 945-0074
	Leonard Derkach Minister of Rural Development 301 Legislative Building, Winnipeg 450 Broadway R3C 0V8	204 945-3788
New Brunswick	Hon. Marcelle Mersereau Minister of Department of the Environment P.O. Box 6000, 364 Argyle Place Fredericton E3B 5H1	506 453-2558
	Hon. Paul Duffie Minister of Municipal Affairs P.O. Box 6000, 364 Marysville Place Fredericton E3B 5H1	506 453-3001
Newfoundland	Hon. Authur Reid Minister of Municipal Affairs and Provincial Affairs P.O. Box 8700, St. John's A1B 4J6	709 729-3048
Northwest Territories	Hon. Richard Nerysoo Min. of Education Culture Employment and Safety and Public Services P.O. Box 1320, Yellowknife X1A 2L9	403 669-2333

Province or territory	Minister address	Phone number
Nova Scotia	Hon. Sandy Jolly Minister of Municipal Affairs P.O. Box 216 1505 Barrington St., 12th Fl. Maritime Centre Halifax B3J 2M4	902 424-5550
Ontario	Hon. Ed Philip Government Housing Leader Director of Management Board 777 Bay Street, 17th Floor Toronto M5G 2E5	416 585-7000
Prince Edward Island	Hon. Alan Buchanan Minister of Provincial Affairs/ Attorney General P.O. Box 2000, Charlottetown C1A 7N8	902 368-5250
Québec	Hon. Claude Ryan Ministre des Affaires Municipales 20 Avenue Chaveau, Sector B, Third Floor, Québec G1R 4J3	418 691-2050
Saskatchewan	Carol Carlson Minister of Municipal Government 303 Legislative Building Regina S4S 0B3	306 787-2635
Yukon	Hon. Micky Fisher Minister for Economic Development and Renewable Resources Yukon Government Administration Building P.O. Box 2703 Whitehorse Y1A 2C6	403 667-5811

Directory 1/5 UNITED STATES AND INTERNATIONAL MUNICIPAL MANAGEMENT ASSOCIATIONS

State, province, or country	Association	President, address, phone number
Alabama	Alabama City Management Association	Donald Marnon City Manager 3001 Fox Ridge Road Dothan 36303 205 794-8226
Alaska	Alaska Municipal Management Association	Paul Day City Manager City of Nome Pouch 281 Nome 99762 907 443-5242
Arizona	Arizona City/County Management Association	Ralph Velez City Manager City of Tolleson 9555 W. Van Buren Tolleson 85353 602 936-7111
Arkansas	Arkansas City Management Association	Lance Hudnell Deputy City Manager City of Hot Springs P.O. Box 700 Hot Springs 71902 501 321-6815
California	City Managers' Department, League of California Cities	John Goss City Manager City of Chula Vista 276 4th Avenue Chula Vista 91910 619 691-5031

State, province, or country	Association	President, address, phone number
Colorado	Colorado City/County Management Association	Roger Fraser City Manager City of Loveland 500 E. 3rd Street Loveland 80537 303 962-2302
Connecticut	Connecticut Town and City Management Association	John Elsesser Town Manager Town of Coventry 1712 Main Street Coventry 06238 203 742-6324
Delaware	City Management Association of Delaware	Robert Ernest Town Manager Town of Delmar 100 S. Penn Avenue Delmar MD/DE 19940 410 896-2777
District of Columbia	District of Columbia Urban Management Association	Larry King Director, Arlington Dept. of Env. Services 2100 Clarendon Blvd. Suite 801 Arlington, VA 22201 202 727-6343
Florida	Florida City and County Management Association	Randall Reid Asst. County Administrator Martin County P.O. Box 1288 Stuart 34995-1288 407 383-9164

Directory 1/5   **UNITED STATES AND INTERNATIONAL**
continued   **MUNICIPAL MANAGEMENT ASSOCIATIONS**

State, province, or country	Association	President, address, phone number	State, province, or country	Association	President, address, phone number
Georgia	Georgia City/County Management Association	Peggy Merriss City Manager City of Decatur P.O. Box 220 Decatur 30031 404 370-4100	Mississippi	Mississippi City and County Management Association	Michael McPhearson Director of Finance and Administration City of Ridgeland 304 Highway 51 P.O. Box 217 Ridgeland 39158 601 856-7113
Idaho	Idaho City Management Association	Roy Rainey City Adm/City Clerk City of Sun Valley P.O. Box 416 Sun Valley 83353 208 622-4438	Missouri	Missouri City Management Association	Martin Corcoran City Manager City of Maplewood 7601 Manchester Maplewood 63143 314 645-3600
Illinois	Illinois City Management Association	Timothy Schuenke Village Manager Village of LaGrange Park 447 N. Catherine Ave. La Grange 60525 708 354-0225	Nebraska	Nebraska City Management Association	Joseph Salitros City Administrator City of Wayne 306 Pearl Street Wayne 68787 402 375-1733
Indiana	Indiana Municipal Management Association	Larry Hopkins Town Manager Town of Fishers 1 Municipal Drive Fishers 46038 317 577-3500	Nevada	Local Government Managers Association of Nevada	Clayton Holstine City Manager City of Reno P.O. Box 1900 Reno 89505
Iowa	Iowa City/County Management Association	Tim Zisoff City Manager City of Indianola 110 N. First Indianola 50125	New Hampshire	New Hampshire Municipal Management Association	John N. Isham Town Administrator Town of Peterborough One Grove St. Peterborough 03458 603 924-3201
Kansas	Kansas Association of City Management	Bob Halloran City Manager City of Garden City P.O. Box 499 Garden City 67846 316 276-1166	New Jersey	New Jersey Municipal Management Association	Dave Kochel Township Administrator Ocean Township 399 Monmouth Rd. Oakhurst 07755 908 531-5000
Kentucky	Kentucky City Management Association	William Fisher, Jr. City Manager City of Ashland P.O. Box 1839 Ashland, KY 41101-1839 606 327-2002	New Mexico	New Mexico City Management Association	Les Montoya City Manager City of Las Vegas P.O. Box 179 Las Vegas 87701 505 454-1401
Maine	Maine Town and City Management Association	Tom Stevens City Manager City of Presque Isle 12 2nd St. P.O. Box 1148 Presque Isle 04769 207 764-4485	New York	Municipal Management Association of New York State	John Crary Deputy Village Manager Village of Scarsdale Village Hall Scarsdale 10583 914 723-5591
Maryland	Maryland City and County Management Association	Marge Wolf City Administrator City of Hyattsville 4310 Gallatin Street Hyattsville 20781 301 985-5000	North Carolina	North Carolina City and County Management Association	Richard McLean NCCCMA 2nd VP P.O. Box 878 Morresville 28115
Massachusetts	Massachusetts Municipal Management Association	Deborah Radway Executive Secretary Town of Montague One Avenue A Turner Falls 01376 413 863-3204	Ohio	Ohio City Management Association	Robert Downey City Manager City of Cleveland Heights 40 Severance Circle Cleveland Heights 44118 216 291-4444
Michigan	Michigan City Management Association	Karl Tomion City Manager City of Midland 333 W. Ellsworth P.O. Box 1647 Midland 48640 616 456-3166	Oklahoma	City Management Association of Oklahoma	Donald Brown City Manager City of Oklahoma City 200 North Walker, #302 Oklahoma City 73102 405 297-2345
Minnesota	Minnesota City/County Management Association	Edward Shukle, Jr. City Manager City of Mound 5341 Maywood Road Mound 55364 612 472-0600	Oregon	Oregon Section of ICMA	Dan Bartlett City Manager City of Milwaukie 10772 SE Main Street Milwaukie 97222 503 659-5171
			Pennsylvania	Association for Pennsylvania Municipal Management	Thomas Fountaine Borough Manager Borough of Hollidaysburg 401 Blair Street Hollidaysburg 16648 814 695-7543

Directory 1/5
continued

UNITED STATES AND INTERNATIONAL
MUNICIPAL MANAGEMENT ASSOCIATIONS

State, province, or country	Association	President, address, phone number
Rhode Island ...	Rhode Island City and Town Managers Association	Dennis Phelan Town Manager Town of Barrington 17 Townsend Street Barrington 02806-2013 401 247-1900
South Carolina ..	South Carolina City and County Management Association	Robert Haynie County Administrator County of Greenwood 600 Monument Street Greenwood 29646 803 942-8502
Tennessee	Tennessee City Management Association	Danny Farmer City Manager City of Mt. Juliet P.O. Box 757 Mt. Juliet 37122 615 754-2552
Texas	Texas City Management Association	Lea Dunn City Manager City of Bellaire 7008 S. Rice Avenue Bellaire 77401 713 662-8222
Utah	Utah City Management Association	Colin Wood City Manager City of North Salt Lake 20 S. Highway 89 North Salt Lake, UT 84054 801 298-3877
Vermont	Vermont Town and City Management Association	William O'Connor Town Manager Town of Westminster Town Offices Westminster 05158
Virginia	Virginia Local Government Management Association	Anton Gardener County Manager County of Arlington, #302 1 Courthouse Plaza 2100 Clarendon Blvd. Arlington 22201 703 358-3120
Washington	Washington City/County Management Association	Roger Crum City Manager City of Spokane 808 W. Spokane Falls Blvd. Spokane 99201 509 625-6262
West Virginia ...	West Virginia City Management Association	Ed Thorne City Manager City of Fairmont 200 Jackson Street Fairmont 26554 304 366-6211
Wisconsin	Wisconsin City Management Association	Paul Webber Administrative Coordinator County of La Crosse 400 N. 4th Street La Crosse 54601
Wyoming, North Dakota, South Dakota, Idaho, and Montana	Great Open Spaces City Management Association	John Lawton City Manager City of Great Falls Civic Center, P.O. Box 5021 Great Falls 59403 406 727-5881
Canada	Canadian Association of Municipal Administrators	Cecil Vincent City Administrative Officer 24 Clarence Ottawa, Ontario K1N 5P3 Canada 613 241-8444 Fax: 613 241-7440 Canada
Australia	The Institute of Municipal Management (Australia)	Stanley B. Fursman Town Clerk Mackay City Council POB 41 Gordon Street Mackay, Queensland Australia 4740 61-79-516466
Europe	European City/County Management Association	A. Jeffrey Greenwell Chief Executive Northamptonshire County Council County Hall Northampton MN1 1DN, England 44 604 236050 FAX 44 604 236223
Germany	Deutscher Städte- und Gemeindebund	Heribert Thallmair Mayor of Starnberg Kaiserswerther Strasse 199/201 Düsseldorf 40474, Germany (49) 211/458-7228 Fax: (49) 211/458-7211
Korea	Korean Urban Management Association	Dr. Choon-Hee Ro 8-3 Jeonnong-Dong Dongdaemun-Gu Seoul, South Korea (82) 2-213-0615 Fax: (82) 2-213-0616
Middle East	Middle East Section of ICMA	IULA-EMME Sultanahmet, Yerebatan Cad. 2 Istanbul, Turkey (90) 1/511-1010 Fax: (90) 1/522-4476
Israel	Union of Local Authorities in Israel	3 Heftman Street P.O. Box 20040 Tel-Aviv 61200 Israel (972) 3/219241 Fax: (972) 3/267447
New Zealand	New Zealand Society of Local Government Managers	Joseph Rudhall Chief Ex. Officer Nelson City Council P.O. Box 645 Nelson, New Zealand 64 354-60200
Sweden	Association of Swedish City Managers	Hans Granquist City Manager Malma Gård 5725 96 Västerås (46) 21 27072
United Kingdom	The Society of Local Authority Chief Executives (SOLACE)	Samuel Jones Town Clerk Corporation of London P.O. Box 270 Guildhall EC2P, 2EJ London, England 44 71 3321400

Directory 1/6 STATE ASSOCIATIONS OF COUNTIES

State	State association and address	Name and title of executive director	Phone number FAX	Year first organized
Alabama	Association of County Commissioners of Alabama 100 North Jackson Street, Montgomery 36104	O. H. "Buddy" Sharpless, Executive Director	205 263-7594 205 263-7678	1929
Alaska	Alaska Municipal League 217 Second Street, Suite 200, Juneau 99801-1267	Kent E. Swisher, Executive Director	907 586-1325 907 463-5480	1950
Arizona	Arizona Association of Counties 1910 West Jefferson, Suite 1, Phoenix 85007	Archie Stephens, Executive Director	602 252-6563 602 254-0969	1968
	County Supervisors Association of Arizona 1570 West Van Buren, Phoenix 85007	P. Jerry Orrick, Executive Director	602 252-5521 602 253-3227	...
Arkansas	Association of Arkansas Counties 314 South Victory Street, Little Rock 72201	James Baker, Executive Director	501 372-7550 501 372-0611	1968
California	California State Association of Counties 1100 K Street, Suite 101, Sacramento 95814	Steve Swendiman, Executive Director	916 327-7500 916 441-5507	1895
Colorado	Colorado Counties, Inc. 1177 Grant Street, Denver 80203-2362	Peter King, Executive Director	303 861-4076 303 861-2818	1915
Delaware	Delaware Association of Counties 414 Federal Street, Dover 19901-3615	...	302 736-2040 302 736-2262	...
Florida	Florida Association of Counties P.O. Box 549, Tallahassee 32302	Vivian Zaricki, Executive Director	904 224-3148 904 222-5839	1929
Georgia	Association of County Commissioners of Georgia 50 Hurt Plaza, Suite 1000, Atlanta 30303	Jerry R. Griffin, Executive Director	404 522-5022 404 525-2477	1914
Hawaii	Hawaii State Association of Counties 200 South High Street, Wailuku 96793-2134	Gwen Yoshimi-Ohashi, Executive Director	808 243-7744 808 243-7686	1959
Idaho	Idaho Association of Counties P.O. Box 1623, Boise 83701	Daniel G. Chadwick, Executive Director	208 345-9126 208 345-0379	1960
Illinois	Illinois Association of County Board Members 413 West Monroe Street, Springfield 62704	Paul Bitschenauer, Executive Director	217 528-5331 217 528-8943	1973
	Urban Counties Council of Illinois 215 East Adams, Suite 300, Springfield 62705	W. Michael McCreery, Executive Director	217 544-5585 217 544-5571	...
Indiana	Association of Indiana Counties, Inc. 101 West Ohio, Suite 710, Indianapolis 46204	Richard J. Cockrum, Executive Director	317 684-3710 317 684-3713	1958
Iowa	Iowa State Association of Counties 701 East Court Avenue, Des Moines 50309	Paul Coates, Executive Director	515 244-7181 515 244-6397	1971
Kansas	Kansas Association of Counties 215 Southeast 8th Street, Topeka 66603-3906	John T. Torbert, Executive Director	913 233-2271 913 233-4830	...
Kentucky	Kentucky Association of Counties 400 King's Daughters Drive, Frankfort 40601-4106	John Griggs, Executive Director	502 223-7667 502 223-1502	1973
Louisiana	Police Jury Association of Louisiana 707 North Seventh Street, Baton Rouge 70802	James T. Hays, Executive Director	504 343-2835 504 343-0050	1923
Maine	Maine County Commissioners Association Three Wade Street, Augusta 04330-6318	Robert Howe, Executive Director	207 623-4697 207 622-4437	1939
Maryland	Maryland Association of Counties 169 Conduit Street, Annapolis 21401	David Bliden, Executive Director	410 269-0043 410 268-1775	1951
Massachusetts	Massachusetts Association of County Commissioners Superior Courthouse, 40 Thorndice Street, Cambridge	Edward Kennedy, Executive Director	617 494-4100 617 577-9722	...
Michigan	Michigan Association of Counties 935 North Washington Street, Lansing 48906	Tim McGuire, Executive Director	517 372-5374 517 482-4599	1898
Minnesota	Association of Minnesota Counties 125 Charles Avenue, St. Paul 55103-2108	James A. Mulder, Executive Director	612 224-3344 612 224-6540	1909
Mississippi	Mississippi Association of Supervisors P.O. Box 1314, Jackson 39215	E. Jack Gregory, Jr., Executive Director	601 353-2741 601 353-2749	1929
Missouri	Missouri Association of Counties P.O. Box 234, Jefferson City 65102	Juanita Donehue, Executive Director	314 634-2120 314 634-3549	1972
Montana	Montana Association of Counties 2711 Airport Road, Helena 59601	Gordon Morris, Executive Director	406 442-5209 406 442-5238	1909
Nebraska	Nebraska Association of County Officials 625 South 14th Street, Suite A, Lincoln 68508	Jack D. Mills, Executive Director	402 434-5660 402 434-5673	1937
Nevada	Nevada Association of Counties 308 North Curry Street, Suite 205, Carson City 89703	Robert S. Hadfield, Executive Director	702 883-7863 702 883-7398	1945
New Hampshire	New Hampshire Association of Counties 16 Centre Street, Concord 03301	John Disko, Executive Director	603 224-9222 603 224-8312	1947
New Jersey	New Jersey Association of Counties 214 West State Street, Trenton 08608	Celeste Carpianoe, Executive Director	609 394-3467 609 989-8567	1921
New Mexico	New Mexico Association of Counties 1215 Paseo De Peralta, Santa Fe 87501	Donna K. Smith, Executive Director	505 983-2101 505 983-4396	1926
New York	New York State Association of Counties 150 State Street, Albany 12207	John R. Zagame, Executive Director	518 465-1473 518 465-0506	1925
North Carolina	North Carolina Association of County Commissioners 215 North Dawson Street, Raleigh 27602-1488	C. Ronald Aycock, Executive Director	919 715-2893 919 733-1065	1908
North Dakota	North Dakota Association of Counties P.O. Box 417, Bismarck 58502	Mark A. Johnson, Executive Director	701 258-4481 701 258-2469	1906

Directory 1/6   STATE ASSOCIATIONS OF COUNTIES
continued

State	State association and address	Name and title of executive director	Phone number FAX	Year first organized
Ohio	County Commissioners Association of Ohio 175 South Third Street, Suite 500, Columbus 43215-5134	Larry L. Long, Executive Director	614 221-5627 614 221-6986	1880
Oklahoma	Association of County Commissioners of Oklahoma 818 N.W. 63rd Street, Oklahoma City 73116-7604	John Ward, Executive Director	405 840-9582 405 840-5122	...
Oregon	Association of Oregon Counties P.O. Box 12729, Salem 97309	Robert Cantine, Executive Director	503 585-8351 503 373-7876	1906
Pennsylvania	County Commissioners Association of Pennsylvania 17 North Front Street, Suite 120, Harrisburg 17101	Douglas E. Hill, Executive Director	717 232-7554 717 232-2162	1886
South Carolina	South Carolina Association of Counties P.O. Box 8207, Columbia 29202-8207	Michael B. Cone, Executive Director	803 252-7255 803 252-0379	1967
South Dakota	South Dakota Association of County Commissioners 207 East Capitol, Suite 203, Pierre 57501	Dennis Hanson, Executive Director	605 224-4554 605 224-4833	1914
Tennessee	Tennessee County Services Association 226 Capitol Boulevard Building, Suite 700, Nashville 37219	Robert M. Wormsley, Executive Director	615 242-5591 615 244-3340	1954
Texas	Texas Association of Counties P.O. Box 2131, Austin 78768	Sam Seale, Executive Director	512 478-8753 512 478-0519	1969
Utah	Utah Association of Counties 4021 South-700 East, Suite 180, Salt Lake City 84107	L. Brent Gardner, Executive Director	801 265-1331 801 265-9485	1923
Virginia	Virginia Association of Counties 1001 East Broad Street, Suite LL20, Richmond 23219	James D. Campbell, Executive Director	804 788-6652 804 788-0083	1935
Washington	Washington Association of County Officials 206 Tenth Avenue S.E., #307, Olympia 98501	Fred Saeger, Executive Director	206 753-7319 206 753-2842	1959
	Washington State Association of Counties 206 Tenth Avenue S.E., Olympia 98501	Gary Lowe, Executive Director	206 753-1886 206 753-2842	1908
West Virginia	West Virginia Association of Counties 2211 Washington East Street, Charleston 25311-2218	John Hoff, Executive Director	304 346-0591 304 346-0592	1960
Wisconsin	Wisconsin Counties Association 802 West Broadway, Suite 308, Madison 53713-1897	Mark Rogacki, Executive Director	608 266-6480 608 221-3832	1935
Wyoming	Wyoming County Commissioners Association P.O. Box 86, Cheyenne 82001	B. G. "Jerry" Michie, Executive Director	307 632-5409 307 632-6533	1968

Directory 1/7   DIRECTORS OF COUNCILS OF GOVERNMENTS
RECOGNIZED BY ICMA[1]

Regional council	Appointed administrator	Phone number
ALABAMA-4		
Birmingham Regional Planning Commission	Paul G. Dentiste	205 251-8139
Central Alabama Regional Planning and Development Commission	...	205 262-4300
East Alabama Regional Planning and Development Commission	James W. Curtis	205 237-6741
South Central Alabama Development Commission	...	205 281-2196
ARIZONA-5		
District 4 COG	...	602 782-1886
Maricopa Association of Governments	John J. DeBolske	602 254-6308
Northern Arizona COG	...	602 774-1895
PIMA Association of Governments	Thomas L. Swanson	602 792-1093
Southeastern Arizona Governments Organization	Joe Brannen	602 432-5301
ARKANSAS-3		
Metroplan	...	501 372-3300
Northwest Arkansas Regional Planning Commission	Larry R. Wood	501 751-7125
White River Planning and Development District	...	501 793-5233
CALIFORNIA-15		
Alameda County Waste Management Authority	Thomas Martinsen	510 639-2481
Association of Bay Area Governments	Revan A. F. Tranter	415 464-7900
Association of Monterey Bay Area Governments	Nicolas Papadakis	408 624-2117
Central Sierra Planning Council	...	209 532-8768
Council of Fresno County Governments	Barbara Goodwin	209 233-4148
Sacramento Area COG	...	916 441-5930
Sacramento Transportation Authority	...	916 323-0850
San Diego Association of Governments	Kenneth E. Sulzer	619 595-5300
San Joaquin County COG	...	805 861-2191

Regional council	Appointed administrator	Phone number
Santa Barbara County Association of Governments	Gerald R. Lorden	805 568-2546
South Bay Regional Public Communications Authority	...	213 973-1802
Southern California Association of Governments	Mark A. Pisano	213 236-1800
Stanislaus Area Association of Governments	...	209 525-7830
Transportation Corridor Agency COG	...	714 557-3298
Tulare County Association of Governments	...	209 733-6303
COLORADO-2		
Denver Regional COG	Robert D. Farley	303 455-1000
Northwest Colorado COG	...	303 668-5445
CONNECTICUT-1		
Connecticut River Estuary Regional Planning Agency	Stanley V. Greimann	203 388-3497
DISTRICT OF COLUMBIA-1		
Metropolitan Washington COG	Ruth R. Crone	202 962-3200
GEORGIA-4		
Atlanta Regional Commission	B. Harry West	404 656-7700
Coastal Georgia Regional Development Center	Vernon D. Martin	912 264-7363
Middle Georgia Regional Development Center	James C. Torr	912 744-6160
Southeast Georgia Regional Development Center	...	912 285-6097
IDAHO-2		
Panhandle Area Council	...	208 772-0584
Southeast Idaho COG	Chuck PRince	208 233-4032
ILLINOIS-10		
Bi-State Regional Commission	Gary B. Vallem	309 793-6300

Regional council	Appointed administrator	Phone number
Champaign County Regional Planning Commission	Robert Soltau	217 328-3313
Greater Egypt Regional Planning and Development Commission	A. S. Kirkikis	618 549-3306
North Central Illinois COG	. . .	815 875-3396
Northeastern Illinois Planning Commission	. . .	312 454-0400
Northwest Municipal Conference	Rita R. Arnas	708 253-6323
South Central Illinois Regional Planning and Development Commission	. . .	618 548-4234
South Suburban Mayors' and Managers' Association	. . .	708 957-6970
Southwestern Illinois Metropolitan Regional Planning Commission	Thomas A. Wobbe	618 344-4250
Tri-County Regional Planning Commission	John F. Boyle	309 694-9330
INDIANA-2		
Michiana Area COG	Charles W. Minkler	219 287-1829
Northwestern Indiana Regional Planning Commission	. . .	219 923-1060
IOWA-4		
East Central Intergovernmental Association	Bill Baum	319 556-4166
Midas COG	Stephen F. Hoesel	515 576-7183
Siouxland Interstate Metropolitan Planning Council	. . .	712 279-6286
Southern Iowa Economic Development Association	. . .	515 682-8741
KANSAS-1		
North Central Regional Planning Commission	. . .	913 738-2218
KENTUCKY-6		
Barren River Area Development District.	. . .	502 781-2381
Big Sandy Area Development District ..	. . .	606 886-2374
Bluegrass Area Development District ...	. . .	606 272-6656
Lincoln Trail Area Development District .	James E. Greer	502 769-2393
Northern Kentucky Area Development District	. . .	606 283-1885
Purchase Area Development District ...	. . .	502 247-7171
LOUISIANA-2		
Lafayette Areawide Planning Commission	Roger K. Hedrick	318 237-0216
Shreve Area COG	J. Kent Rogers	318 226-6488
MAINE-1		
Greater Portland COG	. . .	207 774-9891
MARYLAND-2		
Baltimore Regional COG	. . .	301 383-5830
Tri-County Council for Southern Maryland	Gary V. Hodge	301 884-2144
MASSACHUSETTS-1		
Merrimack Valley Planning Commission	. . .	617 374-0519
MICHIGAN-1		
Southeast Michigan COG	John M. Amberger	313 961-4266
MISSISSIPPI-1		
Central Mississippi Planning and Development District	. . .	601 981-1511
MISSOURI-4		
East-West Gateway Coordinating Council	. . .	314 421-4220
Mid-America Regional Council	David A. Warm	816 474-4240
Ozark Foothills Regional Planning Commission	. . .	314 785-6402
South Central Ozark COG	. . .	417 256-8123
NEW MEXICO-1		
Southwest New Mexico COG	. . .	505 388-1974
NEW YORK-1		
Capital District Regional Planning Commission	Chungchin Chen	518 272-1414
NORTH CAROLINA-7		
Centralina COG	E. Lee Armour	704 372-2416
Land-of-Sky Regional Council	Robert E. Shepherd	704 254-8131
Lumber River COG	James Perry	919 738-8104
Neuse River COG	. . .	919 638-3185
Piedmont Triad COG	Randall Billings	919 294-4950
Region L COG	Greg T. Godard	919 446-0411
Western Piedmont COG	R. Douglas Taylor	704 322-9191

Regional council	Appointed administrator	Phone number
OHIO-4		
Miami Valley Regional Planning Commission	. . .	513 223-6323
Ohio Mid-Eastern Governments Association	John A. Quinlan	614 439-4471
Ohio-Kentucky-Indiana Regional COG ..	. . .	513 621-7060
Toledo Metropolitan Area COG	William L. Knight	419 241-9155
OKLAHOMA-3		
Association of Central Oklahoma Governments	Zach D. Taylor	405 848-8961
Central Oklahoma Economic Development District	Wayne Manley	405 273-6410
Northern Oklahoma Development Association	. . .	405 237-4810
OREGON-6		
Lane COG	George Kloeppel	503 687-4283
Metropolitan Service District	. . .	503 221-1646
Mid-Columbia Economic Development District	. . .	503 296-2266
Mid-Willamette Valley COG	Alan H. Hershey	503 588-6177
Oregon Cascades West COG	William R. Wagner	503 757-6851
Umpqua Regional COG	Richard J. Dolgonas	503 440-4231
PENNSYLVANIA-3		
Allegheny League of Municipalities	. . .	412 355-5986
North Central Pennsylvania Regional Planning and Development Commission	Ronald W. Kuleck	814 773-3162
Northwest Pennsylvania Regional Planning and Development Commission	William R. Steiner	814 437-3024
SOUTH CAROLINA-4		
Central Midlands Regional Planning Council	Donald R. Hinson	803 798-1243
Lower Savannah COG	. . .	803 649-7981
South Carolina Appalachian COG	Robert M. Strother	803 242-9733
Upper Savannah COG	. . .	803 229-6627
SOUTH DAKOTA-2		
Northeast COG	Faye Kann	605 622-2595
Planning and Development District Three	. . .	605 665-4408
TENNESSEE-2		
Chattanooga Area Regional COG/ Southeast Tennessee Development District	Joe Guthrie	615 266-5781
East Tennessee Development District ..	Robert E. Freeman	615 584-8553
TEXAS-17		
Alamo Area COG	. . .	512 225-5201
Ark-Tex COG	James C. Fisher Jr.	501 774-3481
Capital Area Planning Council	. . .	512 443-7653
Central Texas COG	. . .	817 939-1801
Coastal Bend COG	John P. Buckner	512 883-5743
Concho Valley COG	Robert R. Weaver	915 944-9666
Deep East Texas COG	Walter G. Diggles	409 384-5704
East Texas COG	Glynn J. Knight	214 984-8641
Heart of Texas COG	Leon A. Willhite	817 756-6631
Houston-Galveston Area Council	Jack Steele	713 627-3200
Lower Rio Grande Valley Development Council	. . .	512 682-3481
Nortex Regional Planning Commission	. . .	817 322-5281
North Central Texas COG	Mike Eastland	817 461-3300
Panhandle Regional Planning Commission	. . .	806 372-3381
South Plains Association of Governments	. . .	806 762-8721
Texoma Regional Planning Commission	. . .	214 786-2955
West Central Texas COG	. . .	915 672-8544
UTAH-1		
Five County Association of Governments	John S. Williams	801 673-3548
VIRGINIA-8		
Central Shenandoah Planning District Commission	. . .	703 885-5174
Central Virginia Planning District Commission	. . .	804 845-3491
Crater Planning District Commission ...	Dennis K. Morris	804 861-1666
Hampton Roads Planning District Commission	Arthur L. Collins	804 461-3200
Northern Neck Planning District Commission	Joyce Bradford	804 529-7400
Northern Virginia Planning District Commission	G. Mark Gibb	703 642-0700

Directory 1/7 continued — DIRECTORS OF COUNCILS OF GOVERNMENTS RECOGNIZED BY ICMA[1]

Regional council	Appointed administrator	Phone number
Southside Planning District Commission	William Park	804 447-7101
West Piedmont Planning District Commission	. . .	703 638-3987
WASHINGTON-4		
Benton-Franklin Regional Council	Donald P. Morton	509 943-9185
Intergovernmental Resource Center	Dean Lookingbill	206 699-2361
Puget Sound COG	Mary McCumber	206 464-7090
Skagit COG	W. Kelley Moldstad	206 428-1299
WEST VIRGINIA-3		
Bel-O-Mar Regional Council and Interstate Planning Commission	William C. Phipps	304 242-1800

Regional council	Appointed administrator	Phone number
Mid-Ohio Valley Regional Council	. . .	304 485-3801
Region One Planning and Development Council	Norman L. Kirkham	304 425-9508
WISCONSIN-2		
East Central Wisconsin Regional Planning Commission	Kenneth J. Theine	414 729-1100
West Central Wisconsin Regional Planning Commission	. . .	715 836-2918
WYOMING-1		
Fremont County Association of Governments	Mike Morgan	317 856-8589

[1]This directory is limited to those councils of governments that have been recognized by ICMA as of November 1992 as providing for a position of overall professional management.

Directory 1/8 — INTERNATIONAL CHIEF APPOINTED ADMINISTRATORS

Local government	Appointed administrator	Phone number
AUSTRALIA		
New South Wales		
Balranald Shire	Robert J. Foster	615-020-1300
Baulkam Hills Shire	David W. Mead	612-843-0555
Bankstown	Garry J. Payne	612-793-0700
Botany	John F. Patterson	612-317-0555
Drummoyne	Russell J. Lloyd	612-719-0305
Great Lakes	John C. Fitzpatrick	616-554-6277
Hawkesbury	Garry M. McCully	614-587-7000
Hunters Hill	William E. G. Phipson	612-816-1555
Lake Macquarie	Robert John Gray	614-921-0333
Lane Cove	Alan W. Byleveld	612-911-3555
Lismore	Paul T. Muldoon	616-625-0420
Liverpool	John H. Walker	612-821-9222
Manly	Wayne A. Collins	612-976-1500
Mosman	Vivian H. R. May	612-960-0900
Newcastle	William H. Grant	614-929-7830
Penrith	Barry B. Long	614-732-7620
Rockdale	Stephen J. Blackadder	612-567-5573
Ryde	Geraldine M. Brus	612-952-8052
Singleton Shire	John A. Flannery	616-578-7202
Sutherland Shire	John W. Rayner	612-710-0359
Tamworth	Barry F. Pullinger	616-768-4555
Tweed Shire	John F. Griffin	616-672-0415
Wollongong	Roderick J. Oxley	614-227-7111
Wyong Shire	John S. Dawson	614-353-1333
Northern Territory		
Alice Springs	Allan R. McGill	618-950-0500
Darwin	David K. Wormald	618-982-2505
Queensland		
Cairns	Noel P. Briggs	617-050-2419
Miriam Vale Shire	James S. Nixon	617-974-5100
Pine Rivers Shire	John W. Mathews	617-205-0561
Redcliffe	Ronald C. Fennell	617-283-0203
Rockhampton	Robin D. Noble	617-931-1278
Warwick	John P. Cuddihy	617-661-2333
South Australia		
Burnside	Rodney W. S. Donne	618-366-4200
Happy Valley	John D. Christie	618-374-6201
Hindmarsh and Woodville	Geoffrey T. Whitbread	618-348-6111
Noarlunga	Christopher Catt	618-384-0626
Port Adelaide	Keith Beamish	618-479-841
Salisbury	Stephen C. Hains	618-259-1212
Tasmania		
Devonport	David E. Sales	614-240-511
Dorset	Thomas B. Ransom	613-522-444
Hobart	Garry R. Storch	612-382-711
Huon Valley	William D. Perry	610-229-1487
Launceston	Robert G. Campbell	613-371-102
Ulverston	Alfred R. Mott	614-25-1099

Local government	Appointed administrator	Phone number
Victoria		
Altona	John Francis Shaw	613-316-1221
Ballarat	David R. Peile	615-338-602
Ballarat Shire	Jeremy W. M. Johnson	615-338-1477
Barrabool Shire	Mervyn W. Hair	615-261-4202
Benalla	William S. Jaboor	615-762-1533
Bendigo	Ray J. Burton	615-444-9625
Berwick	Neil B. Lucas	613-705-5200
Box Hill	Ian G. Port	613-895-9611
Brighton	Raymond J. Cobain	613-591-8688
Bulla Shire	John W. Watson	613-744-9253
Buninyong Shire	Peter Mangan	. . .
Coburg	Joseph R. Diffen	613-350-0210
Cranbourne Shire	Terence Vickerman	615-996-1000
Creswick Shire	Bruce T. Crago	615-345-2000
Croydon	Terence L. Maher	613-724-3201
Dandenong	Colin G. Dickie	613-212-1010
Eaglehawk	Barry Secombe	615-446-8966
Essendon	Peter R. Seamer	614-332-438888
Flinders Shire	Larry M. Jones	615-986-0111
Frankston	Adrian H. Butler	613-784-1800
Geelong	David Niven	. . .
Gisborne Shire	Terence H. Larkins	. . .
Hamilton	Russell J. Worland	615-573-0444
Hawthorn	Kenneth J. McNamara	613-810-2401
Keilor	Peter J. Black	. . .
Kew	Malcolm D. Hutchinson	613-862-2466
Kilmore Shire	Peter O. Anderson	615-782-1322
Knox	Robert G. Seiffert	618-818-222
Kyabram	John P. Costello	610-585-22166
Malvern	Peter A. Akers	613-823-1222
Marong	Graeme L. Elvey	615-435-2202
Melbourne	Eric W. Howard	613-658-9470
Melton Shire	Lindsay A. Merritt	613-747-7200
Mildura	Damian B. Goss	615-022-2777
Moorabbin	Douglas I. Owens	. . .
Mordialloc	Jonathan F. Edwards	613-584-4366
Morwell	Ronald H. Waters	615-134-4744
Numurkah Shire	Lindsay G. Mitchell	615-862-1222
Nunawading	Barry P. Stow	613-262-6310
Preston	Kelvin L. Spiller	613-479-4602
Richmond	David G. Williams	613-420-9655
Ringwood	John D. Paech	. . .
St. Kilda	Jude R. Munro	613-536-1333
Sale	Graeme L. Pearce	615-144-3644
Sandringham	John L. Purdey	613-598-8111
Sherbrooke Shire	Dennis E. Stevens	613-212-8222
South Melbourne	Noel F. Kropp	613-695-8201
Springvale	Bryan A. Payne	613-549-1117
Strathfieldsaye Shire	Barry W. Edwards	615-441-4000
Tambo Shire	Russ J. Tavener	615-553-100
Warragul	Geoffrey C. Davey	615-623-0211
Warrnambool	Vernon G. Robson	615-554-7800
Waverley	John N. Webster	613-566-0282
Werribee	John T. Kerr	613-742-0703
Whittlesea	Lindsay G. Esmonde	613-401-0333
Woorayl Shire	John F. Dyer	615-662-9200

Directory 1/8   **INTERNATIONAL CHIEF APPOINTED ADMINISTRATORS**
continued

Local government	Appointed administrator	Phone number	Local government	Appointed administrator	Phone number
Western Australia			**Newfoundland**		
Albany Shire	Wayne F. Scheggia	619-841-2311	Gander	Jake Turner	709-651-2949
Gnowangerup Shire	Philip A. Anning	619-827-1007	Labrador City	Cecil E. Vincent	709-944-2621
Kalamunda Shire	Edward H. Kelly	619-293-2111	St. John's	William K. Mann	. . .
Kalgoorlie-Boulder	Leslie P. Strugnell	619-021-2544			
Kwinana	Robert K. Smillie	619-419-2222	**Northwest Territories**		
Mindarie	Ralph H. Fardon	619-332-3867	Yellowknife	Douglas B. Lagore	403-920-5600
Narrogin	Stephen D. Tindale	619-881-1644			
Peppermint Grove Shire	Graham D. Partridge	619-384-0099	**Nova Scotia**		
Perth	Garry G. Hunt	619-265-3260	Argyle District	Robert G. Thibault	902-648-2311
Subiaca	Patrick John Walker	619-381-5000	Dartmouth	Larry Corrigan	902-464-2168
Swan Shire	Eric W. Lumsden	619-274-9801	Halifax	Barry B. Coopersmith	902-421-6500
			Port Hawkesbury	Colin J. MacDonald	902-625-0116
CANADA					
Alberta			**Ontario**		
Airdrie	Deryl Kloster	403-948-5907	Ajax	Barry Malmsten	905-683-4550
Banff	James Bennett	403-762-1200	Ancaster	A. Bruce Davidson	905-648-4419
Brooks	Kevin Bridges	403-362-3333	Aurora	James B. Currier	416-727-1375
Calgary	Paul Dawson	. . .	Burlington	W. Michael Fenn	416-335-7608
Cochrane	Martin J. Schmitke	403-932-2075	Cambridge	Donald N. Smith	519-740-4518
Edmonton	J. Richard Picherack	403-496-8222	Chatham	Hugh J. Thomas	519-436-3241
Fort McMurray	Glen Laubenstein	403-743-7022	Clarence Township	Richard R. Lalonde	613-488-2570
Fort Saskatchewan	Paul Stapleton	403-992-6212	Cobourg	Bryan W. Baxter	905-372-4301
Grande Prairie	Robert W. Robertson	403-538-0312	Durham Region	Garry Cubitt	905-668-7711
Lacombe	Robert D. Jenkins	403-782-6666	Flamborough	Jane Lee	. . .
Leduc	Glenn Pitman	403-980-7101	Fort Erie	Kenneth Paul Zurby	. . .
Lethbridge	Bryan Horrocks	403-320-3901	Guelph	David R. Creech	519-837-5602
Ponoka	Gordon C. Harris	403-783-0121	Hamilton-Wentworth Region	W. McMillin Carson	905-546-4263
Rainbow Lake	Julie M. Burge	. . .	Hawkesbury	Jacques Turgeon	613-632-5613
Red Deer	H. Michael Day	403-342-8156	Kanata	Bert Meunier	613-592-4281
St. Albert	Norbert Van Wyk	403-459-1607	Kingston	John Morand	613-546-4291
Strathmore	Dwight J. Stanford	403-934-3133	Kirkland Lake	Lionel J. Sherratt	705-567-9361
			Kitchener	Tom McKay	519-741-2290
British Columbia			London	John E. Fleming	519-661-5493
Abbotsford District	Rick Beauchamp	604-853-1155	Mississauga	G. Stanley Spencer	905-896-5550
Burnaby	A. L. Parr	604-294-7103	Muskoka District Municipality	Bill Calvert	705-645-2231
Chillowack District	Ted Tisdale	604-793-2943	Nepean	Robert Letourneau	613-727-6602
Coquitlam	Norman A. Cook	604-664-1403	Niagra Falls	Edward Lustig	905-356-7521
Fort St. John	Colin J. Griffith	604-785-4443	Niagara-on-the-Lake	Lew Holloway	905-468-3266
Kamloops	Joseph E. Martignago	604-828-3498	Niagara Regional		
Kelowna	Ronald Born	604-763-6011	Municipality	Michael H. Boggs	905-984-3602
Langley Township	Jim F. Godfrey	604-534-3211	Oakville	Harry E. Henderson	416-845-6601
Maple Ridge District	Jerry A. Sulina	604-463-5221	Oshawa	Nelson Tellis	905-924-2566
Matsqui District	Hedda Cochran	604-853-2281	Ottawa	David S. O'Brien	613-564-1429
Mission District	Glen C. Robertson	604-826-6271	Ottawa-Carleton Regional		
Nanaimo	Gerald D. Berry	604-755-4401	Municipality	C. M. Beckstead	613-560-1214
Nanaimo Regional District	Kelly D. Daniels	604-390-4111	Peel Regional Municipality	Michael R. Garrett	905-791-7800
New Westminster	Larry Kotseff	604-527-4551	Peterborough	David L. Hall	705-748-8811
North Vancouver	A. Kenneth Tollstam	604-985-7761	Richmond Hill	Charles D. Weldon	905-771-2505
Parksville	Grant G. McRadu	604-248-6144	Rockcliffe Park	Murray E. MacLean	613-749-9791
Penticton	Tim Wood	604-490-2401	Rockland	Jean D. Vachon	613-446-6022
Pitt Meadows	Ken J. Wiesner	604-465-2413	Scarborough	Donald W. Roughley	416-396-7278
Port Alberni	D. R. Walker	604-723-2146	Sudbury	William Rice	705-674-3141
Port Hardy District	Phyllis Belaire	. . .	Thunder Bay	Bruce Thom	807-625-2223
Prince George	George Paul	604-561-7607	Waterloo	Robert L. Byron	519-747-8702
Prince Rupert	William J. Smith	604-627-0937	Waterloo Regional		
Richmond	John Y. Carline	604-276-4153	Municipality	Gerald A. Thompson	519-575-4425
Squamish	R. A. (Bob) Miles	604-892-5217	Welland	Volker Kerschl	. . .
Surrey	Douglas A. Lychak	604-591-4122	Whitby	William H. Wallace	905-668-5803
Vancouver	Ken F. Dobell	604-873-7627	Windsor	Hilary G. Payne	519-994-2728
Vancouver Regional District	Ben Marr	604-432-6210	York Regional Municipality	Bob Forhan	416-895-1231
Victoria	Colin F. Crisp	604-385-5711			
West Vancouver District	J. Douglas Allan	604-922-1211	**Prince Edward Island**		
White Rock	Wayne W. Baldwin	604-531-9111	Charlottetown	Harry Gaudet	902-566-5548
			Summerside	Terry Murphy	902-436-4222
Manitoba			West Royalty	Donna Waddell	902-368-1025
Brandon	Earl E. Backman	204-729-2204			
Portage la Prairie	William G. Newell	204-239-8336	**Québec**		
Winnipeg	Richard L. Frost	204-986-2375	Aylmer	Denis Hubert	819-684-5372
			Baie-d'Urfe	Richard White	514-457-5324
New Brunswick			Brossard	Richard Labrècque	514-676-0201
Bathurst	Edward Childs	506-548-0414	Chandler	David C. Johnstone	418-689-2221
Campbellton	Ronald F. Mahoney	506-789-2700	Charlesbourg	Michel Lavoie	418-624-7804
Dalhousie	Michael Allain	506-684-1200	Dollard-des-Ormeaux	Wesley Lancaster	514-684-1010
Edmundston	Jacques Soucy	506-739-2115	Gatineau	Claude Doucet	819-243-2310
Fredericton	Paul Stapleton	506-452-9604	Hull	Paul Preseault	819-595-7131
Moncton	Lawrence E. Strang	506-853-3333	La Salle	Robert Barbeau	514-367-6200
Newcastle	Doug Chase	506-627-2512	Longueuil	Roch Letourneau	514-646-8210
St. Andrews	Jacques Dube	506-529-1820	Mirabel	Yves Lacroix	514-476-0360
St. John	Terrence Totten	506-658-2877	Montreal	Pierre Le François	514-872-2996
			Mount Royal	Duncan E. Campbell	514-734-2911
			Outremont	J. R. Victor Mainville	514-495-6223
			Pointe-Claire	Tom Buffitt	514-630-1200

Directory 1/8   INTERNATIONAL CHIEF APPOINTED ADMINISTRATORS
continued

Local government	Appointed administrator	Phone number
Québec	Denis DeBelleval	418-691-6560
St.-Lambert	Richard J. Shuttleworth	514-672-4444
St.-Laurent	Pierre Lebeau	. . .
Shawinigan-Sud	Charles J. Mills	819-536-5671
Westmount	Bruce St. Louis	514-989-5263
Saskatchewan		
Lloydminster	Roger H. Brekko	306-825-6184
North Battleford	D. McEwen	306-445-1727
Regina	A. R. Linner	306-777-7314
Yukon		
Dawson	Carol Metz-Murray	403-993-5434
Whitehorse	Bryce Walt	403-668-8638
ENGLAND		
Berkshire		
Reading Borough	Sylvie Pierce	44-734-390113
Windsor and Maidenhead Borough	Geoffrey B. Blacker	44-628-796222
Hertfordshire		
Stevenage Borough	Howard L. Miller	44-438-766225
Welwyn/Hatfield	David W. Riddle	44-707-331212
Isle of Wight		
Isle of Wight County	John S. Horsnell	44-983-823102
Kent		
Dover District	John P. Moir	44-304-821199
Kent County	Paul R. Sabin	44-622-694000
Turnbridge Wells	Rodney J. Stone	44-892-526121
Lancashire		
Ribble Valley Borough	Ossie Hopkins	44-810-20025111
Lincolnshire		
South Kesteven District	Kenneth R. Cann	44-4110-476591591
London		
City of London	Samuel Jones	44-713-321400
Merseyside		
Knowsley Metropolitan Borough	David G. Henshaw	44-514-433772
Sefton Metropolitan Borough	Graham J. Haywood	44-519-934-2057
Middlesex		
Spelthorne Borough	Michael B. Taylor	44-784-446250
Norfolk		
South Norfolk District	Adrian Kellett	44-508-533633
Northamptonshire		
Daventry District	Robert J. Symons	44-327-71100
East Northamptonshire District	Roger K. Heath	44-832-742106
Northampton Borough	Roger J. B. Morris	44-604-233500
Northamptonshire County	A. Jeffrey Greenwell	44-604-236050
Nottinghamshire		
Mansfield District	Richard P. Goad	44-623-656656
Oxfordshire		
Cherwell District	Grahame J. Handley	44-295-252535
Shropshire		
Oswestry Castle View Borough	David A. Towers	44-691-654411
Warwickshire		
Stratford-on-Avon District	Ian B. Prosser	44-789-260101
Warwick District	Michael J. Ward	44-926-450000
West Sussex		
Worthing Borough	Michael J. Ball	44-903-239999
Wiltshire		
North Wiltshire	Henry Miles	44-0249-443152

Local government	Appointed administrator	Phone number
Worcester		
Redditch Borough	Stella E. Manzie	44-52-764252
IRELAND		
Cork Corporation	Thomas P. Rice	353-21-966222
ISRAEL		
Beer-Sheva	Josef A. Shelley	972-7-463741
Dimona	Yehoshwa Klein	972-5-7563104
Eilat	Dov Sharf	972-7-374272
Ness Ziona	Nimrod Zach	972-8-404477
NETHERLANDS		
Amsterdam	Klaas Kooiker	31-20-552-3300
NEW ZEALAND		
Auckland	Bruce T. W. Anderson	64-9-379-2020
Buller District	Darryl C. Griffin	64-289-7239
Central Otago District	Patrick T. Cooney	64-3-448-6979
Christchurch	Michael A. Richardson	64-3-3711553
Dunedin	Murray F. Douglas	64-3-477-4000
Hauraki District	I. Keith Laurenson	64-7-862-8609
Kaipara District	Alan J. McKerchar	64-439-7059
Manukau	Colin J. B. Dale	64-9-263-7100
Nelson	Joseph M. Rudhall	64-3-546-0200
New Plymouth District	Kinsley N. Sampson	64-6-758-8099
North Shore	Keven L. Tate	64-9-486-8626
Palmerston North	P. Michael Willis	64-6-351-4435
Papakura	Thomas McLean	64-929-98870
Rotorua District	Allen E. Hansen	64-73-484199
Ruapehu District	Clifford J. Houston	64-7-895-8188
South Taranaki District	Desmond R. Beaven	64-6278-8010
South Waikato	Christopher Hannah	64-7-886-8109
Taranaki Region	Basil G. Chamberlain	64-676-57127
Tararua District	Max C. Griffiths	64-6-374-8068
Tauranga District	Alan N. Bickers	64-757-77010
Timaru District	Leslie Baker	64-3-684-8199
Wairoa	Peter J. Freeman	64-0724-7309
Waitakere	Mark O. Dacombe	64-9-837-3700
Wanganui District	Colin J. Whitlock	64-345-8529
Wellington	Angela C. Griffin	64-4801-3462
SCOTLAND		
Skye and Lochalsh District	David H. Noble	44-478-2341
SOUTH AFRICA		
Durban Corporation	Edward W. H. Norton	031-300-6911
National Transvaal Regional Services Council	Jack A. Botes	27-01521-71015
Pietermartzburg	Granville G. Shenker	27-331-951009
SWEDEN		
Malung	Olof E. Almkleven	46-280-18100
Partille	Ulf C. G. Dermark	46-3136-1138
Vasteras	Hans B. V. Granquist	46-21-161104
SWITZERLAND		
Chur	Dieter Heller	41-81-254-4111
TURKEY		
Iula Eastern Mediterranean/ Middle East Region	Selahattin Yildirim	90-212-511-10-10
WALES		
Cardiff	Roger E. Paine	44-222-822051
Radnorshire District	Geoffrey C. Read	44-597-823737
ZAMBIA		
Lusaka	Wynter M. Kabimba	260-1-250773

Directory 1/9   OFFICIALS IN U.S. MUNICIPALITIES

The data for the directory of municipal officials were collected by ICMA during the summer of 1994 through a mail survey. The 7,217 municipalities surveyed include all incorporated places 2,500 and over, those places under 2,500 that are recognized by ICMA as having either the council-management form of government or a position of overall general management, and those communities whose populations had dropped below 2,500 since the 1986 Census.

In addition to the names of officials (and the municipal phone number), data on race and sex are collected for 20 positions shown in Tables 1/9/a and 1/9/b. Only the names of the chief

elected official, appointed administrator, city clerk, finance officer, fire chief, police chief, and public works director are shown in the municipal directory that follows. All data collected other than the name and phone number are treated with confidentiality, and only aggregate data are presented below.

Sex and Race of Municipal Officials. Tables 1/9/a and 1/9/b present a breakdown of each sex by race and ethnicity for the municipal officials. Given the level of detail shown, it is possible to reaggregate these data for other displays that would show race and sex characteristics for the total number of officials reporting.

The positions shown are most often held by males with the exception of municipal clerk and librarian. Whites are predominant in each position shown. Other than whites, blacks (male and female combined) are more dominant in each of the positions than other minority group members.

The Directory. For convenience, the directory shows the names of municipalities in alphabetical order within each state. Other items indicated in the directory for each municipality are the type of municipality (city, village, town, township, borough, or plantation), form of government, population, and municipal phone number.

Table 1/9/a   MALE MUNICIPAL OFFICIALS BY RACE AND ETHNICITY

	Total reporting (A)	Total males		White		Black		American Indian		Asian		Other		Race not reported		Hispanic	
Position		No. (B)	% of (A)	No.	% of (B)	No.	% of (B)	No.	% of (B)	No.	% of (B)	No.	% of (B)	No.	% of (B)	No.	% of (B)
Chief elected official	4,311	3,698	85.8	3,307	89.4	87	2.4	17	0.5	6	0.2	18	0.5	263	7.1	56	1.5
Chief appointed administrative officer/ manager	3,403	3,024	88.9	2,679	88.6	36	1.2	13	0.4	5	0.2	18	0.6	273	9.0	63	2.1
Assistant manager/assistant CAO	1,102	725	65.8	606	83.6	32	4.4	1	0.1	3	0.4	9	1.2	74	10.2	20	2.8
City clerk/secretary	3,872	966	24.9	626	64.8	13	1.3	1	0.1	1	0.1	3	0.3	322	33.3	12	1.2
Chief financial officer	2,931	1,875	64.0	1,539	82.1	25	1.3	5	0.3	19	1.0	13	0.7	274	14.6	33	1.8
Director of economic development	1,031	834	80.9	681	81.7	33	4.0	5	0.6	2	0.2	7	0.8	106	12.7	19	2.3
Treasurer	2,824	1,458	51.6	1,120	76.8	13	0.9	8	0.5	7	0.5	9	0.6	301	20.6	14	1.0
Director of public works	3,621	3,575	98.7	3,000	83.9	63	1.8	22	0.6	17	0.5	19	0.5	454	12.7	64	1.8
Engineer	1,849	1,817	98.3	1,535	84.5	13	0.7	5	0.3	17	0.9	21	1.2	226	12.4	23	1.3
Police chief	4,068	4,041	99.3	3,336	82.6	101	2.5	27	0.7	3	0.1	26	0.6	548	13.6	57	1.4
Fire chief	3,446	3,441	99.9	2,850	82.8	55	1.6	17	0.5	1	0.0	17	0.5	501	14.6	51	1.5
Planning director	1,947	1,637	84.1	1,349	82.4	38	2.3	6	0.4	10	0.6	10	0.6	224	13.7	42	2.6
Personnel director	2,031	1,128	55.5	883	78.3	56	5.0	4	0.4	1	0.1	14	1.2	170	15.1	29	2.6
Risk manager	954	658	69.0	549	83.4	20	3.0	0	0.0	3	0.5	3	0.5	83	12.6	18	2.7
Director of parks and recreation	2,128	1,827	85.9	1,470	80.5	41	2.2	7	0.4	2	0.1	11	0.6	296	16.2	40	2.2
Superintendent of parks	1,362	1,301	95.5	1,051	80.8	34	2.6	9	0.7	4	0.3	13	1.0	190	14.6	47	3.6
Director of recreation	1,313	513	39.1	323	63.0	15	2.9	1	0.2	0	0.0	8	1.6	166	32.4	12	2.3
Librarian	1,729	564	32.6	286	50.7	2	0.4	2	0.4	1	0.2	0	0.0	273	48.4	9	1.6
Director of data processing/info. serv.	872	622	71.3	496	79.7	11	1.8	0	0.0	8	1.3	4	0.6	103	16.6	15	2.4
Purchasing director	1,356	563	41.5	361	64.1	33	5.9	4	0.7	1	0.2	5	0.9	159	28.2	17	3.0

Table 1/9/b   FEMALE MUNICIPAL OFFICIALS BY RACE AND ETHNICITY

	Total reporting (A)	Total females		White		Black		American Indian		Asian		Other		Race not reported		Hispanic	
Position		No. (B)	% of (A)	No.	% of (B)	No.	% of (B)	No.	% of (B)	No.	% of (B)	No.	% of (B)	No.	% of (B)	No.	% of (B)
Chief elected official	4,311	613	14.2	563	91.8	19	3.1	5	0.8	2	0.3	5	0.8	19	3.1	14	2.3
Chief appointed administrative officer/ manager	3,403	379	11.1	342	90.2	13	3.4	2	0.5	2	0.5	5	1.3	15	4.0	10	2.6
Assistant manager/assistant CAO	1,102	377	34.2	347	92.0	14	3.7	1	0.3	0	0.0	6	1.6	9	2.4	10	2.7
City clerk/secretary	3,872	2,906	75.1	2,702	93.0	77	2.6	22	0.8	11	0.4	24	0.8	70	2.4	77	2.6
Chief financial officer	2,931	1,056	36.0	991	93.8	19	1.8	7	0.7	8	0.8	7	0.7	24	2.3	21	2.0
Director of economic development	1,031	197	19.1	182	92.4	10	5.1	1	0.5	1	0.5	3	1.5	0	0.0	3	1.5
Treasurer	2,824	1,366	48.4	1,291	94.5	28	2.0	7	0.5	6	0.4	6	0.4	28	2.0	21	1.5
Director of public works	3,621	46	1.3	42	91.3	4	8.7	0	0.0	0	0.0	0	0.0	0	0.0	0	0.0
Engineer	1,849	32	1.7	30	93.8	0	0.0	0	0.0	1	3.1	0	0.0	1	3.1	0	0.0
Police chief	4,068	27	0.7	23	85.2	3	11.1	1	3.7	0	0.0	0	0.0	0	0.0	1	3.7
Fire chief	3,446	5	0.1	5	100.0	0	0.0	0	0.0	0	0.0	0	0.0	0	0.0	0	0.0
Planning director	1,947	310	15.9	290	93.5	9	2.9	0	0.0	4	1.3	1	0.3	6	1.9	5	1.6
Personnel director	2,031	903	44.5	820	90.8	57	6.3	2	0.2	4	0.4	7	0.8	13	1.4	27	3.0
Risk manager	954	296	31.0	273	92.2	14	4.7	1	0.3	2	0.7	3	1.0	3	1.0	7	2.4
Director of parks and recreation	2,128	301	14.1	276	91.7	16	5.3	1	0.3	1	0.3	3	1.0	4	1.3	4	1.3
Superintendent of parks	1,362	61	4.5	57	93.4	2	3.3	0	0.0	0	0.0	1	1.6	1	1.6	1	1.6
Director of recreation	1,313	800	60.9	722	90.3	43	5.4	9	1.1	0	0.0	4	0.5	22	2.8	17	2.1
Librarian	1,729	1,165	67.4	1,115	95.7	12	1.0	4	0.3	8	0.7	3	0.3	23	2.0	9	0.8
Director of data processing/info. serv.	872	250	28.7	227	90.8	14	5.6	3	1.2	1	0.4	1	0.4	4	1.6	4	1.6
Purchasing director	1,356	793	58.5	736	92.8	22	2.8	4	0.5	3	0.4	6	0.8	22	2.8	22	2.8

Directory 1/9
continued

OFFICIALS IN U.S. MUNICIPALITIES 2,500 AND OVER IN POPULATION

Form of government
CM Council-manager
CO Commission
MC Mayor-council
RT Representative town meeting
TM Town meeting

Municipal designation
b   borough
pl plantation
t   town
tp township
v   village

Population
Note: The only jurisdictions under 2,500 in population that are listed are those recognized by ICMA.

Population figures are rounded up; 14,500 will appear as 14.

(..) Less than 500 population

Other codes
. . . . Data not reported or not applicable

City, 1990 population figures (000 omitted), form of government	Municipal phone number	Mayor/ chief elected official	Appointed administrator	City clerk/ city secretary	Finance officer	Fire chief	Police chief	Public works director
ALABAMA (135)								
Abbeville (3)	MC 205 585-6444	....	....	....	....	....	....	....
Alabaster (15)	MC 205 664-6800	....	....	....	....	....	....	....
Albertville (15)	MC 205 891-8206	....	....	....	....	....	....	....
Alexander City (15)	MC 205 329-8426	Ben R Cleveland	George H Gordon	....	William R Miller	Marvin L Still	Lynn E Royall	....
Aliceville (3)	MC 205 373-6611	....	....	....	....	....	....	....
Andalusia (9)	MC 205 222-3311	Paul T Armstrong	....	Roland Carter	Roland Carter	Joseph Lee	Jerry Williamson	James B Hogg
Anniston (27)	CM 205 236-3422	David Dethrage	Tom Wright	Alan B Atkinson	Tom Wright	Louis Lefoy	Wayne Chandler	Charles D Johnson
Arab t (6)	MC 205 586-3544	....	....	....	....	....	....	....
Athens (17)	MC 205 233-8720	....	....	....	....	....	....	....
Atmore (8)	MC 205 368-2253	....	....	....	....	....	....	....
Attalla (7)	MC 205 538-9986	....	....	....	....	....	....	....
Auburn (34)	CM 205 887-1900	Jan Dempsey	Douglas J Watson	....	Levi A Knapp	R Blankenship	Edwin D Downing	John A Holmes
Bay Minette (7)	MC 205 937-5502	....	....	....	....	....	....	....
Bessemer (33)	CO 205 424-4060	....	....	....	....	....	....	....
Birmingham (266)	MC 205 254-2000	....	....	....	....	....	....	....
Boaz (7)	MC 205 593-8105	Bruce Sanford	M Montgomery	M Montgomery	M Montgomery	Jackie Nicholson	Bill Robinson	Kenneth Richey
Brent (3)	MC 205 926-4643	Jerry C Pow	....	Linda A Cox	....	Dennis Stripling	Henry Enfinger	....
Brewton (6)	MC 205 867-3281	Ted Jennings	Bernie Wall	....	....	John Martin	Grover Smith	William Henderson
Bridgeport t (3)	MC 205 495-3892	....	....	....	....	....	....	....
Brighton (5)	MC 205 425-8934	....	....	....	....	....	....	....
Brundidge t (2)	MC 205 735-2385	J T Ramage	....	Linda M Holeman	....	David Barbaree	Joe F Connell	David Barbaree
Centreville (3)	MC 205 926-4995	....	....	....	....	....	....	....
Chickasaw (7)	MC 205 452-6450	....	....	....	....	....	....	....
Childersburg (5)	MC 205 378-5521	Billy Joe Meeks	....	Frank Humber	....	Douglas Blair	Kenneth Flowers	....
Citronelle (4)	MC 205 866-7973	Rannel Presnell	....	Diane D Barnett	....	Larry Griffin	Clarence Parker	....
Clanton (8)	MC 205 755-1105	....	....	....	....	....	....	....
Columbiana (3)	MC 205 669-5800	Lewis B Walker	....	Pam Oliver	....	Johnny Howard Jr	....	....
Cordova t (3)	MC 205 483-9266	....	....	....	....	....	....	....
Cullman (13)	MC 205 739-1212	....	....	....	....	....	....	....
Dadeville t (3)	MC 205 825-9242	....	....	....	....	....	....	....
Daleville (5)	MC 205 598-2345	Gene Hughes	....	Angelia Filmore	Angelia Filmore	....	Wess Etheredge	Ray Sartin
Daphne t (11)	CO 205 621-9000	....	....	....	....	....	....	....
Decatur (49)	MC 205 355-7410	....	....	....	....	....	....	....
Demopolis (8)	MC 205 289-0577	Austin Caldwell	....	Dolly S Ward	....	Mike Fuqua	Charles Avery	Clarence Brooker
Dothan (54)	CM 205 793-0152	Alfred Saliba	Don Marnon	Delma Lee	Willie Houston	William McDaniel	....	....
East Brewton t (3)	MC 205 867-6092	Terry Clark	....	Karen Singleton	....	Guyland Langham	Wilson Mallard	Steve Dunaway
Elba (4)	MC 205 897-2333	Ricky Haywood	Henry Clark	....	....	....	Jack Parker	....
Enterprise (20)	MC 205 347-1211	....	....	....	....	....	....	....
Eufaula (13)	MC 205 687-1206	....	....	....	....	....	....	....
Evergreen (4)	MC 205 578-1574	....	....	....	....	....	....	....
Fairfield (12)	MC 205 788-2492	....	....	....	....	....	....	....
Fairhope (8)	MC 205 928-2136	....	....	....	....	....	....	....
Fayette (5)	MC 205 932-5367	....	....	....	....	....	....	....
Florence (36)	MC 205 760-6300	Eddie Frost	....	Steven W Eason	....	Charlie Cochran	Rick Thompson	....
Foley (5)	MC 205 943-1545	....	....	....	....	....	....	....
Fort Payne (12)	MC 205 845-1524	....	....	....	....	....	....	....
Fultondale (6)	MC 205 841-6456	....	....	....	....	....	....	....
Gadsden (43)	CO 205 549-4500	....	....	....	....	....	....	....
Gardendale (9)	MC 205 631-8789	....	....	....	....	....	....	....
Geneva (5)	MC 205 684-2485	Hugh Herring Jr	Sheron Enfinger	....	....	....	Frankie Lindsey	James Dixon
Glencoe t (5)	MC 205 492-1424	John S Sewell	....	Carol Surtees	Billy Jack Gray	....	B J Alexander	Butch White
Graysville (2)	MC 205 674-5643	Wayne Tuggle	....	Judy Flippo	....	Randy Reid	Charles Melton	Paul Busby
Greensboro (3)	MC 205 624-8119	....	....	....	....	....	....	....
Greenville (7)	MC 205 382-2647	C E Smith	....	L Vanden Bosch	....	M Phillips	L Ingram	H Gregory
Gulf Shores (3)	MC 205 968-2425	D L Bodenhamer	A Rivera	R F Ray	S S Bowyer	J L McClusky	A K Bourne	C D Hamilton
Guntersville (7)	MC 205 582-2120	....	....	A M Yarbrough	....	Leon Bridges	Kyle Reogas	....
Haleyville (4)	MC 205 486-3121	Larry Gilliland	....	A M Yarbrough	....	Leon Bridges	Kyle Reogas	....
Hamilton t (6)	MC 205 921-2121	E T Sims Jr	....	Barbara Partain	....	Billy H Loden	Tommy Wooten	Terry Kerr
Hartford (2)	MC 205 588-2245	....	....	....	....	....	....	....
Hartselle (11)	MC 205 773-2535	Samie Wiley	....	Betty Parker	....	Rickey Joe Smith	John Pat Orr	....
Headland (3)	MC 205 693-3365	....	....	....	....	....	....	....
Heflin t (3)	MC 205 463-2291	....	....	....	....	....	....	....
Hokes Bluff t (4)	MC 205 492-2414	....	....	....	....	....	....	....
Homewood (23)	MC 205 877-8600	James K Atkinson	....	Linda J Cook	Linda J Cook	John A Bresnan	William A West	Pierce England
Hoover t (40)	MC 205 444-7500	Frank Skinner	....	Linda Crump	Richard Smith	Thomas Bradley	David Cummings	Steve Brown
Hueytown (15)	MC 205 491-7010	Lillian P Howard	....	Janice Wilhite	....	James Bolin	John Taylor	....
Huntsville (160)	MC 205 532-7332	Stephen Hettinger	John R Holladay	Charles E Hagood	....	Robert C Gareri	Richard V Ottman	W F Stokes Jr
Irondale (9)	MC 205 956-9200	David W Krider	....	Glenda G Cox	Glenda G Cox	John McDanal	Wallace C Gibson	Thomas Anderson
Jackson (6)	MC 205 246-2461	....	....	....	....	....	....	....
Jacksonville (10)	MC 205 435-7611	....	....	....	....	....	....	....
Jasper (14)	MC 205 221-2100	....	....	....	....	....	....	....
Lafayette (3)	MC 205 864-7181	....	....	....	....	....	....	....

Directory 1/9 continued

MUNICIPAL OFFICIALS IN U.S. CITIES OVER 2,500

City, 1990 population figures (000 omitted), form of government	Municipal phone number	Mayor/ chief elected official	Appointed administrator	City clerk/ city secretary	Finance officer	Fire chief	Police chief	Public works director
ALABAMA (135) continued								
Lafayette (3)	MC 205 864-7181	....	....	....	....	....	....	....
Lanett (9)	CM 205 644-2141	Terrell Whaley	Bobby Williams	Shirley B Motley	....	John Garvich Jr	Gene Jones	Larry Ray
Leeds (10)	MC 205 699-2585	Lynn A Maxey	....	Linda T Humber	....	Vester M Arnold	Charles A Hudson	Bob Parker
Linden (3)	MC 205 295-4121	....	....	....	....	....	....	....
Lipscomb (3)	MC 205 428-6374	....	....	....	....	....	....	....
Livingston (4)	CM 205 652-2505	....	....	....	....	....	....	....
Luverne (3)	MC 205 335-3741	John D Harrison	....	Bonnie N King	....	Frank Turner Jr	....	....
Madison (15)	MC 205 772-5600	Charles E Yancura	....	....	Lillie M Causey	Charles P Wallace	Cecil E Moses	Merlyn R Adkins
Marion (4)	MC 205 683-6545	....	....	....	....	....	....	....
Midfield (6)	MC 205 923-7578	....	....	....	....	....	....	....
Millbrook (6)	MC 205 285-6428	Arvil T Minor	....	Arthur E Elsner	Jo Ann Wilkes	Larry Brown	Danny C Pollard	Morris Sherrill
Mobile (196)	MC 205 470-7727	....	....	....	....	....	....	....
Monroeville (7)	MC 205 575-2081	Anne Farish	....	Toni McKelvey	....	Eddie Everette	William Dailey	Lyle Salter
Montevallo (4)	MC 205 665-2555	Ralph W Sears	Steven D Gibbs	Steve D Gibbs	Steven D Gibbs	Alan Blackmon	Allen J Needham	Howard Harkins
Montgomery (187)	MC 205 241-4400	Emory Folmar	Reese McKinney	John L Baker	Hugh S Austin	Wayne Grier	John Wilson	James D Wilder
Moulton t (3)	MC 205 974-5191	....	....	....	....	....	....	....
Mountain Brook (20)	CM 205 870-3532	William Matthews	Sam Gaston	Ann McCutcheon	Sam Collins	Robert Ezekiel	Marty Keely	Cecil Amason
Muscle Shoals t (10)	CO 205 383-5675	Charles Mitchell	....	Clair Stratford	....	Ron Motes	David Underwood	Johnny Wisdom
Northport (17)	CM 205 339-7000	Wayne Rose	Charles Swann	....	Mark Powell	Paul Evans	Dempsey Marcum	Larry Boshell
Oneonta (5)	MC 205 274-2150	Danny B Hicks	....	Martha J Walker	....	C Montgomery	David Odom	Marvin Sloan
Opelika (22)	MC 205 705-5100	Bobby J Freeman	Robert G Shuman	Zane E Burleson	Mitch Price	Charlie Moore	Thomas Mangham	Boalman Johnson
Opp (7)	MC 205 493-4572	....	....	....	....	....	....	....
Oxford t (9)	MC 205 831-3183	Leon Smith	....	Shirley Henson	....	Eugene Smallwood	Stanley Merrill	....
Ozark (13)	MC 205 774-5393	Billy J Blackmon	....	William Blackwell	....	....	Alan Benefield	....
Pelham t (10)	MC 205 663-3901	Bobby Hayes	Bill Overstreet	Peggy Bates	Michael Morgan	Gary Waters	D Allan Wade	Kenneth Holler
Pell City (8)	MC 205 338-3330	Lawrence Fields	....	Peggy Lee	Melanie Doss	Michael Sewell	Joseph Davis	Wayne Duck
Phenix City (25)	CM 205 298-5649	....	....	....	....	....	....	....
Piedmont (5)	MC 205 447-9007	Vera Stewart	Brent Morrison	Brent Morrison	....	Robert Holbrook	Jimmy Trammell	Bill Fann
Pleasant Grove (8)	MC 205 744-7221	....	....	....	....	....	....	....
Prattville (20)	MC 205 361-3600	David Whetstone	....	E M Champion Jr	....	Archie Plyer	Alfred Wadsworth	....
Prichard (34)	MC 205 457-3381	....	....	....	....	....	....	....
Rainbow City t (8)	MC 205 442-2511	....	....	....	....	....	....	....
Rainsville t (4)	MC 205 638-6331	....	....	....	....	....	....	....
Red Bay (3)	MC 205 356-4473	Billy M Bolton	....	Charlene Fancher	....	Thomas Strickland	Charles Garrison	Tommy Nelson
Roanoke (6)	MC 205 863-4129	....	....	....	....	....	....	....
Roosevelt (..)	MC 205 426-1261	....	....	....	....	....	....	....
Russellville (8)	MC 502 726-5000	....	....	....	....	....	....	....
Saraland (12)	MC 205 675-5103	Franklin Pridgen	....	Barbara Timothy	....	Ravon Allen	Gerald Young	Cecil Smith
Satsuma (5)	MC 205 675-1440	....	....	....	....	....	....	....
Scottsboro (14)	MC 205 574-3100	Louis Price	....	Gail Duffey	....	Lonnie Webb	Keith Smith	....
Selma (24)	MC 205 874-2105	....	....	....	....	....	....	....
Sheffield (10)	CO 205 383-0250	....	....	....	....	....	....	....
Southside t (6)	MC 205 442-9775	Grover Hedgspeth	....	Sherry Morgan	....	Fred Christopher	Ed Price	Jimmy Whittemore
Stevenson (2)	MC 205 437-3000	James W Matthews	....	Bettye T Jackson	....	William T Walker	Jim Kerby	....
Sumiton t (3)	MC 205 648-3262	Harry L Ellis Jr	....	Judy M Glover	....	David Waid	Rick A Schultz	Howard Nichols
Sylacauga (13)	MC 205 245-3421	....	....	....	....	....	....	....
Talladega (18)	MC 205 362-8186	....	....	....	....	....	....	....
Tallassee (5)	MC 205 283-6571	....	....	....	....	....	....	....
Tarrant City (8)	MC 205 841-2758	....	....	....	....	....	....	....
Thomasville (4)	MC 205 636-5827	....	....	....	....	....	....	....
Troy (13)	CO 205 566-0177	....	....	....	....	....	....	....
Trussville t (8)	MC 205 655-7478	Charles I Grover	....	Lynn B Huneycutt	....	....	Irving A Nash	Lewis V Simpson
Tuscaloosa (78)	MC 205 349-0125	Alvin P DuPont	....	Bryon Findley	Mike Wright	Tom Davis	Ken Swindle	Richard Curry
Tuscumbia (8)	CO 205 383-5463	....	....	....	....	....	....	....
Tuskegee (12)	MC 205 727-2180	Johnny Ford	....	Hattie King	James C B Samuel	Luther Curry	David Warren	William Foster
Union Springs (4)	MC 205 738-2720	Durden Dean	....	Doris Roten	....	Thomas May	E L Love	Robert Origgers
Valley (8)	MC 205 756-3131	....	....	....	....	....	....	....
Vernon (2)	MC 205 695-7718	....	....	....	....	....	....	....
Vestavia Hills (20)	MC 205 978-1000	....	....	....	....	....	....	....
Warrior (3)	MC 205 647-0521	....	....	....	....	....	....	....
Weaver t (3)	MC 205 820-1125	....	....	....	....	....	....	....
Wetumpka (5)	MC 205 567-5147	Alma S Leak	....	Velma N Gober	....	....	J T Montgomery	Randy Logan
Winfield (4)	MC 205 487-4337	....	....	....	....	....	....	....
York (3)	MC 205 392-5231	Joseph F Stegall	....	Renee Pringle	....	Steven Lang	Cleveland Brown	Edward Stallings
ALASKA (29)								
Anchorage (226)	MC 907 343-4512	Rick Mystrom	Larry Crawford	LeJane Ferguson	Jerry Anderson	....	Kevin O' Leary	....
Barrow (3)	MC 907 852-5211	....	....	....	....	....	....	....
Bethel (5)	CM 907 543-2297	....	....	....	....	....	....	....
Cordova (2)	CM 907 424-6200	Margy Johnson	W S Janke	D Lynda Plant	Cheryl Beckham	Dewey Whetsell	Kevin Clayton	George Keeney
Dillingham (2)	CM 907 842-5211	Thomas Tilden	Chris Hladick	V I Braswell	Paula Bush	Alice Ruby	Ralph Taylor	Steve Hardin
Fairbanks (31)	CM 907 459-6780	James C Hayes	Mark E Boyer	Toni Connor	Barbara Koneczny	....	Michael Pulice	David Jacoby
Fort Yukon (1)	CM 907 662-2479	David M James	David C Smith	Vickie Thomas	....	....	Zelma L Fairchild	Grafton L Bergman
Galena (1)	CM 907 656-1301	....	....	....	....	....	....	....
Homer (4)	CM 907 235-8121	....	....	....	....	....	....	....
Juneau (27)	CM 907 586-5250	Jamie Parsons	Mark Palesh	Patty Ann Polley	Craig Duncan	Charles Lundfelt	Richard Gummow	Ernst Mueller
Kenai (6)	CM 907 283-7530	....	....	....	....	....	....	....
Ketchikan (8)	CM 907 225-3111	Alaire Stanton	Jack Pearson	Karen Miles	Robert E Newell	David O' Sullivan	Daniel Anslinger	Fred Monrean
Kodiak (6)	CM 907 486-8640	Carolyn L Floyd	Gary Bloomquist	Marcella H Dalke	Roy A Deebel	Mike Dolph	Jack McDonald	John E Sullivan
Kotzebue (3)	CM 907 442-3401	Frank Greene	Jeff Smith	Sally Melton	Susan Garner	Ron Monson	....	Ben Brantley
Mountain Village (1)	MC 907 591-2929	....	....	....	....	....	....	....
Nome (4)	CM 907 443-5242	....	....	....	....	....	....	....
Palmer (3)	CM 907 745-3271	Geoge Carte	Tom Smith	....	George Castaneda	Daniel Contini	Ron Otte	James Giyer
Petersburg (3)	CM 907 772-4519	Dave Carlson	Linda Snow	Patricia Curtiss	....	Cris Morrison	Dale Stone	Eli Lucas
Seldovia (..)	CM 907 234-7643	....	....	....	....	....	....	....
Seward (3)	CM 907 224-3331	David Crane	Tyler Jones	Linda Murphy	Rick Gifford	John Gage	Tom Walker	....
Sitka (9)	MC 907 747-3294	....	....	....	....	....	....	....
Skagway (1)	MC 907 983-2297	Stan Selmer	James R Filip	Laurie J Sica	....	Carl Mulvihill	David Sexton	Grant Lawson
Soldotna (3)	CM 907 262-9107	Ken Lancaster	R Underkofler	Patricia Burdick	Joel Wilkins	....	Walter Bonenr	David Bunnell
St. Mary'S (..)	CM 907 438-2515	....	....	....	....	....	....	....
Unalaska (3)	CM 907 581-1251	Frank V Kelty	Mark Earnest	Debra K Mack	Thomas S Graham	Dave Gregory	Glenn Herbst	Roe Sturgulewski
Valdez (4)	CM 907 835-4313	....	....	....	....	....	....	....
Whittier (..)	CM 907 472-2327	Ben Butler	Gary Williams	Debra Burnham	Ray Morris	Alberto Caballero	Richard Powell	Richard Amerman

**Directory 1/9
continued**

MUNICIPAL OFFICIALS
IN U.S. CITIES OVER 2,500

City, 1990 population figures (000 omitted), form of government	Municipal phone number	Mayor/ chief elected official	Appointed administrator	City clerk/ city secretary	Finance officer	Fire chief	Police chief	Public works director
ALASKA (29) continued								
Wrangell (2)	MC 907 874-2381	Raymond McGurk	Duane H Gasaway	Franette Vincent	Jeffry A Jabusch	Timothy Buness	Brent Moody	Robert Caldwell
Yakutat (1)	CM 907 784-3323	....	....	....	....	....	....	....
ARIZONA (68)								
Apache Junction (18)	CM 602 982-8002	Jean Perkins	Michael Lee	Kathleen Connelly	Keith Lewis	....	....	Douglas Dobson
Avondale (16)	CM 602 932-2400	Raymond W Bedoya	Carlos V Palma	Linda M Tyler	Ronald W Brown	John A Walter	Curtis J Stewart	Bill R Bates
Benson (4)	CM 602 586-2245	David Dipeso	Mark Battaglia	Delbert Self	Delbert Self	Max D Jones	Geo McMinimy	....
Bisbee (6)	CM 602 432-5446	....	....	....	....	....	....	....
Buckeye t (5)	CM 602 386-7830	Joseph Schettino	Fred Carpenter	Fred Carpenter	Fred Carpenter	....	Harry Bishop	Ron Long
Bullhead City (22)	CO 602 763-9400	....	....	Dane Bullard	Dane Bullard	....	John Wischmeyer	....
Camp Verde t (6)	CM 602 567-6631	Carter Rogers	....	Dane Bullard	Dane Bullard	....	John Wischmeyer	....
Casa Grande (19)	CM 602 421-8600	Robert D Mitchell	Kent A Myers	Gloria Leija Haro	Frank N Brown	Randy V Baldridge	Don Maxon	Robert M Jackson
Cave Creek t (3)	CM 602 488-1400	R F Bartholomew	Carl Stephani	Carl Stephani	....	....	....	Rodney Richmond
Chandler (91)	CM 602 786-2740	Jay Tibshraeny	John M Pinch	Carolyn H Dunn	Barry H Webber	James P Roxburgh	Bobby Joe Harris	George E Selvia
Chino Valley t (5)	CM 602 636-2646	Daniel O' Connell	Wayne L Smith	Delores Sliger	Wayne L Smith	....	Patricia Huntsman	Roger Pauls
Clifton t (3)	CM 602 865-4146	....	....	....	....	....	....	....
Coolidge (7)	CM 602 723-5361	....	....	....	....	....	....	....
Cottonwood (6)	CM 602 634-5526	Joseph D Jones	Brian S Mickelsen	Marianne Kistner	Robert E Lynch	Donald E Eberle	Roy D Finch	Timothy Costello
Douglas (13)	CM 602 364-7501	Elizabeth Ames	....	Leticia Rodriguez	....	....	Charles Austin	Michael Ortega
Eagar t (4)	CM 602 333-4128	George R Pena	William Greenwood	Karen B Merrill	Cynthia G Snyder	Howard Carlson	Lester James	Douglas Pike
El Mirage (5)	CM 602 972-8116	Maggie Reese	Jose Solarez Jr	Rosalinda Herrera	Jose Solarez Jr	Eddie Rios	Ed Calles	....
Eloy (7)	CM 602 466-9201	....	....	....	....	....	....	....
Flagstaff (46)	CM 602 779-7698	Chris Bavasi	Dave Wilcox	Linda Butler	Mary Jo Jenkins	Dean Treadway	Pat Madden	Bill Menard
Florence t (8)	MC 602 868-5889	Kay Otte	Bill Galletly	....	....	Rick Evans	Tom Rankin	Pat Granillo
Fountain Hills t (10)	CM 602 837-2003	John Cutillo	Paul Nordin	Cassie B Hansen	....	....	....	....
Gila Bend t (2)	MC 602 683-2255	Julius A Fox	....	Beverly Turner	Evelyn Huffine	Gene Merritt	....	Gene Merritt
Gilbert t (29)	CM 602 892-0800	Wilburn Brown	Kent Cooper	Phyllis Alberty	Marc Anderson	John Garcilaso	Fred Dees	Charles Strand
Glendale (148)	CM 602 435-4121	Elaine Scruggs	Martin Vanacour	Lavergne Behm	Arthur Lynch	John Nunes	David Dobrotka	Kenneth Martin
Globe (6)	CM 602 425-7147	David A Franquero	....	Gina Tarango	Teresa Williams	Martin Ricklefs	Frank Baroldy	Steve Stratton
Goodyear (6)	CM 602 932-3910	Carl K Gow	Stephen Cleveland	Barbara A Dunaway	Jean Pace	Mark A Gaillard	Peter J Nick	Lynn Kartchner
Guadalupe t (5)	CM 602 730-3080	Anna R Hernandez	Enrique Serna	Rose M Arellano	Mark Johnson	Henry Bandin	....	Joe Ruiz
Hayden t (1)	CM 602 356-7801	....	....	....	....	....	....	....
Holbrook (5)	CM 602 524-6225	Richard Mester	William A Kelly	William A Kelly	Blaine Hatch	Win Hillebert	Ken Moore	....
Kearny t (2)	CM 602 363-5547	Rose Bradford	Terry Hinton	Lorraine Birkett	Terry Hinton	Dale Hudleston	Terry Wesbrock	Ray Burgess
Kingman (13)	CM 602 753-5561	Carol Anderson	Lou Jorensen	Charlene Ware	James Jordan	Charles Osterman	Carroll Brown	Ed Covington
Lake Havasu City (24)	CM 602 855-2116	Richard L Hileman	Bill Madigan	Ann R Sayne	Carol Mitchell	Robert G Ward	John Alexander	Pete Manderfield
Litchfield Park (..)	CM 602 935-5033	Perry R Hubbard	R Musselwhite	P Maxine Scott	Horatio Skeete	....	....	Robert Gaunt
Mesa (288)	MC 602 644-2365	Willie Wong	C K Luster	Barbara Hogue	Don Ayers	John Oliver	....	Harry Kent
Miami t (2)	MC 602 473-4403	....	....	....	....	....	....	....
Nogales (19)	MC 602 287-6571	Jose L Canchola	Michael Hein	Michael Hein	Darol Cridlebaugh	J L DeLa Ossa	Jose Luis Alday	Manuel Ruiz
Oro Valley t (7)	CM 602 297-2591	....	....	....	....	....	....	....
Page (7)	CM 602 645-8861	Gary Scaramazzo	Curtis Shook	Kaye Findley	Wilkie Miller	....	Richard Obergh	....
Paradise Valley t (12)	CM 602 948-7411	....	....	....	....	....	....	....
Parker t (3)	MC 602 669-9265	....	....	....	....	....	....	....
Payson (8)	CM 602 474-5242	Clifford E Potts	Kenneth Buchanan	Linda J Foster	Wm J Ingram Jr	Charles A Jacobs	Gordon H Gartner	Colin P Walker
Peoria (51)	CM 602 412-7000	Kenneth C Forgia	Peter C Harvey	Janice L Graziano	Jorge G Cruz Aedo	Michael F Fusco	Michael L Strope	Kevin J Kadlec
Phoenix (983)	CM 602 262-6011	Thelda Williams	Frank Fairbanks	Vicky Miel	Kevin Keogh	Alan Brunacini	Dennis Garrett	Ronald Jenson
Pinetop-Lakeside t (2)	CM 602 368-8696	Larry Vicario	Paul M Watson	Leslee M Wessel	Wm A Beecroft	....	Terry J Ringey	....
Prescott (26)	CM 602 445-3500	Daiton Rutkowski	Mark Stevens	Marie Watson	Kayanne Schmitt	....	Robert Reed	Thomas Long
Prescott Valley t (9)	CM 602 772-9207	Harvey Skoog	Ken Rittmer	....	Linda Thorsen	....	Charles Seder	Larry Takowski
Quartzsite t (2)	CM 602 927-4333	....	....	....	....	....	....	....
Queen Creek t (3)	CM 602 987-9887	....	C Seelhammer	....	....	....	....	....
Safford (7)	CM 602 428-2762	Van Talley	Kip Bingham	Sherrie Farar	Ron Jacobson	Dick Bingham	Dennis Thompson	Robert Porter
Scottsdale (130)	CM 602 994-2690	....	....	....	....	....	....	....
Sedona (9)	CM 602 282-0620	....	Kevin M Dunlap	....	....	....	....	....
Show Low (5)	CM 602 537-5203	....	....	....	....	....	....	....
Sierra Vista (33)	CM 602 458-3315	Richard Archer	James Whitlock	Sandra Kenny	Charles Potucek	Bruce Thompson	Arthur Montgomery	George Michael
Snowflake t (4)	CM 602 536-7103	Ray Caldwell	Roy Hunt	Barbra Bigler	....	John Hagelstein	Carl Schafer	Joe Papa
Somerton (5)	MC 602 627-8866	Vivian Robinson	Enrique Castillo	Mark Ryan	Mark Ryan	....	Terry Hollis	Edmundo Mendez
South Tucson (5)	CM 602 792-2424	Shirley Villegas	Rene Gastelum	Dolores Robles	John White	Henry Vega	....	Richard Salaz
St. Johns (3)	CM 602 337-4517	Micheal Pollack	....	Betty Clanton	A Kim Haws	Denis Ashton	R B Overson	William Prentice
Superior t (3)	MC 602 689-5752	....	....	....	....	....	....	....
Surprise t (7)	CM 602 583-1000	Roy Villanueva	Richard McComb	Lucy Fitzpatrick	Vito Tedeschi	Robert Weekley	Garvin Arrell	Robert Zobel
Tempe (142)	CM 602 350-8444	Neil Giuliano	Terry Zerkle	Helen Fowler	Patrick Flynn	Cliff Jones	David Brown	Jim Jones
Thatcher t (4)	MC 602 428-2290	....	....	....	....	....	....	....
Tolleson (4)	CM 602 936-7111	....	....	....	....	....	....	....
Tucson (405)	CM 602 791-4241	....	....	....	....	....	....	....
Wickenburg t (5)	CM 602 684-5451	Dallas C Gant	Ben J Nardelli	Edna C Grieves	Tom Candelaria	Joe T Walters	William Willmann	Coney Orosco
Willcox (3)	CM 602 384-4271	Sandra L Ousley	....	Cristina G Whelan	Stacey Englund	Paul Grant	V E Gene Jones	Rene L Diaz
Williams (3)	CM 602 635-4451	....	....	....	....	....	....	....
Winslow (8)	MC 602 289-2422	Jim Boles	Don McDaniel	Linda Samson	Ken Mitchell	Boney Candeleria	Wayne Wagner	Mike Artz
Yuma (55)	CM 602 783-1271	Marilyn Young	Joyce Wilson	Carrie Fassil	Robert Stull	Phil Mele	William Robinson	Larry Hunt
ARKANSAS (92)								
Alma (3)	MC 501 632-4119	....	....	....	....	....	....	....
Arkadelphia (10)	CM 501 246-9864	....	....	....	....	....	....	....
Ashdown (5)	MC 501 898-2622	....	....	....	....	....	....	....
Atkins (3)	MC 501 641-2900	Stephen Kent	....	Brenda Graves	....	Jim McGee	David Johnston	Alfred Berry
Augusta (3)	MC 501 347-5656	....	....	....	....	....	....	....
Bald Knob (3)	MC 501 724-6371	....	....	....	....	....	....	....
Barling (4)	MC 501 452-1556	Jerry Barling	Rich Haberban	Myra Monchamp	....	Phil Stewart	Paul Rivaldo	Jim Womack
Batesville (9)	MC 501 698-2400	Jim Barnett	....	Denise M Johnston	Denise M Johnston	Bob Davis	....	Sanford E St John
Beebe (4)	MC 501 882-3365	Philip Petray	....	Rebecca P Short	....	Bill Nick	Wayne Gibson	....
Benton (18)	MC 501 776-5900	Jimmy F Presnall	....	Margaret Ramsey	John P Walden	Sam McCallie	Richard Elmendorf	....
Bentonville (11)	MC 501 271-3112	John W Fryer	....	Terry Coberly	Ed Lea	Leon Reece	James Allen	....
Berryville (3)	MC 501 423-4414	Tim McKinney	....	Eugene Allen	....	Gene Chafin	Dave Muniz	Tim Miller
Blytheville (23)	MC 501 763-3602	....	....	....	....	....	....	....
Booneville (4)	MC 501 675-3811	Brian Mueller	....	Melinda Smith	....	David Hardin	Stan Campbell	....
Brinkley (4)	CM 501 734-1382	....	....	....	....	....	....	....
Bryant (5)	MC 501 847-0292	....	....	....	....	....	....	....
Cabot (8)	MC 501 843-3566	....	....	....	....	....	....	....
Camden (14)	CM 501 836-6436	Steve Crumpler	Charles W Bell	Preston L Woods	Peston L Woods	William P Seaton	....	Harlan B Benson
Carlisle (2)	MC 501 552-3120	....	....	....	....	....	....	....

Directory 1/9 continued **MUNICIPAL OFFICIALS IN U.S. CITIES OVER 2,500**

City, 1990 population figures (000 omitted), form of government	Municipal phone number	Mayor/ chief elected official	Appointed administrator	City clerk/ city secretary	Finance officer	Fire chief	Police chief	Public works director
ARKANSAS (92) continued								
Clarksville (6)	MC 501 754-6486	Marvin Vinson	....	Metta Holman	....	Floyd Pledger	Kyn Wilson	....
Conway (26)	MC 501 327-3392	....	....	....	....	....	....	....
Corning (3)	MC 501 857-6716	....	....	....	....	....	....	....
Crossett (6)	MC 501 364-4830	Les Black	....	Nelson Toler	Laura Halley	James Launius	Tommy Sturgeon	Thomas Goree
Dardanelle (4)	MC 501 229-4500	....	....	....	....	....	....	....
De Queen (5)	CM 501 584-3445	....	....	....	....	....	....	....
De Witt (4)	MC 501 946-2191	....	....	....	....	....	....	....
Dermott (5)	MC 501 538-5251	....	....	....	....	....	....	....
Dumas (6)	MC 501 382-2121	Lewis R Baker	....	Mary S Howard	....	David Byrd	Everett Cox	....
Earle (3)	MC 501 792-8909	....	....	....	....	....	....	....
El Dorado (23)	MC 501 862-7911	Mike Dumas	....	Dennis Puckett	....	Ben Blankenship	Donald Tate	Chars R Atkinson
England (3)	MC 501 842-3911	Roy Cox	....	Ruth Baker	....	Gene A Harp	Randy Krablin	....
Eudora (3)	MC 501 355-4436	....	....	....	....	....	....	....
Fayetteville (42)	CM 205 233-8737	Daniel Williams	....	Mignon Bowers	Mignon Bowers	Cliff Christopher	Wayne Harper	Larry Elkins
Fordyce (5)	MC 501 352-2198	....	....	....	....	....	....	....
Forrest City (13)	MC 501 633-1692	....	....	....	....	....	....	....
Fort Smith (73)	CM 501 784-2201	....	....	....	....	....	....	....
Gosnell (4)	MC 501 532-8544	....	....	....	....	....	....	....
Greenwood (4)	MC 501 996-2742	Joe W Siegmund	....	Linda Bryant	....	Eugene Rogers	Robert Hicks	....
Gurdon (2)	MC 501 353-2514	Rick W Smith	....	Tambra D Smith	....	Tillman McBride	David E Childres	....
Hamburg (3)	MC 501 853-5300	Boyce Harrod	....	Brenda Graham	....	Tab Harrod	David Sims	Earle Benson
Harrison (10)	MC 501 741-2525	....	....	....	....	....	....	....
Heber Springs (6)	MC 501 362-3635	Edward L Roper	....	Norma J Martin	....	Frank Valentine	Fred L Byford	....
Helena (7)	MC 501 338-9831	Joann D Smith	....	Louise Galloway	....	Jeff Wages	Boyd S Williams	Dennis Sullivan
Hope (10)	CM 501 777-6701	Dennis Ramsey	David Meriwether	Leneta Hare	Debbie Hall	Joe Don Webb	Richard Thomas	Jim Atchley
Hot Springs (32)	CM 501 321-6800	Helen Selig	....	Lance Hudnell	James Scott	Arval Sanders	Martin White	....
Hoxie (3)	MC 501 886-2742	J M Johnson	....	Joe Douglas	Regina Waterson	Bob Wade	Vernon Moore	....
Jacksonville (29)	MC 501 982-3181	Tommy Swaim	....	Lula Mae Leonard	Paul Mushrush	Rick Ezell	Larry Hibbs	James Spears
Jonesboro (47)	MC 501 932-1052	Hubert Brodell	....	Donna Jackson	Linda Bullock	Wayne Masterson	Floyd Johnson	Guy Lowes
Lake Village (3)	MC 501 265-2228	Joanne H Bush	....	Harolyn Keith	....	Larry Donaldson	Percy L Wilburn	....
Little Rock (176)	CM 501 371-4510	Jim Dailey	Charles Nickerson	Robbie Hancock	John Pryor	Rubin Webb	Louie Caudell	Mike Batie
Lonoke (4)	MC 501 676-7481	Jack W Wheat	Delilah Chivers	John Latimer	Delilah Chivers	Jerry F Brumett	Floyd R Van Horn	Tony Scroggins
Magnolia (11)	MC 501 234-1375	George Wheatley	....	Judy Whitelaw	....	Herschel Hampton	Larry Taylor	Roy Waters
Malvern (9)	MC 501 332-3638	....	....	....	....	....	....	....
Manila (3)	MC 501 561-4437	....	....	....	....	....	....	....
Marianna (6)	MC 501 295-6089	Martin Chaffin	Dorothy Willis	Dorothy Willis	....	Jack Gentry	Barry V Downs	....
Marion (4)	MC 501 739-3071	....	....	....	....	....	....	....
Marked Tree (3)	MC 501 358-3216	L W Ashlock Jr	....	J P Hutchins	....	McDaniel Johnson	Orbie J Crum	....
Maumelle (..)	CM 501 851-2500	....	Gerald C Boon	Beverly Masters	Gerald C Boon	....	Norman Moseley	Robert Cogdell
Mc Gehee (5)	MC 501 222-3160	....	....	....	....	....	....	....
Mena (5)	MC 501 394-4585	....	....	....	....	....	....	....
Monticello (8)	MC 501 367-4400	Harold D West	....	Patricia Nelson	Reva L Abbott	Raymond Chisom	Robert Maxwell	Floyd Fullbright
Morrilton (7)	MC 501 354-3484	....	....	....	....	....	....	....
Mountain Home (9)	MC 501 425-5116	John Ayers	....	Deborah House	....	Dale Harris	Paul Doak	Lester Herring
Nashville (5)	MC 501 845-7400	....	....	....	....	....	....	....
Newport (7)	MC 501 523-2167	....	....	....	....	....	....	....
North Little Rock (62)	MC 501 377-7300	Patrick H Hays	....	Mary L Munns	Robert L Sisson	Charles W Redding	William Nolan	John F Blodgett
Osceola (9)	MC 501 563-5102	....	....	....	....	....	....	....
Ozark (3)	MC 501 667-2238	....	....	....	....	....	....	....
Paragould (19)	MC 501 239-7510	Charles R Partlow	....	Goldie Wise	....	William Brown	Dennis Hyde	Helen Lamb
Paris (4)	MC 501 963-2450	....	....	....	....	....	....	....
Piggott (4)	MC 501 598-2388	Garland M Holcomb	....	Jean Doty	....	John Harlan	Kenneth Parker	....
Pine Bluff (57)	MC 501 543-1840	Jerry Taylor	Betty Massanelli	Katy Heroman	Edward Bogy	William Jacks	Joe Thomas	....
Pocahontas (6)	MC 501 892-3924	....	....	....	....	....	....	....
Prescott (4)	MC 501 887-2210	....	....	....	....	....	....	....
Rogers (25)	MC 501 621-1117	....	....	....	....	....	....	....
Russellville (21)	MC 501 968-2098	Woody Harris	....	Helen Price	....	Ray Hobby	John Waterson	....
Searcy (15)	MC 501 268-2483	....	....	....	....	....	....	....
Sheridan (3)	MC 501 942-3921	....	....	....	....	....	....	....
Sherwood (19)	MC 501 835-5319	Bill Harmon	....	Bobbie Chapman	....	....	James Crockett	Denver Gentry
Siloam Springs (8)	CM 501 524-5136	M L Van Poucke Jr	Mark Latham	Peggy Woody	Winford Mulkey	Wayne Brashear	Al Gregory	....
Springdale (30)	MC 501 756-8200	Charles McKinney	....	Mida Neff	....	Dan White	Gary Payne	....
Stamps (2)	MC 501 533-4771	....	....	....	....	....	....	....
Stuttgart (10)	MC 501 673-3535	....	....	....	....	....	....	....
Texarkana (23)	CM 501 774-3161	....	....	....	....	....	....	....
Trumann t (6)	MC 501 483-5355	....	....	....	....	....	....	....
Van Buren (15)	MC 501 474-1541	....	....	....	....	....	....	....
Waldron (3)	MC 501 637-3181	....	....	....	....	....	....	....
Walnut Ridge (4)	MC 501 886-6638	....	....	....	....	....	....	....
Warren (6)	MC 501 226-6743	R Gregg Reep	....	Bertia Lassiter	....	Bob Stedman	Bob Outlaw	....
West Helena (10)	MC 501 572-2528	Bob Teeter	....	Renee Knowlton	....	Earl Meiers	Waylon Stepp	....
West Memphis (28)	MC 501 732-7601	Keith Ingram	....	Lucinda Greenwood	Wyman D Morgan	Mac Holmes	Bobby Sanders	H T Wilborn
Wynne (8)	MC 501 238-9171	....	....	....	....	....	....	....
CALIFORNIA (433)								
Adelanto (9)	MC 619 246-2300	....	P Chamberlaine	Sharon Gasaway	Michael Sakamoto	Melvin Dorrow	Robert Gardner	Roland Dorvall
Agoura Hills (20)	CM 597-7300	....	....	....	....	....	....	....
Alameda (76)	CM 510 748-4521	E William Withrow	William Norton	Diane Felsch	Zenda James	Robert LaGrone	Burnham Matthews	Robert Warnick
Albany (16)	CM 510 528-5710	....	....	....	....	....	....	....
Alhambra (82)	CM 818 570-5007	Boyd Condie	Julio Fuentes	Frances Moore	Derek Hanway	....	Russell Siverling	Terry James
Alturas (3)	MC 916 233-2512	....	....	....	....	....	....	....
American Canyon (8)	CM 707 647-4360	....	....	....	....	....	....	....
Anaheim (266)	CM 714 254-5100	....	....	....	....	....	....	....
Anderson (8)	CM 916 378-6626	Rodney Jones	William A Murphy	Jacqueline Sharp	Carol Martin	....	William P Raner	Michael Knight
Angels (2)	CM 209 736-2181	....	....	....	....	....	....	....
Antioch (62)	CM 510 779-7020	Joel Keller	David Rowlands Jr	Florence Rundall	John Tasker	....	David Lewis	Stanford Davis
Apple Valley t (..)	CM 619 240-7000	Nick DePrisco	Wayne Lamoreaux	Eunice Puckett	Kevin Smith	....	....	Bruce Williams
Arcadia (48)	CM 818 574-5400	....	....	....	....	....	....	....
Arcata (15)	CM 707 822-5953	Victor Schaub	Alice Harris	....	Daphne Hodgson	....	Mel Brown	Stephen J Leiker
Arroyo Grande (14)	CM 805 489-1303	Pete Gallagher	C Christiansen	Nancy A Davis	David Bacon	Kurt Latipow	Rick Terborch	....
Artesia (15)	CM 310 865-6262	Isidro Menezes	Paul J Philips	Patricia Mitchell	....	....	....	Chuck Bernal
Arvin (9)	CM 805 854-3134	Jess Ortiz	Thomas A Payne	Gola Manasco	....	....	Terry Freeman	Terry Freeman
Atascadero (23)	MC 805 461-5010	R David Bewley	Andrew J Takata	Lee Price	W Bradford Whitty	Mike McCain	R H Bud McHale	....

Directory 1/9 continued — MUNICIPAL OFFICIALS IN U.S. CITIES OVER 2,500

City, 1990 population figures (000 omitted), form of government	Municipal phone number	Mayor/ chief elected official	Appointed administrator	City clerk/ city secretary	Finance officer	Fire chief	Police chief	Public works director
CALIFORNIA (433) continued								
Atherton t (7) CM	415 325-4457	William Conwell	Judy Kelsey	....	Melissa Eddy	....	Patrick Rolle	Scott T Munns
Atwater (22) CM	209 357-6300	Joe Frontella	Dave Adams	Fran Barrett	Bruce Johnson	Dennis Sparks	Tony Altfeld	John Haug
Auburn (11) CM	916 823-4211	....	....	....	....	....	....	....
Avalon (3) CM	310 510-0220	....	....	....	....	....	....	....
Avenal (10) CM	209 386-5766	....	....	....	....	....	....	....
Azusa (41) CM	818 334-5125	Stephen Alexander	Henry Garcia	Adolph Solis	Geoffrey Craig	....	Byron Nelson	Louie Pedroza
Bakersfield (175) CM	805 326-3773	....	....	....	....	....	....	....
Baldwin Park (69) CM	818 813-5207	Fidel A Vargas	....	Linda L Gair	Carl L Yeats	....	Carmine R Lanza	Sid J Mousavi
Banning (21) CM	714 922-1295	....	....	....	....	....	....	....
Barstow (21) CM	619 256-3531	Mal Wessel	Jean Daze Ratelle	Donna Sluder	Evelyn Radel	....	Robert A Sessions	Duane Greenfield
Beaumont (10) CM	909 845-1171	Jan Leja	Dayle Keller	Dayle Keller	Greg Franklin	....	Patrick Smith	Dee Moorjani
Bell (34) CM	213 588-6211	....	....	....	....	....	....	....
Bell Gardens (42) CM	310 806-7700	Frank Duran	Charles Gomez	Ron Hart	Anil Gandhy	....	Andy Romero	S Steinbrecher
Bellflower (62) CM	310 804-1424	....	....	....	....	....	....	....
Belmont (24) MC	415 595-7413	Pam Rianda	Damon Edwards	Dorothy Hall	Sandra Salerno	....	Michael Oliver	John Hopkins
Belvedere (2) CM	415 435-3838	Justin M Faggioli	Edmund San Diego	Edmund San Diego	Edmund San Diego	....	Glenn Accornero	...
Benicia (24) CM	707 746-4200	Ernest Ciarrochi	Michael Warren	Frances D Greco	Alan Nadritch	Ken Hanley	Otto Giuliani	Virgil Mustain
Berkeley (103) CM	510 644-6460	Jeffrey Leiter	Weldon Rucker	Sherry Kelly	Eric Tsao	Gary Cates	Daschel Butler	Vicki Elmer
Beverly Hills (32) CM	310 285-1000	Vicki Reynolds	Mark Scott	....	Don Oblander	Clarence Martin	Marvin Iannone	Dan Webster
Big Bear Lake (5) CM	909 866-5831	Robert C Davies	Henry W Harvey	Kathy Jefferies	Henry W Harvey	Edward Kimbrough	Walt Hanson	Michael Stewart
Bishop (3) CM	619 873-5863	Doug Currie	Richard F Pucci	Richard F Pucci	Richard F Pucci	Phillip Moxley	Frederick Coburn	Andrew Boyd
Blythe (8) CM	619 922-6161	....	....	....	....	....	....	....
Bradbury (1) MC	818 358-3218	B Lapisto Kirtley	Keene Wilson	Claudia Saldana	Claudia Saldana	....	....	....
Brawley (19) CM	619 344-9111	Hoxsie Smith	Rodger Bennett	Janet Smith	Fred Selk	Frank Contreras	David Holt	Behrooz Nikjoo
Brea (33) CM	714 990-7719	Glenn Parker	Frank Benest	Elaine Capps	Lawrence Hurst	William Simpkins	Donald Forkus	P McCarron
Brentwood (8) CM	510 634-6900	William Hill	Jay Corey	Linda Keefer	Jay Corey	....	Larry Shaw	David Bryan
Brisbane (3) CM	415 467-1515	Clara A Johnson	Robin Leiter	Sheri Schroeder	Gul Ramchandani	Scott Kenley	Thomas Hitchcock	James Thompson
Brooktrails (Csd) tp (3) MC	707 459-2494	Randall E Eads	Paul A Williams	Elizabeth Simpson	Patricia Wilson	David J Thomen	....	Wendell M Wilson
Buellton (4) CM	805 686-0137	....	....	....	....	....	....	....
Buena Park (69) CM	714 562-3500	Donald Bone	Kevin O' Rourke	Alcene Cain	Greg Beaubien	Herb Jewell	Richard Tefank	Don Jensen
Burbank (94) CM	818 953-9732	William Wiggins	Robert R Ovrom	Margaret Lauerman	Alvin Holliman	Michael Davis	David Newsham	Ora Lampman
Burlingame (27) CM	415 696-7202	Rosalie O' Mahony	Dennis Argyres	Judy Malfatti	Rahn Becker	Malcolm Towns	Alfred Palmer	Ralph Kirkup
Calabasas (..) CM	818 878-4225	....	....	....	....	....	....	....
Calexico (19) CM	619 768-2110	Richard L Romero	Alejandro C Armen	Lourdes Cordova	Judith A Hashem	Carlos G Escalant	Toriuio Flores	Mariano Martinez
California City (6) MC	619 373-8661	Richard Moser	Stephan West	Helen Dennis	Terry Hicks	Richard Hall	Willie Brown	Kenneth Redfern
Calimesa (12) CM	909 795-9801	Shirley Morton	Dennis R Halloway	Dennis R Halloway	Dennis R Halloway	....	....	W Duane Fessenden
Calipatria (3) MC	714 348-2293	....	....	....	....	....	....	....
Calistoga (4) CM	707 942-2800	LaVerne Ovarzo	John Bahorski	Patt Osborne	Michael Vivrette	....	Leo Peart	Waldo Kolb
Camarillo (52) CM	805 388-5307	Ken Gose	J William Little	Marilyn Thiel	Anita Bingham	....	Ray Abbott	John Elwell
Campbell (36) CM	408 866-2122	Jeanette Watson	Mark Ochenduszko	Anne Bybee	Gretchen Conner	....	James Cost	Robert Kass
Capitola (10) CM	408 475-7300	....	....	....	....	....	....	....
Carlsbad (63) CM	619 434-2852	Claude Lewis	Raymond Patchett	Lee Rautenkranz	James Elliott	D Van Der Maaten	Robert Vales	....
Carmel-By-The-Sea (4) CM	408 624-2781	Ken White	Jere Kersnar	Jeanne Brehmer	....	Bill Hill	Donald P Fuselier	James Cullem
Carpinteria (14) CM	805 684-5405	....	....	....	....	....	....	....
Carson (84) CM	310 952-1736	Michael Mitoma	Lawrence G Olson	Helen Kawngoe	....	....	....	George Schultz
Cathedral City (30) MC	619 770-0340	Carol Englehard	....	Kammy Hill	Dudley Haines	George Truppelli	Bob Ohlemann	....
Ceres (26) CM	209 538-5700	Barbara Hinton	Gary A Napper	Karen Hunter	Carlos Sanchez	Gail W Peterson	Gail W Peterson	Joe Hollstein
Cerritos (53) CM	213 860-0311	....	....	....	....	....	....	....
Chico (40) CM	916 895-4800	James Owens	Thomas Lando	Barbara Evans	Robert Sesnon	Charles Lowden	Michael Dunbaugh	....
Chino (60) CM	909 627-7577	Eunice Ulloa	Richard D Rowe	Kathleen Blomo	Mary O' Neil	....	Patrick Connolly	Robert Beardsley
Chowchilla (6) CM	209 665-8615	David Rogers	David Rickerd	Lori Yanders	Julie DeWall	Harry Turner	Albert Lucchesi	Doug Lackey
Chula Vista (135) CM	619 691-5031	....	....	....	....	....	....	....
Claremont (33) CM	714 399-5440	....	....	....	....	....	....	....
Clayton (7) CM	510 672-3622	Peter Laurence	Thomas Steele	Frances Douglas	....	....	Norm Venturino	....
Clearlake (12) CM	707 994-8201	Rod Mitchell	Dan Obermeyer	Sharon Goode	Les Tyler	....	Bob Chalk	Ron Heim
Cloverdale (5) CM	707 894-2521	Carol Chase	Robert J Perrault	M Winterbottom	Carol Giovanatto	....	Robert Dailey	Frederick Browne
Clovis (50) CM	209 297-2300	William Armstrong	Kathleen Millison	....	Michael Prandini	John Cawelti	Joseph Maskovich	Cecil Leonardo
Coachella (17) CM	619 398-3502	Juan DeLara	Bruce Daniels	Isabel Castillon	Lawrence Ronnow	John Rios	Norman Traub	Thomas Lagier
Coalinga (8) CM	209 935-1533	Alfonso Bonilla	Steven Smith	Cindy Johnson	Dorothy Ingham	Fred Fredrickson	John DeAngelis	Thomas Fossum
Colton (40) CM	714 370-5000	Frank Gonzales	....	Helen Ramos	....	David Hall	....	John Hutton
Colusa (5) CM	916 458-4740	John A Rogers	Gay Rainsbarger	Gay Rainsbarger	....	Randal Dunn	Thomas Gwinnup	....
Commerce (12) CM	213 722-4805	Ruben C Batres	Louis Shepard	Linda K Olivieri	Thomas Bachman	....	....	Samuel Johnson
Compton (90) CM	310 605-5535	Omar Bradley	Howard Caldwell	Charles Davis	Helen Tyler	Milford Fonza	Hourie Taylor	Angel Espiritu
Concord (111) CM	510 671-3000	Michael Pastrick	Edward R James	Lynnet Keihl	Paul R Howard	....	Michael R Maehler	Michael D Vogan
Corcoran (13) CM	209 992-2151	Terry Kwast	Donald F Pauley	Connie Harris	Joyce Venegas	....	Manuel Gonzales	John Cook
Corning (6) CM	916 824-7033	Ross M Turner	Stephen Kimbrough	Darlene Dickison	Stephen Kimbrough	Robert Pryatel	Anthony Cardinas	Terry N Snow
Corona (76) CM	909 736-2200	Bill Miller	William H Garrett	Diedre D Lingenfe	Helen Bell	Mike Warren	John Cleghorn	Joseph Palencia
Coronado (27) CM	619 522-7300	Mary Herron	Homer Bludau	Jacque Wilson	....	Jim Walker	Jack Drown	Andy Anderson
Corte Madera t (8) CM	415 927-5050	....	....	....	....	....	....	....
Costa Mesa (96) CM	714 754-5225	Sandra Genis	Allan Roeder	....	Susan Temple	Frank Fantino	David Snowden	William Morris
Cotati (6) CM	707 792-4600	Richard Cullinen	Bonnie J Long	Bonnie J Long	Jonathan J Ellis	....	Lester W Wasko	Steve Nommsen
Covina (43) CM	818 331-0111	Thomas O' Leary	Francis M Delach	Mary Jo Southall	....	Michael A Marquez	Kenneth R Lavoie	Raymond J Coakley
Crescent City (4) CM	707 464-7483	C Ray Smith	Stephen R Casey	Kathleen A Smith	Carol J Leuthold	Don Olson	Richard Metcalf	David Gustafson
Cudahy (23) CM	213 773-5143	Alex F Rodriguez	Jack M Joseph	Jack M Joseph	Aurora C Martinez	....	....	....
Culver City (39) CM	310 202-5753	Albert Vera	Mary J Hall Esser	Tom Crunk	....	....	Ted Cooke	James Davis
Cupertino (40) CM	408 777-3200	Barbara Koppel	Donald D Brown	Kim Smith	....	....	....	Bert J Viskovich
Cypress (43) CM	714 229-6681	Richard Partin	Darrell Essex	....	Richard Storey	....	Daryl Wicker	Mark Christoffels
Daly City (92) CM	415 991-8000	....	....	....	....	....	....	....
Dana Point (32) CM	714 248-9890	Judy Curreri	Steve Julian	Sharon Waits	Rita Geldert	....	....	Mort August
Danville (31) CM	510 820-4699	....	....	....	....	....	....	....
Davis (46) CM	916 757-5644	David Rosenberg	John Meyer	Bette Racki	Susan Miller	William Berger	Philip Coleman	David Pelz
Del Mar (5) CM	619 755-9313	Jan McMillan	L Brekke Esparza	Mercedes A Martin	Emily G Hobdy	James Baker	....	Richard E Andrews
Del Rey Oaks (2) CM	408 394-8511	....	D Steven Endsley	....	....	....	....	....
Delano (23) CM	805 721-3300	Arthur Armendariz	A DeLa Cerda	Jeanne Bumatay	Wiley Jung	....	Gerald Gruver	Eddie Ahumada
Desert Hot Springs (12) CM	619 329-6411	Mike Segrist	Robert Mack	Colleen Nicol	Marleta Fritz	....	....	Matt Bumguardner
Dinuba (13) CM	209 591-5900	Raymond Millard	Ed Todd	Antonia Marshall	Kenneth Grover	Myles Chute	Emilio Perez	Daniel Meinert
Dixon (10) CM	916 678-7000	Don Erikson	David L Harris	Linda Crisman	Diane Beard	Ric Dorris	Rick Fuller	Ron Tribbett
Dos Palos (4) CM	209 392-2174	Ron Skinner	Darrell Fonseca	Patricia Mann	....	Dewayne Jones	Tom Saavedra	Hub Ballinger
Downey (91) CM	310 904-7293	Barbara Riley	Gerald M Caton	Judith McDonnell	Lowell Williams	Ron Irwin	Gregory Caldwell	Richard Redmayne
Duarte (21) CM	818 357-7931	....	....	....	....	....	....	....
Dublin (23) CM	510 833-6650	....	....	....	....	....	....	....
Dunsmuir (2) CM	916 235-4822	Paul Williams	Alan N Harvey	Ann Smith	Theadore Marconi	Sid Nystrom	....	....
East Palo Alto (23) CM	415 853-3100	....	....	....	....	....	....	....

Directory 1/9
continued

**MUNICIPAL OFFICIALS
IN U.S. CITIES OVER 2,500**

City, 1990 population figures (000 omitted), form of government	Municipal phone number	Mayor/ chief elected official	Appointed administrator	City clerk/ city secretary	Finance officer	Fire chief	Police chief	Public works director
CALIFORNIA (433) continued								
El Cajon (89)	CM 619 441-1736	Joan Shoemaker	Robert Acker	....	James Kell	Richard Hardy	Jack Smith	Marvin Munzenmair
El Centro (31)	CM 619 337-4548	....	....	....	....	....	....	....
El Cerrito (23)	CM 510 215-4300	....	....	....	....	....	....	....
El Monte (106)	MC 818 580-2019	Patricia Wallach	Gregory Korduner	Rose Griffith	Marvin Louie	Leslie George	Wayne Clayton	....
El Paso De Robles (19)	CM 805 237-3888	Walter Macklin	Richard Ramirez	Richard Ramirez	Michael Compton	Doug Hamp	John Nelson	John McCarthy
El Segundo (15)	CM 310 322-4670	Carl Jacobson	James Morrison	Cindy Mortensen	Steven Klotzsche	Jacob Nielson	Tim Grimmond	Eduard Schroder
Emeryville (6)	CM 415 596-4300	....	....	....	....	....	....	....
Encinitas (55)	CM 619 944-5050	....	....	....	....	....	....	....
Escalon (4)	CM 209 838-3556	....	....	....	....	....	....	....
Escondido (109)	CM 619 741-4641	....	....	....	....	....	....	....
Eureka (27)	CM 707 443-7331	....	....	....	....	....	....	....
Exeter (7)	CM 209 592-9244	Willian N Brooks	Roy Chace	Roy Chace	....	....	John Kunkel	Howard Ricks
Fairfax t (7)	CM 415 453-1584	Steven M Vanni	Linda Christman	Judy Anderson	....	....	Jim Anderson	....
Fairfield (77)	CM 707 428-7398	....	....	....	....	....	....	....
Farmersville (6)	CM 209 747-0458	Al Vanderslice	Steve Thompson	Lucille Scott	....	....	Garry Meek	Ron Mathis
Fillmore (12)	CM 805 524-3701	Linda Brewster	Roy Payne	Noreen Withers	Allan Coates	Pat Askren	Richard Diaz	John Kozar
Firebaugh (4)	CM 209 659-2043	Marcia Sablan	L Keyth Durham	Doris Fannon	Nancy K Walker	John Borboa	Rod Lake	David Wilson
Folsom (30)	CM 916 355-7200	....	....	....	....	....	....	....
Fontana (88)	CM 909 350-7600	Gary E Boyles	Gregory Devereaux	Kathleen Montoya	Loron Cox	....	Sam Scott	Ken Jeske
Fort Bragg (6)	CM 707 961-2825	Patricia Campbell	Gary Milliman	Deelynn Carpenter	Roy Mitchell	Wilbur Phenix	Thomas Bickell	Gary Milliman
Fortuna (9)	CM 707 725-6125	Dean Lewis	Dale Neiman	Dale Neiman	Robert Sousa	....	Kent Bradshaw	Tom Cooke
Foster City (28)	CM 415 349-1200	Robert Field	James Hardy	Therese Tyree	Ricardo Santiago	William McDonald	Robert Norman	Charles Loucks
Fountain Valley (54)	CM 714 965-4400	John Collins	Raymond Kromer	Jay Palazzo	Elizabeth Fox	Bernard Heimos	Elvin Miali	Wayne Osborne
Fremont (173)	CM 510 494-4800	Bill Ball	Jan C Perkins	Sharon Whitten	P Garcia Lutz	Daniel Lydon	Craig Steckler	Thomas Blalock
Fresno (354)	CM 209 498-4591	Jim Patterson	Michael Bierman	Jacqueline Ryle	Andrew Souza	Michael Smith	Ed Winchester	Raymond Salazar
Fullerton (114)	CM 714 738-6300	Allen B Catlin	James Armstrong	Anne York	Barbara Henderson	Marc Martin	Patrick McKinley	....
Galt (9)	MC 209 745-9153	Richard Pratt	Peter Cosentini	Carol Cowley	Inez Kiriu	....	Doug Matthews	Bob Kawasaki
Garden Grove (143)	CM 714 741-5000	Frank Kessler	George Tindall	Carolyn Morris	Anthony Andrade	Vince Bonacker	Stan Knee	Dick Conrad
Gardena (50)	CM 310 217-9500	Donald L Dear	Kenneth Landau	May Doi	Richard Roxburgh	Craig Pedego	Richard Propster	Kenneth Ayers
Gilroy (31)	MC 408 848-0400	....	....	....	....	....	....	....
Glendale (180)	CM 818 548-4000	Eileen Givens	David Ramsay	Aileen Boyle	Brian Butler	Richard Hinz	James Anthony	George Miller Jr
Glendora (48)	CM 818 914-8200	Larry Glenn	Arthur Cook	Jo Ann Sharp	L Schroeder	....	Paul Butler	Richard Cantwell
Gonzales (5)	CM 408 675-5000	Harold Wolgamott	Carla L Pew	Carla L Pew	Rene M Vise	Rick Rubbo	L Ray Green	Carlos Lopez
Grand Terrace (11)	CM 714 824-6621	....	....	....	....	....	....	....
Grass Valley (9)	MC 916 274-4310	Bill Hullender	Gene Haroldsen	Bobbi Poznik	Wes Peters	Jeff Brady	Mel Mouser	Rudi Golnik
Greenfield (7)	CM 408 674-5591	Roy F Morris	....	Ann F Rathbun	....	Ed Banvelos	J M Romo	John Alves
Gridley (5)	MC 916 846-5695	Frank Cook	John W Slota	John W Slota	Robin Bertagna	Woody Allshouse	Jack Storne	Ed Melton
Grover Beach (12)	CM 805 473-4567	Fred Munroe	P Culbreth Graft	Patricia Risoldi	Brian Johnson	Robert Cassel	David Brown	Thomas Sullivan
Guadalupe (5)	CM 805 343-1340	....	....	....	....	....	....	....
Gustine (4)	CM 209 854-6471	Thomas Dippel	Mark Melville	Mark Melville	....	Gary Orear	Mark Melville	Gary Davenport
Half Moon Bay (9)	CM 415 726-5566	....	....	....	....	....	....	....
Hanford (31)	CM 209 585-2500	Robert Hill	Jan E Reynolds	Karen McAlister	G Tom Dibble	Wesley P Yeary	Brian L DeCuir	Gary Misenhimer
Hawaiian Gardens (14)	CM 310 420-2641	....	....	....	....	....	....	....
Hawthorne (71)	CM 213 970-7902	....	....	....	....	....	....	....
Hayward (111)	CM 510 293-5000	....	....	....	....	....	....	....
Healdsburg (9)	CM 707 431-7461	Cathleen Harvey	Michael A Wilson	Maria A Curiel	Kurt Hahn	Robert Taylor	Joseph J Palla	Richard J Pusich
Hemet (36)	CM 714 765-2300	....	....	....	....	....	....	....
Hercules (17)	CM 415 799-8200	Eduardo Manuel	Marilyn Leuck	Kay Woodson	Marie Simons	....	Alicia Powers	Ron Richardson
Hermosa Beach (18)	CM 310 318-0239	Sam Y Edgerton	Stephen R Burrell	Elaine Doerfling	Viki Copeland	....	Val Straser	Amy Amirani
Hesperia (50)	CM 619 947-1000	....	....	....	....	....	....	....
Highland (34)	CM 909 864-6861	John P Timmer	Sam J Racadio	Debbie Anderson	Karin Grance	....	Ron Telles	Ernie Wong
Hillsborough t (11)	CM 415 579-3800	....	Robert M Davidson	Eleanor M Giorgi	James F Coyne	Kenneth Newman	Robert McNichol	....
Hollister (19)	CM 408 637-8221	....	....	....	....	....	....	....
Holtville (5)	CM 619 356-2912	Ira Hearen Jr	Karen Stauffer	Jeanne Miller	Jeanne Miller	Charles Cariveau	Robert Weaver	....
Hughson (3)	CM 209 883-4054	....	....	....	....	....	....	....
Huntington Beach (182)	CM 714 536-5265	....	....	....	....	....	....	....
Huntington Park (56)	CM 213 582-6161	Richard V Loya	Donald L Jeffers	Marilyn A Boyetet	Edward S Chow	....	....	Neil B Poole
Huron (5)	CM 209 945-2241	....	....	....	....	....	....	....
Imperial (4)	CM 619 355-4371	Mark T Gran	Paul J Richards	Patricia Cano	Janell Hodgkin	....	A R Moore	Bayani Mauricio
Imperial Beach (27)	CM 619 423-8300	Mike Bixler	Blair King	Cynthia Tjarks	Bob Hain	....	....	C Dave Ewing
Indian Wells (3)	CM 619 346-2489	James Killion	George J Watts	George J Watts	Charles D Francis	....	....	Jeanette Peck
Indio (37)	CM 619 342-6580	Elfrieda L Hall	Frederick Diaz	Karen Dodd	David Culver	Ken Hammond	Roy T Ramirez	Allyn Waggle
Inglewood (110)	CM 213 412-5301	E Vincent	P Eckles	H Harris	N Rives	J Ysais	O Thompson	K Duke
Irvine (110)	CM 714 724-6000	Mike Ward	Paul Brady Jr	Judy Vonada	Jeff Niven	....	Charles Brobeck	Robert W Tracy
Irwindale (1)	CM 818 962-3381	....	....	....	....	....	....	....
Kerman (5)	CM 209 846-9384	T Rodriguez	Ronald J Manfredi	Edith M Forsstrom	Edward Watanabe	....	Raymond L Sands	Kenneth L Moore
King City (8)	CM 408 385-3281	....	....	....	....	....	....	....
Kingsburg (7)	CM 209 897-5821	Gordon Satterburg	Barbara Carpenter	Barbara Carpenter	Don Jensen	Ed Morgan	Jim Taylor	John White
La Canada Flintridge (19)	CM 818 790-8880	....	....	....	....	....	....	....
La Habra (51)	CM 213 905-9700	David Cheverton	Lee Risner	Sharie Apodaca	Sheri Peasley	Ben Wilkins	Steven Staveley	....
La Habra Heights (6)	CM 310 694-6302	Judy Francis	Noelia Chapa	Noelia Chapa	....	Greg Garcia	....	....
La Mesa (53)	CM 619 463-6611	Art Madrid	David Wear	Anita Underwood	Dennis Hackett	Chris Carlson	Walter Mitchell	John Sullivan
La Mirada (40)	CM 310 943-0131	Bob Chotiner	Gary K Sloan	Gail Vasquez	Rick Patton	....	....	Perry Turigliatto
La Palma (15)	CM 714 523-7700	Wally Linn	Pamela Gibson	....	....	....	David Barr	Ismlle Noorbaksh
La Puente (37)	CM 818 855-1500	....	Robert Gutierrez	Linda Groves	Ted Abo	....	....	....
La Quinta (11)	CM 619 777-7000	....	....	....	....	....	....	....
La Verne (31)	CM 909 596-8726	Jon Blickenstaff	Martin Lomeli	Kathleen Hamm	Ron Clark	Robert Miller	Ron Ingels	Brian Bowcock
Lafayette (24)	CM 510 284-1968	....	Robert F D Adams	Susan Jusaitis	....	....	....	....
Laguna Beach (23)	CM 714 497-3311	Ann Christoph	Kenneth Frank	Verna Rollinger	Richard Hasenohrl	Richard Dewberry	Neil Purcell	Terry Brandt
Laguna Niguel (44)	CM 714 362-4300	Janet Godfrey	Timothy Casey	Juanita Zarilla	Dennis Miura	....	....	K Montgomery
Lake Elsinore (18)	CM 714 674-3124	....	....	....	....	....	....	....
Lake Forest (..)	CM 714 707-5583	....	....	....	....	....	....	....
Lakeport (4)	MC 707 263-5615	Howard Van Lente	....	Janel Chapman	Larry Jack	Chuck Hinchcliff	Tom Engstrom	Mike Stevenson
Lakewood (74)	CM 213 866-9771	....	....	....	....	....	....	....
Lancaster (97)	CM 805 723-6000	....	....	....	....	....	....	....
Larkspur (11)	CM 415 927-5110	Ronald Arlas	Jean A Bonander	....	Gail Green	Robert B Sinnott	Phillip D Green	Mark Miller
Lathrop (7)	CM 209 858-2860	....	....	....	....	....	....	....
Lawndale (27)	CM 310 970-2100	Harold Hoffman	Patrick Importuna	Neil Roth	Jan Rush	....	....	Mike Kapanpour
Lemon Grove (24)	CM 619 464-6934	Robert Burns	Douglas A Yount	Christine Taub	Christine Taub	William C Wright	....	Leslie R Ruh
Lemoore (14)	CM 209 924-5398	....	....	....	....	....	....	....
Lincoln (7)	CM 916 645-3314	Roberta Babcock	William J Malinen	Linda Stackpoole	Susan Badgley	Samuel Silvas	Ernest Klevesahl	James McLeod
Lindsay (8)	MC 209 562-7103	Valeriano Saucedo	William R Drennen	Bobbi J Paul	Kenny D Walker	Bert H Garzelli	Bert H Garzelli	Tommy C McCurdy
Live Oak (4)	MC 916 695-2112	Joseph C Berry	....	Lorie A Adams	Steven Kroeger	....	....	Donald Dosser

Directory 1/9 continued — MUNICIPAL OFFICIALS IN U.S. CITIES OVER 2,500

City, 1990 population figures (000 omitted), form of government	Municipal phone number	Mayor/ chief elected official	Appointed administrator	City clerk/ city secretary	Finance officer	Fire chief	Police chief	Public works director
CALIFORNIA (433) continued								
Livermore (57) CM	510 373-5100	Cathie Brown	Lee Horner	Carol Greany	Monica Potter	Stewart Gary	Ron Scott	John Hines
Livingston (7) CM	209 394-8041	Russ Winton	Tim Kerr	Woody Campini	Tim Kerr	....	William Eldridge	Gary Petty
Lodi (52) CM	209 334-5634	....	....	....	....	....	....	....
Loma Linda (17) CM	909 799-2800	Robert Christman	Peter Hills	P Byrnes O' Camb	John Morris	Peter Hills	....	A R Cablay
Lomita (19) CM	310 325-7110	Ben Traina	Walker J Ritter	Dawn Tomita	Walker J Ritter	....	....	....
Lompoc (38) CM	805 736-1261	....	....	....	....	....	....	....
Long Beach (429) CM	310 590-6475	....	....	....	....	....	....	....
Los Alamitos (12) CM	310 431-3538	Anthony Selvaggi	Robert Dunek	....	Richard Patino	....	Michael Skough	Victor Rollinger
Los Altos (26) CM	415 948-1491	Margaret Bruno	Dianne Gershuny	Carol Scharz	Sherry Lambach	Richard Landrum	Lucy Carlton	Bruce Bane
Los Altos Hills t (8) CM	415 941-7222	Elayne Dauber	Les M Jones	Patricia Dowd	Les M Jones	....	....	Jeff Peterson
Los Angeles (3485) MC	213 485-2121	Richard Riordan	Keith Comrie	Elias Martinez	Rick Tuttle	Donald Manning	Willie Williams	....
Los Banos (15) CM	209 827-7000	....	Charles J Martin	Sue Cardoza	Norm Staniec	Chester Guintini	Michael Hughes	Jerry Herman
Los Gatos t (27) CM	408 354-6832	Randy Attaway	David W Knapp	Marian Cosgrove	Michele Braucht	....	Larry Todd	Michael LaRocca
Lynwood (62) CM	310 603-0220	Paul H Richards	Faustin Gonzalez	Andrea Hooper	Alfretta Earnest	Gerald Wallace	....	Emilio Murga
Madera (29) CM	209 661-5400	Marc Scalzo	David Tooley	Evonne Stephenson	Sami Nassar	....	William Colston	Dave Chumley
Mammoth Lakes t (5) CM	619 934-8989	....	Glenn Thompson	Anita Hatter	Tracy Fuller	....	Bruce Mac Afee	Robert Warren
Manhattan Beach (32) CM	310 545-5621	....	....	....	....	....	....	....
Manteca (41) CM	209 239-8400	Franklin Warren	David Jinkins	Joann Tilton	Leticia Espinoza	Charles Rule	W Weatherford	Michael Brinton
Marina (26) CM	408 384-3715	Tak Takali	John L Longley	Joy Junsay	Marty Silguero	....	Roger Williams	Vince DiMaggio
Martinez (32) CM	510 372-3522	Michael Menesini	Jim Jakel	Jim Caroompas	Ronald Peterson	....	Gerald Boyd	....
Marysville (12) MC	916 741-6633	Frank J Crawford	Alan J Bengyel	Alan J Bengyel	Sherri Emitte	John H Ellis	John M Simpson	Benjamin Bramer
Maywood (28) MC	213 562-5000	Henry Santiago Jr	Ronald L Lindsey	Samuel A Pena	Michael Williams	....	Gil Bowman	....
Mc Farland (7) CM	805 792-3091	....	....	....	....	....	....	....
Mendota (7) MC	209 655-3291	Tomas Ramos	Daniel F Ayala	Rosemary Ramirez	Elena R Martin	Ernie Saldivar	Joseph Blohm	Louie Garcia
Menlo Park (28) CM	415 858-3360	....	....	....	....	....	....	....
Merced (56) CM	209 385-6834	Rich Bernasconi	James G Marshall	Dorothy Penner	Bradley Grant	Kenneth Mitten	Patrick Lunney	Nick Pinhey
Mill Valley (13) CM	415 388-4033	Catharine Barnes	Doug Dawson	Mary Herr	Debbie Mills	Peter Brundley	Peter Brindley	Ed Marshall
Millbrae (20) CM	415 259-2334	Janet Fogarty	James Erickson	Alicia Espinoza	Jeffrey Killian	Brian Kelly	Michael Parker	Lou Sandrini
Milpitas (51) CM	408 942-2310	Pete McHugh	Lawrence Moore	Gail Blalock	Lawrence Sabo	Vernon Hamilton	Charles Lawson	....
Mission Viejo (73) CM	714 582-2489	Susan Withrow	Fred Sorsabal	Ivy Joseph	Irwln Bornstein	Rich Witesman	Randy Blair	Dennis Wilberg
Modesto (165) CM	209 577-5200	Richard Lang	J Edward Tewes	Norrine Coyle	Kevin Riper	Larry Hughes	Paul Jefferson	Marshall Elizer
Monrovia (36) CM	818 359-3231	....	....	....	....	....	....	....
Montclair (28) CM	909 626-8571	Larry Rhinehart	Lee McDougal	Margaret Crawford	Ned Crutcher	Loren Pettis	Guy Eisenbrey	Carl Sawtell
Monte Sereno (3) CM	408 354-7635	Pamela Bancroft	Carolyn Lehr	A Chelemengos	Carolyn Lehr	....	....	....
Montebello (60) CM	213 887-1200	Edward C Pizzorno	....	....	....	Robert Fager	Steve Simonian	Ayyad Ghobrial
Monterey (32) CM	408 646-3761	....	....	....	....	....	....	....
Monterey Park (61) CM	818 307-1335	Judy Chu	Chris J Jeffers	David M Barron	David Dong	Ernest M Pruett	Daniel G Cross	Ronald J Merry
Moorpark (25) CM	805 529-6864	Paul Lawrason	Steve Kueny	Lillian Hare	Wayne Boyer	....	....	Kenneth Gilbert
Moraga t (16) CM	510 376-2590	....	....	....	....	....	....	....
Moreno Valley (119) CM	909 243-3000	Bonnie Flickinger	Norm King	Alicia Chavez	Rick Teichert	Bob Green	Sue Hansen	Barry McClellan
Morgan Hill (24) CM	408 779-7271	Jan Smith	David C Biggs	Betty Busk	Michael Shelton	....	Steven Schwab	Gordon Siebert
Morro Bay (10) CM	805 772-6200	William Yates	Dave Howell	Bridgett Davis	Rudy Hernandez	Jeff Jones	Dave Howell	William Boucher
Mount Shasta (3) CM	916 926-3464	Russ Porterfield	Aldo Meneni	Prudence Simon	Keith Samse	Joseph Spini	Robert Montz	Daniel Avila
Mountain View (67) CM	415 903-6309	Robert Schatz	Kevin Duggan	Koliopoulos	....	Hugh Holden	Brown Taylor	Larry Janda
Napa (62) MC	707 257-9500	....	....	....	....	....	....	....
National City (54) CM	619 336-4200	George H Waters	Tom G McCabe	Lori A Peoples	....	Randy Kimball	Kent Reesor	Curtis Williams
Needles (5) CM	619 326-2113	Roy A Mills	Leon H Berger	Leanna Keltner	Virginia Tasker	John Clark	Leroy Morgan	William Cetti
Nevada City (3) CM	916 265-2496	Paul Matson	Beryl R Robinson	C Wilcox Barnes	....	Greg Wasley	Mel McDougal	George Hill
Newark (38) CM	510 793-1400	David Smith	Paul Tong	Thelma Metcalf	Neil Grasso	....	Dennis Gleeson	....
Newman (4) CM	209 862-3725	Janet Carlsen	Stephen Hollister	Stephen Hollister	....	Mel Souza	Larry Bussard	Ernie Garza
Newport Beach (67) CM	714 644-3309	....	....	....	....	....	....	....
Norco (23) CM	714 735-6840	William Vaughan	George Lambert	Dianna Higdon	Carolyn Bartleman	Dave Carlson	....	Joseph Schenk
Norwalk (94) CM	310 929-2677	....	....	....	....	....	....	....
Novato (48) CM	415 897-4311	Cynthia Murray	Roderick Wood	Shirley Gremmels	Richard Hill	....	Brian Brady	V I Grinsteiner
Oakdale (12) CM	209 847-3031	Elmo Garcia	Bruce Bannerman	Rebecca Peluso	Margery Cruz	William Houk	David Sundy	Michael Pettinger
Oakland (372) CM	415 273-3301	....	....	....	....	....	....	....
Oceanside (128) CM	619 966-4485	....	....	....	....	....	....	....
Ojai (8) CM	805 646-5581	Joe DeVito	Andrew S Belknap	Cyndi Reynolds	Cyndi Reynolds	....	....	Warren S Moore
Ontario (133) CM	909 986-1151	Gus J Skropos	Michael Milhiser	D Arterburn	David Bentz	David Lee	Lowell Stark	Michael Teal
Orange (111) CM	714 744-2225	Gene Beyer	David F Nixon	Marilyn J Jensen	....	....	John Robertson	Frank Page
Orange Cove (6) CM	209 626-4488	....	....	....	....	....	....	....
Orinda (17) CM	510 253-4200	Aldo Guidotti	Thomas Sinclair	Mary Ellsworth	Elizabeth Stewart	....	Scott Parsons	John Lisenko
Orland (5) CM	916 865-4741	....	....	....	....	....	....	....
Oroville (12) CM	916 538-2401	....	....	....	....	....	....	....
Oxnard (142) CM	805 385-7430	....	....	....	....	....	....	....
Pacific Grove (16) CM	408 648-3100	Jeanne C Byrne	Michael W Huse	....	Peter Woodruff	Charles G Wilkins	Jon M Reither	Arthur A Andrews
Pacifica (38) CM	415 738-7300	Ellen Castelli	....	....	Pollyann Wallace	Gary Stofan	Charles English	....
Palm Desert (23) CM	619 346-0611	Roy Wilson	Bruce Altman	Sheila Gilligan	Paul Gibson	....	....	Richard Folkers
Palm Springs (40) CM	619 323-8203	Lloyd Maryanov	Rob Parkins	Judith Sumich	Thomas Kanarr	Thomas Robertson	W Valkenburg	David Strecker
Palmdale (69) CM	805 267-5100	James C Ledford	Robert W Toone Jr	Victoria Denham	William Ramsey	....	....	Steve Williams
Palo Alto (56) CM	415 329-2392	....	....	....	....	....	....	....
Palos Verdes Estates (14) CM	310 378-0383	James R Nyman	James Hendrickson	Barbara J Culver	William H Yeomans	....	Gary Johansen	Timothy D' Zmura
Paradise t (25) CM	916 872-6282	....	....	....	....	....	....	....
Paramount (48) CM	310 220-2000	Gerald Mulrooney	Patrick H West	....	....	....	....	Harry Babbitt
Parlier (8) MC	209 646-3545	Arcadio Viveros	Al Puente	Yolanda Padilla	....	....	John Moquin	Leonard Encinas
Pasadena (132) CM	818 405-4000	....	....	....	....	....	....	....
Patterson (9) CM	209 892-2041	Pat Malsetti	Jeffrey Parker	....	Edward Oborn	Richard Galser	William Middleton	Ignaclo Lopez
Perris (21) CM	909 943-6100	Judith Baitinger	James McRea	Betian Hynes	Larry L Weaver	....	Gil Olivarria	....
Petaluma (43) CM	707 778-4345	Patrica Hilligoss	John Scharer	Patricia Bernard	David Spillman	Terry Krout	Dennis Dewitt	....
Pico Rivera (59) MC	310 942-2000	Beatrice Proo	D Courtemarche	C Schaefer	Randy Rassi	....	....	Enrique Acevedo
Piedmont (11) MC	510 420-3040	Milt Kegley	Geoff Grote	Ann Swift	Mark Bichsel	R Christensen	John Moilan	Larry Rosenberg
Pinole (17) CM	510 724-9000	Mary Horton	Donald E Bradley	Elizabeth Grimes	....	Mike Radcliffe	Theodore Barnes	G Keith Freeman
Pismo Beach (8) CM	805 773-4657	....	....	....	....	....	....	....
Pittsburg (48) CM	510 439-4850	Mary Erbez	S Anthony Donato	Lillian J Pride	James F Holmes	Allen Little	Willis A Casey	Robert Soderbery
Placentia (41) CM	714 993-8141	Norman Eckenrode	Robert D' Amato	....	Howard Longballa	....	Manuel Ortega	C Becker
Placerville (8) CM	916 642-5200	Barry Wasserman	Robert W Semple	Robert Gilmore	....	....	Robert S Harmon	....
Pleasant Hill (32) CM	510 671-5270	Terri Williamson	Joseph M Tanner	Doris P Nilsen	Richard J Ricci	....	James R Nunes	Leary B Wong
Pleasanton (51) CM	510 484-8000	....	....	....	....	....	....	....
Pomona (132) CM	909 620-2051	Edward Cortez	Severo Esquivel	E Villeral	....	John Parker	....	Robert Deloach
Port Hueneme (20) CM	805 488-3625	....	....	....	....	....	....	....
Porterville (30) CM	209 782-7466	....	....	....	....	....	....	....
Portola (2) CM	916 832-4216	Joseph Moctezuma	Stacey Mac Donald	Judith Martini	....	....	....	....
Portola Valley (4) CM	415 851-1700	....	....	....	....	....	....	....

Directory 1/9 continued — MUNICIPAL OFFICIALS IN U.S. CITIES OVER 2,500

City, 1990 population figures (000 omitted), form of government		Municipal phone number	Mayor/ chief elected official	Appointed administrator	City clerk/ city secretary	Finance officer	Fire chief	Police chief	Public works director
CALIFORNIA (433) continued									
Poway (44)	CM	619 679-4232	Donald Higginson	James L Bowersox	Marjorie Wahlsten	Peggy Stewart	Mark Sanchez	....	James R Williams
Rancho Cucamonga (101)	CM	909 989-1851	Dennis Stout	Jack Lam	Debra Adams	Susan Neely	Dennis Michael	....	Wm Joe O' Neil
Rancho Mirage (10)	CM	619 324-4511	Sybil Jaffy	Patrick M Pratt	Barbara E Dohn	Scott Morgan	....	....	Eldon K Lee
Rancho Palos Verdes (42)	CM	310 377-0360	Steve Kuykendall	Paul Bussey	Jo Purcell	Brent Mattingly	....	....	Trent Pulliam
Red Bluff (12)	CM	916 527-2605	Eugene F Penne	Dennis W Fischer	Susan M Elston	Beverly Johnson	....	Richard A Bull	Gary B Antone
Redding (66)	CM	916 225-4000	Robert Anderson	R Christofferson	Connie Strohmayer	Linda Downing	Paul Bailey	Robt Blankenship	Robert Galusha
Redlands (60)	CM	909 798-7212	Swen Larson	Gary Luebbers	Lorrie Poyzer	Steve Chapman	Mel Enslow	Lew Nelson	Ron Mutter
Redondo Beach (60)	CM	310 372-1171	Brad Parton	William Kirchhoff	John Oliver	....	Patrick Aust	Melvin Nichols	Desi Alvarez
Redwood City (66)	CM	415 780-7300	....	....	....	....	....	....	....
Reedley (16)	CM	209 637-4212	Don Clark	Nick Pavlovich	Elizabeth Vines	Lori Oken	Bruce Bergthold	Forrest Brown	Mike Olmos
Rialto (72)	CM	909 820-2525	John Longville	Gerald F Johnson	Joseph H Sampson	Andrew M Green	Charles E Skaggs	Dennis J Hegwood	Richard M Scanlan
Richmond (87)	CM	510 620-6602	Rosemary Corbin	Floyd Patterson	Eula Barnes	Jay Goldstone	Floyd Cormier	William Lansdowne	Larry Loder
Ridgecrest (28)	MC	619 371-3700	....	....	....	....	....	....	....
Rio Dell (3)	CM	707 764-3532	Ernie Cannady	Earl D Wilson Jr	Earl D Wilson Jr	Earl D Wilson Jr	....	George Gatto	....
Rio Vista (3)	CM	707 374-6451	....	....	....	....	....	....	....
Ripon (7)	MC	209 599-2108	Marvin Pater	Leon Compton	Lynette Van Laar	....	....	Tom Scheidecker	Dale Ramey
Riverbank (9)	CM	209 869-3671	....	....	....	....	....	....	....
Riverside (227)	CM	714 782-5312	....	....	....	....	....	....	....
Rocklin (19)	CM	916 632-4000	George Magnuson	Carlos A Urrutia	Sandra Tocci	Rex E Miller	James Pennington	Gary A Prince	A Moosakhanian
Rohnert Park (36)	CM	707 795-2411	....	....	....	....	....	....	....
Rolling Hills (2)	CM	310 377-1521	T Heinsheimer	Craig Nealis	Craig Nealis	Nan Huang	....	....	....
Rolling Hills Estates (8)	CM	310 377-1577	....	....	....	....	....	....	....
Rosemead (52)	CM	818 288-6671	....	....	....	....	....	....	....
Roseville (45)	CM	916 774-5204	Millard L Hamel	Allen Johnson	Carolyn Parkinson	Phil E Ezell	William O White	Thomas H Simms	Larry Pagel
Ross t (2)	MC	415 453-1453	....	....	....	....	....	....	....
Sacramento (369)	CM	916 264-5704	Joseph Serna	William Edgar	Valerie Burrowes	Ken Nishimoto	Gary Costamagna	Arturo Venegas	....
Salinas (109)	CM	408 758-7201	Alan D Styles	David R Mora	Ann Camel	John Copeland	Richard Smith	Dan Nelson	John Fair
San Anselmo (12)	CM	415 258-4678	Paul Chignell	Beth Pollard	Caroline Foster	Beth Pollard	....	Bernard Del Santo	Wayne Bush
San Bernardino (164)	MC	714 384-5493	Tom Minor	Shauna Clark	Rachel Clark	Barbara Pachon	William Wright	Daniel Robbins	Roger Hardgrave
San Bruno (39)	CM	415 877-8897	Ed Simon	Frank Hedley	Terri Rasmussen	Molly Smith	Tom Ott	Frank Hedley	....
San Buenaventura (93)	CM	805 654-7800	....	....	....	....	....	....	....
San Carlos (26)	CM	415 593-8011	Tom Davids	Michael Garvey	Margaret Hanley	Brian Moura	Gene Mullins	Cliff Gerst	Parviz Mokhtari
San Clemente (41)	MC	714 361-8324	Truman Benedict	Mike Parness	Myrna Erway	....	Gene Begnell	....	Mike Sorg
San Diego (1111)	CM	619 236-6363	Susan Golding	John R McGrory	Charles Abdelnour	Patricia Frazier	Robert E Osby	Gerald R Sanders	George Loveland
San Dimas (32)	CM	909 394-6200	Terry Dipple	Donald Pruyn	Pamela Jackson	Hertha Nissel	....	....	Frank Basile
San Fernando (23)	CM	818 898-1200	....	....	....	....	....	....	....
San Francisco (724)	MC	415 554-4724	Frank Jordan	Rudolf Nothenberg	John Taylor	Edward Harrington	Joseph Medina	Anthony Ribera	John Cribbs
San Gabriel (37)	CM	818 308-2800	Sabino M Cici	P Michael Paules	Cynthia Bookter	Tracey Butler	Gene E Murry	David A Lawton	John Nowak
San Jacinto (16)	CM	714 654-7337	Henry Hafliger	Pamela S Easter	Dave Anderson	Anna Vega	Gene Price	Nat Holmes	Les Evans
San Jose (782)	CM	408 277-4000	....	....	....	....	....	....	....
San Juan Bautista (..)	CM	408 623-4661	Robert Paradice	Dennis McDuffie	George Rowe Jr	Dennis McDuffie	Rick Cokely	Harvey Nyland	Dennis McDuffie
San Juan Capistrano (26)	CM	714 493-1171	Collene Campbell	G Scarborough	Cheryl Johnson	Cynthia Pendleton	....	....	William Huber
San Leandro (68)	MC	510 577-3200	Ellen Corbett	Michael A Oliver	Alice Calvert	John Jermanis	Stephen Mikinka	Robert Maginnis	Robert Taylor
San Luis Obispo (42)	CM	805 781-7100	Peg Pinard	John Dunn	Diane Gladwell	Bill Statler	Bob Neumann	Jim Gardiner	Mike McClusky
San Marcos (39)	CM	619 744-4020	Lee B Thibadeau	Rick Gittings	Sheila A Kennedy	G L Cano	Harry Townsend	....	Richard Wygant
San Marino (13)	CM	818 300-0700	Bernard Lesage	Keith R Till	Carol Robb	....	Frank J Wills	Frank J Wills	Virgil Nichols
San Mateo (85)	CM	415 377-3350	Gerry Hill	Arne Croce	Norma Gomez	John DeRussy	Gary Schmitz	John Stangl	Arch Perry
San Pablo (25)	CM	510 215-3000	....	....	....	....	....	....	....
San Rafael (48)	CM	415 485-3070	....	....	....	....	....	....	....
San Ramon (35)	CM	415 275-2211	....	....	....	....	....	....	....
Sanger (17)	CM	209 875-2587	....	....	....	....	....	....	....
Santa Ana (294)	CM	714 647-5200	....	....	....	....	....	....	....
Santa Barbara (86)	CM	805 963-0611	Hal Conklin	Sandra Lizarraga	Sandra Lizarraga	Mark Paul	Monroe Rutherford	Richard Breza	David Johnson
Santa Clara (94)	CM	408 984-3000	Everett Souza	J Sparacino	Judy Boccignone	A K Machnick	Gerald Simon	Charles Arolla	Robert Mortenson
Santa Clarita (11)	CM	805 259-2489	George Pederson	George Caravalho	Donna Grindey	Stephen Stark	....	....	Jeffrey Kolin
Santa Cruz (49)	CM	408 429-3616	Scott Kennedy	Richard Wilson	Emma Solden	John Ness	....	....	Larry Erwin
Santa Fe Springs (16)	CM	310 868-0511	Albert L Sharp	Don R Powell	Judy A Chavez	Donald M Nuttall	Norbert Schnable	....	John R Price
Santa Maria (61)	CM	805 925-0951	George S Hobbs Jr	Wayne A Schwammel	Janet R Kalland	Michael D Cox	....	Daniel L Shiner	Reese N Riddiough
Santa Monica (87)	CM	310 458-8246	....	John Jalili	Clarice Dykhouse	Mike Dennis	Richard Bridges	James Butts	Craig Perkins
Santa Paula (25)	CM	805 933-4201	....	....	....	....	....	....	....
Santa Rosa (113)	CM	707 524-5274	....	....	....	....	....	....	....
Santee (53)	CM	619 258-4100	....	....	....	....	....	....	....
Saratoga (28)	CM	408 867-3438	Ann Marie Burger	Harry Peacock	Harry Peacock	Patricia Shriver	....	....	Larry Perlin
Sausalito (7)	CM	415 289-4100	....	....	....	Carl Tregner	Stephen Bogel	William Fraass	....
Scotts Valley (9)	CM	408 438-2324	Peggie Lopez	Chuck Comstock	Judi Coffman	Chuck Comstock	Mel Angel	Stephen Walpole	Ken Anderson
Seal Beach (25)	CM	310 431-2527	George Brown	Jerry Bankston	Joanne Yeo	E Stoddard	....	William Stearns	....
Seaside (39)	CM	408 899-6250	Lancelot McClair	Timothy Brown	Arlene Soto	Michael Brooks	Charles Streeter	C Richardson	Richard Guillen
Sebastapol (7)	CM	707 823-1153	Anne Magnie	Paul Berlant	Paul Berlant	Ron Puccinelli	John Zanzi	Dwight Crandall	Larry Koverman
Selma (15)	CM	209 896-1064	Robert L Allen	Manuel A Esquibel	Melanie Carter	Judy Bier	Roy Peak	Thomas Whiteside	Robert Weaver
Shafter (8)	CM	805 746-6361	Linda Gragg	Wade G McKinney	Dolores Robinson	Jo Barrick	....	Greg Greeson	John D Guinn
Sierra Madre (..)	CM	818 355-7135	M Mac Gillivray	Sean Joyce	N Shollenberger	David Cain	Ed Tracy	Joe Surgent	Kev Tcharkhoutian
Signal Hill (8)	CM	310 989-7300	Michael Noll	Douglas LaBelle	Kathleen Pacheco	Dennis Mac Arthur	....	Michael McCrary	Richard Lundahl
Simi Valley (100)	CM	805 583-6700	Gregory Stratton	M L Koester	....	John McMillan	....	Willard Schlieter	Ronald Coons
Solana Beach (13)	CM	619 755-2998	P Tompkins	....	Deb Harrington	Barb Underwood	William Roebuck	....	....
Soledad (7)	CM	408 678-3963	Fred Ledesma	Belinda Espinosa	....	Hector DeLa Rosa	Graig Stephens	Russ Carlsen	Clarence Nielsen
Solvang (5)	CM	805 688-5575	....	....	....	....	....	....	....
Sonoma (8)	CM	707 938-3681	Anthony Cermak	Brock Arner	Eleanor Berto	....	Michael Cahill	John Gurney	Richard Rowland
Sonora (4)	MC	209 532-4541	Claude Addison	Greg Applegate	....	Pat Perry	Guy Mills	Michael Efford	....
South El Monte (21)	MC	818 579-6540	Vera Valdiviez	Raul T Romero	Kathy L Gonzales	Lou A Delgado	....	....	Steve A Henley
South Gate (86)	CM	213 563-9500	Albert T Robles	Todd W Argow	Nina Banuelos	Karen Plover	....	Ronald George	James Biery
South Lake Tahoe (22)	CM	916 542-6050	Margo Osti	Kerry Miller	Angela Peterson	James Deaton	James Plake	David Solaro	Carol Drawbaugh
South Pasadena (24)	CM	818 799-9101	Amedee Richards	Kenneth Farfsing	Jeannine Gregory	Barbara James	William Eisele	Thomas Mahoney	James Van Winkle
South San Francisco (54)	CM	415 877-8500	Joseph Fernekes	Edward Wohlenberg	Barbara Battaya	Amy Margolis	Andrew Stark	Mark Raffaelli	Ronald Parini
St. Helena (5)	CM	707 963-2741	John Brown	Eugene Armstead	Eugene Armstead	Kevin R Plett	Ronald Ogletree	Sven Johansson	Martin Oldford
Stanton (30)	CM	714 379-9222	....	Greg Hulsizer	Darleen Cordova	John Hartman	....	....	Fred Wickman
Stockton (211)	CM	209 937-8233	Joan Darrah	Dwane Milnes	Frances Hong	L Patrick Samsell	Douglas Ratto	Edward J Chavez	James Giottonini
Suisun City (23)	CM	707 421-7300	James P Spering	Chet J Wystepek	Sharon Ventura	Sergio Fabian	John Malmquist	Ronald Forsythe	George Hicks
Sunnyvale (117)	CM	408 730-7500	Mary F Rowe	Thomas F Lewcock	Thomas F Lewcock	Amy Chan	....	Regan Williams	Marvin Rose
Susanville (7)	MC	916 257-2174	....	....	....	....	....	....	....
Taft (6)	CM	805 763-1222	Ken Knost	Eric G Ziegler	Norma Robinson	Nellie Bazzell	Vance Brannon	Charles R Scott	John W Kytola
Tehachapi (6)	CM	805 822-2200	LaVonne D Booth	Steve Minton	Kathryn L Koski	Ronald Cunningham	Antonio A Anthony	....	Dennis Wahlstrom
Temecula (35)	CM	909 694-1989	....	....	....	....	....	....	....
Temple City (31)	CM	818 285-2171	Harry Budds	Hugh Riley	Lynne Pahner	F Maldonado	....	....	William Hart

Directory 1/9 continued — MUNICIPAL OFFICIALS IN U.S. CITIES OVER 2,500

City, 1990 population figures (000 omitted), form of government	Municipal phone number	Mayor/ chief elected official	Appointed administrator	City clerk/ city secretary	Finance officer	Fire chief	Police chief	Public works director
CALIFORNIA (433) continued								
Thousand Oaks (104) .... CM	805 449-2144	Alexander T Fiore	Grant R Brimhall	Nancy A Dillon	Robert Biery	....	....	Donald Nelson
Tiburon t (8) .... CM	415 435-7373	....	Robert L Kleinert	Therese Hennessy	Richard Stranzl	....	Peter Herley	Tony Iacopl
Torrance (133) .... CM	310 540-0347	Dee Hardison	Leroy Jackson	Sue Herbers	Mary Giordano	Scott Adams	Joe DeLadurantey	Richard Garcia
Tracy (34) .... CM	209 836-2670	Clyde Bland	....	Sharon Smith	Zane H Johnston	Terrell Estes	Jared Zwickey	William Vizza
Truckee t (10) .... CM	915 582-7700	....	....	....	....	....	....	....
Tulare (33) .... CM	209 685-2300	Claude Retherford	W Lynn Dredge	W Lynn Dredge	Edwin Warren	Al Miller	Roger Hill	John Tindel
Turlock (42) .... CM	209 668-5540	Curt Andre	Steve Kyte	Rhonda Greenlee	John Dannewitz	Robert Carlson	Robert Johnson	Cliff Martin
Tustin (51) .... CM	714 573-3000	Thomas Saltarelli	William A Huston	Valerie Whiteman	Ronald Nault	....	W Doug Franks	R Ledendecker
Twentynine Palms (13) .... CM	619 367-6799	....	Jim Hart	....	....	....	....	....
Ukiah (15) .... CM	707 463-6200	Fred Schneiter	Charles Rough	Cathy McKay	Louise Burt	....	Fred Keplinger	Rick Kennedy
Union City (54) .... CM	510 471-3232	Mark Green	Karen A Smith	....	Michael Lynch	....	Albert Guzman	Lawrence Cheeves
Upland (63) .... CM	909 931-4100	Robert Nolan	Kevin Northcraft	Sheryll Schroeder	....	Gary Edwards	Gary Hart	....
Vacaville (71) .... CM	707 449-5100	....	....	....	....	....	....	....
Vallejo (109) .... CM	707 648-4527	Anthony Intintoll	Walter Graham	A Villarante	Kenneth Campo	Stephen Magliocco	Gerald Galvin	John Duane
Victorville (41) .... CM	619 955-5000	....	....	....	....	....	....	....
Villa Park (6) .... CM	714 998-1500	Barry L Denes	Fredric W Maley	J Kaysene Miller	Fredric W Maley	....	....	....
Visalia (76) .... CM	209 738-3318	Basil Perch	Ray Forsyth	Leslie Caviglia	Tim Hansen	Doug Dawson	Bruce McDermott	Britt Fussel
Vista (72) .... CM	619 726-1340	Gloria McClellan	Morris Vance	Jo Seibert	Frank E Rowlen	Roger K Purdie Sr	....	William H Bashan
Walnut (29) .... CM	909 595-7543	Bert Ashley	Linda Holmes	Beverly Sherwood	Chris Londo	....	....	John Davidson
Walnut Creek (61) .... CM	510 943-5800	....	....	....	....	....	....	....
Wasco (12) .... CM	805 758-3003	....	....	....	....	....	....	....
Waterford (5) .... MC	209 874-2328	Ernest Rockwell	L Crist	R Winter	....	R Rinehart	R Michaelsen	H Burris
Watsonville (31) .... CM	408 728-6011	Lowell Hurst	Steven M Salomon	L Washington	Eric Frost	Gary W Smith	Terrence Medina	David Koch
Weed (3) .... CM	916 938-5020	Mel Borcalli	....	D Salvestrin	M Kelly McKinnis	Darin Quigley	Martin Nicholas	....
West Covina (96) .... CM	818 814-8400	Bradley McFadden	James Starbird	Janet Berry	Abraham Koniarsky	Richard Greene	John Distelrath	Patrick Glover
West Hollywood (36) .... CM	310 854-7409	Abbe Land	Paul Brotzman	Vivian Love	Paul Arevalo	....	....	Joan English
West Sacramento (29) .... CM	916 373-5800	Wes Abeers	Joseph M Goeden	Helen M Kanowsky	Leigh P Keicher	Frederick Postel	Larry K Gore	Larry S Gossett
Westlake Village (7) .... CM	818 706-1613	....	....	....	....	....	....	....
Westminster (78) .... CM	714 898-3311	Charles V Smith	Gerald Kenny	Mary Lou Morev	Brian Mayhew	John DeMonaco	James Cook	Donald Vestal
Whittier (78) .... CM	310 945-8200	....	....	....	....	....	....	....
Willits (5) .... CM	707 459-4601	....	....	....	....	....	....	....
Willows (6) .... CM	916 934-7041	....	Russell Melquist	Russell Melquist	Sharon Barker	Bradley Mallory	Robert Shadley	Jon Barker
Windsor t (13) .... CM	707 838-1000	....	....	....	....	....	....	....
Winters (5) .... CM	916 795-4910	J Robert Chapman	Merrell Watts	Nanci G Mills	Merrell Watts	....	Steve Godden	Jon Crawford
Woodlake (6) .... CM	209 564-8055	....	Jack R Justice	Ruth Gonzalez	Alan Christensen	....	Jesse Garcia	....
Woodland (40) .... CM	916 661-5800	Gary Sandy	Kris Kirstensen	Jean Winnop	....	John Buchanan	Russell Smith	Gary Wegener
Woodside t (5) .... CM	415 851-6790	Susan Crocker	Susan George	Ruth Swanson	....	....	....	Kent Dewell
Yorba Linda (52) .... CM	714 961-7100	Barbara Kiley	Arthur Simonian	Carolyn Wallace	Vicki Baker	Larry Holmes	James E Oman	Roy Stephenson
Yountville t (3) .... CM	707 944-8851	Mary Lou Holt	Nancy Weiss	Nancy Weiss	Nancy Weiss	....	....	Nancy Weiss
Yreka (7) .... CM	916 842-4386	James Eckman	James L Dillon	James L Dillon	James L Dillon	Gene Belcastro	Don Callahan	Robert Bly
Yuba City (27) .... CM	916 741-4601	Dennis Nelson	Jeff Foltz	Robyn Kain	Colby Smith	Randy Lavelock	Roy Harmon	John Wright
Yucaipa (..) .... CM	909 797-2489	Dan Crain	John Tooker	Juanita Brown	Mikki Meith	Ray Snodgrass	Monte Lindquist	John McCarty
Yucca Valley t (..) .... CM	619 369-7207	Marge Crouter	Sue Tsuda	Jamie Anderson	Dean Beyer	....	....	....
COLORADO (88)								
Alamosa (8) .... CM	719 589-2593	....	....	....	....	....	....	....
Arvada (89) .... CM	303 431-3089	Robert G Frie	Neal G Berlin	Christine A Koch	Kelly D Colden	....	Ronald C Sloan	Ron K Culbertson
Aspen (5) .... CM	303 920-5240	John Bennett	Amy Margerum	Kathryn Koch	Steve Barwick	Ed Van Walraven	Tom Stephenson	Bob Gish
Aurora (222) .... CM	303 695-7000	Paul E Tauer	John L Pazour	Donna L Young	John Gross	Raymond E Barnes	James F Everett	Darrell R Hogan
Avon t (2) .... CM	303 949-4280	Albert Reynolds	William James	Patty Neyhart	Valerie McCoy	Charles Moore	Gary Thomas	Larry Brooks
Boulder (83) .... CM	303 441-3388	....	....	....	....	....	....	....
Breckenridge t (1) .... CM	303 453-2251	Stephen C West	Gary R Martinez	Mary Jean Loufek	Donald O Taylor	....	A Kiburas	Terry L Perkins
Brighton (14) .... CM	303 654-1643	....	....	....	....	....	....	....
Broomfield (25) .... MC	303 469-3301	....	George D DiCiero	Vicki D Marcy	J Michael Urie	....	Thomas C Deland	Marvin D Thurber
Brush (4) .... MC	303 842-5001	Lawrence Coughlin	Rod Wensing	Cathryn Smith	....	Stanley Krueger	Kenneth Baker	Rowena Pennell
Buena Vista t (2) .... MC	303 395-8643	....	....	....	....	....	....	....
Burlington t (3) .... MC	303 346-8652	....	....	....	....	....	....	....
Canon City (13) .... CM	719 269-9011	Paul Fassler	Steve Thacker	Terry Kimbrel	Jim Allan	....	Martin Stefanic	Jim Patton
Carbondale (3) .... MC	303 963-2733	William K Gray	David Farrar	Suzanne Cerise	Nancy Barnett	....	Alfred Williams	Peter Ware
Castle Rock t (9) .... CM	303 660-1015	Mark C Williams	Ronald Mitchell	Sally A Misare	Dawn Herrington	Joseph Schum	Joseph F Lane	David Hoagland
Cherry Hills Village (5) .... CM	303 789-2541	Joan R Duncan	Charles Coward	Danette Trujillo	Cheryl Bohn	....	Lester Langford	Bob Jaramillo
Colorado Springs (281) .... CM	719 578-6686	Robert Isaac	R Zickefoose	Kathryn Young	David Nickerson	Manuel Navarro	Lorne Kramer	David Zelenok
Commerce City (16) .... CM	303 289-3600	David Busby	Timothy Gagen	Betty Martin	Clarence Kissler	....	James Sanderson	Gregg Clements
Cortez (7) .... CM	303 565-3402	Gerald J Wiltgen	William A Ray Jr	E Reynolds	Kathi Moss	....	Roy Lane	Bruce Smart
Craig (8) .... CM	303 824-9151	Ronald L Ringhand	Donald R Birkner	Shirley M Seely	Albert Hays	....	David P Mawhorter	James E Pankonin
Crested Butte t (1) .... CM	303 349-5338	....	....	....	....	....	....	....
Del Norte t (2) .... MC	719 657-2708	Dennis Murphy	Patsy Moreland	Patsy Moreland	....	....	Jeff Sailee	Vern Paulsen
Delta (4) .... CM	303 874-7566	Gerald Roberts	Les Rumburg	Lynn Williams	Chris Sasse	....	Paul Suppes	Ron Alexander
Denver (468) .... MC	303 640-2613	....	....	....	....	....	....	....
Durango (12) .... CM	303 385-2800	Jasper Welch	Robert Ledger	Linda Yeager	Sherry Eilbes	Michael Dunaway	Albert Bell	Otha Rogers
Eagle t (2) .... CM	303 328-6354	....	Willy Powell	Marilene M Miller	Willy Powell	John Boyd	Phil Biersdorfer	Duston D Walls
Edgewater (5) .... MC	303 238-7803	Roger Mariola	....	....	....	Kent Johnson	Alan Pfeuffer	Robert Martin
Englewood (29) .... CM	303 762-2370	....	....	....	....	....	....	....
Estes Park t (3) .... CM	303 586-5331	H B Dannels	Gary Klaphake	V O' Connor	Monte Vavra	Jack Rumley	David Racine	William Linnane
Evans (6) .... CM	303 339-5344	Dallas Greenfield	Michael J Smith	Kim Betz	Janet Whittet	Gary Johns	Michael Guthrie	James Hewitson
Federal Heights t (9) .... MC	303 428-3526	Mark J Stickel	Eugene C Wieneke	Eugene C Wieneke	Gordon Maddock	James Kroupa	Lester Acker	Lee McDermott
Florence (3) .... CM	303 784-4848	....	....	....	....	....	....	....
Fort Collins (88) .... CM	303 221-6500	....	Steven C Burkett	Wanda Krajicek	Alan Krcmarik	John Mulligan	Fred W Rainguet	....
Fort Lupton (5) .... MC	303 857-6694	Eugene S Reynolds	Gerald Pineau	Barbara Rodgers	Bernadette Kimmey	Richard Hawley	George Ward	Ramon Hernandez
Fort Morgan (9) .... MC	303 867-3001	....	....	....	....	....	....	....
Fountain (10) .... CM	719 382-8521	Judith Christian	Roy Lauricello	Anna L Daugherty	Billy E Clark	William Owens	Larry Baldonado	William Hughes
Frisco t (2) .... CM	303 668-5276	M L Etie	Elizabeth Black	Vivian Touve	....	....	Edward Falconetti	Timothy Mack
Fruita (4) .... MC	303 858-3663	Dan Wilkie	....	Margaret Steelman	Margaret Steelman	....	Kris Monson	Jay Ingelhart
Glendale (2) .... CM	303 759-1513	Steve Ward	Gary L Sears	Jo Ann Skaggs	Jo Ann Skaggs	Richard McGowan	Kenneth E Burge	Robert Taylor
Glenwood Springs (7) .... CM	303 945-2575	Robert Zanella	Michael Copp	Pamela Oliveira	Michael Harman	James Mason	Richard Hollar	Robin Millyard
Golden (13) .... CM	303 279-3331	Marvin L Kay	Michael C Bestor	Susan Brooks	Ann Zelnio	Bob Burrell	Russ Cook	Dan Hartman
Grand Junction (29) .... CM	303 244-1511	R T Mantlo	Mark Achen	Stephanie Nye	Ronald Lappi	Michael Thompson	Darold Sloan	James Shanks
Greeley (61) .... CM	303 350-9710	William Morton	Paul Grattet	Betsy Holder	Tim Nash	Gary Novinger	Ronald Wood	William Sterling
Greenwood Village (8) .... CM	303 773-0252	David Hull	Steven Crowell Jr	Arlene Sagee	Catherine Fromm	....	Richard Waugh	....
Gunnison (5) .... CM	303 641-8000	....	Robert Filson	Peggy Anderson	Terry Lowell	Dennis Spritzer	Stu Ferguson	Ken Coleman
Hayden t (1) .... CM	303 276-3741	Richard D Roberts	Daniel Ellison	Janet L Hays	Janet L Hays	Bryan Rickman	Cyril J Lenahan	Jack A Rickman
Julesburg t (1) .... CM	303 474-3344	Larry L Jones	....	Muriel L Nelson	Muriel L Nelson	Dennis Miller	....	Allen Coyne
La Junta (8) .... CM	719 384-5991	....	....	....	....	....	....	....

Directory 1/9 continued — **MUNICIPAL OFFICIALS IN U.S. CITIES OVER 2,500**

City, 1990 population figures (000 omitted), form of government	Municipal phone number	Mayor/ chief elected official	Appointed administrator	City clerk/ city secretary	Finance officer	Fire chief	Police chief	Public works director
COLORADO (88) continued								
Lafayette (15)	CM 303 665-5588	Michael Romero	Brian Rick	Beverly Smith	M Hornbacher	Dennis James	Leo Carrillo	Tim Paranto
Lakewood (126)	CM 303 987-7700	Linda Morton	Michael Rock	Karen Goldman	Linda O' Banion	....	Charles Johnston	Richard Plastino
Lamar (8)	MC 719 336-4376	Jack Bowman	David Lock	Eric Pearson	Aleta Newman	Jeff Anderson	John Hall	Bill Thrailkill
Las Animas (2)	MC 719 456-1621	Keith E Varner	....	Leslie J Uncel	....	....	Jerry L Butler	John F Trent
Leadville (3)	MC 303 486-0349	....	....	....	....	....	....	....
Limon t (2)	CM 719 775-2346	....	....	....	....	....	....	....
Littleton (34)	CM 303 795-3700	Reynolds Dennis	Andrew McMinimee	Janice Owen	James Woods	Mike Doyle	Craig Camp	Charles Blosten
Longmont (52)	CM 303 776-6050	Leona Stoecker	Gordon Pedrow	Valeria Skitt	James Golden	Steve Trunck	Mike Butler	Barbara Huner
Louisville (12)	CM 303 666-6565	Tom Davidson	....	Margaret Kemper	Asti Caranci	....	Bruce Goodman	Thomas Phare
Loveland (37)	CM 303 962-2000	....	....	....	....	....	....	....
Manitou Springs (5)	MC 719 685-5481	Gherald Ford	James G Pratt	Jeanie Greenman	....	Steve Hart	John Humphrey	Gary Smith
Meeker t (2)	CM 303 878-5344	Jon Hertzke	Sharon Day	Carmen Orris	....	....	Si Woodruff	Dwight Frantz
Monte Vista (4)	CM 719 852-2692	Robert W Olme	Arthur Scibelli	Lucille M Duran	Elaine M Johnsen	....	Frank Martinez	Tony Martinez
Montrose (9)	CM 303 249-4534	....	....	....	....	....	....	....
Morrison t (..)	MC 303 697-8749	....	....	....	....	....	....	....
Northglenn (27)	CM 303 451-8326	Donnie Parsons	James Landeck	Joan Baker	Scott Wright	....	C A Gunderson	Bruce Shipley
Pagosa Springs t (..)	MC 303 294-4151	Ross Aragon	Jay Harrington	Jackie Schick	....	....	Don Volger	....
Palisade tp (2)	CM 303 464-5602	Roger Granat	Larry Clever	Glenda Noble	Larry Clever	Danny Mudge	Greg Kuhn	Larry Clever
Pueblo (99)	CM 719 584-0800	....	....	....	....	....	....	....
Rangely t (2)	MC 303 675-8476	Frances Green	Donald Peach	Daniel Cooley	Daniel Cooley	....	Gerald Reese	John Kenney
Rifle (5)	CM 303 625-2121	David Ling	David Hawker	Ellen Berggren	Nancy Black	....	Daryl Meisner	Bob Whittington
Rocky Ford (4)	MC 719 254-7414	....	....	....	....	....	....	....
Salida (5)	MC 719 539-2311	....	....	....	....	....	....	....
Sheridan (5)	MC 303 762-2200	....	....	....	....	....	....	....
Silverthorne t (2)	CM 303 468-2637	Tom Long	Dallas Everhart	Patty Bierle	....	....	Greg Morrison	Bill Linfield
Snowmass Village t (1)	CM 303 923-3777	....	....	....	....	....	....	....
Steamboat Springs (7)	CM 303 879-2060	William Martin	Harvey Rose	Deborah Carey	Brian Funderburk	James Haugsness	Roger Jensen	Kirk Madsen
Sterling (10)	CM 303 522-9700	Billy G Finch	Randy Gustafson	James Thompson	James Thompson	Charles Miner	Lawrence Graham	Joseph D Kiolbasa
Telluride t (1)	CM 303 728-3071	....	....	....	....	....	....	....
Thornton (55)	CM 303 538-7243	M Carpenter	Jack Ethridge	Nancy Vincent	Keith Tillman	....	James Nursey	Chester Elliot
Trinidad (9)	CM 719 846-9843	....	....	....	....	....	....	....
Vail t (4)	CM 303 479-2100	Peggy Osterfoss	Bob McLaurin	Holly McCutcheon	Steve Thompson	Dick Duran	Ken Hughey	Larry Grafel
Walsenburg (3)	MC 719 738-1048	Jay D Crook	....	P Sterk Conder	H C Summers	Curtis Montoya	Octaviano Vigil	....
Westminster (75)	CM 303 430-2400	Nancy Heil	Bill Christopher	Michele Gallegos	Susann Stubbs	Jim Cloud	Daniel Montgomery	Ron Hellbusch
Wheat Ridge (29)	MC 303 234-5900	Dan Wilde	Robert C Middaugh	Wanda Sang	....	....	Jack Hurst	Robert Goebel
Windsor t (5)	CM 303 686-7476	Thomas Jones	Glen E Welden	Jeanne Nazarenus	....	....	John Michaels	Dennis Wagner
Winter Park t (1)	CM 303 726-8081	Nick Teverbaugh	Daryl Shrum	Nancy Anderson	....	....	....	Tom Russell
Woodland Park (5)	CM 719 687-9246	Clarke D Becker	Don E Howell	Cindy Morse	Cindy Morse	....	John W Hogue	Jim Schultz
Wray (2)	CM 303 332-4431	Pete Brophy	Robert Snedeker	Chuck Murphy	Robert Snedeker	....	Rick Schorzman	Randy Wells
Yuma (3)	CM 303 848-3878	Donald R Starnes	Jim Drinkhouse	Ronda J Wright	Jim Drinkhouse	Dan Baucke	Fred Gonzalez	James Wyrsch
CONNECTICUT (151)								
Ansonia (18)	MC 203 736-5900	....	....	....	....	....	....	....
Ashford t (4)	TM 203 429-2750	William Falletti	....	Barbara B Metsack	....	R Whitehouse	....	John A Balazs
Avon t (14)	CM 203 677-2634	Richard W Hines	Philip K Schenck	Caroline Lamonica	Glenn S Klocko	Harvey Reeser	James A Martino	Rudolph W Fromm
Barkhamsted t (3)	TM 203 379-8285	C Lattizori	Harreit Boyko	Nancy Winn	....	Richard Winn	C Lattizori	Joseph Marek
Beacon Falls t (5)	TM 203 729-4340	Leonard D' Amico	....	Paula Balanda	....	William Lee	Leonard D' Amico	Frank Del Vecchio
Berlin t (17)	TM 201 828-7004	Robert Peters	Janice Serafino	....	Gary Clinton	....	Gerald Charamut	Morgan Seelye
Bethany t (5)	TM 203 393-2100	....	....	....	....	....	....	....
Bethel t (18)	MC 203 794-8501	Clifford Hurgin	....	Jane Shannon	Barry Curina	....	John Basile	Hemraj Khona
Bethlehem t (3)	TM 203 266-7677	Robert Gallo	....	Lucy Palangio	....	Gerald Zarrella	....	James Kacerguis
Bloomfield t (19)	CM 203 769-3538	Faith McMahon	Louie Chapman	M Phillips	William Bailey	....	Anthony Magno	David Gofstein
Bolton t (5)	MC 203 649-8066	Michael W Eremita	John C Guinan	Susan Depold	....	James Preuss	....	Dan Rattazzi
Branford t (28)	RT 203 488-8394	Judy E Gott	....	Georgette Laske	Richard Belden	Peter Buonome	William Holohan	Edward Masotta
Bridgeport (142)	MC 203 576-7600	....	....	....	....	....	....	....
Bristol (61)	MC 203 584-7600	Frank N Nicastro	....	....	Theodore Hamilton	Anthony D Basile	William R Kohnke	Ronald H Smith
Brookfield t (14)	TM 203 775-7300	Bonnie P Smith	....	Ruth B Burr	Raymond Bolek	....	John W Anderson	Ronald Klimas
Brooklyn t (7)	TM 203 779-3411	Donald S Francis	....	Leona A Mainville	Steven Townsend	....	....	Leonard Albee
Burlington t (7)	TM 203 673-6789	....	....	....	....	....	....	....
Canterbury t (4)	TM 203 546-9377	Raymond A Guillet	....	....	Donna M Sharp	....	....	David Veit
Canton t (8)	TM 203 693-4093	Kathleen C Corkum	Terence Sullivan	Shirley Krompegal	Richard Mahoney	....	John LaDucer	Richard Negro
Cheshire (26)	CM 203 271-6660	....	....	....	....	....	....	....
Chester t (3)	TM 203 526-9553	....	....	....	....	....	....	....
Clinton t (13)	TM 203 669-9333	....	....	....	....	....	....	....
Colchester t (11)	TM 203 537-3461	....	....	....	....	....	....	....
Columbia t (5)	TM 203 228-0110	Adella G Urban	....	Eleanor Vickers	Paula Stahl	Jerry James	Adella G Urban	Peter Naumec
Coventry t (10)	CM 203 742-6324	Richard Ashley	John A Elsesser	Ruth E Benoit	John A Elsesser	....	Frank Trzaskos	William Camosci
Cromwell t (12)	TM 203 632-3410	....	....	....	....	....	....	....
Danbury (66)	MC 203 797-4598	Gene F Eriquez	Basil Friscia	E Crudginton	Dominic Setaro	John Murphy	Nelson Macedo	John Schweitzer
Danielson b (4)	RT 203 774-0067	Terry O Sandsbury	....	Bernice Gendreau	Denise A King	....	....	....
Darien t (18)	RT 203 656-7300	....	....	....	....	....	....	....
Deep River t (4)	TM 203 526-6020	Richard H Smith	....	Jeanne Nickse	....	David Steve	Richard H Smith	Richard H Smith
Derby (12)	MC 203 734-9201	Alan Schlesinger	....	Joan Williamson	....	Anthony Gianpoalo	Andrew Cota	Gary Parker
Durham t (6)	TM 203 349-3452	....	....	....	....	....	....	....
East Granby t (4)	TM 203 653-2576	Charles W Chatey	....	E Birmington	....	C Edward Chatey	....	....
East Haddam t (7)	TM 203 873-5020	Susan Merrow	....	Maryjane Plude	....	John Blaschik	....	Andrew Tierney
East Hampton t (10)	CM 203 267-4468	Robert Heidel	Alan H Bergren	Pauline Markham	Carol Souppa	P Visintainer	Eugene Rame	Robert Drewry
East Hartford t (50)	MC 203 291-7100	R DeCrescenzo	Paul Fetherston	Ann Fornabi	Barbara Avard	David Dagon	James Shay	Roger Mullins
East Haven t (26)	MC 203 468-3204	Henry J Luzzi	Louis A Zullo	Elizabeth Leary	Carl Tomchik	Wayne Sandford	James Crisiuolo	Anthony Ferraro
East Lyme t (15)	TM 203 739-6931	....	....	....	....	....	....	....
East Windsor t (10)	TM 203 623-8122	....	....	....	....	....	....	....
Easton t (6)	TM 203 268-6291	....	....	....	....	....	....	....
Ellington t (11)	TM 203 875-0787	....	....	....	....	....	....	....
Enfield t (46)	CM 203 745-0371	Ann Petronella	A Louis Hayward	S Olechnicki	V Santacroce	....	Herbert Foy	Walter Markett
Essex t (6)	TM 203 767-4348	Bruce Glowac	....	Betty Gaudenzi	Richard Gamble	Paul Fazzino	....	Bruce Glowac
Fairfield t (53)	RT 203 256-3000	P Audley	....	M Toth	J Leahy	D Gardiner	R Sullivan	R White
Farmington t (21)	CM 203 673-8200	B Stockwell	Thomas Wontorek	....	....	Vincent DiPietro	Leroy Bangham	James Bonini
Glastonbury t (28)	CM 203 652-7710	Sonya Googins	Richard J Johnson	Ed Friedeberg	G Ted Ellis	....	James Thomas	....
Granby t (9)	CM 203 653-8950	Roger A Hernsdorf	William F Smith	Carol J Smith	Helen C Laraway	Allen Christensen	Jeremiah P Marron	William P Lyons
Greenwich t (58)	RT 203 622-7710	....	....	....	....	....	....	....
Griswold t (10)	TM 203 376-2521	Roland Harris	....	Ellen Dupont	....	....	....	Roland Harris
Groton t (45)	CM 203 441-6600	....	....	....	....	....	....	....
Groton (10)	MC 203 441-2103	....	....	....	....	....	....	....

Directory 1/9
continued

**MUNICIPAL OFFICIALS
IN U.S. CITIES OVER 2,500**

City, 1990 population figures (000 omitted), form of government	Municipal phone number	Mayor/ chief elected official	Appointed administrator	City clerk/ city secretary	Finance officer	Fire chief	Police chief	Public works director
CONNECTICUT (151) continued								
Guilford t (20)	TM 203 453-8015	....	....	....	....	....	....	....
Haddam t (7)	TM 203 345-8531	Marjorie W Debold	....	....	....	....	....	Philip Goff
Hamden t (52)	MC 203 287-2500	....	....	....	....	....	....	....
Hartford (140)	CM 203 722-6340	....	....	....	....	....	....	....
Harwinton t (5)	TM 203 485-9051	Marie M Knudsen	....	P Williamsen	....	....	....	....
Hebron t (7)	TM 203 228-9406	....	....	....	....	....	....	....
Jewett City b (3)	MC 203 376-2443	William Maynard	....	Stephen Stanek	....	Donald Ouillette	Thurston Fields	....
Killingly t (16)	CM 203 774-8601	David Griffiths	R Thomas Homan	Joan Cyr	Michelle Weiss	....	....	....
Killingworth t (5)	TM 203 663-1765	....	....	....	....	....	....	....
Lebanon t (6)	TM 203 642-6100	....	....	....	....	....	....	....
Ledyard t (15)	MC 203 464-8740	Joseph Lozier	Gloria Hosmer	Patricia Karns	Anna Johnson	....	Joseph Lozier	Joseph Lozier
Lisbon t (4)	TM 203 376-3400	....	....	....	....	....	....	....
Litchfield t (8)	TM 203 567-5133	Craig A Miner	....	Evelyn N Goodwin	Steven Hoff	....	Craig A Miner	David P Thompson
Madison t (15)	TM 203 245-5602	Thomas R Rylander	....	Elizabeth Lynch	....	....	James Cameron	S Mac Millan
Manchester t (52)	CM 203 647-3126	....	Richard Sartor	Edward Tomkiel	Alan Desmarais	John Rivosa	Henry S Minor	Peter Lozis
Mansfield t (21)	CM 203 429-3336	....	....	....	....	....	....	....
Marlborough t (6)	TM 203 295-9547	Howard T Dean Jr	....	Ethel Fowler	....	William Lord	....	Thomas Giola
Meriden (59)	CM 203 630-4123	Joseph Marnian	Roger Kemp	Irene Masse	Edward Murphy	Robert Raby	Robert Kosienski	Joseph Franco
Middlebury t (6)	TM 203 758-1770	Edward B St John	....	Alicia H Ostar	James W Henderson	Edmond Bailly	Patrick Bona	....
Middlefield t (4)	MC 203 349-7114	David G Webster	....	Linda R DeMaio	....	Terry Parmelee	David G Webster	John Wyskiel
Middletown (43)	MC 203 344-3401	....	....	....	....	....	....	....
Milford (48)	MC 203 783-3200	....	....	....	....	....	....	....
Monroe t (17)	MC 203 452-5400	Kenneth S Heitzke	....	T Inderdohnen	Jeffry Whone	....	Robert Wesche	Sherwood Lovejoy
Montville t (17)	MC 203 848-3030	Wayne D Scott	....	Margaret Skinner	M Shillsberg	....	....	David King
Naugatuck t (31)	MC 203 729-4571	Robert Paolino	Brian Powell	Kara Keating	John Tedesco	William Mallane	Ned Clisham	Hank Witkowski
New Britain (75)	MC 203 826-3303	....	....	....	....	....	....	....
New Canaan t (18)	TM 203 972-2311	....	....	....	....	....	....	....
New Fairfield t (13)	TM 203 746-8101	Cheryl D Reedy	....	Diana Peck	Gail R Redenz	....	....	Thomas Dube
New Hartford t (6)	TM 203 379-3389	....	....	....	....	....	....	....
New Haven (130)	MC 203 787-8200	....	....	....	....	....	....	....
New London (29)	CM 203 447-5201	Jane Glover	Richard M Brown	Clark Vander Lyke	Donald E Gray Jr	Ronald Samul	Bruce Rinehart	....
New Milford t (24)	MC 203 355-6000	....	....	....	....	....	....	....
Newington t (29)	CM 203 666-4661	Rodney Mortensen	Keith H Chapman	Roberta Jenkins	Joam McGovern	....	Richard Klett	Keith H Chapman
Newtown t (21)	MC 203 270-4201	....	....	....	....	....	....	....
North Branford t (13)	CM 203 488-7203	....	....	....	....	....	....	....
North Canaan t (3)	TM 203 824-7313	Douglas Humes Jr	....	Carolyn O' Connor	....	....	....	Brad R Shook
North Haven t (22)	TM 203 239-5321	Anthony Rescigno	....	Elinor Pedalino	Vincent Palmeri	John Obier	Kevin Connolly	Richard Branigan
North Stonington t (5)	TM 203 535-0793	....	....	....	....	....	....	....
Norwalk (78)	MC 203 854-7900	Frank Esposito	....	Kathryn C Senle	Jack Miller	John Yost	Carl LaBianca	Dominick DiGangi
Norwich (37)	CM 203 886-2381	Harry Jackson	William Tallman	Beverly Muldoon	A San Quedolce	Thomas Kirby	Richard Abele	Walter Wadja
Old Lyme t (7)	TM 203 434-1605	....	....	....	....	....	....	....
Old Saybrook t (10)	TM 203 388-3401	....	....	....	....	....	....	....
Orange t (13)	TM 203 795-0751	Dorothy L Berger	....	Jean V Mitchell	....	Kenneth Mitchell	Joseph Rowley	Jack Kazmarski
Oxford t (9)	TM 203 888-2543	Edward Oczkowski	Carl Serus	C Koskelowski	....	Scott Pelletier	Edward Oczkowski	....
Plainfield t (14)	TM 203 564-4071	....	....	....	....	....	....	....
Plainville t (17)	CM 203 793-0221	Elizabeth Boukus	John P Bohenko	Peter Lennon	Judy Doneiko	Joseph Watkins	Francis Roche	Caryl Bradt
Plymouth t (12)	MC 203 585-4002	....	....	....	....	....	....	....
Pomfret t (3)	TM 203 974-0191	....	....	....	....	....	....	....
Portland t (8)	TM 203 342-2880	Parke C Spicer	....	Hattie Wucik	Morris Fishbone	....	....	Parke C Spicer
Preston t (5)	TM 203 887-5581	....	....	....	....	....	....	....
Prospect t (8)	MC 203 758-4461	R J Chatfield	....	Pat Vaillancourt	R J Chatfield	Ronald Wislocki	....	R J Chatfield
Putnam (9)	MC 203 928-5529	....	....	....	....	....	....	....
Putnam t (..)	TM 203 963-6800	Daniel Rovero	....	Lillian Newth	....	Norman A Bernier	Edward J Perron	Gerard Beausoleil
Redding t (8)	TM 203 938-2002	Henry Bielawa	....	Patricia Creigh	Mary Anne Wiesner	....	....	Roger Harker
Ridgefield t (21)	TM 203 431-2775	Sue Manning	....	Dora Cassavechia	Jay Wahlber	Richard Nagle	Thomas Rotunda	Frank Serfilippi
Rocky Hill t (17)	CM 203 258-2700	Donald W Unwin	O Paul Shew	Barbara R Gilbert	Robert W Metcalf	Harry Kelly	Philip Dunn	Gerry DeRubbo
Salisbury t (4)	TM 203 435-9140	Louis J Trotta Jr	....	Joseph Cleaveland	....	Donald Reid	....	....
Seymour t (14)	TM 203 888-2511	....	....	....	....	....	....	....
Sharon t (3)	MC 203 364-5789	P Robert Moeller	....	Linda Wasley	....	....	....	....
Shelton (35)	MC 203 924-1555	Mark A Lauretti	Sandra Nesteriak	....	Louis Marusic	Richard Tallberg	Robert White	Paul DiMauro
Simsbury t (22)	TM 203 651-3751	....	....	....	....	....	....	....
Somers t (9)	TM 203 763-8200	Robert Percoski	....	Claire Walker	....	Edward Pagani	Robert Percoski	Knneth Anderson
South Windsor t (22)	MC 203 644-2511	Richard Ryan	Jean E Zurbrigen	Liana Kuras	George Spring	William Lanning	Gary Tyler	Michael Gantick
Southbury t (16)	TM 203 264-0606	....	John Weichsel	....	....	....	....	....
Southington t (39)	CM 203 276-6225	....	John Weichsel	....	Edward Brickett	Thomas Murphy	William Perry	Joseph Yurcak
Sprague t (3)	TM 203 822-3000	Thomas McAvoy Jr	....	Mary M Stefon	....	....	....	....
Stafford t (11)	TM 203 684-2130	....	....	....	....	....	....	....
Stafford Springs b (4)	TM 203 684-3827	....	....	....	....	....	....	....
Stamford (108)	MC 203 977-4068	Stanley Esposito	....	Lois Pont Briant	Patrick O' Connor	Ronald Graner	G Patrick Tully	Michael Pavia
Stonington t (17)	TM 203 535-4721	....	....	....	....	....	....	....
Stratford t (49)	CM 203 385-4007	....	Mark Barnhart	P Ulatowski	Edward Gomeau	Roger Macey	Robert Mossman	Michael Hudzik
Suffield t (11)	TM 203 668-7397	....	....	....	....	....	....	....
Thomaston t (7)	TM 203 283-4421	Eugene McMahon	....	Catherine Dupont	....	....	Edward Grabherr	Gerald Grohoski
Thompson t (9)	TM 203 923-9561	....	....	....	....	....	....	....
Tolland t (11)	CM 203 871-3600	....	....	....	....	....	....	....
Torrington (34)	MC 203 489-2228	....	....	....	....	....	....	....
Trumbull t (32)	MC 203 452-5000	....	....	....	....	....	....	....
Vernon t (30)	MC 203 872-8591	Edward Slattery	Robert Dotson	Terri Krawczyk	James Luddecke	Robert Kelley	Rudolf Rossmy	Sherwood Aborn
Wallingford t (41)	MC 203 294-2080	William Dickinson	....	Kathryn Wall	Thomas Myers	Wayne Lefebvre	Douglas Dortenzio	Henry McCully
Washington t (4)	TM 203 868-2786	Alan J Chapin	....	Doris K Welles	....	Mark Lyon	....	....
Waterbury (109)	MC 203 574-6890	Edward D Bergin	Francis Sullivan	Patrick T Drewry	Michael Maunsell	Thomas F Brennan	Edward F Bergin	J Robert Carroll
Waterford t (18)	RT 203 442-0553	....	....	....	....	....	....	....
Watertown t (20)	CM 203 274-5411	....	J Salomone	D Larosa	F Nardelli	O Burrows	J Carroll	P Deleppo
West Hartford t (60)	CM 203 523-3220	Sandra Klebonoff	Barry M Feldman	Nan Glass	Donna Sims	Michael Parker	James Strillacci	Raymond Brignano
West Haven (54)	MC 203 937-3500	H Richard Borer	R Annunziata	William Donegan	Thomas S Hamilton	....	Michael Kelly	Arthur C Ferris
Westbrook t (5)	TM 203 399-6236	Raymond L Jones	....	Tanya Lane	....	....	....	John P Riggio
Weston t (9)	TM 203 222-2656	George C Guidera	Rosemary Cashman	Cynthia Williams	Rosemary Cashman	Frederick Moore	Anthony Land	Joseph Lametta
Westport t (24)	RT 203 226-8311	Joseph P Arcudi	....	Joan Hyde	Donald Miklus	Richard Gough	W Chiarenzelli	Stephen Edwards
Wethersfield t (26)	CM 203 721-2801	Daniel Camilliere	Lee C Erdmann	Dorcas McHugh	Joe Swetcky	John McAuliffe	John Karangekis	Joe Hart
Willington t (6)	TM 203 429-5649	....	....	....	....	....	....	....
Wilton t (16)	TM 203 834-9200	....	....	....	....	....	....	....
Winchester t (12)	CM 203 379-2713	....	....	....	....	....	....	....
Windham t (22)	MC 203 456-3593	....	....	....	....	....	....	....

Directory 1/9 continued

MUNICIPAL OFFICIALS IN U.S. CITIES OVER 2,500

City, 1990 population figures (000 omitted), form of government	Municipal phone number	Mayor/ chief elected official	Appointed administrator	City clerk/ city secretary	Finance officer	Fire chief	Police chief	Public works director
CONNECTICUT (151) continued								
Windsor t (28)	CM 203 688-3675	....	....	....	....	....	....	....
Windsor Locks t (12)	TM 203 627-1444	....	....	....	....	....	....	....
Winsted (..)	MC 203 379-2713	John F Gauger Jr	Paul S Vayer	William T Riiska	Henry L Centrella	John Fratini	Robert Brautigam	Patrick E Hague
Wolcott t (14)	MC 203 879-4666	....	....	....	....	....	....	....
Woodbridge t (8)	TM 203 387-6639	....	....	....	....	....	....	....
Woodbury t (8)	TM 203 263-2141	K Campbell	....	J Sandulli	R Belden	E Kiessling	....	E Lizauskas
Woodstock t (6)	TM 203 928-0208	....	....	....	....	....	....	....
DELAWARE (13)								
Bethany Beach t (..)	CM 302 539-8011	Charles Bartlett	Dean S Phillips	Dean S Phillips	Madalyn J Forrest	....	Clifford Graviet	James Seabrease
Delmar t (1)	CM 410 896-2777	....	....	....	....	....	....	....
Dover (28)	CM 302 736-7000	James L Hutchison	James O' Connor	Debrah J Boaman	Manubhai C Karia	Raymond Osika	Richard J Smith	Richard Scrafford
Elsmere t (6)	CM 302 998-2215	....	....	....	....	....	....	....
Laurel t (3)	MC 302 875-2277	G P Volenik	W S Hitch	D Adkins	R O' Neal	....	J A Harris	A Atkins
Middletown t (4)	MC 302 378-2711	....	....	....	....	....	....	....
Milford (6)	CM 302 422-6616	....	....	....	....	....	....	....
New Castle (5)	CM 302 322-9801	....	....	....	....	....	....	....
Newark (25)	CM 302 366-7000	Ronald Gardner	Carl Luft	Susan Lamblack	Patrick McCullar	....	William Hogan	Richard Lapointe
Rehoboth Beach (1)	CM 302 227-6181	....	....	....	....	....	....	....
Seaford (6)	CM 302 629-9173	G Longo	D Slatcher	S Drugash	....	....	R Miller	J Hedrick
Smyrna t (5)	CM 302 653-3483	George C Wright	Michael S Jacobs	....	....	....	Donald H McGinty	William E Hamburg
Wilmington (72)	MC 302 571-4011	....	....	....	....	....	....	....
DISTRICT OF COLUMBIA								
(607)	MC 202 727-1000	Marion Barry	....	....	....	....	....	....
FLORIDA (240)								
Alachua (5)	CM 904 462-1231	Cleather Hathcock	Charles Morris	Darlene Bond	Francine Jernigan	....	Freddie Dampier	Paul O' Dea
Altamonte Springs (35)	CM 407 830-3800	J Dudley Bates	Phillip D Penland	Patsy Wainright	Mark DeBord	Thomas Siegfried	William A Liquori	Donald Newnham
Apalachicola (3)	MC 904 653-9319	....	....	....	....	....	....	....
Apopka (14)	CM 407 889-1700	John H Land	John H Land	Connie V Major	Jack H Douglas	Richard Anderson	Robert Campbell	....
Arcadia (6)	CM 813 494-4114	Roosevelt Johnson	Edward Strube	Margaret Way	....	Anthony Messina	Bruce Collins	James Bussey
Atlantic Beach (12)	CM 904 247-5800	Lyman T Fletcher	Kim D Leinbach	Maureen King	Ann Meuse	Walter P Rew Jr	David Thompson	Robert S Kosoy
Atlantis (2)	CM 407 965-1744	Clyde F Farmer	E Earl Moore	Betty A Yon	Majella Thornton	....	Robert G Mangold	Steve Mazuk
Auburndale (9)	CM 813 965-5500	....	....	....	....	....	....	....
Avon Park (8)	CM 813 452-2221	....	....	....	....	....	....	....
Bal Harbour v (3)	MC 305 866-4633	....	....	....	....	....	....	....
Bartow (15)	CM 813 533-0911	Reginald Floyd Sr	Joseph J Delegge	Victoria L Troup	John A Nickels	Tim Pitts	M L Roy McKinsey	William Pickand
Bay Harbor Islands t (5)	CM 305 866-6241	Edward Tavlin	Linda Karlsson	Ellen Umans	Cecil Rash	....	John Ross	Kenneth Cassel
Bay Lake (..)	MC 305 828-2034	....	....	....	....	....	....	....
Belle Glade (16)	CM 407 996-0100	Steve Weeks	Lomax Harrelle	Sue Teets	Teresa Guzman	Tony Tuliano	Michael Miller	Mickey McGahee
Belle Isle (5)	MC 407 851-7730	Charles R Scott	Linda M Davidson	Linda M Davidson	Linda M Davidson	....	....	....
Belleair t (4)	CM 813 584-7134	....	....	....	....	....	....	....
Belleair Bluffs (2)	MC 813 584-2151	John E Diller	....	B L Hendrickson	....	....	James W Mangum	David R Sexsmith
Biscayne Park v (3)	CO 305 893-7490	....	....	Patricia A Cerny	Patricia A Cerny	....	Barry J Noe	Thomas S Nunn
Blountstown (2)	CM 904 674-5488	Finley Corbin	Grant Gentry	Grant Gentry	Grant Gentry	Harvey Grantham	Robert W Deason	Grant Gentry
Boca Raton (61)	CM 407 393-7700	....	....	....	....	....	....	....
Bonifay (3)	MC 904 547-4238	....	....	....	....	....	....	....
Boynton Beach (46)	CM 407 375-6000	Edward Harmening	Carrie Parker	Sue Kruse	Grady Swann	Floyd Jordan	Thomas Dettman	Robert Eichorst
Bradenton (44)	MC 813 748-0800	William Evers	....	Paul Esquinaldo	....	Vernon Horne	Vic Badalaminti	Earl Crawley
Brooksville (7)	CM 904 544-5400	John C Tucker	James B Malcolm	Karen M Phillips	Donald E Manges	James E Adkins	Boyce E Tincher	Lyle Titterington
Bushnell (..)	CM 904 793-2591	Joe P Strickland	Vince R Ruano	Judith C Muller	Judith C Muller	....	James D Reed	Ronald D Pitts
Callaway (12)	MC 904 872-7780	Hubert L Rodgers	Judy S Cumbest	Judy S Cumbest	Judy S Cumbest	Tommy J Walls	....	Donald J Minchew
Cape Canaveral (8)	CM 407 868-1200	Joy C Salamone	Bennett Boucher	Faith G Miller	Deborah Haggerty	....	....	Michael Gluskin
Cape Coral (75)	CM 813 574-0401	Roger G Butler	David Sallee	Eula Jorgensen	Howard D Kunik	Thomas Kochheiser	Arnold A Gibbs	Stephen K Kiss
Casselberry (19)	MC 407 831-3551	J Hillebrandt	Jack Schluckebier	Thelma McPherson	Jeffrey Dreier	Paul Algeri	Durbin Gatch	Anthony Segreto
Chattahoochee (4)	MC 904 663-4046	....	....	....	....	....	....	....
Chipley (4)	MC 904 638-6350	....	....	....	....	....	....	....
Clearwater (99)	CM 813 462-6870	....	....	....	....	....	....	....
Clermont (7)	CM 904 394-4081	Robert Pool	Wayne Saunders	....	Joseph Van Zile	Carle Bishop	Prentice Tyndal	Preston Davis
Clewiston (6)	CO 813 983-9191	....	....	....	....	....	....	....
Cocoa (18)	CM 407 639-7585	Lester Campbell	Stephen J Bonczek	Beth A Dabrowski	James R Holt	Fredrick Seawell	Richard H Masten	Wm H Stephenson
Cocoa Beach (12)	CM 407 868-3333	Joseph Morgan	Mark Eckert	Lori Kalaghchy	Janice Bourne	....	Robert Walker	Raj Verma
Coconut Creek (27)	CM 305 973-6770	Ron Greenstein	John Kelly	Angela Bender	Harry Kilgore	....	George Raggio	Scott Sundermeier
Cooper City (21)	CM 305 434-4300	....	....	....	....	....	....	....
Coral Gables (40)	CM 305 446-6800	Raul Valdes Fauli	H C Eads Jr	Virginia Paul	Donald Nelson	David Teems	James Butler	Aurelio Linero
Coral Springs (79)	CM 305 344-1150	....	....	....	....	....	....	....
Crestview (10)	MC 904 682-6131	Ted Mathis	....	Edward Neal	....	Joseph Traylor	Maxie Barrow	General Cox
Crystal River (4)	CM 904 795-4216	Curtis A Rich Sr	Therese C Leary	Shirley L Carroll	George Zoettlein	Brown Dumas Jr	Roger B Krieger	Russell Kreager
Dade City (6)	CM 904 523-5050	Charles McIntosh	Richard Diamond	James Class	James Class	Robert Cabot	Phillip Thompson	Ronald Ferguson
Dania (13)	CM 305 921-8700	Robert Mikes	Robert Flatley	Wanda Mullikin	Marie Jabalee	Thomas Grammer	....	Cliff Taylor
Davenport (..)	CM 813 422-4410	Peter Rust	Wm G Drummond	Marge Williams	F Paula Munro	Fred L Stewart Jr	H B Robinson	Lovit H White
Davie t (47)	CM 305 797-1030	Joan Kovac	Irving Rosenbaum	Gail Reinfeld	....	....	....	....
Daytona Beach (62)	CM 904 258-3187	Paul Carpanella	....	G Azama Edwards	James C Maniak	....	Paul B Crow	T McClelland
Daytona Beach Shores (2)	CM 904 322-5000	....	....	....	....	....	....	....
De Funiak Springs (5)	CM 904 892-8500	Harley Henderson	Michael Standley	Dorothy Donald	Sara Wilson	Bill Yearwood	Clint Hooks	....
De Land (16)	CM 904 738-3900	....	....	....	....	....	....	....
Deerfield Beach (46)	CM 305 480-4200	Albert Capellini	....	Muriel W Rickard	David P Bok	Thomas M Boylston	....	John E Vogel
Delray Beach (47)	CM 407 243-7080	Thomas E Lynch	David T Harden	Alison Harty	Joseph Safford	Robert Rehr	Richard Overman	Richard Corwin
Destin (8)	CM 904 837-4242	Gary Alden	Philip Cook	Lee Garrett	Sandra Zepp	....	....	....
Dundee t (..)	CM 813 439-1086	....	....	....	....	....	....	....
Dunedin (34)	CM 813 733-4151	....	....	....	....	....	....	....
Eagle Lake (2)	CM 813 293-4141	Martin Kellner	Linda Weldon	Linda Culpepper	....	Frank Kehoe	J R Sullivan	Robert Johnson
Edgewater (15)	CM 904 428-3245	Jack Hayman	George McMahon	Susan Wadsworth	Fred Munoz	William Vola	L Schumaker	Hugh Williams
Eustis (13)	MC 904 483-5472	Evelyn Smith	Mike Stearman	Jim Myers	Jim Myers	....	Robert Templin	Chin Khor
Fernandina Beach (9)	CM 904 277-7320	Charles Albert	Larry Myers	Vicki Cannon	May Edwards	William Vanzant	Walter Sturges	Jim Higginbotham
Florida City (6)	CM 305 247-8221	Otis T Wallace	....	Meighan Pier	Mark Ben Asher	....	Earnie Neal	....
Fort Lauderdale (149)	CM 305 761-5000	Jim T Naugle	George L Hanbury	Lucy Olmezer	Damon R Adams	Donald W Harkins	Thomas McCarthy	....
Fort Meade (5)	CM 813 285-8191	Donald R True	William Emmerich	William Emmerich	William Emmerich	Bill Gunter	George M Ferris	....
Fort Myers (45)	MC 813 332-6775	....	....	....	....	....	....	....
Fort Pierce (37)	CM 407 460-2200	W Dannahower	James Powell	Cassandra Steele	George Bergalis	....	....	Robert Morgan
Fort Walton Beach (21)	CM 904 243-3141	Larry Trenary	....	....	Gail Abraham	Ron Williams	Phil Irlsh	Monty Jackson
Frostproof (3)	CM 813 635-2151	John Durant	Roger A Hood	Lillian Amerson	Roger A Hood	Raymond Chatlos	J Neal Byrd	David F Hand

Directory 1/9 continued — MUNICIPAL OFFICIALS IN U.S. CITIES OVER 2,500

City, 1990 population figures (000 omitted), form of government	Municipal phone number	Mayor/ chief elected official	Appointed administrator	City clerk/ city secretary	Finance officer	Fire chief	Police chief	Public works director
FLORIDA (240) continued								
Fruitland Park (3) CM	904 787-6089	William R White	Robert D Proctor	Linda S Rodrick	Lisa M Absher	Thomas L Gamble	J M Isom Sr	Barry J Landstedt
Gainesville (85) CM	904 334-2011	....	....	....	....	....	....	....
Golden Beach t (1) MC	305 932-0744	....	....	....	....	....	....	....
Graceville (3) CO	904 263-3250	....	....	....	....	....	....	....
Green Cove Springs (4) CM	904 284-5621	James Loner	Richard Manfredi	M Robertson	Sue E Heath	Richard Knoff	Gail S Russell	Walter H Rountree
Greenacres City (19) CM	407 642-2000	Samuel J Ferreri	David B Farber	Sondra K Hill	David R Miles	....	John T Treanor	Robert R Flemming
Gulf Breeze (6) CM	904 934-5100	....	....	....	....	....	....	....
Gulfport (12) CM	813 321-1158	....	....	....	....	....	....	....
Haines City (12) CM	813 422-4986	....	....	....	....	....	....	....
Hallandale (31) CM	305 458-3251	Eudyce Steinberg	R J Intlndola	June Depp	Mark Antonio	....	Kenneth Wagner	John Depp
Havana t (2) CM	904 539-6493	T J Davis	Susan Freiden	Anne T Bert	Anne T Bert	Don C Vickers	Phil Fusilier	....
Hialeah (188) MC	305 883-8052	....	....	....	....	....	....	....
Hialeah Gardens (8) MC	305 558-4114	George Hameetman	....	Janice A Tuzzio	George Hameetman	....	Glenn Sime	Pablo Garcia
Highland Beach t (3) CM	407 278-4548	Arlin Voress	Mary Ann Mariano	Anne Kowals	Michael Seaman	....	William Cecere	....
Holly Hill (11) CM	904 947-4120	L Virginia Wine	Ralph K Hester	Sue W Blackwell	Brenda Gubernator	Robert E Lacy	John P Finn	Marcus E Chattin
Hollywood (122) CM	305 921-3218	....	Samuel Finz	Martha Lambos	Susan Miller	James Ward	Richard Witt	Greg Turek
Holmes Beach (5) MC	813 778-2221	Rich Bohnenberger	....	Leslie Ford	....	....	Jay Romine	John Fernandez
Homestead (27) CM	305 247-1801	J W DeMilly	William Rudd	Velva J Burch	H Montes DeOca	....	Curtis K Ivy	Michael Tavano
Indlalantlc t (3) CM	407 723-2242	Bill Vernon	Edward Gross	Carolyn Hazelgrov	Carolyn Hazelgrov	Tom Barker	....	John Eddy
Indlan Creek v (..) CM	305 865-4121	Kenneth Fisher	Kathy Kartsonakis	Susan Doyle	....	....	Rudy Piedra	....
Indlan Harbor Beach (7) CM	407 773-3181	Stephen D Hand	Richard G Edgeton	Ruth H Grigsby	Loren L Rueter	James H Nolan Sr	Frederick Fernez	Gilbert G Grignon
Indlan River Shores t (2) CM	407 231-1771	Robert Schoen	Joseph Dorsky	Virginia Gilbert	Joseph Dorsky	....	Thomas Boisvert	Joseph Dorsky
Indlan Rocks Beach (4) CM	813 595-2517	....	....	....	....	....	....	....
Inverness (6) CM	904 726-2611	Orien J Humphries	Bruce D Banning	Marilyn C Jordan	Joseph Levesque	....	William Vitt	Daniel Sawyer
Jacksonville (635) MC	904 630-1178	....	....	....	....	....	....	....
Jacksonville Beach (18) CM	904 247-6263	William Latham	William Lewis	Bruce Corbitt	Harry Royal	Gary Brown	Bruce Thomason	Stanley Nodland
Jasper (..) CM	904 792-1212	....	....	....	....	....	....	....
Juno Beach t (2) CM	407 626-1122	Frank W Harris	Gail F Nelson	Deborah S Manzo	Joseph F Lo Bello	....	Mitchell L Tyre	Dennis W Barrett
Jupiter t (25) CM	407 746-5134	Karen Golonka	Lee R Evett	Sally M Boylan	Michael A Simmons	....	Richard Westgate	James C Davis
Jupiter Island t (1) CM	407 546-5011	....	....	....	....	....	....	....
Kenneth City t (4) MC	813 544-6655	Harold M Paxton	....	Joan D Musgrave	....	John Karpinecz	Jeff Walkowiak	....
Key Biscayne v (9) CM	305 365-5511	John Festa	C S Kissinger	Guido Inguanzo	Jack Neustadt	W Huddleston	Michael Flaherty	....
Key West (25) CM	305 294-3721	Dennis Wardlow	G Felix Cooper	Josephine Parker	E David Fernandez	Edwin Castro	E R Peterson	P Howanitz
Kissimmee (30) CM	407 847-2821	John B Pollett	Mark E Durbin	Sandra L Yeager	Kenneth Killgore	Larry K Bell	Frank J Ross	George W Mann Jr
Lady Lake t (..) CM	904 753-2212	Lee W Hokr	Robert K McKee	Ellie Whigham	Patricia Land	....	Michael Ross	James Richards
Lake Alfred (4) CM	813 956-3434	Larry Clark	James D Drumm	Ellen M Newbern	....	Larry Cloud	Bruce Efurd	Rudy Banick
Lake Buena Vista (..) CM	407 828-2241	....	....	....	....	....	....	....
Lake City (10) CM	904 752-2031	....	....	....	....	....	....	....
Lake Clarke Shores t (3) MC	407 964-1515	Robert Shalhoub	Stuart Liberman	Joann Hatton	Stuart Liberman	....	Michael Bruscell	....
Lake Mary (6) CM	407 324-3000	Lowry E Rockett	John C Litton	Carol A Foster	Randy B Knight	Duane G Mehl	Richard M Beary	C W Bill Temby
Lake Park t (7) CM	407 848-3460	William H Wagner	George A Long	Barbara Scheihing	Tim W Howard	....	Jeffery Lindskoog	Brian J Sullivan
Lake Wales (10) CM	813 676-2533	....	....	....	....	....	....	....
Lake Worth (29) CM	407 586-1600	....	....	....	....	....	....	....
Lakeland (71) CM	813 499-6007	Ralph L Fletcher	Eugene Strickland	Paula K Hoffer	Jerry Reynolds	Jimmy M Hyatt	Sam V Baca	R Michael Herr
Lantana t (8) CM	407 582-9094	Robert McDonald	Ron Ferris	Mabel D Weiland	Allan Owens	Joseph Coates	Robert Chalman	Dan Reidy
Largo (66) CM	813 587-6700	Thomas D Feaster	Steven B Stanton	Jean P Scott	Kimball R Adams	Daniel J Fries	Richard Kistner	Christian Kubala
Lauderdale Lakes (27) MC	305 731-1212	Alfonso Gereffi	....	Audrey Tolle	....	Cosimo Ricciardi	....	Clifford Goodin
Lauderdale-by-the-Sea t (3) CM	305 776-0576	Thomas D McKane	Phin Horton	Beverly Greene	....	....	Gerald E Leighton	William R Mason
Lauderhill (50) MC	305 739-0100	Ilene Lieberman	....	Muriel Trombley	Donald Giancoli	Charles Faranda	Michael Scott	Jack Clement
Leesburg (15) CM	904 728-9700	David Connelly	Rex A Taylor	James Williams	James Williams	James Works	Charles Idell	Charles L Langley
Lighthouse Point (10) MC	305 943-6500	....	....	....	....	....	....	....
Live Oak (6) MC	904 362-2276	Angus P Nott	J Myron Holmes	Wm J McCullers	Caroline Leonard	Howard Wright	....	Willard Hewiett
Longboat Key t (6) CM	813 383-3721	....	....	....	....	....	....	....
Longwood (13) CM	407 260-3440	....	....	....	....	....	....	....
Lynn Haven (9) CM	904 265-2121	Robert A Gardner	....	Patricia Mercer	Sharon Faile	Jerry Blount	David Messer	....
Macclenny t (4) CM	904 259-6261	T J Raulerson	Gerald Dopson	....	....	Daniel Dugger	....	W Kirkland
Madeira Beach (4) CM	813 391-9951	Tom DeCesare	John M Mulvihill	Denise M Schlegel	Alan Braithwaite	Brian J Turini	Archie B Hatcher	S Thomas Corbett
Madison (3) CM	904 973-4181	Lucy H Pride	Gilbert Donaldson	Pearlie M Pearce	Pearlie M Pearce	Raymond Pinkard	Dennis R White	Bill B Raines
Maitland (9) CM	407 539-6200	Robert Breaux	Phillis Holvey	Donna Williams	William Jones	Daniel Hardester	Edward Doyle	Anthony Leffin
Manalapan t (..) CM	407 585-9477	G Kent Shortz	Charles H Helm	Elizabeth Miller	Beulah G Irwln	....	William W Smith	Mark T Hull
Margate (43) CM	305 972-6454	Mitchell Anton	Leonard Golub	Shirley Baughman	Gail Gargano	Francis Porcella	J Bordenkircher	James Hinds
Marianna (6) CM	904 482-4353	....	....	....	....	....	....	....
Mary Esther t (4) CM	904 243-3566	Randy Stokes	Charles F Dubyak	Cornelia B Taylor	....	Ronald J McArtor	Jeffrey Arrowood	John O Hofstad
Melbourne (60) CM	407 727-2900	Joseph Mullins	....	Zella Gaston	Amy Elliott	Walter Chamberlin	Keith Chandler	Ray Niemi
Melbourne Beach t (3) CM	407 724-5860	James Kelley	William Washburn	Connie Smith	William Washburn	Bill Roffey	Steven Walters	Vince Powers
Miami (359) CM	305 579-6666	....	....	....	....	....	....	....
Miami Beach (93) CM	305 673-7524	Seymour Gelber	Roger Carlton	Roger Brown	Robert Nachlinger	Thomas Sullivan	Lou Guasto	Domingo Rodriguez
Miami Shores v (10) CM	305 758-8000	....	....	....	....	....	....	....
Miami Springs (13) CM	305 885-4581	John A Cavalier	Frank R Spence	Magali Valls	Larry W Napier	....	Earl C Steffen	John W Bergacker
Midway (..) MC	904 574-2355	David M Watson	Chris B Canty	Karen Fitzgerald	....	Randy Harvey	M LaChapelle	....
Milton (7) MC	904 623-3661	Clyde L Gracey	Wm R Whitson	Dewitt Nobles	....	Wm Densmore	R K Young	....
Miramar (41) CM	305 989-6200	Vicki Coceano	Eric M Soroka	Betty Tarno	Stanley Hochman	Michael Murphy	George Atkinson	Lawrence Keating
Monticello (3) MC	904 997-3312	....	....	....	....	....	....	....
Mount Dora (7) CM	904 735-7100	P Alexander	Bernice S Brinson	....	James Schuster	Edward L Spann	Emory B Putman	Rod J Stroupe
Mulberry (3) CM	813 425-1125	Frank R Satchel	Floyd Woods	Patricia Jackson	Floyd Woods	Mitch Carmack	John Hunter	O C Henderson
Naples (20) CM	813 434-4670	Paul Muenzer	Richard Woodruff	Janet Cason	William Harrison	....	Paul C Reble Jr	Danny Mercer
Neptune Beach (7) CM	904 241-3191	....	....	....	....	....	....	....
New Port Richey (14) CM	813 841-4520	....	....	....	....	....	....	....
New Smyrna Beach (17) CM	904 424-2107	George Musson	Frank Roberts	....	Bill Poling	Mike Kelly	Denver Fleming	Melvin Phillips
Niceville (11) CM	904 729-4000	....	....	....	....	....	....	....
North Bay Village (5) CM	305 756-7171	Paul Vogel	James Dipietro	Beatris Arguelles	Patricia Sieber	....	Maynor F Harrell	Micheal Berkman
North Lauderdale (27) CM	305 722-0900	Jack Brady	John Stunson	Milli Dyer	Mark Bates	Rudy Neumann	James Uhde	Micheal Shields
North Miami (50) CM	305 893-6511	Mike Colodny	Lawrence Casey	Simon Bloom	Thomas Schnieders	....	Kenneth Each	Alfred Signore
North Miami Beach (35) CM	305 948-2918	Jeffrey Mishcon	Michael Roberto	Sol Odenz	Marilyn Spencer	....	William Berger	Gary Brown
North Palm Beach v (11) CM	407 848-3474	Gail Vastola	Dennis Kelly	Kathleen Kelly	Shaukat Khan	John Armstrong	Bruce Sekeres	Charles O' Meilia
North Port (12) CM	813 426-8484	Ben Hardin	Robert L Norris	Doris Briggs	Ann Marie Ricardi	Paul G Raskey	David Yurchuck	John J Singer
Oakland Park (26) CM	305 561-6250	Douglas Johnson	....	Carol Gold	Elbert Wrains	Mark Nehiba	Edward Overman	Harry Wimberly
Ocala (42) CM	904 629-8535	Henry Speight	Scotty J Andrews	Mary Jane Milam	Glen Baker	William E Woods	A L McGehee	Charles Amerman
Ocean Ridge t (2) CM	407 732-2635	....	....	....	....	....	....	....
Ocoee (13) CM	407 656-2322	S Van Der Grift	Ellis Shapiro	Jean Grafton	Montye Beamer	Ron Strosnider	....	Ray Brenner
Okeechobee (5) CM	813 763-3372	James E Kirk	John J Drago	Bonnie S Thomas	Lola B Parker	L Keith Tomey	Larry Mobley	Charles Elders
Oldsmar (8) MC	813 855-4693	Jerry Provanzano	Bruce T Haddock	Cheryl Mortenson	Marguerite Burns	Scott McGuff	....	Fred Schildhauer
Opa-Locka (15) CM	305 688-4611	Robert Ingram	L Dennis Whitt	Ronetta Taylor	Neva Reed	....	Melvin L Tooks	Harold Little

Directory 1/9 continued

MUNICIPAL OFFICIALS IN U.S. CITIES OVER 2,500

City, 1990 population figures (000 omitted), form of government	Municipal phone number	Mayor/ chief elected official	Appointed administrator	City clerk/ city secretary	Finance officer	Fire chief	Police chief	Public works director
FLORIDA (240) continued								
Orange City (5)	CM 904 775-3333	Anthony Yebba	Robert Mearns	Linda Fulp	Robert Hague	C Sievert	Arthur Locke	Milton Moritz
Orange Park t (9)	CM 904 264-9565	Edna Griffith	John W Bowles	Joyce G Bryan	Dorothy S Mollnow	....	John C Nelson	William J White
Orlando (165)	MC 407 246-2235	Glenda E Hood	Howard D Tipton	Grace A Chewning	Michael Miller	Robert A Bowman	Thomas D Hurlburt	David L Metzker
Ormond Beach (30)	CM 904 677-0311	Dave Hood	Eugene Miller	Marian Maxwell	Paul Lane	Ronald Jacobs	Robert Stewart	Theodore Mac Leod
Oviedo (11)	CM 407 366-7000	Judy Green	V E Williford	Cindy Bonham	....	Wayne Martin	Dennis Peterson	Charles Smith
Pahokee t (7)	CM 407 924-5534	Ramon Horta Jr	Kenneth N Schenck	Debra N Palmer	William Thrasher	Gary C Burroughs	Carmen Salvatore	Bruce W Miller
Palatka (10)	CM 904 329-0100	Tim Smith	Allen R Bush	Allen R Bush	Allen R Bush	Rudy Howard	Dan R Thies	....
Palm Bay (63)	CM 407 952-3400	Melton Broom	Michael Abels	Alice Passmore	....	David Greene	Paul Rumbley	Robert Nanni
Palm Beach t (10)	CM 407 838-5400	Paul Ilyinsky	Robert Doney	Grace Peters	Marie Crozier	Vincent Elmore	J L Terlizzese	Albert Dusey
Palm Beach Gardens (23)	CM 407 775-8250	David Clark	Bobbie Herakovich	Linda Kosier	Kent Olson	Ed Arrants	James Fitzgerald	Bob Patty
Palm Springs v (10)	CM 407 965-4010	Richard H Jette	Patrick D Miller	Irene L Burroughs	Rebecca L Morse	....	E W Hoagland	William A Leasure
Palmetto (9)	MC 813 723-4570	Gorden Dole	Linda Stearns	Linda Stearns	Susan Dann	....	C Mead Britt	Allen Tusing
Panama City (34)	CM 904 872-3009	Girard L Clemons	Kenneth R Hammons	Michael Bush	....	Terrel Hartzog	David Slusser	Joseph Villadsen
Parker (5)	MC 904 871-4104	....	....	....	....	....	....	....
Parkland (4)	CM 305 753-5040	Sal Pagliara	Harry J Mertz	Susan Armstrong	Judith C Kilgore	....	Ronald Bailey	....
Pembroke Park t (5)	CO 305 966-4600	....	....	....	....	....	....	....
Pembroke Pines (65)	CM 305 431-4500	Charles Flanagan	Charles Dodge	Eileen Tesh	Rene Gonzalez	Vito Splendorio	Martin Rahinsky	Martin Gayeski
Pensacola (58)	CM 904 435-1662	....	Rodney L Kendig	Shirley Law	James Marling	James Dixon	Louis Goss	Helen Chalk
Perry (7)	CM 904 584-7161	Thomas Demps	Wiliam E Brynes	....	Daniel T Porta	Rodney L Lytle	Herman N Putnal	Barney E Johnson
Pinellas Park (43)	CM 813 541-0700	Cecil Bradbury	Ronald Forbes	Grace Kolar	M McGarrity	Kenneth Cramer	David Milchan	Jerry Halstead
Plant City (23)	CM 813 757-9144	Michael Sparkman	....	Martin Wisgerhof	Martin Wisgerhof	Robert Rounds	Troy Surrency	Steve Cottrell
Plantation (67)	MC 305 797-2240	Frank Veltri	....	Barbara Showalter	Robert Brekelbaum	Robert Pudney	Clarence Sharrett	Joseph Spero
Polk City t (1)	CM 813 984-1375	....	....	....	....	....	....	....
Pompano Beach (72)	CO 305 786-4626	Elijah Larking	L McNerney	Mary Chambers	Michael Vizzi	James Bentley	Stanley Tipton	James Pavlick
Ponce Inlet t (2)	CM 904 767-3425	....	Robert C Burns	....	....	....	....	....
Port Orange (35)	CM 904 761-8000	James E Ward	Kenneth W Parker	Kenneth W Parker	John A Shelley	Michael L Ertz	Robert E Ford	Warren J Pike
Port Richey (3)	MC 813 845-7800	Roger Naused	Warren Knowles	Shirley Dresch	....	Tim Fussell	Al Latchford	Al Foley
Port St. Joe (4)	CM 904 229-8261	....	....	....	....	....	....	....
Port St. Lucie (56)	CM 407 871-5225	Robert Minsky	Donald Cooper	Sandra Johnson	Frank Blackwell	....	Charles Reynolds	Cliff Burgess
Punta Gorda (11)	CM 813 575-3302	Rufus Lazzell	William Brady	Ellen Diomedes	Willard Beck	Ed Keeler	Ralph Shoud	Ernie Miles
Quincy (7)	CM 904 627-7681	....	....	....	....	....	....	....
Riviera Beach (28)	CM 407 845-4000	Clara K Williams	Gerald Adams	Gwendolyn Davis	Dennis Widlansky	Richard Wester	Jerry Poreba	....
Rockledge (16)	CM 407 690-3978	John Oates	James McKnight	Betsi Moist	David Henderson	Richard Nix	Richard Kallis	Jimmy Gilliard
Royal Palm Beach v (15)	CM 407 790-5100	Anthony Mas	John Max Weaver	Mary Anne Gould	Peggye Kujanpaa	Karl Combs	Jeff Waites	Chris Stewart
Safety Harbor (15)	CM 813 726-0780	Kent Runnells	Pam Brangaccio	Bonnie Haynes	Joanne Ryan	Wm Jay Stout	....	Kurt Peters
Sanford (32)	CM 407 330-5600	Bettye Smith	William Simmons	Janet Donahoe	Carolyn Small	J Thomas Hickson	Ralph Russell	Robert Herman
Sanibel (5)	CM 813 472-3700	Jerrold A Muench	Gary A Price	....	Renee M Lynch	....	Richard H Plager	Gates D Castle
Sarasota (51)	CM 813 954-4134	Leonore Patterson	D R Sollenberger	Billy E Robinson	Gibson E Mitchell	Julius E Halas	Gordon R Jolly	Gilbert J Leacock
Satellite Beach (10)	CM 407 773-4407	Linda Tisdale	Michael P Crotty	Mary Rogers	Norma Tetrault	Daniel Rocque	Lionel Cote	Vernon McKinney
Sebastian (10)	CM 407 589-5330	Arthur L Firtion	Joel L Koford	K O' Halloran	Marilyn Swichkow	....	Earle Petty	Daniel Eckis
Sebring (9)	MC 813 471-5100	Smith J Rudasill	Robert Hoffman	Shirley Kitchings	....	R E DeLoach	Robert Glick	....
Seminole (9)	MC 813 391-0204	....	....	....	....	....	....	....
South Bay (4)	CO 407 996-6751	Clarence Anthony	Lester Baird	Virginia Walker	Virginia Walker	Roy Humston	Roy Humston	Allen Davis
South Daytona (12)	CM 904 322-3000	Joe Piggotte	Joseph Yarbrough	Patricia Northrup	Robert Holmquist	....	Gary White	Mark Juliano
South Miami (10)	CM 305 663-6300	Neil Carver	William F Hampton	Rosemary Wascura	Hakeem K Oshikoya	....	Perry S Turner	C Patterson
South Pasadena (6)	CO 813 347-4171	Fred G Held	....	Diane E Orloff	D R Perkins	Joseph Novak	....	James Frain
Springfield (9)	MC 904 785-9516	....	....	....	....	....	....	....
St. Augustine (12)	CM 904 825-1005	Gregory E Baker	Joseph Pomar Jr	Paula B Owens	T Burchfield	Jay P Kennedy	William Robinson	Jack E Cubbedge
St. Augustine Beach (4)	MC 904 471-2122	....	....	....	....	....	....	....
St. Cloud (12)	CM 407 892-2161	Ernest G Gearhart	J Paul Wetzel	J Pat Purdy	Michael M Turner	Charlie P Lewis	Leo S Watko Jr	Mark S Luthie
St. Petersburg (239)	CO 813 893-7111	David J Fischer	Richard B Dodge	Jane K Brown	Richard L Ashton	Jerry G Knight	Darrel W Stephens	George W Webb
St. Petersburg Beach (9)	CM 813 367-2735	Michael Horan	Jeffrey Stone	Jane Ellsworth	Stephen Gallaher	Charles Hartman	Thomas Lange	Charles Ames
Starke (5)	CO 904 964-5027	....	....	....	....	....	....	....
Stuart (12)	CM 407 288-5300	Dennis Armstrong	David B Collier	Dianne O' Donnell	William Underwood	Louis Pappitto	Joan Waldron	Dodd Southern
Sunrise (64)	CM 305 741-2580	....	....	....	....	....	....	....
Surfside t (4)	CM 305 861-4863	Paul Novack	Hal Cohen	Jeffrey Naftal	....	....	T Williamson	Chip Cohen
Sweetwater (14)	MC 305 221-0411	Matilde Aguirre	....	Marie Schmidt	Maria Denis	....	Rafael Hernandez	Donald Pucci
Tallahassee (125)	CM 904 891-8120	Penny Shaw Herman	Daniel A Kleman	Robert Inzer	Philip Inglese	Tom Quillin	Tom Coe	....
Tamarac (45)	CM 305 722-5900	N Abramowitz	R S Noe	Carol A Evans	Stanley Hawthorne	James Budzinski	....	Vernon Hargray
Tampa (280)	MC 813 274-8968	Sandy W Freedman	George Pennington	Janett Martin	John Harrell	William Austin	Bennie Holder	Jack Morriss
Tarpon Springs (18)	MC 813 942-5612	Anita E Protos	Carey F Smith	Kathy Alesafis	Robert Bublitz	Alwyn J Carr	Mark G Lecouris	Stanley M Emerson
Tavares (7)	CM 904 742-6220	Eugene Glenn	Tony Otte	Mary Carney	Glenn Irby	Charles Sowers	Nobert Thomas	Charlene Foster
Temple Terrace (16)	CM 813 989-7100	Robert F Woodard	Thomas J Bonfield	Patricia A Jones	Daniel R Klein	James W Bailey	Tom M Matthews	Robert Fernandez
Tequesta v (4)	CM 407 575-6200	Ron T Mackail	Thomas G Bradford	Joann Manganiello	Bill C Kascavelis	James Weinand	Carl R Roderick	Gary Preston
Titusville (39)	CM 407 269-4400	Thomas R Mariani	Randall H Reid	Karan Rounsavall	George Baldwin	Thomas A Harmer	Jerry E Eads	Richard W Lemke
Treasure Island (7)	CM 813 360-0811	Walter Stubbs	Peter Lombardi	Peter Lombardi	Darren LaFrance	Charles Fant	Jos Pelkington	Melton Odom
Valparaiso (5)	MC 904 729-5402	John B Arnold Jr	Alan Gage	Faye B Floyd	John B Arnold Jr	Randy Wilke	Lomax Donaldson	Claude Vanderford
Venice (17)	CM 813 485-3311	Merle L Graser	George N Hunt	Lori A Stelzer	Michael McPhail	Roy C Williams	Joseph P Slapp	Lawrence A Heath
Vero Beach (17)	CM 407 567-5151	Caroline D Ginn	Thomas R Nason	Phyllis Neuberger	Stephen J Maillet	....	James M Gabbard	....
Wakulla (14)	CM 904 926-8876	Sharon Thompson	....	Harold Thurdmond	Harold Thurdmond	Chester Murray	David F Harvey	Cleave Fleming
Wauchula (3)	MC 813 773-3131	Henry Graham	Jerry Conerly	Mavis F Best	....	....	Joey E Brock	Warren E May Jr
West Melbourne (8)	CM 407 727-7700	William A Lane	Mark K Ryan	Janice E Daniels	Charlotte Luikart	....	Brian K Lock	T Ray Bullard
West Miami (6)	CM 305 266-1122	....	....	....	....	....	....	....
West Palm Beach (68)	CO 407 659-8000	Nancy Graham	Michael Wright	....	Elizabeth Bloeser	James Carman	Billy R Riggs	Lee Collum
Wildwood (3)	CM 904 748-0302	Ed Wolf	James R Stevens	Joseph Jacobs	Joseph Jacobs	Thomas L Smart	Don Clark	Eugene Koregay
Wilton Manors (12)	CM 305 390-2100	King Wilkinson	Donald B Lusk	Angela D Scott	Lisa C Rabon	Richard Rothe	Stephen Kenneth	Wm Joe Moss
Winter Garden (10)	CM 407 656-4111	Jack Quesinberry	Hollis Holden	Helen Duckwiler	Betty Swann	Roy LaBossiere	Jimmie Yawn	M Robertson
Winter Haven (25)	CM 813 291-5600	Eleanor Threlkel	Robert C Cheatham	Sarah Lee Shumate	Calvin T Bowen	Charles E Brown	Ronald S Martin	Dale Smith
Winter Park (22)	CM 407 623-3292	Gary A Brewer	James S Williams	Joyce M Swain	Julie Hopper	Dennis M Sargent	James D Younger	....
Winter Springs (22)	CM 305 327-1800	....	....	....	....	....	....	....
Zephyrhills (8)	CM 813 788-2313	James Bailey	Floyd Nichols	Linda Boan	Cathy Familo	Robert Hartwig	William Eiland	Rick Moore
GEORGIA (158)								
Acworth (5)	MC 404 974-3112	Robert Gibson	Ali Bring	Frana Brown	....	....	....	Joseph Griffis
Adel (5)	CM 912 896-2821	....	....	....	....	....	....	....
Albany (78)	CM 912 431-3234	Paul Keenan	Roy Lane	J P Pope	Nelson Rushton	H L Fields	J H Lumpkin Sr	R E Merton
Alma (4)	CM 912 632-8072	....	....	....	....	....	....	....
Alpharetta (13)	CM 404 475-9566	Jimmy Phillips	Michael Wilkes	Sue Rainwater	Linda Dunlap	William Bates	Gordon Dillon	Jarvis Middleton
Americus (17)	MC 912 924-4411	Russell Thomas Jr	Sybil Smith	Charlotte Cotton	....	Stephen Moreno	Edwin Williams	Ronny Smith
Ashburn (5)	MC 912 567-3431	Charles Perry	James Lee	Sandra Strickland	Tina Woodruff	Billy Ray Royal	James Davis	Donald Padgett
Athens (46)	CM 706 613-3090	Gwen O' Looney	H R Crider	Gloria J Spratlin	John S Culpepeer	Wendell Faulkner	Ronald M Chandler	Donald M Loomis
Atlanta (394)	MC 404 330-6000	....	....	....	....	....	....	....
Augusta (45)	MC 706 821-1700	Charles Devaney	Charles Dillard	Lena J Bonner	Aurelia Epperson	Willie L Maddox	Austin McLane	Clifford Goins

Directory 1/9
continued

**MUNICIPAL OFFICIALS
IN U.S. CITIES OVER 2,500**

City, 1990 population figures (000 omitted), form of government	Municipal phone number	Mayor/ chief elected official	Appointed administrator	City clerk/ city secretary	Finance officer	Fire chief	Police chief	Public works director
GEORGIA (158) continued								
Austell (4)	MC 404 944-4300	Joe Jerkins	....	Delores Lockridge	Delores Lockridge	Tim Williams	Clyde Hardin	Clay Hays
Avondale Estates (2)	CM 404 294-5400	John W Lawson	John B Parker	Phyllis D Flowers	....	....	....	....
Bainbridge (11)	CM 912 248-2000	B K Reynolds	Charles B Tyson	William Lanier	William Lanier	Dennis Mock	Larry Funderburk	Tommy King
Barnesville (5)	CM 404 358-0181	James R Matthews	Kenneth D Roberts	Carolyn S Parker	Kenneth D Roberts	Charles Jamerson	Stanley R Rodgers	....
Baxley (4)	CM 912 367-8300	Hilton D Baxley	Jeffrey P Baxley	Jean W Spell	....	Mickey Bass	James Godfrey	David Gore
Blackshear (3)	MC 912 449-7000	Brooks Hampton	Myra Bolden	Myra Bolden	Myra Bolden	Herbert Barber	George Smiley	Herbert Barber
Blakely (6)	MC 912 723-3677	Guy H Dunaway	N Dale Bryant	Sterling P Jones	Sterling P Jones	Kenneth Jones	Charles Middleton	....
Bowdon (2)	MC 706 258-8980	....	....	....	....	....	....	....
Bremen (4)	MC 404 537-2331	....	....	....	....	....	....	....
Brunswick (16)	CM 912 267-5500	....	....	....	....	....	....	....
Buford (9)	CM 404 945-6761	....	....	....	....	....	....	....
Cairo (9)	CM 912 377-1722	....	....	....	....	....	....	....
Calhoun (7)	MC 404 629-0151	....	....	....	....	....	....	....
Camilla (5)	CM 912 336-2220	Jimmy Davis	....	Kathy N Baker	....	Lazelle McCook	Ray Folsom	Mike Pollock
Canton (5)	CM 404 479-2421	James A Cannon	Eddie McCollum	Diana Threewitt	....	Bob Junk	Brad Pope	Tommy Worley
Carrollton (16)	MC 404 830-2000	Joe McGinnis	Danny N Mabry	Jewell Mashburn	....	Casey Coleman	Barry Carroll	Stan Brown
Cartersville (12)	CM 404 387-5684	Alex T Dent	James H Nalley Jr	Helen W Oglesby	Helen W Oglesby	....	James R Willbanks	Roy Southern
Cedartown (8)	CM 706 748-3220	....	....	....	....	....	....	....
Centerville (3)	MC 912 953-4734	Matt Keene	....	Virginia E Abbott	Virginia E Abbott	Frank Wadsworth	Michael Sullivan	Henry Childs
Chamblee (8)	MC 404 986-5010	....	....	....	....	....	....	....
Clarkston t (5)	MC 404 296-6489	....	....	....	....	....	....	....
Claxton (2)	MC 912 739-1712	....	....	....	....	....	....	....
Cochran (4)	MC 912 934-6346	....	....	....	....	....	....	....
College Park (20)	CM 404 767-1537	T Owen Smith	J Scott Miller	Jean C Cress	Jena C Cress	Charles T Dillard	Walter T Sheets	Don E Moore
Columbus-Muscogee (179)	CM 706 571-4700	....	....	....	....	....	....	....
Commerce (4)	MC 404 335-3164	....	....	....	....	....	....	....
Conyers (7)	CM 404 483-4411	Charles C Walker	C Roland Vaughn	Dee Buggay	Rebecca Woolcot	....	Tony Lucas	Bobbie Hill
Cordele (10)	CM 912 273-3102	....	Jack E Miller	....	Steve Fulford	Eugene Stephens	Dwayne Orrick	Jimmy Watson
Cornelia (3)	CM 706 778-8585	....	....	....	....	....	....	....
Covington (10)	MC 404 786-5324	....	....	....	....	....	....	....
Cuthbert (4)	MC 912 732-3761	....	....	....	....	....	....	....
Dahlonega (3)	MC 404 864-6133	....	....	....	....	....	....	....
Dallas (3)	CM 404 443-8110	....	....	....	....	....	....	....
Dalton (22)	MC 706 278-9500	James Middleton	James Sanders	Faye Martin	James Sanders	Treen Coffey	James Chadwick	Ken Boyd
Dawson (5)	CM 912 995-4444	....	....	....	....	....	....	....
Decatur (17)	CM 404 370-4100	....	....	....	....	....	....	....
Donalsonville (3)	MC 912 524-2118	David B Fain	H M Shingler	Linda Faye Gray	Linda Faye Gray	Travis Brooks	Andrew Henry	William Bledsoe
Doraville (8)	MC 404 451-8745	....	....	....	....	....	....	....
Douglas (10)	CM 912 384-3302	Derward Buchan	W Danny Lewis	Hayvene McFall	Terrell Lott	Freddie Davis	Clyde Purvis	....
Douglasville (12)	MC 404 920-3000	Charles L Camp	Bill Osborne	Barbara McCravy	J H Banks	....	J L Whisenant	Keith L Williams
Dublin (16)	CM 912 272-1620	Robert J Walker	George P Roussel	....	Joseph M Kinard	Robert T Drew	Homer W Fuqua	Jimmy D Sawyer
Duluth (9)	MC 404 476-3434	Shirley Lasseter	Larry Rubenstein	Teresa S Lynn	John Paton	....	Randal Belcher	Jerry Fowler
East Dublin t (3)	MC 912 272-6883	George H Gornto	....	Terrie E Drew	Terrie E Drew	Doyle Tanner	Larry N Drew	Dwayne Lake
East Point (34)	CM 404 765-1013	....	....	....	....	....	....	....
Eastman (5)	CM 912 374-7721	....	....	....	....	....	....	....
Eatonton (5)	MC 404 485-3311	James P Marshall	....	Audrey Hightower	Audrey Hightower	O Van Landingham	Kent Lawrence	J R Davis
Elberton (6)	MC 706 283-5321	Iola Stone	Hayden Wiley	Scott Wilson	Scott Wilson	Niles Poole	Mike Seymour	Jimmy Welborn
Fairburn (4)	MC 404 964-2244	Betty W Hannah	Anthony W Cox	Bobbie C Langston	Bobbie C Langston	Mike Brown	John T Cameron Jr	Donald Baxter
Fayetteville (6)	MC 404 461-6029	....	....	....	....	....	....	....
Fitzgerald (9)	MC 912 423-9827	Gerald H Thompson	Alvie L Dorminy	Louise Guardia	Elaine Poole	Robert W Sherrill	William Smallwood	Hubert E Poole
Forest Park (17)	CM 404 366-4720	Charles Hall	....	....	Sarah Davis	....	Joseph Picard	Larry Bateman
Forsyth (4)	MC 912 994-5649	Paul H Jossey Jr	Douglas B White	Carol W Ellerbee	....	Walter Carter	Benjamin Ponder	Alvin Randall
Fort Oglethorpe (6)	CM 706 866-2544	John W Norris	....	J Harold Silcox	Dorothy G Haney	Harold Randy Camp	Charles S Dunn Jr	Phillip B Parker
Fort Valley (8)	MC 912 825-8261	....	....	....	....	....	....	....
Gainesville (18)	CM 404 535-6860	....	....	....	....	....	....	....
Garden City (7)	MC 912 966-7777	....	....	....	....	....	....	....
Glennville (4)	MC 912 654-2461	....	....	....	....	....	....	....
Gordon t (2)	MC 912 628-2222	....	....	....	....	....	....	....
Greensboro (3)	MC 706 453-7967	Andrew Boswell	Glynn Harrison	....	....	Tim Webb	Larry Postell	....
Griffin (21)	CM 404 229-6425	Raymond Head	Richard Crowdis	Richard Crowdis	Lee Poolman	Ronald Ellis	Armand Chapeau	Brant Keller
Grovetown (4)	MC 706 863-4576	Dennis O Trudeau	....	Shirley Beasley	....	....	John Tomberlin	Charles W Newman
Hapeville (6)	MC 404 669-2100	C C Martin	Richard Bray	....	Lisa Bryant	Donald Davis	Leverett Butts	Judy K Nicholson
Hartwell (5)	MC 706 376-4756	Joan H Saliba	Ellis D Foster	Steve Russell	Steve Russell	Terry Vickery	Cecil E Reno	....
Hawkinsville (4)	CM 912 892-3240	....	....	....	....	....	....	....
Hazlehurst (4)	MC 912 375-6680	Wyatt W Spann	....	Ethelyn S Creech	Ethelyn S Creech	Charles Wasdin	Steven Land	David Hughes
Helen (..)	MC 404 878-3382	....	....	....	....	....	....	....
Hinesville (22)	MC 912 876-3564	....	....	....	....	....	....	....
Hogansville (3)	MC 706 637-8629	Calvin Turbyfield	Wesley Duffey	Connie Ellis	....	....	Clarence Martin	James Rippy
Homerville (3)	MC 912 487-2375	Carol W Chambers	....	William C Vest	....	Mike Strickland	Truman Lee	....
Jackson (4)	MC 404 775-7535	Charlie Brown	....	J Fitzgerald	....	Mark Cook	Mike Riley	Dawson Heath
Jesup (9)	CM 912 427-2903	....	....	....	....	....	....	....
Jonesboro (4)	MC 404 478-7407	....	....	....	....	....	....	....
Kennesaw (9)	MC 404 424-8274	J O Stephenson	....	Susan Rackley	....	....	Dwaine Wilson	....
Kingsland (5)	MC 912 729-5613	Keith Dixon	....	Dorothy Peeples	Myrtle Funderburk	Morris Peeples	Wesley Liles	Jim Tarter
La Fayette (6)	MC 706 638-3177	H Neal Florence	David L Aldrich	Glenna J Thomas	....	Jimt Maffett	Chas R Richardson	James McAlister
La Grange (26)	CM 706 883-2028	Eugene H Woodall	James R Hanson	John W Bell	John W Bell	Chris A Smith	George A Yates	David E Brown
Lake City (3)	MC 404 366-8080	Willie R Oswalt	....	Alva O Inman	Alva O Inman	....	Sammy W Banks Sr	Alva O Inman
Lawrenceville (17)	MC 404 963-2414	....	....	....	....	....	....	....
Lilburn (9)	MC 404 921-2210	W Calvin Fitchett	....	Jean A Cole	Jean A Cole	....	Ronald H Houck	G A Nash
Lithonia (2)	MC 404 482-8136	....	....	....	....	....	....	....
Louisville (2)	CM 912 625-3166	Julian L Veatch	J Don Rhodes	Lona F Lane	....	....	James Wm Miller	Clifford T Luckey
Lyons (5)	MC 912 526-6578	....	....	....	....	....	....	....
Macon (107)	MC 912 751-7000	Thomas C Olmstead	Israel G Small	Steven G Durden	John D Thompson	Jimmy E Hinson	Milton J Avera Jr	Larry G Brown
Madison (3)	MC 404 342-1251	....	....	....	....	....	....	....
Manchester (4)	CM 404 846-3141	....	....	....	....	....	....	....
Marietta (44)	CM 404 528-5000	Ansley L Meaders	William J Buckner	Sheila R Hill	Greg Demko	Ken Burris	J Ralph Carter	Ken Clayton
Mc Donough (3)	MC 404 957-3915	....	....	....	....	....	....	....
Mc Rae (3)	MC 912 868-6051	....	....	....	....	....	....	....
Metter (4)	MC 912 685-2527	....	....	....	....	....	....	....
Milledgeville (18)	MC 912 453-9441	....	....	....	....	....	....	....
Millen (4)	MC 912 982-6100	....	....	....	....	....	....	....
Monroe (10)	MC 404 267-7536	....	....	....	....	....	....	....
Montezuma (5)	MC 912 472-8144	....	....	....	....	....	....	....

Directory 1/9 continued **MUNICIPAL OFFICIALS IN U.S. CITIES OVER 2,500**

City, 1990 population figures (000 omitted), form of government	Municipal phone number	Mayor/ chief elected official	Appointed administrator	City clerk/ city secretary	Finance officer	Fire chief	Police chief	Public works director
GEORGIA (158) continued								
Morrow (5)	MC 404 961-4002	....		....	....	....	....	....
Moultrie (15)	CM 912 985-1974	William McIntosh	Robert Arojas	Gary McDaniel	Gary McDaniel	Kenneth Hannon	Richard Crouch	Roger Ruis
Nashville (5)	MC 912 686-5527	Dewey Hall		Johnny Hall	Dewey Hand	Earl Powell	Ira Shealy	Jerry Griner
Newnan (12)	CM 404 253-2682	L Keith Brady	Richard A Bolin	Peggy Dewberry	....		Jerry Helton	....
Norcross (6)	MC 404 448-2122	Maurice Allen	....	Karen Bradley	Meridith Long	....	Richard L Hetzel	Brad Cole
Ocilla (3)	MC 912 468-5141	....	....	....	....	....	....	....
Palmetto (3)	CM 404 463-3377	....		....			....	
Peachtree City (19)	CM 404 487-7657	Robert L Lenox	Jim Basinger	Frances Meaders	Frances Meaders	Gerald Reed	James V Murray	Colin Halterman
Pelham (4)	MC 912 294-7900	....						
Perry (9)	CM 912 987-1911	James E Worrall	F Marion Hay	F Marion Hay	Janice Williams	Gary Hamlin	C Frank Simons	W Hugh Sharp
Pooler (4)	MC 912 748-7261	....		....			....	....
Port Wentworth (4)	MC 912 964-4379	....		....			....	....
Powder Springs (7)	CM 404 943-1666	Richard D Sailors	Wayne P Wricht	Betty G Brady	Lynn F Edwards		Lester K Guthrie	Bobby C Elliott
Quitman (5)	CM 912 263-4166	....	....	....	....		....	....
Rincon t (3)	CM 912 826-5745	....		....			....	....
Riverdale (9)	MC 404 997-8989	....		....			....	....
Rockmart (3)	CM 404 684-5454	Steven B Smith	Ronald S Morgan	Penny J Bratcher	....	Jeff Ellis	Steve Burkhalter	Stewart Mintz
Rome (30)	CM 706 236-4400	George Pullen	John Bennett	Joseph Smith	Gary Burkhalter	Bobbie McKenzie	Hubert Smith	Kirk Milam
Rossville (4)	MC 706 866-1325	....		....			....	
Roswell (48)	MC 404 641-3727	W L Pug Mabry	G W Bill Johnson	G W Bill Johnson	John S Hunter	H N Butterworth	Ed Williams	Frank Mingledorff
Sandersville (6)	MC 912 552-6006	....		....			....	
Savannah (138)	CM 912 651-6481	....		....			....	....
Smyrna (31)	MC 404 434-6600	A Max Bacon	Bob Thomson	Melinda Dameron	Jim Triplett	Larry Williams	Stanley Hook	Larry Dunn
Snellville (12)	MC 404 985-3500	Emmett Clower		Sharon Lowery	Sharon Lowery		John D Hewatt	Alfred Beaver
Social Circle (3)	MC 404 464-2380	Frank W Sherrill	Anne S Peppers	Anne S Peppers		Steve Shelton	....	Kenny Harper
Soperton (3)	MC 912 529-6173	....		....			....	
St. Marys (8)	MC 912 882-5516	Jerry R Brandon	Micheal G Mahaney	Gwendolyn Mungin	Micheal J Fender	Dale Simmons	Ed Wassman	Bennie L Smith
Statesboro (16)	MC 912 764-5468	Hal Averitt	Carter Crawford	Judy McCorkle	Edie Olliff	Joe Beasley	Richard Malone	Bobby Colson
Stone Mountain (6)	CM 404 498-8984	Patricia Wheeler	Wayne Johnson	Wayne Johnson	Carla Tuck		James Rivers	Henry Shoemaker
Sugar Hill (5)	CM 404 945-6716	Gary L Webster	Warren Nevad	Betty B Garbutt	Betty B Garbutt		Chris Robertson	....
Summerville (5)	MC 404 857-3402	....		....			....	
Swainsboro (7)	MC 912 237-7025	....		....			....	
Sylvania (3)	CM 912 564-7411	Sandy Hershey	Roland Stubbs	Mary F Collins		H P Brown	William H Black	Dennis Daley
Sylvester (6)	MC 912 776-8505	H Leroy Wilkerson		Debbie Bridges		Tommy Marchman	Tommy Bozeman	Jimmy Fowler
Tallapoosa (3)	CM 706 574-2345	....		....			....	
Thomaston (9)	CM 706 647-6633	Charles Kersey	Wilbur Avera	Phillip B Adcock	Phillip B Adcock	Jesse Coogler	Tony E McCard	Jesse Walton
Thomasville (17)	CM 912 228-7673	Camille Payne	....	....	....	Charles Anderson	John Perry	John Wood
Thomson (7)	MC 706 595-1781	Robert E Knox Jr	Burton D Patrick	Darleen Plunkett	Kenneth J Pittard	Raymond McHatton	John Hathaway	Harry Johnson
Thunderbolt t (3)	MC 912 354-5533	....		....			....	
Tifton (14)	CM 912 382-6231	....		....			....	....
Toccoa (8)	CM 706 886-8451	Winnie Zeches	James A Calvin	Josephine Gleason	Patti T Joiner	Henry M Thomas	Joseph J Whitmire	Donald E Dye
Union City (8)	MC 404 964-2288	....		....			....	
Valdosta (40)	CM 912 333-1804	James H Rainwater	....	Richard Hamlen	Richard Hamlen	Richard Williams	Charlie Spray	....
Vidalia (11)	CM 912 537-7661	....		....			....	
Vienna (3)	MC 912 268-4744	Willie Davis	Stanley Gambrell	Gail Bembry	....	Tommy Phillips	Bobby Reed	Larry Allen
Villa Rica (7)	CM 404 459-3656	Monroe Spake	Andy Henshaw	Andy Henshaw	Jean Spiva	....	Michael Gibbs	Don McGill
Warner Robins (44)	MC 912 929-1111	....		....			....	....
Washington (4)	CM 706 678-3277	E B Pope	Warren D Sisson	Michael P Eskew		Alan Poss	Roger G Weston	....
Waycross (16)	CM 912 287-2914	....		....			....	
Waynesboro (6)	MC 404 554-8000	....		....			....	
West Point (4)	MC 404 645-2226	....		....			....	
Winder (7)	MC 404 867-3106	....		....			....	
Woodbine (1)	MC 912 576-3211	W Burford Clark	George Hannaford	George Hannaford		Keith Kelley	Edvin W Cooler	Robert Brown
Woodstock (4)	CM 404 926-8852	W David Rogers	D Lamar Hamill	Rhonda L Bishop	D Lamar Hamill	Robby Westbrook	Jimmy Mercer	Bo Ray
Wrightsville (2)	MC 912 864-3303	Willis R Wombles		Jewell R Parker		Stan Garnto	....	Ralph Move
HAWAII (2)								
Hilo (..)	MC 808 961-8361	....		....			....	
Honolulu (836)	MC 808 523-4141	Jeremy Harris	....	Raymond Pua	Russell Miyake	Richard Seto Mook	Michael Nakamura	Kenneth Sprague
IDAHO (42)								
American Falls (4)	MC 208 226-2569	....		....			....	....
Ammon (5)	MC 208 529-4211	C Bruce Ard		Aleen C Jensen		Cal Smith	....	David Wadsworth
Blackfoot (10)	MC 208 785-8600	....		....			....	....
Boise City (126)	MC 208 384-3700	H Brent Coles	James M Thompson	Annette P Mooney	Steven C Purvis	Renn M Ross	Larry A Paulson	William J Ancell
Bonners Ferry (2)	MC 208 267-3105	....		....			....	
Buhl (4)	MC 208 543-5650	....		....			....	
Burley (9)	MC 208 678-2224	Frank Bauman		E E Brinegar		Phillip Heiner	....	Leon Bedke
Caldwell (18)	MC 208 455-3000	Richard Winder	Jim Reames	Betty Jo Keller	Lisa Thompson	Bruce Allcott	Robert Sobba	Gordon Law
Chubbuck (8)	MC 208 237-2400	....		....			....	....
Coeur D'Alene (25)	MC 208 769-2300	Al Hassell	Ken Thompson	Susan Weathers	John F Austin	Frank Sexton	Dave Scates	Rodger Lewerenz
Eagle (3)	MC 208 939-6813	....		....			....	
Emmett (5)	MC 208 365-6050	John LaForde		Cecile Jensen		Orville Wright	Gary Scheihing	Jack Dodson
Garden City (6)	MC 208 377-1831	Ted Ellis		Dave O' Leary		....	T C Brock	Randy Deardon
Gooding (3)	MC 208 934-5669	....		....			....	
Grangeville (3)	MC 208 983-1380	....		....			....	
Hayden (4)	MC 208 772-4411	....		....			....	
Heyburn (3)	MC 208 678-8158	Glen J Loveland	Roger Denker	Ruth Davis	Ruth Davis	Mike Brown	Earl Andrew	Roger Denker
Idaho Falls (44)	MC 208 529-1248	Linda Milam	....	Rose Anderson	S Craig Lords	Richrad Hahn	Monty Montague	Chad Stanger
Jerome (7)	MC 208 324-8189	Gerald M Ostler	Larry Paine	Kathy Miller	John Yon	James Au Claire	James R Dahl	....
Kellogg (3)	MC 208 786-9131	Mervin Hill		Barbara Rinaldi		Dale Costa	John Crawford	Gary Temby
Lewiston (28)	CM 208 746-3671	Gayle McGarry	Janice Vassar	Rebecca Hubbard	Ruth Beck	Thomas Tomberg	Jack Baldwin	Bud Van Stone
Meridian (10)	MC 208 888-4433	....		....			....	
Montpelier (3)	MC 208 847-0824	....		....			....	
Moscow (19)	MC 208 883-7000	Paul C Agidius	William A Smith	C Elaine Russell	James R Wallace	Phillip L Gatlin	William F Brown	Gary J Presol
Mountain Home (8)	MC 208 587-2104	....		....			....	
Nampa (28)	MC 208 465-2270	....		....			....	
Orofino (3)	MC 208 476-4725	H L Clay	Rick Laam	Virginia T Earl		Leonard Eckman		Floyd Williams
Payette (6)	MC 208 642-6024	James E McCue	John P Franks	....		....	Les Cochran	J Mac Gillivra
Pocatello (46)	MC 208 234-6163	Peter Angstadt		Peter McDougall		Richard Wolfe	Lynn Harris	....
Post Falls (7)	MC 208 773-3511	James Hammond	John Hendrickson	Christene Pappas		....	Cliff Hayes	George Wilson
Preston (4)	MC 208 852-1817	....		....			....	
Rexburg (14)	MC 208 359-3020	Nile L Boyle	....	Rose Bagley	Richard Horner	Rex Larsen	Blair K Siepert	Farrell Davidson

Directory 1/9
continued

MUNICIPAL OFFICIALS
IN U.S. CITIES OVER 2,500

City, 1990 population figures (000 omitted), form of government	Municipal phone number	Mayor/ chief elected official	Appointed administrator	City clerk/ city secretary	Finance officer	Fire chief	Police chief	Public works director
IDAHO (42) continued								
Rigby (3)	MC 208 745-8111	Nile H Hall	....	LaRee Rainey	....	Leon Guymon	Larry Anderson	Douglas Nelson
Rupert (5)	MC 208 436-9608	W F Bill Whittom	....	M Fredrickson	....	Thayne Taylor	Kendall Warr	Don Dustin
Salmon (3)	MC 208 756-3214	Patricia A Hauff	Lanny G Sloan	....	....	Don Vial	Bob Nelsen	Don Vial
Sandpoint (5)	MC 208 263-3158	....	....	....	....	....	Alan Dial	Rick Anderson
Shelley (4)	MC 208 357-3390	Heber J Hansen	....	Sandy Hanson	....	....	....	....
Soda Springs (3)	MC 208 547-2600	Kirk L Hansen	Lee Godfrey	Brenda L Erickson	....	Norm Bjorkman	Blynn B Wilcox	Gary L Jensen
St. Anthony (3)	MC 208 624-3494	....	....	....	....	....	....	....
St. Maries (2)	MC 208 245-2577	Ernest Pendell	....	Myrna Linnemeyer	....	Bill Cowin	Fred Cruzan	Phillip Brown
Twin Falls (28)	CM 208 736-2271	....	....	....	....	....	....	....
Weiser (5)	MC 208 549-1965	....	....	....	....	....	....	....
ILLINOIS (403)								
Abingdon (4)	MC 309 462-3182	H Jay Sandercock	....	B Joanne Batson	Richard Boone	Jerry Severns	John Funk	Steve Murfin
Addison v (32)	MC 708 543-4100	....	....	....	....	....	....	....
Aledo (4)	MC 309 582-7241	....	....	....	....	....	....	....
Algonquin v (12)	MC 708 658-4322	Salvatore Spella	William J Ganek	Gerald S Kautz	John R Walde	....	Russell B Laine	Lon D Hawbaker
Alsip v (18)	MC 708 385-6902	....	....	....	....	....	....	....
Alton (33)	MC 618 463-3500	Robert W Towse	....	Mary T Gibson	Mark K Bennett	John L Sowders	Sylvester Jones	William E Moyer
Anna (5)	MC 618 833-8528	....	....	....	....	....	....	....
Antioch v (6)	MC 708 395-1000	....	....	....	....	....	....	....
Arcola (3)	MC 217 268-4966	....	....	....	....	....	....	....
Arlington Heights v (75) ..	CM 708 577-5632	A Mulder	W Dixon	E Corso	J Goral	B Rodewald	R Kath	A Sander
Auburn (4)	MC 207 989-7500	Michael Maybury	Harold F Parks	Arthur C Verow	....	Bruce F Kigas	Eugene P Fizell	Gerald P Bowie
Aurora (100)	MC 708 892-8811	David L Pierce	....	Cheryl Van Hoff	Roger W Cantlin	Gerald Stevens	David L Stover	James Nanninga
Barrington v (10)	CM 708 381-2141	Ronald Hamelberg	Paul C Nicholson	Carol J Smith	Denise M Pieroni	....	Jeffrey Marquette	John M Heinz
Barrington Hills v (4)	MC 708 551-3000	James A Kempe	Robert Kosin	Marla Russo	Charles W Sweet	....	Edgar W Fair	....
Bartlett v (19)	MC 708 837-0800	....	....	....	....	....	....	....
Bartonville v (6)	MC 309 697-2323	....	....	....	....	....	....	....
Batavia (17)	MC 708 879-1424	Jeff Schielke	Ron Podschweit	Jody Haltenhof	Terry Klein	William Darin	Robert Warner	Gary Larsen
Beardstown (5)	MC 217 323-3110	....	....	....	....	....	....	....
Beecher v (2)	CM 708 946-2261	Landis Wehling	Robert O Barber	Janett Conner	Robert O Barber	....	R Wroblewski	William L Merritt
Belleville (43)	MC 618 233-6810	....	....	....	....	....	....	....
Bellwood v (20)	MC 708 547-3500	Donald P Lemm	....	Booker T Brown	I Joseph Lagen	David Stelter	Robert Frascone	John Antonovich
Belvidere (16)	MC 815 544-2612	Rory B Peterson	....	Romelle Cunningha	Richard Stegemann	Paul Moses	Charles Burkhart	Craig Lawler
Bensenville v (18)	CM 708 766-8200	John Geils	Michael Allison	Vera Johnson	Tom Truty	Jack Barba	Walter Hitchuk	Paul Bourke
Benton (7)	CO 618 439-6131	Gale Dawson	....	Michael Malkovich	John Clements	Paul Rogers	Raymond Bain	....
Berkeley v (5)	MC 708 449-8840	Michael Esposito	....	Dawn Furlan	....	Frank Sustr	Timothy Griffin	James Rich
Berwyn (45)	MC 708 788-2660	....	....	....	....	....	....	....
Bethalto v (10)	MC 618 377-8723	Wm F Stephenson	....	Mary A Meyer	....	John Nolte	Anthony Sammis	Joseph Ricci
Bloomingdale v (17)	MC 708 893-7000	Robert Iden	Daniel Wennerholm	Harriet Ford	Gary Szott	....	Gary Schira	Dennis Szaffran
Bloomington (52)	MC 309 828-7361	Jesse Smart	Tom Hamilton	Earlene Nelson	Allan Horsman	Alan Otto	Tim Linskey	Richard Paulson
Blue Island (21)	MC 708 597-8600	....	....	....	....	....	....	....
Bolingbrook v (41)	MC 708 759-0400	Roger C Claar	William Charnisky	Carol Penning	Harriet Allbee	Charles Peterson	Ronald Chruszczyk	Michael Drey
Bourbonnais v (14)	MC 815 937-3570	Grover Brooks	James Bassett	Douglas Warren	....	....	Joseph Beard	Ernest Mooney
Bradley v (11)	MC 815 933-8533	....	....	....	....	....	....	....
Braidwood (4)	CO 815 458-2333	R Peterson	....	C Deterding	....	....	J Kopczick	....
Breese (4)	MC 618 526-7731	....	....	....	....	....	....	....
Bridge View v (14)	MC 708 594-2525	....	....	....	....	....	....	....
Broadview v (9)	MC 708 681-3600	....	....	....	....	....	....	....
Brookfield v (19)	CM 708 485-7344	Thomas Sequens	James R Mann	Kathleen Markland	George R Turdik	Charles LaGreco	Herbert Livermore	....
Buffalo Grove v (36)	CM 708 459-2500	Sidney Mathias	William Balling	Janet Sirabian	William Brimm	Thomas Allenspach	Leo McCann	Gregory Boysen
Burbank (28)	MC 708 599-5500	....	....	....	....	....	....	....
Burnham v (4)	MC 708 862-9150	....	....	....	....	....	....	....
Burr Ridge v (8)	CM 708 654-8181	Emil J Coglianese	Steven Stricker	Patrice Pecora	Hella Tomczak	....	Herbert Timm	....
Bushnell (3)	MC 309 772-2521	Jack Promisson	....	Barb Knott	....	Danny Zook	Merville Hilliard	Delbert Thompson
Cahokia v (18)	MC 618 337-9510	....	....	....	....	....	....	....
Cairo (5)	MC 618 734-4127	....	....	....	....	....	....	....
Calumet City (38)	MC 708 891-8100	....	....	....	....	....	....	....
Calumet Park v (8)	MC 708 389-0850	Buster B Porch	....	Geraldine Galvin	....	T Battistella	Thomas Zielinski	Robert Talaski
Canton (14)	MC 309 647-0020	Donald E Edwards	....	Nancy Whites	....	Robert Derenzy	J Michael Elam	....
Carbondale (27)	CM 618 549-5302	Neil Dillard	Jeff Doherty	Janet Vaught	Paul Sorgen	Cliff Manis	Don Strom	Ed Reeder
Carlinville (5)	MC 217 854-4076	....	....	....	....	....	....	....
Carlyle (3)	MC 618 594-2468	....	....	....	....	....	....	....
Carmi (6)	MC 618 382-8118	....	....	....	....	....	....	....
Carol Stream v (32)	CM 708 665-7606	Ross Ferraro	Gregory Bielawski	....	Stan Helgerson	....	Gary Konzak	John A Turner
Carpentersville v (23)	CM 708 426-3439	John Skillman	Curt Carver	Carol Miller	Don Mazza	Ron Creek	Ben Blake	Scott Killinger
Carrollton (3)	MC 217 942-5517	....	....	....	....	....	....	....
Carterville (4)	MC 618 985-2252	....	....	....	....	....	....	....
Cary v (10)	CM 708 639-0003	Susan McCabe	Carl Tomaso	Mark Shackelford	Jennifer Scott	....	Robert Levitt	....
Casey (3)	MC 217 932-2700	....	....	....	....	....	....	....
Caseyville v (4)	MC 618 344-1234	George Chance	....	Jack Piesbergen	....	G W Scott	Ron Tamburello	....
Centralia (14)	CM 618 533-7622	Mel Hart	Donald Hahn	Gail Simer	....	Roger Sutherland	Arland Speidel	Donald Copple
Centreville (7)	MC 618 332-1021	....	....	....	....	....	....	....
Champaign (64)	CM 217 351-4458	....	....	....	....	....	....	....
Channahon v (4)	CM 815 467-5311	Michael Rittof	Marian T Gibson	Christine Pucel	Robert Guess	....	Steve Admonis	Daniel Werner
Charleston (20)	CO 217 345-7088	Roscoe M Cougill	....	Patsy J Loew	....	Thomas C Watson	H Steidinger	....
Chatham v (6)	MC 217 483-2451	Linda Koester	Del McCord	Penny Moomey	Sandra Farrow	....	Roy Barnett	Meredith Branham
Cherry Valley v (2)	MC 815 332-3441	....	....	....	....	....	....	....
Chester (8)	MC 618 826-2326	Frank Derickson	....	Nancy Eggemeyer	....	M O Atchison	Jack Houghlan	Russ Rader
Chicago (2784)	MC 312 744-4000	....	....	....	....	....	....	....
Chicago Heights (33)	CO 708 756-5300	....	....	....	....	....	....	....
Chicago Ridge v (14)	MC 708 425-7700	....	....	....	....	....	....	....
Chillicothe (6)	MC 309 274-5056	Sherry L Weis	Denise L Passage	Sharon A Crabel	Richard Eckstein	Gail F Myers	Steven Maurer	Clyde S Crabel
Christopher (3)	MC 618 724-7648	....	....	....	....	....	....	....
Cicero t (67)	MC 708 656-3600	....	....	....	....	....	....	....
Clarendon Hills v (7)	MC 708 323-3500	John D Purdy Jr	Joseph Breinig	Mary A Arnold	Kathy Redding	Brian Leahy	Thomas Reasoner	John Hays
Clinton (7)	CO 217 935-9438	....	....	....	....	....	....	....
Coal City v (4)	MC 815 634-8608	....	....	....	....	....	....	....
Coal Valley v (3)	MC 309 799-3604	....	....	....	....	....	....	....
Collinsville (22)	CO 618 344-5252	Fred Dalton	Richard Mays	Louis Jackstadt	Nancy Boeckman	Ken Eichelberger	John Swindle	Brett Hanke
Columbia (6)	MC 618 281-6366	....	....	....	....	....	P Comanda	E Meinheim
Country Club Hills (15) ...	CM 708 798-2616	D Welch	J Muchnik	H Scanan	W Schuessler	....	P Comanda	E Meinheim
Countryside (6)	MC 708 354-7270	Carl W LeGant	John P McDonald	Denise M Likens	W Schuessler	....	Charles D' Urso	Robert Fullar

Directory 1/9 continued

MUNICIPAL OFFICIALS IN U.S. CITIES OVER 2,500

City, 1990 population figures (000 omitted), form of government	Municipal phone number	Mayor/ chief elected official	Appointed administrator	City clerk/ city secretary	Finance officer	Fire chief	Police chief	Public works director
ILLINOIS (403) continued								
Crest Hill (11)	MC 815 741-5100	Donald L Randich	....	Florine Kovalcik	....	....	James A Ariagno	Ted E Bostrom
Crestwood v (11)	MC 708 371-4800	Chester Stranczek	Frank Gassmere	Nancy Benedetto	....	William Boman	John Hefley	....
Crete v (7)	MC 708 672-5431	Michal S Einhorn	Jerold P Ducay	Mariann E Gemper	William R Bruin	Lyle Bachert	David L Wallace	Phillip Hameister
Creve Coeur v (6)	MC 309 699-6714	....	....	....	....	....	....	....
Crystal Lake (25)	CM 815 459-2020	George Wells	Joseph Misurelli	James Kelley	Bruce Raymond	Richard Nebel	Keith Nygren	Clyde Wakefield
Danville (34)	MC 217 431-2200	....	....	....	....	....	....	....
Darien (18)	MC 708 852-5000	Carmen D Soldato	Timothy J Gagen	Joanne F Coleman	....	....	Edward Musial	Arthur Benner
De Kalb (35)	CM 815 748-2000	....	....	....	....	....	....	....
Decatur (84)	CM 217 424-2805	Eric Brechnitz	James C Bacon Jr	Phyllis Sands	Beth Couter	John Plotner	James Williams Jr	Bruce McNabb
Deerfield v (17)	CM 708 945-5000	Bernard Forrest	Robert Franz	Robert Franz	George Valentine	....	Leo Anderson	Jim Soyka
Des Plaines (53)	MC 708 391-5300	Ted Sherwood	T Wallace Douthwa	Donna McAllister	Gregory Peters	Thomas Farinella	John Storm	Scott Shirley
Dixmoor v (4)	MC 708 389-6121	Zeb Lollis	....	Viviane V Young	Michael Cech	Richard Gini	Nickolas Graves	Jerry Smith
Dixon (15)	MC 815 288-1485	Donald Sheets	....	Barbara Graff	....	Jim Hill	Robert Short	Robert Giese
Dolton v (24)	MC 708 849-4000	Donal J Hart	....	Judith Evans	....	Robert Kapusta	David Walker	Robert Myers
Downers Grove v (47)	CM 708 964-0300	....	....	....	....	....	....	....
Du Quoin (7)	CO 618 542-3841	John Rednour	....	Mell Smigielski	....	Richard Fronek	Ken Dement	....
Dupo v (3)	MC 618 286-3280	....	....	....	....	....	....	....
Dwight v (4)	MC 815 584-3077	Daryl N Holt	Daniel A Allen	Barbara Daniels	Barbara Daniels	....	Timothy F Henson	James G Dransfeld
East Alton v (7)	MC 618 259-7714	....	....	....	....	....	....	....
East Dundee v (3)	MC 708 426-2822	....	....	....	....	....	....	....
East Moline (20)	MC 309 752-1599	....	....	....	....	....	....	....
East Peoria (21)	CO 309 698-4715	J Giebelhausen	James D Thompson	Veona I Dinkins	D Giebelhausen	Jim Bevard	Jim Druin	Stephen D Carr
East St. Louis (41)	MC 618 482-6811	....	....	....	....	....	....	....
Edwardsville (15)	MC 618 692-7500	....	....	....	....	....	....	....
Effingham (12)	CO 217 347-5555	John D Thies	....	Rick J Goeckner	....	Nicholas Althoff	John Lange	Lowell Wines
El Paso (2)	MC 309 527-4005	....	....	....	....	....	....	....
Eldorado (5)	CO 618 273-6566	....	....	....	....	....	....	....
Elgin (77)	CM 708 931-6100	G Van DeVoorde	Richard Helwig	Polonna Mecom	James Nowicki	John Henrici	Charles Gruber	James Kristiansen
Elk Grove Village v (33)	CM 708 439-3900	....	....	....	....	....	....	....
Elmhurst (42)	MC 708 530-3000	Thomas D Marcucci	Thomas Borchert	Janet S Edgley	Marilyn K Gaston	John Fennell Jr	John Millner	John Wielebnicki
Elmwood Park v (23)	CM 708 452-7300	Peter Silvestri	John Dalicandro	Elsie Sutter	Carmela Corsini	Kerry Hjellum	F Thomas Braglia	John Zelasco
Eureka (4)	MC 309 467-2113	Joe Serangeli	Benny Arbuckle	Robert Watson	Fred Mall	....	Gerald Reinmann	James Lehman
Evanston (73)	CM 708 328-2100	Lorraine Morton	Eric Anderson	Kirsten Davis	Robert Shonk	James Hunt	Gerald Cooper	David Barber
Evergreen Park v (21)	MC 708 422-1551	Anthony Vacco	....	Ruth Donahue	....	John Hojek	Norbert Smith	Edward Schuth
Fairbury (4)	MC 815 692-2743	Roger L Dameron	....	Brenda E Defries	....	Keith Klitzing	Donald Hedrick	Leroy McPherson
Fairfield (5)	MC 618 842-3871	Kenneth E Wood	....	Annis Lea Doty	....	Larry McCoy	Murrel E Day	Guy L Williams
Fairview Heights (14)	MC 618 397-7743	George A Lanxon	....	Harvey Snoubarian	James Jacob	....	Roger Richards	Robert Hotz
Farmington (3)	MC 309 245-2011	Dorothy M Cox	Roger Woodcock	Donna Degroot	....	....	Fred L Smith	Brad Dilts
Flora (5)	CO 618 662-8313	Lewis L Wolfe	Marion J Long	Laura O' Donnell	Judith C Powless	Bruce E Dickey	Edward McCormick	Marion J Long
Flossmoor v (9)	CM 708 798-2300	Frank J Maher Jr	Peggy Glassford	Jeanne Gummerson	....	Greg Berk	Mike Williams	Bruce Ellis
Ford Heights v (4)	MC 708 758-3131	....	....	....	....	....	....	....
Forest Park v (15)	CO 708 366-2323	Lorraine Popelka	....	Marlene Quandt	Donna Bruenning	Shayne Ryerson	Gary Liesten	Bud Wilkes
Fox Lake v (7)	MC 708 587-2151	Kenneth Hamsher	....	Susan J McNally	....	Stuart C Hoehne	James Busch	....
Fox River Grove v (4)	MC 708 639-3170	....	....	....	....	....	....	....
Frankfort v (7)	MC 815 469-2177	....	....	....	....	....	....	....
Franklin Park v (18)	MC 708 671-4800	....	....	....	....	....	....	....
Freeburg v (3)	MC 618 539-5545	George Prie	Robert Kell	Dora Becker	Dora Becker	....	Victor Logan	Edward Wilson
Freeport (26)	MC 815 235-8200	....	....	....	....	....	....	....
Fulton (4)	CM 815 589-2616	K Ven Huizen	M Joseph Woith	Lavonne Huizenga	....	....	Harvey Meade	Bill Zink
Galena (4)	MC 815 777-1050	....	....	....	....	....	....	....
Galesburg (34)	CM 309 343-4181	Fred Kimble	Robert Knabel	Anita Carlton	Steve Driscoll	....	John Schlaf	Lyman Jensen
Galva (3)	MC 309 932-2555	....	....	....	....	....	....	....
Geneseo (6)	MC 309 944-6419	Thomas P Gorman	....	Tim D Long	....	Jerry Klavohn	Louis J Bervid	....
Geneva (13)	MC 708 232-0854	William T Ottilie	Philip J Page	Dennis A Kabela	Ronald A Steele	Frank D Johnson	William H Kidwell	Thomas W Talsma
Genoa (3)	MC 815 784-2327	Gene Lawrence	Keith Schildt	Jerry Redden	Jerry Redden	....	Joe Zmich	Dale Schepers
Georgetown (4)	MC 217 662-2525	....	....	....	....	....	....	....
Gibson City (3)	MC 217 784-5872	....	....	....	....	....	....	....
Gillespie (4)	MC 217 839-2919	....	....	....	....	....	....	....
Glen Carbon v (8)	MC 618 288-2100	....	....	....	....	....	....	....
Glen Ellyn v (25)	CM 708 469-5000	Johan Demling	Gary Webster	P O' Connor	Sheryl Ligon	Stuart Stone	Howard Thiele	....
Glencoe v (8)	CM 708 835-4111	James O Webb	Peter B Cummins	Ruby Herron	Douglas Merrill	Paul M Harlow	Paul M Harlow	Robert W Hogue
Glendale Heights v (28)	MC 708 260-6000	Ben Fajardo	James Sevcik	Joann Borysiewicz	....	....	James Carroll	....
Glenview v (37)	CM 708 724-1700	Nancy Firfer	Paul McCarthy	Paul McCarthy	Dennis Lauer	John J Robberson	David Kelly	William Porter
Glenwood v (9)	MC 708 758-5150	....	....	....	....	....	....	....
Granite City (33)	MC 618 452-6213	Ron Selph	....	Judy Whitaker	K P Mac Taggart	Keith Talley	David Ruebhausen	....
Grayslake v (7)	MC 708 223-8515	Pat Carey	Michael Ellis	Barb Bacsa	....	....	Dennis Koletsos	Roy Wickersheim
Green Rock (3)	MC 309 792-0571	Terry Van Klavern	....	Lories Graham	Terry Van Klavern	....	Heidi Owen	Leroy Kelley
Greenville (5)	CM 618 664-1644	Eldon Turley	Larry Stoever	Harriet McDonald	....	....	John King	Gary Netzler
Gurnee v (14)	MC 708 623-7650	Richard A Welton	James T Hayner	Norman C Balliet	P Wesolowski	Timothy McGrath	....	James Repp
Hamilton (3)	MC 217 847-2936	Ken DeYong	....	Diann Means	....	Jeff McNeill	Walter Sellens	Bob Allen
Hanover Park v (33)	CM 708 837-3800	....	....	....	....	....	....	....
Harrisburg (9)	MC 618 253-7451	John D Cummins	....	Adele Abraham	....	Bill Summers	Gary Crabtree	....
Harvard (6)	MC 815 943-6468	William Lefew	David Nelson	Chris Ferguson	....	....	Kenneth Mrozek	James Carbonetti
Harvey (30)	CO 708 210-5300	....	....	....	....	....	....	....
Harwood Heights v (8)	MC 708 867-7200	Ray Willas	....	Eugene J Brutto	....	Jack Stefanowicz	William Bagnole	Thomas Schroeder
Havana (3)	MC 309 543-3411	Allan McNeil	....	Mary M Howerter	Edward Ray	Rick Trimpe	Robert Huber	....
Hawthorn Woods v (4)	MC 708 540-5225	....	....	....	....	....	....	....
Hazel Crest v (13)	CM 708 335-9600	S J Rocke	R L Palmer	S Smith	....	D Chappell	H V Moore	R W Fish
Henry (3)	MC 309 364-3056	....	....	....	....	....	....	....
Herrin (11)	MC 618 942-3175	Edward L Quaglia	....	Marlene Simpson	Margaret Boren	Paul Marlo	Tom Cundiff	Joe Lapinski
Hickory Hills (13)	MC 708 598-4800	Daniel A Riley	....	Joann Jackson	....	....	George Dulzo	Larry Boettcher
Highland (8)	CM 618 654-9891	Robert Nagel	Joseph Frei	Lila Manville	Sharon Rusteberg	Michael Kolgore	William Pierce	....
Highland Park (31)	CM 708 432-0800	....	....	....	....	....	....	....
Highwood (5)	MC 708 432-1924	John Sirotti	....	April Powers	....	Ron Pieri	George Smith	Jeff Ponsi
Hillsboro (4)	CO 217 532-5566	....	....	....	....	....	....	....
Hillside v (8)	MC 708 449-6450	....	....	....	....	....	....	....
Hinsdale v (16)	MC 708 789-7000	Joyce E Skoog	Charles O Dobbins	Sharon Henderson	David C Cook	Patrick Kenny	Robert O' Malley	James Kerins
Hoffman Estates v (47)	CM 708 882-9100	....	....	....	....	....	....	....
Hometown (5)	MC 708 424-7500	Donald L Roberton	....	Joan Dobrowits	....	Mark Sikorski	Anthony Wolowicz	Joseph J Madden
Homewood v (19)	CM 708 798-3000	John T Doody Jr	Peter F Hurst	Marjory Dalton	Ray Gosack	Raymond Presnak	Jerald Brandt	Charlie Foulkes
Hoopeston (6)	MC 217 283-5833	....	....	....	....	....	....	....
Indian Head Park v (4)	CM 708 246-3080	....	....	....	....	....	....	....
Inverness v (7)	MC 708 358-7740	Donna Thomas	William Grams	Angie Fridono	....	....	....	....

Directory 1/9 continued

MUNICIPAL OFFICIALS IN U.S. CITIES OVER 2,500

City, 1990 population figures (000 omitted), form of government	Municipal phone number	Mayor/ chief elected official	Appointed administrator	City clerk/ city secretary	Finance officer	Fire chief	Police chief	Public works director
ILLINOIS (403) continued								
Itasca v (7) MC	708 773-0835	Shirley H Ketter	....	Carole Schreiber	....	....	Mike McDonald	Alan Anderson
Jacksonville (19) MC	217 243-3391	....	....	....	....	....	....	....
Jerseyville v (7) CO	618 498-3312	....	....	....	....	....	....	....
Johnston City (4) MC	618 983-6651	Vernon Kee	....	Jean Hatfield	....	Dennis Beaumont	Verlyn Dobbins	....
Joliet (77) CM	815 740-2495	Arthur Schultz	John M Mezera	Nancy M Vallera	Robert D Fraser	Lawrence M Walsh	Joseph P Beazley	Dennis L Duffield
Justice v (11) MC	708 458-2520	Edward C Rusch Jr	....	Judith A Brogdon	....	Ronald Szarzynski	Paul A Wasik	Philip A Depaola
Kankakee (28) MC	815 933-0500	....	....	....	....	....	....	....
Kenilworth v (2) CM	708 251-1666	James McClamroch	Kenneth Terlip	William Sethness	....	....	Gary Wolff	I Fiorentino
Kewanee (13) CM	309 852-2611	Dewey R Colter	John D Kolata	Sandra Murphy	....	Don Karau	Joseph P Dakin	Mike Rapczak
Kildeer v (..) CM	708 438-6000	B Schwietert	Laurel Schreiber	....	....	....	Jay Mills	....
Knoxville (3) MC	309 289-2814	....	....	....	....	....	....	....
La Grange v (15) CM	708 579-2300	Timothy R Hansen	Marlies Perthel	Robert Milne	Thomas Kuehne	Walter Mac Dowall	Ray Kaminskas	C E Ferrell
La Grange Park v (13) CM	708 354-0225	Raymond J Pietrus	Timothy Schuenke	Kerry Brunette	Pierre Garesche	Arthur Tullis	John Dunlop	Jim Schnute
La Salle (10) MC	815 223-4586	....	....	....	....	....	....	....
Lake Bluff v (6) CM	708 234-0774	Fred Wacker	Kent S Street	Donald Patton	Susan M Griffin	Robert B Graham	Fred C Day	Thomas I Cahill
Lake Forest (18) CM	708 234-2600	Rhett Butler	Robert R Kiely Jr	Barbara Douglas	Robert D Shaffer	Robert Wilkins Jr	Robert G Boone	Thomas Naatz
Lake In The Hills v (6) MC	708 658-4213	Tina Thornrose	....	Joyce Arient	....	....	Jim Wales	Dave Gregoria
Lake Zurich v (15) MC	708 438-5141	Deborah Vasels	John Dixon	Marcia Reynolds	Richard Ratkowski	Terry Mastandrea	Frederick Clauser	Robert Mitchard
Lansing v (28) MC	708 895-7200	....	....	....	....	....	....	....
Lawrenceville (5) MC	618 943-2116	Gerald C Harper	....	Helen M Ritchie	....	....	Donald S Foster	Chris Kelly
Lebanon (4) MC	618 537-4976	....	....	....	....	....	....	....
Lemont v (7) MC	708 257-1550	Richard Kwasneski	Steven A Jones	Charlene Smollen	Jean Nona	....	Jack Bluis	Dan Fielding
Leroy (3) MC	309 962-3031	Jerry Davis	....	Juanita Dagley	....	....	Dennis Carter	Gary King
Lewistown (3) MC	309 547-4300	Kendall W Miller	....	Melodee Rudolph	....	....	John Levingston	Jewel Bucy
Libertyville v (19) CM	708 362-2430	Jo Ann Eckmann	Kevin J Bowens	Jane V Curtis	Steven C Noble	John R Reitman	W Dan McCormick	Steven R Magnusen
Lincoln (15) MC	217 735-2815	....	....	....	....	....	....	....
Lincolnshire v (5) CM	708 883-8600	Barbara LaPiana	Robert L Irvln	B Mastandrea	Stanley R Roelker	....	Glenn H Larson	Mathew E Overeem
Lincolnwood v (11) MC	708 673-1540	....	....	....	....	....	....	....
Lindenhurst v (8) MC	708 356-8252	Paul Baumunk	James B Stevens	Carol A Aller	James B Stevens	....	Jack McKeever	Wesley J Welsh
Lisle v (20) MC	708 968-1200	Ronald Ghilardi	Carl Doerr	Melville Handley	Kimberly Schiller	....	Richard Myers	Ray Peterson
Litchfield (7) MC	217 324-2022	....	....	....	....	....	....	....
Lockport (9) MC	815 838-0549	Richard C Dystrup	Gordon McCluskey	Paula Waxweiler	Wendy Cooper	....	James Antole	Larry McCasland
Lombard v (39) CM	708 620-5700	William Mueller	William T Lichter	Lorraine Gerhardt	Leonard Flood	G E Seagraves	Leon Kutzke	Stanley Rickard
Long Grove v (5) CM	708 634-9440	Lenore J Simmons	D M Cal Doughty	Joseph Barry	Alina Althans	....	....	Ronald Damitz
Loves Park (15) MC	815 654-5030	....	....	....	....	....	....	....
Lynwood (7) MC	708 758-6101	....	....	....	....	....	....	....
Lyons v (10) MC	708 447-8886	Glen J Tomlinson	Kevin J Close	William P Polich	Linda Bugielski	Micheal Ehle	Richard Kluk	Richard Wuest
Machesney Park v (19) MC	815 877-5432	Stephen P Kuhn	....	Linda M Vaughn	....	....	....	....
Macomb (20) MC	309 833-2575	Thomas C Carper	Robert A Morris	Lucille Gibson	....	Donald Bytner	Richard Clark	....
Madison (5) MC	618 876-6268	....	....	....	....	....	....	....
Marengo (5) MC	815 568-7112	Thomas Sighoff	....	Betty Struckmeier	....	Peter Bigalke	....	Alvin Liesse
Marion (15) MC	618 993-8575	....	....	....	....	....	....	....
Marissa v (2) MC	618 295-2351	Jerry R Cross	....	Carol Smith	....	Stan Lewis	Michael Kerperien	Danny C Smith
Markham (13) MC	708 331-4905	....	....	....	....	....	....	....
Marquette Heights (3) MC	309 382-3455	James F Steele	....	Susan L Hoover	Michael Therry	Dana Dearborn	Bob Quarello	....
Marseilles (5) CM	815 795-2133	....	....	....	....	....	....	....
Marshall (4) MC	217 826-2112	....	....	....	....	....	....	....
Mascoutah (6) CM	618 566-2965	Vivian Haas	Roderick Wilhelmi	Kathleen Schuetz	Roderick Wilhelmi	Dean R Juenger	Kevin Gordon	....
Mason City (2) MC	217 482-3669	Wilbur L Renken	....	M Joanne Burris	....	....	David N Coulter	Joe T Burris Jr
Matteson v (11) MC	708 748-1559	Mark W Stricker	Daniel E Dubruiel	Donna M Brumfield	James A Spice	Robert H Wilcox	Lawrence Burnson	Frank Denman
Mattoon (18) CO	217 235-5654	....	....	....	....	....	....	....
Maywood v (27) CM	708 681-8846	Joe W Freelon	Bradford Townsend	Eleanor Miller	Keith Bennett	Dennis Hoffman	Willard Jackson	Joseph D Brown
Mc Henry (16) MC	815 363-2100	Steven J Cuda	Gerald R Peterson	Pamela J Althoff	....	Chris Bennett	Patrick J Joyce	Fredric C Batt
Melrose Park v (21) MC	708 343-4000	C August Taddeo	Michael Castaldo	Joseph J Iosco	....	Anthony Maggio	Ronald Belle	Ralph Tolomei
Mendota (7) MC	815 539-7459	....	....	....	....	....	....	....
Metropolis (7) MC	618 524-4016	....	....	....	....	....	....	....
Midlothian v (14) MC	708 389-0200	....	....	....	....	....	....	....
Milan v (6) MC	309 787-8500	Duane Dawson	Steven Seiver	Barbara Lee	....	....	Dennis Baraks	James Larson
Millstadt v (3) MC	618 476-1514	....	....	....	....	....	....	....
Minonk (2) MC	309 432-2558	William Herman Sr	David A Shirley	M Samuelson	....	....	William A Butler	Edward A Shirley
Mokena v (6) CM	708 479-3900	Ronald Grotovsky	John Downs	Jane McGinn	Barb Shryock	Ted Golden	Steve Pollak	Craig Heim
Moline (43) CM	309 797-0735	Stanley F Leach	Alan L Efflandt	Joanne Lambrecht	Kathleen A Carr	Robert J Hearn	Steven Etheridge	George A Stevens
Momence (3) MC	815 472-2001	James A Moody	....	Margaret Clifton	....	....	William DuGuay	....
Monmouth (9) MC	309 734-2141	....	....	....	....	....	....	....
Montgomery v (4) MC	708 896-8080	Gary F Pregel	John J DuRocher	Nan G Cobb	....	....	Dennis Schmidt	Chris J Liveris
Monticello (5) MC	217 762-2583	James Ayers	....	Renee Fruendt	....	Rick Dubson	James O Voss	Ronald Ivall
Morris (10) MC	815 942-4026	....	....	....	....	....	....	....
Morrison (4) MC	815 772-7657	Robert Atherton	Samuel E Tapson	Nancy M Poling	....	....	Robert Snodgrass	Larry Heath
Morton v (14) MC	309 266-5361	....	....	....	....	....	....	....
Morton Grove v (22) MC	708 965-4100	Richard P Hohs	Larry N Arft	Wilma Wendt	Spiro C Hountalas	Ralph Czerwinski	George Incledon	James Dahm
Mount Carmel (8) CO	618 262-4822	Rudy L Witsman	Mark A Bader	Mark A Bader	Mick Mollenhauer	Steve Partee	Dan DeWitt	....
Mount Morris v (3) MC	815 734-6425	Steven Brinker	Sandra Blake	Sandra Blake	....	....	John G Thompson	....
Mount Prospect v (53) CM	708 392-6000	Gerald L Farley	Michael E Janovis	Carol A Fields	David C Jepson	Edward M Cavello	Ronald W Pavlock	Herbert L Weeks
Mount Vernon (17) CM	618 242-5000	Rolland W Lewis	Craig A Olsen	Karl M Powers	John F Lunini	Larry Fally	Ron Massey	Elbert Cain
Mount Zion v (5) CM	217 864-5424	Harry W Ashworth	James F Bowden	Jana L Wood	James F Bowden	....	Paul D Wood	Steven D Simmons
Mundelein v (21) MC	708 949-3200	Marilyn Sindles	K W Marabella	Colleen Kasting	Mary Kay Hatton	Randy Justus	Raymond Rose	Kenneth Miller
Murphysboro (9) MC	618 684-4961	....	....	....	....	....	....	....
Naperville (85) CM	708 420-6044	Samuel Mac Rane	Ronald Miller	Suzanne Gagner	Julia Carroll	Alan Rohlfs	David Dial	Ned Becker
Nashville (3) MC	618 327-3058	....	....	....	....	....	....	....
New Lenox v (10) MC	815 485-6452	John Nowakowski	Russ Loebe	Marjorie Wajchert	Kim Newquist	....	Ken Oldendorf	Ron Sly
Newton (3) MC	618 783-8451	Robert E Burris	....	Jean Ghast	....	....	Mike Swick	....
Niles v (28) CM	708 967-6100	Nicholas Blase	Abe Selman	Kathryn Harbison	George Van Geem	Harry Kinowski	R Giovannelli	Jun Noriega
Nokomis (3) MC	217 563-2514	....	....	....	....	....	....	....
Normal t (40) CM	309 454-2444	Kent Karraker	David S Anderson	Marianne Edwards	Ronald J Hill	George R Cermak	James R Taylor	Ellis G Perl
Norridge v (14) MC	708 453-0800	Joseph Sieb	....	Irene Gdula	....	....	Ervin F Siemers	Brian M Gaseor
North Aurora v (6) MC	708 897-8228	Mike Mudry	Linda Mitchell	Linda Mitchell	....	....	Edward Kelley	James Palmatier
North Chicago (35) MC	708 578-7759	Bobby E Thompson	Evelyn Alexander	C Collins	Kenneth Robinson	Richard Turner	Ernest Fisher	Bill Mayfield
North Riverside v (6) MC	708 447-4211	Richard N Scheck	Wayne E Pesek	Charmaine Kutt	Roger Geske	Dominic Salvino	George Kratochvil	Kenneth Lange
Northbrook v (32) CM	708 272-5050	Mark Damisch	John Novinson	Lona Louis	Dave Kowal	Jay Reardon	Jim Wallace	Jim Reynolds
Northfield v (5) CM	708 446-9200	Richard M Rieser	Mark J Morien	Michael Nystrand	Vivian Perenchio	Michael Nystrand	George A Wagner	Michael Nystrand
Northlake (13) MC	708 343-8700	....	....	....	....	....	....	....
O'Fallon (16) MC	618 624-4500	Robert G Morton	Frank O Miles	Benjamin E Hamm	....	William Henry	Don Slazinik	John Nevenner
Oak Brook v (9) CM	708 990-3000	Karen M Bushy	Stephen B Veitch	Linda K Gonnella	Darrell Langlois	Robert D Nielsen	James R Fleming	Michael J Meranda

City, 1990 population figures (000 omitted), form of government	Municipal phone number	Mayor/ chief elected official	Appointed administrator	City clerk/ city secretary	Finance officer	Fire chief	Police chief	Public works director
ILLINOIS (403) continued								
Oak Forest (26)	MC 708 687-4050	James C Richmond	Bernard J Kelly	R J Fitzpatrick	William Plankis	James Berger	David Griffin	James Chevalier
Oak Lawn v (56)	CM 708 636-4400	E Kolb	J Faber	J Powers	G Paul	T Moran	....	....
Oak Park v (54)	CM 708 383-6400	L Christmas	Allen J Parker	Sandra Sokol	Elizabeth Spencer	Gerald Beeson	Joseph Mendrick	Vincent Akhimie
Oglesby (4)	MC 815 883-3389	....	....	....	....	....	....	....
Olney (9)	CM 618 395-7302	Tom Fehrenbacher	Larry P Taylor	Belinda C Henton	....	Gary D Foster	Elton R Wood	....
Olympia Fields v (4)	MC 708 748-8246	....	....	....	....	....	....	....
Oregon (4)	CO 815 732-6321	James Barnes	....	Julienne Crowley	....	....	Thomas Miller	....
Orland Hills v (6)	MC 708 349-6666	Kyle R Hastings	John A Daly	Curt Petrey	....	....	Joe Miller	Mike Worley
Orland Park v (36)	MC 708 403-6100	D McLaughlin	James Smithberg	James Dodge Jr	S Dianne Kallina	....	Timothy McCarthy	....
Oswego v (4)	MC 708 554-3618	....	....	....	....	....	....	....
Ottawa (17)	MC 815 433-0161	....	....	....	....	....	....	....
Palatine v (39)	CM 708 358-7500	Rita Mullins	Michael Kadlecik	Margaret Duer	Robert Husselbee	Richard Payne	Jerry Bratcher	Andrew Radetski
Palos Heights (11)	MC 708 361-1800	Bonnie Strack	....	Helen Mae Asmus	....	....	Reed Powers	Gerald Martin
Palos Hills (18)	MC 708 598-3400	Gerald R Bennett	Marge Hodek	Rudy Mulderink	Kenneth J Nolan	Richard McKeon	Paul Madigan	George Lutz
Palos Park v (4)	CM 708 448-5200	....	....	....	....	....	....	....
Pana (6)	MC 217 562-3626	Larry J Chaney	....	Terry L Klein	....	Bill Williamson	Michael Harris	....
Paris (9)	CO 217 465-7601	Frank L Clinton	Paul H Ruff	Paul H Ruff	....	Jim Kelly	Gene Ray	....
Park City (5)	MC 708 623-5030	Robert Allen	....	Theresa Oldham	....	....	Robert Williams	....
Park Forest v (25)	CM 708 748-1112	F Patrick Kelly	John Manahan	Elva Ilo	Erica Peterson	Ronald Welch	Robert Maeyama	Benjamin Jordan
Park Ridge (36)	MC 708 318-5200	Ronald W Wietecha	Gerald E Hagman	Betty Henneman	Diane Lembesis	Robert Colangelo	Robert Colangelo	T Fredrickson
Pawnee v (2)	MC 217 625-2951	....	....	....	....	....	....	....
Paxton (4)	MC 217 379-4022	James E Kingston	....	Linda Kellerhals	....	Don Jones	Dennis Schneider	John Curtis
Pekin (32)	CO 309 477-2300	Donald C Williams	....	Robert A Reis	Robert A Reis	John W Hamann	Robert G Burress	Dennis R Kief
Peoria (114)	CM 309 672-8575	James Maloof	Peter Korn	Mary Haynes	Lori Fleming	Ernie Russel	Arthur Kelly	Steve Van Winkle
Peoria Heights v (7)	MC 309 686-2370	Raymond L Picl	Rick Williams	Patricia Honey	....	William Bair	Don Swank	Steve Rettig
Peotone v (3)	MC 708 258-3279	Richard Benson	....	Donna Werner	....	....	Gary Bogart	Thomas Blogg
Peru (9)	MC 815 223-0061	....	....	....	....	....	....	....
Phoenix v (2)	MC 312 331-2636	Terry Wells	....	Johnnie M Lane	Lester Hemingway	Clarence Elmore	Ronnie Berry	Louis McDaniel
Pinckneyville (3)	CO 618 357-6916	Joseph M Holder	....	Frances I Thomas	Thomas Guthrie	Jerry Smith	Tom Denton	Donald Wilkin
Pittsfield (4)	MC 217 285-4484	Rick E Conner	....	Tim Belford	....	Parker Zumwalt	Robert Yelliot	James Blakemore
Plainfield v (5)	MC 815 436-7093	John E Peterson	David P Vanvooren	Susan Janik	....	John Eichelberger	Donald Bennett	....
Plano (5)	MC 708 552-8275	Susan H Nesson	....	Deanna Brown	....	John Dobbs	Steven S Eaves	John P McGinnis
Pontiac (11)	MC 815 844-3396	G Michael Ingles	Robert M Karls	Marjorie M Ripsch	....	David Lopeman	Alvin Lindsay	....
Pontoon Beach v (4)	MC 618 797-9830	Glen R Wilson	....	Louis Whitsell	....	....	Chet Ballew	....
Posen v (4)	MC 708 385-0139	....	....	....	....	....	....	....
Princeton (7)	CO 815 875-2631	Richard L Welte	....	Eugene Wolf	....	Terry Himes	Melvin Hult	Thomas Carr
Prospect Heights (15)	MC 708 398-6070	Edward Rotchford	Kenneth Bonder	Karen Pedersen	Gregory Condell	....	Robert Bonneville	Duane Dobner
Quincy (40)	MC 217 228-4500	Charles W Scholz	Gary Sparks	Janet Hutmacher	Dan Maier	James Doellman	John Wilson	Leon Kowalski
Rantoul v (17)	MC 217 893-1661	....	....	....	....	....	....	....
Red Bud (3)	MC 618 282-2315	....	....	....	....	....	....	....
Richton Park v (11)	CM 708 481-8950	Rudolph Banovich	David Niemeyer	Mary Pierce	Timothy Hammond	Joseph Solick	Richard Labus	Ben Adcock
River Forest v (12)	CM 708 366-8500	Frank M Paris Jr	Charles J Biondo	Emerson K Houser	Lynette K Tuggle	Charles B Henrici	Joseph I Bopp	Gregory W Kramer
River Grove v (10)	MC 708 453-8000	....	....	....	....	....	....	....
Riverdale v (14)	MC 708 841-2200	....	....	....	....	....	....	....
Riverside v (9)	CM 708 447-2700	Joseph N Dinatale	Chester Kendzior	Jane Norman	James Egeberg	Anthony Bednarz	Don Doneske	Patrick Ryan
Riverton v (3)	MC 217 629-9122	....	....	....	....	....	....	....
Riverwoods v (3)	MC 708 945-3990	....	....	....	....	....	....	....
Robbins v (7)	CM 708 385-8940	....	....	....	....	....	....	....
Robinson (7)	MC 618 544-7616	Gilbert Phillippe	....	Sandrea Jared	Gilbert Phillippe	Richard Pearce	Kenneth Watts	William Calvert
Rochelle (9)	CO 815 562-6161	Joseph G Panozzo	....	Linda J Manning	....	Tom McDermott	Al Gorr	Keith Scott
Rock Falls v (10)	MC 815 622-1100	Glen R Kuhlemier	....	Margie C Sommers	Glen R Kuhlemier	James W Larson	Larry G Thoren	....
Rock Island (41)	CM 309 793-3000	Mark Schwiebert	John Phillips	Jeanne Paggen	Bill Scott	Gary Mell	Tony Scott	Bob Hawes
Rockford (139)	MC 815 987-5500	Charles E Box	Samuel J Schmitz	....	Ronald Malmberg	D Wm Robertson	Wm Fitzpatrick	Alan Werner
Rolling Meadows (23)	CM 708 394-8500	Carl Couve	Robert Beezat	....	Edward McKee	Philip Burns	Gerald Aponte	Dennis York
Romeoville v (14)	CM 815 886-7200	Sandra Gulden	Frank Lauro	Judy Canning	Elvira Hogan	Carl J Churulo	Andrew Barto	William Taylor
Roselle v (21)	CM 708 980-2000	Gayle A Smolinski	Robin A Weaver	Linda McDermott	Kathryn M Booth	James Sunagel	Richard Eddington	Robert O Burns
Rosemont v (4)	MC 708 825-4404	....	....	....	....	....	....	....
Round Lake v (4)	MC 708 546-5400	James Lumber	....	Lillian Frost	Margaret Molidor	....	Joseph Trkovsky	Doug Rowley
Round Lake Beach v (16)	MC 708 546-2351	....	....	....	....	....	....	....
Round Lake Park v (4)	MC 708 546-7336	Charlene Beyer	....	Star L Southworth	....	....	Gene Kelly	George Johnson
Rushville (3)	MC 217 322-3833	Dennis R Yates	....	Ina J Patterson	....	Curt Lunt	William White	....
Salem (7)	CM 618 548-2222	....	....	....	....	....	....	....
Sandwich (6)	MC 815 786-9321	Tom Thomas	....	Barbara G Olson	Carmen Dixon	....	Richard Olson	....
Sauk Village v (10)	MC 708 758-3330	Mark Collins	Richard Dieterich	Marjorie Tuley	Beverly Sterrett	Travis Thornhill	Willam Crafton	Wolfgang Nieft
Savanna (4)	MC 815 273-2251	Eugene T Flack	Sheryl L Sipe	Walter I Shrake	....	Harry R Charneski	Robert F Stretton	Paul E Hartman
Schaumburg v (69)	CM 708 894-4500	....	....	....	....	....	....	....
Schiller Park v (11)	MC 708 678-2550	Anna Montana	Glenn Spachman	Claudia Irsuto	....	Walter Preiss	Peter J Puleo	Ronald Sieracki
Shelbyville (5)	CO 217 774-5531	....	....	....	....	....	....	....
Shorewood v (6)	MC 815 725-2150	Bertha J Hofer	Gary C Holmes	Julia A Russell	....	....	Robert P Puleo	Gerald Seil
Silvis (7)	MC 309 792-9181	Bob Steele	....	Barbara J Fox	Wayne Vyncke	Robert Leibovitz	James J Healy	Ron Hall
Skokie v (59)	CM 708 673-0500	Jacqueline Gorell	Albert J Rigoni	Marlene Williams	Robert J Nowak	James C Eaves	William D Miller	Donald Manak
South Beloit (4)	CO 815 389-3023	Alan Palmer	....	Marilyn Hartley	....	Ken Morse	Jack Johnson	....
South Chicago Heights v (4)	MC 708 755-1880	....	....	....	....	....	....	....
South Elgin v (7)	MC 708 742-5780	....	....	....	....	....	....	....
South Holland v (22)	MC 708 333-0572	....	....	....	....	....	....	....
South Jacksonville v (3)	MC 217 245-4803	Glenda Hazelrigg	....	Joann Lindemann	....	S Michael Elliott	Richard A Evans	Garry L Thomas
Sparta (5)	CO 618 443-2917	Tom Maybell	Loren Prest	Ron Cavalier	Judy Crain	Bruce Dahlem	Lyndon Thies	Gregory Aitken
Spring Valley (5)	MC 815 664-4221	James Narczewski	....	Joseph A Taliano	....	Gene Scheri	Douglas Bernabei	Kevin Sawicki
Springfield (105)	MC 217 789-2446	Ossie Langfelder	....	Norma Graves	Carl Forn	Russ Steil	Harvey Davis	Ric Lynch
St. Charles (23)	MC 708 377-4989	Fred T L Norris	....	Jean M Connors	Larry Maholland	Larry Swanson	James Roche	Mark Koenen
Staunton (5)	MC 618 635-2233	Wayne Heinemeyer	....	Marilyn Herbeck	....	....	Ronnie Masinelli	....
Steger v (9)	CM 708 754-3395	....	....	....	....	....	....	....
Sterling (15)	CM 815 622-2221	William Durham	Stephen Berley	Rosemary Coughlin	Sheila Barton	Arlyn Oetting	Cadet Thorp	Vernon Gottel
Stickney v (6)	MC 708 749-4400	....	....	....	....	....	....	....
Stone Park v (4)	MC 708 345-5550	....	....	....	....	....	....	....
Streamwood v (31)	CM 708 837-0200	....	....	....	....	....	....	....
Streator (14)	CM 815 672-2517	Richard E Conner	....	Pamela K Leonard	....	Henry Araujo	James Dutton	Jeff Wilson
Sullivan (4)	CO 217 728-4383	....	....	....	....	....	....	....
Summit v (10)	MC 708 563-4800	....	....	....	....	....	....	....
Swansea v (8)	MC 618 234-0044	Michael Buehlhorn	Lyndon Joost	James Cange	....	David Thacker	Edward Lintzenich	Frank Nadler
Sycamore (10)	MC 815 895-4515	Bernard McMillan	....	Gail Brantner	Kenneth Mundy	Larry Haeffner	Dale N Vesta	Gene Listy
Taylorville (11)	MC 217 824-2101	Dick Adams	....	Pam Peabody	....	Gerald Olive	David Childers	Denny Macke
Thornton v (3)	MC 708 877-4456	Jack C Swan	....	Cheryl L Bult	....	James Swan	Peter J Belos	Peter Den Hartog

Directory 1/9
continued

MUNICIPAL OFFICIALS
IN U.S. CITIES OVER 2,500

City, 1990 population figures (000 omitted), form of government	Municipal phone number	Mayor/ chief elected official	Appointed administrator	City clerk/ city secretary	Finance officer	Fire chief	Police chief	Public works director
ILLINOIS (403) continued								
Tinley Park v (37)	MC 708 532-7700	Edward J Zabrocki	Dennis A Kallsen	Frank W German Jr	....	....	James Wade	Thomas Albright
Trenton (2)	MC 618 224-7323	Virgil E Ripperda	Carol S Metzger	Carol S Metzger	....	....	Timothy J Harris	Roger J Maue
Troy (6)	MC 618 667-6741	Velda Armes	Bud Klaustermeier	Mary Chasteen	David Roady	....	Robert Noonan	Lloyd Wood
Tuscola (4)	MC 217 253-2112	....	....	....	....	....	....	....
University Park v (6)	CM 708 534-6451	Vernon Young	Mike Grubermann	Irma Berry	....	Dave Litton	Tom Leonard	Wes Scholz
Urbana (36)	MC 217 384-2458	Tod Satterthwaite	Bruce Walden	Phyllis Clark	Ronald Eldridge	Dick Dunn	Charles Gordon	Bill Gray
Vandalia (6)	MC 618 283-1196	Rick Walker	....	Norma R Croasdale	....	Merle Adermann	Robert E McCart	David L Reeter
Venice (4)	MC 618 877-2412	Tyrone Echols	Roseann Koelker	Wilbert Glasper	....	Thomas Brent	James R Bennett	Green Jacks
Vernon Hills v (15)	CM 708 367-3700	Roger L Byrne	Larry L Laschen	Kathy Ryg	Larry Nakrin	....	Gary L Kupsak	Ed Laudenslager
Villa Grove (3)	MC 217 832-4721	....	....	....	....	....	....	....
Villa Park v (22)	CM 708 834-8500	Rae Rupp Srch	Wayne L Lulay	....	Michael O' Keefe	Richard Davidson	Ronald Ohlson	Vydas Juskelis
Virden (4)	MC 217 965-5805	Susan Rohrer	....	Judy Berry	....	....	Gary Plessa	John Lewis
Warrenville (11)	MC 708 393-9427	Vivian Lund	James Connors	Rosemary Tierney	Jean McCabe	....	Robert Ladeur	....
Washington (10)	MC 309 444-3196	....	....	....	....	....	....	....
Washington Park v (7)	MC 618 874-2040	....	....	....	....	....	....	....
Waterloo (5)	MC 618 939-8661	....	....	....	....	....	....	....
Watseka (5)	MC 815 432-2017	Wesley R Clement	....	Norma L Martin	Robert L Holt	Dan Adams	M Van Hoveln	....
Wauconda v (6)	MC 708 526-9600	James Eschenbauch	Gerald Sagona Jr	Mary Taylor	Ila Reynolds	....	Andrew Mayer	Jeffery Kuester
Waukegan (69)	MC 708 360-9000	William F Durkin	Donald R Weakley	Sam Filippo	Donald L Schultz	Charles R Perkey	George Bridges	Robert E Johnson
West Chicago (15)	MC 708 293-2200	Steven Lakics	J Donald Foster	Nancy Smith	Warren Warren	....	Gerald Mourning	Ken Dean
West Dundee v (4)	CM 708 551-3800	Calvin Grafelman	Joseph Cavallaro	Barbara Traver	....	Larry McManaman	Alan DeMien	Donald Habermehl
West Frankfort (9)	MC 618 932-3262	John Simmons	....	Barbara Graves	Roger Tippy	Larry Jamrozek	Lindell Blades	....
Westchester v (17)	CM 708 345-0020	John J Sinde	John H Crois	Kathy Hayes	Michael O' Brien	Thomas Rafferty	Donald Musker	Robert Mitchard
Western Springs v (12)	CM 708 246-1800	....	....	....	....	....	....	....
Westmont v (21)	CM 708 829-4400	James A Addington	Raymond P Botch	Elmer Fries	Robert Sterkowitz	Frank Trout	Richard Metzger	Don Thomas
Westville v (3)	MC 217 267-2507	....	....	....	....	....	....	....
Wheaton (51)	CM 708 260-2000	....	....	....	....	....	....	....
Wheeling v (30)	CM 708 459-2612	Sheila H Schultz	Craig G Anderson	Jeanne Selander	....	Keith Mac Isaac	Michael Haeger	Robert Gray
White Hall (3)	MC 217 374-2345	Harold Brimm	....	Beverly Howard	....	Weldon Cooper	Robert McMillen	....
Willow Springs v (5)	MC 708 839-2701	....	....	....	....	....	....	....
Willowbrook v (9)	MC 708 323-8215	Gary Pretzer	Bernard Oglietti	Patrick Spatafore	Jeffrey Rowitz	....	Raymond Arthurs	Philip Modaff
Wilmette v (27)	CM 708 251-2700	John Jacoby	Heidi Voorhees	Heidi Voorhees	Robert Amoruso	Mark Mitchell	George Carpenter	Richard Hansen
Wilmington (5)	MC 815 476-2175	Jerry Hill	....	James C Johnston	Bonita Hill	....	Coralyn Beem	F Richmond
Winfield v (7)	CM 708 665-1778	....	....	....	....	....	....	....
Winnetka v (12)	CM 708 501-6000	Paul F Cruikshank	Douglas Williams	Lois C Resnick	Kenneth A Klein	Ronald Colpaert	William Gallagher	Kenneth R Keene
Winthrop Harbor v (6)	MC 708 872-3846	....	....	....	....	....	Frank Williams	Fred Vogt
Wood Dale (12)	CM 708 766-4900	Jerry C Greer	Rick O Curneal	Geraldine Jacobs	Peter Stefan	....	Frank Williams	Fred Vogt
Wood River (11)	CM 618 251-3100	Lon A Smith	Joey J Tolbert	Jean Bruce	Nancy Schneider	Guy Williams	Charles Nunn	Tim Palermo
Woodridge v (26)	MC 708 852-7000	William F Murphy	John Perry	Dorothy Stahl	Laurie R Hayes	....	Steven List	Joseph Fennell
Woodstock (14)	CM 815 338-4300	William Anderson	Timothy J Clifton	Jean Headley	David Danielson	....	Joseph Marvin	John Isbell
Worth v (11)	MC 708 448-1181	James Bilder	....	Betty Mattera	Steven V Sola	Steve Twining	Frank C Gilbert	Wayne Demonbreun
Yorkville (4)	MC 708 553-4350	Kenneth K Kittoe	James Nanninga	Jackie Allison	Kim King	Mike Hintzeman	Athony Graff	James T Johnson
Zion (20)	CO 708 746-4000	Billy McCullough	....	Judy Smith	....	David McAdams	Lloyd Detienne	....
INDIANA (159)								
Albany t (2)	MC 317 789-6112	....	....	....	....	....	....	....
Alexandria (6)	MC 317 724-4633	....	....	....	....	....	....	....
Anderson (59)	MC 317 646-9685	J Mark Lawler	....	Marie Riggs	Leisa Julian	Dan Edwards	Ronald Rheam	Bill Miller
Angola (6)	MC 219 665-2514	Edwin Selman Jr	....	Margaret Bledsoe	....	Mike Meek	Donald J Wenzel	....
Attica (3)	MC 317 762-2467	....	....	....	....	....	....	....
Auburn (9)	MC 219 925-6450	Norman Rohm	....	Erbecca L Fuller	Rebecca L Fuller	J Bauermeister	Kerry Uhrick	....
Aurora (4)	MC 812 926-1777	....	....	....	....	....	....	....
Austin t (4)	MC 812 794-2877	....	....	....	....	....	....	....
Batesville (5)	MC 812 933-6101	Victor Kaiser	....	Michele D Balser	....	Donald Weigel	Dennis Wallpe	....
Bedford (14)	MC 812 279-6555	....	....	....	....	....	....	....
Beech Grove (13)	MC 317 788-4978	J Warner Wiley	....	....	Marcella L Miceli	James Bright	Michael Johnson	Phil Gurganus
Berne (4)	MC 219 589-8526	Blaine Fulton	....	Gwen Maller	....	Cletus Gifford	Larry Uhrick	....
Bicknell (3)	MC 812 735-4636	....	....	....	....	....	....	....
Bloomington (61)	MC 812 331-6404	Tomilea Allison	....	Patricia Williams	Chuck Ruckman	Larry Fleener	Steve Sharp	Ted Rhinehart
Bluffton (9)	MC 219 824-1520	Everett Faulkner	....	Nancy Hewitt	Nancy Hewitt	Gary Markley	Robert Frantz	....
Boonville (7)	MC 812 897-1230	....	....	....	....	....	....	....
Brazil (8)	MC 812 443-2221	Kenneth L Crabb	....	Ruth Mohr	....	Robert Hayes	John Zuel	David Arnold
Bremen t (5)	MC 219 546-2471	William Garl	Duwaine J Elliott	Joanne Kimmell	....	Jerry Lanning	James Brown	....
Brookville t (3)	CO 317 647-3322	Paul Chaney	....	Alberta Sauerland	....	Daniel Bruns	Thomas Helms	....
Brownsburg t (8)	MC 317 852-1120	Patricia A Lovell	Mark A White	Jeanette Brickler	Jeanette Brickler	Glen Bailey	Frank McCoskey	Dawayne Phillips
Brownstown t (3)	MC 812 358-5500	Robert Millman	....	Patricia Forgey	....	James Renaker	Kenneth Sneed	....
Butler (3)	MC 219 868-5200	....	....	....	....	....	....	....
Carmel (25)	MC 317 844-6433	....	....	....	....	....	....	....
Cedar Lake t (9)	CM 219 374-7000	Robert Carnahan	....	G Kortokrax	....	....	Charles Kouder	....
Chandler t (3)	TM 812 925-6882	Everett L Fisher	Sharon A Gammon	Sharon A Gammon	....	....	Robert M Lockyear	Robert Hess
Charlestown (6)	MC 812 256-3422	....	....	....	....	....	....	....
Chesterfield t (3)	RT 317 378-3331	....	....	....	....	....	....	....
Chesterton t (9)	RT 219 926-1641	Robert E Crone	....	Gayle Polakowski	Gayle Polakowski	Warren Highwood	Geore M Nelson	....
Cicero t (3)	MC 317 984-4900	....	....	....	....	....	....	....
Clarksville t (20)	CO 812 288-7155	....	....	....	....	....	....	....
Clinton (5)	MC 317 832-9880	....	....	....	....	....	....	....
Columbia City (6)	MC 219 244-5141	....	....	....	....	....	....	....
Columbus (32)	MC 812 376-2500	....	....	....	....	....	....	....
Connersville (16)	MC 317 825-4211	Marion Newhouse	....	H Ripberger	....	Bob Wadle	Ken Faw	....
Corydon t (3)	MC 812 738-3958	....	....	....	....	....	....	....
Covington (3)	MC 317 793-2331	....	....	....	....	....	....	....
Crawfordsville (14)	MC 317 362-0805	....	....	....	....	....	....	....
Crown Point (18)	MC 219 663-0257	....	....	....	....	....	....	....
Cumberland t (5)	MC 317 894-3580	Ron Sullivan	....	Kay F Dashley	Greg T Guetterraz	....	Ed Burhenn	Larry Jones
Danville t (4)	CM 317 745-3001	....	Gary D Eakin	Pauletta Frye	....	Jack Willard	William Cope	Terry Myers
De Motte t (2)	MC 219 987-3831	....	....	....	....	....	....	....
Decatur (9)	MC 219 724-7171	....	....	....	....	....	....	....
Dunkirk (3)	MC 317 768-6565	Grant Fager	....	....	Judith Garr	Steve Fields	Arnold Clevenger	Greg Buckner
Dyer t (11)	MC 219 865-6108	....	....	....	....	....	....	....
East Chicago (34)	MC 219 392-1600	....	....	Mary R Drybread	....	Allen J Smith	Patrick L Pankey	Robert L Davis
Edinburg t (5)	CM 812 526-3510	Larry Taulman	....	Mary R Drybread	....	Allen J Smith	Patrick L Pankey	Robert L Davis
Elkhart (44)	MC 219 294-5471	James P Perron	Michelle Fioritto	Sue M Beadle	Maribeth A Hicks	Steven A Gattman	John J Ivory	Gary A Gilot
Ellettsville t (3)	RT 812 876-3860	....	....	....	....	....	....	....

City, 1990 population figures (000 omitted), form of government	Municipal phone number	Mayor/ chief elected official	Appointed administrator	City clerk/ city secretary	Finance officer	Fire chief	Police chief	Public works director
INDIANA (159) continued								
Elwood (9)	MC 317 552-5078	Denny Robinson	....	Sandie Brewer	Sandie Brewer	Milt Gough	Roger Towner	Denny Robinson
Evansville (126)	MC 812 426-5553	Frank McDonald	....	Marsha Abell	Leslie Blenner	Douglas Wilcox	Arthur Gann	Chris Schletzer
Fairmount t (3)	TM 317 948-4632	....	....	....	....	....	....	....
Fort Branch t (2)	CM 812 753-7662	....	....	....	....	....	....	....
Fort Wayne (173)	MC 219 427-1180	W Paul Helmke	Gregory A Purcell	Sandra E Kennedy	Douglas M Lehman	Steven C Hinton	T Neil Moore Jr	Charles E Layton
Fortville t (3)	CM 317 485-4044	....	G Behler	M Manship	....	K Arnold	R Poe	....
Frankfort (15)	MC 317 654-5715	Hrold Woodruff	....	....	Marilyn Chittick	Norman Sterling	James Skinner	....
Franklin (13)	MC 317 736-3602	Charles Littleton	Brenda Matthews	Lena McCracken	Lena McCracken	Jack A Matthews	N Blankenship	Rick Littleton
Garrett (5)	MC 219 357-3836	....	....	....	....	....	....	....
Gary (117)	MC 219 881-1300	....	....	....	....	....	....	....
Gas City (6)	MC 317 677-3079	Eugene Linn	....	Anita Smith	....	Joe Miitsch	H L Leach	....
Goshen (24)	MC 219 533-8621	....	....	....	....	....	....	....
Greencastle (9)	MC 317 653-3100	....	....	....	....	....	....	....
Greendale t (4)	CM 812 537-2125	....	....	....	....	....	....	....
Greenfield (12)	MC 317 462-8510	....	....	....	....	....	....	....
Greensburg (9)	MC 812 663-8582	Sheldon Smith	....	L June Ryle	L June Ryle	Jerry McGuire	Michael Riley	Kathryn Crippen
Greenwood (26)	MC 317 888-2100	M McGovern	....	....	Genevieve Worsham	Paul Kite	Charles Henderson	....
Griffith t (18)	MC 219 924-7500	....	....	....	....	....	....	....
Hammond (84)	MC 219 853-6301	....	....	....	....	....	....	....
Hanover t (4)	MC 812 866-2131	Dennis Stockdale	....	Donna Pettitt	....	....	Willie E Lucas	Dan Kreeger
Hartford City (7)	MC 317 348-0412	....	....	....	....	....	....	....
Hebron t (3)	MC 219 996-4641	Milton Schroader	....	Marcella Mason	Marcella Mason	David Wilson	Keith Foor	Michael Novac
Highland t (24)	MC 219 838-1080	George Georgeff	....	Michael Griffin	Michael Griffin	William Timmer	Lawrence Woods	John Bach
Hobart (22)	MC 219 942-1940	....	....	....	....	....	....	....
Huntingburg (5)	MC 812 683-2211	....	....	....	....	....	....	....
Huntington (16)	MC 219 356-1400	....	....	....	....	....	....	....
Indianapolls-Marion (731)	MC 317 327-3200	Stephen Goldsmith	Anne Shane	....	James Steele Sr	Keith Smith	James Toler	Michael Stayton
Jasper (10)	MC 812 482-4255	William J Schmitt	....	Irls A Gutgsell	Irls A Gutgsell	William Meyer	Richard Gunselman	William J Schmitt
Jeffersonville (22)	MC 812 283-4451	....	....	....	....	....	....	....
Kendallville (8)	MC 219 347-2452	Jeff Smith	....	Kimberly Forker	....	Larry McGahen	William Forker	....
Knox (4)	MC 219 772-3032	....	....	....	....	....	....	....
Kokomo (45)	MC 317 456-7470	Robert Sargent	Nanette Bowling	Brenda Ott	Lawrence Darlin	Joseph Zuppardo	Lynn Rudolph	Charles R Guge
La Porte (22)	MC 219 362-3175	Elmo Gonzalez	....	....	Constance L Ebert	William G Smith	Gene Samuelson	....
Lafayette (44)	MC 317 742-8404	....	....	....	....	....	....	....
Lake Station (14)	MC 219 962-3111	Dewey R Lemley	....	Donna Smelley	....	Robert Janes	Roger Szostek	Eugene Everett
Lawrence (27)	MC 317 549-4804	....	....	....	....	....	....	....
Lawrenceburg (4)	MC 812 537-1676	....	....	....	....	....	....	....
Lebanon (12)	MC 317 482-1218	....	....	....	....	....	....	....
Ligonier (3)	MC 219 894-4113	....	....	....	....	....	....	....
Linton (6)	MC 812 847-7754	Jim Wright	....	Ronald Sparks	....	Henry Mercier	Norman Watson	....
Logansport (17)	MC 219 753-2551	....	....	....	....	....	....	....
Loogootee (3)	MC 812 295-4770	....	....	....	....	....	....	....
Lowell t (6)	CM 219 696-7794	Robert Hatch	George Gray	Marcia Carlson	Marcia Carlson	Dwight Rench	Tom Felder	....
Madison (12)	MC 812 265-8300	....	....	....	....	....	....	....
Marion (33)	MC 317 668-4462	Ron Mowery	Tim Harris	Kathleen Kiley	Evelyn Stephenson	Robert Johnson	David Homer	Owen Gilbert Jr
Martinsville (12)	MC 317 342-6012	....	....	....	....	....	....	....
Merrillville (27)	MC 219 769-3501	David Mirich	Thomas Keilman	John E Petalas	John E Petalas	....	John Shelhart	Daniel Orlich
Michigan City (34)	MC 219 873-1400	Robert J Behler	....	Thomas Fedder	Charles Oberlie	Michael Marciniak	Larry Kunkel	....
Middletown t (2)	CM 317 354-2268	....	....	....	....	....	....	....
Mishawaka (43)	MC 219 258-1600	Robert Beutter	....	Deborah Block	Edwina Kintner	Ronald Watson	George Obren	Philip Miller
Mitchell (5)	MC 812 849-2151	.:.	....	....	R Berkshire	Michael Keever	Patrick Whitaker	....
Monticello (5)	MC 219 583-9889	Richard Cronch	....	....	R Berkshire	Michael Keever	Patrick Whitaker	....
Mooresville t (6)	RT 317 831-1608	Patricia Overhols	....	Ann Whaley	Ann Whaley	Darrell Brown	George Ditton	Joseph Beikman
Mount Vernon (7)	MC 812 838-3317	Jackson L Higgins	....	Laura C Bullard	....	Roger D Waters	Glenn R Boyster	Steven B Wild
Muncie (71)	MC 317 747-4846	David M Dominick	....	Jack E Donati	Joseph W Chance	Gary L Lucas	Carl D Ent	....
Munster t (20)	CM 219 836-8810	Larry Illingworth	Thomas DeGiulio	Phyllis A Hayden	Phyllis A Hayden	Robert Nowaczyk	William Sudbury	Larry Lowery
Nappanee (6)	MC 219 773-2112	....	....	....	....	....	....	....
New Albany (36)	MC 812 948-5333	Douglas B England	Jo Ann R Andres	....	Kathlyn M Garry	Ron Toran	Mathie Anderson	John Mattingly
New Castle (18)	MC 317 529-3502	....	....	....	....	....	....	....
New Chicago t (2)	MC 219 962-1157	....	....	....	....	....	....	....
New Haven (9)	MC 219 749-1911	Lynn H Shaw	....	Caroline R Knepp	....	George Mason	Geoff Robison	Dennis Partridge
New Whiteland t (4)	CM 317 535-9487	Edward J Suding	Maribeth Alspach	Maribeth Alspach	....	Michael Craig	William Withers	Richard L Abbott
Newburgh t (3)	MC 812 853-3578	....	....	....	....	....	....	....
Noblesville (18)	MC 317 773-4614	Mary Sue Rowland	Calvin Kuhn	Marilyn Conner	....	Ken Gilliam	Tim Garner	....
North Manchester t (6) ...	MC 219 982-6536	....	....	....	....	....	....	....
North Vernon (5)	MC 812 346-5907	John G Hall	....	....	....	Roy Matthews	Cecil Gerth Jr	....
Oakland City (3)	MC 812 749-3222	....	....	....	....	....	....	....
Paoli t (4)	MC 812 723-2739	....	....	....	....	....	....	....
Peru (13)	MC 317 472-2400	....	....	....	....	....	....	....
Petersburg (2)	MC 812 354-8511	....	....	....	....	....	....	....
Plainfield t (10)	MC 317 839-2561	Robin G Brandgard	Richard Carlucci	Julie Mitchell	....	Kevin Manning	Jack Miller	Carl Brown
Plymouth (8)	MC 219 936-2124	Jack B Greenlee	....	Beverly J Curtis	....	Wayne Smith	Thomas Chamberlin	....
Portage (29)	MC 219 762-7784	Sammie L Maletta	....	Felix C Kimbrough	Felix C Kimbrough	Daniel Thorn	Warren Lewis	....
Porter t (3)	CM 219 926-2771	....	....	....	....	....	....	....
Portland (6)	MC 219 726-9395	....	....	....	....	....	....	....
Princeton (8)	MC 812 385-4428	....	....	....	....	....	....	....
Rensselaer (5)	MC 219 866-5213	....	....	....	....	....	....	....
Richmond (39)	MC 317 983-7200	....	....	....	....	....	....	....
Rochester (6)	MC 219 223-2510	Edward J Fansler	....	Freda Miller	....	James Cheesman	Richard Roe	Edward J Fansler
Rockville t (3)	MC 317 569-6253	....	....	....	....	....	....	....
Rushville (6)	MC 317 932-2672	....	....	....	....	....	....	....
Salem (6)	MC 812 883-4265	....	....	....	....	....	....	....
Schererville t (20)	CM 219 322-2211	Mary Jaskula	Stephen Z Kil	Larry J Briski	....	Edward Kaeser	Jesse W Cook	Kenneth Crocilla
Scottsburg (5)	MC 812 752-4343	William H Graham	....	Betty Hayes	....	Raymond Jones	Delbert Meeks	William H Graham
Sellersburg t (6)	MC 812 246-3821	....	....	....	....	....	....	....
Seymour (16)	MC 812 522-4020	....	....	....	....	....	....	....
Shelbyville (15)	MC 317 398-6624	Robert E Williams	....	....	....	Kenneth D Scott	Kehrt M Etherton	....
South Bend (106)	MC 219 235-9216	Joseph E Kernan	Ernest J Reed	Irene K Gammon	Kevin C Horton	Luther Taylor	Ronald Marciniak	John Leszczynski
Speedway t (13)	MC 317 241-2566	....	....	....	....	....	....	....
Spencer t (3)	MC 812 829-3213	....	....	Brenda Craig	Brenda Craig	Rick Shields	Jack Loudermilk	....
St. John t (5)	MC 219 365-8636	Carl Brown	....	Judith Companik	Judith Companik	John Geary	Joseph Guzik	Clarence Monix
Sullivan (5)	MC 812 268-6077	Herman A Smith	....	Myrna G Power	....	Robert F Smith	Roy L Dillingham	Herman A Smith
Syracuse t (3)	RT 219 457-3216	Kennth Johson	Mathew Vigneault	Elgie Tatman	....	Jerry Byrd	Robert Ziller	....

Directory 1/9
continued

**MUNICIPAL OFFICIALS
IN U.S. CITIES OVER 2,500**

City, 1990 population figures (000 omitted), form of government	Municipal phone number	Mayor/ chief elected official	Appointed administrator	City clerk/ city secretary	Finance officer	Fire chief	Police chief	Public works director
INDIANA (159) continued								
Tell City (8)	MC 812 547-2349	....	....	....	....	....	....	....
Terre Haute (57)	MC 812 232-9467	....	....	....	....	....	....	....
Tipton (5)	MC 317 675-7561	David Berkemeier	....	....	Beth A Roach	L Mark Herron	Robert Sullivan	....
Trail Creek t (2)	MC 219 872-2422	Daniel W Tompkins	....	Anne M Dobbs	Anne M Dobbs	....	Eugene E Pierce	....
Union City (4)	MC 317 964-6534	Perry E Miller	....	Patricia C Hunt	....	William Mangas	Monte E Poling	Perry E Miller
Upland t (3)	MC 317 998-7439	....	....	....	....	....	....	....
Valparaiso (24)	MC 219 462-1161	....	....	....	....	....	....	....
Vincennes (20)	MC 812 882-7285	Belle Kasting	....	Mary Hurt	....	Michael Siewers	Dennis Holt	Kenneth Burnworth
Wabash (12)	MC 219 563-4171	....	....	....	....	....	....	....
Warsaw (11)	MC 219 372-9545	Jeffrey Plank	....	....	....	Kenny Shepherd	Craig Allebach	Kim Leake
Washington (11)	MC 812 254-5575	Charles T Baumert	....	Rita E Ducharme	....	Larry J Turk	Ronald G Perkins	....
West Lafayette (26)	MC 317 463-3571	Sonya L Margerum	Nicole McMillin	....	Judith C Rhodes	Ronald Ford	Dennis Mitchell	David Downey
Westfield t (3)	MC 317 896-5577	....	Jerry Rosenberger	Mary Lou Thatcher	....	Bob Smith	Bryan Foster	....
Whiting (5)	MC 219 659-7700	Robert J Bercik	....	Margaret Drewniak	....	Mark Kobli	Dennis Weller	....
Winchester (5)	MC 317 584-6845	Jack L Fowler	....	Marilyn Pash	Marilyn Pash	Bill Yost	Ted Jones	Jack L Fowler
Winona Lake t (4)	CM 219 267-7581	David Baker	....	....	Retha S Hicks	Roger Gelbaugh	Terry Howie	....
Yorktown t (4)	CM 317 759-8521	....	....	....	....	....	....	....
Zionsville t (5)	MC 317 873-2469	....	....	....	....	....	....	....
IOWA (133)								
Adel (3)	CM 515 993-4525	Jim Peters	Jim Sanders	Jim Sanders	....	Earl Stucker	Bill Hansen	....
Albia (4)	MC 515 932-2129	Nancy Spaur	....	Carl Gragg	....	John Duorak	Kenneth Powers	Thomas Murph
Algona (6)	MC 515 295-2411	Linda Becker	....	Garlene Schmidt	....	Donald Petersen	Kevin Bangert	Timothy Stovie
Altoona (7)	MC 515 967-5136	Timothy Burget	Thomas Hadden	Robert Fagen	....	....	Ronald Smith	Vernon Willey
Ames (47)	CM 515 239-5199	Larry Curtis	Steven Schainker	Sandra Ryan	Alice Carroll	Mike Childs	Dennis Ballantine	Paul Wiegand
Anamosa (5)	MC 319 462-6055	Dennis Hansen	John Haldeman	Suzanne Marek	....	Mike Shaffer	Richard Stivers	Gary Kula
Ankeny (18)	CM 515 965-6400	John Voigt	Carl M Metzger	Jo Ann Goins	Jo Ann Goins	Thomas Strait	Dennis L Ballard	Richard Ash
Atlantic (7)	MC 712 243-4810	Charles E Smith	....	Debbie L Wheatley	....	Scott Rhoads	Roer Muri	....
Audubon (3)	MC 712 563-3269	....	....	....	....	....	....	....
Belle Plaine (3)	MC 319 444-2200	Tom Hollopeter	....	Kaye Buch	....	Dennis Greenlee	Ron Tippett	Dick Ehlen
Belmond (3)	CM 515 444-3386	....	....	....	....	....	....	....
Bettendorf (28)	MC 319 344-4000	Ann Hutchinson	Decker P Ploehn	Decker P Ploehn	Carol Barnes	Gerald Voelliger	Philip Redington	Gerald Springer
Bloomfield (3)	MC 515 664-2260	H Nardini Crall	....	M McElderry	....	Robert Hougland	Bernard Gutz	Alan D Johnson
Boone (12)	MC 515 432-4211	George F Maybee	Jeffrey Kooistra	Audrey Veldhuizen	Audrey Veldhuizen	Edward Knight	Steven Peasley	James Bustad
Buffalo (1)	MC 319 381-2226	Phil C Hoover	....	Carol A Bernauer	Carol A Bernauer	Terry Adams	Gage D Adams	Dwain G Bollman
Burlington (27)	CM 319 753-8124	J M Heland	M J Wood	K P Salisbury	D J Worden	W L Ell	....	....
Camanche (4)	MC 319 259-8342	....	....	....	....	....	....	....
Carlisle t (3)	MC 515 989-3224	Marvin W Grace	....	Ethe L Lee	....	Mike Prodreborac	Terry B Hardy	....
Carroll (10)	MC 712 792-1000	....	....	....	....	....	....	....
Carter Lake (7)	MC 712 347-6320	....	....	....	....	....	....	....
Cedar Falls (34)	MC 319 273-8600	Ed Stachovic	....	Gary Hesse	Sara Narigon	Arthur Lupkes	Michael Reifsteck	C Budd Curttright
Cedar Rapids (109)	CO 319 398-5000	Larry Serbousek	....	Ann Ollinger	Robert McMahan	Joseph Gorman	William Byrne	Donald Thomas
Centerville (6)	MC 515 437-4339	....	....	....	....	....	....	....
Chariton (5)	CM 515 774-5991	Wm Paul Marner	Edward W Elam	Ruth A Ryun	....	Steve Irving	Jay A Fisher	....
Charles City (8)	MC 515 257-6300	Jeffrey P Sisson	....	Jody J Meyer	Jody J Meyer	Dewayne Meyer	Jim Zirbel	Dan H Barrett
Cherokee (6)	MC 712 225-5749	Bernard Kult	Gilbert Bremicker	Debra Taylor	....	Jack Olson	James Ebert	....
Clarinda (5)	CM 712 542-2136	Frank Snyder	Robert Bailey	Robert Bailey	....	Roger Williams	Joe Newton	Martin Walter
Clarion (3)	MC 515 532-2847	Bernie Case	Vicky J Fluhrer	Vicky J Fluhrer	....	Maurice Riley	Steve Hennigar	Jim Redemske
Clear Lake City (8)	MC 515 357-5267	Lois Kotz	Thomas A Lincoln	Thomas A Lincoln	....	John A Simpson	Daniel J Jackson	Joseph A Weigel
Clinton (29)	CM 319 242-7545	Darrell Smith	George Langmack	Deborah Neels	....	Russell Luckritz	Gene Beinke	James Haag Jr
Clive (7)	MC 515 223-6220	Robert Brownell	Daniel Olson	Marjorie Roberts	....	Vance Riley	Dean Dymond	Willard Wray
Coralville (10)	MC 319 351-1266	Alan Axeen	Kelly Hayworth	Arlys Hannam	....	Gary Kinsinger	Barry Bedford	....
Council Bluffs (54)	CM 712 328-4601	....	....	Sharon Smutzler	....	Vience Hornberger	Tom Heath	Gary Leinhard
Cresco (4)	MC 319 547-3101	Arletta Rose	....	Mary Moore	Joseph G Parker	Melford Johnston	Robert Kessler	Tom Myers
Creston (8)	MC 515 782-2000	Terry Donahue	....	Jackie Ragsdale	Kent Kolwey	Tom Ryan	Donald S Lynn	Dee Bruemmer
Davenport (95)	CM 319 326-7711	Patrick J Gibbs	Cowles Mallory	Sharon Albers	Kay Goddard	John Burken	Richard Peasley	Richard Mohr
De Witt (5)	MC 319 659-3811	Leo Maynard	Cary Conger	Wanda Hemesath	....	Roger Hamilton	Ben Wyatt	D Mac Cormick
Decorah (8)	MC 319 382-3651	Donald Wurtzel	Gerald Freund	M Bretey	....	....	R Bradley	....
Denison (7)	MC 712 263-3143	R Borcherding	....	D Boetel Baker	M Frederickson	Charles Morgan	William Moulder	John Bellizzi
Des Moines (193)	CM 515 283-4500	John Pat Dorrian	Cy Carney	Mary A Davis	Duane Pitcher	William T Miller	John J Mauss	Michael A Koch
Dubuque (58)	CM 319 589-4121	Terrance M Duggan	M Van Milligan	S Steffen Ertl	....	Robert Platz	Allen W Clouse	David J Vorwald
Dyersville (4)	MC 319 875-7724	Robert H Kramer	Gary A Jasper	John M Call	Sue Maier	Gary Lalor	Curt Green	Carl Halverson
Eagle Grove (4)	CM 515 448-4343	Kieth Riley	John M Call	....	....	Bruce Harvey	James K Collins	Tim Hoskins
Eldora (3)	CM 515 858-2393	Bradley Armstrong	Roger Tinklenberg	....	....	....	....	....
Eldridge (3)	MC 319 285-4841	....	....	....	....	....	....	....
Emmetsburg (4)	MC 712 852-4030	Norlyn Stowell	Lee Frederick	R Argabright	....	Virgil Huberty	Eric Hanson	William Dickey
Estherville (7)	MC 712 362-7771	....	....	....	....	....	....	....
Evansdale (5)	MC 319 232-6683	John W Mardis	....	Carol J Wilson	....	Peter Weber	M McConnell	....
Fairfield (10)	MC 515 472-6193	....	....	Paul D Boock	....	....	....	....
Forest City (4)	MC 515 582-3574	Paul L Jefson	....	Paul D Boock	....	Douglas Yeager	Douglas W Book	....
Fort Dodge (26)	MC 515 576-4551	....	....	....	....	....	....	....
Fort Madison (12)	MC 319 372-7700	Arlene J Carlson	John R Pick	Judy A Clark	....	Steve Etka	Jerry Koerber	Scott Peppler
Garner (3)	MC 515 923-2588	....	....	....	....	....	....	....
Glenwood (5)	MC 712 527-4717	....	....	....	....	....	....	....
Graettinger (1)	MC 712 859-3742	....	....	....	....	....	....	....
Grinnell (9)	CM 515 236-2600	Robert E Anderson	Theodore Clausen	Pamela Rupe	....	Jerry Barns	M Birmingham	....
Grundy Center (2)	MC 319 824-6118	Troy Anderson	....	Kenneth Havel	....	Gerald Hoffman	Bruce Stotser	Jim Copeman
Guttenberg (2)	CM 319 252-1161	....	....	....	....	....	....	....
Hampton (4)	MC 515 456-4853	W Roger Palmer	Bruce R Slagle	Bruce R Slagle	....	Ronald Weldin	Selden Nelson	Montey G Halls
Harlan (5)	MC 712 755-5137	....	....	....	....	....	....	....
Hawarden (2)	MC 712 552-2565	....	....	....	....	....	....	....
Hiawatha (5)	MC 319 393-1515	Thomas A Theis	Thomas W Lewis	Roberta A Hamdorf	Roberta A Hamdorf	Mark Powers	David M Saari	....
Humboldt (4)	CM 515 332-3435	Steven N Samuels	Dennis L Pyle	Dennis L Pyle	Dennis L Pyle	Sherman Silbaugh	Jon B Reed	Leroy Clapper
Ida Grove (2)	MC 712 364-2428	Ronald J Powell	....	Diane F Alborn	Diane F Alborn	Jeff Hewitt	....	....
Independence (6)	MC 319 334-2780	Donna K Hansen	....	N Clark Madison	....	Charles Conklin	Randy Miller	N Clark Madison
Indianola (11)	CM 515 961-9410	George Hladky	Tim Zisoff	Mark Ramthun	....	Dean Hutt	Paul Scranton	....
Iowa City (60)	CM 319 356-5000	Susan Horowitz	Stephen Atkins	Marian Karr	Donald Yucuis	James Pumfrey	R J Winkelhake	Charles Schmadeke
Iowa Falls (5)	CM 515 648-2527	Daniel Brown	Michael Hays	Larry Smith	Larry Smith	Marlyn Humphrey	William Reeves	Merlin Clock
Jefferson (4)	CM 515 386-3111	Charles F Davis	Tim Moerman	Diane Kennedy	Diane Kennedy	Eldon Cunningham	Dan Taylor	....
Johnston (5)	MC 515 278-2344	John R Ver Hoef	Robert E Hays	Diane Oltman	Margaret A Sharp	Jerry Smeltzer	Bruce Gaddis	Jerry Meyers
Keokuk (12)	MC 319 524-2050	....	....	....	....	....	....	....
Knoxville (8)	CM 515 828-0550	Mike Cunningham	....	Connie Stevens	Keith Moody	Dwayne Robuck	C Wooldridge	....
Lamoni (2)	MC 515 784-6311	Orville L Hiles	....	Kirk Bjorland	....	Roger Potts	Dale Killpack	....

Directory 1/9 continued

MUNICIPAL OFFICIALS IN U.S. CITIES OVER 2,500

City, 1990 population figures (000 omitted), form of government	Municipal phone number	Mayor/ chief elected official	Appointed administrator	City clerk/ city secretary	Finance officer	Fire chief	Police chief	Public works director
IOWA (133) continued								
Le Claire (3)	CM 319 289-5441	....	....	....	....	....	....	....
Le Mars (8)	MC 712 546-7018	....	....	....	....	....	....	....
Manchester (5)	MC 319 927-3636	....	....	....	....	....	....	....
Maquoketa (6)	CM 319 652-2484	Clifton C Lamborn	Francis Glaser	Francis Glaser	....	Harold Lubben	Mark Brooks	Randy Crouch
Marion (20)	CM 319 377-1581	V Klopfenstein	Jeff Schott	Wesley Nelson	Wesley Nelson	James Ford	Mark Diamond	Rex Parsons
Marshalltown (25)	CM 515 754-5700	T R Thompson Jr	Edward A Geick	Mary J Skartvedt	Edward A Geick	Rex Mundt	Ajmes K Wilkinson	Wayne Hartwig
Mason City (29)	MC 515 421-3604	Carl Miller	Mark McNeill	A Carlene Davis	Charles Hammen	Ron Van Horn	Duane Jewell	Victor Potter
Missouri Valley (3)	MC 712 642-3502	Ronald B Reiff	Robert J Alborn	Robert J Alborn	....	Kenny Athay	Austin O' Brien	....
Monticello (4)	MC 319 465-3577	Bernie B Barker	....	Mary Hunt	....	Clarence Goedken	Burton Walters	....
Mount Pleasant (8)	MC 319 385-1470	Stanley Hill	Scott Neal	Florence Olomon	....	Stewart Kinney	....	Steve Hoyer
Mount Vernon (4)	MC 319 895-8742	Rick Elliott	Michael R Beimer	Michael R Beimer	....	Dan Gaines	Mick Michel	....
Muscatine (23)	CM 319 264-1550	Jeanette Phillips	A J Johnson	....	Dave Casstevens	Steve Dalbey	Gary Coderoni	Randy Hill
Nevada (6)	CM 515 382-5466	James Christy	Dennis Henderson	Sue North	Sue North	Steve Herr	Mark See	Keith Hobson
New Hampton (4)	MC 515 394-5906	A Donald Johnson	....	Suellen Kolbet	....	Pete Willadson	Michael Anderson	Donald J Markle
Newton (15)	CM 515 792-2787	....	....	....	....	....	....	....
Nora Springs (2)	MC 515 749-5315	....	....	....	....	....	....	....
Norwalk (6)	MC 515 981-0228	J L Starkweather	Mark W Miller	Joyce Corton	....	Frank Curtis	Mike Richardson	Dean C Yordi
Oelwein (6)	CM 319 283-5440	Gene M Vine	Steven H Kendall	Steven Kendall	Steven Kendall	Wallace Rundle	John Y Shirkey	Michael Kringlen
Onawa (3)	MC 712 423-1181	Dwight Lamb	Chris R Rustin	Chris R Rustin	Chris R Rustin	Jeffery L Sander	Thomas Vaughn	Jeffery L Sander
Orange City (5)	CM 712 737-4885	....	....	....	....	....	....	....
Osage (3)	MC 515 732-3709	....	....	....	....	....	....	....
Osceola (4)	CM 515 342-2377	....	....	....	....	....	....	....
Oskaloosa (11)	MC 515 673-9431	Norman Zimmerman	Donald Sandor	Marilyn Miller	Marilyn Miller	David Miller	John McGee	Larry Stevens
Ottumwa (24)	MC 515 683-0625	Dale Uehling	Robert Keefe	Ann Cullinan	Michael Heffernan	Dan Thompson	Art LeTourneau	Christy Collicott
Pella (9)	MC 515 628-4173	Johnny A Menninga	Steve Bell	Beverly J Graves	Karen A Shimp	George Carson	Gene Vos	Ron Knoke
Perry (7)	MC 515 465-2481	David Wright	Michael Farley	Cindy McDowell	Thomas Blake	Wilford Roberts	Daniel Brickner	William Simmer
Pleasant Hill (4)	MC 515 262-9368	Phil Hildebrand	Shona Ringgenberg	Shona Ringgenberg	....	Alvin Snyder	Thomas Wilson	Allen Schoemaker
Pocahontas (2)	MC 712 335-4841	Lowell Pedersen	Brian James	Ila Mae Kraus	....	Harold Stoulil	Byran Essing	....
Red Oak (6)	MC 712 623-4908	James A Johnson	Ronald A Crisp	Ronald A Crisp	....	Rick Askey	Dennis Steffensen	....
Rock Rapids (3)	MC 712 472-2511	C J Gustafson	Judy A Weins	....	....	Gary Hunt	James P Kille	....
Rock Valley (3)	MC 712 476-5707	....	....	....	....	....	....	....
Sac City (2)	CM 712 662-7593	Glen L Duncan	Gary C Mahannah	Gary C Mahnnah	....	John Phillips	John Zimmerman	....
Sanborn (1)	MC 712 729-3842	Donald Kroese	John Bird	John Bird	Candice Lyman	D Vanveldhuizen	Gary Grapevine	Randy Lyman
Sheldon (5)	MC 712 324-4651	M Uittenbogaard	....	Sherlene Krogman	....	....	Larry Locke	Eldor Schuerman
Shenandoah (6)	MC 712 246-4411	Robert Creighton	Merrill J Kruse	....	....	Donald Gibson	James Davey	....
Sibley (3)	CM 712 754-2541	....	....	....	....	....	....	....
Sioux Center (5)	MC 712 722-0761	W Dale Den Herder	Brian Gramentz	Brian Gramentz	Eldon Westra	Stan Altena	Paul Adkins	Harold Schiebout
Sioux City (81)	CM 712 279-6200	Robert Scott	Arlen Wiggs	Shirley Brown	John Meyers	Robert Hamilton	Gary Maas	John Arnold
Spencer (11)	MC 712 264-7200	Cleber Meyer	Dan Payne	Donna Fisher	....	Doug Duncan	Marlin Wimmer	Charles Fisher
Spirit Lake (4)	MC 712 336-1871	....	....	....	....	....	....	....
Storm Lake (9)	MC 712 732-8000	Sandra Madsen	Clarence Krepps	Patti Moore	Brian Schaeffer	Ronald Wilson	Mark Prosser	Patrick Kelly
Story City (3)	MC 515 733-2121	Harold A Holm	Mark A Jackson	Pat Twedt	Mark A Jackson	Jim Beck	Brian Haffner	....
Tama (3)	MC 515 484-3822	Richard Gibson	....	Judy Welch	....	Gary Zigler	Rod McCool	Bernrd Brezina
Tipton (3)	MC 319 886-6187	....	Jim Webb	John Foley	Roberta Parker	John Miller	John Soenksen	Don Drager
Urbandale (24)	CM 515 278-3900	....	....	....	....	....	....	....
Vinton (5)	MC 319 472-4707	John Watson	Don Martin	Barb Smith	....	Bob Downs	Jeff Tilson	Don Martin
Washington (7)	MC 319 653-6584	....	Robert Stevenson	....	....	....	....	....
Waterloo (66)	MC 319 291-4311	John R Rooff	....	Diane Sweeney	Diane Sweeney	Frank Magsamen	Bernal Koehrsen	....
Waukon (4)	MC 319 568-3491	Ralph Grotegut	....	....	Jack Bachhuger	Robert Campbell	Loren Fiet	Francis Kessel
Waverly (9)	MC 319 352-4252	Zelle Lester	Richard Crayne	....	....	David Nelson	Art Simpson	Tom Goff
Webster City (8)	CM 515 832-9151	C N Dermand	John Rudd	Gerald K Kent	....	Terry Johnston	Michael Petricca	Greg Malmstrom
West Bend (..)	MC 515 887-2181	Eddie Zinn	Mary J Steil	Laura Montag	....	....	Bill Rasmussen	Robert Mikes
West Burlington (3)	MC 319 752-5451	Hans K Trousil	David Plyman	Terrie Simonson	....	K Beenblossom	....	Daniel Shipley
West Des Moines (32)	CM 515 223-3241	....	....	....	....	....	....	....
West Liberty (3)	CM 319 627-2418	John J Gerstbrein	William T Powers	William T Powers	....	Ken Morrison	Roy Warson	M Joe Stiff
West Point (1)	MC 319 837-6313	Paul Walker	C A White	Mary Winnike	C A White	Dan Schierbrock	Rusty Pavey	....
West Union (2)	MC 319 422-3320	....	....	....	....	....	....	....
Wilton (3)	MC 319 732-2115	....	....	....	....	....	....	....
Windsor Heights (5)	MC 515 279-3662	Donald C Steele	James H Spradling	James H Spradling	....	Albert Hunter	William Hitchcock	John Wiedman
Winterset (4)	MC 515 462-1422	J Schwertfeger	....	Mark Nitchals	Mark Nitchals	R Truckenbrod	Clyde Klave	Randy Jeffs
KANSAS (112)								
Abilene (6)	CM 913 263-2550	John R Zutavern	John A Hier	Mildred E Hanson	....	....	Jim Davis	Cliff Gibbs
Andover (4)	CM 316 733-1303	Jack Finlason	Patricia Stuenkel	Teresa Sexon	....	....	Thomas Mathes	Leslie Mangus
Anthony (3)	CO 316 842-5434	....	Donald F Heidrick	Donald F Heidrick	Donald F Heidrick	Kenny Hodson	John H Blevins	Priscilla Goucher
Arkansas City (13)	CM 316 441-4405	Jerald Hooley	Curtis Freeland	Rod Franz	Ron Franz	Eddie Moore	James Lazelle	Ron Parker
Atchison (11)	CM 913 367-5081	Vicki Hegarty	Joseph Turner	Phyllis Walton	Shirley Moses	Mike McDermed	Mike Wilson	John Hixon
Augusta (8)	CM 316 775-7671	J David Crum	Warren Porter	Elsie George	....	....	David Pate	Frank Dewitt
Baxter Springs (4)	MC 316 856-2114	Terry L Martin	....	Darla Snook	....	Les Page	Gary Allen	....
Belleville (3)	CM 913 527-2288	Doris Beardsley	Roger Mock	C Derowitsch	....	Don Slaughter	Raymond Smee	....
Beloit (4)	MC 913 738-3551	....	....	....	....	....	....	....
Bonner Springs (6)	CM 913 422-1020	T A Stolfus	Thomas Cooley	Sue Stinnett	Sue Stinnett	Warren Hanks	Kenneth Gates	....
Burlington (3)	MC 316 364-5334	Gene L Merry	....	Daniel K Allen	....	Larry Johnson	Steve Timmons	Alfred Mann
Chanute (9)	MC 316 431-5200	Leroy Chard	Robert Walker	James Youngberg	....	....	....	....
Cheney (2)	MC 316 542-3622	....	....	....	....	....	....	....
Cherryvale (2)	CM 316 336-2776	Randy L Wagoner	C Gary Weiland	Ramona Beard	....	Paul Newton	Tim Downum	....
Clay Center (5)	MC 913 632-5454	Donald R Hatfield	....	Calvin Wohler	....	Jerome Dieker	Mark Dunn	....
Clearwater (2)	MC 316 584-2311	Bruce Long	Yvonne E Coon	Debra K Shepard	....	Marvin Schauf	Mike Friday	Jim Peissig
Coffeyville (13)	CM 316 252-6100	Perl S Schmid	Leroy D Alsup	Donna Schoonover	Joyce E Buckner	J D Spohn	Allen Flowers	....
Colby (5)	CM 913 462-3973	R V Van Camp	Carolyn Armstrong	Nola Sloan	Nola Sloan	Ivan Lee	Randall Jones	Michael Albers
Columbus (3)	MC 316 429-2159	....	....	....	....	....	....	....
Concordia (6)	CM 913 243-2670	Gregory L Hattan	Chad C Olsen Jr	Verna Ferguson	....	Jack P Graves	Burl Maley	Tom Fisher
Council Grove (2)	MC 316 767-5417	....	....	....	....	....	....	....
Derby (15)	CM 316 788-1519	K O Lavergne	Phillip Nelson	Patty Kroll	....	Patrick Swaney	Delbert Fowler	Patrick Cillessen
Dodge City (21)	CM 316 225-8100	Robert Carlson	John Deardoff	....	Nannette Lampe	Pat Simpson	Ralph Oakley	Harold Leedom
Edwardsville (4)	CM 913 441-3707	John A McTaggart	Edward E Dawson	Phyllis Freeman	Linda Johnson	Roy Reed	Larry Dixon	....
El Dorado (12)	CM 316 321-9100	Edward L Blake	Stan B Stewart	Adam R Collins	Adam R Collins	....	Victor S Marshall	Oral W Taylor
Ellinwood (2)	MC 316 564-3161	Joe E Hickel	Melvin Waite	Chris Wornkey	....	Art Huslig	Kevin Pe Karek	....
Emporia (26)	CM 316 342-5105	Elvin D Perkins	Steve A Commons	Susan A Mendoza	Larry Bucklinger	James L Woydziak	Robert Rodriguez	Charles F Soules
Eudora (3)	MC 913 542-2153	James Hoover	....	Jo Ann Becker	....	Benny Dean	William Long	Gary Malburg
Eureka (3)	CO 316 583-5611	James H Francis	....	Linda K Martell	....	Allen Hall	....	Gordon Harrison
Fairway (4)	MC 913 262-0350	C Edward Peterson	....	Joni Ripper	Joni Ripper	....	Roy Miller	Henry Lopez
Fort Scott (8)	CM 316 223-0550	Steve Armstrong	Richard Nienstedt	DeElda Coyan	Nancy Calkins	Robert Lowe	Jim Huff	Dennis Kennon

Directory 1/9 continued — MUNICIPAL OFFICIALS IN U.S. CITIES OVER 2,500

City, 1990 population figures (000 omitted), form of government		Municipal phone number	Mayor/ chief elected official	Appointed administrator	City clerk/ city secretary	Finance officer	Fire chief	Police chief	Public works director
KANSAS (112) continued									
Fredonia (3)	CO	316 378-2231	....	....	....	....	....	....	....
Frontenac (3)	MC	316 231-9210	Oscar Deplue	....	Richard Cicero	....	Michael Hagerty	Carl Flora	Fred Bailey
Galena (3)	MC	316 783-5265	Dale Oglesby	....	Jeanie Holstrom	....	Bill Hall	Gerald Hentz	Bud Sills
Garden City (24)	CM	316 276-1172	Dennis Mesa	Robert Halloran	Jean Solze	Melinda Hitz	Alan Shelton	Roger Schroeder	....
Gardner (..)	MC	913 884-7535	....	....	....	....	....	....	....
Garnett (3)	CM	913 448-5496	Michael L Norman	Richard G Doran	Joyce E Martin	Joyce E Martin	Jerry Gettler	Jack Eden	Bill Garrison
Girard (3)	CO	316 724-8918	Jerry D Staton	William Crawford	Carolie J Bennett	....	Ronald E Scales	Randal Pommier	Dave Crumpacker
Goddard (2)	MC	316 794-2441	B J Means	....	Nicki V Vanosdall	....	....	Doyle L Dyer	Larry G Padley
Goodland (5)	CM	913 899-4500	John Golden	Ron Thornburg	Mary Antholz	....	Dean Jensen	Ron Pickman	Gary Newell
Great Bend (15)	MC	316 793-4100	George Drake	Howard Partington	Deborah Durler	Deborah Durler	Marion Root	Dean Akings	....
Hays (18)	CM	913 625-2815	Robert Albers	Hannes Zacharias	Carol Sue Grabbe	Carol Sue Grabbe	Wayne Schwartz	Lawrence Younger	Leo J Wellbrock
Haysville (8)	MC	316 524-3243	Tom Lindsay	....	Carol McBeath	Beverly Rodgers	....	James E Kitchings	John Eaglin
Herington (3)	CM	913 258-2271	Barbara Mastin	John Carder	Debra Wendt	....	....	Dale Kuhn	....
Hesston (3)	MC	316 327-4412	John D Waltner	John T Wieland	Jean Krehbiel	....	Lyle Bitikofer	Mickey DeHook	....
Hiawatha (4)	MC	913 742-7417	James Scherer	Steven King	Laurie Neeman	....	Gary Shear	Jim Wolney	....
Hillsboro (3)	MC	316 947-3162	....	....	....	....	....	....	....
Hoisington (3)	CM	316 653-4125	....	....	....	....	....	....	....
Holton (3)	MC	913 364-2721	Steven Stenger	Bradley Mears	Pat McClintock	....	....	Gale Gakle	....
Horton (2)	CM	913 486-2681	Edwin C Buser	Ted Hauser	Shelia Gibson	....	Kenneth Krug	Lamar Schoemaker	....
Hugoton (3)	MC	316 544-8531	Tom L Greenway	Thomas G Hicks	Thomas G Hicks	Thomas G Hicks	....	Donald L Brown	Jerry Leonard
Hutchinson (39)	CM	316 694-2610	James Fee	Joe Palacioz	Vernon Stallman	James Onello	Dallas Jones	James Heitschmidt	Dennis Clennan
Independence (10)	CM	316 332-2500	G Burks Sherwood	Paul A Sasse	Anthony D Royse	....	Dale A Rail	Lee A Bynum	Earl F Smith Jr
Iola (6)	CO	316 365-4900	Ray Pershall	Weldon Padgett	Carolyn Dreher	Judith Brigham	Wayne Still	Rex Taylor	....
Junction City (21)	CM	913 238-3103	Kevin J Connell	Blaine R Hinds	Rodney D Barnes	Rodney D Barnes	Lawrence E Bruzda	Thomas L Clark Jr	Michael J Fraser
Kansas City (150)	CM	913 573-5000	Joseph Steineger	David Isabell	Tom Roberts	Nancy Zielke	John Bergman	Tom Dailey	Gary Stubbs
Kingman (3)	MC	316 532-3111	Ronald L Kinsler	....	Cindy Conrardy	....	Don Fischer	Paul Kalmar	Frank Smith
Kinsley (2)	MC	316 659-3611	B Montgomery	Janet Freel	Marsha Haxton	....	Buford Brodbeck	Doug Murphy	Newton Baker
La Crosse (1)	CM	913 222-2511	Gerald Washburn	Robert N Barnhart	Sherri Stevens	Robert N Barnhart	Armen Ideker	Leroy Penka	....
Lansing (7)	MC	913 727-3233	....	....	....	....	....	....	....
Larned (4)	CM	316 285-2149	Jerry Larson	Don Gaeddert	Vicki Gillett	....	Ralph Johnson	Charles Orth	Doug Springer
Lawrence (66)	CM	913 832-3000	F Jolene Andersen	H Michael Wildgen	Raymond J Hummert	A Ed Mullins	James McSwain	Wm Ronald Olin	George Williams
Leavenworth (38)	CM	913 682-9201	Frank B Minnis	Mark Pentz	Carol S Sadler	Daniel Williamson	James E Meyers	Lemoine Doehring	Michael McDonald
Leawood (20)	MC	913 642-5555	Marcia Rinehart	Richard Garofano	Martha Heizer	Harry Malnicof	Jerry Strack	J Stephen Cox	Ronald A Brandt
Lenexa (34)	MC	913 492-8800	Richard Becker	David Watkins	Sandra Howell	....	Kenneth Hobbs	Ellen Hanson	Bob Lowry
Liberal (17)	CM	316 626-0102	Joe Bridenburg	Richard Olson	Debra Giskie	Stanley Wilbers	Jach Taylor	Dariel D Hinsdale	Gerald H Memming
Lindsborg (3)	MC	913 227-3355	Don Anderson	Gary Meagher	Gary Meagher	Larry Lindgren	....	Tim Johnson	Tim Dunn
Lyons (4)	MC	316 257-2320	Charles Nichols	Dewey D Breese	Norma A Miller	....	James Miller	Dennis Luck	....
Madison (1)	CO	316 437-2556	Max D Kimberlin	....	Beth A Dains	....	Mike Buce	....	Dale L Haney
Maize (2)	MC	316 722-7561	Stephen Hutchens	Nancy Scott	Karen Bailey	....	....	Robert Circle	....
Manhattan (38)	CM	913 537-0056	Helen G Cooper	James R Pearson	Martha P Scott	Curt Wood	Larry D Reese	....	Bruce McCallum
Marysville (3)	MC	913 562-5331	James L Lindeen	Gerald Cooper	Paula Holle	....	Charles Lindeen	Bryan Davidson	....
Mc Cracken (..)	MC	913 394-2229	....	....	....	....	....	....	....
Mc Pherson (12)	CO	316 241-6300	....	....	....	....	....	....	....
Merriam (12)	MC	913 722-3330	Irene B French	Eric Wade	Connie Schmidt	Michael Scanlon	Jerry Montgomery	Kenneth Sissom	Randall Carroll
Mission (10)	MC	913 722-3685	Sylvester Powell	....	Sue A Grosdidier	....	....	Robert A Sturm	Stephen L Weeks
Mission Hills (3)	MC	913 362-9620	Betty T Keim	Douglas O Cruce	Dianne R Starcke	....	James L W Smith	Charles F Grover	....
Mulvane (5)	MC	316 777-1143	Gerald Wing	Kent L Hixson	Patty Gerwick	Karen Rambo	Robert Welch	Wayne E Brown	Gary Rambo
Neodesha (3)	CM	316 325-2828	Oris Killebrew	James McEwen	Jo Vonnah Boecker	....	Charles Reynolds	James Shue	Jerry Lour
Newton (17)	CM	316 284-6000	Beulah E Day	Philip A Kloster	Sharon K Petersen	James M Heinicke	James E Jackson	Ronald Jackson	Lon W Walker
Norton (3)	MC	913 877-3355	James L Miller	Allen Loyd	Darla R Ellis	....	Mitch Jones	Lynn Menagh	....
Olathe (63)	CM	913 782-2600	Michael Haskin	Michael McCurdy	Howard Pevehouse	....	George F Bentley	Philip J Major	William Ramsey
Osage City (3)	MC	913 528-4325	Richard W Prine	....	Nina Gragg	....	Lawrence Buenger	Douglas Mathey	....
Osawatomie (5)	CM	913 755-2146	Charles R Heckart	Larry L Buchanan	Ann Elmquist	....	....	John Cragg	Howard Goodeyon
Oswego (2)	MC	316 795-4433	Philhip B Blair	Kris McKechnie	Cheri R Peine	....	M T Bringle	George Elliott	Jeff Strickland
Ottawa (11)	CM	913 242-2190	Vicki Cummiskey	Scott M Lambers	Scott D Bird	....	Richard Towe	Jeffrey D Herrman	Donald Haney
Overland Park (112)	CM	913 381-5252	Ed Eilert	Donald Pipes	Norma Moffet	Kristy Cannon	....	Myron Scafe	Dennsi Garrett
Paola (5)	CM	913 294-2397	Floyd J Grimes	Kise K Randall	Jill Ann Holmes	....	Robert T Harris	David E Smail	Joseph L Whitaker
Park City (5)	MC	316 744-2026	....	....	....	....	....	....	....
Parsons (12)	CM	316 421-7000	Robert J Bartelli	James Richardson	Mary E Reed	Mary E Reed	Gordon Fry	Gary Baldwin	Deck Shaver Jr
Phillipsburg (3)	MC	913 543-5234	....	....	....	....	....	....	....
Pittsburg (18)	CM	316 231-4100	Cindy Allen	Larry J Stevens	Karen K Garman	Jon B Garrison	William J Scott	Ralph W Shanks	John D Van Gorden
Prairie Village (23)	MC	913 381-6464	Monroe Talifero	Barbara Vernon	....	Steve Keel	....	Charles Grover	Robert Pryzby
Pratt (7)	CO	316 672-5571	....	....	....	....	....	....	....
Roeland Park (8)	MC	913 722-2600	....	....	....	....	....	....	....
Russell (5)	CM	913 483-6311	Neal Farmer	Judy Sargent	Karen Gates	....	Earl Hemphill	Bob E Tyler	Frank Peirano
Sabetha (2)	CO	913 284-2158	David Emert	Ted Hayden	Beverly Baker	....	Donald Strahm	Michael Hill	....
Salina (42)	CM	913 826-7400	....	....	....	....	....	....	....
Scott City (4)	MC	316 872-5322	Carl Kasten	....	Sharon Ricker	Paul Numrich	Ken Hoover	Alan Stewart	Preston Stewart
Shawnee (38)	CM	913 631-2500	Jim Allen	Gary Montague	Nancy Hodges	H Lee Meyer	H A Hartley	Tom Hayselden	Ron Freyermuth
Spring Hill (2)	MC	913 592-3624	....	....	....	....	....	....	....
St. Marys (2)	CM	913 437-2311	....	....	....	....	....	....	....
Sterling (2)	CM	316 278-3411	....	Randy Riggs	Sandra Fankhauser	Sandra Fankhauser	Bill Calderwood	Ron Groth	Kevin Roach
Stockton (2)	CO	913 425-6703	Leonard E Muir	Dan Pickett	Sandi Rogers	....	Richard Haines	Don Jenkins	Bill Schmitz
Topeka (120)	MC	913 295-3741	....	....	....	....	....	....	....
Ulysses (5)	MC	316 356-4600	Sylvester Hileman	Gary Burr	Paula Shapland	Paula Shapland	....	Lonnie Lee	....
Valley Center (4)	MC	316 755-7310	Robert W Robinson	Robert Finkbiner	Lynn E Ireland	....	M R Tormey	Kelly D Parks	Richard A Dunn
Wamego (4)	CM	913 456-9119	Robert V Johnson	Mark F Arbuthnot	T Leroy Stewart	....	Richard Varnadore	Kenneth W Seager	Claude R Asbury
Wellington (8)	MC	316 326-2811	Satn Gilliland	Carl Myers	Rose Miller	....	John Lloyd	Richard Granger	Rod Conwell
Westwood (2)	MC	913 362-1550	....	....	....	....	....	....	....
Wichita (304)	CM	316 268-4351	Elma Broadfoot	Chris Cherches	Pat Burnett	Ray E Trail	Lawrence Garcia	Rick D Stone	Stephen Lackey
Winfield (12)	CM	316 221-3060	Max Handlin	Richard E Cotton	Diane Rorecrans	....	George Gurley	Ron Gould	Russ Tomevi
KENTUCKY (112)									
Alexandria (6)	MC	606 635-4125	....	....	....	....	....	....	....
Ashland (24)	CM	606 327-2000	A Rudy Dunnigan	William Fisher Jr	Deborah D Musser	David D Johnson	Gary Watts	Ronald W McBride	Joseph P Harris
Barbourville (4)	MC	606 546-6197	Phillip E Connley	James E Tye	Debbie Hammons	....	James E Tye	Johnny E Smith	James M Baker
Bardstown (7)	MC	502 348-5947	....	....	....	....	....	....	....
Beaver Dam (3)	CO	502 274-7106	David Taylor	....	Bonnie Maddox	....	....	Gene Gaither	Roscoe Simpson
Bellevue (7)	MC	606 431-8866	Thomas J Wiethorn	Andrew Riffe	Mary H Scott	Mary H Scott	Ralph Quitter	Rick Sears	Randy Grosch
Benton (4)	MC	502 527-8677	....	....	....	....	....	....	....
Berea (9)	MC	606 986-8528	Clifford F Kerby	Eric A Strahl	Patricia D Abrams	Clifford F Kerby	Bob Davis	D Ray Brandenburg	William Phillips
Bowling Green (41)	CM	502 782-2489	Johnny Webb	Charles Coates	Linda T Leigh	Kirby Ramsey	Vindell Webster	Gary Raymer	William Hays
Campbellsville (10)	MC	502 465-7011	Robert L Miller	....	Sue Smith	....	Jimmy Cox	David K Adams	....

City, 1990 population figures (000 omitted), form of government	Municipal phone number	Mayor/ chief elected official	Appointed administrator	City clerk/ city secretary	Finance officer	Fire chief	Police chief	Public works director
KENTUCKY (112) continued								
Carrollton (4)	MC 502 732-7060	William J Welty	....	Becky H Pyles	....	Jack C Miles	Laman L Stark	Charles C Price
Catlettsburg (2)	MC 606 739-5223	....	....	....	....	....	....	....
Central City (5)	CM 502 754-5097	....	....	....	....	....	....	....
Columbia (4)	MC 502 384-2501	Curtis Hardwick	....	Jane B Akin	....	Charles Sparks	Edwin N Taylor	....
Corbin (7)	CM 606 528-0669	J S Williamson	Dave Hudson	Erin Blount	....	Eugene Rice	J C Mullins	Troy Foley
Covington (43)	CM 606 292-2160	....	....	....	....	....	....	....
Crestview Hills (3)	MC 606 341-7373	Harold A Ries	Joan Weingartner	C R Monhollen	....	....	....	....
Cumberland (3)	MC 606 589-2106	....	....	....	....	....	....	....
Cynthiana (6)	CO 606 234-7150	....	....	....	....	....	....	....
Danville (12)	CM 606 238-1200	John Bowling	Ed Music	Cindi Woolum	....	Donald Harp	Mike Lamb	Ralph Greer
Dawson Springs (3)	MC 502 797-2781	Stacia Peyton	....	Denise W Ridley	....	Kenneth Jackson	Danny Heggen	Roger Rose
Dayton (7)	MC 606 491-1600	B Crittendon	L Wessling	H Lenz	L Wessling	D Lynn	M Hall	J Creekmore
Douglass Hills (6)	MC 502 245-3600	Warren C Walker	....	Faye Tanner	....	....	....	....
Edgewood (8)	MC 606 331-5910	John D Link	Louis A Noll	Lynne Moore	....	....	Charles Dickerson	Stan Goetz
Elizabethtown (18)	MC 502 765-6121	Patricia V Durbin	Charles E Bryant	Wanda W Young	Stephen D Park	Richard A Games	Ruben Gardner	William A Owen
Elsmere (7)	MC 606 342-7911	Al Wermeling	....	Nancy Bowman	....	....	William Hiler	Charles Turner
Erlanger (16)	MC 606 727-2525	Marc T Otto Sr	William L Scheyer	Wilma LaBare	Mary Egan	William Martin	Greg Sandel	David Hahn
Flatwoods (8)	MC 606 836-9661	....	....	....	....	....	....	....
Flemingsburg (3)	MC 606 845-5951	....	....	....	....	....	....	....
Florence (19)	MC 606 371-5491	Evelyn M Kalb	Roger W Rolfes	Betsy Conrad	Ron Epling	Richard Albers	Charles Callen	Greg Tindle
Fort Mitchell (7)	CM 606 331-1212	....	....	....	....	....	....	....
Fort Thomas (16)	MC 606 441-1055	P Steven Pendery	Jeffrey Earlywine	Dorothy A Ivle	Fred W Ewald	William Dieckman	Charles Rogers	Thomas Morrison
Fort Wright (7)	MC 606 331-1700	....	....	....	....	....	....	....
Frankfort (26)	CM 502 875-8500	....	....	....	....	....	....	....
Franklin (8)	MC 502 586-4497	William H Gentry	M T Williams	W Scott Burklow	....	Bobby Turner	James Powell	....
Fulton (3)	CM 502 472-1320	....	....	....	....	....	....	....
Georgetown (11)	MC 502 863-9800	Warren Powers	....	Glenwood Williams	Carolyn Cutshaw	Larry Adkins	Eddie Chesser	R C Linton
Glasgow (12)	MC 502 651-5131	....	....	....	....	....	....	....
Grayson (4)	CO 606 474-6651	....	....	....	....	....	....	....
Greenville (5)	MC 502 338-3966	....	....	....	....	....	....	....
Harlan (3)	MC 606 573-2912	Daniel E Howard	....	Bobbie J Stark	....	William H Simms	Roy W Hatfield	Kenneth Hicks
Harrodsburg (7)	MC 606 734-2383	....	....	....	....	....	....	....
Hartford (3)	MC 502 298-3612	....	....	....	....	....	....	....
Hazard (5)	CM 606 436-3171	....	....	....	....	....	....	....
Henderson (26)	CM 502 831-1200	Glenn L Johnson	James White	Joann Roberts	Sharon Phillips	Bud Trodglen	Ed Brady	Y R Royster
Hickman (3)	CM 502 236-2535	John Shuff	Blake Proctor	Donna Haney	Blake Proctor	Larry Myatt	Dean Parnell	....
Highland Heights (4)	MC 606 441-8575	Charles Roettger	....	Jean A Rauf	....	Brad Derrick	Edgar J Hauger	....
Hillview (6)	MC 502 957-5280	Richard Terry	....	Blenda Weber	....	....	James Perry	Charlie Owens
Hopkinsville (30)	MC 502 887-4000	....	....	....	....	....	....	....
Hurstbourne (4)	CO 502 426-4808	Wm B Bardenwerper	J Schweinhart	J Schweinhart	Diana Isaacs	....	....	Wm Goodknight
Independence (10)	MC 606 356-5302	Ike Gabbard	....	Linda Carter	....	....	Charles Donaldson	....
Irvine (3)	MC 606 723-2554	W T Williams	....	Rhonda Gould	....	Anthony Murphy	Samuel Tipton	....
Jackson (2)	MC 606 666-7069	....	....	....	....	....	....	....
Jeffersontown (23)	MC 502 267-8333	Daniel Ruckriegel	....	Frank G Greenwell	....	....	Fred L Roemele	Richard A Dunn
Jenkins (3)	MC 606 832-2141	Robert Shubert	....	Dennis Dixon	....	Jim Revis Jr	Bill Tackett Jr	Virgil Chavis
La Grange (4)	MC 502 222-1433	Nancy M Steele	....	Zella C Smith	....	Harold Whittaker	Jeffrey R Money	Kirby R Miller
Lakeside Park (3)	MC 606 341-6670	Frank Smith	....	Wanda Wahl	....	....	....	....
Lancaster (3)	MC 606 792-2241	Billy C Moss	....	Shari Lane	....	Kenny Adams	W Schnitzler	....
Lawrenceburg (6)	MC 502 839-5372	....	....	....	....	....	....	....
Lebanon (6)	MC 502 692-6272	....	....	....	....	....	....	....
Leitchfield (5)	MC 502 259-4034	Sherrill Watson	....	Kerry White	....	Ronald Hudson	Elmer Langdon	Darrell Harrell
Lexington-Fayette (225)	MC 606 258-3030	Pam Miller	....	Liz Damrell	Donna Cantrell	Gary McComas	Larry Walsh	James Street
London (6)	MC 606 864-4169	....	....	....	....	....	....	....
Louisville (269)	MC 502 574-3333	Jerry E Abramson	William Summers	....	Robert Schwoeppe	Russell E Sanders	Edward D Hamilton	William E Herron
Ludlow (5)	MC 606 491-1233	Gerald Holloway	Thomas M Kriege	Geneva Palmer	....	....	R Thomas Collins	Andy Beutel
Madisonville (16)	MC 502 824-2100	Philip H Terry	Lloyd Merrell	Gina W Munger	Steven L Ramsey	Glendel Rice	Ron Hunt	....
Marion (3)	MC 502 965-2266	....	....	....	....	....	....	....
Mayfield (10)	MC 502 247-1981	....	....	....	....	....	....	....
Maysville (7)	CM 606 564-9411	....	....	....	....	....	....	....
Middlesborough (11)	MC 606 248-5670	....	....	....	....	....	....	....
Monticello (5)	MC 606 348-8473	Kenneth D Catron	....	Gregory E Latham	....	Jerry S Ferrell	Ralph Miniard	....
Morehead (8)	MC 606 784-8505	....	....	....	....	....	....	....
Morganfield (4)	MC 502 789-2525	....	....	....	....	....	....	....
Mount Sterling (5)	MC 606 498-8725	....	....	....	....	....	....	....
Mount Washington (5)	MC 502 538-7346	....	....	....	....	....	....	....
Murray (14)	MC 502 762-0309	William N Cherry	Tommy Marshall	Jo Crass	Don Leet	Pat Scott	Larry Elkins	Tommy Marshall
Newport (19)	CM 606 292-3682	Tom Guidugli	Jim Parsons	Frank Peluso	Phil Ciafardini	Larry Atwell	Tom Fromme	Peter Hesser
Nicholasville (14)	CO 606 885-9473	....	....	....	....	....	....	....
Olive Hill (2)	MC 606 286-5532	....	....	....	....	....	....	....
Owensboro (54)	CM 502 687-8500	David C Adkisson	Smith G Ted	Carol Blake	Ronald L Payne	John Goins	Arthur Schwartz	....
Paducah (27)	CM 502 444-8530	....	....	....	....	....	....	....
Paintsville (4)	MC 606 789-2600	Robin Cooper	Robert M Conley	Virgie Castle	Robert M Conley	Bob Dixon	Tom Haney	Jim Hopson
Paris (9)	CM 606 987-2110	Douglas F Castle	R L Brunner	Cheryl F Marsh	....	Michael Withrow	Ted C Florence	Archie Miles
Park Hills (3)	MC 606 431-6252	Melissa Worstell	....	Evelyn Fogarty	....	James Kaelin	Ronald Heideman	Dennis Finke
Pikeville (6)	CM 606 437-5100	Steven D Combs	John B Johnson	Karen Harris	Jan Hunt	Tommy L Hall	Eugene Edmonds	....
Pineville (2)	MC 606 337-2958	....	....	....	....	....	....	....
Prestonsburg (4)	MC 606 886-2335	Jerry S Fannin	....	Sue Webb	Brenda Hayes	Thomas Blackburn	Greg Hall	....
Princeton (7)	MC 502 365-9575	....	....	....	....	....	....	....
Providence (4)	MC 502 667-5463	....	....	....	....	....	....	....
Radcliff (20)	MC 502 351-4714	Jennings Smith	....	Frances Johns	....	James Bomar	Roy Easter	Ancil Holbrook
Richmond (21)	CM 606 623-1000	....	....	....	....	....	....	....
Russell (4)	MC 606 836-9666	....	....	....	....	....	....	....
Russellville (7)	MC 502 726-5007	Ken Smith	....	Peggy Jenkins	Paulette Smith	J L Williamson	C R Beard	Ernie Cole
Scottsville (4)	MC 502 237-3238	....	....	....	....	....	....	....
Shelbyville (6)	MC 502 633-1835	Neil S Hackworth	....	Bobbie J Brenner	....	Mike Rodgers	John Miller	Albert Minnis
Shepherdsville (5)	MC 502 543-2923	Sherman Tinnell	....	Neva L Ward	....	James Enlow	Joseph Rogers	Jessie J Walls
Shively (16)	MC 502 449-5000	....	....	....	....	....	....	....
Somerset (11)	MC 606 679-6366	James R Williams	Sheila C Parkey	David Godsey	....	James E Haney Jr	David Gilbert	....
Southgate (3)	MC 606 441-0075	Ronald J Blanchet	....	Rose Welscher	....	John Braun	Charley Hazel	Paul J Krebs
Springfield (3)	MC 606 336-7739	....	....	....	....	....	....	....
St. Matthews (16)	MC 502 895-9444	....	....	....	....	....	....	....
Stanford (3)	MC 606 365-4500	Jack Withrow	....	Wanda Withrow	....	Leroy Lunsford	Don Young	....
Stanton (3)	MC 606 663-2620	....	....	....	....	....	....	....

Directory 1/9
continued

MUNICIPAL OFFICIALS
IN U.S. CITIES OVER 2,500

City, 1990 population figures (000 omitted), form of government	Municipal phone number	Mayor/ chief elected official	Appointed administrator	City clerk/ city secretary	Finance officer	Fire chief	Police chief	Public works director
KENTUCKY (112) continued								
Taylor Mill (6)	MC 606 581-3234	Mark Kreimborg	Edwin Meece	Mary Kordenbrock	....	Dennis Halpin	Steve Knauf	Tom Robke
Tompkinsville (3)	MC 502 487-6776	Windell Carter	....	Clarnell Emberton	....	Charles Landrum	Johnny Graves	J E Petett
Versailles (7)	MC 606 873-5436	Charles R Reed	....	Reata A Buffin	....	Frankie Shuck	Wm A Love	Robert W Stopher
Villa Hills (8)	MC 606 331-4933	....	....	....	....	....	....	....
Vine Grove (4)	MC 502 877-2422	....	....	....	....	....	....	....
Williamsburg (5)	MC 606 549-6035	....	....	....	....	....	....	....
Williamstown (3)	MC 606 824-3633	Robert Hall Jones	....	Deborah A Stacey	....	Mark Courtney	Phil Harney	Gordon Taylor
Wilmore (4)	MC 606 858-4411	Harold Rainwater	....	C Brandenburg	....	James Anderson	Roger Swallows	Donald Grimes
Winchester (16)	CM 606 744-7017	Gene Kincaid	C Y Burtner	Marilyn T Rowe	....	Larry W Potter	W M Jackson	Jay Warden
LOUISIANA (98)								
Abbeville t (11)	MC 318 893-8550	R Brady Broussard	....	S Zaunbrecher	....	Nolan Frederick	Mike Hardy	....
Alexandria (49)	MC 318 449-5026	....	....	....	....	....	....	....
Amite City t (4)	MC 504 748-9850	....	....	....	....	....	....	....
Arcadia t (3)	MC 318 263-8455	....	....	....	....	....	....	....
Baker (13)	MC 504 778-0300	....	....	....	....	....	....	....
Baldwin t (2)	MC 318 923-7523	....	....	....	....	....	....	....
Ball t (3)	MC 318 640-9605	Roy Hebron	....	Willie Bishop	....	Gene Vance	Spencer Williams	....
Basile t (2)	MC 318 432-6693	....	....	....	....	....	....	....
Bastrop (14)	MC 318 283-0250	....	....	....	....	....	....	....
Baton Rouge (220)	MC 504 389-3141	Thomas E McHugh	Grayden Walker	Michael B Mayers	Otha L Schofield	Ronald J Spillman	D Greg Phares	Robert R Canfield
Berwick t (4)	MC 504 384-8858	....	....	....	....	....	....	....
Bogalusa (14)	MC 504 732-6200	Marvin Taylor	Gerald Bailey	....	....	James Dunaway	Wayne Kemp	Billy Daniels
Bossier City (53)	MC 318 741-8501	....	....	....	....	....	....	....
Breaux Bridge (7)	MC 318 332-2171	....	....	Tina Denais	....	John Hebert Jr	Sidney Broussard	....
Broussard t (3)	MC 318 837-6681	C Langlinais	....	Cynthia M Dauzat	....	Joseph Frank	Mary Fanara	Mike Gonzales
Bunkie t (5)	MC 318 346-7663	John Guillory	....	Shirley D Kidder	....	Gene Daigle	Albert J Venable	....
Carencro t (5)	MC 318 896-8481	....	....	Marinne Bloemer	Adrienne Stroble	Julius Holden	Jerome DiFranco	Tommy Mayronne
Church Point t (5)	MC 318 684-5692	J Harold Beaugh	....					
Covington (8)	MC 504 892-1811	Keith J Villere	Adrienne Stroble					
Crowley (14)	MC 318 783-0824	....	....	....	....	....	....	....
De Quincy t (3)	MC 318 786-8241	....	....	....	....	....	....	....
De Ridder (10)	MC 318 462-2461	....	....	....	....	....	....	....
Delhi t (3)	MC 318 878-3792	....	....	....	....	....	....	....
Denham Springs (8)	MC 504 665-8121	....	....	....	....	....	....	....
Donaldsonville (8)	CM 504 473-4247	Bernard Francis	Isaac Dorsey	Isaac Dorsey	Dana Henry	Kirk Landry	....	Raymond Jacobs
Eunice (11)	MC 318 457-7389	Curtis J Joubert	....	Shirley F Vige Sr	....	Gerald E LeJeune	Charles B Manuel	....
Farmerville t (3)	MC 318 368-9242	....	....	....	....	....	....	....
Ferriday t (4)	MC 318 757-3411	....	....	....	....	....	....	....
Franklin (9)	MC 318 828-6303	Sam Jones	Cynthia Hebert	Melissa Thibodeau	Raymond Harris Jr	Timothy Thibodaux	Henry Louviere	Westley Beverly
Franklinton t (4)	MC 504 839-3569	....	....	....	....	....	....	....
Gonzales (7)	MC 504 647-2841	....	....	....	....	....	....	....
Grambling v (5)	MC 318 247-6120	....	....	....	....	....	....	....
Gramercy t (2)	MC 504 869-4403	Herman Bourgeois	....	Lydia Z Louque	Tricia Williamson	Andy Detillier	Carl Spizale Sr	....
Gretna (17)	MC 504 363-1500	....	....	....	....	....	....	....
Hammond (16)	MC 504 542-3400	....	....	....	....	....	....	....
Harahan (10)	MC 504 737-6383	....	....	....	....	....	....	....
Haynesville t (3)	MC 318 624-0911	Tom Crocker	....	Marilyn Bush	....	Tommy Bower	David Mills	Alvin Moss
Homer t (4)	MC 318 927-3555	....	....	Paul Labat	....	Gale LeBoeuf	Jack Smith	Al Levron
Houma (97)	MC 504 873-6401	Barry Bonvillian	Doug Maier					
Jackson t (4)	MC 504 634-7777	....	....	....	....	....	....	....
Jeanerette t (6)	MC 318 256-4587	....	....	Sharon Keel	....	Don Smith	George L King	....
Jena (3)	MC 318 992-2148	Norman Welch	....					
Jennings (11)	MC 318 821-5500	....	....	....	....	....	....	....
Jonesboro t (4)	MC 318 259-2385	....	....	....	....	Ben Adams	Clyde Walker	Robert L Estes
Jonesville t (3)	MC 318 339-8596	Billy Edwards	Yolanda McClure	Yolanda McClure	....			
Kaplan (5)	MC 318 643-8602	....	....	....	....	....	....	....
Kenner (72)	MC 504 468-7200	....	....	....	....	....	....	....
Kentwood t (2)	MC 504 229-3451	....	....	....	....	....	....	....
Kinder t (2)	MC 318 738-2620	....	....	....	....	....	....	....
Lafayette (94)	MC 318 261-8300	Kenneth F Bowen	Aros Mouton	Dee Stanley	Floyd Domingue	Robert Benoit	....	John Raines
Lake Arthur t (3)	MC 318 774-2211	....	....	....	....	....	....	....
Lake Charles (71)	MC 318 491-1200	....	....	....	....	....	....	....
Lake Providence t (5)	MC 318 559-2288	....	....	....	....	....	....	....
Leesville t (8)	CM 318 239-2444	....	....	....	....	....	....	....
Lutcher t (4)	MC 504 869-5564	Guy J Poche	....	Mary Ann Guidry	Mary Ann Guidry	P J Amato	Brian J Melancon	Ray Zeringue
Mamou t (3)	MC 318 468-3272	Warren Pierrotti	Warren Pierrotti	James Butler	James Butler	Randy Young	Jasper Manuel	Spencer Long
Mandeville (7)	MC 504 626-3144	Paul R Spitzfaden	....	Linda P Barnett	Milton G Stiebing	....	Thomas H Buell	Bryan B Clement
Mansfield (8)	MC 318 872-0406	Harold L Cornett	....	Judy Wilkerson	....	Louie Melton	Don R English	James W Ruffin
Many t (3)	MC 318 256-3651	....	....	....	....	....	....	....
Marksville t (6)	MC 318 253-9500	....	....	....	....	....	....	....
Minden (14)	MC 318 377-2144	....	....	....	....	....	....	....
Monroe (55)	MC 318 329-2280	Robert Powell	Billy Pearson	Michelle Robinson	Billy Pearson	George Douglas	Joe Stewart	R D Jefferson
Morgan City (15)	MC 504 385-1770	Timothy Matte	Larry P Bergeron	....	Lorrie Braus	Michael Raymond	Daniel Dossett	George Mikhael
Natchitoches (17)	MC 318 352-2772	Joseph M Sampite	....	Mary Ann Nunley	Charles E Powell	Robert L Hebert	Keith W Thompson	Clifford Walker
New Iberia (32)	MC 318 369-2300	....	....	....	....	....	....	....
New Orleans (497)	MC 504 565-6800	Marc Morial	Marlin Gusman	....	....	Warren McDaniels	Joseph Orticke Jr	....
New Roads t (5)	MC 504 638-7047	....	....	....	....	....	....	....
Oakdale (7)	MC 318 335-3629	Bobby Abrusley	Suzanne S Welch	....	....	Thomas B Moore	V Chamberlain	Kenneth Miller
Opelousas (18)	MC 318 948-2532	John W Joseph	Charles W Ross	Frances C Carron	Mamie C Leach	Robert Trosclair	Larry J Caillier	Michael V Simien
Patterson t (5)	MC 504 395-5205	....	....	....	....	....	....	....
Pineville (12)	MC 318 449-5659	Frederick H Baden	....	Carol Vermillion	Susan Austin	Gary Morrow	P Oestriecher	Robert G Mickels
Plaquemine t (7)	MC 504 687-3116	....	....	....	....	....	....	....
Ponchatoula (5)	MC 504 386-6484	Julian E Dufreche	....	Melinda P Mackey	Ruby P Landry	Erlo McLaurin Jr	Timothy J Gideon	David Opdenhoff
Port Allen (6)	MC 504 348-0441	....	....	....	....	....	....	....
Port Barre t (2)	MC 318 585-7646	....	....	....	....	....	....	....
Rayne (9)	MC 318 334-3121	....	....	....	....	....	....	....
Rayville t (4)	MC 318 728-2011	....	....	....	....	....	....	....
Ruston (20)	MC 318 251-8652	....	....	....	....	....	....	....
Shreveport (199)	MC 318 226-3900	Hazel Beard	Newton Bruce	....	Liz Washington	Bo Roberts	Steve Prator	Tom Dark
Slidell (24)	MC 504 646-4377	Salvatore Caruso	Reinhard Dearing	Davis Dautreuil	Dianne Hanephin	....	Ben Morris	Dan Yeates
Springhill (6)	MC 318 539-5681	J Curtis Smith	....	Jimmie N Murph	....	....	Jerry L Stephens	....
St. Martinville (7)	MC 318 394-5591	....	....	....	....	....	....	....

Directory 1/9
continued

MUNICIPAL OFFICIALS IN U.S. CITIES OVER 2,500

City, 1990 population figures (000 omitted), form of government	Municipal phone number	Mayor/ chief elected official	Appointed administrator	City clerk/ city secretary	Finance officer	Fire chief	Police chief	Public works director
LOUISIANA (98) continued								
Sulphur (20)	MC 318 527-4500	....	....	....	....	....	....	....
Tallulah (9)	MC 318 574-0964	....	....	....	....	....	....	....
Thibodaux (14)	MC 504 447-3767	Alton Roundtree	....	Thomas Eschete	Kenneth Hoffmann	....	Donald Bonvillain	Bert Hebert Jr
Vidalia t (5)	MC 318 336-5206	....	....	....	....	....	....	....
Ville Platte t (9)	MC 318 363-2939	....	....	....	....	....	....	....
Vinton t (3)	MC 318 589-7453	Charles C Coppels	....	Melba Landry	Melba Landry	....	Dennis Drouillard	Raymond Guillory
Vivian t (4)	MC 318 375-3856	....	....	....	....	....	....	....
Walker t (4)	MC 504 664-3123	....	....	....	....	....	....	....
Welsh t (3)	MC 318 734-2231	....	....	....	....	....	....	....
West Monroe (14)	MC 318 396-2600	....	....	....	....	....	....	....
Westlake t (5)	MC 318 433-0691	....	....	....	....	....	....	....
Westwego (11)	MC 504 341-3424	....	....	....	....	....	....	....
Winnfield (6)	MC 318 628-3939	....	....	....	....	....	....	....
Winnsboro t (6)	MC 318 435-9087	....	....	....	....	....	....	....
Zachary (9)	MC 504 654-6871	....	....	....	....	....	....	....
Zwolle t (2)	MC 318 645-6141	Chris Loupe	Larry Cryer	....	....	Kenneth Remedies	Marvin Frazier	....
MAINE (183)								
Amity t (..)	CM 207 532-6862	....	Margaret C Frye	Donna Estabrook	....	....	....	....
Ashland t (2)	CM 207 435-2311	....	....	....	....	....	....	....
Auburn (24)	CM 207 786-2634	Richard Trafton	Steven D Lewis	Mary Lou Magno	William Lundrigan	Clifton Smith	Robert Tiner	Robert Belz
Augusta (21)	CM 207 626-2353	William Burney Jr	Terrence St Peter	Madeline Cyr	Constance Packard	Norman J Arbour	Wayne M McCamish	John H Charest
Baileyville t (2)	TM 207 427-3442	F Doug Jones	Jeff Clukey	Eva J Roberts	Patricia A Coty	Lawrence Gillis	Michael A Coty	William Roehrich
Bangor (33)	CM 207 945-4400	Dennis Soucy	Edward Barrett	Russell McKenna	John Quartararo	John Foley	Randy Harriman	Arthur Stockus
Bar Harbor t (4)	CM 207 288-4098	Robert DeSimone	....	Jean T Barker	Stanley W Harmon	David W Rand	Nathan W Young	Lyle H Dever
Bath (10)	CM 207 443-8330	Dean Almy	Duncan Ballantyne	Beverly Henrikson	George Sargent	Ronald Clark	Lawrence Dawson	Kenneth Murray
Belfast (6)	CM 207 338-3370	Mary Page Worth	Arlo L Redman	Teresa N Crosby	....	James L Richards	Robert B Keating	Wesley A Richards
Berwick t (6)	CM 207 698-1101	Samuel S Mathews	Christopher Rose	Barbara M Martin	....	Dennis R Plante	Peter C Hussey	....
Bethel t (2)	TM 207 824-2669	Arthur Gilbert	Madeleine Henley	Merton Brown	....	James Young	Dale Bellman	Madeleine Henley
Biddeford (21)	MC 207 284-9307	....	....	....	....	....	....	....
Blaine t (1)	TM 207 425-2611	Michael Tweedie	Delmar Clark	Delmar Clark	....	....	....	Eldon Crouse
Boothbay t (3)	TM 207 633-2051	....	....	....	....	....	....	....
Boothbay Harbor t (2)	TM 207 633-3671	Walter Reed	Laurie Smith	Robert Barter	....	Warren Page	Floyd McDunnah	Kevin Mayberry
Bowdoinham t (2)	CM 207 666-5531	....	....	....	....	....	....	....
Brewer (9)	CM 207 989-7500	....	....	....	....	....	....	....
Bridgewater t (1)	CM 207 429-9856	....	....	....	....	....	....	....
Bridgton t (4)	TM 207 647-8786	....	....	....	....	....	....	....
Brownville t (2)	CM 207 965-2561	Robert Hamlin	James Catlin	Jacquline Roy	....	....	Arthur Berce	Arthur Grant
Brunswick t (21)	CM 207 725-6659	Charles R Priest	Donald H Gerrish	Deborah C Cabana	John S Eldridge	Gary W Howard	Jerry A Hinton	John A Foster
Bucksport t (5)	CM 207 469-7368	....	....	....	....	....	....	....
Buxton t (6)	TM 207 929-5191	....	....	....	....	....	....	....
Calais (4)	CM 207 454-2521	....	....	....	....	....	....	....
Camden t (5)	CM 207 236-3353	Morton A Strom	Roger A Moody	Carol Rogers	....	Bruce Hensler	Terry Burgess	Earl Weaver
Cape Elizabeth t (9)	CM 207 799-5251	William H Jordan	Michael McGovern	Debra Lane	....	Phil McGouldrick	David Pickering	Robert C Malley
Caribou (9)	CM 207 493-3324	Robert McMahan	Richard C Mattila	Sylvia Akeley	Paula Harris	Roy Woods	Arthur Gorney	David Bell
Carmel t (2)	TM 207 848-3361	....	....	....	....	....	....	....
Castle Hill t (..)	CM 207 764-3754	Preston Kenney	John Y Edgecomb	John Y Edgecomb	John Y Edgecomb	T McPherson	....	John Y Edgecomb
Chelsea t (2)	TM 207 582-4802	....	....	....	....	....	....	....
Cherryfield t (1)	TM 207 546-2376	....	....	....	....	....	....	....
China t (4)	TM 207 445-2014	....	....	....	....	....	....	....
Clinton t (3)	TM 207 426-8511	Harvey Chesley Jr	Peter A Nielsen	Levina McKechnie	....	Gary Petley	Lee Butler	Dale Bouchard
Corinna t (2)	TM 207 278-4183	Steve Buck	Gary Dorman	Beth Englehardt	Gary Dorman	James Emerson	....	Gary Dorman
Corinth t (2)	TM 207 285-3271	....	....	....	....	....	....	....
Crystal t (..)	TM 207 463-2770	James F D' Angelo	Linda B York	Linda B York	....	Jamie L Main	....	Brian E York
Cumberland t (6)	CM 207 829-5559	E Stephen Murray	Robert B Benson	Klara Norton	Melody S Main	William Fisher	Joseph Charron	Philip Wentworth
Danforth t (1)	CM 207 448-2321	....	....	....	....	....	....	....
Dexter t (4)	CM 207 924-7351	Peter Haskell	Stephen Whitesel	Marcia Delaware	Marilyn A Curtis	Melvin Wyman	David Clukey	Michael Delaware
Dixfield t (3)	CM 207 562-8151	Richard M Pierce	Carol M Granfield	Vickie R Cross	....	Gaetan Bolduc	Rodney C Cross	James W Kidder
Dover-Foxcroft t (5)	CM 207 564-3318	....	....	....	....	....	....	....
Dyer Brook t (..)	TM 207 757-8302	....	....	....	....	....	....	....
Eagle Lake t (1)	CM 207 444-5125	....	....	....	....	....	....	....
Easton t (1)	TM 207 488-6652	Michael Corey	Jackalene Bradley	Cheryl Clark	....	Kim White	....	Jackalene Bradley
Eastport (2)	CM 207 853-2300	Charles Lewis	Mary K Follis	Helen Archer	....	Richard Clark	Charles Shaw	Rene Odell
Eliot t (5)	TM 207 439-1813	Philip Lytle	Daniel Blanchette	J Vittum Clarke	....	Richard Wood	Charles Deguisto	Orland McPherson
Ellsworth (6)	CM 207 667-2563	....	....	....	....	....	....	....
Exeter t (1)	CM 207 379-2191	Reginald Palmer	Jason E Simcock	Jason E Simcock	....	....	....	Jason E Simcock
Fairfield t (7)	CM 207 453-7911	....	Peter McKenney	....	....	Dale Sweet	John Pouliot	G Allen Taylor
Falmouth t (8)	CM 207 781-5253	Lenord Nelson	John D Harris	Nina Oatey	John McNaughton	James Robertson	Craig Hall	Anthony Hays
Farmingdale t (3)	TM 207 582-2225	....	Phyllis H Weeks	Phyllis H Weeks	....	Eugene Proulx	....	Albert E Barry
Farmington t (7)	CM 207 778-6538	Fran Hardy	Alphonse R Dixon	Joan Reid	Bettina Martin	Robert McCleery	John Rogers	Mitchell Boulette
Fort Fairfield t (4)	CM 207 472-3800	Greg Murchison	Scott W Seabury	Susan Levasseur	Lynda Doherty	Dana Mclaughlin	Neil J Saucier	John H Butts
Fort Kent t (4)	CM 207 834-3090	Patrick Plourde	Donald Guimond	Rella Dubois	....	Allan Dow	Kenneth Michaud	Cary Daigle
Freeport t (7)	CM 207 865-4743	Elizabeth Ruff	Dale C Olmstead	Mary Wescott	Hedy Filmore	Duncan Daly	Gerald Schofield	Alton Thompson
Frenchville t (1)	TM 207 543-7301	....	....	....	....	....	....	....
Fryeburg t (3)	TM 207 935-2805	....	....	....	....	....	....	....
Gardiner (7)	CM 207 582-4200	....	....	....	....	....	....	....
Garland t (1)	CM 207 924-6615	....	....	....	....	....	....	....
Gorham t (12)	CM 207 839-5041	Janice Labrecque	David O Cole	D Brenda Caldwell	Shirley Hughes	Robert Lefebvre	Edward Tolan	James Plummer
Gray t (6)	CM 207 657-3339	Anthony Cook	....	Paul Bird	....	Jon Barton	....	Neal Lavallee
Greenbush t (1)	TM 207 732-3644	Robert Carroll	Robert Littlefiel	Robert Littlefiel	Robert Littlefiel	Edward Haverlock	William Flagg	Robert Littlefiel
Greene t (4)	TM 207 946-5146	....	....	....	....	....	....	....
Greenville t (2)	TM 207 695-2421	....	....	....	....	....	....	....
Guilford t (2)	TM 207 876-2202	William Thompson	R Littlefield	Michelle Nichols	Dorene Graf	David Cookson	....	....
Hallowell (3)	CM 207 623-4021	....	....	....	....	....	....	....
Hampden t (6)	CM 207 862-3034	....	....	....	....	....	....	....
Harpswell t (5)	TM 207 833-5771	....	....	....	....	....	....	....
Hartland t (2)	TM 207 938-4401	....	....	....	....	....	....	....
Haynesville t (..)	TM 207 448-2239	....	....	....	....	....	....	....
Hermon t (4)	CM 207 848-3485	Harold Mailman	Kathryn Ruth	Carol Davis	Kathryn Ruth	John Maynard	....	Kathryn Ruth
Hodgdon t (1)	CM 207 532-6498	Randy Lincoln	James D Griffin	Wilma Welton	....	Dana Belyea	....	....
Holden t (3)	TM 207 843-5151	Joel Dearborn	Larry Varisco	Larry Varisco	....	....	....	Bruce Dowling
Hollis t (4)	TM 207 929-8552	....	....	....	....	....	....	....
Houlton t (7)	CM 207 532-7111	M A McLaughlin	R Lewis Bone	C J O' Leary	N J Hanson	M J Cone	D L Malone Sr	R M Cleale

**Directory 1/9
continued**

MUNICIPAL OFFICIALS
IN U.S. CITIES OVER 2,500

City, 1990 population figures (000 omitted), form of government	Municipal phone number	Mayor/ chief elected official	Appointed administrator	City clerk/ city secretary	Finance officer	Fire chief	Police chief	Public works director
MAINE (183) continued								
Island Falls t (1)	TM 207 463-2246	....	....	....	....	....	....	....
Islesboro t (1)	TM 207 734-2253	....	....	....	....	....	....	....
Jackman t (1)	TM 207 668-2111	....	....	....	....	....	....	....
Jay t (5)	TM 207 897-6785	....	....	....	....	....	James Lavalle	John D Dickens
Kennebunk t (8)	TM 207 985-2102	Richard A Erb	....	Ethelyn Marthia	....	....		
Kennebunkport t (3)	TM 207 967-4243	....	....	....	....	....	....	....
Kittery t (9)	CM 207 439-1633	Maria Barth	Philip McCarthy	Maryann Place	Philip McCarthy	George Varney	Edward Strong	Richard Rossiter
Lebanon t (4)	TM 207 457-1171	Gilbert D Zinck	....	Lorraine A Patch	Ethel Lizotte	Gilbert Gerrish	....	John F Hayden
Lewiston (40)	CM 207 784-2951	John T Jenkins	Robert J Hulready	Gerald P Berube	Richard Metivier	Michel A Lajoie	Michael F Kelly	C Branch
Limestone t (10)	TM 207 325-4704	....	....	....	....	Burton Weed	Larry Merrithew	David Washburn
Lincoln t (6)	CM 207 794-3372	Deirdra Trask	Clifton Barker	Lisa Goodwin	....	Michael Eugley	Richard Osgood	....
Lincolnville t (2)	TM 207 763-3555	Ernest F Littlefi	Joshua T Day	Doris F Weed	....	Stephen Bither		
Linneus t (1)	CM 207 532-6182	A Andrew Brennan	F Hutchinson	F Hutchinson	....	....	....	....
Lisbon Falls t (9)	CM 207 353-5958	....	....	....	....	....	....	....
Litchfield t (3)	TM 207 268-4721	....	....	....	....	....	....	....
Littleton t (1)	TM 207 538-9862	....	....	....	....	....	....	....
Livermore Falls t (3)	CM 207 897-2016	....	....	....	....	....	....	....
Lubec t (2)	CM 207 733-2341	Jed Coggins	Mark D Decoteau	Jill Mulholland	....	Joe O' Brian	....	Mark F Decoteau
Ludlow t (..)	CM 207 532-7743	....	....	....	....	....	....	....
Lyman t (3)	TM 207 499-7562	....	....	....	....	....	....	....
Machias t (3)	CM 207 255-6621	S Altmannsberger	C Loughlin	Martha A Bagley	C Loughlin	Colby Dennison	Robbie E Dirsa	Carlo Coletti
Madawaska t (5)	TM 207 728-6351	....	....	....	....	Walter Hayden	Harley G Dunlap	Philip A Curtis
Madison t (5)	TM 207 696-3971	Jeffery A Lloyd	Richard R Michaud	Lisa F Paine	....	T McPherson	....	John Y Edgecomb
Mapleton t (2)	TM 207 764-3754	Jeffrey O Smith	John Y Edgecomb	John Y Edgecomb	John Y Edgecomb	....	....	....
Mars Hill t (2)	CM 207 425-3731	David Caron	Raymond Mersereau	Raymond Mersereau	....	Barry Dorr	....	Wallace Boyd
Masardis t (..)	TM 207 435-2841	....	....	....	....	....	....	....
Mechanic Falls t (3)	CM 207 345-2871	....	....	....	....	....	....	....
Merrill t (..)	CM 207 757-8286	....	....	....	....	....	....	....
Mexico t (3)	TM 207 364-7971	....	....	....	....	....	....	....
Milbridge t (1)	TM 207 546-2422	....	....	....	....	....	....	....
Millinocket t (7)	CM 207 723-7000	James Mingo	James Kotredes	Diane Lombard	....	Milan Thornton	Wayne Scarano	Robert Lander
Milo t (3)	CM 207 943-2202	Glenn Ricker	Jane S Jones	Melinda Sherburne	....	David Preble	Todd Lyford	Harold Burton
Monmouth t (3)	TM 207 933-2206	Richard Milligan	Steven A Dyer	Steven A Dyer	Steven A Dyer	Laurence Folsom	Kenneth Latulippe	Herbert Whittier
Monroe t (1)	TM 207 525-3515	Daniel Lawson	Valerie J Moody	Lois N Aitken	....	Marshall T Moody	....	....
Monson t (1)	TM 207 997-3641	....	....	....	....	....	....	....
Monticello t (1)	TM 207 538-9500	....	....	....	....	....	....	....
Mount Desert t (2)	TM 207 276-5531	John Butler	Edward Storey Jr	Kimberly Walker	....	Douglass Gray Jr	John C Doyle	Ernest Coombs
New Canada t (..)	CM 207 834-6673	....	....	....	....	....	....	....
New Gloucester t (4)	TM 207 926-4126	....	....	....	....	....	....	....
New Portland t (1)	TM 207 628-4441	....	....	....	....	....	....	....
Newport t (3)	TM 207 368-4410	Albert Worden	Arthur Ellingwood	Janet Atkinson	....	Charles Erickson	James Ricker	Jack Wilson
Norridgewock t (3)	TM 207 634-2252	....	Rodney C Lynch	Charlotte Curtis	Faye Stevens	....	....	Milford Witham
North Berwick t (4)	TM 207 676-3353	Harland Roberts	Kayellen P Glaze	Janet Belmain	....	Jim Moore	Randy Jones	Donald Folsom
Norway t (5)	TM 207 743-6651	....	....	....	....	....	....	....
Oakfield t (1)	TM 207 757-8479	....	....	....	....	....	....	....
Oakland t (6)	CM 207 465-7357	Ralph Farnham	Robert J Quinn	Janice Porter	....	Charles Pullen	Kevin O' Leary	Jeff Higgins
Ogunquit t (1)	CM 207 646-5139	Dennis E Andrews	L Raymond Empey	Judy S Kagiliery	....	Bruce A Bernard	Michael W Pardue	Jonatan L Webber
Old Orchard Beach t (8)	CM 207 934-5714	James Abennett	Alice Leveris	Maureen O' Leary	....	Philip Laporte	Dana Kelley	Theodore Dydowicz
Old Town (8)	CM 207 827-6148	Roberta Fowler	Ron Singel	Patricia Ramsey	Constance Murray	Edwin Pollard	D O' Halloran	John Ellis
Orono t (11)	CM 207 866-2556	George J Gonyar	Gerald S Kempen	Wanda J Thomas	....	Robert J Burke	Daniel J Lowe	Calvin Smith
Orrington t (3)	TM 207 825-3340	Joseph Coffin	Candace Guerette	Carole A Hardin	....	....	....	John Hodgins
Oxford t (4)	CM 207 539-4431	Roger Smedberg	Howard Munday	Leslie Hennessey	....	Fred Knightly	Ron Kugell	Howard Munday
Paris t (4)	TM 207 743-2501	Janet Jamison	John White	Elizabeth Larson	....	John Bryant	Stephen Cobbett	Galen Curtis
Patten t (1)	TM 207 528-2215	....	....	....	....	....	....	....
Phillips t (1)	TM 207 639-3561	Timothy Abbott	Laura Toothaker	Anna Teele	Laura Toothaker	Daniel Arms	....	Stephen Haines
Pittsfield t (4)	TM 207 487-3136	....	....	....	....	....	....	....
Poland t (4)	TM 207 998-4601	....	....	....	....	....	....	....
Portage Lake t (..)	CM 207 435-4361	....	....	....	....	....	....	....
Portland (64)	CM 207 874-8300	....	....	....	....	....	....	....
Presque Isle (11)	CM 207 764-4485	Roger Thibodeau	Thomas R Stevens	Konni Munson	....	James Krysiak	James Ferland	John Carrier
Rangeley t (1)	TM 207 864-3326	Walter Davenport	Edward M Barrett	Patricia Raymond	Susan L Cushman	Harold Schaetzle	Edward M Barrett	Edward M Barrett
Reed pl (..)	CM 207 456-7546	....	....	....	....	....	....	....
Richmond t (3)	CM 207 737-4305	....	Phil Nadeau	....	....	John Carver	....	Gregory Blackwell
Rockland (8)	CM 207 594-8431	Thomas Molloy	Cathy Sleeper	Stuart Sylvester	James Frankowski	Raymond Wooster	Alfred Ockenfels	Stephen Beveridge
Rockport t (3)	TM 207 236-9648	Robert G Duke Jr	Don Willard	Brenda Richardson	Frances Hernandez	Bruce Woodward	Leforest Doucette	Robert C Welch
Rumford t (7)	CM 207 364-4576	James Thibodeau	Robert Welch	Mary Ann Prue	....	J Arthur Boivin	Timothy Bourassa	....
Sabattus t (4)	MC 207 375-4331	....	....	....	....	....	....	....
Saco (15)	CM 207 282-1032	....	....	....	....	....	....	....
Sanford t (20)	RT 207 324-9100	Faith Ballenger	John Webb	Claire Morrison	Karen Stevens	Daniel Hart	Gordon Paul	Richard Wilkins
Sangerville t (1)	TM 207 876-2814	....	....	....	....	....	....	....
Scarborough t (13)	CM 207 883-4301	Michael J Martin	Carl L Betterley	Laurel R Nadeau	Ruth D Porter	Robert S Carson	Hollis G Dixon	William D Giguere
Searsport t (3)	CM 207 548-6372	Walter P Sarnacki	Fred T Breslin	Suzan M Cotter	....	Gary W Collins	James S Gillway	Lewis Seekins
Sherman t (1)	TM 207 365-4260	Ernest I Elder	Debra J O' Roak	Debra J O' Roak	Debra J O' Roak	Douglas N Clark	....	....
Skowhegan t (9)	TM 207 474-6900	Edward Conley Jr	Patricia A Dickey	Rhonda L Stark	....	Winton T Keene Jr	Harold C Brown	Gregory A Dore
Smyrna t (..)	CM 207 757-8286	....	....	....	....	....	....	....
South Berwick t (6)	CM 207 384-3300	G Mac Pherson	Richard Brown	Meredith Clark	Fern Houliares	George Gorman	Dana Lajoie	Jon St Pierre
South Portland (23)	CM 207 767-3201	Susan Avery	Jerre Bryant	Linda Cohen	Ralph St Pierre	John True	Robert Schwartz	Arvin Erskine
Southwest Harbor t (2)	CM 207 244-5404	....	....	....	....	....	....	....
St. Agatha t (1)	TM 207 543-7305	....	....	....	Larry Post	David Crocker	....	Ronnie Finson
St. Albans t (2)	CM 207 938-4568	Brian Hanson	Larry Post	Stacey Desrosiers	Larry Post	....	....	....
Stacyville t (..)	TM 207 365-4195	....	....	....	....	....	....	Roger Mosley
Standish t (8)	CM 207 642-3461	....	Scott Cole	Mary Chapman	Barbara Kollander	Kevin Warren	....	....
Stockholm t (..)	TM 207 896-5659	David Sterris	Kathleen Lausier	Albertne Dufour	Kathleen Lausier	John Hotelling	John Teager	....
Stonington t (1)	TM 207 367-2351	....	....	....	....	....	....	....
Thomaston t (3)	CM 207 354-6107	Lee Ann Upham	Valmore Blastow	Joan Linscott	....	Malcolm Hyler	James Hosford	David Taylor
Topsham t (9)	TM 207 725-5821	Peter J Lepari	Larry D Cilley	Ruth Lyons	....	Clayton Baker	Paul Lessard	Tad Hunter
Tremont t (1)	CM 207 244-7204	Eric Lanpher	Fay A Lawson	Diane E Huff	....	....	....	David N Elvin
Turner t (4)	TM 207 225-3416	....	....	....	....	....	....	....
Van Buren t (3)	CM 207 868-2886	....	....	....	....	....	....	....
Vassalboro t (4)	TM 207 872-2826	....	....	....	....	....	....	....
Veazie t (2)	CM 207 947-2781	Rod Hathaway	Bill Reed	Bill Reed	Guyla Downing	Roger Sirois	Frank Crowley	George Free
Waldoboro t (5)	TM 207 832-5369	William Blodgett	Lee L Smith	Rebecca B Maxwell	....	Robert M Maxcy	Leroy L Jones	John R Daigle
Wallagrass t (1)	CM 207 834-5894	....	Judy Stadig	Elaine Labbe	....	....	....	....

MUNICIPAL OFFICIALS
IN U.S. CITIES OVER 2,500

City, 1990 population figures (000 omitted), form of government	Municipal phone number	Mayor/ chief elected official	Appointed administrator	City clerk/ city secretary	Finance officer	Fire chief	Police chief	Public works director
MAINE (183) continued								
Warren t (3)	CM 207 273-2421	....	....	....	....	....	....	....
Washburn t (2)	CM 207 455-8485	....	....	....	....	....	....	....
Waterboro t (5)	TM 207 247-5166	Dennis Abbott	....	Dianne Holden	....	Michael Emmons	....	....
Waterville (17)	MC 207 873-7131	Thomas J Brazier	Scott Shanley	Linette Dostie	Nancy Orr	Darrel Fournier	John Morris	Kenneth Ryder
Wells t (8)	TM 207 646-5113	Robert Foley	Jonathan Carter	Marion Noble		John Dean	William Zackular	Jonathan Carter
Westbrook (16)	MC 207 854-9105	....				....		
Wilton t (4)	CM 207 645-4961	Clint Cushman	Richard P Davis	Linda P Jellison	Richard P Davis	Theodore Baxter	James C Parker	Kenneth L Vining
Windham t (13)	CM 207 892-1907	Tom Burtell	Glenn Fratto	Rita Bernier	Debra Taber	Charles Hammond	Richard Lewsen	Steve Walker
Winslow t (8)	CM 207 872-2776	Bernard McCaslin	Edward A Gagnon	Elizabeth Furman	....	William Page	Ronald Whary	Ernest Baker
Winter Harbor t (1)	TM 207 963-2235	....					....	....
Winterport t (3)	TM 207 223-5055	Samuel Butler Jr	Scott M Tilton	Scott M Tilton	Scott M Tilton	Creighton Parker		
Winthrop t (6)	CM 207 377-2286	David W Maxwell	Edward I Heath	Judyann Ward	Jan A Tewksbury	Hartley Palleschi	Joseph E Young Sr	Edward I Heath
Wiscasset t (3)	TM 207 882-6331	....	....	....	....	....	....	....
Yarmouth t (8)	CM 207 846-9036	....				....	....	....
York t (10)	CM 207 363-1000	James Bartlett	Mark Green	Mary Szeniawski	Tom Marcoux	....	William Foster	Leon Moulton
MARYLAND (55)								
Aberdeen t (13)	CM 410 272-1600	Charles R Boutin	Peter A Dacey	....	....	Edward Budnick	John R Jolley	William G McKean
Annapolis (33)	MC 410 263-7998	Alfred A Hopkins	Michael Mallinoff	Patricia L Bembe	William S Tyler	Edward Sherlock	....	John E C Patmore
Baltimore (736)	MC 410 396-3860	Kurt Schmoke	Lynnette Young		William Brown	Herman Williams	Thomas Frazier	George Balog
Bel Air t (9)	CM 410 638-4550	Russell Poole	William McFaul	Joyce Oliver	....	....	Leo Matrangola	Chris Schlehr
Berwyn Heights t (3)	MC 301 474-5000	Thomas Love	Karen Nelson	Patricia Barber	....	....	James Artis	Joseph Coleman
Bladensburg t (8)	MC 301 927-7048	Susanna C Yatman	Eric Morsicato	Elsie S Morrison	....	....	Robert Zidek	John A Parker
Bowie (38)	CM 301 262-6200	....	....	....	....	....	....	....
Brentwood t (3)	MC 301 927-3344	George D Denny Jr	Roylene M Roberts	Mary E Reed	....	Leonard Johnson	....	....
Brunswick t (5)	MC 301 834-7500	....	Richard Weldon	....	....	....	Lance Miller	Kevin Brawner
Cambridge (12)	MC 301 228-4020	....		....	....			
Capitol Heights t (4)	CM 301 336-0626	....	....	....	....	....	....	....
Centreville t (2)	CM 410 758-1186	Florence Walls	Denise M Rose	Doris M Payne	Doris M Payne	....	Douglas Crites	Paul I Roberts
Chestertown t (4)	MC 410 778-4378	Margo G Bailey	William Ingersoll	....	....	....	Wayne Bradley	Medford Capel
Cheverly t (6)	CM 301 773-8360	Larry Beyna	David Warrington	Lenore Lerch	....	....	Gilbert Jones Jr	Juan Torres
Chevy Chase v (3)	CM 301 654-7300	Margot Anderson	Jerry Schiro	....	....	....	George Winkel	Jerry Lesesne
Chevy Chase t (2)	CM 301 654-7144	Mier Wolf	Susan G Robinson	Andrea J Silverst	....	....	....	....
College Park (22)	CM 301 864-8667	Joseph E Page	Richard N Conti	Miriam P Wolff	John M Markowski	....	....	James C Johnson
Crisfield (3)	MC 410 968-1333	Donald W Gerald	....	....	....	....	....	....
Cumberland (24)	MC 301 722-2000	Edward C Athey	Jeffrey E Repp	Audrey C Wolford	Mark Alderton	Russell Livengood	James R Dick	Dennis McCormick
Delmar t (1)	CM 410 896-2777	Douglas Niblett	Roberta Neilson	Wendy Foxwell	Roberta Neilson	....	Harold Saylor	Robert Handy
District Heights t (7)	MC 301 336-1402	Mary Pumphrey	....	Marie E Gibbs	Daniel R Baden	....	Michael W Conboy	Jim McGill
Easton t (9)	MC 410 822-2525	George Murphy	....	Robert Karge	....	....	R Edward Blessing	John Larrimore
Elkton t (9)	CM 301 398-0970	....	....	....	....	....	....	....
Forest Heights t (3)	MC 301 839-1030	....	....	....	....	....	....	....
Frederick (40)	MC 301 694-1440	....	....	....	....	....	....	....
Friendship Heights v (..)	MC 301 656-2797	Alfred Muller	Leslie Strathmann	....	....	....	....	....
Frostburg (8)	CO 301 689-6000	....	....	....	....	....	....	....
Fruitland (4)	MC 410 548-2800	Valerie J Mann	Richard M Pollitt	Richard M Pollitt	....	Robin Townsend	Paul R Jackson	P Cooper Townsend
Gaithersburg (40)	CM 301 258-6310	W Edward Bohrer	Sanford W Daily	....	Roger Anderson	....	Maryann Viverette	James D Arnoult
Glenarden t (5)	CM 301 773-2100	....	....	....	....	....	....	....
Greenbelt (21)	CM 301 474-8000	Antoinette Bram	Daniel G Hobbs	Dorothy Lauber	....	....	James R Craze	Carl Hirsch
Hagerstown (35)	CM 301 739-8577	Steven Saber	Bruce Zimmerman	Georgiann Lucas	Alfred Martin	Gary Hawbaker	Dale Jones	Douglas Stull
Havre de Grace (9)	MC 410 939-1800	....	....	....	....	....	....	....
Hyattsville (14)	MC 301 985-5000	Thomas L Bass	Marge Wolf	....	....	Donald Moltrup	Robert T Perry	Daniel Jones
Indian Head t (4)	CM 301 743-5511	Dennis Scheessie	Joseph A Mangini	....	Dorothy Smith	....	....	James P Chase
La Plata t (6)	MC 301 870-3377	....	....	....	....	....	....	....
Landover Hills t (2)	MC 301 773-6401	....	....	....	....	....	....	....
Laurel t (19)	MC 301 725-5300	....	....	....	....	....	....	....
Mount Rainier t (8)	MC 301 927-0104	....	....	....	....	....	....	....
New Carrollton (12)	MC 301 459-6100	....	....	....	....	....	....	....
Ocean City t (5)	CM 410 289-8221	Roland E Powell	Denis W Dare	Carol Jacobs	Martha Bennett	....	David Massey	Hal Adkins
Pocomoke City (4)	MC 410 957-1333	Curt Lippoldt	Russell Blake	Janet Stewart	Sharon Beyma	....	Frank White	Dwight Campbell
Poolesville t (4)	CO 301 428-8927	....	....	....	....	....	....	....
Princess Anne t (2)	CM 410 651-1818	Garland R Hayward	Johanna B Volandt	....	....	....	Samuel D Howser	Thomas R Starr
Riverdale t (5)	MC 301 927-6381	....	....	....	....	....	....	....
Rockville (45)	CM 301 309-3000	....	....	....	....	....	....	....
Salisbury (21)	MC 410 548-3100	W Paul Martin	Patrick J Fennell	V Crawford	R Baskerville	W Higgens	C Dykes	....
Seat Pleasant (5)	CM 301 336-2600	Eugene Kennedy	Wendy Watkin	Evelyn Nighengale	Robert L Ashton	....	Ronald Harvey	....
Snow Hill t (2)	MC 410 632-2080	....	....	....	....	....	....	....
Takoma Park (17)	MC 301 270-1700	Edward F Sharp	Beverly K Habada	Cathrine Sartoph	....	....	Robert A Phillips	Richard Knauf
Taneytown (4)	CM 410 751-1100	Henry I Reindolla	John L Kendall	Linda M Hess	....	....	Melvin E Diggs	Bruce P Eyler Jr
Thurmont t (3)	MC 301 271-7313	Terrence R Best	Richard K May	....	....	....	Neil F Bechtol	....
University Park t (2)	MC 301 927-4262	Margaret Mallino	....	....	Daniel Baden	....	Richard Ashton	Warren Hall
Westernport t (2)	MC 301 359-3932	....	....	....	....	....	....	....
Westminster (13)	MC 410 848-9000	....	....	....	....	....	....	....
MASSACHUSETTS (271)								
Abington t (14)	TM 617 878-0805	....	....	....	....	....	....	....
Acton t (18)	TM 508 264-9621	Norman Lake	Don Johnson	Cathy Belbin	Roy Wetherby	Robert Craig	George Robinson	Richard Howe
Acushnet t (10)	TM 508 998-0200	Jackie Brightman	Elaine Miranda	Leanne Nichols	Alan Coutinho	Paul Cote	Michael Pointras	Richard Provencal
Adams t (9)	RT 413 743-9344	....	....	....	....	....	....	....
Agawam t (27)	MC 413 786-0400	....	....	....	....	....	....	....
Amesbury t (15)	RT 508 388-8100	Sally A McKay	Henry E Fournier	Josephine Jacques	Charles Benevento	Arthur R Gaudet	Gary P Ingham	Timothy H Haskell
Amherst t (35)	RT 413 256-4001	Bryan Harvey	Barry Delcastilho	Cornelia D Como	Nancy G Maglione	Victor Zumbruski	Donald N Maia	Noel J Tyan
Andover t (29)	TM 508 470-3800	Gerald Silverman	R Stapczynski	Randall Hanson	Anthony Torrisi	Harold Hayes	James Johnson	Robert McQuade
Arlington t (45)	MC 617 646-1000	....	....	....	....	....	....	....
Ashburnham t (5)	TM 508 827-5548	....	Christopher Rathy	Wes Landry	....	Paul Zibkowski	Ronald Leplante	William Brenna
Ashland t (12)	TM 508 881-0100	Teresa Evans	Dexter Blois	Cindy Giles	....	....	Robert Gonfrade	Silvio Baruzzi
Athol t (11)	RT 508 249-2368	....	....	....	....	....	....	....
Attleboro (38)	MC 508 223-2222	Judith H Robbins	....	Susan Flood	....	Ronald Churchill	Roland Sabourin	Houshang Hamarahi
Auburn t (15)	RT 508 832-7720	George Jewell	....	Elizabeth Prouty	....	Roger Belhumeur	Ronald Miller	....
Avon t (5)	TM 508 588-0414	....	....	....	....	....	....	....
Ayer t (7)	TM 617 772-2072	....	....	....	....	....	....	....
Barnstable t (41)	CM 508 790-6200	....	....	....	....	....	....	....
Barre t (5)	TM 508 355-2504	....	....	....	....	....	....	....
Bedford t (13)	TM 617 275-1111	....	....	....	....	....	....	....

Directory 1/9
continued

**MUNICIPAL OFFICIALS
IN U.S. CITIES OVER 2,500**

City, 1990 population figures (000 omitted), form of government	Municipal phone number	Mayor/ chief elected official	Appointed administrator	City clerk/ city secretary	Finance officer	Fire chief	Police chief	Public works director
MASSACHUSETTS (271) continued								
Belchertown t (11)	TM 413 323-0403	....	....	....	....	....	....	....
Bellingham t (15)	TM 508 966-0040	....	....	....	....	....	....	....
Belmont t (25)	RT 617 489-8213	A Taubes Warner	Melvin A Kleckner	C Stafford	....	James Murphy	Ronald Blanchette	....
Berkley t (4)	TM 508 822-3348	....	....	....	....	....	....	....
Beverly (38)	MC 508 921-6000	....	....	....	....	....	....	....
Billerica t (38)	RT 508 671-0942	Ralph M Krau	Robert A Mercier	Shirley E Schult	Valarie M Connor	Anthony E Capaldo	John M Barretto	Richard Bento
Blackstone t (8)	TM 508 883-7289	....	....	....	....	....	....	....
Bolton t (3)	TM 617 779-2297	....	....	....	....	....	....	....
Boston-Suffolk (574)	MC 617 725-4000	....	....	....	....	....	....	....
Bourne t (16)	TM 508 759-0600	Robert Parady	....	Linda Marzelli	Irene Sundquist	Steven Philbrick	John Ford	Louis Pellegrini
Boxborough t (3)	TM 617 263-1116	....	....	....	....	....	....	....
Boxford t (6)	TM 508 887-8181	....	....	....	....	....	....	....
Boylston t (4)	TM 617 869-2234	....	....	....	....	....	....	....
Braintree t (34)	RT 617 848-1870	....	....	Joan Cole	Lisa Souve	Roy Jones	James Ehrhart	Allan Tkaczyk
Brewster t (8)	TM 508 896-3701	John Mitchell	Charles Sumner	....	....	....	....	....
Bridgewater t (21)	TM 508 697-0919	....	....	....	....	....	....	....
Brockton (93)	MC 508 580-7123	Michael W Merrill	Richard T Leary	Patrick J Ward	Harvey Beth	Robert D English	Howard A Brackett	A Thomas Demaio
Brookline t (55)	CM 617 730-2000	Robert P Marrano	David W Owen	Jane L Chew	Patrick J Mullin	Paul Thibault	William Soda	Syamal Chaudhuri
Burlington t (23)	RT 617 270-1635	Kenneth Reeves	Robert Healy	Margaret Drury	James Maloney	Kevin Fitzgerald	Perry Anderson	Ralph Dunphy
Cambridge (96)	CM 617 349-4000	George F Jenkins	William T Friel	Ralph Eames	Christine Tague	James Fitzpatrick	John F Ruane	Joseph Campo
Canton t (19)	TM 617 821-5000	Ralph P Anderson	Paul E Cohen	Sarah Andreassen	Sarah Andreassen	Robert J Koning	David T Galvin	Gary R Davis
Carlisle t (4)	TM 508 369-6136	....	....	....	....	....	....	....
Carver t (11)	TM 617 866-4551	R Kwiatkowski	Guy E Helander	Helene Caplette	Evelyn Murkland	Ralph Harris	Philip Stevens	William Foley
Charlton t (10)	TM 508 248-5900	....	....	....	....	....	....	....
Chatham t (7)	TM 508 945-2100	Roger Blomgren	Bernard Lynch	Mary E St Hilaire	Charles F Mansfie	John Parow	Armand Caron	James Pearson
Chelmsford t (32)	TM 508 250-5201	Louis H Spence	S McGoldrick	Lucy Zbikowski	Edward Cyr	Louis Addonizio	Edward Flynn	Ted Sobolewski
Chelsea (29)	MC 617 889-8294	....	....	....	....	....	....	....
Cheshire t (3)	TM 413 743-2826	Joseph J Chessey	....	Nancy A Mulvey	Norman J Ritchott	Robert J Nunes	John F Ferraro Jr	Stanley W Kulif
Chicopee (57)	MC 413 594-4711	Mary Dickhaut	Paul B Jensen	Earl Wilson	Mary Dickhaut	Richard Hart	Mark Laverdore	Bill Gilmore
Clinton t (13)	TM 508 365-4120	....	....	....	....	....	....	....
Cohasset t (7)	TM 617 383-9900	....	....	....	....	....	....	....
Concord t (17)	TM 617 369-2100	Paul C Carter	Donna L Boryta	Barbara L Suriner	Richard Charon	Thomas Murray	Daniel Filiault	Terry Young
Dalton t (7)	TM 413 684-6111	....	....	....	....	....	....	....
Danvers t (24)	RT 508 777-0001	....	....	....	....	....	....	....
Dartmouth t (27)	RT 508 999-0700	....	....	....	....	....	....	....
Dedham t (24)	RT 617 326-5770	E Kirkwood	....	William Leno	....	....	M Wozniakewicz	Harold Eaton
Deerfield t (5)	RT 413 665-4645	Heidi Schadt	Stephen Lombard	Elinor Slade	....	Paul Tucker	John Symington	Dennis Hanson
Dennis t (14)	TM 508 394-8300	....	....	....	....	....	....	....
Dighton t (6)	TM 508 669-6431	....	....	....	....	....	....	....
Douglas t (5)	TM 508 476-4000	....	....	....	....	....	....	....
Dover t (5)	TM 508 785-2269	James O' Loughlin	Dennis E Piendak	Gary McCarthy	Joseph H Harper	Robert Kohanski	Louis Panas	Paul G Dillon
Dracut t (26)	TM 508 452-1227	....	....	....	....	....	....	....
Dudley t (10)	TM 617 943-2792	Margaret Kearney	Rocco J Longo	Nancy Oates	....	Kenneth Erickson	Enrico Cappucci	Walter Tonazuck
Duxbury t (14)	CM 617 934-6586	....	....	....	....	....	....	....
East Bridgewater t (11)	TM 508 378-1601	....	....	....	....	....	....	....
East Longmeadow t (13)	TM 413 525-5400	Thomas L Newton	Sheila Vanderhoef	Lillian Lamperti	Carolyn Gifford	John E Austin	Donald Watson	Steven Douglas
Eastham t (4)	TM 508 255-0333	....	....	....	....	....	....	....
Easthampton t (16)	RT 413 527-0818	Patricia Hunt	Kevin Paicos	Janet Andrus	....	Phillip Blye	Stanley Bates	Paul Wollenhaupt
Easton t (20)	TM 508 230-3300	J McCarthy	....	J Hanlon	K Flynn	P Colameta	J Bonnel	D Risteen
Essex t (3)	TM 508 768-7111	John R Mitchell	Robert L Connors	Joseph Doran	Raymond Reynolds	Edward Dawson	Francis McDonald	Ronald Costa
Everett (36)	MC 617 394-2280	Edward Marks Jr	Peter F Boyer	Carol Martin	....	George Packish	Gene Kulander	William B Owen
Fairhaven t (16)	RT 508 992-5416	....	Andrew A Gala Jr	Arlene M Crimmins	Todd K Hassett	Hobart H Boswell	Edward T O' Leary	Robert E Federico
Fall River (93)	MC 508 324-2000	....	Edgar Gadbois	George King	....	Michael Smith	Brent Larrabee	John McMahon
Falmouth t (28)	RT 508 548-7611	....	....	....	....	....	....	....
Fitchburg (41)	MC 508 345-9550	....	....	....	....	....	....	....
Foxborough t (15)	TM 508 543-1200	Lawrence Ogden	....	Kenneth Owens	....	Glen Silva	Richard Spencer	John Moultrie
Framingham t (65)	RT 508 620-4847	....	....	....	....	....	....	....
Franklin t (22)	CM 508 520-4949	....	....	....	....	....	....	....
Freetown t (9)	TM 508 644-2201	....	....	....	....	....	....	....
Gardner (20)	MC 617 632-4350	David A Smith Jr	Joseph A Kellogg	Mary Ellen Siok	Lauren Sartori	Michael Fitzpatrk	William Walsh	Donald Chester
Georgetown t (6)	TM 508 352-5755	....	....	....	....	....	....	....
Gloucester (29)	MC 508 281-9700	....	....	....	....	....	....	....
Grafton t (13)	TM 508 839-5335	....	....	....	....	....	....	....
Granby t (6)	TM 413 467-7177	Candace T Kniffen	....	Marcia K Cole	M Fitzgerald	Kenneth Calvin	Michael Manoogian	Ralph Hayward
Great Barrington t (8)	MC 413 528-1623	....	....	....	....	....	....	....
Greenfield t (19)	RT 413 774-7441	....	....	....	....	....	....	....
Groton t (8)	TM 508 448-9818	....	....	....	....	....	....	....
Groveland t (5)	TM 617 372-6861	....	....	....	....	....	....	....
Hadley t (4)	TM 413 586-3354	Joseph Frisoli	Joseph Nugent	Sandra Harris	Barbara Gomez	Peter Huska	Eugene Berry	Richard Harris
Halifax t (7)	TM 617 293-5761	....	....	....	....	....	....	....
Hamilton t (7)	TM 508 468-4455	....	....	....	....	....	....	....
Hampden t (5)	TM 413 566-3713	....	....	....	....	....	....	....
Hanover t (12)	TM 617 826-2261	Martin Crane	Charles Cristello	Thomas Hall	Allan J Masison	Richard K Wehter	Joachim Borowski	Brian J Sullivan
Hanson t (9)	TM 617 293-2131	....	....	....	....	....	....	....
Harvard t (12)	TM 508 456-3995	....	....	....	....	....	....	....
Harwich t (10)	TM 508 430-7513	....	....	....	....	....	....	....
Hatfield t (3)	TM 413 247-9200	Frederick Misilo	Brian J Bullock	Kathleen Peterson	Marion E Hewson	Edward R Oberg	Charles R Hicks	Alan R Berg
Haverhill (51)	MC 508 374-2300	....	....	....	....	....	....	....
Hingham t (20)	TM 617 741-1400	....	....	....	....	....	....	....
Holbrook t (11)	RT 617 767-4312	....	....	....	....	....	....	....
Holden t (15)	CM 508 829-0225	Joseph Strazzulla	Theodore D Kozak	Mary Nealon	Stephen Roomian	R Mac Millian	William McRobert	Robert Bartlet
Holliston t (13)	TM 508 429-0608	....	....	....	....	....	....	....
Holyoke (44)	MC 413 534-2176	....	....	....	....	....	....	....
Hopedale t (6)	TM 508 634-2203	....	....	....	....	....	....	....
Hopkinton t (9)	TM 508 497-9700	William George	George E Howe	Frances Richards	Donna M Walsh	....	Charles Surpitski	Armand Michaud
Hudson t (17)	TM 508 562-9963	....	....	....	....	....	....	....
Hull t (10)	TM 617 925-2000	....	....	....	....	....	....	....
Ipswich t (12)	TM 508 356-6609	....	....	....	....	....	....	....
Kingston t (9)	TM 617 585-0500	....	....	....	....	....	....	....
Lakeville t (8)	TM 617 947-3400	....	....	....	....	....	....	....
Lancaster t (7)	TM 508 365-3326	....	....	....	....	....	....	....
Lanesborough t (3)	TM 413 442-1167	....	....	....	....	....	....	....
Lawrence (70)	MC 508 794-5803	....	....	....	....	....	....	....

Directory 1/9 continued

MUNICIPAL OFFICIALS IN U.S. CITIES OVER 2,500

City, 1990 population figures (000 omitted), form of government	Municipal phone number	Mayor/ chief elected official	Appointed administrator	City clerk/ city secretary	Finance officer	Fire chief	Police chief	Public works director
MASSACHUSETTS (271) continued								
Lee t (6)	RT 413 243-2100	....	....	....	....	....	....	....
Leicester t (10)	TM 508 892-8210	....	....	....	....	....	....	....
Lenox t (5)	TM 413 637-0144	....	....	....	....	....	....	....
Leominster (38)	MC 617 537-6311	....	....	....	....	....	....	....
Lexington t (29)	CM 617 861-2773	William Dailey	Richard J White	Bernice Fallick	John Ryan	John Bergeron	Christopher Casey	Richard Spiers
Lincoln Center t (8)	TM 617 259-8850	Harriet B Todd		Nancy Zuelke	Betty Lang	D James Arena	D James Arena	Vincent Deamicis
Littleton t (7)	TM 508 952-2311	Paul J Tiernan	Mark W Haddad	Mary Crory	Bernard W Meyler	A McCurdy	Thomas W Odea Jr	Eric K Durling
Longmeadow t (15)	TM 413 567-5433	Arlene C Miller	Patricia A Vinche	Louise W Lines	Paul J Pasterczyk	Peter Marcotte	Richard A Marches	Douglas W Barron
Lowell (103)	CM 508 970-4105	Richard Howe	M Boisvert	....	Barbara Hagg	Andrew Lacourse	Edward Davis	Edward Walsh
Ludlow t (19)	RT 413 589-7511	....	....	....	....	....	....	....
Lunenburg t (9)	TM 508 582-6853	....	....	....	....	....	....	....
Lynn (81)	MC 617 598-4000	....	....	....	....	....	....	....
Lynnfield t (11)	CM 617 334-3180	....	....	....	....	....	....	....
Malden (54)	MC 617 324-6600	....	....	....	....	....	....	....
Manchester t (5)	TM 508 526-1712	Ronald G Kelley	Paul Bockelman	Gretchen Wood	Charles Lane	Joseph O' Malley	Ronald Ramos	Robert Moroney
Manchester-by-the-Sea t (5)	MC 508 526-1712							
Mansfield t (17)	CM 508 261-7370	Amos Robinson	William Williams	....	....	Edward Sliney	Arthur O' Neill	Daniel Clifford
Marblehead t (20)	TM 617 631-0000	Thomas A McNulty	J Von Sternberg	....	....	....	....	....
Marion t (4)	TM 508 748-3500	....	....	....	....	....	....	....
Marlborough (32)	MC 508 460-3700	....	....	....	....	....	....	....
Marshfield t (22)	TM 617 837-5141	Faith A Jean	Richard A Montori	Sheila Sullivan	....	Roy McNamee	William Sullivan	William Burke
Mashpee t (8)	MC 508 539-1408	....	....	....	....	....	....	....
Mattapoisett t (6)	TM 508 758-4100	....	....	....	....	....	....	....
Maynard t (10)	TM 508 897-1001	Frank Ignachuck	Michael Giamotis	Judith Peterson	Harry Gannon	Ronald Cassidy	Edward Lawton	Walter Sokolowski
Medfield t (11)	TM 508 359-8505	....	....	....	....	....	....	....
Medford (57)	CM 617 396-5500	....	....	....	....	....	....	....
Medway t (10)	TM 201 627-2000	Joseph L Lebar	Joyce Hubschman	Joyce Hubschman	Frank J Augustine	Tom Slockbower	Michael Bahnatka	Gilbert Graner
Melrose (28)	MC 617 665-4500	Richard D Lyons	P Dellorusso	P Dellorusso	P Dellorusso	Charles Sheridan	Frank A Fiandaca	Joseph H Mac Kay
Mendon t (4)	TM 508 473-2312	Joseph Reed		Jean Bavosi		Gioachino Deluca	Dennis Grady	
Merrimac t (5)	TM 617 346-8862	....	....	....	....	....	....	....
Methuen t (40)	CM 617 794-3210	Dennis DiZoglio	....	James Maloney	Thomas Kelly	James Clarke	Donald DeSantis	Kenneth Martin
Middleborough t (18)	TM 508 947-0928	Michele Grenier	John F Healey	Sandra L Bernier	Lorraine Reilly	Carl Reed Sr	William E Warner	Donald Boucher
Middleton t (5)	TM 508 777-3617	Richard Ajootian	Ira S Singer	....	Robert Murphy	Henry Michalski	Robert Peachey	Dennis Roy
Milford t (25)	RT 508 634-2303	....	....	....	....	....	....	....
Millbury t (12)	TM 508 865-4710	....	....	....	....	....	....	....
Millis t (8)	TM 508 376-2634	....	....	....	....	....	....	....
Millville t (3)	MC 508 883-8433	....	....	....	....	....	....	....
Milton t (26)	RT 617 698-0100	....	....	....	....	....	....	....
Monson t (5)	TM 413 267-4100	....	....	....	....	....	....	....
Montague t (8)	RT 413 863-3204	Hutch Hammond	Deborah Radway	John Zywna	C Martin	....	Patrick O' Bryan	Edward Mleczko
Nahant t (4)	TM 617 581-0088	....	....	....	....	....	....	....
Nantucket t (6)	TM 508 228-7255	Timothy R Madden	Suzanne K Kennedy	Rebecca J Lohmann	Bruce Miller	Bruce L Watts	Randolph P Norris	Jeff Willett
Natick t (31)	RT 508 651-7230	....	....	....	....	....	....	....
Needham t (28)	RT 617 455-7500	H Phillip Garrity	Carl F Valente	Theodore Eaton	Carl F Valente	Robert DiPoli	William Slowe	Richard Merson
New Bedford (100)	MC 508 979-1444	Rosemary Tierney	....	Janice Davidian	Daniel Patten	Henry Openshaw	Richard Benoit	Lawrence Worden
Newbury t (6)	TM 508 465-9241	....	....	....	....	....	....	....
Newburyport (16)	MC 508 465-4413	Lisa L Mead	....	Michael Sullivan	Nolan Morris	John Cutter	Francis O' Connor	Joseph Keefe
Newton (83)	MC 617 552-7000	....	....	....	....	....	....	....
Norfolk t (9)	TM 617 528-1408	....	....	....	....	....	....	....
North Adams (17)	MC 413 663-6685	John Barrett	Fred Holmes	Maryann Abuisi	....	Craig Rougeau	Rodney Prevey	....
North Andover t (23)	TM 508 682-6483	Kenneth C Crouch	James P Gordon	Daniel Long	Kevin F Mahoney	William V Dolan	Richard M Stanley	George Perna
North Attleborough t (25)	RT 508 699-0100	Luis Lema	Sally Melo	....	....	Robert Coleman	John Coyle	Raymond Payson
North Brookfield t (5)	TM 508 867-0200	John J Lane	Melanie A Jenkins	Sheila Buzzell	Scott Usher	James Black	Nelson Barrett	Raymond Blake
North Reading t (12)	MC 508 664-6000	Rosalie A Senior	Stephen J Daly	Betty Vullo	George Dow	Edward O' Brien	Henry Purnell	David Hanlon
Northampton (29)	MC 413 586-6950	Mary L Ford	Thomas Hedderick	Christine Skorups	Michael Lyons	Lawrence Jones	Russel Sienkiewic	Samuel Brindis
Northborough t (12)	TM 508 393-5040	Fred George	Charles Kellner	Adele Beatty	....	Brian Duggan	Ken Hutchins	John Schunder
Northbridge t (13)	CM 617 234-2095	....	....	....	....	....	....	....
Norton t (14)	TM 508 285-0210	Clarence Rich	Walter Lindberg	Diane Casagni	Muriel Robbins	George Burgess	Benton Keene Jr	Carl Jacobs
Norwell t (9)	TM 617 659-8000	....	....	....	....	....	....	....
Norwood t (29)	CM 617 762-1240	....	John Carroll	Robert Thornton	....	William Sullivan	George DiBlasi	Joseph Welch
Orange t (7)	TM 508 544-2254	....	....	....	....	....	....	....
Orleans t (6)	TM 508 240-3700	Francis E Suits	N Schwinn	Jean Wilcox	David Withrow	Raphael Merrill	William Stone	Richard Gould
Oxford t (13)	TM 508 987-6030	Thomas F Spooner	Dennis A Power	Lori A Kelley	Donald Kaminski	Michael Plante	James B Triplett	John Phillips
Palmer t (12)	TM 413 283-2603	Lawrence M Jasak	Beverly A Lund	Patricia Donovan	Carol Sugrue	Alan Roy	Howard E Case	Philip Sampson
Paxton t (4)	TM 508 753-2803	Joseph McKay	....	June T Herron	....	Brian Murphy	Michael Ahearn	Paul Palumbo
Peabody (47)	MC 508 532-3000	Peter Torigian	....	....	Patricia Schaffer	Joseph Russell	Robert Champagne	Richard Carnevale
Pembroke t (15)	TM 617 293-3844	....	....	....	....	....	....	....
Pepperell t (10)	TM 508 433-6359	....	....	....	....	....	....	....
Pittsfield (49)	MC 413 499-9340	....	....	....	....	....	....	....
Plainville t (7)	TM 508 695-3142	Andrea Soucy	Joseph Fernandes	Kathleen Sandland	....	Robert Skinner	Edward Merrick	Ron Fredrickson
Plymouth t (46)	RT 508 746-1620	Peter Paulding Jr	William R Griffin	Lawrence Pizer	Michael Daley	Thomas Fugazzi	Robert J Pomeroy	Leighton F Peck
Provincetown t (4)	CM 508 487-7000	Irene Rabinowitz	Keith A Bergman	Sheila Silva	Jon Richardson	Michael S Trovato	Robert P Anthony	Joseph J Borgesi
Quincy (85)	MC 617 376-1000	James A Sheets	....	Joseph Shea	Robert Foy	Thomas Gorman	Francis Mullen	David A Colton
Randolph t (30)	RT 617 963-3212	....	....	....	....	....	....	....
Raynham t (10)	TM 508 824-2707	Donald McKinnon	Randall A Buckner	Helen A Lounsbury	Belcher Stanley	George Andrews	Peter King	J Michael Silvia
Reading t (23)	CM 617 942-9001	George V Hines	P Hechenbleikner	Catherine Quimby	Elizabeth Klepeis	Donald Wood	Edward Marchand	Edward McIntlre
Rehoboth t (9)	TM 508 252-3758	....	....	....	....	....	....	....
Revere (43)	MC 617 284-3600	....	....	....	....	....	....	....
Rochester t (4)	TM 508 763-3871	David L Hughes	....	Naida L Parker	....	Joseph Clapp	Walter V Denham	Jeffrey Eldridge
Rockland t (16)	TM 617 871-1874	Patricia Murphy	Kevin R Donovan	Mary Pat Kaszanek	....	Kevin Henderson	Kevin M Donovan	Kevin Carrico
Rockport t (7)	TM 508 546-6894	....	....	....	....	....	....	....
Rowley t (4)	TM 508 948-2705	Robert W Morse	Lawrence Cameron	Jeanne Grover	J Vigeant	Scott McKenzie	Kevin Barry	Scott Leavitt
Rutland t (5)	TM 508 886-4103	....	....	....	....	....	....	....
Salem (38)	MC 508 745-9595	Neil Harrington	....	Deb Burkinshaw	Paul Dooley	Robert Turner	Robert St Pierre	Charles Quigley
Salisbury t (7)	CM 508 465-2310	Hattie Stoltzfus	Michael W Basque	Wilma Mahoney	....	Robert Cook	Lawrence Streeter	David W Keithly
Sandwich t (15)	TM 508 888-4910	....	....	....	....	....	....	....
Saugus t (26)	RT 617 231-4126	Janette Fasano	Edward J Collins	Marcia Wallace	Richard Cardillo	Walter Newbury	Cornelius Meehan	Joseph Attubato
Scituate t (17)	TM 617 545-6700	Joseph Norton	Richard H Agnew	Barbara Maffucci	....	James E Breen	Thomas R Neilen	A Antoniello
Seekonk t (13)	RT 508 336-7400	....	....	....	....	....	....	....
Sharon t (16)	TM 617 784-1515	Norman Katz	Benjamin E Puritz	Shirley Davenport	....	James Polito	Joseph Bernstein	John Sulik
Sheffield t (3)	CM 413 229-2335	Thomas Leigh	Robert Weitz	Natalie Fonk	....	John Vilrich	James McGarry	Ronald Bassett
Sherborn t (4)	TM 508 651-7850	James J Norton	Susan Adler	Lucy Almasian	Kenneth Crowell	Francis Heffron	Gary Hendron	Michael Pakstis
Shirley t (6)	TM 508 425-4331	....	....	....	....	....	....	....

Directory 1/9
continued

MUNICIPAL OFFICIALS IN U.S. CITIES OVER 2,500

City, 1990 population figures (000 omitted), form of government	Municipal phone number	Mayor/ chief elected official	Appointed administrator	City clerk/ city secretary	Finance officer	Fire chief	Police chief	Public works director
MASSACHUSETTS (271) continued								
Shrewsbury t (24)	CM 508 842-7471	Edward Fitzgerald	Richard D Carney	Donald R Gray	Mary E Thompson	George A Duhamel	Robert McGinley	....
Somerset t (18)	TM 508 646-2800	Christopher Matte	Arthur Marchand	Patricia Hart	....	Stephen Rivard	James Smith	....
Somerville (76)	MC 617 625-6600	Michael E Capuano	Michael Gorman	Arthur McCue	Michele Gigli	John Gover	Robert Carroll	Robert Trahan
South Hadley t (17)	RT 413 538-5017	Constance Clancy	Normand Cloutier	....	....	....	William Schenker	Greg Kereakaglow
Southampton t (4)	TM 413 527-4741	....	....	....	....	....	....	....
Southborough t (7)	TM 508 485-0710	....	....	....	....	....	....	....
Southbridge t (18)	CM 508 764-5405	....	....	....	....	....	....	....
Southwick t (8)	TM 413 569-5504	F Paul Saler	Karl J Stinehart	John R Zanolli	Linda D Carr	Donald Morris	Henry LaBombard	Arthur Chevalier
Spencer t (12)	TM 508 885-7500	....	....	....	....	....	....	....
Springfield (157)	MC 413 787-6100	....	....	....	....	....	....	....
Sterling t (6)	TM 508 422-8111	....	....	....	....	....	....	....
Stoneham t (22)	TM 617 279-2600	John F Mahoney	Jeffrey D Nutting	Annamae Arsenault	Ronald F Florino	W G McLaughlin	Eugene M Passaro	Robert E Grover
Stoughton t (27)	CM 617 341-1300	Mark Kelley	Philip Farrington	Jeanne Fleming	Arti Mehta	John Soave	Philip Dineen	Lawrence Barrett
Stow t (5)	TM 508 897-4514	Jean H Lynch	William J Wrigley	Ann L Allison	Linda S Stokes	Bruce E Fletcher	Charles C Mayo	Bruce E Fletcher
Sturbridge t (8)	TM 508 347-2500	Michael Hager	....	Susan Blair	....	Leonard Senecal	Kevin Fitzgibbons	Makrom Megalli
Sudbury t (14)	TM 508 443-8891	Lawrence Blacker	Richard Thompson	Jean Mac Kenzie	James Vanar	Michael Dunne	Peter Lembo	Robert A Noyes
Sunderland t (3)	TM 413 665-4414	....	....	....	....	....	....	....
Sutton t (7)	CM 508 865-5078	....	....	....	....	....	....	....
Swampscott t (14)	RT 617 596-8850	....	....	....	....	....	....	....
Swansea t (15)	TM 508 678-2981	....	....	....	....	....	....	....
Taunton (50)	MC 508 821-1057	....	....	....	....	....	....	....
Templeton t (6)	TM 508 939-8801	....	....	....	....	....	....	....
Tewksbury t (27)	TM 508 640-4300	Richard Hanson	David G Cressman	Elizabeth Carey	Thomas Berube	Thomas Ryan	John Mackey	William Burris
Tisbury t (3)	TM 508 696-4200	....	....	....	....	....	....	....
Topsfield t (6)	TM 617 887-8571	....	....	....	....	....	....	....
Townsend t (8)	TM 508 597-2837	....	....	....	....	....	....	....
Truro t (2)	CM 508 349-3635	....	....	....	....	....	....	....
Tyngsborough t (9)	TM 508 649-2300	Warren W Allgrove	Robert Griffin Jr	D Dunderdale	....	Timothy Madden	C Chrnopoulo	Ronald Corcoran
Upton t (5)	TM 617 529-6901	....	....	....	....	....	....	....
Uxbridge t (10)	TM 617 278-2041	....	....	....	....	....	....	....
Wakefield t (25)	TM 617 246-6390	Peter G Melanson	Thomas P Butler	V Zingarelli	Matthew J Burns	David Parr	Stephen Doherty	Donald Onusseit
Walpole t (20)	RT 508 660-7294	Joanne Damish	James Merriam	Louis Hoegler	Cynthia Moore	Leonard Anderson	Joseph Betro	Martin Feeney
Waltham (58)	MC 617 893-4040	William Stanley	John Langley	Peter Koutoujian	Dennis Quinn	Thomas Keough	Stephen Unsworth	John Snedeker
Ware t (10)	TM 413 967-5289	....	....	....	....	....	....	....
Wareham t (19)	CM 508 291-3100	Sarah D Woods	Joseph F Murphy	Elizabeth Pezolli	Robert Bliss	....	Thomas Joyce	Mark Gifford
Warren t (4)	TM 413 436-5701	....	....	....	....	....	....	....
Watertown t (33)	CM 617 972-6465	....	....	....	....	....	....	....
Wayland t (12)	TM 508 358-7701	Dennis Berry	Tom Landry	Judy St Croix	Robert Hilliard	Michael Murphy	Gerry Galvin	Toma Duhani
Webster t (16)	TM 617 943-0033	....	....	....	....	....	....	....
Wellesley t (27)	RT 617 431-1019	Barbara Shanahan	....	Joan Regan	Judy Curby	Robert Waters	Tom O' Loughlin	Pat Berdan
Wellfleet t (2)	TM 508 349-0300	Carolina Kiggins	Julia Enroth	Dawn Rickman	Patricia Eagar	Roger Henson	Richard Rosenthal	Richard Fressilli
Wenham t (4)	TM 508 468-5522	....	....	....	....	....	....	....
West Boylston t (7)	TM 617 835-6091	....	....	....	....	....	....	....
West Bridgewater t (6)	TM 508 588-4820	Eldon F Moreira	Elizabeth Faricy	Marion L Leonard	Marilyn Gordon	Leonard T Hunt	Howard R Anderson	Donald Newman
West Brookfield t (4)	TM 508 867-6874	Edward Sauer	W Frangiamore	Nancy Korsec	....	Ron Gresty	John Zabek	Dan Santos
West Newbury t (3)	TM 508 363-5487	....	....	....	....	....	....	....
West Springfield t (28)	RT 413 781-7550	....	....	....	....	....	....	....
Westborough t (14)	TM 508 366-3030	Denzil Drewry	Lee Bourgoin	Elizabeth Amoroso	Leah Talbot	James Parker Jr	Glenn Parker	John Walden
Westfield (38)	MC 413 568-9181	....	....	....	....	....	....	....
Westford t (16)	CM 508 692-5501	Madonna McKenzie	Robert Halpin	Elaine McKenna	Frank Messer	George Rogers	Robert Welch	Richard Barrett
Westminster t (6)	TM 508 874-2184	....	....	....	....	....	....	....
Weston t (10)	TM 617 893-7320	Ann G Leibowitz	J Ward Carter	M Elizabeth Nolan	....	John E Thorburn	James J McShane	....
Westport t (14)	TM 508 636-1003	....	....	....	....	....	....	....
Westwood t (13)	TM 617 326-6450	Robert W Uek	Michael A Jaillet	Edith McCracken	Pamela M Dukeman	John J Sheehy	Robert C Haas	J Timothy Walsh
Weymouth t (54)	RT 617 335-2000	....	....	....	....	....	....	....
Whitman t (13)	TM 617 447-2561	....	....	....	....	Daniel P Merritt	Allen M Stratton	Edmond Miga
Wilbraham t (13)	TM 413 596-2805	Terry L Nelson	William J Fogarty	Beverly Radner	....	Edward Migowan	S Michael Kennedy	Timothy Kaiser
Williamstown t (8)	CM 413 458-3500	Paul M Humora	Steven L Ledoux	Mary C George	Charles St John	Daniel R Stewart	Bobby N Stewart	Robert P Palmer
Wilmington t (18)	TM 508 658-3311	Michael V McCoy	Michael A Caira	Kathleen Scanlon	Michael Morris	Richard Williams	Steven D Thompson	Michael P Murphy
Winchendon t (9)	TM 508 297-2766	Lorenzo J Sordoni	Richard S Lak	Lois A Regan	Eleanor Black	....	....	....
Winchester t (20)	RT 617 721-7133	....	....	....	....	....	....	....
Winthrop t (18)	RT 617 846-1077	....	....	....	....	....	....	....
Woburn (36)	MC 617 932-4400	....	....	....	....	....	....	....
Worcester (170)	CM 508 799-1030	....	....	Joan Embree	Tom Brady	Dan Brock	....	Jay Fink
Wrentham t (9)	TM 508 384-5400	Michael Carroll	....	George Barabe	Susan Milne	David Akin	Robert Chapman	George Allaire
Yarmouth t (21)	TM 508 398-2231	Herbert Schnitzer	Robert C Lawton					
MICHIGAN (273)								
Adrian (22)	CM 517 263-2161	Joe Wagley	Alden Smith	Marsha Rowley	Larry Opelt	Larry Liedel	David Emerson	Keith Richard
Albion (10)	CM 517 629-5535	Mike Williams	Lewis Steinbrecher	Jim Bonamy	Jim Bonamy	....	Harold Hoaglin	Leroy Schmidt
Algonac (5)	CM 810 794-9361	Raymond J Martin	Marilyn Manning	Rose Perricone	....	Charles Johnson	Ken L Canode	Paul Jarmolowicz
Allegan (5)	CM 616 673-5511	David Ferber	Aaron Anthony	Aaron Anthony	....	Kevin Blanchard	Edward Cone	Dale Commans
Allen Park (31)	MC 313 928-1400	Gerald Richards	Richard Huebler	Bernice Weiss	Daniel Cassidy	James Cabadas	Leo Lanctot	Ted Jaroslawski
Alma (9)	CM 517 463-8336	Stewart McDonald	Doug Thomas	William Stuckey	Phillip Moore	George Blyton	Robert Lombardi	Kenneth Feldt
Almont v (2)	CM 810 798-8528	....	David Murphy	Sally McCrea	Sally McCrea	....	Leonard Everitt	Fred Treutle
Alpena (11)	CM 517 354-4158	William LaHaie	Peter Parker	Alan Bakalarski	....	....	Thad Taylor	David Nordquist
Ann Arbor (110)	CM 313 994-2700	Ingrid Sheldon	Alfred Gatta	Winnie Northcross	A Dean Moore	George Markus	....	Roye Burr
Auburn (2)	MC 517 662-6761	Steve Samborn	Jeffery B Lawson	Lucy Wiesenauer	Jeffery B Lawson	Russ Pickelman	James Klann	....
Auburn Hills (17)	CM 810 370-9400	James McDonald	Dennis McGee	Veronica New	Lisa Banes	Mark Walterhouse	John Dalton	Bruce Pothoff
Bad Axe (3)	CM 517 269-7681	....	....	....	....	....	William Barczak	Roy Hill
Bangor (2)	CM 616 427-8506	David Rigozzi	....	Wanda Rissley	....	....	....	....
Battle Creek (54)	CM 616 966-3378	John J Gallagher	Rance Leaders	Deborah Owens	Merrill Stanley	Charles Owens	Thomas Pope	Ken Tsuchiyama
Bay City (39)	CM 517 894-8146	....	....	Kareen Thomas	....	....	D Roger Mason	....
Belding (6)	CM 616 794-1900	David Greene	Alan Hartley	Agnes Frisch	....	Jack Loria	....	....
Belleville (3)	CM 313 697-9323	Glen Silvenis	....	....	....	....	....	....
Benton Harbor (13)	CM 616 927-8400	....	....	Leona Garrett	Michael P Tyler	....	William Rechlin	Richard Shepler
Berkley (17)	CM 810 546-2410	Jerold Durst	Calvin Teague	Bruce Carlson	Isabelle Haapoja	August Semmerling	....	....
Bessemer (2)	CM 906 663-4311	Vivian Coleman	Bruce Carlson	Roberta R Cline	....	....	Kevin Courtney	Tim Vogel
Big Rapids (13)	CM 616 592-4001	Kay Farrow	Steve Stilwell	Laura Neuman	James Wonacott	....	Arthur Gunter	Mark Strahan
Birmingham (20)	CM 313 644-1800	....	....	....	....	....	....	....
Blissfield v (3)	MC 517 486-4347	Patrick Hinde	James Wonacott	....	....	....	....	....
Bloomfield Hills (4)	CM 313 644-1520	....	....	....	....	....	....	....

Directory 1/9 continued **MUNICIPAL OFFICIALS IN U.S. CITIES OVER 2,500**

City, 1990 population figures (000 omitted), form of government		Municipal phone number	Mayor/ chief elected official	Appointed administrator	City clerk/ city secretary	Finance officer	Fire chief	Police chief	Public works director
MICHIGAN (273) continued									
Boyne City (3)	CM	616 582-6597	....	....	....	....	....	....	....
Brighton (6)	CM	810 227-1911	James A Winchel	Dana W Foster	Theresa Swiecicki	David C Gajda	Richard J Shinske	Mike D Kinaschuk	David C Blackmar
Bronson (2)	CM	517 369-7334	Len Kolcz	Gerald Hollister	Karen Smith	Gerald Hollister	Chuck Somerlott	Richard Stout	Carl Ransbottom
Brown City (1)	CM	810 346-2325	Dan Loutzenhiser	Thomas F McCoy	Toni Loutzenhiser	....	Rodger Wood	....	Gary Gorsline
Buchanan (5)	CM	616 695-3844	....	....	....	....	....	....	....
Buena Vista tp (11)	CM	517 754-6536	Frances Hayes	Grady Holmes Jr	Willie C Jenkins	Tracy L Cormier	....	Michael Rembisz	Renee Johnson
Burton (28)	MC	313 743-1500	....	....	....	....	....	....	....
Cadillac (10)	CM	616 775-0181	....	....	....	....	....	....	....
Capac v (2)	MC	313 395-4355	....	....	....	....	....	....	....
Carleton v (3)	MC	313 654-6255	....	....	....	....	....	....	....
Caro v (4)	MC	517 673-7671	Wes Frederick	Don Duggar	Charles Spaulding	Don Duggar	David Mattlin	Ron Iseler	Don Duggar
Caseville v (1)	CM	517 856-2102	....	Gary Kuckel	....	....	....	....	....
Caspian (1)	CM	906 265-2514	Joe Sabal	Rosalie King	....	....	....	....	....
Cassopolis v (2)	CM	616 445-8648	....	....	....	....	....	....	....
Cedar Springs (3)	CM	616 696-1330	John Teusink	Frank Walsh	Amber Bailey	....	Mark Strpko	Marvin Weinrich	Gerald Hall
Center Line (9)	CM	810 757-6800	Louis J Nardi Jr	Ronald Reiterman	Ronald Reiterman	....	....	Gerald M Solai	Patrick W Cross
Charlevoix (3)	CM	616 547-3270	....	Michael Wiesner	Jo Anne Patrick	Richard Brandi	Doug Carver	Dennis Halverson	....
Charlotte (8)	CM	517 543-2750	David L Brown	Larry R Deetjen	Deborah L Granger	....	Kevin Fullerton	Tom Potter	Bruce Nichols
Cheboygan (5)	CM	616 627-5280	....	....	....	....	....	....	....
Chelsea v (4)	MC	313 475-1771	....	....	....	....	....	....	....
Chesaning v (3)	CM	517 845-3800	Gary E Klein	Milan D Stasa	Mary Beth Reiber	....	Daniel J Ryan	Howard R Ormes	Joseph Pacek
Clare (3)	CM	517 386-7541	....	Vincent Pastue	Patty Lemm	....	....	Anthony Smolinski	Robert Bonham
Clawson (14)	CM	313 435-4500	....	....	....	....	....	....	....
Clio (3)	CM	313 686-5850	Alice Boyse	George N Atkin Jr	Alice Grigar	....	James Bronson	Dale W Moore	....
Coldwater (10)	CM	517 279-9501	Robert Rumsey	William Stewart	Gerald Boguth	Michael Ashley	....	Gary Chester	David Sattler
Constantine v (2)	CM	616 435-2085	Robert Coryn	Wm R Commenator	D H Al Kharusy	....	Tom Robinson	Robert Brewer	....
Coopersville (3)	CM	616 837-9731	Randy Laug	Tom O' Malley	Tom O' Malley	Patricia Bush	....	Paul Davis	Ken Ortquist
Corunna (3)	MC	517 743-4411	....	....	....	....	....	....	....
Croswell (2)	MC	810 679-2299	Kate Meneghin	Jimmie W Hanes Jr	April Johnston	....	Tom Dickensheets	Jeffery Dawson	Harley Wright
Crystal Falls (2)	CM	906 875-3212	Lawrence Hegstrom	Walter E Hagglund	Dorothea Olson	....	John Ahola	Jack Bicigo	Dennis Fabbri
Davison (6)	CM	810 653-2191	Kay Ann Adair	Jack N Abernathy	Rosemary Simpson	....	Jack Somers	Robert D Johnson	Keith Skellenger
De Witt (4)	MC	517 669-2441	Gerald M Nester	Michael J Czymbor	Margie N Lotre	....	Brent Newman	Wendell D Myers	Michael J Czymbor
Dearborn (89)	MC	313 943-2000	....	....	....	....	....	....	....
Dearborn Heights (61)	MC	313 277-7219	Ruth A Canfield	John Zadikian	Helene Sheridan	Donald Barrow	Errol Lewis	S DiPrima	John Preston
Delta Charter tp (26)	CM	517 323-8590	Joseph Drolett	Richard Watkins	Janice Vedder	Lawrence Kallio	Victor Hilbert	Mark O' Donnell	....
Detroit (1028)	MC	313 224-3270	Dennis W Archer	Nettie Seabrooks	Jackie Currie	Eric M Tucker	Harold D Watkins	Islah McKinnon	Clyde Dowell
Dexter v (..)	CM	313 426-8303	....	....	....	....	....	....	....
Dowagiac (6)	CM	616 782-2195	James E Burke	James M Palenick	James E Snow	David A Pilot	Wayne K Mattix	Gary L Dumeney	Melvin L Lyons
Dundee v (3)	CM	313 529-3430	John R Williams	Patrick H Burtch	Mary C Miller	....	Tom Harwick	....	Dale Goetz
Durand (4)	CM	517 288-3113	Denny Stokes	Lynn Markland	Amy Roddy	....	Wayne McGuire	Robert Eldridge	Kevin McDonald
East Grand Rapids (11)	CM	616 949-2110	Nyal Deems	Brian Donovan	Sally Bode	....	....	Peter Gallagher	William Baragar
East Lansing (51)	CM	517 337-1731	Robert Phipps	....	Marie S Donnell	Gary Murphy	Jack Gregg	Lawton Connelly	Peter Eberz
East Tawas (3)	CM	517 362-6161	....	....	....	....	....	....	....
Eastpointe (35)	CM	313 445-5016	....	....	....	....	....	....	....
Eaton Rapids (5)	MC	517 663-8118	Donald Colestock	....	Marietta White	....	Richard Freer	Michael Seeley	Howard Hillard
Ecorse (12)	MC	313 386-5887	James Tassis	....	Robin Underwood	Richard Eva	Manuel Salas	Rubin Trevino	Charles Weber
Elk Rapids v (2)	MC	616 264-9274	Joseph Yuchasz	Marc Bergman	Elaine Glowicki	....	....	Jack Blesma	Robert Loper
Escanaba (14)	CM	906 786-9402	Charles Vader	Rosalind Allis	Robert Richards	Michael Dewar	....	Wayne Heikkila	Allen Newman
Essexville (4)	CM	517 893-7192	John B Freel	Mary Monville	Mary Monville	Mary Monville	....	Terrence Hugo	C Donald Lowe
Evart (..)	CM	616 734-2181	Roger Elkins	Daniel Elliott	Diane Faber	....	....	Randy Kruse	R D Trembath
Farmington (10)	CM	313 474-5500	Arnold T Campbell	Frank J Lauhoff	Patsy K Cantrell	Patsy K Cantrell	....	Gary M Goss	Kevin G Gushman
Farmington Hills (75)	CM	810 474-6115	Lawrence Litchman	William Costick	Kathryn Dornan	Charles Rosch	Richard Marinucci	William Dwyer	Dan Rooney
Fenton (8)	CM	810 629-2261	Patricia Lockwood	....	Lucille Little	....	Gerald Palmer	Gerald Cattaneo	Leslie P Bland
Ferndale (25)	CM	810 546-2360	P McCullough	Jess R Soltess	Dorothy L Fuller	Jaynmarie Reddie	David T Laprairie	S Joseph Sullivan	Kenneth G Bautel
Flat Rock (7)	MC	313 782-2455	Richard C Jones	....	Thomas W Burbo Jr	Thomas W Burbo Jr	William Vack	Charles Humphriss	Bruce Hammond
Flint (141)	MC	810 766-7280	W Stanley	D Ready	L Hawkins	M Pockett	P Garrison	C Duncan	F Watts
Flushing (9)	CM	810 659-3130	Beverley A Martin	Peter Von Drak	Nancy G Parks	....	Leon V Noack	Fay E Peek	Patrick Creighton
Fowlerville v (3)	CM	517 223-3771	John B Hyden	....	Muriel J Bohm	....	John Wright	Gary Kraus	Ronald L Hanna
Frankenmuth (4)	CM	517 652-9901	Gary C Rupprecht	Charles B Graham	Charles B Graham	....	Gene Rittmueller	James R Petteys	Randy Braeutigam
Franklin v (3)	MC	313 626-9666	....	....	....	....	....	....	....
Fraser (14)	CM	810 293-1877	Joseph Blanke	Frank Rubino	Frank Rubino	Karoline Kulas	....	Ronald Wolber	B J Van Fleteren
Fremont (4)	CM	616 924-2101	Raymond E Rathbun	Chris Yonker	Michael R Pohlod	Michael R Pohlod	Michael Pranger	Galen Brookens	Jim Vedders
Garden City (32)	CM	313 525-8800	Michael T Breen	Steven R Aynes	Ronald Showalter	Ronald Showalter	Kenneth Hines	David Kocsis	Richard Lang Jr
Gaylord (3)	CM	517 732-4060	Ernest Grocock	Dave Siegel	Rebecca Curtis	....	....	John Jenkins	....
Gibraltar (4)	MC	313 676-3900	....	....	....	....	....	....	....
Gladstone (5)	CM	906 428-2311	Dale Jamison	Dals Soumis	Linda Gray	....	....	Randall Walter	Michael Albrecht
Gladwin (..)	MC	517 426-9231	Earl Schuster	Robert McConkie	E Barnebee	....	....	John Simpson	Scott Stanley
Grand Blanc (8)	MC	810 694-1118	Gregory L Crane	Randall D Byrne	Richard Saathoff	Richard Saathoff	James Harmes	Mark D Heidel	Jack Kipp
Grand Haven (12)	CM	616 842-5988	John Nortier	William D Cargo	Kathryne E Olds	Gary L Schreiber	Terry E French	....	Mark Verberkmoes
Grand Haven tp (..)	CM	616 847-6216	....	William D Cargo	....	....	....	....	....
Grand Ledge (8)	CM	517 627-2149	Lynda Trinklein	Davdi Rich	Christine Hnatiw	....	Graydon Briggs	Ronald Flitton	Harold Jolley
Grand Rapids (189)	CM	616 456-3000	John Logie	Kurt Kimball	Sandra Wright	Robert White	Albert Conners	William Hegarty	Don Joswick
Grandville (16)	CM	616 531-3030	James R Buck	W David Boehm	Sharon Streelman	....	Harvey Veldhouse	Kenneth Madejczyk	Jerald Postema
Grayling (2)	CM	517 348-2131	Robert Golnick	Jerry W Morford	Jerry W Morford	Verna M Maharg	Russell Strophaul	Peter Stephan	Thomas Dunham
Greenville (8)	CM	616 754-5645	Jon Aylsworth	George Bosanic	David Moore	....	Bruce Schnepp	Bruce Schnepp	Gary Stacey
Grosse Pointe (6)	CM	313 885-5800	Susan Wheeler	T W Kressbach	T W Kressbach	Dennis C Foran	....	Bruce Kennedy	Joseph Dube
Grosse Pointe Farms (10)	CM	313 885-6600	Gregg Berendt	Richard Solak	Shane Reeside	James Nash	....	Robert Ferber	John DeFoe
Grosse Pointe Park (13)	CM	313 822-6200	Palmer T Heenan	Dale Krajniak	Jane Blahut	Peter Dobrzenieck	....	Richard Caretti	Muzaffar Lakhani
Grosse Pointe Shores v (3)	CM	313 881-6565	John Huetteman	Michael Kenyon	Ronald Laskowski	Rhonda Gaskill	Dan Healy	Dan Healy	Brett Smith
Grosse Pointe Woods (18)	CM	313 343-2440	Robert E Novitke	Peter A Thomas	Louise Warnke	Clifford Maison	Jack Patterson	Jack Patterson	Thomas Whitcher
Hamtramck (18)	MC	313 876-7766	....	....	....	....	....	....	....
Hancock (5)	CM	906 482-2720	Mary J Tuisku	Ron M Howell	Karen S Haischer	....	Scott Dickson	Michael Beaudoin	Roland Kyllonen
Harbor Beach (2)	MC	517 479-3363	Dave Hunter	Tom Youatt	Tom Youatt	....	....	Sid Schock	Dale Schultz
Harbor Springs (2)	CM	616 526-2104	Jean Jardine	Frederick Geuder	Ronald McRae	Ronald McRae	Gerald Hoffman	C Dean Rye	Donald Gregory
Harper Woods (15)	CM	313 343-2505	James R Haley	James E Leidlein	Mickey D Todd	....	Robert Delor	Larry W Semple	Robert Slawinski
Hart (2)	CM	616 873-2488	William Wells	Terry Hofmeyer	Terry Hofmeyer	Louise Stevens	Jerry Schaner	Daniel Leimback	Jerry Verschueren
Hartford (..)	MC	616 621-2642	....	....	....	....	....	....	....
Hastings (7)	MC	616 945-2468	....	....	....	....	....	....	....
Hazel Park (20)	CM	810 546-4060	Jeffrey A Keeton	Frank L Meyers	Ruth Ann Hines	Raymond J Lambert	James D Carene	Albert H Sadow	William R Stroup
Highland Park (20)	MC	313 252-0022	Lindsey Porter	Scott Wainwright	Mattie Carter	Elaine Terrell	Ridley Robinson	Ridley Robinson	....
Hillsdale (8)	MC	517 437-7312	Nicholas Ferro	Roy Adams	Herbert Hine	Tim Vagle	Larry Eichler	Chris Gutowski	Michael Pilarski
Holland (31)	CM	616 394-1300	Al McGeehan	Soren Wolff	Jodi Syens	Larry Sandy	Dan Henderson	Charles Lindstorm	Tim Morawski
Holly v (6)	MC	313 634-9571	....	....	....	....	....	....	....

Directory 1/9 continued — MUNICIPAL OFFICIALS IN U.S. CITIES OVER 2,500

City, 1990 population figures (000 omitted), form of government	Municipal phone number	Mayor/ chief elected official	Appointed administrator	City clerk/ city secretary	Finance officer	Fire chief	Police chief	Public works director
MICHIGAN (273) continued								
Homer v (..) CM	517 568-4721	Donna Bowser	Lyle Dickson	Leaanne Crague	....	....	John Kirkbride	Jim Nowlin
Houghton (7) CM	906 482-1700	....	....	....	....	....	....	....
Howell (8) CM	517 546-3500	Paul B Streng	Michael S Herman	....	....	James Reed	Michael Oyler	Terry J Wilson
Hudson (3) CM	517 448-8983	Gerald Blackburn	....	Freda Rodehaver	....	Dick Opsal	Albert Clements	Sheldon Peltier
Hudsonville (6) CM	616 669-0200	....	....	....	....	....	....	....
Huntington Woods (6) CM	810 541-4300	Ronald F Gillham	Alex R Allie	Janet M Wayne	Richard T Lehmann	....	David Danaher	Larry Page
Imlay City (3) CM	810 724-2135	Rod Dewey	Dennis W Collison	Amy Stryker	Kim Liponoga	Warner Hoeksema	Arlan Winslow	Larry Lloyd
Inkster (31) CM	313 563-4232	Edward Bivens Jr	Margie C Rose	Delphine G Oden	....	Victor Boulanger	Terry Colwell	John Lyons
Ionla (6) MC	616 527-4170	Daniel Balice	Tom Wieczorek	Jean Barker	Robin Marhofer	....	Roger Frazee	Dan Czarnecki
Iron Mountain (9) CM	906 774-8530	Ed Koerschner	James Urbany	Lou Ann Hagen	James Brinker	Bill Rocheleau	David Lee	James Urbany
Iron River (2) CM	906 265-4719	George Treado	Gary Shimun	Peggy Benson	....	....	Russell Westman	Gary Shimun
Ironwood (7) CM	906 932-5050	James Lorenson	Edward Bailey	Anita Zak	Eero Haukkala	....	Leroy Johnson	Wallace Magdziak
Ishpemlng (7) CM	906 485-1091	James F Tobin Jr	John D Korhonen	Corbin S Hytinen	....	Daniel Gaboury	John A Healey	Richard Burke
Ithaca (3) CM	517 875-3200	John C Thomas	Troy L Feltman	Todd M Blake	....	Gordon Larry	Lee Schlappi	....
Jackson (37) CM	517 788-4046	Richard Dirlam	Gary L Dickson	Sandy Price	Philip Hones	D Braunreiter	Robert L Johnson	Anton Raykovich
Jonesville v (..) MC	517 849-2104	Bill Hendrick	Kristine B Silver	S McKitterick	Kristine B Silver	Gordon Turner	Brian Corbett	Claude Russell
Kalamazoo (80) CM	616 337-8052	....	....	....	....	....	....	....
Kalkaska v (2) MC	616 258-9191	Jeffrey E Fitch	Scott Yost	Virginia Thomas	Virginia Thomas	....	Melvin F Hill	Craig Wood
Keego Harbor (3) CM	313 682-1930	....	....	....	....	....	....	....
Kentwood (38) MC	616 698-9610	Bill Hardiman	....	Beverly Bacon	Thomas Chase	James Carr	Richard Mattice	John Heitman
Kingsford (5) CM	906 774-3526	Michael Church	Darryl Wickman	Darryl Wickman	....	....	Dennis Charette	Anthony Edlebeck
L'Anse v (2) MC	906 524-6116	....	....	....	....	....	....	....
Lake Orion v (3) CM	810 693-8391	....	John D Berchtold	Arlene Nichols	Kelly Carter	....	James Leach	John Ranville
Lansing (127) MC	517 483-4004	David C Hollister	David M Wiener	Marilynn Slade	Douglas L Rubley	Andrew F Jackson	Jerome G Boles	Lenora K Jadun
Lapeer (8) CM	810 664-5231	Al Gelhausen	George Strand	George Strand	Paul Boucher	Louis Finsterwald	Mike Robinet	....
Lathrup Village (4) CM	313 557-2600	....	....	....	....	....	....	....
Laurium v (2) CM	906 337-1600	....	....	....	....	....	....	....
Leslie (2) CM	517 589-8236	....	....	....	....	....	....	....
Lincoln Park (42) MC	313 386-1800	Frank Sall	....	Donna Breeding	John Martin	Dave Silvani	Joseph Vago	Donald Mandernach
Linden (..) MC	810 735-7980	Douglas Wagner	Joseph Murray	Martha Wills	....	David McDaniel	Pete Van Driesche	James Letts
Litchfield (1) MC	517 542-2921	Edwin J Smith	Clarence F Wolfe	Marguerite Dooley	Marguerite Dooley	Dick Wade	John Michelin	Dean Wooden
Livonia (101) MC	313 421-2000	Robert D Bennett	....	Joan McCotter	Michael T Slater	Ronald J Engle	Lee B Grieve	Robert J Beckley
Lowell (4) CM	616 897-8457	James D Maatman	David M Pasquale	David M Pasquale	David M Pasquale	Frank W Martin	James B Valentine	Art Gall
Ludington (9) MC	616 845-6237	Jack R Scott	James H Miller	Gerry P Klaft	....	Mike McDonald	Walter Taranko	John H Verboam
Mackinaw City v (1) CM	616 436-5351	....	....	....	....	....	....	....
Madison Heights (32) CM	810 588-1200	George W Suarez	Jon R Austin	Geraldine A Case	Margaret P Birach	William A Donahue	Ronald F Pearce	Peter J Connors
Manistee (7) CM	616 723-2558	Beth Adams	R Ben Bifoss	Kenneth Oleniczak	Kenneth Oleniczak	....	Robert Hornkohl	Robert Hornkohl
Manistique (3) CM	906 341-2290	....	....	....	....	....	....	....
Marine City (5) CM	810 765-8846	Larry Aspenleiter	Michael LaChance	Carol Ouellette	....	Gregory Merrill	John Kelly	Richard Ames
Marlette (2) CM	517 635-7448	Kenneth L Babich	Robert A Ellisor	Carol Goodrich	....	Rick Vanderpoel	Steven Schaub	Robert Foster
Marquette (22) CM	906 228-0480	....	Dale E Iman	Norman L Gruber	Donna M Kohut	Thomas Belt	George G Johnson	....
Marquette tp (..) CM	906 228-6220	Max H Muelle	George LaBlonde	Kathe A Thill	....	Ronald E DeMarse	....	Kirk E Page
Marshall (7) CM	616 781-5183	Joseph Schroeder	Maurice Evans	Sue Kelly Hecht	Sue Kelly Hecht	....	Roger Graves	Tom Tarkiewicz
Marysville (9) CM	810 364-6613	W Deem Boldyreff	Jack M Schumacher	Sharon Schess	Bradley S Hool	Roger Bundy	P T O' Boyle	Steve Kerr
Mason (7) CM	517 676-9155	Sue Ann Parsons	Patrick M Price	Patrick M Price	Norman L Austin	James Pelton	Roger Fleming	Les Bruno Jr
Melvindale (11) MC	313 389-2000	Thomas J Coogan	....	Alice M Whitaker	Fred Zorn	Robert Harris	James Brophy	Eric Witte
Menominee (9) MC	906 863-2656	John B Baker	....	Anthony D Furton	Anthony D Furton	Robert Falkenberg	Joseph Posepheny	George Krah
Meridian tp (36) CM	517 349-1200	....	Jeffrey H Minor	Virginia L White	....	Phillip Johnson	Jay Kohn	Bert Teitzel
Midland (38) CM	517 835-7711	Donald Taylor	Karl Tomion	Penny Kovacevich	Robert Fisher	Daniel Hargarten	James St Louis	Martin McGuire
Milan (4) MC	313 439-1501	Alan Israel	Patrick McShane	Ann M Lindsay	....	Gerald Straits	Herbert Mahoney	Timothy Ard
Milford v (6) MC	810 684-1515	R R Danley	A Shufflebarger	D Bridgers	....	....	J Daly	F Morin
Monroe (23) MC	313 243-0700	C D Cappuccilli	....	E Dickey	J E Sherburne	R Soleau	H Kanavel	....
Montrose (2) CM	810 639-6168	Nancy Persons	Marcia Strong	Kathy Parsons	....	Al Rush	Ronald Steinhorst	Matthew Fejedelem
Mount Clemens (18) CM	810 469-6804	Quinnie E Cody	Warren D Renando	Frances Pietrzak	William N Ringler	Michael D Coyle	....	....
Mount Morris (3) CM	313 686-2160	....	Brian M Bulthuis	....	....	....	....	....
Mount Pleasant (23) CM	517 773-7971	Robert Trullinger	Paul L Preston Jr	Rick J Sanborn	Rick J Sanborn	Andrew Mayer	Martin E Trombley	Duane F Ellis
Munising (3) CM	906 387-2095	Bert Gorbutt	Judy Slancik	Betty A Williams	....	Theodore Belfry	Douglas Miron	Eugene Faucette
Muskegon (40) CM	616 724-6713	James W Prium	David L Wendtland	Theresa S Malik	Timothy J Paul	Larry D Robbins	Edward E Griffin	Robert H Kuhn
Muskegon Heights (13) CM	616 739-1331	Robert A Warren	Melvin C Burns	Lynne A Mahan	Craig Loudermill	Ivory B Morris	Johnnie Capehart	Henry Witherspoon
Negaunee (5) CM	906 475-7700	Terry Talo	Ken Huber	Joan DuShane	....	Tom Gordyko	Paul Waters	Bob Johnson
New Baltimore (6) MC	810 725-2151	Greg Bayer	Lauren Wood	Ann Billock	....	Larry Marcero	Leo Parrott	Ed Santo
New Buffalo (2) CM	616 469-1500	....	....	....	....	....	....	....
Newaygo (1) CM	616 652-1657	....	....	....	....	....	....	....
Niles (12) MC	616 683-4700	Dan Excleshyner	Bernard Vanosdale	Ruth Harte	Susan B Coulston	Richard Davidson	Myron Galchutt	Brian Day
North Muskegon (4) CM	616 744-1621	....	....	....	....	....	....	....
Northville (6) CM	810 349-1300	Chris Johnson	Gary Word	Delphine Dudick	Nickie Bateson	Jim Allen	Rodney Cannon	Ted Mapes
Norton Shores (22) MC	616 798-4391	....	....	....	....	....	....	....
Norway (3) CM	906 563-8015	....	....	....	....	....	....	....
Novi (33) CM	810 347-0452	K McLallen	Edward Kriewall	Geraldine Stipp	Les Gibson	Arthur Lenaghan	Douglas Shaeffer	Anthony Nowicki
Oak Park (30) CM	810 691-7400	Gerald E Naftaly	D Fitzpatrick	Sandra K Gadd	James Ghedotte	....	G Robert Seifert	S Michael Santo
Ontonagon v (2) CM	906 884-2305	Kurt Giesau	Glenn Anderson	Joan Nygard	....	Dennis O' Brien	Timothy Guzek	....
Ortonville v (1) MC	313 627-4976	....	....	....	....	....	....	....
Otisville v (..) CM	313 631-4680	....	....	....	....	....	....	....
Otsego (4) CM	616 692-3391	Joel Thompson	Curtis Holt	Paula Baker	Matthew Storbeck	James Clark Jr	Elton Goswick	Darl Gilliland
Owosso (16) CM	517 723-8844	....	....	....	....	....	....	....
Oxford v (3) CM	810 628-2543	Peter C Burke	Darwin D Parks	....	....	....	John LeRoy	Michael Rider
Parchment (2) CM	616 349-3785	John H Bultje	Richard J Rice	Curtis E Flowers	....	Timothy Bourgeois	Ralph G Herrick	Russell Veldt
Paw Paw v (3) CM	616 657-3148	....	....	....	....	....	....	....
Petoskey (6) CM	616 347-2500	Jeremy Wills	George Korthauer	....	Alan Terry	....	Tom Postelnick	Walter Goodwin
Pinconning (1) CM	517 879-2360	Michael Duranczyk	Bradley Noeldner	Karen Waterman	....	Buck Schumman	Art Hopp	Tim Stalker
Plainwell (4) CM	616 685-5460	Lori Snyder	Richard G Runnels	Ruth A King	....	....	Frank Post	Thomas Seymour
Pleasant Ridge (3) CM	313 541-2900	....	....	....	....	....	....	....
Plymouth (10) CM	313 453-1234	Douglas Miller	Steven Walters	Linda Langmesser	William Graham	Alan Matthews	Robert Scoggins	Paul Sincock
Pontiac (71) MC	810 857-7611	Charlie Harrison	....	Mary Williams	James Miriani	Jeff Hawkins	Ronald Gracey	K Joseph Young
Port Huron (34) CM	810 984-9723	James Relkin	Gerald Bouchard	Pauline Repp	Bruce Seymore	Robert Carmichael	William Corbett	....
Portage (41) CM	616 329-4400	....	....	....	....	....	....	....
Portland (4) CM	517 647-7531	Joseph Tichvon	Rex Wambaugh	Rex Wambaugh	Wm Trierweiler	Jon Hyland	Richard White	Jon Hyland
Reed City (2) CM	616 832-2245	....	Phillip Rathbun	Judith Utrup	....	Ralph Westerburg	William Riemersma	Kevin Rambadt
Richland tp (..) MC	517 642-2097	Frederick Clark	David D McKeage	David Schafer	....	Gary H Wade	....	Timothy Rohn
Richmond (4) CM	313 727-7571	....	....	....	....	....	....	....
River Rouge (11) MC	313 842-0801	....	....	....	....	....	....	....
Riverview (14) MC	313 281-4200	Peter Rotteveel	Robert Elliott	Michael J Steklac	C Abercrombie	Robert C Hale	James A Bartus	Gerald N Perry
Rochester (7) CM	810 651-9061	Thomas L Werth	Kenneth A Johnson	Nancy D Hill	....	William Gray	Theodore Glynn	....

Directory 1/9 continued

MUNICIPAL OFFICIALS IN U.S. CITIES OVER 2,500

City, 1990 population figures (000 omitted), form of government		Municipal phone number	Mayor/ chief elected official	Appointed administrator	City clerk/ city secretary	Finance officer	Fire chief	Police chief	Public works director
MICHIGAN (273) continued									
Rockford (4)	CM	616 866-1537	Betty Combs	Daryl J Delabbio	Daryl J Delabbio	John L Strauss	Robert Vandermey	John V Porter	Michael Chesher
Rockwood (3)	MC	313 379-9496	Mary Kay Metzger	Curt B Seditz	Nancy Dvorak Rich	James B Herzog	Frank Hinzmann	Dennis R Anderson	Curt B Seditz
Rogers City (4)	CM	517 734-2191	Gary M Chappell	....	Theresa A Heinzel	....	Keith E Froelich	Garnet P Robinson	Vernon E Langlois
Romeo v (4)	MC	313 752-3565	....	....	....	....	....	....	....
Romulus (23)	MC	313 942-7571	Beverly McAnally	....	Linda Choate	Donavon McGuire	W Greenslait	Robert Brown	James Panos
Roosevelt Park (4)	CM	616 755-3721	M Sherry White	William K Gleason	Barbara S Smith	....	....	Thomas M Kelenske	Terry Sladick
Roseville (51)	CM	810 445-5410	Gerald Alsip	Thomas Van Damme	Charles LaGrant	John Knapp	Keith Weisgerber	William Lucas	Larry Snelling
Royal Oak (65)	CM	810 546-1000	Dennis Cowan	William Baldridge	Mary C Haverty	John L Dagiau	William Crouch	John Tyler Jr	Thomas Trice
Saginaw (70)	CM	517 759-1570	Gary L Loster	J Marvin Baldwin	Bevelyn Bradley	Jon Bayless	Donald Couturier	Alex Perez	Tom Darnell
Saginaw tp (38)	MC	517 791-9800	George Olson	Ronald Lee	Timothy Braun	Virginia Gottscha	Richard Powell	Kenneth Ott	Gerald Francis
Saline (7)	MC	313 429-4907	Patrick J Little	David M White	Dianne S Hill	David M White	R Weisenreder	Paul Bunten	George Danneffel
Sault Ste. Marie (15)	CM	906 635-5261	....	....	....	....	....	....	....
Scottville (1)	CM	616 757-4729	Duane Slagle	Bob Peterson	....	....	Rick Gleason	Larry Nichols	Chuck Smith
South Haven (6)	CM	616 637-0700	David Paull	Alan Vanderberg	Gary Simpson	Gary Simpson	Jerry Bridges	Rod Somerlott	Robert Stickland
South Lyon (6)	CM	810 437-1735	Jeffrey L Potter	Rodney L Cook	Julie Zemke	....	Craig Kaska	Gerald Smith	Linden Beebe
Southfield (76)	CM	810 354-1000	Donald F Fracassi	Robert R Block	Mary A Bonner	James G Scharret	Robert E Ozias	Joseph E Thomas	Thomas P Vukonich
Southgate (31)	MC	313 246-1305	....	....	....	....	....	....	....
Sparta v (4)	MC	616 887-8251	Paul C Schulz	Daniel P Chargo	Sue Vander Mey	....	Gary Hall	Robert W Smith	Byron Bloom
Spring Lake v (3)	CM	616 842-1393	Victoria Verplank	Eric R Delong	Robert G Lucking	J Van Bemmelen	....	William Kaufman	John Hansen
Springfield (6)	CM	616 965-2354	....	....	....	....	....	....	....
St. Charles v (2)	CM	517 865-8287	Thomas Krawczak	Kristine Neumann	Robert J Grnak	....	....	David J Sickle	Hal W Mead
St. Clair (5)	CM	810 329-7121	Bernard E Kuhn	Patrick Greve	Janice DiGiusto	....	William Beaudua	Wayne Goralski	....
St. Clair Shores (68)	CM	810 445-5200	Ted Wahby	Mark Wollenweber	Jack L Fields	Timothy P Haney	Frank Turner	Lawrence Germain	Robert Sawicki
St. Ignace (3)	CM	906 643-9671	Bruce J Dodson	Gary L Heckman	Larry E Morris	Larry E Morris	John Robinson Jr	Timothy Matelski	....
St. Johns (7)	CM	517 224-8944	....	....	....	....	....	....	....
St. Joseph (9)	CM	616 983-5541	Jeffrey Richards	William Sinclair	Ronald S Momany	....	Elwood Munson	Francis Fleisher	Gary M Soper
St. Louis (4)	CM	517 681-2137	George T Kubin	Larry W Burkhart	Nancy L Roehrs	Nancy L Roehrs	Larry Parsons	Howard R Teed	Robert McCormick
Stambaugh (1)	CM	906 265-4213	Garold Ward	Albert Silfven	Albert Silfven	....	....	....	Richard Anderson
Standish (1)	CM	517 846-9588	....	....	....	....	....	....	....
Sterling Heights (118)	CM	810 977-6123	Richard Notte	Steve Duchane	Mary Zander	Virginia Fette	....	Thomas Derocha	Guy Kebbe
Sturgis (10)	CM	616 651-2321	Carl Holsinger	Jerome Kisscorni	Carol Rambadt	Jerome Kisscorni	Paul Trinka	Gene Allie	Ray McKersher
Swartz Creek (5)	CM	313 635-4464	....	....	....	....	....	....	....
Sylvan Lake (2)	CM	313 682-1440	....	....	....	....	....	....	....
Tawas City (2)	CM	517 362-8688	James J Lansky	Thomas M Chatel	Judith A Werth	Thomas M Chatel	Brian Lansky	Dennis A Frank	Robert E Werth
Taylor (71)	MC	313 287-6550	Cameron G Priebe	....	Dorothy West	Dean Philo	Robert Diel	Thomas Bonner	James Boardman
Tecumseh (7)	CM	517 423-2107	Vera Gardner	Frank L Crosby	Laura Caterina	....	Joseph Tuckey	L Van Alstine	Steven Johnston
Three Rivers (7)	CM	616 273-1075	Taylor Snow	David Richards	Barbara Redford	Wendy Kowalski	Steven Sullivan	Kenneth Baker	Mark Glessner
Tittabawassee tp (5)	CM	517 695-9512	Kenneth A Kasper	George A Brown	Robert DuCharme	Jo Ella Krantz	....	Robert C Harken	Kenneth D Hoff
Traverse City (15)	CM	616 922-4481	Jack Boynton	Richard Lewis	Debbra Curtiss	W Twietmeyer	....	Ralph Soffredine	Michael Slater
Trenton (21)	MC	313 675-6500	Thomas Boritzki	Larry Fitch	Kyle Stack	Ralph Lesko	Glenn Spry	Gerald Brown	Lawrence Dusincki
Troy (73)	CM	810 524-3300	Jeanne Stine	Frank Gerstenecke	Tamara Renshaw	John Lamerato	William Nelson	Lawrence Carey	Michael Culpepper
Utica (5)	MC	810 739-1600	Jacqueline Noonan	....	M C McGrail	....	Robert Beck	Bruce Bissonnette	Joseph Francis
Vassar (3)	CM	517 823-8517	....	....	....	....	....	....	....
Vicksburg v (2)	MC	616 649-1919	Robert J Philipp	Donald R Flanders	Mercer D Munn	Don Flanders	William Sillaman	M Descheneau	Roy Hodgman
Wakefield (2)	CM	906 229-5132	....	....	....	....	....	....	....
Walker (17)	MC	616 791-6860	Don E Knottnerus	James M Hatch	Linda Wiser	W Van Tuinen	William Schmidt	Walter Sprenger	John Kinney
Walled Lake (6)	CM	810 624-4847	William T Roberts	Phillip Vawter	M Cornelius	Joyce Golden	Thomas Bennett	Kenneth Borico	Ralph Smith
Warren (145)	MC	313 574-4670	....	....	....	....	....	....	....
Wayland (3)	CM	616 792-2265	Michael Deweerd	H A Stull	....	....	Hugh Deweerd	Daniel Miller	David Long
Wayne (20)	CM	313 722-2000	....	John J Zech	Doris Nall	Thomas Norwood	Thomas O' Brien	John Colligan	Gary Clark
West Branch (2)	CM	517 345-0500	Todd Thompson	Patrick McGinnis	Jane Tennant	....	....	Howard Hanft	Thomas Brindley
Westland (85)	MC	313 467-3200	Robert Thomas	....	Diane Fritz	Michael Gorman	Larry Lane	Emery Price	Carl Clark
Whitehall (3)	CM	616 894-4048	Wallace Weesies	Gerald Homminga	Scott Huebler	Laurie Audo	....	James Bartholomew	Jack Van Gelson
Williamston (3)	CM	517 655-2774	John Coe	Milford Mellon	Rebecca Ruttan	....	Kirt Hunt	James LaClear	Ellis Wygant
Wixom (9)	CM	313 624-0885	....	....	....	....	....	....	....
Wolverine Lake v (5)	CM	810 624-1710	Jim Allen	Michael Cain	Sharon Miller	....	....	James Davis	....
Woodhaven (12)	MC	313 675-4925	John S Zarotney	David W Flaten	Karen M Mazo	David W Flaten	Dennis M Andrew	Richard C Foster	Charles A Horn Jr
Wyandotte (31)	MC	313 246-4500	....	....	....	....	....	....	....
Wyoming (64)	CM	616 530-7225	Jack Magnuson	Donald Mason	James Miller	Joseph Bommarito	James Austin	Lowell Henline	Gerald Snyder
Ypsilanti (25)	CM	313 483-1100	Michael Homel	Herbert Gilsdorf	Robert Slone Jr	Kerreen Gellert	James Roberts	L J McKeown	Charles White Jr
Zeeland (5)	MC	616 772-6400	Lester Hoogland	....	Nancy Tuls	John Leisenring	William Gruppen	Robert Metzger Jr	David Langhorst
Zilwaukee (2)	CM	517 755-0931	....	Rolland C Spencer	C E Langschwager	....	Douglas Luplow	Joel J Dobis	Dennis Mahan
MINNESOTA (205)									
Afton (3)	MC	612 436-5090	....	....	....	....	....	....	....
Albert Lea (18)	CM	507 377-4300	Marvin Wangen	Paul Sparks	Sandra Behrens	John Bennett	Orrion Roisen	Clarence Ayres	David Olson
Alexandria (8)	MC	612 763-6678	Karl Glade	Arlan E Johnson	Arlan E Johnson	....	Pat Ellingson	Charles Nettestad	Al Growser
Andover (15)	MC	612 755-5100	J E McKelvey	Richard Fursman	Victoria Volk	Daryl E Sulander	Dale Mashuga	....	....
Annandale (2)	CM	612 274-3055	Marian Harmoning	Garrison L Hale	....	Sylvia J Onstad	....	Myron A Morris	William McNellis
Anoka (17)	CM	612 421-6630	....	Mark Nagel	....	James Knutson	Ronald Bickford	Andrew Revering	Ray Schultz
Apple Valley (35)	MC	612 953-2500	Willis Branning	John B Gretz	Mary E Mueller	George Ballenger	Marvin Calvin	....	Dennis Miranowski
Arden Hills v (9)	MC	612 633-5676	....	....	....	....	....	....	....
Aurora v (2)	MC	218 229-2614	Alan R Hodnik	....	Linda Cazin	Linda Cazin	Chris Vreeland	Gary Loberg	Gerald Kaeter
Austin (22)	MC	507 437-7671	John O' Rourke	Patrick McGarvey	Lucy Johnson	Richard Benzkofer	Daniel Wilson	Paul Philipp	Jon Erichson
Baxter (4)	MC	218 829-7161	....	....	....	....	....	....	....
Bayport (3)	MC	612 439-2530	Beverly Schultz	Kenneth Hartung	....	....	....	Peter Vollmer	John Burkhart
Becker (1)	CM	612 261-4302	Norman Jensen	Joe Rudberg	Janet Boettcher	Joe Rudberg	Larry Woolhouse	Kevin Rieland	James Boettcher
Belle Plaine (3)	MC	612 873-5553	Gerald J Meyer	David R Iverson	David R Iverson	David R Iverson	Terry Gregory	Steve Rost	Robert Kruse
Bemidji (11)	CM	218 759-3560	Douglas Peterson	Phil Shealy	Shirley Kubian	Dale Page	Bill Rabe	Bob Tell	....
Benson (3)	CM	612 843-4775	R Christenson	Charles Whiting	Glen Pederson	Glen Pederson	Greg Lee	....	Brian Flynn
Biwabik (1)	CM	218 865-4183	....	....	....	....	....	....	....
Blaine (39)	CM	612 784-6700	Elwyn Tinklenberg	Donald Poss	Joyce Twistol	Bill Stawarski	....	Ron Nicholas	Ken Irvln
Bloomington (86)	CM	612 887-9610	Neil Peterson	Mark Bernhardson	Evelyn Woulfe	Lyle Olson	Ulysses Seal	Robert Lutz	Charles Honchell
Blue Earth (4)	MC	507 526-7336	Jonas Schwab	David Urbia	....	....	Mark Mensing	Donald Ficken	Jeff Jansen
Brainerd (12)	MC	218 828-2307	Bonnie Cumberland	Daniel J Vogt	Daniel J Vogt	Daniel J Vogt	Ron Johnson	Frank Ball	Walt Sjolund
Branch (..)	MC	612 674-7401	....	....	....	....	....	....	....
Breckenridge (4)	MC	218 643-1431	Kalvin Michels	....	Blaine Hill	....	Michael Dohman	Dennis Milbrandt	Jeffrey Muehler
Brooklyn Center (29)	CM	612 569-3300	....	....	....	....	....	....	....
Brooklyn Park (56)	CM	612 493-8000	Jesse Ventura	Craig R Rapp	Myrna L Maikkula	Alan J Erickson	James W Driste	Donald E Davis	Jon M Thiel
Buffalo (7)	CM	612 682-1181	....	....	....	....	....	....	....
Burnsville (51)	CM	612 895-4400	Daniel McElroy	Gregory Konat	Susan Olesen	Leslie Anderson	Ronald Payne	Michael DuMoulin	Craig Eberling
Caledonia (3)	MC	507 724-3450	Robert H Burns	....	Robert L Nelson	....	Anthony J Klug	Duane L St Mary	....
Cambridge v (5)	CM	612 689-3211	....	....	....	....	....	....	....

Directory 1/9 continued

MUNICIPAL OFFICIALS IN U.S. CITIES OVER 2,500

City, 1990 population figures (000 omitted), form of government	Municipal phone number	Mayor/chief elected official	Appointed administrator	City clerk/city secretary	Finance officer	Fire chief	Police chief	Public works director
MINNESOTA (205) continued								
Cannon Falls (3)	MC 507 263-3954	....	....	....	....	....	....	....
Champlin (17)	MC 612 421-8100	Steven E Boynton	Kurtis G Ulrich	Joanne M Brown	P Boedigheimer	Ronald Bickford	Allen Garber	Bret Heitkamp
Chanhassen (12)	CM 612 937-1900	Donald Chmiel	Don Ashworth	Don Ashworth	Thomas Chaffee	James McMahon	Scott Harr	Charles Folch
Chaska (11)	CM 612 448-2851	Robert Roepke	David Pokorney	....	Noel Graczyk	Daryl Brengman	Gregory Schol	Richard Schalow
Chisholm (5)	MC 218 254-3353	....	....	....	....	....	....	....
Circle Pines (5)	MC 612 784-5898	L Osbun Miller	James Keinath	....	Peggy Link	Milo Bennet	David Van Burkleo	Bert Caverson
Cloquet (11)	MC 218 879-3347	....	....	....	....	....	....	....
Cokato (2)	MC 612 286-5505	....	....	....	....	....	....	....
Columbia Heights (19)	CM 612 782-2800	Joseph Sturdevant	Patrick Hentges	William Elrite	William Elrite	Charles Kewatt	....	Mark Winson
Coon Rapids (53)	CM 612 780-6486	William Thompson	Robert Svehla	Betty Backes	Sharon Legg	....	Steve Ahrens	W Ottensmann
Corcoran (5)	MC 612 420-2288	....	....	....	....	....	....	....
Cottage Grove (23)	MC 612 458-2800	Jack Denzer	Kevin Frazell	Caron Stransky	Diane Archer	Denis Ericksen	Dennis Cusick	Les Burshten
Crookston (8)	MC 218 281-1232	....	....	....	....	....	....	....
Crystal (24)	CM 612 531-1000	Peter Meintsma	Jerry Dalgar	Darlene George	James Otto	Kevin McGinty	James Mossey	William Monk
Dawson (2)	CM 612 769-2154	Richard Pollei	David A Bovee	Melva Larson	....	Larry Stangeland	William Stock	Brent Powers
Dayton (4)	CM 612 427-4589	Phillip Forseth	Shirley Slater	Sandra Borders	....	Dave Carson	Gary Kroells	....
Deephaven (4)	MC 612 474-4755	Howard Bennis Myr	....	Sandra Langley	....	....	Harlan Johnson	Raymond Williams
Delano (3)	MC 612 479-1135	Dwight A Poss	....	Marlene E Kittock	Marlene E Kittock	Robert C Van Lith	....	Daniel M Alger
Detroit Lakes (7)	MC 218 847-5658	....	....	....	....	....	....	....
Dilworth (3)	MC 218 287-2313	....	....	....	....	....	....	....
Duluth (85)	MC 218 723-3291	Gary Doty	Karl Nollenberger	Jeffrey Cox	Elaine Hansen	Duane Flynn	Scott Lyons	Richard Larson
Eagan (47)	CM 612 681-4600	Thomas Egan	Thomas Hedges	E J Van Overbeke	E J Van Overbeke	Dale Nelson	Patrick Geagan	Thomas Colbert
East Bethel (8)	MC 612 434-9569	....	....	....	....	....	....	....
East Grand Forks (9)	MC 218 773-2483	....	....	....	....	....	....	....
Eden Prairie (39)	CM 612 937-2262	....	....	....	....	....	....	....
Edina (46)	CM 612 927-8861	F Richards	Kenneth Rosland	Marcella Daehn	John Wallin	Ted Paulfranz	Wm Bernhjelm	Francis Hoffman
Elk River (11)	MC 612 441-7420	Henry Duitsman	Patrick Klaers	Sandra Thackeray	Lori Johnson	....	Thomas Zerwas	....
Ely (4)	MC 218 365-3224	....	....	....	....	....	....	....
Eveleth (4)	MC 218 744-2501	W Tom Coombe Jr	....	Raymond J Eck	....	....	James Bozicevich	John J Palo
Excelsior (2)	CM 612 474-5233	....	....	....	....	....	....	....
Eyota (..)	MC 507 545-2135	....	....	....	....	....	....	....
Fairmont (11)	CM 507 238-9461	Marlin Gratz	David Schornack	Lois J Cairns	James Zarling	Roger Carlson	Erwin Thiel	Larry Read
Falcon Heights (5)	MC 612 644-5050	Tom Baldwin	Susan Hoyt	....	Tom Kelly	Clement Kurhajetz	....	Vincent Wright
Faribault (17)	CM 507 334-2222	....	....	....	....	....	....	....
Farmington (6)	MC 612 463-7111	....	....	....	....	....	....	....
Fergus Falls (12)	MC 218 739-2251	....	....	....	....	....	....	....
Forest Lake (6)	MC 612 464-3550	....	....	....	....	....	....	....
Franklin (..)	MC 507 557-2259	Ronald Degner	....	Laurie Sherman	....	Ronald Zempel	Roger Degner	Kevin Kokesch
Fridley (28)	CM 612 571-3450	William J Nee	William W Burns	William A Champa	Richard D Pribyl	Charles McKusick	David H Sallman	John G Flora
Gilbert (2)	MC 218 741-9443	Ed Schneider Sr	Gary Mackley	Gary Mackley	Gary Mackley	Michael Bradach	Allan Olsen	Ken Kuitunen
Glencoe (5)	CM 612 864-5586	....	....	....	....	....	....	....
Golden Valley (21)	CM 612 593-8000	Blair Tremere	William S Joynes	Shirley J Nelson	Donald G Taylor	Mark Kuhnly	Dean Mooney	Fredrick Salsbury
Goodview (3)	MC 507 452-1630	Jack Weimerskirch	....	Daryl Zimmer	....	Robert Matzke	Reed Schmidt	Greg Volkart
Grand Rapids (8)	MC 218 326-7600	Jim Hoolihan	Craig Mattson	Karlene Gale	Jean Lane	Greg Taylor	Harvey Dahline	Jeff Davies
Granite Falls (3)	CM 612 564-3011	....	....	....	....	....	....	....
Ham Lake (9)	MC 612 434-9555	....	....	....	....	....	....	....
Hastings (15)	MC 612 437-4127	Michael Werner	David Osberg	Barbara Thompson	Lori Webster	Donald Latch	Nick Wasylik	Thomas Montgomery
Hermantown (7)	CM 218 729-6331	Wallace Loberg	Lynn Lander	Nancy Sirois	....	....	Terry Ulshafer	Jim Olson
Hibbing (18)	CM 218 262-3486	Ronald Dicklich	John A Fedo	Patrick Garrity	Jeri L Brysch	Douglas Moberg	Leroy Davidson	Clyde W Busby
Hopkins (17)	CM 612 935-8474	Chuck Redepenning	Steve Mielke	James Genellie	John Schedler	George Magdal	Earl Johnson	Lee Gustafson
Hoyt Lakes (2)	RT 218 225-2344	Ronald Nemanic	Richard Bradford	Richard Bradford	Richard Bradford	Steven Stoks	Steven Stoks	Paul Forlan
Hugo (4)	CM 612 429-6676	Walter Stoltzman	Robert A Museus	Mary Ann Creager	Ron Otkin	....	....	Roger Bacon
Hutchinson (12)	CM 612 587-5151	Marlin Torgerson	Gary D Plotz	....	Kenneth B Merrill	Brad Emans	Steven Madson	John Rodeberg
Independence (3)	MC 612 479-0527	....	....	....	....	....	....	....
International Falls (8)	MC 218 283-9484	....	....	....	....	....	....	....
Inver Grove Heights (22)	CM 612 450-2500	Joseph Atkins	James Willis	Loretta Garrity	Daniel Maiers	Robert Gamlain	Stanley Troyer	Gary Johnson
Isantl (2)	MC 612 444-5512	Ken Kahle	Michael Robertson	Michael Robertson	....	Lester Peterson	Norris Sorenson	Harlen Stecker
Jackson (4)	MC 507 847-4410	David Fell	....	....	Marilyn Ailts	Albert Winrich	Richard Seim	....
Janesville (..)	MC 507 234-6265	....	....	....	....	....	....	....
Jordan (3)	MC 612 492-2535	Ronald Jabs	Kay Kuhlmann	....	Kathy Lapic	William Busch	Alvin Erickson	Dave Bendzick
Kasson (4)	MC 507 634-7071	Folmer Carlsen	....	Dolores Meyer	Barbara Pike	Randy Fjerstad	David Johnson	Burt Fjerstad Jr
Kenyon (2)	MC 507 789-6415	John L Cole	Duane Hebert	Duane Hebert	Duane Hebert	Gary Pavek	Bob Vanderheiden	Leroy Eischens
La Crescent (4)	MC 612 895-2595	Richard Wieser	....	Marlene Butzman	....	Bernard Buehler	Vern Yolton	Harris Waller
Lake City (4)	MC 612 345-5383	....	....	....	....	....	....	....
Lake Elmo (6)	MC 612 777-5510	John Wyn	Mary Kueffner	Mary Kueffner	Marilyn Banister	....	....	Dan Olinger
Lakeville (25)	CM 612 469-4431	Duane R Zaun	Robert A Erickson	Charlene Friedges	Dennis D Feller	Barry Christensen	Donald Gudmundson	James R Robinette
Le Sueur (4)	CM 612 665-6401	....	....	....	....	....	....	....
Lino Lakes (9)	MC 612 464-5562	....	....	....	....	....	....	....
Litchfield (6)	CM 612 693-7201	Ron Ebnet	Bruce Miller	Betty Anderson	....	....	Bruce Dicke	....
Little Canada (9)	CM 612 484-2177	Raymond Hanson	Joel Hanson	....	....	....	....	David Harris
Little Falls (7)	CM 612 632-2341	Ron Hinnenkamp	Richard Carlson	Susan Haugen	Richard Carlson	Fred Tabatt	Michael Pender	Gerald Lochner
Long Prairie (3)	CM 612 732-2167	....	....	....	....	....	....	....
Luverne (4)	CM 507 283-2388	William V Weber	Douglas Bunkers	Marianne Ouverson	Barbara Berghorst	Jim Johannsen	Keith Aanenson	Darrell Huiskes
Madison (2)	CM 612 598-7373	Norma Larsen	David Huseman	....	....	Bob Buer	Stan Ross	Harold Hodge
Mahtomedi (6)	CM 612 426-3344	....	....	....	....	....	....	....
Mankato (31)	CM 507 387-8600	Stan Christ	William Basset	Sandra Paulson	Harley Mohr	....	....	Paul Baker
Maple Grove (39)	CM 612 420-4000	....	....	....	....	....	....	....
Maplewood (31)	CM 612 770-4500	Gary Bastian	Michael McGuire	Lucille Aurelius	Daniel Faust	....	Ken Collins	Ken Haider
Marshall (12)	MC 507 537-6763	Robert J Byrnes	Michael J Johnson	....	T Meulebroeck	David Marks	Marvin Bahn	....
Medina v (3)	MC 612 473-4643	Anne Theis	....	Jeffrey Karlson	....	....	Richard Rabenort	James Dillman
Mendota Heights (9)	MC 612 452-1850	C Mertensotto	M Thomas Lawell	Kathleen Swanson	Larry Shaughnessy	John Maczko	Dennis Delmont	James Danielson
Milaca (2)	CM 612 983-3141	Randy Furman	John Hill	....	....	David Oistad	Michael Mott	Steve Burklund
Minneapolis (368)	MC 612 673-3000	S Sayles Belton	Kathleen O' Brien	Merry Keefe	John Moir	Thomas Dickinson	John Laux	Richard Straub
Minnetonka (48)	CM 612 939-8200	....	....	....	....	....	....	....
Minnetrista (3)	MC 612 446-1660	Scott W Carlson	Charlotte Erickso	Charlotte Erickso	Charlotte Erickso	....	....	Richard Bialon
Montevideo (5)	CM 612 269-6575	....	....	....	....	....	....	....
Monticello (5)	CM 612 295-2711	Bradley Fyle	Rick Wolfsteller	Rick Wolfsteller	Rick Wolfsteller	Jerry Wein	....	John Simola
Moorhead (32)	CM 218 299-5301	Morris Lanning	James Antonen	Kaye Buchholz	Harlyn Ault	Gary Schulz	Leslie Sharrock	Robert Martin
Mora (3)	CM 612 679-1511	....	....	....	....	....	....	....
Morris (6)	CM 612 589-3141	Merlin Beyer	Edward Larson	....	Gene Krosschell	....	Curt Wiese	Bill Storck
Mound (10)	CM 612 472-0600	Skip Johnson	Edward J Shucle	Fran Balrk	Gino Businaro	Steve Erickson	Len Harrell	Greg Skinner
Mounds View (13)	MC 612 784-3055	Jerry Linke	Samantha Orduno	....	Don Brager	Ron Fagerstrom	Tim Ramacher	Mike Ulrich
Mountain Iron (3)	MC 218 735-8267	William Mattila	Peter Abbey	Jill Forseen	....	Tom Cvar	....	Don Kleinschmidt

Directory 1/9 continued **MUNICIPAL OFFICIALS IN U.S. CITIES OVER 2,500**

City, 1990 population figures (000 omitted), form of government	Municipal phone number	Mayor/ chief elected official	Appointed administrator	City clerk/ city secretary	Finance officer	Fire chief	Police chief	Public works director
MINNESOTA (205) continued								
New Brighton (22) CM	612 633-0056	Bob Benke	Matthew Fulton	....	Margaret Egan	Mark Friedan	John Kelley	Les Proper
New Hope (22) CM	612 531-5100	Edward Erickson	Daniel Donahue	Valerie Leone	Larry Watts	Doug Smith	Colin Kastanos	Roger Paulson
New Prague (4) MC	612 758-4401	Jerry Flicek	Jerry Bohnsack	....	....	....	Dennis Rohloff	Bob Vohnoutka
New Ulm (13) CM	507 359-8235	Carl Wyczawski	Richard Salvati	Bruce Kessel	Bruce Kessel	David Clancy	Richard Gulden	....
Newport (4) MC	612 459-5677	Timoty Geraghty	Larry Bodahl	Wanda Swarthout	Sharon Hanestad	Robert Engen	Stephan Sawyer	Bruce Hanson
North Branch (2) CM	612 674-8113	....	....	....	....	....	....	....
North Mankato (10) CM	507 625-4141	....	....	....	....	....	....	....
North Oaks (3) MC	612 484-5777	....	....	....	....	....	....	....
North St. Paul (12) CM	612 770-4450	William Sandberg	....	....	Al Mahlum	David Zick	Dan Scott	....
Northfield (15) MC	507 645-8832	Marvin Grundhofer	Peter Stolley	Karl Huber Jr	Karl Huber Jr	John Machacek	Ronald Pieri	....
Oak Park Heights (3) CM	612 439-4439	Barbara O' Neal	Lavonne Wilson	....	Judy Holst	....	Lindy Swanson	Roger Benson
Oakdale (18) CM	612 739-5086	Ted Bearth	Craig Waldron	Susan Barry	Suzanne Warren	....	William Sullivan	Rollie Harrington
Olivia (3) MC	612 523-2361	John R Stumpf	Don W Frederick	Mary Jo Halliday	Kathy Herdina	Steve Kirtz	Don Davern	Larry Baumgartner
Orono (7) MC	612 473-7357	Edward Callahan	Ronald Moorse	Dorothy Hallin	Thomas Kuehn	....	Stephen Sullivan	John Gerhardson
Ortonville (2) MC	612 839-3428	....	....	....	....	....	....	....
Osseo (3) MC	612 425-2624	....	....	....	....	....	....	....
Owatonna (19) MC	507 451-4540	Wayne Klinkhammer	Richard Hierstein	Richard Hierstein	James Moeckly	Gerald Rosendahl	Roger Brown	Arnold Putnam
Park Rapids (3) MC	218 732-3163	....	....	....	....	....	....	....
Perham (2) CM	218 346-4455	Marlin Zitzow	Robert Louiseau	....	Linda Bjelland	Thomas Hammers	Terry Shannon	Dwight Lundgren
Pine City (..) MC	612 629-2575	....	....	....	....	....	....	....
Pine Island (2) MC	507 356-4591	....	....	....	....	....	....	....
Pipestone (5) MC	507 825-3324	Barbara Hansen	Terry Berg	....	....	Marlin Taubert	James Carstensen	Paul Miersma
Plymouth (51) CM	612 550-5000	Joy Tierney	Dwight Johnson	Laurie Ahrens	Dale Hahn	....	Craig Gerdes	Fred Moore
Princeton (4) CM	612 389-2040	Greg Furzland	William Schimmel	William Schimmel	Steven Jackson	Gerald Bieringer	David Warneke	Thomas Mismash
Prior Lake (11) CM	612 447-4230	Lydia I Andren	Frank F Boyles	....	Ralph G Teschner	Allen A Borchardt	Richard H Powell	Larry J Anderson
Proctor (3) MC	218 624-3641	Steven Elder	....	John Foschi	Brian Grave	Ellsworth Lind	Scott Schneider	....
Ramsey (12) CM	612 427-1410	James Gilbertson	Ryan Schroeder	Ryan Schroeder	Jessie Hart	Dave Griffin	Mike Auspos	Steve Jankowski
Red Wing (15) MC	612 388-6734	....	....	....	....	....	....	....
Redwood Falls (5) MC	507 637-5755	Gary Revier	Jeffrey Weldon	Elaine Jenniges	Christine Jones	Marshall Messer	Terrill Hutson	Ronald Mannz
Renville (1) CM	612 329-8366	....	....	....	....	....	....	....
Richfield (36) CM	612 861-9700	Martin J Kirsch	James D Prosser	Thomas P Ferber	Steven L Devich	....	John D Erskine	Donald A Fondrick
Robbinsdale (14) CM	612 537-4534	Joy J Robb	Francis D Hagen	....	R Gangelhoff	Tom Sipe	John Spetch	Fran Hagen
Rochester (71) MC	507 285-8074	Charles Hazama	Stevan Kvenvold	Carole Grimm	Dale Martinson	David Kapler	Patrick Farrell	Richard Freese
Rosemount (9) CM	612 423-4411	E B McMenomy	Thomas D Burt	Susan Walsh	Jeffrey May	....	Elliel Knutsen	Henry Osmundson
Roseville (33) CM	612 490-2200	Vern Johnson	Steve Sarkozy	....	Ed Burrell	Joel Hewitt	Jim Zelinsky	Karl Keel
Rush City (1) CM	612 358-4743	Mike Skalsky	Daniel P Hoffman	....	....	Curt Burda	Floyd Pinotti	Leon Kruse
Sandstone (2) MC	612 245-5241	....	....	....	....	....	....	....
Sartell (5) MC	612 253-2171	....	....	....	....	....	....	....
Sauk Centre (4) MC	612 352-2203	Robert Polipnick	....	Joe Heinen	....	Virgil Marthaler	G Trierweiler	Harold Wessel
Sauk Rapids (8) MC	612 251-1022	Thomas Braun	Robert Haarman	....	Julie Braun	Andrew Hovanes	John Welsh	Richard Gronau
Savage (10) MC	612 890-1045	Don Egan	Stephen P King	Jan Saarela	Ron Hedberg	....	Gordon Vlasak	....
Shakopee (12) MC	612 445-3650	....	....	....	....	....	....	....
Shoreview (25) CM	612 490-4600	James Chalmers	Terry C Schwerm	Terry C Schwerm	Jeanne Haapala	Daniel Winkel	Jerry Bergeron	....
Shorewood (6) MC	612 474-3236	Barbara Brancel	James C Hurm	Theresa L Naab	Alan J Rolek	....	....	Donald Zdrazil
Silver Bay (2) MC	218 226-4408	Robert Kind	....	Gary Brumberg	....	John Fredrickson	Robert Sando	....
Sleepy Eye (4) MC	507 794-3731	James J Broich	Edwin V Treml	Edwin V Treml	....	Robert Zinniel	Ronald Ellevold	....
South Internatl Falls (..) MC	218 283-9461	....	....	....	....	....	....	....
South St. Paul (20) MC	612 450-8700	....	....	....	....	....	....	....
Spring Lake Park v (7) MC	612 784-6491	Harley Wells	....	Donald Busch	Donald Busch	....	Bruce Porter	Gary Peterson
Spring Valley v (2) MC	507 346-7367	....	....	....	....	....	....	....
St. Anthony (8) CM	612 789-8881	Clarence Ranallo	Michael Mornson	Connie Kroeplin	Roger Larson	Richard Johnson	Richard Engstrom	Lawrence Hamer
St. Cloud (49) MC	612 255-7200	Charles Winkleman	Chris Hagelie	Gregg Engdahl	John Norman	Bill Graham	Dennis O' Keefe	John Dolentz
St. James (4) CM	507 375-3241	....	....	....	....	....	....	....
St. Joseph (3) MC	612 363-7201	Donald Reber	....	Rachel Stapleton	....	Richard Taufen	Bradley Lindgren	Richard Taufen
St. Louis Park (44) CM	612 924-2500	Lyle Hanks	Charlie Meyer	Beverly Flanagan	Kathleen McBride	Bob Gill	Mancel Mitchell	Jim Grube
St. Paul (272) MC	612 298-4221	....	....	....	....	....	....	....
St. Paul Park (5) CM	612 459-9785	....	....	....	....	....	....	....
St. Peter (9) CM	507 931-4840	Ellery O Peterson	Daniel Jordet	....	David Stutelberg	Art Zuhlsdorf	Bradley Kollmann	Lewis Giesking
Staples (3) MC	218 894-2550	....	....	....	....	....	....	....
Stewartville (5) MC	507 533-4745	Larry Gray	Larry Hansen	....	....	Joe Himmer	....	Kenneth Kraft
Stillwater (14) MC	612 439-6121	....	....	....	....	....	....	....
Thief River Falls (8) MC	218 681-2943	Bob Reeve	....	....	Roger Delap	David Tjorkman	Ken Froschheiser	....
Tracy (2) MC	507 629-3460	....	....	....	....	....	....	....
Two Harbors (4) CM	218 834-5631	W Sletten	R Simonson	....	L Klein	R Sellman	R Hogenson	R Leroy
Vadnais Heights (11) MC	612 429-5343	Mark Haider	Gerald Urban	....	....	....	....	Joseph Momsen
Virginia (9) CM	218 741-3890	Leroy Guss	N Dragisich	....	Susan Lemieux	Ed Clark	Thomas Yarick	....
Waconia (3) MC	612 442-2184	Michael R Zender	Bruce Eisenhauer	Mary Johnson	Wendy Moldenhauer	Randall Sorensen	....	Randall Sorensen
Wadena (4) MC	218 631-2383	James Lundquist	Bradley Swenson	Bradley Swenson	Lloyd Lanz	Tom Reger	Lane Waldahl	Mark Petsche
Waite Park v (5) MC	612 252-6822	....	....	....	....	....	....	....
Waseca (8) CM	507 835-9700	Judy Kozan	Michael McCauley	Mary Buenzow	Julie A Linnihan	Bob Johnson	James Staloch	....
Watertown (2) MC	612 955-2681	Norman A Bauer	Michael A Ericson	Marilyn Paschka	....	Hubert D Widmer	....	K Gulbrandson
Waterville (2) MC	507 362-8300	Lawrence Meskan	Nickie Roberge	Maria Stoering	....	Steve Anderson	Arlie Bluhm	....
Wayzata (4) CM	612 473-0234	....	....	....	....	....	....	....
Wells (2) MC	507 553-6371	Jim Prust	....	Dolly Schultz	....	Jack Horntasch	Gary Robbins	....
West St. Paul (19) CM	612 552-4100	Michael P Bisanz	William P Craig	Dianne R Krogh	John W Remkus	Richard B Krogh	Thomas Iago	Philip Stefaniak
White Bear Lake (25) CM	612 429-8526	Harry Mares	Mark Sather	....	Don Rambew	Tim Vadnais	Todd Miller	Mark Burch
Willmar (18) MC	612 235-4913	Richard Hoglund	Michael Schmit	Kevin Halliday	Steven Okins	Douglas Lindblad	Daniel Strootman	Lowell Gjelhaug
Windom (4) CM	507 831-2363	John Galle Sr	....	Dennis W Nelson	....	Jack Rogers	Elton Wagner	....
Winnebago (2) CM	307 893-4774	....	Daniel L Mundahl	....	....	....	....	....
Winona (25) CM	507 457-8200	Thomas J Slaggie	Eric B Sorensen	James G Pomeroy	Darrel Johnson	Edward Krall	Frank Pomeroy	Robert J Bollant
Woodbury (20) CM	612 739-5972	Bill Hargis	Barry Johnson	....	Tom Wright	Ken Southorn	Greg Orth	David Jessup
Worthington (10) MC	507 372-8600	....	....	....	....	....	....	....
Young America (1) MC	612 467-2603	....	....	....	....	....	....	....
MISSISSIPPI (88)								
Aberdeen (7) MC	601 369-4165	....	....	....	....	....	....	....
Amory (7) MC	601 256-5635	Thomas Griffith	....	Suzanne C Mobley	....	Jimmy Bost	Ronnie Bowen	....
Baldwyn t (3) MC	601 365-2383	....	....	....	....	....	....	....
Batesville (6) MC	601 563-4576	....	....	....	....	....	....	....
Bay St. Louis (8) MC	601 467-9092	....	....	....	....	....	....	....
Belzoni (3) MC	601 247-1343	....	....	....	....	....	....	....
Biloxi (46) MC	601 435-6254	A J Holloway	David Nichols	Brenda Johnston	William Lanham	Floyd Thibodeaux	Tommy Moffett	Jerry Morgan
Booneville t (8) MC	601 728-6810	....	....	....	....	....	....	....

Directory 1/9 continued

MUNICIPAL OFFICIALS IN U.S. CITIES OVER 2,500

City, 1990 population figures (000 omitted), form of government	Municipal phone number	Mayor/ chief elected official	Appointed administrator	City clerk/ city secretary	Finance officer	Fire chief	Police chief	Public works director
MISSISSIPPI (88) continued								
Brandon (11)	MC 601 825-5021	M L Whittington	Billy C Smith	....	Mary Anne Magee	Byron P McDaniel	Eudene Adcock	George L Bobo
Brookhaven (10)	MC 601 833-2362	....	....	....	....	....	....	....
Canton (10)	MC 601 859-4331	....	....	....	....	....	....	....
Carthage t (4)	MC 601 267-8322	....	....	....	....	....	....	....
Charleston (2)	MC 601 647-5841	Robert Rowe	....	Diane Stanford	....	Phil Shook	Jerry Williams	....
Clarksdale (20)	CO 601 627-8400	Henry Espy	....	Sylvia H Burton	....	S Washington	Danny L Vick	Robert H Gaston
Cleveland (15)	MC 601 846-1471	....	....	....	....	....	....	....
Clinton (22)	MC 601 924-5462	Rosemary Aultman	Nelson Byrd	Nelson Byrd	Wayne Derrick	Jeffrey Landrum	Donald Byington	Harold Alderman
Columbia (7)	MC 601 736-8201	....	....	....	....	....	....	....
Columbus (24)	MC 601 328-7021	Jimmy Fannon	....	....	Dorothy Pridmore	James Massey	Edward H Bowen	....
Corinth (12)	MC 601 286-6644	E S Bishop Sr	James Billingsley	James Billingsley	Vickie Roach	Gerald Horner	Larry Brinkley	Billy Ray Briggs
Crystal Springs (6)	MC 601 892-1212	....	....	Bettie Dickey	....	Ricky Jenkins	Burner Smith	Mac Benson
Drew (2)	MC 601 745-8556	Eugene Wakham	....	Bettie Dickey	....	Ricky Jenkins	Burner Smith	Mac Benson
Durant (3)	MC 601 653-3221	Bennie Killebrew	....	....	Rosie Hill	Houston Kyzer	Martin Frazure	R C Umphers
Ellisville (4)	MC 601 477-3323	Ernest P Todd	....	Kathy Brewer	....	Stan Kinmon	R L Jenkins	Howell Beech
Forest (5)	MC 601 469-2921	....	....	....	....	....	....	....
Fulton t (3)	MC 601 862-4929	....	....	....	....	....	....	....
Gautier (10)	CM 601 497-2332	Charles A Keith	Ronald L Waller	Pearl B Mercer	Johnny A Roberts	....	C Allen Johnson	....
Greenville (45)	MC 601 378-1567	C C Self	....	T G Jefcoat	....	Ely Nelson	Dennis Blass	John Ventura
Greenwood (19)	MC 601 453-2246	....	....	....	....	....	....	....
Grenada (11)	CM 601 226-8820	L D Boone Jr	L R Kegley	Valleria Blaylock	....	Eugene Doss	Ben Simmons	Ken Mixon
Gulfport (41)	MC 601 868-5831	Ken Combs	Havard Jordan Jr	Sandra Baylor	Havard Jordan Jr	George Bordeaux	George Payne	Buddy Broadway
Hattiesburg (42)	MC 601 545-4501	J Ed Morgan	....	Clarice Wansley	Joe Townsend	George Herrington	Wayne Landers	Bennie Sellers
Hazlehurst (4)	MC 601 894-3131	....	....	....	....	....	....	....
Hernando (3)	MC 601 429-9092	....	....	....	....	....	....	....
Hollandale (4)	MC 601 827-2241	Oscar C Peace	....	Jo Ann Boykin	....	Mitchell Baugh	Green Townsend	Lee O Edwards
Holly Springs (7)	MC 601 252-4280	Eddie L Smith Jr	....	Sandra R Young	....	Kenneth Holbrook	William V Hasty	....
Horn Lake (9)	MC 601 393-6178	Mike Thomas	....	Diane Stewart	Diane Stewart	Leroy Bledsoe	Darryl Whaley	Jim McKell
Houston (4)	MC 601 456-2328	....	....	....	....	....	....	....
Indianola (12)	MC 601 887-3101	....	....	....	....	....	....	....
Itta Bena t (2)	MC 601 254-7231	....	....	....	....	....	....	....
Iuka (3)	MC 601 423-3781	....	....	....	....	....	....	....
Jackson (197)	MC 601 960-1005	....	....	....	....	....	....	....
Kosciusko (7)	MC 601 289-1226	George E Lewis	....	Janet P Baird	....	Roy Frazier	Dirk Thayer	Edgar Taylor
Laurel (19)	CO 601 428-6401	Susan Vincent	T G Myrick	Jolyn Sellers	....	Marvin Overstreet	James E Bush	....
Leland (6)	MC 601 686-4136	Sam Thomas	....	Mickey Fratesi	....	Junior Walker	Michael H Dees	....
Lexington (2)	MC 601 834-1261	....	....	....	....	....	....	....
Long Beach (16)	MC 601 863-1556	....	....	....	....	....	....	....
Louisville (7)	MC 601 773-9201	....	....	....	....	....	....	....
Magee t (4)	MC 601 849-3344	....	....	....	....	....	....	....
Mc Comb (12)	MC 601 684-4000	Ronnie Wilkinson	Sam Mims	Donna Ladner	Donna Ladner	Richard Coglan	Billie Hughes	Ronnie Lindsey
Mendenhall t (2)	MC 601 847-1212	....	....	....	....	....	....	....
Meridian (41)	MC 601 485-1927	John Robert Smith	Kenneth R Storms	Lawrence Skipper	....	Joseph S Taylor	William D Sollie	Benny Wolfe
Moorhead t (2)	CM 601 246-5461	....	....	....	....	....	....	....
Morton (3)	MC 601 732-8609	....	....	....	....	....	....	....
Moss Point (18)	MC 601 475-0300	....	....	....	....	....	....	....
Mound Bayou (2)	MC 601 741-2193	Nerissa Norman	....	Milburn J Crowe	....	Eugene Brown	Shelton Woodley	Joseph Woods
Natchez (19)	MC 601 445-7500	Larry L Brown	....	Frances Trosclair	....	Gary Winborne	Willie Huff	Richard Burke
New Albany (7)	MC 601 534-1010	Tom Cooper	....	Anne Neal	....	William Douell	David Grisham	....
Newton (4)	MC 601 683-6181	Preston H Beatty	Geraldine M Seal	Geraldine M Seal	....	Charles Vance	Joe R Mowdy	Daryl W Ford
Ocean Springs (15)	MC 601 875-4236	Kevin V Alves Sr	....	Sandra F Jenkins	....	James Murray	Carolyn Frayser	Robert Powell
Okolona (3)	MC 601 447-5461	....	....	....	....	....	....	....
Oxford (10)	MC 601 236-1310	John O Leslie	....	V Chrestman	....	Terry McDonald	Billy White Sr	David N Bennett
Pascagoula (26)	CM 601 762-1020	Wayne Savell	Conrad Bird	Brenda Reed	Kenneth McKeown	Jewell McMillian	Michael Whitmore	Garland Lear
Pass Christian (6)	MC 601 452-3310	....	....	....	....	....	....	....
Pearl (20)	MC 601 932-2262	....	....	....	....	....	....	....
Petal (8)	MC 601 545-1776	Jack Gay	....	Priscilla Daniel	Priscilla Daniel	L Aubra Evans	Billy W Murphy	....
Philadelphia (7)	MC 601 656-3612	Harlan Majure	Brenda H Mills	....	....	Kenneth Coleman	James A Gentry	....
Picayune (11)	CM 601 798-9770	J Woody Spiers	James M Young	Howard Parker	....	Jackie Mitchell	Freddy Drennan	Ray Pearson
Pontotoc (5)	MC 601 489-4321	....	....	....	....	....	....	....
Poplarville (3)	MC 601 795-8161	Billy W Spiers	Brenda T Burge	....	....	Benjie Wells	Joe Stuart	John E Davis
Quitman t (3)	MC 601 776-3728	....	....	....	....	....	....	....
Richland (4)	MC 601 932-3000	Lester Spell Jr	....	Donna Diffrient	Donna Diffrient	Maurice J Joy	W F Fortenberry	Glen Thomas
Ridgeland (12)	MC 601 856-7113	....	....	....	....	....	....	....
Ripley (5)	MC 601 837-8578	....	....	....	....	....	....	....
Rolling Fork (2)	MC 601 873-2814	John Pippin Jr	....	Dorothy K Pearson	....	Larry Harris	Charles McPhail	Billy G Johnson
Ruleville (3)	MC 601 756-2791	....	....	....	....	....	....	....
Senatobia (5)	MC 601 562-4474	Steve Hale	....	Kay Minton	....	....	Al Dodson	Robert Morris
Shelby (3)	MC 601 398-5156	Robert D Gray	....	Carmere Scott	....	Dan Harris	William Crocker	....
Southaven (18)	MC 601 393-5931	Joseph A Cates	....	Marlene Sprinkle	B Hendrichovsky	Vernon McCammon	Tom Long	Michael Forsythe
Starkville (18)	CM 601 324-4011	Jesse Greer	....	Vivian Collier	Larry Murphy	Willie H Johnson	James L Sisk	H W Webb
Tupelo (31)	MC 601 841-6487	....	....	....	....	....	....	....
Vicksburg (21)	CO 601 634-4554	Joseph Loviza	....	Paul Rogers	Paul Rogers	Doris Sprouse	Herman Redick	James Rainer
Water Valley (4)	MC 601 473-2431	....	....	....	....	....	....	....
Waveland (5)	MC 601 467-4134	Stella Frilot	Mike Barnes	Betsy Phillips	....	David Garcia	James Varnell	John R Woodall
Waynesboro t (5)	MC 601 735-4874	....	....	....	....	....	....	....
West Point (8)	MC 601 494-2573	Kenneth D Dill	Dewel G Brasher	....	....	Richard Stripling	William Ladd	....
Wiggins t (3)	MC 601 928-7221	....	....	....	....	....	....	....
Winona (6)	MC 601 283-1232	....	....	....	....	....	....	....
Yazoo City (12)	MC 601 746-1401	....	....	....	....	....	....	....
MISSOURI (185)								
Arnold (19)	MC 314 296-2100	....	....	....	....	....	....	....
Aurora (6)	CM 417 678-5121	....	....	....	....	....	....	....
Ava (3)	MC 417 683-4122	....	....	....	....	....	....	....
Ballwin (22)	CM 314 227-8580	Richard G Andrews	Robert Kuntz	....	Donette Johnson	....	Donald J Loehr	....
Bel-Ridge v (3)	MC 314 429-2878	....	....	....	....	....	....	....
Bellefontaine Neighbrs (11)	MC 314 867-0076	Marty Rudloff	....	C Youngman	Lawrence Abeln	....	David Erker	Lou Roth
Belton (18)	CM 816 331-4331	Steve Farmer	Ronald Trivitt	Patricia Ledford	Leon Ellis	H K Denkler	James Person	....
Berkeley (12)	CM 314 524-3313	William Miller	Arbon Hairston	Lorraine Batton	Arbon Hairston	Roosevelt Sims	Robert Stewart	....
Bethany (3)	MC 816 425-3511	Dorthy Premer	David L Haugland	Marilyn Smith	....	John Gannan	John Findley	Larry Starmer
Black Jack (6)	MC 314 355-0400	....	....	....	....	....	....	....
Blue Springs (40)	CM 816 228-0110	Gregory O Grounds	Frederick R Siems	Dianne Gardner	Isabel Stoecklein	....	Howard L Brown	....

City, 1990 population figures (000 omitted), form of government	Municipal phone number	Mayor/ chief elected official	Appointed administrator	City clerk/ city secretary	Finance officer	Fire chief	Police chief	Public works director
MISSOURI (185) continued								
Bolivar (7)	MC 417 326-5298	....	....	....	....	....	....	....
Bonne Terre (4)	CM 314 358-2254	Wayne Weber	Terry Rickard	Sandra Wells	....	David Pratte	Fred Mallow	Butch Keen
Boonville (7)	CM 816 882-2332	Bernard V Kempf	Steven Goehl	Kim Gerlach	....	Van Warrick	Irvin Drew	Steven Goehl
Bowling Green (3)	MC 314 324-5451	Leonard M Grote	Joseph Smith	Martha Jane Bell	....	Don Nacke	Jack Floyd	....
Branson (4)	MC 417 334-3345	....	....	....	....	....	....	....
Breckenridge Hills v (5)	MC 314 427-6868	....	....	....	....	....	....	....
Brentwood (8)	MC 314 962-4800	Mark Kurtz	Chris Seemayer	Chris Seemayer	Susan Zimmer	Robert Niemeyer	William Karabas	Willie Wright
Bridgeton (18)	MC 314 739-7500	Conrad Bowers	....	Carole Stahlhut	....	....	Warren Runge	Richard Houchin
Brookfield (5)	CM 816 258-3377	Jack Forbes	....	Dana Tarpening	....	Walter Gordon Jr	David Hane	....
Buckner (3)	MC 816 249-3191	Joyce Neasham	Judy Buttress	Kelly Gilgour	....	....	C Micheal Seibert	Carl Williams
Butler (4)	MC 816 679-4013	Joe Fuller	Bob Bridges	Janet Kirtley	....	Jim Henry	Steve Brochoff	....
Cabool (2)	MC 417 962-3136	Edwin R Hardy	M Mac Pherson	Tracy L Upton	M Mac Pherson	Jerry Miller	Lynn L Jones	....
California (3)	MC 314 796-2500	Carol Rackers	....	Sue A Kuhn	....	Allen Smith	Jerry McCarty	Gary Wells
Camdenton (..)	MC 314 346-3600	Kay Cyrus	....	Brenda Colter	Kay Boillot	David Stonitsch	Elmer Meyer	Bob Marshall
Cameron (5)	CM 816 632-2177	....	Phil Lammers	Barbara O' Connor	....	....	Harold Riddle	James Roach
Cape Girardeau (34)	MC 314 334-1212	Albert Spradling	J Ronald Fischer	Mary F Thompson	John R Richbourg	Robert L Ridgeway	Howard H Boyd Jr	Douglas K Leslie
Carl Junction (4)	MC 417 649-7237	....	....	....	....	....	....	....
Carrollton (4)	MC 816 542-1414	Jack B Mathis	....	Carol Pink	....	Wayne Shirk	Don King	Lowell Anderson
Carthage (11)	MC 417 358-5904	....	....	....	....	....	....	....
Caruthersville (7)	CM 314 333-2142	....	....	....	....	....	....	....
Centralia (3)	MC 314 682-2139	Deanna Richman	Lynn P Behrns	Kathy Colvin	....	Lannie Patton	James McNabb	Randy McDowell
Chaffee (3)	MC 314 887-3558	Ronald Moyers	....	Diane Eftink	....	Steve Graham	Jerry Bledsoe	John Martin
Charleston (5)	CM 314 683-3325	Brett Mathews	Herb Llewellyn	Marsh Hart	....	....	Robert Richey	Dave Teeters
Chesterfield (38)	MC 314 537-4000	Jack Leonard	Michael Herring	Marty Demay	Jan Hawn	....	Ray Johnson	Michael Geisel
Chillicothe (9)	MC 816 646-2267	....	....	....	....	....	....	....
Clayton (14)	CM 314 746-0449	B Uchitelle	Steven Hoffner	Linda Huffman	Dale Dickmann	Richard Morris	Richard Morris	Bryan Pearl
Clinton (9)	MC 816 885-6121	....	....	....	....	....	....	....
Columbia (69)	CM 314 874-7111	Maryann McCollum	Raymond Beck	Launa Daniel	Harold Boldt	William Markgraf	Ernest Barbee	Lowell Patterson
Crestwood (11)	CM 314 966-4700	Patricia Killoren	Kent Leichliter	C Schneiderhahn	Robert Wuebbels	William Kramer	Don Greer	Mark Payken
Creve Coeur (12)	CM 314 432-6000	William E Winter	T M McDowell	LaVerne Collins	Jeffrey J Steiner	....	Richard E Schnarr	Vijay K Bhasin
Crystal City (4)	MC 314 937-4614	....	....	....	....	....	....	....
De Soto (6)	CM 314 586-3326	Elizabeth Mueller	....	Arlene Burt	Dan Blanchfield	John Wood	Lloyd Davis	....
Dellwood (5)	MC 314 521-4339	....	....	....	....	....	....	....
Des Peres (8)	MC 314 966-4600	Sharon Burkhardt	Douglas J Harms	....	....	....	Ronald Martin	Denis G Knock
Desloge (4)	MC 314 431-3700	....	....	....	....	....	....	....
Dexter (8)	MC 314 624-5959	Willis Conner	....	Joann Steinbrueck	....	Al Banken	Rick Walker	Tom Espey
East Prairie (3)	MC 314 649-3057	....	....	....	....	....	....	....
El Dorado Springs (4)	CM 417 876-2521	C E Morlan	Bruce Rogers	Lisa Janes	Jill Smith	Eugene Elliott	Jimmy Luster	Clay Sanders
Eldon (4)	CM 314 392-3654	Kevin D Simpson	James A Link	Laverne Belk	James A Link	Charles Wilson	Robert Hurtubise	....
Ellisville (8)	CM 314 227-9660	Dennis N Smith	Setphen A Arbo	Catherine Demeter	....	....	B Wayne Prince	Terrence Keran
Eureka (5)	MC 314 938-5233	Barney Nelson	Craig Sabo	Ralph Lindsey	Ralph Lindsey	Michael McMurray	Michael Wiegand	Michael Schlereth
Excelsior Springs (10)	CM 816 630-0761	Michael Robertson	Craig Hubler	Frances Smith	Richard Crimbly	William Stewart	John McGovern	Rex Brinker
Farmington (12)	MC 314 756-1701	....	....	....	....	....	....	....
Fayette (3)	MC 816 248-5246	Ken O' Brian	Michael P Brown	Robin Overstreet	....	Wally Eaton	Bryan Kunze	....
Ferguson (22)	CM 314 521-7721	Michael James	Robert B Burns	Dorris S Carter	Jo Ann Bordeleau	Donald G Parrotte	James E Carter	Danny D Fain
Festus (8)	CM 314 937-4694	John Graham	Richard T Turley	Charlene I Byers	....	Donald Declue	Ronald Scaggs	....
Flat River (5)	CM 314 431-3577	Leonard Henson	Larry Hughes	Carla Johnson	....	Jim Easter	William Holloway	Paul Richardson
Florissant (51)	MC 314 921-5700	James J Eagan	....	Carol Fritschie	Randal McDaniel	....	Robert Lowery	Louis B Jearls
Fredericktown (4)	MC 314 783-3683	Jerry R Foster	Joseph R Smith	Linda S Stevens	....	Darryl Asher	Roy Roberts	....
Frontenac (3)	MC 314 994-3200	....	....	....	....	....	....	....
Fulton (10)	MC 314 642-6826	....	....	....	....	....	....	....
Gladstone (26)	CM 816 436-2200	George Nodler	James H Norris	Marilyn Ahnefeld	E Sue Henning	....	William Adamo	Gerald Menefee
Glendale (6)	MC 314 965-3600	....	....	....	....	....	....	....
Grain Valley (2)	CM 816 229-6275	Duard L Coombs	Timothy R Ryan	Jere J Chieppo	Timothy R Ryan	....	Skipper R Hedges	Garry R Edwards
Grandview (25)	CM 816 763-3900	....	....	....	....	....	....	....
Hannibal (18)	MC 314 221-0111	....	....	....	....	....	....	....
Harrisonville (8)	MC 816 884-3285	William F Mills	Damon Bartles	Cheri Powell	Vernon Chalfant	Joe Gerke	Norman Schnorf	....
Hayti (3)	MC 314 359-0632	Herbert DeWeese	....	Terri Merrell	....	Milford Chism	Barry McKay	Leonard Plunkett
Hazelwood (15)	CM 314 839-3700	David Farquharson	Edwin Carlstrom	Norma Caldwell	Edwin Carlstrom	James Matthies	Carl Wolf	Thomas Manning
Hermann (3)	MC 314 486-5400	....	....	....	....	....	....	....
Higginsville (5)	MC 816 584-2106	....	....	....	....	....	....	....
Holts Summit (2)	MC 314 896-5600	R C Miller	John Watkins	Linda Batye	....	....	Andrew Goldman	....
Houston (2)	MC 417 967-3348	....	....	....	....	....	....	....
Independence (112)	CM 816 325-7000	Rondell F Stewart	Larry N Blick	Bruce E Lowery	James C Harlow	Larry B Hodge	Donald L Carey	Howard B Penrod
Jackson (9)	MC 314 243-3568	....	....	....	....	....	....	....
Jefferson City (35)	MC 314 634-6300	....	....	....	....	....	....	....
Jennings (16)	MC 314 388-1164	William D Tharp	....	Cheryl Balke	Beverly Roche	James Sutphin	James Trentham	Richard Perry
Joplin (41)	CM 417 624-0820	Ronald Richard	Steven Lewis	Mary Davis	Linda Sharp	Harry Guinn	David Niebur	Harold McCoy
Kansas City (435)	CM 816 274-1724	Emanuel Cleaver	Larry Brown	Catherine Rocha	Verlyn Leiker	Charles Fisher	Steven Bishop	George Wolf
Kearney (2)	CM 816 635-4142	....	....	....	....	....	....	....
Kennett (11)	CM 314 888-9001	Charles B Brown	....	Leverna S Moore	....	John H Mallott	Mike Damron	....
Kinloch (3)	MC 314 521-3335	....	....	....	....	....	....	....
Kirksville (17)	CM 816 627-1224	Bob Funk	Scot Wrighton	Vickie Parrish	Kathleen Rogers	Ronald Stewart	David Pingel	Mark Gaugh
Kirkwood (27)	CM 314 822-5800	Marge Schramm	Michael G Brown	....	Carolyn J Schmidt	Richard P Daly Jr	Daniel B Linza	Kenneth D Yost
Knob Noster (..)	MC 816 563-2595	....	....	....	....	....	....	....
La Plata (1)	MC 816 332-7166	Stephen A Sawyer	....	B Richardson	....	Jerry Thomas	Dexter Brookhart	....
Ladue (9)	MC 314 993-3439	Edith J Spink	....	John T Williams	George O Pelt	Robert Leroy	Calvin Dierberg	Dennis Bible
Lake Saint Louis (7)	CM 314 625-1200	Ed Hajek	Ron Nelson	Marylou Von Blohn	Jean McDonough	....	Mike Force	Freddy Williams
Lamar (4)	MC 417 682-5554	Gerald W Gilkey	Lynn B Calton	Carolyn Taffner	....	Bill Rawlings	Ron Hager	....
Lawson (..)	CM 816 580-3217	....	....	....	....	....	....	....
Lebanon (10)	MC 417 532-2157	....	....	....	....	....	....	....
Lee'S Summit (46)	CM 816 251-2300	Karen Messerli	Arthur Davis	Denise Chisum	Conrad Lamb	Richard Dyer	Daniel Rettig	W Stockhausen
Lexington (5)	MC 816 259-4633	Robert L Estill	Abigail Tempel	Carla Ghisalberti	....	Scott Wandell	Ron Bahl	P Winningham
Liberty (20)	CM 816 781-7100	Robert J Saunders	Gary W Jackson	....	Arthur Dewitt	Richard Lehmann	Bruce Davis	Steve Hansen
Louisiana (4)	MC 314 754-4132	Bill Wunderlich	....	Kathy Walker	....	Richard A Murry	Daniel Sedivec	....
Macon (6)	MC 816 385-3173	Dale Whitley	Gary Quick	Vicky McLeland	....	Ray Blomberg	Scott Ziebarth	Gary Quick
Malden (5)	MC 314 276-4502	Clark Duckett	....	Mary Lou Bearden	....	Winford German	Norman McMillion	....
Manchester (7)	CM 314 227-1385	Frank McGuire	Michael Leavitt	Michael Leavitt	Diana Madrid	....	John Quinn	Edward Blattner
Maplewood (10)	CM 314 645-3600	Jane Moeller	Martin J Corcoran	Charlotte First	Martin J Corcoran	Merv Feick	Tom Holland	Mike Doi
Marceline (3)	CM 816 376-3528	....	....	....	....	....	....	....
Marshall (13)	MC 816 886-2226	....	....	....	....	....	....	....
Marshfield (4)	MC 417 468-2310	....	....	....	....	....	....	....
Maryland Heights (25)	MC 314 291-6550	Michael O' Brien	Mark M Levin	Carol Turner	David V Watson	....	Neil Kurlander	Martin Macke

Directory 1/9 continued — MUNICIPAL OFFICIALS IN U.S. CITIES OVER 2,500

City, 1990 population figures (000 omitted), form of government	Municipal phone number	Mayor/chief elected official	Appointed administrator	City clerk/city secretary	Finance officer	Fire chief	Police chief	Public works director
MISSOURI (185) continued								
Maryville (11)	CM 816 562-2811	Dale Mathes	David Angerer	Jo E Gill	Denise Town	....	Keith Wood	Ronald Franz
Mexico (11)	CM 314 581-2100	Donald Magnus	Dan Parrott	Donna Barnes	Joe Kernell	....	Don Bolli	Glenn Phillips
Moberly (13)	CM 816 263-4420	Larry Noel	Don Tuley	Carole Kehoe	Nick Burton	Dave Lacy	Mike Garbulski	Ron Wilson
Moline Acres (3)	MC 314 868-2533	....	....	....	....	....	....	....
Monett (7)	CO 417 235-3763	....	....	....	....	....	....	....
Monroe City (3)	MC 314 735-4585	....	....	....	....	....	....	....
Montgomery City (2)	MC 314 564-3160	John J O' Fallon	James K Koshmider	James K Koshmider	James K Koshmider	Thomas J O' Keefe	Michael D Frye	Emory Gerken
Mount Vernon (4)	MC 417 466-2122	Neal Underwood	....	Mary Walker	....	Melvin Owens	W F Turk	Jack Swearingen
Mountain Grove (4)	CM 417 926-4162	Delbert Crewse	Joe Rodery	Judy Kjellberg	Joe Rodery	Norman Jarrett	Tommy Gaddis	....
Neosho (9)	CM 417 451-8050	....	....	....	....	....	....	....
Nevada (9)	CM 417 448-2700	Dick Meyers	Wayne Neal	Reni Geiger	Ronald Chandler	William Gillette	Larry Moore	....
New Madrid (3)	MC 314 748-2866	Lawrence H Rost	Furgison Hunter	Shelby S Desmore	....	Frank Hadder	Denson J Taylor	....
Nixa (5)	CM 417 725-3785	Sharon Whitehill	Jan M Blase	Coralee Patrick	Coralee Patrick	....	John Burdick	....
Normandy (4)	MC 314 385-3300	E Houlihan	....	Jackie Iocca	Jackie Iocca	....	Jerome Burke	John Hutchison
North Kansas City (4)	MC 816 274-6000	Elizabeth Short	George DeFrench	Virginia Viar	Frank Henderson	Frank Smith	Wm Biggerstaff	Carl Elshire
Northwoods (5)	MC 314 385-8000	Charlie A Dooley	Emma F Weaver	Collette Bass	Tracy Y Williams	....	Kevin Neal	....
O'Fallon (19)	CM 314 240-2000	E Griesenauer	Patrick A Nasi	Sandra Stokes	Laura Chiles	....	Michael Kernan	Benny Hedden
Oak Grove (5)	MC 816 625-4012	....	....	....	....	....	....	....
Odessa (4)	MC 816 230-5577	Leo V Thompson	Michael Tholen	Kathy Massie	....	....	Robert Kinder	....
Olivette (8)	CM 314 993-0444	Joan Markow	Jerome Feldman	Tim Clark	Jerome Feldman	Al Wedel	Henry Davenport	Gene Kunzie
Osage Beach (3)	MC 314 348-3151	Gary Martin	Pat McCourt	Diann Warner	Brett Vuagniaux	....	Roland Trautman	Pat McCourt
Overland (18)	MC 314 428-4321	Frank Munsch	....	Gail Waggoner	Gail Waggoner	....	Eddy Williams	Charles Karam
Ozark (4)	MC 417 485-2407	Donald R Watts	Steven T Horton	Mary Lou Erhart	Alice R Edwards	William McKnabb	Steven Marler	Robert L Snider
Pacific (4)	MC 314 257-7200	....	....	....	....	....	....	....
Pagedale (4)	MC 314 726-1200	....	....	....	....	....	....	....
Palmyra (3)	MC 314 769-2223	William D Huffman	....	Shirley J Nix	....	Charles Hoehne	James Beadle	Raymond Houston
Perryville (7)	MC 314 547-2594	Robert J Miget	Craig M Lindsley	Marilyn Dobbelare	....	Wayne Walker	Eugene Besand	Charles Larose Jr
Pevely (3)	MC 314 475-4452	John Knobloch	Betty A Stackley	Marilyn A Green	....	....	Ronnie E Weeks	William A Heyse
Pine Lawn (5)	MC 314 261-5500	....	....	....	....	....	....	....
Pleasant Hill (4)	CM 816 987-3135	Clarence Hall	Mark R Randall	Sandi Beatty	Sandi Beatty	....	John Harris	Jerry Barbarick
Poplar Bluff (17)	CM 314 686-8620	Calvin Rutledge	Thomas J Lawson	William Pettet	....	Gerald Garrett	Bill Adams	....
Portageville (3)	MC 314 379-5789	....	....	....	....	....	....	....
Potosi (3)	MC 314 438-2767	....	....	....	....	....	....	....
Raymore (6)	MC 816 331-0488	Robert W Moore	Robert J Frank	....	....	....	Walter Buck	....
Raytown (31)	MC 816 737-6000	....	....	....	....	....	....	....
Republic (6)	MC 417 732-6065	Harold Tindell	....	Karen Cline	Jane Medlin	Don Murray	Sam Hartsell	Ronnie Smith
Richland (2)	MC 314 765-4421	....	....	....	....	....	....	....
Richmond (6)	MC 816 776-5304	Monroe Evert	Rick Outersky	Dolores Elliston	Rick Outersky	Lonnie Quick	Doug Porter	Dale Minnick
Richmond Heights (10)	CM 314 645-0404	B W LaTourette	Carl L Schwing	M Khamlaksana	Carl L Schwing	Larry Drexler	Ronald Pfeiffer	Byrl Engel
Riverside (3)	MC 816 741-3993	....	....	....	....	....	....	....
Riverview v (3)	CM 314 868-0700	Elizabeth Morris	....	Jean Wolford	....	Al Marhanka	Carl Schulze	Sharon Shoults
Rock Hill (5)	MC 314 968-1410	....	....	....	....	....	....	....
Rolla (14)	MC 314 364-1835	Elwyn E Wax	Merle L Strouse	Carol L Daniels	Daniel L Murphy	William T Oliver	Michael W Snavely	Steve L Hargis
Salem (4)	CM 615 272-7497	Jim Sells	William H Lyons	....	....	Hal Price Jr	Larry Lawson	....
Savannah (4)	MC 816 324-3315	Dave Ingersoll	Guy Speckman	Janice Hatcher	....	James Edwards	George Birdsong	Kenny Lance
Scott City (4)	MC 314 264-2157	Larry J Forhan	....	Nona M Walls	....	Les Crump	Danny Clubb	Harold J Uelsman
Sedalia (20)	MC 816 827-3000	Jane A Gray	Irl Tessendorf	Shirley Collins	Pamela Burlingame	Michael Ditzfeld	Philip Bue	Gary Johnson
Shrewsbury (6)	MC 314 647-5795	Bert L Gates	Wayne R Behney	....	Barbara Smeener	William P Fox	James E Roth	Jeffery Baumann
Sikeston (18)	CM 314 471-2512	Mike Moll	S Borgsmiller	Carroll Couch	Carroll Couch	....	James Leist	Doug Friend
Slater (2)	MC 816 529-2271	....	....	....	....	....	....	....
Smithville (3)	MC 816 532-0500	....	....	....	....	....	....	....
Springfield (140)	CM 417 864-1000	N L McCartney	Tom Finnie	Brenda Cirtin	Fred Fantauzzi	Jim Dancy	Lynn Rowe	Marc Thornsberry
St. Ann (14)	MC 314 427-8009	....	....	....	....	....	....	....
St. Charles (55)	MC 314 949-3200	....	....	....	....	....	....	....
St. Clair (4)	MC 314 629-0333	James A Barns	Marv S Harman	Darlene J Coons	....	....	Tom A Yoden	....
St. James (3)	MC 314 265-7011	Nelson A Hart	....	Marilyn S Linke	Ladonna S Bailey	Nick Green	Richard Woolsey	Kenneth A Young
St. John (7)	CM 314 427-8700	....	....	....	....	....	....	....
St. Joseph (72)	CM 816 271-4610	Larry R Stobbs Sr	Ryne P Lilly	Paula Heyde	Pamela Windsor	John McGarry	Arthur Kelly	Jerry Burris
St. Louis (397)	MC 314 622-3561	Freeman Bosley Jr	Lloyd Jordan	....	Virvus Jones	Neil Svetanics	Clarence Harmon	Dave Visintainer
St. Peters (46)	MC 314 928-1800	....	....	....	....	....	....	....
Ste. Genevieve (4)	CM 314 883-5400	William Anderson	....	Betty A Seibel	....	Jerry P Roth	David Beckermann	....
Sugar Creek (4)	MC 816 252-4400	....	....	....	....	....	....	....
Sullivan (6)	MC 314 468-4612	Elmer Cowan	John Butz	Janice Nolie	John Butz	....	George R Counts	....
Sunset Hills (5)	MC 314 849-3400	....	....	....	....	....	....	....
Town And Country (10)	MC 314 432-6606	Peggy Symes	James Robinson	Joan Klinghammer	Betty Cotner	....	Salvador Delmar	Douglas Hopkins
Trenton (6)	MC 816 359-2013	Nick McHargue	David Blackburn	Cindy Simpson	....	Bill Vaughn	Eddie Koenig	....
Union (6)	MC 314 583-3600	....	....	....	....	....	....	....
University City (40)	CM 314 862-6767	Janet Majerus	Frank Ollendorff	Dolores A Miller	Willie Norfleet	Bob Metcalf	Lee Payne	Allan Dieckgraefe
Valley Park (4)	MC 314 225-5171	....	....	....	....	....	....	....
Vandalia (3)	CM 314 594-6186	Ramon Barnes	Todd Hileman	Kimberly Wood	Sharon Myers	Ramon Barnes	George Hannaford	....
Warrensburg (15)	CM 816 747-9131	....	....	....	....	....	....	....
Warrenton (4)	MC 314 456-3535	Greg Costello	....	Eileen Boehm	Anita Koelling	....	Ray Clark	Denneth Schwerdt
Washington (11)	MC 314 390-1006	Bernie Hillermann	James A Briggs	Dolly Gerstenkorn	Janet Braun	Willard Halmich	Dan Rowden	Gary Thornhill
Waynesville (3)	MC 314 774-6171	Bill Ransdall	John T Tinsley	Barbara A Stinson	....	Danny Fry	John Mellan	John T Tinsler
Webb City (7)	MC 417 673-4651	....	....	....	....	....	....	....
Webster Groves (23)	CM 314 963-5300	Terri Williams	Carl E Ramey	Lynne N Greene	Carl E Ramey	Jack R Buechler	Gene A Young	Dennis L Wells
Wellston (4)	MC 314 385-1015	Robert Powell	....	Kate Cole	Rose Jackson	....	Robert Young	Eldright White
Wentzville (5)	MC 314 327-5101	Darrel B Lackey	H Joe McReynolds	Lou Ann Wibe	Dennis Walsh	....	Kenneth T Conlee	Roger Cox
West Plains (9)	CO 417 256-7176	Harry Kelly	Gerald Elmore	Constance Shelton	Constance Shelton	Hubert Redburn	James Boze	Jim Davidson
Windsor (3)	MC 816 647-3512	....	....	....	....	....	....	....
Woodson Terrace (4)	MC 314 427-2600	William Ratchford	....	Dorothy Rickard	....	....	Thomas A McKay	Stephen Wipfler
MONTANA (29)								
Anaconda-Deer Lodge (10)	CM 406 563-8421	....	....	....	....	Tom Shagina	....	....
Billings (81)	CM 406 657-8204	Richard L Larsen	Mark S Watson	Marita R Herold	Nathan R Tubergen	Lorren L Ballard	David C Ward	Kenneth L Haag
Bozeman (23)	CM 406 586-3321	John Vincent	James E Wysocki	Robin S Sullivan	....	Aaron E Holst	Charles R Boyer	Phillip J Forbes
Butte-Silver Bow (33)	MC 406 723-8262	....	....	....	....	....	....	....
Columbia Falls (3)	MC 406 892-4391	Lyle Christman	Roger W Hopkins	Connie Konopatzke	Connie Konopatzke	Don Barnhart	....	Claude Tesmer
Conrad (3)	MC 406 278-3623	Tom Hammerbacker	....	Mike Eve	....	....	Gary Dent	Steve Ruhd
Cut Bank (3)	MC 406 873-5526	William McCauley	....	Marie B Mitch	....	Robert J Taylor	Joseph A Gauthier	Lorin N Lowry
Deer Lodge (3)	MC 406 846-3649	....	....	....	....	....	....	....
Dillon (4)	MC 406 683-4245	....	....	....	....	....	....	....
Forsyth (2)	MC 406 356-2521	....	....	....	....	....	....	....

Directory 1/9 continued

MUNICIPAL OFFICIALS IN U.S. CITIES OVER 2,500

City, 1990 population figures (000 omitted), form of government	Municipal phone number	Mayor/ chief elected official	Appointed administrator	City clerk/ city secretary	Finance officer	Fire chief	Police chief	Public works director
MONTANA (29) continued								
Glasgow (4)	MC 406 228-2476	....	....	....	....	....	....	....
Glendive (5)	MC 406 365-3318	....	....	....	....	....	....	....
Great Falls (55)	CM 406 771-1180	Gayle Morris	John Lawton	Peggy Bourne	Timothy Magee	Richard Meisinger	Robert Jones	Erling Tufte
Hamilton (3)	MC 406 363-2101	Laurel Hegstad	Don Williamson	L Higginbotham	Don Williamson	Buzz Greenup	Allan Auch	Don Williamson
Hardin (3)	MC 406 665-2113	Ron Adams	....	....	Nancy Young	Ron Johnson	....	Larry Vandersloot
Havre (10)	MC 406 265-6719	....	....	....	....	....	....	....
Helena (25)	CM 406 447-8404	H Kay McKenna	William Verwolf	Debbie Pulliam	Shelly Laine	Don Hurni	William Ware	Kim Milburn
Kalispell (12)	MC 406 752-6600	Douglas D Rauthe	Bruce Williams	Deborah Gifford	Amy H Robertson	Ted A Waggener	Addison Clark	Robert H Babb
Laurel (6)	MC 406 628-8791	Chuck Rodgers	....	Don Hackmann	....	Darrell McGillen	Mike Atkinson	....
Lewistown (6)	MC 406 538-2302	....	....	....	....	....	....	....
Libby (3)	MC 406 293-2731	Fred A Brown	....	Kim D Aarstad	....	Charle Comer	....	Bill Kemp
Livingston (7)	CM 406 222-6120	....	....	....	....	....	....	....
Miles City (8)	CM 406 232-3462	....	....	....	....	....	....	....
Missoula (43)	MC 406 523-4700	....	....	....	....	....	....	....
Polson (3)	MC 406 883-2131	....	....	....	....	....	....	....
Shelby (3)	MC 406 434-5222	Larry J Bonderud	....	....	Jo Ann Wright	....	....	John B Boettcher
Sidney (5)	MC 406 482-2809	....	....	....	....	....	....	....
Whitefish (4)	CM 406 862-2640	....	....	....	....	....	....	....
Wolf Point (3)	MC 406 653-1852	....	....	....	....	....	....	....
NEBRASKA (57)								
Alliance (10)	CM 308 762-5400	Mike Dafney	Bret A Jones	Linda Jines	....	Howard Taylor Jr	Robert Jatczak	....
Auburn (3)	MC 402 274-3420	....	....	....	....	....	....	....
Aurora (4)	MC 402 694-6992	Kenneth Harter	Michael Bair	Erma Luth	Erma Luth	Harlan Schafer	Wm Gage	Wm Vandeman
Beatrice (12)	MC 402 223-3569	David I Maurstad	James W Bauer	Gwen D Grabouski	....	Darrell Eastin	Bruce E Lang	James W Bauer
Bellevue (31)	MC 402 293-3000	....	....	....	....	....	....	....
Blair (7)	MC 402 426-4191	Jerome Jenny	Rodney A Storm	Alice Diedrichsen	....	....	Marvin Doeden	Warren Whitaker
Broken Bow (4)	MC 308 872-5831	....	....	....	....	....	....	....
Central City (3)	MC 308 946-3806	Vernie Smith	Fritz Behring	David H Rish	....	Tim Bolling	Dennis Wagner	Mel Burkhardt
Chadron (6)	CM 308 432-4444	Cliff Hanson	Carl Dierks	Donna Rust	....	Robert Geister	Theodore Vastine	Milo Rust
Columbus (19)	MC 402 564-8584	....	....	....	....	....	....	....
Cozad (4)	MC 308 784-3907	....	....	....	....	....	....	....
Crete (5)	MC 402 826-4311	Harlyn Crisman	....	Gary L Yank	....	Arthur Henning Jr	Rick Nettifee	George Beyer
Dakota City (1)	MC 402 987-3448	Ron Brunton	Austin Edmondson	Austin Edmondson	....	John Norris	....	Danny Rager
David City (3)	MC 402 367-3135	Stephen Smith	Douglas C Rix	Joan E Kovar	....	Michael C Hiatt	Stephen M Sunday	....
Fairbury (4)	MC 402 729-2476	Lewis Mason	....	Lila Hannappel	....	Ronald Southwick	Rick Carmichael	Michael Beachler
Falls City (5)	CM 402 245-2707	Stephen P Kottich	Martin R Gist	Martin R Gist	....	Alan Romine	Norman Hemmerling	Larry R Merz
Fremont (24)	MC 402 727-2630	....	....	....	....	....	....	....
Fullerton (1)	MC 308 536-2893	....	Bob Higel	....	....	....	....	....
Geneva (2)	MC 402 759-3109	Gaylord Songster	Bob Higel	Barbara Whitley	M Christiancy	Bob Hofferber	Bob Taylor	Bob Higel
Gering (8)	MC 308 436-5096	....	....	....	....	....	....	....
Gordon (2)	CM 308 282-0837	....	....	....	....	....	....	....
Gothenburg (3)	MC 308 537-3677	Richard L Blase	Bruce Clymer	Connie Stull	....	Dale Franzen	Randell Olson	William J Crouch
Grand Island (39)	MC 308 385-5444	Ernest L Dobesh	Zachary Z Zoul	Cindy Cartwright	Chuck D Haase	Jim Rowell	Eugene Q Watson	Wayne Bennett
Grant (1)	MC 308 352-2100	....	Robert G Francis	....	....	....	....	....
Hastings (23)	MC 402 461-2309	J Phillip Odom	Barbara Bramblett	Connie Hartman	....	James Mitera	....	Dave Wacker
Holdrege (6)	MC 308 995-8681	James Van Marter	Norman Melton	Norman Melton	....	James Wagner	Ken Jackson	Larry Duval
Kearney (24)	CM 308 233-3215	Ron Larsen	Gary Greer	Michaelle Trembly	Wendell Wessels	Gene Rains	Steve Lamken	Tom Murray
Kimball (3)	MC 308 235-3639	Thomas Wilson	Bruce Smith	Harold Farrar	....	Art McEntee	Billy Shank	....
La Vista (10)	MC 402 331-4343	Harold Anderson	Donald Eikmeier	Dorothy McGinnis	Judy Nemetz Jr	....	John Packett	Ed McGinnis
Lexington (7)	CM 308 324-2341	....	....	....	....	....	....	....
Lincoln (192)	MC 402 471-7171	Michael Johanns	Polly McMullen	Paul Malzer	Jamie Warner	Michael Merwick	Thomas Casady	Richard Erixson
Madison (2)	CM 402 454-3412	Wayne Glasser	Donald Barnhart	George Moehnert	....	Raymond Keifer	....	Jim Lewis
Mc Cook (8)	CM 308 345-2022	Philip Lyons	John E Carter	Lea Ann Doak	....	Cliff Clapp	Richard Brunswick	Marty Conroy
Minden (3)	MC 308 832-1820	Peter M Jensen	Brent Lewis	Dick Young	Dick Young	Ralph Layton	James Huff	Brent Lewis
Nebraska City (7)	CO 402 873-5515	Larry Rawlings	....	Kay Dammast	Kay Dammast	Charles Swanson	Kent Roumpf	William Brockley
Norfolk (21)	MC 402 644-8720	Harley Rector	Michael Nolan	Elizabeth Deck	Randy Gates	Michael Smith	William Mizner	Dennis Smith
North Platte (23)	MC 308 534-2610	G Keith Richadson	Mark Roath	Bill May	Bill May	Richard Pedersen	Martin Gutschenri	Larry Linstrom
O'Neill (4)	MC 402 336-3640	Dennis Shannahan	....	James Schwartz	....	Scott Menish	Gary Smith	....
Ogallala (5)	CM 308 284-6001	....	Gary Rimington	Louis Kinnan	....	Buck Bassett	Joe Humphrey	Toney Krajewski
Omaha (336)	MC 402 444-5000	....	....	....	....	....	....	....
Ord (2)	MC 308 728-5791	Roger Goldfish	....	Sandy Kruml	....	Doug Sedlacek	John Young	Paul Markowski
Papillion (10)	MC 402 339-3376	....	....	....	....	....	....	....
Plainview (1)	MC 402 582-4928	Michael Bernecker	Mark Kober	Jayne Gentzler	....	Doug Nissen	Bruce Yosten	....
Plattsmouth (6)	MC 402 296-2522	Ronald Buethe	Howard C Parrott	Rosalyn Covert	Howard C Parrott	Bob Wagner	Ronald Duckworth	....
Ralston (6)	MC 402 331-6677	....	....	....	....	....	....	....
Scottsbluff (14)	CM 308 632-4136	Donald Overman	Keith Jantz	Lynn Gibb	Margaret Elder	Jon Surbeck	James Livingston	....
Seward (6)	MC 402 643-2928	Roger E Glawatz	Daniel Berlowitz	Debra Schaefer	....	Terry Kamprath	C Marlin Sturgis	....
Sidney (6)	CM 308 254-5300	Robert Van Vleet	Marlan V Ferguson	G F Anthony	....	Keith Stone	Richard T Willis	Lawrence Heinrich
South Sioux City (10)	MC 402 494-7500	Vernie A Larson	Lance A Hedquist	Brenda Westphalen	....	Jerry Stolze	Scot E Ford	Jeff Harcum
Superior (2)	MC 402 879-4713	Lloyd Rust	....	Dewayne L Aberg	....	Mike Fenimore	Robert Allgood	Richard Elliott
Sutton (..)	MC 402 773-4225	Virgil D Ulmer	Malcolm L Tilberg	Sherrie Bartell	....	Larry T Nuss	Richard Fringer	Kevin Finnegan
Valentine (3)	CM 402 376-2323	Donn Peterson	Rick Medema	John Hanzlicek	....	Allen Brott	James Lutter	....
Wahoo (4)	MC 402 443-3222	Donald Virgl	....	Phyllis Nozicka	....	Rodney Kuss	John Kolterman	Brian Skeahan
Wakefield (1)	MC 402 287-2080	....	....	....	....	....	....	....
Wayne (5)	MC 402 375-1733	Robert A Carhart	Joseph H Salitros	Betty A McGuire	....	Ken Sitzman	Vern Fairchild	Vern Schulz
West Point (3)	MC 402 372-2468	....	....	....	....	....	....	....
York (8)	MC 402 362-4407	Ken Kunze	Jack R Kidder	C Jean Thiele	Jack R Kidder	Mark M Grosshans	Donald D Kluge	Orville Davidson
NEVADA (12)								
Boulder City (13)	CM 702 293-9202	Irls Bletsch	George Forbes	Vicki Bergdale	Robert Boyer	Dean Molburg	David Mullin	Alan Gove
Carson City-Ormsby (40)	CM 702 887-2103	....	....	....	....	....	....	....
Elko (15)	CM 702 738-5176	Jim Polkinghorne	Lorry Liparelli	Giuliana Murphy	....	Orvis Cash	Robert Songer	Charles Williams
Ely (5)	MC 702 289-2430	Joann Macone	David Olsen	Jolynn Pescio	....	....	....	Max Vigil
Fallon (6)	MC 702 423-5104	Robert Erickson	....	Gary Cordes	....	James Allison	Louis Fetheroff	Larry White
Henderson (65)	CM 702 565-2070	Robert Groesbeck	Philip Speight	Colleen Bell	Steven Hanson	Lester Haskett	James Goff	Mark Calhoun
Las Vegas (258)	CM 702 229-6011	Janis L Jones	Larry K Barton	Kathy Tighe	Steven P Houchens	Clell A West	....	Richard D Goecke
North Las Vegas (48)	CM 702 649-5811	James K Seastrand	Michael H Dyal	Eileen M Sevigny	Vytas Vaitkus	Michael A Massey	Ronald E Lusch	Gary W Holler
Reno (134)	CM 702 334-2000	....	....	....	....	....	....	....
Sparks (53)	CM 702 353-2345	Bruce Breslow	Terry J Reynolds	Deborine Peebles	Terri Thomas	Ron Irwln	John Dotson	Shaun Carey
Wells (1)	MC 702 752-3355	George Sh Yan	Michael Cosgrove	....	Mary Lou Ray	Randy Dedman	L James Hertz	Frederick Schacht
Winnemucca (6)	MC 702 623-6339	Paul Vesco	Stephen West	Mary Echeverria	....	Walter Johnstone	Donnell Wright	Eugenio Bernardi

Directory 1/9 continued — MUNICIPAL OFFICIALS IN U.S. CITIES OVER 2,500

City, 1990 population figures (000 omitted), form of government		Municipal phone number	Mayor/ chief elected official	Appointed administrator	City clerk/ city secretary	Finance officer	Fire chief	Police chief	Public works director
NEW HAMPSHIRE (84)									
Allenstown t (5)	TM	603 485-4276	....	....	....	....	....	....	....
Amherst t (9)	TM	603 673-6041	....	....	....	....	....	....	....
Atkinson t (5)	TM	603 362-5266	....	....	....	....	....	....	....
Auburn t (4)	TM	603 483-5052	Paula Marzloff	....	Nancy Gagnon	....	Bruce Phillips	Edward Picard	....
Barrington t (6)	TM	603 664-9007	Peter Royce	John F Dolan	Muriel Leocha	....	Russell Hayes	Richard Conway	Ronald Landry
Bedford t (13)	CM	603 472-5242	Edward P Moran	Artie L Robersen	Edith Schmidtchen	Anthony T Plante	Robert A Fabich	David C Bailey	Edward S Kelly
Belmont t (6)	TM	603 267-8300	David A Rolfe	Frederick W Welch	Doralyn M Harper	Brenda Paquette	Albert Akerstrom	Michael McCarty	Luther M Brown
Berlin (12)	CM	603 752-7532	Yvonne Coulombe	M Berkowitz	Lise Malia	Aline Boucher	Paul Fortier	Alan Tardif	Maurice Wheeler
Boscawen t (4)	RT	603 796-2426	Thomas Danko	Sherlene Fisher	Jodi Welch	Patricia Knight	Roland Bartlett	Mark Pepler	Richard Hollins
Bow t (6)	TM	603 228-1187	Eric Anderson	Albert R St Cyr	C Batchelder	....	H Dana Abbott	Peter Cheney	....
Candia t (4)	TM	603 483-8101	Peter J Onksen	....	Christine Dupere	Carolyn Emerson	Leonard Wilson	S Agrafiotis	Ronald Severino
Charlestown t (5)	RT	603 826-4400	Jon B LeClair	Marianne S Marsha	....	....	Robert W Burns	Frederick Domini	....
Chesterfield t (3)	TM	603 363-4624	....	....	....	....	....	....	....
Claremont (14)	CM	603 542-7002	Allen Whipple	Robert W Jackson	Doris J Nelson	Jeannine T Perry	Thomas G Ford	Michael Prozzo Jr	Peter G Goewey
Concord (36)	CM	603 225-8570	William Veroneau	Julia N Griffin	Eliz Campbell	James Howard	John M Dionne	David G Walchak	John Forrestall
Conway t (8)	TM	603 447-3811	John A Cuddy	James Somerville	John D Stevens	Mary E Conlon	Larry B Wade	Robert Mullen	Paul Degliangeli
Derry t (30)	MC	603 432-6100	Arthur McLean	William Jackson	Pauline Myers	Grace Collette	Ronald Gagnon	Edward Garone	Alan Swan
Dover (25)	CM	603 743-6000	Patricia Torr	Paul G Beecher	Karen Larson	J J Harrington	David F Bibber	William Fenniman	....
Durham t (12)	CM	603 868-5571	William J Healy	Laurence R Wood	Linda Exdahl	Clara Varney	Robert Wood	Paul Gowan	Joseph Grady
Enfield t (4)	TM	603 632-4201	C James Martel	S DeMontigny	Ilene P Reed	....	David J Crate	Peter H Giese	....
Epping t (5)	TM	603 679-5441	Kim Sullivan	....	Linda Foley	....	Richar Marcotte	Gregory Dodge	....
Epsom t (4)	TM	603 736-9002	John F Hickey	Gloria J Reeves	M Ellsworth	....	R Stewart Yeaton	....	Gregory Bowen
Exeter t (12)	TM	603 778-0591	Paul Binette	George N Olson	Linda Hartson	....	J Carbonneau	S Mac Kinnon	Keith Noyes
Farmington t (6)	TM	603 755-2208	Barbara Spear	Richard Magnifico	Kathy Vickers	....	Richard Moolton	Barry Carr	Clark Hackett
Franklin (8)	MC	603 934-3900	Thomas P Matzke	James C Pitts	Elaine S Rayno	James Fenn	Scott Clarenbach	Douglas Boyd	Alfred Elliott
Gilford t (6)	RT	603 524-7438	Philip D Labonte	David R Caron	Debra Eastman	Geoffrey Ruggles	Michael Mooney	Evans Juris	Sheldon Morgan
Goffstown t (15)	TM	603 497-5701	Vivian Blondeau	John Scruton	Marlene Ganans	Twila Barss	Richard Fletcher	Stephen Monier	Donald Hambidge
Gorham t (3)	TM	603 466-3322	Yves Zornio	Kelly Goddard	Grace Savage	Diane Legere	Raymond Chandler	Rodney Collins	Roger Guilmette
Hampstead t (7)	TM	603 329-5011	....	....	....	....	....	....	....
Hampton t (12)	TM	603 926-6766	Thomas Gillick	Hunter Rieseberg	Jane Kelley	John Adams	William Sullivan	Robert Mark	John Hangen
Hanover t (9)	TM	603 643-4123	Marilyn W Black	Clifford Vermilya	Elizabeth B Banks	B Michael Gilbar	Roger Bradley	Nicholas Giaccone	Richard Hauger
Haverhill t (4)	TM	603 747-3318	....	....	....	....	....	....	....
Henniker t (4)	RT	603 428-3221	W Belanger	E Wojnowski	K Johnson	....	B Ayer	T Russell	T Woodley
Hillsborough t (4)	TM	603 464-3877	Joseph M Eaton Jr	James Coffey	Deborah McDonald	....	Richard Ritter	Frank P Cate	....
Hinsdale t (4)	RT	603 336-5401	....	....	....	....	....	....	....
Hollis t (6)	RT	603 465-2209	....	....	....	....	....	....	....
Hooksett t (9)	TM	603 485-8471	Joe Wilson	Gerald Cottrell	Leslie Nepveu	Matt Shevenell	Ray O' Brien	James Oliver	Roger Bergeron
Hopkinton t (5)	TM	603 746-3170	John Prewitt	Alice Monchamp	Thomas Johnson	....	Peter Russell	Ira Migdal	David Story
Hudson t (20)	CO	603 886-6024	Ann Seabury	Paul Sharon	Cecile Nichols	Lydia Angell	Brian Mason	Richard Gendron	....
Jaffrey t (5)	CM	603 532-7445	Jeanne L Labrie	Jonathan Sistare	Maria Chamberlain	....	John A White	Gary A Phillips	Floyd N Roberts
Keene (22)	CM	603 357-9804	....	....	....	....	....	....	....
Kingston t (6)	TM	603 642-3342	....	....	....	....	....	....	....
Laconia (16)	CM	603 524-1520	....	....	....	....	....	....	....
Lancaster t (4)	TM	603 788-3391	....	....	....	....	....	....	....
Lebanon (12)	CM	603 448-1720	....	....	....	....	....	....	....
Lincoln t (1)	CM	603 745-2757	Deanna Huot	Kalene H Roberts	Sandy Dovholuk	....	Clifton Dauphine	R Craig Ohlson	Clifton Dauphine
Litchfield t (6)	TM	603 424-4045	....	....	....	....	....	....	....
Littleton t (6)	TM	603 444-3996	Kathryn Taylor	Michael Farrell	Faye White	Melodie Hodgdon	Fred Whitcomb	Louis Babin	Larry Jackson
Londonderry t (20)	TM	603 432-1110	Arthur E Rugg	Richard Plante	....	Peter Curro	Alan J Sypek	Richard J Bannon	....
Manchester (100)	MC	603 624-6500	....	....	....	....	....	....	....
Meredith t (5)	TM	603 279-4538	James F Hughes	Peter G Russell	....	....	Fred Copp	John P Curran	Barry Cotton
Merrimack t (22)	TM	603 424-2331	Edward J Silva	Richard S Borden	Betty Spence	Robert T Levan	Charles Q Hall	Joseph R Devine	Earle M Chesley
Milford t (12)	TM	603 673-2257	John E Ruonala	Lee F Mayhew	Wilfred Leduc	K Chambers	R Tortorelli	Steven C Sexton	Robert E Courage
Nashua (80)	MC	603 880-3300	....	....	....	....	....	....	....
New London t (3)	TM	603 526-4821	....	....	....	....	....	....	....
Newmarket t (7)	CM	603 659-3617	Priscilla Shaw	Frank Edmunds	Judith Harvey	....	Charles Clark	Charles Reynolds	David Walker
Newport t (6)	TM	603 863-1877	Virginia Irwln	Daniel O' Neill	Karlene Stoddard	Paul Brown	John Marcotte	David Hoyt	Larry Wiggins
Newton t (3)	TM	603 382-4405	....	....	....	....	....	....	....
North Hampton t (4)	TM	603 964-8087	Mary B Herbert	Beverley Frenette	Delores Chase	....	....	Frank Beliveau	Robert Strout
Northfield t (4)	TM	603 286-7039	Thomas Jordan	Joyce Johnson	Eliza Conde	Roland Seymour	Harold Harbour	Paul Leary	Albert Cross
Northumberland t (2)	CM	603 636-1450	David Goulet	John Normand	....	....	James Sanborn	Harry L Rice Jr	John Normand
Pelham t (9)	RT	603 635-8233	William McDevitt	Peter R Flynn	Linda M Lavallee	Doris S Mannies	E David Fisher	David F Rowell	....
Pembroke t (7)	TM	603 485-4747	John B Goff	David L Stack	James F Goff	....	Richard Chase	Thomas F Iverson	Henry Malo
Peterborough t (5)	TM	603 924-3201	Jefferson Allen	John Isham	Robert Lambert	....	Stephen Black	Quentin Estey Jr	John Isham
Pittsfield t (4)	TM	603 435-6773	....	....	....	....	....	....	....
Plaistow t (7)	CM	603 382-5200	Mary M Collins	Donald W Whitman	Barbara Tavitian	....	Donald Petzold	Stephen Savage	....
Plymouth t (6)	RT	603 536-1731	Richard M Piper	M O' Connor	....	....	Brian Thibeault	W Daniel Libby	Richard J Gonsalv
Portsmouth (26)	CM	603 431-2000	Eileen Foley	James McSweeney	Daphne Savramis	T Jankowski	Randal Sage	William Burke	Steven Parkinson
Raymond t (9)	TM	603 895-4735	Edward Varney	Martha S Roy	....	Lavaughn Wikstrom	Kevin Pratt	James Murphy	Dennis McCarthy
Rindge t (5)	TM	603 899-5181	....	....	....	....	....	....	....
Rochester (27)	CM	603 335-7503	Roland Roberge	Gary Stenhouse	Gail Varney	R LaRochelle	Mark Dellner	Donald Vittum	Martin Laferte
Rye t (5)	TM	603 964-5523	Martin S Quirk	Janet C Thompson	Jane E Ireland	....	Ronald M Lima	Bradley B Loomis	C Moynahan
Salem t (26)	TM	603 893-5731	Robert Campbell	Barry M Brenner	Barbara Lessard	Frances Bernard	John Nadeau	Stephen McKinnon	George Sealy
Seabrook t (7)	RT	603 474-3311	E Thibodeau	E Russell Bailey	Virginia L Small	....	Jerry W Brown	Paul J Cronin	Veron G Dow
Somersworth (11)	CM	603 692-4262	....	....	....	....	....	....	....
Stratham t (5)	TM	603 772-4741	Martin Wool	Paul R Deschaine	Joyce Rowe	....	Ralph S Walker	Michael Daley	Fred Hutton Jr
Swanzey t (6)	RT	603 352-7411	Bonnie J Tolman	Elizabeth Fox	Carol Frazier	....	Jeffrey Hurt	Larss Ogren	Elton Blood
Tilton t (3)	TM	603 286-4521	Kenneth Money	Betty Pierce	Gayle Twombly	Thomas Gallant	Harold Harbour	Charles Chase	David Wadleigh
Walpole t (3)	TM	603 756-3672	James M Freeman	....	Elaine Wheeler	Sheila Turner	....	....	Robert Smith
Weare t (6)	TM	603 529-7525	Merrill J Shepard	....	Evelyn Conner	....	C Rhodenizer	David M Mason	Lloyd Bailey
Wilton t (3)	TM	603 654-9451	....	....	....	....	....	....	....
Winchester t (4)	RT	603 239-4951	Vernon A Jones	Patricia B Rogers	Marjorie M Austin	....	Richard Lapoint	James E Harrison	Dale R Gray
Windham t (9)	RT	603 432-7732	....	....	....	....	....	....	....
Wolfeboro t (5)	TM	603 569-8161	K Mac Donald	Paul J Skowron	Patricia Waterman	Carroll D Piper	Michael Howard	Stanley E Stevens	Marty Bilafer
NEW JERSEY (357)									
Aberdeen tp (17)	CM	908 583-4200	Brian P Murphy	James M Cox	Ann T Barker	Robert Daetsch	Louis Auriemma	Brian G Dougherty	James Lauro
Absecon (7)	MC	609 641-0663	Peter C Elco	Edward N Perugini	Doris Pauciello	Theodore Nell	....	Richard Mulvihill	Angelo Giorano
Allendale b (6)	MC	201 818-4400	Albert H Klomburg	Thomas F Carroll	Lorraine Stark	Paula Favata	R Cauwenberghs	Robert Herndon	George Higbie
Alpha b (3)	MC	908 454-0088	Thomas Fey	....	Alicia Konolash	....	....	John Hajdu	Clarence Deemer
Andover tp (5)	MC	201 383-8299	....	....	....	....	....	....	....
Asbury Park (17)	CM	201 775-2100	....	....	....	....	....	....	....
Atlantic City (38)	MC	609 347-5300	....	....	....	....	....	....	....
Atlantic Highlands b (5)	MC	908 291-1444	R Schoelffing	W Bishof	P Puza	C Campbell	W Curry	C Mazzarella	W Bishof

Directory 1/9 continued

MUNICIPAL OFFICIALS IN U.S. CITIES OVER 2,500

City, 1990 population figures (000 omitted), form of government	Municipal phone number	Mayor/ chief elected official	Appointed administrator	City clerk/ city secretary	Finance officer	Fire chief	Police chief	Public works director
NEW JERSEY (357) continued								
Audubon b (9)	CO 609 547-0711	Alfred W Murray	....	Lee C Daniels	Margaret Meekins	....	William V Taulane	Anthony Pugliese
Barrington b (7)	MC 609 547-0706	....	....	....	....	....	....	....
Bayonne (61)	MC 201 858-6010	....	....	....	....	....	....	....
Beachwood b (9)	MC 201 286-6000	....	....	....	....	....	....	....
Belleville tp (34)	CM 201 450-3300	James Messina	Stephen J Cuccio	Mary Lou Hood	Arthur Minsky	Robert Caruso	Raymond Kimble	Charles Cerami
Bellmawr b (13)	MC 609 933-1313	....	....	....	....	....	....	....
Belmar b (6)	MC 908 681-1176	K Pringle	J Ascione	C Ormsbee	C Ormsbee	T Mihalic	R Lynch	P Greco
Bergenfield b (24)	CM 201 387-4055	Chas F McDowell	Gerard V Leary	Gerard V Leary	Norman L Gust	Gerard Naylis	Richard Baroch	Robert Bartley
Berkeley Heights tp (12)	MC 908 464-2700	Jeanne P Viscito	Joseph V Cara	Gertrude Gonnelli	Angela Rica	....	Theodore P Rica	Frederick Miller
Berlin b (6)	MC 609 767-7777	....	....	....	....	....	....	....
Bernards tp (17)	MC 908 766-2510	Jerome E Kienlen	H Steven Wood	Rita M Osborne	Dorothy J Stikna	....	C Fortenbacher	Michael Beale
Bernardsville b (7)	MC 908 766-3000	Peter S Palmer	Ralph A Maresca	Sandra G Jones	Ralph A Maresca	James Pickell	Thom J Sciaretta	Allan Rome
Beverly (3)	MC 609 387-1881	Frank R Costello	....	Theresa M Lowden	Janice Johnsen	George Meredith	Harry G Craythorn	....
Bloomfield tp (45)	MC 201 680-4000	....	....	....	....	....	....	....
Bloomingdale b (8)	MC 201 838-0778	Anne DuHaime	Edward Pomerantz	Jane Febbi	Robert Hammer	Richard Boud	Edward Fletcher	Kenneth Barrett
Bogota b (8)	MC 201 342-1736	....	....	....	....	....	....	....
Boonton t (8)	MC 201 299-7724	Daniel Gregory	William B Wahl	Ann Marie Fitch	William B Wahl	Mark Janton	Robert L Banks	Stephen Koval
Bordentown (4)	CO 609 298-0604	....	....	....	....	....	....	....
Bound Brook b (9)	MC 908 356-0833	Ronald Fasanello	....	Thomas R Brodbeck	....	....	Anthony Cimino	Mark Cassebaum
Bradley Beach b (4)	CO 908 776-2999	Stephen Schueler	....	Phyllis Quixley	Charles Ormsbee	Keith Dilello	Robert Denardo	Leroy Christensen
Branchburg tp (11)	MC 908 526-1300	....	....	....	....	....	....	....
Bridgeton (19)	MC 609 455-3230	....	....	....	....	....	....	....
Bridgewater tp (33)	MC 201 725-6300	James T Dowden	William O' Neill	Bette Nuse	Peter P Sepelya	Gary Ewald	Richard Voorhees	Hugh McCluskey
Brielle b (4)	MC 908 528-6600	Thomas B Nicol	Thomas F Nolan	Thomas F Nolan	Karen S Brisben	Anthony Scarano	Harry Whelan	William Burkhardt
Brigantine (11)	CM 609 266-7600	Philip J Guenther	Thom E Ciccarone	Lois O' Connor	George McDermott	Darryl Platt	Guy Wilkins	Harold W Lakes
Buena b (4)	MC 609 697-1780	....	....	....	....	....	....	....
Burlington (10)	MC 609 386-1195	Robert Vandegrift	Barry Moore	Alexader Shultz	K Mac Millan	Ernest Schroeder	Leroy Breece	Vincent Calisti
Butler b (7)	MC 201 838-7200	....	....	....	....	....	....	....
Byram tp (8)	CM 201 347-2500	....	....	....	....	....	....	....
Caldwell tp (8)	MC 201 226-6100	....	....	....	....	....	....	....
Camden (87)	MC 609 757-7150	Arnold W Webster	Patrick J Keating	Dorothy A Burley	Richard Cinaglia	Kenneth L Penn	George D Pugh	Carl E Bowles
Cape May (5)	CM 609 884-9525	....	....	....	....	....	....	....
Carlstadt b (6)	MC 201 939-2850	....	....	....	....	....	....	....
Carteret b (19)	MC 908 541-3800	Peter J Sica	....	Kathleen Barney	Patrick Deblasio	Richard Greenberg	Joseph Sica	Ted Surick
Cedar Grove tp (12)	CM 201 239-1410	....	....	....	....	....	....	....
Chatham b (8)	MC 201 635-0674	Barbara L Hall	Henry M Underhill	Henry M Underhill	Dorothy Klein	Greg Henrich	Donald Cardinal	Thomas Zilinek
Cherry Hill tp (69)	MC 609 488-7800	....	....	....	....	....	....	....
Cinnaminson tp (15)	MC 609 829-6000	....	....	....	....	....	....	....
Clark tp (15)	MC 908 388-3600	....	....	....	....	....	....	....
Clayton b (6)	MC 609 881-2882	Ken Landis	R DeVilla Santa	R DeVilla Santa	R DeVilla Santa	Al Freck	Frank Winters	Edward Bell
Clementon b (6)	MC 609 783-0284	....	....	....	....	....	....	....
Cliffside Park b (20)	MC 201 945-3456	....	....	....	....	....	....	....
Clifton (72)	CM 201 470-5800	....	....	....	....	....	....	....
Clinton tp (11)	MC 908 735-5328	....	....	....	....	....	....	....
Closter b (8)	MC 201 784-0760	Edward Rogan	Robert Anderson	Loretta Castano	Robert Anderson	Alfonso Young	John Rose	Harry Lampman
Collingswood b (15)	CO 609 854-0720	Frank F Law Jr	Jean DiGennaro	Joanne McCormack	Sandra Leahy	Robert Eckert	John Spavlik	Frank F Law Jr
Colts Neck t (9)	MC 908 462-5470	....	....	....	....	....	....	....
Cranford tp (23)	CM 908 709-7200	Carolyn J Vollero	John F Laezza	John F Laezza	Thomas J Grady	Arthur A Kiamie	Harry W Wilde	Robert Maiberger
Cresskill b (8)	MC 201 569-5400	John Bergamini	....	Dorothy M Giguere	Robert V Camasto	Thomas Lepore	Frank V Tino Jr	Gerald Crum
Delran tp (13)	MC 609 461-7734	Thomas DiLauro	Jeffrey S Hatcher	B Porreca	Louis Kaniecki	Craig Manning	Arthur Saul	Edward Bart
Demarest b (5)	MC 201 768-0167	Richard Schooler	....	Carol A Kroepke	Maureen Neville	Richard Motta	James Powderley	Fred Shaffer
Denville tp (14)	MC 201 627-1234	....	....	....	....	....	....	....
Deptford tp (24)	CM 609 845-5300	....	....	....	....	....	....	....
Dover t (15)	MC 201 366-2200	....	....	....	....	....	....	....
Dumont b (17)	MC 201 387-5022	Donald C Winant	Marvin Katz	Beth Shafer	Marvin Katz	John Ruggero	Michal Affrunti	John Cook
Dunellen b (7)	MC 908 968-3033	Lawrence Anzovino	John B Cahill	John B Cahill	G Ross Babal	William Drake	Joseph DeBiase	Brian O' Neill
East Brunswick tp (44)	MC 908 390-6820	Ira Oskowsky	Raymond Stone	Elizabeth Kiss	Lou Mason Neely	....	John Cross	Michael Opaleski
East Hanover tp (10)	MC 201 887-5454	....	....	....	....	....	....	....
East Orange (74)	MC 201 266-5100	Cardell Cooper	Leroy J Jones Jr	Constance Newton	Linda Munro	Elliot C Peterkin	Harry Harman	....
East Rutherford b (8)	MC 201 933-3444	James L Plosia	....	Darlene A Sawicki	Anthony V Bianchi	Dennis Rodgers	Gilbert Logatto	Robert Roth
East Windsor tp (22)	CM 609 443-4000	Clifford Eberle	Barry Larson	Elizabeth Nolan	John Milano	....	Barry Barlow	Robert DiMarco
Eastampton tp (5)	CM 609 267-5723	Marie N Potter	David O' Brien	Mary Jane Jones	Gerald Mingin	....	Gerald Mingin	Richard Parks
Eatontown b (14)	MC 908 389-7600	J Joseph Frankel	Michael L Trotta	Margaret L Smith	Adeline F Schmidt	Dane Richards	William Barnshaw	Warren P Ceres
Edgewater b (5)	MC 201 943-1700	....	....	....	....	....	....	....
Edison tp (89)	MC 908 248-7240	George Spadoro	Stephen Sasala	Theodore Gierlich	G Ross Bobal	Albert Lamkie	Edward Costello	Robert Heck Sr
Egg Harbor tp (..)	MC 609 926-4000	Robert V Burns	Peter Miller	Patricia Indrlerl	Charlene Canale	....	Alfred Lisicki	N Ciarlante
Egg Harbor City (5)	MC 609 965-0081	....	....	....	....	....	....	....
Elizabeth (110)	MC 908 820-4000	J C Bollwage	N Milan Rivera	Anthony Pillo	Joseph Mularz	William Neafsey	Gene Mirabella	Blaise Lapolla
Elmwood Park b (18)	MC 201 796-1457	....	....	....	....	....	....	....
Emerson b (7)	MC 201 262-6086	Harvey Truppi	Arlene Raymond	Sandra Plicinski	Ann Burns	Brian Yhele	Peter Mazzeo	Raymond Donnelly
Englewood (25)	CM 201 871-6658	....	....	....	....	....	....	....
Englewood Cliffs b (6)	MC 201 569-5252	Joseph C Parisi	Joseph Favaro	Joseph Favaro	Joseph Iannaconl	....	Patrick Farley	Rodney Bialko
Essex Fells tp (2)	MC 201 226-3400	D McWilliams	Robert Ditommaso	Robert Ditommaso	William Homa	James Egan	George Haydu	Robert Gervasi
Evesham tp (35)	CM 609 983-2900	Augustus Tamburro	Florence Ricci	Florence Ricci	Thomas Tontarski	Thaddeus Lowden	Nicholas Matteo	David Buchanan
Ewing tp (34)	MC 609 883-2900	Linda Lengyel	Fred Walters	Ted Yim	Joe Monzo	....	Ed Schaller	....
Fair Haven b (5)	MC 908 747-0241	T David Hinton	Michael Pellechio	Michael Pellechio	Michael Pellechio	Barry Brett	Richard Towler	John Riley
Fair Lawn b (31)	CM 201 796-1700	....	....	....	....	....	....	....
Fairfield tp (8)	MC 201 882-2700	Anna M Rotonda	Sanford A Kaplan	Meyghan Weber	Ken Sesholtz	Anthony Gerardi	W Vanderhoff	Larry Gonnello
Fairview b (11)	MC 201 943-3300	....	....	....	....	....	....	....
Fanwood b (7)	MC 908 322-8236	....	....	....	....	....	....	....
Flemington b (4)	MC 908 782-8840	Austin H Kutscher	....	Robert B Hauck	Raymond Krov	Francis Gilmartin	Peter Tirpok	....
Florham Park b (9)	MC 201 377-5800	....	....	....	....	....	....	....
Fort Lee b (32)	MC 201 592-3546	Jack Alter	Peggy Thomas	Gladys Brunell	Joseph Iannaconl	Peter Manchise	John Orso	Daniel Kingcaid
Franklin tp (43)	CM 908 873-2500	Richard Tornquist	John C Lovell	Jean Pellicane	George Ramsey	....	Daniel Livak	C Andy Twiford
Franklin b (5)	MC 201 827-9280	....	....	....	....	....	....	....
Franklin Lakes b (10)	MC 201 891-0048	W Vichiconti	Rosemary Martin	Rosemary Martin	Harold E Laufeld	Len Van Ess	William Holland	Brian Peterson
Freehold b (11)	MC 908 462-1410	....	....	....	....	....	....	....
Freehold tp (25)	CM 908 294-2000	Raymond Kershaw	Thomas E Antus	Romeo Cascaes	Debrah DeFeo	....	John Willis	Richard Warren
Galloway tp (23)	CM 609 652-3700	Calvin D Brads	Joseph Picardi	Karen A Bacon	Jill A Gougher	Thomas Culleny Sr	Charles Bellino	Stephen Bonanni
Garfield (27)	CM 201 340-2000	James Krone	John A Nunno	Andrew J Pavlica	John A Nunno	Stanley Pikul	Alessi P Cimino	Nunzio Santora
Garwood b (4)	MC 908 789-0710	Michael Crincoli	....	Doris Polidore	Doris Polidore	Joseph Peluscio	Robert Ryan	....
Gibbsboro b (2)	MC 609 783-6655	....	....	....	....	....	....	....
Glassboro b (16)	MC 609 881-9230	....	....	....	....	....	....	....

Directory 1/9 continued — MUNICIPAL OFFICIALS IN U.S. CITIES OVER 2,500

City, 1990 population figures (000 omitted), form of government		Municipal phone number	Mayor/ chief elected official	Appointed administrator	City clerk/ city secretary	Finance officer	Fire chief	Police chief	Public works director
NEW JERSEY (357) continued									
Glen Ridge tp (7)	MC	201 748-8400	Carolyn W Bourne	Vincent Belluscio	Vincent Belluscio	Vincent Belluscio	....	Thomas Dugan	Maurits Modin
Glen Rock b (11)	MC	201 670-3956	Jacqueline Kort	Robt Freudenrich	Jean L Malone	Lenora Benjamin	Walter Perry	Steven Cherry	Roy Nordstrand
Gloucester tp (54)	MC	609 228-4000	Sandy Love	Thomas C Cardis	Rose M Stortini	Candy Prince	....	John Stollsteimer	Gabriel Bush
Gloucester City (13)	MC	609 456-0205	Walter W Jost	John J Holman	Mary A Moran	Jeffrey M Coles	William Glassman	Theodore Howarth	James J Johnson
Guttenberg t (8)	MC	201 868-2315	W O' Donnell	....	Linda Martin	Nicholas Goldsack	George Malik	John Broking	Edward Huebsch
Hackensack (37)	CM	201 646-3980	Jack Zisa	James Lacava	Doris Dukes	M Mariniello	Richard Johnson	John Aletta	Jesse D' Amore
Hackettstown t (8)	MC	908 852-3130	....	....	....	....	....	....	....
Haddon tp (15)	CO	609 854-1176	William J Park Jr	Joanne M Schaefer	Denise P White	Joanne M Schaefer	....	Charles E Gooley	Daniel F Aaron
Haddon Heights b (8)	MC	609 547-7164	Robert Battersby	....	Joan Young	Ernest J Merlino	Gene Dannenfelser	Donald Wilson	Gary Geserick
Haddonfield b (12)	CM	609 429-4700	John J Tarditi Jr	Richard B Schwab	Janet G Betley	Richard B Schwab	George Cox	William Ostrander	Letitia G Colombi
Haledon b (7)	MC	201 595-7766	....	....	....	....	....	....	....
Hamilton tp (87)	MC	609 890-3500	....	....	....	....	....	....	....
Hammonton t (12)	MC	609 567-4300	....	....	....	....	....	....	....
Hardyston tp (5)	CM	201 697-4987	....	....	....	....	....	....	....
Harrington Park b (5)	MC	201 768-1700	....	....	....	....	....	....	....
Harrison t (13)	MC	201 268-2425	....	....	....	....	....	....	....
Hasbrouck Heights b (11)	MC	201 288-0195	....	....	....	....	....	....	....
Haworth b (3)	MC	201 384-4785	John DeRienzo	Ann E Fay	Ann E Fay	Rebecca Overgaard	Ronald Green	Donald Galgano	Martin Mahon
Hawthorne b (17)	MC	201 427-1167	Paul Englehardt	Larry Worth	Sally Genova	Mary J Hewitt	Vincent Tamburro	David Noble	....
Hazlet tp (22)	MC	908 264-1700	John J Bradshaw	M J Margiotta	Patricia Johnson	Patricia M Frank	Francis Baumann	Holmes Gormerley	James Boehler
High Bridge b (4)	MC	908 638-6455	Alfred Schweikert	....	Claire R Knapp	Randy Bahr	Jeffrey Smith	Joseph M Lacey	Mark Banks
Highland Park b (13)	MC	908 572-3400	H James Polos	Evelyn Sedehi	Valerie Thompson	Jose Agosto	....	Ronald Haskins	Lloyd Young
Highlands b (5)	MC	201 872-1515	....	....	....	....	....	....	....
Hightstown b (5)	MC	609 490-5100	Ernest B Turp	John J Kennedy	Marie Pellecchia	John J Kennedy	Lawrence Blake	Kevin Hopkins	Lawrence Blake
Hillsdale b (10)	MC	201 666-4800	Douglas Groner	Joseph S Rompala	Robert P Sandt	Joseph S Rompala	James R Fisher	Frank A Mikulski	Keith I Durie
Hillside tp (21)	MC	201 926-3000	Ann C Lord	....	C DeFilippo	Rosemary McClave	James Dill	Frank DeSanto	Scott Anderson
Hoboken (33)	MC	201 420-2084	....	....	....	....	....	....	....
Hohokus b (4)	MC	201 652-4400	Richard M Sayers	Cathern Henderson	Judith Odo	Cathern Henderson	John Ludwig	Russell Berke	Thomas Dawson
Holmdel tp (12)	MC	908 946-2820	Henry Ferris	Carol Williams	Sheila Van Winkle	Joseph Annecharic	Ron Pontrelli	Robert Phillips	James Allocco
Hopatcong b (16)	MC	201 770-1200	....	....	....	....	....	....	....
Hopewell tp (12)	MC	609 737-0605	William H Cane	Robert Pellegrino	Annette Bielawski	Deborah Smith	....	Robert J Ferrarin	....
Irvington tp (61)	MC	201 399-6622	Michael G Steele	David W Fuller	Harold E Wiener	Gregory Della Pia	Joseph Gallagher	Bernard DeLucia	James Racz
Jackson tp (33)	CO	908 928-1200	Kenneth Bressi	William Santos	David T Miller Sr	Philip Del Turco	....	Richard Chinery	John Smatusik Jr
Jamesburg b (5)	MC	908 521-2222	Joseph Tonkery	....	Gretchen Schauer	Jo Ann Olenik	....	Victor Knowles	....
Jefferson tp (18)	MC	201 697-1500	....	....	....	....	....	....	....
Jersey City (229)	MC	201 547-5000	Bret Schundler	Robert Lombard	Robert Byrne	Serafina Sengco	F Constantinoble	Robert Sabo	Kevin Sluka
Keansburg b (11)	CM	201 787-0215	....	....	....	....	....	....	....
Kearny t (35)	MC	201 955-7400	Leo R Vartan	....	James Cantlon	Russell Murray	Vincent DiRenzo	Chester Bielski	Richard Ferraioli
Kenilworth b (8)	MC	908 276-9090	Joseph J Rego	....	Margaret Adler	Dianne Kurutza	Gary Walck	Brent David	Frank Plummer
Keyport b (8)	MC	908 739-3900	John J Merla	Judith L Poling	Judith L Poling	....	Marc Thailheimer	Howard J Ruth	Arthur S Rooke
Kinnelon b (8)	MC	201 838-5401	....	....	....	....	....	....	....
Lakehurst b (3)	CM	908 657-4141	....	....	....	....	....	....	....
Lakewood tp (45)	CM	908 364-2500	Robert W Singer	G Fehrenbach	Bernadette Work	Carl A Innlss	....	Michael J Lynch	Larry Branch
Lambertville (4)	MC	609 397-0110	David Del Vecchio	....	Mary E Sheppard	Linda Monteverde	Millard Thornton	Jack M Venettone	Paul A Cronce
Lawnside b (3)	MC	609 573-6200	Mark Bryant	Jessie G Harris	Gwen Watson	Jessie G Harris	Michael Harper	....	Alex Barr
Lawrence tp (26)	CM	609 844-7005	Gretel Gatterdam	William J Guhl	D Simonelli	Richard Krawczun	....	John Prettyman	Joseph Maher
Leonia b (8)	MC	201 592-5743	....	....	....	....	....	....	....
Lincoln Park b (11)	MC	201 694-6100	Lorelei N Mottese	....	Annette Maida Smi	Robert Benecke	Ira Kronenfeld	Kenneth West	Thomas Piorkowski
Linden (37)	MC	908 474-8400	John T Gregorio	....	Val D Imbrlaco	Joseph Suliga	William Konecny	John E Miliano	John Brozana Jr
Lindenwold b (19)	MC	609 783-2121	....	....	....	....	....	....	....
Linwood (7)	MC	609 927-4108	Donald B Vass	Gary Gardner	Gary Gardner	F Bonie Tiemann	Donald Dagrossa	A Jerry Ferguson	George Jones
Little Falls tp (11)	MC	201 256-0170	....	....	....	....	....	....	....
Little Ferry b (10)	MC	201 641-9234	....	....	....	....	....	....	....
Little Silver b (6)	TM	201 842-2400	....	....	....	....	....	....	....
Livingston tp (27)	CM	201 992-5000	....	....	....	....	....	....	....
Lodi b (22)	MC	201 365-4005	....	....	....	....	....	....	....
Long Branch (29)	MC	908 222-7000	Adam Schneider	Francis Hayes	Irene Joline	Ronald Mehlhorn	Irven Miller	....	Anthony Critelli
Lower tp (21)	CM	609 886-2005	....	....	....	....	....	....	....
Lyndhurst tp (18)	CO	201 804-2457	Louis J Stellato	....	Josephine Oleske	Deborah Ferrato	Bryan Hennig	John A Scalese	John P Beirne
Madison b (16)	MC	201 593-3000	....	....	....	....	....	....	....
Magnolia b (5)	MC	609 783-1520	....	....	....	....	....	....	....
Mahwah tp (18)	MC	201 529-5757	....	....	....	....	....	....	....
Manalapan tp (27)	MC	908 446-3200	....	....	....	....	....	....	....
Manasquan b (5)	MC	201 223-0544	....	....	....	....	....	....	....
Manville b (11)	MC	908 725-9478	Angelo Corradino	Daniel Palladino	....	Roger Pribush	Kenneth Otrimski	Michael Moschak	Bruce Kosensky
Maple Shade tp (19)	CM	609 779-9610	Joseph P Dugan	George D Haeuber	Marlene McVeigh	Kathleen Anderson	....	James Ryan	Arthur Dees
Maplewood tp (22)	MC	201 762-8120	....	....	....	....	....	....	....
Margate City (8)	CO	609 822-2605	....	....	....	....	....	....	....
Matawan b (9)	MC	201 566-3898	....	....	....	....	....	....	....
Maywood b (9)	MC	201 845-2900	John A Stevert Jr	....	Mary A Rampolla	Charles Cuccia	Peter Casamento	Andrew Costa	Sam Pernetti
Medford tp (21)	CM	609 654-2608	Judith F Adams	Constance Lauffer	Jean K Lobach	N Janet Cooper	....	E John Foulk	John W Crafchun
Medford Lakes b (4)	CM	609 654-8898	C Philip Murray	Paul E Thomas Jr	Paul E Thomas Jr	Paul E Thomas Jr	Clarence Wingert	Roger N Smith	P McCorriston
Mendham b (5)	MC	201 543-7152	C W Steelman	Victor L Woodhull	Denise V B Fuchs	Susan Giordano	F Scharfenberg	George Vanderbush	C David Crotsley
Merchantville b (4)	MC	609 662-2474	....	....	....	....	....	....	....
Metuchen b (13)	MC	908 632-8540	Susan Marshall	William E Boerth	Reina A Murphy	Lori Majeski	George Wallace	Frederick E Hall	C DiLorenzo
Middlesex b (13)	MC	908 356-7400	Ronald S Dobies	....	Ruth Yambor	A Collins	Barry Procter	James Benson	Jerry Schaefer
Middletown tp (68)	CM	908 615-2000	Joseph Oxley	Joseph P Leo	Elaine Wallace	Robert Roth	Stan Midose	William Fowlie	Paul Linder
Midland Park b (7)	MC	201 445-5720	....	....	....	....	....	....	....
Millburn tp (19)	CM	201 564-7075	William J Caveney	Timothy P Gordon	Lynn Rogers	Martin M McElroy	Terrence Murray	F Warren Ebert	Michael T Rella
Milltown b (7)	MC	908 828-2100	....	....	....	....	....	....	....
Millville (26)	CO	609 825-7000	....	....	....	....	....	....	....
Monmouth Beach b (3)	CO	201 229-2204	....	....	....	....	....	....	....
Montclair tp (38)	CM	201 509-4939	....	....	....	....	....	....	....
Montgomery tp (10)	CM	908 359-8211	....	....	....	....	....	....	....
Montvale b (7)	CM	201 391-5700	David Metlitz	Helene V Fall	Betty McLaughlin	Dawn L Babcock	J Dellabella	J Marigliani	Alvin Walters
Montville tp (16)	MC	201 334-2370	Robert C Auriemma	Edward J Pullan	Gladys C Jarombek	F L Vanderhoof	....	Carl DeBacco	Robert A Cook
Moonachie b (3)	MC	201 641-1813	....	....	....	....	....	....	....
Moorestown tp (16)	CM	609 235-0912	Walter T Maahs	John T Terry	Margie P Murphy	John Schoenberg	....	W Wesolowski	Jack R Lallier
Morris Plains b (5)	MC	201 538-2284	Frank J Druetzler	....	June R Uhrin	David E Banks	Mark Van Orden	William E Pierson	Robert Sturtevant
Morristown t (16)	MC	201 292-6600	....	....	....	....	....	....	....
Mount Arlington b (4)	MC	201 398-6832	....	....	....	....	....	....	....
Mount Ephraim b (5)	CO	609 931-1546	Joseph E Wolk	....	Catherine Pepe	C Humphreville	John West	Nicholas Salamone	J Blocklinger
Mount Holly tp (11)	CM	609 267-0170	James Logan	John Tegley	Joan Boas	Christina Chamber	Bruce E Matthews	James Hansen	....

Directory 1/9 continued

MUNICIPAL OFFICIALS IN U.S. CITIES OVER 2,500

City, 1990 population figures (000 omitted), form of government		Municipal phone number	Mayor/ chief elected official	Appointed administrator	City clerk/ city secretary	Finance officer	Fire chief	Police chief	Public works director
NEW JERSEY (357) continued									
Mount Laurel tp (30)	CM	609 234-0001	....	....	....	....	....	....	....
Mount Olive tp (21)	MC	201 691-0900	James E Schiess	L V Corea Jr	Lisa M Lashway	Randall W Carter	....	Edward A Kane	....
Mountain Lakes b (4)	CM	201 334-3131	....	....	....	....	....	....	....
Mountainside b (7)	MC	908 232-2400	Robert Viglianti	Kathleen Tuland	Judith Osty	Michelle Swisher	....	William Alder	Robert Wyckoff
National Park b (3)	MC	609 845-3891	....	....	....	....	....	....	....
Neptune tp (28)	CO	908 988-5200	....	....	....	....	....	....	....
Neptune City b (5)	MC	908 776-7224	Robert Deeves	....	Joel Popkin	Charles Ormsbee	Mark Lane	James Johnson	Gerrit DeVos
Netcong b (3)	MC	201 347-0252	....	....	....	....	....	....	....
New Brunswick (42)	MC	908 745-5004	James M Cahill	Thomas Loughlin	Ludwig Previte	Alice Anne Pareti	Horace Jordan	M Beltranena	Steven Zarecki
New Hanover tp (10)	CO	609 758-7149	....	....	....	....	....	....	....
New Milford b (16)	MC	201 967-5044	Theresa M King	Richard N Shuss	Kathy A Sayers	Richard N Shuss	Alan Silverman	J R Costello	Robert K Chester
New Providence b (11)	MC	908 665-1400	Harold Weideli Jr	Edward M Bien	Wendi B Barry	Richard O Burr	Kevin Kennedy	James J Venezia	John A Meyer
Newark (275)	MC	201 733-6400	Sharpe James	Glenn Grant	Robert Marasco	Ronald Jean	Stanley Kossup	William Celester	....
Newton t (8)	CM	201 383-3521	Raymond A Torm	Camille Furgiuele	Douglas L Cummins	Camille Furgiuele	Edmund Zukowski	James J Kilduff	Christopher Bond
North Arlington b (14)	MC	201 955-5660	....	....	....	....	....	....	....
North Bergen tp (48)	CO	201 392-2000	....	....	....	....	....	....	....
North Brunswick tp (31)	MC	908 247-0922	....	....	....	....	....	....	....
North Caldwell tp (7)	MC	201 228-4444	....	....	....	....	....	....	....
North Haledon b (8)	MC	201 427-7793	Renate Lampe	Robert J Pacca	Lucille B Debiak	Rosalie M Tebbs	....	Joseph Rutkowski	William Graham
North Plainfield b (19)	MC	908 769-2902	....	....	....	....	....	....	....
North Wildwood (5)	MC	609 522-2030	Aldo A Palombo	D Robert Heal	Jane Parson	Jame G Nicola	William Callahan	Anthony Sittineri	Timothy O' Leary
Northfield (7)	MC	609 641-2832	....	....	....	....	....	....	....
Northvale b (5)	MC	201 767-3330	....	....	....	....	....	....	....
Norwood b (5)	MC	201 767-7200	....	....	....	....	....	....	....
Nutley tp (27)	CO	201 284-4951	Carmen A Orechio	....	Lucille Simonian	Rosemary Costa	Charles Kucinski	Robert Delitta	Peter C Scarpelli
Oakland b (12)	MC	201 337-8111	John Peter Kendal	Robert Hammer	Robert Hammer	Steven Schwager	Edward Proskey	James O Connor	N David Fagerlund
Oaklyn b (4)	MC	609 858-2457	....	....	....	....	....	....	....
Ocean tp (25)	CM	908 531-5000	Terrance Weldon	David Kochel	Virginia Bergeron	Herbert Kushner	....	William Koch	William Taylor
Ocean City (16)	MC	609 399-6111	Henry S Knight	Richard W Deaney	Angela H Pilleggi	John J Hansen	Todd E Bower	Dominic Longo	George Savastano
Oceanport b (6)	MC	201 222-8221	....	....	....	....	....	....	....
Ogdensburg b (3)	MC	201 827-3444	A J Rutkowski	....	Jean Dickson	Margaret A Alfano	Richard Keslo	James Duke	Ronald Search
Old Bridge tp (56)	MC	908 721-5600	Barbara Cannon	John Coughlin	R Saracino	Himanshu Shah	....	Jerry Palumbo	Rocco Donatelli
Old Tappan b (4)	MC	201 664-1849	Edward Gallagher	Marie Koehler	Marie Koehler	Christine Cauvet	Charles Anders	John Kramer	George Pomponio
Oradell b (8)	MC	201 261-8200	....	....	....	....	....	....	....
Orange Township (30)	MC	201 266-4005	Robert L Brown	Thomas J Morrison	Dwight Mitchell	John Kelly	John Gamba	....	....
Palisades Park b (15)	MC	201 585-4100	....	....	....	....	....	....	....
Palmyra b (7)	MC	609 829-6100	....	....	....	....	....	....	....
Paramus b (25)	MC	201 265-2100	Cliff Gennarelli	....	Ian I Shore	Joseph Citro	William A Rice	M McCormack	Brian Koenig
Park Ridge b (8)	MC	201 573-1800	R Mancinelli	Charles E Gasior	Anne Krouse	Ann F Kilmartin	....	Robert Minugh	Alvin Roehrer
Parsippany-Troy Hills tp (48)	MC	201 263-4266	Joseph Weisberg	Paula Cozzarelli	Judith Silver	Robert Griffith	Bruce Wingate	M Filippello	Jerry Rhodes
Passaic (58)	MC	201 365-5500	Margie Semler	Robert Czech	Tina Fiorellino	Edward Routel	Louis Imparato	Richard Wolak	Bernard Geminder
Paterson (141)	MC	201 881-3343	William Pascrell	Edward Cotton	Jane Williams	Margaret Cherone	John Mauro	Richard Munsey	Juan Santana
Paulsboro b (7)	MC	609 423-1500	....	....	....	....	....	....	....
Pemberton tp (31)	MC	609 894-8201	Thalia C Kay	Michael Spurgeon	Charlotte Newhart	Douglas B Ayrer	Craig Augustoni	Paul Tuliano	Paul Leary Sr
Penns Grove b (5)	MC	609 299-0098	....	....	....	....	....	....	....
Pennsauken tp (35)	CM	609 665-1000	....	....	....	....	....	....	....
Pequannock tp (13)	CM	201 835-5700	E Cass Schmidt	T Kane	E Eley	T Kane	H Bradley	J Reeves	A Barile Jr
Perth Amboy (42)	MC	908 826-0290	....	....	....	....	....	....	....
Phillipsburg t (16)	MC	908 454-5500	Gloria A Decker	Frank J Tolotta	Michele Broubalow	Joseph Hriczak	Richard A Hay	James F Mac Aulay	Frank J Tolotta
Pine Hill b (10)	MC	609 783-0374	....	....	....	....	....	....	....
Piscataway tp (47)	MC	908 562-2300	....	....	....	....	....	....	....
Pitman b (9)	MC	609 589-3522	....	Jay Todd	Jay Todd	Earl Kelly	Coxie Brown	Chuck Walker	Edward Lewis
Plainfield (47)	CM	908 753-3219	Mark A Fury	Henry C Kita	Laddie Wyatt	Jerome Reddy	Henry Lariccia	John Waldron	Eric Watson
Plainsboro tp (14)	MC	609 799-0909	Peter Cantu	Patrick Guilfoyle	Patricia Hullfish	Jayne McGuigan	....	David Lyon	Jeff Cramer
Pleasantville (16)	MC	609 484-3600	....	....	....	....	....	....	....
Point Pleasant b (18)	MC	908 892-3434	....	....	....	....	....	....	....
Point Pleasant Beach b (5)	MC	908 892-1118	....	....	....	....	....	....	....
Pompton Lakes b (11)	MC	201 835-0143	....	....	....	....	....	....	....
Princeton b (12)	MC	609 924-3118	Marvin R Reed	Thomas B Shannon	P Edwards Carter	Decimus Marsh	Benjamin R Warren	Thomas B Michaud	Wayne Carr
Princeton tp (13)	CM	609 924-5176	Phyllis Marchand	James Pascale	Patricia Shuss	John Clawson	....	Anthony Gaylord	Robert Kiser
Prospect Park b (5)	MC	201 790-7903	....	....	....	....	....	....	....
Rahway (25)	MC	908 381-8000	....	....	....	....	....	....	....
Ramsey b (13)	MC	201 825-3400	....	....	....	....	....	....	....
Randolph tp (20)	CM	201 989-7100	John P Finnerin	J Peter Braun	Frances Bertrand	Michael J Soccio	Joseph Dolan	James McLagan	Carl Bressan
Raritan tp (16)	MC	908 806-6100	Edward Dougherty	Allan Pietrefesa	Dorothy Gooditis	Allan Pietrefesa	Christopher Petit	William Meytrott	Robert Kling
Raritan b (6)	MC	908 231-1300	Anthony Decicco	Daniel Jaxel	Louise Salerno	Jack Hurst	Chris Jensen	Joseph Sferra	A DiGuiseppa
Red Bank b (11)	MC	908 530-2740	Edward McKenna	Sally Levine	Carol Vivona	Bruce Loversidge	Robert Talerico	Robert Clayton	J Buonaquista
Ridgefield b (10)	MC	201 943-5215	....	....	....	....	....	....	....
Ridgefield Park v (12)	CO	201 641-4950	....	....	....	....	....	....	....
Ridgewood v (24)	CM	201 670-5500	Patrick Mancuso	Rodney Irwin	Heather Mailander	James M Ten Hoeve	Robert Missel	Louis Mader	David Baker
Ringwood b (13)	CM	201 962-7002	....	....	....	....	....	....	....
River Edge b (11)	MC	201 599-6300	James T Kirk	Alan P Negreann	Grace Gutekunst	Alan P Negreann	Clay Marcoux	Kenneth J Quinn	John Pusterla
River Vale tp (9)	MC	201 664-2346	Walter V Jones	Roy S Blumenthal	Corinne Verhille	Ann Olivarius	....	Vincent Lally	Peter Wayne
Riverdale b (2)	MC	201 835-4060	....	....	....	....	....	....	....
Riverside tp (8)	CO	609 461-0284	....	....	....	....	....	....	....
Riverton b (3)	MC	609 829-0120	....	....	....	....	....	....	....
Rochelle Park tp (6)	CO	201 587-7727	Richard Lo Cascio	Joseph Manzella	Virginia DeMaria	Joseph Manzella	Douglas Watson	William Betten	John Tanucilli
Rockaway tp (20)	MC	201 627-7200	Frank Maddaloni	A Guadagnino	Almira Salvesen	Charles Wood Jr	James Henderson	Steven J Dachisen	Gerald Kunkel
Rockaway b (6)	MC	201 627-2000	....	....	....	....	....	....	....
Roseland b (5)	MC	201 226-8080	Louis Debell	Gloria C Floyd	Gloria C Floyd	Molly Cusano	Robert Kozlowski	Walter Critchett	Vincent E Toma
Roselle b (20)	MC	908 245-5600	....	....	....	....	....	....	....
Roselle Park b (13)	MC	908 245-2300	....	....	....	....	....	....	....
Roxbury tp (20)	CM	201 927-2000	Robert Badini	Gary Webb	B Johannsen	Gary Rieth	John Feneck	Mark Noll	Joseph Femia
Rumson b (7)	MC	908 842-3300	....	....	....	....	....	....	....
Runnemede b (9)	MC	609 939-5161	....	....	....	....	....	....	....
Rutherford b (18)	MC	201 939-0020	Andrew E Bertone	Robert A Gorman	Mary P Kirston	Edward Cortright	A Dombrowski	Edward P Caughey	Douglas Adamo
Saddle Brook tp (13)	MC	201 587-2900	R Santa Lucia	....	Joyce Larena	Robert Calise	....	Paul Jacob	Charles Cerone
Saddle River b (3)	MC	201 327-2609	....	....	....	....	....	....	....
Salem (7)	MC	609 935-0372	Leon F Johnson	....	Barbara A Wright	Darla J Timberman	Fred Shipley	Harold G May	Kenneth Homan
Sayreville b (35)	MC	201 390-7000	....	....	....	....	....	....	....
Scotch Plains tp (21)	CM	908 322-6700	W McClintock	Thomas E Atkins	Barabra Riepe	Ulrich Steinberg	Jonathan P Ellis	Robert Luce	Walter DiNizo
Sea Girt b (2)	MC	908 449-9433	....	....	....	....	....	....	....
Sea Isle City (3)	CO	609 263-4461	....	....	....	....	....	....	....

Directory 1/9
continued

**MUNICIPAL OFFICIALS
IN U.S. CITIES OVER 2,500**

City, 1990 population figures (000 omitted), form of government	Municipal phone number	Mayor/ chief elected official	Appointed administrator	City clerk/ city secretary	Finance officer	Fire chief	Police chief	Public works director
NEW JERSEY (357) continued								
Secaucus t (14)	MC 201 330-2000	Anthony E Just Sr	Philip J Kieffer	Claire Grecco	Margaret Barcala	Gus Mangin	Alfred Cormann	Michael Gonnelli
Shrewsbury b (3)	MC 908 741-4200	Raymond Mass	....	Marlene Hotaling	Jane Longo	Samuel Johnson	James Hagan	Samuel Johnson
Somerdale b (5)	MC 609 783-6320	....	....	....	....	....	....	....
Somers Point (11)	MC 609 927-8938	....	....	....	....	....	....	....
Somerville b (12)	MC 908 725-2300	John Kobiela	Ralph Sternadori	Ralph Sternadori	Janet Kelk	Steve Fetko	Charles Niles	Peter Hendershot
South Amboy (8)	MC 201 727-4600	....	....	....	....	....	....	....
South Bound Brook b (4)	MC 908 356-0258	Russ Reynolds	....	Donald E Kazar	Catherine A Hoats	....	Ronald Henry	....
South Brunswick tp (26)	CO 908 329-4000	Roger E Craig	Louis C Goetting	Kathleen Thorpe	Ralph Palmieri	Robert Davidson	Michael Paquette	Thomas Evans
South Orange Village tp (16)	CO 201 378-7715	....	....	....	....	....	....	....
South Plainfield b (20)	MC 908 754-9000	....	....	....	....	....	....	....
South River b (14)	MC 201 257-1999	....	....	....	....	....	....	....
South Toms River b (4)	MC 908 349-0403	Joseph T Barone	....	E Silvestri	Lily Ann Farley	....	Andrew Izatt	Joseph Jubert
Sparta tp (15)	CM 201 729-8485	Delores Blackburn	David J Ferguson	Miriam Tower	Nicklas Lella	....	Frederick Geffken	Charles Ryan
Spotswood b (8)	MC 908 251-3378	....	....	....	....	....	....	....
Spring Lake b (3)	MC 908 449-0800	....	....	....	....	....	....	....
Spring Lake Heights b (5)	MC 908 449-3500	....	....	....	....	....	....	....
Springfield tp (13)	RT 201 912-2200	....	....	....	....	....	....	....
Stanhope b (3)	MC 201 347-0159	Michael Bender	John Arntz	Audrey Dressel	Allan Dickinson	Harry Peterson	Douglas Waldron	James Floyd
Stratford b (8)	MC 609 783-0600	....	....	....	....	....	....	....
Summit (20)	MC 908 273-6400	Janet L Whitman	Reagan Burkholder	David L Hughes	Ronald J Angelo	C Cotter	William Schneller	Michael R Townley
Teaneck tp (38)	CM 201 837-4816	....	Gary A Saage	Elizabeth Clay	Sandra L Kaye	Wm Hillermeir	Donald Giannone	Howarth Gilmore
Tenafly b (13)	MC 201 568-6100	....	....	....	....	....	....	....
Tinton Falls b (12)	MC 908 542-3400	Ann Y McNamara	Anthony Muscillo	Karen M Taylor	Stephen G Pfeffer	....	Anthony Muscillo	Louis Buono
Totowa b (10)	MC 201 956-1000	....	....	....	....	....	....	....
Trenton (89)	MC 609 989-3030	....	....	....	....	....	....	....
Union tp (50)	MC 908 688-2800	Jerome Petti	Louis Giacona	Nancy Issenman	....	Frederic Fretz	Dennis Farrell	George Salzmann
Union Beach b (6)	MC 201 264-2277	....	....	....	....	....	....	....
Union City (58)	CO 201 348-5754	....	....	....	....	....	....	....
Upper Saddle River b (7)	MC 201 327-2196	....	....	....	....	....	....	....
Ventnor City (11)	CO 609 823-7900	....	....	....	....	....	....	....
Verona tp (14)	MC 201 239-3220	James Treffinger	Vincent DiMauro	Vincent DiMauro	Dorothy Trimmer	Charles Magotti	Douglas Huber	James Helb
Vineland (55)	MC 609 794-4000	Joseph E Romano	Linda M Dechen	Keith Petrosky	Edward Rochetti	Biaggio Ciulla	Mario R Brunetta	William Rich
Waldwick b (10)	MC 201 652-5070	Rick Vander Wende	Gary Kratz	Paula Jaegge	Mary Ann Viviani	James O' Connell	Daniel Lupo	Joseph Agugliaro
Wall tp (20)	MC 908 449-8444	Gerald Nelson	Joseph Verruni	Beatrice Gassner	Stephen Mayer	....	Francis Hall	James White
Wallington b (11)	MC 201 779-4879	....	....	....	....	....	....	....
Wanaque b (10)	MC 201 839-3000	....	....	....	....	....	....	....
Warren tp (11)	RT 908 753-8000	....	Mark M Krane	Doris Lortie	Carolyn J Gara	James Herlich	Michael G Lach	Ewald Friedrich
Washington b (6)	CM 908 689-3600	Karen E Tucker	Alan M Fisher	Linda Hendershot	Bernadette Tuttle	Stesve Alpaugh	Stephen B Speirs	....
Washington (Bergen) tp (9)	MC 201 664-4404	....	....	....	....	....	....	....
Washington (Glcstr) tp (42)	MC 609 589-0520	....	....	....	....	....	....	....
Washington (Morris) tp (16)	MC 908 876-3315	M Nordstrom	Dianne S Gallets	Dianne S Gallets	Kevin Lifer	....	George Kluetz	Ralph DeFranzo
Washington (Warren) tp (5)	MC 908 689-7200	....	....	....	....	....	....	....
Watchung b (5)	MC 201 756-0080	Anthony Addario	Lyn Evers	Adele Widin	Raymond Krou	....	George King	....
Wayne tp (47)	MC 201 694-1800	David Waks	Neal Bellet	John O' Brien	John Aitken	....	Donald Pavlak	Anthony Buzzoni
Weehawken tp (12)	CO 201 867-1707	....	....	....	....	....	....	....
West Caldwell tp (10)	MC 201 226-2300	....	....	....	....	....	....	....
West Deptford tp (19)	CM 609 845-4004	....	....	....	....	....	....	....
West Long Branch b (8)	MC 908 229-1756	....	....	....	....	....	....	....
West Milford tp (25)	CM 201 728-7000	Carl Richko	Kevin J Byrnes	Kevin J Byrnes	Theresa Benack	....	James Breslin	Gerald Storms
West New York t (38)	CO 201 861-7000	....	....	....	....	....	....	....
West Orange tp (39)	MC 201 325-4050	Samuel A Spina	Richard Giuditta	Patrick J Melvin	Edward J Coleman	Frank J Capron	Edward M Palardy	Leonard R Lepore
West Paterson b (11)	MC 201 345-8100	....	....	....	....	....	....	....
West Windsor tp (16)	MC 609 799-2400	....	....	....	....	....	....	....
Westfield t (29)	MC 908 789-4230	....	....	....	....	....	....	....
Westville b (5)	MC 609 456-0030	....	....	....	....	....	....	....
Westwood b (10)	MC 201 664-7100	Henry G Geier	Donald Rainey	Teresa Massood	Rebecca Overgaard	Christopher Mayer	Robert Burroughs	Robert Woods
Wharton b (5)	MC 201 361-8444	Harry R Shupe	Susan R Best	Susan R Best	Marie A Goble	John Craven	Anthony Fernandez	Arnold Boyer
Wildwood (4)	MC 609 522-2444	....	....	....	....	....	....	....
Wildwood Crest b (4)	CO 609 522-7788	....	....	....	....	....	....	....
Willingboro tp (36)	CM 609 877-2200	Doreathea Campbel	Saide Johnson	R Lichtenstadter	Joanne Diggs	Jeff Silagy	Benjamin Braxton	Harry McFarland
Wood-Lynne b (3)	MC 609 962-8300	J Drew Coyle	....	Veronica M Gitto	Donna Conda	Kenneth Steward	John Ragan	Richard D' Adamo
Wood-Ridge b (8)	MC 201 939-0254	Paul Calocino	Janet L Lynds	Janet L Lynds	Doris A Marek	Ronald Phillips	John Frank	John Sabia
Woodbine b (3)	MC 609 861-2153	William Pikolycky	....	Frances Pettit	....	Anthony Mayshura	....	Clarence Ryan
Woodbridge tp (93)	MC 908 634-4500	James McGreevey	James Davy	Philip Cerria	John McCormac	....	William Trenery	Timothy Daly
Woodbury (11)	MC 609 845-1300	....	....	....	....	....	....	....
Woodbury Heights b (3)	MC 609 848-2832	....	....	....	....	....	....	....
Woodcliff Lake b (5)	MC 201 391-4977	Bernard Kettler	John T Doyle	John T Doyle	John T Doyle	Bruce Mautz	Dennis Winters	Edward Barboni
Woodstown b (3)	MC 609 769-2200	Jan Edwards	....	I McAllister	James Hackett	Gary Walsh	Walt Simpkins	M DeMarcantonio
Wrightstown b (4)	MC 609 723-4450	....	....	....	....	....	....	....
Wyckoff tp (15)	MC 201 891-7000	....	....	....	....	....	....	....
NEW MEXICO (43)								
Alamogordo (28)	CM 505 437-4530	....	....	....	....	....	....	....
Albuquerque (385)	MC 505 768-3700	Martin Chavez	Lawrence Rael	Milli Santillanes	Sylvia Baca	Gregory Chavez	Joseph Polisar	Robert Gurule
Angel Fire v (..)	MC 505 377-3232	....	....	....	....	....	....	....
Artesia (11)	MC 505 746-2122	Ernest Thompson	....	Shirley Clark	....	Ray Castleberry	Ernest Chavez	Thomas Howell
Aztec (5)	CM 505 334-9456	Michael Padilla	Debi Lee	Jackie Jordan	Andy Mason	Kevin Simpson	Clay Morris	Steve Christensen
Bayard v (3)	MC 505 537-3327	Jovita Gonzales	Zeke Santa Maria	....	....	Eddie Arrey	A C Manzano	Eddie Sedillos
Belen t (7)	CM 505 864-8221	....	....	....	....	....	....	....
Bernalillo t (6)	MC 505 867-3311	....	....	....	....	....	....	....
Bloomfield (5)	MC 505 632-8096	Art Kittel	Albert Keller	Carol Miller	Shirley Ross	George Duncan	Bill Goodman	James Moore
Bosque Farms v (4)	MC 505 869-2358	Carl R Allen	Sue Padilla	....	....	Burl Cox	Hastings Hutchins	....
Carlsbad (25)	CM 505 887-1191	....	....	....	....	....	....	....
Clayton t (2)	MC 505 374-8331	....	....	....	....	....	....	....
Clovis (31)	CM 505 769-7828	James B Moss	Donald E Clifton	Terri G McCully	Terri G McCully	Bill Morey	Harry Boden	Joe Thomas
Corrales v (5)	MC 505 897-0502	Gary Kanin	Phillip Rios	Tina Dominguez	Phillip Rios	Bob Bone	Mike Tarter	Tony Tafoya
Deming (11)	MC 505 546-8848	Sam D Bala	John G Strand	....	Steve A Duran	Fred Rossiter	Mike Carillo	Louis Jenkins
Espanola (8)	MC 505 753-2377	Ross Chavez	Fred J Rivera	Alice Lucero	Lillian Brooks	Manuel Vigil	....	....
Eunice (3)	MC 505 394-2576	Edgar T Pearcy	....	Harriet Reed	....	Gary Colvin	Wilbert F Johnson	....
Farmington (34)	CM 505 327-7701	Thomas C Taylor	Daniel R Dible	Mary L Banks	Hilary Parker	Carl J Peskor	Richard G Melton	Joseph A Schmitz
Gallup t (19)	CM 505 863-1220	George Galanis	David Ruiz	Ruth Ruiz	Helen Kirk	Michael Lovato	Danny Ross	Joshua Richardson
Grants (9)	MC 505 287-7927	....	....	....	....	....	....	....
Hobbs (29)	CM 505 397-9200	Randy Owensby	....	Joyce Edmiston	Lawrence Jones	Mike Gray	Bill Morrill	....

Directory 1/9 continued

MUNICIPAL OFFICIALS IN U.S. CITIES OVER 2,500

City, 1990 population figures (000 omitted), form of government	Municipal phone number	Mayor/ chief elected official	Appointed administrator	City clerk/ city secretary	Finance officer	Fire chief	Police chief	Public works director
NEW MEXICO (43) continued								
Jal (2)	MC 505 395-2222	....		....		....	....	....
Las Cruces (62)	CM 505 526-0350	Ruben Smith	Bruno Zaldo	Karen Stevens	Barbara Willis	Louis Roman	William Hampton	James Ericson
Las Vegas (15)	CM 505 454-1401	....		....		....	....	....
Lordsburg (3)	MC 505 542-3421	Arthur C Smith		Irene A Galvan	Theodoro Castillo	John Hill	John McDonald	John Hill
Los Lunas v (6)	MC 505 865-9689	Louis Huning	Phillip Jaramillo	Phillip Jaramillo		Atilano Chavez	Nick Balido	J Eddie Saiz
Los Ranchos De Alb v (4)	MC 505 344-6582	John S O' Connor		A Martinez	Sylvia Pesce	Jose Jaramillo		Jose Jaramillo
Lovington (9)	CM 505 396-2884	Troy Harris	Bob G Carter	Kristi Mannan		Jack Davis	Archie Cunningham	....
Milan v (2)	MC 505 285-6694	....		....		....		
Portales (11)	CM 505 356-6662	Donald W Davis	Kendel G Goslee	J Martinez Terry		Johnny J Johnson	Jeffrey M Gill	Hillrey E Beggs
Raton (7)	CM 505 445-9551	....		....		....	....	
Rio Rancho (33)	MC 505 891-7201	Thomas Swisstack	Harold Donovan	Tina Gonzales	Gene Waite		Dencil Haycox	Jerry Fossenier
Roswell (45)	MC 505 624-6700	Thomas Jennings	John Capps	Ruth May	Larry Fry	Paul Sorensen	Raymond Mounts	Roger Cooper
Ruidoso (5)	MC 505 258-4014	....		....		....	....	....
Santa Fe (56)	CM 505 984-6500	....		....		....	....	....
Santa Rosa (2)	MC 505 472-3404	....		....		....	....	....
Silver City t (11)	CM 505 538-3731	....		....		....	....	....
Socorro (8)	MC 505 835-0240	....		....		....	....	....
Sunland Park (8)	MC 505 589-7565	Irene Aguirre		Concepcion Medina		Benito Hernandez	Eduardo Medina	Kurt Moffatt
Taos v (4)	MC 505 751-2000	Frederick Peralta	Gustavo Cordova	Lorraine Gallegos	Uvaldo Mondragon	Jim Fambro	Neil Curran	Walter Vigil
Truth Or Consequences (6)	CM 505 894-6673	....		....		....	....	....
Tucumcari (7)	CM 505 461-3451	Mark Lehnick	Bernadette Moya	Rachel Dominguez		Mike Cherry	Robert Velasco	Robert Welch
Tularosa v (3)	MC 505 585-2771	....		....		....	....	....
NEW YORK (275)								
Akron v (3)	MC 716 542-9636	....		....		....	....	....
Albany (101)	MC 518 434-5075	Gerald D Jennings		Pamela A Mineaux	Nancy Burton	James Larson	John Dale	Michael F Conners
Albion v (6)	MC 716 589-9176	David Albanese		Kathleen Ludwick			James Proietty	Quincy Washburn
Alfred v (5)	MC 607 587-9188	William Hall		Linda Burlingame	Linda Burlingame		Randal Belmont	Roger Mullen
Amityville v (9)	MC 516 264-6000	Emil G Pavlik Jr	Bruce E Mac Gill	Bruce E Mac Gill	Anne Mackin	Stanley Allen	Kenneth Greguski	Kendall W Muncy
Amsterdam (21)	MC 518 841-4311	Mareo Villa		Jane DiCaprio	Kim Brumley	James LaConte	Kenneth Trzaskos	....
Ardsley v (4)	CM 914 693-1550	John Morehouse	George F Calvi	Mary Kamens	Marion Demaio	Robert Reid	Louis D' Aliso	Louis Pascone
Attica v (3)	MC 716 591-0898	....		....		....	....	....
Auburn (31)	CM 315 255-4146	Guy Cosentino	James E Malone	Paul Norman	Beatrice O' Hora	Michael Harmon	John Ecklund	Francis Deorio
Avon v (3)	MC 716 226-8118	....		....		....	....	....
Babylon v (12)	MC 516 669-1212	....		....		....	....	....
Baldwinsville v (7)	MC 315 635-3521	....		....		....	....	....
Ballston Spa v (5)	MC 518 885-5711	James L Capasso		Patricia A Bowers			Charles Koenig	Joseph Thompson
Batavia (16)	CM 716 343-8180		William Reemtsen	Rebecca Swanson	William Reemtsen	Keith Hunt	Mark Robinson	Dennis Larson
Batavia t (..)	MC 716 343-1729	....		....		....	....	....
Bath v (6)	MC 607 776-3811	Warren Hopkins		Kathleen Dimmick			Larry Barnes	Jeffrey Muller
Bayville v (7)	MC 516 628-1439	....		....		....	....	....
Beacon (13)	MC 914 831-0302	Clara Lou Gould	Joseph H Braun	Helen Nuccitelli	Linda Greenough	Steven Van Buren	Richard Sassi	Randy Casale
Bellport v (3)	MC 516 286-0327	Frank C Trotta		Stephen Yacubich				Louis Cardimone
Binghamton (53)	MC 607 772-7000	....		....		....	....	....
Blasdell v (3)	MC 716 822-1921	....		....		....	....	....
Briarcliff Manor v (7)	CM 914 941-4800	....		....		....	....	....
Brighton t (34)	MC 716 473-8800	....		....		....	....	....
Brightwaters v (3)	MC 516 665-1280	Robert L Cox		Anna M Garbedian				Harry L Weed
Brockport v (9)	MC 716 637-5300	Mary Ann Thorpe		Scott Rightmyer		Kenneth Rombaut	Arthur Zimmer	Elliott Reynolds
Bronxville v (6)	CM 914 337-6500	Nancy D Hand	William T Regan	William T Regan			A Divernieri	Peter J Woodcock
Brookville v (4)	MC 516 626-1792	....		....		....	....	....
Buffalo (328)	MC 716 851-4841	Anthony Masiello		Charles Michaux	Joel Giambra	Cornelius Keane	R Kerlikowski	Joseph Giambra
Camden v (3)	MC 315 245-0560	John P Murray		Tamara Bourgeois	Robin L Mitchell	Roy Scoville	Richard D Paul Sr	Karl Keil Jr
Canandaigua (11)	CM 716 396-5000	Ellen Polimeni	William Bridgeo	Joseph Delforte	William Bridgeo	James Farrell	Patrick McCarthy	Louis Loy Jr
Canastota v (5)	MC 315 697-7559	Mark Lavonas		Sena C Clarke		John Massarotti	Richard Haumann	Joseph Capparelli
Canisteo v (2)	MC 607 698-4553	....		....		....	....	....
Canton v (6)	MC 315 386-2871	David T Button		Marlene Thompson	Charles Carvel	Dale Gardner	Ronald Houle	Charles Carvel
Carthage v (4)	CO 315 493-1060	....		....		....	....	....
Catskill v (5)	MC 518 943-3830	....		....		....	....	....
Cayuga Heights v (3)	MC 607 257-1238	....		....		....	....	....
Cazenovia v (3)	MC 315 655-3041	....		....		....	....	....
Cedarhurst v (6)	MC 516 295-5770	....		....		....	....	....
Chestnut Ridge v (8)	MC 914 425-2805	....		....		....	....	....
Chittenango v (5)	MC 315 687-3936	....		....		....	....	....
Cobleskill v (5)	MC 518 234-3891	....		....		....	....	....
Cohoes (17)	MC 518 237-7641	Robert Signoracci		M Archambeault	Michael Gagnon	Andrew Gisondi	Raymond Heslin	John Stackrow
Colonie v (8)	MC 518 869-7562	....		....		....	....	....
Corinth v (3)	MC 518 654-2012	....		....		....	....	....
Corning (12)	MC 607 962-0721	James G Bacalles		Rose M Blackwell	James G Bacalles	Gary C Brown	Richard T Faulisi	Ronald J Majesky
Cornwall-On-Hudson v (3)	MC 914 534-4200	Edward C Moulton		Roberta Hirsch		Tim McCarty	Richard Douglass	Robert C Gilmore
Cortland (20)	MC 607 756-7312	....		....		....	....	....
Coxsackie v (3)	MC 518 731-2718	Margaret Chaloner		Angela D Wilsey			Gary Grigalus	John Halsted
Croton-On-Hudson v (7)	CM 914 271-4781	Robert W Elliott	Richard F Herbek	Richard F Herbek	Richard Campbell		Dennis Coxen	Lawrence Black
Dannemora v (4)	MC 518 492-7000	H Philip Maynard		Donna D Taylor	H Philip Maynard	Byron Wing		Richard R Scholl
Dansville v (5)	MC 716 335-5330	....		....		....	....	....
Delhi v (3)	MC 607 746-2258	Eric J Greenfield		Margaret Reinmann		William Fields	Francis J Harmer	Ronald Pagerie
Depew v (18)	MC 716 683-1400	....		....		....	....	....
Dobbs Ferry v (10)	MC 914 693-2203	Donald P Marra	Margaret Slavin	Mathew P Carey	Mathew P Carey	Jack Krocian	Geore Longworth	James W Dunn
Dolgeville v (2)	MC 315 429-3112	Philip Dahlia		Donna L Cammann		Richard Levonski	Douglas Murphy	Robert R Sheppard
Dunkirk (14)	MC 716 366-1600	....		....		....	....	....
East Aurora v (7)	CM 716 652-6000	John Pagliaccio	Jerry C Hiller	Jerry C Hiller		David Meyer	William Nye	Robert Urban
East Hills v (7)	MC 516 621-4251	Michael R Kublenz		Marlene Bettman				Angelo DeCurtis
East Rochester v (7)	CM 716 586-3553	....		....		....	....	....
East Rockaway v (10)	MC 516 599-1211	Irving F Shaw		Phyllis J Rand		Thomas Harding		John H Conklin
East Syracuse v (3)	MC 315 437-3541	....		....		....	....	....
East Williston v (3)	MC 516 746-0782	....		....		....	....	....
Ellenville v (4)	CM 914 647-7080	....		....		....	....	....
Elmira (34)	CM 518 737-5644	Howard F Townsend	Samuel F Iracl Jr	Kathryn Peterson	Joy J Bates	Donald Harrison	Joseph Michalko	Ronald Hawley
Elmira Heights v (4)	MC 607 734-7156	Allen L Rice				Mahlon B Baldwin	Robert N Hamptman	Jean Cazarola
Elmsford v (4)	MC 914 592-6555	....		....		....	....	....
Endicott v (14)	MC 607 757-2428	David J Archer		Christine Mullins		Paul J Ripic	Gary F O' Neill	Eugene A Kudgus
Fairport v (6)	MC 716 223-0313	Clark T King	Kenneth W Moore	Nancy E Loughney	Kenneth W Moore		Brian T Page	Douglas Waite
Falconer v (3)	MC 716 665-4400	....		....		....	....	....

**Directory 1/9
continued**

**MUNICIPAL OFFICIALS
IN U.S. CITIES OVER 2,500**

NEW YORK (275) continued

City, 1990 population figures (000 omitted), form of government	Municipal phone number	Mayor/chief elected official	Appointed administrator	City clerk/city secretary	Finance officer	Fire chief	Police chief	Public works director
Fallsburg t (11)	CM 914 434-8810							
Farmingdale v (8)	MC 516 249-0093							
Fayetteville v (4)	MC 315 637-9864	Marian S Loosmann		Martin E Lynch		James Craw		Robert Grevelding
Floral Park v (16)	MC 516 326-6300							
Flower Hill v (4)	MC 516 627-2253							
Fort Edward v (4)	MC 518 747-4023							
Fort Plain v (2)	MC 518 993-4271	Albert T Nalli		Susanne Mahn		David Bowman	Harold Wilday Jr	Raymond Pedrick
Frankfort v (3)	MC 315 894-8811							
Fredonia v (10)	MC 716 673-1325							
Freeport v (40)	MC 516 378-4000	Arthur W Thompson	Michael Williams	Nora Sudars	Thomas J Preston	Michael Sotira	Joseph W King Jr	David R Lovejoy
Fulton (13)	MC 315 592-7330							
Garden City v (22)	MC 516 742-5800	Allen S Mathers	Robert L Schoelle	Robert L Schoelle	Robert L Schoelle	Michael C Hayes	Ernest J Cipullo	Robert J Mangan
Gates t (29)	TM 716 247-6100							
Geneseo v (7)	MC 716 243-1177	Richard Hatheway			Gerald R Youtzy	Craig Moses	Joseph Guarino	
Geneva (14)	CM 315 789-2603	Frank J Cecere Jr	Sanford I Miller	Margaret Cass	David M Stowell	Ralph E Debolt	Frank Pane	Robert W Helstrom
Glen Cove (24)	MC 516 676-2000	Thomas R Suozzi	Kathleen Tooher	Carol Nowicki			Timothy Edwards	Gerald Gardrvits
Glens Falls (15)	MC 518 761-3820	Vincent DeSantis		Tambrie Alden		Ronald Cote	Carl Carlton	Lawrence Fredella
Gloversville (17)	MC 518 773-4500							Conrad Kroll
Goshen v (5)	MC 914 294-6750	George M Lyons		Ronald J Bally	Jennifer Stauder		John Egbertson	Conrad Kroll
Gouverneur v (5)	MC 315 287-1720	D Scozzafava	Scott A Hudson	Sheryl E Simmons		Dale Johnson	David C Whitton	Ronald D Cochrane
Gowanda v (3)	MC 716 532-3353							
Granville v (3)	MC 518 642-2640							
Great Neck v (9)	MC 516 482-0019							
Great Neck Estates v (3)	MC 516 482-8283							
Great Neck Plaza v (6)	MC 516 482-4500	Robert Rosegarten	Patricia Wolfe	Jane Nitzky			Michael Sweeney	Michael Simone
Green Island v (2)	MC 518 273-2201	John J McNulty	James D Finning	Anne M Strizzi		Michael Carlow	Kenneth T Davis	Henry Carl Jr
Greenwood Lake v (3)	MC 914 477-9215							
Hamburg v (10)	MC 716 649-0200							
Hamilton v (4)	MC 315 824-1111	Lawrence Baker		Paul Kogut		Robert Reed	James Tilbe	John Rathbone
Harrison (23)	MC 914 835-2000	P A Marraccini		N Brunner Ponce		Vito Faga		
Hastings-On-Hudson v (8)	CM 914 478-3400							
Haverstraw v (9)	MC 914 429-0300	Thos L Watson		Deborah P Smith		Robert Sullivan	John J Reilly	Andrew M Connors
Hempstead v (49)	MC 516 489-3400							
Herkimer v (8)	MC 315 866-3303							
Highland Falls v (4)	MC 914 446-3400							
Hilton v (5)	MC 716 392-4144	Larry Garsslin	James Ingham	Janet Surridge	Janet Surridge			Thomas Tilebein
Homer v (3)	MC 607 749-3322	Mary A Bellardini		Jo Anne Williams		James Reif	David V Sampson	Robert Lottridge
Hoosick v (3)	MC 518 686-7072							
Hornell (10)	MC 607 324-7421							
Horseheads v (7)	CM 607 739-5691	Patricia Gross	Chris Lawrick	S Cunningham		Richard Sullivan	R Craig Banfield	James Stevens
Hudson (8)	MC 518 828-1030	Richard Scalera		Bonita J Colwell	John Pryshlak	Joseph Pulver	Edward A Eisley	C Butterworth
Hudson Falls v (8)	MC 518 747-5426							
Ilion v (9)	MC 315 895-7449	Stephen Canipe	Marilyn Slaughter	Gale Hatch	Gale Hatch	Karl Tripple	Lloyd Wadsworth	James Rowland
Irondequolt t (52)	MC 716 467-8840							
Irvington v (6)	MC 914 591-7070	Dennis Flood	Stephen McCabe	Lawrence Schopfer	Lawrence Schopfer	Michael Colantuono	Richard Denike	Robert Bauer
Island Park v (5)	MC 516 431-0600	J Papatsos		Ann M Leonard		Steve Ruscio		Joseph Didomenico
Islandla v (3)	MC 516 348-1133							
Ithaca (30)	MC 607 274-6501	Benjamin Nichols		C Paolangeli	D Cafferillo	Brian Wilbur	Harlin R McEwen	William J Gray
Jamestown (35)	MC 716 483-7610	Richard Kimball		Shirley Sanfilipo	Richard Cole	Charles Hajduk	Andrew Johnson	Jeffrey Lehman
Johnson City v (17)	MC 607 798-7861							
Johnstown (9)	MC 518 762-3911							
Kenmore v (17)	MC 716 873-5700	John W Beaumont		Edmund J O' Grady	John W Beaumont	Mark Belis	Elmer Arnet	Charles Sottile
Kings Point v (5)	MC 516 482-7872							
Kingston (23)	MC 914 331-0080	T R Gallo		M Theresa Duross		John E Reinhardt	James K Riggins	Jay Hogan
Lackawanna (21)	MC 716 827-6464	K Staniszewski	Annie Swygert	Dorothy Wojcik	Robert Marciniak	Stanley Kaminski	Joseph Deren	Leo Murphy
Lake Grove v (10)	MC 516 585-2000	Lillian B Griffin		Marian Zetterberg				Douglas J Colino
Lake Success v (2)	MC 516 482-4411	Roberta Chavis	Roberta Penchina	Roberta Penchina	Roberta Penchina		William Roberts	Richard Faraci
Lakewood v (4)	MC 716 763-8557							
Lancaster v (12)	MC 716 683-2105							
Lansing v (3)	MC 607 257-0424	Theodore C Wixom		Sylvia S Smith				Dennis K Reinhart
Larchmont v (6)	MC 914 834-6202	Cheryl Lewy		Eileen Finn		Joseph Russo	William Keresey	
Lawrence v (7)	MC 516 239-4600							
Le Roy v (5)	CM 716 768-2527							
Lewiston v (3)	MC 716 754-8271							
Liberty v (4)	CM 914 292-2250	Ron F Gozza		Judy Zurowski	Ron F Gozza	Carlton Fritz	Micael Ward	Marv Cox
Lindenhurst v (27)	MC 516 957-7500							
Little Falls (6)	MC 315 823-2400							
Liverpool v (3)	MC 315 457-3441	F A Bobenhausen		Nancy K O' Brien		Robert Cussen	Gerald Neri	Patrick Babcock
Lloyd Harbor v (3)	MC 516 423-9044						Bernard J Welsh	
Lockport (24)	MC 716 439-6676	Kenneth Swan		Richard Mullaney		Gary Millhollen	Henry Newman	John Claypool
Long Beach (34)	CM 516 431-1000							
Lowville v (4)	MC 315 376-6711							
Lynbrook v (19)	MC 516 599-8300							
Lyons v (4)	MC 315 946-4531	Gabriel Vardabash		Diana Marro		Melvin Briggs	John Lese	Charles Bowers
Malone v (7)	MC 518 483-4570							
Malverne v (9)	MC 516 599-1200	Joseph J Hennessy		Carolyn E Knauer		John O' Brien	Raymond Garrigan	Vincent Gebbia
Mamaroneck t (17)	CM 914 381-7810							
Manlius v (5)	MC 315 682-9171							
Manorhaven v (6)	MC 516 883-7000							
Massapequa Park v (18)	MC 516 798-0244	George Nussbaum	M Capobianco	M Capobianco	M Capobianco			William Colfer
Massena v (12)	MC 315 769-7052	Charles R Boots				Thomas LaCombe	Tim Currier	Hassan A Fayad
Mechanicville (5)	CO 518 664-9884	Thomas J Higgins		Clara Pitcheralle	James J Levesque	Louis Alonzo		Francis A Rubino
Medina v (7)	MC 716 798-0710							
Menands v (4)	MC 511 427-7303	John Weidman	William J Jones	William J Jones	William J Jones	Donald Caswell	Michael McCauley	William Treacy
Middletown (24)	MC 914 343-4189							
Mineola v (19)	MC 516 746-0750		Richard M DeVoe			William Mahoney		Louis DiDomenico
Minoa v (4)	MC 315 656-3100							
Mohawk v (3)	MC 315 866-4312	Leo Kinville		Judy Bray		James Hennings	Daniel Spatto	Michael Hess
Monroe v (7)	MC 914 782-8341	Robert R Bonney		Virginia Carey	Marcella Hopwood		Dominic Giudice	
Montebello v (..)	MC 914 368-2211							
Monticello v (7)	CM 914 794-6130							
Morrisville v (3)	MC 315 684-3214							
Mount Kisco v (9)	CM 914 241-0500							

Directory 1/9
continued

MUNICIPAL OFFICIALS
IN U.S. CITIES OVER 2,500

City, 1990 population figures (000 omitted), form of government	Municipal phone number	Mayor/ chief elected official	Appointed administrator	City clerk/ city secretary	Finance officer	Fire chief	Police chief	Public works director
NEW YORK (275) continued								
Mount Morris v (3)	MC 716 658-4160	....	....	....	....	....	....	....
Mount Vernon (67)	MC 914 665-2300	....	....	....	....	....	....	....
Munsey Park v (3)	MC 516 365-7790	....	....	....	....	....	....	....
Muttontown v (3)	MC 516 364-2240	....	....	....	....	....	....	....
New Hempstead v (4)	MC 914 354-8100	....	....	....	....	....	....	....
New Hyde Park v (10)	MC 516 354-0022	....	....	....	....	....	....	....
New Paltz v (5)	MC 914 255-0130	Thomas E Nyquist	Estelle Wilson	Estelle Wilson	Thomas E Nyquist	David Weeks	....	Garry Thomsen
New Rochelle (67)	CM 914 654-2140	Timothy Idonl	C Indellcato	Gwendolyn Byrd	Howard Rattner	Raymond Kiernan	Patrick Carroll	George Lee
New York City (7323)	MC 212 566-5700	....	....	....	....	....	....	....
New York Mills v (4)	MC 315 736-9212	....	....	....	....	....	....	....
Newark v (10)	MC 315 331-4770	....	....	....	....	....	....	....
Newburgh (26)	CM 914 561-4873	A Carey	H Porr	N D' Addio	H Patel	R Paden	W Bloom	....
Niagara Falls (62)	CM 716 286-4300	Jacob Palillo	Thomas Lizardo	Elsie Paradise	Patrick Brown	John Gabriele	Thomas Zwelling	Richard Lucinski
North Syracuse v (7)	MC 315 458-0900	James A Hotchkiss	....	E Jane Visell	....	Paul Linnertz	....	Michael Abruzzese
North Tarrytown v (8)	MC 914 631-1440	Sean Treacy	Linda E David	Linda E David	....	John Morabito	James Brophy	Joseph Defeo
North Tonawanda (35)	MC 716 695-8555	James A McGinnis	....	John W Wylucki	David Jakubasek	David Rogge	Lloyd Graves	Gary J Franklin
Northport v (8)	MC 516 261-7502	Peter J Nolan	....	Judith Zahm	....	Terry Koch	Robert Howard	Joseph Correia
Norwich (8)	MC 607 334-1200	Joseph L Biviano	....	Jody Zakrevsky	Harold Hutton	Timothy Ashcraft	Robert Mason	Joseph Loscavio
Nyack v (7)	MC 914 358-0548	....	....	....	....	....	....	....
Ocean Beach v (..)	MC 516 583-5940	....	....	....	....	....	....	....
Ogdensburg (14)	CM 315 393-6100	Richard Lockwood	John Krol	Rebecca J Claxton	Philip A Cosmo	Albert Livingston	Lorne H Fairbairn	James W Farrell
Old Westbury v (4)	MC 516 626-0800	....	....	....	....	....	....	....
Olean (17)	MC 716 372-2200	....	....	....	....	....	....	....
Oneida (11)	MC 315 363-4800	Army Carinci	....	Grace Perretta	Joan Cukierski	Erwin Smith	John McClellan	James Bacher
Oneonta (14)	MC 607 432-0670	David Brenner	....	James Koury	David Martindale	Robert Barnes	John Donadio	Ted Christman
Orchard Park v (3)	MC 716 662-9327	....	....	....	....	....	....	....
Ossining v (23)	CM 914 941-3554	John Pasquerella	Gennaro J Faiella	Marie Fuesy	Pat D' Imperlo	Louis DiLoreto	Joseph Burton	Robert Emerick
Oswego (19)	MC 315 342-8160	Terrence Hammill	Kathryn E Torba	Thomas M Ryan	Paul R Miller	James C Borden	Frederick Waters	John F McHale
Owego v (4)	MC 607 687-3555	Charlene Caldwell	....	Lynne Mieczkowski	....	Ken Zaston	Robert Williams	Charles Lohmeyer
Palmyra v (4)	MC 315 597-4849	....	....	....	....	....	....	....
Patchogue v (11)	MC 516 475-4300	F S Leavandosky	....	Rose Marie Berger	....	Joseph Gallitelli	....	....
Peekskill (20)	CM 914 737-3400	....	....	....	....	....	....	....
Pelham v (6)	MC 914 738-2015	Joseph E Durnin	Michael S DeLong	Lisa Stiefvater	Michael S DeLong	....	Joseph Benefico	Harry Pallett
Pelham Manor v (5)	MC 914 738-4754	Valentine Taubner	Richard Blessing	Richard Blessing	....	Archelle Petrucci	Dennis Carroll	....
Penn Yan v (5)	MC 315 536-3015	Gerald A Nissen	....	Joyce E Benedict	Joyce E Benedict	Jens Jensen	Stephen Hill	....
Perry v (4)	MC 716 237-2216	Steve Moultrup	....	Paula Parker	....	....	Gary Jurkowski	Phil Cowie
Plattsburgh (21)	MC 518 563-7702	....	....	....	....	....	....	....
Pleasantville v (7)	CM 914 769-1900	M Gail Grimaldi	Patricia Dwyer	Judith Weintraub	....	....	A Chiarlitti	Stephen A Johnson
Port Chester v (25)	CM 914 939-2200	John Branca	Michael Graessle	Richard Falanka	Robert Reardon	Thomas Gallagher	Carl Verrastro	Wiliam Summa
Port Jefferson v (7)	MC 516 473-4724	....	....	....	....	....	....	....
Port Jervis (9)	MC 914 858-4014	R Michael Worden		....	James J Hinkley	Russell Potter	William Wagner	Vincent Lopez
Port Washington N v (3)	MC 516 883-5900	....	....	....	....	....	....	....
Potsdam v (10)	MC 315 265-7480	Ruth F Garner	Robert R Burns	Margaret Robinson	....	Steven A Keleher	Terry McKendree	....
Poughkeepsie (29)	CM 914 451-4035	Sheila Newman	Joseph Chiseri	Barbara Schelin	Mark Newton	Jack Forbes	Neil Polay	Michael Murphy
Ravena v (4)	MC 518 756-8233	John T Bruno	....	Josephine Dority	....	Brian Dunican	Frank McCabe	Ronald Burns
Rensselaer (8)	MC 518 462-9511	....	....	....	....	....	....	....
Rhinebeck v (3)	MC 914 876-7015	Peter F Sipperley	....	Valerie S Kilmer	Valerie S Kilmer	....	....	Raymond G Warman
Rochester (232)	MC 716 428-7000	William Johnson	Daniel Benitez	Carolee Conklin	Vincent Carfagna	David L Griffith	Robert S Warshaw	Edward Doherty
Rockville Centre v (25)	MC 516 678-9300	....	....	....	....	....	....	....
Rome (44)	MC 315 336-6000	Joseph A Griffo	....	Jeanette Denton	....	Ronald Swinney	Merino Ciccone	Robert Comis
Rye (15)	CM 914 967-5400	Edward B Dunn	Frank J Culross	Alice K Conrad	C Martino	Peter Cotter	William A Pease	Joseph M Carlucci
Rye Brook (8)	CM 914 939-1121	S Cresenzi	Christopher Russo	Christopher Russo	....	....	Robert Santoro	Rocco Circosta
Sag Harbor v (2)	MC 516 725-0222	Pierson W Hance	....	R Winchell	Pierce W Hance	Robert Bori	Joseph Ialaccl	James Early
Salamanca (7)	MC 716 945-4620	Rosalyn Hoag	....	A Vecchiarella	Linda Rychcik	Jack McClune	Edward Gimbrone	A Pascarella
Sands Point v (2)	MC 516 883-3044	Leonard Wurzel	....	Linda H Mitchell	....	....	Michael Connolly	Dominick Gallucio
Saranac Lake v (5)	CM 518 891-4150	W F Madden	J P Fitzgerald	M C Clement	....	R Girard	K Peer	S Natoli
Saratoga Springs (25)	CO 518 587-3550	A C Dake	....	Edward Valentine	J M O' Connell	Vincent Camarro	Kenneth King	Joseph O' Neill
Saugerties v (4)	MC 914 246-2321	Anthi Chorvas	....	Jean C Turner	....	Gary Anderson	William B Kimble	John Kolano
Scarsdale v (17)	CM 914 723-5591	Walter Handelman	Lowell Tooley	Lowell Tooley	David Coldrick	Walter Felice	Donald Ferraro	William Cooke
Schenectady (66)	MC 518 382-5010	Frank J Duci	William Fyvie	Carolyn Friello	Fred Bartz	Thomas Varno	Charles Mills	Milton Mitchell
Scotia v (7)	MC 518 374-1071	....	....	....	....	....	....	....
Sea Cliff v (5)	MC 516 671-0080	....	....	....	....	....	....	....
Seneca Falls v (7)	MC 315 568-8107	....	....	....	....	....	....	....
Sherrill (3)	CM 315 363-2440	....	....	....	....	....	....	....
Sidney v (5)	MC 607 561-2324	Elwood Davis	....	Denise Singlar	....	....	Craig Whitten	Frank Holley
Silver Creek v (3)	MC 716 934-3240	E Turzillo	....	Cynthia Klocko	....	Richard Bartlett	John M Yannie	John L Burt
Skaneateles v (3)	MC 315 685-3440	Martin L Hubbard	....	Sally L Sheehan	....	....	Jack McNeil	John O Abbott
Sloan v (4)	MC 716 897-1560	Adeline Sicignano	Patricia Krzemien	Patricia Krzemien	Patricia Krzemien	Joseph Coffta	....	Anthony Sisti
Sloatsburg v (3)	MC 914 753-2727	Samuel J Abate	....	Thomas F Bollatto	....	Anthony Massaro	....	John Dobrinski Sr
Solvay v (7)	MC 315 468-1679	....	....	....	....	....	....	....
South Glens Falls v (4)	MC 518 793-1455	Robert Phinney	....	Karin Blood	....	Ronald Quinn	Kevin Judd	John Dixon
South Nyack v (3)	MC 914 358-0287	Charles Cross	....	Mary G Martini	Wallace B Martini	Joseph Dellilio	Alan B Colsey	James F Johnson
Southampton v (4)	MC 516 283-0247	Douglas Murtha	Howard McElroy	Howard McElroy	....	Stephen Phillips	James Sherry	Robert Brown
Spencerport v (4)	MC 716 352-4771	Clyde W Carter	....	Gina M Tojek	....	Gerald Smith	....	Roy G Hill
Spring Valley v (22)	MC 914 352-1100	Allan A Thompson	....	Sam Hershkowitz	....	Jack Ahlf	Howard Goldin	John Ackerson
Springville v (4)	MC 716 592-4936	....	....	....	....	....	....	....
Suffern v (11)	MC 914 357-1600	....	....	....	....	....	....	....
Syracuse (164)	MC 315 448-8077	....	....	....	....	....	....	....
Tarrytown v (11)	MC 914 631-1106	Eileen Pilla	Michael Blau	Louise Camillieri	Gerald Barbelet	....	Scott Brown	B Salanitro
Thomaston v (3)	MC 516 482-3110	....	....	....	....	....	....	....
Ticonderoga v (3)	MC 518 585-7404	....	....	....	....	....	....	....
Tonawanda (17)	MC 716 695-1800	....	....	....	....	....	....	....
Troy (54)	CM 518 270-4401	....	....	....	....	....	....	....
Tuckahoe v (6)	MC 914 961-3100	Philip A White	....	Susan Ciamarra	L Kalkstein	....	Gerard Mignone	Anthony Cacciola
Tupper Lake v (4)	MC 518 359-3341	....	....	....	....	....	....	....
Union t (60)	MC 607 754-2102	....	....	....	....	....	....	....
Utica (69)	MC 315 792-0300	....	....	....	....	....	....	....
Valley Stream v (34)	MC 516 825-4200	George A Donley	Vincent W Ang	Vincent W Ang	....	William Howley	....	Robert J Gunther
Voorheesville v (3)	MC 518 765-2692	....	....	....	....	....	....	....
Walden v (6)	CM 914 778-2177	Andrew Uszenski	John Kelly	Nancy Mitchell	Jan Weiner	Ed Pimm	Jeffrey Holmes	Walter Sweed
Walton v (3)	MC 607 865-4358	....	....	....	....	....	....	....
Wappingers Falls v (5)	MC 914 297-8773	....	....	....	....	....	....	....
Warsaw v (4)	MC 716 786-2120	....	....	....	....	....	....	....

Directory 1/9 continued

MUNICIPAL OFFICIALS IN U.S. CITIES OVER 2,500

City, 1990 population figures (000 omitted), form of government		Municipal phone number	Mayor/ chief elected official	Appointed administrator	City clerk/ city secretary	Finance officer	Fire chief	Police chief	Public works director
NEW YORK (275) continued									
Warwick v (6)	MC	914 986-2031	....	....	....	....	....	....	....
Waterloo v (5)	MC	315 539-9131	....	....	....	....	....	....	....
Watertown (29)	CM	315 785-7730	Jeffrey E Graham	Karl R Amylon	Donna M Dutton	James M McCauley	Ronald Chisamore	Michael Hennegan	Eugene P Hayes
Watervliet (11)	CM	518 270-3810	J Leo O' Brien	Paul S Murphy	Bruce A Hidley	Robert A Fahr	....	....	N J Ostapkovich
Waverly v (5)	MC	607 565-8106	Daniel F Leary	....	Mary Ann Laman	....	....	Larry Preston	Micheal Steck
Webster v (5)	MC	716 265-3770	....	....	....	....	....	....	....
Wellsville v (5)	MC	716 593-1121	Susan Goetschius	....	Janice A Givens	Janice A Givens	James Meehan	James A Cicirello	Robert Chaffee
Wesley Hills v (..)	MC	914 354-0400	Robert H Frankl	....	Dorothy L France	....	....	....	....
West Haverstraw v (9)	MC	914 947-2800	Edward P Zugibe	....	O Fred Miller	....	Bruce Carver	....	George E Wargo Sr
West Seneca t (48)	MC	716 674-5600	....	....	....	....	....	....	....
Westbury v (13)	MC	516 334-1700	....	....	....	....	....	....	....
Westfield v (3)	MC	716 326-4961	Joseph Pagano	....	Richard Clawson	....	John Lindstrom	Kenneth Machemer	....
White Plains (49)	MC	914 422-1257	S J Schulman	Kevin Fish	Janice Minieri	John Powell	John Cullen	James Bradley	Joseph Nicoletti
Whitehall v (3)	MC	518 499-0871	....	....	....	....	....	....	....
Whitesboro v (4)	MC	315 736-1613	....	....	....	....	....	....	....
Williamsville v (6)	MC	716 632-4120	....	....	....	....	....	....	....
Williston Park v (8)	MC	516 746-2193	....	....	....	....	....	....	....
Woodridge v (1)	CM	914 434-7447	....	....	....	....	....	....	....
Yonkers (188)	MC	914 377-6000	Terence Zaleski	....	Joan Deierlein	William Thomas	Neil Curry	Robert Olson	....
Yorkville v (3)	MC	315 736-0263	....	....	....	....	....	....	....
NORTH CAROLINA (173)									
Ahoskie t (4)	CM	919 332-5146	James Hutcherson	Russell W Overman	Edith Merritt	Edith Merritt	Kenneth Dilday	Stephen B Hoggard	Terry Padgett
Albemarle (15)	CM	704 982-0131	Roger F Snyder	Raymond I Allen	Raymond I Allen	Robert N Stewart	George McDaniel	Charles McManus	James C Coble
Angier tp (2)	CO	919 639-2071	Ty Cobb	John Moore	Jean Matthews	Linda Williams	....	Leslie Halpin	Emory Brooks
Apex t (5)	CM	919 362-7300	Everette Edwards	William Sutton	Georgia Parker	Lee Smiley	....	Ronald Hearn	....
Archdale (7)	CM	910 431-9141	Donald L Hancock	Carl W Howie	Maxine V Renn	Carl W Howie	....	Larry Allen	Shelton Bradshaw
Asheboro (16)	CM	910 626-1200	W Joseph Trogdon	David B Leonard	Carol J Cole	Darrell Rich	James W Smith	James C Finch	Dumont Bunker
Asheville (62)	CM	704 251-1122	Russ Martin	....	William Wolcott	Larry A Fisher	John Rukavina	Will Annarino	James Ewing
Atlantic Beach t (2)	CM	919 726-2121	....	Don E Holycross	....	....	....	....	....
Ayden t (5)	CM	919 746-7030	M C Baldree Jr	Rick Benton	Dorothy Bridges	Cathy Wilson	Jeff Tripp	Roger Paul	Jim Westbrook
Beaufort t (4)	CM	919 728-2141	....	....	....	....	....	....	....
Beech Mountain t (..)	CM	704 387-4236	Fred Pfohl	Seth Lawless	Barbara Mooradian	Sally Rominger	....	Marvin Hefner	Joe Perry
Belhaven t (2)	CM	919 943-3055	Charles O Boyette	Timothy M Johnson	Marie A Johnston	Jerry L Lamaster	Jessie Taylor	Mark S Smith	Carroll Hearring
Belmont (8)	CM	704 825-5586	Kevin B Loftin	Mitchell B Moore	M Lingafeldt	....	Jimmy Austin	Charles B Flowers	....
Benson t (3)	MC	919 894-4953	Charles W Matthew	Keith R Langdon	Carolyn Nordan	Carolyn Nordan	Tony Barnes	Donald Miller	Steve Barefoot
Bessemer City (5)	CM	704 629-5542	William D Wise	Ralph S Messera	Janice M Costner	Mary Ann Hook	David Ford	Ken Hunsucker	Eddie Sykes
Biltmore Forest t (1)	CM	704 274-0824	E Glenn Kelly	Nelson E Smith	Nelson E Smith	Nelson E Smith	....	Eugene L Ray	Swain M Ballard
Black Mountain t (5)	CM	704 669-9102	....	....	....	....	....	....	....
Boone t (13)	CM	704 262-4530	Velma Burnley	Greg Young	Freida Van Allen	Joyce Watson	Reggie Hassle	Zane Tester	Blake Brown
Brevard (5)	CM	704 884-4123	John Peterson	Dee Freeman	Glenda Sansosti	Dot Angel	....	Lud Vaughan	Don Owen
Burlington (39)	CM	910 222-5000	Joe P Barbour	William R Baker	Jondeen D Terry	Billy K Truett	W F Andrews	John M Glenn	Arthur R Kornegay
Canton t (4)	CM	704 648-2363	Robert M Phillips	William G Stamey	Jimmy L Flynn	William G Stamey	Phillip Smathers	William M Guillet	Roger M Lyda
Carolina Beach t (4)	MC	910 458-2992	Anthony A Loreti	Laurence Flindsey	Lona B Thompson	E Schneider	Robert E Weeks	B H Woods	....
Carrboro t (12)	CM	919 942-8541	Eleanor Kinnaird	Robert Morgan	Sarah Williamson	William Gibson Jr	Rodney Murray	Benjamin Callahan	Monty Peterson
Cary t (44)	CM	919 469-4070	Koka Booth	James Westbrook	Sue Rowland	Karen Mills	Macon House	David Fortson	Robert Fisher
Chadbourn t (2)	CM	910 654-4148	Paul Avant	Howard A Jones	Marie Williamson	Marie Williamson	Allen Yates	Kelly Rogers	Spurgeon Duncan
Chapel Hill t (39)	CM	919 968-2700	Kenneth Broun	W Calvin Horton	Peter Richardson	James Baker	Daniel Jones	Ralph Pendergraph	Bruce Heflin
Charlotte (396)	CM	704 336-2285	Richard Vinroot	O Wendell White	Brenda Freeze	Richard Martin	Luther Fincher	Dennis Nowicki	....
Cherryville (5)	CM	704 435-1710	J Ralph Beam Jr	Janice Hovis	Jean Beam	Janice Hovis	Jeff Cash	Johnny Wehunt	Ted Mace
Claremont (1)	CM	704 459-7009	Joseph M Chander	Marion McGinnis	Patricia C Miller	Patricia C Miller	Gary W Sigmon	Gerald R Tolbert	Billy R Henson
Clayton t (5)	CM	919 553-5866	....	....	....	....	....	....	....
Clinton t (8)	CM	910 592-1961	A E Kennedy Jr	Tommy M Combs	Betty Fortner	Peggy B Wiggins	Leonard Edge	Alton Hunter	Wayne Hollowell
Concord (27)	CM	704 786-6161	George Liles	Leonard Sossamon	Vickie C Weant	Joyce A Allman	T Randy Holloway	Robert E Cansler	C W Barringer
Conover (5)	CM	704 464-1191	Bruce R Eckard	L B Beasley Jr	Frances L Kincaid	Vickie K Yandle	J Reid Poovey Jr	Dale C Stewart	Jimmy A Clark
Cornelius t (3)	CM	704 892-6031	....	....	....	....	....	....	....
Dallas t (3)	MC	704 922-3176	C H Cloninger	....	N E Vlaservich	N E Vlaservich	D Callahan	H Guffey	J D Ferguson
Davidson t (4)	MC	704 892-7591	Russell B Knox	Leamon B Brice	Peggy W Smith	Peggy W Smith	Robert W Gurley	Henry McKiernan	James T Treadaway
Drexel t (2)	CM	704 437-7421	Richard Propst	Morris Baker	Sherri Bradshaw	Morris Baker	Benny Orders	Terry Yount	Bill Dowdle
Dunn (8)	CM	910 892-2633	Oscar Harris	Carl Dean	Joyce Valley	Teresa Haney	Austin Tew	Kenneth Sills	Ronnie Autry
Durham (137)	CM	919 560-4214	Sylvia Kerckhoff	Orville W Powell	Margaret M Bowers	John G Pedersen	N L Thompson	Jackie W McNeil	A T Rolan
Eden (15)	CM	910 623-9707	Phillip Price	James Pennington	Mary Lambert	William R Sharp	Ronald Overby	Gary Benthin	Steven Branz
Edenton t (5)	CM	919 482-2155	Roy L Harrell	Anne Marie Kelly	....	Janet P Hines	Lynn C Perry	Charles Williams	Michael Rayner
Elizabeth City (14)	CM	919 338-3981	H Rick Gardner	Ralph Clark	Dianne Pierce	Sarah Blanchard	Tedd Melvin	H L Bunch	Ray Rogerson
Elizabethtown t (4)	MC	910 862-2067	Wallace Leinwand	James Freeman	Marion Morrisey	....	Tim Sessoms	Mike Royston	Dan Harbaugh
Elkin t (4)	CM	910 835-9800	Thomas Gwyn	Joseph Huffman	Joe Layell	Joe Layell	Tommy Wheeler	Stephen Hampton	Tim Darnel
Elon College t (4)	CM	910 584-3601	Jerry R Tolley	Michael A Dula	Sabrina M Oliver	Michael A Dula	Walter E King	Dan W Ingle	Donald K Wagoner
Enfield t (3)	CM	919 445-3146	E Kai Hardaway	....	Julius G Woody	....	James P Ellen	Theodore H Mayer	Bobby E Davis
Erwin t (4)	MC	910 897-5140	George R Joseph	Charles S Simmons	Ramona O Warren	....	....	Thomas Chandler	Mark W Byrd
Fairmont t (2)	CM	910 628-9766	Jeffrey G Lewis	....	Shirley Price	Helen Lockley	John Jackson	Terry Hunt	Ben Hill
Farmville t (4)	CM	919 753-5774	Robert E Winborn	Richard N Hicks	Michelle Creech	Michelle Creech	John Baker	Robert Smith	W R Oakley
Fayetteville (76)	CM	919 433-1990	J L Dawkins	John P Smith	Bobbie Joyner	Kai Nelson	Duke Piner	Ronald Hansen	....
Forest City t (7)	CM	704 245-0148	Charles E Butler	Charles R Summey	Sandra P Mayse	F Pruett Walden	L Mark McCurry	Randy G Chapman	Herbert R Toms Jr
Franklin t (3)	MC	704 524-2516	Wm Steele Smith	James Williamson	Janet A Anderson	Janet A Anderson	William Jamison	....	Alvin L Ledford
Franklinton t (2)	CM	919 494-2520	Charles Draughn	Bill Vance	Kim Worley	Bill Vance	....	Ray Gilliam	Raymond Bragg
Fuquay-Varina t (5)	CM	919 552-3178	Alfred M Johnson	Larry W Bennelt	Rachel B Turner	Rachel B Turner	....	Stacy Pleasant	T C O' Connell
Gamewell (3)	MC	704 754-6242	John D Wootton Jr	....	Carolyn K Warren	Jack F Roberts	....	....	....
Garner t (15)	CM	919 772-4688	Don Rohrbaugh	Peter Bine	Mary Lou Rand	Linwood Jones Jr	....	Tom Moss	Bill Rudy
Gastonia (55)	MC	704 866-6859	James B Garland	Danny O Crew	Susan C Kluttz	John A Philyaw	Robert L Murray	Jackie S Postell	Donald Carmichael
Gibsonville t (3)	CM	910 449-4144	William Moricle	DeLeno Flynn	DeLeno Flynn	Connie Woody	James R Tomas	Morris McPherson	Coy L May
Goldsboro (41)	CM	919 751-6121	Hal Plonk	Richard Slozak	Lura Ray	Richard Durham	Willard Herring	Chester Hill	C R Southerland
Graham (10)	CM	910 228-8362	Victor Euliss	Ray Fogleman	Eydie May	Ray Fogleman	Kenneth Evans	....	Donnie Braxton
Granite Falls t (3)	CM	704 396-3131	A W Huffman Jr	Linda Story	Judy L Mackie	....	Thomas B Laws	Jerry Bumgarner	William Hamilton
Greensboro (184)	CM	910 373-2065	Carolyn Allen	Wm H Carstarphen	Nancy McPeak	Richard Lusk	Ray Flowers	Syl Daughtry	....
Greenville (45)	CM	919 830-4432	Nancy M Jenkins	Ronald R Kimble	Wanda T Elks	Bernita W Demery	Raymond L Carney	Charles E Hinman	Thomas N Tysinger
Hamlet (6)	CM	910 582-2651	Abbie Covington	Lee Matthews	Lisa Vierling	Michael Deese	David Fuller	Terry Moore	Ralph Yates
Havelock (20)	CM	919 444-6402	Jimmy A Sanders	....	Kathleen Townsend	Diane Scarborough	....	Michael Campbell	Robert S Collins
Henderson (16)	CM	919 492-6111	Robert G Young Jr	Eric M Williams	Dianne White	Jerry L Moss	Thomas Wilkerson	Steve Kincheloe	James Morgan
Hendersonville (7)	MC	704 697-3000	Fred H Niehoff Jr	Chris A Carter	Barbara W Porter	Jim Rudisill	Charles King	Donnie R Parks	Don Sides
Hickory (28)	CM	704 323-7400	William McDonald	B Gary McGee	Patricia Williams	Julie McCollum	Herman R Bishop	Floyd W Lucas	W Jerry Twiggs
High Point (69)	CM	919 883-3259	....	....	....	....	....	....	....
Hillsborough t (4)	CM	919 732-2104	Horace H Johnson	Eric P Swanson	Donna F Ray	Sherry Carter	Jimmy Summey	Larry Biggs	....
Holden Beach t (1)	CM	910 842-6488	Gay Matkins	Gustav M Ulrich	Joyce B Shore	Sylvia B Bissell	....	Robert L Cook	John R Hickman

Directory 1/9 continued — **MUNICIPAL OFFICIALS IN U.S. CITIES OVER 2,500**

City, 1990 population figures (000 omitted), form of government	Municipal phone number	Mayor/ chief elected official	Appointed administrator	City clerk/ city secretary	Finance officer	Fire chief	Police chief	Public works director
NORTH CAROLINA (173) continued								
Hope Mills t (8)	CM 910 424-4555	Edwin S Deaver	Steven L Routh	Phyllis Register	Erika U Santiago	Merrill O Naylor	John W Hodges	Robert C Cox
Hudson t (3)	CM 704 728-8272	....	....	....	....	....	....	....
Jacksonville (30)	CM 910 455-2600	Joe M C Choate	Jerry Bittner	S McMurtrey	Debra Bailey	Franklin Barger	Roger Halbert	Michael Ellzey
Jonesville t (2)	CM 910 835-3426	....	Mark Mcdonald	....	....	....	....	....
Kannapolis (30)	MC 704 938-5131	C R Anderson	R Gene McCombs	Bridgette Laws	Michael W Shinn	Larry C Phillips	Paul D Brown	Melvin W Rape
Kenly t (2)	MC 919 284-2116	Scott A Turik	Edison E Temple	Sharon A Bailey	....	Steve Brinchek	Larry G Carter	Terry Strickland
Kernersville t (11)	CM 910 996-3121	Thomas W Prince	Randy E McCaslin	Diane S Cook	John W Cater	Jimmy L Barrow	Grady C Stockton	Charles Hamilton
Kill Devil Hills t (4)	CM 919 480-4000	Terence L Gray	Debora P Diaz	Mary E Quidley	Teresa Pickrel	William Gard	James Gradeless	Charles A Smith
King (4)	CM 910 983-8265	Joel B New	R Randy Martin	Jolene H Massie	Christine Whicker	....	T A Patrick	Thomas F New
Kings Mountain (9)	CM 704 734-0333	Scott Neisler	Charles Nance	Marilyn Sellers	....	Frank Burns	Warren Goforth	Karl Moss
Kinston (25)	CM 919 559-4200	O A Ritch	Anthony Barrett	Peggy Boone	Edward Pierce	Tony Kelly	John Wolford	J T Pratt
La Grange t (3)	MC 919 566-3186	....	....	....	....	....	....	....
Lake Lure t (..)	CM 704 625-9983	Max E Lehner	Tom Hord	Mary A Flack	Sam A Karr	Donny Ruff	Jake Gamble	Tony Hennessee
Laurinburg (12)	CM 910 276-8324	William R Purcell	Peter Vandenberg	Betty R Childress	Phillip L Robey	James A Lytch	Robert L Malloy	Harold Smith
Lenoir (14)	CM 704 757-2200	Robert A Gibbons	James H Hipp	Lynn P Martin	Elizabeth Wilson	Bobby H Coffey	Jack F Warlick	....
Lewisville t (..)	CM 910 945-5558	Hank Chilton	John A Whitson	Janet Wrights	John A Whitson	....	....	....
Lexington (17)	CM 704 243-2489	Vernon Price Jr	Duke Whisenant	Martha Hoffman	Richard Ratcliff	William Deal	Leroy Pearson	Jeffrey Edmonds
Lincolnton t (7)	CM 704 732-2281	Jerry L Campbell	David E Lowe	Kay B Polhill	George E Heavner	Donald Wise	Terry Burgin	Stephen Peeler
Long Beach t (4)	CM 910 278-5011	Joan P Altman	Jerry A Walters	Patricia Brunell	Cathy Harvell	Tim Pittman	Danny Laughren	Charles Derrick
Long View t (3)	CM 704 322-3921	Norman E Cook	E Bruce Morgan	Amy Hall	Roxanne Brittain	Ernest Riley	David Turner	Teddy Franklin
Louisburg t (3)	MC 919 496-4145	....	....	....	....	....	....	....
Lowell (3)	MC 704 824-3518	....	....	....	....	....	....	....
Lumberton (19)	CM 910 671-3800	Ray B Pennington	Robert W Hites	Janie Revels	Timothy Inch	Ronald Parker	Harry P Dolan	Dixon Ivey
Madison t (2)	CM 910 427-0221	Arthur R Gwaltney	Bradley K Smith	Brenda D Moore	Philip M Pulliam	William W Wall	Jerry H Welch	Keith R Tucker
Maiden t (3)	CM 704 428-5000	Robert L Smyre	Doris C Bumgarner	Sharon Sipe	Doris C Bumgarner	Rick Cansler	Donald R Walker	Billy R Price
Marion (5)	CM 704 652-3551	A Everette Clark	J Earl Daniels	J Earl Daniels	J Earl Daniels	Thomas S Milligan	Thomas B Pruett	Glen Sherlin
Maxton t (2)	MC 910 844-5231	Robert B Midgette	Paul G Davis	....	Paul G Davis	....	Ronald L Wagner	Shelton McNair
Mayodan t (2)	CM 919 427-0241	Jeffrey Bullins	Jerry Carlton	Debra Cardwell	Debra Cardwell	Donald Case	Edwin Shelton	....
Mebane t (5)	CM 919 563-5901	G Stephenson	Robert Wilson	....	....	....	Gary Bumgarner	James Jobe Jr
Mint Hill t (12)	MC 704 545-9726	Joseph V Hamilton	James F Owens	Beth Q Hamrick	William H Sirakos	Paul E Campbell	....	....
Mocksville t (3)	CM 704 634-2259	D J Mando	Terry L Bralley	Jeff White	Terry L Bralley	Jimmy Kelly	Richard Sink	Danny Smith
Monroe (16)	CM 704 282-4500	Lewis Fisher	Jerry E Cox	Jeanne Deese	Sonia Vizcaino	....	Bobby G Kilgore	J Ronald Griffin
Mooresville t (9)	CM 704 663-3800	Joe V Knox	Richard A McLean	B Whittington	Thomas Nixon	Doug Nantz	Joe Puett	Frankie White
Morehead City t (6)	MC 919 726-6848	William Horton	David Walker	Joanne Spencer	Ellen Sewell	Jerry Leonard	Sammie Turner	David McCabe
Morganton (15)	CM 704 437-8863	Mel L Cohen	Michael C Cronk	Debbie Ogle	Sally Sandy	....	Robert W Williams	....
Morrisville t (1)	CM 919 469-1426	Ernest Lumley	William W Cobey	Evelyn Lumley	Julia Powell	Tony Chiotakis	Bruce Newnam	....
Mount Airy (7)	CM 910 786-3501	Emily Taylor	Ronald Niland	Barbara Jones	John Overton	Wesley Greene	Leo Shores	Elmer Dawson
Mount Holly (8)	CM 704 827-3931	Charles B Black	Phillip G Ponder	Phillip G Ponder	Phillip G Ponder	Ray Massey	Jerry Bishop	Winton Nichols
Mount Olive t (5)	CM 919 658-9536	....	....	....	....	....	....	....
Murfreesboro t (3)	MC 919 398-5904	....	....	....	....	....	....	....
Nags Head t (2)	CM 919 441-5508	Renee Cahoon	J Webb Fuller	Connie Hardee	Anna McGinnis	Douglas Remaley	Lonnie Dickens	Harry Lange
Nashville t (4)	CM 919 459-2193	Warren Evans	Tony Robertson	Gail Thomas	Barbara Woodall	Ross Strickland	Donald Skinner	Edward White
New Bern (17)	MC 919 636-4000	Thomas Bayliss	Walter Hartman	Vickie H Johnson	Mary Bratcher	Robert Aster	Ken Bumgarner	Danny Meadows
Newton (9)	CM 704 465-7400	Horace T Rowe	Thomas L Radford	Rita K Williams	Dorothy Bumgarner	Charles R Doty	James C Masters	Dwight E Wilson
North Wilkesboro t (3)	CM 910 667-7129	Conley Call	....	Gail M Harris	Gail M Harris	Edgar Harris	Barry Brown	Charles Billings
Oxford t (8)	CM 919 603-1100	Allie G Ellington	H T Ragland Jr	Ann S Parrott	Kelway L Howard	John B Norris	James H Waugh	Jimmy D Crews
Pembroke t (2)	CM 919 521-9758	....	....	....	....	....	....	....
Pinehurst v (5)	CM 919 295-1900	....	....	....	....	....	....	....
Pineville t (3)	MC 704 889-2291	....	....	....	....	....	....	....
Pittsboro t (1)	MC 919 542-4621	Charles Devinney	Ken Cornatzer	Alice J Lloyd	....	....	Larry O Hipp	....
Plymouth t (4)	CM 919 793-9101	Jarahnee H Bailey	....	Tammie G Smith	Sandra H Smith	Truitt Johnson	Ronald McKimmey	Paul Fonville
Princeville t (2)	CM 919 823-1057	....	....	....	....	....	....	....
Raeford (3)	CM 910 875-8161	Bob M Gentry	Thomas A Phillips	Betty S Smith	Helen H Huffman	Crawford L Thomas	James E Murdock	James M McNeill
Raleigh (208)	CM 919 890-3100	Tom Fetzer	Dempsey E Benton	Gail Smith	Z Brian Hill	Sherman Pickard	Mitchell Brown	William L Baird
Red Springs t (4)	CM 910 843-5241	George T Paris	Thomas W Horne	R Sue Humphrey	R Sue Humphrey	William McPhaul	Olin Levi Powers	Cleveland Parker
Reidsville (12)	CM 910 349-1035	W Clark Turner	....	Ann S Bradsher	Bernice Phillips	Charlie E King	James K Festerman	Jerry W Rothruck
Roanoke Rapids (16)	CM 919 535-2031	R Allan Welch	Victor H Denton	Lisa B Vincent	Phyllis P Lee	Kenny R Carawan	Drewery N Beale	Richard Parnell
Rockingham (9)	CM 910 997-5546	G R Kindley Jr	Monty R Crump	William Reynolds	Monty R Crump	Charles D Trotter	Eddie R Martin	....
Rocky Mount (49)	CM 919 972-1111	Frederick Turnage	William Batchelor	Jean Bailey	Craig Kivett	John Hawkins	Joseph Brown	Douglas Roberson
Roxboro (7)	CM 910 599-3116	Lois M Winstead	Thomas G Hogg	Dorothy B Harris	Bertha L Thomas	Roy W Hall	Terry L Hill	James P Whitfield
Rutherfordton t (4)	MC 704 287-3520	W Fred Williams	Karen Andrews	Karen Andrews	Janet Nix	Jim Hall	Randy Greenway	Glenn Cash
Salisbury (23)	CM 704 638-5226	Margaret H Kluttz	David W Treme	Virginia P Petrea	John A Sofley Jr	Samuel I Brady	Jeffrey M Jacobs	Vernon E Sherrill
Sanford (14)	CM 919 775-8200	Winston Hester	Pat LaCarter	Lois Oldham	Glenda Tomlinson	Floyd Caviness	Ronnie Yarborough	Larry Thomas
Scotland Neck t (3)	MC 919 826-3152	Ferd Harrison	Scott Buffkin	Patsy Faithful	Scott Buffkin	Bruce Josey	John Hodnett	Douglas Braddy
Selma t (5)	CM 919 965-9841	Joe Moore	Bruce Radford	Fran Davis	Debbie Holloman	Joe Price	Roy Godwin	Terry Keen
Seven Devils t (..)	CM 704 963-5342	Harold Buzzy Wolf	Chess Hill	Chess Hill	Barbara Presnell	Keith Cook	Joe Buchanan	Gary Fox
Shelby (15)	CM 704 484-6801	George W Clay Jr	David M Wilkison	S E Carouthers	E Warren Newton	Boyd Anthony	....	Roy Wellmon
Siler City t (5)	CM 919 742-4731	Earl Fitts	Leonard Barefoot	Wanda Ingold	Wanda Ingold	Billy Scott	Lewis Phillips	Joel Brower
Smithfield t (8)	CM 919 934-2116	Norwood Worley	Ron Owens	Debra Pierce	Robert Plowman	Norman Johnson	Pete Peterson	Jimmy Llapp
Southern Pines t (9)	CM 910 692-7021	Michael D Fields	Kyle Sonnenberg	Eleanore Ogletree	Melissa Miller	Peter Rapatas	Gerald Galloway	Bobby Teague
Southern Shores t (1)	CM 919 261-2394	Kern P Pitts	Carole E Cross	....	....	David Sanders	Danny W Beasley	....
Southport (2)	CM 919 457-7900	Norman R Holden	Rob Gandy	....	S Butterworth	Greg Cumbee	Bob Gray	Ed Honeycutt
Spencer (3)	CM 704 633-2231	Buddy Gettys	Steve Leary	Lisa Perdue	Steve Leary	Jody Everhart	Steve Schenk	Scott Benfield
Spindale t (4)	CM 704 286-3466	....	....	....	....	....	....	....
Spring Lake t (8)	MC 910 436-0241	B Manning	R Higgins	C Nunes	M B Clayton	P Stevens	G Campbell	R Dickerson
Statesville (18)	CM 704 878-3570	John E Marshall	John D King	Mary L Kerley	Ralph S Staley	James R Campbell	....	A Wayne Lambert
Stoneville t (1)	MC 919 573-9393	....	....	....	....	....	....	....
Sugar Mountain v (..)	MC 704 898-9292	Marjory C Unrath	R Robert Patton	Katy Sudderth	Carlene Garrison	....	Marvin E Sharpe	David G Webb
Tabor City t (2)	CM 919 653-3458	....	....	....	....	....	....	....
Tarboro t (11)	CM 919 641-4200	Moses A Ray	....	William L Corbett	William L Corbett	George G Cherry	Danny D Hayes	John H Chapman
Thomasville (16)	CM 910 475-4210	Hubert M Leonard	J Michael Moore	Mary G Hill	Tony C Jarrett	C R Cranford	Larry A Murdock	H Layton Paul
Topsail Beach t (..)	CM 910 328-5841	....	Eric Peterson	S Rivenbark	....	....	Rickey Smith	Frank Ricks
Troy t (3)	CM 910 572-3661	Roy Maness	Matt Bernhardt	Cathy Maness	Cathy Maness	Joe Huntley	E J Phillips Jr	Gray Walls
Tryon t (2)	CM 704 859-6654	....	....	....	....	....	....	....
Valdese t (4)	CM 704 879-2120	Jim Draughn	Jeff Morse	Frances Hildebran	Bill Chapman	Ernest Bertalot	Danny Barus	Jim Stockton
Wadesboro t (4)	CM 704 694-5171	....	....	....	....	....	....	....
Wake Forest t (6)	CM 919 556-2024	Dick Monteith	Mark Williams	Joyce Wilson	Aileen Staples	Jimmy Keith	Greg Harrington	Roe O' Donnell
Wallace t (3)	CM 910 285-4136	G Arnold Duncan	J Douglas Drymon	J Douglas Drymon	J Douglas Drymon	Thomas Townsend	Bobby Maready	Darret Ezzell
Warrenton t (1)	MC 919 257-3315	....	....	....	....	....	....	....
Warsaw t (3)	MC 919 293-7814	....	....	....	....	....	....	....
Washington (9)	CM 919 975-9318	Floyd Brothers	Ed Burchins	Rita Thompson	Carol Williams	Hugh Sterling	John Crone	Russell Waters
Waynesville t (7)	CM 704 456-3515	Henry Foy	A Lee Galloway	Phyllis McClure	Edward Caldwell	Bill Fowler	Coleman Moody	Fred Baker
Weaverville t (2)	CM 704 645-7116	....	Michael J Morgan	Shelby G Shields	Brenda T Ayers	John V Penley	Howard G Higgins	Larry T Sprinkle

Directory 1/9
continued

MUNICIPAL OFFICIALS
IN U.S. CITIES OVER 2,500

City, 1990 population figures (000 omitted), form of government	Municipal phone number	Mayor/ chief elected official	Appointed administrator	City clerk/ city secretary	Finance officer	Fire chief	Police chief	Public works director
NORTH CAROLINA (173) continued								
Wendell t (3)	CM 919 365-4444	Lucius S Jones	Ira C Fuller	....	Barbara A Raper	....	Joe A Privette	Donnie Ayscue
Whiteville (5)	CM 910 642-8046	Horace B Whitley	Jeff B Emory	Susan D Rhodes	Jean Babson	Terry R McCall	Randall Aragon	Stanlil Davis
Williamston t (6)	MC 919 792-5142	Tommy Roberson	John T Boykin Jr	Mary P Jackson	Ronnie R Wilson	James B Peele	Richard Holloman	Willie M Long Jr
Wilmington (56)	CM 910 341-7810	Donald H Betz	Mary M Gornto	Agnes P Spicer Si	William B McAbee	Samuel C Hill Sr	Robert C Wadman	....
Wilson (37)	CM 919 399-2200	C Bruce Rose	Eward A Wyatt	Ana I Heder	Gordon R Baker	Donald R Oliver	Thomas C Younce	Charles W Pittman
Winston-Salem (143)	CM 910 727-2123	Martha Wood	Bryce Stuart	Marie Matthews	Loris Colclough	Otis Cooper	George Sweat	Paschal Swann
Woodfin t (3)	MC 704 253-4887	Stephen R Henders	Andren Honeycutt	Cheryl W Mears	....	....	Darell Rathburn	Bill Rice
Wrightsville Beach t (3)	CM 910 256-7900	Herbert McKim	Anthony N Caudle	Linda Askew	Linda Askew	Everett K Ward Jr	Eorge M Antley	John T Nesbitt
Zebulon t (3)	CM 919 269-7455	Robert Matheny	Charles Horne	Wanda Price	Carla Stephens	Sidney Perry	Wayne Medlin	....
NORTH DAKOTA (18)								
Beulah (3)	MC 701 873-4637	....	....	....	....	....	....	....
Bismarck (49)	CO 701 222-6471	Bill Sorensen	....	....	....	Jack Hegedus	Robert Matzke	Robert Gausvik
Bottineau (3)	MC 701 228-3232	....	....	....	....	....	....	....
Carrington (2)	MC 701 652-2911	....	....	....	....	....	....	....
Devils Lake (8)	CO 701 662-7600	Fred Bott	....	Todd E Dalziel	Todd E Dalziel	William Oehlke	Bruce Kemmet	Glenn Olson
Dickinson (16)	CO 701 225-6765	....	....	....	....	....	....	....
Fargo (74)	MC 701 241-1300	....	....	....	....	....	....	....
Grafton (5)	MC 701 352-1561	....	....	....	....	....	....	....
Grand Forks (49)	MC 701 746-2666	Michael Polovitz	....	Alice Fontaine	John Schmisek	Richard Aulich	Chet Paschke	Mark Lambrect
Harvey (2)	MC 701 324-2000	Alfred Weisser	Corey Leintz	....	....	Gary Keller	Larry Hoffer	Robert Weninger
Jamestown (16)	MC 701 252-5900	Frank Chase	....	....	Jeff Fuchs	Bert Gray	David Donegan	....
Mandan (15)	CO 701 667-3215	Robert Dykshoorn	....	....	Kevin Christ	Pete Gartner	Dennis Rohr	Pete Snider
Minot (35)	CM 701 857-4777	Orlin Backes	Robert Schempp	David Waind	Robert Frantsvog	Duwayne Ward	Carroll Erickson	Alan Walter
Rugby (3)	MC 701 776-6181	David Cichos	Howard Burns	Judy Heintz	Howard Burns	Mark Johnson	Boyd Eagleson	Jerome Voeller
Valley City (7)	CO 701 845-1700	....	....	....	....	....	....	....
Wahpeton (9)	MC 701 642-6565	Dan Rood Jr	....	Arden C Anderson	....	B Langendorfer	Delano Lotzer	Jerry C Lein
West Fargo (12)	CO 701 282-3843	....	....	....	....	....	....	....
Williston (13)	CO 701 572-8161	....	....	....	....	....	....	....
OHIO (355)								
Ada v (5)	MC 419 634-4045	Donald L Traxler	James A Meyer	Kathryn J Gulbis	....	....	Wayne E Seely	....
Akron (223)	MC 216 375-2320	Don Plusquellic	....	Vince Ciraco	Richard Merolla	Thomas Alexander	Larry Givens	William Mullen
Alliance (23)	MC 216 821-3110	....	....	....	....	....	....	....
Amberley v (3)	CM 513 531-8675	Richard Kerstine	Bernard Boraten	Evelyn Dumont	Ada Keller	John Monahan	John Monahan	John Platter
Amherst (10)	MC 216 988-4380	....	....	....	....	....	....	....
Archbold v (3)	CM 419 445-4726	Chuck Rychener	Nolan Tuckerman	Gladys Winzeler	....	Richard Erbskorn	Martin Schmidt	....
Ashland (20)	MC 419 289-8622	....	....	....	....	....	....	....
Ashtabula (22)	MC 216 992-7103	....	....	....	....	....	....	....
Athens (21)	MC 614 592-3338	....	....	....	....	....	....	....
Aurora (9)	MC 216 562-6131	....	....	....	....	....	....	....
Avon (7)	MC 216 934-1200	....	....	....	....	....	....	....
Avon Lake (15)	MC 216 933-6141	Vincent M Urbin	....	Kathleen Lynch	Donald A Shupek	Gary E Fryfogle	David Owad	Wade M Mertz
Baltimore v (3)	MC 614 862-4491	....	....	....	....	....	....	....
Barberton (28)	MC 216 753-6611	....	....	....	....	....	....	....
Barnesville v (4)	MC 614 425-1880	....	....	....	....	....	....	....
Bay Village (17)	MC 216 871-2200	....	....	....	....	....	....	....
Beachwood (11)	MC 216 464-1070	....	....	....	....	....	....	....
Beavercreek (34)	CM 513 426-5100	Paul T Dunnigan	....	Lucia W Ball	Jon W Stoops	....	Warner Huston	Ronald Huff
Bedford (15)	CM 216 232-1600	D Grossenbaugh	Vilas S Gamble	Gayle C Pastor	Frank C Gambosi	Jeffrey L Duber	Robert R Reid	Clinton E Bellar
Bedford Heights (12)	MC 216 439-1600	....	....	....	....	....	....	....
Bellaire v (6)	MC 614 676-6538	V Esposito	....	Mary Nixon	Lawrence Gress	Michael Wallace	Robert Wallace	Vince DiFabrizio
Bellbrook (7)	CM 513 848-4666	....	....	....	....	....	....	....
Bellefontaine (12)	MC 513 592-4376	....	....	....	....	....	....	....
Bellevue (8)	MC 419 483-6399	George J Branco	R C Salkowitz	Vickie Dauch	Ethel R Foti	Sherrard Barr	Ronald Zerman	....
Belpre (7)	MC 614 423-7592	....	....	....	....	....	....	....
Berea (19)	MC 216 826-5800	....	....	....	....	....	....	....
Bexley (13)	MC 614 235-8694	....	....	....	....	....	....	....
Blanchester (4)	MC 513 783-2431	Lee Miller	....	Bernice Hoggatt	....	....	Richard Payton	Donald Walker
Blue Ash (12)	CM 513 745-8500	Walter L Reuszer	Marvin D Thompson	Mary Malone	Nancy Hennel	Glen Ross	Michael W Allen	Woody Cauble
Bluffton v (3)	MC 419 358-2066	....	....	....	....	....	....	....
Bowling Green (28)	MC 419 354-6200	Wesley K Hoffman	Colleen J Smith	Kay Scherreik	Rebecca Underwood	Joseph Burns	Galen Ash	William Blair
Brecksville (12)	MC 216 526-2610	J Hruby	....	M Scullin	D Wood	R Clark	D Kancler	J Smith
Bridgeport v (2)	MC 614 635-2424	....	....	....	....	....	....	....
Broadview Heights (12)	MC 216 526-4357	Leo H Bender	....	Annette M Phelps	Linda Pertz	Lee Ippollto	Fred Carmichael	Raymond Mack
Brook Park (23)	MC 216 433-1300	Thomas J Coyne Jr	....	P Eckerfield	Shelby Lawhun	Neal Donnelly	Thomas Dease	Brian Higgins
Brooklyn (12)	MC 216 351-2133	John M Coyne	....	Jeff Harwood	John M Coyne	Dennis Corrigan	James F Maloney	Kenneth Patton
Brookville v (5)	CM 513 833-2135	Michael A Duncan	John R Wright	E Eugene Roeser	E Eugene Roeser	James Nickel	Andrew J Papanek	Ronald Brandt
Brunswick (28)	CM 216 225-9144	J Beadell Rapp	Robert A Trimble	Betty Taller	Margaret Thesling	....	Patrick Beyer	Gregory L Crane
Bryan (8)	MC 419 636-4232	....	....	....	....	....	....	....
Buckeye Lake v (3)	MC 614 928-7100	James F Bartoe	....	Antoinette Yarman	Antoinette Yarman	Ken Johnson	Ron Small	....
Bucyrus (13)	MC 419 562-6767	....	....	....	....	....	....	....
Byesville v (2)	MC 614 685-5901	....	....	....	....	....	....	....
Cadiz v (3)	MC 614 942-8844	Raymond Jones	....	Carolyn Davidson	....	....	Dwight Spaar	Mary Banks
Cambridge (12)	MC 614 439-1240	C Charles Schaub	Richard D Giroux	Sharon Cassler	Donna Gander	Ermal Shimp	James Grubbs	Jerry Williams
Campbell (10)	MC 216 755-1451	....	....	....	....	....	....	....
Canal Fulton v (4)	MC 216 854-2225	....	....	....	....	....	....	....
Canal Winchester v (3)	MC 614 837-7493	....	....	....	....	....	....	....
Canfield (5)	CM 216 533-1101	F McLaughlin	Charles Tieche	Pat Matevich	Sandra Mayberry	....	David Blystone	Ron Wiant
Canton (84)	MC 216 489-3378	....	....	....	....	....	....	....
Carey v (4)	MC 419 396-7681	Dallas K Risner	John A Windau	Sara M Nye	Sara M Nye	Kenneth E Myers	Dennis L Yingling	Roy L Coppler
Carlisle v (5)	CM 513 746-0555	Patrick Long	Matthew W Coppler	Flo Cracraft	Dan Muldowney	Greg Wallace	Gary Long	Gaylon Brown
Carrollton v (3)	MC 216 627-2411	Harold K Laizure	....	Betty Davis	....	Robert Herron	Ronald A Yeager	....
Cedarville v (3)	MC 513 766-2061	Robert Preston	Nelson McKeever	Ronald Corry	Ronald Corry	....	Keith Stigers	....
Celina (10)	MC 419 586-6464	J Mustard	T Schwartz	....	P Smith	....	D Slusser	D Zahn
Centerville (21)	CM 513 433-7151	Shirley Heintz	Gregory B Horn	M McLauchlin	William Bettcher	....	John W Lickert	....
Chagrin Falls v (4)	MC 216 247-5050	....	....	....	....	....	....	....
Chardon v (4)	CM 216 285-3585	John Reid	David A Lelko	Jeffrey Smock	Jeffrey Smock	....	David Hyslop	Gayland Moore
Cheviot (10)	MC 513 661-2700	J Michael Laumann	Steven O Neal	....	Debra Gooch	Donald B Clark	David Voss	Thomas L Braun
Chillicothe (22)	MC 614 773-1211	Joseph P Sulzer	Beverly Riley	....	William Morrissey	Larry Thompson	Timothy Crawford	....
Cincinnati (364)	CM 513 352-3000	Roxanne Qualls	John Shirey	Sandy Sherman	Frank Dawson	Thomas Steidel	Michael Snowden	John Hamner
Circleville (12)	MC 614 477-2551	Thomas Royster	....	Patricia Fouch	Madeline Sanders	Wayne Malott	Jon Kinney	James Stanley
Cleveland (506)	MC 216 664-2000	Michael R White	Lavonne S Turner	Benny Bonanno	Kathy Burrer Hyer	William E Lee	Patrick Oliver	Michael G Konicek

Directory 1/9 continued

MUNICIPAL OFFICIALS IN U.S. CITIES OVER 2,500

City, 1990 population figures (000 omitted), form of government	Municipal phone number	Mayor/ chief elected official	Appointed administrator	City clerk/ city secretary	Finance officer	Fire chief	Police chief	Public works director
OHIO (355) continued								
Cleveland Heights (54)	CM 216 291-4444	Carol Edwards	Robert Downey	....	Robert Certner	Stanley Powaski	Martin Lentz	Spencer Caress
Clyde (6)	CM 419 547-6898	....	Dennis E Albrinck	Virginia Cullen	Dennis Tuck	David Moyer	Dan Weaver	Lonnie Dick
Coal Grove v (2)	MC 614 532-7447	....						
Coldwater v (4)	MC 419 678-4881	Walter C Weigel	Raymond Kremer	J Billerman	J Billerman	John Moorman	Les Langdon	....
Colerain Township t (..)	MC 513 385-7500	Patricia Clancy	David Foglesong	Kathy Mohr	Kathy Mohr	Bruce Smith	Edmund Phillips	....
Columbiana v (5)	CM 216 482-2173	....	....	....	....	....	....	....
Columbus (633)	MC 614 645-7671	....		....	....	....	....	....
Conneaut (13)	MC 216 593-4357	Judith Parlongo	Robert Herron	Norma Sass	Julia Sanger	Bim Orrenmaa	Rocco Russo	George Adams
Cortland v (6)	MC 216 637-3916	....						
Coshocton (12)	MC 614 622-1373	Charles A Turner	Ray T Miskimens	Marlene Griffith	Lois Murphy	Chuck Turner Jr	....	....
Covington v (3)	MC 513 473-2102	M C Longendelpher		Kay McKinney	....	Bill Westfall	Rick Wright	....
Crestline (5)	MC 419 683-3800	....						
Crooksville v (3)	MC 614 982-2656	....	....	....	....	....	....	....
Cuyahoga Falls (49)	MC 216 971-8000	Don L Robart	....	Kenneth Lahn	Vic Nogalo	Robert Leonard	Donald Smith	Gerald Pursley
Dayton (182)	CM 513 443-4000	....						
Deer Park (6)	MC 513 791-1081	....	....	....	....	....	....	....
Defiance (17)	MC 419 784-2101	Rita Kissner	Joel Daniels	....	Jeff Leonard	Robert Marihugh	Norman Walker	....
Delaware (20)	CM 614 368-1640	Dennis D Davis	Frank A Ciarochi	Elizabeth Speese	Dean Stelzer	Thomas Macklin	Randy Martz	Dave Bilsing
Delhi tp (30)	MC 513 922-3111	Carol A Espelage	Joseph R Morency	Robert Bedinghaus	Robert Bedinghaus	Harold E Edwards	Howard R Makin	Robert W Bass
Delphos (7)	MC 419 695-4010	....						
Delta v (3)	CM 419 822-3190	Lorraine Clair	Gary Baker	Valerie Edwards	....	George Dick	Robert Taylor	Gary Baker
Dennison v (3)	MC 614 922-2861	Paul Collins		Ronnie Vinci	....	Paul Vance	Craig Kohler	....
Dover (11)	MC 216 343-7725	R P Homrighausen	Matthew Kline	....	Zoe Ann Kelley	W Fred Nixon	Ronald Johnson	....
Dublin (16)	CM 614 761-6500	Joel R Campbell	Timothy C Hansley	Anne C Clarke	Marsha I Grigsby	....	Ronald G Ferrell	....
East Cleveland (33)	CM 216 681-2265	Wallace D Davis	....	....	Gayle G Smith	Paul Blockson	Mitchel Buyton	C Clinkscale
East Liverpool (14)	MC 216 385-3381	....						
East Palestine (5)	MC 216 426-4367	Mark L Rhodes	John K Francis	Bruce Van Fossen	Connie Robinson	Merle Stewart	Gary Clark	....
Eastlake (21)	MC 216 951-1416	....						
Eaton (7)	CM 513 456-4125	....	....	....	....	....	....	....
Elmwood Place v (3)	MC 513 242-2578	....						
Elyria (57)	MC 216 322-1829	....						
Englewood (11)	CM 513 836-5106	Edward S Kemper	Eric A Smith	Karen E Sodders	Mark B Brownfield	....	Michael J Dickey	....
Enon v (3)	MC 513 864-7870	....						
Euclid (55)	MC 216 289-2700	....						
Fairborn (31)	CM 513 879-1730	Lynn E Wolaver	Michael Hammond	Daniel N Smith	Daniel N Smith	Robert Sponseller	Anthony A Slifka	R Frank Loy
Fairfield (40)	CM 513 867-5352	Robert J Wolpert	Cheryl A Hilvert	....	James A Hanson	Donald Bennett	Gary Rednour	David A Bock
Fairfield tp (49)	MC 513 863-5414	....	....	....	....	....	....	....
Fairlawn (6)	MC 216 666-8875	....						
Fairport v (3)	MC 216 352-3620	....						
Fairview Park (18)	MC 216 333-2200	....						
Findlay (36)	MC 419 424-7137	Keith Romick	David J Wobser	Becky Greeno	Janet Wobser	Roy DeVore	Daniel Routzon	....
Forest Park (19)	CM 513 595-5200	Cathy Barret	Ray Hodges	Kathy Lives	Fred Watterson	Bob Stegeman	Steve Vollmar	Dave Buesking
Fort Shawnee v (4)	MC 419 991-2015	Douglas C Harris	....	Diane L Barnes	Diane L Barnes	....	M Harnishfeger	....
Fostoria (15)	MC 419 435-8282	Barbara L Marley	Eugene R Kinn	Paul W Allison	Cortland Heykoop	David DiCesare	Dennis G Day	....
Franklin (11)	CM 513 746-9921	Jim Mears	Samuel L Coxson	Jane McGee	Sandy Morgan	Hugh Depew	Don Fry	Sonny Lewis
Fremont (18)	MC 419 334-2687	Terry Overmyer		Linda Swartz	Fred Recktenwald	Daniel Devanna	Robert Dorsey	Kenneth Myers
Gahanna (28)	MC 614 471-4103	James McGregor	....	Peg Cunningham	W J Isler	....	Daniel Stumpf	Wayne Murphy
Galion (12)	MC 419 468-1857	....						
Gallipolis (5)	CM 614 446-2489	....						
Garfield Heights (32)	MC 216 475-1503	Thomas Longo	....	Margaret Johnston	Richard Obert	Anthony Collova	Thomas Murphy	Charles Goedecke
Geneva (7)	CM 216 466-4675	....	Charles V Bowman	Nancy J Bowdler	Nancy J Bowdler	Gary J Farley	Jame C Pearson	....
Georgetown v (4)	MC 513 378-6395	Joseph C Rose	Michael D Miller	Idella Bauer	Idella Bauer	Joe Brookbank	Harry Lee Graves	Michael D Miller
Germantown (5)	CM 513 855-6567	Theodore Landis	Edward Schwaberow	Karen Epperson	Robyn Charlton	Gary Nesslage	James Desch	....
Girard (11)	MC 216 545-3879	Vincent Schuyler	....	L Dutcher Casale	Sam Lamancusa	Daniel Merwin	Anthony Ross	Ralph Ruggiero
Golf Manor (4)	MC 513 531-7491	....						
Grandview Heights (7)	MC 614 488-3159	John R Leutz	Julia A Gafford	J Mikal Townsley	J Mikal Townsley	Henry K Kauffman	Ronald C Treon	Salvatore Troiano
Granville v (4)	CM 614 587-0707	Arnold Eisenberg	Douglas Plunkett	Carie Miller	Shirley Robertson	....	Steven Cartnal	....
Green tp (53)	MC 513 574-4848	William J Seitz	Thomas R Maley	Marilyn Wagner	....	Robert J Weitzel	James L Suder	Adam B Goetzman
Greenfield (5)	MC 513 981-3500	....						
Greenhills v (4)	MC 513 825-2100	Oscar A Hoffmann	David B Moore	M Joy Hoffmann	Kathryn L Brokaw	Thomas P Eberle	Donald Slaughter	....
Greenville (13)	MC 513 548-4435	Richard A Rehmert	Terry Emery	Marvella Fletcher	Marvella Fletcher	Steve Birt	Eric Hughes	....
Grove City (20)	MC 614 871-6331	Richard L Stage	Charles W Boso Jr	Tami Kelly	Robert E Behlen	....	James M McKean	James M Blackburn
Groveport v (3)	MC 614 836-5301	J Harold Carley	Philip D Honsey	Julie Fisher	Nanisa K Osborn	....	Roger Adams	Thomas Simkins
Hamilton (61)	CM 513 868-5891	....	....	....	....	....	....	....
Harrison v (8)	MC 513 367-2111	Harry Folfes	....	....	Mary Lou Dawson	Alan Kinnett	Gary Foust	Michael Hunter
Heath (7)	MC 614 522-1420	John C Geller		....	Carolyn J Broyles	Rick Taylor	Gordon Ellis	....
Hicksville v (4)	MC 419 542-6138	....						
Highland Heights (6)	MC 216 461-2440	....						
Hilliard (12)	MC 614 876-7361	Roger A Reynolds	....	....	Lynn A Skeels	....	Rodney Garnett	....
Hillsboro (6)	MC 513 393-5219	....						
Hubbard (8)	MC 216 534-3090	....						
Huber Heights (39)	CM 513 233-1423	Jack Hensley	James W Pierce	Margaret Stivers	C Armocida	Thomas J Grile	Michael D' Amico	....
Hudson v (5)	CM 216 650-1799	....						
Huron (7)	CM 419 433-5268	....						
Independence (7)	MC 216 524-4131	....						
Indian Hill v (5)	CM 513 561-6500	Donald P Klekamp	Michael W Burns	....	Paul C Riordan	....	William C Wiebold	David M Couch
Ironton (13)	MC 614 532-3833	James Tordiff				Donald Delong	Rodney McFarland	James Meyers
Jackson (6)	MC 614 286-3224	John T Evans	....	....	Carl A Barnett Jr	Richard Eubanks	Teddy Penix	Ronald B Speakman
Jefferson v (3)	MC 216 576-3941	....						
Jefferson (Madison) v (5)	MC 614 879-7363	....						
Johnstown v (3)	MC 614 967-3177	Steven M Wingo		Charles Williams	....	....	Reginald Dotson	....
Kent (29)	CM 216 678-8100	Kathleen Chandler	P J Blanchard	Linda Mauck	Barbara Rissland	Barry Blankenship	William Lillich	Michael Y Sepi
Kenton (8)	MC 419 674-4850	Clay Flinn		Brenda Keckler	Michael Bacon	Arnold Downey	Reginald Slack	Byron J Pfeiffer
Kettering (61)	CM 513 296-2400	Richard Hartmann	Steven C Husemann	Virginia Schulke	Nancy H Gregory	James C Frey	James M O' Dell	James H Graham
Kirtland (6)	MC 216 256-3332	Mario V Marcopoli	....	Valerie Beres	Keith W Martinet	Richard Martincic	Dennis Yarborough	....
Lakemore v (3)	MC 216 733-6125	....						
Lakewood (60)	MC 216 521-7580	David R Harbarger	....	....	Gale W Fisk	Lawrence Mroz	Matthew Biscotti	David J Coyle
Lancaster (35)	MC 614 687-6600	A Wallace	E Strawn	S Eckman	M Green	J Rupe	T Chilcote	....
Lebanon (10)	CM 513 932-3060	Jackson Hedges	Richard Hayward	Debbie Biggs	Debbie Biggs	Mike Hannigan	Ken Burns	Bill Marshall
Leipsic v (2)	MC 419 943-2009	Judith Crawford	James Russell	Jeanne Baumeier	Jeanne Baumeier	David Herring	Edward Long	James Russell
Lexington v (4)	MC 419 884-0765	Eugene Parkison	Charles Pscholka	Elaine Browning	Bobbi Ann Huffman	....	Richard Hamrick	Charles Pscholka
Lima (46)	MC 419 228-5462	David J Berger	....	Sally Clemans	Alan McDougle	John Brookman	Frank Catlett	Howard Elstro
Lincoln Heights (5)	CM 513 733-5900	James E Mobley	John C McConn	....	Dennis Strayhorn	Ernie McCowen	Roger Reynolds	....

Directory 1/9 continued — MUNICIPAL OFFICIALS IN U.S. CITIES OVER 2,500

City, 1990 population figures (000 omitted), form of government		Municipal phone number	Mayor/ chief elected official	Appointed administrator	City clerk/ city secretary	Finance officer	Fire chief	Police chief	Public works director
OHIO (355) continued									
Lisbon v (3)	MC	216 424-5503	Willis L Coleman	....	Kathy Raneri	....	Harold Adams	Charles Carlisle	Mike Ours
Lockland v (4)	MC	513 761-1124	....	....	....	....	....	....	....
Lodi v (3)	MC	216 948-2040	Russell Bell	....	Annette Geissman	Annette Geissman	Carl Stewart	Stephen Sivard	Donald Eaken
Logan (7)	MC	614 385-8310	....	....	....	....	....	....	....
London (8)	MC	614 852-1263	David Eades	Elmer Olsen	Arlene Duffey	Kathy McClelland	Richard Minner	Michael Creamer	Paul Maddux
Lorain (71)	MC	216 244-3204	Alex M Olejko	....	Stephen W Bansek	L Craig Foltin	Donald R Poprock	Craig A Casteel	Mark J Mihok
Lordstown v (3)	MC	216 824-2507	....	....	....	....	....	....	....
Loudonville v (3)	MC	419 994-3214	Thomas R Miller	....	Susan R Kern	....	Ronald C Hans	William Porter	....
Louisville (8)	CM	216 875-3321	Thomas Zwick	Stephen Townley	Peggy Brazelton	Robert Miller	Denny Myers	Ross Riggs	Walt Metzger
Loveland (10)	CM	513 683-0150	Roland Boike	Wayne Barfels	Linda Cox	Bill Taphorn	Jim Hunter	Howard Espelage	Joe Geers
Lyndhurst (16)	MC	216 442-5777	Leonard M Creary	....	Joseph G Mirtel	Joseph G Mirtel	Joseph A Sweeney	Sherwood Eldredge	William Moviel
Macedonia (8)	MC	216 468-1300	Joseph Migliorini	....	....	Tom DiLellio	Daniel Gagliardi	James Popovich	....
Madeira (9)	CM	513 561-7228	....	....	....	....	....	....	....
Mansfield (51)	MC	419 755-9626	....	....	....	....	....	....	....
Maple Heights (27)	MC	216 662-6000	....	....	....	....	....	....	....
Mariemont v (3)	MC	513 271-3246	Donald L Shanks	....	S L Bahler	S L Bahler	Thomas A Driggers	Richard A Pope	....
Marietta (15)	MC	614 373-1387	....	....	....	....	....	....	....
Marion (34)	MC	614 387-2020	Jack L Kellogg	....	Joan Steward	Robert Cramer	Allen Gruber	Frank Arnold	Tracy Mercer
Martins Ferry (8)	MC	614 633-2876	....	....	....	....	....	....	....
Marysville (10)	MC	513 642-6015	Thomas Kruse	Kenneth Kraus	Lois Reese	Ivan L Schrock	Rick Collins	Rick E Coutts	....
Mason (11)	CM	513 398-8010	Dick Staten	Scot Lahrmer	Betty Baysore	Betty Baysore	....	Arthur Scott	John Saar
Massillon (31)	MC	216 830-1700	....	....	....	....	....	....	....
Maumee (16)	MC	419 897-7100	Stepen J Pauken	Richard A Krieger	Richard L Pfaff	Richard L Pfaff	Frederick R Burdo	Robert E Bunce	F Joseph Cory
Mayfield v (3)	MC	216 461-2210	Bruce G Rinker	....	Donna J Heath	....	David Mohr	Donald Stevens	....
Mayfield Heights (20)	MC	216 442-2626	M A Egensperger	....	....	Robert G Tribby	Michael J Forte	Thomas J Slivers	Andrew D Fornaro
Mc Donald v (4)	MC	216 530-5472	Thomas J Hannon	Virginia Evans	Barbara J Urban	....	Michael Badila	Jimmy Tyree	E Domitrovich
Medina (19)	MC	216 725-8861	James S Roberts	....	Catherine Horn	Wayne Hamilton	Leland Codding	Thomas Steyer	Joseph Walker
Mentor (47)	CM	216 255-1100	Jim Struna	Julian Suso	Maureen Russo	John Aten	John Preuer	Richard Amiott	Rob Pauley
Mentor-On-The-Lake (8)	MC	216 257-7216	John S Crocker	Kip L Molenaar	....	....	Robert Mahoney	Edward Wild	Bert A Guinn
Miami tp (28)	MC	513 248-3725	Jean Schmidt	David D Duckworth	Eric Ferry	Eric Ferry	James H Whitworth	Harry Snyder	Walter D Fischer
Miamisburg (18)	CM	513 866-3303	Richard Church Jr	John K Weithofer	Judy Barney	George S Perrine	Robert Bobbitt	Thomas Schenck	Claude Berry
Middleburg Heights (15)	MC	216 234-8811	Gary W Starr	....	....	Timothy Pope	James McCarthy	John Maddox	Frank Castelli
Middleport v (3)	CM	614 992-6424	....	....	....	....	....	....	....
Middletown (46)	CM	513 425-7730	Geoffrey Kimball	Ronald L Olson	Bettie J Arthur	John T Lyons	John J Sauter	Earl R Smith Jr	Preston M Combs
Milford (6)	CM	513 831-4192	Craig Kolb	....	Rose Fredwest	Stephen Wagner	John Cooper	Daniel Chilton	Elmer Weigel
Millersburg v (3)	CM	216 674-1886	Douglas Polen	Jim Andrick	Karen Shaffer	Karen Shaffer	....	S Thomas Vaughn	....
Minerva v (4)	CM	216 868-7705	....	....	....	....	....	....	....
Mingo Junction v (4)	MC	614 535-1511	....	....	....	....	....	....	....
Minster v (3)	MC	419 628-2595	Ted Purpus	Donald Harrod	John Stechschulte	....	Donald Lampert	Lawrence Murtz	Carl Wuebker
Mogadore v (4)	MC	216 628-4896	....	....	....	....	....	....	....
Monroe v (4)	CM	513 539-7374	E R Tannreuther	A Seth Johnston	Linda L Egelston	Frank C Pahr	Mark A Neu	Ernest Howard	....
Montgomery (10)	CM	513 891-2424	Donald Hess	Jon Bormet	Susan Hamm	Terri Mayle	....	Don McGlothlin	....
Montpelier v (4)	MC	419 485-5543	....	....	....	....	....	....	....
Moraine (6)	CM	513 299-7312	Paul Beardsley	....	Rita Krell	Marty Brown	Harold Sigler	David Hicks	....
Moreland Hills v (3)	MC	216 248-1188	....	....	....	....	....	....	....
Mount Gilead v (3)	MC	419 946-3926	....	....	....	....	....	....	....
Mount Healthy (8)	MC	513 931-8840	Steve Wolf	Bill Kocher	Vera Adkins	Al Peters	C McDanials	Al Scheafer	George Rouse
Mount Vernon (15)	MC	614 393-9517	....	....	....	....	....	....	....
Munroe Falls v (5)	MC	216 688-7491	Gerald L Hupp	....	....	....	James Bowery	Steve Stahl	James C Brown
Napoleon (9)	CM	419 599-1235	Robert G Heft	Terry Dunn	....	R W Schweinhagen	Allan Woo	George Schmidt	....
Nelsonville (5)	MC	614 753-1314	....	....	....	....	....	....	....
New Boston (3)	MC	614 456-4103	....	....	....	....	....	....	....
New Carlisle (6)	CM	513 845-9493	Darryl Bauer	Madge Shellhaas	Clair Miller	Connie Barney	Charles Harvey	....	Harry Taynor
New Lebanon v (4)	MC	513 687-1341	....	....	....	....	....	....	....
New Lexington (5)	MC	614 342-1633	Delmar Danison	John Johnson	....	....	Edmund Kinsel	Jeff Newlon	Dan Hammer
New Miami v (3)	MC	513 896-7337	Eugene Rogers	....	April Whissen	....	Jerry Cook	Dannay Shultz	....
New Philadelphia (16)	MC	216 364-4491	Timothy A Hurst	Richard A Rausch	....	Betty L Gleitsman	Charles E Caton	Thomas R Staggers	John R Grasselli
New Richmond v (2)	MC	513 553-4146	....	....	....	....	....	....	....
Newark (44)	MC	614 349-6747	Frank Stare	....	Diana Eshelman	Lenord Feightner	Earl Whittington	Paul Green	Tim Matheny
Newburgh Heights v (2)	MC	216 641-4650	Kathleen Edwards	Bev Pereces	Christine Smetana	....	John Martin	Gerald Hoehn	....
Newcomerstown v (4)	MC	614 498-6313	Wayne McFarland	....	Donald L Porcher	....	....	James A Friel	....
Newton Falls (5)	CM	216 872-0806	Patrick Layshock	Dennis L Kirkland	Cindy L Magargle	Cheryl B Bucy	Kenneth E Whetzel	Robert T Carlson	Harry J Shaver
Niles (21)	MC	216 652-3415	....	....	....	....	....	....	....
North Baltimore v (3)	MC	419 257-2394	....	....	....	....	....	....	....
North Canton (15)	MC	216 499-8223	....	....	....	....	....	....	....
North College Hill (11)	MC	513 521-7413	....	....	....	....	....	....	....
North Kingsville v (3)	MC	216 224-0091	....	....	....	....	....	....	....
North Olmsted (34)	MC	216 777-8000	Edward Boyle	Nancy Wlodarski	Barbara Seman	James Burns	Roger Osterhouse	Dennis Sefcek	Ralph Bohlmann
North Ridgeville (22)	MC	216 353-0819	Jeffry Armbruster	....	Sandra Lewis	C Costin	Ray Diederich	Ron Bauer	....
North Royalton (23)	MC	216 237-5686	Gary D Skorepa	....	Darlene Thomas	Christine May	Michael Fabish	Paul Bican	Leon Darby
Northfield v (4)	MC	216 467-7139	Carmen Consolo	....	Winifred Malone	....	Donald Burger	Donald Barney	....
Northwood (6)	MC	419 693-9326	John P Donegan	....	Lynn Richey	Marsha J Kurek	William St Clair	Douglas Breno	Herman Warnke
Norton (11)	MC	216 825-7815	....	....	....	....	....	....	....
Norwalk (15)	MC	419 663-6740	....	....	....	....	....	....	....
Norwood (24)	MC	513 396-8102	Joe Sanker	Darrell Maxwell	....	Don Jones	Dave Walters	Vern Costello	....
Oak Harbor v (3)	MC	419 898-5561	....	....	....	....	....	....	....
Oakwood (9)	CM	513 298-0600	D Jeffrey Ireland	Michael J Kelly	Cathy D Blum	Calie M Rehrig	John Hohensee	John Hohensee	John C Chain
Oakwood v (3)	MC	216 232-9988	....	....	....	....	....	....	....
Oberlin (8)	CM	216 775-1531	Frances Baumann	Gary W Goddard	Sharon Miller	Kelly E Clark	Doyle J Jones	Robert K Jones	Michael Sigg
Obetz v (3)	MC	614 491-1080	....	....	....	....	....	....	....
Olmsted Falls (7)	MC	216 235-5550	Tom Jones	....	Barbara Walker	Dan Patrick	Wm Fisher	Richard Krusinski	Stan Wares
Ontario v (4)	MC	419 529-3723	....	....	....	....	....	....	....
Oregon (18)	MC	419 698-7045	....	....	....	....	....	....	....
Orrville (8)	MC	216 684-5000	Howard Wade	William Stocker	Julia Leathers	Charles Horst	Robert Ballentine	Wesley Morris	Dan Preising
Ottawa v (4)	MC	419 523-5020	Kenneth Maag	John Williams	Harold Schierloh	....	Eugene Diemer	John Kottenbrock	....
Ottawa Hills v (5)	CM	419 536-1111	Jean Youngen	Marc Thompson	Gay Mac Arthur	Karen Urbanik	Donald Farley	Ronald Jornd	....
Oxford (19)	CM	513 523-2171	Alan Kyger	James C Collard	....	Thomas Peterson	Len Endress	Stephan Schwein	Mark S Tate
Painesville (16)	CM	216 639-4890	....	Lester N Nero	Shirley Onderisin	....	Jack A Martin	Jerry T White	Raymond L Dray
Parma (88)	MC	216 885-8000	....	....	....	....	....	....	....
Parma Heights (21)	MC	216 884-9600	Paul W Cassidy	....	Carla Binder	Terry Hickey	Kay Diamond	Michael Mlecik	M Kronenberger
Paulding v (3)	MC	419 399-4011	Vera M Miles	Harry Wiebe	Janice K Phlipot	....	Rex Ankney	Paul Keeler	....
Pepper Pike (6)	MC	216 831-8500	Bruce Akers	....	Anne Jerina	....	Chris Roseboro	John Guarino	John Hanigofsky
Perrysburg (13)	MC	419 872-8000	Reeve Kelsey	James Bagdonas	David D Creps	David D Creps	Dean Woods	William Dhondt	....

Directory 1/9 continued

MUNICIPAL OFFICIALS IN U.S. CITIES OVER 2,500

OHIO (355) continued

City, 1990 population figures (000 omitted), form of government	Municipal phone number	Mayor/ chief elected official	Appointed administrator	City clerk/ city secretary	Finance officer	Fire chief	Police chief	Public works director
Pickerington v (6)	CO 614 837-3974	Lee A Gray	Joyce E Bushman	Lynda Yartin	Linda Fersch	....	Don Pruden	....
Piqua (21)	CM 513 778-2051	Lucinda L Fess	Frank Patrizio Jr	Rebecca J Cool	Robert N Slagle	Gregory L Fashner	Philip K Potter	Thomas R Zechman
Plain tp (34)	MC 216 492-4689	Claude Shriver	Vincent Marion	Michael Cirelli	....	John A Sabo	....	....
Poland v (3)	MC 216 757-2112	....	....	....	....	....	....	....
Pomeroy v (2)	MC 614 992-2246	....	....	....	....	....	....	....
Port Clinton (7)	MC 419 734-5522	Jeanne Huskey	Max E McLaury	Loretta Eberle	Nancy O' Neal	John Drummer	Walter Bahnsen	....
Portsmouth (23)	MC 614 354-8807	Franklin Gerlach	....	Joann Aeh	Patrica Jenkins	Robert Storey	Thomas Bihl	William Rush
Powell v (2)	CM 614 885-5380	....	....	....	....	....	....	....
Ravenna (12)	MC 216 296-9629	....	....	....	....	....	....	....
Reading (12)	MC 513 733-3725	Frank Carnevale	Frank Sherman	Midge Brown	Doug Sand	Stephan Ashbrock	Robert Huelsman	G R Glaser Jr
Reynoldsburg (26)	MC 614 866-9523	Robert McPherson	....	....	....	....	Jeanne Miller	Mel Clemens
Richfield v (3)	MC 216 659-9201	Ralph R Waszak Sr	Eleanor Lukovics	Joyce Remec	Eleanor Lukovics	Russell English	John Walsh	....
Richmond Heights (10)	MC 216 486-2474	....	....	....	....	....	....	....
Rittman (6)	CM 216 925-2045	....	....	....	....	....	....	....
Rocky River (20)	MC 216 331-0600	Don Umerley	Jim Linden	Gretchen Burt	Susan Wollenzier	Dale Kraus	Bernard Barrett	....
Rossford (6)	MC 419 666-0210	....	....	....	....	....	....	....
Sabina v (3)	MC 513 584-2123	....	....	....	....	....	....	....
Salem (12)	MC 216 332-4482	Alvahn Mondell	....	Stacey Darner	Frances Dickey	Dwight Stacy	John Sommers	Donald Weingart
Sandusky (30)	CM 419 627-5844	....	....	....	....	....	....	....
Sebring (5)	CM 216 938-9340	....	....	....	....	....	....	....
Seven Hills (12)	MC 216 524-4421	....	....	....	....	....	....	....
Shadyside (4)	MC 614 676-5972	....	....	....	....	....	....	....
Shaker Heights (31)	MC 216 491-1400	....	....	....	....	....	....	....
Sharonville (13)	MC 513 563-1144	Paul Kattelman	Rex Baysore	....	K Greensfelder	Dale Duermit	Michael Schappa	Audrey Privett
Sheffield Lake (10)	MC 216 949-7141	Charles Kelly	....	....	Robert Hamilton	Eugene Rouse	Thomas Schmidt	Frances Schremp
Shelby (10)	MC 419 347-5131	James Henkel	....	....	John Devito	Scott Hartman	John Van Wagner	....
Sidney (19)	CM 513 498-2335	Thomas R Miller	William P Barlow	Jocele Fahnestock	Michael Puckett	Stanley Crosley	Steven Wearly	Richard Hohman
Silver Lake v (3)	MC 216 923-5233	....	....	....	....	....	....	....
Silverton (6)	MC 513 793-7980	Arthur Hackett Jr	....	William M Kuhr	....	Paul J Steman	Dennis Race	Paul J Steman
Solon (19)	MC 216 248-1155	Robert Paulson	....	Dianne Bartoshek	Dennis Tellep	Frank Zugan	Robert Bruckner	Everett McDaries
South Charleston v (2)	MC 513 462-8888	Marilyn Jarvis	Sarah Wildman	Bonnie White	Bonnie White	....	Beryl McCloud	Sarah Wildman
South Euclid (24)	MC 216 381-0400	John T Kocevar	....	Celeste DiCillo	Celeste DiCillo	Larry Huston	James Farrell	....
South Lebanon v (3)	MC 513 494-2296	....	....	....	....	....	....	....
South Point v (4)	MC 614 377-4838	....	....	....	....	....	....	....
South Russell v (3)	MC 216 338-7843	....	....	....	....	....	....	....
Springboro (7)	CM 513 748-1041	Robert Schaefer	Edward Doczy	Gayle Bennett	Sam Steadman	....	R Hochstrasser	George Brackney
Springdale (11)	MC 513 346-5700	Ronald Pitman	Cecil W Osborn	....	Doyle H Webster	Robert Posega	James I Freland	Robert Sears
Springfield (70)	CM 513 324-7300	Dale A Henry	Matthew J Kridler	Connie J Chappell	Sandra L Gaier	Donald J Lee	Roger L Evans	Leonard Hartoog
St. Bernard (5)	MC 513 242-7770	....	....	....	....	....	....	....
St. Clairsville (5)	MC 614 695-1324	....	....	....	....	....	....	....
St. Marys (8)	MC 419 394-3303	William T Sell	Michael L Weadock	Betty A Wehrman	Pamela J Edgar	Wilbur Drummond	William Applegate	Steve Opperman
Steubenville (22)	CM 614 283-6133	Domenick Mucci Jr	Gary J Dufour	Pamela L Orlando	Robert P Corabi	Richard F Blair	James McCartney	....
Stow (28)	MC 216 688-8206	....	....	....	....	....	....	....
Streetsboro (10)	MC 216 626-4942	Sally Henzel	....	Catherine Hamilto	D William Weber	Gerald Vicha	James Brown	Gregory Solarz
Strongsville (35)	MC 216 238-5720	....	....	....	....	....	....	....
Struthers (12)	MC 216 755-2181	....	....	....	....	....	....	....
Swanton v (4)	CM 419 826-9515	Richard Ueberroth	John Syx	Ardys Slaninka	Nancy E Spaulding	Lewis Taylor	Homer Chapa	Ray Walters
Sycamore tp (20)	MC 513 791-8447	....	....	....	....	....	....	....
Sylvania (17)	MC 419 885-8932	James E Seney	....	Margaret T Rauch	John W Plock	David Drake	Gerald A Sobb	Jeffrey P Ballmer
Tallmadge (15)	MC 216 633-0857	....	....	....	....	....	....	....
Tiffin (19)	MC 419 448-5402	David A Martien	Howard L Magers	....	Larry Clausing	Thomas A Huss	Wayne A Stephens	John A Baker
Tipp City (6)	CM 513 667-8425	Carol S Cook	William Nelson Jr	Neva B Hufford	Richard Drennen	David Imler	Thomas Davidson	M J Eichman
Toledo (333)	CO 419 245-1500	Carty Finkbeiner	John Alexander	Larry Brewer	Russell Martin	Michael Bell	James Wiegand	Bernard Leite
Toronto (6)	MC 614 537-3743	....	....	....	....	....	....	....
Trenton (6)	CM 513 988-6304	Roy Wilham	Melvin Ruder	Katherine Richard	Gregory Watson	Kenneth Achberger	Joe Richard	Ron Phelps
Trotwood (9)	CM 513 837-7771	Richard Haas	Michael Ratcliff	Lois Singleton	Darryl Kenning	....	Michael Etter	Roland Zellers
Troy (19)	MC 513 335-1725	Peter E Jenkins	N Lawrence Wolke	J Sue Knight	....	Robert Counts	Charles Frank	Stephen Weaver
Twinsburg (10)	MC 216 425-7161	James R Karabec	....	Cynthia Kaderle	Joanne Terry	Daniel Simecek	Anthony Frank	....
Uhrichsville (6)	MC 614 922-1242	....	....	....	....	....	....	....
Union tp (33)	CM 513 752-1741	....	....	....	....	....	....	....
Union tp (40)	CM 513 777-5900	Dick Alderson	David Gully	Patricia Williams	....	James Detherage	Lynn Brown	Bob McGuire
Union (6)	CM 513 836-8624	Robert Packard	John P Applegate	Denise Winemiller	Denise Winemiller	....	Dan Gessner	....
University Heights (15)	MC 216 932-7800	Beryl Rothschild	....	Nancy E Moore	Anthony Ianlro	Richard Kosmerl	Charles Lo Bello	Christopher Vild
Upper Arlington (34)	CM 614 457-5080	John R Allen	Richard A King	Margie Halk	Pete Rose	Michael Gibbons	Thomas Kulp	Larry Helscel
Upper Sandusky (6)	MC 419 294-3862	....	....	....	....	....	....	....
Urbana (11)	MC 513 653-3736	Thomas Crowley	John Kane	Patricia King	Dale Miller	James McIntosh	Bill Lingrell	....
Van Wert (11)	MC 419 238-6976	....	....	....	....	....	....	....
Vandalia (14)	CM 513 898-5891	Joy A Clark	Bruce E Sucher	....	William H Hoffman	Robert Treiber	Douglas Knight	Ted Rusen Jr
Vermilion (11)	MC 216 967-6989	Elizabeth Sheehe	....	Gwen Fisher	Laurence Rush	Gene Kropf	Nicholas Mayer	Jim Lenthe
Versailles v (2)	CM 513 526-3294	....	....	....	....	....	....	....
Wadsworth (16)	MC 216 335-1521	John Hanna	William Lyren	Lynda Gehring	Lynda Carrino	Richard Hontert	Michael King	....
Walbridge v (3)	MC 419 666-1830	....	....	....	....	....	....	....
Wapakoneta (9)	MC 419 738-3011	....	....	....	....	....	....	....
Warren (51)	MC 216 841-2610	....	....	....	....	....	....	....
Warrensville Heights (16)	MC 216 587-6500	....	....	....	....	....	....	....
Washington (13)	CM 614 335-5200	Gordon Davis	Mark Rohr	Tom Riley	Tom Riley	Dan Fowler	Larry Walker	....
Washington tp (8)	CM 513 433-0152	....	....	....	....	....	....	....
Waterville v (5)	CM 419 878-8107	Charles P Duck Jr	Thomas L Mattis	Claudia Guimond	Gary Langenderfer	....	Lance W Martin	Kenneth B Blair
Wauseon (6)	MC 419 335-9022	Jerry G Matheny	....	Margaret A Murphy	Wayne J Badenhop	James E Gamber	Paul A Arruda	John R Sanderson
Waverly (4)	MC 614 947-5162	H Blaine Beekman	....	Christin Barnhart	Mary Lou Hopkins	R R Armbruster	Michael D Corwin	....
Wellington v (4)	MC 216 647-4626	....	....	....	....	....	....	....
Wellston (6)	MC 614 384-2725	....	....	....	....	....	....	....
Wellsville (5)	MC 216 532-2510	Wayne Elliott	....	Thomas A Lascola	Thomas A Lascola	David Lloyd	Martin K Thorn	....
West Carrollton (14)	CM 513 859-5183	Maxine Gilman	G Tracy Williams	Roberta Donaldson	Roberta Donaldson	....	Bill Przybylek	Don Hill
West Milton v (4)	CM 513 698-4191	Howard L DeHart	Bradley C Vath	Linda L Cantrell	Donna R Clark	Dennis L Frantz	David R Mote	Robert D Sowers
West Union v (3)	MC 513 544-5326	....	....	....	....	....	....	....
Westerville (30)	CM 614 890-8542	John P Parimuha	G David Lindimore	Sharon L Hahn	John P Winkel	Richard Morrison	James J Whitney	Karl P Craven
Westlake (27)	MC 216 871-3300	Dennis Clough	....	....	William Fritzsche	Franklin Kunz	John Kreps	John Lehlbach
Whitehall (21)	MC 614 237-8611	....	....	....	....	....	....	....
Whitehouse v (3)	MC 419 877-5383	Diane McGilvery	James C Fox	B Wielinski	Linda L Snyder	Kenneth Rupp	Norbert J Miller	Mark G Weber
Wickliffe (15)	MC 216 943-7117	Julie Morales	....	C Theophl Actos	Joseph Unetic	David Geosano	Robert Dion	Darryl Crossman
Willard (6)	CM 419 933-2591	....	Christian Morris	Joann Jones	Anne Fritz	George Painter	David Sattig	William Smiley
Willoughby (21)	MC 216 951-2800	David E Anderson	....	Loretta Radebaugh	Chalmers H Glover	Melvin House	Conrad Straube	Dean R Keller

Directory 1/9
continued

**MUNICIPAL OFFICIALS
IN U.S. CITIES OVER 2,500**

City, 1990 population figures (000 omitted), form of government	Municipal phone number	Mayor/ chief elected official	Appointed administrator	City clerk/ city secretary	Finance officer	Fire chief	Police chief	Public works director
OHIO (355) continued								
Willoughby Hills (8)	MC 216 946-1234	....	....	....	....	....	....	....
Willowick (15)	MC 216 585-3700	....	....	....	....	....	....	....
Wilmington (11)	MC 513 382-5458	Clifford Evaland	L S Eichelberger	....	D Hollingsworth	Joseph Spicer	Michael Hatten	Robert W Holmes
Windham v (3)	MC 216 326-2622	M D Archon	....	R W Barrett	....	D G Miller	....	W J Szymanski
Wintersville v (4)	MC 614 264-5533	....	....	....	....	....	....	....
Woodlawn v (3)	MC 513 771-6130	S Upton Farley	Lucius L Ware	Beverly Harris	Roy Borneman	Robert Mynatt	John Williams	....
Woodsfield v (3)	MC 614 472-0418	....	....	Sheila Stanley	James Pyers	Vic Haugh	Robert Merillat	Robert Holland
Wooster (22)	MC 216 263-5200	J Clyde Breneman	....	Sheila Stanley	James Pyers	Vic Haugh	Robert Merillat	Robert Holland
Worthington (15)	CM 614 436-3100	John P Coleman	David B Elder	Janice Yarrington	Barry A Brooks	Bruce A Moore	Wayne I McCoy	David W Groth
Wyoming (8)	CM 513 821-7600	David Savage	Shari S Haldeman	Rozetta Roberts	Mary Ann Engel	John Wirtz	Timothy World	John Wirtz
Xenia (25)	CM 513 376-7273	....	....	....	....	....	....	....
Yellow Springs v (4)	CM 513 767-7202	....	....	....	....	....	....	....
Youngstown (96)	MC 216 742-8700	....	....	....	....	....	....	....
Zanesville (27)	MC 614 455-0600	....	....	....	....	....	....	....
OKLAHOMA (129)								
Ada (16)	CM 405 436-6300	Barbara Young	Patrick Copeland	Joe Ann Dean	Donna Coolen	John Ryan	Wayne McElhannon	David Hathcoat
Altus (22)	MC 405 477-1950	Edythe J McMahan	William C Martin	C Richardson	Charles Reagan	Jack Smiley	Michael Patterson	....
Alva (5)	MC 405 327-1340	....	....	....	....	....	....	....
Anadarko (7)	CM 405 247-2481	Jerry Marcum	Bill R Rowton	Teresa Allen	D Littlechief	Johnnie Beeler	E M Salmon	Bill R Rowton
Antlers t (3)	MC 405 298-3756	Roy E Jackson	Joel Taylor	Athelta Harmon	Robin Byrum	Randy Janoe	Dwayne Morgan	Craig Wilson
Ardmore (23)	CM 405 223-2933	....	....	....	....	....	....	....
Atoka (3)	CM 405 889-3341	Bill Miller	Martha Yates	Sharon Lang	....	Donnie Allen	John Smithart	Stephen Smith
Bartlesville (34)	CM 918 336-0000	Harvey Little	Robert Metzinger	....	George Jones	O Harrington	Steve Brown	....
Bethany (20)	CM 405 789-2146	Don Willis	Richard Gertson	John Shugart	....	....	Mike Baskin	Charles Smoot
Bixby (10)	CM 918 366-4430	Joe Williams	Micky Webb	Vicki R Robinson	Judy Ehlinger	Terry Bowlin	Mike Webster	....
Blackwell (8)	CM 405 363-5490	Bill J Coussens	Robert G Annis	Sara J Norris	....	Terry K Bonewell	Edward L Smith	....
Bristow (4)	MC 918 367-6233	....	....	....	....	....	....	....
Broken Arrow (58)	CM 918 251-5311	James C Reynolds	John T Vinson	Brenda F Rinehart	Thomas L Caldwell	Melvin Mashburn	James R Stover	David Wooden
Broken Bow (4)	CM 405 584-2282	....	....	....	....	....	....	....
Chandler (3)	CM 405 258-3200	....	....	....	....	....	....	....
Checotah (3)	MC 918 473-5411	....	....	....	....	....	....	....
Cherokee (2)	CM 405 596-3326	....	....	....	....	....	....	....
Chickasha (15)	CM 405 222-6020	Harold Jackson	Larry Shelton	Sharon Chapman	....	John Clift	Dany Sterling	Larry Fuchs
Choctaw (9)	CM 405 390-8198	Ruth Ann Luke	Robert L Floyd	Aneata R McBride	....	David Newby	John Whetsel	Bernie Nauheimer
Claremore (13)	MC 918 341-1325	Tom Pool	....	Carlene Webber	....	Chris Neal	Mickey Perry	....
Cleveland (3)	CM 918 358-3506	Jim King	....	Virginia Grantham	....	Granville Wilcox	Marvin D Howard	Floyd E Johnson
Clinton (9)	CM 405 323-0217	Don Rodolph	Dan Galloway	Glendene Goucher	....	Leon Kinder	Bill Weedon	Alvin Knauf
Coalgate (2)	CM 405 927-2241	....	....	....	....	....	....	....
Collinsville (4)	MC 918 371-2811	....	....	....	....	....	....	....
Comanche (2)	CM 405 439-8832	Larry Jones	James Beene	Janice Willis	....	Austin Martin	George Newton	James Beene
Commerce (2)	MC 918 675-4373	....	....	....	....	....	....	....
Coweta (6)	CM 918 486-2189	Vertis Watkins	Steven C Whitlock	Joyce Terry	....	Bill Osburn	Dale Bradley	John Kirkpatrick
Crescent (1)	CM 405 969-2538	....	....	....	....	....	....	....
Cushing (7)	CM 918 225-2394	....	....	....	....	....	....	....
Davis (3)	CM 405 369-2323	Delford Fox	Buck Wilson	Sandra Webb	....	Norman Shiplett	Louise Wall	R Thomasson Jr
Del City (24)	CM 405 671-2802	Joe Nichols	Stan Griel	Reba Basinger	....	Tom Tollison	Leon Rippee	Steve Beck
Dewey (3)	CM 918 534-2272	Jim Eppler	Bill Atkinson	Judy McMurtrey	....	Craig Epps	Lester Rogers	Dewayne Lowe
Drumright (3)	CM 918 352-2610	....	....	....	....	....	....	....
Duncan (22)	CM 405 252-0250	Phil Leonard	Lloyd Rinderer	Clyde Shaw	Clyde Shaw	Robert E Emmons	Dale Anderson	....
Durant (13)	CM 405 924-7200	Steve Wright	Paul Buntz	Tommy Bradburn	Tommy Bradburn	Haskell Manners	Jack Jones	Leonard Morgan
Edmond (52)	CM 405 348-8830	Randel C Shadid	Leonard A Martin	Nancy C Nichols	Roy L Moeller	Dwight L Maker	G Mike Meador	Ronald V Shaw
El Reno (15)	CM 405 262-4070	Phil Todd	Lawrence C Palmer	John P Wiewel	John P Wiewel	Ronald G Martin	Lloyd D Blaine	Donald R Goucher
Elk City (10)	CM 405 225-3230	....	....	....	....	....	....	....
Enid (45)	CM 405 234-0400	Norman Grey	Jim Ferree	Linda Parks	Bill Pritchard	Duane Doney	George Stover	Geoff Brueggemann
Eufaula (3)	MC 918 689-2532	....	....	....	....	....	....	....
Fairview (3)	CM 405 227-4416	....	....	....	....	....	....	....
Frederick (5)	CM 405 335-7551	Leo J Fallon	Robert B Johnston	Yvonne Rector	....	Louis Hickerson	Jack Whitson	....
Glenpool (7)	CM 918 322-5409	....	....	....	....	....	....	....
Grandfield (1)	CM 405 479-5215	Charles Hyman	Richard Harriman	Donna Nill	....	Don Spradlin	Donnie Rowe	....
Grove (4)	CM 918 786-6107	....	....	....	....	....	....	....
Guthrie (11)	CM 405 282-0493	....	....	....	....	....	....	....
Guymon (8)	CM 405 338-3396	Jess Nelson	Wayne Hill	Marcy Twyman	Marcy Twyman	Quinten Smith	Duane Boren	Nolan Bowers
Harrah t (4)	CM 405 454-2951	Kevin Spaeth	Robert Wherry	Bill C Knox	....	Sammy Martin	Richard J Reier	Greg Hill
Healdton (3)	CM 405 229-1283	....	....	....	....	....	....	....
Heavener (3)	CM 918 653-2217	....	....	....	....	....	....	....
Henryetta (6)	CM 918 652-3348	....	....	....	....	....	....	....
Hobart (4)	MC 405 726-3100	....	....	....	....	....	....	....
Holdenville (5)	MC 405 379-3397	Jack Barrett	....	Frenola Janes	....	Orville Reid	Robert Horton	....
Hollis (3)	CM 405 688-2167	....	....	....	....	....	....	....
Hominy (2)	CM 918 885-2164	Cha Fairweather	Bret R Sholar	Pat Wikel	Bret R Sholar	....	Joe Lucas	Jr Goebel
Hugo (6)	MC 405 326-2722	....	....	....	....	....	....	....
Idabel (7)	MC 405 286-7608	....	....	....	....	....	....	....
Jenks (7)	CM 918 299-5883	Mike Tinker	V R Ewing	Kenda Rice	Kenda Rice	Bob Douglas	Lloyd Ruddell	Sam Balsiger
Kingfisher (4)	CM 405 375-3705	Vernie Snow	Reuben Pulis	Hallo Jean Shults	....	Garold Post	Tom Jones	....
Konawa (2)	CM 405 925-3775	....	....	....	....	....	....	....
Lawton (81)	CM 405 581-3500	John T Marley	Gil Schumpert	Brenda Smith	Steve Livingston	Mike Carter	Bill Adamson	J B Howle
Lindsay (3)	CM 405 756-2019	....	....	....	....	....	....	....
Lone Grove (4)	CM 405 657-3111	Clayton Redding	Ron Holt	Vonnie Updike	Peggy Thomason	Terry Ferrel	Danny Howard	Ron Holt
Madill (3)	CM 405 795-3378	....	....	....	....	....	....	....
Mangum (3)	CM 405 782-2256	....	....	....	....	....	....	....
Marlow (4)	CM 405 658-5401	....	....	....	....	....	....	....
Mc Alester (16)	CM 918 423-9300	....	Randy Green	Bobbie Lanz	....	Larry Ketchum	G Dale Nave	George Marcangeli
Mc Loud t (2)	MC 405 964-5264	....	....	....	....	....	....	....
Medford (1)	CM 405 395-2823	Louise McGregor	Warern A Beggs	Frances E Mark	Frances E Mark	Dennis Brittain	Chester Black	Dennis Brittain
Miami (13)	MC 918 542-6685	Louis E Mathia	H Alton Rivers Jr	....	Charle A Tomlin	Keith Manion	Bill G Melton	....
Midwest City (52)	CM 405 732-2281	Eddie Reed	Charles Johnson	Tommy Melton	Tommy Melton	Mike Bower	Clovis Davis	Tommy Canfield
Moore (40)	CM 405 793-5000	Glenn Lewis	Huey P Long	Priscilla Hargis	Priscilla Hargis	John Knight	Bruce Storm	....
Muldrow t (3)	MC 918 427-3226	....	....	....	....	....	....	....
Muskogee (38)	CM 918 682-6602	....	....	....	....	....	....	....
Mustang (10)	CM 405 376-4521	....	....	....	....	....	....	....
New Cordell (3)	MC 405 832-3825	....	....	....	....	....	....	....
Newcastle (4)	CM 405 387-4427	Lloyd A Gramling	Stan Patty	Loycie Kerr	....	Philip Thompson	Jim Greene	Virgil Fielding

Directory 1/9
continued

**MUNICIPAL OFFICIALS
IN U.S. CITIES OVER 2,500**

City, 1990 population figures (000 omitted), form of government	Municipal phone number	Mayor/ chief elected official	Appointed administrator	City clerk/ city secretary	Finance officer	Fire chief	Police chief	Public works director
OKLAHOMA (129) continued								
Newkirk (2)	MC 405 362-2117	....	....	....	....	....	....	....
Nichols Hills (4)	CM 405 843-6637	Stewart E Meyers	Douglas D Henley	Douglas D Henley	Cathy Keller	Keith Bryan	James P Stoddard	Russell Fields
Nicoma Park t (2)	MC 405 769-5673	....						
Noble t (5)	CM 405 872-9251	Dee Downer	Harry Hill	James E Hunt	James E Hunt	James Stufflebean	Paul Boyd	Elza Harris
Norman (80)	CM 405 366-5482	Willim Nations	Ron Wood	Mary Hatley	Karen Montgomery	John Dutch	David Boyett	Jimmy Berry
Nowata (4)	CM 918 273-3538	John Carroll Jr	Nancy C Shipley	Nancy C Shipley	Nancy C Shipley	Richard Pugh	Timothy Wilson	Clifton Nickell
Okemah (3)	CM 918 623-1050	....	....	....	....	....	....	....
Oklahoma City (445)	CM 405 297-2345	....	....	....	....	....	....	....
Okmulgee (13)	CM 918 756-4060	....	....	....	....	....	....	....
Owasso (11)	CM 918 272-2251	Jerry Duke	Rodney J Ray	....	Sherry Bishop	Bob Allen	Maria Alexander	F Robert Carr Jr
Pauls Valley (6)	CM 405 238-3308	Kirk Dunham	Rick Wickenkamp	Florence Johnson		Buck Pearson	James Frizell	
Pawhuska (4)	CM 918 287-3040	Preston D Landrum	Bruce O Decker	Lucile Smith	Lucile Smith		John W Boone	Dean Branson
Perry (5)	MC 405 336-9360	....	....	....	....	....	....	....
Pocola t (4)	MC 918 436-2388	....						
Ponca City (26)	CM 405 767-0322	Marilyn Andrews	Gary Martin	Don Wolfe	....	Martin Smith	Raymond Ham	Ken Parr
Poteau (7)	MC 918 647-4191	Donald J Barnes		Launa Pate		Richard F Couri	Bobby Hendricks	Shirley Weatherfo
Prague (2)	CM 405 567-2270	J Ted McBride	Daniel D Gibson	Christi Riddle	Christi Riddle	Tony Simek	James Bartlett	Louis Devereaux
Pryor (8)	MC 918 825-0888	Lucy B Schultz	....	Patricia Morgan		David Harrison	Dennis Nichols	....
Purcell (5)	CM 405 527-6561	....		....	....			
Sallisaw (7)	CM 918 775-6241	George Glenn	James R Hudgens	Elton W Rogers		Gus Fullbright	Wayne Craghead	
Sand Springs (15)	CM 918 245-8751	E Bruce Ford	Loy Calhoun	Mary Sue Overbey	Mary Sue Overbey	Wayne Bennett	Tom Lewallen	Ken Hill
Sapulpa (18)	CM 918 224-3040	Brian Bingman	....	Shirley Burzio	Mary Wesson	Jackie Carner	Ron Sole	Elmer Grisham
Sayre (3)	MC 405 928-2260	....	....	....	....	....	....	....
Seminole (7)	CM 405 382-4330	M McCreight	Thomas DeArman	Diane Johnson	....	Howard Allen	....	....
Shawnee (26)	CM 405 273-1250	Pierre Taron	Terry Powell	Diana Hallock	James Wilsie	James Roberts	Joe Lahue	James Cole
Skiatook t (5)	MC 918 396-2797	....	....	....	....	....	....	....
Spencer (4)	CM 405 771-3226	....	....	....	....	....	....	....
Stigler (3)	CM 918 967-2164	Larry Godfrey	James W Smith	Leann Lassiter		Wayne Cantrell	Manuel Ballard	....
Stillwater (37)	CM 918 372-0025	Terry Miller	Carl Weinaug	....	Marcy Alexander	Jim Smith	Norman McNickle	Jeff Hough
Stroud (3)	CM 918 968-2571	....	....	....	....	....	....	....
Sulphur (5)	MC 405 622-5096	....	....	....	....	....	....	....
Tahlequah (10)	MC 918 456-0651	Eunice Ross	Jerry Latty	Jo Ann Bradley		Robert Adrian	Norman Fisher	....
Tecumseh (6)	CM 405 598-2188	....	....	....	....	....	....	....
The Village (10)	CM 405 751-8861	....	....	....	....	....	....	....
Tishomingo (3)	MC 405 371-2369	....	....	....	....	....	....	....
Tonkawa (3)	CM 405 628-2508	....	....	....	....	....	....	....
Tulsa (367)	MC 918 596-7440	S Susan Savage	Robert Lemons	Michael Kier	Michael Kier	Thomas L Baker	Ronald D Palmer	Charles Hardt
Tuttle t (3)	CM 918 381-2335	James O Cobble	Bruce A Drawdy	Geri L Scott	....	David Williams	Bill Murr	T J Chester
Vinita (6)	MC 918 256-6468	Joe Johnson	....	Faye Jones	....	Roy Faulconer	Larry Parrish	....
Wagoner (7)	MC 918 485-2554	Kenneth Peters	....	Linda Gaylor	....	Gerald McCuhn	Jim Parker	Alua Smith
Walters (3)	CM 405 875-3337	....	....	....	....	....	....	....
Warr Acres (9)	MC 405 789-2892	....	....	....	....	....	....	....
Watonga (3)	MC 405 623-4669	....	....	....	....	....	....	....
Waurika (2)	CM 405 228-2713	Dewey Richardson	Nolan Combs	Donna Brown		Ed Keith	Ken Ferreira	Ken Ferreira
Weatherford (10)	MC 405 772-7451	Gary Rader	George Wilkinson	....	A G Davenport	Dean Brown	Paul Gaines	Arnold Miller
Wetumka (1)	CM 405 452-3251	....	....	....	....	....	....	....
Wewoka (4)	CM 405 257-2413	....	....	....	....	....	....	....
Wilburton (3)	MC 918 465-2262	....	....	....	....	....	....	....
Woodward (12)	CM 405 256-2280	George Goetzinger	Gary Lyon	Harry Sever	....	Ronald Waggoner	Harvey Rutherford	Harry Sever
Wynnewood (2)	CM 405 665-2307	....	....	....	....	....	....	....
Yale (1)	CM 918 387-2405	William Jester	Carl W Hensley	Sharon Crisjohn	Carl W Hensley	Richard Adsit	Hogart Simpson	Wes Thurman
Yukon (21)	CM 405 354-2163	Ray Wright	....	Mary Huckaba	Mary Huckaba	Robert Noll	James Huffman	Dwyane Whitner
OREGON (92)								
Albany (29)	CM 503 967-4300	Eugene Belhumeur	Steve Bryant	....	D Gary Holliday	Darrel Tedisch	Pat Merina	Mark Yeager
Ashland (16)	MC 503 482-3211	Catherine Golden	Brian L Almquist	Nan Franklin	Jill Turner	Keith Woodley	Gary Brown	Steve M Hall
Astoria (10)	CM 503 325-5821	Willis Van Dusen	Robert DeLong	....	John Snyder	Lane Wintermute	Robert Deu Pree	
Baker City (9)	CM 503 523-6541	Lawrence Griffith	Arthur Reiff	....	Roland Campbell	Donald Everson	Douglas Humphress	Randall Jones
Bandon (2)	MC 503 347-2437	Judith Densmore	Matthew J Winkel	Denise Skillman	Chele Gamble	Lanny Boston	Richard Lewis	
Beaverton (53)	MC 503 526-2222	Rob Drake	....	....		Gary Nees	David Bishop	Steve Baker
Bend (20)	CM 503 388-5505	John Wujack	Larry Patterson	....	A Andrew Parks	Larry Langston	R David Malkin	Tom L Gellner
Boardman (1)	MC 503 481-9252	....	....	....	....	....	....	....
Brookings (4)	CM 503 469-2163	Tom Davis	Dennis Cluff	Beverly Shields	Beverly Shields	....	Kent Owens	Dennis Barlow
Brownsville (1)	CM 503 466-5666	Joe Dezurney	Diane J Rinks	Sandi Jensen	Diane J Rinks	....	....	Joe Anthony
Burns (3)	MC 503 573-5255	Joe Hayse	Harvey Barnes	Norma Hill	Harvey Barnes	Chris Briels	Aaron Richardson	David Cullens
Canby (9)	CM 503 266-4021	Scott Taylor	Michael Jordan	Marilyn Perkett	Virginia Biddle	....	Jerry Giger	Roy Hester
Cannon Beach (1)	CM 503 436-1581	Herb Schwab	John Williams		John Williams	....	Dave Rouse	Dave Kinash
Cascade Locks (1)	CM 503 374-8484	Ken Lambert	George Lewis	Kate Mast		Neil McCormick	....	Richard McCulley
Central Point (8)	CM 503 664-3321	Roger Westensee	Dave Kucera	....	Gary Lawing	Mark Servatius	Laddie Hancock	Larry Blanchard
Clatskanie (2)	CM 503 728-2622	....	William McDonald	Arlene Long	....	William Mellinger	Wayne Smith	David True
Coos Bay (15)	CM 503 269-8912	Joanne Verger	Jim Watson	....	Gail George	Cliff Vaniman	Marc Adams	Ralph Dunham
Coquille (4)	CM 503 396-2115	Mike Swindall	Joseph Wolf	Shirley Patterson	....	Jerry McCue	Dave Knapp	John Higgins
Cornelius (6)	CM 503 357-9112	Neal Knight	Harold Schilling	....	....	Chris Asanovic	Charles Standley	Frank Neys
Corvallis (45)	CM 503 757-6900	....	....	....	....	....	....	....
Cottage Grove (7)	CM 503 942-5501	Jean Sinclair	Jeffrey Towery	Joan Hoehn	Linda Gardner	Stephen Allen	Michael Grover	Robert Sisson
Dallas (9)	CM 503 623-2338	G Van Den Bosch	Roger Jordan	....	Del Funk	Maark Stevens	James Harper	David M Shea
Eagle Point (3)	MC 503 826-4212	Walter B Barker	John Luthy	Carmen Bernhardt	....	Dennis Jordan	Leon C Sherman	Jim Robertson
Estacada (2)	CM 503 630-8270	Dave Vail	Shelley Jones	Denise Carey	Shelley Jones	....	....	William Strawn
Eugene (113)	CM 503 687-5010	....	....	....	....	....	....	....
Florence (5)	MC 503 997-3436	....	....	....	....	....	....	....
Forest Grove (14)	CM 503 359-3200	Richard Kidd	Ivan Burnett	....	Jeff Hecksel	Bob Davis	Tom Lowther	John Burdett
Gladstone (10)	CM 503 656-5225	Wade Byers	Ronald J Partch	Verna Howell	Ronald J Partch	Wayne L Hauck	Robert M King	....
Gold Beach (2)	CM 503 247-7029	Marlyn Schafer	Bill Curtis	Norma Rath	Bill Curtis	Bruce Floyd	Mark Coltrane	Richard Eccleston
Grants Pass (17)	CM 503 474-6360	Gordon Anderson	William Peterson	Joanne Stumpf	Joanne Stumpf	....	Eric Millgren	David Wheaton
Gresham (68)	CM 503 669-2300	Gussie McRobert	Bonnie Kraft	Phyllis Brough	Roy Wall	Joe Parrott	Art Knori	Greg DiLoretto
Hermiston (10)	MC 503 567-5521	Frank Harkenrider	Ed Brookshier	Robert D Irby	Robert D Irby	James E Stearns	Grant E Asher	
Hillsboro (38)	CM 503 681-6100	....	....	....	....	....	....	....
Hood River (5)	MC 503 386-1488	....	....	....	....	....	....	....
Independence (4)	MC 503 838-1212	....	....	....	....	....	....	....
Junction City (4)	MC 503 998-2153	John W Peterson	Roberta L Likens	Barbara A Scott	Barbara A Scott	Dave Harlacher	Michael Cahill	Robert L Fountain
Keizer (22)	CM 503 390-3700	Dennis Koho	Dorothy Tryk	Tracy Davis	Kimberly Krause	....	Charles Stull	Wally G Mull
Klamath Falls (18)	CM 503 883-5317	....	....	....	....	....	....	....
La Grande (12)	CM 503 962-1302	K Larsen Hill	Larry Dalrymple	....	Eldon Slippy	Doug Perry	John Courtney	Ron Gross

Directory 1/9 continued — MUNICIPAL OFFICIALS IN U.S. CITIES OVER 2,500

City, 1990 population figures (000 omitted), form of government	Municipal phone number	Mayor/ chief elected official	Appointed administrator	City clerk/ city secretary	Finance officer	Fire chief	Police chief	Public works director
OREGON (92) continued								
Lake Oswego (31) .... CM	503 635-0220	Alice Schlenker	Doug Schmitz	Kris Hitchcock	Bruce Griswold	Phil Sample	Les Youngbar	Jerry Baker
Lakeview t (3) .... MC	503 947-2029	Bob Alger	....	Sherry Landers	Sherry Landers	Del Lepley	John Bush	Ron Wilkie
Lebanon (11) .... MC	503 451-7422	....	....	....	....	....	....	....
Lincoln City (6) .... CM	503 996-2152	Sam Cribbs	Kathleen Stockton	D W Works	D W Works	....	Michael Holden	....
Mc Minnville (18) .... CM	503 472-9371	....	....	....	....	....	....	....
Medford (47) .... CM	503 770-4432	Jerry Lausmann	Harold Anderson	Kathleen Ishlara	Jonathan Jalali	David Bierwiler	Oscar Shipley	Donald Walker
Milton-Freewater (6) ..... CM	503 938-5531	Mary Nicholson	James A Swayne	....	Linda K Carter	William Saager	Don Witt	Howard Moss
Milwaukie (19) .... CM	503 659-5171	Craig Lomnicki	Dan R Bartlett	....	Angus Anderson	Dan Olsen	Brent Collier	R Tim Corbett
Molalla (4) .... CM	503 829-6855	....	....	....	....	....	....	....
Monmouth (6) .... CM	503 838-0722	....	....	....	....	....	....	....
Mt. Angel (3) .... MC	503 845-9291	Randy Traeger	Richard Van Orman	Marilyn Ross	Phyllis Gustin	Joe Traeger	Pete Kelly	Phil Meissner
Myrtle Creek (3) .... CM	503 863-3171	Robert Cotterell	Leroy Blodgett	Charity Hays	Jeanne Babcock	Bill Leming	David Oelrich	Steven Johnson
Myrtle Point (3) .... CM	503 572-2626	....	....	....	....	....	....	....
Newberg (13) .... MC	503 538-9421	Donna Proctor	Duane Cole	....	Katherine Tri	Michael Sherman	Robert Tardiff Jr	Charles Liebert
Newport (8) .... CM	503 265-5331	....	....	....	....	....	....	....
North Bend (10) .... CM	503 756-0405	Timm Slator	Jim C Allan	Terri Tori	Carol Bender	....	Gil Zaccaro	Ron Stillmaker
Nyssa (3) .... MC	503 372-2264	J R Shuster	Gordon Zimmerman	Hilda Contreras	....	Tony Frost	Terry Thompson	Ray Page
Oakridge (3) .... CM	503 782-2258	Richard Culbertson	Wes Hare	Holly Lee	Sharon O' Brien	James Archer	Michael Reaves	Jerry Shanbeck
Ontario (9) .... CM	503 889-7684	Robert Switzer	Allen Brown	....	Roger Dexter	Mike Sopkis	Mitchell Lawson	William Critz
Oregon City (15) .... CM	503 657-0891	....	....	....	....	....	....	....
Pendleton (15) .... CM	503 276-1811	Robert E Ramig	Larry L Lehman	....	Carol A James	Richard D Hopper	Edwin S Taber	Jerry Odman
Philomath (3) .... CM	503 929-6148	Van O Hunsaker	Harry L Million	Terri J Phillips	Phyllis G Beggs	....	Richard K Raleigh	Richard Clark
Pilot Rock (1) .... MC	503 443-2811	John Standley	....	Amanda Howard	Jackie Carey	....	Ronnie Layton	Steve Draper
Portland (437) .... CO	503 823-4352	....	....	....	....	....	....	....
Prineville (5) .... CM	503 447-5627	Todd M Vallie	Henry Hartley	....	....	Dave Fields	Jim Soules	....
Redmond (7) .... CM	503 548-2148	Jerry C Thackery	Joe Hannan	Nancy Blankenship	David Reeves	Bob Garrison	Jim Carlton	Mary Meloy
Reedsport (5) .... CM	503 271-3603	Steven W Wilson	Nolan K Young	Sandra K Hanson	Sandra K Hanson	John Cable	John Smart	J McIlvenna
Roseburg (17) .... CM	503 672-7701	Jeri Kimmel	Randy A Wetmore	Sheila R Taucher	C Lance Colley	Ford G Swauger	John R Hodgson	Chris S Berquist
Salem (108) .... CM	503 588-6255	....	Larry Wacker	....	George Shelley	James Bone	Brian Riley	Frank Mauldin
Sandy (4) .... CM	503 668-5533	Mark Mullins	Scott Lazenby	....	June Peterson	....	Fred Punzel	Mike Walker
Scappoose (4) .... CM	503 543-7146	Rita Bernhard	James Minard	....	....	....	Scott Woods	Carl Dentler
Seaside (5) .... CM	503 738-5511	....	....	....	....	....	....	....
Sheridan (4) .... CM	503 843-2347	Val Adamson	Michael Saverweln	Joan D Williams	....	....	....	Lonnie Hinchcliff
Sherwood (3) .... CM	503 625-5522	Walter Hitchcock	James H Rapp	....	P Blankenbaker	....	Larry A Laws	Ron Hudson
Silverton (6) .... CM	503 873-5321	Ken Hector	Michael J Scott	....	Becky Hein	....	Randy Lunsford	Richard Barstad
Springfield (45) .... CM	503 726-3700	Bill Morrisette	Michael Kelly	Eileen Stein	Robert Duey	Dennis Murphy	Bill Deforrest	Dan Brown
St. Helens (8) .... MC	503 397-6272	D Kallberg	B Little	D Gruenhagen	M Peterson	....	R Roth	....
Stayton (5) .... MC	503 769-3425	Willmer Van Vleet	David W Kinney	....	Elaine Fisk	....	Michael D Healy	....
Sutherlin (5) .... CM	503 459-2856	Stan McKnight	Bruce Long	....	Roy Stulken	Tom Wells	Duane Parnell	Don Moore
Sweet Home (7) .... CM	503 367-5128	Craig Fentiman	Dan Dean	....	Patricia Gray	Joseph Mengore	Gary David	David Sypher
Talent (3) .... CM	503 535-1566	Leo Lomski	Tony Paxton	Tony Paxton	Tony Paxton	Jim Flynn	Dale D Kinnan	Timothy Connolly
The Dalles (11) .... CM	503 296-5481	Les Cochenour	William B Elliott	Julie Krueger	Donald Gower	Robert Palmer	Darrell Hill	William Keyser
Tigard (29) .... CM	503 639-4171	John Schwartz	....	C Wheatley	R Wayne Lowry	....	Ronald Goodpaster	Edward Wegner
Tillamook (4) .... CM	503 842-2472	J R McPheeters	Michael Mahoney	....	....	Tom Weber	Roy White	Michael Mahoney
Toledo (3) .... CM	503 336-2247	Floyd D Ferguson	Jim Landon	Renee Ballinger	....	David Simmons	Jerry Pryor	Lance Burke
Troutdale (8) .... CM	503 665-5175	Paul Thalhofer	Pamelia Christian	George Martinez	Robert Gazewood	....	Mark Berrest	Jim Galloway
Tualatin (15) .... CM	503 692-2000	Steven L Stolze	Stephen A Rhodes	....	Stephen A Rhodes	....	Steve Winegar	Dan Boss
Umatilla (3) .... MC	503 922-3226	George Hash	Bonnie Parker	Linda Gettmann	Shannon Vannett	Don Drayton	Travis Eynon	Roger Frances
Warrenton (3) .... CM	503 861-2233	....	....	....	....	....	....	....
West Linn (16) .... CM	503 657-0331	Jill Thorn	Scott A Burgess	....	William Gin	....	Terry Hart	David Monson
Wilsonville (7) .... CM	503 682-1011	....	....	....	....	....	....	....
Winston (4) .... CM	503 679-6739	James McClellan	Bruce Kelly	Margo Moore	....	....	Bruce Justis	Eric Wilson
Woodburn (13) .... CM	503 982-5222	Len Kelley	C Childs	Mary Tennant	Nancy Gritta	....	Kenneth L Wright	Girjesh S Tiwari
PENNSYLVANIA (555)								
Abington tp (56) .... MC	215 884-5000	Richard E Fluge	Burton T Conway	Burton T Conway	Allyn R Larash	Kenneth Clark	William J Kelly	Ed Micciolo
Abington tp (2) .... MC	717 586-0111	Alfred G Rice Jr	Ronald G Bray	....	....	....	Daniel J Mooney	Harry F Derr Jr
Akron b (4) .... MC	717 859-1600	....	....	....	....	....	....	....
Aldan b (5) .... MC	215 626-3553	....	....	....	....	....	....	....
Aliquippa b (13) .... CO	412 375-5188	Daniel Britza	Charles Bergensky	Rodna Casto	Rebecca Bradley	Oresto Costanza	William Alston	Anthony Battalini
Allentown (105) .... MC	610 437-7523	William Heydt	....	Michael Hanlon	....	David Novosat	John Stefanik	Neal Kern
Altoona (52) .... CM	814 949-2428	Raphael J Voltz	Robert F Hagemann	Amy J Hanna	Arthur E Wilkin	Reynold D Santone	John J Reilly	Robert C McPhee
Ambler b (7) .... MC	215 646-1000	....	....	....	....	....	....	....
Ambridge b (8) .... CM	412 266-4070	....	....	....	....	....	....	....
Amity tp (6) .... CM	215 689-9415	....	....	....	....	....	....	....
Archbald b (6) .... MC	717 876-1800	....	....	....	....	....	....	....
Arnold (6) .... MC	412 337-4441	....	....	....	....	....	....	....
Ashland b (4) .... MC	717 875-2411	....	....	....	....	....	....	....
Ashley b (3) .... MC	717 824-1364	John J Jablowski	....	Kathleen Krofchok	....	Phillip Collotty	Thomas Engle	....
Aspinwall b (3) .... MC	412 781-0213	Arthur G Esser	....	Georgene C Veltri	....	Nicholas J Scheid	William L Eckert	....
Aston tp (15) .... MC	610 494-1636	J DiGiacomo	Richard Lehr	Bridget Thomas	Joan Brunner	....	James McCarthy	Richard Lehr Jr
Athens b (3) .... MC	717 888-2120	....	....	....	....	....	....	....
Avalon b (6) .... CM	412 761-5820	....	....	....	....	....	....	....
Avoca b (3) .... MC	717 457-4011	....	....	....	....	....	....	....
Baden b (5) .... MC	412 869-3700	....	....	....	....	....	....	....
Baldwin b (22) .... MC	412 882-9600	John N Bova	Shirley A Kuchta	....	....	....	Christopher Kelly	....
Bally b (1) .... MC	610 845-2351	Phil Ferrizzi	Robert Moll	Judith Krebs	....	....	....	....
Bangor b (5) .... MC	610 588-2216	Carol Cuono	Joseph Dweleski	Melissa Raisner	....	Robert Owens	Donald Gillingham	....
Barnesboro b (3) .... MC	814 948-8230	....	....	....	....	....	....	....
Beaver b (5) .... MC	412 773-6700	....	....	....	....	....	....	....
Beaver Falls (11) .... CO	412 847-2803	Thomas Berger	Perry C Wayne	....	Perry C Wayne	Robert Butler	Donald Burdine	Ted A Krzemienski
Beavertown b (1) .... MC	717 658-2505	Cloyd W Wagner	Thomas Wagner	....	....	Michael Mattern	....	Thomas Wagner
Bedford b (3) .... MC	814 623-8192	William R Newman	John L Montgomery	Lisa Merritt	....	Jay Speicher	Earl Packer	....
Bellefonte b (6) .... CM	814 355-1501	Candace Dannaker	Walter B Peterson	....	....	....	Lester McCellan	Dick Brown
Bellevue b (9) .... CM	412 766-6164	Rosemary Heflin	Robert Grimm	....	....	Charles Amrhein	Michael Bookser	Robert Kusserow
Bensalem tp (57) .... CM	215 633-3600	J DiGirolamo	James White	William Cmorey	James White	....	Frank Friel	James Nolan
Bentleyville b (3) .... MC	412 239-2112	....	....	....	....	....	....	....
Benzinger tp (9) .... MC	814 781-1274	....	....	....	....	....	....	....
Berwick b (11) .... CM	717 752-2723	Lou Biacchi	Matthew Kulhanek	....	Matthew Kulhanek	Charles East	James Comstock	James Gavitt
Bethel Park (34) .... CM	412 831-6800	Alan Hoffman	William Spagnol	....	Timothy Babik	John Foster	Joseph Kletch	Marshall Scurlock
Bethlehem (71) .... MC	610 865-7049	Kenneth R Smith	Robert C Wilkins	C Biedenkopf	Robert C Wilkins	Carmen J Oliver	John W Yerk	Wendell S Sherman
Bethlehem tp (16) .... CM	215 865-5563	....	....	....	....	....	....	....
Big Beaver b (2) .... MC	412 827-2416	Donald Wachter	Janet E Kolson	....	John Nugent	Jeff Pinkerton	J Diffenbacher	Willis Androlia

**Directory 1/9
continued**

**MUNICIPAL OFFICIALS
IN U.S. CITIES OVER 2,500**

City, 1990 population figures (000 omitted), form of government	Municipal phone number	Mayor/ chief elected official	Appointed administrator	City clerk/ city secretary	Finance officer	Fire chief	Police chief	Public works director
PENNSYLVANIA (555) continued								
Birdsboro b (4)	CM 610 582-6030	Donald R Lebo	Ronald M Ewing	Michele Crammer	Ronald M Ewing	Craig Seidel	Robert Rothhardt	Ronald M Ewing
Blairsville b (4)	CM 412 459-9100	....	....	....	....	....	....	....
Blakely b (7)	MC 717 383-3340	Robert Klinko	Harold McCusker	....	Dennis Corvo	Dana DeLeo	Thomas K Dubas	....
Bloomsburg t (12)	MC 717 784-7703	....	....	....	....	....	....	....
Blossburg b (2)	MC 717 638-2452	....	....	....		....	....	
Boyertown b (4)	CM 215 367-2688	....	....					
Brackenridge b (4)	MC 412 224-0800	William Beale	Kristen Geyer	Carol Jones	....	Daniel Brestensky	Guy Gula	
Braddock b (5)	MC 412 271-1018	....	....	....				
Braddock Hills b (2)	MC 412 241-5080	....	....					
Bradford (10)	CM 814 368-3232	Arvid R Nelson	J F Roslinski	....	Connie Cavallaro	Frank Frontino	R J Cavallero	J F Roslinski
Brentwood b (11)	MC 412 884-1500	....	....	....	....	....	....	....
Bridgeport b (4)	MC 215 272-1811	....	....	....	....		....	....
Bridgeville b (5)	CM 412 221-6012	....	....	....	....	....	....	....
Brighton tp (7)	MC 412 774-4803	Roy E Harden	Bryan K Dehart	....	....	John Curtaccio	Jack E Erath	....
Bristol tp (57)	MC 215 785-5884	Anthony Cipullo	Carmen Raddi	....	Sharon Rendeiro	Edward Copper	Thomas Mills	William Surrick
Bristol b (10)	MC 215 788-3828	....	....	....	....	....	....	....
Brookhaven b (9)	MC 215 874-2557	....	....	....	....	....	....	....
Brookville b (4)	MC 814 849-5325	....	....	....	....		....	....
Brownsville b (3)	MC 412 785-5761	Samuel J Nicola	....	....	....	....	Richard A Gordon	....
Buckingham tp (9)	CM 215 794-8834	....	Beverly J Curtin	....	Nancy L Saxe	....	Steven P Daniels	Donald G Naylor
Butler (16)	CO 412 285-4124	Richard J Schontz	Glenn P Crytzer	Glenn P Crytzer	....	Donald Acquaviva	Paul A Cornibe Jr	Pete Zissi
Butler tp (17)	MC 412 283-3430	....	....	....	....		....	....
California b (6)	MC 412 938-8878	....	....	....	....		....	....
Callimont b (..)	MC							
Caln tp (12)	MC 215 384-0600	....	....	....	....	....	....	....
Cambridge Springs b (2)	CM 814 398-2311	Robert Repa	Carol Powell	Judy Wikris	....	Gayle Wolfe	John Yanc	Kenneth Dine
Camp Hill b (8)	MC 717 737-3456	T Prosser	E J Knittel	....	....	....	G A Ammons	T Maro
Canonsburg b (9)	CM 412 745-1800	Daniel A Caruso	Jack C Haney	....	....	Harold Coleman	R T Bell	Chester Osiecki
Carbondale (11)	MC 717 282-4110	....	....	....	....	....	....	....
Carlisle b (18)	CM 717 249-4422	Kirk Wilson	Fredrick Bean	....	R Fahnestock	David Boyles	Stephen Margeson	Michael Keiser
Carnegie b (9)	MC 412 276-1414	Robert R Heinrich	....	Carol Goldbach	....	John Kandracs	Jeffrey Harbin	John Kandracs
Carroll Valley b (1)	MC 717 642-8269	Grady Edwards	Virginia Ciliotta	Barbara Hertz	....	....	Douglas Kiel	....
Castle Shannon b (9)	CM 412 561-9200	Thomas O' Malley	E R McFadden	....	....	....	Harold C Lane	George Fuss
Catasauqua b (7)	CM 610 264-0571	Robert C Boyer	Eugene Goldfeder	Eugene Goldfeder	....	Samuel W Burrows	Wayne W Muffley	Joseph I Nicklas
Center tp (11)	MC 412 774-0271	....	....	....	....	....	....	....
Centerville b (4)	MC 412 757-6307	....	....	....	....	....	....	....
Chalfont b (3)	MC 215 822-0991	....	....	....	....	....	....	....
Chambersburg b (17)	MC 717 264-5151	Robert P Morris	Julio D Lecuona	Tanya Mickey	C Forrester	William Sheppard	Michael DeFrank	Robert Wagner
Charleroi b (5)	MC 412 483-6011	....	....	....	....	....	....	....
Cheltenham tp (35)	CM 215 887-1000	....	....	....	....	....	....	....
Chester (42)	MC 215 447-7700	....	....	....	....	....	....	....
Chippewa tp (7)	CM 412 843-8177	Dale S Laughner	Stephen L Johnson	....	Stephen L Johnson	Robert E Beatty	Robert Berchtold	Dale R Morgan
Churchill b (4)	MC 412 241-7113	William Richards	Louis Bruwelheide	Anna C Sekela	....	Louis Bruwelheide	Richard H James	....
Clairton (10)	CM 412 233-8113	D Serapiglia	Kenneth L Weaver	....	David James	John A Lattanzi	William S Scully	Francis A Geletko
Clarion b (6)	CM 814 226-7707	....	....	....	....	....	....	....
Clarks Summit b (5)	CM 717 586-9316	Anthony Perry	James G Vones	....	....	Frank Miller Jr	Wesley Dunn	Neil Bartholome
Clearfield b (7)	MC 814 765-7817	....	....	....	....	....	....	....
Clifton Heights b (7)	MC 215 623-1000	....	....	....	....	....	....	....
Coaldale b (3)	RT 717 645-7986	....	....	....	....	....	....	....
Coatesville (11)	CM 610 384-0300	Ernest Campos	Jeffrey Braun	....	Lewis Gay	Francis Pilotti	Dennis Alexander	David Gay
College tp (7)	CM 814 234-7200	....	....	....	....	....	....	....
Collegeville b (4)	MC 215 489-9208	....	....	....	....	....	....	....
Collingdale b (9)	MC 215 586-0500	....	....	....	....	....	....	....
Columbia b (11)	CM 717 684-2468	....	....	....	....	....	....	....
Colwyn b (3)	MC 610 461-2000	Diane McGonigle	Daniel McEnhill	Mary Martin	....	....	....	....
Concord tp (7)	CM 215 459-8911	Howard Gallagher	John W Cornell	....	....	Steven Cooper	....	Harry T Shinn
Connellsville (9)	MC 412 628-2020	....	....	....	....	....	....	....
Conshohocken b (8)	MC 215 828-1092	....	....	....	....	....	....	....
Conway b (2)	MC 412 869-5550	Jack Andolina	S Brandenburg	Dorothy Work	....	....	Anthony Blum	Edward Tolbert
Coopersburg b (3)	MC 610 282-3307	Thelma M Kiess	Roberta M Shelly	Carol F Anderson	....	Calvin Sharrer	James M Lawrence	Dennis G Nace
Coplay b (3)	MC 610 262-6088	J Shemanski	Carol A Schleder	Carol A Schleder	....	Jay Ambearle	Donald Hill	Richard Bundra
Coraopolis b (7)	MC 412 264-3002	....	....	....	....	....	....	....
Cornwall b (3)	MC 717 274-3436	....	....	....	....	....	....	....
Corry (7)	CO 814 663-7041	....	....	....	....	....	....	....
Coudersport b (3)	MC 814 274-9776	....	....	....	....	....	....	....
Crafton b (7)	MC 412 921-0752	....	P Kozlowski	....	....	....	Harold Rost	....
Cranberry tp (15)	CM 412 776-4806	....	....	....	....	....	....	....
Cumru tp (13)	CO 215 777-1343	....	....	....	....	....	....	....
Curwensville b (3)	MC 814 236-1840	....	....	....	....	....	....	....
Dallas b (3)	MC 717 675-1389	Paul J Labar	Milton Lutsey	Mary F Gill	....	Brett Slocum	John R Fowler	Charles Shurites
Dallastown b (4)	MC 717 244-6626	....	....	....	....	....	....	....
Danville b (5)	MC 717 275-3091	....	....	....	....	....	....	....
Darby b (11)	MC 215 586-1100	....	....	....	....	....	....	....
Darby tp (11)	CO 610 586-1514	L Patterson	John B Ryan Jr	Donna Mollichella	Michael DiPaolo	....	Robert Thompson	Charles Joyner
Derry tp (18)	CM 717 533-2057	....	Craig R Zins	....	Marian Gerber	....	Jim Negley	Scott Graubard
Derry b (3)	MC 412 694-2030	Olie F Merlin	....	Mary Jane Geary	....	....	Lawrence Brodrick	....
Dickson City b (6)	MC 717 489-5758	....	....	....	....	....	....	....
Dillsburg b (2)	CM 717 432-9969	....	....	....	....	....	....	....
Donora b (6)	MC 412 379-6600	....	....	....	....	....	....	....
Dormont b (10)	MC 412 561-8900	....	....	....	....	....	....	....
Dover tp (16)	CM 717 292-3634	....	....	....	....	....	....	....
Downingtown b (8)	MC 215 269-0344	....	....	....	....	....	....	....
Doylestown tp (15)	MC 215 348-9915	....	David R Jones	....	William R Wigtman	....	Stephen White	Richard John
Doylestown b (9)	MC 215 345-4140	William E Neis	John H Davis	....	Caroline Brinker	Steve Walther	Paul P Brady	....
Dravosburg b (2)	MC 412 466-5200	....	....	....	....	....	....	....
Du Bois (8)	CM 814 371-2000	William H Reay	Patrick A Nuzzo	Lamarr Adamson	Lamarr Adamson	....	Darrell Clark	James North
Duncannon b (1)	CM 717 834-4311	....	....	....	....	....	....	....
Dunmore b (15)	CM 717 344-4590	Patrick Lughney	Richard Carr	....	....	Vince Arnone	Sal Mecca	Sal Maglio
Dupont b (3)	MC 717 655-6216	....	....	....	....	....	....	....
Duquesne (9)	MC 412 469-3770	....	....	....	....	....	....	....
Duryea b (5)	MC 717 457-6784	....	....	....	....	....	....	....
East Caln tp (3)	CM 610 269-1989	William Van Roden	Edwin R Hill	....	....	....	....	Edwin R Hill
East Goshen tp (15)	CM 215 692-7171	....	....	....	....	....	....	....

Directory 1/9 continued — MUNICIPAL OFFICIALS IN U.S. CITIES OVER 2,500

City, 1990 population figures (000 omitted), form of government	Municipal phone number	Mayor/ chief elected official	Appointed administrator	City clerk/ city secretary	Finance officer	Fire chief	Police chief	Public works director
PENNSYLVANIA (555) continued								
East Lampeter tp (..)	CM 717 393-1567	....	....	J E McDevitt	James Bonner	James Carr	Thomas Pearlingi	....
East Lansdowne b (3)	MC 610 623-7131	Robert L Dimond	....	....	....	....	....	....
East Mc Keesport b (3)	MC 412 824-2531	William Correll	Rosemarie Mazur	....	Rita Lavella	Thomas Hubinsky	....	Samuel E Pack
East Norriton tp (13)	CM 610 275-2800	John B Gourley	Helmuth Baerwald	Helmuth Baerwald	....	James Staufenberg	John D McGowan	Joseph P Sorgini
East Pennsboro tp (15)	CO 717 732-0711	....	Robert L Gill	....	....	....	Richard Dougherty	....
East Petersburg b (4)	MC 717 569-9282	....	....	....	....	....	....	....
East Stroudsburg b (9)	CM 717 421-8300	Charles A Garris	Kenneth R Brown	....	....	William L Miller	Charles McDonald	Thomas Sekula
East Whiteland tp (8)	CM 610 648-0600	Glenn H Cockerham	J Reimenschneider	....	J Reimenschneider	Darin Fitzgerald	....	Edward W Galante
Easton (26)	MC 610 250-6622	Thomas Goldsmith	Michael McFadden	Joseph Mauro Sr	Michael McFadden	Frederick May	John Border	Edgar Sales
Easttown tp (10)	MC 215 644-9000	....	....	....	....	....	....	....
Ebensburg b (4)	MC 814 472-8930	....	....	....	....	....	....	....
Economy b (10)	MC 412 869-4779	Kenneth Campbell	Randy S Kunkle	Marie Hagg	....	....	Tom Harrington	Larry Guerrierro
Eddystone b (2)	MC 215 874-9325	....	....	....	....	....	....	....
Edgewood b (4)	MC 412 242-4824	Ruth W Pickering	Peter D Messina	Michael S Bowen	Ruth Walter	Theodore Hale	Peter D Messina	R Christenson
Edgeworth b (2)	CM 412 741-2866	....	....	....	....	....	....	....
Edinboro b (8)	CM 814 734-1812	....	....	....	....	....	....	....
Edwardsville b (5)	MC 717 288-6484	....	....	....	....	....	....	....
Elizabethtown b (10)	CM 717 367-1700	C Bud Greiner	Nick Viscome	....	Peter Whipple	Ed Powl	Robert Ardner	Wayne DeVan
Ellwood City b (9)	CM 412 758-5576	....	....	....	....	....	....	....
Emmaus b (11)	MC 610 965-9292	....	Bruce Fosselman	Laura G Rieder	Bruce Fosselman	Robert Reiss	Frank Taylor	Daniel Delong
Emporium b (3)	CM 814 486-0768	....	....	....	....	....	....	....
Emsworth b (3)	MC 412 761-1161	....	....	....	....	....	....	....
Ephrata b (12)	CM 717 738-9232	....	....	....	....	....	....	....
Erie (109)	MC 814 870-1234	Joyce A Savocchio	Herbert Herriman	James E Klemm	Herbert Herriman	Gregory E Martin	Paul J Dedionisio	John T Barzano
Etna b (4)	MC 412 781-0569	William Dougherty	Mary E Cavlovic	....	....	Robert Ettmyer	Ronald Harris	Joseph Ferraro
Exeter tp (17)	MC 215 779-5660	....	....	....	....	....	....	....
Exeter b (6)	MC 717 654-3001	....	....	....	....	Alan L Heck	Eric A Bistline	....
Fairview tp (13)	CM 717 774-3190	Arvel Freydenfelt	E R McCollum	....	....	....	James Kettler	E R McCollum
Falls tp (35)	CM 215 736-5308	Walter Almond	James J Dillon	....	Elaine M Gibbs	....	....	....
Farrell (7)	CM 412 983-2700	....	....	....	....	....	....	....
Ferguson tp (9)	CM 814 238-4651	....	Mark A Kunkle	....	....	....	Edward J Connor	Ronald A Seybert
Fleetwood b (3)	MC 215 944-8220	....	....	....	....	....	....	....
Folcroft b (8)	MC 215 522-1305	....	....	....	....	....	....	....
Ford City b (3)	MC 412 763-3081	John Zanetti	....	....	....	Ron Wojcik	Jan Lysakowski	Henry Fijal
Forest Hills b (7)	CM 412 351-7330	Elmer Incheck	Richard J Branzel	....	Marian Horsmon	Raymond Heller	Michael Conroy	Richard J Branzel
Forty Fort b (5)	MC 717 287-8586	....	....	....	....	....	....	....
Foster tp (5)	CO 814 362-4656	....	....	....	....	....	....	....
Fountain Hill b (5)	MC 215 867-0301	....	....	....	....	....	....	....
Fox Chapel b (5)	CM 412 963-1100	....	....	....	....	Orval Palsgrove	John Morgan Jr	....
Frackville b (5)	MC 717 874-3860	Charles Brayford	....	....	....	....	Paul Hunsberger	Franklin Kerver
Franconia tp (7)	CM 215 723-1137	Merrill Bergey	J Delton Plank	....	....	....	Lynn D McMasters	Robert E Heller
Franklin (7)	CM 814 437-1485	Jack C Sanford	E William Gabrys	E William Gabrys	Cheryl A Carson	....	....	....
Franklin Park b (10)	CM 412 364-4115	....	....	....	....	....	....	....
Freeland b (4)	MC 717 636-0111	....	....	....	....	....	....	....
Geistown b (3)	MC 814 266-8313	....	....	....	....	....	....	....
Gettysburg b (7)	MC 717 334-1160	....	....	....	....	....	....	....
Girard b (3)	CM 814 774-9683	....	....	....	....	....	....	....
Glassport b (6)	MC 412 672-7400	....	....	....	....	....	....	....
Glenolden b (7)	MC 215 583-3221	....	....	....	....	....	....	....
Green Tree b (5)	CM 412 921-1110	....	....	....	....	....	....	....
Greencastle b (4)	CM 717 597-7143	Frank Mowen	Kenneth E Myers	....	....	....	Terry L Sanders	David W Nichols
Greensburg (16)	MC 412 838-4324	Daniel J Fajt	R Edward Jackson	....	C Moonis	Edward Hutchinson	Paul J Burkey	Rick Hoyle
Greenville b (7)	CM 412 588-4193	Clifford Harriger	Marie Julian	....	....	Walter Sankey	Barry Williams	Paul Boyer
Grove City b (8)	CM 412 458-7060	....	....	....	....	....	....	....
Hamburg b (4)	CM 215 562-7821	....	....	....	....	....	....	....
Hampden tp (20)	CO 717 761-0119	....	....	....	....	....	....	....
Hampton tp (16)	CM 412 486-0400	Donald Wolfe	W C Lochner	Susan Bernet	Irene Reaghard	....	Chester J Kline	E J Berzonski
Hanover b (14)	CM 717 637-3877	....	....	....	....	....	....	....
Hanover tp (2)	CM 610 264-1069	Eleanore M Hayden	Sandra A Pudliner	Clara W Masessa	....	Robin J Yoder	....	Bruce C Pudliner
Harmony tp (4)	CO 412 266-1910	....	....	....	....	....	....	....
Harris tp (4)	CM 814 466-6228	John B Tait	Thomas C Miller	....	Linda S Carter	Norman Spackman	....	Allen P Klinger
Harrisburg (52)	MC 717 255-3011	....	....	....	....	....	....	....
Harrison tp (12)	CO 412 226-1393	George E Conroy	Faith A Payne	Susan Motosicky	....	....	Michael A Klein	Harry B Gourley
Hatboro b (7)	MC 215 443-9100	Thomas McMackin	Albert L Herrmann	....	....	....	Frank Campbell	W Robert Stauch
Hatfield tp (15)	CM 215 855-0900	Jean Vandegrift	Stan Seitzinger	....	....	....	W Robert Stanley	Fred Leister
Hatfield b (3)	MC 215 855-0781	Herbert Flosdorf	Mark A Curfman	....	Lola K Bridi	Ralph Rehrig	Robert Stanley	Robert F Hickson
Haverford tp (50)	CM 610 446-1000	Fred C Moran	Thomas J Bannar	....	Timothy L Sander	James Marino	Gary E Hoover	Al DiGirolamo
Hazleton (25)	MC 717 459-4960	John Quigley	Samuel Monticello	Carol Destefano	....	John Andeara	Joseph James	John Mundie
Hellertown b (6)	CM 610 838-7041	Ben Muschlitz	James Sigworth	....	D Campanella	Gerald Malone	....	Lorrain Cawley
Hempfield tp (43)	CO 412 834-7232	....	....	....	....	....	....	....
Hermitage (15)	CM 412 981-0800	James White	Gary P Hinkson	Gary P Hinkson	....	Robert S Goeltz	John A Marriott	Peter D' Orazio
Highspire b (3)	CM 717 939-3303	James G Baker	Cyndi Montgomery	Patricia Julian	....	....	Timothy L Roth	Dennis Bailey
Hollidaysburg b (6)	CM 814 695-7543	James L Shoemaker	Thomas Fountaine	Ann M Andrews	Robert Kuntz	Robert E Kerns	Edward L Plowman	Kenneth Holsinger
Homer City b (2)	CM 717 479-8005	John Griffith	Judith Nipps	Peggy Citeroni	....	Carl Filler	....	....
Homestead b (4)	MC 412 461-1340	Gary Graham	John Cornelius	Lynette Mariner	....	Robert Stuart	Ellsworth Ford	....
Honesdale b (5)	MC 717 253-0731	....	....	....	....	....	....	....
Hopewell tp (13)	CO 412 378-1460	Matt DeLuca	James Eichenlaub	....	....	Gary Newkirk	Fred David	Edward Shaffer
Horsham tp (22)	CM 215 643-3131	....	....	....	....	....	....	....
Hughesville b (2)	CM 717 584-5272	....	....	....	....	....	....	....
Hummelstown b (4)	MC 717 566-2555	....	....	....	....	....	....	....
Huntingdon b (7)	CM 814 643-3966	Sharon L Gutshall	Willis L Shore	Karen A Brown	Willis L Shore	....	....	James Cutshall
Indiana b (15)	MC 412 465-6691	....	....	....	....	....	....	....
Indiana b (6)	MC 412 767-5333	....	....	....	....	....	....	....
Ingram b (4)	CM 412 921-3625	Charles Mitsch Jr	Cynthia L Baccaro	Chrissy Testa	....	Roy McGee	Robert Clark	Ray Cato
Irwin b (5)	CM 412 864-3100	Daniel T Rose	Joseph R Plues	Mary L Benko	....	Harry Neil	John R Karasek	Arthur Youngstead
Jeannette (11)	MC 412 527-4000	Glenn D Hoak	....	Richard S Laskey	Richard Demarcki	Timothy Stape	Carl J Matt	John J Orange Jr
Jefferson b (10)	CM 412 655-7735	Pat Capolopo	Richard Clark	Saundra Walsh	....	....	John Maple	....
Jenkintown b (5)	MC 215 885-0700	....	....	....	....	....	....	....
Jersey Shore b (4)	MC 717 398-0104	....	....	....	....	....	....	....
Jessup b (5)	MC 717 489-0411	Rocco Valvano	....	....	....	Steve Pitoniak	Patrick Kane	....
Jim Thorpe b (5)	MC 717 325-3025	....	....	....	....	....	....	....
Johnsonburg b (3)	CM 814 965-5682	Nancy Rekowski	Richard Beaver	Mary Polaski	Richard Beaver	Bob Dickey	Bryan Parana	James Dilullo
Johnstown (28)	MC 814 533-2001	....	....	....	....	....	....	....

Directory 1/9
continued

**MUNICIPAL OFFICIALS
IN U.S. CITIES OVER 2,500**

City, 1990 population figures (000 omitted), form of government	Municipal phone number	Mayor/ chief elected official	Appointed administrator	City clerk/ city secretary	Finance officer	Fire chief	Police chief	Public works director
PENNSYLVANIA (555) continued								
Kane b (5)	CM 814 837-9240	....	....	....	....	....	....	....
Kenhorst b (3)	CM 215 777-7327	....	....	....	....	....	....	....
Kennett Square b (5)	CM 215 444-4590	....	....	....	....	....	....	....
Kingston (15)	MC 717 288-4576	Gary R Reese	James S Keiper	....	Carol K Urban	Raymond Novitski	Gerald O' Donnell	Daniel Thomas
Kingston tp (7)	CM 717 696-3809	....	....	....	....	....	....	....
Kittanning b (5)	MC 412 543-2091	....	....	....	....	....	....	....
Kulpmont b (3)	MC 717 373-1521	....	....	....	....	....	....	....
Kutztown b (5)	MC 610 683-6131	James W Schwoyer	Keith A Hill	....	Richard B Landis	Robert L Hauck	Edmund F Pilarski	....
Lancaster (56)	MC 717 291-4711	Janice C Stork	Ginger L Bucher	....	Robert I Bolton	Charles Welcomer	Walter T Goeke	Richard B Nissley
Lancaster tp (13)	MC 717 291-1213	....	....	....	....	....	....	....
Lansdale b (16)	CM 215 368-1691	Michael Dinunzio	F Lee Mangan	....	Frank Celona	Jay Daveler	Frank Heinze	Jacob Ziegler
Lansdowne b (12)	CM 610 623-7300	John J Rankin Jr	R J Robinson	....	Joseph F Gorman	Darryl Harris	Charles L Lausch	Clarence Steward
Lansford b (5)	MC 717 645-3900	....	....	....	....	....	....	....
Larksville b (5)	MC 717 288-6619	....	....	....	....	....	....	....
Latrobe b (9)	MC 412 539-8548	James Gebicki	Robert L Barto	Kathy Baum	....	John Orzehowski	John J Smetanka	David H Williams
Laureldale b (4)	MC 215 929-8700	....	....	....	....	....	....	....
Lebanon (25)	CO 717 273-6711	....	....	....	....	....	....	....
Leechburg b (3)	MC 412 842-8511	....	....	....	....	....	....	....
Lehighton b (6)	CM 215 377-4002							
Lemoyne b (4)	CM 717 737-6843							
Lewisburg b (6)	MC 717 523-3614	....	....	....	....	....	....	....
Lewistown b (9)	CM 717 248-1361	....	....	....	....	....	....	....
Liberty b (3)	MC 717 324-3461	....	....	....	....	....	....	....
Limerick tp (7)	CM 610 495-6432	....	L B Gregory	Florence R Chomyn	....	....	Douglas Weaver	Edward J Fink
Lititz b (8)	MC 717 626-2044	Russell Pettyjohn	Sue Barry	....	Sue Barry	....	Douglas Shertzer	Nevin Koch
Littlestown b (3)	MC 717 359-5101	Charles Bridinger	Richard E Selby	Samuel B Michael	....	M Sneeringer	Donald F Baker Jr	Michael Dillman
Lock Haven (9)	CM 717 893-5900	R A Edmonston	Paul K Cornell	Paul K Cornell	C G Beers	Norman F Wolfrom	J C Frazier	Richard C Ardner
Logan tp (12)	MC 814 944-5349	Larry Barton	J E Adams	....	Bonnie Lewis	Joseph Lynch	Stephen Jackson	....
Lower Allen tp (15)	CM 717 737-8681	John H Paulding	Ronald J Mull	....	Thomas Vernau	James Polly	Raymond Rhodes	....
Lower Burrell (12)	MC 412 335-9875	D L Kowalski	Edward A Kirkwood	....	....	....	William Newell	Ottis Quarles
Lower Gwynedd tp (10)	MC 215 646-5302	Kate Harper	Edward Clifford	....	Ruth Dunn	....	Edward Hancock	Robert Pierson
Lower Makefield tp (25)	CM 215 493-3646	....	....	....	....	....	....	....
Lower Merion tp (58)	CM 215 649-4000	....	....	....	....	....	....	....
Lower Moreland tp (12)	MC 215 947-3100	....	....	....	....	....	....	....
Lower Paxton tp (39)	CM 717 657-5600	....	....	....	....	....	....	....
Lower Pottsgrove tp (9)	MC 610 323-0436	Gerald Richards	Gregory Prowant	Patricia Mazeski	....	R Sierocinski	Richard Lengel	Richard Yoder
Lower Providence tp (19)	CM 610 539-8020	Richard Brown	Rick C Schnaedter	....	Alva Stead	Steve Makowiak	Edward P McDade	David H Shaffer
Lower Saucon tp (8)	MC 610 865-3291	Priscilla DeLeon	Robt G Anckaitis	....	Martha L Chase	....	Guy L Lesser	Charles Senich
Lower Southampton tp (20)	CO 215 357-7300	Steven Pizzollo	Kathleen Goldhahn	....	Raymond Schaefer	....	Edward Donnelly	John Murphy
Lower Swatara tp (7)	CM 717 939-9377	....	....	....	....	....	....	....
Luzerne b (3)	MC 717 287-7633	Walter Yablonski	Bonnie Arnone	Linda Ziegenfus	....	David White	Charles J Urban	Howard Fox Jr
Mahanoy City b (5)	MC 717 773-2150	John J McFarland	David I Weisberg	....	....	Randy Kalce	John W Lewis	....
Malvern b (3)	MC 610 644-2602	Dominic Pisano	Patrick McGuigan	Mary Morelli	....	....	John Rychlak Jr	Ira Dutter Jr
Manchester b (8)	CM 717 764-4646	Dale W Linebaugh	David A Raver	....	....	Richard R Shank	....	Larry E Gross
Manheim tp (29)	CM 717 569-6408	Nelson Rohrer	James Martin	....	Valerie Calhoun	....	Paul Rager	Carl Neff
Manheim b (5)	CM 717 665-2463	Ralph B Martin	James R Williams	....	....	Rick J Carpenter	John C Winters	....
Mansfield b (4)	CM 717 662-2315	....	....	....	....	....	....	....
Marcus Hook b (3)	MC 215 485-1341	....	....	....	....	....	....	....
Marietta b (3)	MC 717 426-4143	....	....	....	....	....	....	....
Marple tp (23)	MC 215 356-4040	....	....	....	....	....	....	....
Marysville b (2)	CM 717 957-3110	B Blair Huling	Larry N Wilfong	Anita E Wilfong	Larry N Wilfong	Kenneth B Seitz	....	....
Masontown b (4)	MC 412 583-7731	....	....	....	....	....	....	....
Mc Adoo b (2)	MC 717 929-1182	....	....	....	....	....	....	....
Mc Candless t (29)	CM 412 364-0616	Robert J Powers	Tobias M Cordek	....	Edith Liguori	....	Ralph J LeDonne	Mark E Sabina
Mc Donald b (2)	MC 412 926-8711	Michael S Nagy Jr	....	Gloria J Stroop	....	Douglas Cooper	Mark E Dorsey	....
Mc Kees Rocks b (8)	MC 412 331-2498	Michael Kaminski	William C Beck	....	....	Nicholas Radoycis	Robert Martineau	Richard Naughton
Mc Keesport (26)	MC 412 675-5050	....	....	....	....	....	....	....
Mc Sherrystown b (3)	MC 717 637-1838	....	....	....	....	....	....	....
Meadville (14)	CM 814 724-7633	Anthony G Petruso	Gregory A Knowles	Ronald L Rushton	Timothy C Groves	Larndo L Hedrick	Harold C Tubbs	Joseph Chriest
Mechanicsburg b (9)	CM 717 691-3310	Harold Hertzler	Scott T Eppley	Nancy C Hanlon	....	Patrick Neff	Rodney Whitcomb	Ronald Adams
Media b (6)	MC 215 566-5210	....	....	....	....	....	....	....
Mercer b (2)	MC 412 662-3980	....	....	....	....	....	....	....
Mercersburg b (2)	CM 717 328-3116	Thomas L Ralston	Judith R Chambers	....	Judith R Chambers	....	Larry E Thomas Sr	Leeroy Beck
Meyersdale b (3)	CM 814 634-5110	....	....	....	....	....	....	....
Middletown tp (43)	MC 215 943-0300	....	....	....	....	....	....	....
Middletown tp (14)	CM 610 565-2700	Lawrence Hartley	W Bruce Clark	....	Celeste M Dunion	....	....	Arthur W Rothe
Middletown b (9)	CM 717 948-3051	....	....	....	....	....	....	....
Midland b (3)	CM 412 643-4170	....	....	....	....	....	....	....
Mifflinburg b (3)	CM 717 966-1013	Thomas A Muchler	George M Steese	Margaret Metzger	....	....	Douglas I Lauver	....
Millcreek tp (47)	MC 814 833-1111	....	....	....	....	....	....	....
Millersburg b (3)	MC 717 692-4713	R Koppenhaver	H Randall Dilling	Edra S Carvell	Edra S Carvell	Robert Lehman	H Randall Dilling	....
Millersville b (8)	MC 717 872-4645	....	....	....	....	....	....	....
Millvale b (4)	MC 412 821-2777	....	....	....	....	....	....	....
Milton b (7)	CM 717 742-8759	....	....	....	....	....	....	....
Minersville b (5)	MC 717 544-2149	....	....	....	....	....	....	....
Monaca b (7)	CM 412 775-9600	....	....	....	....	....	....	....
Monessen (10)	MC 412 684-9712	....	....	....	....	....	....	....
Monongahela (5)	MC 412 258-5500	....	....	....	....	....	....	....
Monroeville (29)	CM 412 856-1000	....	....	....	....	....	....	....
Montgomery tp (12)	CM 215 855-1771	....	....	....	....	....	....	....
Montgomery b (2)	CM 717 547-1671	....	Fred Pfeiffer	Andrea Rowe	....	....	Terry Lynn	....
Montoursville b (5)	MC 717 368-2486	....	....	....	....	....	....	....
Moon tp (20)	CM 412 262-1700	....	....	....	....	....	....	....
Moosic b (5)	MC 717 457-5480	Bill McDonough	Christine Heil	Pat Breymeier	Robert Gronski	Dominick Lombardi	Charles Maurer	Willard Hughes
Morrisville b (10)	CM 215 295-8181	....	....	....	....	....	....	....
Mount Carmel b (7)	CM 717 339-4486	....	....	....	....	....	....	....
Mount Joy b (6)	CM 717 653-2300	....	....	....	....	....	....	....
Mount Joy tp (..)	CM 717 367-8917	Harvey Nauss Jr	Jack Hadge	Richard Forry	Richard Forry	....	Charles Kraus	David Hummer
Mount Oliver b (4)	MC 412 431-8107	John W Smith	Joanne M Malloy	....	Jean F Miller	David P Herold	John V Hindmarch	Donald Froehlich
Mount Penn b (3)	MC 610 799-5151	D R Skrincosky	Mary Sue Buss	....	....	Michael Vogt	....	....
Mount Pleasant b (5)	MC 412 547-6745	....	....	....	....	....	....	....
Mount Union b (3)	MC 814 542-4051	....	....	....	....	....	....	....
Mt. Lebanon (33)	CM 412 343-3400	....	Wilmer K Baldwin	....	G David Egler	S Darcangelo	Frank M Brown	James W Harrod

Directory 1/9
continued

MUNICIPAL OFFICIALS
IN U.S. CITIES OVER 2,500

City, 1990 population figures (000 omitted), form of government	Municipal phone number	Mayor/chief elected official	Appointed administrator	City clerk/city secretary	Finance officer	Fire chief	Police chief	Public works director
PENNSYLVANIA (555) continued								
Muncy b (3)	MC 717 546-3952	....	....	....	....	....	....	....
Munhall b (13)	MC 412 464-7310	....	....	....	....	....	....	....
Murrysville (17)	MC 412 327-2100	....	....	....	....	....	....	....
Myerstown b (3)	MC 717 866-5038	Glenn E Miller	Edward H Treat	John S Brown	....	Fredrick L Shaak	Phillip W Stark	Randall L Brown
Nanticoke (12)	MC 717 735-2200	....	....					
Nanty-Glo b (3)	MC 814 749-0331	James P Bracken	Dorothy Kozlovac			Thomas Waltz	Richard Miller	
Narberth b (4)	CM 610 664-2840	Dennis J Sharkey	William J Martin	....	William J Martin	John R Thomas		
Nazareth b (6)	MC 215 759-0202	....	....					
Nesquehoning b (3)	MC 717 669-9588	Joseph Staivecki	Joseph G Greco Jr			Michael Kravelk	Joseph Tout	
Nether Providence tp (13)	CO 215 566-4516	....	....	....	....	....	....	....
New Brighton b (7)	CM 412 846-1870	....	....					
New Britain tp (9)	CM 215 822-1391	....	....					
New Britain t (2)	CM 215 348-4586	Robert Snavely	John K Wolff	Robin Trymbiski		Austin Brown	David Sempowski	Edward Deschamps
New Castle (28)	MC 412 656-3500	....	....					
New Cumberland b (8)	CM 717 774-0404	Robert W Henning	S C Sultzaberger			Walter Sral	Oren H Kauffman	
New Eagle b (2)	MC 412 258-4477	....	....					
New Hanover tp (6)	MC 215 323-1008	Gerald Reege	Anita B Turner		Janice Keyser	William C Moyer	Michael A Dykie	C Ray Batchelder
New Holland b (4)	CM 717 354-4567		J Richard Fulcher				Edward Sprecher	Barry G Eitnier
New Hope b (1)	CM 215 862-3347	James Magill		Helen Williams	Helen Williams	Thomas Markey	Robert Brobson	Russell Vender
New Kensington (16)	CO 412 337-4523	....	....					
New Stanton b (2)	MC 412 925-9700	Wilbur Bussard	Faith Thomas	Margaret Kelly	Karl Stinebiser	Paul Todd		Barbara Burtyk
New Wilmington b (3)	MC 412 946-8167	....	....					
Newtown tp (11)	CM 610 356-0200	Suzanne Mathes	Larry M Comunale	Deborah O' Rourke		Robbie Robinson	Michael A Mallon	Paul McDonald
Newtown b (3)	MC 215 968-2109	Harold Bud Smith		Lois B Saurman		Dennis Forsyth	J H Feeney	
Norristown b (31)	MC 215 272-8080	....	....					
North Braddock b (7)	CM 412 271-1306	....	....					
North Catasauqua b (3)	MC 215 264-1504	....	....					
North Coventry tp (8)	MC 215 323-1694	....	....					
North East b (5)	MC 814 725-8611	Alison Schmidt	Thomas J Murray	Barbara Bessetti		Darrell Meyers	Terry Still	
North Huntingdon tp (28)	CM 412 863-3806	....	....					
North Londonderry tp (6)	MC 717 838-1373	....	....					
North Middleton tp (10)	MC 717 243-8550	....	....					
North Strabane tp (8)	CM 412 745-8880	Brian Spicer	Frank R Siffrinn		Frank R Siffrinn	Gary Zimak	Dan L Strimel	Walter Klamut
North Versailles tp (12)	MC 412 823-6602	....	....					
North Wales b (4)	MC 215 699-4424	Herbert Schlegel	Susan Patton	Christa Liebel		Willam Goltz	Kenneth C Veit	Thomas Costella
Northampton tp (35)	CM 215 357-6800	Peter F Palestina	D Bruce Townsend			Adam Selisker	M Barry Pilla Jr	Pasquale Giradi
Northampton b (9)	MC 610 262-2576	Robert Hantz	Gene Zarayko		Gene Zarayko	Michael Holtzman	R Fenstermaker	David Marsh
Northumberland b (4)	MC 717 473-3414	Ernest Gessner	Thomas Propst	Jane G Sanders	Charles Smeltz	Michael Reedy	Larry Redington	Norman E Williams
Norwood b (6)	MC 215 586-5800	....	....					
O'Hara tp (9)	CM 412 782-1400		Douglas Arndt		Susan Hockenberry		Raymond Schafer	Charles K Clinton
Oakmont b (7)	CM 412 828-3232	....	....					
Ohio tp (2)	CO 412 364-6321	....	....					
Ohioville b (4)	MC 412 643-1920	Darryl R Michael	Diane M Kemp		John Anderson	Clarence Dawson	Ronald H Lutton	Bruce A Thorne
Oil City (12)	CM 814 678-3012	Barbara F Davison	Thomas Rockovich		C Marshall	John Huey	Fredrick Weaver	James Hicks
Old Forge b (9)	MC 717 457-8852	Edward V Kania	Anthony Giordano			Robert Aulisio	Frank Avvisato	Leonard Zupon
Olyphant b (5)	MC 717 489-2135	....	....					
Orwigsburg b (3)	MC 717 366-3103	....	....					
Oxford b (4)	MC 610 932-2500	Harold Gray	Jon Walker				Noel Roy	Thomas Hindman
Palmerton b (5)	CM 215 826-2505	....	....					
Palmyra b (7)	MC 717 838-6361	Ross W Watts	Karen L Koncle	Carol L Light	Karen L Koncle	Edward Berkhimer	Stanley Jasinski	
Parkesburg b (3)	MC 215 857-2616	....	....					
Patton tp (10)	MC 814 234-0271	Philip Park	Thomas Kurtz	Connie Thomas	Cindy Rollins		Gary Davenport	John Miknis
Pen Argyl b (3)	MC 610 863-4119	James F Wilson		Dolores B Savitz		Dean Parsons	David Matlock	Dennis J Miller
Penbrook b (3)	MC 717 232-3733	....	....					
Penn tp (12)	CM 717 630-8460	Frederick W Stine	Jeffrey R Garvick	Sharon A Lance		Anthony Clouser	Joseph H Maddox	
Penn Hills (51)	CM 412 798-2100	William DeSantis	Harry R McIndoe	Harry R McIndoe	E Schrecengost	Jack Mason	Kenneth Sechoka	Jerry Nosal
Penndel b (2)	MC 215 757-5152	....	....					
Perkasie b (8)	MC 215 257-5065	Jay Godshall	Paul A Leonard			Tim Metzler	Paul T Dickinson	Neil Fosbenner
Peters tp (14)	CM 412 941-4180	O Forrest Morgan	Michael Silvestri	M Silvestri	P Lauer	Daniel Coyle	Harry Fruecht	Peter Overcashier
Philadelphia (1586)	MC 215 686-1776	Edward Rendell	Joseph Certaine		Ben Hayllar	Harold Hairston	Richard Neal	
Philipsburg b (3)	MC 814 342-3440	....	....					
Phoenixville b (15)	CM 215 933-8801	....	....					
Pine tp (4)	CM 412 625-1591	Dominic Navarro	Gary J Koehler	Joni L Preston		Kenneth M Young	Rudolph Vojtko	Jack C Fasick
Pitcairn b (4)	MC 412 372-6500	Margaret Stevick	Josephine Higgins				David McIntyre	
Pittsburgh (370)	MC 412 255-2100	Tom Murphy				Charles Dickinson	Earl Buford	Ralph Kraszewski
Pittston (9)	CO 717 654-0513	....	....					
Pleasant tp (3)	MC 814 723-5240	....	....					
Pleasant Hills b (9)	MC 412 655-3300	....	....					
Plum b (26)	CM 412 795-6800	Alfred Franci	Martha L Perego				Terry Focareta	John Walters
Plymouth tp (16)	CM 215 277-4100	....	....					
Plymouth b (7)	MC 717 779-1011	....	....					
Port Allegany b (2)	CM 814 642-2526	....	....					
Port Carbon b (2)	MC 717 622-2255	....	....					
Port Vue b (5)	MC 412 664-9323	....	....					
Portage b (3)	MC 814 736-4330	....	....					
Pottstown b (22)	CM 610 970-6500	Anne M Chomnuk	Robert C Jones			Richard Lengel	C Carlile	Douglass M Yerger
Pottsville (17)	CO 717 622-1234	....	....					
Prospect Park b (7)	MC 215 532-1007	....	....					
Punxsutawney b (7)	CM 814 938-4480	....	....					
Quakertown b (9)	CM 215 536-5001	Dennis A Hallman	David L Woglom			Ray Stever	James McFadden	Rick Ostvedt
Radnor tp (29)	CM 610 688-5600	C Stuntebeck	Robert M Crofford	Concetta Clayton	David A Bashore	Donald Wood	Henry P Jansen	Daniel E Malloy
Rankin b (3)	MC 412 271-1027	....	....					
Red Lion b (6)	CM 717 244-3475	....	....					
Reynoldsville b (3)	MC 814 653-2110	....	....					
Richland tp (..)	CM 215 536-4066	....	....					
Richland tp (9)	MC 412 443-5921	....	....					
Ridgway b (5)	CM 814 776-1125	James D Martin	Martin R Schuller			John Brown	Burton Shaver	J Rosenhoover
Ridley tp (31)	CM 610 534-4800	Timothy Murtaugh	Anne S Howanski		Daniel E Mingis		Richard J Herron	Louis DiPetro
Ridley Park b (8)	MC 215 532-2100	....	....					
Roaring Spring b (3)	MC 814 224-4814	Paul I Holsinger	Barbara Wagner				Kenneth Bathurst	
Robinson tp (11)	CO 412 788-8120	William Blumling	Bernard Dudash	Mildred Cvengros				Joseph Bonkowski
Rochester b (4)	CM 412 775-1200	....	....					
Ross tp (33)	MC 412 931-7055	Thomas G Lawlor	Thomas D Lavorini	Linda Gillespie	Sarah A Scharding	Frank Stright	Carl M Zotter	Gary Gorajewski

City, 1990 population figures (000 omitted), form of government	Municipal phone number	Mayor/ chief elected official	Appointed administrator	City clerk/ city secretary	Finance officer	Fire chief	Police chief	Public works director
PENNSYLVANIA (555) continued								
Royersford b (4)	MC 215 948-3737	....	....		....	....	....	....
Salisbury tp (13)	CM 610 797-4000	Francis Walter	Clifford Steff	....	Janice Walz	....	Allen Stiles	Ronald Gantert
Sayre b (6)	CM 717 888-7739	....	....	....	....	....	....	....
Schuylkill Haven b (6)	CM 717 385-2841	....	....		....	....	....	....
Scott tp (17)	CO 412 276-5300	J P Mulligan	G L Williard		....	....	S Butkus	L Dellana
Scottdale b (5)	CM 412 887-8220	....	....		....	....	....	....
Scranton (82)	MC 717 348-4100	James P Connors	John Cawley	Frank Naughton	....	Richard Pica	George Murphy	Joseph Loughney
Selinsgrove b (5)	CM 717 374-2311	Garry F Beaver	George R Kinney	Ann M Wochley	....	Fred Ulrich	James W Hartley	Gary L Klingler
Sellersville b (4)	CM 215 257-5075	Joseph E Hufnagle	Richard D Coll		....	Craig Wilhelm	William Heim	Robert Coll
Sewickley b (4)	CM 412 741-4015	Kenneth E Johns	Kevin M Flannery	....	Fran Frakewicz	George Edel	John F Mook	Ray Wolfgang
Sewickley Heights b (1)	CM 412 741-5111	G W Snyder	William P Rohe	Julienne Giuliani	William P Rohe	George Edel	Alan E Farrier	Herbert C Ford
Shaler tp (31)	MC 412 486-9700	....	....	....	....	....	....	....
Shamokin (9)	MC 717 644-0876	Daniel Strausser	William Strausser		Betsy Richardson	Charles Carpenter	Ronald W Yeager	Barry W Weikel
Sharon (17)	MC 412 983-3220	Robert T Price	....	Mary Beth Fragle	Michael Gasparich	Arthur Scarmack	David O Ryan	Gary R Douglas
Sharon Hill b (6)	MC 610 586-8200	Albert Cortese	William Scott		....	William Scott	Joseph Kelly Jr	William Scott
Sharpsburg b (4)	MC 412 781-0546	....	....		....	....	....	....
Sharpsville b (5)	CM 412 962-7896	Kenneth Robertson	Michael Wilson		....	....	Willard Thompson	....
Shenandoah b (6)	MC 717 462-1918	....	....		....	....	....	....
Shillington b (5)	CM 215 777-1338	....	....		....	....	....	....
Shippensburg b (5)	CM 717 532-2147	Timothy Costanza	Wilkliam Wolfe		....	Edward S Goodhart	Dennis McMaster	William Wolfe
Shrewsbury b (3)	MC 717 235-4371	....	....		....	....	....	....
Silver Spring tp (8)	MC 717 766-0178	....	....		....	....	....	....
Sinking Spring b (2)	MC 215 678-4903	....	....		....	....	....	....
Slatington b (5)	CM 610 767-2131	Robert Keegan	Stephen Sechriest		....	Jeff Schmick	Arthur Kistler	....
Slippery Rock b (3)	MC 412 794-6391	....	....		....	....	....	....
Somerset b (6)	CM 814 443-2661	....	Benedict Vinzani	Mathilda Brown	Mathilda Brown	Jay R Lehman	Ronald L Stern	Elwood J Hutzel
Souderton b (6)	CM 215 723-4371	....	....		....	....	....	....
South Fayette tp (10)	CM 412 221-8700	Ken Chambon	Rich Kasmer	Claudia Smelko	Marion Thomas	....	Ted Villani	Steve Zeman
South Greensburg b (2)	MC 412 837-8858	....	....		....	....	....	....
South Hanover tp (5)	MC 717 566-0224	....	....		....	....	....	....
South Lebanon tp (7)	CM 717 274-0481	....	....		....	....	....	....
South Park tp (14)	CM 412 831-7000	....	....		....	....	....	....
South Strabane tp (8)	CM 412 225-9055	Frank Brown Jr	John Stickle	John Stickle	John Stickle	....	Donald Zofchak	Reed Mankey
South Whitehall tp (18)	CO 610 398-0401	Steven C Seyer	Gerald J Gasda	....	Ronnie J Rice	....	D Mac Connell	Ralph H Kocher Sr
South Williamsport b (6)	CM 717 322-0158	....	....		....	....	....	....
Southmont b (2)	MC 814 255-3104	....	....		....	....	....	....
Southwest Greensburg b (2)	MC 412 834-0360	....	....		....	....	....	....
Spring tp (19)	MC 215 678-5393	....	....		....	....	....	....
Spring City b (3)	CM 610 948-3660	Timothy Hoyle	D Rittenhouse	....	....	Keith Bliss	Clarence Collopy	Daniel Beutler
Spring Garden tp (11)	CM 717 848-2858	Joseph K Bath	William J Conn	....	Glenda L Alwine	Joseph F Barron	Walter R Groom	Edward C Salabsky
Springdale b (4)	MC 412 274-8366	....	....		....	....	....	....
Springettsbury tp (22)	CM 717 757-3521	....	....		....	....	....	....
Springfield tp (24)	CM 215 544-1300	....	....		....	....	....	....
Springfield tp (20)	CM 215 836-7600	Michael Cassidy	Donald Berger	Carol Holcomb	....	Earl Hopkins	....	John Connor
St. Clair b (4)	MC 717 429-0640	Richard Tomko	....	Roland Price Jr	....	R Shellhammer	Robert Wapinski	Don Hosler
St. Marys b (6)	CM 814 781-1718	Anne Grosser	Kenneth Gabler	....	....	Michael Bauer	Gary Eckert	Steve Samick
State College b (39)	CM 814 234-7100	William L Welch	Peter S Marshall	Barbara J Natalie	Michael S Groff	....	Thomas R King	Lee L Lowry
Steelton b (5)	MC 717 939-9842	....	....	....	....	....	....	....
Stowe tp (8)	CO 412 331-4050	....	....		....	....	....	....
Stroudsburg b (5)	MC 717 421-5444	Jonathan Mark	Pamela S Caskie		Pamela S Caskie	Clement Kochanski	Kevin Kelly	Frank Labar Jr
Sugar Creek b (6)	CM 814 432-4717	....	....		....	....	....	....
Summit Hill b (3)	MC 717 645-2305	....	....		....	....	....	....
Sunbury (12)	CO 717 286-7820	David L Persing	....	S McKinney	Joseph G Halko	Richard Neff	Charles McAndrew	William Rohrbach
Susquehanna tp (19)	MC 717 545-4751	....	....		....	....	....	....
Swarthmore b (6)	MC 610 543-4599	G Guy Smith	Jane C Billings	....	Mark Duperberg	Cris Hansen	Donald H Lee	Charles Rowles
Swatara tp (20)	MC 717 564-2551	Anthony Spagnolo	James Brokenshire	Dolores Rubinic	Florence Bingaman	....	Ronald Mellott	Harlow Emerick
Swissvale b (11)	MC 412 271-7101	Martin Busch	Thomas J Esposito	....	....	Kenneth Johnston	James Ohrman	Michael Viglietta
Swoyersville b (6)	MC 717 288-6581	Vince Dennis	Gene Breznay	Shirley Gavlick	....	....	John Shemo	Ed Volack
Tamaqua b (8)	CM 717 668-0300	Jerome P Knowles	Donald Matalavage	Pauline Boettgen	Joan D Snyder	Art Connely	Donald Gerber	....
Tarentum b (6)	MC 412 224-1818	James E Wolfe	....	....	....	....	Frank Prazenica	David Hilliard
Taylor b (7)	MC 717 562-1400	....	....		....	....	....	....
Telford b (4)	CM 215 723-5000	Jay Stover	Charles Feindler	Charles Feindler	Erma Slemmer	Joseph Rausch	Douglas Bickel	Donald Beck
Throop b (4)	MC 717 489-8311	Stanley Lukowski	....		....	....	Neil Furiosi	....
Titusville (6)	CM 814 827-5303	Tim McGregor	Carolyne F Ford	....	Leslie Fulton	Richard Barker	C M Anderson	Robert Lytle
Tobyhanna (4)	CM 717 646-1212	Alfred A Kerrick	Kelly L Biddle	....	....	John E Kerrick	Robert Martz	....
Towamencin tp (14)	MC 215 368-7602	Richard Lanning	John A Granger	....	Beth DiPrete	....	Joseph Kirschner	John Reinhart
Towanda b (3)	CM 717 265-2696	....	....		....	....	....	....
Trafford b (3)	MC 412 372-6559	Reynold Peduzzi	Thomas Moore	Christine Perovic	....	Tom Grills	Charles Noll	Mike Bayko
Tredyffrin tp (28)	CM 215 644-1400	....	....		....	....	....	....
Troy b (1)	CM 717 297-2966	....	....		....	....	....	....
Turtle Creek b (7)	MC 412 824-2500	....	....		....	....	....	....
Tyrone b (6)	CM 814 684-1330	....	....		....	....	....	....
Union tp (3)	MC 717 935-2890	....	....		....	....	....	....
Union City b (4)	CM 814 438-2331	Ray Whitney Jr	Cheryl R Capela	....	....	Ed Eastman	Marvin Tubbs	Scott Sweeney
Uniontown (12)	MC 412 430-2900	Charles Machesky	Harvey C King	Grace Giachetti	Odilia A John	C William Sneddon	Ronald Machesky	Charles Ellis
Upland b (3)	MC 215 874-7317	....	....		....	....	....	....
Upper Allen tp (13)	CM 717 766-0756	Ray Trimmer	Robert Sabatini	....	....	Karl Kunkel	Richard Hammon	George Anderson
Upper Chichester tp (..)	MC 215 855-5881	....	....		....	....	....	....
Upper Darby tp (81)	MC 215 352-4100	....	....		....	....	....	....
Upper Dublin tp (24)	CM 215 643-1600	Richard R Rulon	Gregory N Klemick	....	Jonathan Bleemer	Edward Hurt	....	William B Grove
Upper Gwynedd tp (12)	CM 215 699-7777	....	....		....	....	....	....
Upper Merion tp (26)	CM 610 265-2600	Ed Wilkes	Ron Wagenmann	....	Ken Pennoyer	....	Clement Reedel	Roman Pronczak
Upper Moreland tp (25)	CM 215 659-3100	Jack Tarman	Brian L Mook	....	Patricia A Burns	Edward O Stauch	Lee Perlmutter	John Snyder
Upper Providence tp (10)	CM 215 933-9179	....	....		....	....	....	....
Upper Providence tp (10)	CM 215 565-4944	....	Elizabeth Crane		Maxine Burkholder	....	Thomas Davis	Elizabeth Crane
Upper Saucon tp (10)	CM 215 282-1171	....	....		....	....	....	....
Upper Southampton tp (16)	MC 215 322-9700	Charles Martin	Paul Janssen	....	Anoop Tolani	Gary Edwards	David Schultz	Wayne Crompton
Upper St. Clair tp (20)	CM 412 831-9000	Charles R Molzer	Douglas A Watkins	....	August G Stache	....	Ronald J Pardini	F Kyle Robinson
Upper Yoder tp (5)	CM 814 255-5243	....	....		....	....	....	....
Uwchlan tp (13)	MC 610 363-9450	John J Mahoney	Douglass Hanley	Rebecca Hertwig	....	Richard Ruth	J Patrick Davis	Martin Sorensen
Vandergrift b (6)	CM 412 567-7818	....	....		....	....	....	....
Verona b (3)	MC 412 828-8080	Leonard Brennan	Bonnie Conway		....	Thomas Tihey	Michael Zampogna	William Futules
Warminster tp (33)	MC 215 443-5414	....	....	....	....	....	....	....

MUNICIPAL OFFICIALS
IN U.S. CITIES OVER 2,500

City, 1990 population figures (000 omitted), form of government	Municipal phone number	Mayor/ chief elected official	Appointed administrator	City clerk/ city secretary	Finance officer	Fire chief	Police chief	Public works director
PENNSYLVANIA (555) continued								
Warren b (11)	CM 814 723-6300	....	....	....	....	....	....	....
Warrington tp (12)	CM 215 822-1318	....	....	....	....	....	....	....
Warwick tp (12)	CM 717 626-8900	....	....	....	....	....	....	....
Washington (16)	MC 412 223-4200	Francis L King	....	Cathy B Voytek	Susanne E Gomez	John A Manning	Ronald Rossi	Robert Nicolella
Watsontown b (2)	MC 717 538-1000	....	....	....	....	....	....	....
Waynesboro b (10)	CM 717 762-2101	Louis M Barlup	Lloyd R Hamberger	Sonia Medevich	....	Donald Ringer	Glenn Phenicie	Paul Doub
Waynesburg b (4)	MC 412 627-8111	John McCall	Richard C Provo	....	....	....	Timothy Hawfield	....
Weatherly b (3)	MC 717 427-8640	....	....	....	....	....	....	....
Wellsboro b (3)	CM 717 724-3186	R Robert Decamp	Patricia Russell	....	....	Clair Pierce	John E Wheeler	Martin Beck
Wesleyville b (4)	MC 814 899-9124	....	....	....	....	....	....	....
West Bradford tp (10)	CM 610 269-4174	John Haiko	Jack M Hines Jr	Andrea Procter	Karen Vogt	John Carbo	....	Francis Fry
West Caln tp (6)	CM 215 384-5643	....	....	....	....	....	....	....
West Chester b (18)	CM 610 692-7574	Eleanor E Loper	Ernie B McNeely	....	Douglas K Kapp	David Smiley	John O Green	Robert Wilpizeski
West Goshen tp (18)	CM 610 696-5266	Robert E Lambert	Patricia Guernsey	L Joan Rivell	....	....	Michael Carroll	....
West Hazleton b (4)	MC 717 455-3694	....	....	....	....	....	....	....
West Homestead b (2)	MC 412 461-1844	....	....	....	....	....	....	....
West Manchester tp (14)	CM 717 792-3505	Bradley C Jacobs	Jan R Dell	....	Betty L Keller	John J Bierling	Robert D March	William Bollinger
West Mifflin b (24)	CM 412 461-5619	Kenneth Ruffing	Howard J Bednar	Justine Zak	Howard J Bednar	....	John Andzelik	Donald Finney
West Newton b (3)	MC 412 872-6860	....	....	....	....	....	....	....
West Norriton tp (15)	CO 215 631-0450	....	....	....	....	....	....	....
West Pittston b (6)	MC 717 654-6567	....	....	....	....	....	....	....
West Pottsgrove tp (4)	MC 215 323-7717	....	....	....	....	....	....	....
West Reading b (4)	CM 610 374-8273	E David Wenger	C George Dilllo	....	....	Ed Fabriziani	Jerry R Kantner	....
West View b (8)	MC 412 931-2800	....	....	....	....	....	....	....
West Whiteland tp (12)	CM 610 363-9525	David F Bortner	Stephen J Ross	....	....	William Miller	Robert P Bitter	Joseph P Roscioli
West Wyoming b (3)	MC 717 693-1311	....	....	....	....	....	....	....
West York b (4)	MC 717 846-8889	....	....	....	....	....	....	....
Westmont b (6)	MC 814 255-3865	....	....	....	....	....	....	....
White Oak b (9)	CM 412 672-9727	Robert Massie	Robert R Kipp	Vicki L McNamee	Janet L Gerber	....	Bruce R Greenland	Ronald Baldridge
Whitehall b (14)	MC 412 884-0505	....	....	....	....	....	....	....
Whitehall tp (23)	MC 610 437-5524	E L Buchmiller	....	....	John D Meyers	Robert F Benner	James G Walsh	John Rackus
Whitemarsh tp (15)	CM 610 825-3535	P Bruce Ferguson	Lawrence J Gregan	....	Thomas Mullin	C Bonenberger	Richard Zolko	....
Whitpain tp (16)	CM 215 277-2400	....	....	....	....	....	....	....
Wilkes-Barre (48)	MC 717 826-8200	Lee Namey	Richard Muessig	William Brace	John Rollman	George Soltis	Joseph Coyne	Albert Clocker
Wilkins tp (8)	CM 412 824-6650	Michael J Madden	Bruce D Jamison	....	Bruce D Jamison	....	Elias Sejko	Paul A Vargo
Wilkinsburg b (21)	CM 412 244-2900	Sylvia LaFranchi	....	....	Virginia Finnegan	Sammie Coley	Paul Wood	Theodore Hatcher
Williamsport (32)	MC 717 327-7500	Phillip Preziosi	....	Diane Ellis	....	Randy Goodbrod	Anthony Evans	John Grado
Willistown tp (9)	CM 610 647-5300	Jack Weber Jr	W Rosenberry	Lorraine Kline	....	....	Charles Bennett	John DiMascio
Wilson b (8)	MC 215 258-6142	....	....	....	....	....	....	....
Wind Gap b (3)	MC 215 863-7288	....	....	....	....	....	....	....
Windber b (5)	CM 814 467-9014	....	....	....	....	....	....	....
Windsor tp (9)	CM 717 244-3512	....	....	....	....	....	....	....
Wormleysburg b (3)	MC 717 763-4483	George Sellers	Gary W Berresford	Barbara Harlacher	....	Ronald Frank	Russel Lukens	....
Wyoming b (3)	MC 717 693-0291	Gladys Wilson	Kathy Nalewajko	....	....	John Pascucci	John Gilligan	Joseph Cook
Wyomissing b (7)	CM 215 376-7481	....	....	....	....	....	....	....
Yardley b (2)	MC 215 493-6832	....	....	....	....	....	....	....
Yeadon b (12)	MC 215 284-1606	....	....	....	....	....	....	....
York (42)	MC 717 849-2251	Charles Robertson	Valerie Bortner	Miriam Neff	Joseph Robinson	George E Kroll	William E Smith	....
York tp (19)	MC 717 741-3861	....	....	....	....	....	....	....
Youngsville b (2)	CM 814 563-4604	....	....	....	....	....	....	....
Youngwood b (3)	MC 412 925-3660	....	....	....	....	....	....	....
Zelienople b (4)	MC 412 452-6610	....	....	....	....	....	....	....
RHODE ISLAND (39)								
Barrington t (16)	CM 401 247-1900	....	Dennis M Phelan	Lorraine A Derois	David B Okun	Edward J Carey	John T Lazzaro	Peter DeAngelis
Bristol t (22)	TM 401 253-7000	Halsey Herreshoff	....	Diane C Mederos	....	David Sylvaria	Thomas Moffatt	Paul E Romano
Burrillville t (16)	CM 401 568-4300	....	Thomas Bercher	Robert E Potter	John Mainville	....	....	....
Central Falls (18)	MC 401 724-4500	....	....	....	....	....	....	....
Charlestown t (6)	CM 401 364-1200	....	George C Hibbard	Marcia D Carsten	....	....	Michael T Brady	Alan A Arsenault
Coventry t (31)	CM 401 821-6400	James J Kiley	Francis A Frobel	Roberta Johnson	Barry L Yeaw	....	Roger J Laliberte	Sheila B Patnode
Cranston (76)	MC 401 461-1000	M Traficante	Phillip Loscoe	Robert Moretti	....	Albert Tedeschi	Augustine Comella	Peter Alviti
Cumberland t (29)	MC 401 728-2400	....	....	....	....	....	....	....
East Greenwich t (12)	CM 401 886-8665	....	....	....	....	....	....	....
East Providence (50)	CM 401 434-3311	....	....	....	....	....	....	....
Exeter t (5)	RT 401 294-3891	....	....	....	....	....	....	....
Foster t (4)	RT 401 392-9200	....	....	....	....	....	....	....
Glocester t (9)	MC 401 568-6206	Patricia Hayward	....	Barbara Robertson	John Driscoll	....	Joseph Green	Paul Bilsky
Hopkinton t (7)	TM 401 377-2220	....	....	....	....	....	....	....
Jamestown t (5)	CM 401 423-7220	Fred Pease	Frances H Shocket	Theresa C Donovna	Maryanne Crawford	Prescott Freberg	Thomas P Tighe	Steve J Goslee
Johnston t (27)	MC 401 351-6618	....	....	....	....	....	....	....
Lincoln t (18)	MC 401 333-1100	Burton Stallwood	....	Sue Sheppard	Claudette Paine	....	William Strain	Robert Schultz
Little Compton t (3)	MC 401 635-4658	....	....	....	....	....	....	....
Middletown t (19)	CM 401 849-2898	George L Andrade	Michael E Embury	Barbara L Nash	William Hanlon	Donald Ardito	William Burns	Francis Santos
Narragansett t (15)	CM 401 789-1044	Ted Wright	S A Hancock	Mary Beck	David Krugman	L J Miller	J O' Donnell	....
New Shoreham t (1)	CM 401 466-3200	Edward McGovern	David C Holt	Susan R Shea	Mary Jane Balser	R Batchelder	William McCombe	....
Newport (28)	CM 401 846-9600	David Roderick Jr	Francis Edwards	Jane McManus	Joel Johnson	John Booth	Steven Weaver	Susan Cooper
North Kingstown t (24)	CM 401 294-3331	David R Burnham	Richard I Kerbel	James D Marques	Cynthia J Olobri	Roger F Walsh	James L Wynne	Richard J Crenca
North Providence t (32)	MC 401 232-0900	....	....	....	....	....	....	....
North Smithfield t (10)	MC 401 767-2202	Kenneth Bianchi	....	Joan Mowry	Henritta Delage	....	Roger Remillard	P Kaczorowski
Pawtucket (73)	MC 401 728-0500	Robert E Metivier	William Noonan	Richard Goldstein	John Rahill	Robert Forsher	Richard DeLyon	F Ihenacho
Portsmouth t (17)	MC 401 683-2101	....	....	....	....	....	....	....
Providence (161)	MC 401 421-7740	....	....	....	....	....	....	....
Richmond t (5)	RT 401 539-2497	....	....	....	....	....	....	....
Scituate t (10)	MC 401 647-2822	....	....	....	....	....	....	....
Smithfield t (19)	MC 401 233-1012	....	....	....	....	....	....	....
South Kingstown t (25)	CM 401 789-9331	....	....	....	....	....	....	....
Tiverton t (14)	TM 401 625-6700	Louise Durfee	Paul B Northrup	Hannibal F Costa	....	Peter J Lamb	Alton H Conn Jr	Joseph Farias Jr
Warren t (11)	TM 401 245-7340	....	....	....	....	....	....	....
Warwick (85)	MC 401 738-2000	Lincoln D Chafee	Edmund B Sarno	Marie T Bennett	Peder A Schaefer	George Noble	Wesley Blanchard	Charles T Sheahan
West Greenwich t (3)	TM 401 397-5016	....	....	....	....	....	....	....
West Warwick t (29)	TM 401 822-9219	....	....	....	....	....	....	....
Westerly t (22)	CM 401 596-0341	....	....	....	....	....	....	....
Woonsocket (44)	MC 401 762-6400	Francis L Lanctot	Vincent P Ward	Pauline S Payeur	John P Kuzmiski	Henry A Renaud	Rodney C Remblad	Illdlo Azinheira

Directory 1/9 continued — MUNICIPAL OFFICIALS IN U.S. CITIES OVER 2,500

City, 1990 population figures (000 omitted), form of government		Municipal phone number	Mayor/ chief elected official	Appointed administrator	City clerk/ city secretary	Finance officer	Fire chief	Police chief	Public works director
SOUTH CAROLINA (94)									
Abbeville (6)	CM	803 459-5017	Joe Savitz	David H Krumwiede	Thomas W Chandler	....	Mason Speer	Robin D Rucker	Franklin E Lewis
Aiken (20)	CM	803 642-7654	Fred B Cavanaugh	Steven Thompson	Sara Ridout	Anita Lilly	....	Carrol Busbee	Roger Leduc
Allendale t (4)	MC	803 584-4619	William Holmes	Wilbur Cave	....	Dwight Williams	Marshall Lawson	James Henry Grant	....
Anderson (26)	CM	803 231-2200	Darwin H Wright	John R Moore Jr	Peggy G Maxwell	Peggy G Maxwell	Odis F Gilreath	James E Burriss	M Anthony Norris
Andrews t (3)	MC	803 264-8666	....	....	....	....	....	....	....
Bamberg t (4)	MC	803 245-5128	....	....	....	....	....	....	....
Barnwell (5)	MC	803 259-3266	....	....	....	....	....	....	....
Batesburg-Leesville t (6)	CM	803 532-1198	....	Olin E Gambrell	....	....	....	....	....
Beaufort (10)	CM	803 525-7045	David M Taub	Gary M Cannon	Beverly Gay	Ross A Jones	Wendell O Wilburn	William R Neill	....
Belton (5)	MC	803 338-7773	Leo Fisher	....	Edna H Cason	....	Michael Smith	David Dockins	Bobby E Burriss
Bennettsville (9)	CM	803 479-9001	Wanda Stanton	Marty K Lawing	....	Wesley D Park	Harvey D Odom Jr	Richard A Nagy	Thomas P Bostick
Bishopville t (4)	MC	803 484-9418	Thomas Alexander	David R Bushyager	....	....	Ronald Williams	Robert Nesbitt	Leon Arnold
Blackville t (3)	MC	803 284-2444	....	....	....	....	....	....	....
Camden (7)	CM	803 432-2421	Philip Minges	G Frank Broom Jr	Maedele Brown	Philip W Jackson	Bobby Parnell	Jack Cobb	Jimmy Parnelle
Cayce (11)	MC	803 796-9020	Avery B Wilkerson	Rachel L Scioscia	....	John Sharpe	....	A G Dantzler	Frank Robinson
Charleston (80)	MC	803 724-7388	Joseph P Riley Jr	....	Mary Wrixon	James Etheredge	Russell Thomas Jr	Reuben Greenberg	Douglas Smits
Cheraw t (6)	MC	803 537-8400	Andrew R Ingram	J William Taylor	Helen Funderburk	....	Donald J Baker	J A Graves	James T Lewis Jr
Chester (7)	CM	803 581-2123	....	....	....	....	....	....	....
Clemson (11)	MC	803 653-2030	....	....	....	....	....	....	....
Clinton (8)	CM	803 833-7505	Myra Nichols	Steven L Harrell	Barbara Sumpter	Steven L Harrell	Troy Bentley	Carroll Barker	C Litchfield
Clover t (3)	MC	803 222-9495	John M Smith	....	Betty R Ferguson	....	....	David P Milligan	Mack E McCarter
Columbia (98)	CM	803 733-8200	Robert Coble	Miles Hadley	Zenda Leaks	Susan Busbice	John Jansen	Charles Austin	Mark McCain
Conway (10)	MC	803 248-7351	Ike G Long Jr	Stephen J Sobers	Carolyn C Stevens	J Larry Lewis	Tony D Hendrick	Gary C Michell	Freddie DuBose
Darlington (7)	MC	803 393-5838	....	....	....	....	....	....	....
Denmark t (4)	MC	803 793-3734	Elona C Davis	Jewel B Davis	....	....	Otis P Sandifer	Joseph S Jenkins	J P Robinson
Dillon (7)	CM	803 774-0040	Howard Cutler	James D Corl	....	Stephen Daulton	Billy Caines	Joe Rogers	....
Easley (15)	MC	803 859-3890	....	....	....	....	....	....	....
Edgefield t (3)	MC	803 637-3935	....	....	....	....	....	....	....
Florence (30)	CM	803 665-3158	....	....	....	....	....	....	....
Folly Beach (1)	MC	803 588-2447	....	....	....	....	....	....	....
Forest Acres (7)	CM	803 782-9475	Joseph Drawdy	Ron Garbinsky	....	....	....	Gene Sealy	....
Fort Mill t (5)	MC	803 547-2034	....	....	....	....	....	....	....
Fountain Inn t (4)	MC	803 862-4221	....	....	....	....	....	....	....
Gaffney (13)	MC	803 487-8505	V L Sanders	J McDonough	....	S D Holly	D Parris	J Scates	J Watkins
Georgetown (10)	MC	803 546-2000	Thomas J Rubillo	L Boyd Johnson	Joseph C Steen Jr	R Cobb Bell	Kenneth E Gaiser	Roger C Haddix	Elder B Holmes
Goose Creek (25)	MC	803 797-6220	Michael Heitzler	Dennis Harmon	Sherry Ferguson	Lee Moulder	Barfield Holland	Harvey Becker	John Askins
Great Falls t (2)	MC	803 482-2055	Marcus Ray	....	Rose B Alexander	....	Joseph E Ransom	John G Brown Sr	Richard Collins
Greenville (58)	CM	803 467-4500	William Workman	Aubrey V Watts	Cheryl Cofie	Giles Dodd	Robert Capps	Michael D Bridges	James Greer
Greenwood (21)	CM	803 942-8410	Floyd Nicholson	Steven J Brown	Mary E Edwards	....	Harold G Hinton	Gerald L Brooks	Danny Polatty
Greer (10)	CM	803 877-9061	C Don Wall	K L Westmoreland	Lucia Polson	Mary P Greer	W H Brissey	H Dean Crisp	....
Hampton t (3)	MC	803 943-2951	John B Rhoden	Ernie D Glynn	....	....	Wade Freeman	Jerry Thomas	Caskell Hudson
Hanahan (13)	MC	803 554-4221	William L Cobb	Daniel W Davis	....	Berlino D Veloso	David B Peterson	M C Bellew	Jerry W Stegall
Hardeeville t (..)	CM	803 784-2231	Rodney T Cannon	C P Boyles	Jeanie P Bennett	Jeanie P Bennett	D L Hubbard	R J Fialkowski	Stephen W Murdock
Hartsville (8)	CM	803 383-3018	Flora C Hopkins	William F Bruton	Sherron L Skipper	Pam P Sansbury	Tommy Livingston	Richard F Ritch	Mike A Welch
Hemingway t (1)	MC	803 558-2824	....	....	....	....	....	....	....
Hilton Head Island t (24)	CM	803 842-8900	Frank R Chapman	Michael O' Neill	Sandi Santaniello	Shirley A Freeman	David Mac Lellan	....	Charles O Hoelle
Honea Path t (4)	CM	803 369-2466	....	....	....	....	....	....	....
Irmo t (11)	CM	803 781-7050	John Gibbons	P McMahon	Terri Saxon	P McMahon	....	Everett Howard	....
Isle Of Palms (4)	MC	803 886-6428	Carmen R Bunch	Mark M Williams	Nellie McDuffie	....	Ann G Corbett	James B Arnold Jr	Andrew J Parrish
Johnston t (3)	MC	803 275-2488	....	....	....	....	....	....	....
Kershaw t (2)	MC	803 475-6065	William Clyburn	....	Phyllis Dorman	....	Mike Gardner	Emerson Coates	Todd Knight
Kingstree t (4)	CM	803 354-7484	....	....	....	....	....	....	....
Lake City (7)	MC	803 394-5421	William Sebnick	Adalia A Sova	Cherline Miles	Ann Locke	Walter L Moody	Michael Brumbles	Donald Parrott
Lancaster (9)	MC	803 283-8426	Joe Shaw	Richard Graves	....	....	Dennis Cole	William Sumner	William Summerlin
Laurens (10)	MC	803 984-0144	....	....	....	....	....	....	....
Liberty t (3)	MC	803 850-3505	Marvin E Kelley	....	Elizabeth G Roper	....	Patrick P Turner	Robert E Moore Sr	Robert F Chappell
Manning (4)	CM	803 435-8477	....	....	....	....	....	....	....
Marion t (8)	MC	803 423-5961	Bobby Gerald	L Frazier Waldrop	Mary C Batson	Wanda G Lee	William R Jones	Willie L Smith	Mitchell Dew
Mauldin (12)	MC	803 288-4910	L S Green Sr	David M Bates	....	....	James Moore	Harold Sherbert	....
Mc Coll t (3)	MC	803 523-5341	....	....	....	....	....	....	....
Moncks Corner t (6)	MC	803 761-6650	John S West	Marion T Graham	Marilyn M Baker	....	David A Miller	Gregory A Hoover	James H Bodiford
Mount Pleasant t (30)	MC	803 884-8517	C Woods Flowers	R Mac Burdette	Carol Hunter	Colleen Jernigan	Fred Tetor	Thomas Sexton	Furman Reynolds
Mullins t (6)	MC	803 464-9583	....	....	....	....	....	....	....
Myrtle Beach (25)	CM	803 626-7645	Robert M Grissom	Thomas E Leath	Joan Grove	Maria E Baisden	Lynwood O Womack	Samuel H Killman	Larry S Kerr
Newberry (11)	CM	803 276-4193	....	....	....	....	....	....	....
North Augusta (15)	MC	803 279-0333	....	....	....	....	....	....	....
North Charleston (70)	MC	803 554-5700	Kenneth McClure	....	Amelia Greer	Harley Henderson	Alvar Rissanen	....	....
North Myrtle Beach (9)	CM	803 280-5555	Philip Tilghman	A William Moss	Beverly Franz	Randy Wright	....	Johnny Causey	Jerry Pierce
Orangeburg (14)	CM	803 533-6000	Martin C Cheatham	John H Yow	Sharon G Fanning	Sharon G Fanning	....	Wendell Davis	B Reese Earley
Pageland t (3)	MC	803 672-7292	....	....	....	....	....	....	....
Pendleton t (3)	MC	803 646-9409	H B Durham	....	Joyce Elrod	....	....	James Cleveland	Richard Bork
Pickens t (3)	MC	803 878-6421	Norman L Kennemer	....	....	Mary A Childs	Thomas H Nealy	Wendal E Jenkins	Joe E Davis
Port Royal t (3)	MC	803 524-5125	Henry Robinson	John P Perry	Cecilia Short	....	....	George D Smith	Harvey Cawthorn
Ridgeland t (1)	MC	803 726-3351	Joseph N Malphrus	Carl F Lehmann	Penelope B Daley	Sharon W Boyles	Thomas Jenkins	Harry D Dibiase	James R Mixson Jr
Rock Hill (42)	CM	803 329-5570	Elizabeth Rhea	Russell Allen	....	Gerry Schapiro	Dickie Hoffman	Larry Nowery	Jim Villano
Saluda t (3)	MC	803 445-3522	....	....	....	....	....	....	....
Seneca t (8)	MC	803 885-2700	John W Fields	Tommy Grant	Walter Smith	Walter Smith	Richard Timms	....	Benny Burrell
Simpsonville t (12)	MC	803 963-3461	....	....	....	....	....	....	....
Spartanburg (43)	MC	803 596-2062	James Talley	Wayne Bowers	Mandy Merck	L Gray Brewton	Thomas Ivey	W C Bain	Michael Garrett
Springdale t (3)	CM	803 794-0408	Pat G Smith	C G Robinson	Esta Wetherley	Ross I Beebe	....	Thomas A Lucas	Gary Wilson
Summerville t (23)	MC	803 871-6000	Berlin G Myers	John F Wilbanks	Kara Silva	Gracie L Smith	Richard G Waring	Ray Nash	James Avant
Sumter (42)	CM	803 773-3371	Stephen M Creech	C Talmadge Tobias	Sherry Evans	Julia Muldrow	Eli C Parnell Jr	Harold B Johnson	William Ed Davis
Surfside Beach t (4)	MC	803 238-2590	Dick M Johnson	H Neil Ferguson	Elaine K Cowart	Sharon D Cashion	Dan Thomas	John M Lloyd	Ron Peaks
Travelers Rest (3)	CM	803 834-8740	....	....	....	....	....	....	....
Union (10)	MC	803 429-1700	T B Williamson	Charles Potts	Pat Hicks	Walker Gallman	....	Russell Roark	Perry Harmon
Walhalla t (4)	MC	803 638-4343	Julian Stoudemire	V Satterfield	....	....	....	Broadus Albertson	....
Walterboro (5)	CM	803 549-2548	W Harry Cone	Eric G Budds	Betty Hudson	Brenda B Colson	Ashton Syfrett	Kenneth Arthur	Charlie Chewning
West Columbia (11)	CM	803 791-1880	....	William E Unthank	....	....	....	....	....
Westminster t (3)	MC	803 647-5071	....	....	....	....	....	....	....
Williamston t (4)	MC	803 847-7473	....	....	....	....	....	....	....
Williston t (3)	MC	803 266-7015	....	....	....	....	....	....	....
Winnsboro t (3)	CM	803 635-4943	....	....	....	....	....	....	....
Woodruff (4)	CM	803 476-8154	Guy S Blakely Sr	Julian L Jackson	Beverley M Maddox	Julian L Jackson	W T Westmoreland	Michael E Cromer	Gerald E Bailey
York (7)	CM	803 684-2341	W Roddey Connolly	Karen S Carter	Nelle J Pittman	....	Domenico M Manera	C David Morton	Charles G Helms

Directory 1/9
continued

MUNICIPAL OFFICIALS
IN U.S. CITIES OVER 2,500

City, 1990 population figures (000 omitted), form of government	Municipal phone number	Mayor/ chief elected official	Appointed administrator	City clerk/ city secretary	Finance officer	Fire chief	Police chief	Public works director
SOUTH DAKOTA (24)								
Aberdeen (25)	CO 605 622-7013	Timothy Rich	....	Candace Lindskov	Bruce Nelson	....	Allen Aden	....
Belle Fourche (4)	MC 605 892-2494	....	....	....	....	....	....	....
Box Elder (3)	MC 605 923-1403	....	....	....	....	....	Phil Youngdale	Leo Narum
Brandon (4)	MC 605 582-6515	D Kleinvachter	Dennis E Olson	Ellaine Henriksen	Dennis E Olson	....	Dennis Falken	Andy Jensen
Brookings (16)	CO 605 692-6281	Wayne Hauschild	....	....	Theodore Kryger	Curtis Jensen	Dennis Johnson	Palmer L Ericksen
Canton (3)	CO 605 987-2881	David R Gard	....	....	Daniel P Amert	Norris Elke	Alvin Merchen	....
Hot Springs (4)	MC 605 745-3135	D J DeVries	....	....	Cheryl Wait	Gale Harkless		
Huron (12)	CO 605 352-6791	....	....	....	....	....	....	....
Lead (4)	CO 605 584-1401	Dennis J York	....	....	Harley Lux	David Tesch	Steven Palmer	Cillford Rook
Madison (6)	CO 605 256-4586	....	....	....	....	....	....	....
Milbank (4)	MC 605 432-9575	Rudolph Nef	....	Cynthia Schultz	Craig Wellnitz	Ron Bjerke	Bob Eide	Dave Zinter
Mitchell (14)	MC 605 996-6452	Don Dailey	....	....	Michele Franey	Robert Miller	Doug Kirkus	Tim McGannon
Mobridge (4)	MC 605 845-3509	....	....	....	....	....	....	....
Pierre (13)	CO 605 224-5921	Gary L Drewes	....	....	Kenneth L Hericks	Stan Mikkonen	Bill Abernathy	Bruce Pier
Rapid City (55)	MC 605 394-2511	E McLaughlin	....	....	Richard Wahlstrom	Owen Hibbard	Thomas Hennies	....
Redfield (3)	MC 605 472-0660	Duane Sanger	Sharon Jungwirth	....	Sharon Jungwirth	Gordon Schroeder	....	Royce Bush
Sioux Falls (101)	CO 605 339-7112	Jack White	....	Dianne Metli	Manfred Szameit	Kirk Anderson	Terry Satterlee	....
Sisseton (2)	CM 605 698-3391	....	....	....	....	....	....	....
Spearfish (7)	MC 605 642-7775	Fred W Romkema	....	....	Elizabeth Benning	Mark Heggem	Rick Mowell	Ted Vore
Sturgis (5)	MC 605 347-4422	....	....	....	....	....	....	....
Vermillion (10)	CM 605 624-5641	William J Radigan	Jeffrey Pederson	Michael D Carlson	Michael D Carlson	Doug Brunick	Gary Wright	Rollie Isaacson
Watertown (18)	MC 605 886-4057	....	....	....	....	....	....	....
Winner (3)	MC 605 842-2606	....	....	....	....	....	....	....
Yankton (13)	MC 605 665-4501	Terry Crandall	William Ross	....	Jerald Knodel	Patrick Smith	Leon Cantin	Eugene Hoag
TENNESSEE (134)								
Adams t (1)	MC 615 696-2593	Omer G Brooksher	Rachel Nolen	....	....	Ray Brown	....	....
Alamo t (2)	MC 901 696-4515	....	....	....	....	....	....	....
Alcoa (6)	CM 615 981-4100	Donald R Mull	Carl L Overman	....	Ray E Richesin	Larry L Graves	Wayne M Chodak	Kenneth D Wiggins
Athens (12)	CM 615 745-3140	L Roseberry	Mel Barker	Kaye Burton	....	Robert Miller	Charles Ziegler	Mark Miller
Bartlett t (27)	MC 901 385-6400	Bobby K Flaherty	Jeannine Lukaszes	....	Stephen Smith	Paul Smith	Robert Paudert	Bill Kilp
Beersheba Springs t (1)	CO 615 692-3314	Glen Richardson	....	Lonnie Whitman	....	Donald Boyd	....	....
Belle Meade (3)	CM 615 297-6041	T S Fillebrown	W D Brinton Jr	Dianne G Borum	....	....	Vince Perry	George Bartlett
Berry Hill (1)	CM 615 292-5531	Charles McKelvey	Glenn H Delzell	....	....	....	Herman Jett	....
Bolivar t (6)	MC 901 658-2020	Charles L Frost	James R Sain	Mary Ann Russell	James R Sain	John D Baker	Johnny R Anthony	Lloyd Bell
Brentwood (16)	CM 615 371-0060	Brian J Sweeney	Michael Walker	....	Randy L Sanders	Kenneth Lane	Howard Buttrey	Louis J Baltz
Bristol (23)	CM 615 989-5500	John S Gaines	Frank W Clifton	June Sparger	June Sparger	Phil Vinson	David E Wampler	Bill Sorah
Brownsville t (10)	MC 901 772-1212	Webb Banks	Jerry Taylor	....	Webb Banks	Jimmy White	Dan Singleton	Howard Wyatt
Camden t (4)	MC 901 584-4656	Wendel Oglesby	....	Phyllis Woodard	....	Tom Bordonaro	James Woodard	....
Carthage t (2)	MC 615 735-1881	David H Bowman	Joyce M Rash	Brenda McKinley	Joyce M Rash	Edward Stallings	Scotty L Lewis	Charle E Hunt
Centerville t (4)	MC 615 729-4246	Kenneth R Wright	Kenneth R Wright	....	Mildred D Jones	Kenneth Thompson	Roger T Livengood	Wayne Prince
Charleston t (1)	CM 615 336-1483	....	....	....	....	....	....	....
Chattanooga (152)	CO 615 757-5200	....	....	....	....	....	....	....
Church Hill t (5)	MC 615 357-6161	....	....	Sylvia Skinner	Wilbur Berry	Eugene Keel	Johnny Rosson	....
Clarksville (75)	MC 615 645-7444	Donald Trotter	....	Janice S Casteel	....	David W May Jr	Lee Reese	Richard T Lyles
Cleveland (30)	CO 615 472-4551	J Thomas Rowland	George A Wood	Janice S Casteel	....	David W May Jr	Lee Reese	Richard T Lyles
Clifton City t (1)	CM 615 676-3370	....	....	....	....	....	....	....
Clinton t (9)	MC 615 457-0424	Frank Diggs	Steve Queener	Sharon Antrican	Patsy Meredith	Ernest Payne	Clifton Melton	Wendell Ward
Collegedale (5)	CM 615 396-3135	....	....	....	....	....	....	....
Collierville t (14)	MC 901 853-3200	....	....	....	....	....	....	....
Collinwood (1)	CM 615 724-9107	James A Dicus	Robert M Vandiver	Willodean Hill	Robert M Vandiver	Sherman Martin	Jerry Benedict	William Thompson
Columbia (29)	CM 615 388-5432	Larry Smithson	William E Gentner	....	Betty Modrall	Don Martin	James Boyd	....
Cookeville (22)	CM 615 526-9591	....	....	....	....	....	....	....
Covington (7)	MC 901 476-9613	R B Bailey	....	....	J H Hadley	J W Craig	R J Gagnon	R D Stockman
Crossville (7)	CM 615 484-7060	Earl Dean	Robert R Collins	Sally Oglesby	....	Mike Turner	Robert Foutch	James K Knott
Dayton (6)	CM 615 775-1818	....	....	....	....	....	....	....
Dickson t (9)	MC 615 441-9570	Don L Weiss Jr	Alton E Brown	....	....	Clay Tidwell	Rick Chandler	....
Dunlap (4)	MC 615 949-2115	....	....	....	....	....	....	....
Dyersburg (16)	MC 901 286-7607	Bill Revell	....	Barbara Luft	....	Billy Taylor	Bobby Williamson	Charles Asbridge
East Ridge t (21)	CO 615 867-7711	....	....	....	....	....	....	....
Elizabethton (12)	CM 615 543-3551	Pat Red Bowers	Charles Stahl	....	Sidney Cox	Bill Carter	Roger Deal	Rodney Trent
Erwin t (5)	MC 615 743-6231	....	....	....	....	....	....	....
Etowah (4)	CM 615 263-2202	E Burke Garwood	Richard Whitehead	Yvonne Derreberry	Jean B James	....	Marty Aderhold	Larry Lanning
Fairview (4)	CM 615 799-2484	....	....	....	....	....	....	....
Farragut t (13)	CM 615 966-7057	W Edward Ford	Jack S Hamlett	Alexis Williamson	....	....	....	William McKelvey
Fayetteville t (7)	MC 615 433-6154	....	....	....	....	....	....	....
Forest Hills (4)	CO 615 383-8447	....	Tom Balthrop	....	....	....	....	....
Franklin t (20)	MC 615 794-4572	Jerry W Sharber	James R Johnson	....	Judy G Kennedy	Samuel M Liggett	M Fred Wisdom	....
Gallatin (19)	MC 615 452-5400	Robert W Landford	....	Connie Kittrell	Peggy Vantrease	Joe Womack	Wayne Womack	Lynn Patillo
Gatlinburg (3)	CM 615 436-1400	Charles Bradley	Cindy Cameronogle	....	David A Beeler	Terry Reagan	Harry Montgomery	....
Germantown (33)	MC 901 757-7274	Charles Salvaggio	Patrick Lawton	Judy Simerson	John Dluhos	James Smith	Eddie Boatwright	Sam Beach
Goodlettsville (11)	CM 615 859-4078	....	....	....	....	....	....	....
Greenbrier t (3)	MC 615 643-4531	....	....	....	....	....	....	....
Greeneville t (14)	MC 615 639-7105	....	....	....	....	....	....	....
Harriman (7)	MC 615 882-3960	....	....	....	....	....	....	....
Hartsville (2)	MC 615 374-3074	....	....	....	....	....	....	....
Henderson (5)	MC 901 989-4628	Charles Patterson	....	Jim E Garland	....	Prince A Burkeen	Jerome P Hurst	Jerry L King
Hendersonville (32)	MC 615 822-1000	R J Hank Thompson	....	....	James Young	Charles Black	David Key	Bob Freudenthal
Hohenwald (4)	MC 615 796-2231	Guy Nicholson	....	Peggy Dye	....	....	Robert Conner	....
Humboldt (10)	MC 901 784-2511	....	....	....	....	....	....	....
Huntingdon t (4)	MC 901 986-8211	....	....	....	....	....	....	....
Jackson (49)	MC 901 425-8252	Charles Farmer	....	....	Russ Truell	Owen Collins	Rick Staples	Jerry Gist
Jasper t (3)	MC 615 942-3180	....	Don Darden	....	Monica Myers	Bob Kinder	Will Clark	Mike Jones
Jefferson City (5)	CM 615 475-9071	Bill Bales	Don Darden	Betty R Hurst	Monica Myers	George Deuel	Ned Smiddy	Howard Asher
Jellico (2)	MC 615 784-6351	Wm Forster Baird	....	Betty R Hurst	....	Doug Buckles	Ron Street	Phil Pindzola
Johnson City (49)	CM 615 929-9171	Jeff Anderson	John Campbell	....	Laura Hamilton	Roger Perkins	Craig Ford	....
Jonesborough t (3)	CM 615 753-6128	Kevin B McKinney	Robert E Browning	Laura Hamilton	Anthony R Massey	John C Moser	James F Keesling	B R Wilkerson
Kingsport (36)	CM 615 229-9400	Hunter Wright	Peter T Connet	....	Carolyn Brewer	....	Gary Humphrys	....
Kingston (5)	CM 615 376-6584	Don Woody	Edwin Smith	Eleanor Neal	Randolph Vineyard	A Bruce Cureton	Phillip E Keith	Robert M Whetsel
Knoxville (165)	MC 615 521-2106	Victor Ashe	....	Cindy Mitchell	Bob Joines	A C Wintemeyer	Michael Patrick	Ron Darden
La Follette (7)	CM 615 562-4961	....	....	....	....	....	....	....
La Vergne (7)	MC 615 793-6295	Shirley Winfree	Daniel Briddle	Bruce Richardson	Bob Joines	A C Wintemeyer	Michael Patrick	Ron Darden
Lafayette (4)	MC 615 666-2194	....	....	....	....	....	....	....
Lake City t (2)	CO 615 426-2838	....	....	....	....	....	....	....

Directory 1/9
continued

**MUNICIPAL OFFICIALS
IN U.S. CITIES OVER 2,500**

City, 1990 population figures (000 omitted), form of government	Municipal phone number	Mayor/ chief elected official	Appointed administrator	City clerk/ city secretary	Finance officer	Fire chief	Police chief	Public works director
TENNESSEE (134) continued								
Lakewood (2)	CM 615 847-2187	....	....	....	....	....	....	....
Lawrenceburg (10)	CO 615 762-4459	Lindsey Garner	....	J Ralph Cross	....	Roy Holloway	Louis Fite	....
Lebanon (15)	MC 615 443-2839	....	....	....	....	....	....	....
Lenoir City (6)	MC 615 986-2715	....	....	....	....	....	....	....
Lewisburg (10)	MC 615 359-1544	....	....	....	....	....	....	....
Lexington (6)	MC 901 968-6657	....	....	....	....	....	....	....
Livingston t (4)	MC 615 823-1269	....	....	....	....	....	....	....
Loudon (4)	MC 615 458-2033	Bernie Swiney	Barry Baker	S Putkonen	....	Rondel Branam	Bill Grimes	Bill Fagg
Madisonville t (3)	MC 615 442-9416	....	....	....	....	....	....	....
Manchester (8)	MC 615 728-4652	Lonnie J Norman	....	....	Nina H Moffitt	J Sam Miller	Ross Simmons	Edward Anderson
Martin (9)	MC 901 587-3126	Larry W Taylor	Richard L Tidwell	Linda A Walker	Richard L Tidwell	N B Williams	Jackie R Moore	James W Crocker
Maryville (19)	MC 615 981-1300	Stanley Shields	Gary H Hensley	....	Mark Johnson	Kenneth Abbott	Terry Nichols	Richard Whaley
Maynardville (1)	CM 615 992-3821	William P Graves	Edgar Cook	....	Hazel Gillenwater	Darrell White	Edgar Cook	....
Mc Kenzie (5)	MC 901 352-2292	....	....	....	....	....	....	....
Mc Minnville (11)	MC 615 473-1200	....	....	....	....	....	....	....
Memphis (610)	MC 901 576-6403	....	....	....	....	....	....	....
Milan t (8)	MC 901 686-3301	....	....	....	....	....	....	....
Millington (18)	MC 901 872-2211	....	....	....	....	....	....	....
Monterey t (3)	MC 615 839-2323	Jack Phillips	Debbie Stephens	Jo Nelda Stamps	....	Richard Milligan	Bruce Breedlove	....
Morristown (21)	CM 615 581-0100	John R Johnson	R Keith Jackson	R Keith Jackson	Michael W Lutche	Rick E Reynolds	Joel K Seal	Carl Gilbert
Mount Carmel t (4)	CM 615 357-7311	....	....	....	....	....	....	....
Mount Juliet (5)	CM 615 754-2552	David J Waynick	Danny C Farmer	....	Sheila Luckett	....	Charles McCrary	James Evetts
Mount Pleasant (4)	CM 615 379-7717	William H Boyd	Robert A Murray	Carolyn Douglas	....	M H Massey	Tom Wilson	Larry Holden
Murfreesboro (45)	CM 615 893-5210	Joe B Jackson	Roger G Haley	....	James B Penner	David Baxter	Billy Jones	Ricky Cantrell
Nashville-Davidson (511)	MC 615 862-6650	Philip Bredesen	....	Marilyn Swing	Eugene Nolan	Norman Dozier	Robert Kirchner	William Keel
Newbern (3)	MC 901 627-3221	Joe Adams	Judy Steelman	Judy Steelman	....	Bill Berry	Harold Dunivant	....
Newport t (7)	MC 615 623-7323	....	....	....	....	....	....	....
Norris (1)	CM 615 494-7645	Richard Dyer	Benny Carden	Darlene Buckner	....	Dorman Scarbrough	Dorman Scarbrough	William Pointer
Oak Hill (4)	CM 615 371-8291	Warren Wilkerson	George W Morris	....	George W Morris	....	....	....
Oak Ridge (27)	CM 615 482-8316	Edmund A Nephew	Jeffrey Broughton	Jacquelyn Bernard	Steven W Jenkins	W Mack Bailey	David H Beams	Gary M Cinder
Oliver Springs t (3)	CM 615 435-7722	....	....	....	....	....	....	....
Oneida t (4)	MC 615 569-4295	....	....	....	....	....	....	....
Paris (9)	CM 901 642-1212	John T Van Dyck	Carl G Holder Jr	....	Evonne J Phifer	George C Atkins	Thomas A Cooper	....
Pigeon Forge (3)	CM 615 453-9061	Ralph Chance	Earlene M Teaster	Mable O Ellis	Elsie Cole	Denny Clabo	Jack H Baldwin	Garland C Harmon
Portland t (5)	CM 615 325-6776	Robert Wilkinson	....	Nancy Keen	....	....	Robert West	Wayne Walker
Pulaski (8)	MC 513 561-7228	Clyde Dorn	Thomas W Moeller	Donna J Goens	Sharon E King	Robert Coy	Gerald L Beckman	Floyd Poppenhouse
Red Bank (12)	CM 615 877-1103	....	....	....	....	....	....	....
Ripley (6)	MC 901 635-4000	Richard Douglas	....	Donna Buckner	Richard Douglas	Ronnie Crawford	Dennis King	Leamon Pennington
Rockwood (5)	CO 615 354-0163	....	....	....	....	....	....	....
Rogersville t (4)	MC 615 272-7497	....	....	....	....	....	....	....
Samburg t (..)	MC 901 538-2735	....	....	....	....	....	....	....
Savannah (7)	CM 901 925-3300	....	....	....	....	....	....	....
Selmer t (4)	MC 901 645-3242	....	....	....	....	....	....	....
Sevierville (7)	CM 615 453-5504	....	....	....	....	....	....	....
Shelbyville (14)	CM 615 684-2691	Henry Feldhaus	Thomas Christie	....	Dana Thomas	Garland King	Austin Swing	William Sullivan
Signal Mountain t (7)	CM 615 886-2177	....	....	....	....	....	....	....
Smithville t (4)	MC 615 597-4745	....	....	....	....	....	....	....
Smyrna t (14)	MC 615 459-2553	Paul Johns	Mike Woods	Mike Woods	....	Bill Culbertson	Charles Vance	Ben Andrews
Soddy-Daisy (8)	CM 615 332-5323	Leroy Grant	Don Pickard	....	Sara Burris	Steve Grant	Douglas M Everett	Jack Parker
South Fulton (3)	CM 901 479-2151	Kent Greer	George Gunter	Debbie Beadles	....	Tommy Smith	Andy Crocker	Roy Coley
South Pittsburg (3)	CM 615 837-7511	....	....	....	....	....	....	....
Sparta (5)	MC 615 836-3248	....	....	....	....	....	....	....
Spring City t (2)	CM 615 365-6441	....	....	....	....	....	....	....
Springfield (11)	CM 615 382-2200	Dave Fisher	Doug Bishop	Janice Frey	Bobby Lehman	David Greer	Mike Wilhoit	Allan Ellis
St. Joseph (1)	CM 615 845-4141	....	....	....	....	....	....	....
Sweetwater (5)	MC 615 337-6979	....	....	....	....	....	....	....
Tennessee Ridge t (1)	CM 615 721-3385	....	....	....	....	....	....	....
Trenton (5)	MC 901 855-2013	Tommie Goodwin	Sammy Dickey	Marilyn Zarecor	Kathy Stewart	Barry Green	Tommy Litton	Paul Bennett
Tullahoma (17)	CM 615 455-2648	....	....	....	....	....	....	....
Tusculum (2)	MC 615 638-6211	....	....	....	....	....	....	....
Union City (11)	CM 901 885-1341	Terry Hailey	Don Thornton	Mildred Roberts	Mildred Roberts	Dale Burress	Joe Garner	Bobby Grimes
Watauga (..)	CM 615 928-3490	John Skeans	Herbert Keller	Hattie Skeans	Ethel Wilhoit	....	John Bolus	....
Waverly t (4)	CM 615 296-2101	....	....	....	....	....	....	....
Waynesboro (2)	CM 615 722-5458	Loyd Howell	Howard Riley	Darlene Skelton	Flora E Lacher	Doug Gobbell	Gene Seitz	Gilbert Cole
Whitwell (2)	CM 615 658-5151	....	....	....	....	....	....	....
Winchester t (6)	MC 615 967-4771	....	....	....	....	....	....	....
TEXAS (427)								
Abernathy (3)	CM 806 298-2546	....	....	....	....	....	....	....
Abilene (107)	CM 915 676-6245	Gary McCaleb	....	Jo A Moore	David M Wright	J Deloss Edwards	Melvin Martin	Marva Pritchett
Addison (9)	CM 214 450-7000	Rich Beckert	Ronald Whitehead	....	Randolph Moravec	R Wallingford	James McLaughlin	John Baumgartner
Alamo (8)	MC 210 787-0006	Marcelino Medina	H G Lumbreras	Gloria B Gonzales	Reymundo Ortiz Jr	Harold G Nunn	Noe Garza	Jose Villescas
Alamo Heights (7)	MC 210 822-3331	William Balthrope	Susan Rash	....	Susan Rash	William E Renken	Jack Summey	Steve Steinmetz
Alice (20)	CM 512 668-7200	....	....	....	....	....	....	....
Allen (18)	CM 214 727-0100	Joe Farmer	Jon McCarty	Judy Morrison	Charlotte Smith	Ron Gentry	Richard Carroll	George Conner
Alpine t (6)	MC 915 837-3301	William J Sohl	Jerry Carvajal	Annabel M Holguin	Tomi J McDaniel	Paul Loeffler	Henry Ogletree	Ted Scown
Alton (3)	MC 210 581-2793	Salvador Vela	Israel Sagredo	Melinda Mendoza	Lydia Elizondo	Ron Sturchio	Fred Horner	Rene Trevino
Alvarado (3)	MC 817 783-3351	....	....	....	....	....	....	....
Alvin (19)	CM 713 388-4200	Elmer Dezso	Marvin P Norwood	Wynette Stoner	Fred Mendoza	Donald R Eernisse	Michael Merkel	Douglas Wilson
Amarillo (158)	CM 806 378-3000	Kel Seliger	John Ward	Donna Deright	Dean Frigo	Curtis Richards	Jerry Neal	Mike Kennedy
Andrews (11)	CM 915 523-4820	Greg Sweeney	Len Wilson	Kitty Bristow	Kitty Bristow	Henry Cook	Dolphus Bud Jones	Larry Fleming
Angleton (17)	CM 409 849-4364	....	....	....	....	....	....	....
Anson (3)	MC 915 823-2411	....	....	....	....	....	....	....
Anthony (3)	MC 915 886-3944	Art Franco	....	Nila J Stillwell	Keith Puhlman	....	Hal B Caldwell	Jesus Almaraz
Aransas Pass (7)	CM 512 758-5301	Billy St Clair	Rick Ewaniszyk	Natalia Smith	....	Gilbert Ritz	Melvin Shedd	Allen Berna
Arlington (262)	CM 817 275-3271	....	....	....	....	....	....	....
Athens (11)	CM 903 675-9225	C R Stonier	Donald Manning	....	Joanne Glasgow	Waylen Padgett	Davie W Harris	Don O Herriage
Atlanta (6)	CM 903 796-7153	Peyton Childs	Andre Wimer	Janice Elliott	Andre Wimer	David Burden	Mike Scott	Jeff Buzbee
Austin (466)	CM 512 499-2000	Bruce Todd	Jesus Garza	Elden Aldridge	Betty Dunkerley	Robin Paulsgrove	Elizabeth Watson	Bill Stockton
Azle (9)	CM 817 444-2541	Cy Rone	Harry Dulin	Kim Shelton	Robert Horton	Robert Fowler	Marvin Ivy	Darrell Riding
Balch Springs (17)	CM 214 557-6070	David Haas	Anelia Warner	Tresa Davis	Anelia Warner	Mike Cooper	Ed Leach	James Glover
Balcones Heights (3)	MC 210 735-9148	Lucille Wohlfarth	Roy Miller	....	....	Charles Matthies	Kenneth Menn	Don Gourley
Ballinger (4)	CM 915 365-3511	Dan Morelock	Judy Miller	Bonita F Shields	....	Timmy Kresta	William P Boggess	Tommy New

Directory 1/9
continued

MUNICIPAL OFFICIALS
IN U.S. CITIES OVER 2,500

City, 1990 population figures (000 omitted), form of government	Municipal phone number	Mayor/chief elected official	Appointed administrator	City clerk/city secretary	Finance officer	Fire chief	Police chief	Public works director
TEXAS (427) continued								
Bastrop (4)	MC 512 321-3941	David Lock	Michael H Talbot	Shawnda Sanders	Joann Wilcoxen	Mike Fisher	Ronnie Duncan	Marvin Patterson
Bay City (18)	MC 409 245-2137	....	....	....	....	....	....	....
Baytown (64)	CM 713 422-8281	Pete Alfaro	Bobby Rountree	Eileen Hall	Monte Mercer	Robert Leiper	Charles Shaffer	Herb Thomas
Beaumont (114)	CM 409 880-3777	David W Moore	Ray A Riley	R Chiappetta	....	Chester A Shelton	Thomas J Scofield	John R Labrie
Bedford (44)	CM 817 952-2100	Rick Hurt	Jim Walker	Rita Frick	Charles Gardner	E M Bilger Jr	Jimmy Simpson	Don Burnes
Beeville (14)	CM 512 358-4641	....	....	....	....	....	....	....
Bellaire (14)	CM 713 662-8222	Harold Penn	Lea Dunn	Roena Loftin	Norma Quinn	Rufus Summers	Jerry Loftin	Richard Larsen
Bellmead (8)	CM 817 799-2436	....	S G Radcliffe	....	E W Dieterich	James Karl	Bob Harold	Mike Willis
Bellville (3)	MC 409 865-3136	....	....	....	....	....	....	....
Belton (12)	CM 817 939-5851	Charley Powell	Jeff Holberg	Connie Torres	Cristy Daniell	Roy Harmon	Roy Kneese	Lou Griffin
Benbrook (20)	CM 817 249-3000	Jerry Dunn	Ken Neystel	Joanna King	David Ragsdale	....	Sam Horan	Chuck Rogers
Big Lake t (4)	MC 915 884-2511	....	....	....	....	....	....	....
Big Spring (23)	CM 915 264-2348	Tim Blackshear	Lanny S Lambert	....	Thomas Ferguson	Frank Anderson	Jerry Edwards	Tom Decell
Bishop t (3)	CM 512 584-2567	Janie Shafer	....	Cynthia Contreras	....	Mark Wilkerson	Francisco Garcia	Juan G Puente
Boerne (4)	MC 210 249-9511	Patrick R Heath	Ronald C Bowman	Bernell Norton	Ronald C Bowman	....	Gary Miller	John Moring
Bonham (7)	CM 903 583-7555	Bob McCraw	Jim Stiff	....	Jim Stiff	....	Mike Bankston	....
Borger (16)	CM 806 273-2881	Judy Flanders	Alyn Rogers	Wanda Klause	Glynn Carlock	W McWilliams	Michael Smith	Henry Veach
Bowie (5)	CM 817 872-1114	Bert Cunningham	James Cantwell	Linda Shelton	James Cantwell	Kelly Tomlin	Mike Gentry	....
Brady (6)	MC 915 597-2152	H L Bud Gober Jr	Raymond H Kendall	....	Lindell L Estes	Garon L Salter	James D Ledford	Gary L Broz
Brazoria (3)	CM 409 798-2489	William V James	K Timmermann	Betty M Wilson	K Timmermann	Marcus Rabren	Neal Longbotham	W J Humphery
Breckenridge (6)	CM 817 559-8287	Bruce W Curry	Gary G Ernest	Linda Knight	Linda Knight	Roger McMullen	Ronnie Pendleton	Joe Brown
Brenham (12)	MC 409 836-7911	....	....	....	....	....	....	....
Bridge City (8)	CM 409 735-6801	....	....	....	....	....	....	....
Bridgeport (4)	MC 812 683-5906	....	....	....	....	....	....	....
Brownfield (10)	CM 806 637-4547	Graham Swain	R C Fletcher	Zelma Miller	....	Marvin Dawson	Bill Avera	....
Brownsville (99)	CM 210 548-6000	Henry Gonzalez	Andres Vega Jr	Melissa Morales	Pete Gonzalez Jr	Ramiro Torres	Victor Rodriguez	....
Brownwood (18)	CM 915 646-6056	....	....	....	....	....	....	....
Bryan (55)	CM 409 361-3600	Marvin Tate	Michael A Conduff	Mary L Galloway	Kathy Davidson	James Bland	Lee Freeman	Ed Ilschner
Bunker Hill Village (3)	MC 713 467-9764	G Stubblefield	David F Eby	Gloria A Drabek	Eileen O' Leary	Anthony Calagna	Chris Price	James L Williams
Burkburnett (10)	CM 817 569-2263	Pat Norriss	Gary Bean	Tamara Burchett	Gary Bean	Troy Mills	Curtis Salyer	John Brookman
Burleson (16)	CM 817 295-1113	Rick Roper	Kay Godbey	Jean Phillips	Charles Harris	Kerry Kinney	Harvey Hightower	Bill Davison
Burnet t (3)	CM 512 756-6093	....	....	....	....	....	....	....
Caldwell (3)	CM 409 567-3271	Bernard E Rychlik	William Broaddus	....	William Broaddus	Douglas Beavers	Willie J Kovar	William Broaddus
Cameron (6)	MC 817 697-6646	James E Lafferty	Lanny C French	Janet Sheguit	Lanny C French	Thomas Harwell	Leonard Doskocil	Lanny C French
Canadian t (2)	CM 806 323-6473	....	....	....	....	....	....	....
Canton (3)	CM 903 567-2826	....	....	....	....	....	....	....
Canyon (11)	CM 806 655-5000	Lois Rice	Glen R Metcalf	James W Glenn	Howard Morris	Joe Rice	Bobby Griffin	Mark Clark
Carrizo Springs (6)	CM 210 876-2476	Maria B Mendiola	Richard Cantu	Mario A Martinez	....	Jose L Rodriguez	....	....
Carrollton (82)	CM 214 466-3000	Gary Blanscet	Dan Johnson	Janice Carroll	Bob Scott	Bruce Varner	David James	Bobby Atteberry
Carthage (6)	CM 903 693-3868	....	....	....	....	....	....	....
Castle Hills (4)	MC 512 342-2341	....	....	....	....	....	....	....
Cedar Hill (20)	CM 214 291-5100	....	....	....	....	....	....	....
Cedar Park (5)	CM 512 258-4121	Dorthey Duckett	Daron K Butler	Nancy Faulkner	Wesley J Vela	....	Robert L Young	Sam P Roberts
Center (5)	CM 409 598-2941	....	Jeff K Ellington	Shirley Green	Melinda Brittain	Tommie Fenley	Jimmy Matthews	Dallon Permentor
Childress (5)	CM 817 937-3684	....	....	....	....	....	....	....
Cisco (4)	CM 817 442-2111	Joe Wheatley	Michael Moore	Ginger Johnson	Maryann Perry	Joe Jarvis	Douglas Fairbanks	Leon Boles
Clarksville (4)	CM 903 427-3834	Mark Lewis	Robert E Moore	Melissa Gibson	....	....	....	....
Cleburne (22)	CM 817 645-0917	Katherine Raines	Joel Victory	Jean Hamilton	Greg Wilmore	Lloyd McVicker	Tom Cowan	Larry Barkman
Cleveland (7)	CM 713 592-2667	....	W N Petropolis	Carol Sherrard	Caroline Cox	Steve Wheeler	Ike Hines	Alton D Alford
Clifton (3)	MC 817 675-8337	....	....	....	....	....	....	....
Clute (9)	MC 713 265-2541	....	....	....	....	....	....	....
Clyde t (3)	MC 915 893-4234	Robert J Gwilt	....	C Jean Gilmore	....	Rick Gilmore	Ronald L Young	Norman Smith
Cockrell Hill (4)	MC 214 330-6333	....	....	....	....	....	....	....
Coleman (5)	CM 915 625-5114	Woodrow J Maddox	David S Sooter	Joe E Faries	....	Larry Robinson	Larry Titsworth	....
College Station (52)	CM 409 764-3500	Larry Ringer	Ron Ragland	Connie Hooks	Glenn Schroeder	William Kennedy	Edgar Feldman	Mark Smith
Colleyville (13)	CM 817 281-4044	....	....	....	....	....	....	....
Colorado City (5)	CM 915 728-3464	....	....	....	....	....	....	....
Columbus (3)	MC 409 732-2366	Dwain Dungen	John Brasher	Jill Ready	Jill Ready	Robert C Walla	Robert E Connor	Milton Wavra
Comanche (4)	MC 915 356-2616	....	....	....	....	....	....	....
Commerce (7)	CM 903 886-1100	Marna Martinez	Roger McKinney	Carol Roberts	Sue Porter	....	....	James Turney
Conroe (28)	MC 409 539-4431	Carter Moore	Craig Lonon	Marla Porter	Hattie Weisinger	David Miller	John Lindon	Dean Towery
Converse (9)	CM 210 658-5356	Richard Maas	Samuel Hughes	Gracie Beane	Samuel Hughes	Jack Doughtery	Mark D' Spain	Keith Dickerson
Coppell (17)	CM 214 462-0022	Tom Morton	Jim Witt	Dorothy Timmons	Alan Johnson	Clay Phillips	....	Steve Goram
Copperas Cove (24)	CM 817 547-4221	Skip Darossett	....	....	L Leslie Ledger	Ray E Ashcraft	Stephen Klempa	Daniel McIntIre
Corpus Christi (257)	CM 512 880-3000	Mary Rhodes	Jaun Garza	Armando Chapa	Rosie G Vela	Juan J Adame	Henry C Garrett	....
Corsicana (23)	CM 903 654-4803	....	....	....	....	....	....	....
Cotulla (4)	MC 512 879-2367	....	....	....	....	....	....	....
Crane (4)	MC 915 558-3563	....	....	....	....	....	....	....
Crockett (7)	CM 409 544-5156	....	....	....	....	....	....	....
Crowley (7)	MC 817 297-2201	Nancy Behrens	Jay Singleton	....	....	Jeff Stubbs	Armen Tamakian	Jim McDonald
Crystal City (8)	CM 512 374-3477	....	....	....	....	....	....	....
Cuero (7)	CM 512 275-6114	Michael Thamm	John M Trayhan	Corlis Riedesel	John Washburn	Eldred Schultz	W T Allen Jr	....
Daingerfield (3)	CM 903 645-3906	William L Thorne	Margie J Hargrove	Margie J Hargrove	....	Tony Hall	Joe Farino	Marion D Clayton
Dalhart (6)	MC 806 249-5511	Gene Rahl	Greg Duggan	Jan Alexander	Kurt Presley	Max Stipe	Stan Simmons	Steve Fisk
Dallas (1007)	CM 214 670-3563	Steve Bartlett	John L Ware	Robert S Sloan	Jeniffer S Varley	D J Miller	Bennie Ray Click	Ramon F Miguez
Dayton t (5)	CM 409 258-2642	....	....	....	....	....	....	Gordon Mayer
De Soto (31)	CM 214 223-4120	David Doyle	....	Jean Garner	Daniel Crawford	....	....	....
Decatur (4)	MC 817 627-2741	Bobby Wilson	Brett Shannon	Brett Shannon	Brett Shannon	Kevin Burns	Rex Hoskins	Robert Gage
Deer Park (28)	CM 713 479-2394	Jimmy Burke	Ronald Crabtree	Shirley Koym	Glenn Windsor	....	Donald Little	Paul Pondish
Del Rio (31)	CM 512 774-8652	Alfredo Gutierrez	Florencio Sauceda	Jayne Douglas	Yvonne Gomez	Howard Baughman	Charlie Bruce	Robert Sifuentez
Denison (22)	CM 903 465-2720	Wayne Cabaniss	Larry Cruise	Barbara Forrest	Andy Wilkins	Bill Taylor	Jimmy Lovell	Jerry White
Denton (66)	CM 314 965-3600	Anthony Monaco	Michael P Pounds	Shirley L Richter	Lori Davis	Gillyette Soffner	Richard Black	Edward Veazey
Denver City t (5)	MC 806 592-5426	....	....	....	....	....	....	....
Devine (4)	MC 210 663-2804	Jerry Beck	Jim Mangum	Delia Ambriz	Sharon Neuman	Gilbert Rodriguez	Doyle Eads	Marshall Davis
Diboll (4)	MC 409 829-4757	....	....	....	....	....	....	....
Dickinson v (9)	MC 713 337-6190	John Mitchiner	Don E Taylor	Patrice Fogarty	Debra Wennagel	Jasper Liggio	Wayne Broussard	Ed Barmore
Dilley t (3)	MC 210 965-1624	John Moore	Irma Rodriguez	....	....	Gerald Burris	Santos Martinez	Raymond Castaneda
Dimmitt t (4)	MC 806 647-2155	Wayne Collins	Reeford Burrous	Dolores Baldridge	Jo Hamilton	Randy Griffitt	Dewayne Haney	James Killough
Donna (13)	CM 210 464-3314	Hilda Adame	R Diaz DeLeon	Rosa Rodriguez	Holly Mettlach	David Simmons	Steve Gurski	Tomas Garcia
Dublin (3)	MC 817 445-3331	....	....	....	....	....	....	....
Dumas (13)	MC 806 935-4101	....	....	....	....	....	....	....
Duncanville (36)	CM 214 780-5000	Ed Purcell	Dan Savage	Pam Schmidt	Jerry Striplin	Jackie Walton	Michael Courville	Dennis Schwartz
Eagle Lake (4)	CM 409 234-2640	....	....	....	....	....	....	....

City, 1990 population figures (000 omitted), form of government	Municipal phone number	Mayor/ chief elected official	Appointed administrator	City clerk/ city secretary	Finance officer	Fire chief	Police chief	Public works director
TEXAS (427) continued								
Eagle Pass (21)	CM 512 773-1111	Raul Trevino Jr	Susana Gomez	....	Manuel Contreras	Guadalupe Cardona	Juan A Castaneda	Jose O Sanchez
Early (2)	CM 915 643-5451	Earl Rhea	Ken Thomas	Deloris Walker	Deloris Walker	Bryan Chambers	Charles Thomas	Raymond Edwards
Eastland (4)	CM 817 629-8321	C W Hoffman Jr	Paul Catoe	Karen Moore	Juanita Grisham	....	Cecil Funderburgh	Steve Jameson
Edcouch t (3)	CM 512 262-2140	....	....	Linda Crump	....	....	....	....
Edgecliff Village t (3)	MC 817 293-4313	Bill Sherman	....	Linda Crump	....	....	....	Michael Duehring
Edinburg (30)	CM 210 383-5661	Joe Ochoa	John R Milford	Maria M Corona	Jose H Gonzalez	Johnny Economedes	Quirino Munoz	Arnoldo Vera
Edna (5)	CM 512 782-3122	Joe D Hermes	Nicholas P Caruso	Becky Ratliff	Nicholas P Caruso	....	Norman Glaze	....
El Campo (11)	CM 409 543-5361	....	Terry Roberts	Diane Kaluza	John Steelman	Jack Roberts	Jimmy Elliott	Larry Keesler
El Lago (3)	MC 713 326-1951	....	....	....	....	....	....	....
El Paso (515)	MC 915 541-4000	Larry G Francis	Kenneth E Beasley	Carole A Hunter	William Chapman	Andrew F Mehl	....	....
Electra (3)	CM 817 495-2146	Jim Bentley	David Vestal	Tracey Lowe	Bob Meeks	Johnny Thompson	J W Mayfield	Ed Helton
Elgin (5)	MC 512 285-5721	Eric W Carlson	Jack A Harzke	....	Loren Mayfield	Wayne Siegmund	William Smith	Gary N Cooke
Elsa (5)	CM 512 262-2127	....	....	....	....	....	....	....	....
Ennis (14)	CM 214 875-1234	Bill Lewis	Steve Howerton	....	Wynell Rose	David Hopkins	Dale Holt	Roy Callahan
Euless (38)	CM 817 685-1400	Mary Lib Saleh	Tom Hart	Susan Crim	Debra B Forte	Lee Koontz	Gary McKamie	Randy Byers
Everman (6)	MC 817 293-0525	Cathey Thurston	David Hunnicutt	Donna Anderson	David Hunnicutt	Donnie Hurd	Randy Sanders	....
Fairfield (3)	MC 903 389-2633	Luke Ward Jr	Ted Mayo	Judy Sneed	Amanda Carroll	Steve James	Jim Kellum	Charles Myers
Falfurrias (6)	CO 512 325-2420	....	....	....	....	....	....	....	....
Farmers Branch (24)	CM 214 247-3131	Dave Blair	Richard Escalante	....	Charles Cox	Kyle King	Jimmy Fawcett	Mark Pavageaux
Farmersville (3)	CM 214 782-6151	George G Crump	Randall E Holly	Paula Jackson	Shirley Horton	....	Gregory A Gorden	Alan Hein
Flatonia t (1)	CM 512 865-3548	....	....	....	....	....	....	....	....
Floresville (5)	MC 512 393-3105	....	....	....	....	....	....	....	....
Flower Mound t (16)	CM 214 539-6006	Larry W Lipscomb	Van James	Ruth DeShaw	Linda Truitt	Eric Metzger	Paul Griffith	Robert Stengele
Floydada t (4)	CM 806 983-2834	Hulon Carthel	Gary Brown	Sharon Quisenberr	Gary Brown	Bobby Welborn	James Hale	Jim Green
Forest Hill (11)	CM 817 568-3000	Donald Walker	Edward Badgett	Janie Willman	Cecil Berry	Paul Philbin	Rebecca Coleman	William McDonald
Fort Stockton (9)	CM 915 336-8525	....	....	....	....	....	....	....	....
Fort Worth (448)	CM 817 871-8900	Kay Granger	Robert Terrell	Alice Church	Charles Boswell	H L McMillen	Thomas Windham	....
Fredericksburg t (7)	MC 512 997-7521	....	....	....	....	....	....	....	....
Freeport (11)	CM 409 233-3526	James Barnett	Gary Stone	Jan Spencer	J Vandergrifft	Bob Johnson	Pedro Flores	Meryl Walters
Freer (3)	MC 512 394-6612	Malloy A Hamilton	....	Hilda Rosales	....	James Finney	George Gomez Jr	....
Friendswood (23)	CM 713 482-6491	E Newman	R Cox	D McKenzie	....	....	J Stout	M Meinecke
Friona (4)	CM 806 247-2761	....	....	....	....	....	....	....	....
Frisco (6)	MC 214 335-5555	Bob Warren	George Purefoy	Nan Parker	Patrica Reinhart	Mack Borchardt	Todd Renshaw	Gary Hartwell
Fritch (2)	CM 806 857-3143	....	....	....	....	....	....	....	....
Gainesville (14)	CM 817 665-4523	Jim J Hatcher	Lyle H Dresher	Rita Gray	Phill Conner	Steve Boone	Carl Dunlap	Jim Gray
Galena Park (10)	MC 713 672-2556	James B Havard	Barbara Nugent	....	Barbara Nugent	Bruce Glover	Johnny McDonald	E C Day
Galveston (59)	CM 409 766-2113	Barbara Crews	Douglas Matthews	Anna Lee	Bob Richardson	Willie Wisko	Dale Rodgers	Kathi Flowers
Garland (181)	CM 214 205-2000	James Ratliff	....	Ranette Boyd	George E Kauffman	Daniel Grammer	....	....
Gatesville (11)	CM 817 865-8951	Wyllis Ament	Bob Stevens	Darleen Hodges	Evelyn Thomas	Billy Vaden	Carroll Duke	Robert Patterson
George West (3)	CM 512 449-1556	August Caron Jr	Jack Fendley	Terri Garza	....	Bob Wientjes	Roy Kraus	....
Georgetown (15)	CM 512 930-3636	Leo Wood	Edwin R Hart	Sandra D Lee	Susan L Morgan	....	Larry M Hesser	James H Briggs
Giddings (4)	CM 409 542-2311	Lavonne D Morrow	James E Dover	Dianne Schneider	....	Robert Kuehn	Dennis R Oltmann	Serapio Garza
Gilmer (5)	CM 903 843-2552	Roy Owens	R Timothy Gump	Peggy J Smith	....	Mike Waller	A L McAllister	Donnie Bond
Gladewater (6)	CM 903 845-2196	Jackie D Wood	Sharon Johnson	Sandra Rhea	Barbara Kennedy	Wayne Smith	Jimmy Davis	Roy Perryman
Gonzales (7)	CM 512 672-2815	....	....	....	....	....	....	....	....
Graham (9)	CM 817 549-3324	....	....	....	....	....	....	....	....
Granbury (4)	CM 817 573-1114	....	....	....	....	....	....	....	....
Grand Prairie (100)	CM 214 660-8000	....	....	....	....	....	....	....	....
Grand Saline (3)	MC 903 962-1322	....	....	....	....	....	....	....	....
Grapevine (29)	CM 817 481-0300	W D Tate	Trent Petty	Linda Huff	Larry Koonce	Bill Powers	Tom Martin	Jerry Hodge
Greenville (23)	CM 903 457-3100	Sue Ann Harting	Edward Thatcher	Patricia Merrell	Lee Maness	Robert Wood	Barry Paris	Massoud Ebrahim
Gregory (2)	MC 512 643-6562	Louis Galvan	....	Olivia Saldivar	....	....	Dan DeLeon	Mario Zapata
Groesbeck (3)	MC 817 729-3293	Jim Longbotham	....	Martha Stanton	....	Dwain Funderburk	Charles Walker	Keith Tilley
Groves (17)	CM 409 962-4471	....	....	....	....	....	....	....	....
Hallettsville (3)	MC 512 798-3681	Don R Jones	David J Drury Jr	....	Sharon Rose	Anthony Ludwig	Elmo Grant	William Cardiff
Haltom City (33)	CM 817 834-7341	Trae Fowler	Bill Eisen	Helen Harris	Patrick Elfrink	Jerry McEntire	Andrew Burt	Kenneth Slovak
Hamilton (3)	MC 817 386-8116	....	....	....	....	....	....	....	....
Hamlin (3)	MC 915 576-2711	Melvin J Scott	....	Oletha Waldrop	....	Holman Jones	Ronnie Hill	....
Harker Heights (13)	CM 817 699-2301	Stewart Meyer	Steve Carpenter	Patricia Brunson	Alberta Barrett	Leon Charpentier	John Drake	Joe Goodman
Harlingen (49)	CM 210 427-8700	H William Card Jr	Natalie Prim	....	Jerry Dale	Sigfredo Cantu	James Scheopner	Ruben Diaz
Haskell (3)	MC 817 864-2355	Ken Lane	Sam Watson	Loretta Gray	Sam Watson	E J Stewart	Tom Bassett	Dave Miller
Hearne (5)	MC 409 279-3461	....	....	....	....	....	....	....	....
Hedwig Village (3)	MC 713 465-6009	Robert I Goehrs	Lana Rizzuto	Lana Rizzuto	Lana Rizzuto	Anthony Calagna	William G Rush	Paul H Addington
Hempstead (4)	MC 409 826-2486	....	....	....	....	....	....	....	....
Henderson (11)	CM 903 657-6551	Chester Johnson	Earl Heath	Patsy Farley	Nancy Jackson	Dwayne Pirtle	Randall Freeman	Connie Monk
Henrietta t (3)	CM 817 538-4316	Scott Catlin	Joe Pence	Betty Thorn	Joe Pence	Tom Griffin	Tom Griffin	R D McAlister
Hereford (15)	CM 806 364-2123	Bob Josserand	Chester Nolen	....	Mike Hatley	Jadie Spain	David Wagner	....
Hewitt (9)	CM 817 666-6171	Pike Anderson	Dennis Woodard	Betty A Orton	Dennis Woodard	Tom Lucenay	Jack L Caswell	Paul Holroyd
Highland Park t (9)	CM 214 521-4161	Wade C Smith	L A Patterson	....	Bill Pollock	Darrel Fant	Darrel Fant	James Fisher Jr
Highland Village (7)	CM 214 317-2558	Bruce Lockhart	Robert McDaniel	Paula Lawrence	Alan Dickerson	Glen Harris	....	Chris Curry
Hillsboro (7)	CM 817 582-3271	Henry Moore	Gene Cravens	....	Frankie Lahr	....	Jackie Halbert	Terry Hafer
Hitchcock (6)	MC 409 986-5591	....	....	....	....	....	....	....	....
Hollywood Park (3)	MC 512 494-2023	....	....	....	....	....	....	....	....
Hondo (6)	MC 210 426-3378	Mary J Lopez	Scott Wall	Beatric Cervantez	....	....	....	....
Houston (1631)	MC 713 247-1000	Bob Lanier	Richard Lewis	Anna Russell	Richard Lewis	Edward Corral	Samuel Nuchia	J Schindewolf
Humble (12)	MC 713 446-3061	Hayden E McKay	....	Georgia B Fields	James P Baker	Max W Cullum	Jack W Fulbright	Barry K Brock
Hunters Creek Village (4)	MC 713 465-2150	....	....	....	....	....	....	....	....
Huntsville (28)	CM 409 295-6471	William Hodges	Gene Pipes	Dana Welter	Patricia Allen	Joe French	Hank Eckhardt	Boyd Wilder
Hurst (34)	CM 817 281-6160	....	....	....	....	....	....	....	....
Hutchins (3)	MC 214 225-6121	....	....	....	....	....	....	....	....
Ingleside (6)	CM 512 776-2517	M C Rittiman Jr	Steve Fitzgibbons	Marilyn Hall	Gayle Goble	Claude Perkins	Randy Wright	George Kneuper
Iowa Park (6)	MC 817 592-2131	Wayne House	Michael C Price	Janice Newman	Donna Koehler	Danny Skinner	Ray Smock	Belvin Lytle
Irving (155)	CM 214 721-2600	....	....	....	....	....	....	....	....
Jacinto City (9)	CM 713 674-8424	David Gongre	Joann Griggs	Joyce Raines	Joann Griggs	Guadalupe Azocar	Joseph Clark	John Cooper
Jacksboro (3)	CM 817 567-6321	Jerry Craft	Leroy Lane	Oneta Tanner	Oneta Tanner	Larry Weaver	Arthur Reaves	John Ash
Jacksonville (13)	CM 903 586-3510	Larry Durrett	Jim Anderson	Shine Chancellor	Dewey Jones	Rodney Kelley	Floyd Stiefer	....
Jasper (7)	CM 409 384-4651	Frank R Lindsey	Kerry M Lacy	Betty B Glenn	Judy C Nash	James Gunter	Harlan Alexander	Joe Matthews
Jefferson (2)	MC 214 665-3922	....	....	....	....	....	....	....	....
Jersey Village (5)	CM 713 466-6159	B Michael Descant	R Dale Brown	Laverne M Hale	....	Kathleen Hutchens	Michael G Lindsey	John T Horton
Jones Creek v (2)	MC 409 233-1826	Wayne DuBose	Tamie Schmidt	Araveila Ortiz	....	....	Howard Rape	....
Jourdanton (3)	CM 512 769-3589	....	....	....	....	....	....	....	....
Junction (3)	CO 915 446-2622	....	....	....	....	....	....	....	....
Karnes City t (3)	MC 210 780-3422	Don Tymrak	David Carrothers	Amelia Martinez	....	Charles Malik	Nolan Jonas	Michael Theriot

Directory 1/9
continued

MUNICIPAL OFFICIALS
IN U.S. CITIES OVER 2,500

City, 1990 population figures (000 omitted), form of government	Municipal phone number	Mayor/ chief elected official	Appointed administrator	City clerk/ city secretary	Finance officer	Fire chief	Police chief	Public works director
TEXAS (427) continued								
Katy (8)	MC 713 391-9181	....	....	....	....	....	....	....
Kaufman (5)	CM 214 932-2216	Jess M Murrell	Dennis Berry	Joann Talbot	Patrica Garrett	Eddie Brown	Johnny Riggins	....
Keene (4)	MC 817 641-3336	Gary Heinrich	....	Carol Landau	....	David Wilkes	Regan Scherencel	Ronald Bradley
Keller (14)	CM 817 431-1517	John Buchanan	....	Sheila Stephens	Beverly Queen	Kelly King	William Griffith	Mike Barnes
Kenedy (4)	MC 210 583-2230	Ruhman C Franklin	Joe Ed Ponish	Debbie Theuret	....	....	Dennis Fenner	Gary Wegner
Kennedale (4)	CM 817 478-5418	Bill Abbott	Ted Rower	Kathy Turner	Vicki Thompson	David Arnold	David Geeslin	Joey Highfill
Kermit (7)	CM 915 586-3460	Ted Westmoreland	A Wayne Reynolds	Melody Salmons	Lynette Burleson	Bobby Arnold	David Norwood	Jon R Ford
Kerrville (17)	CM 210 257-8000	....	Glenn Brown	Sheila Brand	Dane Tune	Raymond Holloway	Chuck Dickerson	George Kerr
Kilgore (11)	CM 903 984-5081	Bob Barbee	Ron Stephens	Karen Brock	....	....	Ronnie Moore	Charles Overbeck
Killeen (64)	CM 817 634-2191	Raul Villaronga	Talmadge Buie	Paula Miller	Connie Green	Ken Arnold	F L Giacomozzi	Bennie Heddon
Kingsville (25)	CM 512 595-8017	....	Carlos Lerma	Diana Ramirez	Hector Hinojosa	Juan Torres	Felipe Garza	Meg Conner
Kirby (8)	CM 512 661-3198	....	....	....	....	....	....	....
Kountze (2)	MC 409 246-3463	....	....	....	....	....	....	....
La Feria (4)	MC 210 797-2261	Paul F Beechner	Sunny K Philip	Alberto Martinez	Reynaldo Burnias	Mario Prado	Gerald P Senk	Javier Martinez
La Grange (4)	CM 409 968-5805	....	....	....	....	....	....	....
La Marque (14)	CM 409 938-9202	Pete W Rygaard	Nicholas Finan	Carol McLemore	Terry Knudsen	....	Larry Crow	Rick Malbrough
La Porte (28)	CM 713 471-5020	Norman L Malone	Robert T Herrera	Sue Lenes	Jeff Litchfield	Joe Sease	Bobby Powell	Steve Gillett
Lacy-Lakeview (4)	MC 817 799-2458	Charles W Doherty	....	Jean Perkins	Jean Perkins	Donnie Garner	Terry Fiene	John W Powell
Lake Dallas (4)	MC 817 497-2226	Jerry McCutcheon	....	Donna Hamilton	....	....	Nick Ristagno	....
Lake Jackson (23)	CM 409 297-2481	Doris Williams	William P Yenne	Charles Smith	Pam Eaves	Steve S Hultz	P C Miller	Dyson Campbell
Lake Worth Village (5)	MC 817 237-1211	J T Hinkle	Mark Todd	....	....	Mark Cone	Ron Wadkins	Monte Taylor
Lamesa (11)	CM 806 872-2124	....	....	....	....	....	....	....
Lampasas (6)	CM 512 556-6831	Jack Calvert	Kim Foutz	Cherry Hargrove	Greg Westerfield	John Rathman	L D Bender	Randy Clark
Lancaster (22)	CM 214 227-2111	Margie Waldrop	William Gaither	Jackie Denman	Pauline Hodges	Donald McMullan	Malcolm McGuire	Robert Foster
Laredo (123)	CM 512 791-7300	....	....	....	....	....	....	....
League City (30)	MC 713 332-3431	....	Henry Brummett	Gretchen Black	Henry Brummett	Walton Daugherty	Bill Stannard	James Malone
Leon Valley (10)	MC 210 684-1391	....	Greg Ingham	Chris Wade	Judy Stephens	Thurman Davis	Ted Holder	Kenneth Rumbaugh
Levelland (14)	CM 806 894-0113	Raymond Dennis	Charles Owens	Alan E Guard	Joseph C Barrett	George R Corbin	Steve McFadden	Steven L Bacchus
Lewisville (47)	CM 214 219-3450	Bobbie Mitchell	Norman W Dykes	....	Bruce Mintz	Jamie Galloway	Billy Tidwell	....
Liberty (8)	CM 409 336-3684	Paul J Henry	Marty Mangum	Amalia Martinez	....	Don Huckabey	Gary Lightfoot	Jimmy Durham
Littlefield (6)	CM 806 385-5161	Ray G Keeling	Douglas G Faseler	Marian H Elbel	....	Brian D Elbel	Mark A Wagster	Mark A Wagster
Live Oak (10)	CM 210 653-9140	Ray Hildebrand	Sam Gordon	Marilyn Sutton	Marilyn Sutton	Corky Cochran	Dennis Clifton	Richard Walker
Livingston (5)	CM 409 327-4311	Ben R Ogletree Jr	Tom Donaldson	....	....	Beverly Harden	Stacey Nobles	Harold Underwood
Llano (3)	MC 915 247-4158	Jeffrey Hope	Joe Michie	Gwen Barrett	Mike McElhaney	John Walters	Mark Hinnenkamp	Ralph Gerald
Lockhart (9)	CM 512 398-3461	M Louis Cisneros	....	Lois G McCaleb	Al L Milligan Jr	Walter L Fort	Johnny Upton	Pedram Farahnak
Longview (70)	CM 903 237-1000	I J Patterson	Bob N Cass	Betty M Johnson	Robert Massengale	Donald L Stevens	Ken A Walker	....
Lubbock (186)	CM 806 767-3000	David R Langston	C G Mac Lin	Atha Stokes	Darryl Mayfield	Fenton Prowit	E Sherman Collins	Ron Wesch
Lufkin (30)	CM 409 634-8881	Louis Bronaugh	Randy G Thomas	Ruby L White	Pat Jackson	Paul Stahl	Travis Thomas	Sam Jernigan
Luling (5)	CM 210 875-2481	John A Moore	....	....	....	....	....	....
Madisonville (4)	CM 409 348-2748	....	Clayton Chandler	Judy Howard	Tommie Johnson	Bob Looney	Coy Martin	....
Mansfield (16)	CM 817 473-9371	Duane Murray	....	....	....	Steve Del Bello	John Rose	....
Manvel (4)	MC 713 489-0630	Merl Bradley	....	....	....	....	....	....
Marble Falls t (4)	CM 512 693-3615	....	....	....	....	....	....	....
Marlin (6)	MC 817 883-5542	....	....	....	....	....	....	....
Marshall (24)	CM 903 935-4416	....	....	....	....	Lucio Munoz	Rene Rios	Fred F Farias
Mathis (5)	MC 512 547-3343	Eva F Medrano	Pedro Cavazos	....	....	....	A Longoria	Alvaro Gonzalez
Mc Allen (84)	CM 210 686-6551	Othal E Brand	Mike R Perez	Letty Vacek	Guillermo Seguin	Everett Derr	Mike Cook	Dave Faubion
Mc Gregor (5)	CM 817 840-2806	Felix Morris	Bill Dake	Christine Otter	Bill Dake	Ronnie Spradley	....	....
Mc Kinney (21)	CM 214 542-2675	John Gay	Donald E Paschal	Jennifer Smith	Nell Lange	Robert Hultkrantz	....	....
Meadows (5)	MC 806 539-2377	Dale Wylie	....	Jerry Blair	....	Joe Perez	....	....
Memphis (2)	MC 806 259-3001	....	....	....	....	....	....	....
Menard (2)	CM 915 396-4616	....	....	....	....	....	....	....
Mercedes (13)	CM 512 565-3114	....	....	....	....	....	....	....
Mesquite (101)	CM 214 288-7711	Cathye Ray	James A Prugel	....	....	Don R Nelson	Travis L Hass	Morris Bishop
Mexia (7)	CM 817 562-4100	Stanley Cotton	James K White	Nancy Ridge	....	Aaron Thompson	Rodger Cotton	Tommy Vaughan
Midland (89)	CM 915 685-7100	Bobby Burns	Michael McGregor	Bill Clanton	Troy Gifford Jr	James Roberts	Richard Czech	Harvey Hansen
Midlothian (5)	CM 214 775-3481	....	....	....	....	....	....	....
Mineola (4)	MC 214 569-6183	....	....	....	....	....	....	....
Mineral Wells (15)	CM 817 328-1478	Myron Crawford	Lance Howerton	Neta Mason	K Archambault	Jerry Vannatta	Jerry White	Don Dietrich
Mission (29)	CM 210 580-8681	Richard Perez	John Vidaurri	Ramona Martinez	J R Gonzalez	Armando Ocana	Patrick Dalager	Juan Barrera
Missouri City (36)	CM 713 261-4260	....	David Mills	Sheri Lord	....	....	Dave Watts	Bobby Sinclair
Monahans (8)	CM 915 943-4343	David B Cutbirth	Brad Stafford	....	....	Jerry Arthur	....	....
Morton t (3)	MC 806 266-8850	Ray Lewis	Richard E Chaffin	Brenda Reynolds	Brenda Reynolds	Larry McRae	Ted Gibson	Pete Donnelly
Mount Pleasant (12)	CM 903 572-3412	Jim Blanchard	Dave Marr Jr	Mary Hicks	....	Donald Harrison	Julian Dominguez	Cleve Bland
Muleshoe (5)	CM 806 272-4528	Robert Montgomery	David K Stall	Vicky L Hawkins	....	James McGee	Richard Holden	Phil Briscoe
Nacogdoches (31)	CM 409 564-4693	....	Harold Underwood	....	Geraldine Binford	Ronald Busse	Chris P Siracusa	Gary E Johnson
Nassau Bay (4)	CM 713 333-4211	Donald Johnson	Bill Storey	Ladonna Floyd	....	Mike Lovelady	Billy Neal	Steve Hamilton
Navasota (6)	CM 409 825-6475	Bill Miller Jr	....	Carol Ensey	....	Billy R House	Kerry Pinkham	R C Thomas
Nederland (16)	CM 409 723-1501	Carl N Leblanc	Mike Shands	Veronica Sarkozi	Sharon Day	Phil Baker	C R Headen	Mike Shands
New Boston t (5)	MC 903 628-5596	Hubert C May	....	....	....	....	....	....
New Braunfels (27)	CM 210 608-2100	Paul Fraser	Rodger N Line	Jeanette Rewis	Larry Cunningham	Stan Gertz	Jerry McGlasson	Greg Dickens
Nocona (3)	MC 817 825-3281	....	....	....	....	....	....	....
North Richland Hills (46)	MC 817 581-5500	Tommy Brown	Jerry McGuire	Jerri Sullivan	James Zentner	James Wiggs	James Jenkins	Matt Squyres
Oak Ridge North (2)	MC 713 292-4648	....	....	....	....	....	....	....
Odessa (90)	CM 915 337-7381	Lorraine Perryman	Byron E Hollinger	Terry E Strickler	....	Vincent Lancaster	Michael K Ullevig	....
Olmos Park (2)	CM 210 824-3281	Gerald Z Dubinski	Jack Northrup	Lee Ann Campbell	Jean Clifton	Garry Keeter	Cliff Blackstock	Ronnie Stroud
Olney (4)	MC 817 564-2102	Marc Wipperman	Charles W Pinto	Judy Davis	Gail English	Jerry Wimberly	Sam Kittrell	James P Foyle
Orange (19)	CM 409 886-3611	Dan Cochran	....	....	....	....	....	....
Palacios (4)	MC 512 972-3605	....	....	....	....	....	....	....
Palestine (18)	CM 903 729-2181	....	....	....	....	....	....	....
Pampa (20)	CM 806 669-5700	....	Thomas J Blazek	....	....	Richard Robinson	Kenneth J Rogers	Len Jennings
Panhandle (2)	CM 806 537-3517	Les McNeill	Larry Smith	Tracy Norr	Mary Harrison	Doug Davis	Doug Davis	Ronnie Gibson
Pantego t (2)	CM 817 274-1381	Bob Surratt	....	....	....	....	....	....
Paris (25)	CM 903 785-7511	....	....	....	....	....	....	....
Pasadena (119)	MC 713 477-1511	....	Paul Grohman	Pat Jones	Janet Eastburn	Larry Steed	P M Hogg	Ronald McWhirter
Pearland (19)	CM 713 485-2411	Vic Coppinger	....	....	....	....	....	....
Pearsall (7)	CM 512 334-3676	....	David A Landis	Janice M Henson	Don D Jennings	C B Luther	Joseph E Hannon	Teb B Dodd
Pecos (12)	CM 915 445-2421	....	....	....	....	....	....	....
Perryton (8)	MC 806 435-4014	David Hale	....	....	....	....	....	....
Pharr (33)	CO 512 787-2703	....	....	....	....	....	....	....
Pinehurst (3)	CM 409 886-2221	....	....	....	....	....	....	....
Piney Point Village (3)	MC 713 782-0271	....	Ned C Muse	Sue Sharp	Sue Sharp	David Abernathy	Weldon Reynolds	Wayne Hadderton
Pittsburg (4)	MC 903 856-3621	D H Abernathy						

Directory 1/9 continued — **MUNICIPAL OFFICIALS IN U.S. CITIES OVER 2,500**

City, 1990 population figures (000 omitted), form of government		Municipal phone number	Mayor/ chief elected official	Appointed administrator	City clerk/ city secretary	Finance officer	Fire chief	Police chief	Public works director
TEXAS (427) continued									
Plainview (22)	CM	806 296-1100	....	....	....	....	....	....	....
Plano (129)	CM	214 424-6531	James Muns	T Muehlenbeck	J Blakely	John McGrane	William Peterson	Bruce Glasscock	James R Hogan
Pleasanton (8)	CM	512 569-3867	Bob Hurley	Larry Pippen	Kathy McMullen	....	Chunck Garris	Keith Blair	Bill Lamb
Port Aransas (2)	CM	512 749-4111	James Sherrill	Tommy Brooks	Esther O Arzola	Judy Lyle	Mark Young	Don R Perkins	Carl Castell
Port Arthur (59)	CM	409 983-8101	Mary E Summerlin	Cornelius Boganey	Carolyn Dixon	Walter Thomas	Clifford Barbay	Melbourne Gorris	Leslie McMahen
Port Isabel (4)	CM	210 943-2682	Calvin Byrd	Manuel Hinojosa	Ernestina Barrera	Loretta Streif	Robert Harris	Charles Londrie	....
Port Lavaca (11)	CM	512 552-9795	Tiney Browning	C J Webster	....	John Iles	Larry Steen	Allen Tharling	Bob Coen
Port Neches (13)	CM	409 727-2181	....	....	....	....	....	....	....
Portland (12)	CM	512 643-6501	Billy G Webb	Patrick Conner	Norma S Lockhart	Sarah Murphy	....	Harrold White	Kim Parker
Post (4)	MC	806 495-2811	Jim Jackson	Rick L Hanna	Wyvonne Kennedy	Rick L Hanna	Ronny Menser	....	Mike Sanchez
Poteet (3)	MC	512 742-3574	....	....	....	....	....	....	....
Prairie View (4)	MC	409 857-3711	....	....	....	....	....	....	....
Premont (3)	MC	512 348-2022	....	....	....	....	....	....	....
Princeton t (2)	MC	214 736-2416	Bill Caldwell	....	....	....	Bill Caldwell	Allen Gibson	....
Quanah (3)	MC	817 663-5336	....	....	....	....	....	....	....
Ranger (3)	CO	817 647-3522	Ronnie Ainsworth	Barbara Wheat	Billy Gene Tedfor	Buddy Vinson	Darrell Fox	Clark Crane	Samuel Sanchez
Raymondville (9)	CM	512 689-2443	C M Crowell	Jose L Lopez	....	Jose L Lopez	Fred Ramirez	Rene R Martin	Octavio A Correa
Refugio (3)	MC	512 526-5361	....	....	....	....	....	....	....
Richardson (75)	CM	214 238-4150	Gary Slagel	Bob Hughey	Ina Garber	Daniel Parker	Bobby Holley	Kenneth Yarbrough	Marshall Haney
Richland Hills t (8)	CM	817 595-6600	C F Kelley	Stephen D Hughes	....	....	Greg Tucker	Barbara Childress	Robert Osborn
Richmond t (10)	CM	713 342-5456	Hilmar G Moore	R Glen Gilmore	Mona Matak	....	Stephen Noto	A M Gibson	Mark Zgabay
Richwood (3)	MC	409 265-2082	James M Vera	....	Karen B Schrom	Karen B Schrom	Rick Cary	Glenn Patton	Ralph M Harper
River Oaks (7)	MC	817 626-5421	....	....	....	....	....	....	....
Robinson (7)	MC	817 662-1425	....	....	....	....	....	....	....
Robstown (13)	MC	512 387-4589	Hector Gallegos	Jesse B Guerra	Norma Nunez	Jesse B Guerra	Julio M Flores	Rene DeAlejandro	Roy L Gutierrez
Rockdale (5)	MC	512 446-2511	Bill T Avrett	Sue Foster	....	....	Elvis McQuinn	R D Wilmeth	J P Voyles
Rockport (5)	CM	512 729-2213	Raymond O' Brien	M H Gildon	Myrna L Mokry	Debbie Littleton	Mitchel Ammons	Lowell T Jayroe	Billy Dick
Rockwall (10)	CM	214 771-7700	Alma Williams	Julie Couch	....	Mike Phemister	Mark Poindexter	Bill Watkins	Rick Crowley
Roma (8)	CM	210 849-1411	Alonzo H Alvarez	Rogeio Salinas	Elodia Cruz	....	Gabriel E Recio	Jose H Garcia	....
Rosebud (2)	CM	817 583-7926	....	....	....	....	....	....	....
Rosenberg (20)	MC	713 342-3850	....	....	....	....	....	....	....
Round Rock (31)	CM	512 255-3612	Charles Culpepper	Robert Bennett	....	David Kautz	Lynn Bizzel	Wes Wolff	Jim Nuse
Rowlett (23)	CM	214 412-6100	Mark Enoch	James M Gibson	Glenna Bean	Ron Hutchison	Joe Howard	Randall Posey	Nathan Stewart
Rusk t (4)	CM	903 683-2213	Mike Crysup	Brenda Williams	Fran Wendeborn	Brenda Williams	Wayne Morgan	Larry Robertson	Billy Ballard
Sachse (5)	CM	214 495-1212	Larry Holden	Lloyd Henderson	....	Pam Dennis	Doug Kendrick	Tom Fenley	Daniel Martin
Saginaw (9)	CM	817 232-4640	John Ed Keeter	Pat Moffatt	....	Nan Stanford	James England	Gene Springer	....
San Angelo (84)	CM	915 657-4221	Dick Funk	Stephen Brown	Carol Rigby	Roland Howard	Daryl Eddy	Russell Smith	Will Wilde
San Antonio (936)	CM	210 299-8360	Nelson Wolff	Alexander Briseno	Norma Rodriguez	Nora Chavez	Robert Ojeda	William O Gibson	John L German
San Augustine t (2)	MC	409 275-2121	Curt Goetz	Alton Shaw	Amelia Jeanes	....	Keith Bradford	John Cartwright	....
San Benito (20)	CM	210 361-3800	Charles Weekley	Richard Torres	Lupita Passement	Ida C Martinez	Armando Lucio	Richard Clark	Hector Jalomo
San Diego (5)	MC	512 279-3341	Alfredo Cardenas	Jose H Jimenez	....	Agapita Everett	Sergio H Garcia	A Escalante	....
San Juan (11)	CM	512 787-9923	Arturo Guajardo	Gilbert Hernandez	Vicki Ramirez	Pete Maldonado	Eddie Garcia	Jorge A Arcaute	Ted Trevino
San Marcos (29)	CM	512 353-4444	Kathy Morris	Larry D Gilley	Janis Womack	William White	Don O' Leary	Larry Kendrick	George Boeker
Sanger (4)	MC	817 458-7930	Nel Armstrong	John Hamilton	Etta Stogsdill	....	Bill Murrell	Benny Erwin	Chuck Tucker
Sansom Park Village (4)	MC	817 626-3791	Merle Easterling	Deana Keplinger	....	Deana Keplinger	Mike Wasser	Ronnie Mackey	Garland Hicks
Santa Fe (8)	CM	409 925-6412	George Willoughby	Vince DiPiazza	Janet Davis	....	Tommy Anderson	Michael Barry	....
Schertz (11)	CM	210 658-7477	Hal Baldwin	Kerry R Sweatt	June G Krause	Debra Kline	Johnny J Woodward	Norman Agee	John Bierschwale
Seabrook (7)	CM	713 474-3201	....	....	....	....	....	....	....
Seagoville (9)	CM	214 287-2050	Neal Wooley	Odis Lacey	Ruth Sorrells	Linnie Weaver	David Maroney	I D Smith	Mike Hitt
Seagraves (2)	MC	806 546-2593	....	....	....	....	....	....	....
Sealy (5)	CM	409 885-3511	Betty Reinbeck	Roger Carlisle	Pauline Small	Roger Carlisle	....	Ronald Novosad	John Maresh
Seguin (19)	CM	210 379-3212	Edward Gotthardt	....	....	LeAnn Piatt	Terry Mayfield	Gary Hopper	....
Selma (1)	MC	210 651-6661	H Friesenhahn	Margie Lubianski	Margie Lubianski	....	Scott Lee	Mark Riffe	Scott Lee
Seminole (6)	CM	915 758-3676	Wayne Mixon	Tommy Phillips	Teresa Howell	Anna Smith	Ricky Strickland	Michael Browne	Gary Duncan
Seymour (3)	MC	817 888-3148	Dick Wirz	Scott Thompson	Judy S Gilbert	Judy S Gilbert	Gene P Robinson	Floyd C Burke	Carl H Parker
Shamrock (2)	CM	806 256-3281	....	....	....	....	....	....	....
Sherman (32)	CM	903 892-4545	....	....	....	....	....	....	....
Silsbee (6)	CM	409 385-2863	Wesley C Latham	Ronald Hickerson	Edna E Brown	Cesar Dominguez	R D Welborn	Dennis M Allen	....
Sinton t (6)	CM	512 364-2381	Jose Gutierrez	Ron Garrison	....	Dennis Lindeman	....	Joe Schumann	Ruben Fonseca
Slaton (6)	MC	806 828-6505	Don Kendrick	Mitch Grant	Kay E Bruedigam	....	Bob Kern	Mike James	Doyce Field
Smithville (3)	CM	512 237-3282	Vernon Richards	Gerald Decker	Brenda Page	Blanda Butler	Mike Davis	E Lee Nusbaum	Jack Page
Snyder (12)	CM	915 573-4957	Paul Zeck	John Gayle	....	Jeanne Johnson	Terry McDowell	Lannie Lee	....
Sonora (3)	MC	915 387-2558	....	....	....	....	....	....	....
South Houston t (14)	MC	713 947-7700	....	....	....	....	....	....	....
South Padre Island t (2)	MC	512 761-6456	....	....	....	....	....	....	....
Southlake (7)	MC	817 481-5581	Gary Fickes	Curtis E Hawk	Sandra L LeGrand	Lou Ann Heath	....	Billy Campbell	Robert Whitehead
Spearman (3)	CM	806 659-2524	Burl Buchanan	Kelvin Knauf	Cheryl Gibson	Kelvin Knauf	Ronnie Antalek	....	....
Spring Valley (3)	CM	713 465-8308	....	....	....	....	....	....	....
Stafford t (8)	MC	713 499-4537	....	....	....	....	....	....	....
Stamford (4)	CM	915 773-2591	....	....	....	....	....	....	....
Stephenville (14)	MC	817 965-7887	....	....	....	....	....	....	....
Sugar Land (25)	CM	713 275-2700	Lee M Duggan	David E Neeley	Glenda Gundermann	Susanne G Barnett	Diane P Breedlove	Earnest B Taylor	Tommy G Haynes
Sulphur Springs (14)	CM	903 885-7541	....	....	....	....	....	....	....
Sundown (2)	MC	806 229-3131	....	....	....	....	....	....	....
Sunray (2)	CM	806 948-4111	....	....	....	....	....	....	....
Sweeny t (3)	MC	409 548-3321	....	....	....	....	....	....	....
Sweetwater (12)	CM	915 236-6313	Jay Lawrence	David Maddox	Russell J Thoma	Russell J Thoma	Jerry Huffman	James Kelley	Dewey Teel
Taft (3)	MC	512 528-3512	....	....	....	....	....	....	....
Tahoka (3)	CM	806 998-4211	....	....	....	....	....	....	....
Taylor (11)	CM	512 352-3675	....	....	....	....	....	....	....
Taylor Lake Village (3)	MC	713 474-2843	....	....	....	....	....	....	....
Teague (3)	MC	817 739-2547	Jereld Sartor	Wm G Wasserman	Stacii Steen	Wm G Wasserman	....	Roger Brookes	Fred Davis
Temple (46)	CM	817 770-5700	J W Perry	David Taylor	Geraldine Goebel	Sam Huey	Edward Clanton	Thomas Vannoy	Leonard Henry
Terrell (12)	CM	214 551-6604	Don L Lindsey	Jim Mullins	....	Bobby Bishop	Michael Roscoe	Geoffrey Whitt	Steve Rogers
Terrell Hills (5)	CM	210 824-7401	Barbara Christian	Cal D Johnson	Edyth E Warren	Cal D Johnson	Arnold G Rose	Barney R Flowers	Juan B Camacho
Texarkana (32)	CM	903 794-0912	....	....	....	....	....	....	....
Texas City (41)	MC	409 948-3111	Charles T Doyle	....	....	....	Gerald J Grimm	Jerry D Purdon	Thomas E Kessler
The Colony (22)	CM	214 625-4756	William Manning	Johnny P Smith	Patti Hicks	James England	Van Morrison	Bruce Stewart	Tom Cravens
Tomball t (6)	CM	713 351-5484	H G Harrington	Warren K Driver	Julie A Stafford	Ben F Griffin	Bruce Preckwinkle	Paul Michna	Robert L Johnson
Tulia (5)	CM	806 995-3547	John C Emmitt	Bryan S Easum	Barbara B Cabe	Barbara C Cabe	Wayne Nevins	Jimmy McCaslin	Foy Campbell
Tyler (75)	CM	903 531-1100	Smith Reynolds	Ernest Clark	Ann Lanier	H V Bryan	Paul White	Larry Robinson	....
Universal City (13)	CM	512 659-0333	....	....	....	....	....	....	....
University Park (22)	CM	214 363-1644	Felix Goldman	Robert Livingston	Bobbie Sharp	Robert Hicks	....	Robert Dixon	Gene Smallwood

Directory 1/9 continued — MUNICIPAL OFFICIALS IN U.S. CITIES OVER 2,500

City, 1990 population figures (000 omitted), form of government		Municipal phone number	Mayor/ chief elected official	Appointed administrator	City clerk/ city secretary	Finance officer	Fire chief	Police chief	Public works director
TEXAS (427) continued									
Uvalde (15)	CM	210 278-3315	Bill McWhorter	Cale Diaz	Rosa Martinez	Janis Erwin	Jim Surber	John W Looper	....
Van Horn (3)	MC	915 283-2050	....	....	....	....	....	....	....
Vernon (12)	CM	817 552-2581	....	....	....	....	....	....	....
Victoria (55)	CM	512 573-2401	Ted B Reed	....	Virginia Yeater	Charles Windwehen	Henry Juenke	Timothy Braaten	....
Vidor (11)	MC	409 769-5473	....	....	....	....	....	....	....
Waco (104)	CM	817 750-5600	Robert Sheehy	James Holgersson	Nana Cornwell	Robert Salter	Robert Mercer	Gilbert Miller	Wayne Dickens
Wake Village (5)	MC	903 838-0515	Mike Huddleston	Bob Long	Maxine Orr	....	Tommy Seale	Tony Estes	Bob Long
Watauga (20)	CM	817 581-4327	A W Girtman	W E Keating	Nancy J Meadows	Debra Maness	....	Bobby R Whitmire	Carlton Addy
Waxahachie (18)	CM	214 937-7330	Mackey Morgan	Robert W Sokoll	Nancy Ross	Carl Wessels	David Hudgins	Allwin Barrow	Frank Davis
Weatherford (15)	CM	817 594-5441	Sherry Watson	Kenneth Reneau	Gloria Wood	Bill Davis	George Teague	Jerry Blaisdell	Ed Banks
Weimar (2)	CM	409 725-8554	....	....	....	....	....	....	....
Wellington (2)	CM	806 447-2544	Gary Brewer	Loretta McKinney	Anne Langford	Jon Sessions	Danny Gray	....	Paul Davis Jr
Weslaco (22)	CM	210 968-3181	Gene A Braught	Wai Lin Lam	Amanda Elizondo	Enrique Guzman	Tony Abrigo	William Roach	Juan Flores
West Columbia (4)	CM	409 345-3123	....	....	....	....	....	....	....
West Orange (4)	MC	409 883-3468	Carl K Thibodeaux	Walter Schexnyder	Linda Morvant	....	Tommy Aven	Bruce Simpson	....
West University Place (13)	CM	713 668-4441	Bill Watson	Michael A Tanner	Kaylynn Holloway	C Taylor	Terry Stevenson	Stephen Griffith	Edward Menville
Westworth Village (2)	MC	817 738-3673	....	....	....	....	....	....	....
Wharton (9)	CM	409 532-2491	Dennis Voulgaris	Andres Garza Jr	....	Lewis M Daws	Everett J Wendel	Timothy Guin	Phillip M Bush
White Oak t (5)	MC	903 759-3936	....	....	....	....	....	....	....
White Settlement (15)	CM	817 246-4971	James Herring	Bob Salinas	Frances Colwell	Joel Welch	....	Richard Mills	Paul Bounds
Whitesboro t (3)	MC	903 564-3311	Alfred C Miller	Joe N West	Lila Beste	....	J T Brown	Larry Macomber	Earnest Moore
Wichita Falls (96)	CM	817 761-7615	Michael Lam	James Berzina	Lydia Torres	Fred Werner	Ronnie James	Curtis Harrelson	George Bonnett
Wills Point (3)	CM	903 873-2578	Bobby Mitchell	C C Girdley	Lillian Samples	....	C C Girdley	Richard Koonce	Scott Drake
Windcrest (5)	MC	210 655-0022	Watson Burnfield	....	Nancy Cain	....	Thomas Winn	F R Cain	Walton Melson
Winnsboro (3)	MC	903 342-3654	....	....	....	....	....	....	....
Winters (3)	CM	915 754-4424	....	....	....	....	....	....	....
Woodville t (3)	MC	409 283-2234	Billy W Rose	Donald W Shaw	Donald W Shaw	Wes Whitworth	Charles Boettcher	Scott Yosko	Donald W Shaw
Woodway (9)	CM	817 772-4480	....	....	Margie Barker	Linda Klump	....	Yousry Zakhary	Dean Conner
Wylie (9)	CM	214 442-2236	Jim Swartz	Steven P Dorwood	Mary Nichols	Brady Snellgrove	Shan English	David Brungardt	Jack Jones
Yoakum (6)	CM	512 293-6321	M W Harbus Jr	A J Veselka	Gladys M Jiral	Charlotte Morrow	David Ferry	Ronald L Leck	Calvin Cook
UTAH (67)									
Alpine (3)	MC	801 756-6347	Joel S Hall	Janis H Williams	Janis H Williams	....	John R Pool	John G Lilly	William H Devey
American Fork (16)	MC	801 756-3571	....	....	....	....	....	....	....
Blanding (3)	CM	801 678-2791	James K Slavens	Norman L Johnson	Rona Flannery	Norman L Johnson	Gorden Hawkins	Mike Halliday	Philip L Palmer
Bountiful (37)	MC	801 298-6140	John R Cushing	Thomas R Hardy	Arden F Jenson	....	Jerry Lemon	Larry Higgins	Jack P Balling
Brian Head t (..)	MC	801 677-2029	....	....	....	....	....	....	....
Brigham City (16)	MC	801 734-2001	Clark N Davis	Roger K Handy	....	Dennis Sheffield	Rodney Romer	Charles G Earl	Bruce Leonard
Cedar City (13)	MC	801 586-2950	Harold Shirley	Joe Melling	Bonnie Moritz	....	Clint Neilsen	J Peter Hansen	....
Centerville (12)	CM	801 295-3477	Priscilla Todd	David Hales	Marilyn Holje	Blaine Lutz	....	Jim Oswald	Randy Randall
Clearfield (21)	CM	801 774-7200	....	....	....	....	....	....	....
Clinton (8)	CM	801 825-5098	....	....	....	....	....	....	....
Draper (7)	MC	801 576-6500	Elaine Redd	David Campbell	Barbara Sadler	LaMont Smith	Boyd Johnson	....	Gordon Haight
Ephraim (3)	MC	801 283-4631	....	....	....	....	....	....	....
Farmington (9)	CM	801 451-2383	....	....	....	....	....	....	....
Fruit Heights (4)	MC	801 546-0861	....	....	....	....	....	....	....
Grantsville (5)	MC	801 884-3411	....	....	....	....	....	....	....
Heber (5)	MC	801 654-0757	Scott Wright	Mark K Anderson	Mark K Anderson	Mark K Anderson	....	Jimmy J Matthews	A Lance Higgs
Helper (2)	MC	801 472-5391	....	....	....	....	....	....	....
Hyrum (5)	MC	801 245-6033	....	....	....	....	....	....	....
Kaysville (14)	CM	801 546-1235	....	....	....	....	....	....	....
Layton (42)	MC	801 546-8500	Jerry Stevenson	Alex Jensen	....	Steven Ashby	Allan Peek	Doyle Talbot	Terry Coburn
Lehi (8)	MC	801 768-8467	....	....	....	....	....	....	....
Lindon (4)	MC	801 785-5043	Scott J Cullimore	E Ray Brown	C Inger Cordner	....	....	....	Don C Peterson
Logan (33)	MC	801 750-9800	Darla D Clark	James Ferguson	....	Donald L Fulton	Danny L Dever	Richard Hendricks	Rod Blossom
Mapleton (4)	MC	801 489-5655	....	....	....	....	....	....	....
Midvale (12)	MC	801 561-1418	J Donald Poulsen	Michael L Siler	....	Ruth Wollshleger	Merrill H Ross	Gerald W Maughan	Duane D Goodyear
Moab (4)	MC	801 259-5121	....	....	....	....	....	....	....
Monticello (2)	MC	801 587-2271	Jack N Young	....	Rita Walker	....	Joe Slade	Kent Adair	Clyde Christensen
Murray (31)	MC	801 264-2656	Lynn Pett	....	....	Don Whetzel	Lee Daugherty	Ken Killian	Charles Clay
Nephi (4)	MC	801 623-0822	Robert L Steele	J Randy McKnight	J Corrine Garrett	R Blair Painter	Boyd Park	Chad M Bowles	Gary Howarth
North Ogden (12)	MC	801 782-7211	....	....	....	....	....	....	....
North Salt Lake (6)	MC	801 298-3877	Clare A Jones	Collin H Wood	Collin H Wood	....	....	Val Wilson	Rodney Wood
Ogden City (64)	MC	801 629-8100	Glenn Mecham	Rocky J Fluhart	Gloria Berrett	L Nate Pierce	Jon Williams	Michael Empey	Causen Anderson
Orem (68)	CM	801 224-7070	....	....	....	....	....	....	....
Panquitch (1)	MC	801 676-8585	Maloy Dodds	Allen K Henrie	Shirley Chidester	....	Russell Bulkley	Martin Nay	David Owens
Park City (4)	MC	801 645-5000	Bradley Olch	Toby Ross	....	Kent Parker	....	Frank Bell	Jerry Gibbs
Payson (10)	MC	801 465-5200	Russell Hillman	Keith Morey	J Prousgard	....	Robert Riding	Mike Openshaw	....
Pleasant Grove (13)	MC	801 785-5045	....	....	....	....	....	....	....
Pleasant View (4)	MC	801 782-8529	....	....	....	....	....	....	....
Price (9)	MC	801 637-5010	....	....	....	....	....	....	....
Providence (3)	MC	801 752-9441	Alma Leonhardt	Brent Speth	Kathleen Gale	....	....	....	Leroy Barnes
Provo (87)	MC	801 379-6182	George O Stewart	Thomas A Martin	Marilyn Perry	George J Karlsven	Rodney C Jones	Swen C Nielsen	Merril Bingham
Richfield (6)	MC	801 896-6439	....	....	....	....	....	....	....
Riverdale (6)	MC	801 394-5541	Ben Jones	Dean Steel	Glenna Stump	Lynn Fortie	Steve Carter	Wayne Hoaldridge	Lynn Moulding
Riverton (11)	MC	801 254-0704	....	....	....	....	....	....	....
Roosevelt (4)	MC	801 722-5001	....	....	....	....	....	....	....
Roy (25)	CM	801 774-1000	Glade Nielsen	Randy Sant	....	Gail Hill	Stan Robins	J R Hammon	Mike Mansfield
Salem (2)	MC	801 423-2770	....	....	....	....	....	....	....
Salt Lake City (160)	MC	801 535-7900	Deedee Corradini	Bryan Hatch	....	Gordon Hoskins	Frank Florence	Ruben Ortega	Catherine Hofmann
Sandy City (75)	MC	801 566-1561	....	....	....	....	....	....	....
Smithfield (6)	MC	801 563-6226	....	....	....	....	....	....	....
South Jordan (12)	MC	801 254-3742	....	....	....	....	....	....	....
South Ogden (12)	MC	801 399-4413	....	....	....	....	....	....	....
South Salt Lake (10)	MC	801 483-6000	Randy Fitts	....	Karen Rynearson	Gail Carlson	Robert Adams	Robert Gray	....
Spanish Fork (11)	CM	801 798-5000	Marie W Huff	David A Oyler	....	Kent R Clark	Lloyd Miller	Dee Rosenbaum	Richard J Heap
Springville (14)	MC	801 489-2700	....	....	....	....	....	....	....
St. George (29)	MC	801 634-5800	Dan McArthur	Gary Esplin	Barbara Hunt	Joe Vincent	Wayne Houston	Jon Pollie	Larry Bulloch
Sunset (5)	MC	801 825-1628	Carol Belmon	....	Vicki Wise	....	Rod Bockwoldt	Philip Olmstead	Mickey Hennessee
Syracuse (5)	MC	801 825-1477	Michael R Garrett	J Michael Moyes	Kathy Holt	J Michael Moyes	Tom Jensen	Brian Wallace	Blaine McDermott
Tooele (14)	MC	801 882-0110	....	....	....	....	....	....	....
Tremonton (4)	MC	801 257-3324	....	....	....	....	....	....	....
Vernal (7)	CM	801 789-2255	Leonard E Heeney	Kenneth L Bassett	Roxanne Behunin	Harley Hales	Dennis Paulson	Michael Hamner	....

Directory 1/9 continued

MUNICIPAL OFFICIALS IN U.S. CITIES OVER 2,500

City, 1990 population figures (000 omitted), form of government	Municipal phone number	Mayor/ chief elected official	Appointed administrator	City clerk/ city secretary	Finance officer	Fire chief	Police chief	Public works director
UTAH (67) continued								
Washington (4)	CM 801 628-1666	Terrill Clove	Ralph McClure	Laura Johnston	....	Richard Wilcox	....	John Van Staveren
Washington Terrace (8)	MC 801 393-8681	....	....	....	....	....	....	....
West Bountiful (4)	MC 801 292-4486	....	....	....	....	....	....	....
West Jordan (43)	CM 801 561-1463	....	....	....	....	....	....	....
West Valley City (87)	CM 801 966-3600	....	....	....	....	....	....	....
Woods Cross (5)	CM 801 292-4421	....	....	....	....	....	....	....
VERMONT (70)								
Barre (9)	CM 802 476-0240	Harry Monti	Michael A Welch	James F Milne	....	Douglas Brent	Edward Fish	Reginald Abare
Barre t (7)	CM 802 479-9331	....	....	....	....	....	....	....
Barton t (3)	TM 802 525-6222	Rupert Chamberlin	....	Katherine H White	....	....	....	....
Bellows Falls v (3)	CM 802 463-3964	....	Paul McGinley	Evelyn Weeks	Lynn Dunn	William Weston	Gary Derosia	Maurice Kelly
Bennington t (16)	TM 802 442-1037	Lodie Colvin	Stuart Hurd	Mary Hodeck	David Essaff	Mark Sawyer	David Woodin	Joseph Sokul
Bethel t (2)	TM 802 234-9340	John Washborn	Geneva Gaiko	Jean Burnham	....	Robert Dean	Wendell Wills	Gary Slack
Brandon t (4)	CM 802 247-3635	Bill Heath	Brannon Godfrey	Bill Dick	....	....	Joe Arduca	Bruce Rounds
Brattleboro t (12)	TM 802 254-4541	Peter J Duff	Glenn E Hill	Annette Cappy	David Fredenburgh	David Emery	Bruce G Campbell	Jerome Remillard
Bristol t (4)	CM 802 453-2410	....	....	....	....	....	....	....
Bristol v (2)	CM 802 453-2410	....	....	....	....	....	....	....
Burlington (39)	MC 802 865-7145	Peter Brownell	....	Ruth Stokes	Brendan Keleher	Richard Desautels	Kevin Scully	Scott Johnstone
Castleton t (4)	CM 802 468-5319	....	....	....	....	....	....	....
Cavendish t (1)	CM 802 226-7291	Thomas Lazetera	Richard Svec	Jane Pixley	Jane Pixley	....	....	Richard Svec
Charlotte t (3)	TM 802 425-3071	Maurice Harvey	....	Mary Bown	....	Jonathan Foote	....	....
Chester t (3)	TM 802 875-2173	....	....	....	....	....	....	....
Colchester t (15)	CM 802 655-0811	William Mac Leay	David Timmons	Joyce Sweeney	Coral Coleman	....	Charles Kirker	Bryan Osborne
Derby t (4)	TM 802 766-4906	....	....	....	....	....	....	....
Dorset t (2)	CM 802 362-4571	John P Stannard	....	Denise Hebert	....	....	....	....
Essex t (16)	TM 802 878-1341	Martin Myers	Patrick Scheidel	Rosa Lee Crewdson	Douglas Fisher	Larry Ransom	John Terry	Dennis Lutz
Essex Junction v (8)	CM 802 878-6944	....	....	....	....	....	....	....
Fair Haven t (3)	TM 802 265-3010	Robert Richards	Patricia Paolillo	Suzanne Ruest	Patricia Paolillo	H Kenneth Ward	Andrew Brown	Richard Reid
Hardwick t (3)	TM 802 472-6120	Richard Brochu	Charles Safford	Gerald Hall	....	Ronald Bellavance	Leslie Dimick	Michael Leonard
Hartford t (9)	CM 802 295-9353	Richard Ballou	Ralph W Lehman	Deborah Adams	....	John Wood Jr	Joseph Estey	Michael Lavalla
Hartland t (3)	TM 802 436-2236	Patricia B Peat	Hiram E Allen	Clyde A Jenne	Carolyn Trombley	....	....	Hiram E Allen
Hinesburg t (4)	TM 802 482-2281	....	....	....	....	....	....	....
Jericho t (4)	TM 802 899-4936	....	....	....	....	....	....	....
Johnson t (3)	TM 802 635-2611	....	....	....	....	....	....	....
Ludlow t (2)	CM 802 228-2841	Keith Arlund	Paul W Hughes	Jane Creaser	....	Richard Harrison	Jeffrey Billings	....
Ludlow v (1)	TM 802 228-2841	Diana O' Connor	Paul Hughes	Dorothy S Bragg	Paul Hughes	....	....	....
Lyndon t (5)	TM 802 626-5785	....	....	....	....	....	....	....
Manchester t (4)	CM 802 362-1313	Ivan Beattie	Jeffrey D Wilson	Barbara Cross	Ruth Skuse	Thomas Ouellette	Manfred Wessner	....
Middlebury t (8)	TM 802 388-4041	Timothy Buskey	Betty Wheeler	Richard Goodro	....	Roger Young	Thomas Hanley	William Hageman
Milton t (8)	TM 802 893-6655	....	....	....	....	....	....	....
Montpelier (8)	CM 802 223-9502	Ann E Cummings	....	Charlotte L Hoyt	John R Kroll	Norman J Lewis	Douglas S Hoyt	Stephen A Gray
Morristown t (5)	TM 802 888-3534	....	....	....	....	....	....	....
Newport (4)	CM 802 334-5136	....	....	....	....	....	....	....
North Troy v (1)	CM 802 988-2663	....	....	....	....	....	....	....
Northfield t (6)	TM 802 485-6121	....	....	....	....	....	....	....
Northfield v (2)	CM 802 485-6121	....	....	....	....	....	....	....
Poultney t (3)	CM 802 287-9751	....	....	....	....	....	....	....
Poultney v (2)	CM 802 287-4003	Richard Frank	Paul H Hermann	W R Beer	....	....	....	....
Pownal t (3)	TM 802 823-7757	....	....	....	....	....	....	....
Randolph t (5)	CM 802 728-5433	....	....	....	....	....	....	....
Richmond t (4)	TM 802 434-2221	Wright Preston	Ronald Rodjenski	Velma Godfrey	....	Tom LeVesque	John O' Hara	Kendall Chamberli
Rockingham t (5)	CM 802 463-3964	....	Paul McGinley	Rita Bruce	Lynn Dunn	....	....	Maurice Kelly
Rutland (18)	MC 802 773-1800	....	....	....	....	....	....	....
Rutland t (4)	TM 802 773-2528	....	....	....	....	....	....	....
Shaftsbury t (3)	TM 802 442-4038	....	....	....	....	....	....	....
Shelburne t (6)	CM 802 985-5110	Alice Winn	William Finger	Colleen Haag	Colleen Haag	Craig Wooster	James Warden	....
Sherburne t (1)	CM 802 422-3241	....	....	....	....	....	....	....
South Burlington (13)	CM 802 658-7953	W Cimonetti	C Hafter	M Picard	....	W Possich	B Searles	A Audette
Springfield t (10)	CM 802 885-2104	....	....	....	....	....	....	....
St. Albans (7)	CM 802 524-1500	Peter Deslauriers	William Cioffi	Dianna R Baraby	....	Gary G Palmer	Timothy Datig	William H Scott
St. Albans t (5)	CM 802 524-2415	....	....	....	....	....	....	....
St. Johnsbury t (8)	CM 802 748-3926	....	....	....	....	....	....	....
Stowe t (3)	TM 802 253-7350	Richard Marrow	Greg Federspiel	....	Karla Spaulding	Wendall Mansfield	Kenneth Kaplan	....
Swanton t (6)	TM 802 868-4421	Earl Fournier	....	Doris Raleigh	....	....	....	....
Swanton v (2)	CM 802 868-3397	Leon Babbie	George Lague	Carol Winchester	....	Al Kinzinger	Michael McCarthy	Michael Menard
Troy t (2)	TM 802 988-2663	....	....	....	....	....	....	....
Waterbury t (5)	TM 802 244-7033	....	....	....	....	....	....	....
Weathersfield t (3)	CM 802 674-2626	Fred Crowley	C Peter Cole	Carol Daniels	....	Rodney Spaulding	Richard Poland	C Peter Cole
West Rutland t (2)	TM 802 438-2263	....	....	....	....	....	....	....
Westminster t (3)	CM 802 722-4255	William A Noyes	William O' Connor	Janette Holton	....	....	....	Mark C Lund
Williamstown t (3)	TM 802 433-6671	Roland Tousignant	Linda Riddell	Doreen Townsend	....	Edward Eaton	....	Mark Simon
Williston t (5)	TM 802 878-5121	Herb Goodrich	Bert Moffatt	Arlene Degree	Susan Sieg	Kenneth Morton	Osburn Glidden	Neil Boyden
Wilmington t (2)	TM 802 464-8591	Ann Manwaring	Sonia Alexander	Janice Karwoski	Laurie Boyd	Brian Johnson	Thomas Donnelly	....
Windsor t (4)	CM 802 674-6786	William Hochstin	David Battistoni	Gloria Tansey	....	Lewis Gage	Patric Foley	....
Winooski (7)	CM 802 655-6410	William Norful	Michael D Letcher	Pauline Schmoll	....	David Bergeron	Walter Nieliwocki	Steve Woodworth
Woodstock t (3)	TM 802 457-3456	....	....	....	....	....	....	....
Woodstock v (1)	CM 802 457-3456	....	....	....	....	....	....	....
VIRGINIA (94)								
Abingdon t (7)	CM 703 628-3167	Joe T Phipps	G M Newman	G M Newman	Mark Godbey	H M McCormick Jr	Cecil Kelly	C M Vernon Jr
Alexandria (111)	CM 703 838-4000	Patricia S Ticer	Vola T Lawson	Beverly I Jett	Arthur S Gitajn	Thomas M Hawkins	Charles E Samarra	Thomas F O' Kane
Altavista t (4)	CM 804 369-5001	J R Burgess	S I Goldsmith	Myra M Chism	....	S H Belvin	T L Neal	C E Dawson
Appalachia t (2)	CM 703 565-3900	Gary A Bush	Bobby L Dorton	Diane Reece	Bobby L Dorton	Robert Anderson	Roy Munsey	Bobby G Reynolds
Appomattox t (2)	MC 804 352-8268	....	....	....	....	....	....	....
Arlington (171)	CM 703 358-3000	....	....	....	....	....	....	....
Ashland t (6)	CM 804 798-9219	....	....	....	....	....	....	....
Bedford (6)	CM 703 586-7102	....	....	....	....	....	....	....
Berryville t (3)	MC 703 955-1099	Rick Sponseller	R John Hogan	Nancy L Tinsman	Desiree A Ellmore	....	Elden Nesselrodt	James E O' Brien
Big Stone Gap t (5)	CM 703 523-0115	....	....	....	....	....	....	....
Blacksburg t (35)	CM 703 961-1188	Roger E Hedgepeth	Ronald A Secrist	Donna B Caldwell	....	....	William H Brown	S Kelly Mattingly
Blackstone t (3)	CM 804 292-7251	....	....	....	....	....	....	....
Bluefield t (5)	CM 703 322-4626	Cecile S Barrett	Art Mead	Art Mead	Art Mead	Jim Hardy	Jack W Asbury	James F Mayo

Directory 1/9 continued **MUNICIPAL OFFICIALS IN U.S. CITIES OVER 2,500**

City, 1990 population figures (000 omitted), form of government		Municipal phone number	Mayor/ chief elected official	Appointed administrator	City clerk/ city secretary	Finance officer	Fire chief	Police chief	Public works director
VIRGINIA (94) continued									
Bowling Green t (1)	MC	804 633-6212	....	....	....	....	....	....	....
Bridgewater t (4)	CM	703 828-3390	Roland Z Arey	Bob F Holton	Doris S Kennedy	Melvin D Wampler	....	Mark L Payne	Jerry Oakes
Bristol (18)	CM	703 645-7300	Jerry A Wolfe	Paul D Spangler	Daniel Johnson	Daniel Johnson	Charles Denton	Wm H Price	Wm A Dennison Jr
Brookneal t (1)	MC	804 376-3124	Ronald Cox	....	Elizabeth Elder	....	Bryan Owen	James Hires	James Marstin
Buena Vista (6)	CM	703 261-6121	....	....	....	....	....	....	....
Cape Charles t (1)	CM	804 331-3259	....	....	....	....	....	....	....
Charlottesville (40)	CM	804 971-3490	....	....	....	....	....	....	....
Chase City t (2)	CM	804 372-5136	Charles Duckworth	Rickey G Reese	....	....	Winthy Hatcher Jr	Fred A Parsons	Stanley Duckworth
Chatham t (1)	MC	804 432-8153	....	....	....	....	....	....	....
Chesapeake (152)	CM	804 547-6166	....	....	....	....	....	....	....
Christiansburg t (15)	CM	703 382-6128	Harold Linkous	John E Lemley	Imogene Brumfield	John E Lemley	James W Epperly	Ronald L Lemons	Robert Gearheart
Clarksville t (1)	MC	804 374-8177	Kathleen Walker	Melinda Moran	Tara Glover	....	Raymond Hite	Ricky Wilkinson	Terry Hite
Clifton Forge (5)	CM	703 863-2500	Johnny S Wright	Stephen A Carter	Craig Hudson	....	Thomas Fitch	Barry G Balser	Brandon Nicely
Coeburn t (2)	CM	703 395-3323	Harold L Ringley	Terry L Gibson	Sherry Bise	Terry L Gibson	Clinton Hawkins	F Harold Markham	Danny Jordan
Colonial Heights (16)	CM	804 520-9265	James B McNeer	Robert E Taylor	Rita C Schiff	William E Johnson	A G Moore Jr	Steven Sheffield	Kurt E Ankrom
Covington (7)	CM	703 965-6300	....	....	....	....	....	....	....
Crewe t (2)	CM	804 645-9453	Garland R Redford	R Martin Long	R Martin Long	R Martin Long	Sammy Jarrell	William C Abel	Ralph T Shelton
Culpeper t (9)	CM	703 825-1120	Waller P Jones	Jerry Davis	Donna B Foster	....	....	C B Jones	W T Beales
Danville (53)	CM	804 799-5240	Seward Anderson	Ray Griffin	....	Aubrey Dodson	David Lampley	Neal Morris	Ric Drazenovich
Dumfries t (4)	MC	703 221-3400	Samuel W Bauckman	Michael E Long	Retta S Ladd	....	....	James K Habern	Daniel L Lycan
Emporia (5)	CM	804 634-3332	....	....	....	....	....	....	....
Fairfax (20)	CM	703 385-7855	John Mason	Robert Sisson	Jackie Henderson	Edward Cawley	Gary Mesaris	John Skinner	John Veneziano
Falls Church (10)	CM	703 241-5025	Jeffery Tarbert	David Lasso	Elizabeth Shawen	Douglas Scott	....	Robert Murray	Richard Durgin
Farmville t (6)	CM	804 392-5686	J David Crute	Gerald J Spates	....	....	Phillip F Gay	Otto S Overton	Eugene M Philbeck
Franklin (8)	CM	804 562-8500	C Franklin Jester	John J Jackson	John J Jackson	John J Jackson	James M Wagenbach	Robert K Eubanks	William W Fleming
Fredericksburg (19)	CM	703 372-1028	Lawrence A Davies	Marvin Bolinger	Deborah Ratliffe	Clarence Robinson	Denny W Kelly	James Powers	Thomas Slaydon
Front Royal t (12)	CM	703 635-7799	Stan W Brooks Jr	M Lyle Lacy	Rhonda S North	John B O' Neill	Elmer D McIntosh	Larry W Daniel	Eugene R Tewalt
Galax (7)	CM	703 236-5773	C M Mitchell	Daniel Campbell	Myrna Holder	Doris Bedwell	Mike Coomes	B R Melton	Waymon Dalton
Glasgow t (1)	CM	703 258-2246	Samuel Blackburn	William S Knick	William S Knick	....	Richard Spangler	Richard Hostetter	....
Grundy t (1)	MC	703 935-2551	....	....	....	....	....	....	....
Hampton (134)	CM	804 727-6407	James L Eason	Robert J O' Neill	Diana T Hughes	James A Peterson	Gregory B Cade	....	Edmond Panzer
Harrisonburg (31)	CM	703 434-6776	John N Neff	Steven E Stewart	Bonnie Ryan	Lester O Seal	Larry Shifflett	Donald Harper	James Baker
Herndon t (16)	CM	703 435-6800	Thomas Davis Rust	Robert A Stalzer	Viki Wellershaus	Mary C Kemp	....	George E Kranda	John E Moore
Hopewell (23)	CM	804 541-2245	D Paul Karnes	Clinton H Strong	Mary Frances Pito	Elesteen Hager	Steve Brown	Wilbur R Clarke	Henry Wilde
Lebanon t (3)	MC	703 889-7200	....	....	....	....	....	....	....
Leesburg t (16)	CM	703 777-2420	James E Clem	Steven C Brown	Barbara Messinger	Paul E York	....	James M Kidwell	Thomas A Mason
Lexington (7)	CM	703 463-7133	H E Derrick Jr	T Jon Ellestad	Georgiana M Vita	Curtis F Higgins	Kenneth Hall Jr	Bruce Beard	David A Woody
Luray t (5)	CM	703 743-5511	Ralph Dean	Ronald Good	Cynthia Bushey	....	Dan Seal	Albert Judd	Jimmie Griffith
Lynchburg (66)	CM	804 847-1400	James S Whitaker	Charles F Church	Patricia W Kost	Michael W Hill	William Anderson	....	Raymond A Booth
Manassas (28)	CM	703 257-8200	Robert L Browne	John G Cartwright	Linda A Hawley	M Joy Ringler	....	Christopher Tutko	....
Manassas Park (7)	CM	703 335-8800	Ernest Evans	Frank McDonough	Lana Conner	Brett Shorter	Gerald Grove	William Kiefer	Karl Rudolph
Marion t (7)	CM	703 783-4113	....	....	....	....	....	....	....
Martinsville (16)	CM	703 656-5180	George B Adams	Earl B Reynolds	Lance G Heater	Richard D Fitts	W Lewis Reeves	Terry L Roop	Leon E Towarnicki
Middleburg t (1)	CM	703 687-5152	Caroline Bowersck	Alice Love	Betty Patterson	....	....	David Simpson	James Triplett
Narrows t (2)	CM	703 726-2423	....	....	....	....	....	....	....
Newport News (175)	MC	804 247-8444	Barry E Duval	Edgar E Maroney	Bernice I Berry	Kamal C Doshi	Larry L Orie	....	Max T Palmer
Norfolk (261)	CM	804 441-2549	....	....	....	....	....	....	....
Norton (4)	CM	703 679-1160	B Robert Raines	E W Ward	Mary D Brown	E W Ward	David Mullins	Samuel A Mongle	James C Hall
Orange t (3)	CM	703 672-1020	Frederick Sherman	Doyle W Frye	Sabrina Martyn	....	Bert Roby	Alexander Clary	William Smith
Pearisburg t (2)	CM	703 921-1222	John H Givens Jr	Kenneth F Vittum	Judy R Harrell	....	Daryl Scott	William Whitsett	Steven W Stafford
Petersburg (38)	CM	804 733-2324	....	....	....	....	....	....	....
Poquoson (11)	CM	804 868-3510	L Cornell Burcher	Robert M Murphy	Judy F Wiggins	Carol O Davis	C E Ward	John T White	J Montgomery
Portsmouth (104)	CM	804 393-8874	Gloria O Webb	V Wayne Orton	Shiela P Pittman	....	Donald Newberry	Dennis A Mook	Richard A Hartman
Pulaski t (10)	CM	703 980-1000	Andrew Graham	Thomas Combiths	Ruth Harrell	Mildred Bolen	H Jeff Hall	....	Mike Jenkins
Purcellville t (2)	MC	703 338-7421	....	....	....	....	....	....	....
Radford (16)	CM	703 731-3603	Thomas Starnes	Robert P Asbury	Roy I Lloyd Jr	Jess Cantline	Martin R Roberts	A C Earles	James H Hurt Jr
Richlands t (4)	CM	703 964-2566	Kenneth Wysor	Timothy Taylor	Elva L Van Dyke	Timothy Taylor	Charles A Puckett	Jack Young	Donald Van Dyke
Richmond (203)	CM	804 780-5660	Leonidas B Young	Robert C Bobb	Edna Williams	Max Bohnstedt	Ronald C Lewis	Marty M Tapscott	Jerry Ellett
Roanoke (96)	CM	703 981-2000	David Bowers	W Robert Herbert	Mary Parker	James Grisso	Raleigh W Quarles	M David Hooper	William Clark
Rocky Mount t (4)	CM	703 483-7660	B Shively	M Henne	P Hooke	D Fecher	P Dillon	B Jenkins	C Mason
Salem (24)	CM	703 375-3060	James Taliaferro	Randolph M Smith	Forest G Jones	Frank P Turk	Danny W Hall	Harry T Haskins	....
Smithfield t (5)	CM	804 357-3247	James Chapman	Kenneth McLawhon	Suzzann S Pittman	Suzzann S Pittman	I N Jones	Mark A Marshall	W R Batten
South Boston (7)	CM	804 575-4200	George H Bagwell	Gary F Christie	Gary F Christie	....	William R Murray	James E Hall	G C Carrington
South Hill t (4)	CM	804 447-3191	Earl Horne	G Morris Wells	....	....	James E Crowder	Norman Hudson	Hunter J Chavis
Staunton (24)	CM	703 332-3825	Gianfranco Avoli	Bernard J Murphy	Deborah L Sutton	Jeanne R Colvin	William A Shaver	Grafton L Wells	Frank S Wiggins
Strasburg t (4)	CM	703 465-9197	Harry Applegate	Kevin Fauber	Mary Price	Mary Price	William Walton	Thomas Wilson	John Rhodes
Suffolk (52)	CM	804 934-3111	S Chris Jones	Richard L Hedrick	Henry L Murden	C Lee Acors	Mark R Outlaw	Gilbert F Jackson	Thomas G Hines
Tappahannock t (2)	CM	804 443-3336	E L Hammond	G G Belfield Jr	B J Corrieri	....	Wayne Thompson	J H Barrett Jr	T P Wyatt
Tazewell t (4)	CM	703 988-2501	Jerry G Wood	John E B Clark Jr	Linda S Griffith	....	A D Buchanan	Daniel H Martin	Flint McAmis
Victoria t (2)	MC	804 696-2343	....	....	....	....	....	....	....
Vienna t (15)	CM	703 255-6300	C A Robinson Jr	J H Schoeberlein	C Orndorff	P Grant	....	D Kerr	J Stockton
Vinton t (8)	CM	703 983-0601	Charles R Hill	B Clayton Goodman	Carolyn S Ross	....	Barry L Fuqua	Riley R Foutz	Cecil W Stacy
Virginia Beach (393)	CM	804 427-4242	....	....	....	....	....	....	....
Warrenton t (5)	CM	703 347-1101	J W Lineweaver	John A Anzivino	Evelyn J Weimer	F K Timberlake	....	Dale L Koglin	Michael C Moon
Waynesboro (19)	CM	703 942-6600	Thomas L Gorsuch	Jerry L Gwaltney	Wilma M Zeh	Frank M Fletcher	Harvey Kelley	Philip Broadfoot	Jax Bowman
West Point t (3)	MC	804 843-3330	R Tyler Bland	Watson M Allen	Watson M Allen	Watson M Allen	Stephen Ogg	W Wayne Healy	Edward L Haurand
Williamsburg (12)	CM	804 220-6100	Trist McConnell	Jackson C Tuttle	Lois Bodie	Raymond Adams	Terrill K Weiler	Larry Vardell	Daniel Clayton
Winchester (22)	CM	703 667-1815	....	....	....	....	....	....	....
Wise t (3)	CM	703 328-6013	Caynor Smith Jr	Bevely L Collins	Robin Bryant	....	Conley Holbrook	Anthony Bates	....
Woodstock t (3)	CM	703 459-3621	J Timothy Dalke	Larry D Bradford	Michelle M Lohr	....	Gary Yew	Jerry P Miller	Robert L Neff
Wytheville t (8)	CM	703 223-3333	Trent Crewe	Wayne Sutherland	Sharon Cassell	....	....	Albert Newberry	Dennis Hackler
WASHINGTON (103)									
Aberdeen (17)	MC	206 533-4100	Chuck Gurrad	....	Fred J Thurman	Fred J Thurman	Lowell Killen	Bill Ellis	Robert A Salmon
Anacortes (11)	MC	206 293-5131	....	....	....	....	....	....	....
Arlington (4)	MC	206 435-5785	Robert Kraski	Thomas R Myers	Kathy Peterson	....	Dean Olson	Steven Robinson	Terry Castle
Auburn (33)	MC	206 931-2105	Charles Booth	....	Robin Wohlheuter	Francis Thompson	Robert Johnson	David Purdy	Frank Currie
Battle Ground (4)	MC	206 687-7131	Marvin Brothers	....	Judie Kastner	....	....	Ron Johnson	Frank Hodgson
Bellevue (87)	CM	206 462-4585	Donald Davidson	Phillip Kushlan	Myrna Basich	Edward Oberg	Peter Lucarelli	Joseph Smith	William Guenzler
Bellingham (52)	MC	206 676-6979	Tim Douglas	....	....	Lynn Carpenter	Jay Gunsauls	Donald Pierce	John M Garner
Blaine (2)	CM	206 332-8311	....	....	....	....	....	....	....
Bonney Lake (7)	MC	206 862-8602	Rex Pulfrey	....	Kathleen Clayton	Kathleen Clayton	Alden Dobson	Donald Frazier	Bruce Gould
Bothell (12)	CM	206 486-3256	John Curtin	Anne L Pflug	Terry A Briscoe	Maryann Ness	Richard O Duncan	Mark Ericks	Lynn Guttmann

**MUNICIPAL OFFICIALS
IN U.S. CITIES OVER 2,500**

City, 1990 population figures (000 omitted), form of government	Municipal phone number	Mayor/ chief elected official	Appointed administrator	City clerk/ city secretary	Finance officer	Fire chief	Police chief	Public works director
WASHINGTON (103) continued								
Bremerton (38)	MC 206 478-5290	Lynn Horton	....	K McKluskey	....	Mike McKinney	Delbert McNeal	Eddy Chu
Brier (6)	MC 206 775-5440	Sharon L Walker	Norma L Wilds	Norma L Wilds	....	....	Dan Elfenson	Alan Hammerquist
Buckley (4)	MC 206 829-1921	John Blanusa	Merlin Reynolds	....	Sheila Hulett	Robert Roy	Arthur McGehee	Mikel Brendel
Burlington (4)	MC 206 755-0531	Raymond C Henery	Phillip M Messina	Richard A Patrick	Richard A Patrick	Glen H Staheli	Edward M Goodman	Rodney D Garrett
Camas (6)	MC 206 834-2462	Dean E Dossett	Lloyd N Halverson	....	Dale E Scarbrough	David G Artz	Michael C Slyter	Douglas A Quinn
Centralia (12)	CM 206 736-5827	Vondean Thompson	Carig Nelson	Sacia Graber	Mark Griffen	Chuck Newbury	Toni Breckel	Terry Calkins
Chehalis (7)	CM 206 748-6664	T F Bud Hatfield	David Campbell	Joann Hakola	Joann Hakola	....	Randy Hamilton	Barry Heid
Chelan (3)	MC 509 682-4037	Joyce Stewart	John Greiner	Robert Daykin	....	William Greenway	Edwin Bush	William Greenway
Cheney (8)	MC 509 235-7211	Al Ogdon	Jim Reinbold	Grant Murie	Grant Murie	John Montague	Jerry Gardner	Paul Schmidt
Clarkston (7)	CO 509 758-5541	Gwen Schwane	....	Vickie Storey	....	Robert Berreman	....	....
Clyde Hill t (3)	MC 206 453-7800	....	....	....	....	....	....	....
Colfax (3)	MC 509 397-3861	Norma Becker	Myrt Webb	Emily Adams	Vic Roberts	James Krouse	Barney Buckley	Myrt Webb
College Place (6)	MC 509 529-1200	....	....	....	....	....	....	....
Colville (5)	MC 509 684-5094	Duane Scott	Harlan Elsasser	Lynne Somerville	....	Rick Naff	Damond Meshishnek	....
Connell (2)	MC 509 234-2701	Jim Klindworth	Arthur Tackett	C Seachriest	Joan Eckman	....	Ricky Rochleau	John Klein
Dayton (2)	MC 509 382-2361	Gale Davis	Don Avery	Don Avery	....	....	Larry Groom	Gus Hawks
Des Moines (17)	CM 206 878-4595	Richard Kennedy	Greg Prothman	Denis Staab	Jim Hathaway	....	Martin Pratt	Dale Schroeder
Edmonds (31)	MC 206 775-2525	Laura M Hall	....	Rhonda March	Art Housler	Michael Springer	Thomas Miller	Paul Mar
Ellensburg (12)	CM 509 962-7220	Mollie E Edson	Cynthia M Curreri	Coreen Reno	Larry M Carpenter	Steve Alder	Hal Rees	Thomas E Chini
Elma t (3)	MC 206 482-2212	William Bilsland	....	Ingrld M Daniels	....	Craig Nelson	Les N Bonfield	C Quentin Boyer
Enumclaw (7)	MC 206 825-3591	George Rossman	Michael Quinn	Marcia Basham	J Richard Scott	Joseph Kolisch	Richard Williams	Mark Bauer
Ephrata (5)	MC 509 754-4601	....	....	....	....	....	....	....
Everett (70)	MC 206 259-8700	Edward D Hansen	James L Langus	Donna Rider	William Cushman	Terrill Ollis	Michael Campbell	Clair Olivers
Federal Way (..)	CM 206 661-4000	Mary Gates	Ken Nyberg	Maureen Swaney	Iwen Wang	....	....	Philip Keightley
Ferndale (5)	CM 206 384-4302	....	....	....	....	....	....	....
Fircrest t (5)	CM 206 564-8901	David M Viafore	Jill Monley	Susan Clough	Pam Gardner	Jan Chamberland	Ron Ames	Bob Shelton
Forks t (3)	MC 206 374-5412	Phil Arbeiter	....	Dan Leinan	....	Phil Arbeiter	Vern Johnson	Dave Zellar
Gig Harbor (3)	MC 206 851-8136	Gretchen Wilbert	Mark Hoppen	Mark Hoppen	Tom Enlow	....	Dennis Richards	Ben Yazici
Goldendale (3)	CM 509 773-3771	Skip Grimes	Ehman Sheldon	Betty Smith	....	Terry Campbell	Robert Hampshire	Ehman Sheldon
Grandview (7)	MC 509 882-9200	Jesse Palacios	C J Sewell	D Jean Wallar	....	Jerry Donaldson	David Charvet	Cus Arteaga
Hoquiam (9)	MC 206 532-9330	Phyllis Shrauger	Pete Wall	....	Pete Wall	Lance Talley	Scott Finlayson	....
Issaquah (8)	MC 206 557-3217	Rowan Hinds	Leon Kos	Linda Ruehle	Jim Blake	Jim Rankin	D A Garrison	Victor Salemann
Kelso (12)	CM 206 423-0900	Don Gregory	Doug Robinson	Veryl Anderson	Veryl Anderson	Joe Valenzuela	Tony Stoutt	Bob Gregory
Kennewick (42)	CM 509 586-4181	Bruce Showalter	Robert M Kelly	Marge Price	Robert F Noland	Bobby F Kirk	Marc Harden	Roy Cross
Kent (38)	CM 206 859-3300	....	....	....	....	....	....	....
Kirkland (40)	CM 206 828-1100	David Russell	Terrence Ellis	Janice Perry	Tom J Anderson	Tom F Fieldstead	Ron Burns	Jim Arndt
Lacey (19)	CM 206 491-3214	....	....	....	....	....	....	....
Longview (31)	CM 206 577-3310	John H Crocker	Edwin R Ivey	C Sue Marsh	....	Ron Spreadborough	Jan Duke	Leroy E Gower
Lynden (6)	MC 206 354-4270	Jim Kaemingk Sr	Stephan J Jilk	J Halderman	....	Jim Top	Jack Foster	Terry Klimpel
Lynnwood (29)	MC 206 775-1971	....	....	....	....	....	....	....
Marysville (10)	MC 206 659-8477	....	....	....	....	....	....	....
Medical Lake (4)	MC 509 299-7712	....	....	....	....	....	....	....
Medina (3)	CM 206 454-9222	Dewey Taylor	....	Lynn Batchlor	....	....	Joe Race	Anne M Weigle
Mercer Island (21)	CM 206 236-5300	Judy Clibborn	Paul Lanspery	Debra Symmonds	Joanne Sylvis	Jan Deveny	Jan Deveny	....
Mill Creek (7)	CM 206 745-1891	Timothy Austin	John Sims Jr	Debra Tarry	Debra Tarry	....	John Klei	Michael Monken
Milton t (5)	MC 206 922-8733	....	....	....	....	....	....	....
Monroe (4)	MC 206 794-7400	Gordon Tjerne	Doug Jacobson	Betty King	Carol Grey	Tom Healy	Collen Wilson	Doug Jacobson
Montesano (3)	MC 206 249-3021	....	....	....	....	....	....	....
Moses Lake (11)	CM 509 766-9201	R Wayne Rimple	Joseph Gavinski	....	Walter Fry	Elvis Swisher	Fred Haynes	Gary Harer
Mount Vernon (18)	MC 206 336-6207	....	....	....	....	....	....	....
Mountlake Terrace (19)	CM 206 776-1161	Roger Bergh	Walter Fehst	Ron Swanson	Ron Swanson	Pat Vollandt	John Turner	Marv Seabrands
Mukilteo (..)	MC 206 355-4151	Brian Sullivan	Jerald Osterman	....	Linda Miller	Dennis Hixon	Jon Walters	Warren Gray
Normandy Park (7)	CM 206 248-7603	Bob Davis	Jim Murphy	Brenda Trent	Brenda Trent	....	Al Teeples	Chuck Heit
Oak Harbor (17)	CM 206 679-5551	Al Koetje	Pat Nevins	Rosemary Morrison	....	Mark Soptich	Tony Barge	....
Ocean Shores (2)	CM 206 289-2488	Bruce Wolgemuth	Michael L Pence	....	....	David H Cowardin	Michael F Wilson	John L Gow
Olympia (34)	CM 206 753-8447	....	....	....	....	....	....	....
Omak (4)	MC 509 826-1170	E Walt Smith	....	Trish Sieker	....	Cal Bowling	Ron Bailey	Fred Sheldon
Othello (5)	MC 509 488-5686	Milo Hirschi	Rex Mather	Debbie Kudrna	Teresa Potter	Duane Van Beek	Bill McDonell	Howard Johnston
Pasco (20)	CM 509 545-3408	Joyce Defelice	Gary Crutchfield	Daniel Underwood	Daniel Underwood	Larry Dickinson	Donald Francis	James Ajax
Port Angeles (18)	MC 206 457-0411	Joan Sargent	Jeffrey Pomeranz	Becky Upton	Katherine Godbey	Larry Glenn	Steve Ilk	Jack Pittis
Port Orchard (5)	MC 206 876-4407	Leslie Weatherill	....	Patricia Parks	....	Joseph Snow	Joseph Mathews	Lawrence J Curles
Port Townsend (7)	MC 206 385-3000	....	....	....	....	....	....	....
Poulsbo (5)	MC 206 779-3901	R Mitchusson	....	Karol Jones	....	Jim Shields	Jeff Doran	Milt Ludington
Prosser (4)	MC 509 786-2332	Wayne Hogue	Ken Carter	Regina Williams	....	Doug Merritt	Scott Hamilton	Charles George
Pullman (23)	MC 509 334-4555	Alfred Halvorson	John F Sherman	....	John D Tonkovich	Patrick E Wilkins	William Weatherly	James J Hudak
Puyallup (24)	CM 206 841-4321	Michael Deal	....	Barbara Price	Dean Driver	Merle Frank	Lockheed Reader	Tom Heinecke
Quincy t (4)	MC 509 787-3523	Patricia A Martin	....	Linda B Mead	....	....	Merle S Wilson	Peter M Smith
Raymond (3)	CO 206 942-3451	....	....	....	....	....	....	....
Redmond (36)	MC 206 556-2900	Rosemarie M Ives	Linda A Herzog	Doris A Schaible	Lenda M Crawford	Rand Scott Coggan	Steven R Harris	Carol E Osborne
Renton (42)	MC 206 235-2556	Earl Clymer	Jay Covington	Marilyn Peterson	Victoria Runkle	Austin L Wheeler	Alan Wallis	Gregg Zimmerman
Richland (32)	CM 509 943-7396	Jim Hansen	Joseph C King	Kenneth Bays	Ron D Musson	Robert T Panuccio	David Lewis	....
Seattle (516)	MC 206 684-4000	....	....	....	....	....	....	....
Sedro-Woolley (6)	MC 206 855-1661	William Stendal	....	Patricia Brooks	....	Dean Klinger	David Cooper	....
Selah (5)	MC 509 698-7326	John Sweesy	Frank Sweet	Nancy Whalen	....	John Soden	Steve Robertson	Dale Nobel
Sequim (4)	MC 206 683-4139	....	....	....	....	....	....	....
Shelton (7)	CO 206 426-4491	Joyce Jaros	Michael McCarty	....	....	Dan Ward	Johnny Johnston	Gary Rhoades
Snohomish (6)	CM 206 568-3115	Stephen Dana	Kelly Robinson	Molly Linville	....	....	Patrick Murphy	Lawrence W Waters
Spokane (177)	CM 509 625-6267	Jack Geraghty	Roger Crum	M Montgomery	Pete Fortin	Bobby Williams	Terry Mangan	Irving Reed
Stanwood (2)	MC 206 629-2181	Donald K Moa	....	Ray L Nielsen	....	....	Robert Kane	Gary A Armstrong
Steilacoom t (6)	MC 206 581-1900	Janda Volkmer	David Moseley	Susan Wilson	Paul Menter	....	Michael Campbell	Jim Richards
Sumner (6)	MC 206 863-8300	Robert Moltke	Alan Nygaard	Barbara Hughes	Alan Nygaard	R Wade Joyner	Ron Hyland	Marwan Salloum
Sunnyside (11)	CM 509 837-3997	Don Hughes	Leo S Fancey	Hugo R Schatz	Hugo R Schatz	Gary L Cole	Wallace Anderson	Gary Potter
Tacoma (177)	CM 206 591-5000	Harold G Moss	Ray E Corpuz Jr	Genelle Birk	Peter Luttropp	Richard E Moore	Raymond Fjetland	William L Pugh
Toppenish (7)	CM 509 865-5000	Norman Johnson	James Southworth	LuHumphrey	....	Keith Yamane	James Andrews	Jo Miles
Tukwila (12)	MC 206 433-1800	John W Rants	John M McFarland	Jane Cantu	Alan Doerschel	Tom Keefe	Ron Waldner	Ross Earnst
Union Gap (3)	MC 509 248-0432	....	....	....	....	....	....	....
Vancouver (46)	CM 206 696-8142	Bruce Hagensen	John Fischbach	Kent Shorthill	Kent Shorthill	Dan Fraijo	Rod Frederiksen	John Ostrowski
Walla Walla (26)	CM 509 527-4522	....	....	....	....	....	....	....
Wapato (4)	MC 509 877-2334	....	....	....	....	....	....	....
Washougal (5)	MC 206 835-8501	....	....	....	....	....	....	....
Wenatchee (22)	CO 509 664-3300	Earl Tilly	Glenn Haugo	Glenn Haugo	....	Bill Edwardson	Ken Badgley	James Ajax
West Richland (4)	MC 509 967-3431	....	....	....	....	....	....	....
Yakima (55)	CM 509 575-6090	Patricia A Berndt	Dick A Zais	Karen S Roberts	John R Hanson	Keith Chronister	Pleas Green Jr	Jerry D Copeland

Directory 1/9
continued

**MUNICIPAL OFFICIALS
IN U.S. CITIES OVER 2,500**

City, 1990 population figures (000 omitted), form of government	Municipal phone number	Mayor/ chief elected official	Appointed administrator	City clerk/ city secretary	Finance officer	Fire chief	Police chief	Public works director
WEST VIRGINIA (60)								
Barboursville v (3)	MC 304 736-8994	Nancy Cartmill	....	Ann Reed	Charles Woolcock	Paul Ritchie	Frank Simpson	Steve Parsons
Beckley (18)	MC 304 256-1768	....	....	....	....	....	....	....
Bethlehem v (3)	MC 304 242-4180	....	....	....	....	....	....	....
Bluefield (13)	CM 304 327-2401	J Rudolph Brammer	Wm H Looney Jr	Beverly Tresch	Charles Cromer	Richard Poe	Mike Poe	Willard Agee
Bridgeport t (7)	MC 304 842-8232	Carl E Furbee Jr	Harold E Weiler	Judy Lawson	Keith Boggs	Kelley Blackwell	Jack Clayton	Dale Shields
Bridgeport (8)	CM 304 842-8233	....	Harold E Weiler	....	....	....	....	....
Buckhannon (6)	MC 304 472-1651	....	....	....	....	....	....	....
Charles Town (3)	MC 304 725-2311	....	....	....	....	....	....	....
Charleston (57)	MC 304 348-8033	....	....	....	....	....	....	....
Chester (3)	MC 304 387-2820	....	....	....	....	....	....	....
Clarksburg (18)	CM 304 624-1683	Louis Iqulnto	Paul Shives	Jeanine Fultz	Frank Ferrari	Bill Spencer	Tom Durrett	George Duffer
Dunbar (9)	MC 304 766-0222	....	....	....	....	....	....	....
Elkins (7)	MC 304 636-1414	Jimmy Hammond	....	Philip J Graziani	....	Roger Bolyard	Dale Kelley	....
Fairmont (20)	CM 304 366-6211	Wayna A Stutler	Edwin J Thorne	Janet L Keller	....	David L Wimer	Theodore Offutt	Michael A DeMary
Fayetteville t (2)	MC 304 574-0101	Thomas E Woodrum	Cecil J Gibson Jr	....	....	John Vernon	James J Smith	....
Follansbee (3)	CM 304 527-1330	....	....	....	....	....	....	....
Grafton (6)	CM 304 265-1412	Daniel E Mankins	Donna C Hoyler	Shirley Dougherty	Larry Richman	William Roy	Thomas Broadstock	Gerald Weber
Hinton (3)	CM 304 466-3255	James A Leslie Jr	Cynthia S Cooper	Cynthia S Cooper	....	Leon R Pivont Jr	....	Ralph Trout Jr
Huntington (55)	MC 304 696-5540	Jean Dean	David Harrington	Ann Shaye	Glenn White	Allen Cremeans	Gary Wade	George Burgess
Hurricane v (4)	MC 304 562-5896	Raymond Peak	Karen S Lilly	Alwilda Johnson	....	....	L D Foster	Douglas Peak
Kenova (4)	MC 304 453-1571	....	....	....	....	....	....	....
Keyser (6)	MC 304 788-1511	....	....	....	....	....	....	....
Kingwood t (3)	MC 304 329-1225	....	....	....	....	....	....	....
Lewisburg (4)	MC 304 645-2080	James R Matheny	....	Pat Pennington	....	Wayne Pennington	Richard Weikel	Herb Montgomery
Logan t (2)	MC 304 752-4044	....	....	....	....	....	....	....
Madison (3)	MC 304 369-2762	....	....	....	....	....	....	....
Mannington t (2)	MC 304 986-2700	....	....	....	....	....	....	....
Martinsburg (14)	CM 304 264-2131	Earnest L Sparks	Philip F Hertz	Sharon Flick	Mark Spickler	Douglas Fellers	....	Jack Leonard
Montgomery t (2)	MC 304 442-5181	Ben Carson	....	....	....	Larry Robinson	Dave Stephenson	....
Morgantown (26)	CM 304 284-7405	Charlene Marshall	Dan Boroff	Linda Little	Donna Frum	Larry Rose	James McCabe	Marwan Rayan
Moundsville (11)	CM 304 845-3394	....	....	....	....	....	....	....
Mullens t (2)	MC 304 294-7132	....	....	....	....	....	....	....
New Martinsville (7)	MC 304 455-9120	....	....	....	....	....	....	....
Nitro t (7)	MC 304 755-0701	....	....	....	....	....	....	....
Oak Hill (7)	CM 304 469-9541	....	....	....	....	....	....	....
Paden City t (3)	MC 304 337-2295	....	....	....	....	....	....	....
Parkersburg (34)	MC 304 424-8400	....	....	....	....	....	....	....
Philippi (3)	CM 304 457-3700	Don Baughman	Joe Mattaliano	Doris Mundy	Joe Mattaliano	....	Gerald Gaynor	Mike Scott
Point Pleasant (5)	MC 304 675-2360	....	....	....	....	....	....	....
Princeton (7)	CM 304 487-5020	Wm H Draper	Richard J Shakman	Kelly F Davis	Richard J Shakman	John W Howell	Charles A Kassay	Wayne C Shumate
Ranson (3)	MC 304 725-1010	....	....	....	....	....	....	....
Ravenswood (4)	CM 304 273-2621	....	....	....	....	....	....	....
Richwood (3)	MC 304 846-2596	Jimmy Gladwell	....	Dixie A Cornell	Millie Stinnett	John Greer	Larry Tinney	Frank White
Ripley (3)	MC 304 372-3482	....	....	....	....	....	....	....
Shinnston (3)	MC 304 592-5631	....	....	....	....	....	....	....
South Charleston (14)	MC 304 744-5301	....	....	....	....	....	....	....
Spencer (2)	MC 304 927-1640	....	....	....	....	....	....	....
St. Albans (11)	MC 304 722-3391	A Eddie Bassitt	Donald Cheek	Bennett Burgess	....	Bob Fitch	Homer Clark	Donald Cheek
St. Marys (2)	MC 304 684-2401	....	....	....	....	....	....	....
Summersville t (3)	MC 304 872-1211	....	....	....	....	....	....	....
Vienna (11)	MC 304 295-4541	....	....	....	....	....	....	....
Weirton (22)	MC 304 797-8500	....	....	....	....	....	....	....
Welch (3)	CM 304 436-3113	Martha H Moore	....	Debora L Bias	....	James R Ingole Jr	Hubert C Leslie	Robert L Lee
Wellsburg (3)	CM 304 737-2104	....	....	....	....	....	....	....
Weston (5)	MC 304 269-6141	John C Burkhart	....	Joyce A Brown	....	Edward Griffin	George Blake	....
Westover (4)	MC 304 296-6860	....	....	....	....	....	....	....
Wheeling (35)	CM 304 234-3617	....	....	....	....	....	....	....
White Sulphur Springs (3)	MC 304 536-1035	Barbara S Wooding	....	Margaret Lewis	....	Roger White	Emmett W Sullivan	....
Williamson (4)	MC 304 235-1510	....	....	....	....	....	....	....
Williamstown (3)	MC 304 375-7761	....	....	....	....	....	....	....
WISCONSIN (175)								
Algoma (3)	MC 414 487-2163	....	....	....	....	....	....	....
Allouez v (14)	MC 414 448-2800	Cameron McCain	Dave Waffle	Susan L Foxworthy	....	Jeff Roemer	....	Thomas C Meier
Altoona (6)	CM 715 839-6092	....	....	....	....	....	....	....
Amery (3)	MC 715 268-7486	Jerome Wittstock	Julie Riemenschne	Julie Riemenschne	....	Rick Van Blaricom	Mike Holmes	John Frisco
Antigo (8)	MC 715 623-3033	Miles R Stanke	Gary G Rogers Jr	Eleanor Hoerman	....	Len Vander Wyst	Robert Brehm	P Vander Leest
Appleton (66)	MC 414 832-6425	....	....	....	....	....	....	....
Ashland (9)	MC 715 682-7071	Lowell J Miller	Tony Murphy	Carol A Larson	Patrick Onderak	Keith Tveit	Gordon Gilbertson	Steve Stadler
Ashwaubenon v (16)	MC 414 435-3751	....	....	....	....	....	....	....
Baraboo (9)	MC 608 356-8361	Dean Steinhorst	Mark Howard	Pat Seaberg	....	Al Swayze	Tom Lobe	....
Barron (3)	MC 715 537-5631	....	....	....	....	....	....	....
Bayside v (5)	CM 414 351-8811	....	Scott A Botcher	....	....	....	Bruce Resnick	Harry Hohmann
Beaver Dam (14)	MC 414 885-5541	....	....	....	....	....	....	....
Beloit (36)	CM 608 364-6610	....	Daniel Kelley	Diane Henry	Henry Schreve	Gerald Buckley	Terry Fell	Michael Slavish
Berlin (5)	CM 414 361-0800	....	....	....	....	....	....	....
Black River Falls (3)	MC 715 284-2315	....	....	....	....	....	....	....
Bloomer (3)	MC 715 568-3032	Randy Summerfield	....	Desiree L Roff	....	Rod Schmidt	Wayne Geist	....
Boscobel (3)	MC 608 375-5001	Paul Bloyer	....	John DuCharme	....	....	Jerry Staskal	Mike Reynolds
Brillion (3)	CM 414 756-2250	....	....	....	....	....	....	....
Brodhead (3)	MC 608 897-4018	Allan Herrington	....	Nancy Schoeller	....	Philip McManus	David Wickstrum	Randy Rosheisen
Brookfield (35)	MC 414 782-9650	Kathryn Bloomberg	....	Gary Rasmussen	Arlin Wesner	James Mehring	Robert Jacobs	William Muth Jr
Brown Deer v (12)	CM 414 357-0100	....	....	....	....	....	....	....
Burlington (9)	MC 414 763-3717	Jeannie Hefty	Mark Fitzgerald	Christine Kerkman	....	Richard Lodle	Ronald V Patla	....
Butler v (2)	MC 414 783-2525	Richard Ensslin	Larry Plaster	Larry Plaster	....	Ron Worgull	Ernie Rosenthal	....
Cedarburg (10)	MC 414 375-7600	John P Kuerschner	Clinton P Gridley	Jacquelyn Dekker	....	R Van Dinter	George R Rees	Robert R Dreblow
Chilton (3)	MC 414 849-2451	....	....	....	....	....	....	....
Chippewa Falls (13)	MC 715 726-2719	....	....	....	....	....	....	....
Clintonville (5)	MC 715 823-7600	Gib Johnson	Wallace Thiel	Chris Vollrath	....	John Krubsack	Gerald Bartelt	Mike McCord
Columbus (4)	MC 414 623-5900	Joseph A Marks	....	Anne Donahue	....	Fred Dartt	Anthony Brus	....
Combined Locks v (2)	MC 414 788-2059	....	....	....	....	....	....	....
Cudahy (19)	MC 414 769-2200	....	....	....	....	....	....	....
De Forest v (5)	CM 608 846-6751	Rex Yankee	Duane A Gau	Kim Manley	Duane A Gau	Joel Rider	James Culbertson	Jean Hale
De Pere (17)	CM 414 339-4050	Nancy Nusbaum	Jerome Smits	David Minten	....	Ted Pagels	David Tellock	Carl Weber

Directory 1/9 continued — MUNICIPAL OFFICIALS IN U.S. CITIES OVER 2,500

City, 1990 population figures (000 omitted), form of government		Municipal phone number	Mayor/ chief elected official	Appointed administrator	City clerk/ city secretary	Finance officer	Fire chief	Police chief	Public works director
WISCONSIN (175) continued									
Delafield (5)	MC	414 646-3395	E J McAleer	Lois Jensen	Lois Jensen	Lois Jensen	Harold Roberts	Jack Arndt	Michael Scaff
Delavan (6)	MC	414 728-5585	Ronald Henriott	Timothy Freitag	Betty L Wassel	....	Neill Flood	Lawrence H Malsch	Lyle A Smith
Dodgeville (4)	MC	608 935-5228	....	....	....	....	....	....	....
East Troy v (3)	MC	414 642-5338	....	....	....	....	....	....	....
Eau Claire (57)	CM	715 839-4921	Mark D Lewis	Don Norrell	Carol Schumacher	Rebecca Noland	Ron Brown	Dave Malone	William Bittner
Edgerton (4)	MC	608 884-3341	Eugene V Gruna	Richard A Schultz	Richard A Schultz	L Wandschneider	....	Keith Burdick	Stanley Strandlie
Elkhorn (5)	MC	414 723-2219	....	....	....	....	....	....	....
Elm Grove v (6)	CM	414 782-6700	Thomas E Vavra	John L Klaiber	James J Pellowski	....	William Selzer	Jeffrey W Haig	Kenneth Blaedow
Evansville (3)	MC	608 882-4424	....	....	....	....	....	....	....
Fitchburg t (16)	MC	608 275-7141	D Morrissette	Daniel Elsass	....	....	Larry Huber	Terry Askey	Paul Woodard
Fond Du Lac (38)	CM	414 929-3320	....	Jack Howley	Thomas Lehman	G A Rebensburg	David Flagstad	Daniel J Bord	J William Roemer
Fort Atkinson (10)	CM	414 563-7760	Ken Pattow	R C Martin	John Wilmett	John Wilmett	Steven Mode	Greg Gilbert	Jeff Woods
Fox Point v (7)	CM	414 351-8900	Mark B Pollack	Allan Medoff	Constance McHugh	....	Mark B Hayes	Mark B Hayes	Michael Lynett
Franklin (22)	MC	414 425-7500	Fred F Klimetz	James C Payne	James C Payne	Gene Strizek	David Bublitz	Norm Pollman	John Bennett
Germantown v (14)	CM	414 253-8250	Charles Hargan	Steve Kubacki	Jane Wilms	Robert Reis	Gary Pollpeter	Gerald Blum	Lloyd Turner
Glendale (14)	MC	414 228-1700	....	....	....	....	....	....	....
Grafton v (9)	MC	414 375-5300	Rodney Schroeder	Darrell Hofland	Teri Dylak	Shirley Ritger	....	Howard Thiede	Mark Gottlieb
Green Bay (96)	MC	414 448-3147	Sam Halloin	....	Paul Janquart	Jim Blumreich	John Troeger	Bob Langan	Dick Hall
Greendale v (15)	CM	414 423-2100	....	....	....	....	....	....	....
Greenfield (33)	MC	414 545-5500	James Besson	....	Donna Rynders	....	Roland Poppy	Francis Springob	Richard Andresen
Hales Corners v (8)	CM	414 529-6161	James R Ryan	Michael F Weber	Michael F Weber	....	Richard L Demien	....	Ronald J Romeis
Hartford (8)	MC	414 673-8204	James H Core	Kevin O' Donnell	John C Spielmann	Gary Koppelberger	Robert Baus	Tom Jones	Lucian Darin
Hartland v (7)	CM	414 367-2714	David Lamerand	Charles Erickson	Connie Casper	Joicelyn Schwager	Allen Wilde	Morton Hetznecker	James Wilson
Horicon (4)	MC	414 485-3500	Richard Greshay	....	David J Pasewald	....	Gordon Schwartz	Douglas Glamann	....
Hortonville v (2)	MC	414 779-6011	Alfred Handrich	M Schiedermayer	Joan Dockter	....	Lyle Otto	Kenneth Hansen	Robert Henrickson
Howard v (10)	CM	414 434-4640	George Speaker	Kevin Anderson	Kevin Anderson	C Haltom	John O' Connor	....	Bruce Boykin
Hudson (6)	MC	715 386-4765	Jack Breault	....	Gerald Berning	Gerald Berning	Dean Rossing	Dick Trende	Hank Paulson
Janesville (52)	CM	608 755-3080	....	Steve E Sheiffer	Jean A Wulf	Herbert Stinski	Larry J Grorud	George Brunner	Thomas O Rogers
Jefferson (6)	MC	414 674-7700	Arnold Branders	Karl P Frantz	Karl P Frantz	....	Donald D Wegner	Michael P Besel	Reuben F Schulz
Kaukauna (12)	MC	414 766-6312	John Lambie	....	Susan Duda	Stephen Giebel	Thomas Jansen	Patrick Campbell	....
Kenosha (80)	MC	414 656-8124	John Antaramian	Nick Arnold	Gail Procarione	Carol Stancato	Richard Thomas	Gerald Schuetz	Fred Haerter
Kewaskum v (3)	MC	414 626-8484	Robert H Wagner	Daniel S Schmidt	Daniel S Schmidt	....	Mark E Groeschel	Richard L Knoebel	Jerry E Gilles
Kewaunee (3)	MC	414 388-5000	Jerome Zelten	Joan Boyer	Joan Boyer	Joan Boyer	....	Dave DeCramer	Dave Suchocki
Kiel (3)	MC	414 894-2909	....	....	....	....	....	....	....
Kimberly v (5)	CM	414 734-9441	James J Siebers	Rick J Hermus	Rick J Hermus	....	Eugene Vandenberg	Dennis L Jansen	D Vanden Boogaard
La Crosse (51)	MC	608 789-7579	....	....	....	....	....	....	....
Ladysmith (4)	MC	715 532-2600	Ronald Moore	Alan Christianson	Kathleen Stewart	....	Scott Bingham	Norman Rozak	Bill Christianson
Lake Geneva (6)	MC	414 248-3673	Jane Brandley	James Stadler	Colleen Alexander	....	Thomas Derrick	Richard Newberry	....
Lake Mills (4)	CM	414 648-2344	....	Vernon C Johnson	James E Heilman	....	Richard J Heinz	Ronald W Klick	....
Lancaster (4)	MC	608 723-4246	J Pebworth	....	Vanda Vorwald	Gregg Berry	....	Rodger Janssen	Jerry Carroll
Little Chute v (9)	CM	414 788-7380	Donald DeGroot	Russel Van Gompel	Russel Van Gompel	Dale Haug	Martin Marasch	David Peterson	Gene Hojan
Madison (191)	MC	608 266-4671	....	....	....	....	....	....	....
Manitowoc (33)	MC	414 683-4432	Kevin Crawford	....	June Fetzer	Michael Easker	Charles Herzog	Richard Brey	Michael Hawley
Maple Bluff v (..)	CM	608 244-3048	Robert Cooper	Andrea S Crawford	Andrea S Crawford	....	Richard Reiter	Randolph Swingen	Ed Koval
Marinette (12)	MC	715 735-7427	....	....	....	....	....	....	....
Marshfield (19)	MC	715 387-6597	Richard E Daniels	Randy Allen	Carolyn Kautzer	Michael E Brehm	Gregg Cleveland	Clem Spencer	David C Patek
Mauston (3)	MC	608 847-6676	David E Pelton	....	....	....	Richard Hale	O J Foster	P Geisendorfer
Mayville (4)	MC	414 387-7900	John Lippert	....	Ken Jaeger	....	Lynn Cundy	Merlin Kahlhamer	Vern Hilker
Mc Farland v (5)	MC	608 838-3154	Doris Hanson	....	Ann Davis	....	....	Mike Larson	Dennis Dancker
Medford (4)	MC	715 748-4321	....	....	....	....	....	....	....
Menasha (15)	MC	414 751-5100	Joseph Laux	....	Joan Smogeleski	Tom Stoffel	Tom Miller	Bob Stanke	Mark Radtke
Menomonee Falls v (27)	CM	414 255-8300	Joseph Greco	R Farrenkopf	Patricia Struve	Diane Conrad	John Fulcher	David Steingraber	Max Vogt
Menomonie (14)	MC	715 232-2187	Charles Stokke	Lowell Prange	Jo Ann Kadinger	Lowell Prange	Charles Vind	Dennis Beety	....
Mequon (19)	MC	414 242-3100	James Moriarty	Harry Kollman	L Rzentkowski	Doug Bates	Curt Witzlib	Patrick Call	Jon Garms
Merrill (10)	MC	715 536-5594	....	....	....	....	....	....	....
Middleton (13)	MC	608 836-7481	....	....	....	....	....	....	....
Milton (4)	MC	608 868-6900	Richard Dabson	....	Doris Viney	....	....	Terry Hawkins	Howard Robinson
Milwaukee (628)	MC	414 286-3751	John O Norquist	Anne S Kinney	Ronald Leonhardt	Waldemar M Morics	August G Erdmann	Philip Arreola	James C Kaminski
Mondovi (2)	MC	715 926-3866	Allen R Whelan	....	Daniel Lauersdorf	....	Dennis Brion	Terry M Pittman	Gary D Risen
Monona (9)	CM	608 222-2525	V Thomas Metcalfe	Kevin M Brunner	Nanette K Ursino	....	Everette Pettey	Paul Welch	....
Monroe (10)	MC	608 325-4101	....	....	....	....	....	....	....
Mosinee (4)	MC	715 693-2275	James B Jacobson	Larry Saeger	Marcella Sitko	....	B Rheinschmidt	M Grzadzielewski	Kevin Breit
Mount Horeb v (4)	MC	608 437-3084	Peter J Waltz	Patrick E Dann	Mickey Deneen	....	....	Geore Mayerhofer	Laurel Grindle
Mount Pleasant t (20)	RT	414 554-8750	....	....	....	....	....	....	....
Mukwonago v (4)	MC	414 363-6420	Jerry Gasser	....	Bernard W Kahl	....	Jeff Rolfe	James Frank	Jerome Dettmann
Muskego (17)	MC	414 679-4100	David DeAngelis	....	Jean K Marenda	....	....	John Johnson	John Loughney
Neenah (23)	MC	414 751-4604	....	....	....	....	....	....	....
Neillsville (3)	MC	715 743-2105	....	....	....	....	....	....	....
Nekoosa (3)	MC	715 886-3811	....	....	....	....	....	....	....
New Berlin (34)	MC	414 786-8610	Mary Claire Cera	....	William Bowers	....	....	Mike Neuens	....
New Holstein (3)	MC	414 898-5766	....	....	....	....	....	....	....
New London (7)	MC	414 982-8500	Gregory Mathewson	L Steinbrecher	James Villiesse	James Villiesse	Wayne Wilfeur	David Neumann	Chris Zoppa
New Richmond (5)	MC	715 246-4268	H William Smith	Dennis A Horner	Helen E Demulling	....	Francis B Otto	David H Levi	John R Berends
North Fond Du Lac v (4)	CM	414 929-3765	C Engebregtsen	Don Peterson	Don Peterson	....	Mark Wiener	Larry Wodack	Mike Tolustad
Oak Creek (20)	MC	414 768-6500	Dale J Richards	Robert L Kufrin	Beverly A Buretta	....	Lyle L Brossman	Michael Younglove	....
Oconomowoc (11)	MC	414 569-2175	M Schumacher	Richard Mercier	Ardyce Senflebten	Hal Wortman	....	Hugh Martin	George Langohr
Oconto (4)	MC	414 834-7711	Dwaine M Konshak	....	Linda M Belongia	....	Michael Hoppe	Oren Woodworth	Robert Mommaerts
Omro (3)	MC	414 685-5693	Raymond Hoeft	Janet Schettl	Janet Schettl	....	David Treleven	John Vonderloh	Mike Domke
Onalaska (11)	MC	608 781-9530	George Osterhout	Rickert Durst	Orlene Hough	....	Robert Ritger	Randy Williams	Paul Johnson
Oregon v (5)	MC	608 835-3118	....	....	....	....	....	....	....
Oshkosh (55)	CM	414 236-5000	Richard Wollangk	William D Frueh	Donna Serwas	Edward Nokes	Stanley Tadych	James Thome	Gerald Konrad
Park Falls (3)	MC	715 762-2436	....	....	....	....	....	....	....
Peshtigo (3)	MC	715 582-3041	J F Dale Berman	....	Mary Ann Rodgers	....	Steven R Anderson	Thomas F Strouf	Steven A Cota
Pewaukee v (5)	MC	414 691-5660	John Laimon	Frank M Paulus	E Williams	Frank M Paulus	James Babe	Edward Baumann	Louis Thibault
Platteville (10)	CM	608 348-9741	....	Rosemary Kulow	Annette Dutcher	Duane Borgen	Robert Leieghty	James Enfelt	Ronald Mueller
Pleasant Prairie v (..)	MC	414 694-1400	Thomas W Terwall	Michael Pollocoff	Teresa M Matheny	Teresa M Matheny	Paul Guilbert Jr	James Horvath	Michael Foran
Plover v (8)	MC	715 345-5250	....	....	....	....	....	....	....
Plymouth (7)	MC	414 892-4474	....	....	....	....	....	....	....
Port Washington (9)	MC	414 284-5585	Joseph Dean	Mark Grams	....	....	Marc Eernisse	Edward Rudolph	....
Portage (9)	MC	608 742-2176	....	....	....	....	....	....	....
Prairie Du Chien (6)	MC	608 326-6406	William Farnum	Gary Koch	....	....	Michael DeMuth	Gary Knickerbocke	Roger Grunow
Prescott (3)	CM	715 262-5544	Jim Richman	Janet S Huppert	Connie M Gilles	....	Donald Johnson	Bill Cook	Jeff Kittleson
Racine (84)	MC	414 636-9103	N Owen Davies	....	Karen M Norton	Jerome J Maller	....	Richard Polzin	Richard M Jones

MUNICIPAL OFFICIALS
IN U.S. CITIES OVER 2,500

City, 1990 population figures (000 omitted), form of government	Municipal phone number	Mayor/ chief elected official	Appointed administrator	City clerk/ city secretary	Finance officer	Fire chief	Police chief	Public works director
WISCONSIN (175) continued								
Reedsburg (6)	MC 608 524-6404	....	....	....	....	....	....	....
Rhinelander (7)	MC 715 369-1657	Gordon Waldvogel	....	Deborah Breivogel	....	David E Lehman	James C Sebestyen	Gary R Knutson
Rice Lake (8)	MC 715 234-7088	Frank Ferguson	Curtis Snyder	Kathleen Morse	....	James Resac	Bradley Beffa	....
Richland Center (5)	MC 608 647-3466	Thomas McCarthy	....	Jude Elliott	....	David Foth	Craig Chicker	William McCorkle
Ripon (7)	MC 414 748-7771	John Haupt	Philip Deaton	....	Barbara Mashack	Mike Fredrick	Dave Lukoski	Jim Kaiser
River Falls (11)	MC 715 425-0900	Duane Pederson	Neil Ruddy	Dorothy Frederick	Julie Bergstrom	Dan Reis	Roger Leque	David Wisdorf
River Hills v (2)	CM 414 352-8213	....	Joseph T Szyper	Kathleen Pellerin	....	....	Michael Downing	Kurt Fredrickson
Rothschild v (3)	MC 715 359-3660	Neal C Torney	....	Sheila Pudelko	....	Jeffrey Hanson	Joseph E Toth	James E Hahn
Sauk City v (3)	CM 608 643-3932	....	....	....	....	....	....	....
Saukville v (4)	CM 414 284-9423	Jeffery P Knight	Christopher Lear	Sandy Garbarek	....	Glenn Dickmann	Bell Meloy	....
Seymour (3)	MC 414 833-2209	Ervin Conradt	....	Susan Garsow	....	Tom Seidl	Don Raymakers	Mike Pepin
Shawano (8)	MC 715 526-6138	Lee M Schrader	....	Marlene I Brath	....	Doug Knope	Donald Thaves	Rick J Stautz
Sheboygan (50)	MC 414 459-3373	....	....	....	....	....	....	....
Sheboygan Falls (6)	MC 414 459-3191	....	....	....	....	....	....	....
Shorewood v (14)	CM 414 963-6990	Michael R Schulte	Edward C Madere	Joanne Woodford	Denise Vandenbush	....	Alvin J Berndt	James F Bartnicki
Shorewood Hills v (2)	CM 608 266-4781	Gard Strother	Tom Popp	Tom Popp	....	Tom DeMeuse	Terry Ninneman	Dennis Lybeck
South Milwaukee (21)	MC 414 762-2222	Dave Kieck	Jon Syndergaard	Jackie Johnson	....	Don Egner	Erick Slamka	....
Sparta (8)	MC 608 269-4340	Milo D Seubert	Stephen J Gunty	Janice E Foss	Stephen J Gunty	Scott D Lindemann	Ray G Harris	Larry K Brown
St. Francis (9)	MC 414 481-2300	....	....	....	....	....	....	....	....
Stevens Point (23)	MC 715 346-1594	Orville Halverson	....	Barbara Kranig	....	Peter Ugorek	Robert Kreisa	Jon Van Alstine
Stoughton (9)	MC 608 873-6677	Helen J Johnson	....	Judy A Kinning	....	Odean Teigen	Patrick O' Connor	Robert Kardasz
Sturgeon Bay (9)	MC 414 746-2900	N Schachtner	Dennis Jordan	Paul Bellin	Paul Bellin	Gary Drexler	Michael Nordin	John Kolodziej
Sturtevant v (4)	MC 414 886-7200	Clay Morgan	....	Barbara Pauls	....	John Theama	Ronald R Kittel	....
Sun Prairie (15)	MC 608 837-2511	Jo Ann C Orfan	Patrick A Cannon	Edna Markstahler	Margaret Powers	Robert Krause	Frank Sleeter	Larry Herman
Superior (27)	MC 715 394-0212	Herbert Bergson	....	Margaret Ciccone	Timothy Nelson	Steven Gotelaere	Doyle Barker	Jeffrey Vito
Sussex v (5)	CM 414 246-5200	....	....	....	....	....	....	....
Thiensville v (3)	CO 414 242-3720	Roy Wetzel	....	John R Gibbons	....	William F Rausch	Richard W Preston	....
Tomah (8)	MC 608 374-7420	Frances M Pollard	David Berner	Phillis Zimmerman	....	Thomas Flock	Steven Rinzel	Kenneth Patterson
Tomahawk (3)	MC 715 453-4040	....	....	....	....	....	....	....
Twin Lakes v (4)	MC 414 877-2858	John Staudemeyer	....	Dorothy E Sandona	William Porps	Wayne Trongeau	Dale Crichton	Carol Paus
Two Rivers (13)	CM 414 793-5528	....	....	....	....	....	....	....
Union Grove v (4)	MC 414 878-1818	....	....	....	....	....	....	....
Verona (5)	MC 608 845-6495	Arthur R Cresson	Beverly J Beyer	Beverly J Beyer	....	....	Edward E Moffett	Ronald R Rieder
Viroqua (4)	MC 608 637-7154	Charles F Dahl	....	Patricia Griffin	....	....	John Thompson	Thomas Henry
Washington t (6)	CM 715 834-3257	....	....	....	....	....	....	....
Watertown (19)	MC 414 262-4000	Frederick H Smith	....	Mike H Hoppenrath	Mike H Hoppenrath	Dick Gallup	Chuck McGee	Joe Radocay
Waukesha (57)	MC 414 524-3500	Carol A Opel	....	Thomas E Neill	Robert H Wolf	Robert W Stedman	Thomas H Stigler	R Vanden Noven
Waunakee v (6)	MC 608 849-5626	....	....	....	....	....	....	....
Waupaca (5)	MC 715 258-2044	....	....	Kyle J Clark	....	Norman Lenz	Thomas Winscher	Bruce Zellner
Waupun (8)	MC 414 324-7900	Harold Nummerdor	....	Gary Klingbeil	Carla Manthe	K Szeklinski	W Brandimore	David Koch
Wausau (37)	MC 715 843-1000	John D Hess	....	Janice Simonsen	Ronald Braier	Donald Pekel	Barry Weber	Howard Young
Wauwatosa (49)	MC 414 471-8400	Maricolette Walsh	James Grassman	Eldon Rinka	Gary Schmid	Raymond Schrader	John Butorac	Michael Pertmer
West Allis (63)	MC 414 256-8200	John Turck	Paul Ziehler	Barbara Barringer	....	Brian Mayer	James Schwartz	Terry Kieckhaefer
West Bend (24)	MC 414 335-5100	Michael R Miller	Dennis W Melvin	Jadell Ferge	....	....	Eugene Oldenburg	Jack Russell
West Milwaukee v (4)	MC 414 645-1530	Ronald Hayward	....	Teresa Schnitzler	Kenneth R Knutson	Donald Buisman	Dennis Abbott	Jack Twining
West Salem v (4)	MC 608 786-1858	Robert Machotka	Kenneth R Knutson	Barbara Patin	Edmund Henschel	....	Gary Mikulec	R Vanden Noven
Whitefish Bay v (14)	CM 414 962-6690	James Gormley	Edmund Henschel	....	....	....	Robert Ziegert	James Borski
Whitewater (13)	CM 414 473-0502	....	....	....	....	....	....	....
Wisconsin Dells (2)	MC 608 254-2012	....	....	....	....	....	....	....
Wisconsin Rapids (18)	MC 715 421-8200	Vernon Verjinsky	....	Vernon Borth	....	James Gignac	Robert Ziegert	James Borski
WYOMING (25)								
Buffalo t (3)	MC 307 684-5566	Nels B Lofgren	....	Kay L Wertz	....	Robert Hancock	Terry Barnhart	Robert Borgialli
Casper (47)	CM 307 235-8400	....	Thomas Forslund	....	Calvin Chadsey	....	Art DeWerk	Philip Stuckert
Cheyenne (50)	MC 307 637-6200	....	....	....	....	....	....	....
Cody (8)	MC 307 527-7511	Jack T Skates	....	James S Smiley	....	Ken Reiter	Daniel F Kelsey	....
Douglas (5)	CM 307 358-3462	Ray Haskins	Bobbe Fitzhugh	Janet Dahmke	V H McDonald	William Roberts	Larry Majerus	Steve Bennett
Evanston t (11)	MC 307 789-9690	Dennis J Ottley	....	Don U Welling	Stephen D Widmer	....	Russell D Harvey	Brian Honey
Evansville t (1)	MC 307 234-6530	....	....	....	....	....	....	....
Gillette (18)	CM 307 686-5203	Edd Collins	John Darrington	Mildred Huravitch	David Layden	....	Jeff Pfau	Bill Carson
Glenrock t (2)	MC 307 436-9294	....	....	....	....	....	....	....
Green River (13)	MC 307 875-5000	....	....	....	....	....	....	....
Jackson t (4)	MC 307 733-3932	....	....	....	....	....	....	....
Kemmerer (3)	CM 307 877-9007	....	....	....	....	....	....	....
Lander (7)	MC 307 332-2870	Arland Carlson	....	Paul J Freese	....	....	Richard G Currah	Laurence Ashdown
Laramie (27)	CM 307 721-5200	Amber Travsky	F McConnaughey	Susan Vosseller	....	Jim Noel	Mark Bridgemon	....
Lyman t (2)	MC 307 786-4898	....	....	....	....	....	....	....
Newcastle (3)	MC 307 746-3535	....	....	....	....	....	....	....
Powell (5)	CM 307 754-5106	Janna F Harkrider	Duane F Wroe	Ardyce Busboom	Duane F Wroe	....	John Cox	Robert Brock
Rawlins (9)	CM 307 328-4500	Judy Dixon	David Crow	Alice Garvin	David Derragon	....	Tony Rose	Bruce Florovist
Riverton (9)	MC 307 856-2227	Albert T Brown	....	Marie Burkhalter	....	....	Mike Hays	Harry C Labonde
Rock Springs (19)	MC 307 362-2330	Paul S Oblock	....	....	Marlene E Kudar	Harvey Cozad	Matt Bider	Glenn Sugano
Sheridan (14)	MC 307 674-6483	Della Herbst	....	Art Elkins	Art Elkins	Jim Wenzel	Charlie Hendren	Tony Pelesky
Thermopolis t (3)	MC 307 864-9285	....	....	....	....	....	....	....
Torrington t (6)	MC 307 532-5666	....	....	....	....	....	....	....
Wheatland t (3)	MC 307 322-2962	Maurice Berger	Scott A Sikes	....	....	Ron McCormick	Steven Gilmore	....
Worland (6)	MC 307 347-2486	....	....	....	....	....	....	....

Directory 1/10   **COUNTY OFFICIALS IN U.S. COUNTIES**

The data for the directory of county officials were collected by ICMA in the summer of 1994 through a mail survey. The 3,107 counties surveyed include all counties with populations of 2,500 and over and those under 2,500 that are recognized by ICMA as providing for a professional management position.

In addition to the names of officials (and the county phone number), data on race and sex were collected for the county chief elected official, judge or president, the appointed administrator, clerk to the governing board, chief financial officer, county health officer, planning director,

county engineer, director of welfare/human services, chief law enforcement officer, purchasing director, and personnel director. The positions of planning director, director of welfare, purchasing director, health officer, and engineer are not shown in the individual county directory that follows. All data collected other than the names and phone numbers are treated with complete confidentiality, and only aggregate data are presented below.

Sex and Race of County Officials. Tables 1/10/a and 1/10/b present a breakdown of each sex by race and ethnicity for the county officials.

Given the level of detail shown, it is possible to reaggregate these data for other displays that would show race and sex characteristics of the total number of officials reporting.

The Directory. For convenience, the directory shows the names of counties in alphabetical order within each state. Other items indicated in the directory for each county-type government are the population and county phone number.

Table 1/10/a   MALE COUNTY OFFICIALS BY RACE AND ETHNICITY

Position	Total reporting (A)	Total males No. (B)	Total males % of (A)	White No.	White % of (B)	Black No.	Black % of (B)	American Indian No.	American Indian % of (B)	Asian No.	Asian % of (B)	Other No.	Other % of (B)	Race not reported No.	Race not reported % of (B)	Hispanic No.	Hispanic % of (B)
Chief elected official	1,538	1,389	90.3	1,283	92.4	40	2.9	9	0.6	0	0.0	9	0.6	48	3.5	21	1.5
Chief appointed administrative officer	725	592	81.7	545	92.1	14	2.4	4	0.7	3	0.5	9	1.5	17	2.9	12	2.0
Clerk to the governing board	1,426	424	29.7	384	90.6	8	1.9	2	0.5	3	0.7	4	0.9	23	5.4	9	2.1
Chief financial officer	1,209	644	53.3	590	91.6	10	1.6	4	0.6	8	1.2	3	0.5	29	4.5	10	1.6
County health officer	937	600	64.0	519	86.5	13	2.2	3	0.5	8	1.3	5	0.8	52	8.7	9	1.5
Planning director	783	654	83.5	607	92.8	7	1.1	1	0.2	3	0.5	2	0.3	34	5.2	6	0.9
County engineer	806	793	98.4	735	92.7	7	0.9	1	0.1	4	0.5	6	0.8	40	5.0	12	1.5
Director health/human services	806	441	54.7	385	87.3	15	3.4	2	0.5	2	0.5	2	0.5	35	7.9	12	2.7
Chief law enforcement official	1,544	1,535	99.4	1,404	91.5	19	1.2	10	0.7	2	0.1	12	0.8	88	5.7	34	2.2
Purchasing director	626	377	60.2	336	89.1	14	3.7	4	1.1	1	0.3	5	1.3	17	4.5	12	3.2
Personnel director	754	404	53.6	353	87.4	21	5.2	4	1.0	3	0.7	4	1.0	19	4.7	6	1.5

Table 1/10/b   FEMALE COUNTY OFFICIALS BY RACE AND ETHNICITY

Position	Total reporting (A)	Total females No. (B)	Total females % of (A)	White No.	White % of (B)	Black No.	Black % of (B)	American Indian No.	American Indian % of (B)	Asian No.	Asian % of (B)	Other No.	Other % of (B)	Race not reported No.	Race not reported % of (B)	Hispanic No.	Hispanic % of (B)
Chief elected official	1,538	149	9.7	137	91.9	5	3.4	2	1.3	0	0.0	0	0.0	5	3.4	2	1.3
Chief appointed administrative officer	725	133	18.3	119	89.5	4	3.0	2	1.5	0	0.0	0	0.0	8	6.0	4	3.0
Clerk to the governing board	1,426	1,002	70.3	937	93.5	19	1.9	9	0.9	2	0.2	11	1.1	24	2.4	24	2.4
Chief financial officer	1,209	565	46.7	541	95.8	5	0.9	2	0.4	0	0.0	4	0.7	13	2.3	9	1.6
County health officer	937	337	36.0	314	93.2	9	2.7	0	0.0	4	1.2	5	1.5	5	1.5	3	0.9
Planning director	783	129	16.5	121	93.8	5	3.9	1	0.8	1	0.8	0	0.0	1	0.8	1	0.8
County engineer	806	13	1.6	12	92.3	0	0.0	0	0.0	1	7.7	0	0.0	0	0.0	1	7.7
Director welfare/human services	806	365	45.3	327	89.6	29	7.9	0	0.0	1	0.3	2	0.5	6	1.6	8	2.2
Chief law enforcement official	1,544	9	0.6	8	88.9	1	11.1	0	0.0	0	0.0	0	0.0	0	0.0	0	0.0
Purchasing director	626	249	39.8	226	90.8	14	5.6	2	0.8	0	0.0	3	1.2	4	1.6	9	3.6
Personnel director	754	350	46.4	315	90.0	23	6.6	3	0.9	0	0.0	1	0.3	8	2.3	10	2.9

Directory 1/10 OFFICIALS IN U.S. COUNTIES 2,500 AND OVER IN POPULATION
continued

County designation
c City-county consolidation
i Independent city
b Borough
p Parish

Population
Note: The only jurisdictions under 2,500 in population that are listed are those recognized by ICMA.

Population figures are not rounded up; 14,500 will appear as 14.

(..) Less than 500 population

Other codes
. . . . Data not reported or not applicable

County, county seat, 1990 population figures (000 omitted)	County telephone number	Chief elected official	Appointed administrator	Clerk to the governing board	Chief financial officer	Personnel director	Chief law enforcement official
ALABAMA (67)							
Autauga (Prattville) (34)	205 361-3701	....	....	....	....	....	....
Baldwin (Bay Minette) (98)	205 937-9561	C Dean Hansen	James W Zumwalt	Lori Ruffin	Locke Williams	Byron C Calhoun	James Johnson
Barbour (Clayton) (25)	205 775-3203	....	....	....	....	....	....
Bibb (Centreville) (17)	205 926-4823	....	....	....	....	....	....
Blount (Oneonta) (39)	205 274-9111	....	....	....	....	....	....
Bullock (Union Springs) (11)	205 738-3883	....	....	....	....	....	....
Butler (Greenville) (22)	205 382-3512	....	....	....	....	....	....
Calhoun (Anniston) (116)	205 236-3521	....	....	....	....	....	....
Chambers (Lafayette) (37)	205 864-8823	....	....	....	....	....	....
Cherokee (Centre) (20)	205 927-3668	....	....	....	....	....	....
Chilton (Clanton) (32)	205 755-1551	Bobby L Agee	Sharon G Sumrall	Sharon G Sumrall	Sharon G Sumrall	Cathy B Martin	Paul N Strength
Choctaw (Butler) (16)	205 459-2100	Charles V Ford	Alice C Smith	Alice C Smith	Alice C Smith	....	Donald Lolley
Clarke (Grove Hill) (27)	205 275-3251	....	....	....	....	....	....
Clay (Ashland) (13)	205 354-2198	....	....	....	....	....	....
Cleburne (Heflin) (13)	205 463-2951	....	....	....	....	....	....
Coffee (Elba) (40)	205 987-5430	....	....	....	....	....	....
Colbert (Tuscumbia) (52)	205 383-4981	....	....	....	....	....	....
Conecuh (Evergreen) (14)	205 578-2095	....	....	....	....	....	....
Coosa (Rockford) (11)	205 377-2420	....	....	....	....	....	....
Covington (Andalusia) (36)	205 222-3613	....	....	....	....	....	....
Crenshaw (Luverne) (14)	205 335-6568	Johnny Smith	....	Linda Williamson	Linda Williamson	Linda Williamson	Robert Colquett
Cullman (Cullman) (68)	205 739-3530	....	....	....	....	....	....
Dale (Ozark) (50)	205 774-6262	....	....	....	....	....	....
Dallas (Selma) (48)	205 875-4401	....	....	....	....	....	....
De Kalb (Fort Payne) (55)	205 845-0541	....	....	....	....	....	....
Elmore (Wetumpka) (49)	205 567-2571	....	....	....	....	....	....
Escambia (Brewton) (36)	205 867-6261	William C America	Kenneth Taylor	Kenneth Taylor	Kenneth Taylor	....	Timothy A Hawsey
Etowah (Gadsden) (100)	205 549-5301	W A Lutes	David Akins	....	David Akins	Mike Naugher	James Hayes
Fayette (Fayette) (18)	205 932-4510	Joe Stewart	....	Johnny Humber	....	Bobbie Kemp	James Turner
Franklin (Russellville) (28)	205 332-3814	....	....	....	....	....	....
Geneva (Geneva) (24)	205 684-2276	....	....	....	....	....	....
Greene (Eutaw) (10)	205 372-3349	....	....	....	....	....	....
Hale (Greensboro) (15)	205 624-4257	Riley Lucas	Nell McMillan	Nell McMillan	Nell McMillan	....	Larry Johnson
Henry (Abbeville) (15)	205 585-2753	....	....	....	....	....	....
Houston (Dothan) (81)	205 677-4700	....	....	....	....	....	....
Jackson (Scottsboro) (48)	205 259-6617	....	....	....	....	....	....
Jefferson (Birmingham) (652)	205 325-5311	....	....	....	....	....	....
Lamar (Vernon) (16)	205 695-7333	....	....	....	....	....	....
Lauderdale (Florence) (80)	205 760-5750	....	....	....	....	....	....
Lawrence (Moulton) (32)	205 974-0663	....	....	....	....	....	....
Lee (Opelika) (87)	205 745-6471	....	....	....	....	....	....
Limestone (Athens) (54)	205 232-1320	....	....	....	....	....	....
Lowndes (Haynesville) (13)	205 548-2331	....	....	....	....	....	....
Macon (Tuskegee) (25)	205 727-5120	....	....	....	....	....	....
Madison (Huntsville) (239)	205 532-3492	....	....	....	....	....	....
Marengo (Linden) (23)	205 295-2200	....	....	....	....	....	....
Marion (Hamilton) (30)	205 921-3172	Scott Alldredge	....	Gearldean Lindsey	....	....	J Max Brasher
Marshall (Guntersville) (71)	205 571-7701	....	....	....	....	....	....
Mobile (Mobile) (379)	205 470-7727	Freeman Jockish	W C Helveston	Geraldine Griffin	Susan Morrison	Shannon Weekley	Tom Purvis
Monroe (Monroeville) (24)	205 743-3782	....	....	....	....	....	....
Montgomery (Montgomery) (209) ..	205 832-4950	William F Joseph	David T Stockman	....	Donnie Mims	Barbara M Montoya	James D Jones
Morgan (Decatur) (100)	205 351-4737	....	....	....	....	....	....
Perry (Marion) (13)	205 683-6886	....	....	....	....	....	....
Pickens (Carrollton) (21)	205 367-2020	William Latham	....	S Keith Powell	....	....	David Abston
Pike (Troy) (28)	205 566-6374	Ronald M Morgan	Britt Thomas	....	....	....	Harold Anderson
Randolph (Wedowee) (20)	205 357-4551	....	....	....	....	....	....
Russell (Phenix City) (47)	501 968-6064	C Doug Luningham	....	Don Johnson	Gail Lutrell	....	Jay Winters
Shelby (Columbiana) (99)	205 669-3741	....	....	....	....	....	....
St. Clair (Ashville) (50)	205 594-3641	....	....	....	....	....	....
Sumter (Livingston) (16)	205 652-2731	....	....	....	....	....	....
Talladega (Talladega) (74)	205 362-2112	....	....	....	....	....	....
Tallapoosa (Dadeville) (39)	205 825-4268	....	....	....	....	....	....
Tuscaloosa (Tuscaloosa) (151)	205 349-3870	W Hardy McCollum	....	Robert Johnston	William M Lamb	Melvin L Vines	Edmund M Sexton
Walker (Jasper) (68)	205 384-7230	Joseph C Kimbrell	Jean Franklin	....	Ray Bradford Jr	Linda A Armstrong	Joe B Robertson
Washington (Chatom) (17)	205 847-2208	Tom W Turner	Mary K Carpenter	....	....	....	William J Wheat
Wilcox (Camden) (14)	205 682-9112	Bobby Jo Johnson	Ira Bradford	....	....	Bobby Jo Johnson	Prince Arnold
Winston (Double Springs) (22)	205 489-5026	Roger Hayes	....	Lola Gilbreath	....	....	Hobby Walker
ALASKA (12)							
Anchorage (Anchorage) c (226)	907 343-4425	....	....	....	....	....	....
Bristol Bay (Naknek) b (1)	907 246-4224	....	....	....	....	....	....
Fairbanks North Star (Fairbanks) b (78)	907 459-1202	Jim Sampson	Ralph Malone	Mona Lisa Drexler	Judith Slajer	Diane Thacker	....
Haines (Haines) b (2)	907 766-2711	....	....	....	....	....	....
Juneau (Juneau) c (27)	907 586-5240	....	Mark Palesh	Patty Ann Polley	Craig Duncan	Kenneth Kareen	Richard Gummow
Kenai Peninsula (Soldotna) b (41) ..	907 262-4441	....	....	Gaye Vaughan	Ross Kinney	Richard Campbell	....

Directory 1/10 **OFFICIALS IN U.S. COUNTIES**
continued

County, county seat, 1990 population figures (000 omitted)	County telephone number	Chief elected official	Appointed administrator	Clerk to the governing board	Chief financial officer	Personnel director	Chief law enforcement official
ALASKA (12) continued							
Ketchikan Gateway (Ketchikan) b (14)	907 228-6625	Jim Carlton	Michael Rody	G Zimmerle	Alvin Hall	....	....
Kodiak Island (Kodiak) b (13)	907 486-9301	....	....	....	....	....	....
Matanuska Susitna (Palmer) b (40)	907 745-4801	Ernest W Brannon	Donald L Moore	Linda Dahl	R Desmond Mayo	Ann K Stokes	....
North Slope (Barrow) b (6)	907 852-2611	....	....	....	....	....	....
Northwest Arctic (Kotzebue) b (6)	907 442-2500	Reggie Cleveland	Chuck Greene	Paulette Lambert	....	Linda Joule	....
Sitka (Sitka) c (9)	907 747-3294	....	....	....	....	....	....
ARIZONA (15)							
Apache (St. Johns) (62)	602 337-4364	Michael Nelson	Clarence Bigelow	Clarence Bigelow	John Smith	Rick McRoy	C Arthur Lee
Cochise (Bisbee) (98)	602 432-9200	....	....	....	....	....	....
Coconino (Flagstaff) (97)	602 774-5011	Tony Gabaldon	James R Keene	Ethel Ulibarri	Holly Lindfors	Donna P Patterson	Joe Richards
Gila (Globe) (40)	602 425-3231	Cruz Salas	Steven Besich	Steven Besich	....	Susan Mitchell	Joe Rodriquez
Graham (Safford) (27)	602 428-3250	....	....	....	....	....	....
Greenlee (Clifton) (8)	602 865-2072	Hector Ruedas	Robert K Stokes	Deborah K Gale	Robert K Stokes	Robert K Stokes	Allen Williams
La Paz (Parker) (14)	602 669-6115	Gregory Q Upton	Daniel G Field	Daniel G Field	Sandra J Dodge	....	Marvin Hare
Maricopa (Phoenix) (2122)	602 506-3236		Paul G Ahler				
Mohave (Kingman) (93)	602 753-9141	Joan Ward	David J Grisez	Pat Chastain	Robert L Kenney	Joyce Clifton	Joe Cook
Navajo (Holbrook) (78)	602 524-6161	Marlin Gillespie	Edward Koury	S Keene Wright	Clinton Shreeve	Gilbert Gonzales	Gary Butler
Pima (Tucson) (667)	602 740-8661	Mike Boyd	C Huckelberry	Jane Williams	Carol Bonchalk	Carol Bonchalk	Clarence Dupnik
Pinal (Florence) (116)	602 868-6000	Sandra L Smith	Stanley D Griffis	Stanley D Griffis	Terry L Doolittle	Robert L Keiser	Frank R Reyes
Santa Cruz (Nogales) (30)	602 761-7800	Robert Damon	Dennis Miller	Fran Decillis	Dennis Miller	Fran Decillis	Tony Estrada
Yavapai (Prescott) (108)	602 771-3100	Bill Feldmeier	Jim Holst	Bev Staddon	Mike Danowski	Carol Berra	G C Buck Buchanan
Yuma (Yuma) (107)	602 329-2104	Kathryn Prochaska	James R Stahle	James R Stahle	Donald P Wicks	Cherlene Penilla	Ralph E Ogden
ARKANSAS (75)							
Arkansas (Stuttgart) (22)	501 673-3181	....	....	....	....	....	....
Ashley (Hamburg) (24)	501 853-5144	....	....	....	....	....	....
Baxter (Mountain Home) (31)	501 425-2755	....	....	....	....	....	....
Benton (Bentonville) (97)	501 271-1000	....	....	....	....	....	....
Boone (Harrison) (28)	501 741-5760	Dale Wagner	....	David Witty	Linda Brown	....	Kenneth Foley
Bradley (Warren) (12)	501 226-3853	....	....	....	....	....	....
Calhoun (Hampton) (6)	501 798-4818	....	....	....	....	....	....
Carroll (Berryville) (19)	501 423-2967	....	....	....	....	....	....
Chicot (Lake Village) (16)	501 265-2208	....	....	....	....	....	....
Clark (Arkadelphia) (21)	501 246-5847	Frank Taylor	Deborah McMaster	....	....	....	Troy Tucker
Clay (Piggott) (18)	501 598-2667	Travis Boyd	....	Charles Pollard	Betty Haley	....	Darvin Stow
Cleburne (Heber Springs) (19)	501 362-8141	....	....	....	....	....	....
Cleveland (Rison) (8)	501 325-6214	Joe W Rauls	....	John T Reed	Nancy L Saeler	....	Joe P King
Columbia (Magnolia) (26)	501 234-4194	....	....	....	....	....	....
Conway (Morrilton) (19)	501 354-9640	D H Pettingill	....	Beverly Paladino	Roy B Bane	....	Carl Poteete
Craighead (Jonesboro) (69)	501 933-4520	Roy C Bearden	....	Jane Todd	Roy C Bearden	Jane Todd	Larry Emison
Crawford (Van Buren) (42)	501 474-1312	....	....	....	....	....	....
Crittenden (Marion) (50)	501 739-3383	....	....	....	....	....	....
Cross (Wynne) (19)	501 238-3373	....	....	....	....	....	....
Dallas (Fordyce) (10)	501 352-2307	....	....	....	....	....	....
Desha (Arkansas City) (17)	501 877-2426	....	....	....	....	....	....
Drew (Monticello) (17)	501 460-6200	Dale L Hughes	....	....	....	....	Tommy C Free
Faulkner (Conway) (60)	501 450-4900	....	....	....	....	....	....
Franklin (Ozark) (15)	501 667-4726	Joe Powell	Laura Rudolph	Mary Williams	Jane Ferguson	Joe Powell	Kenneth Ross
Fulton (Salem) (10)	501 895-3310	....	....	....	....	....	....
Garland (Hot Springs) (73)	501 622-3600	Bud Williams	Larry Williams	Nancy Johnson	Jo West Taylor	Larry Williams	Larry Selig
Grant (Sheridan) (14)	501 942-2551	....	....	....	....	....	....
Greene (Paragould) (32)	501 239-6300	David Lange	....	Nadine Jamison	Denna Napier	....	James Danley
Hempstead (Hope) (22)	501 777-6164	....	....	....	....	....	....
Hot Spring (Malvern) (26)	501 332-2261	....	....	....	....	....	....
Howard (Nashville) (14)	501 845-7500	Conrad Bagley	....	Shirley Dildy	Diana Shaw	....	Richard Wakefield
Independence (Batesville) (31)	501 793-8829	....	....	....	....	....	....
Izard (Melbourne) (11)	501 368-4328	....	....	....	....	....	....
Jackson (Newport) (19)	501 523-7400	Jerry Carlew	....	Geneva White	Donna Lewis	....	Donald Ray
Jefferson (Pine Bluff) (85)	501 541-5360	....	....	....	....	....	....
Johnson (Clarksville) (18)	501 754-2175	Mike Jacobs	....	....	....	....	Charles Nicklas
Lafayette (Lewisville) (10)	501 921-4858	Frank Scroggins	George H Turner	Diane Fletcher	Sue Ormand Lanie	....	Harlis Camp
Lawrence (Walnut Ridge) (17)	501 886-2167	....	....	....	....	....	....
Lee (Marianna) (13)	501 295-2339	....	....	....	....	....	....
Lincoln (Star City) (14)	501 628-4147	....	....	....	....	....	....
Little River (Ashdown) (14)	501 898-5021	....	....	....	....	....	....
Logan (Paris) (21)	501 963-3601	....	....	....	....	....	....
Lonoke (Lonoke) (39)	501 676-2368	....	....	....	....	....	....
Madison (Huntsville) (12)	501 738-6721	....	....	....	....	....	....
Marion (Yellville) (12)	501 449-6231	....	....	....	....	....	....
Miller (Texarkana) (38)	501 774-1301	....	....	....	....	....	....
Mississippi (Blytheville) (58)	501 763-3212	Karen Green	Paul Sullins	Jo Ann Morgan	Eva Gill	Brenda Burke	Leroy Meadows
Monroe (Clarendon) (11)	501 747-3632	....	....	....	....	....	....
Montgomery (Mount Ida) (8)	501 867-3114	....	....	....	....	....	....
Nevada (Prescott) (10)	501 887-3115	John Henry	....	Julie Stockton	Sydney DuCharme	....	William A Morman
Newton (Jasper) (8)	501 446-5127	....	....	....	....	....	....
Ouachita (Camden) (31)	501 837-2210	Paul A Lucas	Loren Strickland	Evelon Holeman	....	....	Ben Garner
Perry (Perryville) (8)	501 889-5126	....	....	....	....	....	....
Phillips (Helena) (29)	501 338-5500	....	....	....	....	....	....
Pike (Murfreesboro) (10)	501 285-2231	....	....	....	....	....	....
Poinsett (Harrisburg) (25)	501 578-5333	....	....	....	....	....	....
Polk (Mena) (17)	501 394-4945	....	....	....	....	....	....
Pope (Russellville) (46)	501 968-6064	....	....	....	....	....	....
Prairie (Des Arc) (10)	501 256-3741	Guyman Devore	....	Nancy Gutrie	Dorothy Flangan	....	Dale Madden
Pulaski (Little Rock) (350)	501 372-8305	....	....	....	....	....	....
Randolph (Pocahontas) (17)	501 892-5264	....	....	....	....	....	....
Saline (Benton) (64)	501 776-5600	....	....	....	....	....	....
Scott (Waldron) (10)	501 637-2155	Booster Hawkins	....	Evelyn Ammons	Verna Rogers	....	James Isham
Searcy (Marshall) (8)	501 448-3554	....	....	....	....	....	....
Sebastian (Fort Smith) (100)	501 783-6139	....	....	....	....	....	....
Sevier (De Queen) (14)	501 642-2425	O H Durham	....	Sandra Dunn	....	....	John Partain
Sharp (Ash Flat) (14)	501 994-7338	Franklin Arnold	....	Tommy Estes	Norman Girtman	....	T J Sonny Powell

Directory 1/10 OFFICIALS IN U.S. COUNTIES
continued

County, county seat, 1990 population figures (000 omitted)	County telephone number	Chief elected official	Appointed administrator	Clerk to the governing board	Chief financial officer	Personnel director	Chief law enforcement official
ARKANSAS (75) continued							
St. Francis (Forrest City) (28)	501 261-1700	Gazzola Vaccaro	Elizabeth Smith	Dick Krablin	Wayne Courtney	....	David Parkman
Stone (Mountain View) (10)	501 269-3106	R C Alexander	....	Donna Wilson	Donna Passmore	....	Dave Barnum
Union (El Dorado) (47)	501 863-5244	....	....	....	....	....	....
Van Buren (Clinton) (14)	501 745-2443	....	....	....	....	....	....
Washington (Fayetteville) (113)	501 521-8400	....	....	....	....	....	....
White (Searcy) (55)	501 268-2950	....	....	....	....	....	....
Woodruff (Augusta) (10)	501 347-2871	John Davis	....	Pat Rives	....	....	Jack Caperton
Yell (Danville) (18)	501 495-2414	Gary M Moore	....	Carolyn Morris	Dorothy Keathley	....	Loyd Maughn
CALIFORNIA (58)							
Alameda (Oakland) (1279)	510 272-6425	Edward Campbell	Steven C Szalay	Bill Mehrwein	P O' Connell	Naomi O Burns	Charles C Plummer
Alpine (Markleeville) (1)	916 694-2287	....	....	....	....	....	....
Amador (Jackson) (30)	209 223-6456	Edward Bamert	....	C Giannini	John Kirkpatrick	C Giannini	Kenneth Blake
Butte (Oroville) (182)	916 538-7631	Ed McLaughlin	John Blacklock	Carol Roach	David Houser	....	Mick Grey
Calaveras (San Andreas) (32)	209 754-6303	M Dell' Orto	Brent Harrington	Karen Varni	Joann Long	Jalynne Tobias	William Nuttall
Colusa (Colusa) (16)	916 458-2101	....	....	....	....	....	....
Contra Costa (Martinez) (804)	510 646-4064	....	....	....	....	....	....
Del Norte (Crescent City) (23)	707 464-7214	Bob Bark	R S Holden	Karen Walsh	R S Holden	R S Holden	Mike Ross
El Dorado (Placerville) (126)	916 621-5565	John Upton	Paul McIntosh	Dixie Foote	Joe Harn	Kathryn Libicki	Don McDonald
Fresno (Fresno) (667)	209 488-3364	Vernon Conrad	William Randolph	Shari Greenwood	Gary Peterson	....	Steve Magarian
Glenn (Willows) (25)	916 934-6451	Marilyn Baker	....	Carolyn Davis	Joseph Sites	John Greco	Roger Roberts
Humboldt (Eureka) (119)	707 445-7509	Bonnie Neely	Chris Arnold	Laura Frediani	Neil Prince	D McClelland	David Renner
Imperial (El Centro) (109)	619 339-4488	Wayne Vandegraaf	Richard H Inman	Linda K Weaver	Raymond Comstock	Hoyl E Belt	Oren Fox
Inyo (Independence) (18)	619 878-2411	....	....	....	....	....	....
Kern (Bakersfield) (543)	805 861-2095	Ben Austin	Joseph E Drew Jr	T Pickett Davis	Scott E Jones	Kay F Madden	C L Sparks
Kings (Hanford) (101)	209 582-3211	Joe Hammond	Larry Spikes	Rose Martinez	Darrell Warnock	Dennis Berry	Tommy Clark
Lake (Lakeport) (51)	707 263-2213	Walter Wilcox	Kelly Cox	Sharon Lewis	Judy Murray	Glenn Walters	James Wright
Lassen (Susanville) (28)	916 257-8311	Claud Neely	William Bixby	Theresa Nagel	Irene Doyle	Christine Beard	Ronald Jarrell
Los Angeles (Los Angeles) (8863)	213 974-1101	....	....	....	....	....	....
Madera (Madera) (88)	209 675-7705	Jess Lopez	Stell Manfredi	Wanda Gavello	Robert Dewall	Earl Eckert	Glen Seymour
Marin (San Rafael) (230)	415 499-7331	....	....	....	....	....	....
Mariposa (Mariposa) (14)	209 966-3222	Arthur G Baggett	Mike Coffield	Margie Williams	Don Z Phillips	....	Roger Matlock
Mendocino (Ukiah) (80)	707 463-4261	Elmer McMichael	Michael Scannell	Joyce A Beard	Dennis L Huey	Steven R Smith	James T Tuso
Merced (Merced) (178)	209 385-7682	Gerald O' Banion	Clark G Channing	Kenneth L Randol	James L Ball	Marvin J Bolling	Thomas C Sawyer
Modoc (Alturas) (10)	916 233-6413	....	....	....	....	....	....
Mono (Bridgeport) (10)	619 932-5228	Daniel A Paranick	William T Mayer	Nancy Wells	Annika Wilkes	William T Meyer	Martin Strelneck
Monterey (Salinas) (356)	408 755-5115	....	....	....	....	....	....
Napa (Napa) (111)	707 253-4303	Fred Negri	Jay Hull	Mary McLaughlin	Pam Kindig	Bill Carden	Gary Simpson
Nevada (Nevada City) (79)	916 265-1218	Karen Knecht	Douglas Latimer	Cathy Thompson	....	Lori Walsh	Paul Rankin
Orange (Santa Ana) (2411)	714 834-5400	Thomas Riley	Ernie Schneider	Phyllis Henderson	Steve Lewis	Russ Patton	Brad Gates
Placer (Auburn) (173)	916 889-4000	....	....	....	....	....	....
Plumas (Quincy) (20)	916 283-6246	....	....	....	....	....	....
Riverside (Riverside) (1170)	714 275-1000	....	....	....	....	....	....
Sacramento (Sacramento) (1041)	916 440-7097	....	....	....	....	....	....
San Benito (Hollister) (37)	408 636-4000	Mike Graves	David Edge	John Hodges	John Hodges	David Edge	Harvey Nyland
San Bernardino (San Bernardino) (1418)	714 387-5563	....	....	....	....	....	....
San Diego (San Diego) (2498)	619 236-2191	Pam Slater	David E Janssen	Thomas Pastuszka	Manuel Lopez	Ethel M Chastain	Jim Roache
San Francisco c (724)	415 558-6161	....	....	....	....	....	....
San Joaquin (Stockton) (481)	209 468-3370	Douglass Wilhoit	David Baker	Lois M Sahyoun	A J Van Houten	P Huarte Pechan	Temple B Dunn
San Luis Obispo (San Luis Obispo) (217)	805 781-5959	Evelyn Delaney	Robert Hendrix	Frances Cooney	Gere Sibbach	Robert W Conen	Edward Williams
San Mateo (Redwood City) (650)	415 363-4000	Tom Huening	John Maltbie	Richard Silver	Gerry Trias	Mary Welch	Don Horsley
Santa Barbara (Santa Barbara) (370)	805 681-4200	....	....	....	....	....	....
Santa Clara (San Jose) (1498)	408 299-2011	....	....	....	....	....	....
Santa Cruz (Santa Cruz) (230)	408 425-2171	....	....	....	....	....	....
Shasta (Redding) (147)	916 225-5515	Francie Sullivan	John W McCamman	Carolyn Taylor	Edward B Davis	Harry E Albright	James J Pope
Sierra (Downieville) (3)	916 289-3295	....	....	....	....	....	....
Siskiyou (Yreka) (44)	916 842-8005	Roger Zwanziger	Robt W Sellman	Sherrie Bennett	David Elledge	Benton A Angove	Charles Byrd
Solano (Fairfield) (340)	707 421-6170	William Carroll	Michael Johnson	Linda Terra	William Eldridge	Susan Harrington	Albert Cardozo
Sonoma (Santa Rosa) (388)	707 527-2331	....	....	....	....	....	....
Stanislaus (Modesto) (371)	209 525-6333	Raymond Simon	Reagan Wilson	Christine Ferraro	Byron Bystrom	....	Leslie Weidman
Sutter (Yuba City) (64)	916 741-7100	....	....	....	....	....	....
Tehama (Red Bluff) (50)	916 527-4655	....	....	....	....	....	....
Trinity (Weaverville) (13)	916 623-1325	Stan Plowman	Donald Benedetti	Dero Forslund	John Larkin	Jeanne Gravette	Paul Schmidt
Tulare (Visalia) (312)	209 733-6531	....	....	....	....	....	....
Tuolumne (Sonora) (48)	209 533-5511	Kathi Campana	Mark A Mitton	Edna Bowcutt	Tim R Johnson	Mark A Mitton	Richard Nutting
Ventura (Ventura) (669)	805 654-5000	Vicky Howard	R Wittenberg	Richard Dean	Thomas Mahon	Ron Komers	Larry Carpenter
Yolo (Woodland) (141)	916 666-8055	....	....	....	....	....	....
Yuba (Marysville) (58)	916 741-6281	Jay Palmquist	Fred Morawcznski	Terry Hansen	Jim Kennedy	Roger Carey	Gary Tindel
COLORADO (63)							
Adams (Brighton) (265)	303 659-2120	G Deherrera	John Bramble	Robert Sack	Terry Funderburk	....	Edward Camp
Alamosa (Alamosa) (14)	719 589-3841	Robert Zimmerman	Harold E Andrews	Holly Z Lowder	Harold E Andrews	Peggy R Curto	James P Drury
Arapahoe (Littleton) (392)	303 795-4400	....	....	....	....	....	....
Archuleta (Pagosa Springs) (5)	303 264-2536	....	....	....	....	....	....
Baca (Springfield) (5)	303 523-4521	....	....	....	....	....	....
Bent (Las Animas) (5)	719 456-1600	Harrell Ridley	Virley Burkhalter	Patti Nickell	Janice Keenan	Virley Burkhalter	Gregorio Trujillo
Boulder (Boulder) (225)	303 441-3500	Ronald K Stewart	Arlen Stokes	Charlotte Houston	Virginia Aragon	Peggy Jackson	George E Epp
Chaffee (Salida) (13)	719 539-2218	Thomas M Eve	Frank M Thomas	Mary Ellen Belmar	Sharna Graves	....	George Chavez
Cheyenne (Cheyenne Wells) (2)	303 767-5685	Jerry L Allen	....	Rita M Holthus	....	....	James L Blain
Clear Creek (Georgetown) (8)	303 569-3251	Nelson Fugate	Jack Benson	Bobbie Hawkes	Carl Small	Gail Buckley	Robert Cahill
Conejos (Conejos) (7)	303 376-5772	Leroy Velasquez	Miguel Lujan	Andrew Perea	T Martinez	....	Gerald Rivera
Costilla (San Luis) (3)	303 672-3962	....	....	....	....	....	....
Crowley (Ordway) (4)	719 267-4643	Melvin Odea	Joe Kinard	Marilou Geringer	....	....	Dale Anderson
Custer (Westcliffe) (2)	719 783-9067	John Coleman	Francis R Ferron	Mary Kattnig	John Piquette	Francis R Ferron	Fred Jobe
Delta (Delta) (21)	303 874-2100	Ted H Hayden	Susan S Hansen	Josephine M Gore	Susan S Hansen	Gwendolyn Braddt	William Blair
Denver (Denver) c (468)	303 640-2721	....	....	....	....	....	....
Dolores (Dove Creek) (2)	303 677-2383	....	....	....	....	....	....
Douglas (Castle Rock) (60)	303 660-7427	M Michael Cooke	....	Wanda Bailey	Barbara Krohta	Ken Milano	Stephen Zotos
Eagle (Eagle) (22)	303 328-8790	Johnette Phillips	Jack Lewis	Sara Fisher	Allen Sartin	Chris Armstead	A J Johnson
El Paso (Colorado Springs) (397)	719 520-6426	Jeri Howells	....	Eileen Gilbert	William Houghton	Marvin R Adams Sr	Bernard Barry
Elbert (Kiowa) (10)	303 621-2341	Robert Morrison	Trish Gilbert	Geri Sheidt	Suzie Graeff	Sheri Shrader	Walley Wessel

Directory 1/10   OFFICIALS IN U.S. COUNTIES
continued

County, county seat, 1990 population figures (000 omitted)	County telephone number	Chief elected official	Appointed administrator	Clerk to the governing board	Chief financial officer	Personnel director	Chief law enforcement official
COLORADO (63) continued							
Fremont (Canon City) (32)	719 275-1515	....	....	....	....	....	....
Garfield (Glenwood Springs) (30)	303 945-1377	Buckey Arbaney	Charles Deschenes	Mildred Alsdorf	Charles Deschenes	Charles Deschenes	Verne Soucie
Gilpin (Central City) (3)	303 582-5214	....	....	....	....	....	....
Grand (Hot Sulphur Springs) (8)	303 725-3347	....	....	....	....	....	....
Gunnison (Gunnison) (10)	303 641-8505	Fred Field	Gary Tomsic	Judy Goodman	John McBride	....	Richard Murdie
Hinsdale (Lake City) (..)	303 944-2225	Claire Jessee	Don Van Wormer	Linda Ragle	Don Van Wormer	Don Van Wormer	Frank Wilcox
Huerfano (Walsenburg) (6)	719 738-2370	William Reiners	Andrew P Nigrini	Albert P Vigil	Andrew P Nigrini	....	Harold Martinez
Jackson (Walden) (2)	303 723-4334	....	....	....	....	....	....
Jefferson (Golden) (438)	303 271-8676	....	....	....	....	....	....
Kiowa (Eads) (2)	719 438-5810	Cardon G Berry	Gloria Peck	Betty V Crow	Gary Woodward	Gloria Peck	Gary Rehm
Kit Carson (Burlington) (7)	719 346-8133	Leroy Herndon	....	Della Calhoon	....	Nancy Baker	Jim Hetland
La Plata (Durango) (32)	303 382-6202	Frank Joswick	Robert Brooks	Betty Fox	Wayne Bedor	....	William Gardner
Lake (Leadville) (6)	719 486-1410	James Martin	Nancy Hilleary	June Ossman	Nancy Hilleary	Nancy Hilleary	David Duarte
Larimer (Fort Collins) (186)	303 498-7000	Janet Duvall	....	Myrna Rodenberger	Robert Grewell	Ralph Jacobs	Richard Shockley
Las Animas (Trinidad) (14)	303 846-3314	....	....	....	....	....	....
Lincoln (Hugo) (5)	719 743-2444	Charles Covington	....	Roxana Devers	James R Covington	....	Leroy Yowell
Logan (Sterling) (18)	303 522-0888	Lyle Schumacher	....	....	....	Richard Snook	Don Bollish
Mesa (Grand Junction) (93)	303 244-1800	John Crouch	J Michael Casey	....	William Voss	Nancie Flenard	Riecke Claussen
Mineral (Creede) (1)	719 658-2331	....	....	....	....	....	....
Moffat (Craig) (11)	303 824-5517	Chuck Sis	....	Jessie Rowley	....	....	Jeff Corriveau
Montezuma (Cortez) (19)	303 565-8317	....	....	....	....	....	....
Montrose (Montrose) (24)	303 249-7755	....	....	....	....	....	....
Morgan (Fort Morgan) (22)	303 867-2761	John Crosthwait	....	Fay Johnson	....	Lori Navarette	W Gale Davey
Otero (La Junta) (24)	719 384-7785	Robert Bauserman	Barry Shioshita	Stella Sedillo	Barry Shioshita	Val Manweiler	John Eberly
Ouray (Ouray) (2)	303 325-4961	....	....	....	....	....	....
Park (Fairplay) (7)	719 836-2771	....	....	....	....	....	....
Phillips (Holyoke) (4)	303 854-3778	....	....	....	....	....	....
Pitkin (Aspen) (13)	303 920-5240	Robert Child	Reid Haughey	Silvia Davis	Thomas Oken	Cheryl Cumnock	Robert Braudis
Prowers (Lamar) (13)	719 336-9001	Robert R Tempel	DeAnne J Tyner	Dorothy McCaslin	Barbara Barrow	DeAnne J Tyner	James Hamilton
Pueblo (Pueblo) (123)	719 583-6000	Kathy Farley	....	Chris Munoz	Dorothy Hewitt	Jeanette O' Quin	Dan Corsentino
Rio Blanco (Meeker) (6)	303 878-5001	Joe Collins	....	Nancy Amick	Tom Judd	Rob Munger	Peter Larson
Rio Grande (Del Norte) (11)	719 657-2744	....	....	....	....	....	....
Routt (Steamboat Springs) (14)	303 879-0108	Benjamin Beall	....	Dorothy Mariano	Dan Strnad	Kelly Udall	Edgar Burch
Saguache (Saguache) (5)	719 655-2231	Rod Hines	Brad Jones	Mary Moore	Brad Jones	Shirley Anderson	Daniel Pacheco
San Juan (Silverton) (1)	303 387-5766	Ernest F Kuhlman	William C Norman	Dorothy Zanoni	....	....	Greg Leithauser
San Miguel (Telluride) (4)	303 728-3954	Leslie Sherlock	....	Darlene Frieman	Gordon Glockson	Gordon Glockson	William Masters
Sedgwick (Julesburg) (3)	303 474-3346	....	....	....	....	....	....
Summit (Breckenridge) (13)	303 453-2561	....	....	....	....	....	....
Teller (Cripple Creek) (12)	719 689-2988	Carol Vayhinger	Greg Winkler	Constance Joiner	Laurie Litwin	....	Gary Shoemaker
Washington (Akron) (5)	303 345-2701	Cynthia S Hickert	....	Garland M Wahl	....	....	William L Wood
Weld (Greeley) (132)	303 356-4000	Connie Harbart	Donald D Warden	Donald D Warden	Donald D Warden	David Worden	Ed Jordan
Yuma (Wray) (9)	303 332-5796	....	....	....	....	....	....
DELAWARE (3)							
Kent (Dover) (111)	302 736-2000	Ron Smith	Robert McLeod	Edie Hemphill	Stephen Cimo	Michael Adams	Carl Wright
New Castle (Wilmington) (442)	302 571-7500	Dennis Greenhouse	Robert Maxwell	Shirley Agnor	Anne Elder	William F Steele	Thomas P Gordon
Sussex (Georgetown) (113)	302 855-7741	Dale R Dukes	Robert L Stickles	Robin A Griffith	David B Baker	Dennis V Cordrey	William L Jones
WASHINGTON D.C. (1)							
Washington (Washington) i (607)	202 727-1000	....	....	....	....	....	....
FLORIDA (66)							
Alachua (Gainesville) (182)	904 374-5219	Kate Barnes	Robert Fernandez	J K Buddy Irby	Steve Carr	Colleen Hayes	Steve Oelrich
Baker (Macclenny) (18)	904 259-3613	....	....	....	....	....	....
Bay (Panama City) (127)	904 784-4013	Carol Atkinson	Dan Duda	Harold Bazzel	Joseph Rogers	Joy Bates	Guy Tunnell
Bradford (Starke) (23)	904 964-6280	....	....	....	....	....	....
Brevard (Melbourne) (399)	407 633-2000	T Scarborough Jr	T Jenkins	B Talbert	K Wall	F Abbate	J Miller
Broward (Fort Lauderdale) (1255)	305 357-7585	Sylvia Poitier	B Jack Osterholt	....	Phillip Allen	Philip Rosenberg	....
Calhoun (Blountstown) (11)	904 674-4545	....	....	....	....	....	....
Charlotte (Port Charlotte) (111)	813 743-1260	....	Thomas W Frame	....	Kenneth Meade	Karen Morinelli	....
Citrus (Inverness) (94)	904 637-9400	Frank Schiraldi	Anthony Shoemaker	Betty Strifler	Gary Herndon	Dwight Small	Charles Dean
Clay (Green Cove Springs) (106)	904 284-6300	....	....	....	....	....	....
Collier (Naples) (152)	813 774-8460	T J Constantine	W N Dorrill	D E Brock	M A McNees	T C Whitecotton	D C Hunter
Columbia (Lake City) (43)	904 755-4100	Ronald Williams	Dale Williams	Dewitt Cason	Dewitt Cason	Dale Williams	Tom Tramel
Dade (Miami) (1937)	305 375-5311	....	....	....	....	....	....
De Soto (Arcadia) (24)	813 993-4800	....	....	....	....	....	....
Dixie (Cross City) (11)	904 498-5806	....	....	....	....	....	....
Escambia (Pensacola) (263)	904 444-8610	Mike Whitehead	Barry Evans	Joe A Flowers	Joe A Flowers	A Larry Maltby	Jim Lowman
Flagler (Bunnell) (29)	904 437-7414	....	....	....	....	....	....
Franklin (Apalachicola) (9)	904 653-8861	....	....	....	....	....	....
Gadsden (Quincy) (41)	904 875-8650	Edward Dixon	James Carter	Nicholas Thomas	....	Arthur Lawson	W A Woodham
Gilchrist (Trenton) (10)	904 463-2341	....	....	....	....	....	....
Glades (Moore Haven) (8)	813 946-0949	William Petersen	Richard Corley	Jerry Beck	Jerry Beck	....	Barry Walbourn
Gulf (Port Saint Joe) (12)	904 229-6113	....	....	....	....	....	....
Hamilton (Jasper) (11)	904 792-1288	Wendell Wynn	....	Elaine Rozier	Elaine Rozier	....	J Harrell Reid
Hardee (Wauchula) (19)	813 773-6952	....	....	....	....	....	....
Hendry (La Belle) (26)	813 675-5217	....	....	....	....	....	....
Hernando (Brooksville) (101)	904 754-4000	June Ester	Charles Hetrick	Karen Nicolai	Robert Simpson	Yvonne D Taylor	Thomas Mylander
Highlands (Sebring) (68)	813 385-2581	Audrey Vickers	Carl Cool Sr	Luke Brooker	Rick Helms	Phil Wickstrom	Howard Godwin
Hillsborough (Tampa) (834)	813 272-5750	Joe Chillura	Fred Karl	Richard Ake	Richard Ake	Gene Gardner	Cal Henderson
Holmes (Bonifay) (16)	904 547-5055	....	....	....	....	....	....
Indian River (Vero Beach) (90)	407 567-8000	John Tippin	James Chandler	Jeff Barton	....	Jack Price	Gary Wheeler
Jackson (Marianna) (41)	904 482-9633	Alban Green	Harold Emrich	Daun Crews	Larry Spivey	Marilyn Pittman	John Sullivan
Jacksonville-Duval (Jacksonville) c (635)	904 630-1106	Donald R Moran	L A Hester	Henry Cook	Michael Weinstein	C Wm Marshall Jr	James E McMillan
Jefferson (Monticello) (11)	904 997-3596	....	....	....	....	....	....
Lafayette (Mayo) (6)	904 294-1600	....	....	....	....	....	....
Lake (Tavares) (152)	904 343-9694	Catherine Hanson	Peter F Wahl	James C Watkins	Barbara Lehman	Lois R Martin	George E Knupp
Lee (Fort Myers) (335)	813 335-2245	Ray Judah	Donald D Stilwell	Charlie Green	Bruce Loucks	George Bradley	John McDougall
Leon (Tallahassee) (192)	904 487-2220	....	....	....	....	....	....
Levy (Bronson) (26)	904 486-4311	....	....	....	....	....	....
Liberty (Bristol) (6)	904 643-5404	John T Sanders	....	Vernon Ross	Vernon Ross	Vernon Ross	W L Burke
Madison (Madison) (17)	904 973-3179	Michael W Salls	Cohen L Bond	Tim Sanders	Tim Sanders	Karen Botino	Joe C Peavy

Directory 1/10   OFFICIALS IN U.S. COUNTIES
continued

County, county seat, 1990 population figures (000 omitted)	County telephone number	Chief elected official	Appointed administrator	Clerk to the governing board	Chief financial officer	Personnel director	Chief law enforcement official
FLORIDA (66) continued							
Manatee (Bradenton) (212)	813 748-4501	Stanley Stephens	William Estabrook	R B Shore	James Seuffert	Frank Gilbert	Charles B Wells
Marion (Ocala) (195)	904 620-3380	Jeff Gann	Joseph Cone	Frances E Thigpin	Frances E Thigpin	Sarah McCarroll	Ken Ergle
Martin (Stuart) (101)	407 288-5437	Marshall Wilcox	Peter Cheney	Marsha Stiller	Danny Hudson	Stephen Novak	Robert Crowder
Monroe (Key West) (78)	305 294-4641	Jack London	James Roberts	Danny Kolhage	Eva Limbert	Rochelle Leonard	Richard Roth
Nassau (Fernandina Beach) (44) ...	904 321-5700	John A Crawford	....	T J Greeson	T J Greeson	T J Greeson	W Ray Geiger
Okaloosa (Ft Walton Beach) (144) ..	904 651-7515	Raymond E Sansom	Chris Holley	Newman C Brackin	Robert McGuire	Bette Wells	Larry Gilbert
Okeechobee (Okeechobee) (30)	813 763-6441	Charles W Harvey	Chris W Chinault	Gloria J Ford	Gloria J Ford	Chris W Chinault	O L Raulerson
Orange (Orlando) (677)	407 836-5660	Linda Chapin	Jean Bennett	Martha Haynie	Martha Haynie	Sandra Price	Kevin E Beary
Osceola (Kissimmee) (108)	407 847-1200	Charles Owen	William Goaziou	William Goaziou	T J Allen	Dave Apfelbaum	Charles Croft
Palm Beach (West Palm Beach) (864)	407 355-2040	Mary McCarty	Robert Weisman	....	....	Brad Merriman	....
Pasco (Newport Richey) (281)	813 847-2411	....	....	....	....	....	....
Pinellas (Clearwater) (852)	813 464-3367	Bruce Tyndall	Fred Marquis	Karleen DeBlaker	C Richard Short	Jack J Houk	Everett S Rice
Polk (Bartow) (405)	813 534-6030	....	....	....	....	....	....
Putnam (Palatka) (65)	904 329-0200	Samuel Taylor	Gary D Adams	Edward L Brooks	Robert D Moore	Donna L Gunn	Talor Douglas
Santa Rosa (Milton) (82)	904 623-0135	....	John Wesley White	....	Peter Ramsden	H Skeet Surrency	Geoff Monge
Sarasota (Sarasota) (278)	813 951-5200	Wayne L Derr	John Wesley White	Karen Rushing	Peter Ramsden	H Skeet Surrency	Geoff Monge
Seminole (Sanford) (288)	407 321-1130	Dick Vanderweide	Ron Rabun	Maryanne Morse	Bob Wilson	German Romero	Don Eslinger
St. Johns (St. Augustine) (84)	904 824-8131	....	....	....	....	....	....
St. Lucie (Fort Pierce) (150)	407 466-1100	Havert Fenn	Thomas Kindred	Joann Holman	Dan Kurek	Patricia Clute	Robert Knowles
Sumter (Bushnell) (32)	904 793-0200	Jim Allen	Bernard Dew	Sara H Mason	Sara H Mason	....	Jamie Adams
Suwannee (Live Oak) (27)	904 364-3400	W W Jernigan	Edward Allen	Randy Henderson	Randy Henderson	Luanne Mixon	Robert Leonard
Taylor (Perry) (17)	904 584-3531	Vance Howell	Michael Mathews	Annie Mae Murphy	Tammy L Taylor	Laura Johnson	John W Walker
Union (Lake Butler) (10)	904 496-3711	....	....	....	....	....	....
Volusia (De Land) (371)	904 736-2700	....	Thomas C Kelly	Dorothy Buckles	Donald Butler	Michael Lary	Robert Vogel
Walton (De Funiak Springs) (28) ...	904 892-3137	....	....	....	....	....	....
Washington (Chipley) (17)	904 638-6200	....	....	....	....	....	....
GEORGIA (159)							
Appling (Baxley) (16)	912 367-8100	William L Leggett	Mike Cleland	Ann Jones	Mike Cleland	Mike Cleland	Lewis Parker
Atkinson (Pearson) (6)	912 422-3391	....	....	....	....	....	....
Bacon (Alma) (10)	912 632-5214	Virgil Taylor	....	Mary Edna Wheeler	....	....	Johnny Hayes
Baker (Newton) (4)	912 734-5294	....	....	....	....	....	....
Baldwin (Milledgeville) (40)	912 453-4007	....	....	Avis Lewallen	....	....	....
Banks (Homer) (10)	706 677-2320	Milton Patterson	....	Avis Lewallen	....	....	Allen Venable
Barrow (Winder) (30)	404 867-7581	....	....	....	....	....	....
Bartow (Cartersville) (56)	404 382-4766	Clarence Brown	Stephen Bradley	Lane McMillan	....	Sandra Southern	Donald Thurman
Ben Hill (Fitzgerald) (16)	912 423-2455	....	....	....	....	....	....
Berrien (Nashville) (14)	912 686-5421	Grady Williams	Randall Dowling	Elaine Smithwick	Randall Dowling	Randall Dowling	Jerry Brogdon
Bibb (Macon) (150)	912 749-6343	....	....	....	....	....	....
Bleckley (Cochran) (10)	912 934-3200	....	....	....	....	....	....
Brantley (Nahunta) (11)	912 462-5256	....	....	....	....	....	....
Brooks (Quitman) (15)	912 263-5561	....	....	....	....	....	....
Bryan (Pembroke) (15)	912 653-4681	Thomas H Bacon	Waverly P Jones	Donna M Waters	....	....	Clyde Smith
Bulloch (Statesboro) (43)	912 764-6245	....	....	....	....	....	....
Burke (Waynesboro) (21)	706 554-2324	Ellis Godbee	C W Hopper Jr	C W Hopper Jr	C W Hopper Jr	C W Hopper Jr	Gregg Coursey
Butts (Jackson) (15)	404 775-8200	Russ Crumbley	H Thomas Williams	Jackie Cavender	Jackie Cavender	Dianne Holloway	Gene Pope
Calhoun (Morgan) (5)	912 849-4835	Calvin Schramm	....	Priscilla Boyce	....	Priscilla Boyce	Jimmy Camp
Camden (Woodbine) (30)	912 576-5601	....	....	Pam Holland	....	....	....
Candler (Metter) (8)	912 685-2835	George W Bird	....	Pam Holland	....	....	....
Carroll (Carrollton) (71)	404 830-5800	Horrie B Duncan	....	Kim B Jones	Kathy Chapman	Kim B Jones	Jack T Bell
Catoosa (Ringgold) (42)	404 935-4047	....	....	Rosa Mae Brooks	Rosa Mae Brooks	....	Ernest H Conner
Charlton (Folkston) (8)	912 496-2549	William J Carter	....	Rosa Mae Brooks	Rosa Mae Brooks	....	Ernest H Conner
Chatham (Savannah) (217)	912 652-7174	....	....	....	....	....	....
Chattahoochee (Cusseta) (17)	706 989-3602	Walter F Rosso	....	Annelle D Harp	....	....	Glynn Cooper
Chattooga (Summerville) (22)	706 857-4021	Jim Parker	....	Martha A Latta	Jim Parker	....	Ralph Kellett
Cherokee (Canton) (90)	404 479-1953	John Brandenburg	Ken Vanderslice	Karen Huey	Sandra Brown	Renay W Phillips	Roger Garrison
Clarke (Athens) (88)	706 613-3020	....	....	....	....	....	....
Clay (Fort Gaines) (3)	912 768-2631	....	....	....	....	....	....
Clayton (Jonesboro) (182)	404 477-3208	....	....	....	....	....	....
Clinch (Homerville) (6)	912 487-2667	....	....	....	....	....	....
Cobb (Marietta) (448)	404 528-2541	William Byrne	David Hankerson	Carol Myers	J Virgil Moon	Shelia L Buckner	Bill Hutson
Coffee (Douglas) (30)	912 384-4799	Frank Jackson	James R Bramblett	Joann Metts	....	....	....
Colquitt (Moultrie) (37)	912 985-6859	Joe G Clark	Robert M Cobb	Deborah Cox	Robert M Cobb	Robert M Cobb	William F Howell
Columbia (Evans) (66)	706 868-3300	Richard Reynolds	Steven Szablewski	Phebe J Dent	George M Crawford	Ed E Wade	Otis L Hensley
Columbus-Muscogee (Columbus) c (179)	404 571-4740	....	....	....	....	....	....
Cook (Adel) (13)	912 896-2266	....	....	....	....	....	....
Coweta (Newnan) (54)	404 254-2601	James Millians	L Theron Gay	Roxie H Clark	Eva J Wagner	Charles Crawford	Michael S Yeager
Crawford (Knoxville) (9)	912 836-3328	....	....	....	....	....	....
Crisp (Cordele) (20)	912 276-2672	J Reginald Barry	W D Goff Jr	....	....	....	Donald Haralson
Dade (Trenton) (13)	706 657-4625	Bill Wallin	Jefferson D Kirby	Ronda Gold	Jefferson D Kirby	....	Philip Street
Dawson (Dawsonville) (9)	404 265-3164	....	....	....	....	....	....
De Kalb (Decatur) (546)	404 371-2332	Liane Levetan	....	David W Joyner	David W Joyner	Richard E Conley	Robert P Jarvis
Decatur (Bainbridge) (26)	912 248-3030	....	....	....	....	....	....
Dodge (Eastman) (18)	912 374-4361	J Don McCranie	....	Glenda G Williams	....	....	Jackson Jones
Dooly (Vienna) (10)	912 268-4228	....	....	....	....	....	....
Dougherty (Albany) (96)	912 431-2121	....	....	....	....	....	....
Douglas (Douglasville) (71)	404 920-7264	Rita Rainwater	....	Aida Tullis	....	Gloria Turner	Tommy Waldrop
Early (Blakely) (12)	912 723-4304	....	....	....	....	....	....
Echols (Statenville) (2)	912 559-6538	J Lamar Raulerson	....	Brenda Stalvey	....	....	Charles E Carter
Effingham (Springfield) (26)	912 754-6071	....	....	....	....	....	....
Elbert (Elberton) (19)	404 283-4702	....	....	....	....	....	....
Emanuel (Swainsboro) (21)	912 237-8911	....	....	....	....	....	....
Evans (Claxton) (9)	912 739-1141	....	....	....	....	....	....
Fannin (Blue Ridge) (16)	404 632-2039	....	....	....	....	....	....
Fayette (Fayetteville) (62)	404 461-6041	Steve Wallace	Billy P Beckett	....	Emory McHugh	Connie L Boehnke	Randall Johnson
Floyd (Rome) (81)	706 291-5156	Pete Odillon	R McCullough	Sue Broome	Bob McCollum	Larry Johnson	James Free
Forsyth (Cumming) (44)	404 781-2100	....	....	....	....	....	....
Franklin (Carnesville) (17)	706 384-2483	Roger W Roper	....	Yvette C Eavenson	....	....	....
Fulton (Atlanta) (649)	404 730-6710	Mitch Skandalakis	John H Stanford	Avarita L Hanson	Peter Cunningham	Robert O Brandes	Jacquelyn Barrett
Gilmer (Ellijay) (13)	404 635-4361	....	....	....	....	....	....
Glascock (Gibson) (2)	706 598-2671	Joe Dean Usry	....	Denise L Kent	....	....	James English

Directory 1/10 OFFICIALS IN U.S. COUNTIES
continued

County, county seat, 1990 population figures (000 omitted)	County telephone number	Chief elected official	Appointed administrator	Clerk to the governing board	Chief financial officer	Personnel director	Chief law enforcement official
GEORGIA (159) continued							
Glynn (Brunswick) (62)	912 267-5600	....	....	....	....	....	....
Gordon (Calhoun) (35)	706 629-3795	....	....	....	....	....	....
Grady (Cairo) (20)	912 377-1512	Jack C Drew	M I Stephenson	Ann W Mobley	Bonnie H Amdahl	....	Sydney Turner
Greene (Greensboro) (12)	404 453-7716	....	....	....	....	....	....
Gwinnett (Lawrenceville) (353)	404 822-8000	Wayne Hill	Bill Northquest	Barbara Bruce	Charlotte Nash	Harry Owens	Jim Carsten
Habersham (Clarkesville) (28)	706 754-6264	Fred T Parker	Lewis Canup	Ruby S Fulbright	....	....	Harrison Nix
Hall (Gainesville) (95)	404 531-7000	Brenda Branch	Harry W Hayes	Jill A Lambert	Arlin W Pitts	Phillip H Sutton	Robert G Vass
Hancock (Sparta) (9)	404 444-5746	....	....	....	....	....	....
Haralson (Buchanan) (22)	404 646-2002	Jim McBrayer	....	Charlene Smith	....	....	Kenneth Spearman
Harris (Hamilton) (18)	706 628-4958	George E Elmore	Marian T Young	Carol A Silva	Carol A Silva	Diane Goodman	Mike Jolley
Hart (Hartwell) (20)	404 376-2024	....	....	....	....	....	....
Heard (Franklin) (9)	706 675-3821	Larry A Pike	....	June Yates	....	....	Franklin Crook
Henry (Mc Donough) (59)	404 954-2400	William Gardner	Aubrey Harvey	Sara B Austin	Sara B Austin	Gene Morris	William D Chaffin
Houston (Perry) (89)	912 542-2115	Sherrill Stafford	Stephen Engle	Stephen Engle	Sandra Stalnaker	Harold H Wilson	Cullen Talton
Irwin (Ocilla) (9)	912 468-9441	....	....	....	....	....	....
Jackson (Jefferson) (30)	404 367-9838	....	....	....	....	....	....
Jasper (Monticello) (8)	404 468-2812	....	....	....	....	....	....
Jeff Davis (Hazlehurst) (12)	912 375-6611	Lonnie Waters	Lonnie V Roberts	Lonnie V Roberts	Lonnie V Roberts	Lonnie V Roberts	Jimmy Boatright
Jefferson (Louisville) (17)	912 625-3332	....	....	....	....	....	....
Jenkins (Millen) (8)	912 982-2563	....	....	....	....	....	....
Johnson (Wrightsville) (8)	912 864-3388	....	....	....	....	....	....
Jones (Gray) (21)	912 986-6405	....	....	....	....	....	....
Lamar (Barnesville) (13)	404 358-5146	Bobby Burnette	....	Patty Johnston	....	....	Frank Monaghan
Lanier (Lakeland) (6)	912 482-2088	V L Moore	....	Bonnie R Ganas	....	....	Clyde Brogdon
Laurens (Dublin) (40)	912 272-4755	....	....	....	....	....	....
Lee (Leesburg) (16)	912 759-6000	John L Leach	William R Dean	Carolyn Bowers	Esther R Griffith	William R Dean	Harold N Breedon
Liberty (Hinesville) (53)	912 876-2164	M L Coffer	Joseph W Brown	E Faye Beasley	....	....	J Don Martin
Lincoln (Lincolnton) (7)	706 359-4444	Walker T Norman	Roxanne B Ashmore	Roxanne B Ashmore	....	Roxanne B Ashmore	Edwin Bentley
Long (Ludowici) (6)	912 545-2143	Randall T Wilson	Lisa R Long	Mary Ann Odum	Lisa R Long	Lisa R Long	Cecil Nobles
Lowndes (Valdosta) (76)	912 245-5210	G Norman Bennett	Michael J Stewart	Inez M Pendleton	Marcus Cambell	Mickey Tillman	Ashley Paulk
Lumpkin (Dahlonega) (15)	404 864-3742	....	....	....	....	....	....
Macon (Oglethorpe) (13)	912 472-7021	....	....	....	....	....	....
Madison (Danielsville) (21)	706 795-3351	William C Madden	....	Junne B Temple	....	....	Jack D Fortson
Marion (Buena Vista) (6)	912 649-2603	....	....	....	....	....	....
Mc Duffie (Thomson) (20)	706 595-2100	Joyce Blevins	....	Ann Roberts	Preston Newton	....	Logan Marshal
Mc Intosh (Darien) (9)	912 437-6671	....	....	....	....	....	....
Meriwether (Greenville) (22)	404 672-1314	....	....	....	....	....	....
Miller (Colquitt) (6)	912 758-4104	....	....	....	....	....	....
Mitchell (Camilla) (20)	912 336-2000	Benjamin Hayward	Bennett W Adams	Shelia Cannon	Bennett W Adams	Bennett W Adams	William Bozeman
Monroe (Forsyth) (17)	912 994-7000	James V Ham	....	Gail M King	Linda J Jiles	....	John Cary Bittick
Montgomery (Mount Vernon) (7)	912 583-4401	....	....	....	....	....	....
Morgan (Madison) (13)	706 342-0725	Henry G Carson	C Rosebrough	Doris Harris	Doris Harris	C Rosebrough	Kenny Pritchett
Murray (Chatsworth) (26)	706 695-2413	Jimmie Witherow	Stephen North	Arlene Gibson	....	Marla Bearden	Howard Ensley
Newton (Covington) (42)	404 784-2005	Davis C Morgan	Brian Allen	Mildred M Johnson	....	Jesse L Knight	Gerald Malcom
Oconee (Watkinsville) (18)	706 769-5120	Wendell Dawson	Peter Mallory	Gina Lindsey	....	....	Scott Berry
Oglethorpe (Lexington) (10)	404 743-5270	....	....	....	....	....	....
Paulding (Dallas) (42)	404 443-7521	Bobby H Hollis	....	Pat C Brannum	Pat C Brannum	Lillian T Norton	Bruce Harris
Peach (Fort Valley) (21)	912 825-2535	....	....	....	....	....	....
Pickens (Jasper) (14)	404 692-2121	....	....	....	....	....	....
Pierce (Blackshear) (13)	912 449-2022	Robert N Howard	....	Nicole Y Carter	....	....	Richard T King
Pike (Zebulon) (10)	706 567-3406	James Lester	....	....	....	....	James Gibson
Polk (Cedartown) (34)	404 748-1305	....	....	....	....	....	....
Pulaski (Hawkinsville) (8)	912 783-1911	....	....	....	....	....	....
Putnam (Eatonton) (14)	706 485-5826	Donald Ridley	Frank Brantley	Helen J Carnes	Helen J Carnes	....	Carlton E Resseau
Quitman (Georgetown) (2)	912 334-2159	....	....	....	....	....	....
Rabun (Clayton) (12)	404 782-5271	....	....	....	....	....	....
Randolph (Cuthbert) (8)	912 732-6440	....	....	....	....	....	....
Richmond (Augusta) (190)	706 821-2300	William Mays	Linda Beazley	....	Albert McKie	Minor J Etheridge	Charles Webster
Rockdale (Conyers) (54)	404 929-4000	Randolph Poynter	Jean Hambrick	....	Sarah Alexander	John Meyers	Guy Norman
Schley (Ellaville) (4)	912 937-2101	....	....	....	....	....	....
Screven (Sylvania) (14)	912 564-7535	....	....	....	....	....	....
Seminole (Donalsonville) (9)	912 524-2878	....	....	....	....	....	....
Spalding (Griffin) (54)	404 228-9900	Larry Kelly	Michael M Ruffin	Maureen C Jackson	....	Elaine M Bonds	Richard H Cantrel
Stephens (Toccoa) (23)	706 886-9491	Samuel Sosebee	Charles Whitworth	Nancy Downs	....	....	Don Shirley
Stewart (Lumpkin) (6)	912 838-6769	....	....	....	....	....	....
Sumter (Americus) (30)	912 924-6725	....	....	....	....	....	....
Talbot (Talbotton) (7)	404 665-3220	....	....	....	....	....	....
Taliaferro (Crawfordville) (2)	706 456-2494	Jesse L Brown	....	Ruby Randolph	....	....	James M Leslie
Tattnall (Reidsville) (18)	912 557-4335	....	....	....	....	....	....
Taylor (Butler) (8)	912 862-3336	....	....	....	....	....	....
Telfair (Mc Rae) (11)	912 868-5688	....	....	....	....	....	....
Terrell (Dawson) (11)	912 995-4476	Wilbur T Gamble	....	Deborah Crawford	....	....	John Bowens
Thomas (Thomasville) (39)	912 225-4100	John Bulloch	Rick Morrison	Ruth M Jones	....	....	R Carlton Powell
Tift (Tifton) (35)	912 386-7850	Charles Kent	....	Imogene Register	....	....	Edd Walker
Toombs (Lyons) (24)	912 526-3311	....	....	....	....	....	....
Towns (Hiawassee) (7)	706 896-2276	....	....	....	....	....	....
Treutlen (Soperton) (6)	912 529-3664	Jim L Gillis Jr	....	Sylvia Norris	....	....	Wayne Hooks
Troup (La Grange) (56)	404 883-1610	....	....	....	....	....	....
Turner (Ashburn) (9)	912 567-4313	....	....	....	....	....	....
Twiggs (Jeffersonville) (10)	912 945-3629	....	....	....	....	....	....
Union (Blairsville) (12)	706 745-9655	Glen Gooch	Tammy Rusk	Tammy Rusk	Tammy Rusk	Tammy Rusk	S Richardson
Upson (Thomaston) (26)	706 647-7012	J Irvin Hendricks	....	Lakeitha Reeves	....	Lakeitha Reeves	Mountain Greene
Walker (La Fayette) (58)	706 638-1437	Roy E Parrish Jr	....	Bebe Heiskell	....	Bebe Heiskell	Albert Millard
Walton (Monroe) (39)	404 267-4571	....	....	....	....	....	....
Ware (Waycross) (35)	912 287-4300	Roger Strickland	Joseph Pritchard	Gail Barron	James Johnson	....	Herbert E Bond
Warren (Warrenton) (6)	706 465-2171	Bobby W Johnson	....	Lynette Johnson	....	....	Joseph Peebles
Washington (Sandersville) (19)	912 552-2325	....	....	....	....	....	....
Wayne (Jesup) (22)	912 427-5900	Richard Madray	Robert Honsted	Nancy Jones	....	....	David Herrin
Webster (Preston) (2)	912 828-5775	....	....	....	....	....	....
Wheeler (Alamo) (5)	912 568-7137	....	....	....	....	....	....
White (Cleveland) (13)	706 865-2235	....	....	....	....	....	....
Whitfield (Dalton) (72)	400 275-7500	....	....	....	....	....	....
Wilcox (Abbeville) (7)	912 467-2737	Homer L Conner	....	Hazel Keen	....	....	C E Bloodsworth

Directory 1/10   OFFICIALS IN U.S. COUNTIES
continued

County, county seat, 1990 population figures (000 omitted)	County telephone number	Chief elected official	Appointed administrator	Clerk to the governing board	Chief financial officer	Personnel director	Chief law enforcement official
GEORGIA (159) continued							
Wilkes (Washington) (11)	404 678-2511	....	....	....	....	....	....
Wilkinson (Irwinton) (10)	912 946-2236	J M Howell	....	Charlene Stuckey	....	....	T Lloyd Gibbs
Worth (Sylvester) (20)	912 776-8200	Billy McDonald	Jack H Powell	Nell Ford	....	Jack H Powell	Freddie Tompkins
HAWAII (4)							
Hawaii (Hilo) (120)	808 961-8361	Spencer K Schutte	William G Davis	Robin J Yahiku	Harry A Takahashi	Michael R Ben	Victor V Vierra
Honolulu (Honolulu) c (836)	808 523-4809	Gary Gill	Jeremy Harris	Raymond K Pua	Russell W Miyake	Cynthia M Bond	Michael Nakamura
Kauai (Lihue) (51)	808 245-3385	....	....	....	....	....	....
Maui (Wailuku) (100)	808 243-7711	....	....	....	....	....	....
IDAHO (44)							
Ada (Boise) (206)	208 364-2330	V Bisterfeldt	....	J David Navarro	Barbara Bauer	Terry L Johnson	Vaughn Killeen
Adams (Council) (3)	208 253-4561	....	....	....	....	....	....
Bannock (Pocatello) (66)	208 236-7211	T Katsilometes	C Fisher	J Jensen	P Wilson	W H Lloyd	W T Lynn
Bear Lake (Paris) (6)	208 945-2212	....	....	....	....	....	....
Benewah (St. Maries) (8)	208 245-3212	....	....	....	....	....	....
Bingham (Blackfoot) (38)	208 785-5005	....	....	....	....	....	....
Blaine (Hailey) (14)	208 788-5505	....	....	....	....	....	....
Boise (Idaho City) (4)	208 392-4431	....	....	....	....	....	....
Bonner (Sandpoint) (27)	208 265-1438	Eugene Brown	....	Marie Scott	Karen Weldon	Jan Morrison	Chip Roos
Bonneville (Idaho Falls) (72)	208 529-1100	....	....	....	....	....	....
Boundary (Bonners Ferry) (8)	208 267-2242	....	....	....	....	....	....
Butte (Arco) (3)	208 527-3021	James O Andreason	....	Judith R Bailey	Lori Beck	....	Cary D Vanetten
Camas (Fairfield) (1)	208 764-2242	Jack Renfrow	....	Rollie Bennett	Rollie Bennett	Rollie Bennett	Harold P Lee
Canyon (Caldwell) (90)	208 454-7300	....	....	....	....	....	....
Caribou (Soda Springs) (7)	208 547-4342	....	....	....	....	....	....
Cassia (Burley) (20)	208 678-7302	....	....	....	....	....	....
Clark (Dubois) (1)	208 374-5304	Charles R Vadnais	....	Jo Ann Tavenner	Jo Ann Tavenner	....	Craig King
Clearwater (Orofino) (9)	208 476-5615	V James Wilson	....	Robin Christensen	Robin Christensen	....	Nick Albers
Custer (Challis) (4)	208 879-2360	....	....	....	....	....	....
Elmore (Mountain Home) (21)	208 587-2130	Bud Riddle	....	Dolores Robison	....	....	Rick Layher
Franklin (Preston) (9)	208 852-1090	Jeff Olson	....	LaRae E Johnson	LaRae E Johnson	....	Don Beckstead
Fremont (St. Anthony) (11)	208 624-7332	....	....	....	....	....	....
Gem (Emmett) (12)	208 365-4561	Richard R Welch	....	Thelma Kolodziej	Edith M Sawyer	....	Mark D John
Gooding (Gooding) (12)	208 934-4841	Don Morrow	....	John A Myers	John A Myers	....	Jim Jax
Idaho (Grangeville) (14)	208 983-2751	....	....	....	....	....	....
Jefferson (Rigby) (17)	208 745-7756	Paul D Walker	....	Connie M Keller	....	Margaret E Poole	Blair Olsen
Jerome (Jerome) (15)	208 324-8811	....	....	....	....	....	....
Kootenai (Coeur D'Alene) (70)	208 769-4400	....	....	....	....	....	....
Latah (Moscow) (31)	208 882-8580	....	....	....	....	....	....
Lemhi (Salmon) (7)	208 756-2815	Denny Hawley	....	A Wiederrick	Shirley Hoy	A Wiederrick	Brett Barsalou
Lewis (Nezperce) (4)	208 937-2661	....	....	....	....	....	....
Lincoln (Shoshone) (3)	208 886-7641	Jerry Nance	....	Dana Sturgeon	Dana Sturgeon	....	Stephen Southwick
Madison (Rexburg) (24)	208 356-3662	Del Barney	....	Beth Reese	Beth Reese	....	Greg Moffat
Minidoka (Rupert) (19)	208 436-9511	Norman Seibold	....	Duane Smith	Duane Smith	....	Paul Fries
Nez Perce (Lewiston) (34)	208 799-3020	....	....	....	....	....	....
Oneida (Malad City) (3)	208 766-4116	....	....	....	....	....	....
Owyhee (Murphy) (8)	208 495-2421	Richard Bass	....	Barbara Jayo	Barbara Jayo	....	Tim Nettleton
Payette (Payette) (16)	208 642-9371	....	....	....	....	....	....
Power (American Falls) (7)	208 226-7611	Ralph Wheeler	....	Carol Schreiber	....	....	Howard Sprague
Shoshone (Wallace) (14)	208 752-3331	....	....	....	....	....	....
Teton (Driggs) (3)	208 354-2905	Keith J Kunz	....	Asa J Drake	Asa J Drake	....	Kim Cooke
Twin Falls (Twin Falls) (54)	208 736-4000	James Fraley	....	Robert Fort	Robert Fort	Renee Robbins	Wayne Tousley
Valley (Cascade) (6)	208 382-4297	Tom Olson	....	Leland G Heinrich	Leland G Heinrich	....	Lewis Pratt
Washington (Weiser) (9)	208 549-2092	Don Stephens	....	Mary Kautz	Sharon Widner	....	Michael Wadley
ILLINOIS (102)							
Adams (Quincy) (66)	217 223-6300	....	....	....	....	....	....
Alexander (Cairo) (11)	618 734-7000	....	....	....	....	....	....
Bond (Greenville) (15)	618 664-1966	....	....	....	....	....	....
Boone (Belvidere) (31)	815 547-4770	....	....	....	....	....	....
Brown (Mount Sterling) (6)	217 773-3421	Robert E Koch	....	Judy J Woodworth	Joseph Ray	....	Michael Myers
Bureau (Princeton) (36)	815 875-2014	....	....	....	....	....	....
Calhoun (Hardin) (5)	618 576-2351	....	....	....	....	....	....
Carroll (Mount Carroll) (17)	815 244-9171	....	....	....	....	....	....
Cass (Virginia) (13)	217 452-7217	....	....	....	....	....	....
Champaign (Urbana) (173)	217 384-3772	Lyle E Shields	Jacquelin A White	Dennis R Bing	Gerrie Parr	Lyle E Shields	David J Madigan
Christian (Taylorville) (34)	217 824-4969	William C Curtin	....	Terry E Ryan	Colleen M Hadley	....	Richard E Mahan
Clark (Marshall) (16)	217 826-8311	David Schiver	....	Bill Downey	....	....	Dan Crumrin
Clay (Louisville) (14)	618 665-3626	....	....	....	....	....	....
Clinton (Carlyle) (34)	618 594-2464	Virgil Schrage	....	David V Lampe	Ferd W Mueller Jr	....	Donald Krohn
Coles (Charleston) (52)	217 348-0595	Eli Sidwell Jr	....	Betty Coffrin	William Grimes	....	Jim Kimball
Cook (Chicago) (5105)	312 443-5500	....	....	....	....	....	....
Crawford (Robinson) (19)	618 546-1212	A L Earleywine	....	Ruth E Knoblett	Doris Gill	....	Tom W Weger
Cumberland (Toledo) (11)	217 849-2631	....	....	....	....	....	....
De Kalb (Sycamore) (78)	815 895-7127	Robert Hutcheson	Ray Bockman	Sharon Holmes	Gary Hanson	....	Roger Scott
De Witt (Clinton) (17)	217 935-2119	....	....	....	....	....	....
Douglas (Tuscola) (19)	217 253-2411	....	....	....	....	....	....
Du Page (Wheaton) (782)	708 682-7000	....	....	....	....	....	....
Edgar (Paris) (20)	217 465-5264	Jim McCulloch	....	Rebbeca R Kraemer	Linda Lane	....	Karl Farnham
Edwards (Albion) (7)	618 445-2115	....	....	....	....	....	....
Effingham (Effingham) (32)	217 342-4990	J Pat Green	....	Robert Behrman	Joseph Green	....	Art Kinkelaar
Fayette (Vandalia) (21)	618 283-5000	Jean B Finley	....	Isabelle B Brandt	....	....	Michael Kleinik
Ford (Paxton) (14)	217 379-2721	Jean R Herriott	....	Ronald A Rasmus	Nancy Krumwiede	....	Ralph E Henson
Franklin (Benton) (40)	618 438-3221	....	....	....	....	....	....
Fulton (Lewistown) (38)	309 547-3041	William Danner	....	Randal L Rumler	Bernard J Oaks	....	Dan Daly
Gallatin (Shawneetown) (7)	618 269-3025	....	....	....	....	....	....
Greene (Carrollton) (15)	217 942-5443	....	....	....	....	....	....
Grundy (Morris) (32)	815 941-3215	Donald Kaufman	....	Lana J Phillips	Betty J Olson	....	James L Olson
Hamilton (Mc Leansboro) (8)	618 643-2721	Ronald Ewald	....	Lovella Craddock	Keith Botsch	....	William Warren
Hancock (Carthage) (21)	217 357-3911	David Leffler	....	Kerry Asbridge	Kerry Asbridge	....	Dick Yager
Hardin (Elizabethtown) (5)	618 287-2251	Ronald Armstrong	....	Sue McMaster	David M Humphrey	....	Lowell D Lasater
Henderson (Oquawka) (8)	309 867-2911	Larry Dowell	....	Joyce Meloan	....	....	Daryl Thompson

Directory 1/10 OFFICIALS IN U.S. COUNTIES
continued

County, county seat, 1990 population figures (000 omitted)	County telephone number	Chief elected official	Appointed administrator	Clerk to the governing board	Chief financial officer	Personnel director	Chief law enforcement official
ILLINOIS (102) continued							
Henry (Cambridge) (51)	309 937-5192	....	....	John M Kuntz	Shelby J Townsend	....	....
Iroquois (Watseka) (31)	815 432-6963	D Widholm	....	Robert B Harrell	Shirley D Booker	....	Joseph V Mathy
Jackson (Murphysboro) (61)	618 687-7240	David E Conrad	....				William Kilquist
Jasper (Newton) (11)	618 783-3124	....	....	....	....	....	....
Jefferson (Mount Vernon) (37)	618 244-8000	....	....	....	....	....	....
Jersey (Jerseyville) (21)	618 498-5571	....	....	....	....	....	....
Jo Daviess (Galena) (22)	815 777-0161	William McFadden	....	Pam Miller	....	....	Steven Allendorf
Johnson (Vienna) (11)	618 658-3611	Max Ray	....	Jerry R Simmons	....	....	Elry Faulkner
Kane (Geneva) (317)	708 208-3836	Warren Kammerer	....	Lorraine Sava	Thomas Walter	Randy Bullock	John Randall
Kankakee (Kankakee) (96)	815 937-2910	....	....	....	....	....	....
Kendall (Yorkville) (39)	708 553-4142	James Boan	Jay D Young	Paul Anderson	Thomas Holbrook	Jay D Young	Richard Randall
Knox (Galesburg) (56)	309 343-3121	Richard D Allen	....	Yvonne Tabb	Carolyn Griffith	....	Mark J Shearer
La Salle (Ottawa) (107)	815 434-8242	....	....	....	....	....	....
Lake (Waukegan) (516)	708 360-6600	Robert W Depke	Dwight A Magalis	Linda Ianuzl Hess	Raymond A Amadei	Cliff Van Dyke	Clinton Grinnell
Lawrence (Lawrenceville) (16)	618 943-2346	Harold Benson	....	Will Gibson	....	....	Eddie Ryan
Lee (Dixon) (34)	815 288-3309	Ronald Conderman	....	Nancy Nelson	....	....	Tim Bivins
Livingston (Pontiac) (39)	815 844-5166	Charles M Brady	....	Arnold E Natzke	Sylvia L Bashore	....	C Keith Mills
Logan (Lincoln) (31)	217 732-4148	Ronald L Sparks	....	Weldon B Frantz	....	....	Robert Patterson
Macon (Decatur) (117)	217 424-1470	Kevin L Kehoe	Marilyn A Riley	Stephen M Bean	David A Sapp	....	H Lee Holsapple
Macoupin (Carlinville) (48)	217 854-3214	....	....	....	....	....	....
Madison (Edwardsville) (249)	618 692-6200	Nelson Hagnauer	James K Monday	Debbie Saltich	Frederick Bathon	Chris Aldridge	Bob Churchich
Marion (Salem) (42)	618 548-3400	....	....	....	....	....	....
Marshall (Lacon) (13)	309 246-6325	Andrew L Placher	....	Marjorie Rossetti	....	....	James Frawley
Mason (Havana) (16)	309 543-6661	Henry W Imlg	....	Willim R Blessman	....	....	Richard E Walker
Massac (Metropolis) (15)	618 524-5213	....	....	....	....	....	....
Mc Donough (Macomb) (35)	309 837-2308	Charles Gilbert	Janet Hurtgen	Shirley Simpkins	Patricia Waggoner	....	John Bliven
Mc Henry (Woodstock) (183)	815 338-2040	Dianne L Klemm	Bill Barron	Katherine Schultz	Albert Jourdan	....	William T Mullen
Mc Lean (Bloomington) (129)	309 888-5001	Gary C Riss	John M Zeunik	Jeanette Barrett	James Boylan	Edward Williams	Stephen Brienen
Menard (Petersburg) (11)	217 632-2415	....	....	....	....	....	....
Mercer (Aledo) (17)	309 582-7021	Wayne Anderson	....	Thomas L Hanson	....	....	Larry Glancey
Monroe (Waterloo) (22)	618 939-8681	....	....	....	....	....	....
Montgomery (Hillsboro) (31)	217 532-2552	....	....	....	....	....	....
Morgan (Jacksonville) (36)	217 245-4619	....	....	....	....	....	....
Moultrie (Sullivan) (14)	217 728-4389	....	....	....	....	....	....
Ogle (Oregon) (46)	815 732-3201	Jerry Daws	....	Jean Wolfe	Chris Martin	....	Melvin Messer
Peoria (Peoria) (183)	309 672-6947	Sharon Kennedy	....	Mary E Harkrader	Edward O' Connor	John A Saxton	Alan H Misener
Perry (Pinckneyville) (21)	518 357-5116	Leonard Heisner	....	Don Hirsch	Frak L Mangin	....	Samuel D Hiller
Piatt (Monticello) (16)	217 762-9487	....	....	....	....	....	....
Pike (Pittsfield) (18)	217 285-6812	Don Apps Sr	....	Carrol K Hoover	....	....	Mike Lord
Pope (Golconda) (4)	618 683-8101	....	....	....	....	....	....
Pulaski (Mound City) (8)	618 748-9360	....	....	....	....	....	....
Putnam (Hennepin) (6)	815 925-7129	William G Urnikis	....	Gudmund Jessen Jr	....	....	Donald J A Maggi
Randolph (Chester) (35)	618 826-5000	Dan Reitz	....	William Rabe	....	....	Ben Picou
Richland (Olney) (17)	618 392-3111	Dan Sulsberger	....	Michael T Buss	....	....	Gary W Dowty
Rock Island (Rock Island) (149)	309 786-4451	Paul E Mulcahey	....	Margaret Bennett	Donald L Jacobs	Lester R Carlson	Michael Grchan
Saline (Harrisburg) (27)	618 253-8197	Eric E Gregg	....	Jim Fowler	Jay D Williams	....	George Henley
Sangamon (Springfield) (178)	217 753-6600	Larry K Bomke	....	Joseph T Aiello	Joseph Bonefeste	....	J William Demarco
Schuyler (Rushville) (7)	217 322-4734	Maurice Ross	....	....	....	....	C DeWayne Bond
Scott (Winchester) (6)	217 742-3178	....	....	....	....	....	....
Shelby (Shelbyville) (22)	217 774-4421	....	....	....	....	....	....
St. Clair (Belleville) (263)	618 277-6600	John Baricevic	Daniel Maher	Janice Delaney	John Driscoll	Betty L Martz	Mearl Justus
Stark (Toulon) (7)	309 286-5901	E Musselman	....	L Pyell	P Becket	....	L Dennison
Stephenson (Freeport) (48)	815 235-8277	F Dean Danner	Russell J Mulnix	Dean W Amendt	Edith M Dadez	....	Samuel J Volkert
Tazewell (Pekin) (124)	309 477-2274	George A Saal Jr	David A Nelson	Lori Stead	Christie Webb	David A Nelson	Mary Drexler
Union (Jonesboro) (18)	618 833-5711	....	....	....	....	....	....
Vermilion (Danville) (88)	217 431-2554	Max Call	....	Lynn Foster	Josie Divan	Edie Hesser	Patrick Hartshorn
Wabash (Mount Carmel) (13)	618 262-4561	Donald W Kennard	....	Joan E Wolfe	....	....	Randy Grounds
Warren (Monmouth) (19)	309 734-8592	William Reichow	....	Janet Rutledge	....	....	Gary Higbee
Washington (Nashville) (15)	618 327-8314	John D Schubert	....	Thomas Ganz	David Meyer	David Jasper	John Mierkowski
Wayne (Fairfield) (17)	618 842-5182	Donnie Barnard	....	Gladys Onstott	....	....	Bennie Suddarth
White (Carmi) (17)	618 382-7211	James P Taylor	....	Paula Dozier	....	....	Jerry O' Neal
Whiteside (Morrison) (60)	815 772-5100	Tony Arduini	J R Gallagher Jr	Dan Heusinkveld	Karen Mulnix	Deborah L Workman	Roger A Schipper
Will (Joliet) (357)	815 722-5515	Charles Adelman	....	Janice Gould	Mary Brown	....	Thomas Fitzgerald
Williamson (Marion) (58)	618 997-1301	....	....	....	....	....	....
Winnebago (Rockford) (253)	815 987-3000	....	....	....	....	....	....
Woodford (Eureka) (33)	309 467-2822	Gary Jones	....	Peggy Rapp	Patricia Eckhoff	....	Bill Myers
INDIANA (92)							
Adams (Decatur) (31)	219 724-2600	William Baker	....	James Hill	....	....	Tom Coolman
Allen (Fort Wayne) (301)	219 428-7555	....	....	....	....	....	....
Bartholomew (Columbus) (64)	812 379-1515	....	....	....	....	....	....
Benton (Fowler) (9)	317 884-0760	....	....	....	....	....	....
Blackford (Hartford City) (14)	317 348-1620	Marjorie I Young	....	David A Troyer	....	....	Jerry J Brown
Boone (Lebanon) (38)	317 482-2940	James R Detamore	Paul H Green	....	Connie J Lamar	....	Ern K Hudson
Brown (Nashville) (14)	812 988-5486	....	....	....	....	....	....
Carroll (Delphi) (19)	317 564-3172	William E Duff	....	Kenneth I Red Elk	Kenneth I Red Elk	....	Lee Noard
Cass (Logansport) (38)	219 753-7727	Merlyn Raikes	....	Keneta Musall	Chod Gibson	....	Ron Woolley
Clark (Jeffersonville) (88)	812 285-6218	Steven Fleece	....	Richard Jones	Keith Groth	....	Michael Becher
Clay (Brazil) (25)	812 448-8044	....	....	....	....	....	....
Clinton (Frankfort) (31)	317 659-6309	....	....	....	....	....	....
Crawford (English) (10)	812 338-2601	....	....	....	....	....	....
Daviess (Washington) (28)	812 254-1090	....	....	....	....	....	....
De Kalb (Auburn) (35)	219 925-2362	....	....	....	....	....	....
Dearborn (Lawrenceburg) (39)	812 537-1040	....	....	....	....	....	....
Decatur (Greensburg) (24)	812 663-2570	John Moore	....	....	Mary M Doggett	....	Larry Snyder
Delaware (Muncie) (120)	317 747-7730	....	....	....	....	....	....
Dubois (Jasper) (37)	812 481-7000	....	....	Donna Schroeder	Marge Gadlage	....	Terry Tanner
Elkhart (Goshen) (156)	219 535-6400	....	David Hess	Joyce Rowe	Charles Miller	Kathy Brewton	Randall Yohn
Fayette (Connersville) (26)	317 825-8987	....	....	....	....	....	....
Floyd (New Albany) (64)	812 948-5491	Larry R Denison	....	Betty J Hammond	William B Jenks	Wiliam Burkhart	Leland Watson
Fountain (Covington) (18)	317 793-2243	Vince Grogg	....	....	....	Suzette Burgner	Teryl Martin
Franklin (Brookville) (20)	317 647-4631	....	....	Bonita Back	....	....	Lee V Davidson
Fulton (Rochester) (19)	219 223-2912	Stephen Hartzler	....	Judith A Reed	Judith A Reed	Sherry Porterfied	Bruce Bauer

Directory 1/10   OFFICIALS IN U.S. COUNTIES
continued

County, county seat, 1990 population figures (000 omitted)	County telephone number	Chief elected official	Appointed administrator	Clerk to the governing board	Chief financial officer	Personnel director	Chief law enforcement official
INDIANA (92) continued							
Gibson (Princeton) (32)	812 386-8401	....	....	....	....	....	....
Grant (Marion) (74)	317 668-8871	....	....	....	....	....	....
Greene (Bloomfield) (30)	812 384-3537	....	....	....	....	....	....
Hamilton (Noblesville) (109)	317 776-8401	William Karns	Jon M Ogle	Jon M Ogle	Jon M Ogle	....	Dan Stevens
Hancock (Greenfield) (46)	317 462-1105	William Silvey	....	Marilyn Counter	Marilyn Counter	Marilyn Counter	James Bradbury
Harrison (Corydon) (30)	812 738-8241	....	....	....	....	....	Edward L Davis
Hendricks (Danville) (76)	317 745-9341	Richard P Myers	....	Marthalyn Pearcy	....	Susan K Fair	Thomas Underwood
Henry (New Castle) (48)	317 529-4705	....	....	....	....	....	....
Howard (Kokomo) (81)	317 456-2215	....	....	....	....	....	....
Huntington (Huntington) (35)	219 356-0692	....	....	....	....	....	....
Indianapolls-Marion (Indianapolls) c (731)	317 236-3200	....	....	....	....	....	....
Jackson (Brownstown) (38)	812 358-6122	....	....	....	....	....	....
Jasper (Rensselaer) (25)	219 866-4930	....	....	Kenneth Brooks	Donya G Jordan	....	Steve Reames
Jay (Portland) (22)	219 726-9575	....	....	....	....	....	....
Jefferson (Madison) (30)	812 265-8900	....	....	....	....	....	....
Jennings (Vernon) (24)	812 346-2131	....	....	....	....	....	....
Johnson (Franklin) (88)	317 736-3065	Jeffrey Eggers	....	Betty Stringer	....	....	Doran Miller
Knox (Vincennes) (40)	812 885-2552	....	....	....	....	....	Donald Kirkham
Kosciusko (Warsaw) (65)	219 267-4444	W E Creighton	....	Marsha McSherry	Patrica Brown	Ron Robinson	Al Rovenstine
La Porte (La Porte) (107)	219 326-6808	....	....	....	....	....	....
Lagrange (Lagrange) (29)	219 463-7801	Freeman Lambright	....	....	Billie E Wiard	....	Randy Merrifield
Lake (Crown Point) (476)	219 755-3000	....	....	....	....	....	....
Lawrence (Bedford) (43)	812 275-3111	....	....	....	....	....	Chester Hall
Madison (Anderson) (131)	317 641-9470	....	....	....	....	....	....
Marshall (Plymouth) (42)	219 935-8555	Ray Borggren	....	Mary Lou Leavell	Mary Lou Leavell	....	Charles Criswell
Martin (Shoals) (10)	812 247-3731	....	....	....	....	....	....
Miami (Peru) (37)	317 472-3901	William Page	....	Karen Large	Karen Large	....	Jack Rich
Monroe (Bloomington) (109)	812 333-3550	....	....	....	....	....	....
Montgomery (Crawfordsville) (34)	317 364-6400	James M Kirtley	....	Nelda J Hester	Carolyn Swank	....	Dennis Rice
Morgan (Martinsville) (56)	317 342-1001	....	....	....	....	....	....
Newton (Kentland) (14)	219 474-6081	Russell Collins	....	....	....	....	Charles Mulligan
Noble (Albion) (38)	219 636-2658	Samuel W Patton	....	Anita Huff	....	....	Gary Dial
Ohio (Rising Sun) (5)	812 438-2062	....	....	....	....	....	....
Orange (Paoli) (18)	812 723-3600	....	....	....	....	....	....
Owen (Spencer) (17)	812 829-2260	....	....	....	....	....	....
Parke (Rockville) (15)	317 569-3422	J Gene Jones	....	Catherine Cooper	Dale Gerrish	....	Mark Bridge
Perry (Cannelton) (19)	812 547-2758	Donald H Etienne	Loretta Cassidy	Marietta Dauby	....	....	Oscar Ballis Jr
Pike (Petersburg) (13)	812 354-8448	Arvel Grubb	....	Gayle Bradfield	....	....	William Scales
Porter (Valparaiso) (129)	219 465-3440	....	....	....	....	....	....
Posey (Mount Vernon) (26)	812 838-1300	....	....	....	....	....	....
Pulaski (Winamac) (13)	219 946-3653	Stanley Boehning	....	Carolyn Kruger	Betsy Matthews	....	Carl Freeman
Putnam (Greencastle) (30)	317 653-4603	....	....	....	....	....	....
Randolph (Winchester) (27)	317 584-7070	Jan Chalfant	....	Shirley A Wright	....	....	Ralph Harris
Ripley (Versailles) (25)	812 689-6311	....	....	....	Virginia Busching	....	....
Rush (Rushville) (18)	317 932-2077	Marvin L Cole	....	....	....	....	Douglas Gosser
Scott (Scottsburg) (21)	812 752-4745	....	....	....	....	....	....
Shelby (Shelbyville) (40)	317 392-6310	....	....	....	....	....	....
Spencer (Rockport) (19)	812 649-4376	Wayne A Roell	....	....	....	....	Sheldon R Tharp
St. Joseph (South Bend) (247)	219 235-9547	....	....	....	....	....	....
Starke (Knox) (23)	219 772-9101	Clifford Allen	....	M Houston	M Houston	....	Randall Wakefield
Steuben (Angola) (27)	219 665-3014	Dale Hughes Jr	....	Linda Hansen	Cheryl A Beck	....	L McClelland
Sullivan (Sullivan) (19)	812 268-4491	....	....	....	....	....	....
Switzerland (Vevay) (8)	812 427-3302	....	....	....	....	....	....
Tippecanoe (Lafayette) (131)	317 423-9376	William D Haan	Vickie Rhine	....	Betty J Michael	Frank Cederquist	David Heath
Tipton (Tipton) (16)	317 675-2795	....	....	....	....	....	....
Union (Liberty) (7)	317 458-5464	Judge McCarty	....	....	....	....	Charles Marcum
Vanderburgh (Evansville) (165)	812 426-5241	....	....	....	....	....	....
Vermillion (Newport) (17)	317 492-3570	James R Young	....	Phyllis Orman	Ruth A Swinford	....	Larry Jones
Vigo (Terre Haute) (106)	812 462-3367	Charles McCrory	....	Patricia Mansard	William Decker	....	James R Jenkins
Wabash (Wabash) (35)	219 563-0661	Brian Haupert	....	....	Jean Gilbert	....	William Wheatley
Warren (Williamsport) (8)	317 762-3275	....	....	....	....	....	....
Warrick (Boonville) (45)	812 897-6120	....	....	....	....	....	....
Washington (Salem) (24)	812 883-4805	David Bagshaw	....	Douglas Campbell	Mingon Marshall	....	James Watson
Wayne (Richmond) (72)	317 973-9200	Max A Smith	....	Joseph L Kaiser	Doris E Miller	June Clements	Dennis Andrews
Wells (Bluffton) (26)	219 824-6470	....	....	....	....	....	....
White (Monticello) (23)	219 583-5761	....	....	....	....	....	....
Whitley (Columbia City) (28)	219 248-3101	....	....	....	....	....	....
IOWA (99)							
Adair (Greenfield) (8)	515 743-2546	Don Johnson	....	Jenice Wallace	Constance Sheriff	....	Fred Skellenger
Adams (Corning) (5)	515 322-3340	James Amdor	....	Donna L West	....	....	Merlin Dixon
Allamakee (Waukon) (14)	319 568-3522	David D Snitker	....	Bill Roe Jr	Elsa Hager	....	Neil Becker
Appanoose (Centerville) (14)	515 856-6191	Wayne L Sheston	....	Linda S Demry	....	....	Gerald Banks
Audubon (Audubon) (7)	712 563-2584	Harold F Akers	....	....	K W Slothouber	....	Bill Shaw
Benton (Vinton) (22)	319 472-2365	Norman Sackett	....	Jill Marlow	....	....	K Popenhagen
Black Hawk (Waterloo) (124)	319 291-2422	Brian Quirk	....	....	Grant Veeder	Thomas Pounds	Michael Kubik
Boone (Boone) (25)	515 433-0502	David Reed	....	Philippe Meier	....	....	Ronald Fehr
Bremer (Waverly) (23)	319 352-5040	David Busch	....	Kathy Thoms	John DeVries	....	W Westendorf
Buchanan (Independence) (21)	319 334-3578	....	....	....	....	....	....
Buena Vista (Storm Lake) (20)	712 749-2542	....	....	....	....	....	....
Butler (Allison) (16)	319 267-2670	Melvin Bakker	....	Donald G Johnson	....	....	Timothy A Junker
Calhoun (Rockwell City) (12)	712 297-7741	Dean Hoag Sr	....	Judy Howrey	Joyce Toms	....	Bill Davis
Carroll (Carroll) (21)	712 792-9802	....	....	Paul Fricke	....	....	Douglas Bass
Cass (Atlantic) (15)	712 243-4570	Charles Rieken	....	....	Dale Sunderman	....	Larry Jones
Cedar (Tipton) (17)	319 886-3168	Edward Compton	....	Patricia Meixner	Gary Jedlicka	....	Keith Whitlatch
Cerro Gordo (Mason City) (47)	515 421-3021	Jay Urdahl	....	Sandy Sievers	Ken Kline	Larry Phearman	Bob Balek
Cherokee (Cherokee) (14)	712 225-4890	William G Hurd	....	Barbara A Huey	....	....	Larry Simon
Chickasaw (New Hampton) (13)	515 394-2100	....	....	....	....	....	....
Clarke (Osceola) (8)	515 342-3315	William B Oehlert	....	Anita Chandler	....	....	Mark A Addison
Clay (Spencer) (18)	712 262-1569	....	....	....	....	....	....
Clayton (Elkader) (19)	319 245-1106	Ron Willie	....	Dennis Freitag	Dorothy Samuelson	....	Verdean Dietrich
Clinton (Clinton) (51)	319 243-6210	....	....	....	....	....	....

County, county seat, 1990 population figures (000 omitted)	County telephone number	Chief elected official	Appointed administrator	Clerk to the governing board	Chief financial officer	Personnel director	Chief law enforcement official
IOWA (99) continued							
Crawford (Denison) (17)	712 263-3045	Virgil E Anderson	....	Leo J Remmes	....	....	Thomas Hogan
Dallas (Adel) (30)	515 993-5806	Joe E Reece	....	Carole Bayeur	Bev Kimrey	Shirley Marker	Arthur Johnson
Davis (Bloomfield) (8)	515 664-2101	David W Burns	....	....	....	....	D Wayne Rogers
Decatur (Leon) (8)	515 446-4323	Linda Rouse	....	William Greenwood	Goldie Martin	....	Fred Buckingham
Delaware (Manchester) (18)	319 927-2515	Eldon Koeneke	....	Sharon McCrabb	Sharon McCrabb	....	Ronald Wilhelm
Des Moines (Burlington) (43)	319 753-8232	Thomas Elmore	J V Leonard	....	....	....	Joel Behne
Dickinson (Spirit Lake) (15)	712 336-3356	....	....	....	....	....	....
Dubuque (Dubuque) (86)	319 589-4440	Alan Manternach	Jan Hess	Denise M Dolan	Denise M Dolan	Jan Hess	Leo Kennedy
Emmet (Estherville) (12)	712 362-4261	Donald Heerdt	....	Beverly Juhl	Betty Anderson	....	Larry Lamack
Fayette (West Union) (22)	319 422-6061	Marilyn Rubner	....	Larry Popenhagen	Phyllis Massman	....	E Dietzenbach
Floyd (Charles City) (17)	515 257-6131	....	....	....	....	....	....
Franklin (Hampton) (11)	515 456-5622	Leonard Worden	....	Bob Davies Jr	Jane Lubkeman	....	Duane Payne
Fremont (Sidney) (8)	712 374-2031	Keith Hickey	....	....	....	....	Steven Mac Donald
Greene (Jefferson) (10)	515 386-2552	....	....	....	....	....	....
Grundy (Grundy Center) (12)	319 824-3122	Donald Schildroth	....	Mary L Schmidt	Susan Kitzman	....	Rick Penning
Guthrie (Guthrie Center) (11)	515 747-3619	James L Petersen	Darwin Hall	....	Harriet Sloss	....	Stuart Stringham
Hamilton (Webster City) (16)	515 832-9510	Marvin D Johnson	....	Mary Shultz	Deborah Leksell	....	Scott Anderson
Hancock (Garner) (13)	515 923-3163	....	....	....	....	....	....
Hardin (Eldora) (19)	515 858-3461	Linn Adams	....	Renee McClellan	Renee McClellan	Renee McClellan	Loren Goodknight
Harrison (Logan) (15)	712 644-2401	....	....	....	....	....	....
Henry (Mount Pleasant) (19)	319 385-0756	Mike Hampton	....	Carol McCulley	Marjorie Burden	....	Terry Morrow
Howard (Cresco) (10)	319 547-2880	Chuck Malek	....	Deborah Gaul	Warren Steffen	Craig Fencl	Gary Cleveland
Humboldt (Dakota City) (11)	515 332-1571	Keith O' Donnell	....	Jerry C Diedrick	Pat Albrecht	....	Marvin Andersen
Ida (Ida Grove) (8)	712 364-2626	Joseph Cronin	....	Joy Sharkey	Shirley Palm	....	Don Bremer
Iowa (Marengo) (15)	319 642-3923	Perah Read	....	Linda Griggs	Donna Akerman	....	James Slockett
Jackson (Maquoketa) (20)	319 652-3144	Jason E Haynes	....	T M Cotton	T M Cotton	....	Robert P Lyons
Jasper (Newton) (35)	515 792-9808	....	....	....	....	....	....
Jefferson (Fairfield) (16)	515 472-2851	....	....	....	....	....	....
Johnson (Iowa City) (96)	319 356-6000	Stephen Lacina	....	....	....	....	Robert Carpenter
Jones (Anamosa) (19)	319 462-2282	Miles M Tredway	....	Michael S Albers	Michael S Albers	....	John W Cook
Keokuk (Sigourney) (12)	515 622-2320	Maryl Grove	....	Marilyn Wells	Arlene Nilles	....	Ron George
Kossuth (Algona) (19)	515 295-2718	Lennon Brandt	....	Delores Thilges	....	....	K Van Otterloo
Lee (Fort Madison) (39)	319 372-6557	....	....	....	....	....	....
Linn (Cedar Rapids) (169)	319 398-3958	James M Houser	....	Linda Langenberg	Stephen B Tucker	Trude J Elliott	Dennis H Blome
Louisa (Wapello) (12)	319 523-3371	Warren Kemper	....	....	....	....	Herbert Eutsler
Lucas (Chariton) (9)	515 774-2018	James Wright	....	Linda Reed	G Patterson	....	James Swarthout
Lyon (Rock Rapids) (12)	712 472-3713	Jerry Stubbe	Kenneth Mellema	Kenneth Mellema	Richard Heidloff	....	Kevin Hammer
Madison (Winterset) (12)	515 462-3914	....	....	....	....	....	....
Mahaska (Oskaloosa) (22)	515 673-7148	Daryl Denney	....	Kay Swanson	Kay Swanson	Kay Swanson	Charles Van Toorn
Marion (Knoxville) (30)	515 828-2217	Willard Prather	....	Delores DeVries	Delores DeVries	....	M Van Haaften
Marshall (Marshalltown) (38)	515 754-6300	A E Bill Minner	....	Martha Isaacson	Deane Adams	....	Ted Kamatchus
Mills (Glenwood) (13)	712 527-4729	Naomi Christensen	....	....	....	....	Mack Taylor
Mitchell (Osage) (11)	515 732-5861	....	....	....	....	....	....
Monona (Onawa) (10)	712 423-2191	Wilbur Mann	....	Benita J Davis	Roger Blatchford	....	Dennis K Smith
Monroe (Albia) (8)	515 932-7706	Paul V Koffman	....	C M Brothers	....	....	Wayne Messamaker
Montgomery (Red Oak) (12)	712 623-5127	Bernard Palmquist	....	Donna Mae Smith	Anita Walker	....	Jeffrey Smith
Muscatine (Muscatine) (40)	319 263-5317	Sandra Huston	....	Richard Crooks	Richard Crooks	Nancy Schreiber	Ron Hazen
O'Brien (Primghar) (15)	712 757-3225	Carl Struve	....	Barb Kreibaum	Barb Kreibaum	....	Michael Anderson
Osceola (Sibley) (7)	712 754-2441	Gale Howe	....	....	....	....	Mitchell Watters
Page (Clarinda) (17)	712 542-2219	Robert Anderson	....	Judy Clark	....	....	Robert Rank
Palo Alto (Emmetsburg) (11)	712 852-2924	Charley Naig	....	Gary Leonard	Kathleen Thompson	....	Russell Jergens
Plymouth (Le Mars) (23)	712 546-6100	Herman Kluver	....	K Kae Meyer	Norman Kehrberg	....	Mike Vanotterloo
Pocahontas (Pocahontas) (10)	712 335-3361	....	....	....	....	....	....
Polk (Des Moines) (327)	515 286-3000	....	....	....	....	....	....
Pottawattamie (Council Bluffs) (83)	712 328-5700	Stanley Grote	Lois Haines	Marilyn Jo Drake	Judy Ann Miller	....	Jeffery Danker
Poweshiek (Montezuma) (19)	515 623-5443	....	....	....	....	....	....
Ringgold (Mount Ayr) (5)	515 464-3239	Ethel Campbell	....	Eloise Brown	....	....	Lyle Minnick
Sac (Sac City) (12)	712 662-7401	....	....	....	....	....	....
Scott (Davenport) (151)	319 326-8611	Bill Fennelly	F Glen Erickson	Karen Fitzsimmons	C Ray Wierson	David C Whan	Mike Bladel
Shelby (Harlan) (13)	712 755-3831	....	....	....	....	....	Gene Cavenaugh
Sioux (Orange City) (30)	712 737-2216	....	....	....	....	....	....
Story (Nevada) (74)	515 382-6581	....	....	....	....	....	....
Tama (Toledo) (17)	515 484-3980	R Kim Wilson	....	John Adams	....	....	Mike Richardson
Taylor (Bedford) (7)	712 523-2280	....	....	....	....	....	....
Union (Creston) (13)	515 782-7218	Gerald McLain	....	....	....	....	John Coulter
Van Buren (Keosauqua) (8)	319 293-3129	John R Whitaker	....	Jon P Finney	....	....	Hugh H Hardin
Wapello (Ottumwa) (36)	515 683-0020	John Richards	....	Mary A Gaskill	....	....	Buddy C Erwin
Warren (Indianola) (36)	515 961-1001	....	....	....	....	....	....
Washington (Washington) (20)	319 653-7715	....	....	....	....	....	....
Wayne (Corydon) (7)	515 872-2242	Larry Andrews	....	Sue Ruble	Dean Besco	....	Gilbert Sanders
Webster (Fort Dodge) (40)	515 573-7175	....	....	....	....	....	....
Winnebago (Forest City) (12)	515 582-3412	Gorden Anderson	....	Robert D Paulson	Ruth Bachman	....	Thomas Lillquist
Winneshiek (Decorah) (21)	319 382-5085	Linus Rothmeyer	....	G Schweinefus	....	....	Floyd Ashbacher
Woodbury (Sioux City) (98)	712 279-6525	....	....	....	....	....	....
Worth (Northwood) (8)	515 324-2316	....	....	....	....	....	....
Wright (Clarion) (14)	515 532-3262	Caye Chelesvig	....	Gladys Riley	Bernice Valley	....	Vernon Elston
KANSAS (105)							
Allen (Iola) (15)	316 365-1407	Dick Works	....	Laura Baker	Betty Daniels	....	Ron Moore
Anderson (Garnett) (8)	913 448-6841	....	....	....	....	....	....
Atchison (Atchison) (17)	913 367-1653	....	....	....	....	....	....
Barber (Medicine Lodge) (6)	316 886-3961	R Sternberger	....	Linda S McGuire	Linda K Hamilton	....	Tommy Tomson
Barton (Great Bend) (29)	316 793-1800	Marlin Isern	Mike Leighton	Coleen Murphy	Mike Leighton	Mike Leighton	Jim Daily
Bourbon (Fort Scott) (15)	316 223-3800	Carey Lockwood	....	Barbara Wood	Opal Hess	Doylene Kennedy	Harold Coleman
Brown (Hiawatha) (11)	913 742-2581	Frank W Davis	....	Grace L Miller	Judy Grathwohl	....	Rob Hendricks
Butler (El Dorado) (51)	316 321-1960	....	....	....	....	....	....
Chase (Cottonwood Falls) (3)	316 273-6423	....	....	....	....	....	....
Chautauqua (Sedan) (4)	316 725-3370	Mike Champlin	....	Lori Martin	Peggy McAfee	....	Harry Williams
Cherokee (Columbus) (21)	316 429-2042	....	....	....	....	....	....
Cheyenne (St. Francis) (3)	913 332-2401	Roger Faulkender	....	Elaine Kehlbeck	Elaine Kehlbeck	....	Ray Lee
Clark (Ashland) (2)	316 635-2813	Michael Myatt	....	Rebecca Mishler	....	....	Bradley Harris
Clay (Clay Center) (9)	913 632-2552	....	....	....	....	....	....
Cloud (Concordia) (11)	913 243-8110	....	....	....	....	....	....

Directory 1/10 OFFICIALS IN U.S. COUNTIES
continued

County, county seat, 1990 population figures (000 omitted)	County telephone number	Chief elected official	Appointed administrator	Clerk to the governing board	Chief financial officer	Personnel director	Chief law enforcement official
KANSAS (105) continued							
Coffey (Burlington) (8)	316 364-2191	....	....	....	....	....	....
Comanche (Coldwater) (2)	316 582-2361	Bill Bayne	....	Alice Smith	....	....	Jene Allen
Cowley (Winfield) (37)	316 221-5400	Gerald Lawrence	....	H Joe Gaston	Robert Odell	H Joe Gaston	Robert Odell
Crawford (Girard) (36)	316 724-6115	Anthony Pichler	....	Dan Brunetti	John Kovacic	....	Lynn Fields
Decatur (Oberlin) (4)	913 475-2132	....	....	....	....	....	....
Dickinson (Abilene) (19)	913 263-7157	....	....	....	....	....	....
Doniphan (Troy) (8)	913 985-3513	Dana Foley	....	B Schoenfelder	....	....	Mark Long
Douglas (Lawrence) (82)	913 841-7700	....	....	....	....	....	....
Edwards (Kinsley) (4)	316 659-3121	....	....	....	....	....	....
Elk (Howard) (3)	316 374-2490	....	....	....	....	....	....
Ellis (Hays) (26)	913 628-9410	Neil W Dreiling	....	Peggy McCullick	Mike Billinger	....	Frank Reese
Ellsworth (Ellsworth) (7)	913 472-4161	....	....	....	....	....	....
Finney (Garden City) (33)	316 272-3542	Robert Jones	Peter H Olson	Carol Brown	Raylene Nelson	....	Grover Craig
Ford (Dodge City) (27)	316 227-4550	Don C Wiles	....	Rita A Slattery	....	....	Arlyn Leaming
Franklin (Ottawa) (22)	913 242-1471	....	....	....	....	....	....
Geary (Junction City) (30)	913 238-3912	F Whitebread	....	Joyce Bielefeld	....	....	William L Deppish
Gove (Gove) (3)	913 938-2300	....	....	....	....	....	....
Graham (Hill City) (4)	913 674-3453	Darrol Irby	....	Darlene Riggs	Jerilyn Keith	....	Don E Scott
Grant (Ulysses) (7)	316 356-1335	....	....	....	....	....	....
Gray (Cimarron) (5)	316 855-3618	....	....	....	....	....	....
Greeley (Tribune) (2)	316 376-4256	Ron L Lehman	....	Linda K Firner	Diane Gentry	....	Steve A Schmidt
Greenwood (Eureka) (8)	316 583-8121	Gus Carpenter Jr	....	Carol E Pope	....	....	Lowell Parker
Hamilton (Syracuse) (2)	316 384-5629	Terryl Spiker	....	Beverly Holdren	....	....	Daniel Levens
Harper (Anthony) (7)	316 842-5555	Bob Wohlschlegel	....	Tanis L Lieurance	Carmen Alldritt	Cheryl Adelhardt	Terry G Bane
Harvey (Newton) (31)	316 284-6806	Charles Benjamin	Craig Simons	Margaret Wright	James Reber	Evelyn Reimer	Byron Motter
Haskell (Sublette) (4)	316 675-2263	....	....	....	....	....	....
Hodgeman (Jetmore) (2)	316 357-6421	....	....	....	....	....	....
Jackson (Holton) (12)	913 364-2891	Jerry A Harter	....	Kathy L Mick	....	Kathy L Mick	Phil McManigal
Jefferson (Oskaloosa) (16)	913 863-2272	William K Rhodes	....	Shirley Walbridge	....	Shirley Walbridge	Roy Dunnaway
Jewell (Mankato) (4)	913 378-4020	Doyle Alchorn	....	Wes Moore	Lynn Scarrow	....	John Owen
Johnson (Olathe) (355)	913 764-8484	Bruce R Craig	Eugene H Denton	Beverly L Baker	Ronald F Cousino	Cheryl Leichliter	F Allenbrand
Kearny (Lakin) (4)	316 355-6422	....	....	Donna R Brown	....	....	Robert M Bayack
Kingman (Kingman) (8)	316 532-2521	Walter J Harbert	....	Donna R Brown	....	....	Robert M Bayack
Kiowa (Greensburg) (4)	316 723-3366	Robert Mitchum	....	Evelyn Grimm	....	....	Thomas Boman
Labette (Oswego) (24)	316 795-2138	....	....	....	....	....	....
Lane (Dighton) (2)	316 397-5356	Thomas J Bennett	....	Sarah J Fuller	Patricia A Sharp	....	Donald L Wilson
Leavenworth (Leavenworth) (64)	913 684-0400	....	....	Doris White	Joyce Walker	....	Anne Branda
Lincoln (Lincoln) (4)	913 524-4757	Allan D Serrien	....	Doris White	Joyce Walker	....	Anne Branda
Linn (Mound City) (8)	913 795-2668	Frank Gable	....	Donald L Proffitt	Patricia E Davey	....	Richard O' Bryant
Logan (Oakley) (3)	913 672-4244	Robert K Scott	....	Patricia M Miller	Harvene Hoeb	....	Ronald Keith
Lyon (Emporia) (35)	316 342-4950	....	....	Marquetta Eilerts	Jannine Bateman	....	Edward Davies
Marion (Marion) (13)	316 382-2185	Leon Suderman	....	Marquetta Eilerts	Jannine Bateman	....	Edward Davies
Marshall (Marysville) (12)	913 562-5361	....	....	....	....	....	....
Mc Pherson (Mc Pherson) (27)	316 241-8149	....	....	....	....	....	....
Meade (Meade) (4)	316 873-2581	....	....	....	....	....	....
Miami (Paola) (23)	913 294-9500	Lawrence Guenther	Jay Newton Jr	Kathy Peckman	Mary Lou Bricker	....	Ken Davis
Mitchell (Beloit) (7)	913 738-3652	William P Bunger	....	Joleen Walker	....	....	Douglas Daugherty
Montgomery (Independence) (39)	316 331-2710	....	....	....	....	....	....
Morris (Council Grove) (6)	316 767-5518	James Lee	....	Michelle Garrett	Patty Carson	....	Gary Carrier
Morton (Elkhart) (3)	316 697-2157	....	....	....	....	....	....
Nemaha (Seneca) (10)	913 336-2170	....	....	....	....	....	....
Neosho (Erie) (17)	316 244-3293	....	....	....	....	....	Gary W O' Brien
Ness (Ness City) (4)	913 798-2401	Paul D Pavlu	....	Ramona Meis	....	....	Gary W O' Brien
Norton (Norton) (6)	913 877-5710	Dean Esslinger	....	Dorothy Shearer	Valerie Babcock	....	Myron H Cochran
Osage (Lyndon) (15)	913 828-4812	....	....	....	....	....	....
Osborne (Osborne) (5)	913 346-2431	Donald S Kiper	....	Gloria B Wood	Gloria B Wood	Gloria B Wood	Curtis L Miner
Ottawa (Minneapolis) (6)	913 392-2279	....	....	....	....	....	....
Pawnee (Larned) (8)	316 285-3721	Donna Pelton	....	Ruth Searight	....	....	Charles Shearrer
Phillips (Phillipsburg) (7)	913 543-6825	Leonard Archer	....	Linda McDowell	....	....	Leroy Stephen
Pottawatomie (Westmoreland) (16)	913 457-3314	Wes Holt	....	Gwen Harris	Bryan Kidney	....	Anthony Metcalf
Pratt (Pratt) (10)	316 672-5181	....	....	....	....	....	....
Rawlins (Atwood) (3)	913 626-3351	....	....	....	....	....	....
Reno (Hutchinson) (62)	316 694-2929	Joe Stucky	....	Roxanne Wheatley	Larry Tucker	Monica Holtsclaw	Larry Leslie
Republic (Belleville) (6)	913 527-5691	....	....	....	....	....	....
Rice (Lyons) (11)	316 257-2232	Mary Bolton	Joan Davison	....	....	....	Jeffrey Baker
Riley (Manhattan) (67)	913 537-0700	Karen McCulloh	....	Ilene Colbert	Eileen King	Janee Roche	Alvan Johnson
Rooks (Stockton) (6)	913 425-6391	Jack Turnbull	....	Clara Strutt	....	....	David S Denton
Rush (La Crosse) (4)	913 222-2731	Bob Tammen	....	Linda M Bott	....	....	Jack Mendenhall
Russell (Russell) (8)	913 483-4641	....	....	....	....	....	....
Saline (Salina) (49)	913 826-6555	Gary L Hindman	....	Shirley J Jacques	Charles K Lilly	Rita A Deister	Darrell L Wilson
Scott (Scott City) (5)	316 872-2420	....	....	....	....	....	....
Sedgwick (Wichita) (404)	316 383-7400	Betsy Gwin	William Buchanan	Susan Spoon	Terry Coltrain	Maryann Mamoth	Michael Hill
Seward (Liberal) (19)	316 626-3200	....	....	....	....	....	....
Shawnee (Topeka) (161)	913 233-8200	....	....	Patsy McDonald	Marty Bloomquist	Donna Allen	Dave Meneley
Sheridan (Hoxie) (3)	913 675-3361	Stanley Rogers	....	Paula Bielser	....	....	James Johnson
Sherman (Goodland) (7)	913 899-6125	....	....	....	....	....	....
Smith (Smith Center) (5)	913 282-6832	....	....	....	....	....	....
Stafford (St. John) (5)	316 549-3509	....	....	....	....	....	....
Stanton (Johnson) (2)	316 492-2140	....	....	....	....	....	....
Stevens (Hugoton) (5)	316 544-2541	Richard Farrar	....	Opal Hall	....	....	Russ DeWitt
Sumner (Wellington) (26)	316 326-3395	Keith Yearout	....	Sibyl P Whipple	....	....	Tony Schwaubauer
Thomas (Colby) (8)	913 462-4500	John P Bremenkamp	....	Rosalie Seemann	....	....	Thomas W Jones
Trego (Wakeeney) (4)	913 743-5773	Leary J Johnson	....	Kathleen Conness	Gary Watson	Kathleen Conness	Jerry White
Wabaunsee (Alma) (7)	913 765-3414	Fred H Howard	....	Ruth Diepenbrock	....	....	Mike Watson
Wallace (Sharon Springs) (2)	913 852-4282	Blaine A Rohn	....	Jacalyn Mai	....	....	Raymond Garcia
Washington (Washington) (7)	913 325-2974	John L' Ecuyer	....	LaVon Hornbostel	....	....	J Wiley Kerr
Wichita (Leoti) (3)	316 375-2731	Elmer Ridder	....	Berneice Gilmore	Sharen Altman	....	D Wayne Collins
Wilson (Fredonia) (10)	316 378-2186	Glenn Jones	....	Maurine Burns	Rita Githens	....	Paul Ammann
Woodson (Yates Center) (4)	316 625-8605	Gordon McNitt	....	Sandra Solander	....	....	....
Wyandotte (Kansas City) (162)	913 573-2800	....	....	....	....	....	....
KENTUCKY (120)							
Adair (Columbia) (15)	502 384-4703	....	....	....	....	....	....

Directory 1/10
continued
OFFICIALS IN U.S. COUNTIES

County, county seat, 1990 population figures (000 omitted)	County telephone number	Chief elected official	Appointed administrator	Clerk to the governing board	Chief financial officer	Personnel director	Chief law enforcement official
KENTUCKY (120) continued							
Allen (Scottsville) (15)	502 237-3631	....	....	....	....	....	....
Anderson (Lawrenceburg) (15)	502 839-3471	Thomas D Cotton	Ann Cheek	....	W Dudley Shryock	Ann Cheek	Harold Cornish
Ballard (Wickliffe) (8)	502 335-5177						
Barren (Glasgow) (34)	502 651-3338	David A Dickerson	K Steenbergen	Howard M Jones	Sherry J Jones		Barney Jones
Bath (Owingsville) (10)	606 674-6346	....	....	....	....	....	....
Bell (Pineville) (32)	606 337-3076	....	....	....	....	....	....
Boone (Burlington) (58)	606 334-2100	....	....	....	....	....	....
Bourbon (Paris) (19)	606 987-3010	....	....	....	....	....	....
Boyd (Catlettsburg) (51)	606 739-4134	Billy Joe Ross	Charles Pelfrey	Debbie Jones	Linda Cassity	Linda Cassity	Phillip Sturgill
Boyle (Danville) (26)	606 238-1100	....	....	....	....	....	....
Bracken (Brooksville) (8)	606 735-2300	....	....	....	....	....	....
Breathitt (Jackson) (16)	606 666-2818	....	....	....	....	....	....
Breckinridge (Hardinsburg) (16)	502 756-2269	....	....	....	....	....	....
Bullitt (Shepherdsville) (48)	502 543-2262	....	....	....	....	....	....
Butler (Morgantown) (11)	502 526-3433	....	....	....	....	....	....
Caldwell (Princeton) (13)	502 365-6660	....	....	....	....	....	....
Calloway (Murray) (31)	502 753-2920	J D Williams	....	....	....	....	Stan Scott
Campbell (Newport) (84)	606 292-3838	....	....	....	....	....	....
Carlisle (Bardwell) (5)	502 628-5451	....	....	....	....	....	....
Carroll (Carrollton) (9)	502 732-7000	Gene McMurry	Traci Courtney	Bill Lyles	Jackie Willhoite	Gene McMurry	Charles Maiden Jr
Carter (Grayson) (24)	606 474-5366	Joe D Kitchen	....	Hugh R McDavid	Joy C Nolan	Joe D Kitchen	Coleman Binion
Casey (Liberty) (14)	606 787-6154	....	....	....	....	....	....
Christian (Hopkinsville) (69)	502 887-4104	Philip S Tribble	....	....	Frank T Mason	....	Thomas E Scillian
Clark (Winchester) (29)	606 745-0200	....	....	....	....	....	....
Clay (Manchester) (22)	606 598-2071	....	....	....	....	....	....
Clinton (Albany) (9)	606 387-5234	....	....	....	....	....	....
Crittenden (Marion) (9)	502 965-5251	John C May	....	Danny Byford	....	....	Floyd Andrews
Cumberland (Burkesville) (7)	502 864-3444	....	....	....	....	....	....
Daviess (Owensboro) (87)	502 685-8424	....	....	....	....	....	....
Edmonson (Brownsville) (10)	502 597-2819	....	....	....	....	....	....
Elliott (Sandy Hook) (6)	606 738-5821	David Blair	....	....	Melanie Blair	....	C Pennington
Estill (Irvine) (15)	606 723-7524	....	....	....	....	....	....
Fleming (Flemingsburg) (12)	606 845-8461	....	....	....	....	....	....
Floyd (Prestonsburg) (44)	606 886-9193	....	....	....	....	....	....
Franklin (Frankfort) (44)	502 875-8751	Bob Arnold	Paula M Smith	Paula M Smith	Duane V Ellis	....	Ted Collins
Fulton (Hickman) (8)	502 236-2594	....	....	....	....	....	....
Gallatin (Warsaw) (5)	606 567-5691	Clarence Davis	....	Cathy Adams	Opaline Moore	....	Clifford Higgins
Garrard (Lancaster) (12)	606 792-3531	Ray Hammonds	....	....	Louise Robinson	Dana Hensley	Buddy Rogers
Grant (Williamstown) (16)	606 823-7561	Shirley Howard	....	Evalene Davis	Katsia J Baird	....	Charles Hudson
Graves (Mayfield) (34)	502 247-3626	....	....	....	....	....	....
Grayson (Leitchfield) (21)	502 259-3159	....	....	....	....	....	....
Green (Greensburg) (10)	502 932-4024	....	....	....	....	....	....
Greenup (Greenup) (37)	606 473-3151	....	....	....	....	....	....
Hancock (Hawesville) (8)	502 927-8137	....	....	....	....	....	....
Hardin (Elizabethtown) (89)	502 765-2350	Glen D Dalton	....	David L Logsdon	Margie Ree Oliver	....	Robert E Thomas
Harlan (Harlan) (37)	606 573-2600	....	....	....	....	....	....
Harrison (Cynthiana) (16)	606 234-7136	Charles Swinford	....	....	....	....	....
Hart (Munfordville) (15)	502 524-9474	....	....	....	....	....	....
Henderson (Henderson) (43)	502 826-3971	Sandy L Watkins	Phylis Martin	Suzanne D Cravens	Cathy L Davis	....	Dennis Clary
Henry (New Castle) (13)	502 845-2891	....	....	....	....	....	....
Hickman (Clinton) (6)	502 653-4369	Gregory D Pruitt	Carol N Malugin	Sophia P Barclay	Nancy C Pruitt	Scott Smith	J W Moran
Hopkins (Madisonville) (46)	502 821-7361	....	....	....	....	....	....
Jackson (Mc Kee) (12)	606 287-8562	....	....	....	....	....	....
Jefferson (Louisville) (665)	502 574-6161	David L Armstrong	Wendell P Wright	Mary W Bolton	Steve J Rowland	Patricia M Childs	Leon E Jones Sr
Jessamine (Nicholasville) (31)	606 885-4500	Wm Neal Cassity	Phyllis Bradshaw	Eva McDaniel	Dorothy Ward	....	Joe Walker
Johnson (Paintsville) (23)	606 789-2550	....	....	....	....	....	....
Kenton (Covington) (142)	606 491-2800	Clyde W Middleton	George Neack	Carol A Brockell	Ivan Frye	Ralph L Bailey Jr	Jeffrey L Butler
Knott (Hindman) (18)	606 785-5592	....	....	....	....	....	....
Knox (Barbourville) (30)	606 546-6192	....	....	....	....	....	....
Larue (Hodgenville) (12)	502 358-4400	....	....	....	....	....	....
Laurel (London) (43)	606 864-5158	....	....	....	....	....	....
Lawrence (Louisa) (14)	606 638-4108	....	....	....	....	....	....
Lee (Beattyville) (7)	606 464-3678	....	....	....	....	....	....
Leslie (Hyden) (14)	606 672-3200	Onzie Sizemore	....	James Lewis	Margie Asher	....	Ford Bowling
Letcher (Whitesburg) (27)	606 633-2129	Carroll A Smith	Linda J Bailey	Charlie Wright	Phillip Hampton	....	Steve Banks
Lewis (Vanceburg) (13)	606 796-3062	George M Plummer	....	Shirley A Hinton	....	....	Virgle Cole
Lexington-Fayette (Lexington) c (225)	606 258-3030	....	....	....	....	....	....
Lincoln (Stanford) (20)	606 365-2534	....	....	....	....	....	....
Livingston (Smithland) (9)	502 928-4522	Ralph Smith	....	James Jones	....	....	....
Logan (Russellville) (24)	502 726-3116	....	....	....	....	....	....
Lyon (Eddyville) (7)	502 388-7311	....	....	....	....	....	....
Madison (Richmond) (58)	606 624-4700	....	....	....	....	....	....
Magoffin (Salyersville) (13)	606 349-2313	....	....	....	....	....	....
Marion (Lebanon) (16)	502 692-3451	....	....	....	....	....	....
Marshall (Benton) (27)	502 527-3388	....	....	....	....	....	....
Martin (Inez) (13)	606 298-2800	Kelly Callaham	Mike Cassday	Carol Mills	Lou Blackburn	....	Darryl Young
Mason (Maysville) (17)	606 564-6706	J L Gallenstein	....	....	P Heflin	....	T Wenz
Mc Cracken (Paducah) (63)	502 444-4707	Danny Orazine	M Annet Lofton	Martha N Bradford	Mary M Hoffman	Danny Orazine	Frank Augustus
Mc Creary (Whitley City) (16)	606 376-2413	Jimmie W Greene	Bruce Murphy	Jo Kidd	John A Crabtree	....	McArthur Swain
Mc Lean (Calhoun) (10)	502 273-3082	....	....	....	....	....	....
Meade (Brandenburg) (24)	502 422-3967	....	....	....	....	....	....
Menifee (Frenchburg) (5)	606 768-3482	Hershell L Sexton	....	....	Marcia Peck	....	Sam Swartz
Mercer (Harrodsburg) (19)	606 734-5135	....	....	....	....	....	....
Metcalfe (Edmonton) (9)	502 432-4821	....	....	....	....	....	....
Monroe (Tompkinsville) (11)	502 487-5505	....	....	....	....	....	....
Montgomery (Mount Sterling) (20)	606 498-8707	B D Wilson	Brenda Jackson	Judy L Witt	Brenda Mapel	Brenda Jackson	Bob Bellamy
Morgan (West Liberty) (12)	606 743-3949	....	....	....	....	....	....
Muhlenberg (Greenville) (31)	502 338-2520	Rodney Kirtley	....	Gaylan Spurlin	Charles R Lewis	....	Jerry Mayhugh
Nelson (Bardstown) (30)	502 348-5941	....	....	....	....	....	....
Nicholas (Carlisle) (7)	606 289-2404	....	....	....	....	....	....
Ohio (Hartford) (21)	502 298-4400	Dudley Cooper	....	Lessie R Johnson	Sue Hitchel	Dudley Cooper	Elvis Doolin
Oldham (La Grange) (33)	502 222-9311	....	....	....	....	....	....
Owen (Owenton) (9)	502 484-3405	....	....	....	....	....	....

Directory 1/10
continued

OFFICIALS IN U.S. COUNTIES

County, county seat, 1990 population figures (000 omitted)	County telephone number	Chief elected official	Appointed administrator	Clerk to the governing board	Chief financial officer	Personnel director	Chief law enforcement official
KENTUCKY (120) continued							
Owsley (Booneville) (5)	606 593-6202	....	....	....	....	....	....
Pendleton (Falmouth) (12)	606 654-4321	....	....	....	....	....	....
Perry (Hazard) (30)	606 436-4513	....	....	....	....	....	....
Pike (Pikeville) (73)	606 432-6247	....	....	....	....	....	....
Powell (Stanton) (12)	606 663-2834	....	....	....	....	....	....
Pulaski (Somerset) (49)	606 678-4853	Louie Floyd	Robert Roland	Willard Hansford	Arlene Phelps	....	Sam Catron
Robertson (Mount Olivet) (2)	606 724-5615	G Wayne Buckler	....	S Hendricks	Janet England	....	Randy Insko
Rockcastle (Mount Vernon) (15)	606 256-2856	Buzz Carloftis	....	Anna Rose Mullins	Joseph B Clontz	....	Shirley Smith
Rowan (Morehead) (20)	606 784-5151	....	....	....	....	....	....
Russell (Jamestown) (15)	502 343-2112	Charles M Smith	Pam Smith	Pam Smith	Anita Tucker	....	Larry Bennett
Scott (Georgetown) (24)	502 863-7875	....	....	....	....	....	....
Shelby (Shelbyville) (25)	502 633-1220	....	....	....	....	....	....
Simpson (Franklin) (15)	502 586-7184	....	....	....	....	....	....
Spencer (Taylorsville) (7)	502 477-3205	Larry S Lawson	Karen Curtsinger	Robin Greenwell	Doug Williams	Larry S Lawson	Steve Coulter
Taylor (Campbellsville) (21)	502 465-7729	....	....	....	....	....	....
Todd (Elkton) (11)	502 265-2363	....	....	....	....	....	....
Trigg (Cadiz) (10)	502 522-8459	Berlin Moore Jr	....	Wanda Thomas	Elsie Tinsley	....	Randy Clark
Trimble (Bedford) (6)	502 255-7196	....	....	....	....	....	....
Union (Morganfield) (17)	502 389-1081	James D Veatch	....	Vicki V O' Nan	Jane R Hite	....	James R Girten
Warren (Bowling Green) (77)	502 843-4146	....	....	....	....	....	....
Washington (Springfield) (10)	606 336-5410	....	....	....	....	....	....
Wayne (Monticello) (17)	606 348-4241	....	....	....	....	....	....
Webster (Dixon) (14)	502 639-5042	James R Townsend	James C Whitledge	Becky Sharp	Paula Guinn	James R Townsend	Kenneth Storey
Whitley (Williamsburg) (33)	606 549-1330	....	....	....	....	....	....
Wolfe (Campton) (7)	606 668-3040	....	....	....	....	....	....
Woodford (Versailles) (20)	606 873-4139	....	....	....	....	....	....
LOUISIANA (64)							
Acadia (Crowley) p (56)	318 783-0953	....	....	....	....	....	....
Allen (Oberlin) p (21)	318 639-4396	Tommy Ballard	....	Carolyn Bush	Judy E Young	....	....
Ascension (Donaldsonville) p (58)	504 473-9866	....	....	....	....	....	....
Assumption (Napoleonville) p (23)	504 369-7435	....	....	....	....	....	....
Avoyelles (Marksville) p (39)	318 253-9208	....	....	....	....	....	....
Baton Rouge (Baton Rouge) c (220)	504 389-3141	Tom Ed McHugh	Graydon Walker	Michael B Mayers	Otha L Schofield	Jerald L Boykin	D Greg Phares
Beauregard (De Ridder) p (30)	318 463-7019	....	....	....	....	....	....
Bienville (Arcadia) p (16)	318 263-2019	....	....	....	....	....	....
Bossier (Benton) p (86)	318 965-2329	....	....	....	....	....	....
Caddo (Shreveport) p (248)	318 226-6780	....	....	....	....	....	....
Calcasieu (Lake Charles) p (168)	318 437-3500	....	....	....	....	....	....
Caldwell (Columbia) p (10)	318 649-2273	....	....	....	....	....	....
Cameron (Cameron) p (9)	318 775-5718	....	....	....	....	....	....
Catahoula (Harrisonburg) p (11)	318 744-5435	H C Peck Jr	Emmett Book	Emmett Book	Emmett Book	Emmett Book	Joe Tom Trunzler
Claiborne (Homer) p (17)	318 927-9601	....	....	....	....	....	....
Concordia (Vidalia) p (21)	318 336-5953	Fred Falkenheiner	Robbie Shirley	Clyde Webber	Cathy Darden	Don Glynn	Randy Maxwell
De Soto (Mansfield) p (25)	318 872-0738	Persley White Jr	....	Shirley C Wheless	Betty A Woods	S Mayweather	Hugh Bennett Jr
East Carroll (Lake Providence) p (10)	318 559-2256	....	....	....	....	....	....
East Feliciana (Clinton) p (19)	504 683-8577	James F Hunt	Clarence Payne	Judith G Kelly	Judith G Kelly	....	T R Maglone
Evangeline (Ville Platte) p (33)	318 363-5651	....	....	....	....	....	....
Franklin (Winnsboro) p (22)	318 435-9429	Ray Young	....	Kaye Cupp	Colleen Hammons	....	Eugene Parker
Grant (Colfax) p (18)	318 627-9907	....	....	....	....	....	....
Iberia (New Iberia) p (68)	318 365-8246	....	....	....	....	....	....
Iberville (Plaquemine) p (31)	504 687-5190	....	....	....	....	....	....
Jackson (Jonesboro) p (16)	318 259-2795	....	....	....	....	....	....
Jefferson (Gretna) p (448)	504 736-6400	Michael J Yenni	Timothy P Coulon	Terrie Rodrigue	Dennis DiMarco	Martin Schwegmann	Harry Lee
Jefferson Davis (Jennings) p (31)	318 824-4792	....	....	....	....	....	Bob Garifo
La Salle (Jena) p (14)	318 992-2158	John Carter	Patsye Breithaupt	....	....	....	Donald Breaux
Lafayette (Lafayette) p (165)	318 233-6220	Walter Comeaux	John Warner Smith	Lloyd Rochon	James Dorton	Rudolph Bourg	Donald Breaux
Lafourche (Thibodaux) p (86)	504 446-8427	Steven D Wilson	Marie F Borne	Sheila Boudreaux	Craig Roussel	Jackie W Jackson	Craig Webre
Lincoln (Ruston) p (42)	318 251-5150	H F Delony	Richard I Durrett	Sue Sanderson	Jerry Smith	Annie Hamlin	Wayne Houck
Livingston (Livingston) p (71)	504 686-2266	....	....	....	....	....	....
Madison (Tallulah) p (12)	318 574-3451	....	....	....	....	....	....
Morehouse (Bastrop) p (32)	318 281-4132	Lee E Loche	E A Greer	E A Greer	E A Greer	....	Frank Carroll
Natchitoches (Natchitoches) p (37)	318 352-2714	....	....	....	....	....	....
New Orleans c (497)	504 565-6000	....	....	....	....	....	....
Ouachita (Monroe) p (142)	318 327-1340	....	....	....	....	....	....
Plaquemines (Pointe a la Hache) p (26)	504 682-0081	....	....	....	....	....	....
Pointe Coupee (New Roads) p (23)	504 638-9556	Clement Guidroz	David E Cifreo	....	....	....	Preston Chuztz
Rapides (Alexandria) p (132)	318 473-6660	Steve Bordelon	Jack Dewitt	Angie Richmond	Tim Ware	....	William Hilton
Red River (Coushatta) p (9)	318 932-5719	....	....	....	....	....	....
Richland (Rayville) p (21)	318 728-2061	....	....	....	....	....	....
Sabine (Many) p (23)	318 256-5637	....	....	....	....	....	....
St. Bernard (Chalmette) p (67)	504 278-4200	Lynn B Dean	John L Carney	Myra Kattengell	Lewis Heston	Eleanor Lefebvre	Jack Stephens
St. Charles (Hahnville) p (42)	504 783-5000	Chris A Tregre	Timothy J Vial	....	R A Becnel Jr	Sandra W Zimmer	....
St. Helena (Greensburg) p (10)	504 222-4549	....	....	....	....	....	....
St. James (Convent) p (21)	504 562-2387	Dale Hymel	....	Lena Kliebert	Arile Laiche	Sidney Oubre Jr	....
St. John the Baptist (Laplace) p (40)	504 652-9569	....	....	....	....	....	....
St. Landry (Opelousas) p (80)	318 948-3688	....	....	....	....	....	....
St. Martin (St. Martinville) p (44)	318 394-3711	....	....	....	....	....	....
St. Mary (Franklin) p (58)	318 828-4100	Oray P Rogers	Connie M Fournet	Kim Pusateri	D Sue Carter	Tammy Charpentier	....
St. Tammany (Covington) p (145)	504 898-2362	....	Allan R Cartier	....	Lynn W Cox	....	....
Tangipahoa (Amite) p (86)	504 748-3211	....	....	....	....	....	....
Tensas (St. Joseph) p (7)	318 766-3542	Thomas Hale	Ronnie W Hopkins	Ronnie W Hopkins	Ronnie W Hopkins	....	Jeff Britt
Terrebonne (Houma) c (..)	504 873-6401	Barry Bonvillain	Doug Maier	Paul Labat	Doug Maier	Lawrence Robinson	Jerry Carpenter
Union (Farmerville) p (21)	318 368-8687	Don Acree	Patty Allen	....	....	....	....
Vermilion (Abbeville) p (50)	318 898-4300	....	....	....	....	....	....
Vernon (Leesville) p (62)	318 239-2444	....	....	....	....	....	....
Washington (Franklinton) p (43)	504 839-4582	....	....	....	....	....	....
Webster (Minden) p (42)	318 377-2144	....	....	....	....	....	....
West Baton Rouge (Port Allen) p (19)	504 383-4755	....	....	....	....	....	....
West Carroll (Oak Grove) p (12)	318 428-3390	....	....	....	....	....	....
West Feliciana (St. Francisville) p (13)	504 635-3794	....	....	....	....	....	....

County, county seat, 1990 population figures (000 omitted)	County telephone number	Chief elected official	Appointed administrator	Clerk to the governing board	Chief financial officer	Personnel director	Chief law enforcement official
LOUISIANA (64) continued							
Winn (Winnfield) p (16)	318 628-5824	Loyd E Vines	Thelma Jarnagin	Thelma Jarnagin	Thelma Jarnagin	Thelma Jarnagin	James E Jordan
MAINE (16)							
Androscoggin (Auburn) (105)	207 784-8390	Emile Jacques	....	Patricia Fournier	Richard Fournier	Patricia Fournier	Ronald Gagnon
Aroostook (Caribou) (87)	207 493-3318	Norman Fournier	Roland D Martin	Roland D Martin	Roland D Martin	Roland D Martin	Edgar Wheeler
Cumberland (Portland) (243)	207 871-8380	....	....	....	....	....	....
Franklin (Farmington) (29)	207 778-6614	....	....	....	....	....	....
Hancock (Ellsworth) (47)	207 667-9542	....	....	....	....	....	....
Kennebec (Augusta) (116)	207 622-0971	George M Jabar	Wesley Kieltyka	Charles G Dow Sr	Sandi Pelletier	....	Bryan Lamoreau
Knox (Rockland) (36)	207 594-0420	....	....	....	....	....	....
Lincoln (Wiscasset) (30)	207 882-6311	Rupert C Stevens	....	Ann M Merry	Rupert Neily Sr	....	William C Carter
Oxford (South Paris) (53)	207 743-6359	....	....	....	....	....	....
Penobscot (Bangor) (147)	207 942-8535	Thomas J Davis Jr	....	Donna L Keim	Irene A Burke	....	Edward J Reynolds
Piscataquis (Dover-Foxcroft) (19) ...	207 564-2161	....	....	....	....	....	....
Sagadahoc (Bath) (34)	207 443-8200	J Franklin Howe	....	Barry M Sturgeon	Gloria P Barnes	....	Mark A Westrum
Somerset (Skowhegan) (50)	207 474-9861	....	....	....	....	....	....
Waldo (Belfast) (33)	207 338-3282	....	....	....	....	....	....
Washington (Machias) (35)	207 255-3127	Preston E Smith	....	Joyce E Thompson	Joyce E Thompson	Joyce E Thompson	John B Crowley
York (Alfred) (165)	207 324-1571	....	....	....	....	....	....
MARYLAND (24)							
Allegany (Cumberland) (75)	301 777-5911	John W Stotler	Daniel McMullen	Carol A Gaffney	Jerry L Frantz	Monty Pagenhardt	Gary W Simpson
Anne Arundel (Annapolis) (427) ...	410 222-7000	Ed Middlebrooks	Walter Chitwood	Judith C Holmes	John R Hammond	....	Robert P Russell
Baltimore (Baltimore) i (736)	410 396-3880	....	Lynnette Young	....	William Brown	Jesse Hoskins	Thomas Frazier
Baltimore (Towson) (692)	410 887-3139	....	Merreen E Kelly	....	James Gibson	Richard Holloway	Michael Gambrill
Calvert (Prince Frederick) (51)	410 535-1600	Hagner R Mister	Richard L Holler	Mary S Watson	James J Allman	G Davis Bourdon	Lawrence Stinnett
Caroline (Denton) (27)	301 479-0660	....	....	....	....	....	....
Carroll (Westminster) (123)	410 848-4500	Donald I Dell	Robert A Bair	Shawn D Reese	Eugene C Curfman	Jimmie L Saylor	John H Brown
Cecil (Elkton) (71)	410 996-5200	W Edwin Cole Jr	Edward L Sealover	Christine A Main	Lewis R Jackson	....	Rodney Kennedy
Charles (La Plata) (101)	301 645-0550	Thomas Middleton	Thomas Fritz	Shirley Gore	Richard Winkler	Ann Pokora	James Gartland
Dorchester (Cambridge) (30)	410 228-1700	....	....	....	....	....	....
Frederick (Frederick) (150)	301 694-9000	Ron Sundergill	Dawn Hatzer	....	Tom Fox	Mitchell Hose	Carl Harbaugh
Garrett (Oakland) (28)	301 334-8970	....	....	....	....	....	....
Harford (Bel Air) (182)	410 638-3201	Jeffrey D Wilson	Larry W Klimovitz	Doris Poulsen	James M Jewell	Randall J Schultz	Robert E Comes
Howard (Ellicott City) (187)	410 313-2033	Charles Ecker	Raquel Sanudo	....	Raymond Servary	P William Herndon	James Robey
Kent (Chestertown) (18)	410 778-4600	William S Sutton	Charles Mac Leod	Janice F Fletcher	Jennifer J Miller	Charles Mac Leod	William T Bright
Montgomery (Rockville) (757)	301 217-1000	William H Hanna	Eugene R Lynch	....	Timothy Firestine	William P Garrett	Clarence Edwards
Prince George'S (Upper Marlboro) (729)	301 952-3000	....	....	....	....	....	....
Queen Annes (Centreville) (34)	410 758-4406	William V Riggs	Robert D Sallitt	Lynda H Palmatary	Joseph Zimmerman	Robert D Sallitt	Charles Crossley
Somerset (Princess Anne) (23)	410 651-0320	Phillip L Gerald	Charles E Massey	Charles E Massey	Charles L Muir	Debbie M Massey	Robert Jones
St. Marys (Leonardtown) (76)	301 475-5621	Carl M Loffler	Edward V Cox	....	Charles H Wade	George A Foster	Wayne L Pettit
Talbot (Easton) (31)	410 822-2401	Robert D Higgins	Blenda Armistead	Fran Levanios	Blenda Armistead	Blenda Armistead	Thomas G Duncan
Washington (Hagerstown) (121) ...	301 791-3090	....	....	....	....	....	....
Wicomico (Salisbury) (74)	301 548-4800	....	....	....	....	....	....
Worcester (Now Hill) (35)	410 632-0090	....	John A Yankus	....	Gerald Mason	Matthew Azzolini	G D McAllister
MASSACHUSETTS (14)							
Barnstable (Barnstable) (187)	508 362-2511	....	....	....	....	....	....
Berkshire (Pittsfield) (139)	413 448-8424	....	....	....	....	....	....
Boston-Suffolk (Boston) c (574) ...	617 725-4000	....	....	....	....	....	....
Bristol (Taunton) (506)	508 824-9681	Maria F Lopes	....	....	P Harrington	....	David R Nelson
Dukes (Edgartown) (12)	617 627-5535	....	....	....	....	....	....
Essex (Salem) (670)	508 741-0200	John O' Brien	Janis C Simard	James D Leary	K O' Leary	Ann Jean	Charles Reardon
Franklin (Greenfield) (70)	413 774-3167	....	....	....	....	....	....
Hampden (Springfield) (456)	413 781-8100	....	....	....	....	....	....
Hampshire (Northampton) (147) ...	413 584-0557	....	....	....	....	....	....
Middlesex (East Cambridge) (1398)	617 494-4000	....	....	....	....	....	....
Nantucket (Nantucket) c (6)	508 228-7255	....	....	....	....	....	Harry E Clute
Norfolk (Dedham) (616)	617 461-6100	W P O' Donnell	Henry W Ainslie	N Barbadoro	Robert D Hall	....	Clifford Marshall
Plymouth (Plymouth) (435)	508 830-9100	Patricia A Lawton	....	Francis R Powers	John F McLellan	....	Peter Y Flynn
Worcester (Worcester) (710)	508 798-7700	Francis Holloway	James P Purcell	Loring Lamoureux	Michael Donoghue	....	John M Flynn
MICHIGAN (83)							
Alcona (Harrisville) (10)	517 724-6807	....	....	....	....	....	....
Alger (Munising) (9)	906 387-2076	....	....	....	....	....	....
Allegan (Allegan) (91)	616 673-0205	David Babbitt	Joanne Jones	Joyce Watts	P Birkholtz	Christine Jurkas	David Haverdink
Alpena (Alpena) (31)	517 356-0930	Cameron Habermehl	....	B Smolinski	Dale A Huggler	R Donakowski	Thomas Male
Antrim (Bellaire) (18)	616 533-8607	....	....	....	....	....	....
Arenac (Standish) (15)	501 673-3181	....	....	....	....	....	....
Baraga (L'Anse) (8)	906 524-6183	Roland Sweeney	....	Nelda Robillard	Nelda Robillard	....	Bob Teddy
Barry (Hastings) (50)	616 948-4891	Orvin H Moore	Judith A Peterson	Nancy L Boersma	Judith A Peterson	....	David O Wood
Bay (Bay City) (112)	517 895-4098	Edward L Rivet	Thomas L Hickner	Barbara Albertson	Michael Regulski	Brian Redmond	Gerald Vanalst
Benzie (Beulah) (12)	616 882-9671	David Mead	....	Jean Bowers	Ronald Mead	....	Paul Stiles
Berrien (St. Joseph) (161)	616 983-7111	R J Burkholz	John M Henry	M Louise Stine	Carol Stockman	....	Robert Kimmerly
Branch (Coldwater) (42)	517 279-8411	Charlene Burch	John C Dean	Judy Elliott	Sandra Thatcher	....	Ted Gordon
Calhoun (Marshall) (136)	616 781-0700	Michael Nofs	Peter Herlofsky	Anne Norlander	....	Roger Likkel	James Roberts
Cass (Cassopolis) (49)	616 445-4420	R James Guse	Terry L Proctor	Ann Simmons	Sharon Hansell	John Murphy	Joseph Underwood
Charlevoix (Charlevoix) (21)	616 547-7200	....	....	....	....	....	....
Cheboygan (Cheboygan) (21)	616 627-8808	....	....	....	....	....	....
Chippewa (Sault Ste. Marie) (35) ...	906 635-6330	Leno Pianosi	Gordon Newland	Margaret Kaunisto	Dave Carpenter	Gordon Newland	Edward Berkompas
Clare (Harrison) (25)	517 539-7131	Ed Howland	....	Donna M Carr	....	....	Howard Haskin
Clinton (St. Johns) (58)	517 224-5120	Robert D Ditmer	David D Benda	Jane Swanchara	David D Benda	Jeanette Smith	Donald Hengesh
Crawford (Grayling) (12)	517 348-2841	Dennis Long	....	Elizabeth Wieland	Joseph Wakeley	....	David Lovely
Delta (Escanaba) (38)	906 786-2237	....	....	....	....	....	....
Dickinson (Iron Mountain) (27) ...	906 774-2573	Ernest Mariucci	William Marchetti	Dolly Cook	Joanne Johnson	....	D Charlevoix
Eaton (Charlotte) (93)	517 543-7500	....	....	....	....	....	....
Emmet (Petoskey) (25)	616 347-2801	James Tamlyn	Lyn Johnson	Irene Granger	Martin Krupa	Lyn Johnson	Jeff Budzick
Genesee (Flint) (430)	313 257-3034	Daniel Kildee	....	Michael Carr	Leonard Smorch	Steven Statton	Joseph Wilson
Gladwin (Gladwin) (22)	517 426-4821	Roy O' Hare	....	Laura E Flach	Roy O' Hare	....	Michael Hargrave
Gogebic (Bessemer) (18)	906 667-0411	....	....	....	....	....	....
Grand Traverse (Traverse City) (64)	616 922-4599	Tony Buday	K Ross Childs	Virginia Watson	Glenn Peroceschi	Marilyn Brown	Harold Barr
Gratiot (Ithaca) (39)	517 875-3343	Floyd DeMott	Roger Cook	Pauline Merchant	Mary L Sullivan	....	Michael Vetter

Directory 1/10 OFFICIALS IN U.S. COUNTIES
continued

County, county seat, 1990 population figures (000 omitted)	County telephone number	Chief elected official	Appointed administrator	Clerk to the governing board	Chief financial officer	Personnel director	Chief law enforcement official
MICHIGAN (83) continued							
Hillsdale (Hillsdale) (43)	517 437-3932	....	....	....	....	....	....
Houghton (Houghton) (35)	906 482-8307	....	....	....	....	....	....
Huron (Bad Axe) (35)	517 269-8242	....	....	....	....	....	....
Ingham (Lansing) (282)	517 887-4327	Jean McDonald	Gerald Ambrose	Lingg Brewer	Mary Barnes	Harold Hailey	G Wrigglesworth
Ionia (Ionia) (57)	616 527-5300	....	....	....	....	....	....
Iosco (Tawas City) (30)	517 362-4212	Clyde L Soucie	....	Michael A Welsch	E Shellenbarger	....	Craig Herriman
Iron (Crystal Falls) (13)	906 875-3301	....	....	....	....	....	....
Isabella (Mount Pleasant) (55)	517 772-0911	Sandra Caul	....	Betty Prout	Steve Pickens	....	Barry DeLau
Jackson (Jackson) (150)	517 788-4333	James Shotwell	Randolph Terronez	Mickey Mortimer	Janet Rochefort	Phyllis Way	Henry Zavislak
Kalamazoo (Kalamazoo) (223)	616 384-8111	Richard D Kleiman	Wesley K Freeland	James O Youngs	William L Dundon	Richad L Kinas	Thomas Edmonds
Kalkaska (Kalkaska) (13)	616 258-3336	Melvin F Hill	....	Patricia Rodgers	Frank Wright	Frank Wright	Nelson J Cannon
Kent (Grand Rapids) (501)	616 774-3679	....	....	....	....	....	....
Keweenaw (Eagle River) (2)	906 337-2229	....	....	....	....	....	....
Lake (Baldwin) (9)	616 745-4641	....	....	....	....	....	....
Lapeer (Lapeer) (75)	810 667-0366	Richard Blonde	John Biscoe	Marlene Bruns	Craig Horton	....	Ron Kalanquin
Leelanau (Leland) (17)	616 256-9711	G Henshaw	D Beard	D Wunderlich	J Blackburn	D Beard	C Johnson
Lenawee (Adrian) (91)	517 263-8831	....	....	....	....	....	....
Livingston (Howell) (116)	517 546-3520	....	....	....	....	....	....
Luce (Newberry) (6)	906 293-5521	Rodney Richards	....	Kathy Mahar	Lois Fighter	....	Kevin Erickson
Mackinac (St. Ignace) (11)	906 643-7300	Dale Webber	....	Mary Kay Tamlyn	....	....	Lawrence Leveille
Macomb (Mount Clemens) (717)	313 469-5100	Mark A Steenbergh	....	Carmella Sabaugh	David M Diegel	William Israel	William Hackel
Manistee (Manistee) (21)	616 723-4575	Carl Rutske	Thomas Kaminski	Dorlene Schudlich	Alan Verheek	Thomas Kaminski	Edward Haik
Marquette (Marquette) (71)	906 228-1501	....	....	....	....	....	....
Mason (Ludington) (26)	616 843-8202	....	....	....	....	....	....
Mecosta (Big Rapids) (37)	616 796-2505	J Michael Shaw	Charles Randolph	Ruth M Hess	Shirley Johnson	....	Henry Wayer
Menominee (Menominee) (25)	906 863-7779	Lloyd Benson	Kevin Hamann	Barbara Morrison	Kevin Hamann	Kevin Hamann	Dennis Kenney
Midland (Midland) (76)	517 832-6780	Tony Stamas	Marc A McGill	Jeffrey P Porter	....	Richard J Busch	John S Reder
Missaukee (Lake City) (12)	616 839-4967	Gary Birgy	....	Carolyn Flore	Carolyn Flore	....	James Bosscher
Monroe (Monroe) (134)	313 243-7053	Raymond Noble	Charles A Londo	Geraldine Allen	James F Beck	Peggy A Howard	Carl E Van Wert
Montcalm (Stanton) (53)	517 831-5226	Mark O Stevens	Nancy Hansing	Joyce Ehle	John Chapin	Nancy Hansing	Donald Godell
Montmorency (Atlanta) (9)	517 785-3358	Dick Hermanson	Connie Marlatt	Nancy Cunningham	Gloria Marlatt	....	Daniel Braun
Muskegon (Muskegon) (159)	616 724-6211	Kenneth Hulka	Frank Bednarek	Ruth Stevens	....	James Delaney	Robert Carter
Newaygo (White Cloud) (38)	616 689-7200	....	....	....	....	....	....
Oakland (Pontiac) (1084)	810 858-0542	Larry P Crake	L B Patterson	Suzette M Vogt	Robert J Daddow	C Vincent Luzi	John F Nichols
Oceana (Hart) (22)	616 873-4835	Loyd Van Sickle	Paul E Inglls	Phylis J Schlee	Paul E Inglls	Paul E Inglls	Fred Korb
Ogemaw (West Branch) (19)	517 345-0215	....	....	....	....	....	....
Ontonagon (Ontonagon) (9)	906 884-4255	Allan Slye	....	Judith Roehm	Diana Killoran	....	Gerald Kitzman
Osceola (Reed City) (20)	616 832-3261	Rick Johnson	....	Karen J Bluhm	E Stafford	....	David Needham
Oscoda (Mio) (8)	517 826-3241	....	....	....	....	....	....
Otsego (Gaylord) (18)	517 732-6484	James H Jacobs	Lambert L Chard	Evelyn M Pratt	....	....	Donald W Anderson
Ottawa (Grand Haven) (188)	616 846-8306	David Vanderkool	Robert Oosterbaan	Daniel Krueger	Rosemary Zink	Rich Schurkamp	Gary Rosema
Presque Isle (Rogers City) (14)	517 734-3288	....	....	....	....	....	....
Roscommon (Roscommon) (20)	517 275-8021	Richard Kobman	....	Robert W Smith	....	....	Thomas McKindles
Saginaw (Saginaw) (212)	517 790-5200	....	....	....	....	....	....
Sanilac (Sandusky) (40)	313 648-2933	Helen B Takacs	Richard F Lessner	Linda I Kozfkay	Richard F Lessner	Richard F Lessner	Virg Stricler
Schoolcraft (Manistique) (8)	906 341-3618	Louis L Lauzon	....	Sigrid I Hedberg	Terri A Evonich	....	Gary Maddox
Shiawassee (Corunna) (70)	517 743-2279	Jana L Kurrle	Paul J Brake	John S Pajtas	Judith Kingsbury	Paul J Brake	A James LaJoye
St. Clair (Port Huron) (146)	313 985-2001	....	....	....	....	....	....
St. Joseph (Centreville) (59)	616 467-5533	Art Renner	Judy West	Pattie S Bender	Bradley M Whaley	Bradley M Whaley	Matthew J Lori
Tuscola (Caro) (55)	517 673-5999	....	....	....	....	....	....
Van Buren (Paw Paw) (70)	616 657-8253	Daniel Ruzick	Douglas Cultra	Shirley Jackson	....	....	H Cal Rosema
Washtenaw (Ann Arbor) (283)	313 994-2400	Mary Egnor	....	Peggy Haines	Peter Ballios	Verna McDaniel	Ron Schebil
Wayne (Detroit) (2112)	313 224-5900	....	....	Alfred Montgomery	Lester Robinson	Thomas Bednarski	Robert Ficano
Wexford (Cadillac) (26)	616 779-9453	Robert M Lee	Larry Huebner	Elaine Richardson	Larry Huebner	Larry Huebner	Gary Finstrom
MINNESOTA (87)							
Aitkin (Aitkin) (12)	218 927-7276	....	....	....	....	....	....
Anoka (Anoka) (244)	612 421-4760	Dan W Erhart	John McLinden	....	Terry L Johnson	Ronald B Welde	Ken G Wilkinson
Becker (Detroit Lakes) (28)	218 846-7301	Jack Murray	M Williams	M Williams	R Thompson	D Dougherty	C Parrus
Beltrami (Bemidji) (34)	218 759-4156	Gail Skare	Gregory Lewis	Gregory Lewis	Christine Patten	Marilyn Nelson	Dwight Stewart
Benton (Foley) (30)	612 968-6254	Ken Neeser	....	Wm Scott	....	Roxanne Chmielews	Frank Wippler
Big Stone (Ortonville) (6)	612 839-2525	....	....	....	....	....	....
Blue Earth (Mankato) (54)	507 389-8100	....	....	....	....	....	....
Brown (New Ulm) (27)	507 359-7900	Richard Petersen	Jerome Bentz	Jerome Bentz	Marlin Helget	Leah Crabtree	Larry Pedersen
Carlton (Carlton) (29)	218 384-4281	Gordon Aanerud	....	Paul Gassert	Paul Gassert	Michael Stafford	David Seboe
Carver (Chaska) (48)	612 361-1500	Tracy Swanson	Richard Stolz	....	Frederc Boethin	Pamela Peters	Allen Wallin
Cass (Walker) (22)	218 547-3300	....	....	....	....	....	....
Chippewa (Montevideo) (13)	612 269-7447	....	....	....	....	....	....
Chisago (Center City) (31)	612 257-0451	Bob Vande Kamp	James Thoreen	....	Dennis Freed	....	Randy Schwegman
Clay (Moorhead) (50)	218 299-5002	Charles Brantner	Vijay Sethi	Vijay Sethi	Pauline Sarbaum	Terry Jacobson	Larry Costello
Clearwater (Bagley) (8)	218 694-6177	....	....	....	....	....	....
Cook (Grand Marais) (4)	218 387-2282	Chet Lindskog	....	Carol Gresczyk	Carol Gresczyk	Janet Iverson	John Lyght
Cottonwood (Windom) (13)	507 831-1905	Marlowe Nelsen	....	William Mielke	....	....	Glen Ward
Crow Wing (Brainerd) (44)	218 828-2932	....	....	....	....	....	....
Dakota (Hastings) (275)	612 438-4418	Donald Maher	Brandt Richardson	Richard Neumann	Richard Neumann	Wilfried Volk	Rodney Boyd
Dodge (Mantorville) (16)	507 635-6239	Don Gray	Curt Kephart	Curt Kephart	Curt Kephart	Curt Kephart	William Weber
Douglas (Alexandria) (29)	612 762-2381	William Collins	....	Harvey Tewes	A C Olsen	K LeBrasseur	Bill Ingebrigtsen
Faribault (Blue Earth) (17)	507 526-6225	Jerald Niebuhr	....	Nan Crary	John Thompson	Nan Crary	Scott Campbell
Fillmore (Preston) (21)	507 765-4701	....	....	....	....	....	....
Freeborn (Albert Lea) (33)	507 377-5116	George Hajek	Eugene Smith	Eugene Smith	Harold Olson	Susan Phillips	Donald Nolander
Goodhue (Red Wing) (41)	612 385-3001	Lyle Lexvold	Stephen Bloom	Stephen Bloom	Jeff Cole	Stephen Bloom	Forest Wipperling
Grant (Elbow Lake) (6)	218 685-4520	Dennis Anderson	....	Patricia Shearer	Patricia Shearer	Patricia Shearer	Greg Schelin
Hennepin (Minneapolis) (1032)	612 348-3000	....	....	....	....	....	....
Houston (Caledonia) (18)	507 724-5803	David Corcoran	....	A Peter Johnson	A Peter Johnson	Tim Comstock	Dennis Swedberg
Hubbard (Park Rapids) (15)	218 732-1451	Larry Burgoon	....	....	....	Gene O' Brien	Larry Johnson
Isantl (Cambridge) (26)	612 689-3859	Glenn E Johnson	Robyn M Sykes	Robyn M Sykes	....	Robyn M Sykes	Larry Southerland
Itasca (Grand Rapids) (41)	218 327-2847	....	....	....	....	....	....
Jackson (Jackson) (12)	507 847-2763	Gerald D Benjamin	....	Luther F Glaser	Luther F Glaser	Ben Pribyl	Peter Eggimann
Kanabec (Mora) (13)	612 679-1030	Melvin Pearson	....	....	....	....	Von Thompson
Kandiyohi (Willmar) (39)	612 231-6215	....	....	....	....	....	....
Kittson (Hallock) (6)	218 843-2655	....	....	....	....	....	....
Koochiching (International Falls) (16)	218 283-6252	Wade Pavleck	....	Teresa Jaksa	....	Teresa Jaksa	William Elliott
Lac Qui Parle (Madison) (9)	612 598-7444	Albert Hoffman	....	Stan Bjorgan	Stan Bjorgan	....	Graylen Carlson

Directory 1/10 **OFFICIALS IN U.S. COUNTIES**
continued

County, county seat, 1990 population figures (000 omitted)	County telephone number	Chief elected official	Appointed administrator	Clerk to the governing board	Chief financial officer	Personnel director	Chief law enforcement official
MINNESOTA (87) continued							
Lake (Two Harbors) (10)	218 834-8320	Lee Ramsdell	....	Richard A Sigel	Steven McMahon	....	Harold Paulseth
Lake Of the Woods (Baudette) (4)	218 634-2836	....	....	....	....	....	....
Le Sueur (Le Center) (23)	612 357-2251	Bill Stangler	....	Terry Overn	Terry Overn	....	Patrick W Smith
Lincoln (Ivanhoe) (7)	507 694-1529	....	....	....	....	....	....
Lyon (Marshall) (25)	507 537-6727	Robert Fenske	....	C Sheffield	....	....	Don Stokke
Mahnomen (Mahnomen) (5)	218 935-5669	....	....	....	....	....	....
Marshall (Warren) (11)	218 745-4851	....	....	....	....	....	....
Martin (Fairmont) (23)	507 235-3261	....	....	....	....	....	....
Mc Leod (Glencoe) (32)	612 864-5551	....	....	....	....	....	....
Meeker (Litchfield) (21)	612 693-6329	George Rice	Paul Virnig	D Groskreutz	Allan Knutson	Paul Virnig	Michael Hirman
Mille Lacs (Milaca) (19)	612 983-2561	....	....	....	....	....	....
Morrison (Little Falls) (30)	612 632-2941	Paul Nieman Jr	....	Russ Nygren	Russ Nygren	Paul Froncak	Paul Tschida
Mower (Austin) (37)	507 437-9535	Richard Cummings	Craig Oscarson	Craig Oscarson	Ruth Harris	Craig Oscarson	Wayne Goodnature
Murray (Slayton) (10)	507 836-6163	Berneva Johnson	....	....	....	....	Ronald McKenzie
Nicollet (St. Peter) (28)	507 931-6800	....	....	....	....	....	....
Nobles (Worthington) (20)	507 372-8231	....	....	....	....	....	....
Norman (Ada) (8)	218 784-2101	Don C Anderson	....	Jack A Deitz	Jack A Deitz	....	Larry Miller
Olmsted (Rochester) (106)	507 285-8115	Carol Kamper	....	Richard Devlin	Robert Bendzick	David Griffin	Steven Borchardt
Otter Tail (Fergus Falls) (51)	218 739-2271	....	....	....	....	....	....
Pennington (Thief River Falls) (13)	218 681-4011	Ken Murphy	....	Kenneth Olson	Vickie Bjorgaard	....	Gerald Moe
Pine (Pine City) (21)	612 629-6781	Glenn S Danelski	....	L Perreault	L Perreault	....	Donald Faulkner
Pipestone (Pipestone) (10)	507 825-4494	Clayton C Ihlen	....	Gordon Baden	Steven Weets	Judith Oldemeyer	Ronald Smidt
Polk (Crookston) (32)	218 281-5408	....	....	....	....	....	....
Pope (Glenwood) (11)	612 634-5301	....	....	....	....	....	....
Ramsey (St. Paul) (486)	612 266-8500	Hal Norgard	Terry Schutten	Bonnie Jackelen	James Van Houdt	Richard Brainerd	Patricia Moen
Red Lake (Red Lake Falls) (5)	218 253-4281	....	....	....	....	....	....
Redwood (Redwood Falls) (17)	507 637-3207	....	....	....	....	....	....
Renville (Olivia) (18)	612 523-2071	Mary Page	James Tersteeg	James Tersteeg	James Tersteeg	Jerald Brustuen	Jerry Agre
Rice (Faribault) (49)	507 332-6100	....	....	....	....	....	....
Rock (Luverne) (10)	507 283-4173	Willis Brakke	Kyle Oldre	Kyle Oldre	Margaret Cook	Kyle Oldre	Ronnal McClure
Roseau (Roseau) (15)	218 463-2541	....	....	....	....	....	....
Scott (Shakopee) (58)	612 496-8103	Edwin Mackie	Clifford McCann	Jane Hansen	James Berg	Thomas Longmire	William Nevin
Sherburne (Elk River) (42)	612 241-2700	Lyle Smith	Dave Loch	Dave Loch	Ramona Doebler	Dave Loch	Dick Witschen
Sibley (Gaylord) (14)	612 237-2369	Leo Bauer	....	Gene Solmonson	Waldo Reckdahl	Roseann Nagel	Roger Graham
St. Louis (Duluth) (198)	218 726-2562	Steve Rauker	John J Kachmar Jr	Karen Erickson	Gordon McFaul	Anthony J Bruno	Gary Waller
Stearns (St. Cloud) (119)	612 656-3600	Robert A Gambrino	George Rindelaub	Henry Kohorst	Henry Kohorst	Irene Koski	James Kostreba
Steele (Owatonna) (31)	507 451-8040	Les Oeltjenbruns	Dave Severson	Laura Ihrke	Steve Rohlik	Dave Severson	Bill Hildebrandt
Stevens (Morris) (11)	612 589-7417	Steven Sherstad	Gene Wiegand	....	Richard Bluth	....	Larry Sayre
Swift (Benson) (11)	612 843-4069	Lawrence Stock	....	Byron L Giese	Byron L Giese	....	Kenneth Hanson
Todd (Long Prairie) (23)	612 732-4469	G Jagush	....	J Rosenow	K Gresser	J Rosenow	D Asmus
Traverse (Wheaton) (4)	612 563-4242	....	....	....	....	....	....
Wabasha (Wabasha) (20)	612 565-2648	....	....	....	....	....	....
Wadena (Wadena) (13)	218 631-2425	Ralph Lorentz	....	Robert Fort	....	....	H Michael Carr
Waseca (Waseca) (18)	507 835-0630	....	....	....	....	....	....
Washington (Stillwater) (146)	612 439-3220	Mary Hauser	Jim Schug	....	John Devine	Judy Honmyhr	Ken Boyden
Watonwan (St. James) (12)	507 375-3341	Noren Durheim	Donald Kuhlman	Donald Kuhlman	Donald Kuhlman	Donald Kuhlman	Jack Keech
Wilkin (Breckenridge) (8)	218 643-4981	Robert Perry	....	Carolyn Ellingson	Carolyn Ellingson	....	Thomas Richels
Winona (Winona) (48)	507 457-6350	M J McCauley	P Blaisdell	....	Cherie Mac Lennan	Colleen Schultz	Richard Johnson
Wright (Buffalo) (69)	612 682-3900	Pat Sawatzke	Richard Norman	Richard Norman	Darla Groshens	Richard Norman	Don Hozempa
Yellow Medicine (Granite Falls) (12)	612 564-3132	....	....	....	....	....	....
MISSISSIPPI (82)							
Adams (Natchez) (35)	601 446-6684	....	....	....	....	....	....
Alcorn (Corinth) (32)	601 286-6265	....	....	....	....	....	....
Amite (Liberty) (13)	601 657-8022	....	....	....	....	....	....
Attala (Kosciusko) (18)	601 289-2921	....	....	....	....	....	....
Benton (Ashland) (8)	601 224-6611	....	....	....	....	....	....
Bolivar (Cleveland) (42)	601 843-9413	....	....	....	....	....	....
Calhoun (Pittsboro) (15)	601 983-3117	....	....	....	....	....	....
Carroll (Carrollton) (9)	601 237-9274	....	....	....	....	....	....
Chickasaw (Houston) (18)	601 456-2513	....	....	....	....	....	....
Choctaw (Ackerman) (9)	601 285-6329	....	....	....	....	....	....
Claiborne (Port Gibson) (11)	601 437-4992	....	....	....	....	....	....
Clarke (Quitman) (17)	601 776-2126	....	....	....	....	....	....
Clay (West Point) (21)	601 494-3124	....	....	....	....	....	....
Coahoma (Clarksdale) (32)	601 624-3000	....	....	....	....	....	....
Copiah (Hazlehurst) (28)	601 894-3011	....	....	....	....	....	....
Covington (Collins) (17)	601 765-4242	....	....	....	....	....	....
De Soto (Hernando) (68)	601 429-5011	Paul L Riley	Clovis B Reed Jr	William E Davis	William E Davis	Ginger K Allison	James A Riley
Forrest (Hattiesburg) (68)	601 545-6000	....	....	....	....	....	....
Franklin (Meadville) (8)	601 384-2330	....	....	....	....	....	....
George (Lucedale) (17)	601 947-7506	Norman C Howell	....	Jerry R Harvey	....	....	Eugene Howell
Greene (Leakesville) (10)	601 394-2377	....	....	....	....	....	....
Grenada (Grenada) (22)	601 226-1821	....	....	....	....	....	....
Hancock (Bay St. Louis) (32)	601 467-5404	....	....	....	....	....	....
Harrison (Gulfport) (165)	601 865-4194	....	....	....	....	....	....
Hinds (Jackson) (254)	601 968-6501	....	....	....	....	....	....
Holmes (Lexington) (22)	601 834-2508	....	....	....	....	....	....
Humphreys (Belzoni) (12)	601 247-1740	....	....	....	....	....	....
Issaquena (Mayersville) (2)	601 873-2761	W E Fleeman Jr	....	Erline Fortner	....	....	Arthur Lawler
Itawamba (Fulton) (20)	601 862-3421	Danny Holley	Gary Franks	Jim Witt	Jim Witt	Gary Franks	Leon Hayes
Jackson (Pascagoula) (115)	601 769-3000	Carroll Clifford	George Touart	Lynn Presley	Cheryl Jacobs	George Touart	Donald Pope
Jasper (Bay Springs) (17)	601 764-3368	....	....	....	....	....	....
Jefferson (Fayette) (9)	601 786-3021	Robert Ballard	Delorise Frye	Charles Evers	Charles Evers	Freddie Oliver	Peter Walker
Jefferson Davis (Prentiss) (14)	601 792-4204	J E O' Connell	....	Jack D Berry	Jack D Berry	Faye Bedwell	Hall Magee
Jones (Laurel) (62)	601 428-0527	....	....	....	....	....	....
Kemper (De Kalb) (10)	601 743-2460	....	....	....	....	....	....
Lafayette (Oxford) (32)	601 234-2131	....	....	....	....	....	....
Lamar (Purvis) (30)	601 794-8504	....	....	....	....	....	....
Lauderdale (Meridian) (76)	601 482-9701	....	....	....	....	....	....
Lawrence (Monticello) (12)	601 587-7351	....	....	....	....	....	....
Leake (Carthage) (18)	601 267-8002	Ben Parker Ganann	Glenn C Thomas	Sheila H Crawford	....	Margaret Smith	James L Callahan
Lee (Tupelo) (66)	601 841-9110	....	....	....	....	....	....

Directory 1/10 **OFFICIALS IN U.S. COUNTIES**
continued

County, county seat, 1990 population figures (000 omitted)	County telephone number	Chief elected official	Appointed administrator	Clerk to the governing board	Chief financial officer	Personnel director	Chief law enforcement official
MISSISSIPPI (82) continued							
Leflore (Greenwood) (37)	601 453-1041	....	....	....	....	....	....
Lincoln (Brookhaven) (30)	601 833-4911	....	....	....	....	....	....
Lowndes (Columbus) (59)	601 327-7880	....	....	....	....	....	....
Madison (Canton) (54)	601 859-8241	David Richardson	Debbie Montgomery	Steve Duncan	Steve Duncan	Debbie Montgomery	Jessie Hopkins
Marion (Columbia) (26)	601 736-2691	....	....	....	....	....	....
Marshall (Holly Springs) (30)	601 252-4431	....	....	....	....	....	....
Monroe (Aberdeen) (37)	601 369-8143	....	....	....	....	....	....
Montgomery (Winona) (12)	601 283-2333	....	....	....	....	....	....
Neshoba (Philadelphia) (25)	601 656-3581	....	....	....	....	....	....
Newton (Decatur) (20)	601 683-6181	....	....	....	....	....	....
Noxubee (Macon) (13)	601 726-4243	....	....	....	....	....	....
Oktibbeha (Starkville) (38)	601 323-5834	....	....	....	....	....	....
Panola (Batesville) (30)	601 563-6200	Mike Darby	David Chandler	Sally H Fisher	David Chandler	David Chandler	David M Bryan
Pearl River (Poplarville) (39)	601 795-4539	....	....	....	....	....	....
Perry (New Augusta) (11)	601 964-8398	....	....	....	....	....	....
Pike (Magnolia) (37)	601 783-5289	....	....	....	....	....	....
Pontotoc (Pontotoc) (22)	601 489-3451	....	....	....	....	....	....
Prentiss (Booneville) (23)	601 728-8151	....	....	....	....	....	....
Quitman (Marks) (10)	601 326-2661	Mack Young	Butch Scipper	Butch Scipper	Butch Scipper	Butch Scipper	Jack Harrison
Rankin (Rankin) (87)	601 825-2217	....	....	....	....	....	....
Scott (Forest) (24)	601 469-1926	Johnny D Owens	....	James E Johnston	James E Johnston	....	W S Richardson
Sharkey (Rolling Fork) (7)	601 873-2755	Joe Carson	Sandra Oxner	Sandra Oxner	....	Sandra Oxner	Joe W Ford
Simpson (Mendenhall) (24)	601 847-1418	....	....	....	....	....	....
Smith (Raleigh) (15)	601 782-4463	Benjie K Ford	....	C Gary Crumpton	C Gary Crumpton	Dennis R Robinson	Keith E Bounds
Stone (Wiggins) (11)	601 928-5266	....	....	....	....	....	....
Sunflower (Indianola) (33)	601 887-4703	....	....	....	....	....	....
Tallahatchie (Charleston) (15)	601 647-5551	....	....	....	....	....	....
Tate (Senatobia) (21)	601 562-5661	....	....	....	....	....	....
Tippah (Ripley) (20)	601 837-7374	Denise Grisham	....	Danny Shackelford	....	....	Paul Gowdy
Tishomingo (Iuka) (18)	601 423-6021	....	....	....	....	....	....
Tunica (Tunica) (8)	601 363-1465	....	....	....	....	....	....
Union (New Albany) (22)	601 534-5284	....	....	....	....	....	....
Walthall (Tylertown) (14)	601 876-3553	....	....	....	....	....	....
Warren (Vicksburg) (48)	601 636-4415	....	....	....	....	....	....
Washington (Greenville) (68)	601 332-1595	....	....	....	....	....	....
Wayne (Waynesboro) (20)	601 735-6242	C Fred Andrews	....	H H Hardee	....	....	Marvin Farrior
Webster (Walthall) (10)	601 258-4131	....	....	....	....	....	....
Wilkinson (Woodville) (10)	601 888-4381	....	....	....	....	....	....
Winston (Louisville) (19)	601 773-3319	....	....	....	....	....	....
Yalobusha (Water Valley) (12)	601 473-2091	Moyle Surrette	Robert Chandler	Robert Chandler	Robert Chandler	Robert Chandler	Lloyd Defer
Yazoo (Yazoo City) (26)	601 746-2661	....	....	....	....	....	....
MISSOURI (115)							
Adair (Kirksville) (25)	816 665-2283	....	....	....	....	....	....
Andrew (Savannah) (15)	816 324-3624	Wilton H Adkins	....	Rose Latham	Janet Shell	....	Gary Howard
Atchison (Rockport) (7)	816 744-6214	....	....	....	....	....	....
Audrain (Mexico) (24)	314 473-5822	J W Toalson	....	John B Jesse	....	....	Stuart Miller
Barry (Cassville) (28)	417 847-2561	....	....	....	....	....	....
Barton (Lamar) (11)	417 682-3529	....	....	....	....	....	....
Bates (Butler) (15)	816 679-3371	....	....	....	....	....	....
Benton (Warsaw) (14)	816 438-7326	Duane Brodersen	....	....	....	....	....
Bollinger (Marble Hill) (11)	314 238-2126	....	....	....	....	....	....
Boone (Columbia) (112)	314 886-4305	Don Stamper	....	Wendy S Noren	June E Pitchford	....	Theodore P Boehm
Buchanan (St. Joseph) (83)	816 271-1503	Thomas J Mann	....	Patrick Conway	....	Kendra Ezzell	Mickey Gill
Butler (Poplar Bluff) (39)	314 686-8050	....	....	....	....	....	....
Caldwell (Kingston) (8)	816 586-2571	Dale Hartley	....	Shari Lee	....	....	Wayne Atkison
Callaway (Fulton) (33)	314 642-0730	....	....	....	....	....	....
Camden (Camdenton) (27)	314 346-4440	....	....	....	....	....	....
Cape Girardeau (Jackson) (62)	314 243-1052	....	....	....	....	....	....
Carroll (Carrollton) (11)	816 542-0615	....	....	....	....	....	....
Carter (Van Buren) (6)	314 323-4527	James E Grassham	....	Rebecca M Simpson	....	....	Jerry Reyolds
Cass (Harrisonville) (64)	816 884-5100	....	....	....	....	....	....
Cedar (Stockton) (12)	417 276-3514	....	....	....	....	....	....
Chariton (Keytesville) (9)	816 288-3273	....	....	....	....	....	....
Christian (Ozark) (33)	417 485-6360	Frank Thomas	....	Junior Combs	....	....	Steve Whitney
Clark (Kahoka) (8)	816 727-3283	....	....	....	....	....	....
Clay (Liberty) (153)	816 792-7600	Bill Brandom	Gary Panethiere	Ella Bowles	Gary Panethiere	....	Bob Boydston
Clinton (Plattsburg) (17)	816 539-3713	....	....	....	....	....	....
Cole (Jefferson City) (64)	314 634-9100	Donald C Stockman	....	William J Deeken	L Steinkeuhler	L Steinkeuhler	John C Hemeyer
Cooper (Boonville) (15)	816 882-2114	Darlene Boehm	....	Darryl Kempf	....	....	Paul Milne
Crawford (Steelville) (19)	314 775-2376	....	....	....	....	....	....
Dade (Greenfield) (7)	417 637-2724	....	....	....	....	....	....
Dallas (Buffalo) (13)	417 345-2632	....	....	....	....	....	....
Daviess (Gallatin) (8)	816 663-2641	....	....	....	....	....	....
De Kalb (Maysville) (10)	816 449-5402	Jerry Popplewell	....	Mary Berry	....	....	Jerry Smith
Dent (Salem) (14)	314 729-4144	....	....	....	....	....	....
Douglas (Ava) (12)	417 683-4714	J G Heinlein	....	William Merritt	Kathleen Potter	....	Roldan Turner
Dunklin (Kennett) (33)	314 888-2796	....	....	....	....	....	....
Franklin (Union) (81)	314 583-6355	Tom Fenner	....	Tom Herbst	Alvin Marquart	Tom Herbst	Gary Toelke
Gasconade (Hermann) (14)	314 486-5427	Wilford Kallmeyer	....	Roger Prior	Ralph Grannemann	....	Robert Mathis
Gentry (Albany) (7)	816 726-3525	....	....	....	....	....	....
Greene (Springfield) (208)	417 868-4000	H C Mike Compton	....	R Struckhoff	Ernest Frisch	Sherri Murdaugh	John Pierpont
Grundy (Trenton) (11)	816 359-6305	Dwaine Meservey	....	L D Gibson	....	....	Greg A Coon
Harrison (Bethany) (8)	816 425-6424	Isaac N Cox	....	Barbara J Gates	....	....	George W Martz
Henry (Clinton) (20)	816 885-6963	....	....	....	....	....	....
Hickory (Hermitage) (7)	417 745-6450	....	....	....	....	....	....
Holt (Oregon) (6)	816 446-3303	John Killin	....	Jim Luce	....	....	....
Howard (Fayette) (10)	816 248-2284	....	....	....	....	....	....
Howell (West Plains) (31)	417 256-2591	....	....	....	....	....	....
Iron (Ironton) (11)	314 546-2912	....	....	....	....	....	....
Jackson (Kansas City) (633)	816 881-3000	Marsha J Murphy	Marsha M Campbell	Mary J Brogoto	Susan A Sweeney	Joanne R Mossie	James D Anderson
Jasper (Carthage) (90)	417 358-0416	....	....	....	....	....	....
Jefferson (Hillsboro) (171)	314 789-3911	....	....	....	....	....	....

Directory 1/10 **OFFICIALS IN U.S. COUNTIES**
continued

County, county seat, 1990 population figures (000 omitted)	County telephone number	Chief elected official	Appointed administrator	Clerk to the governing board	Chief financial officer	Personnel director	Chief law enforcement official
MISSOURI (115) continued							
Johnson (Warrensburg) (43)	816 747-6161	Ray Maring	....	Wendell Davis	Ray Maring	....	Glenn Seymour
Knox (Edina) (4)	816 397-2104	....	....	....	....	....	....
Laclede (Lebanon) (27)	417 532-5471	....	....	....	....	....	....
Lafayette (Lexington) (31)	816 259-4315	James R Strodtman	....	Linda Nolting	James R Strodtman	Linda Nolting	Robert Teichman
Lawrence (Mount Vernon) (30)	417 466-3666	....	....	....	....	....	....
Lewis (Monticello) (10)	314 767-5205	Dennis McCutchan	....	Sharon Schlager	....	....	B Lavern Whitaker
Lincoln (Troy) (29)	314 528-4415	....	....	....	....	....	....
Linn (Linneus) (14)	816 895-5417	....	....	....	....	....	....
Livingston (Chillicothe) (15)	816 646-2293	....	....	....	....	....	....
Macon (Macon) (15)	816 385-2913	....	....	....	....	....	....
Madison (Fredericktown) (11)	314 783-2176	....	....	....	....	....	....
Maries (Vienna) (8)	314 422-3388	James Kleffner	....	Joseph C Crum	Joseph C Crum	....	Roy L Bassett
Marion (Palmyra) (28)	314 769-2549	Drex Rothweiler	Lawrence Golden	R J Ravenscraft	Brock Phillips	....	Daniel C Campbell
Mc Donald (Pineville) (17)	417 223-4717	....	....	....	....	....	....
Mercer (Princeton) (4)	816 748-3425	Russell Hobbs	....	Jane Lowrey	Ray Woodward	....	Duane Hobbs
Miller (Tuscumbia) (21)	314 369-2317	....	....	....	....	....	....
Mississippi (Charleston) (14)	314 683-2146	Fred Defield	....	Hubert Delay Jr	Hubert Delay Jr	Hubert Delay Jr	Larry Turley
Moniteau (California) (12)	314 796-4661	....	....	....	....	....	....
Monroe (Paris) (9)	816 327-5817	....	....	....	....	....	....
Montgomery (Montgomery City) (11)	314 564-3357	....	....	....	....	....	....
Morgan (Versailles) (16)	314 378-4644	....	....	....	....	....	....
New Madrid (New Madrid) (21)	314 748-2524	....	....	....	....	....	....
Newton (Neosho) (44)	417 451-8220	Jerry G Owen	....	Robert R Bridges	....	....	Ronald L Doerge
Nodaway (Maryville) (22)	816 582-2251	....	....	....	....	....	....
Oregon (Alton) (9)	417 778-7475	....	....	....	....	....	....
Osage (Linn) (12)	314 897-2139	....	....	....	....	....	....
Ozark (Gainesville) (9)	417 679-3516	....	....	....	....	....	....
Pemiscot (Caruthersville) (22)	314 333-4203	....	....	....	....	....	....
Perry (Perryville) (17)	314 547-4242	....	....	....	....	....	....
Pettis (Sedalia) (35)	816 826-4892	....	....	....	....	....	....
Phelps (Rolla) (35)	314 364-1891	....	....	....	....	....	....
Pike (Bowling Green) (16)	314 324-2412	....	....	....	....	....	....
Platte (Platte City) (58)	816 858-2232	Carol Tomb	Hattie Forbes	Doris Gerner	L Robert Griffith	....	Tom Thomas
Polk (Bolivar) (22)	417 326-4031	....	....	....	....	....	....
Pulaski (Waynesville) (41)	314 774-6609	Bobby L Miller	....	Stephanie Leuthen	....	....	J T Roberts
Putnam (Unionville) (5)	816 947-2674	....	....	....	....	....	....
Ralls (New London) (8)	314 985-7111	....	....	....	....	....	....
Randolph (Huntsville) (24)	816 277-4717	....	....	....	....	....	....
Ray (Richmond) (22)	816 776-3184	....	....	....	....	....	....
Reynolds (Centerville) (7)	314 648-2494	....	....	....	....	....	....
Ripley (Doniphan) (12)	314 996-3215	Wm D Kennon Jr	....	Marian Dalton	....	Marian Dalton	Dennis K Cox
Saline (Marshall) (24)	816 886-3331	....	....	....	....	....	....
Schuyler (Lancaster) (4)	816 457-3842	....	....	....	....	....	....
Scotland (Memphis) (5)	816 465-7027	....	....	....	....	....	....
Scott (Benton) (39)	314 545-3549	....	....	....	....	....	....
Shannon (Eminence) (8)	314 226-3414	....	....	....	....	....	....
Shelby (Shelbyville) (7)	314 633-2181	....	....	....	....	....	....
St. Charles (St. Charles) (213)	314 949-7320	Gene Schwendemann	Gerald Ohlms	Jim Primm	James Hodges	William Kauffman	Ray Runyon
St. Clair (Osceola) (8)	417 646-2315	....	....	....	....	....	....
St. Francois (Farmington) (49)	314 756-4551	....	....	....	....	....	....
St. Louis (Clayton) (994)	314 889-2000	George R Westfall	Lawrence E Mooney	John A Grellner	James E Baker	Sandra J Edwards	Ronald A Battelle
St. Louis (St. Louis) i (397)	314 622-3561	Freeman Bosley Jr	Lloyd Jordan	....	Virvus Jones	William C Duffe	Clarence Harmon
Ste. Genevieve (Ste. Genevieve) (16)	314 883-5589	....	....	....	....	....	....
Stoddard (Bloomfield) (29)	314 568-3339	....	....	....	....	....	....
Stone (Galena) (19)	417 357-6127	....	....	....	....	....	....
Sullivan (Milan) (6)	816 265-3786	....	....	....	....	....	....
Taney (Forsyth) (26)	417 546-2241	....	....	....	....	....	....
Texas (Houston) (21)	417 967-2112	....	....	....	....	....	....
Vernon (Nevada) (19)	417 448-2500	Jime Earnest	....	Wava Halcomb	....	....	Ted Thomas
Warren (Warrenton) (20)	314 456-3331	John D Miller	....	Janis Meyer	....	....	Michael Baker
Washington (Potosi) (20)	314 438-4901	Robert L Simpson	....	Theresa E West	....	....	Chris G Harmon
Wayne (Greenville) (12)	314 224-3513	....	....	....	....	....	....
Webster (Marshfield) (24)	417 468-2223	....	....	....	....	....	....
Worth (Grant City) (2)	816 564-2219	....	....	....	....	....	....
Wright (Hartville) (17)	417 741-6661	....	....	....	....	....	....
MONTANA (56)							
Anaconda-Deer Lodge (Anaconda) c (10)	406 563-8421	Jane Anderson	Cheryl Beatty	Jim Glover	....	....	James P Connors
Beaverhead (Dillon) (8)	406 683-2642	....	....	....	....	....	....
Big Horn (Hardin) (11)	406 665-1506	....	....	....	....	....	....
Blaine (Chinook) (7)	406 357-3250	....	....	....	....	....	....
Broadwater (Townsend) (3)	406 266-3443	James V Hohn	....	Elaine Graveley	....	....	Richard Thompson
Butte-Silver Bow (Butte) c (33)	406 723-8262	....	....	....	....	....	....
Carbon (Red Lodge) (8)	406 446-1595	....	....	....	....	....	....
Carter (Ekalaka) (2)	406 775-8749	Milton Markuson	....	P J Castleberry	....	....	Rusty Jardee
Cascade (Great Falls) (78)	406 761-6700	....	....	....	....	....	....
Chouteau (Fort Benton) (5)	406 622-3631	K Engellent	....	Jo Ann L Johnson	L C Siebenaler	....	Paul F Williams
Custer (Miles City) (12)	406 232-7800	Duane Mathison	....	Julie A Coder	....	Julie A Coder	Tony Harbaugh
Daniels (Scobey) (2)	406 487-5561	C William Tande	....	Carol Malone	Lorraine Jerome	....	James P Kramer
Dawson (Glendive) (10)	406 365-3562	Richard Shoopman	....	Patricia P Boje	....	....	Pat Denning
Fallon (Baker) (3)	406 778-2883	Donald Rieger	....	Mary Lee Dietz	Afye M Koenig	....	Leland E Gundlach
Fergus (Lewistown) (12)	406 538-5119	....	....	....	....	....	....
Flathead (Kalispell) (59)	406 752-5300	....	....	....	....	....	....
Gallatin (Bozeman) (50)	406 585-1383	A D Pruitt	....	Shelley M Cheney	Edward Blackman	Kathy Nowierski	Bill Slaughter
Garfield (Jordan) (2)	406 557-2760	John J Pluhar	....	Jo Ann Stanton	....	....	Charles A Phipps
Glacier (Cut Bank) (12)	406 873-5063	....	....	....	....	....	....
Golden Valley (Ryegate) (1)	406 568-2231	Edgar E Lewis	....	Aileen Mattheis	....	....	Richard Zaharko
Granite (Philipsburg) (3)	406 859-3771	Frank Waldbillig	....	Jo Bayer	....	....	Don Dee Kennedy
Hill (Havre) (18)	406 265-5481	Kathy Bessette	....	Diane Mellem	....	Donna Ahlert	Tim Solomon
Jefferson (Boulder) (8)	406 225-4251	....	....	....	....	....	....
Judith Basin (Stanford) (2)	406 566-2301	....	....	....	....	....	....
Lake (Polson) (21)	406 883-6211	Gerald Newgard	....	Jeanne Doepke	Maureen Sweeney	....	Joe Geldrich

Directory 1/10 OFFICIALS IN U.S. COUNTIES
continued

County, county seat, 1990 population figures (000 omitted)	County telephone number	Chief elected official	Appointed administrator	Clerk to the governing board	Chief financial officer	Personnel director	Chief law enforcement official
MONTANA (56) continued							
Lewis And Clark (Helena) (47)	406 447-8200	Blake Wordal	Tim Burton	Paulette DeHart	Ed Blackman	Sheila Cozzie	Charles O' Reilly
Liberty (Chester) (2)	406 759-5365	....	....			....	
Lincoln (Libby) (17)	406 293-7781	Noel E Williams	....	Coral M Cummings	Coral M Cummings		Ray H Nixon
Madison (Virginia City) (6)	406 843-5392						
Mc Cone (Circle) (2)	406 485-3505	Kenton Larson	....	Leanne K Switzer	Janet L McCabe	....	Robert A Jensen
Meagher (White Sulphur Springs) (2)	406 547-3612	....	....	....	....	....	....
Mineral (Superior) (3)	406 822-4541	....	....	....	....	....	....
Missoula (Missoula) (79)	406 721-5700	....	....	....	....	....	....
Musselshell (Roundup) (4)	406 323-1104	Sue M Olson	....	Jane E Mang	Mary E Nelson	....	G Paul Smith
Park (Livingston) (15)	406 222-6120	E James Hunt	....	B Dean Holmes	Debra B Frazier	....	Charley Johnson
Petroleum (Winnett) (1)	406 429-5551	....	....	....	....	....	....
Phillips (Malta) (5)	406 654-2423	Eugene Cowan	....	Laurel Hines	....	....	Eugene Peigneux
Pondera (Conrad) (6)	406 278-7681	Bill Rappold	....	Elsie Lamma	....	....	Leon Simpson
Powder River (Broadus) (2)	406 436-2657	Ted Fletcher	....	Karen Amende	Nancy Klapmeier	Karen Amende	Ken Rogge
Powell (Deer Lodge) (7)	406 846-3680	....	....	....	....	....	....
Prairie (Terry) (1)	406 637-5575	....	....	....	....	....	....
Ravalli (Hamilton) (25)	406 363-4790	....	....	....	....	....	....
Richland (Sidney) (11)	406 482-1708	....	....	....	....	....	....
Roosevelt (Wolf Point) (11)	406 653-1590	....	....	....	....	....	....
Rosebud (Forsyth) (11)	406 356-7318	....	....	....	....	....	....
Sanders (Thompson Falls) (9)	406 827-4391	....	....	....	....	....	....
Sheridan (Plentywood) (5)	406 765-2310	....	....	....	....	....	....
Stillwater (Columbus) (7)	406 322-4546	Vicki Hyatt	....	....	....	....	Clifford Brophy
Sweet Grass (Big Timber) (3)	406 932-5152	Elaine Allestad	....	Alta Scholten	Alta Scholten	....	George Ames
Teton (Choteau) (6)	406 466-2151	Arnold Gettel	....	Joan Pierce	Diane Ameline	Gigi Mathis	George O Anderson
Toole (Shelby) (5)	406 434-2232	John Alstad	....	Melodee Robins	....	Jewel Moritz	Vernon Anderson
Treasure (Hysham) (1)	406 342-5547	Ole Redland	....	Lavon Adair	Kathleen Thomas	....	Bill W Hedges
Valley (Glasgow) (8)	406 228-8221	Eleanor D Pratt	....	Mary Lou Eide	....	....	Clifton C Cook
Wheatland (Harlowton) (2)	406 632-4891	....	....	....	....	....	....
Wibaux (Wibaux) (1)	406 795-2481	Leif Bakken	....	Marlene J Blome	Sandra F Evans	....	Arleigh H Meek
Yellowstone (Billings) (113)	406 256-2701	....	....	....	....	....	....
NEBRASKA (93)							
Adams (Hastings) (30)	402 461-7104	Morris B Ellerbee	....	Phyllis Newell	Julia Moeller	....	Gregg Magee
Antelope (Neligh) (8)	402 887-4410	Barbara Finn	Gordon Baker	E Holm Brady	Donna Payne	....	Ralph Black
Arthur (Arthur) (..)	308 764-2203	....	....	....	....	....	....
Banner (Harrisburg) (1)	308 436-5265	George I Van Pelt	....	Barbara Stoddard	....	....	K Patrick Mooney
Blaine (Brewster) (1)	308 547-2222	Dennis Wyckoff	....	Edna D Spencer	Sue Clark	....	Tim Sierks
Boone (Albion) (7)	402 395-2055	....	....	....	....	....	....
Box Butte (Alliance) (13)	308 772-6565	Clifford Bartels	....	Kathryn M Hood	Karel Essex	....	....
Boyd (Butte) (3)	402 775-2391	Kenneth Boettcher	....	Phyllis Black	....	....	Duane Pavel
Brown (Ainsworth) (4)	402 387-2705	....	....	....	....	....	....
Buffalo (Kearney) (37)	308 236-1200	....	....	....	....	....	....
Burt (Tekamah) (8)	402 374-1955	....	....	....	....	....	Leo F Meister
Butler (David City) (9)	402 367-7430	Morris T White	....	Chris Meysenburg	....	....	Wm Brueggemann
Cass (Plattsmouth) (21)	402 296-2164	Dale Sharp	....	Alan D Wohlfarth	Richard Wassinger	....	Elliot Arens
Cedar (Hartington) (10)	402 254-7411	Marlen Kraemer	....	David Dowling	Roger Schwartz	....	Elliot Arens
Chase (Imperial) (4)	308 882-5266	Dale Bischoff	....	Geoff Clark	Kay J Hazard	....	Craig D Fokken
Cherry (Valentine) (6)	402 376-2420	....	....	....	....	....	....
Cheyenne (Sidney) (9)	308 254-2080	Frank Rauner	....	Dianne Cook	....	....	Darrell Johnson
Clay (Clay Center) (7)	402 762-3463	Lawrence Griess	....	....	....	....	Richard Marsh
Colfax (Schuyler) (9)	402 352-3434	Don Trojan	....	Lamar J Brdicko	....	....	Lynn L Blum
Cuming (West Point) (10)	402 372-2144	....	....	....	....	....	....
Custer (Broken Bow) (12)	308 872-5701	....	....	....	....	....	....
Dakota (Dakota City) (17)	402 987-2126	Jack Bobier	....	Theodore H Piepho	....	....	James Wagner
Dawes (Chadron) (9)	308 432-2863	....	....	....	....	....	....
Dawson (Lexington) (20)	308 324-2127	....	....	....	....	....	....
Deuel (Chappell) (2)	308 874-3308	....	....	....	....	....	....
Dixon (Ponca) (6)	402 755-2208	Russell Fleury	....	Diane Mohr	....	....	Dean Chase
Dodge (Fremont) (35)	402 727-2767	Dean T Lux	Fred Mytty	Fred Mytty	....	....	Dan Weddle
Douglas (Omaha) (416)	402 444-7025	Ray Simon	Dean Sykes	Tom Cavanaugh	Steve Walker	John Taylor	Dick Roth
Dundy (Benkelman) (3)	308 423-2058	Larry Williams	....	Tony Lutz	....	....	Robert Bellamy
Fillmore (Geneva) (7)	402 759-4931	....	....	....	....	....	....
Franklin (Franklin) (4)	308 425-6202	Claudette Russell	....	Marcia Volk	....	....	Jerry L Archer
Frontier (Stockville) (3)	308 367-8641	Robert D Jack	....	Twila P Johnson	....	....	Lannie L Roblee
Furnas (Beaver City) (6)	308 268-4145	....	....	....	....	....	....
Gage (Beatrice) (23)	402 223-1300	....	....	....	....	....	....
Garden (Oshkosh) (2)	308 772-3924	Charles Chadwick	....	....	....	....	....
Garfield (Burwell) (2)	308 346-4161	....	....	....	....	....	....
Gosper (Elwood) (2)	308 785-2611	....	....	....	....	....	....
Grant (Hyannis) (1)	308 458-2488	Lewis A Anderson	....	Delores M Blakey	Regina J Stumpff	....	Kenneth B McCune
Greeley (Greeley Center) (3)	308 428-3625	B J Meyer	....	Margaret Sorensen	....	....	Doyal Keller
Hall (Grand Island) (49)	308 381-5083	Richard L Hartman	....	Marjorie Haubold	Doris A Mason	....	Emmett C Arnett
Hamilton (Aurora) (9)	402 694-3443	....	....	....	....	....	....
Harlan (Alma) (4)	308 928-2173	....	....	....	....	....	....
Hayes (Hayes Center) (1)	308 286-3413	....	....	....	....	....	....
Hitchcock (Trenton) (4)	308 334-5646	Donald L Keller	....	Margaret Pollmann	....	....	D Bryan Leggott
Holt (O'Neill) (13)	402 336-1762	....	....	....	....	....	....
Hooker (Mullen) (1)	308 546-2244	....	....	....	....	....	....
Howard (St. Paul) (6)	308 754-4343	....	....	....	....	....	....
Jefferson (Fairbury) (9)	402 729-2323	Ivan Zimmerman	....	Sandra Stelling	Alice Nelson	....	Rex Southwick
Johnson (Tecumseh) (5)	402 335-3246	Howard Wilkinson	....	Kathleen Nieveen	....	....	David Wieting
Kearney (Minden) (7)	308 832-2723	Wayne A Roesler	....	Pat Osterbuhr	....	....	Marshall S Nelson
Keith (Ogallala) (9)	308 284-4726	Richard Lindauer	....	Donna Messersmith	Paul Schwasinger	....	Wayne Young
Keya Paha (Springview) (1)	402 497-3791	....	....	....	....	....	....
Kimball (Kimball) (4)	308 235-2241	Vernon Bourlier	....	Elaine Sandridge	Diana Quicke	....	Wm John Thacker
Knox (Center) (10)	402 288-4282	....	....	....	....	....	....
Lancaster (Lincoln) (214)	402 471-7447	Marcia Malone	Kerry Eagan	....	David Kroeker	....	Sam Van Pelt
Lincoln (North Platte) (33)	308 534-4350	....	....	....	....	....	....
Logan (Stapleton) (1)	308 636-2311	Glen D Barner	....	Pat Harvey	....	....	James E Wonch
Loup (Taylor) (1)	308 942-3135	....	....	....	....	....	....
Madison (Madison) (33)	402 454-3311	Duane Reeves	....	Nancy Scheer	....	....	Vern Hjorth

County, county seat, 1990 population figures (000 omitted)	County telephone number	Chief elected official	Appointed administrator	Clerk to the governing board	Chief financial officer	Personnel director	Chief law enforcement official
NEBRASKA (93) continued							
Mc Pherson (Tryon) (1)	308 587-2363	....	....	....	....	....	....
Merrick (Central City) (8)	308 946-2881	....	....	....	....	....	....
Morrill (Bridgeport) (5)	308 262-0860	Peggy J Golden	....	Dorothy P Lanik	....	....	John D Edens
Nance (Fullerton) (4)	308 536-2331	Vernon Olson	....	Dianne Carter	....	....	Sam King
Nemaha (Auburn) (8)	402 274-4213	....	....	....	....	....	....
Nuckolls (Nelson) (6)	402 225-4361	Joe Sullivan	....	Selma Ferguson	....	....	James R Marr
Otoe (Nebraska City) (14)	402 873-3586	John J Hoges	....	Marcina Cody	Jacqueline Smith	....	James M Gress
Pawnee (Pawnee City) (3)	402 852-2962	John Snyder	....	Sonya Lave	....	....	John Scholze
Perkins (Grant) (3)	308 352-4643	....	....	....	....	....	....
Phelps (Holdrege) (10)	308 995-4469	Willard Peterson	....	Lois E Young	Sharon Rupe	....	Dwayne C Newman
Pierce (Pierce) (8)	402 329-4225	....	....	....	....	....	....
Platte (Columbus) (30)	402 563-4904	B Brandenburgh	....	Diane C Pinger	....	....	Jon Zavadil
Polk (Osceola) (6)	402 747-5431	Jerome H Reisdorf	....	Ruth N Stromberg	Coral R Boden	....	Steven L Cherry
Red Willow (Mc Cook) (12)	308 345-1552	....	....	....	....	....	....
Richardson (Falls City) (10)	402 245-2911	....	....	....	....	....	....
Rock (Bassett) (2)	402 684-3933	....	....	....	....	....	....
Saline (Wilber) (13)	402 821-2374	Phil Weber	....	Norma Kripa	Lila Witt	....	Byron Buzek
Sarpy (Papillion) (103)	402 593-4155	Drew Miller	Mark Wayne	Debra Houghtaling	Brian Hanson	....	Pat Thomas
Saunders (Wahoo) (18)	402 443-8101	Doris M Karloff	....	Patti J Lindgren	....	....	Ronald Poskochic
Scotts Bluff (Gering) (36)	308 436-6600	....	....	....	....	....	....
Seward (Seward) (15)	402 643-2883	....	....	....	....	....	....
Sheridan (Rushville) (7)	308 327-2633	....	....	....	....	....	....
Sherman (Loup City) (4)	308 745-1513	....	....	....	....	....	....
Sioux (Harrison) (2)	308 668-2443	Harold Keener	....	M Wasserburger	....	....	James Robertson
Stanton (Stanton) (6)	402 439-2222	Kenneth Wolverton	....	Rita Roenfeldt	Sandy Zoubek	....	Mike Unger
Thayer (Hebron) (7)	402 768-6126	Russel L Loontjer	....	Marilynn K Free	....	....	Gary R Young
Thomas (Thedford) (1)	308 645-2261	Stan Pettit	....	Marilyn Maseberg	....	Marilyn Maseberg	Steve Petersen
Thurston (Pender) (7)	402 385-2343	Mark E Casey	....	Pat Higgins	....	....	Harold Obermeyer
Valley (Ord) (5)	308 728-3700	....	....	....	....	....	....
Washington (Blair) (17)	402 426-6822	John Lutz	....	C Petersen	Kay Erwin	....	DeWayne Flora
Wayne (Wayne) (9)	402 375-2288	Merlin Beiermann	....	Debra Finn	Leon Meyer	....	Leroy Janssen
Webster (Red Cloud) (4)	402 746-2716	....	....	....	....	....	....
Wheeler (Bartlett) (1)	308 654-3235	....	....	....	....	....	....
York (York) (14)	402 362-7759	Dean D Buller	....	Pat Bredenkamp	....	....	Steve A Rediger
NEVADA (17)							
Carson City-Ormsby (Carson City) c (40)	702 887-2103	....	John Berkich	K Nishikawa	Mary Walker	Judie Fisher	Paul McGrath
Churchill (Fallon) (18)	702 423-5136	....	....	....	....	....	....
Clark (Las Vegas) (741)	702 455-4565	Jay Bingham	Donald L Shalmy	Lorretta Bowman	Guy Hobbs	Cheryl Miller	John Moran
Douglas (Minden) (28)	702 782-9860	David G Pumphrey	Julio Aveal	Barbara J Reed	C Springmeyer	Neldon G Demke	Jerry Maple
Elko (Elko) (34)	702 753-7073	Lee Chapman	George Boucher	Karen Vasquez	Linda Ritter	....	Neil Harris
Esmeralda (Goldfield) (1)	702 485-3406	....	....	....	....	....	....
Eureka (Eureka) (2)	702 237-5262	....	....	....	....	....	....
Humboldt (Winnemucca) (13)	702 623-6300	John H Milton	Kerry Hawkins	Susan Harrer	Belle Bundy	Kerry Hawkins	Gene Hill
Lander (Austin) (6)	702 964-2447	....	....	....	....	....	....
Lincoln (Pioche) (4)	702 962-5495	....	....	....	....	....	....
Lyon County (Yerington) (20)	702 463-3341	Rene Cardinal	Stephen Snyder	Marian Pinkerton	Rita Evasovic	Rita Evasovic	Sid Smith
Mineral (Hawthorne) (6)	702 945-2446	....	....	....	....	....	....
Nye (Tonopah) (18)	702 482-8191	Cameron McRae	William L Offutt	Juanita Robb	Geneva Neuhauser	Debra L Jeffrey	Wade Lieseke
Pershing (Lovelock) (4)	702 273-2208	....	....	....	....	....	....
Storey (Virginia City) (3)	702 847-0577	....	....	....	....	....	....
Washoe (Reno) (255)	702 328-2000	Diane Cornwall	John Mac Intyre	Judi Bailey	Robert Jasper	Joanne Ray	Vince Swinney
White Pine (Ely) (9)	702 289-8841	Julio Costello	....	P Heinbaugh	....	....	Bernardino Romero
NEW HAMPSHIRE (10)							
Belknap (Laconia) (49)	603 524-3579	Norman C Marsh	....	....	Philip Daigneault	....	Stephen G Hodges
Carroll (Ossipee) (35)	603 539-7751	....	....	....	....	....	....
Cheshire (Keene) (70)	603 352-8215	....	....	....	....	....	....
Coos (Berlin) (35)	603 752-2144	....	....	....	....	....	....
Grafton (Woodsville) (75)	603 787-6941	Betty Jo Raffe	Ernest Towne	Raymond Burton	Kathleen W Ward	Tracy Allbee	Charles Barry
Hillsborough (Manchester) (336)	603 627-5600	....	....	....	....	....	....
Merrimack (Concord) (120)	603 228-0331	Stuart D Trachy	Carol A Haessly	....	Charles T Carroll	Barry L Cox	Chester L Jordon
Rockingham (Epping) (246)	603 679-2256	Ernest P Barka	....	Warren Henderson	Theresa Young	Roy E Morrisette	Wayne Vetter
Strafford (Dover) (104)	603 742-1458	....	....	....	....	....	....
Sullivan (Newport) (39)	603 863-2560	....	....	....	....	....	....
NEW JERSEY (21)							
Atlantic (Atlantic City) (224)	609 345-6700	....	....	....	....	....	....
Bergen (Hackensack) (825)	201 646-2000	....	....	....	....	....	....
Burlington (Mount Holly) (395)	609 265-5020	Vincent Farias	Frederick F Galdo	Frederick F Galdo	Arthur J Collins	Frederick F Galdo	Edward A Cummings
Camden (Camden) (503)	609 757-8000	....	....	....	....	....	....
Cape May (Cape May Court House) (95)	609 465-1060	....	....	....	....	....	....
Cumberland (Bridgeton) (138)	609 453-2121	....	....	....	....	....	....
Essex (Newark) (778)	201 621-4977	Sara Bost	Donald Biase	Adrianne Davis	Vincent Foti	Brenda Veltri	Armando Fontoura
Gloucester (Woodbury) (230)	609 853-3200	....	....	....	....	....	....
Hudson (Jersey City) (553)	201 795-6255	....	....	....	....	....	....
Hunterdon (Flemington) (108)	908 788-1102	....	Dorothy K Bertany	Denise B Doolan	Charles Balogh Jr	....	James Marino
Mercer (Trenton) (326)	609 989-6636	Robert D Prunetti	John F Ricci	Cathy DiCostanzo	Steven Zielinski	Lewis Goldstein	Samuel Plumeri
Middlesex (New Brunswick) (672)	908 745-3000	David Crabiel	....	Dorothy Power	Albert Kuchinskas	J Thomas Cross	Joseph Spicuzzo
Monmouth (Freehold) (553)	201 431-7384	....	....	....	....	....	....
Morris (Morristown) (421)	201 285-6000	....	....	....	....	....	....
Ocean (Toms River) (433)	908 244-2121	....	Steven L Pollock	Daniel J Hennessy	James T Mullins	Keith J Goetting	William Polhemus
Passaic (Paterson) (453)	201 881-4405	....	....	....	....	....	....
Salem (Salem) (65)	609 935-7510	John M Lake Jr	....	Gilda T Gill	Erma Halstead	....	Norris Williams
Somerset (Somerville) (240)	908 231-7000	....	....	....	....	....	....
Sussex (Newton) (131)	201 579-0350	....	....	....	....	....	....
Union (Elizabeth) (494)	201 527-4200	....	....	....	....	....	....
Warren (Belvidere) (92)	908 475-6500	Jacob Matthenius	Melinda Carlton	Melinda Carlton	Robert Leudo	Jerry Coyle	....
NEW MEXICO (33)							
Bernalillo (Albuquerque) (481)	505 768-4000	....	....	....	....	....	....

Directory 1/10   OFFICIALS IN U.S. COUNTIES
continued

County, county seat, 1990 population figures (000 omitted)	County telephone number	Chief elected official	Appointed administrator	Clerk to the governing board	Chief financial officer	Personnel director	Chief law enforcement official
NEW MEXICO (33) continued							
Catron (Reserve) (3)	505 533-6423	Carl Livingston	Danny Fryar	Sharon Armijo	Janet Porter	Danny Fryar	Robert Wellborn
Chaves (Roswell) (58)	505 624-6600	Joe Velasquez	Hubert Quintana	Rhoda Goodloe	Joe Baca	Hubert Quintana	Terrell Tucker
Cibola (Grants) (24)	505 287-9431	....	....	....	....	....	....
Colfax (Raton) (13)	505 445-9661	Frank Cimino Jr	Whitney Hite	Barbara Castillo	....	....	Jim Maldonado
Curry (Clovis) (42)	505 763-6016	Paul D Barnes	Geneva Cooper	Coni Jo Lyman	Geneva Cooper	Geneva Cooper	James M Jackson
De Baca (Fort Sumner) (2)	505 355-2601	Frank McRee	....	Shana Kenyon	Lahonda Fox	Shana Kenyon	Champ Landrum
Dona Ana (Las Cruces) (136)	505 525-6600	Everardo Chavez	Don Brooks	Rita Torres	Robert Pena	Don Brooks	Ray Storment
Eddy (Carlsbad) (49)	505 887-9511	Nancy C Brantley	Stephen D Massey	Karen S Davis	Louise L Greene	....	Jack R Childress
Grant (Silver City) (28)	505 538-3338	....	....	....	....	....	....
Guadalupe (Santa Rosa) (4)	505 472-3306	....	....	....	....	....	....
Harding (Mosquero) (1)	505 673-2927	Michael Lewis	Arlene Aragon	E Martinez	E Martinez	....	Raymond Gutierrez
Hidalgo (Lordsburg) (6)	505 542-9213	....	....	....	....	....	....
Lea (Lovington) (56)	505 396-8521	....	....	....	....	....	....
Lincoln (Carrizozo) (12)	505 648-2385	Monroy Montes	Martha Guevara	Martha M Proctor	Charlene Schlarb	Martha Guevara	James M McSwane
Los Alamos (Los Alamos) (18)	505 662-8080	Lawry Mann	James M Flint	Bettie Kerr	Max Baker	Karen Willis	Allen Kirk
Luna (Deming) (18)	505 546-0494	Bert Irwin	Scott Vinson	Natalie Pacheco	Victor Kostelnik	....	Jim Clay
Mc Kinley (Gallup) (61)	505 722-3868	Earnest C Becenti	Irvin Harrison	Milton Gabaldon	Steven Baumgardt	Pat Holloway	Frank Gonzales
Mora (Mora) (4)	505 387-5279	....	....	....	....	....	....
Otero (Alamogordo) (52)	505 437-7427	Robt Bishop	David Weitzel	Mary Quintana	....	Jeanette Abney	John Lee
Quay (Tucumcari) (11)	505 461-2112	Glenn Briscoe	Sandra P Garley	J Maddaford	Nadine Angel	....	James Knight
Rio Arriba (Tierra Amarilla) (34)	505 588-7255	....	....	....	....	....	....
Roosevelt (Portales) (17)	505 356-8562	David Sanders	Michael Miller	Maudene Haragan	....	....	Bobby Dodgin
San Juan (Aztec) (92)	505 334-9481	....	....	....	....	....	....
San Miguel (Las Vegas) (26)	505 425-9333	....	....	....	....	....	....
Sandoval (Bernalillo) (63)	505 867-2341	....	....	....	....	....	....
Santa Fe (Santa Fe) (99)	505 986-6200	Linda Grill	Gilbert Tercero	Jona Armijo	Peter Garcia	Paul O' Donoghue	Benjamin Montano
Sierra (Truth Or Consequences) (10)	505 894-6215	Ralph Gooding	Ella Chandler	Lupe Carrejo	....	....	Ron Brown
Socorro (Socorro) (15)	505 835-0589	Daniel Romero	Tony J Jaramillo	Carmen Gallegos	....	....	....
Taos (Taos) (23)	505 758-8834	Celestino Romero	Samuel O Montoya	Carmen Medina	Mary Lou Chacon	....	Glenn D Weathers
Torrance (Estancia) (10)	505 384-2418	Bill Williams	Patricia Marciano	Carla Clayton	Marilyn Autry	Paula Rodriguez	Robert Chavz
Union (Clayton) (4)	505 374-8896	D E Carter	Della Wetsel	Freida J Birdwell	Carolyn L Wright	Della Wetsel	Jesse L Yeargain
Valencia (Los Lunas) (45)	505 866-2003	....	....	....	....	....	....
NEW YORK (58)							
Albany (Albany) (293)	518 447-7040	....	....	....	....	....	....
Allegany (Belmont) (50)	716 268-7612	....	....	....	....	....	....
Broome (Binghamton) (212)	607 778-2185	....	....	....	....	....	....
Cattaraugus (Little Valley) (84)	716 938-9111	Don Winship	Donald Furman	Donald Furman	Joseph Keller	Howard Peterson	Jerry Burrell
Cayuga (Auburn) (82)	315 253-1284	Ralph Standbrook	....	Lester Brew	David A Farrell	....	Peter J Pinckney
Chautauqua (Mayville) (142)	716 753-4000	John Ward	R Gilbert Randell	Robert White	Robert Beckman	....	....
Chemung (Elmira) (95)	607 737-2918	John Flory	....	Linda Palmer	Mimlton Sydney	Michael Krusen	Charles Houper
Chenango (Norwich) (52)	607 337-1700	Clifford Crouch	....	Thomas Whittaker	William Evans	Bonnie Carrier	Thomas Loughren
Clinton (Plattsburgh) (86)	518 565-4679	Melvin Bruno	William Bingel	William Bingel	Janet Duprey	Carol Wallett	Russell Trombly
Columbia (Hudson) (63)	518 828-1527	....	....	....	....	....	....
Cortland (Cortland) (49)	607 753-5049	Richard Tupper	....	Deanna Lincoln	Alex Fumarola	Bethany O' Rourke	Duane Whiteman
Delaware (Delhi) (47)	607 746-2603	....	....	....	....	....	....
Dutchess (Poughkeepsie) (259)	914 431-2169	....	....	....	....	....	....
Erie (Buffalo) (969)	716 858-8500	Leonard Lenihan	....	Laurie Manzella	Nancy Naples	Richard Slisz	Thomas Higgins
Essex (Elizabethtown) (37)	518 873-3363	Joyce W Morency	Kim Higgs	Peter R Mends	S Egglefield	Peter R Mends	....
Franklin (Malone) (47)	518 483-6767	....	....	....	....	....	....
Fulton (Johnstown) (54)	518 762-0540	....	....	....	....	....	....
Genesee (Batavia) (60)	716 344-2550	Carl Perkowski	Jay Gsell	Carolyn Pratt	John Flint	Martha Standish	Gary Maha
Greene (Catskill) (44)	518 943-3080	....	....	....	....	....	....
Hamilton (Lake Pleasant) (5)	518 548-6651	William Farber	....	Natalie Williams	Nancy Rhoads	Zereda Bastian	Douglas Parker
Herkimer (Herkimer) (66)	315 867-1002	....	....	....	....	....	....
Jefferson (Watertown) (111)	315 785-3075	William Walldroff	John V Hartzell	John V Hartzell	Jane T Jenkins	Stephen R Miller	Donald F Newberry
Lewis (Lowville) (27)	315 376-5325	....	....	....	....	....	....
Livingston (Geneseo) (62)	716 243-7000	James Steele	Dominic Mazza	Virginia Amico	Arlene Johnston	Elizabeth Sliker	John York
Madison (Wampsville) (69)	315 366-2201	....	....	....	....	....	....
Monroe (Rochester) (714)	716 428-5301	Robert L King	....	....	Gerald Mecca	Richard Mackey	Andrew Meloni
Montgomery (Fonda) (52)	518 853-3431	....	....	....	....	....	....
Nassau (Mineola) (1287)	516 535-3131	....	....	....	....	....	....
New York City (New York) c (7323)	212 566-5700	....	....	....	....	....	....
Niagara (Lockport) (221)	716 439-7000	John Tylec	....	James K McGinnis	David S Broderick	Frank G Caputo	Thomas A Beilein
Oneida (Utica) (251)	315 798-5790	John J Williams	....	Susan Crabtree	Anthony Carvelli	Mary Lou Berie	Gerald Washburn
Onondaga (Syracuse) (469)	315 435-3537	William Sanford	Edward Kochian	Nancy Skahen	Michael Sullivan	Elaine Walter	John Dillon
Ontario (Canandaigua) (95)	716 396-4465	Raymond Barend	John T Hicks	L Marchildon	Alan Bubb	John E Garvey	Philip C Povero
Orange (Goshen) (308)	914 294-5151	Joseph Rampe	Chris Dunleavy	Gail Sicina	Ruth McMorrow	Joseph Dwyer	James Garvey
Orleans (Albion) (42)	716 589-7004	Lyndon Billings	Stanley Dudek	Kathleen Ahlberg	....	Sandra Bower	David Green
Oswego (Oswego) (122)	315 349-8230	....	....	....	....	....	....
Otsego (Cooperstown) (61)	607 547-4200	Carl Higgins	....	Laura Child	Thedora Moore	Nancy Morton	....
Putnam (Carmel) (84)	914 225-0860	Robert Bondi	....	Jean LePere	William Carlin	Paul Eldridge	Robt Thoubboron
Rensselaer (Troy) (154)	518 270-2700	....	....	....	....	....	....
Rockland (New City) (265)	914 638-5000	....	....	....	....	....	....
Saratoga (Ballston Spa) (181)	518 885-5381	....	....	....	....	....	....
Schenectady (Schenectady) (149)	518 388-4270	....	....	....	....	....	....
Schoharie (Schoharie) (32)	518 295-8369	James Brown	....	David Hallock	Lawrence Tague	Craig Mausler	Harvey Stoddard
Schuyler (Watkins Glen) (19)	607 535-2051	Angeline Franzese	....	Doris Craig	Nancy Peters	Margaret Jensen	Michael Maloney
Seneca (Waterloo) (34)	315 539-5655	....	....	....	....	....	....
St. Lawrence (Canton) (112)	315 379-2210	Stephen Teele	Allen Rishe	Allen Rishe	Robert McNeil	Donald Brining	Keith Knowlton
Steuben (Bath) (99)	607 776-9631	John E Clifford	Mark R Alger	Christine Kane	John W Young	Robert F Biehl	Jerry A Dartt
Suffolk (Hauppauge) (1322)	516 853-4000	Robert J Gaffney	D Blydenburgh	Elisabeth Taibbi	Joseph R Caputo	Alan Schneider	Peter Cosgrove
Sullivan (Monticello) (69)	914 794-3000	Andrew Boyar	Linda Green	Robert Krutman	Daniel Briggs	Richard L Green	Joseph Wasser
Tioga (Owego) (52)	607 687-0100	Vincent Squeglia	Ronald Dougherty	Maureen Dougherty	James McFadden	Jan K Pierson	Roger Besser
Tompkins (Ithaca) (94)	607 274-5526	Stuart Stein	Scott Heyman	Catherine Covert	David Squires	Anita Fitzpatrick	Emery Guest
Ulster (Kingston) (165)	914 331-9300	Daniel L Alfonso	William Darwak	Randall V Roth	Lewis C Kirchner	Thomas J Costello	Michael LaPaglia
Warren (Lake George) (59)	518 761-6535	....	....	....	....	....	....
Washington (Fort Edward) (59)	518 746-2210	R Harry Booth	Kevin G Hayes	Carrie A Whitney	Phyllis Cooper	Margaret L Wright	Robert Endee Jr
Wayne (Lyons) (89)	315 946-5400	....	....	....	....	....	....
Westchester (White Plains) (875)	914 285-2000	....	....	....	....	....	....
Wyoming (Warsaw) (43)	716 786-8800	Howard W Payne	Kevin D Defebbo	Michelle J Millen	John B Edwards	Sally Wing	Allen Capwell
Yates (Penn Yan) (23)	315 536-5100	Robert Multer	Amy Manley	Connie Hayes	Bonnie Percy	....	Ronald Spike

Directory 1/10 continued **OFFICIALS IN U.S. COUNTIES**

County, county seat, 1990 population figures (000 omitted)	County telephone number	Chief elected official	Appointed administrator	Clerk to the governing board	Chief financial officer	Personnel director	Chief law enforcement official
NORTH CAROLINA (100)							
Alamance (Graham) (108)	919 228-1312	....	....	....	....	....	....
Alexander (Taylorsville) (28)	704 632-9332	....	....	....	....	....	....
Alleghany (Sparta) (10)	910 372-4179	John Hampton	Daniel McMillan	Daniel McMillan	Wanda Edwards	Daniel McMillan	Mike Caudill
Anson (Wadesboro) (23)	704 694-2796	Herman K Little	Steve D Carpenter	Bonnie Huntley	Dorothy Tyson	....	Tommy Allen
Ashe (Jefferson) (22)	910 246-8841	Jerry Powers	Wm Jeff Miller	Sandra Richardson	Patricia Fowler	Wm Jeff Miller	James Hartley
Avery (Newland) (15)	704 733-8201	....	....	....	....	....	....
Beaufort (Washington) (42)	919 946-0079	Frank Bonner	Donald Davenport	Sharon Singleton	Donald Davenport	....	Nelson Sheppard
Bertie (Windsor) (20)	919 794-5300	Joseph W Spruill	John E Whitehurst	John E Whitehurst	Lydia M Hoggard	John E Whitehurst	Jame W Perry
Bladen (Elizabethtown) (29)	910 862-6700	Delilah B Blanks	Alexis H Jones	Alexis H Jones	Ann A Weeks	Phoebe McGavock	Earl Storms
Brunswick (Bolivia) (51)	910 253-4331	Donald Warren	William W Yelton	Joyce C Johnson	Lithia B Hahn	Margaret Grissett	John C Davis
Buncombe (Asheville) (175)	704 255-5702	....	....	....	....	....	....
Burke (Morganton) (76)	704 439-4357	Larry Huffman	Bobby White	Frances McKinney	Paul Ijames	Jacqueline Kanipe	Ralph E Johnson
Cabarrus (Concord) (99)	704 788-8100	Jeffrey Barnhart	John Witherspoon	Frankie Bonds	Blair Bennett	Donald Moorhead	Robert Canaday
Caldwell (Lenoir) (71)	704 757-1300	William S Stone	Dave Flaherty Sr	Betty Blankenship	Robert R Query Jr	David Hill	Roger L Hutchings
Camden (Camden) (6)	919 338-1919	Larry G Lamb	John T Smith	Phyllis Timmerman	Clarann Mansfield	John T Smith	Joe G Jones
Carteret (Beaufort) (53)	919 728-8400	....	....	....	....	....	....
Caswell (Yanceyville) (21)	910 694-4193	G Satterfield	Paul C Tax	Wanda P Smith	Faye T Mise	Paul C Tax	J I Smith
Catawba (Newton) (118)	704 465-8200	Robert Hibbitts	J Thomas Lundy	Virginia Sobotkin	Michael Talbert	Janith Huffman	L David Huffman
Chatham (Pittsboro) (39)	919 542-8200	Henry H Dunlap	Benjamin T Shivar	Sandra Lee	Vicki McConnell	Kim R Bush	Donald J Whitt
Cherokee (Murphy) (20)	704 837-5527	Robert Gibson	William M Green	R Scott Lindsay	Tammy Johnson	....	Jack Thompson
Chowan (Edenton) (14)	919 482-8431	....	....	....	....	....	....
Clay (Hayesville) (7)	704 389-6301	Howard Walker	....	Donna Crowell	Donna Crowell	....	Tony Woody
Cleveland (Shelby) (85)	704 484-4800	....	....	....	....	....	....
Columbus (Whiteville) (50)	910 642-5700	Samuel G Koonce	Roy L Lowe	Ida L Smith	Gayle B Godwin	Roy L Lowe	Harold L Rains
Craven (New Bern) (82)	919 636-6600	Earl Wright	Harold Blizzard	Gwendolyn Bryan	Richard Hemphill	Ray Moser	Calton Bland
Cumberland (Fayetteville) (275)	910 678-7700	Lee Warren	C Strassenberg	Marsha Fogle	John Nalepa	Patricia Jones	Morris Bedsole
Currituck (Currituck) (14)	919 232-2075	B U Evans	W S Richardson	Gwendolyn H Tatem	Daniel F Scanlon	Barbara C Long	William N Newbern
Dare (Manteo) (23)	919 473-1101	R V Owens Jr	Terry L Wheeler	Frances W Harris	John D Clawson	Shawn R Murphy	Albert L Austin
Davidson (Lexington) (127)	704 242-2000	Stanley Bingham	L Norman Shronce	Garry Frank	William Bryan	Virginia Lou May	Jimmy Johnson
Davie (Mocksville) (28)	704 634-5513	Joe Long	Kenneth Windley	Brenda Hunter	James Stockert	Kenneth Windley	William Wooten
Duplin (Kenansville) (40)	910 296-2100	H C Powers	Russell Tucker	Russell Tucker	Teresa Lanier	Judy C Brown	George Garner Jr
Durham (Durham) (182)	919 560-7900	William Bell	George Williams	Garry Umstead	Arthur Lord Jr	Jacqueline Knight	Albert Hight
Edgecombe (Tarboro) (57)	919 641-7832	....	....	....	....	....	....
Forsyth (Winston-Salem) (266)	910 727-2851	Wayne G Willard	Graham Pervier	Jane F Cole	Paul L Fulton Jr	Dwight D Defee	Ronald N Barker
Franklin (Louisburg) (36)	919 496-5994	George T Wynne	David P Hodgkins	Jean P Gordon	....	David P Hodgkins	Robert G Redmond
Gaston (Gastonia) (175)	704 866-3100	....	....	....	....	....	....
Gates (Gatesville) (9)	919 357-1240	....	....	....	....	....	....
Graham (Robbinsville) (7)	704 479-7961	Hall Jenkins	Pat S Irons	Janet C Lequire	Sharon Crisp	....	Melvin Howell
Granville (Oxford) (38)	919 693-5240	Zelodis Jay	John W Lewis Jr	Bobbie R Wilson	Phyllis R Vick	John W Lewis Jr	Marion Grissom
Greene (Snow Hill) (15)	919 747-3446	....	....	....	....	....	....
Guilford (Greensboro) (347)	910 373-3324	Wallace Harrelson	Hector A Rivera	Norma H Bodsford	Brenda L Jones	Irls W Roberson	Walter A Burch Jr
Halifax (Halifax) (56)	919 583-1131	William B Hux	Neal C Phillips	Peggy H Hudson	Linda E Taylor	Neal C Phillips	Mallie Stallings
Harnett (Lillington) (68)	910 893-7500	H L Sorrell	N Emory	V Young	V Young	Y E Siefert	Larry Knott
Haywood (Waynesville) (47)	704 452-6625	Edwin Russell	C Jack Horton	C Jack Horton	Donna Clark	C Jack Horton	Tom Alexander
Henderson (Hendersonville) (69)	704 697-4809	Vollie Good	David Thompson	Elizabeth Corn	J C McLelland	....	Albert Jackson
Hertford (Winton) (23)	919 358-7805	Dupont Davis	Donald Craft	Patricia Weaver	Robbin Stephenson	Patricia Weaver	Winfred Hardy
Hoke (Raeford) (23)	910 875-8751	L E McLaughlin	Michael N Wood	Oleta K Lopez	Charles Davis	Michael Wood	Wayne Byrd
Hyde (Swanquarter) (5)	919 926-5711	Troy L Mayo	....	Linda M Basnight	Emily C Thomas	....	David T Mason
Iredell (Statesville) (93)	704 878-3000	Sara Haire	Joel Mashburn	Alice Fortner	Susan Blumenstein	Carolyn Harris	Clyde Lloyd
Jackson (Sylva) (27)	704 586-4055	....	....	....	....	....	....
Johnston (Smithfield) (81)	919 989-5100	Norman C Denning	Richard B Self	Joyce H Ennis	Richard B Self	Jan M Whitley	Freddy Narron
Jones (Trenton) (9)	919 448-7571	Nolan B Jones	Larry P Meadows	Cora Davenport	Judy Smith	Larry P Meadows	Ralph W Mallard
Lee (Sanford) (41)	919 774-8403	Bertha L Matthews	William K Cowan	Gaynell M Beal	Lisa G Minter	Patsy E Rogers	William A Bryant
Lenoir (Kinston) (57)	919 523-7659	George W Graham	Bob I Snapp	Pamela McLawhorn	Nola D Tyndall	....	William Smith
Lincoln (Lincolnton) (50)	704 732-9000	C Harry Huss	Richard L French	H Lineberger	J Leon Harmon	Jackie L Moore	Joe Kiser
Macon (Franklin) (23)	704 524-6421	Cecil Poindexter	Richard Honeycutt	Richard Honeycutt	Evelyn Southard	....	Homer Holbrooks
Madison (Marshall) (17)	704 649-2521	James T Ledford	....	Larry Leake	Michael R Worley	....	James D Brown
Martin (Williamston) (25)	919 792-1901	....	....	....	....	....	....
Mc Dowell (Marion) (36)	704 652-7121	Dean Buff	Charles Abernathy	Carrie Padgett	Alison Morgan	Lesa Gragg	Bob R Haynes
Mecklenburg (Charlotte) (511)	704 336-2931	H Parks Helms	Gerald G Fox	Janice Paige	J Harry Weatherly	Susan B Hutchins	C Kidd
Mitchell (Bakersville) (14)	704 688-2139	....	....	....	....	....	....
Montgomery (Troy) (23)	910 576-4221	D T Scarborough	Gary S McCaskill	Sally M Morris	Janice G Shaw	Gary S McCaskill	Wayne Wooten
Moore (Carthage) (59)	910 947-6363	Robert Ewing	David McNeill	Carol Thomas	Michael Griffin	Allison Dandar	James Wise
Nash (Nashville) (77)	919 459-9800	J Claude Mayo Jr	J Wayne Deal	Wayne Moore	Steve Walters	....	Frank Brown
New Hanover (Wilmington) (120)	910 341-7178	Robert G Greer	M Allen O' Neal	Lucie F Harrell	Bruce T Shell	Andre R Mallette	Joseph McQueen
Northampton (Jackson) (21)	919 534-2501	Jasper Eley	W E Daniels	Rose R Sumner	W E Daniels	W E Daniels	John Wood
Onslow (Jacksonville) (150)	919 347-4717	....	....	....	....	....	....
Orange (Hillsborough) (94)	919 732-8181	Moses Carey	John Link	Beverly Blythe	Ken Chavious	Elaine Holmes	Lindy Pendergrass
Pamlico (Bayboro) (11)	919 745-3133	Johnnie Tripp	William R Rice	William R Rice	William R Rice	William R Rice	Danny Miller
Pasquotank (Elizabeth City) (31)	919 335-0865	W C Witherspoon	Randy Keaton	Karen Jennings	Hilda Ward	....	Davis Sawyer
Pender (Burgaw) (29)	910 259-1200	Robert S Murray	John A Bauer	John A Bauer	John A Bauer	John A Bauer	Michae M Harvell
Perquimans (Hertford) (10)	919 426-8484	Mack E Nixon	N Paul Gregory Jr	Sharon S Ward	N Paul Gregory Jr	N Paul Gregory Jr	Joseph L Lothian
Person (Roxboro) (30)	910 597-1720	H G Stonbraker	Barry J Reed	Faye T Fuller	Andrew Davenport	Barry J Reed	Dennis Oakley
Pitt (Greenville) (108)	919 830-6300	Edward B Bright	Thomas B Robinson	Susan J Banks	Margaret Roberts	Vivian J Stanley	Billy L Vandiford
Polk (Columbus) (14)	704 894-3301	Benny Smith	W Lane Bailey	Pam Thomas	C Sullivan	W Lane Bailey	Boyce Carswell
Randolph (Asheboro) (107)	910 318-6602	Philip D Kemp	William F Willis	L Alice Dawson	Jane H Leonard	Hal L Scott	Litchard D Hurley
Richmond (Rockingham) (45)	910 997-8200	Jimmy L Maske	Richard O Tillis	Marian S Savage	Roger K Lowery	Richard O Tillis	Dale B Furr
Robeson (Lumberton) (105)	910 671-3016	Bobby D Locklear	James E Martin	Linda A Hedgpeth	Leo Hunt	Cynthia Neloms	Hubert Stone
Rockingham (Reidsville) (86)	910 342-8100	Clarence E Tucker	Jerry D Myers	Pamela Robertson	Michael W Apple	Ben L Neal	Clinton D Vernon
Rowan (Salisbury) (111)	704 636-0361	Newton Cohen	Tim Russell	Kelly Dickinson	Brady Frick	Ken Deal	Bob Martin
Rutherford (Rutherfordton) (57)	704 287-6145	Robert Z Hawkins	John W Condrey	Hazel Haynes	Stella Womack	Joe L Swing	Daniel J Good
Sampson (Clinton) (47)	910 592-7181	Kermit Williamson	Jerry Hobbs	Susan Holder	Sylvia Robichaud	Jerry Hobbs	O L McCullen
Scotland (Laurinburg) (34)	910 277-2406	J D Willis Jr	Scott Sauer	Annie J Kohnen	Charles Williams	Susan Butler	Wayne Bryant
Stanly (Albemarle) (52)	704 983-7200	Dwight Smith	John Munn	Nancy M Litaker	Marie Boger	Cemita H Gibbs	Joseph Lowder
Stokes (Danbury) (37)	910 593-2811	Robert Robertson	W Craig Greer	W Craig Greer	Julia Edwards	W Craig Greer	Mike Joyce
Surry (Dobson) (62)	910 401-8201	Fred O' Neal	Dennis Thompson	Linda H Wilkins	Betty Taylor	....	Bill Hall
Swain (Bryson City) (11)	704 488-9273	Donald Bunn	Linda Cable	Linda Cable	Janine Crisp	Karen Ledford	William D Lewis
Transylvania (Brevard) (26)	704 884-3100	....	....	....	....	....	....
Tyrrell (Columbia) (4)	919 796-1371	Thomas Spruill	James Brickhouse	Joann Cahoon	James Brickhouse	....	Darryl Liverman
Union (Monroe) (84)	704 283-3500	Parker Mills	Ron Lewis	Barbara Moore	Michael Wilson	....	Frank McGuirt
Vance (Henderson) (39)	919 492-2141	....	....	....	....	....	....
Wake (Raleigh) (423)	919 856-6090	....	....	....	....	....	....
Warren (Warrenton) (17)	919 257-3115	....	....	....	....	....	....
Washington (Plymouth) (14)	919 793-5823	Andrew B Allen	William Lee Smith	Lois C Askew	Gayle T Critcher	William Lee Smith	Jim Whitehurst

Directory 1/10   OFFICIALS IN U.S. COUNTIES
continued

County, county seat, 1990 population figures (000 omitted)	County telephone number	Chief elected official	Appointed administrator	Clerk to the governing board	Chief financial officer	Personnel director	Chief law enforcement official
NORTH CAROLINA (100) continued							
Watauga (Boone) (37)	704 264-1300	....	....	....	....	....	....
Wayne (Goldsboro) (105)	919 731-1435	....	....	....	....	....	....
Wilkes (Wilkesboro) (59)	910 651-7300	John A Garwood	Cecil E Wood	Alene E Faw	Melba L Wood	....	Dane C Mastin
Wilson (Wilson) (66)	919 399-2803	Frank Emory	Ellis Williford	Willie Best	Evelyn Roberts	Shirley C Howard	Wayne Gay
Yadkin (Yadkinville) (30)	910 679-4200	Michael D Crouse	Jimmy M Varner	Jimmy M Varner	Geraldine V Nance	....	Jackie Henderson
Yancey (Burnsville) (15)	704 682-3971	....	....	....	....	....	....
NORTH DAKOTA (53)							
Adams (Hettinger) (3)	701 567-4363	....	....	....	....	....	....
Barnes (Valley City) (13)	701 845-0881	....	....	....	....	....	....
Benson (Minnewaukan) (7)	701 473-5340	....	....	....	....	....	....
Billings (Medora) (1)	701 623-4491	....	....	....	....	....	....
Bottineau (Bottineau) (8)	701 228-2225	....	....	....	....	....	....
Bowman (Bowman) (4)	701 523-5421	....	....	....	....	....	....
Burke (Bowbells) (3)	701 377-2861	Lavern Chrest	....	Ranae C Ehlke	Ranae C Ehlke	....	Fred Marquardt
Burleigh (Bismarck) (60)	701 222-6718	....	....	....	....	....	....
Cass (Fargo) (103)	701 241-5720	....	....	....	....	....	....
Cavalier (Langdon) (6)	701 256-2229	....	....	....	....	....	....
Dickey (Ellendale) (6)	701 349-3249	Earl H Redlin	....	....	Lawrence Hoffman	....	Jim Bohannon
Divide (Crosby) (3)	701 965-6351	....	....	....	....	....	....
Dunn (Manning) (4)	701 573-4448	....	....	....	....	....	....
Eddy (New Rockford) (3)	701 947-2434	Dick Turcotte	....	Wanda Lee Kurtz	Wanda Lee Kurtz	....	Lawrence Schagunn
Emmons (Linton) (5)	701 254-4807	....	....	....	....	....	....
Foster (Carrington) (4)	701 652-2441	John Murphy	....	....	Roger Schlotman	....	John Statema
Golden Valley (Beach) (2)	701 872-3243	....	....	....	....	....	....
Grand Forks (Grand Forks) (71)	701 780-8200	....	....	....	....	....	....
Grant (Carson) (4)	701 622-3275	Wendel Dawson	....	Ervin H Schatz	Ervin H Schatz	....	Darwin D Roth
Griggs (Cooperstown) (3)	701 797-3117	....	....	....	....	....	....
Hettinger (Mott) (3)	701 824-2515	....	....	....	....	....	....
Kidder (Steele) (3)	701 475-2632	....	....	....	....	....	....
La Moure (La Moure) (5)	701 883-5301	....	....	....	....	....	....
Logan (Napoleon) (3)	701 754-2425	....	....	....	....	....	....
Mc Henry (Towner) (7)	701 537-5724	....	....	....	....	....	....
Mc Intosh (Ashley) (4)	701 288-3347	William Wald	....	Luella Blumhardt	Luella Blumhardt	....	Milton O Wiest
Mc Kenzie (Watford City) (6)	701 842-3616	Harold Rolfsrud	....	....	Frances M Olson	....	Paul Larson
Mc Lean (Washburn) (10)	701 462-8541	....	....	....	....	....	....
Mercer (Stanton) (10)	701 745-3292	Lynn Amsden	....	Leora Retterath	Leora Retterath	Lynn Amsden	Ronald Kessler
Morton (Mandan) (24)	701 667-3300	....	....	....	....	....	....
Mountrail (Stanley) (7)	701 628-2145	Kenneth O Lystad	....	Karen H Eliason	Karen H Eliason	....	Kenneth Halvorson
Nelson (Lakota) (4)	701 247-2463	....	....	....	....	....	....
Oliver (Center) (2)	701 794-8777	....	....	....	....	....	....
Pembina (Cavalier) (9)	701 265-4231	....	....	....	....	....	....
Pierce (Rugby) (5)	701 776-6161	....	....	....	....	....	....
Ramsey (Devils Lake) (13)	701 662-7007	Robert Freije	Byrdia M Spidahl	Byrdia M Spidahl	....	....	Perry R Horner
Ransom (Lisbon) (6)	701 683-5823	....	....	....	....	....	....
Renville (Mohall) (3)	701 756-6301	Charles Routledge	....	Susan A Ritter	Susan A Ritter	....	Robert F Thomas
Richland (Wahpeton) (18)	701 642-7700	....	....	....	....	....	....
Rolette (Rolla) (13)	701 477-3816	....	....	....	....	....	....
Sargent (Forman) (5)	701 724-6241	....	....	....	....	....	....
Sheridan (Mc Clusky) (2)	701 363-2205	Armin Erdmann	....	....	Shirley A Murray	....	Arlen Schatz
Sioux (Fort Yates) (4)	701 854-3481	....	....	....	....	....	....
Slope (Amidon) (1)	701 879-6276	Ralph Urlacher	....	....	Robert Strommen	....	Pat Lorge
Stark (Dickinson) (23)	701 264-7630	Leo Jahner	....	Eileen Leiss	Eileen Leiss	....	James Rice
Steele (Finley) (2)	701 524-2110	Sherman Thykeson	....	Ruth Gullicks	Ruth Gullicks	....	Wayne Beckman
Stutsman (Jamestown) (22)	701 252-9035	....	....	....	....	....	....
Towner (Cando) (4)	701 968-4340	Darwin Baerwald	....	Verna M Martz	....	....	Howard Soderberg
Traill (Hillsboro) (9)	701 436-4458	G E Thoreson	....	Joanne Haugen	Joanne Haugen	....	Merle Haisley
Walsh (Grafton) (14)	701 352-2851	....	....	....	....	....	....
Ward (Minot) (58)	701 857-6420	John Pence	Gregory R Nelson	Dave Senger	Dave Senger	Gregory R Nelson	Vern Erck
Wells (Fessenden) (6)	701 547-3521	....	....	....	....	....	....
Williams (Williston) (21)	701 572-1700	Donald Arnson	Beth M Innis	....	Dan Kalil	....	Stan Lyson
OHIO (88)							
Adams (West Union) (25)	513 544-3286	....	....	....	....	....	....
Allen (Lima) (110)	419 228-3700	....	Fred Eldridge	Kelli Singhaus	Richard Ditto	....	Daniel Beck
Ashland (Ashland) (48)	419 289-0000	C R Meyers	....	Susan Norris	S E Ryland	....	Larry Overholt
Ashtabula (Jefferson) (100)	216 576-9090	....	....	....	....	....	....
Athens (Athens) (60)	614 592-3224	Robert B Irwin	....	Joyce A Longworth	Peter G Couladis	....	John H Hicks
Auglaize (Wapakoneta) (45)	419 738-3612	Dow Wagner	Kurt Kuffner	Connie Cordonnier	Karyn Schumann	....	Larry Longsworth
Belmont (St. Clairsville) (71)	614 695-2121	Michael Bianconi	....	P Bittengle	Joseph Pappano	....	Tom McCort
Brown (Georgetown) (35)	513 378-3956	....	....	....	....	....	....
Butler (Hamilton) (291)	513 887-3247	....	....	....	....	....	....
Carroll (Carrollton) (27)	216 627-5177	....	....	....	....	....	W Offenberger Sr
Champaign (Urbana) (36)	513 653-2701	Marilyn Foulk	....	Carolyn Poe	Bonnie Warman	....	Paul Williams
Clark (Springfield) (148)	513 328-2413	R D Tackett	W D Howard	S White	G Sodders	....	G A Kelly
Clermont (Batavia) (150)	513 732-7300	....	....	....	....	....	....
Clinton (Wilmington) (35)	513 382-2250	....	....	....	....	....	....
Columbiana (Lisbon) (108)	216 424-9511	....	....	....	....	....	....
Coshocton (Coshocton) (35)	614 622-1753	Alice S Moore	....	M Jean Clark	Richard Tompkins	....	David Corbett
Crawford (Bucyrus) (48)	419 562-5876	....	....	....	....	....	....
Cuyahoga (Cleveland) (1412)	216 443-7190	....	....	....	....	....	....
Darke (Greenville) (54)	513 547-7300	Tony F Walters	Margaret Hile	Robin Blinn	Norma Knick	....	Toby Spencer
Defiance (Defiance) (39)	419 782-4761	....	....	....	....	....	....
Delaware (Delaware) (67)	614 368-1800	Roy Jackson	Brian Stanfill	Jeannie Hatfield	Jon Peterson	Dewey Fittro	Al Myers
Erie (Sandusky) (77)	419 627-7682	....	....	....	....	....	....
Fairfield (Lancaster) (103)	614 687-7190	Steven L Goodyear	....	Mary K Webb	Jon Slater	....	Gary DeMastry
Fayette (Washington Ct Hse) (27)	614 335-0720	....	....	....	....	....	....
Franklin (Columbus) (961)	614 462-3322	....	....	....	....	....	....
Fulton (Wauseon) (38)	419 337-9255	....	....	....	....	....	....
Gallia (Gallipolis) (31)	614 446-4612	....	....	....	....	....	....
Geauga (Chardon) (81)	216 285-2222	Tony Gall	John B Murray	B McGunnigle	R J Makowski	....	George R Simmons
Greene (Xenia) (137)	513 376-5002	....	....	....	....	....	....
Guernsey (Cambridge) (39)	614 432-9200	....	....	....	....	....	....

Directory 1/10 continued   OFFICIALS IN U.S. COUNTIES

County, county seat, 1990 population figures (000 omitted)	County telephone number	Chief elected official	Appointed administrator	Clerk to the governing board	Chief financial officer	Personnel director	Chief law enforcement official
OHIO (88) continued							
Hamilton (Cincinnati) (866)	513 632-8841	Guy Guckenberger	David Krings	Jacqueline Paniot	William Rhodes	James Lowry	Simon Leis
Hancock (Findlay) (66)	419 424-7044	....	....	....	....	....	....
Hardin (Kenton) (31)	419 674-2205			....	....		....
Harrison (Cadiz) (16)	614 942-4623	Carl Sparling	....	Cindy Heisler	Patrick Moore		Rihcard Rensi
Henry (Napoleon) (29)	419 592-4876	....		....	....		....
Highland (Hillsboro) (36)	513 393-1911	....	....	....	....	....	
Hocking (Logan) (26)	614 385-5195	Gary Starner	....	Karen Walker	Leonard Myers	....	James Jones
Holmes (Millersburg) (33)	216 674-0286	Leah Miller	....	Judith Miller	Richard Graven		Timothy Zimmerly
Huron (Norwalk) (56)	419 668-3092	James Seitz	Russel Sword	Ann Winters	John Elminger		R Sutherland
Jackson (Jackson) (30)	614 286-3301	A Dale Neal	....	Jane D Romeo	Edward Jarvis		Gregg Kiefer
Jefferson (Steubenville) (80)	614 283-4111	....	....	....	....	....	
Knox (Mount Vernon) (47)	614 393-6703						
Lake (Painesville) (215)	216 350-2749	Bob Gardner	Ken Gauntner Jr	Philip Dolan	Dale Langbehn	....	Daniel Dunlap
Lawrence (Ironton) (62)	614 533-4300	Terry Null	Kathleen R Fraley	Tami L Goody	Ray T Dutey		Roy J Smith
Licking (Newark) (128)	614 349-6066	....	....	....	....	....	....
Logan (Bellefontaine) (42)	513 599-7283	....	....	....	....		
Lorain (Elyria) (271)	216 329-5000	....	....	....	....	....	....
Lucas (Toledo) (462)	419 245-4500	Sandra Isenberg	Edward Ciecka	Nancy Poskar	Larry Kaczala	Barbara Walker	James Telb
Madison (London) (37)	614 852-9717	Herbert C Markley	....	Carol Sue Ames	Raymond M Weimer	....	Stephen Saltsman
Mahoning (Youngstown) (265)	216 740-2130	....	....	....	....	....	....
Marion (Marion) (64)	614 387-5871	....	....	....	....	....	....
Medina (Medina) (122)	216 723-3641	....	....	....	....	....	....
Meigs (Pomeroy) (23)	614 992-2895	....	....	....	....	....	
Mercer (Celina) (39)	419 586-3178	Jerry Laffin	....	Joan Bollenbacher	R Schwieterman	....	Carl Eichar
Miami (Troy) (93)	513 332-6800	....	....	....	....	....	....
Monroe (Woodsfield) (15)	614 472-0873	....	....	....	....	....	....
Montgomery (Dayton) (574)	513 225-4690	....	....	....	....	....	....
Morgan (Mc Connelsville) (14)	614 962-4752	....	....	....	....	....	....
Morrow (Mount Gilead) (28)	419 947-4085	....	....	....	....	....	....
Muskingum (Zanesville) (82)	614 455-7100	Larry E Merry	....	Rebecca J Cooper	Norma J Bowman	....	Bernard Gibson
Noble (Caldwell) (11)	614 732-2969	....	....	....	....	....	....
Ottawa (Port Clinton) (40)	419 734-6700	....	....	....	....	....	
Paulding (Paulding) (20)	419 399-3786	....	....	....	....	....	
Perry (New Lexington) (32)	614 342-2074	Michael Heavener		Sheri Starner	Joann N Hankinson		William R Barker
Pickaway (Circleville) (48)	614 474-6093	....	....	....	....	....	....
Pike (Waverly) (24)	614 947-4817	....	....	....	....	....	....
Portage (Ravenna) (143)	216 296-6466	....	....	....	....	....	....
Preble (Eaton) (40)	513 456-8143	....	....	....	....	....	....
Putnam (Ottawa) (34)	419 523-3656	....	....	....	....	....	....
Richland (Mansfield) (126)	419 755-5500	....	....	....	....	....	....
Ross (Chillicothe) (69)	614 773-5115	....	....	....	....	....	....
Sandusky (Fremont) (62)	419 332-6411	....	....	....	....		
Scioto (Portsmouth) (80)	614 355-8202	Walter Lytten	Inez Bloomfield	Inez Bloomfield	Dorothy Deemer	....	James Sutterfield
Seneca (Tiffin) (60)	419 447-4550	Janet A Dell	....	Lucinda S Keller	Rick Smith	....	Larry D Stephens
Shelby (Sidney) (45)	513 498-7226	....	....	....	....	....	....
Stark (Canton) (368)	216 438-0371	....	....	....	....	....	
Summit (Akron) (515)	216 643-2500	Tim Davis	William Hartung	Peggy A Spraggins	John A Donofrio	Nancy L Wilson	David W Troutman
Trumbull (Warren) (228)	216 841-0400	....	....	....	....	....	
Tuscarawas (New Philadelphia) (84)	216 364-8811	John Zion	....	Jane Clay	John Bietzel	....	Harold McKimmie
Union (Marysville) (32)	513 645-3012	Glenn W Irwln	....	Rebecca Roush	Eloise Dowell	....	John G Overly
Van Wert (Van Wert) (30)	419 238-0238	George Ropp	....	Larry Clouse	Nancy Dixon	Jane Harris	Stan Owens
Vinton (Mc Arthur) (11)	614 596-4571	Jerry M Fee	....	Barbara Radekin	Barbara Radekin	....	Donald Peters
Warren (Lebanon) (114)	513 933-1251	Larry Crisenbery	Robert D Price	Tina A Davis	Nick Nelson	Sandra Stevens	William Ariss
Washington (Marietta) (62)	614 373-6623	Dick Young	....	Mary Patterson	Winifred Merritt	....	Bob Schlicher Jr
Wayne (Wooster) (101)	216 287-5400	Mark Wiest	....	Susan Bender	Sueann Fouche	....	Loran Alexander
Williams (Bryan) (37)	419 636-2059	....	....	....	....	....	....
Wood (Bowling Green) (113)	419 354-9100	Marilyn Baker	Richard Edwards	Kristy Muir	Mike Sibbersen	....	John Kohl
Wyandot (Upper Sandusky) (22)	419 294-3836	....	....	....	....	....	....
OKLAHOMA (77)							
Adair (Stillwell) (18)	918 696-7198	....	....	....	....	....	....
Alfalfa (Cherokee) (6)	405 596-2392	....	....	....	....	....	
Atoka (Atoka) (13)	405 889-5157	Johnny Self	....	Troy Gammon	....	....	Gary McCool
Beaver (Beaver) (6)	405 625-3151	....	....	....	....	....	....
Beckham (Sayre) (19)	405 928-2457	....	....	....	....	....	
Blaine (Watonga) (11)	405 623-5890	....	....	....	....	....	
Bryan (Durant) (32)	405 924-2201	Tony Morrison	....	Glenda Williams	....	....	Bill Sturch
Caddo (Anadarko) (30)	405 247-6609	....	....	....	....	....	....
Canadian (El Reno) (74)	405 262-1070	....	....	....	....	....	....
Carter (Ardmore) (43)	405 223-8414	....	....	....	....	....	....
Cherokee (Tahlequah) (34)	918 456-3171	....	....	....	....	....	....
Choctaw (Hugo) (15)	405 326-5331	....	....	....	....	....	....
Cimarron (Boise City) (3)	405 544-2251	John H Twyman	....	Dwilene Holbert	Gayla James	....	Ken C Miller
Cleveland (Norman) (174)	405 366-0200	Leroy Krohmer	....	Pat Dodson	Carol Lowery	....	Dewayne Beggs
Coal (Coalgate) (6)	405 927-3122	....	....	....	....	....	....
Comanche (Lawton) (111)	405 353-3717	....	....	....	....	....	....
Cotton (Walters) (7)	405 875-3026	....	....	....	....	....	....
Craig (Vinita) (14)	918 256-3564	....	....	....	....	....	....
Creek (Sapulpa) (61)	918 224-4084	Darrel Newman	....	Betty Rentz	Dessa Hammontree	....	Doug Nichols
Custer (Arapaho) (27)	405 323-4420	....	....	....	....	....	....
Delaware (Jay) (28)	918 253-4520	Howard Payton	....	Jim Swinford	....	....	Jim Swinford
Dewey (Taloga) (6)	405 328-5361	Bobby Logan	....	Patricia Riley	Cindy Farris	....	Ivan Evans
Ellis (Arnett) (4)	405 885-7301	....	....	....	....	....	....
Garfield (Enid) (57)	405 237-0227	Wendell Vencl	....	Darla Hisey	Shirley Lorenz	....	Bill Addington
Garvin (Pauls Valley) (27)	405 238-2772	....	....	....	....	....	....
Grady (Chickasha) (42)	405 224-7388	....	....	....	....	....	....
Grant (Medford) (6)	405 395-2214	....	....	....	....	....	....
Greer (Mangum) (7)	405 782-3664	....	....	....	....	....	....
Harmon (Hollis) (4)	405 688-3658	....	....	....	....	....	....
Harper (Buffalo) (4)	405 735-2870	....	....	....	....	....	....
Haskell (Stigler) (11)	918 967-2107	....	....	....	....	....	....
Hughes (Holdenville) (13)	405 379-2746	....	....	....	....	....	....
Jackson (Altus) (29)	405 482-4420	....	....	....	....	....	....

Directory 1/10
continued
OFFICIALS IN U.S. COUNTIES

County, county seat, 1990 population figures (000 omitted)	County telephone number	Chief elected official	Appointed administrator	Clerk to the governing board	Chief financial officer	Personnel director	Chief law enforcement official
OKLAHOMA (77) continued							
Jefferson (Waurika) (7)	405 228-2029	....	....	....	....	....	....
Johnston (Tishomingo) (10)	405 371-3184	J W Reed	....	Delores Muse	....	....	....
Kay (Newkirk) (48)	405 362-2537	....	....	....	....	....	....
Kingfisher (Kingfisher) (13)	405 375-3887	Jim Shimanek	....	Jane Hightower	Albert Post	....	Danny Graham
Kiowa (Hobart) (11)	405 726-5286	Wayne Barker	....	Geanea Watson	Deanna Beamon	....	Tommy Denton
Latimer (Wilburton) (10)	918 465-3543	....	....	....	....	....	....
Le Flore (Poteau) (43)	918 647-2527	....	....	....	....	....	A T Brixey Jr
Lincoln (Chandler) (29)	405 258-0080	Riley Miller Jr	....	Sharon K Turk	Don E Sporleder	....	....
Logan (Guthrie) (29)	405 282-2124	....	....	....	....	....	....
Love (Marietta) (8)	405 276-3059	Lee Lemons	....	Dora Jackson	Langdon Spivey	....	Wesley Liddell
Major (Fairview) (8)	405 227-4732	Skip Wood	....	Janie Cravens	....	....	John C Davis
Marshall (Madill) (11)	405 795-3165	....	....	....	....	....	....
Mayes (Pryor) (33)	918 825-2426	Jimmy Montgomery	....	Laurel Rabon	....	....	Harold Berry
Mc Clain (Purcell) (23)	405 527-3360	W C Shofner	....	Phyllis Bennett	....	....	Dwayne Anderson
Mc Curtain (Idabel) (33)	405 286-2370	Aubrey Thompson	....	Karen S Conaway	....	....	Richard McPeak
Mc Intosh (Eufaula) (17)	918 689-2741	....	....	....	....	....	....
Murray (Sulphur) (12)	405 622-3920	....	....	....	....	....	....
Muskogee (Muskogee) (68)	918 682-9601	Gene Bullard	....	Betty Pace	Dorothy Lawson	....	David Crater
Noble (Perry) (11)	405 336-2141	....	....	....	....	....	....
Nowata (Nowata) (10)	918 273-2480	Jack C Dugger	....	Teresa Jackson	Helen Jo Baldwin	....	Lewis R Arnold
Okfuskee (Okemah) (12)	918 623-0939	....	....	....	....	....	....
Oklahoma (Oklahoma City) (600)	405 278-1864	Richard Freeman	....	John J Garvey	John J Garvey	Medhi Azimi	J D Sharp
Okmulgee (Okmulgee) (36)	918 756-0788	Charlie Chapman	....	Martha Fuller	....	....	Dayle James
Osage (Pawhuska) (42)	918 287-2615	....	....	....	....	....	....
Ottawa (Miami) (31)	918 542-9408	James E Leake	....	Carol J Randall	Brenda Conner	....	James Ed Walker
Pawnee (Pawnee) (16)	918 762-3741	....	....	....	....	....	....
Payne (Stillwater) (62)	405 624-9300	....	....	....	....	....	Don Hass
Pittsburg (Mc Alester) (41)	918 423-6865	Oben Weeks	....	Debbie Lenox	....	....	Jeff Glase
Pontotoc (Ada) (34)	405 332-1425	Sam Hunt	....	Lynn Lofton	Larry Heard	....	Weldon Cantrell
Pottawatomie (Shawnee) (59)	405 273-8222	Buck Day	....	Nancy Bryce	Steve Sanders	....	....
Pushmataha (Antlers) (11)	405 298-2512	....	....	....	....	....	....
Roger Mills (Cheyenne) (4)	405 497-3365	....	....	....	....	....	....
Rogers (Claremore) (55)	918 341-2518	....	....	....	....	....	....
Seminole (Wewoka) (25)	405 257-2450	Noble Hays	....	Tim Anderson	Jim Hardin	....	Charles Sisco
Sequoyah (Sallisaw) (34)	918 775-5539	....	....	....	....	....	....
Stephens (Duncan) (42)	405 255-8460	....	....	....	....	....	....
Texas (Guymon) (16)	405 338-3233	Gary Winters	....	Linda Bowman	Anne L Scott	....	Arnold Peoples
Tillman (Frederick) (10)	405 335-3421	Dewayne Stout	....	Delores Haynie	Kim Lamb	....	Billy Hanes
Tulsa (Tulsa) (503)	918 596-5000	....	....	....	....	....	....
Wagoner (Wagoner) (48)	918 485-2216	....	....	....	....	....	....
Washington (Bartlesville) (48)	918 336-0330	....	....	....	....	....	....
Washita (Cordell) (11)	405 832-2284	....	....	....	....	....	....
Woods (Alva) (9)	405 327-0998	....	....	....	....	....	....
Woodward (Woodward) (19)	405 256-8097	....	....	....	....	....	....
OREGON (36)							
Baker (Baker) (15)	503 523-8200	Steve M Bogart	....	Julia Woods	Peggy L Vernholm	Sherry L Jurd	Terry Speelman
Benton (Corvallis) (71)	503 757-6802	Pamela Folts	Neil Richardson	....	Clark Ruggles	Frank Dieu	David Cook
Clackamas (Oregon City) (279)	503 655-8011	Ed Lindquist	Mike Swanson	Penny Morrison	Nancy McClain	Mike Webby	Riz Bradshaw
Clatsop (Astoria) (33)	503 325-1000	Eric Olsen	William B Barrons	Lori Davidson	Keith Moes	William B Barrons	John Raichl
Columbia (St. Helens) (38)	503 397-3796	....	....	....	....	....	....
Coos (Coquille) (60)	503 396-3121	Jack Beebe	....	....	Mary Barton	Janis Silveus	Michael Cook
Crook (Prineville) (14)	503 447-6555	Fred Rodgers	....	Kathleen Eby	Mary Johnson	....	Rodd Clark
Curry (Gold Beach) (19)	503 247-7011	Rocky McVay	....	Renee Kolen	Peter Hatfield	Peter Hatfield	Chuck Denney
Deschutes (Bend) (75)	503 388-6570	....	....	....	Tom Eckerd	Jim Bruce	John Pardon
Douglas (Roseburg) (95)	503 440-4405	Doug Robertson	....	Debby Mendenhall	Alcenia Byrd	....	Paul D Barnett
Gilliam (Condon) (2)	503 384-2311	Laura M Pryor	....	Rena J Kennedy	....	....	....
Grant (Canyon City) (8)	503 575-0059	....	....	Dolores Swisher	....	Ladene Hurd	Dave Glerup
Harney (Burns) (7)	503 573-8372	Dale White	....	Donna Layman	Dan Chamness	....	Joe Wampler
Hood River (Hood River) (17)	503 386-3970	Jerry Routson	Jim Azumano	....	Gary Cadle	....	C W Smith
Jackson (Medford) (146)	503 776-7248	Hank Henry	Burke M Raymond	Elaine Henderson	Bonnie K Namenuk	....	Mike Throop
Jefferson (Madras) (14)	503 475-2449	Daniel J Aherr	....	Harlene Darkins	Alan Hudson	David Dickman	Daniel Calvert
Josephine (Grants Pass) (63)	503 474-5100	Harold Haugen	....	Bonnie Grant	Melodee Spiker	Dennis Engelhard	Carl Burkhart
Klamath (Klamath Falls) (58)	503 883-4296	Wesley Sine	....	Karen O' Conner	Nancy Hall	....	Charles Withers
Lake (Lakeview) (7)	503 947-6003	Robert M Pardue	Ray Simms	....	M A Drivas	G H Russell	R L McManus
Lane (Eugene) (283)	503 687-4203	G H Rust Jr	W A Van Vactor	....	Glen Morris	Robert Huddleston	John O' Brien
Lincoln (Newport) (39)	503 265-6611	Donald Linly	....	....	Shannon Willard	....	Art Martinak
Linn (Albany) (91)	503 967-3825	David R Schmidt	Ralph E Wyatt	S Druckenmiller	....	....	....
Malheur (Vale) (26)	503 473-5183	....	....	....	....	Randy Curtis	Robert Prinslow
Marion (Salem) (228)	503 588-5165	Gary Heer	Ken Roudybush	Alan Davidson	Ken Roudybush	Andrea Denton	Roy Drago
Morrow (Heppner) (8)	503 676-9061	Louis Carlson	....	Barbara Bloodswor	Lisanne Currin	Curtis Smith	Robert Skipper
Multnomah (Portland) (584)	503 248-3511	Beverly Stein	....	....	David Boyer	Andrew K Nelson	Ray E Steele
Polk (Dallas) (50)	503 623-8179	Ronald S Dodge	John K Anderson	....	....	....	....
Sherman (Moro) (2)	503 565-3606	....	....	....	....	....	....
Tillamook (Tillamook) (22)	503 842-3418	Gina Mulford	....	Josephine Veltri	Karen Richards	Darlene Cherry	Tom Dye
Umatilla (Pendleton) (59)	503 276-7111	William S Hansell	Marcia Wells	Tom Grant	Bruce Peet	....	Larry Rowan
Union (La Grande) (24)	503 963-1001	Lorence Savage	Marlene Perkins	Shelley Burgess	Phil Kohfeld	....	Steve Oliver
Wallowa (Enterprise) (7)	503 426-4543	....	....	....	....	....	....
Wasco (The Dalles) (22)	503 296-2276	John Mabrey	Kathy McBride	Kathy McBride	Karen Lebreton	Robb Van Cleave	Art Labrousse
Washington (Hillsboro) (312)	503 648-8611	Bonnie Hays	Charles Cameron	....	....	Sandy Zodrow	Jim Spinden
Wheeler (Fossil) (1)	503 763-2400	....	....	....	....	....	....
Yamhill (Mc Minnville) (66)	503 472-9371	Dennis Goecks	John Krawcyk	Charles Stern	John Krawcyk	Steve Mikami	Lee Vasquez
PENNSYLVANIA (67)							
Adams (Gettysburg) (78)	717 334-6781	....	....	....	....	....	....
Allegheny (Pittsburgh) (1336)	412 355-5300	....	....	....	....	....	....
Armstrong (Kittanning) (73)	412 543-2500	....	....	....	....	....	....
Beaver (Beaver) (186)	412 728-5700	James Albert	Robert W Cyphert	Robert W Cyphert	Richard Towcimak	William P Greer	Frank Policaro
Bedford (Bedford) (48)	814 623-4807	....	....	....	....	....	....
Berks (Reading) (337)	215 378-8000	....	....	....	....	....	....
Blair (Hollidaysburg) (131)	814 695-5541	....	....	Terry L Wagner	Richard J Peo	W T Williams	Larry D Field
Bradford (Towanda) (61)	717 265-5700	....	....	....	....	....	....
Bucks (Doylestown) (541)	215 348-6000	....	....	....	....	....	....

Directory 1/10 **OFFICIALS IN U.S. COUNTIES**
continued

County, county seat, 1990 population figures (000 omitted)	County telephone number	Chief elected official	Appointed administrator	Clerk to the governing board	Chief financial officer	Personnel director	Chief law enforcement official
PENNSYLVANIA (67) continued							
Butler (Butler) (152)	412 285-4731	James A Green	....	W O' Donnell	Arthur Shuker	Eileen McCue	Dennis Rickard
Cambria (Ebensburg) (163)	814 472-5440	....	....	....	....	....	....
Cameron (Emporium) (6)	814 486-2315	....	....	....	....	....	....
Carbon (Jim Thorpe) (57)	717 325-3611	Dean E W Delong	Mortimer Smedley	Marie A Midas	....	Mary L Kelshaw	Peter P Hoherchak
Centre (Bellefonte) (124)	814 355-6700	Vicki L Wedler	Evan B Smith	....	Donald A Asendorf	Oliver C Goodman	Dennis Nau
Chester (West Chester) (376)	215 344-6100	....	....	....	....	....	....
Clarion (Clarion) (42)	814 226-4000	Linda V McCarthy	....	Donna Hartle	Nancy Murray	J A Hollingsworth	Vern Smith
Clearfield (Clearfield) (78)	814 765-2641	....	....	....	....	....	....
Clinton (Lock Haven) (37)	717 893-4000	Robert Ohl	....	Linda Bickford	....	....	Keith Eichenlaub
Columbia (Bloomsburg) (63)	717 389-5600	William Soberick	Gail S Kipp	Gail S Kipp	Shirley F Drake	Janet Weeks	Harry Roadarmel
Crawford (Meadville) (86)	814 333-7300	Morris W Waid	William E Harry	William E Harry	Robyn Sye	William E Harry	Robert Stevens
Cumberland (Carlisle) (195)	717 240-6100	....	....	....	....	....	....
Dauphin (Harrisburg) (238)	717 255-2740	Russell Sheaffer	Jeffrey Haste	Jeffrey Haste	C E Henery	Jeffrey Haste	Wm Livingston
Delaware (Media) (548)	610 891-4852	Mary Ann Arty	Edwin B Erickson	Joyce A Lamont	Edwin B Erickson	Leonard J Maloney	Ann Osborne
Elk (Ridgway) (35)	814 776-1161	Christine Gavazzi	Peggy Aharrah	Peggy Aharrah	Peggy Aharrah	Peggy Aharrah	Alfred Gausman
Erie (Erie) (276)	814 451-6000	....	....	....	....	....	....
Fayette (Uniontown) (145)	412 430-1200	Fred L Lebder	....	Joseph P Korona	Harry J Fike	....	Norma J Santore
Forest (Tionesta) (5)	814 755-3537	Samuel J Wagner	....	Virginia M Call	Pamela Millin	Farley Wright	Harry E Tucker
Franklin (Chambersburg) (121)	717 264-4125	....	....	....	....	....	....
Fulton (Mc Connellsburg) (14)	717 485-4212	....	....	....	....	....	....
Greene (Waynesburg) (40)	412 852-5221	Pauline Crumrine	....	Gene Lee	John Stets	Connie Rush	Richard Ketchem
Huntingdon (Huntingdon) (44)	814 643-3091	Harold L Lockhoff	Eydie S Miller	Eydie S Miller	....	....	Harry E Ersek
Indiana (Indiana) (90)	412 465-3800	Thomas Coyne	Helen C Hill	Helen C Hill	Sandra Kirkland	Margaret J Karp	Donald Beckwith
Jefferson (Brookville) (46)	814 849-8031	Lugene Inzana	....	Julie Coleman	Paul Corbin	....	Harry Dunkle
Juniata (Mifflintown) (21)	717 436-8991	Dale S Shelley	....	Gladys M Boyer	Margaret L Lyter	....	H Thomas Lyter
Lackawanna (Scranton) (219)	717 963-6800	James Walsh	Gerald Stanvitch	....	Steve Barcoski	Anthony Bernardi	John Szymanski
Lancaster (Lancaster) (423)	717 299-8000	James Huber	Sherri Heller	Doris Kiehl	Benjamin H Hess	J Thomas Myers	Theodore Sattler
Lawrence (New Castle) (96)	412 658-2541	Glenn McCracken	....	Charlene Micco	....	Gertrude Blight	Robert Clark
Lebanon (Lebanon) (114)	717 274-2801	R M Swanger	Donald J Rhine	Donald J Rhine	Lynn Nelson	Gary B Robson	Michael Deleo
Lehigh (Allentown) (291)	215 820-3306	....	....	....	....	....	....
Luzerne (Wilkes-Barre) (328)	717 825-1500	....	....	....	....	....	....
Lycoming (Williamsport) (119)	717 327-2314	Henry F Frey	David D Winterle	David D Winterle	David Raker	Ann M Gehret	Charlie Brewer
Mc Kean (Smethport) (47)	814 887-5571	Harrijane Hannon	....	Audrey Irons	Connie Eaton	....	Donald Morey
Mercer (Mercer) (121)	412 662-3800	Olivia M Lazor	....	Freida Eakman	Ambrose Rocca	Ambrose Rocca	William Romine
Mifflin (Lewistown) (46)	717 248-6733	Ora H Sunderland	....	Peggy Finkenbiner	....	....	Jay R Laub
Monroe (Stroudsburg) (96)	717 420-3450	Janet Weidensaul	Zenia Citsay	....	Donald Chase	Richard Bielat	Forrest Sebring
Montgomery (Norristown) (678)	610 278-3000	Mario Mele	Nicholas Melair	Kathryn Canavan	Jon Ganser	....	Francis Lalley
Montour (Danville) (18)	717 271-3000	Darla J Gill	Susan M Kauwell	Susan M Kauwell	Luther L Cooke	Susan M Kauwell	Fred Shepperson
Northampton (Easton) (247)	215 559-3000	....	....	....	....	....	....
Northumberland (Sunbury) (97)	717 988-4100	Eleanor Kuhns	....	Joseph Warner	Chet Stesney	Joseph Warner	Russell Wolfe
Perry (New Bloomfield) (41)	717 582-8984	Billy M Roush	....	....	Richard Long	June D Smith	G Frownfelter
Philadelphia (Philadelphia) c (1586)	215 686-1776	Edward G Rendell	....	....	Ben Hallar	Philip River	....
Pike (Milford) (28)	717 296-7613	Donald C Brink	Centa T Quinn	Centa T Quinn	Robert C Phillips	....	Harry L Geiger
Potter (Coudersport) (17)	814 274-8290	....	....	....	....	....	....
Schuylkill (Pottsville) (153)	717 622-5570	....	....	....	....	....	....
Snyder (Middleburg) (37)	717 837-0691	....	....	....	....	....	....
Somerset (Somerset) (78)	814 443-1434	Robert J Will	....	Kay F Slope	....	....	Ronald J Delano
Sullivan (Laporte) (6)	717 946-5201	Pemala K Arthur	....	Lynne A Stabryla	Kathy A Robbins	Lynne A Stabryla	Burton Adams
Susquehanna (Montrose) (40)	717 278-4600	Warren Williams	Jerry A Myers	Jerry A Myers	Jerry A Myers	....	Dick Pelicci
Tioga (Wellsboro) (41)	717 724-1906	....	....	....	....	....	....
Union (Lewisburg) (36)	717 524-8631	Ruth W Zimmerman	Diana L Robinson	Diana L Robinson	Diana L Robinson	Diana L Robinson	Donald Everitt
Venango (Franklin) (59)	814 432-9501	Walter L Schafer	....	Denise W Jones	....	Connie A Hazelton	E Eugene Price
Warren (Warren) (45)	814 723-7550	Richard Campbell	Eunice Herrington	Avis Valentine	Robert L Hansen	Clare Morrison	Larry Kopko
Washington (Washington) (205)	412 228-6738	....	....	....	....	....	....
Wayne (Honesdale) (40)	717 253-5970	....	....	....	....	....	....
Westmoreland (Greensburg) (370)	412 830-3786	Richard Vidmer	....	Elaine Oravets	Dennis Adams	Betsy Griffin	Dennis Genard
Wyoming (Tunkhannock) (28)	717 836-3200	Willard Baker	William Gaylord	....	Carl Smith	William Gaylord	Robert Truesdale
York (York) (340)	717 771-9614	George Trout	Allan Dameshek	....	Mike Gingerich	Patrick McFadden	Kenneth Markel
SOUTH CAROLINA (46)							
Abbeville (Abbeville) (24)	803 459-5312	....	....	....	....	....	....
Aiken (Aiken) (121)	803 642-2013	....	....	....	....	....	....
Allendale (Allendale) (12)	803 584-3438	....	....	....	....	....	....
Anderson (Anderson) (145)	803 260-4000	G Fred Tolly Jr	Gary A Smoak	Linda N Gilstrap	G Jacky Hunter	Nancy O Baxter	Gordon E Taylor
Bamberg (Bamberg) (17)	803 245-5191	Isaiah Odom	Mark D Baskin	Rose R Shepherd	Booker Patrick	Susan D Hiers	J Edward Darnell
Barnwell (Barnwell) (20)	803 541-1000	Jim Kearse	....	Jane O Bradley	Elaine D Bryan	Alice L Martin	Joseph Zorn
Beaufort (Beaufort) (86)	803 525-7100	Thomas C Taylor	Michael G Bryant	Suzanne M Rainey	Thomas A Henrikso	Marie S Smalls	David J Lucas Jr
Berkeley (Moncks Corner) (129)	803 761-6900	James H Rozier Jr	....	Betty Lou Hanna	Betty Jo Fondren	Bryan O Sorensen	Raymond O Isgett
Calhoun (St. Matthews) (13)	803 874-2435	....	....	....	....	....	....
Charleston (Charleston) (295)	803 723-6716	R Keith Summey	Ernest E Fava	Beverly T Craven	Harold Bisbee	Barbara DeMarco	James A Cannon Jr
Cherokee (Gaffney) (45)	803 487-2561	Hoke Parris	Joey R Preston	Doris Pearson	Elmer Huskey	Frances Fowler	Billy Blanton
Chester (Chester) (32)	803 385-5133	....	....	....	....	....	....
Chesterfield (Chesterfield) (39)	803 623-2535	Bruce E Rivers	Jody C McKinney	Denise S Hubbard	....	Peggy E Miller	Ralph C Freeman
Clarendon (Manning) (28)	803 435-8424	Betty Roper	Robert T Boland	Thomas Harvin Jr	....	Linda J Taylor	Hoyt Collins
Colleton (Walterboro) (34)	803 549-5221	Floyd Buckner	Hank Veleker	Jacqueline Holmes	....	....	Cecil E Chasteen
Darlington (Darlington) (62)	803 398-4100	James C Stone Jr	James H Schafer	Jessie J Blow	Phyllis Griffitts	Brenda P Broach	Walter G Campbell
Dillon (Dillon) (29)	803 774-1400	....	....	....	....	....	....
Dorchester (St. George) (83)	803 563-0199	....	Jack Langston	Myrtle Barten	Anthony Ogliettt	Anne S Ayer	John Southerland
Edgefield (Edgefield) (18)	803 637-4000	C Monroe Kneece	Thomas C McCain	Thomas C McCain	James W McCord	Thomas C McCain	R Billy Parker
Fairfield (Winnsboro) (22)	803 635-1415	Carnell Murphy	William A Frick	Shryll M Brown	Deborah Simmons	Callie S Bell	Herman W Young
Florence (Florence) (114)	803 665-3099	....	....	....	....	....	....
Georgetown (Georgetown) (46)	803 546-4189	James Nichols	Gordon Hartwig	....	David Parks	Mary Graham	A Lane Cribb
Greenville (Greenville) (320)	803 467-7156	C Wade Cleveland	Gerald Seals	Elizabeth Hanzey	John F Hansley	Beverly R Pruitt	Johnny Mack Brown
Greenwood (Greenwood) (60)	803 942-8501	Pat Brennan	Robert M Haynie	Lisa Emily	Reel Robertson	Faye Ridge	Sam Riley
Hampton (Hampton) (18)	803 943-4951	....	....	....	....	....	....
Horry (Conway) (144)	803 248-1207	....	....	....	....	....	....
Jasper (Ridgeland) (15)	803 726-3173	....	....	....	....	....	....
Kershaw (Camden) (44)	803 425-1500	....	....	....	....	....	....
Lancaster (Lancaster) (55)	803 285-1565	Ray Gardner	J Chappell Hurst	Irene Plyler	Jerry Witherspoon	Judy Chavis	Williford Faile
Laurens (Laurens) (58)	803 984-5214	....	....	....	....	....	....
Lee (Bishopville) (18)	803 484-5341	....	....	....	....	....	....
Lexington (Lexington) (168)	803 359-8000	....	....	....	....	....	....
Marion (Marion) (34)	803 423-3904	Jasper Eaddy	Claude W Graham	Landis H Baxley	....	Cheryl S Rogers	L C Richardson

Directory 1/10   **OFFICIALS IN U.S. COUNTIES**
continued

County, county seat, 1990 population figures (000 omitted)	County telephone number	Chief elected official	Appointed administrator	Clerk to the governing board	Chief financial officer	Personnel director	Chief law enforcement official
SOUTH CAROLINA (46) continued							
Marlboro (Bennettsville) (29)	803 479-4462	....	....	....	....	....	....
Mc Cormick (Mc Cormick) (9)	803 465-2231	Alonzo Harrison	Paul H Bjorkman	Mary Beckwith	Ferrel Percival	....	George Reid
Newberry (Newberry) (33)	803 321-2100	....			....		....
Oconee (Walhalla) (57)	803 638-4242	Norman D Crain	....	Opal O Green	George Hunnicutt	Merle P Orr	James E Singleton
Orangeburg (Orangeburg) (85)	803 533-1000	Vernon Ott	Donnie Hilliard	Susan Matthews	Avis Butler	Bill Clark	Cameron Smith
Pickens (Pickens) (94)	803 898-5900	....			....		....
Richland (Columbia) (286)	803 748-4616	Harriet G Fields	T Cary McSwain	Brenda R Fuller	Deborah F Ashe	Robin Owens	Allen F Sloan
Saluda (Saluda) (16)	803 445-2635	....			....		....
Spartanburg (Spartanburg) (227) ...	803 596-2525	David G Dennis	Roland H Windham	Carolyn P Parris	Alfred G Rickett	Bonnie H Hammond	William Coffey
Sumter (Sumter) (103)	803 773-1581	....		Linda G Jolly	Dianne Wilkins	....	W Howard Wells
Union (Union) (30)	803 429-1600	M Dale Robinson		Lisha B Graham			Jack McCrea
Williamsburg (Kingstree) (37)	803 354-9321	Alex Chatman	E Nelson Brown	Nancy Moore	Anne Bunton	David Larson	Joseph Mitchell
York (York) (131)	803 684-8512	Carl Gullick	Clay Killian				
SOUTH DAKOTA (66)							
Aurora (Plankinton) (3)	605 942-7752	....	....	Connie R Muth	Evie Hofer	....	Tom Beerman
Beadle (Huron) (18)	605 352-8436	Randy Ziegeldorf	....				....
Bennett (Martin) (3)	605 685-6969	....		Katherine Horacek			Steven Knakmuhs
Bon Homme (Tyndall) (7)	605 589-3391	Allen Sternhagen	....	Sara Kneip	Debra Hanson	....	Gordon Ribstein
Brookings (Brookings) (25)	605 692-6284	Don Larson	Dennis Biegler	Maxine Taylor	Sheila Enderson		Stephen Oakes
Brown (Aberdeen) (36)	605 622-7110	Dennis Feickert		Bette Shields	Bette Shields		Darrell Miller
Brule (Chamberlain) (5)	605 734-6521	Ronald Bairey		Elaine J Wulff	Janice Voneye	Elaine Wulff	Wayne Willman
Buffalo (Gannvalley) (2)	605 293-3217	Hugh W Sedgwick	....	Sally Pflaumer	....		Richard Davis
Butte (Belle Fourche) (8)	605 892-4485	William J Hannah					
Campbell (Mound City) (2)	605 955-3366	....	....	....	....	....	....
Charles Mix (Lake Andes) (9)	605 487-7131	....	....	....	....	....	....
Clark (Clark) (4)	605 532-5921	....	....	....	....	....	....
Clay (Vermillion) (13)	605 624-2281	....	....	....	....	....	....
Codington (Watertown) (23)	605 886-8497	....	....	....	....	....	....
Corson (Mc Intosh) (4)	605 273-4229	....	....	....	....	....	....
Custer (Custer) (6)	605 673-4815	....	....	John Oster	John Oster		Lyle Swenson
Davison (Mitchell) (18)	605 996-2474	Thomas Greenway	....				....
Day (Webster) (7)	605 345-3102	....					Lynn Pederson
Deuel (Clear Lake) (5)	605 874-2330	Oscar Bren		Adele Enright	Adele Enright	Adele Enright	Jim Fisher
Dewey (Timber Lake) (6)	605 865-3672	Bob Berndt	....				....
Douglas (Armour) (4)	605 724-2423	....					....
Edmunds (Ipswich) (4)	605 426-6762	....		Sherrill A Dryden	Shirley Green		Leo W Bray
Fall River (Hot Springs) (7)	605 745-5130	Erv Heimbuck	....				....
Faulk (Faulkton) (3)	605 598-6224	....		Karen Layher	Maureen Dinter	....	Michael McKernan
Grant (Milbank) (8)	605 432-6711	George Dummann	....	Julie Bartling	Sara Grim		Damon Wolf
Gregory (Burke) (5)	605 775-2664	Gilbert Frank	....				....
Haakon (Philip) (3)	605 859-2800	....		Dixie Opdahl			Dan Mack
Hamlin (Hayti) (5)	605 783-3201	Robert Ward		Betty Morford	Betty Morford		Jerry Miller
Hand (Miller) (4)	605 853-2182	Larry Hurd		Janet Ibls			Robert Brown
Hanson (Alexandria) (3)	605 239-4714	Sherman Letcher	....				....
Harding (Buffalo) (2)	605 375-3313	....		Shellie Baker	Maggie Oliva		Arlo Mortimer
Hughes (Pierre) (15)	605 224-2181	Jerry Hawkins		Jerome Hoff			Raymond Zeeb
Hutchinson (Olivet) (8)	605 387-2835	LuVerne N Locken	....		Sandra Blair		Charles Wortman
Hyde (Highmore) (2)	605 852-2519	Elton Vilhauer	Connie Konrad	....	Vicki D Wilson		Arlo B Madsen
Jackson (Kadoka) (3)	605 837-2422	Larry A Byrd	....	....			....
Jerauld (Wessington Springs) (2) ...	605 539-1202	....	....	....	....		....
Jones (Murdo) (1)	605 669-2242	....					....
Kingsbury (De Smet) (6)	605 854-3832	Wm Cronkhite		Audrey Penney	Betty Zell		Norman Lee
Lake (Madison) (11)	605 256-2068	....					....
Lawrence (Deadwood) (21)	605 578-1941	Gerald Apa		Marlene Barrett	Connie Atkinson		Charles Crotty
Lincoln (Canton) (15)	605 987-2581	....					....
Lyman (Kennebec) (4)	605 869-2247	Raymond Boe		Joan Brinckmeyer	Adelia B Olsen		John H Michalek
Marshall (Britton) (5)	605 448-2401	Connie Williams	....	Caro Christianson			Dale Eisen
Mc Cook (Salem) (6)	605 425-2791	Harold Heitgen	....	Geralyn Sherman	Joan Matthaei		Eugene Taylor
Mc Pherson (Leola) (3)	605 439-3314	Michael Rath		Steven Serr	Sylvia Arioso		Keith Kunz
Meade (Sturgis) (22)	605 347-4513	....		....	....		....
Mellette (White River) (2)	605 259-3291	....		....			
Miner (Howard) (3)	605 772-4671	Thomas Dold	....	Cindy Callies	Cindy Callies	Cindy Callies	Tim Reisch
Minnehaha (Sioux Falls) (124)	605 335-4206	James Zweep	Ken McFarland	Deb Johnson	Sue Roust	Nora Buckman	Les Hawkey
Moody (Flandreau) (7)	605 997-3161	Larry Miles	....	Laurie Johnson	....		Jerry Hoffman
Pennington (Rapid City) (81)	605 394-2153	....		....			....
Perkins (Bison) (4)	605 244-5624	Robert Jangula		Fern Brockel	Dolores Chapman		Kelly Serr
Potter (Gettysburg) (3)	605 765-9408	....		....	....		....
Roberts (Sisseton) (10)	605 698-7336	....		....			....
Sanborn (Woonsocket) (3)	605 796-4513	....		....			
Shannon (Hot Springs) (10)	605 745-3996	C Whirlwindhorse	....	Sherrill A Dryden	Shirley Green		Leo W Bray
Spink (Redfield) (8)	605 472-1825	Richard C Mueller		Rosemary Parker	Rose Nelson		Gary Newman
Stanley (Fort Pierre) (2)	605 223-2673	Bob Wilco		Phyllis Kenzy	Patty McGee		Bradley Rathbun
Sully (Onida) (2)	605 258-2541	William Floyd		Patty McGee	Patty McGee	Patty McGee	Bill Stahl
Todd (Winner) (8)	605 842-3727	Harold W Whiting	....	Kathleen Flakus	Donna D Trego		Larry Christensen
Tripp (Winner) (7)	605 842-3727	Louis Polasky		Kathleen Flakus	Donna D Trego		C Schroeder
Turner (Parker) (9)	605 297-3153	Luverne Langerock	....	Sheila Hagemann	Marlys Andersen		Paul Morehouse
Union (Elk Point) (10)	605 356-2101	M C Bak		Carol Klumper	Winna Lanning		Dan Limoges
Walworth (Selby) (6)	605 649-7878	Dean W Lemburg		Mary L Bucklin	Julie Lundquist	Mary L Bucklin	James Spiry
Yankton (Yankton) (19)	605 665-2143	Bennett Van Osdel		....			Dave Hunhoff
Ziebach (Dupree) (3)	605 365-5157	Clinton Farlee	....	Cindy Longbrake	Cindy Longbrake	Cindy Longbrake	Robert Menzel
TENNESSEE (95)							
Anderson (Clinton) (68)	615 457-5400	....	....	....	....	....	....
Bedford (Shelbyville) (30)	615 684-1921	....	....	....	....	....	....
Benton (Camden) (15)	901 584-6011	....	....	....	....	....	....
Bledsoe (Pikeville) (10)	615 447-6855	....	....	....	....	....	....
Blount (Maryville) (86)	615 982-1302	William A Crisp	....	Roy D Crawford	John M Troyer		James Berrong
Bradley (Cleveland) (74)	615 476-0600	....	Carl Shrewsbury	....	Donna J Hubbard	Kay Montgomery	Dan Gilley
Campbell (Jacksboro) (35)	615 562-6201	Tommy C Stiner	Jeff Marlow	Don Nance	Tommy C Stiner	Tommy C Stiner	Ron McClellan
Cannon (Woodbury) (10)	615 563-2320	Harold Patrick	....	Robert P Smith	Joe Rogers		Robert Simpson
Carroll (Huntingdon) (28)	901 986-3762	....	....	....	....	....	....
Carter (Elizabethton) (52)	615 542-1801	....	....	....	....	....	....

Directory 1/10 **OFFICIALS IN U.S. COUNTIES**
continued

County, county seat, 1990 population figures (000 omitted)	County telephone number	Chief elected official	Appointed administrator	Clerk to the governing board	Chief financial officer	Personnel director	Chief law enforcement official
TENNESSEE (95) continued							
Cheatham (Ashland City) (27)	615 792-4316	....	....	....	....	....	....
Chester (Henderson) (13)	901 989-5672	....	....	....	....	....	....
Claiborne (Tazewell) (26)	615 626-5236	....	....	....	....	....	....
Clay (Celina) (7)	615 243-2161	Coell Hickman	....	Patricia Hix	Coell Hickman	Coell Hickman	Cecil Anderson
Cocke (Newport) (29)	615 623-8791	....	....	....	....	....	....
Coffee (Manchester) (40)	615 723-5100	James R Wilhelm	....	Charles E Wells	James R Wilhelm	....	Freddie Conn
Crockett (Alamo) (13)	901 696-5451	....	....	....	....	....	....
Cumberland (Crossville) (35)	615 484-6165	....	....	....	....	....	....
De Kalb (Smithville) (14)	615 597-5177	....	....	....	....	....	....
Decatur (Decaturville) (10)	901 852-2131	....	....	....	....	....	....
Dickson (Charlotte) (35)	615 789-4171	....	....	....	....	....	....
Dyer (Dyersburg) (35)	901 286-7800	....	....	....	....	....	....
Fayette (Somerville) (26)	901 465-5202	Wm David Smith	....	Dell T Graham	Betty L Bobbitt	....	Billy G Kelley
Fentress (Jamestown) (15)	615 879-7713	....	....	....	....	....	....
Franklin (Winchester) (35)	615 967-1279	Clinton Williams	Jo Ann Brinkley	....	Susan Wall	Annette Sisk	Teddy McCallie
Gibson (Trenton) (46)	901 855-4550	....	....	....	....	....	....
Giles (Pulaski) (26)	615 363-5300	....	....	....	....	....	....
Grainger (Rutledge) (17)	615 828-3513	....	....	....	....	....	....
Greene (Greeneville) (56)	615 638-8118	....	....	....	....	....	....
Grundy (Altamont) (13)	615 692-3718	Michael Partin	....	Jimmy Rogers	Keith McBee	Michael Partin	Bill Reid
Hamblen (Morristown) (50)	615 586-1931	Stancil L Ford	....	Wilburn Beck	Paul L Bruce	Sonia R Miller	Charles E Long
Hamilton (Chattanooga) (286)	615 757-2496	....	....	....	....	....	....
Hancock (Sneedville) (7)	615 733-4341	....	....	....	....	....	....
Hardeman (Bolivar) (23)	901 658-3266	....	....	....	....	....	....
Hardin (Savannah) (23)	901 925-9078	Kim Stricklin	....	Connie Stephens	Kim Stricklin	....	Sammy Davidson
Hawkins (Rogersville) (45)	615 272-7359	....	....	....	....	....	....
Haywood (Brownsville) (19)	901 772-1432	....	....	....	....	....	....
Henderson (Lexington) (22)	901 968-7141	....	....	....	....	....	....
Henry (Paris) (28)	901 642-5212	Herman Jackson	....	Jerry Bomar	Herman Jackson	....	Tom Jenkins
Hickman (Centerville) (17)	615 729-2492	Steve Gregory	....	Randell Totty	Scott Powers	....	Dwight England
Houston (Erin) (7)	615 289-3633	....	....	....	....	....	....
Humphreys (Waverly) (16)	615 296-7795	....	....	....	....	....	....
Jackson (Gainesboro) (9)	615 268-9888	....	....	....	....	....	....
Jefferson (Dandridge) (33)	615 397-3800	....	....	....	....	....	....
Johnson (Mountain City) (14)	615 727-9696	....	....	....	....	....	....
Knox (Knoxville) (336)	615 521-2000	Dwight Kessel	Patsy Miller	Mike Padgett	Kathy Hamilton	Joe Hamby	Tim Hutchison
Lake (Tiptonville) (7)	901 253-7382	....	....	....	....	....	....
Lauderdale (Ripley) (23)	901 635-3500	....	....	....	....	....	....
Lawrence (Lawrenceburg) (35)	615 762-7700	Marty Dunkin	....	Kenneth Weathers	Robin A Roberts	....	Bruce Durham
Lewis (Hohenwald) (9)	615 796-3378	....	....	....	....	....	....
Lincoln (Fayetteville) (28)	615 433-3045	....	....	....	....	....	....
Loudon (Loudon) (31)	615 458-4663	....	....	....	....	....	....
Macon (Lafayette) (16)	615 666-2363	....	....	....	....	....	....
Madison (Jackson) (78)	901 423-6020	....	....	....	....	....	....
Marion (Jasper) (25)	615 942-2552	....	....	....	....	....	....
Marshall (Lewisburg) (22)	615 359-1279	Sam D Kennedy	....	Nancy Thompson	A C Howell	....	J Wade Matheny
Maury (Columbia) (55)	615 381-3690	Jack Powers	....	....	Ed Fiegle	....	Geore Rogers
Mc Minn (Athens) (42)	615 745-4103	....	....	....	....	....	....
Mc Nairy (Selmer) (22)	901 645-3511	....	....	....	....	....	....
Meigs (Decatur) (8)	615 334-5850	....	....	....	....	....	....
Monroe (Madisonville) (31)	615 442-3981	....	....	....	....	....	....
Montgomery (Clarksville) (100)	615 648-5787	....	....	....	....	....	....
Moore (Lynchburg) (..)	615 759-7076	....	....	....	....	....	....
Morgan (Wartburg) (17)	615 346-6288	....	....	....	....	....	....
Nashville-Davidson (Nashville) c (511)	615 862-6640	....	....	Marilyn Swing	Eugene Nolan	John W Lynch	Robert Kirchner
Obion (Union City) (32)	901 885-9611	....	....	....	....	....	....
Overton (Livingston) (18)	615 823-5638	Richard Mitchell	....	Hugh L Ogletree	Richard Mitchell	....	Herman Moody
Perry (Linden) (7)	615 589-2216	....	....	....	....	....	....
Pickett (Byrdstown) (5)	615 864-3798	....	....	....	....	....	....
Polk (Benton) (14)	615 338-2841	....	....	....	....	....	....
Putnam (Cookeville) (51)	615 526-6321	....	....	....	....	....	....
Rhea (Dayton) (24)	615 775-7803	....	....	....	....	....	....
Roane (Kingston) (47)	615 376-5578	....	....	....	....	....	....
Robertson (Springfield) (41)	615 384-2476	Emerson Meggs	....	....	Larry Morris	....	Taylor T Emery
Rutherford (Murfreesboro) (119) ...	615 898-7745	....	....	....	....	....	....
Scott (Huntsville) (18)	615 663-2355	....	....	....	....	....	....
Sequatchie (Dunlap) (9)	615 949-3479	....	....	....	....	....	....
Sevier (Sevierville) (51)	615 453-6136	....	....	....	....	....	....
Shelby (Memphis) (826)	901 576-4500	Charles Perkins	Richard Swiggart	....	Henry Marmon	H L Hilbun	A C Gilless
Smith (Carthage) (14)	615 735-2294	....	....	....	....	....	....
Stewart (Dover) (9)	615 232-5371	....	....	....	....	....	....
Sullivan (Blountville) (144)	615 323-6409	Wm H J McKamey	....	Gay B Feathers	Harry P Trent	....	Keith Carr
Sumner (Gallatin) (103)	615 452-4282	....	....	....	....	....	....
Tipton (Covington) (38)	901 476-2604	....	....	....	....	....	....
Trousdale (Hartsville) (6)	615 374-2461	....	....	....	....	....	....
Unicoi (Erwin) (17)	615 743-9391	Paul C Monk	....	Ruby McLaughlin	....	....	Peter DeStefano
Union (Maynardville) (14)	615 992-3061	Gerald E Simmons	Glenn E Coppock	Roy Carter	James Phillips	....	Thomas Keaton
Van Buren (Spencer) (5)	615 946-2314	....	....	....	....	....	....
Warren (Mc Minnville) (33)	615 473-2505	....	....	....	....	....	....
Washington (Jonesborough) (92) ...	615 753-1666	George Jaynes	....	Roy Phillips	George Jaynes	....	Ronald England
Wayne (Waynesboro) (14)	615 722-3653	....	....	....	....	....	....
Weakley (Dresden) (32)	901 364-5413	....	....	....	....	....	....
White (Sparta) (20)	615 836-3216	Tommy Denton	....	Connie Jolley	Keith Ryder	....	Charles Anderson
Williamson (Franklin) (81)	615 790-5700	Robert Ring	....	Charlie Fox Jr	Bill Giddens	....	Lance Saylor
Wilson (Lebanon) (68)	615 444-1383	Don Simpson	....	Jim Goodall	Don Simpson	....	Terry Ashe
TEXAS (254)							
Anderson (Palestine) (48)	903 723-7427	John B McDonald	....	Jo Huddleston	Mary E Cox	Mary E Cox	Mickey Hubert
Andrews (Andrews) (14)	915 523-3062	....	....	....	....	....	....
Angelina (Lufkin) (70)	409 634-5413	Joe Berry	....	Pauline Grisham	E H Bush Jr	....	Michael Lawrence
Aransas (Rockport) (18)	512 790-0100	Agnes A Harden	....	Peggy L Frieble	Stanley Svehla	Stanley Svehla	David Petrusaitis
Archer (Archer City) (8)	817 574-4811	....	....	....	....	....	....
Armstrong (Claude) (2)	806 226-3221	....	....	....	....	....	....

Directory 1/10   **OFFICIALS IN U.S. COUNTIES**
continued

County, county seat, 1990 population figures (000 omitted)	County telephone number	Chief elected official	Appointed administrator	Clerk to the governing board	Chief financial officer	Personnel director	Chief law enforcement official
TEXAS (254) continued							
Atascosa (Jourdanton) (31)	512 769-3093	....	....	....	....	....	....
Austin (Bellville) (20)	409 865-5911	....	....	....	....	....	....
Bailey (Muleshoe) (7)	806 272-3077	Marilyn Cox	....	Barbara McCamish	Dorothy Turner	....	Jerry N Hicks
Bandera (Bandera) (11)	210 796-3781	Ray F Mauer	....	Bernice Bates	Elizabeth James	....	James Mac Millan
Bastrop (Bastrop) (38)	512 321-2460	Randy Fritz	....	....	....	....	Fred W Hoskins
Baylor (Seymour) (4)	817 888-2662	Joe Dickson	....	Doris Rushing	Pat Coker	....	Jerry Barton
Bee (Beeville) (25)	512 362-3200	Jay Kimbrough	....	Julia Torres	Bonnie M White	....	Robert L Horn
Bell (Belton) (191)	817 939-3521	John Garth	....	Vada Sutton	Bert Liles	Bert Liles	Dan Smith
Bexar (San Antonio) (1185)	210 220-2011	C T Krier	J O Garza	R D Green	S O Lewis	M Vargas McCabe	R Lopez
Blanco (Johnson City) (6)	512 868-4266	....	....	....	....	....	....
Borden (Gail) (1)	806 756-4391	....	....	....	....	....	....
Bosque (Meridian) (15)	817 435-2382	E W Reinke Jr	....	Patsy Mize	Randy Pullin	....	Timothy S Gage
Bowie (New Boston) (82)	903 628-2571	James M Carlow	....	....	Tom Kesterson	....	Mary Choate
Brazoria (Angleton) (192)	409 849-5711	James W Phillips	....	Dolly Bailey	Connie Garner	....	Joe King
Brazos (Bryan) (122)	409 775-7400	R J Holmgreen	....	Mary Ann Ward	Sandie Walker	....	Bobby Riggs
Brewster (Alpine) (9)	915 837-2412	....	....	....	....	....	....
Briscoe (Silverton) (2)	806 823-2131	....	....	....	....	....	....
Brooks (Falfurrias) (8)	512 325-5604	....	....	....	....	....	....
Brown (Brownwood) (34)	915 643-2828	E Ray West	....	....	Rex Bessent	....	William B Donahoo
Burleson (Caldwell) (14)	409 567-4161	....	....	....	....	....	....
Burnet (Burnet) (23)	512 756-5420	Martin E McLean	....	Janet K Parker	Katy Gilmore	Katy Gilmore	Joe F Pollock
Caldwell (Lockhart) (26)	512 398-1809	....	....	....	....	....	....
Calhoun (Port Lavaca) (19)	512 553-4600	....	....	....	....	....	....
Callahan (Baird) (12)	915 854-1155	....	....	....	....	....	....
Cameron (Brownsville) (260)	512 544-0830	....	....	....	....	....	....
Camp (Pittsburg) (10)	214 856-3845	....	....	....	....	....	....
Carson (Panhandle) (7)	806 537-3622	Jay R Roselius	....	Sue Persons	....	....	Loren Brand
Cass (Linden) (30)	903 756-5181	....	....	....	....	....	....
Castro (Dimmitt) (9)	806 647-5534	Pollyanna Simpson	....	Frances Joy Jones	Oleta Merle Raper	Oleta Merle Raper	C D Fitzgearld
Chambers (Anahuac) (20)	409 267-8295	Oscar F Nelson Jr	....	Norma W Rowland	Jimmie Moorhead	....	P Burkhalter
Cherokee (Rusk) (41)	214 683-2324	Craig Caldwell	....	Fairy Upshaw	Craig Caldwell	....	James Campbell
Childress (Childress) (6)	817 937-2221	....	....	....	....	....	....
Clay (Henrietta) (10)	817 538-5911	Bill Nobles	Romana Seward	Kay Hutchison	Sue Brock	Sue Brock	John P Bevering
Cochran (Morton) (4)	806 266-5508	Robert Yeary	....	Rita Tyson	....	....	Royce Fred
Coke (Robert Lee) (3)	915 453-2641	Royce Lee	....	Ettie Hubbard	Stover Taylor	Royce Lee	Marshall Millican
Coleman (Coleman) (10)	915 625-4218	....	....	....	....	....	....
Collin (Mc Kinney) (264)	214 548-4100	....	....	....	....	....	....
Collingsworth (Wellington) (4)	806 447-5408	Thomas Zook	....	Karen Coleman	Yvonne Brewer	....	Dale Tarver
Colorado (Columbus) (18)	409 732-2604	H O Strunk	Raymie Kana	Darlene Hayek	Raymie Kana	Raymie Kana	Billy Esterling
Comal (New Braunfels) (52)	210 620-5501	Carter Casteel	....	....	Bate Bond	Tom Corlette	John Bremer
Comanche (Comanche) (13)	915 356-2466	....	....	....	....	....	....
Concho (Paint Rock) (3)	915 732-4321	....	....	....	....	....	....
Cooke (Gainesville) (31)	817 668-5435	....	....	....	....	....	....
Coryell (Gatesville) (64)	817 865-5911	....	....	....	....	....	....
Cottle (Paducah) (2)	806 492-3613	Billy J Gilbert	....	Becky J Tucker	Athea Prater	....	Frank Taylor
Crane (Crane) (5)	915 558-3581	....	....	....	....	....	....
Crockett (Ozona) (4)	915 392-2022	....	....	....	....	....	....
Crosby (Crosbyton) (7)	806 675-2011	....	....	....	....	....	....
Culberson (Van Horn) (3)	915 283-2059	John Conoly	Francisco R Gomez	Linda Urias	Norma Hernandez	....	Placido Nunez
Dallam (Dalhart) (6)	806 249-2450	David D Field	....	LuAnn Taylor	Jiggs Payne	....	E H Little
Dallas (Dallas) (1853)	214 653-7668	Lee Jackson	Jon A Clemson	....	Phil Scheps	Mario Malacara	James Bowles
Dawson (Lamesa) (14)	806 872-7544	....	....	....	....	....	....
De Witt (Cuero) (19)	512 275-3478	Ben Prause	....	Ann Drehr	Phyllis Massey	....	David Dodge
Deaf Smith (Hereford) (19)	806 364-1451	....	....	....	....	....	....
Delta (Cooper) (5)	903 395-2611	....	....	....	....	....	....
Denton (Denton) (274)	817 565-8553	Jeff Moseley	Don Alexander	Tim Hodges	James Wells	Fred Rozell	Weldon Lucas
Dickens (Dickens) (3)	806 623-5532	Woodie McArthur	....	Helen Arrington	Drulene Rape	....	Doyle King
Dimmit (Carrizo Springs) (10)	512 876-2323	....	....	....	....	....	....
Donley (Clarendon) (4)	806 874-3625	W R Christal	....	Fay Vargas	Wanda Smith	....	Willam Thompson
Duval (San Diego) (13)	512 279-3322	Gilberto Uresti	....	Oscar Garcia Jr	Rosie G Chapa	....	Santiago Barrera
Eastland (Eastland) (18)	817 629-1583	....	....	....	....	....	....
Ector (Odessa) (119)	915 335-3099	Jim T Jordan	....	Barbara Bedford	David Austin	Pat Mac Allister	O A Brookshire
Edwards (Rocksprings) (2)	512 683-2235	....	....	....	....	....	....
El Paso (El Paso) (592)	915 546-2218	Alicia R Chacon	....	....	Steve Seely	Nita Corral Nava	Leo Samaniego
Ellis (Waxahachie) (85)	214 937-8620	....	....	....	....	....	....
Erath (Stephenville) (28)	817 965-4310	....	....	....	....	....	....
Falls (Marlin) (18)	817 883-2961	....	....	....	....	....	....
Fannin (Bonham) (25)	903 583-7451	Jimmy L Doyle	....	Margaret Gilbert	Kathy Moss	Kathy Moss	Talmage Moore
Fayette (La Grange) (20)	409 968-3055	....	....	....	....	....	....
Fisher (Roby) (5)	915 776-2443	....	....	....	....	....	....
Floyd (Floydada) (8)	806 983-2244	....	....	....	....	....	....
Foard (Crowell) (2)	817 684-1424	....	....	....	....	....	....
Fort Bend (Richmond) (225)	713 341-8619	Roy Cordes Jr	....	Dianne Wilson	Robert Grayless	Richard Selleh	R George Molina
Franklin (Mount Vernon) (8)	214 537-2342	A Wayne Foster	....	Wanda Johnson	Sue Ann Harper	....	Charles J White
Freestone (Fairfield) (16)	214 389-2635	....	....	....	....	....	....
Frio (Pearsall) (13)	512 334-2154	....	....	....	....	....	....
Gaines (Seminole) (14)	915 758-3521	....	....	....	....	....	....
Galveston (Galveston) (217)	713 762-8621	....	....	....	....	....	....
Garza (Post) (5)	806 495-2521	....	....	....	....	....	....
Gillespie (Fredericksburg) (17)	210 997-7502	Jay Weinheimer	....	Doris Lange	Janice Menking	....	Milton Jung
Glasscock (Garden City) (1)	915 354-2415	....	....	....	....	....	....
Goliad (Goliad) (6)	512 645-3337	John Barnhill	....	Gail Turley	Lauren Henry	....	James McMahan
Gonzales (Gonzales) (17)	512 672-2327	....	....	....	....	....	....
Gray (Pampa) (24)	806 669-8004	....	....	....	....	....	....
Grayson (Sherman) (95)	214 868-9515	....	....	....	....	....	....
Gregg (Longview) (105)	214 758-6181	....	....	....	....	....	....
Grimes (Anderson) (19)	409 873-2111	Larry Snook	Paul Yount	David Pasket	Alvina Schroeder	Alvina Schroeder	William Foster
Guadalupe (Seguin) (65)	512 379-4188	....	....	....	....	....	....
Hale (Plainview) (35)	806 293-8488	Bill Hollars	Jackie Latham	Mildred Tucker	Bill Hollars	....	Charles Tue
Hall (Memphis) (4)	806 259-2511	Kenneth Dale	....	Raye Bailey	Marion Bownos	....	Garvin Speed
Hamilton (Hamilton) (8)	817 386-3815	....	....	....	....	....	....
Hansford (Spearman) (6)	806 659-2626	Jim Brown	....	Amelia Johnson	Elaine Morris	....	R L McFarlin
Hardeman (Quanah) (5)	817 663-2911	Kenneth McNabb	....	Judy Cokendolpher	Van R White	....	Randy Akers

Directory 1/10   OFFICIALS IN U.S. COUNTIES
continued

County, county seat, 1990 population figures (000 omitted)	County telephone number	Chief elected official	Appointed administrator	Clerk to the governing board	Chief financial officer	Personnel director	Chief law enforcement official
TEXAS (254) continued							
Hardin (Kountze) (41)	409 246-3371	....	....	....	....	....	....
Harris (Houston) (2818)	713 755-5000	Jon Lindsay	Jack Thompson	Beverly Kaufman	Richard Raycraft	Janie Reyes	J Klevenhagen
Harrison (Marshall) (57)	903 938-4805	....	....	....	....	....	....
Hartley (Channing) (4)	806 235-3442	....	....	....	....	....	....
Haskell (Haskell) (7)	817 864-2851	B O Roberson	....	Rhonda Moeller	....	....	Johnny Mills
Hays (San Marcos) (66)	512 392-4858	....	....	....	....	....	....
Hemphill (Canadian) (4)	806 323-6521	....	....	....	....	....	....
Henderson (Athens) (59)	903 675-6119	Tommy Smith	....	Gwen Moffeit	Carolyn Sorrell	Carolyn Sorrell	Howard Alfred
Hidalgo (Edinburg) (384)	210 318-2000	J Edgar Ruiz	....	William R Leo	Stephen F Austin	....	Brijido Marmolejo
Hill (Hillsboro) (27)	817 582-2371	Tommy J Walker	....	Ruth Pelham	Jewel Burton	....	Brent Button
Hockley (Levelland) (24)	806 894-6070	Don Avery	Gene Rush	Mary K Walker	Jo Beth Hittson	....	Leroy Schulle
Hood (Granbury) (29)	817 579-3209	Don Cleveland	....	Anjanette Ables	Don Cleveland	Reva Hendrix	Rodney Jeanis
Hopkins (Sulphur Springs) (29)	214 885-3926	....	....	....	....	....	....
Houston (Crockett) (21)	409 544-3255	....	....	....	....	....	....
Howard (Big Spring) (32)	915 264-2218	Ben Lockhart	....	....	Jackie Olson	Bonnie Franklin	A N Standard
Hudspeth (Sierra Blanca) (3)	915 369-2321	Billy R Love	....	P Bramblett	....	....	Arcadio Ramirez
Hunt (Greenville) (64)	214 455-4504	....	....	....	....	....	....
Hutchinson (Stinnett) (26)	806 878-2171	....	....	....	....	....	....
Irion (Mertzon) (2)	915 835-4361	....	....	....	....	....	....
Jack (Jacksboro) (7)	817 567-2241	....	....	....	....	....	....
Jackson (Edna) (13)	512 782-3402	A H Stafford	Caroline Pitzer	Martha Knapp	Laverne Ellison	Marcell Maresh Jr	Kelly R Janica
Jasper (Jasper) (31)	713 384-2632	Whitehead Corbit	....	Evelyn Stott	Jonetta Nash	....	Roscoe Davis
Jeff Davis (Fort Davis) (2)	915 426-3968	....	....	....	....	....	....
Jefferson (Beaumont) (239)	409 839-2391	Richard LeBlanc	....	Lolita Ramos	Mindy Nantz	Cary Erickson	Carl Griffith
Jim Hogg (Hebbronville) (5)	512 527-3015	....	....	....	....	....	....
Jim Wells (Alice) (38)	512 668-5706	....	....	....	....	....	....
Johnson (Cleburne) (97)	817 645-2292	....	....	....	....	....	....
Jones (Anson) (16)	915 823-3741	Brad Rowland	Louise Peacock	....	Dennis Brown	Irene Hudson	Mike Middleton
Karnes (Karnes City) (12)	210 780-3732	Robert H Thonhoff	....	Elizabeth Swize	Clem R Cannon	....	Terry Schmidt
Kaufman (Kaufman) (52)	214 932-4331	....	....	....	....	....	....
Kendall (Boerne) (15)	210 249-9343	James Gooden	....	Darlene Herrin	Barbara J Schwope	....	Lee D' Spain Jr
Kenedy (Sarita) (..)	512 294-5224	....	....	....	....	....	....
Kent (Jayton) (1)	806 237-3373	Tommy Stanaland	....	Cornelia Cheyne	Linda McCurry	....	Larry Rider
Kerr (Kerrville) (36)	210 257-7972	William G Stacy	....	Patricia Dye	Barbara Nemec	Barbara Nemec	Frances A Kaiser
Kimble (Junction) (4)	915 446-2724	....	....	....	....	....	....
King (Guthrie) (..)	806 596-4411	....	....	....	....	....	....
Kinney (Brackettville) (3)	512 563-2521	....	....	....	....	....	....
Kleberg (Kingsville) (30)	512 592-2411	....	....	....	....	....	....
Knox (Benjamin) (5)	817 454-2191	....	....	....	....	....	....
La Salle (Cotulla) (5)	512 879-3033	....	....	....	....	....	....
Lamar (Paris) (44)	903 737-2417	....	....	....	....	....	....
Lamb (Littlefield) (15)	806 385-4222	....	....	....	....	....	....
Lampasas (Lampasas) (14)	512 556-8271	Norris Monroe	....	Connie Hartmann	....	....	Gordon Morris
Lavaca (Hallettsville) (19)	512 798-2301	Charles J Rother	....	Henry J Sitka	Dolores T Kyle	....	Robert E Wurm
Lee (Giddings) (13)	713 542-3178	....	....	....	....	....	....
Leon (Centerville) (13)	214 536-2352	....	....	....	....	....	....
Liberty (Liberty) (53)	409 336-8071	....	....	....	....	....	....
Limestone (Groesbeck) (21)	817 729-3810	....	....	....	....	....	....
Lipscomb (Lipscomb) (3)	806 862-4131	Willis V Smith	....	Coeta Sperry	Pat Wyatt	....	Calvin Babitzke
Live Oak (George West) (10)	512 449-2733	....	....	....	....	....	....
Llano (Llano) (12)	915 247-5054	....	....	....	....	....	....
Loving (Mentone) (..)	915 377-2511	Donald C Creager	Clay Patrick	Juanita E Busby	Jaime A Jones	....	Richard N Putnam
Lubbock (Lubbock) (223)	806 767-1004	....	....	....	....	....	....
Lynn (Tahoka) (7)	806 998-4222	J F Brandon	....	Ima Robinson	Janet Porterfield	....	Dennis Diggs
Madison (Madisonville) (11)	409 348-2670	James R Fite	Mary A Turner	Joyce M Coleman	Judy G Weathers	....	Travis E Neeley
Marion (Jefferson) (10)	214 665-3971	....	....	....	....	....	....
Martin (Stanton) (5)	915 756-3631	....	....	....	....	....	....
Mason (Mason) (3)	915 347-5556	Fritz E Landers	....	Bea Langehennig	Jane Hoerster	....	Don Grote
Matagorda (Bay City) (37)	409 244-7611	....	....	....	....	....	....
Maverick (Eagle Pass) (36)	210 773-3824	....	Guillermo Mancha	Linda G Sumpter	Carlos A Pereda	Manuel Reyes Jr	Salvador Rios
Mc Culloch (Brady) (9)	915 597-0733	Randy Young	....	Rose M Luttrell	Norma G Holloway	....	Dwain Hensley
Mc Lennan (Waco) (189)	857 757-5000	....	....	....	....	....	....
Mc Mullen (Tilden) (1)	512 274-3215	....	....	....	....	....	....
Medina (Hondo) (27)	512 426-5381	....	....	....	....	....	....
Menard (Menard) (2)	915 396-4682	....	....	....	....	....	....
Midland (Midland) (107)	915 688-1000	....	....	....	....	....	....
Milam (Cameron) (23)	817 697-2932	Roger Hashem	....	....	M Michalka	....	Leroy Broadus
Mills (Goldthwaite) (5)	915 648-2222	....	....	....	....	....	....
Mitchell (Colorado City) (8)	915 728-8439	....	....	....	....	....	....
Montague (Montague) (17)	817 894-2401	Jack Winn	....	Gayle Edwards	James M Johnson	....	Kevin Benton
Montgomery (Conroe) (182)	409 756-0571	Alan B Sadler	....	Roy Harris	Martha Gustavsen	Diane J Bass	Guy L Williams
Moore (Dumas) (18)	806 935-5588	....	....	....	....	....	....
Morris (Daingerfield) (13)	214 645-3691	Vandy Boozer	....	....	....	....	Ricky Blackburn
Motley (Matador) (2)	806 347-2334	Laverna M Price	....	Lucretia Campbell	Joe E Campbell	....	Jim Meador
Nacogdoches (Nacogdoches) (55)	409 560-7755	....	....	....	....	....	....
Navarro (Corsicana) (40)	903 654-3090	....	....	....	....	....	....
Newton (Newton) (14)	409 379-5691	....	....	....	....	....	....
Nolan (Sweetwater) (17)	915 235-2263	....	....	....	....	....	....
Nueces (Corpus Christi) (291)	512 888-0111	Robert N Barnes	....	....	Margaret L Hayes	Sandra Clarkson	James P Luby
Ochiltree (Perryton) (9)	806 435-8075	....	....	....	....	....	....
Oldham (Vega) (2)	806 267-2607	....	....	....	....	....	....
Orange (Orange) (81)	409 883-7740	John C McDonald	....	Molly Theriot	W Tod Mixson	J L Masciarelli	Huel R Fontenot
Palo Pinto (Palo Pinto) (25)	817 659-1253	....	....	....	....	....	....
Panola (Carthage) (22)	214 693-0391	....	....	....	....	....	....
Parker (Weatherford) (65)	817 599-6591	....	....	....	....	....	....
Parmer (Farwell) (10)	806 481-3383	....	....	....	....	....	....
Pecos (Fort Stockton) (15)	915 336-7264	Fredie Capers	Charlotte Carey	....	B McCallister	B McCallister	Bruce Wilson
Polk (Livingston) (31)	409 327-6813	John Thompson	....	Jo Anne Hopkins	Karen Remmert	Betty Rundell	Billy Ray Nelson
Potter (Amarillo) (98)	806 379-2200	Arthur H Ware	....	Sue S Daniel	L Youngblood	L Youngblood	Jimmy D Boydston
Presidio (Marfa) (7)	915 729-4452	....	....	....	....	....	....
Rains (Emory) (7)	214 473-2461	....	....	....	....	....	....
Randall (Canyon) (90)	806 655-6255	C W McMenamy	....	Leroy Hutton	Joella McPherson	Geneva Bagwell	Harold Hooks
Reagan (Big Lake) (5)	915 884-2665	Mike Elkins	....	Hazel S Carr	Jane H Gay	....	Efrain Gonzales

Directory 1/10 OFFICIALS IN U.S. COUNTIES
continued

County, county seat, 1990 population figures (000 omitted)	County telephone number	Chief elected official	Appointed administrator	Clerk to the governing board	Chief financial officer	Personnel director	Chief law enforcement official
TEXAS (254) continued							
Real (Leakey) (2)	512 232-5304	G W Twilligear	....	Rosemary Brice	Kathy Brooks	Kathy Brooks	James Brice
Red River (Clarksville) (14)	214 427-2680	L D Williamson	....	Mary Hausler	Shirley Anderson	....	Bob Storey
Reeves (Pecos) (16)	915 445-5418	....	....	....	....	....	....
Refugio (Refugio) (8)	512 526-2245	....	....	....	....	....	....
Roberts (Miami) (1)	806 868-3721	Vernon H Cook	....	Jackie Jackson	Sarah Gill	....	Bill Britton
Robertson (Franklin) (16)	409 828-3542	....	....	....	....	....	....
Rockwall (Rockwall) (26)	214 771-5152	....	....	....	....	....	....
Runnels (Ballinger) (11)	915 365-2221	M Murchison	D Smith	L Bruchmiller	M Smith	....	W Baird
Rusk (Henderson) (44)	214 657-5584	....	....	....	....	....	....
Sabine (Hemphill) (10)	409 787-3543	....	....	....	....	....	....
San Augustine (San Augustine) (8)	409 275-2762	....	....	....	....	....	....
San Jacinto (Coldspring) (16)	409 653-2353	Joe L McMurrey	Joe Cronin	Joyce Hogue	Charlene Everitt	Charlene Everitt	James L Rogers
San Patricio (Sinton) (59)	512 364-6120	Josephine Miller	....	Dottie Maley	David W Wendel	Norma J Gonzales	Leroy Moody
San Saba (San Saba) (5)	915 372-3635	....	....	....	....	....	....
Schleicher (Eldorado) (3)	915 853-2593	Johnny Griffin	....	Helen Blakeway	Karen Henderson	....	Richard Harris
Scurry (Snyder) (19)	915 573-8576	....	....	....	....	....	....
Shackelford (Albany) (3)	915 762-2232	....	....	....	....	....	....
Shelby (Center) (22)	409 598-3863	Floyd A Watson	....	Peaches Conway	Wanda Smith	Wanda Smith	Carl Shofner
Sherman (Stratford) (3)	806 396-5551	....	....	....	....	....	....
Smith (Tyler) (151)	903 535-0500	....	....	....	....	....	....
Somervell (Glen Rose) (5)	817 897-2322	....	....	....	....	....	....
Starr (Rio Grande City) (41)	210 487-2307	Jose M Martinez	....	Omar J Garza	Joaquin Gutierrez	Elisa Y Barrera	Eugenio Falcon Jr
Stephens (Breckenridge) (9)	817 559-3700	....	....	....	....	....	....
Sterling (Sterling City) (1)	915 378-5191	....	....	....	....	....	....
Stonewall (Aspermont) (2)	817 989-3393	....	....	....	....	....	....
Sutton (Sonora) (4)	915 387-2711	Carla Garner	....	Bobbie Smith	Carla Garner	....	W W Webster
Swisher (Tulia) (8)	806 995-3294	....	....	....	....	....	....
Tarrant (Fort Worth) (1170)	817 884-1188	Tom Vandergriff	G K Manius	....	....	Gerald Wright	David Williams
Taylor (Abilene) (120)	915 674-1235	Lee Hamilton	....	Janice Lyons	Bridget McDowell	Larry G Bevill	Jack Dieken
Terrell (Sanderson) (1)	915 345-2391	....	....	....	....	....	....
Terry (Brownfield) (13)	806 637-6421	Douglas Ryburn	....	Ann Willis	Alan Bayer	....	Jerry Johnson
Throckmorton (Throckmorton) (2)	817 849-3081	....	....	....	....	....	....
Titus (Mount Pleasant) (24)	214 572-8891	....	....	....	....	....	....
Tom Green (San Angelo) (98)	915 659-6507	William R Moore	....	Judith K Hawkins	Rebecca Papazian	....	U E Pete Skains
Travis (Austin) (576)	512 473-9555	....	....	....	....	....	....
Trinity (Groveton) (11)	409 642-1443	....	....	....	....	....	....
Tyler (Woodville) (17)	409 283-2141	Jerome Owens	....	Donece Gregory	Joyce Moore	Tina Bump	Gary Hennigan
Upshur (Gilmer) (31)	903 843-3083	....	....	....	....	....	....
Upton (Rankin) (4)	915 693-2321	....	....	....	....	....	....
Uvalde (Uvalde) (23)	512 278-3216	....	....	....	....	....	....
Val Verde (Del Rio) (39)	512 774-7500	....	....	....	....	....	....
Van Zandt (Canton) (38)	214 567-2551	....	....	....	....	....	....
Victoria (Victoria) (74)	512 575-4558	....	....	....	....	....	....
Walker (Huntsville) (51)	409 291-9500	Frank Robinson	....	James Patton	Dan Clower	Lois Brown	Dale Myers
Waller (Hempstead) (23)	713 826-3357	....	....	....	....	....	....
Ward (Monahans) (13)	915 943-3209	Sam G Massey	....	Pat V Finley	Barbra Walsh	....	Ben A Keele
Washington (Brenham) (26)	409 836-9374	....	....	....	....	....	....
Webb (Laredo) (133)	210 721-2500	Mercurio Martinez	....	Henry Flores	Mercurio Martinez	....	Juan Garza
Wharton (Wharton) (40)	409 532-4612	....	....	....	....	....	....
Wheeler (Wheeler) (6)	806 826-5544	....	....	....	....	....	....
Wichita (Wichita Falls) (122)	817 766-8100	Nick Gipson	....	Theresa Mawson	Marsha Watson	James Burgess	Tom Callahan
Wilbarger (Vernon) (15)	817 552-5486	....	....	....	....	....	....
Willacy (Raymondville) (18)	512 689-2710	....	....	....	....	....	....
Williamson (Georgetown) (140)	512 863-3585	....	....	....	....	....	....
Wilson (Floresville) (23)	512 393-7303	....	....	....	....	....	....
Winkler (Kermit) (9)	915 586-2526	Frances Clark	....	Sonja Fullen	Dawn McLennan	Dawn McLennan	Robert L Roberts
Wise (Decatur) (35)	817 627-3540	....	....	....	....	....	....
Wood (Quitman) (29)	903 763-4186	Lee Williams	Barbara L Statser	Brenda C Taylor	D June Robinson	....	Charles F White
Yoakum (Plains) (9)	806 456-2721	....	....	....	....	....	....
Young (Graham) (18)	817 549-2030	....	....	....	....	....	....
Zapata (Zapata) (9)	210 765-9920	David Morales	....	Arnoldo Flores	Alejandro Ramirez	Sylvia Mendoza	S Gonzalez
Zavala (Crystal City) (12)	210 374-2442	Pablo Avila	....	Teresa P Flores	....	Susie Perez	Jose Serna
UTAH (29)							
Beaver (Beaver) (5)	801 438-2352	....	....	....	....	....	....
Box Elder (Brigham City) (36)	801 734-2031	....	....	....	....	....	....
Cache (Logan) (70)	801 752-5935	....	M Lynn Lemon	Stephen Erickson	Tamra Stones	M Lynn Lemon	Sidney P Groll
Carbon (Price) (20)	801 637-4700	....	....	....	....	....	....
Daggett (Manila) (1)	801 784-3154	Elbert Steinaker	....	Gene Briggs	....	....	Gaylen Jarvie
Davis (Farmington) (188)	801 451-3415	Gayle Stevenson	....	Margene Isom	....	G Steven Baker	Glenn T Clary
Duchesne (Duchesne) (13)	801 738-2435	....	....	....	....	....	....
Emery (Castle Dale) (10)	801 381-2119	....	....	....	....	....	....
Garfield (Panguitch) (4)	801 676-8826	Thomas V Hatch	....	Hazel W Rich	....	....	Than Cooper
Grand (Moab) (7)	801 259-1321	Paul Menard	Earl Sires	Fran Townsend	Fran Townsend	Peggy Taylor	Jim Nyland
Iron (Parowan) (21)	801 477-3375	Robert L Gardner	....	David I Yardley	Merna H Mitchell	Dennis A Lowder	Ira M Schoppmann
Juab (Nephi) (6)	801 623-0271	Joseph A Bernini	....	Pat P Greenwood	Joyce C Pay	....	David L Carter
Kane (Kanab) (5)	801 644-2551	Glen Martin	....	Karla Johnson	Karla Johnson	Karla Johnson	Maxwell Jackson
Millard (Fillmore) (11)	801 743-6223	....	....	....	....	....	....
Morgan (Morgan) (6)	801 829-6811	Joan M Patterson	....	Penny P Taylor	Gloria B Anderson	Marsha A Martin	Bert C Holbrook
Piute (Junction) (1)	801 577-2840	....	....	....	....	....	....
Rich (Randolph) (2)	801 793-2415	Blair R Francis	....	Pamela Shaul	....	....	Farren R Floyd
Salt Lake (Salt Lake City) (726)	801 468-3000	....	....	....	....	....	....
San Juan (Monticello) (13)	801 587-3223	....	....	....	....	....	....
Sanpete (Manti) (16)	801 835-2131	....	....	....	....	....	....
Sevier (Richfield) (15)	801 896-9262	Merlin Ashman	....	Steven C Wall	Steven C Wall	....	John L Meacham
Summit (Coalville) (16)	801 336-4451	Ron Perry	....	Kent H Jones	Blake L Frazier	....	D Fred Eley Jr
Tooele (Tooele) (27)	801 882-9157	Leland J Hogan	....	Dennis Ewing	Glenn Caldwell	Pamela Loth	Donald Proctor
Uintah (Vernal) (22)	801 781-0770	....	....	....	....	....	....
Utah (Provo) (264)	801 370-8000	Malcolm H Beck	....	J Bruce Peacock	Leonard Ellis	Mikeil Callahan	David Bateman
Wasatch (Heber City) (10)	801 654-3211	T Laren Provost	Sherry L Bond	Sherry L Bond	Jeff Bradshaw	Sherry L Bond	Mike Spanos
Washington (St. George) (49)	801 634-5700	Gayle M Aldred	....	Calvin R Robison	Alis M Ritz	Alis M Ritz	G Humphries
Wayne (Loa) (2)	801 836-2731	....	....	....	....	....	....

Directory 1/10 OFFICIALS IN U.S. COUNTIES
continued

County, county seat, 1990 population figures (000 omitted)	County telephone number	Chief elected official	Appointed administrator	Clerk to the governing board	Chief financial officer	Personnel director	Chief law enforcement official
UTAH (29) continued							
Weber (Ogden) (158)	301 399-8401	Joan Hellstrom	....	Greg Haws	Greg Haws	....	Craig Dearden
VERMONT (14)							
Addison (Middlebury) (33)	802 388-7741	....	....	....	....	....	....
Bennington (Bennington) (36)	802 442-8528	....	....	....	....	....	....
Caledonia (St. Johnsbury) (28)	802 748-6600	Eugene D Lowrey	....	....	Edward Senecal	....	....
Chittenden (Burlington) (132)	802 863-3467	....	....	....	....	....	....
Essex (Guildhall) (6)	802 254-6857	....	....	....	....	....	....
Franklin (St. Albans) (40)	802 524-3863	....	Roger N Luneau	Roger N Luneau	....	....	Dale Messier
Grand Isle (North Hero) (5)	802 372-8350	Herman C Brown	Sherri Potvin	Sherry L Little	....	....	....
Lamoille (Hyde Park) (20)	802 888-2207	....	....	....	....	....	Gardner G Manosh
Orange (Chelsea) (26)	802 685-4610	Patricia Davis	....	Mary Kennedy	....	....	Samuel Frank
Orleans (Newport) (24)	802 334-2711	....	....	....	....	....	....
Rutland (Rutland) (62)	802 775-4394	....	....	....	....	....	....
Washington (Montpelier) (55)	802 223-7066	....	....	....	....	....	....
Windham (Newfane) (42)	802 254-4994	....	....	....	....	....	....
Windsor (Woodstock) (54)	802 457-2121	....	....	....	....	....	....
VIRGINIA (135)							
Accomack (Accomac) (32)	804 787-4289	....	....	....	....	....	....
Albemarle (Charlottesville) (68)	804 296-5827	Walter F Perkins	Robert W Tucker	Ella W Carey	Melvin A Breeden	R B Brandenburger	John F Miller
Alexandria (Alexandria) i (111)	703 838-4699	....	....	....	....	....	....
Alleghany (Covington) (13)	703 965-1600	L J Rose Jr	Eston Burge	Melissa Meadows	Susan Myers	Eston Burge	T D Warlitner
Amelia (Amelia Court House) (9)	804 561-3039	Edward T Hurley	John R Wallace	John R Wallace	John R Wallace	John R Wallace	Jimmy E Weaver
Amherst (Amherst) (29)	804 946-9400	Roy C Wood	Stewart E Shaner	Stewart E Shaner	Donald T Wood	Stewart E Shaner	Michael E Cox
Appomattox (Appomattox) (12)	804 352-2637	Dennis W Torrence	Aileen T Ferguson	Aileen T Ferguson	....	....	J E Richardson
Arlington (Arlington) (171)	703 358-3000	Mary M Whipple	Anton S Gardner	Sabra L Jones	Mark B Jinks	Alan Christenson	William K Stover
Augusta (Verona) (55)	703 245-5600	J Donald Hinger	Patrick Coffield	Patrick Coffield	Joseph W Davis	....	Glenn P Lloyd
Bath (Warm Springs) (5)	703 839-7221	Richard B Byrd	Claire A Collins	Claire A Collins	Claire A Collins	Claire A Collins	James W Bryan
Bedford (Bedford) (46)	703 586-7601	....	William C Rolfe	William C Rolfe	Kathleen D Guzi	Kathleen D Guzi	Carl H Wells
Bedford (Bedford) i (6)	703 586-7102	....	....	....	....	....	....
Bland (Bland) (7)	703 688-4622	William R Ramsey	Gary L Cutlip	Gary L Cutlip	Karen W Harman	Gary L Cutlip	Melvin M Cox
Botetourt (Fincastle) (25)	703 473-8220	Robert E Layman	Gerald A Burgess	Gerald A Burgess	C Benton Bolton	....	B Reed Kelly
Bristol i (18)	703 466-5252	....	Paul D Spangler	Daniel L Johnson	Daniel L Johnson	Marilyn F Carmody	Eddie Barnes
Brunswick (Lawrenceville) (16)	804 848-3107	....	....	....	....	....	....
Buchanan (Grundy) (31)	703 935-2745	....	....	....	....	....	....
Buckingham (Buckingham) (13)	804 969-4242	....	....	....	....	....	....
Buena Vista (Buena Vista) i (6)	703 261-6121	....	....	....	....	....	....
Campbell (Rustburg) (48)	804 332-5161	Eddie Gunter Jr	E F Talbert Jr	E F Talbert Jr	Barbara T Farmer	....	Robert E Maxey Jr
Caroline (Bowling Green) (19)	804 633-5380	Calvin Taylor	Thomas Foley	....	....	....	Homer Johnson
Carroll (Hillsville) (27)	703 728-3331	....	....	....	....	....	....
Charles City (Charles City) (6)	804 829-2401	....	....	....	....	....	....
Charlotte (Charlotte Crt House) (12)	804 542-5117	....	....	....	....	....	....
Charlottesville (Charlottesville) i (40)	804 971-3490	David Toscano	Don C Hendrix	Jeanne O Cox	Rita K Scott	Bruce Keith	J W Rittenhouse
Chesapeake (Chesapeake) i (152)	804 547-6166	....	....	....	....	....	....
Chesterfield (Chesterfield) (209)	804 748-1211	Whaley Colbert	Lane B Ramsey	Theresa M Pitts	J L Stegmaier	Frederick Willis	Joseph E Pittman
Clarke (Berryville) (12)	703 955-5100	John D Hardesty	David L Ash	....	Thomas J Judge	....	Dale Gardner
Clifton Forge (Clifton Forge) i (5)	703 863-2500	James D Morris	....	T G Ailstock	....	Retha Scialoia	Russell Smith
Colonial Heights (Colonial Heights) i (16)	804 520-9265	James B McNeer	Robert E Taylor	Rita C Schiff	William E Johnson	Robert E Taylor	Steven Sheffield
Covington (Covington) i (7)	703 965-6300	....	....	....	....	....	....
Craig (New Castle) (4)	703 864-5010	Zane M Jones	Richard C Flora	Richard C Flora	Richard C Flora	....	Billy McPherson
Culpeper (Culpeper) (28)	703 825-3035	....	....	....	....	....	....
Cumberland (Cumberland) (8)	804 492-3625	Robert L Rigsby	Judy O Whaley	Judy O Whaley	....	....	Claude B Meinhard
Danville (Danville) i (53)	804 799-5240	....	Ray Griffin Jr	....	Aubrey Dodson	Lundy Shackelford	Neal Morris
Dickenson (Clintwood) (18)	703 926-1676	Damon Rasnick	Vickie Garrett	Vicki Garrett	Gary Artrip	Betty R Hill	F Childress
Dinwiddie (Dinwiddie) (21)	804 469-4500	Leenora Everett	Charles W Burgess	Charles W Burgess	Glenice Townsend	Charles W Burgess	Bennie M Heath
Emporia (Emporia) i (5)	804 634-3332	....	....	....	....	....	....
Essex (Tappahannock) (9)	804 443-4331	Robert S Handly	R Gary Allen	R Gary Allen	Frances W Ellis	....	Damon E Davis
Fairfax (Fairfax) (819)	703 324-3346	T M Davis	M J Leidinger	Nancy J Vehrs	Susan S Planchon	Peter J Schroth	Michael Young
Fairfax (Fairfax) i (20)	703 385-7855	John Mason	Robert Sisson	Jackie Henderson	Edward Cawley	David Sudduth	John Skinner
Falls Church (Falls Church) i (10)	703 241-5001	....	....	....	....	....	....
Fauquier (Warrenton) (49)	703 347-8699	James Brumfield	G Robert Lee	D Gouldthorpe	Dennis Hunsberger	Deborah Johnson	Joe Higgs
Floyd (Floyd) (12)	703 745-9300	Jerry Boothe	Randal Arno	Randal Arno	Randal Arno	Terri Morris	Charles Higgins
Fluvanna (Palmyra) (12)	804 589-3138	....	....	....	....	....	....
Franklin (Rocky Mount) (40)	703 483-3030	Lois H English	Macon C Sammons	Sharon K Tudor	Elaine H Chitwood	Macon C Sammons	W Q Overton
Franklin (Franklin) i (8)	804 562-8508	C Franklin Jester	John J Jackson	John J Jackson	John J Jackson	Baucom Hinson	Robert K Eubanks
Frederick (Winchester) (46)	703 665-5666	Richard G Dick	John R Riley Jr	John R Riley Jr	Cheryl B Shiffler	Ann K Kelican	Bob Williamson
Fredericksburg (Fredericksburg) i (19)	703 372-1028	....	....	Deborah Ratliffe	Clarence Robinson	Melissa B Webb	James W Powers
Galax (Galax) i (7)	703 236-3441	....	....	....	....	....	....
Giles (Pearisburg) (16)	703 921-2525	L J Williams	J E Tuckwiller	D R Altizer	....	....	L W Falls
Gloucester (Gloucester) (30)	804 693-4042	Burton M Bland	William H Whitley	William H Whitley	R Edward Brown Jr	William H Whitley	Robin P Stanaway
Goochland (Goochland) (14)	804 556-5300	Andrew W Pryor	Gregory K Wolfrey	Cynthia Clements	Geraldine Parrish	....	James Agnew
Grayson (Independence) (16)	703 773-2471	Raymond L Carico	Donald G Young	Donald G Young	....	....	Herbert McKnight
Greene (Stanardsville) (10)	804 985-5201	Joanne Burkholder	Julius Morris	Julius Morris	Mary Garth	Julius Morris	William Morris
Greensville (Emporia) (9)	804 348-4205	Peggy R Wiley	David Whittington	David Whittington	....	....	Earl Sasser
Halifax (Halifax) (29)	804 476-3300	Joe C Satterfield	William D Sleeper	....	Linda S Foster	....	Eugene G Shortt
Hampton (Hampton) i (134)	804 727-6407	....	....	....	....	....	....
Hanover (Hanover) (63)	804 730-6000	William Bolling	John F Berry	....	Joseph Casey	Nan S Eddleton	V Stuart Cook
Harrisonburg (Harrisonburg) i (31)	703 434-6776	....	....	....	....	....	....
Henrico (Richmond) (218)	804 672-4000	James B Donati	Virgil R Hazelett	Martha A Joiner	Dennis W Kerns	George H Cauble	Richard G Engels
Henry (Collinsville) (57)	703 634-4601	Sandra Hodges	Robert P Lawler	Robert P Lawler	Jimmie L Wright	Veronica Venable	Frank Cassell
Highland (Monterey) (3)	703 468-2447	....	....	....	....	....	....
Hopewell (Hopewell) i (23)	804 541-2245	....	....	....	....	....	....
Isle Of Wight (Isle Of Wight) (25)	804 357-3191	O A Spady	Myles E Standish	Myles E Standish	M C Ledford	Donald Robertson	C W Phelps
James City (Williamsburg) (35)	804 253-6600	Perry Depue	David B Norman	....	John E McDonald	Carol M Luckam	Robert C Key
King And Queen (King & Queen Ct. Hse.) (6)	804 785-7955	....	....	....	....	....	....
King George (King George) (14)	703 775-9181	Michael Geraghty	L Eldon James Jr	L Eldon James Jr	Lisa M Baxter	....	C W Dobson
King William (King William) (11)	804 769-3011	James E Mickens	David S Whitlow	David S Whitlow	Terri E Hale	David S Whitlow	W Wayne Healy
Lancaster (Lancaster) (11)	804 462-5129	Charles A Kenner	William H Pennell	William H Pennell	William H Pennell	William H Pennell	Ronald D Crockett
Lee (Jonesville) (24)	703 346-7714	....	....	....	....	....	....
Lexington (Lexington) i (7)	703 463-7133	....	....	....	....	....	....

Directory 1/10 OFFICIALS IN U.S. COUNTIES
continued

County, county seat, 1990 population figures (000 omitted)	County telephone number	Chief elected official	Appointed administrator	Clerk to the governing board	Chief financial officer	Personnel director	Chief law enforcement official
VIRGINIA (135) continued							
Loudoun (Leesburg) (86)	703 777-0563	George Barton	Kirby M Bowers	Patsye L Matthews	M E Poole Jr	Julie Withrow	John Isom
Louisa (Louisa) (20)	703 967-0401	....	....	....	....	....	....
Lunenburg (Lunenburg) (11)	804 696-2142	....	....	....	....	....	....
Lynchburg (Lynchburg) i (66)	804 847-1315	....	....	....	....	....	....
Madison (Madison) (12)	703 948-6102	....	....	....	....	....	....
Manassas (Manassas) i (28)	703 257-8200	....	....	....	....	....	....
Manassas Park (Manassas Park) i (7)	703 361-0124	....	....	....	....	....	....
Martinsville (Martinsville) i (16)	703 638-3971	....	....	....	....	....	....
Mathews (Mathews) (8)	804 725-7172	Dorothy D Foster	Frank A Pleva	Frank A Pleva	Judy Burroughs	Frank A Pleva	K H Jordan Jr
Mecklenburg (Boydton) (29)	804 738-6191	....	....			....	....
Middlesex (Saluda) (9)	804 758-4330	....	....			....	....
Montgomery (Christiansburg) (74) ..	703 382-6954	Larry J Linkous	Betty S Thomas	....	J J Lunsford	E Randall Wertz	Kennard L Phipps
Nelson (Lovingston) (13)	804 263-4873	John W Ponton	M Douglas Powell	M Douglas Powell	J Marvin Davis	....	Ronald R Wood
New Kent (New Kent) (10)	804 966-9861	....	....	....	....	....	....
Newport News (Newport News) i (175)	804 247-8444	....	Edgar E Maroney	....	Kamal C Doshi	Caroline D Hurt	....
Norfolk i (261)	804 441-5185	Paul D Fraim	James B Oliver Jr	Robert Daughtrey	Sterling Cheatham	Robert Robinette	Robert J McCabe
Northampton (Eastville) (13)	804 678-0440	Thomas H Dixon	Thomas E Harris	Thomas E Harris	E B Savage	Thomas E Harris	W Wayne Bradford
Northumberland (Heathsville) (11) ..	804 580-7666	....	....	....	....	....	....
Norton (Norton) i (4)	703 679-1160	....	....	....	....	....	....
Nottoway (Nottoway) (15)	804 645-8696	James D Coleburn	Ronald E Roark	Ronald E Roark	Barbara L Senger	Ronald E Roark	Larry J Parrish
Orange (Orange) (21)	703 672-3313	R Duff Green	Brenda G Bailey	....	Phyllis M Yancey	Janice Crockett	W D Spence
Page (Luray) (22)	703 743-4142	T Leon Rickard	Ron Wilson	Ron Wilson	Gerald Judd	Geraldine Cubbage	Edward Sedwick
Patrick (Stuart) (17)	703 694-6094	D Philip Plaster	David R Hoback	David R Hoback	N Louise Harris	....	Jay E Gregory
Petersburg i (38)	804 733-2324	Rosalyn R Dance	Valerie A Lemmie	Barbara W Moore	Thomas R Blount	M Angela White	Willie R Williams
Pittsylvania (Chatham) (56)	804 432-2041	James B Williams	George E Supensky	George E Supensky	Glenn A Brown	....	G Harold Plaster
Poquoson (Poquoson) i (11)	804 868-3510	L C Burcher	Robert M Murphy	Judy F Wiggins	Carol O Davis	....	John T White
Portsmouth (Portsmouth) i (104) ...	804 393-8874	....	V Wayne Orton	Shiela P Pittman	....	C A Fletcher	Dennis A Mook
Powhatan (Powhatan) (15)	804 598-5600	....	....	....	....	....	....
Prince Edward (Farmville) (17)	804 392-8837	Hugh E Carwile Jr	Mildred B Hampton	Mildred B Hampton	Mable Shanaberger	....	Gene A Southall
Prince George (Prince George) (27)	804 733-2600	Marion B Williams	John G Kines Jr	John G Kines Jr	Jean N Barker	John G Kines Jr	Perry A Lewis
Prince William (Woodbridge) (216) .	703 792-6636	Kathryn Seefeldt	James Mullen	James Agbayani	John Wenderski	Cleil Fitzwater	Charlie Deane
Pulaski (Pulaski) (34)	703 980-7705	Jerry White	Joseph N Morgan	....	Rose Marie Tickle	Nancy M Burchett	Ralph Dobbins
Radford (Radford) i (16)	703 731-3603	....	....	....	....	....	John H Woodward
Rappahannock (Washington) (7) ...	703 675-3342	Hubert S Gilkey	John W McCarthy	John W McCarthy	....	....	....
Richmond (Richmond) i (203)	804 780-5660	Leonidas B Young	Robert C Bobb	Edna Williams	Max Bohnstedt	Johnel Bracey	Marty M Tapscott
Richmond (Warsaw) (7)	804 333-3415	....	....	Mary Allen	Diane Hyatt	D Keith Cook	Gerald Holt
Roanoke (Roanoke) (79)	703 772-2018	Lee B Eddy	Elmer C Hodge	Don Austin	Don Austin	Don Austin	Robert Day
Rockbridge (Lexington) (18)	703 463-4361	Dasniel Snider	Don Austin	William O' Brien	Larry T Garber	William O' Brien	G Weatherholtz
Rockingham (Harrisonburg) (57) ...	703 564-3000	Charles W Ahrend	William O' Brien	James A Gillespie	Helen Baker	James A Gillespie	Trigg Fields
Russell (Lebanon) (29)	703 889-8000	Frank Horton	James A Gillespie				
Salem (Salem) i (24)	703 375-3060	....	....	....	....	....	....
Scott (Gate City) (23)	703 386-6521	....	....	....	....	....	....
Shenandoah (Woodstock) (32)	703 459-6165	William Pence	John Cutlip	John Cutlip	Vincent Poling	Janet Kilby	Marshall Robinson
Smyth (Marion) (32)	703 783-3298	M Jay Hubble	Kenneth C Noble	Kenneth C Noble	Ruth D Albert	Kenneth C Noble	John H Grubb Jr
South Boston (South Boston) i (7) .	804 575-4200	....	....	....	....	....	....
Southampton (Courtland) (18)	804 653-3015	A M Felts	R L Taylor	R L Taylor	D K Britt	R L Taylor	V W Francis Jr
Spotsylvania (Spotsylvania) (57) ...	703 582-7000	Emmitt Marshall	L Kimball Payne	....	Tammy D Petrie	Susan Reynolds	T C Waddy Jr
Stafford (Stafford) (61)	703 659-8603	Lyle R Smith	C M Williams Jr	C M Williams Jr	James M K Reid	Robert W Clark	Ralph M Williams
Staunton i (24)	703 332-3825	....	....	....	....	....	....
Suffolk (Suffolk) i (52)	804 934-3111	....	....	....	....	....	Harold D Brown
Surry (Surry) (6)	804 294-5271	Ray D Peace	Terry D Lewis	Terry D Lewis	....	....	E Stuart Kitchen
Sussex (Sussex) (10)	804 246-5511	Roslyn C Tyler	George N Walker	George N Walker	Onnie L Woodruff	George N Walker	D J Joe Johnson
Tazewell (Tazewell) (46)	703 988-7541	James L Jones	Richard Farthing	Richard Farthing	Norman Cook	Patricia Green	....
Virginia Beach (Virginia Beach) i (393)	804 427-4242	....	....	....	....	....	....
Warren (Front Royal) (26)	703 636-4600	....	....	....	....	....	....
Washington (Abingdon) (46)	703 676-6203	James T Osborne	Bruce E Bentley	Bruce E Bentley	Mark W Seamon	Cecile Rosenbaum	Joe D Mitchell
Waynesboro i (19)	703 942-6600	....	....	....	....	....	....
Westmoreland (Montross) (15)	804 493-0130	William O Sydnor	Norm Risavi	Norm Risavi	Vicki M Douglas	....	Charles W Jackson
Williamsburg (Williamsburg) i (12) .	804 220-6100	....	....	....	....	....	....
Winchester (Winchester) i (22)	703 667-1815	Gary Chrisman	Edwin Daley	Joan Spicer	Bill Ewing	Sharen Gromling	Allen Borley
Wise (Wise) (40)	703 328-2321	J Fred Tate	Scott H Davis	Annette Underwood	Shannon C Scott	....	William F Kelley
Wythe (Wytheville) (25)	703 223-6020	....	....	....	....	....	....
York (Yorktown) (42)	804 890-3690	....	....	....	....	....	....
WASHINGTON (39)							
Adams (Ritzville) (14)	509 659-0090	Dean Judd	....	Linda Reimer	....	....	Ron Snowden
Asotin (Asotin) (18)	509 243-4160	....	....	....	....	....	....
Benton (Prosser) (113)	509 786-5600	Sandi Strawn	Donna Noski	Jeri Lynn Cabbage	....	....	James Kennedy
Chelan (Wenatchee) (52)	509 663-1147	....	....	....	....	....	....
Clallam (Port Angeles) (56)	206 452-7831	Lawrence Gaydeski	Jim Rumpeltes	Karen Flores	....	Marge Upham Rood	W J Hawe
Clark (Vancouver) (238)	206 699-2000	....	....	....	....	....	....
Columbia (Dayton) (4)	509 382-4542	George Wood	....	....	....	....	James Latour
Cowlitz (Kelso) (82)	206 577-3065	Van Youngquist	....	Vickie Musgrove	Frank Bishop	Dick Anderson	Brian Pederson
Douglas (Waterville) (26)	509 745-8527	....	....	....	....	....	....
Ferry (Republic) (6)	509 775-5200	Gary Kohler	....	Shilah Moores	....	....	Richard Baldwin
Franklin (Pasco) (37)	509 545-3535	....	....	....	....	....	....
Garfield (Pomeroy) (2)	509 843-1391	....	....	....	....	....	....
Grant (Ephrata) (55)	509 754-2011	Helen Fancher	....	Peggy Grigg	Robert Mosher	....	William Wiester
Grays Harbor (Montesano) (64)	206 249-3731	....	....	....	....	....	....
Island (Coupeville) (60)	206 679-7300	Mike Shelton	....	Arthur Hyland	....	Connie Henwood	William Norton
Jefferson (Port Townsend) (20)	206 385-9100	Robert Hinton	David R Goldsmith	Lorna L Delaney	Ila Mikkelsen	....	Melvin Mefford
King (Seattle) (1507)	206 296-0100	....	....	....	....	....	....
Kitsap (Port Orchard) (190)	206 876-7053	Win Granlund	Deborah Broughton	Holly Anderson	Saron Shrader	Bert Furuta	Pat Jones
Kittitas (Ellensburg) (27)	509 962-7508	Don Sorenson	....	Anita Kazee	B Allenbaugh	....	Robert McBride
Klickitat (Goldendale) (17)	509 773-4612	....	....	....	....	....	....
Lewis (Chehalis) (59)	206 748-9121	....	....	....	....	....	....
Lincoln (Davenport) (9)	509 725-3031	Deral Boleneus	....	Shelly Johnston	Doris Hein	....	Dan Berry
Mason (Shelton) (38)	206 427-9670	Marv L Faughender	....	Rebecca S Rogers	....	....	Robert Shepherd
Okanogan (Okanogan) (33)	509 422-7100	Ed Thiele	Dan Powers	Brenda White	Pat Lovell	....	Jim Weed
Pacific (South Bend) (19)	206 875-9300	Pat Hamilton	Vyrle Hill	Kathy Noren	....	....	Jerry Benning
Pend Oreille (Newport) (9)	509 447-4119	Mike Hanson	....	Alice Mitchell	....	....	Doug Malby
Pierce (Tacoma) (586)	206 591-7477	Dennis Flannigan	....	Gerri G Rainwater	Patrick L Kenney	Robert H Weaver	John H Shields
San Juan (Friday Harbor) (10)	206 378-2898	....	....	....	....	....	....

Directory 1/10   **OFFICIALS IN U.S. COUNTIES**
continued

County, county seat, 1990 population figures (000 omitted)	County telephone number	Chief elected official	Appointed administrator	Clerk to the governing board	Chief financial officer	Personnel director	Chief law enforcement official
WASHINGTON (39) continued							
Skagit (Mount Vernon) (80)	206 336-9300	Harvey Wolden	Robert Taylor	Patti Owen	Mike Woodmansee	Shelley Holt	Gary Frazier
Skamania (Stevenson) (8)	509 427-9447	Dean Evans	....	Brenda Sorenson	....	....	Ray Blaisdell
Snohomish (Everett) (466)	206 388-3411	Robert J Drewel	Joan Earl	Kathryn Morton	Dan Clements	Bridget Clawson	James I Scharf
Spokane (Spokane) (361)	509 456-5750	Steven Hasson	Marhsall Farnell	Rosanne Montague	John D Ogden	Charles C Wright	Lawrence Erickson
Stevens (Colville) (31)	509 684-3751	Fran Bessermin	....	Polly Buckner	....	....	Richard Andres
Thurston (Olympia) (161)	206 754-3800	....	....	....	....	....	....
Wahkiakum (Cathlamet) (3)	206 795-3219	Leon J Almer	....	Mary J Baldwin	Paula Holloway	....	Eugene Strong
Walla Walla (Walla Walla) (48)	509 525-6161	....	....	....	....	....	....
Whatcom (Bellingham) (128)	206 676-6690	....	....	....	....	....	....
Whitman (Colfax) (39)	509 397-6200	James W Potts	....	Maribeth Becker	Richard Brown	Jean M Conger	Steve Tomson
Yakima (Yakima) (189)	509 575-4061	....	....	....	....	....	....
WEST VIRGINIA (55)							
Barbour (Philippi) (16)	304 457-2232	....	....	....	....	....	....
Berkeley (Martinsburg) (59)	304 264-1923	William Kisner	Daniel O' Donnell	John Small	....	....	Preston Gooden
Boone (Madison) (26)	304 369-3925	....	....	....	....	....	....
Braxton (Sutton) (13)	304 765-2833	....	....	....	....	....	....
Brooke (Wellsburg) (27)	304 737-3661	....	....	....	....	....	....
Cabell (Huntington) (97)	304 525-7754	....	....	....	....	....	....
Calhoun (Grantsville) (8)	304 354-6725	....	....	....	....	....	....
Clay (Clay) (10)	304 587-4259	Jerry C Bird	....	Judy R Moore	....	....	Clarence Douglas
Doddridge (West Union) (7)	304 873-2631	....	....	....	....	....	....
Fayette (Fayetteville) (48)	304 574-1200	....	....	....	....	....	....
Gilmer (Glenville) (8)	304 462-7641	....	....	....	....	....	....
Grant (Petersburg) (10)	304 257-4422	....	....	....	....	....	....
Greenbrier (Lewisburg) (35)	304 645-2373	....	....	....	....	....	....
Hampshire (Romney) (16)	304 822-5112	Stephen R Haines	....	Nancy C Feller	....	....	Philip E Nixon Sr
Hancock (New Cumberland) (35)	304 564-3311	David O Miller	Sharon L Ulbright	Eleanor Straight	Naomi Balt	Sharon L Ulbright	Warren L Watkins
Hardy (Moorefield) (11)	304 538-2929	....	....	....	....	....	....
Harrison (Clarksburg) (69)	304 624-8500	....	....	....	....	....	....
Jackson (Ripley) (26)	304 372-2011	Donald Stephens	Sandra Garrett	Jeff Waybright	....	....	Janette McVay
Jefferson (Charles Town) (36)	304 725-9761	R Gregory Lance	Leslie D Smith	John E Ott	....	....	Wm Senseney
Kanawha (Charleston) (208)	304 357-0101	Louis H Bloom	Stephen Zoeller	....	....	....	Arden Ashley
Lewis (Weston) (17)	304 269-8200	....	....	....	....	....	....
Lincoln (Hamlin) (21)	304 824-3336	....	....	....	....	....	....
Logan (Logan) (43)	304 752-2000	....	....	....	....	....	....
Marion (Fairmont) (57)	304 367-5400	....	....	....	....	....	....
Marshall (Moundsville) (37)	304 845-1220	Malcolm M Shimp	....	Norma G Sine	....	....	Robert L Lightner
Mason (Point Pleasant) (25)	304 675-1110	....	....	....	....	....	....
Mc Dowell (Welch) (35)	304 436-8344	....	....	....	....	....	....
Mercer (Princeton) (65)	304 487-8311	....	....	....	....	....	....
Mineral (Keyser) (27)	304 788-5921	Robert D Harman	Michael C Bland	Ruby L Staggs	Patrick L Nield	....	Patrick L Nield
Mingo (Williamson) (34)	304 235-1638	....	....	....	....	....	....
Monongalia (Morgantown) (76)	304 291-7257	Elizabeth Martin	Diane DeMedici	Thelma Gibson	Joseph Bartolo	....	Joseph Bartolo
Monroe (Union) (12)	304 772-3096	W C Sibold	....	Donnie Evans	....	....	Gerald Crosier
Morgan (Berkeley Springs) (12)	304 258-8547	Richard G Gay	William R Clark	Ralph N Shambaugh	Debra A Kesecker	....	Kermit M Ambrose
Nicholas (Summersville) (27)	304 872-3630	....	....	....	....	....	....
Ohio (Wheeling) (51)	304 234-3628	....	....	....	....	....	....
Pendleton (Franklin) (8)	304 358-7573	....	....	....	....	....	....
Pleasants (St. Marys) (8)	304 684-3542	Joseph Troisi	....	....	....	....	David Kelly
Pocahontas (Marlinton) (9)	304 799-4604	....	....	....	....	....	....
Preston (Kingwood) (29)	304 329-1805	....	....	....	....	....	....
Putnam (Winfield) (43)	304 586-9036	....	....	....	....	....	....
Raleigh (Beckley) (77)	304 255-9146	....	....	....	....	....	....
Randolph (Elkins) (28)	304 636-0543	....	....	....	....	....	....
Ritchie (Harrisville) (10)	304 643-2164	....	....	....	....	....	....
Roane (Spencer) (15)	304 927-2860	....	....	....	....	....	....
Summers (Hinton) (14)	304 466-4235	....	....	....	....	....	....
Taylor (Grafton) (15)	304 265-1401	....	....	....	....	....	....
Tucker (Parsons) (8)	304 478-2606	....	....	....	....	....	....
Tyler (Middlebourne) (10)	304 758-2102	Robert D Wable	....	Donna J Tomas	....	....	Michael K Griffin
Upshur (Buckhannon) (23)	304 472-0535	....	....	....	....	....	....
Wayne (Wayne) (42)	304 272-5101	....	....	....	....	....	....
Webster (Webster Springs) (11)	304 847-5780	Ernest F Ayers	....	....	....	....	....
Wetzel (New Martinsville) (19)	304 455-8224	Shirley Michael	....	Mary Riggenbach	N E Higginbotham	....	N E Higginbotham
Wirt (Elizabeth) (5)	304 275-4271	Paul Bumgarner	....	Barbara Cheuvront	Darrell Null	....	Darrell Null
Wood (Parkersburg) (87)	304 424-1984	Holmes R Shaver	Mary R Rader	Jamie Six	....	....	Kenneth Merritt
Wyoming (Pineville) (29)	304 732-8000	....	....	....	....	....	....
WISCONSIN (72)							
Adams (Friendship) (16)	608 339-4267	....	....	Beverly Ward	....	Michael McKenna	Robert Farber
Ashland (Ashland) (16)	715 682-7000	Michael Ellias	Thomas Kieweg	Elaine Stibbe	....	....	John Kovach
Barron (Barron) (41)	715 537-3212	....	....	....	....	....	....
Bayfield (Washburn) (14)	715 373-6100	....	....	....	....	....	....
Brown (Green Bay) (195)	414 448-4071	....	....	....	....	....	....
Buffalo (Alma) (14)	608 685-4940	....	....	....	....	....	....
Burnett (Siren) (13)	715 349-2181	....	....	....	....	....	....
Calumet (Chilton) (34)	414 849-2361	....	....	....	....	....	....
Chippewa (Chippewa Falls) (52)	715 723-1831	....	....	....	....	....	....
Clark (Neillsville) (32)	715 743-5148	....	....	....	....	....	....
Columbia (Portage) (45)	608 742-2191	Ed Riley	....	Cathy Lathrop	Lois Schepp	Jim Aiello	James Smith
Crawford (Prairie Du Chien) (16)	608 326-0200	Robert Dillman	....	Patricia Benish	....	....	William Fillbach
Dane (Madison) (367)	608 266-4114	....	....	....	....	....	....
Dodge (Juneau) (77)	414 386-3600	Charles Swain	....	Dorothy Ebert	Roger Gorst	....	S Fitzgerald
Door (Sturgeon Bay) (26)	414 743-5511	Lyle Hill	....	Nancy Bemmann	....	James Jetzke	Charles Brann
Douglas (Superior) (42)	715 394-0483	David Ohmke	....	Ray Sommerville	Larry Kroll	John Mulder	Marvin Arneson
Dunn (Menomonie) (36)	715 232-2429	Raymond Score	Patrick Thompson	Lorraine Hartung	....	Joann Olson	Robert Zebro
Eau Claire (Eau Claire) (85)	715 839-5106	Howard Ludwigson	Ronald T Wampler	Joanne Lester	Richard Roe	Marvin Niese	Richard Hewitt
Florence (Florence) (5)	715 528-3201	Vaughn Neuens	....	Robert Anderson	....	....	Jeffrey Rickaby
Fond Du Lac (Fond Du Lac) (90)	414 929-3000	G Stanchfield	....	Joyce Buechel	Dick Celichowski	Rich Brzozowski	Jim Gilmore
Forest (Crandon) (9)	715 478-2422	....	....	....	....	....	....
Grant (Lancaster) (49)	608 723-2675	....	....	....	....	....	....
Green (Monroe) (30)	608 328-9430	Robert M Hoesly	....	Michael J Doyle	Rhonda Hunter	....	Patrick J Conlin

Directory 1/10 OFFICIALS IN U.S. COUNTIES
continued

County, county seat, 1990 population figures (000 omitted)	County telephone number	Chief elected official	Appointed administrator	Clerk to the governing board	Chief financial officer	Personnel director	Chief law enforcement official
WISCONSIN (72) continued							
Green Lake (Green Lake) (19)	414 294-4005	Donald Bartol	....	Marge Bostelmann	Kathleen Morris	....	Lance Buchholtz
Iowa (Dodgeville) (20)	608 935-5445	Richard Scullion	....	David D Meudt	....	....	Thomas DeVoss
Iron (Hurley) (6)	715 561-3375	Louis P Leoni	....	George G Reed	....	....	Richard Ekmark
Jackson (Black River Falls) (17)	715 284-7441	....	....	....	....	....	....
Jefferson (Jefferson) (68)	414 674-7100	Wendell Wilson	Willard Hausen	Barbara Geyer	....	Willard Hausen	Orval Quamme
Juneau (Mauston) (22)	608 847-9300	Barrett James	....	Carl Wilke	Lori Chipman	Vi Ann C Cabezal	Richard McCurdy
Kenosha (Kenosha) (128)	414 653-6422	....	....	....	....	....	....
Kewaunee (Kewaunee) (19)	414 388-3580	....	....	....	....	....	....
La Crosse (La Crosse) (98)	608 785-9641	James A Ehrsam	Paul Webber	Sharon M Lemke	Gerald Seubert	Robert B Taunt	Karl W Halverson
Lafayette (Darlington) (16)	608 776-4850	....	....	....	....	....	....
Langlade (Antigo) (20)	715 627-6200	....	....	....	....	....	....
Lincoln (Merrill) (27)	715 536-0310	Robert Sumnicht	Roger Schmoldt	Marlene Fox	Jan Lemmer	Roger Schmoldt	Harvey Woodward
Manitowoc (Manitowoc) (80)	414 683-4060	....	B Peterson	Daniel Fischer	Todd Reckelberg	Sharon Cornils	Thomas Kocourek
Marathon (Wausau) (115)	715 847-5000	Gary Wyman	Mort McBain	Louann Fenhaus	Byron Karow	Brad Karger	Gerald Kittel
Marinette (Marinette) (41)	715 732-7400	William Setunsky	S M Fredericks	Don E Phillips	Roger DeGroot	S Fredericks	James Kanikula
Marquette (Montello) (12)	608 297-9114	....	....	....	....	....	....
Menominee (Keshena) (4)	715 799-3311	Chantel Otradovec	Ray Deperry	Kathryn White	....	....	Kenneth M Fish
Milwaukee (Milwaukee) (959)	414 278-4148	Robert Jackson Jr	....	Rod Lanser	Earl Hawkins	Gary J Dobbert	Richard Artison
Monroe (Sparta) (37)	608 269-8719	Wayne Selbrede	....	David Hering	Annette Erickson	Ken Kittleson	Dale Trowbridge
Oconto (Oconto) (30)	414 834-5322	....	....	....	....	....	....
Oneida (Rhinelander) (32)	715 369-6143	William Korrer	....	Bob Bruso	Margie Coffen	Carey Jackson	Charlie Crofoot
Outagamie (Appleton) (141)	414 832-5051	....	....	Harold Dobberpuhl	Karen Makoutz	Michael J Puksich	Michael Milas
Ozaukee (Port Washington) (73)	414 284-9411	Leroy Bley	....	....	....	....	John C Andrews
Pepin (Durand) (7)	715 672-8704	Bernard Milliren	....	....	....	....	James Hines
Pierce (Ellsworth) (33)	715 273-3531	Richard Wilhelm	....	David Sorenson	....	....	Craig Benware
Polk (Balsam Lake) (35)	715 485-3161	Gerald Handlos	....	Sharon Schiebel	....	Thomas Wishman	Ronald Borski
Portage (Stevens Point) (61)	715 346-1351	Clarence Hintz	....	....	Jerome Glad	Gerald Lang	Wayne Wirsing
Price (Phillips) (16)	715 339-3325	Douglas Moquin	....	Clarence Cvengros	Clarence Cvengros	....	....
Racine (Racine) (175)	414 636-3118	....	....	....	....	....	....
Richland (Richland Center) (18)	608 647-2197	....	....	....	....	....	....
Rock (Janesville) (140)	608 757-5520	Donald Upson	Craig Knutson	....	Jeffrey Smith	James Bryant	F Joseph Black
Rusk (Ladysmith) (15)	715 532-2100	....	....	....	....	....	....
Sauk (Baraboo) (47)	608 356-5581	Roger Shanks	J Thomas McCarty	Beverly Mielke	Dona Newman	Michael Wolfe	Virgil Steinhorst
Sawyer (Hayward) (14)	715 634-6463	....	....	....	....	....	....
Shawano (Shawano) (37)	715 526-9135	....	....	....	....	....	....
Sheboygan (Sheboygan) (104)	414 459-3000	Wm Jens	....	Patricia Meyer	Robert Danforth	Louella Conway	Wm Spelshaus
St. Croix (Hudson) (50)	715 386-4609	Robert Boche	John Krizek	Sue Nelson	Richard Loney	Debra Kathan	Ralph Bader
Taylor (Medford) (19)	715 748-1400	Edwin H Ahlers	....	Roger L Emmerich	Roger L Emmerich	Charles A Rude	William Breneman
Trempealeau (Whitehall) (25)	715 538-2311	John C Killian	....	Paul Syverson	....	....	R Weisenberger
Vernon (Viroqua) (26)	608 637-3569	Gerald Sandry	....	Roger Novy	S Vold Brudos	Nancy Murphy	Geoffrey Banta
Vilas (Eagle River) (18)	715 479-6469	....	....	....	....	....	....
Walworth (Elkhorn) (75)	414 741-2590	Larry Scharine	....	....	Nicole Andersen	Janice St John	Dean McKenzie
Washburn (Shell Lake) (14)	715 468-7808	....	....	....	....	....	....
Washington (West Bend) (95)	414 335-4488	Kenneth Miller	....	Marilyn Merten	Susan Haag	Gary G Moschea	Robert Schulteis
Waukesha (Waukesha) (305)	414 548-7902	Daniel Finley	....	Patricia Madden	Norman Cummings	Allan Walsch	Arnold Moncada
Waupaca (Waupaca) (46)	715 258-6200	....	....	....	....	....	....
Waushara (Wautoma) (19)	414 787-4631	George Sorenson	Debra Behringer	John Benz	....	Debra Behringer	Patrick Fox
Winnebago (Oshkosh) (140)	414 236-4747	Joseph Maehl	....	Linda Wolfe	Charles Orenstein	William Wagner	Robert Kraus
Wood (Wisconsin Rapids) (74)	715 421-8400	Al A Reynolds	....	Anthony Ruesch	David M Goetz	Douglass F Maurer	Brian Illingworth
WYOMING (23)							
Albany (Laramie) (31)	307 721-2541	Pat Gabriel	....	Jackie R Gonzales	Betty Prahl	....	Gary Puls
Big Horn (Basin) (11)	307 568-2357	....	....	....	....	....	....
Campbell (Gillette) (29)	307 682-7283	Willis Chrans	....	Vivian E Addison	....	....	Byron F Oedekoven
Carbon (Rawlins) (17)	307 328-2699	Artlin Zeiger	....	W E Harshman	....	....	Chet Engstrom
Converse (Douglas) (11)	307 358-2244	....	....	....	....	....	....
Crook (Sundance) (5)	307 283-1323	....	....	....	....	....	....
Fremont (Lander) (34)	307 332-2405	Tom Satterfield	....	Alma Nicol	H S Harnsberger	....	Joe Lucero
Goshen (Torrington) (12)	307 532-4051	....	....	....	....	....	....
Hot Springs (Thermopolis) (5)	307 864-3515	....	....	....	....	....	....
Johnson (Buffalo) (6)	307 684-7272	....	....	....	....	....	....
Laramie (Cheyenne) (73)	307 638-4260	....	....	....	....	....	....
Lincoln (Kemmerer) (13)	307 877-9056	....	....	....	....	....	....
Natrona (Casper) (61)	307 235-9200	....	....	....	....	....	....
Niobrara (Lusk) (2)	307 334-2211	Donna I Ruffing	....	Suzanne R Sturman	....	....	Eldon R Alexander
Park (Cody) (23)	307 587-2204	....	....	....	....	....	....
Platte (Wheatland) (8)	307 322-2315	....	....	....	....	....	....
Sheridan (Sheridan) (24)	307 674-6722	Kenneth D Kerns	....	Ronald L Dailey	Janet L Lewis	....	Robert Shelley
Sublette (Pinedale) (5)	307 367-4372	Monte B Skinner	....	Mary Lankford	Mary Lankford	....	Jack Cain
Sweetwater (Green River) (39)	307 875-7602	....	....	....	....	....	....
Teton (Jackson) (11)	307 733-4430	....	....	....	....	....	....
Uinta (Evanston) (19)	307 789-1780	....	....	....	....	....	....
Washakie (Worland) (8)	307 347-3131	....	....	....	....	....	....
Weston (Newcastle) (7)	307 746-4744	Ted Elliott	....	Paulette Thompson	Joann Fassbender	....	Donal Howell

D 2

Professional, Special Assistance and Educational Organizations Serving Local and State Governments

This article briefly describes 76 organizations that provide services of particular importance to cities, counties, and other local and state governments. Most of the organizations are membership groups for school administrators, health officers, city planners, city managers, public works directors, city attorneys, and other administrators who are appointed rather than elected. Several are general service and representational organizations for states, cities, counties, and administrators and citizens. Some organizations provide distinctive research, technological, consulting, and educational programs on a cost-of-service basis and have been established to meet specific needs of state and local governments. The others support educational activities in urban affairs or government administration and conduct research and other educational activities in urban affairs or government administration and conduct research and other educational activities thereby indirectly strengthening professionalism in government administration.

The assistance available through the secretariats of these national organizations provides an excellent method of obtaining expert advice and actual information on specific problems. The information secured in this way enables local and state officials to improve administrative practices, organization, and methods and thus to improve the quality of services rendered to the people. Many of these organizations also are active in raising the professional standards of their members through inservice training, special conferences and seminars, and other kinds of professional development.

Research on current problems is a continuing activity of many of these groups, and all issue a variety of publications ranging from a newsletter and occasional bulletins to diversified books, monographs, research papers, conference proceedings, and regular and special reports.

These organizations provide many of the services that in other countries would be the responsibility of the national government. They arrange annual conferences, publish newsletters and magazines, answer inquiries, provide in-service training and other kinds of professional development, provide placement services for members, and develop service and cost standards for various activities.

Most of the organizations listed have individual memberships, and several also have agency or institutional memberships. Some of these organizations have service memberships that may be based on the population of the jurisdiction, the annual revenue of the jurisdiction or agency, or other criteria that roughly measure the costs of providing service.

In addition to these kinds of membership fees, some of the organizations provide specialized consulting, training, and information services both by annual subscription and by charges for specific projects.

LISTING OF ORGANIZATIONS

Academy for State and Local Government, 444 North Capitol Street, N.W., Room 345, Washington, D.C. 20001. (202) 434-4850. Director: Enid Beaumont. Major publications: Publications list available on request. Purpose: To serve as the research, training, and policy center for joint projects and programs of Council of State Governments, International City/County Management Association, National Association of Counties, National Conference of State Legislatures, National Governors' Association, National League of Cities, and U.S. Conference of Mayors. An arm of the Academy, the State and Local Legal Center, is devoted to the interests of state and local governments in the Supreme Court. The Academy's International Center facilitates the exchange of people and ideas between the international community and state and local governments. Established 1971.

Airports Council International-North America, 1775 K Street, N.W., Suite 500, Washington, D.C. 20006. (202) 293-8500; Fax (202) 331-1362. President: George Howard. Major publications: Airport Highlights, studies, surveys, and reports. Purpose: To promote sound policies dealing with financing, construction, management, operations, and development of airports; to provide reference and resource facilities and information for airport operators; and to act as the "voice" of airports to governmental agencies, officials, and the public on the problems and solutions concerning airport operations. Established 1948.

American Association of Airport Executives, 4212 King Street, Alexandria, Virginia 22302. (703) 824-0500. President: Charles M. Barclay. Major publications: Airport Report; Airport Magazine. Purpose: To assist the airport managers in performing their complex and diverse responsibilities for the airport and community through an airport management reference library; a consulting service; publications containing technical, administrative, legal, and operational information; an electronic bulletin board system; a professional accreditation program for airport executives; and a private satellite broadcast network, Aviation News and Training Network (ANTN), for airport employee training and news. Established 1928.

American Association of Port Authorities, 1010 Duke Street, Alexandria, Virginia 22314. (703) 684-5700. President: Erik Stromberg. Purpose: The American Association of Port Authorities (AAPA) is the alliance of ports of the Western Hemisphere. The association promotes the common interests of the port community and provides leadership on trade, transportation, environmental, and other issues related to port development and operations. AAPA furthers public understanding of the essential role fulfilled by ports within the global transportation system. The association serves as a resource to help members accomplish their professional responsibilities.

American Association of School Administrators, 1801 North Moore Street, Arlington, Virginia 22209. (703) 528-0700. Executive Director: Paul D. Houston. Major publications: The School Administrator; Leadership News; Critical Issues Series. Purpose: To develop qualified educational leaders and support excellence in educational administration; to initiate and support laws, policies, research, and practice that will improve education; to promote programs and activities that focus on leadership for learning and excellence in education; and to cultivate a climate in which quality education can thrive. Established 1865.

American College of Healthcare Executives, One North Franklin Street, Suite 1700, Chicago, Illinois 60606-3491. (312) 424-2800. President/CEO: Thomas C. Dolan, Ph.D., FACHE. Major publications: *Hospital & Health Services Administration*; *Healthcare Executive; Frontiers, Directory* (biennial); and miscellaneous task force, committee, and seminar reports. Purpose: The mission of the American College of Healthcare Executives is to be the professional membership society for healthcare executives; to meet its members' professional, educational, and leadership needs; to increase the effectiveness of healthcare management; and to advance healthcare management excellence.

American Institute of Architects, 1735 New York Avenue, N.W., Washington, D.C. 20006. (202) 626-7300. Executive Vice President/CEO: James P. Cramer, Hon. AIA. Major publications: *AIA Memo*. Purpose: The objectives of the American Institute of Architects shall be to organize and unite in fellowship the members of the architectural profession of the United States of America; to promote the aesthetic, scientific, and practical efficiency of the profession; to advance the science and art of planning and building by advancing the standards of architectural education, training, and practice; to coordinate the building industry and the profession of architecture to ensure the advancement of the living standards of people through their improved environment; and to make the profession of ever-increasing service to society.

American Library Association, 50 East Huron Street, Chicago, Illinois 60611. (312) 944-6780. Executive Director: Elizabeth Martinez. Major publications: *American Libraries*; *Book-list*; *Choice*. Purpose: To assist libraries and librarians in promoting and improving library service and librarianship. Established 1876.

American Planning Association, Including the American Institute of Certified Planners (AICP). 1776 Massachusetts Avenue, N.W., Washington, D.C. 20036. (202) 872-0611. With an office also at 1313 East 60th Street, Chicago, Illinois 60637. (312) 955-9100. Executive Director: Michael Barker. Major publications: *Journal of the APA*; *Planning*; *Planning Advisory Service Reports*; *Land-Use Law & Zoning Digest*; *Zoning News*; *Environment & Development*. Purpose: To advance the art and science of urban and regional planning; to promote effective techniques for development in cities, regions, and states; to provide research for planners and information on new developments; and to bring together the professional planner, citizen, elected official, developer, and private practitioner. AICP provides an examination for

certification, promotes professional continuing education, establishes ethical standards, and sponsors accreditation of university planning programs. Established 1909.

American Public Gas Association, Suite 102, 11094-D Lee Highway, Fairfax, Virginia 22030. (703) 352-3890. Executive Director: Robert S. Cave. Major publications; *Newsletter*; *Publicly Owned Natural Gas System Directory* (annual). Purpose: To provide professional assistance to publicly owned natural gas systems. Established 1961.

American Public Health Association, 1015 15th Street, N.W., Washington, D.C. 20005. (202) 789-5600. Executive Director: Fernando M. Treviño, Ph.D., M.P.H. Major publications: *American Journal of Public Health*; *The Nation's Health*. Purpose: To protect the health of the public through the maintenance of standards for scientific procedures, legislative education, and practical application of innovative health programs. Established 1872.

American Public Power Association, 2301 M Street, N.W., Washington, D.C. 20037. (202) 467-2900. Executive Director: Larry Hobart. Major publications: *Public Power*; *Weekly Newsletter*. Purpose: To promote the efficiency of publicly owned electric systems; to achieve greater cooperation among public systems; to protect the interest of publicly owned utilities; and to provide services in the fields of management and operation, energy conservation, consumer services, public relations, engineering, design, construction, research and accounting practice. Established 1940.

American Public Transit Association, 1201 New York Avenue, N.W., Washington, D.C. 20005. (202) 898-4000. Executive Vice President: Jack R. Gilstrap. Major publications: *Passenger Transport*; *Transit Fact Book*. Purpose: To represent the operators of and suppliers to public transit; to provide a medium for exchange of experiences, discussion, and comparative study of industry affairs; to research and investigate methods to improve public transit; to provide assistance in dealing with special issues; and to collect, compile, and make available data and information relative to public transit. Established 1882.

American Public Welfare Association, 810 First Street, N.E., Washington, D.C. 20002. (202) 682-0100. Executive Director: A. Sidney Johnson, III. Major publications: *Public Welfare*; *Public Welfare Directory*; *This Week in Washington*; *W-Memo*; *APWA News*. Purpose: To work for more effective federal policy in human services, including income assistance, social services, health care, and employment services, and to promote the professional development of persons working in the field of public welfare. Established 1930.

American Public Works Association, 106 W. Eleventh Street, Suite 1800, Kansas City, Missouri 64105-1806. Executive Director: William J. Bertera. Major publications: *APWA Reporter* (monthly); research reports; technical publications and manuals. Purpose: To advance the theory and practice of all aspects

of public works facilities and services; to disseminate information on improved practices; to encourage high professional standards; and to promote cooperation in the field of public works. Established 1894.

American Society for Public Administration, 1120 G Street, N.W., Suite 700, Washington, D.C. 20005. (202) 393-7878. Executive Director: John P. Thomas. Major publications: *Public Administration Review*; *PA Times*. Purpose: To improve the management of public service at all levels of government; to advocate on behalf of public service; to advance the science, processes, and art of public administration; and to disseminate information and facilitate the exchange of knowledge among persons interested in the practice or teaching of public administration. Established 1939.

American Water Works Association, 6666 West Quincy Avenue, Denver, Colorado 80235. (303) 794-7711. Executive Director: J. B. Mannion. Major publications: *Journal AWWA*; *MainStream*; *OpFlow*; *WaterWeek*. Purpose: To promote public health, safety, and welfare through the improvement of the quality and quantity of drinking water for the public. Established 1881.

Association of Public-Safety Communications Officials–International, Inc., 2040 S. Ridgewood Avenue, South Daytona, Florida 32119. (904) 322-2500. Executive Director: Ronnie Rand. Major publications: *APCO BULLETIN*; *The Journal of Public Safety Communications*; *APCO Reports Newsletter*; *Public Safety Operating Procedures Manual*; *APCO Training Courses*. Purpose: To promote the development and progress of public safety telecommunications through research, planning, and training; to promote cooperation among public safety agencies; to perform frequency coordination for radio services administered by the Federal Communications Commission; and to act as a liaison with federal regulatory bodies. Established 1935.

Building Officials and Code Administrators International, 4051 West Flossmoor Road, Country Club Hills, Illinois 60478-5795. (708) 799-2300. Chief Executive Officer: Paul K. Heilstedt, P.E. Major publications: National Code Series; *The Building Official and Code Administrator*; *BOCA Bulletin*; Research Reports; Professional Development Series. Publications catalog available on request. Purpose: To promulgate a complete package of performance model codes; to assist the user through training and educational services; and to provide technical services such as plan reviews, product evaluations, inspections, and administrative and management reviews. Established 1915.

Cable Television Information Center, 1700 Shaker Church Road, N.W., Olympia, Washington 98502. (206) 866-2080. President: Harold E. Horn. Purpose: To help local officials make informed decisions about cable television; to provide a centralized cable resource and information center to local governments across the country; to provide information, valuable contacts, and suggestions to local governments; and to represent local government interests in the formation of cable policy at the federal level. Established 1972.

Canadian Association of Municipal Administrators, 24 Clarence Street, Ottawa, Ontario K1N 5P3 Canada. (613) 241-8444. Executive Director: Marja Hughes. Purpose: To achieve greater communication and cooperation between municipal administrators across Canada and to focus the talents of its members on the preservation and advancement of local government through enhancing the quality of municipal management and administration in Canada. Established 1972. An affiliate, the Canadian Municipal Personnel Association, serves as a major resource group in the area of personnel administration in municipal government and labor relations. Established 1975.

Council of State Community Development Agencies, 444 North Capitol Street, Room 224, Washington, D.C. 20001. (202) 393-6435. Executive Director: John Sidor. Major publications: *The State Line*; *The National Line*; *Put Up or Give Way: States, Economic Competitiveness and Poverty*; *Linking Housing and Human Services: Guide to Completing a CHAS*; *1990 Compendium of State Housing Initiatives*; *Role of CDBG Funds in Rural Development*; *Assisting Rural Development*; and others. Purpose: To help state agencies keep abreast of state and federal initiatives in community and economic development, housing, public facilities, and local assistance and to improve state programs through interstate coordination. Established 1974.

Council of State Governments. Iron Works Pike, P.O. Box 11910, Lexington, Kentucky 40578. (606) 244-8000. Executive Director: Dan Sprague. Major publications: *Book of the States*; *SPECTRUM: The Journal of State Government*; *State Government News; State Trends and Forecasts*. Purpose: To strengthen state government and preserve its role in the federal system via research, information, and leadership programs; to assist states in improving their legislative, administrative, and judicial practices; to promote state, local, regional, and interstate cooperation; and to facilitate state-federal relations. Established 1933.

Federation of Canadian Municipalities, 24 Clarence Street, Ottawa, Ontario KIN 5P3, Canada. (613) 237-5221. FAX (613) 237-2965. Executive Director: James W. Knight. Purpose: To represent the national interest of local governments in Canada and to act as a spokesman for Canadian local governments and as a clearinghouse for the collection, exchange, and dissemination of statistical data and information on Canadian municipal practices and procedures. Major publications: *FCM Forum* (newsletter); two reports on the physical condition of Canada's municipal infrastructure; *FCM Policy Development*; *At Your Service: In Both Official Languages*; *FCM: 50 Years of Making History* (1987), briefs on goods and services tax, municipal

infrastructure, federal payment of property taxes (grants in lieu of taxes), social housing, transportation, municipal liability insurance, race relations, tax reform, radio license fees, etc., presented to federal government departments and agencies; Municipal Economic Development Publications: *Management and Planning Capabilities in Small Communities*; *Community Crossroads*; *"How to ..."* manuals; *International Office 1992–1993*; *1993–1994 Annual Review*; *FCM International Bulletin*; *Youth Violence and Youth Gangs*; *"How to...."* manuals on race relations; A-C-T brochures (Affordability and Choice Today-housing initiatives). Established 1937.

Government Finance Officers Association, 180 North Michigan Avenue, Suite 800, Chicago, Illinois 60601. (312) 977-9700. FAX (312) 977-4806. With an office at 1750 K Street, N.W., Suite 650. Washington, D.C. 20006. (202) 429-2750. FAX (202) 429-2755. Executive Director: Jeffrey L. Esser. Major publications: *GFOA Newsletter*; *Government Finance Review Magazine*; *Public Investor*; *GAAFR Review*; *Governmental Accounting, Auditing and Financial Reporting*; *Investing Public Funds*; *Elected Official's Series*; *Local Government Finance: Concepts and Practices*. Purpose: To enhance and promote the professional management of governmental financial resources by identifying, developing, and advancing fiscal strategies, policies, and practices for the public benefit. Established 1906.

Government Management Information Sciences, P.O. Box 926, Wichita Falls, Texas 76307-0926. (817) 692-3707. Executive director: Dorothy G. Harrison. The organization is committed to cooperation; mutual assistance; and sharing ideas, talent, research, and systems. Network of over 400 agencies in 43 states, Canada, and Holland. Membership is limited to city, county, and state government agencies and educational institutions dealing in government activities. Publications: Newsletter and results of annual survey that provides demographic data and types of hardware, software, and applications used by member agencies.

Governmental Accounting Standards Board, 401 Merritt 7, P.O. Box 5116, Norwalk, Connecticut 06856-5116. (203) 847-0700. Chairman: James Antonio. The Governmental Accounting Standards Board was organized by the Financial Accounting Foundation to establish standards of financial accounting and reporting for state and local governmental entities. Its standards guide the preparation of external financial reports of those entities. Interested parties are invited to read and comment on discussion documents of proposed standards. One copy of a discussion document can be obtained free of charge by calling the order department during the comment period. For automatic mailings of discussion and final documents, contact the order department to subscribe. Established 1984.

Governmental Research Association, 315 Samford Hall, Birmingham, Alabama 35229. (205) 870-2482. President: Donald C. Berno. Major publications: *GRA Directory*; *GRA Reporter*. Purpose: To promote and coordinate the activities of governmental research agencies; to encourage the development of effective organization and methods for the administration and operation of government; to encourage the development of common standards for the appraisal of results; to facilitate the exchange of ideas and experiences; and to serve as a clearinghouse. Established 1914.

ICMA, 777 North Capitol Street, N.E., Washington, D.C. 20002-4201. (202) 289-4262. FAX (202) 962-3500. Executive Director: William H. Hansell, Jr. Major publications: *Public Management*; *ICMA Newsletter*; *Municipal Management Series*; *Municipal Year Book*; Special Data Issues; Management Information Service Reports; Practical Management Series; *Compensation*. Purpose: To enhance the quality of local government through professional management; to support and assist professional local government managers internationally. Provides training and development programs and publications for local government professionals that improve their skills, increase their knowledge of local government, and strengthen their commitment to the ethics, values, and ideals of the profession. Serves as a clearinghouse for the collection, analysis, and dissemination of local government information and data to enhance current practices and serve as a resource to public interest groups in the formulation of public policy. Established 1914.

ICMA Retirement Corporation, 777 North Capitol Street, N.E., Washington, D.C. 20002. President: Girard Miller. (800) 669-7400. Purpose: To provide and administer retirement plans as aids to units of government in their overall management benefits programs. Included are qualified and deferred compensation programs for all personnel, plus investment management services for employers. Established 1972.

Institute of Internal Auditors, Inc., 249 Maitland Avenue, Altamonte Springs, Florida 32701-4201. (407) 830-7600. FAX (407) 831-5171. President: William G. Bishop III, C.I.A. Major publication: *Internal Auditor*. Purpose: To provide comprehensive professional development activities and the standards for the practice of internal auditing and to research, disseminate, and promote knowledge and information about internal auditing and internal control. Of special interest to government auditors are the Institute's activities in governmental and public affairs. (Special memberships available for government organizations.) Established 1941.

Institute of Public Administration, 55 West 44th Street, New York, New York 10036. (212) 730-5480. President: David Mammen. Luther H. Gulick Scholar in Residence: Annmarie H. Walsh. Major publications: list of publications available on request. Purpose: To provide research, training, education, consulting, and advisory services in the United States and abroad in areas of public policy, government structure, public policy, government structure, public authorities, public enterprises, government procurement, personnel management and training, public-private sector improvements, economic development, charter revision, local government legislative bodies, planning and management, intergovernmental program responsibilities and relationships, and public ethics. Established 1906.

Institute of Transportation Engineers (formerly Institute of Traffic Engineers), 525 School Street, S.W., Washington, D.C. 20024. (202) 554-8050. FAX (202) 863-5486. Executive Director: Thomas W. Brahms. Major publications: *ITE Journal*; *Traffic Engineering Handbook*; *Transportation Planning Handbook*; *Residential Street Design and Traffic Control*; *Traffic Safety Toolbox, A Primer on Traffic Safety*; *Transportation and Land Development*; *Toolbox for Alleviating Traffic Congestion*; *Manual of Traffic Signal Design*; *Manual of Transportation Engineering Studies*; *Trip Generation*; *Parking Generation*; *Parking Handbook for Small Communities*. Purpose: To promote professional development in the field through support and encouragement of education, research, development of public awareness, and exchange of information. Established 1930.

International Association of Assessing Officers, 130 East Randolph Street, Chicago, Illinois 60601. (312) 819-6100. Executive Director: John Eckenrod. Major publications: *Assessment Digest*; *Property Tax Journal*; *Improving Real Property Assessment: A Reference Manual*; *Property Appraisal and Assessment Administration*; Bibliographic Series; Research and Information Series; Assessment Standards. Purpose: To provide leadership in accurate property valuation, property tax administration, and property tax policy through out the world. Established 1934.

International Association of Auditorium Managers, 4425 W. Airport Freeway, Suite 590, Irving, Texas 75062-5835. (214) 255-8020. FAX (214) 255-9582. Executive Director: John Swinburn. Major publications: *Crowd Management*; *Facility Manager*; *IAAM Guide to Members and Services*; *IAAM News*. Purpose: To promote professional development in the public assembly field and provide assistance to members. Membership consists of the managers of arenas, convention centers, auditoriums, exhibit halls, amphitheaters, performing arts theaters, and stadiums. Established 1924.

International Association of Chiefs of Police, 515 N. Washington Street, Alexandria, Virginia 22314-2357. (703) 836-6767. Executive Director: Dan Rosenblatt. Major publications: *Police Chief*; *Training Keys*. Purpose: To advance the art of police science through development and dissemination of improved administrative, technical, and operational practices and to promote their use in police work; to foster police cooperation and exchange of information and experience among police administrators; to recruit and train qualified persons; and to encourage adherence of all police officers to high professional standards of performance and conduct. Established 1893.

International Association of Fire Chiefs, 4025 Fair Ridge Drive, Fairfax, Virginia 22033-2868. (703) 273-0911. Executive Director: Garry L. Briese, C.A.E. Major publications: *On Scene* (twice-monthly newsletter). Purpose: To provide information and assistance to those charged with the task of administering fire prevention, protection and suppression efforts, and emergency medical services in the United States, Canada, and abroad. Established 1873.

Operation Life Safety is an affiliate organization. It is a consortium of public, government, and private sector agencies that promote life safety from fire through public awareness and education, use of smoke detector and alarm systems, installation of quick response residential fire sprinklers, and development of community programs to support these objectives.

International Conference of Building Officials, 5360 Workman Mill Road, Whittier, California 90601-2298. (310) 699-0541. President: Jon S. Traw, P.E. Major publications: Uniform Building Code and related codes, mechanical, plumbing, housing, signs, dangerous buildings, and fire prevention; textbooks on building department administration, building inspection, building code community, plan review, mechanical inspection, concrete inspection; instructor guides and student workbooks on fire protection, building department administration, all phases of building inspection; video training films; *Building Standards* magazine; and newsletter. Purpose: To develop and maintain uniform codes for the benefit of member city, county, and state agencies; to provide through its subsidiary, ICBO Evaluation Service, Inc., an evaluation service on new building products and systems; to develop educational programs and seminars and certification programs for inspectors; to provide management studies of building department operations; and to provide engineering consultative services on code matters, including plan review and interpretation and application of code requirements. Established 1922.

International Institute of Municipal Clerks, 1206 North San Dimas Canyon Road, San Dimas, California 91773. (909) 592-4462. Executive Director: John Devine. Major publications: *IIMC News Digest*; Case Study Packets; Technical Bulletins; *Meeting Administration Handbook*; *The Language of Local Government*; *Role Call: Strategy for a Professional Clerk*. Purpose: To improve administration of state, provincial, county, and local government through the position of clerk, secretary, or recorder—by maintaining central facilities for study and research devoted to improvement of methods and procedures relating to the municipal clerk's duties; by sponsoring professional career development institutes in 46 universities; by maintaining an Academy for Advanced Education with seminars at 46 universities; by offering a self-study course in supervision and records and information management; and by administering a professional certification program. Established 1947.

International Personnel Management Association—United States, 1617 Duke Street, Alexandria, Virginia 22314. (703) 549-7100. Executive Director: Donald K. Tichenor. Major publications: *Public Personnel Management*; *Agency Issues*; *IPMA News*; Public Employee Relations Library (PERL) Series. Purpose: To improve service to the public by promoting quality human resource management in the public sector. Established 1973.

League of Women Voters. 1730 M Street, N.W., Washington, D.C. 20036. (202) 429-1965. President: Becky Cain. Executive Director: Gracia Hillman. Purpose: The League of Women Voters of the United States is a nonpartisan, political organization that encourages the informed and active participation of citizens in government and influences public policy through education and advocacy. The League's current advocacy priorities are health care, early intervention for children at risk, crisis in the community, and opening government to citizens. Major publications: *The National Voter, Report from the Hill*. Established 1920.

The League of Women Voters Education Fund, a separate but complementary organization, provides research and citizen education services to League members and to the public to encourage and enable citizen participation in government. Current citizen education programs involve health care, the environment, the right of privacy in reproductive choices, electoral participation, and emerging democracies. Major publications: *Getting into Issues*; *VOTE, the First Steps*; *Pick a Candidate*; *Getting out the Vote*; *The Nuclear Waste Primer*; *The Garbage Primer*; and *The Plastics Primer*. Established 1957.

Maritime Municipal Training and Development Board, 6100 University Avenue, Halifax, Nova Scotia, Canada B3H 3J5. (902) 494-3712. FAX (902) 494-1961. Executive Director: A. Donald Smeltzer. The Maritime Municipal Training and Development Board (MMTDB) was established in 1974 as an agency of the Council of Maritime Premiers. Its purpose, within the Maritime region, is to improve municipal government administration, management, and decision-making through training, education, and professional development.

The MMTDB is a coordinator, a facilitator, and a catalyst for positive change. The organization and activity of this agency are unique in Canada and have helped to establish the Maritime region as a pioneer and leader in the training, education, and development of both elected and appointed municipal officials.

Among its many activities, the MMTDB initiates and coordinates training; promotes the use of new technologies for municipal decision makers; encourages the sharing of scarce resources; provides assistance and counsel to municipal officials; encourages innovative and progressive management practices; promotes professional study in public administration; provides a forum for discussion of important issues; builds consensus and encourages cooperation.

Municipal Treasurers Association, 1229 19th Street, N.W., Washington, D.C. 20036. (202) 833-1017. Executive Director: Stacey L. Crane. Major publications: *Technical Topics*; *Treasury Notes*. Purpose: To enhance local treasury management by providing educational training, technical assistance, legislative services, and a forum for treasurers to exchange ideas and develop policy papers and positions.

National Animal Control Association, P.O. Box 480851, Kansas City, Missouri 64148-0851. (800) 828-6474. Executive Director: John Mays. Major publications: *The NACA News*, newsletter; *The NACA Training Guide*. Purpose: To provide training for animal control personnel; to provide consultation and guidance for local governments on animal control ordinances, animal shelter design, budget and program planning, and staff training; and to provide public education. Established in 1978.

National Association of Counties, 440 First Street, N.W., Washington, D.C. 20001. (202) 393-6226. Executive Director: Larry Naake. Major publication: *County News*. Purpose: To serve as the voice of county government at the national level; to improve county government; to serve as a liaison between county and other levels of government; to achieve public understanding of the role of counties in the intergovernmental system; to provide information and analysis of data. Two-thirds of the nation's counties are members of NACo and its 25 affiliated organizations. Established 1935. Through the National Association of Counties Research Foundation, Inc. (NACoR, Inc.), NACo undertakes grant and contract funded research and maintains expertise in major problems and programs of county government.

National Association of Housing and Redevelopment Officials, 1320 18th Street, N.W., Suite 500, Washington, D.C. 20036. (202) 429-2960. FAX (202) 429-9684. Executive Director: Richard Y. Nelson, Jr. Major publications: *Journal of Housing*; *NAHRO Monitor*; *Directory of Local Agencies*; *Commissioners Dictionary; Commissioners Handbook*. Purpose: To serve as a professional membership organization representing local housing authorities, community development agencies, and individual professionals in the housing, community development, and redevelopment fields. Divided into 8 regions and 43 chapters, NAHRO works to provide safe, decent, and affordable housing for low- and moderate-income persons.

NAHRO provides its 9,000 members with information on federal policy, legislation, regulations, and funding. NAHRO also provides professional development and training programs in all phases of agency operations, including management, maintenance, and procurement. Established 1933.

National Association of Regional Councils, 1700 K Street, N.W., Washington, D.C. 20006. (202) 457-0710. FAX (202) 296-9352. Executive Director: John W. Epling. Major publications: *Directory of Regional Councils*; *The Regional Reporter*; *The Regionalist*. Purpose: To promote the development and understanding of regional councils; to provide up-to-date information and technical assistance to councils; to assist in the expansion of regional council program opportunities; to develop and communicate national policy proposals on issues of regional impact; and to act as a liaison with federal and state agencies in order to promote the use of regional councils and present their needs. Established 1967.

National Association of Schools of Public Affairs and Administration, Suite 730, 1120 G Street, N.W., Washington, D.C. 20005. (202) 628-8965. FAX (202) 626-4978. Executive Director: Alfred M. Zuck. Major publications: *Directory of Programs in Public Affairs and Administration 1994*; *Newsletter*; *MPA Standards*; *Doctoral Policy Statement*; *MPA Career Brochure*; *Peer Review and Accreditation* documents. Purpose: To serve as a national center for information about programs and developments in the area of public affairs and administration; to foster goals and standards of educational excellence; to represent members' concerns and interests in the formulation and support of national, state, and local policies for education and research; and to serve as a specialized accrediting agency for MPA degrees. Established 1970.

National Association of State Information Resource Executives, 167 West Main Street, Suite 600, Lexington, Kentucky 40507. (606) 231-1905. Staff Director: Louise Spieler. Major publications: *NASIRE Exchange* (newsletter); *NASIRE Biennial Report*. Purpose: To strengthen state government through the application of information systems technology; to act as a liaison with federal agencies; to promote the development and transferral of information systems technology between states. Established 1969.

National Association of Towns and Townships, 1522 K Street, N.W., Suite 600, Washington, D.C. 20005. (202) 737-5200. Director of Communications: Bruce G. Rosenthal. Major publication: *NATaT's Reporter*. Purpose: To offer technical assistance, educational services, and public policy support to local government officials from towns, townships, and other small communities across the country; through its National Center for Small Communities to conduct research and to develop public policy recommendations scaled to the unique needs and nature of rural governments and small towns; to keep local officials

abreast of decisions and actions of national import. Established 1963.

National Civic League, 1445 Market Street, Suite 300, Denver, Colorado 80202. (303) 571-4343. FAX (303) 571-4404. Internet: jparr@NCL.org. President: John Parr. Major publications: *NATIONAL CIVIC REVIEW*; *Civic Action*; *Model County Charter*; *Model City Charter*; *Healthy Communities Resource Guide*. Purpose: To create communities that work for everyone. NCL provides technical assistance to communities in consensus-based decision-making, collaborative problem solving, and healthy communities implementation and strengthening. Also acknowledges 10 communities annually through the All-American City Award Program. Celebrates 100th anniversary in 1994.

National Conference of State Legislatures, 1560 Broadway, Suite 700, Denver, Colorado 80202. (303) 830-2200. Executive Director: William Pound. Major publication: *State Legislatures*. Purpose: To improve the quality and effectiveness of state legislatures; to assure states a strong, cohesive voice in the federal decision-making process; and to foster interstate communication and cooperation. Established 1975. The Conference's Office of State-Federal Relations, 444 North Capitol Street, Suite 515, Washington, D.C. 20001 (202) 624-5400, produces *Federal Update* and *Mandate Monitor*.

National Council for Urban Economic Development, 1730 K Street, N.W., Suite 915, Washington, D.C. 20006. (202) 223-4735. Executive Director: Jeffrey A. Finkle. Major publications: *Urban Economic Developments*; *Economic Development Commentary*; *Economic Development Abroad*; and *Legislative Report*. Purpose: To serve public and private participants in economic development across the United States and in international settings; to provide information to its members, who build local economies through job creation, attraction, and retention and who include public economic development directors, chamber of commerce staff, utility executives, academicians, and many other professionals. Established 1967.

National Environmental Health Association, 720 South Colorado Boulevard, Suite 970, South Tower, Denver, Colorado 80222. (303) 756-9090. FAX (303) 691-9490. Executive Director: Nelson E. Fabian. Major publications: *Journal of Environmental Health* and more than 170 other publications. Purpose: To advance the professional who works in the environmental field by promoting and encouraging research, education, professional meetings, and the dissemination of information; to publish information relating to environmental health and protection; and to promote professionalism in the field. Established 1937.

National Fire Protection Association, Batterymarch Park, P.O. Box 9101, Quincy, Massachusetts 02269-9101. (617) 770-3000. President: George D. Miller. Major publications: *National Electrical Code®*; *National*

Fire Codes®; *Fire Protection Handbook*; *Life Safety Code®*; *NFPA Journal*; *Fire Technology*; textbooks, manuals, training packages, detailed analyses of important fires, fire officers guides, and others. Purpose: To safeguard people and their environment from destructive fire using scientific and engineering techniques and education; to develop and publish consensus standards intended to minimize the possibility and effects of fire; and to educate the public in ways to avoid loss of life and property from fire by making fire safety habits a way of life. Established 1896.

National Governors' Association, Hall of the States, 444 North Capitol Street, Suite 267, Washington, D.C. 20001-1512. (202) 624-5300. Executive Director: Raymond C. Scheppach. Major publications: *Governors' Bulletin*; *Fiscal Survey of the States*; *Directory of Governors*; *Governors' Staff Directory*; reports on a wide range of state issues. Purpose: To act as a liaison between the states and the federal government and to serve as a clearinghouse for information and ideas on state and national issues. Established 1908.

National Housing Conference, 815 15th Street, N.W., Suite 601, Washington, D.C. 20005. (202) 393-5772. Executive Director: Robert J. Reid. Major publications: *NHC News*. Purpose: To promote better communities and housing for Americans through legislative action. Established 1931.

National Institute of Governmental Purchasing, 11800 Sunrise Valley Drive, Suite 1050, Reston, Virginia 22091-5302. (703) 715-9400. FAX (703) 715-9897. Executive Vice President: J. E. Brinkman, CPPO. Major publications: *Government Procurement* magazine; *NIGP Technical Bulletin*; *Dictionary of Purchasing Terms*; *General Public Purchasing*; *Public Purchasing and Materials Management*; *Public PROcurement Management, Parts 1 & 2*; *Annual Governmental Procurement Research Survey*; *Annual Survey of In-State (Buy-Local), Buy American Practices, and Recycle Preferences*; *Commodity/Service Code Index* (a numbering system). Seminars on the foregoing, plus: Competitive Sealed Proposals/Competitive Negotiations; Standardization and Specification Writing. Also, on-site technical and consulting services; research projects and reports; NGIP Commodity/Service Coding System (2 Parts: Class-Item Code and Detailed Item Description Code); Certification for Public Purchasing Personnel. Purpose: To raise the standards of the public purchasing profession through the interchange of information and ideas. Established 1944.

National Institute of Municipal Law Officers, 1000 Connecticut Avenue, N.W., Suite 902, Washington, D.C. 20036. (202) 466-5424. FAX (202) 785-0152. General Counsel: Benjamin L. Brown. Major publication: *The Municipal Attorney*. Purpose: To provide an organization for cooperation on litigation of nationwide municipal concern, law information, research, library services, and publications on law information to municipal attorneys of member municipalities. Established 1935.

National League of Cities, 1301 Pennsylvania Avenue, N.W., Washington, D.C. 20004. (202) 626-3000. Executive Director: Donald J. Borut. Major publications: *Nation's Cities Weekly*; *Issues and Options*; guide books, directories, and research reports. Purpose: To serve as an advocate for its members in Washington in the legislative, administrative, and judicial processes that affect them; to develop and pursue a national urban policy that meets the present and future needs of the nation's urban communities and the people who live in them; to offer training, technical assistance, and information to local government and state league officials to help them improve the quality of local government in our urban nation; and to undertake research and analysis on policy issues of importance to urban America. Established 1924.

National Public Employer Labor Relations Association, 1620 Eye Street, N.W., 4th Floor, Washington, D.C. 20006. (202) 296-2230. President: R. Sue Weller. Executive Director: Roger E. Dahl. Major publications: *NPELRA Newsletter*; contract clause reference manual; strike contingency planning manual; family and medical leave guide; labor relations supervisor's training manual; and drug testing monographs. Purpose: To further the professional interests of federal, state, county, school/special district, and municipal government managers in the area of labor and employee relations through training programs and the dissemination and exchange of information and policy pertaining to all areas of public sector labor relations; and to promote cooperation among members and professional standards in the field. Established 1971.

National Recreation and Park Association, 2775 South Quincy Street, Arlington, Virginia 22206-2204. (703) 820-4940. Executive Director: R. Dean Tice, Major publications: *Parks & Recreation*; *Journal of Leisure Research*; *Therapeutic Recreation Journal*; *Recreation & Parks Law Reporter*; *Park Practice Program*; *Dateline: NRPA* (newsletter); *Programmers Information Network, Recreation . . . Access in the 90s*. Worldwide NRPA/SCHOLE™ computer network. Purpose: To improve and expand park and recreation systems and leisure services for the public through assisting park and recreation officials in the development and administration of physical, human, and financial resources. Parent organization established 1898.

National School Boards Association, 1680 Duke Street, Alexandria, Virginia 22314. (703) 838-6722. FAX (703) 683-7590. Executive Director: Thomas A. Shannon. Major publications: *The American School Board Journal*; *The Executive Educator*; *The School Administrator's Policy Portfolio*; *Leadership Reports*; *School Board News*. Purpose: To work with and through all of its federation members to foster excellence and equity in public education through school board leadership. Established 1940.

National Society for Experiential Education. 3509 Haworth Drive, Suite 207, Raleigh, North Carolina 27609. (919) 787-3263. Executive Director: Allen J. Wutzdorff. Major publications: *NSEE Quarterly*; *The National Directory of Internships*; *Strengthening Experiential Education within Your Institution*; *The Experienced Hand: A Student Manual for Making the Most of an Internship*; *Combining Service and Learning: A Resource Book for Community and Public Service*; *A Guide to Environmental Internships: How Environmental Organizations Can Utilize Internships Effectively*; Resource papers on issues of quality program design and administration. Purpose: As a community of individuals, institutions, and organizations, NSEE is committed to fostering the effective use of experience as an integral part of education, in order to empower learners and promote the common good. Established 1971.

Police Foundation, 1001 22nd Street, N.W., Washington, D.C. 20037. (202) 833-1460. President: Hubert Williams. Major publications: research and technical assistance reports on a wide range of issues related to law enforcement and public safety; list of publications available upon request. Purpose: To improve policing in America through research and technical assistance. The foundation offers state and local governments assistance in such areas as community policing, strategic planning, civil disorder preparedness, operational and administrative review, program evaluation, community and race relations, illegal drug control, and police chief selection. Created and operates the National Center for the Study of Police and Civil Disorder. Established 1970.

Public Administration Service, 8301 Greensboro Drive, Suite 420, McLean, Virginia 22102. (703) 734-8970. President and Executive Director: Theodore Sitkoff. Purpose: To provide management and specialized consulting services and conduct research for public jurisdictions and public managers—domestic and international—in order to improve the quality and delivery of public services. Consulting and research services provided include the development and installation of modern management systems, methods, techniques, and practices in many different functional fields such as local, state, and federal organization and reorganization; human resource administration; criminal justice; public works; intergovernmental relations; telecommunications; data processing and office automation; and public sector productivity and responsiveness and privatization. Nonprofit organization. Established 1933.

Public Risk Management Association, 1815 North Fort Myer Drive, Suite 1020, Arlington, Virginia 22209. (703) 528-7701. Executive Director: Dennis Kirschbaum. Major publications: Public Risk magazine; *Riskwatch newsletter*; *Public Sector Risk Management manual*; *Tort Liability Today*; *Public*

Official Liability Decisions in Federal Courts (subscription series); *Risk Management Behind the Blue Curtain: A Primer on Law Enforcement Liability.* Special Reports: *State of the Profession Survey; Employee Assistance Programs: Strategies for Local Government Workplaces; 1991–92 Risk Financing Survey; Workers' Compensation Cases: Local Government.* Purpose: To increase the proficiency of risk management in local government by providing an information network between government officials and employees involved in risk management, by assisting in the establishment of effective risk-management programs, and by conducting research projects and training programs to aid in the development of more effective techniques. Established 1978.

Public Technology, Inc., 1301 Pennsylvania Avenue, N.W., Washington, D.C. 20004. (202) 626-2400. FAX (202) 626-2. President: Costis Toregas. Purpose: With ICMA, NLC, and NACO as sponsors, PTI works with 150 progressive member cities and counties to identify and create technologies and management approaches for providing the best possible services to citizens and business communities. Three priorities of PTI are 1) to make communities 'well-connected' by advancing communication capabilities, 2) to develop tools and processes for wise decision-making, and 3) to create approaches to ensure a balance between economic development and a clean, quality environment. A research and development program combined with a strong Public Enterprise program are the means by which PTI priorities are carried forward. The PTI member program provides a local government executive information service including LEX (an electronic information and communications system), ANSWER (a research service), publications, executive briefings, and an extensive consultation service. Recent major publications: *The Enterprising Government: Improving Services and Generating Revenues; Solutions for Technology Sharing Networks* (annual); *The Local Government Guide to Geographic Information Systems.* The Public Enterprise Program integrates three elements to help member cities and counties create new revenues: a how-to guide and training for local leaders, expert business planning assistance, and access to venture capital for the PTI In-

vestment Fund and other capital sources. Established 1971.

Solid Waste Association of North America, P.O. Box 7219, Silver Spring, Maryland 20907. (301) 585-2898. Executive Director: H. Lanier Hickman, Jr., PE, DEE. Purpose: To advance the practice of environmentally and economically sound municipal solid waste management in North America. Established 1961.

Southern Building Code Congress International, Inc., 900 Montclair Road, Birmingham, Alabama 35213. (205) 591-1853. Chief Executive Officer: William J. Tangye, P.E. Major publications: *The Standard Codes; A Directory of Services* listing other publications and services and a membership directory are available on request. Purpose: To provide a forum for governments, design professionals, and industry to join together to democratically promulgate and maintain a set of model regulatory construction codes. Established 1940.

Special Libraries Association, 1700 18th Street, N.W., Washington, D.C. 20009-2508. (202) 234-4700. Executive Director: David R. Bender. Major publications: *Special Libraries; SpeciaList;* publications catalog available on request. Purpose: To provide an association of individuals and organizations having a professional, scientific, or technical interest in library and information science, especially as these are applied in the recording, retrieval, and dissemination of knowledge and information in areas such as the physical, biological, technical and social sciences, the humanities, and business; and to promote and improve the communication, dissemination, and use of such information and knowledge for the benefit of libraries or other educational organizations. Established 1909; membership 14,000.

Town Affiliation Association of the United States (Sister Cities International), 120 S. Payne Street, Alexandria, Virginia 22314. (703) 836-3535. Major publications: *Your City and the World; A Sister City Handbook; Sister City News; Directory of Sister Cities by State and Country.* Purpose: To provide a national forum for the interchange of ideas and resources to help local communities further their international programs. Established 1956.

United States Conference of Mayors, 1620 Eye Street, N.W., Washington, D.C. 20006. (202) 293-7330. Executive Director: J. Thomas

Cochran. Major publications: *U.S. Mayor; Mayors of America's Principal Cities.* Purpose: To act as the official nonpartisan organization of cities with populations of 30,000 or more; to aid the development of effective national urban policy; to serve as a legislative action force in federal-city relations; to ensure that federal policy meets urban needs; and to provide mayors with leadership and management tools of value in their cities. Each city is represented in the Conference by its chief elected official, the mayor. Established 1932.

Urban Affairs Association, University of Delaware, Newark, Delaware 19716. (302) 831-1681. Executive Director: Mary Helen Callahan. Major publications: *Urban Affairs; Journal of Urban Affairs; Directory of University Urban Programs;* selected papers of annual meetings; other special studies and reports. Purpose: To encourage the dissemination of information and research findings about urbanism and urbanization; to support the development of university education, research, and service programs in urban affairs; and to foster the development of urban affairs as a professional and academic field. Established 1969.

The Urban Institute, 2100 M Street, N.W., Washington, D.C. 20037. (202) 833-7200. President: William Gorham. Major publication: *Policy and Research Report;* publication catalog and annual report available on request. Purpose: To respond to needs for objective analyses and basic information regarding social and economic problems confronting the nation and government policies and programs designed to alleviate such problems. Established 1968.

Water Environment Federation, 601 Wythe Street, Alexandria, Virginia 22314. (703) 684-2400. Executive Director: Quincalee Brown. Major publications: *Water Environment Research; Water Environment and Technology; Operations Forum; Industrial Wastewater; Water Environment Regulation Watch;* series of Manuals of Practice. Purpose: To develop and disseminate technical information concerning the preservation and enhancement of the global water environment. The Federation has held as an integral component of its mandate the pledge to act as a source of education to the general public as well as to individuals engaged in the field of water pollution control. Established 1928.

E References

1 Sources of Information

Sources of Information

Anne Maura English
Researcher/Bibliographer

The following reference listings are compiled primarily for urban administrators, staff members of government or research bureaus and other research and service organizations, and staff members of state and federal government agencies directly involved in urban affairs.

This edition's basic and functional area references have been compiled by Anne Maura English, independent researcher/bibliographer. The "Basic Statistical Resources Section" was prepared by Grace Waibel, information analyst at the U.S. Bureau of the Census.

Few sources listed in *The 1995 Municipal Year Book* were included in preceding editions. Nearly all sources listed have been published since January 1993. For a complete picture of publications issued during the past several years in this field, use this edition in conjunction with the Sources of Information in the preceding editions of *The Municipal Year Book*.

This updated bibliography includes a section on Basic References and another on Basic Statistical Resources, followed by 15 functional area subject headings. Under each subject are three sections: the first includes books, reports, monographs, bibliographies, and reference works and is intended to keep the urban administrator informed of the latest thinking in various fields. Annotations appear as necessary. The second section lists periodicals and includes magazines, journals, and newsletters. Frequency of publication is indicated as follows: (W)

weekly, (BW) biweekly, (M) monthly, (BM) bimonthly, (Q) quarterly, (SM) semimonthly, (SA) semiannually, (BA) biannually, (IRR) irregularly. A third section lists databases.

Many references listed here are written and published by well-known public interest groups or professional associations. In these cases, the name of the organization is not written in full. An abbreviation of the organization's name is used. For example, APA refers to the American Planning Association; IPMA refers to the International Personnel Management Association, etc. All abbreviations are included in the publishers' list at the end of this bibliography. Where they appear, they precede the full name of the organization and are followed by the word *see*. The publishers' list also provides the full names and addresses of other publishers whose publications have been listed in the bibliography.

The publications are not available from ICMA unless so noted in the entry or unless ICMA is the publisher.

Many ICMA publications are included in this bibliography. The notation BDR refers to Baseline Data Reports, SDI refers to Special Data Issues, and MIS refers to the reports of the Management Information Service. These reports are available by subscription and by individual copy. Information on how to order ICMA reports may be obtained by telephoning 1-800-745-8780.

Subject headings (2 basic reference headings followed by 15 functional area headings) used in this bibliography are

Basic References
Basic Statistical Resources
Emergency Management
Environment and Energy
Fire Protection
Housing
Human Services
Information Technologies
Intergovernmental Relations
Law Enforcement and Criminal Justice
Local Government Organization and
    Management
Personnel and Labor Relations
Planning and Development
Public Finance
Public Works and Utilities
Recreation and Leisure
Transportation and Roads

BASIC REFERENCES

BOOKS, REPORTS, MONOGRAPHS, BIBLIOGRAPHIES, AND REFERENCE SOURCES

Acronyms and Abbreviations of Computer Technology and Telecommunications. David Tavaglione. Dekker. 1993. 291p.

Associations Canada: An Encyclopedic Directory. Canadian Almanac and Directory. 1994. 1200p. The 20,000 entries in this directory encompass Canadian organizations or international associations active in Canada. Articles and statistics on association activity, convention information, and speakers' bureaus listings complete the text.

Buttress's World Guide to Abbreviations of Organizations. 10th ed. Jean C.M. Swinbank, Henry J. Heaney. Blackie Academic. 1993. 1048p.

Canadian Directory to Foundations. Norah McClintock. Canadian Centre for Philanthropy. 1994. 600p.

Companion to Contemporary Architectural Thought. Ben Farmer, Hentie Louw, eds. Routledge. 1993. 640p.

The Complete Directory for People with Disabilities. 3rd ed. Leslie MacKenzie, Amy Lignor. Grey House Publishing. 1994. 749p. Associations, organizations, media resources, products, and programs are covered in this exhaustive manual. Both a geographical index and an index by specific disability are provided.

Criminal Victimization in the United States: 1973–92 Trends. U.S. Bureau of Justice Statistics. 1994. 136p.

Demography of Aging. National Research Council. National Academy Press. 1994. 350p.

Dictionary of Legal Terms: A Simplified Guide to the Language of Law. 2nd ed. Stephen H. Gifis. Barron. 1993. 520p.

Dictionary of Professional Management: Fifty Thousand New Terms and Concepts Used in Private, Public and Third Sector Organizations. Systems Research Institute. 1994. 1500p.

Dictionary of Scientific and Technical Terms. Sybil P. Parker. McGraw-Hill. 1994. 2194p.

Directory of Organizations Engaged in Urban and Regional Research in Canada. ICURR. 1993. 120p. Both private and public agencies are listed.

Encyclopedia of Associations: Regional, State, Local. 4th ed. Niles Eldridge. Gale. 1994. Varied paging. The five volumes may be purchased separately. Each volume covers a different section of the U.S.

Encyclopedia of Business Information Sources. 10th ed. James B. Way. Gale. 1994. 877p. Here, managers and supervisors will find periodicals, trade associations, handbooks, bibliographies, and CD-ROM databases oriented to the needs of the manager.

Encyclopedia of Drugs and Alcohol. Edward Jerome Jaffe. Macmillan. 1994. 750p.

Encyclopedia of Environmental Control. Vol. 7: Work Area Hazards. Paul N. Chremesinoff, ed. Gulf. 1994. 768p.

Encyclopedia of Violence: Origins, Attitudes, Consequences. Margaret Dicanio. Facts on File. 1993. 416p.

Energy and American Society: A Reference Handbook. E. Willard Miller, Ruby M. Miller. ABC/CLIO. 1993. 418p. This book opens with a brief but thorough overview of the most common energy sources and a shorter look at alternate fuels. Other sections offer a chronology of the development of fuel use, a guide to energy-related laws and regulations in the U.S., a listing of pertinent U.S. governmental and intergovernmental agencies, and an annotated bibliography.

Every Manager's Guide to Information Technology: A Glossary of Key Terms and Concepts for Today's Business Leader. 2nd ed. Peter G. W. Keen. Harvard Business School Press. 1994. 232p.

Fax USA: A Directory of Facsimile Numbers for Business and Organizations Nationwide. Kay Gill, ed. Omnigraphics, Inc. 1994. 652p.

Federal Disability Law in a Nutshell. Bonnie Tucker. West. 1994. 437p.

The Foundation Center's Guide to Proposal Writing. Jane C. Geever, Patricia McNeill. The Foundation Center. 1993. 191p.

Guide to Federal Funding for Governments and Nonprofits. Elizabeth Basch, Heather C. Bodell, Charles J. Edwards, et al. Government Information Services. 1994. 3 vols., looseleaf, various paging. The introduction to this extensive guide covers such topics as meeting proposal requirements and locating appropriate sources. Funding resources are arranged by subject.

Guide to Multicultural Resources. Charles A. Taylor. Highsmith and Praxis. 1994. 476p.

HIV/AIDS Resources—The National Directory of Resources on HIV Infection/AIDS: The Professional's Reference. 5th ed. Mitchell F. Nauffts, ed. National Directory of Children, Youth and Families Services. 1994. 624p.

Homelessness: A Sourcebook. Rick Fantasia, Maurice Isserman. Facts on File. 1994. 320p.

International Acronyms, Initialisms and Abbreviations Dictionary. 3rd ed. Jennifer Mossman. Gale. 1993. 1211p.

Mastering NEPA: A Step-by-Step Approach. Ronald E. Bass, Albert Herson. Solano. 1993. 250p. This book walks the reader through the provisions of the National Environmental Policy Act (NEPA) and the environmental review process. NEPA mandates all government agencies to analyze and disclose the environmental impact of their decisions. This book provides guidelines for determining which actions come under NEPA, which situations require an Environmental Impact Statement, and how to prepare an EIS that meets legal requirements.

The National Association of State Information Resource Executives (NASIRE) 1994 Directory. NASIRE. 1994. The directory includes state information resource management officials, related federal officials and national information policy and management organizations.

Newnes Communications Technology Handbook. Geoffrey E. Lewis. Butterworth. 1994. 456p.

Non-Profit Corporations, Organizations, and Associations. 6th ed. Howard L. Okeck, Martha E. Stewart. Prentice-Hall. 1994. 1632p.

Owners and Officers of Private Companies. Mark W. Scott, Jacqueline K. Barrett. Taft. 1994. 2 vol. 3000p. Arranged by state, this directory lists chief executives of 113,000 companies with for annual sales over $5 million.

Ten Steps to Effective Presentations Training Workbook. ICMA. 1994. 127p. Planning is identified as the key to effectiveness with ten pointed steps given for the preparation, for the actual speech, and for effective visual aids and handouts.

Think Tank Directory: A Guide to Nonprofit Public Policy Research Organizations. Lynn Hellebust. Government Research Services. 1993. 350p.

Training and Development Organizations Directory. Janice McLean. Gale. 1994. 677p. This is a detailed listing of centers, organizations, and consulting groups that provide managerial training.

Understanding the Nature of Poverty in Urban America. James Jennings. Praeger. 1994. 209p. The past several decades have seen varied attempts to deal with poverty. This volume provides a thorough but readable overview of those approaches, analyzing their successes and failures from the combined perspective of academic research and the concrete insights of practitioners.

Violence in Urban America: Mobilizing a Response. Committee on Law and Justice. National Academy Press. 1994. 118p.

U.S. Industrial Outlook: An Almanac of Industry, Technology and Services. U.S. Department of Commerce/Bernan. 1994. 650p. After a brief review of trends and characteristics, this guide focuses on forecasts for job opportunities in an exhaustive listing of work fields.

PERIODICALS

Administration and Society. (Q) Sage.

COGEL Guardian. (BM) Council on Governmental Ethics Laws.

Congressional Quarterly Service Weekly Report. (W) CQ.

Governing. (M) CQ.

Government Executive. (M) National Journal.

Index to Current Urban Documents. (Q) Greenwood.

Management Information Service. (M) ICMA.

National Civic Review. (Q) National Civic League.

National Journal. (W) National Journal.

PAIS International in Print. (M) PAIS.

Planning. (M) APA.

Political Woman. (11/yr) Political Woman.

Public Administration Review. (BM) ASPA.

Public Affairs Quarterly. (Q) Bowling Green State University Philosophy Documentation Center.

Public Management. (M) ICMA.

Public Productivity and Management Review. (Q) Jossey-Bass.

Sage Urban Studies Abstracts. (Q) Sage.

Social Sciences Index. (Q) H. W. Wilson.

Urban Affairs Abstracts. (M) NLC.

Urban Affairs Quarterly. (Q) Sage.

DATABASE RESOURCES

Foundation Directory Database

Type: Directory

Coverage: 34,000 private and governmental sources for funding which can be searched by organization, area of interest, or type of support offered.

Scope: Updated annually.

Producer: The Foundation Center.

Available: DIALOG. Computer printout.

Local Government Information Network (LOGIN)

Type: Directory, full text.

Coverage: An information exchange service offering experience and expertise in technical data, how-to instructions, and information sources. Emphasis on innovation and efficiency. Bibliographic citations pertinent to local government.

Scope: Predominantly U.S. Updated daily. 1979—.

Producer: Login Services Corporation.

Available: Producer.

Management Information Service (MIS)

Type: Reference.

Coverage: A fee-based annual subscription service open to local governments. In addition to receiving selected ICMA publications, users may borrow documents or utilize Inquiry Service, which provides answers to specific research requests from a database of 12,000 documents.

Scope: Current.

Producer: ICMA.

Available: Producer.

Newsletters in Print (NIP)

Type: Directory

Coverage: Descriptions of over 11,000 subscription, membership, and free newsletters, bulletins, digests, and updates from public and private organizations.

Scope: U.S. and Canada. Updated every two years.

Producer: Gale

Available: HRIN

Newspaper and Periodical Abstracts

Type: Bibliographic

Coverage: Almost 2.5 million citations and abstracts to articles from 25 major newspapers, 1600 general interest, professional and scholarly journals, and 70 current affairs television programs.

Scope: U.S. Updated daily. 1989—.

Producer: UMI.

Available: CARL, CitaDel, DIALOG, Infomart, OCLC.

PAIS International

Type: Bibliographic

Coverage: Index to the public policy literature of business, economics, finance, law, international relations, government, political science, and other social sciences. Journal articles, books, government documents at all levels, pamphlets, and reports.

Scope: International. Updated monthly. 1976—.

Producer: Public Affairs Information Service.

Available: CompuServe, Data-Star, DIALOG. CD-ROM, magnetic tape.

Washington Post

Type: Full text.

Coverage: Newspaper articles offering in-depth coverage of government affairs.

Scope: Updated daily. 1989—.

Producer: Washington Post News Research Center.

Available: DataTimes, DIALOG, Dow Jones, Legi-Slate, News/Retrieval, NEXIS. CD-ROM.

Urban Data Service (UDS)

Type: Bibliographic, statistical.

Coverage: Subscription service package that includes six Special Data Issues each year with responses to survey data and *The Municipal Year Book*.

Scope: 1964—.

Producer: ICMA.

Available: Producer.

BASIC STATISTICAL RESOURCES

Grace Waibel

Population Division

U.S. Bureau of the Census

BOOKS, REPORTS, MONOGRAPHS, BIBLIOGRAPHIES, AND REFERENCE SOURCES

ICMA often receives requests from urban administrators concerning the availability of data sources. In response to these requests, we have compiled the following list of selected publications of the U.S. Departments of Commerce and Labor. The publications are divided into Employment, Finance, Population, and Housing, followed by the 1992 Census of Governments with descriptions of each volume and number. Other basic data sources are included at the end of this list. All publications that appear in this section of the *Year Book* are available from the GPO.

EMPLOYMENT

U.S. Department of Labor Bureau of Labor Statistics

Analysis of Work Stoppages. Annual statistical analysis.

Current Wage Developments. Monthly report summarizing wage and benefit changes in major collective bargaining situations. Compiled primarily from newspapers and other secondary sources.

National Survey of Professional, Administrative, Technical, and Clerical Pay. Annual bulletin summarizing the bureau's annual survey of selected professional, administrative, technical, and clerical pay in industry.

State and Local Government Employment and Payrolls. Monthly publication.

Work Stoppages. Preliminary statistical estimates of work stoppages for the entire year.

U.S. Department of Commerce Bureau of the Census

City Employment in (year). National and population size group statistics on October employment and payrolls of municipal governments, by function, with individual figures for about 460 cities and selected townships that have 50,000 population or more. GE (yr), No. 2.

Public Employment in (year). National totals on October employment and payrolls of all governments (including the federal government), by function, and by type of government. GE (yr), No. 1.

Survey of Governments, (year). Annual employment statistics. (Available from Customer Services, Census Bureau.)

FINANCE

U.S. Department of Labor Bureau of Labor Statistics

The Consumer Price Index. Monthly report on consumer price movements. Includes statistical tables and technical notes.

U.S. Department of Commerce Bureau of the Census

City Government Finances in (year). National and size-group totals of municipal government finances, with comparative totals for previous years. Supplies financial statistics for each of the approximately 460 cities and selected townships having 50,000 population or more, and additional detail for each of the 50 largest cities having 300,000 population or more. GF (yr), No. 4.

Finances of Employee-Retirement Systems of State and Local Governments in (year). Figures for the nation, by states, and for major individual systems, on the receipts, payments, and financial assets of employee-retirement systems administered by state and local governments. GF (yr), No. 2.

Government Finances in (year). National totals of revenue, expenditure, indebtedness, and assets covering all governments—federal, state, and local—with comparative summary data for previous years, and statistics for state and local governments, by states. GF (yr), No. 5.

Quarterly Summary of Federal, State, and Local Tax Revenue (quarter). These reports provide nationwide figures on tax revenue by level of government and type of tax, data on property tax collections for county areas with a population of 200,000 or more, and data for individual state governments of selected major taxes. GT (qr), Nos. 1–4.

POPULATION

U.S. Department of Commerce
Bureau of the Census

1990 Census

Public Law 94-171, the Legislative Redistricting Program. Selected population and housing unit counts for all states and the District of Columbia by geographic areas, ranging from states to Census blocs. Provided to all state legislatures and governors for legislative redistricting. P.L. 94-171 tapes, listings, and maps available for purchase; data also released on CD-ROM.

1990 Census of Population and Housing

Printed Reports

Summary Population and Housing Characteristics. (1990 CPH-1). Provides total population and housing unit counts, as well as summary statistics on age, sex, and race. Provides Hispanic origin, household relationship, units in structure, value and rent, number of rooms, tenure, and vacancy characteristics for local governments, including American Indian and Alaska Native areas.
Population and Housing Unit Counts. (1990 CPH-2 Series). Provides total population and housing unit counts for 1990 and previous censuses. Counts provided for most geographic units.
Population and Housing Characteristics for Census Tracts and Block Numbering Areas. (1990 CPH-3 Series). Statistics on 100 percent and sample population and housing subjects.
Population and Housing Characteristics for Congressional Districts of the 103rd Congress. (1990 CPH-4 Series). One report for each state and the District of Columbia showing population and housing data for Congressional districts, as well as other geographic units.
Summary Social, Economic, and Housing Characteristics. (1990 CPH-5 Series). These reports provide sample population and housing data for local governments, including American Indian and Alaska Native areas.

Computer Tape Files

STF 1. Includes 100 percent population and housing counts and characteristics similar in subject content to the 1980 STF 1 but with expanded detail.
STF 2. Contains 100 percent population and housing characteristics similar to the 1980 STF 2 but with expanded detail.
STF 3. Includes sample population and housing

characteristics similar in subject to the 1980 STF 3 but with expanded detail.
STF 4. Contains sample population and housing characteristics similar in content to 1980 STF 4 but with more subject detail than STF 3.

1990 Census of Population

General Population Characteristics. (1990 CP-1 Series). Detailed statistics on age, sex, race, Hispanic origin, marital status, and household relationship characteristics for various geographic areas, including states, counties, place of 1,000 or more inhabitants, and other geographic areas. Separate reports issued for each state and the United States.
General Population Characteristics for American Indian and Alaska Native Areas. (1990 CP-1-1A).
General Population Characteristics for Metropolitan Areas. (1990 CP-1-1B).
General Population Characteristics for Urbanized Areas. (1990 CP-1-1C).
Social and Economic Characteristics. (1990 CP-2 Series). These reports, one for each state and the U.S. summary, focus on the population subjects collected on a sample basis in 1990. Data shown for states, counties, and other geographic areas.
Social and Economic Characteristics for American Indian and Alaska Native Areas. (1990 CP-2-1A).
Social and Economic Characteristics for Metropolitan Areas. (1990 CP-2-1B).
Social and Economic Characteristics for Urbanized Areas. (1990 CP-2-1C).
Population Subject Reports. (1990 CP-3 Series). More than twenty reports (in print or tape or both) are planned covering population subjects and subgroups, including migration, income, and the older population.
(1990 CPH-L-Selected population and housing data paper listings). A series of works in progress. Listings compiled to meet needs of potential users. Covers various geographic areas and subjects; may include rankings, changes, etc. Available from Statistical Information Staff, Population Division, Bureau of the Census, Washington, DC 20233; (301) 763-5002.

Current Population Reports

In addition to the findings of the Census of Population conducted every ten years, the Bureau of the Census publishes continuing and up-to-date statistics on population counts, characteristics, and other special studies on the American people (described below). All issued under the general title *Current Population Reports.*
Local Population Estimates. (P-26 Series). Population estimates for counties and metropolitan areas for selected states. Figures prepared by a state agency as part of the Federal-State Cooperative Program for Local Population Estimates.
Population Characteristics. (P-20 Series). Current national and, in some cases, regional data on geographic residence and mobility,

fertility, education, school enrollment, marital status, numbers, and characteristics of households and families.
Population Estimates and Projections. (P-25 Series). Monthly estimates of the total population of the United States. Annual midyear state population estimates. Projections of the future population of the United States and individual states.
Special Censuses. (P-28 Series). Summary of population censuses generally taken at the request and expense of city or other local governments. Data are also available in Current Populations Survey Data Files. Subjects include personal and labor force data, estimates of after-tax money income, and non-cash benefit value. For complete description and list, see the *Census Catalog and Guide, 1992.*
Special Studies. (P-23 Series). Studies on methods, concepts, and specialized data. Includes occasional reports on the black population and other categories.

HOUSING

U.S. Department of Commerce
Bureau of the Census

1990 Census of Housing

General Housing Characteristics. (1990 CH-1 Series). Presents detailed statistics on units in structure, value and rent, number of rooms, tenure, and vacancy characteristics for states, counties, and other geographic areas.
General Housing Characteristics for American Indian and Alaska Native Areas. (1990 CH 1-1A).
General Housing Characteristics for Metropolitan Areas. (1990 CH-1-1B).
General Housing Characteristics for Urbanized Areas. (1990 CH-1-1C).
Detailed Housing Characteristics. (1990 CH-2 Series). These reports will focus on the housing subjects collected on a sample basis in 1990. Data will be shown for states, counties, and other geographic areas.
Detailed Housing Characteristics for American Indian and Alaska Native Areas. (1990 CH-2-1A).
Detailed Housing Characteristics for Metropolitan Areas. (1990 CH-2-1B).
Detailed Housing Characteristics for Urbanized Areas. (1990 CH-2-1C).
Housing Subject Reports. (1990 CH-3 Series). Ten housing subject reports are planned for items such as structural characteristics and space utilization. Geographic areas shown in the report generally will include the United States, regions, and divisions.

Products of the 1990 Census have been issued since 1991 with PL 94-171 reports. More complete descriptions of the reports as published can be found in the annual *Census Catalog and Guide* and the Monthly Report Announcement, issued by the Bureau of the Census and for sale by the Superintendent of Documents. For more information, call or write Customer Services, Bureau of the Census, Washington, DC 20233, or see these publications from the Bureau of the Census:

1990 Census of Population and Tabulation and Publication Program. A free report describing 1990 Census products, comparing 1990 with those of 1980, and more. Request from Customer Services, Bureau of the Census.

Census '90 Basics. A free booklet covering how 1990 Census data were collected and processed, data products, and more, available from Customer Services, Bureau of the Census.

AMERICAN HOUSING SURVEY

The American Housing Survey, published every other year in odd-numbered years, continues the Annual Housing Survey published annually until 1984. It provides current information on (1) size and composition of the housing inventory, (2) characteristics of its occupants, (3) changes in the inventory resulting from new construction, (4) indicators of housing and neighborhood quality, and (5) characteristics of recent movers.

1992 CENSUS OF GOVERNMENTS

U.S. Department of Commerce
Bureau of the Census

The 1992 Census of Governments, similar to those taken every 5 years since 1957, covers four major subject fields relating to state and local governments—government organization, taxable property values, public employment, and government finances.

The results are issued in six volumes, described below. Publication of individual reports/volumes is announced in the *Monthly Product Announcement*, issued by the Bureau of the Census. Publications order forms for specific reports may be obtained from any Department of Commerce district office or from Customer Services (publications), Bureau of the Census, Washington, DC 20233.

The 1992 Census of Governments began publication in 1993. For details, see the *Monthly Product Announcement* issued by the Data User Services Division, Bureau of the Census, Washington, DC 20233, or call Customer Services, (301) 763-4100.

Vol. 1. Government Organization.

No. 1. Government Organization. Data for the nation and by states on county, municipal, and township governments by size classes; on public school systems by size of enrollment, grades provided, and number of schools provided; and on special district governments by function and by amount of outstanding debt. Also shown is the number of local governments, by type, in each county area in the nation. This report also includes a description of local government structure in each state.

Vol. 2. Taxable Property Values.

Figures for the nation, states, counties, and selected cities having a population of 25,000 or more, on numbers of realty parcels and amounts of assessed value distributed by major property use categories.

Vol. 3. Public Employment.

No. 1. Employment of Major Local Governments. Statistics on October 1992 employment and payrolls for all county governments; municipalities and northeast townships having 10,000 or more population; school systems having 5,000 or more enrollment; and special district governments having 100 or more full-time employees.

No. 2. Compendium of Public Employment. Employment and payroll data are shown by government function for the nation, by states, and by type of government. Local government employment and payrolls are also summarized by county area.

No. 3. Labor-Management Relations. National and state-by-state statistics on the number of employees belonging to an employee organization; contractual agreements and employees covered; and employee bargaining units.

No. 4. Government Costs for Employee Benefits. A report providing statistics on state and local government costs for providing selected employee benefits. Data are presented by type of employee benefit, by state, and by type of government. Selected benefits include federal Social Security, retirement, unemployment insurance, disability insurance, life insurance, hospital/medical insurance, uniform and equipment allowances, bonuses and cash awards, and other benefits. The report also includes information on the number of current state and local government employees determined by federal Social Security.

Vol. 4. Government Finances.

No. 1. Finances Public School Systems. Statistics on revenue, expenditure, debt, and financial assets of school systems, presented for the nation, for states, and for school systems having 5,000 or more enrollment.

No. 2. Finances of Special Districts. Statistics on finances of special district governments by states and for selected large districts.

No. 3. Finances of County Governments. Statistics on revenue, expenditure, debt, and financial assets of county governments in summary for the nation, by size group and state, and for all individual county governments.

No. 4. Finances of Municipal and Township Governments. Statistics on revenue, expenditure, debt, and financial assets of municipalities and townships in summary for the nation, by size and state, and for all individual municipalities and northeast townships with a population of 10,000 or more.

No. 5. Compendium of Government Finances. A summary of census findings on government finances for federal, state, and local governments including derived data on per capita amounts and percentage distributions. Data are presented for the nation, for state areas by type of government, and local governments in each individual county area.

No. 6. Employee Retirement Systems of State and Local Governments. Membership, receipts, expenditure, number of beneficiaries, and financial assets of state and local government employee-retirement systems. Data are shown for the nation, for states, and for individual retirement systems having 200 or more members.

Vol. 6. Guide to the 1992 Census of Governments. A compilation of samples of tables published in the 1992 Census of Governments report series.

OTHER BASIC DATA SOURCES

U.S. Department of Commerce
Bureau of the Census

County and City Data Book, 1994. Statistical data for counties, states, regions, divisions, and cities.

Guide to Recurrent and Special Governmental Statistics. Summarizes the tabular presentations produced as part of the Census Bureau's program of state and local government statistics. Covers governmental finances, public employment, city employment, etc. Includes tabular presentation of summary statistics on a wide variety of subjects.

State and Local Government Special Studies. Irregular series of publications based on data collected through the Census Bureau's program of state and local government statistics.

State and Metropolitan Area Data Book, 1991. Presents a variety of statistical information for states and metropolitan areas, including population, vital statistics, education, labor, employment and earnings, business enterprises, and various economic data. Includes state, metropolitan, and area ranking tables.

Statistical Abstract of the United States. Annual. National data book and guide to sources. Standard summary of statistics on social, political, and economic organizations of the United States.

EMERGENCY MANAGEMENT

BOOKS, REPORTS, MONOGRAPHS, BIBLIOGRAPHIES, AND REFERENCE SOURCES

The Army's Role in Domestic Disaster Support: An Assessment of Policy Choices. John Y. Schrader. Rand. 1993. 33p.

At Risk: Natural Hazards, People's Vulnerability and Disasters. Piers Blaikie, Terry Cannon, Ian Davis, Ben Wisner. Routledge, 1994. 320p. For the authors, social, political, and economic factors are what turn a natural phenomenon into a "disaster." They advocate recognition of human vulnerability and willingness to take common action as first steps to disaster mitigation. Practical action and policy implications flow from this.

Bibliography on Dam Safety Practices. Association of State Dam Safety Officials. ASDSO. 1993. 167p.

Children and Disasters. C. F. Saylor, ed. Plenum Press. 1993. 237p. A comprehensive presentation of theory, therapeutic interventions, networking, cultural considerations, exercises, and networking, this book covers a broad range of specific situations from war and natural disasters to the witnessing of shootings or hostage takings.

Cross Training: Light the Torch. Association of State Floodplain Managers. NHRAIC. 1993. 264p. Proceedings from the 1993 ASFPM meeting address numerous aspects of flood hazard preparedness, mitigation, and recovery.

Current Practices in Modelling the Management of Stormwater Impacts. William James, ed. Lewis. 1994. 481p.

Disaster Evacuation and the Tourist Industry. Thomas E. Drabek. Institute of Behavioral Science, NHRAIC. 1994. 268p.

Disaster Response Guide: The Unique Role of the Religious Community in Disaster Response. Craig Paterson. Santa Clara Council of Churches. 1993. 246p. Aimed at grassroots religious leaders, this book urges the religious community to appreciate their role. General recommendations are supplemented by discussions of grief counseling, emergency shelter operation, and interfaith/interagency action.

Disaster Survival Planning Guides. Judy K. Bell. Disaster Survival Planning. 1944. 4 vols.: 25–72p. Detailed instructions and forms are provided in four volumes devoted to each step of the planning process: organizing, preparing, implementing, and testing. Software templates are available.

Earth Shock: Hurricanes, Volcanoes, Earthquakes, Tornadoes and Other Forces of Nature. Andrew Robison. Thames and Hudson. 1993. 304p.

Earthquake Recovery: A Survival Manual for Local Government. Association of Bay Area Governments. 1993. 483p. Each of the 30 sections of this handbook focuses on a specific recovery issue which a local government might face after an earthquake. Numerous concrete suggestions from California communities are included, as are the complete forms, procedures, and ordinances which these governments have developed.

Emergency Media Relations Guide: Implementation Resource and Training Guide for Spokespersons. James E. Lukaszewski. Phillips. 1993. Various paging.

Emergency Planning for Water Utility Management (M19). 3rd. AWWA. 1994. 108p.

Emergency Services Sourcebook. 3rd ed. Daniel G. Smith, ed. Specialized Publication Services. 1993. 1212p. Volume I provides an extensive listing of emergency training programs, national associations, clearinghouses, and relevant public agencies at each governmental level. Volume II is a directory to over 6,000 periodicals, books, audiovisuals, and software packages.

Environmental Risks and Hazards. Susan L. Cutter, ed. Prentice-Hall. 1994. 429p. This book draws together the research of various social sciences to examine hazards, disasters, and risk management. A final section highlights increasingly important dangers of human origin: chemical contamination, global environmental change, and warfare.

Flooding: Canada Water Book. Economics and Conservation Branch, Environment Canada. Canada Communication Group. 1993. 182p. One of Canada's contributions to the International Decade of Natural Disaster Reduction, this volume examines Canadian flooding of the last 200 years with examples from each province and territory. Flood responses from forecasting and preparedness to assistance programs are also scrutinized.

The Great Flood of 1993. Natural Disaster Survey Report. Office of Hydrology, National Weather Service. 1994. 348p. This report of the National Weather Service's performance during the flood concludes that most of the problems uncovered can be ascribed to technological flaws, rather than human error. Areas covered include the impacts of the flooding, forecast methodology, telecommunications and computer system, coordination, and preparedness.

Handbook of Emergency Chemical Management. D. R. Quigley. CRC Press. 1994. 727p.

Heat Wave Preparedness Task Force Preliminary Report. Commonwealth of Pennsylvania, Dept. of Aging. 1993. 62p.

Household and Community Recovery after Earthquakes. Robert C. Bolin. NHRAIC. 1994. 112p.

Improving Disaster Planning and Response Efforts: Lessons from Hurricanes Andrew and Iniki. Louis J. Levy, Llewellyn M. Toulman. Booz-Allen & Hamilton. 1993. 58p.

Landslides/Landslide Mitigation. J. E. Slosson, A. G. Kene, J. A. Johnson, eds. Geological Society of America. 1993. 124 p.

Learning from Disaster: Risk Management after Bhopal. Sheila Jasanoff, ed. University of Pennsylvania Press. 1994. 291p.

Natural Disasters. David Alexander. Chapman and Hall. 1993. 650p. This book provides a comprehensive analysis of the full spectrum of geophysical disasters and their impact on human society.

A New Species of Trouble: Explorations in Disaster, Trauma, and Community. Kai T. Erikson. W.W. Norton. 1994. 263p. Increasing complexity and industrialization are seen to complicate disasters and disaster recovery and to generate their own distinctive hazards.

Practical Lessons from the Loma Prieta Earthquake. Geotechnical Board, National Research Council. National Academy Press. 1994. 280p.

Preventing Chaos in a Crisis: Strategies for Prevention, Control and Damage Limitation. Patrick Lagadec. McGraw-Hill. 1993. 363p. The author offers theoretically-based practical recommendations to contemporary decision-makers who must factor a knowledgeable public and omnipresent media into their disaster management planning.

Retaining and Flood Walls. ASCE. 1994. 313p.

Seismic Awareness, Transportation Facilities: A Primer for Transportation Managers on Earthquake Hazards and Measures for Reducing Vulnerability. U.S. Department of Transportation. 1993. 220p.

Symposium: Women in Emergencies and Disasters. Bureau of Emergency Services, Queensland. 1993. 75p. These symposium proceedings draw on case studies to examine the special needs of women during disasters and to make recommendations.

The Utilization of Amateur Radio in Disaster Communications. Lynn Ellen Edwards. NHRAIC. 1994. 88p. On the basis of case studies examined here, the author concludes that amateur radio use should be included in agency disaster training and preparedness planning. She offers concrete recommendations for improved cooperation between operators and disaster response agencies.

PERIODICALS

Aware: Warning Coordination and Hazard Awareness Report. (Q) National Oceanic and Atmospheric Administration.

Disaster Management. (Q) Joint Assistance Centre.

Disaster Volunteer. (M) Cher Amie.

Disasters: The Journal of Disaster Relief and Management. (Q) Basil Blackwell.

Earthquake Spectra. (Q) Earthquake Engineering Research Institute.

Earthquakes and Volcanos. (BM) U.S. Geological Survey. GPO.

Emergency Preparedness Digest. (Q) Emergency Preparedness Canada.

Emergency Preparedness News. (BW) Business Publishers.

Hazard. (10/yr) EIS International.

Hazard Technology: News on Crisis Management Systems and Applications. (BM) EIS International.

Hazardous Materials Control. (BM) Hazardous Materials Control Resources Institute.

Hazardous Materials Newsletter. (BM) Hazardous Materials Publishing.

Hazardous Waste News. (W) Business Publishers.

Journal of Civil Defense. (Q) American Civil Defense Association.

Natural Hazards. (6/yr) Kluwer.

Natural Hazards Observer. (BM) NHRAIC.

NCCEM Bulletin (M) National Coordinating Council on Emergency Management.

Phenomenal News. (Q) Natural Phenomena Hazards Project.

Rescue. (BM) JEMS.

Response! The Journal of Search, Rescue, and Emergency Response. (Q) National Association of Search and Rescue Headquarters.

SARScene: The Canadian Search and Rescue Newsletter. (Q) National Search and Rescue Secretariat

Watermarks. (3–4/yr) Center for Research in Water Resources, University of Texas-Austin.

DATABASE RESOURCES

Disaster Management Information System (DMIS)

Type: Reference, directory.

Coverage: A series of files including the Automated Disaster Reporting System, Damage Survey Report, Disaster Field Office/Disaster Assistance, and separate files on numerous aspects of disaster relief benefits.

Scope: English language. Most files are updated daily or as changes occur.

Producer: FEMA, Office of Information Resources Management.

Available: Producer.

Emergency Management Information Center (EMIC)

Type: Loan program.

Coverage: Case studies, both print and audio-visual, that document specific natural or man-made disasters, including floods, hurricanes, tornadoes, earthquakes, urban fires, and transportation accidents.

Scope: National Emergency Training Center.

Producer: FEMA.

Available: FEMA.

National Earthquake Information Center (NEIC)

Type: Digital and analog data.

Coverage: Data on earthquakes that have occurred around the world including time, location, depth, magnitude, and other characteristics.

Scope: Updated as events occur.

Producer: U.S. Geological Survey, Denver, CO.

Available: Producer.

National Emergency Training Center. Learning Resource Center, FEMA

Type: Reference.

Coverage: A library rather than a database. Access to personnel who will answer inquiries, perform literature searches, compile bibliographies and, within copyright limitations, provide documentation.

Producer: National Emergency Training Center, Learning Resource Center.

Available: Producer

National Fire Incident Reporting System (NFIRS)

Type: Statistical.

Coverage: Data that can be used in determining the magnitude and characteristics of fire problems, in decision-making, and in developing a local fire data system.

Scope: U.S. 1982.

Producer: FEMA

Available: Producer. Magnetic tape.

Urban Search and Rescue Database

Type: Directory.

Coverage: Names and addresses of persons and organizations who work with heavy collapse search and rescue operations.

Scope: Current information.

Producer: NIUSR.

Available: Labels available for purchase from producer.

ENVIRONMENT AND ENERGY

BOOKS, REPORTS, MONOGRAPHS, BIBLIOGRAPHIES, AND REFERENCE SOURCES

Air Pollution and Climate Change: The Biological Impact. Alan Wellburn. Halsted. 1994. 288p.

Applied Wetlands Science and Technology. Donald M. Kent, ed. Lewis. 1994. 436p. Topics covered include wetland management, wastewater and stormwater drainage, water quality renovation, wetlands for wildlife, and wetlands education.

Arsenic in the Environment. Jerome O. Nriagu, ed. Wiley. 1994. Pt. 1, 560p, Pt. 2, 345p.

Clean Ships, Clean Ports, Clean Oceans: Controlling Garbage and Plastic Wastes at Sea. National Research Council. National Academy. 1994. 300p. This book examines both progress toward and obstacles to compliance with MARPOL, 73/78 Annex V, the international treaty for garbage control at sea. Industry, military, and shoreside residents all get a chance to speak up.

Culture, Conflict, and Communication in the Wildland Urban Interface. A.W. Ewert, D.J. Chavez, A.W. Magill. International Association of Wildland Fire. 1993. 410p. Articles in this volume address such issues as fostering a land ethic among non-traditional wildland users, communicating effectively with different cultures, and managing destructive behavior.

Defense Environmental Cleanup Program Annual Report to Congress for Fiscal Year 1993. GPO. 1994. 734p. Progress to date on the cleanup of hazardous wastes at defense sites is presented, arranged alphabetically by the name of the military base or installation.

Degrees of Disaster—Prince William Sound: How Nature Reels and Rebounds. Jeff Wheelwright. Simon & Schuster. 1994. 348p. While not trivializing long term effects, the author notes the amazing recuperative signs in this post-Valdez site.

Energy Management Guide for Government Buildings. Albert Thumann, Robert Nashide, eds. Prentice-Hall. 1994. 551p. Numerous concrete recommendations are made for making public buildings more energy efficient.

Energy Management Handbook. 2nd ed. Wayne C. Turner, ed. Fairmont. 1993. 627p. This book treats an exhaustive spectrum of energy management topics: codes, standards and legislation; energy auditing and maintenance for systems boilers through air conditioning. Alternative energy sources are also examined.

Environmental Analysis, Air Quality, Noise, Energy, and Alternative Fuels. TRB. 1994. 130p.

Environmental Impacts of Mining: Monitoring, Restoration, and Control. M. Sengupta. Lewis. 1993. 494p.

Environmental Regulatory Process: Does It Work? Dredging U.S. Ports. TRB. 1994. 62p.

Environmental Restoration and Waste Management: A Guide to the Issues. Linda Murakami, David Furneaux, Asiyih Davis, Sean Cavanaugh. NCSL Conference. 1994. 115p.

Everything You Wanted to Know about Environmental RegulationsBut Were Afraid to Ask: A Guide for Small Communities. Rev. ed. EPA. 1993. 85p.

Glaciers and Environmental Change. W. H. Theakstone, J. A. Matthews, C. Harris. Edward Arnold. 1994. 320p. The latest research is used to discuss how glaciers figure in climatic changes over time and in current concerns about climate change and global warming.

Implementing a Stormwater Management Program. David S. Pyzoha. Lewis. 1994. 170p.

Industrial Environmental Control: Pulp and Paper Industry. Tappi, Water Quality Committee. Tappi. 1993. 650p.

Innovative Energy and Environmental Applications. Marilyn Jackson, ed. Fairmont. 1993. 625p. Papers presented at the World Energy Engineering Conference bring case study and technical analysis to a wide range of topics from wastewater treatment to manufactured housing.

International Conference on Emerging Natural Gas Technologies: Implications and Applications. International Energy Agency. OECD. 1993. 219p.

Introduction to Oil and Gas Environmental Project Management. Tim Marler. PennWell. 1994. 320p.

Keys to Success: Ten Case Studies of Effective Weatherization Programs. M.A. Brown, L.G. Berry, J.O. Kolb, et al. NTIS. 1993. 206p. This report is a careful analysis of the characteristics which underlie the proven success of these ten programs.

Local Prosecution of Environmental Crime. Theodore M. Hammett, Joel Epstein. Diane. 1994. 111p.

Low-Level Radioactive Waste: A Legislator's Guide. L. Cheryl Runyon, James B. Reed, Barbara Foster. NCSL. 1994. 98p.

No Turning Back: Dismantling the Fantasies of Environmental Thinking. Wallace Kaufman. Basic. 1994. 210p. The author, a noted environmental activist, argues that the environmental crisis cannot be solved merely by returning contemporary civilization to a simpler lifestyle. Technological advances must be accepted and utilized to address the problems.

Phosphate Fertilizers and the Environment: A Discussion Paper. James J. Schultz, D. Ian Gregory, Orvis P. Engelstad. International Fertilizer Development Center. 1993. 51p.

Polluting for Pleasure. This book examines the environmental aspects of boats and boating on coastal and inland waterways. Audre Merle. W. W. Norton. 1993. 224p.

Power from Plants: The Global Implications of New Technologies for Electricity from Biomass. Walt Patterson, Roger Booth, Philip Elliot. Brookings. 1994. 80p.

Toxic Substances in the Environment. B. Magnus Francis. Wiley. 1994. 376p.

Tree Conservation Ordinances: Land-Use Regulations Go Green. Christopher Duerksen. Planning Advisory Service Report. APA. 1993. 446p.

Water: Opposing Viewpoints. Greenhaven. 1994. 191p. Diverse perspectives are offered for a wide range of problems from acid rain to water management.

PERIODICALS

Air and Waster: Journal of the Air and Waste Management Association. (M) Air and Waste Management Association.

Coastal Management: An International Journal of Marine Environment, Resources, Law and Society. (Q) Taylor and Francis.

Environmental Communique of the States. (BM) CSG.

Environmental Viewpoints. (A) Gale.

From the State Capitals: Environmental Regulation. (W) Wakeman/Walworth.

Garbage: The Practical Journal for the Environment. (6-yr) Old House Journal.

International Journal of Environment and Pollution. (Q) Inderscience Enterprises.

Journal of Energy and Development. (SA) International Research Center for Energy and Economic Development.

Journal of Environmental Engineering. (BM) American Society of Civil Engineers.

Land Economics. (Q) Land Tenure Center, University of Wisconsin-Madison.

Resources, Conservation and Recycling. (M) Elsevier (New York).

Wasteline. (Q) New York State Department of Environmental Conservation.

DATABASE RESOURCES

Energy, Science, and Technology
Type: Bibliographic
Coverage: Wide range of topics related to energy: nuclear, wind, fossil, geothermal, tidal, and solar.
Scope: Updated biweekly. 1974—.
Producer: U.S. Department of Energy.
Available: DIALOG

Energyline
Type: Bibliographic.
Coverage: Books, journals, congressional committee reprints, conference proceedings, speeches, statistics.
Scope: International. Updated monthly. 1971—
.
Producer: Congressional Information Service.
Available: Data-Star, DIALOG, ESA-IRS, FIZ, ORBIT. CD-ROM, magnetic tape.

Enviroline
Type: Bibliographic
Coverage: Comprehensive, interdisciplinary, worldwide collection of periodicals, government documents, industry reports, proceedings, newspaper articles, films, monographs, patents, judicial rulings.
Scope: Updated monthly. 1971—.

Producer: Bowker A&I Publishing.
Available: Data-Star, DIALOG, DIMDI, ESA-IRS, FIZ, ORBIT. CD-ROM, magnetic tape.

Hazardous Waste News
Type: Full Text
Coverage: Legislative, regulatory, and judicial decisions at state and federal levels
Scope: International. English language. Updated weekly. 1982—.
Producer: Business Publishers
Available: NewsNet

Pollution Abstracts
Type: Bibliographic
Coverage: Worldwide technical and nontechnical literature on pollution research sources and controls: air, water, land, thermal, noise, and radiological pollution; pesticides; sewage and waste treatment; toxicology and health.
Scope: Updated bimonthly. 1970—.
Producer: Cambridge Scientific Abstracts
Available: CompuServe, Data-Star, DIALOG, ESA-IRS, STN International. CD-ROM, magnetic tape.

RecycleLine
Type: Bulletin Board
Coverage: Upcoming events in the recycling field, markets, prices, and recycled products.
Scope: Current
Producer: American Recycling Market
Available: Producer

Water Resources Abstracts
Type: Bibliographic
Coverage: Citations, with abstracts, to scientific and technical literature on all aspects of water, including quality, quantity, conservation, control, use, and management of water resources.
Scope: International. Updated monthly. 1968—.
Producer: U.S. Geological Survey. Water Resources Scientific Information Center.
Available: DIALOG. CD-ROM, magnetic tape.

FIRE PROTECTION

BOOKS, REPORTS, MONOGRAPHS, BIBLIOGRAPHIES, AND REFERENCE SOURCES

Advanced Life Support Skills. E. Jackson Allison, ed. Mosby. 1994. 274p.

Advances in Detection and Suppression Technology. Proceedings of the Society of Fire Protection Engineers Engineering Seminars. SFPE. 1994. 135p.

Crash, Fire, and Rescue Handbook. Charles Bellomo, John Lynch. IAP. 1994. 94p. The special problems of responding to airplane crashes are discussed in this book.

Critical Incident Stress Debriefing—CISD: An Operations Manual for the Prevention of Traumatic Stress among Emergency Services and Disaster Workers. Jeffrey T. Mitchell. Chevron. 1993. 223p. This work also outlines procedures for setting up a CISD team.

Development of a Machine Vision Fire Detec-

tion System. A. D. Goedeke, G. Healey, B. Drda. NTIS. 1994. 81p.

Fighting Fires with Foam. Steven P. Woodworth, John A. Frank. Van Nostrand Reinhold. 1994. 228p. The authors, experienced crash and structural firefighters, provide an in-depth but highly readable discussion of situations in which foam fighting is desirable, as well as techniques and logistics for its use. A planning guide and checklist are provided.

Fire Apparatus Purchasing Handbook. William C. Peters. Fire Engineering Books & Videos. 1994. 450p.

The Fire Department Water Supply Handbook. William F. Eckman. Fire Engineering Books & Videos. 1994. 440p.

Fire Litigation Sourcebook. 2nd ed. Alexander J. Patton. Wiley. 1994. 445p. Focused primarily on legal issues, this book includes a detailed examination of the information needed from the scene for cases from flammable material to arson.

Fire Protection Systems. Justin Duncan. Business News Publishing. 1994. 312p.

Fire Service Administration. Nancy K. Grant, David M. Hoover. NFPA. 1994. 442p. This text and reference is geared to help fire officers develop the skills and techniques which field research has identified as needed by fire service administrators.

Fire Suppression and Detection Systems. 3rd ed. John L. Bryan. Macmillan. 1993. 608p.

Fire-raising: Its Motivation and Management. Herschel Prins. Routledge. 1994. 224p.

Firefighting Lore: Strange but True Stories from Firefighting History. W. Fred Conway. Fire Buff House. 1993. 188p.

First Responder. 3rd ed. David Bergeron, Gloria J. Bizjak, David M. Wall. Brady. 1994. 382p. This newly revised manual for emergency medical technicians now includes a section on protection from airborne pathogens.

Forest Wildfire. Canadian Forestry Association. International Association of Wildland Fire. 1994. 96p. This reprint of a special edition of *Forestry on the Hill* contains 30 articles devoted to problems and strategies concerning forest wildfires.

Handbook of Pediatric Emergencies. 2nd ed. Gregory A. Baldwin, M.D., ed. Little, Brown, & Co. 1994. 601p. This edition expands treatment of resuscitation, cardiac and respiratory emergencies, environmental emergencies, and trauma. It includes a new chapter on transportation of the critically ill child.

Hazardous Material Dictionary. 2nd ed. Ronny J. Coleman. Technomic. 1994. 209p. This guide is aimed at the communication needs of emergency dispatchers and service personnel. It provides some attention to code enforcement and hazmat programs.

Instructional Methods in Emergency Services: A Resource Text Designed for EMS, Fire, and Rescue Instructors. William D. McClincy. Prentice-Hall. 1994. 336p.

International Translation Guide for Emergency Medicine. G. G. Bodiwala, A. W. McCaskie, M. M. Thomson. Butterworth-Heinemann. 1993. 227p.

Introduction to a Civil Disturbance: Survival in a Hostile Environment. Jerry Smith. International Consulting System. 1993. 40p. Prompted by experience during the LA riots, this book draws on the plans and experiences of six localities to discuss issues of fireground tactics, rescue, and personal safety under extreme conditions.

Making & Managing Money: A Financial Planning Workbook for Volunteer Departments. Howard Chatterton, Margaret Chatterton. Fire Engineering Books and Videos. 1994. 109p.

Performance-Based Fire Safety Engineering. Proceedings of the Society of Fire Protection Engineers Engineering Seminars. SFPE. 1994. 85p.

Presuppression of Roadside Fires. D. S. Hauser, W. G. McCully. NTIS. 1993. 31p.

Psycheresponse: Psychological Skills for Optimal Performance by Emergency Responders. Michael J. Asken. Brady. 1993. 172p. The author, a consultant and instructor with fire service programs, draws extensively on sports comparisons to train emergency responders to manage stress *during* crisis situations.

Rural Rescue and Emergency Care. Robert A. Worsing. American Academy of Orthopaedic Surgeons. 1993. 368p. Much of this book is devoted to the problems of extrication, with separate chapters on agricultural equipment, tractors, combines, grain and silage storage facilities.

Safe Fire Fighter Staffing: Critical Considerations. Department of Research and Labor Issues. International Association of Fire Fighters. 1993. 37p. This book provides standards to use in making decisions about level of service. It encourages fire service leadership to take the offensive in informing the public about the relationship between funding, staffing, and service.

Wilderness Medicine: Beyond First Aid. 4th ed. William W. Forguy, ed. I.C.S. Books. 1994. 192p. Wilderness Society practice guidelines for wilderness emergency.

PERIODICALS

American Fire Journal. (M) Fire Publications.
The Canadian Firefighter. (BM) Canadian Firefighter.
Emergency. (M) Hare.
Emergency Medical Services. (10/yr) Creative Age.
Fire and Arson Investigator. (Q) International Association of Arson Investigators.
Fire and Police Personnel Reporter. (M) Public Safety Personnel Research Institute.
Fire Chief. (M) Communications Channels.
Fire Engineering. (M) PennWell, NJ.
Fire Safety Engineering. (BM) Paramount Publishing, U.K.
Fire Technology. (Q) NFPA.
Firefighting in Canada. (9/yr) NCC.
Firehouse. (M) PTN Publishing.
JEMS: A Journal of Emergency Medical Services. (M) JEMS Publishing.

Journal of Fire Protection Engineering. (Q) SFPE.
Journal of Fire Sciences. (BM) Technomic.
NFPA Journal. (BM) NFPA.
Sprinkler Age. (M) American Fire Sprinkler Association.
Sprinkler Quarterly. (Q) National Fire Sprinkler Association.
VOICE. (M) International Society of Fire Service Instructors.
Wildfire. (Q) International Association of Wildland Fire.
Wildfire News and Notes. (4/yr) NFPA.

DATABASE RESOURCES

Applied Science and Technology Index.
Type: Bibliographic.
Coverage: Basic index to 390 science and technology journals.
Scope: Updated twice weekly. Oct 1983—.
Producer: H. W. Wilson.
Available: CDP, OCLC, Wilsonline. CD-ROM, magnetic type.

BRIX/FLAIR
Type: Bibliographic.
Coverage: Citations, with abstracts, to books, journals, and reports on construction and fire science. The FLAIR file covers fire detections, ignition, growth, extinction and suppression, special fire hazards in industries and materials, structural aspects of fire in buildings, firefighting, and fire statistics.
Scope: International, English language. Updated monthly. 1950—.
Producer: Great Britain Department of the Environment.
Available: ESA-IRS.

Fire Research Computer bulletin board
Type: Computer bulletin board.
Coverage: Computer programs developed by the Center for Fire Research, its activities, information about FIREDOC, and simulation programs. No fee or password is necessary, but telephone costs are paid by user.
Scope: Center for Fire Research Activities. Current.
Producer: U.S. National Institute of Standards and Technology. Center for Fire Research.
Available: Producer.

FIREDOC
Type: Bibliographic.
Coverage: Over 35,000 citations to reports, articles, books, conference proceedings, and audiovisual materials.
Scope: Fire Research Information Service holdings. Updated daily. 1974—.
Producer: U.S. National Institute of Standards and Technology. Building and Fire Research Laboratory.
Available: Producer.

FIREfacts
Type: Computer bulletin board.
Coverage: Information from NFPA's *Fire News*, notices of meetings, and public education materials.

Scope: Current.
Producer: NFPA.
Available: Accessed via Connect and Connect software.

ICHIEFS
Type: Computer bulletin board.
Coverage: Master calendar of events and conferences; *Fire Flash* (news and studies of local incidents); the ICHIEF library; hazardous materials information; and discussion, issues, drills, product support, and troubleshooting tips for Computer-Aided Management of Emergency Operations (CAMEO).
Scope: Current.
Producer: IAFC.
Available: Accessed via Connect and Connect software.

HOUSING

BOOKS, REPORTS, MONOGRAPHS, BIBLIOGRAPHIES, AND REFERENCE SOURCES

The Affordable City: Toward a Third Sector Housing Policy. Lawrence B. Joseph, ed. Temple University Press. 1994. 311p. This book uses the Boston experience to explore the roles of state, local government, and community-based nongovernmental organizations in addressing the housing crisis.

Affordable Housing and Public Policy: Strategies for Metropolitan Chicago. John Emmeus Davis. Center for Urban Research and Policy Studies, University of Chicago. 1993. 371p. Chicago's experience illustrates the effect of a new emphasis on the affordability of privately-owned housing. involvement of public sector in producing, assisting and promoting. New models of social ownership community-owned and non-profit.

American Homelessness: A Reference Handbook. 2nd ed. Mary Ellen Hombs. ABC-CLIO. 1994. 230p.

Breakthroughs: Re-creating the American City. Neal R. Peirce, Robert Guskind. Center for Urban Policy Research. Rutgers. 1994. 203p. Despite the award title—Rudy Bruner Award for Excellence in the Urban Environment—two of the six winners showcased here are small rural towns. Their successes are examined as models for how neighborhoods can be transformed by collective action.

Building Code Quick Reference Guide: A Schematics Building Design Timesaver. William J. Brummett, Alec W. Johnson. Professional Publications. 1993. 118p.

Capital and Communities in Black and White. Gregory D. Squires. SUNY. 1994, 166p. This book examines central structural characteristics that contribute to patterns of separation in housing and urban development.

Developing Affordable Housing: A Practical Guide for Nonprofit Organizations. Bennett L. Hecht. Wiley. 1994. 499p.

Development, Marketing and Operation of

Manufactured Home Communities. George Allen, David Alley, Edward Hicks, Joseph Owens. Wiley. 1994. 456p.

Down and Out in Canada: Homeless Canadians. Thomas O'Reilly-Fleming. Canadian Scholars Press. 1993. 202p.

Drug Enforcement in Public Housing: Signs of Success in Denver. Sampson O. Annan. Police Foundation. 1993. 47p.

Element of Risk: The Politics of Radon. Leonard A. Cole. Oxford University Press. 1994. 246p.

Final Report: National Commission on Manufactured Housing. GPO. 1994. 195p. The Commission will submit recommendations from these findings as proposed legislation.

Homelessness: An Annotated Bibliography. James M. Henslin. Garland. 1993. 1104p.

Housing on the Block: Disinvestment and Abandonment Risks in New York City. Victor Bach, Sherece Y. West. Community Services Society of New York. 1993. 134p. This book analyzes the cycle of property tax loss.

Local Historic Preservation Plans: A Selected Annotated Bibliography. Neil Gagliardi. U.S. Department of the Interior. 1993. 26p.

Managing the Residential Treatment Center in Troubled Times. Northrup Gordon, ed. Haworth Press. 1994. 124p. This book considers ideas for major restructuring as well as service contracting to independent agencies. It includes a successful example of the placement of a treatment home for girls in a highly resistant neighborhood.

Ownership, Control, and the Future of Housing Policy. R. Allen Hays, ed. Greenwood Press. 1993. 257p. This book brings a comparative perspective to such issues as converting multi-family housing to cooperatives, tenant control, and the role of neighborhood-based nonprofit housing organizations, attempting to assess their significance for the future of housing policy.

Paths to Homelessness: Extreme Poverty and the Urban Housing Crisis. Doug A. Timmer, D. Stanley Eitzen, Kathryn D. Talley. Westview Press. 1994. 210p. Through individual case studies this book seeks to change the reader's focus from the characteristics of individuals to the structural conditions which are the root causes of homelessness.

Post-Disaster Residential Rebuilding. Mary C. Comerio, John D. Landis, Yodan Rofe. Institute of Urban and Regional Development. 1994. 93p. Inadequacies in current recovery programs are highlighted by a follow-up on Loma Prieta. Although multifamily and residential rental property accounted for 60–70% of the housing destroyed, recovery programs continue to focus on middle- and upper-income homeowners.

Rehabilitating Apartments: A Recycling Process. Robert A. Cagann. Institute of Real Estate Management. 1994. 193p.

Report on Emerging Resident Management Corporations in Public Housing. GPO. 1993. 52p. A number of key policy conclusions are drawn from this study of 80 resident man-

agement corporations which received HUD assistance grants between 1988–1990.

Shelter Burden: Local Politics and Progressive Housing Policy. Edward G. Goetz. Temple University. 1993. 250p. This book chronicles the results of the federal withdrawal from housing support in the past decade. It analyzes the resultant transformation of housing policy.

Tenants' Rights: California. 12th edition. Myron Moskovitz. Nolo Press. 1994. Various paging.

The Uptown Kids: Struggle and Hope in the Projects. Terry M. Williams. Putnam. 1994. 256p. Research begun in 1989 in Harlem is used to combat stereotypes about project youth. Without minimizing the real problems, these interviews demonstrate that projects can be good places to raise children, providing a better environment than surrounding tenements.

Urbanization: An Introduction to Urban Geography. Paul L. Knox. Prentice-Hall. 1994. 436p. The need to achieve a balance between residential needs and corporate priorities in urban development is the focus here. Eight of the 15 chapters focus on how neighborhoods change.

PERIODICALS

Architecture. (M) BPI Communications.

Association for Preservation Technology-Communique. (Q) Association for Preservation Technology International.

Builder. (M) NAHB.

Building Official and Code Administrator. (BM) BOCA.

Current Construction Reports. (Q) U.S. Bureau of the Census.

Current Housing Reports. (Q) U.S. Bureau of the Census.

Historic Preservation. (BM) National Trust for Historic Preservation.

Housing and Development Reporter. (BW) Warren, Gorham & Lamont.

Journal of Housing. (BM) NAHRO.

Journal of Social Distress and the Homeless. (Q) Human Sciences.

NAHRO Monitor. (SM) NAHRO.

Town and Country Planning. (M) Town and Country Planning Association, England.

DATABASE RESOURCES

CENDATA
Type: Statistical, full text.
Coverage: U.S. population and demographic figures drawn from all U.S. Bureau of the Census programs, including housing.
Scope: U.S. Updated daily, 1980—.
Producer: U.S. Bureau of the Census. Data Users Services Division.
Available: CompuServe, DIALOG.

DRI Housing Forecast
Type: Numeric.

Coverage: Projections of new and existing single-family homes in the U.S. Thirteen quarterly historical and forecast time series show housing sales and prices.
Scope: U.S. Updated quarterly, 1970—.
Producer: DRI/McGraw-Hill. Data Products Division.
Available: Producer.

State Housing and Construction
Type: Time series.
Coverage: Housing, demographics, financial and economic data, and construction expenditures in 36,000 weekly, monthly, quarterly, and annual time series for U.S., states, and regions.
Scope: U.S. Time and updating vary by series.
Producer: WEFA Group.
Available: Producer. Diskette, magnetic tape.

HUMAN SERVICES

BOOKS, REPORTS, MONOGRAPHS, BIBLIOGRAPHIES, AND REFERENCE SOURCES

Barrios and Borderlands: Cultures of Latinos and Latinas in the United States. Denis Lynn Daly Heyck. Routledge. 1994. 448p. This volume uses interviews and oral histories to explore Latino culture in various walks of life and various geographic areas.

The Chronically Disabled Elderly in Society. Merna J. Alpert. Greenwood. 1994. 141p.

Collaborating for Comprehensive Services for Young Children and Their Families: The Local Interagency Coordinating Council. William W. Swan, Janet L. Meyer. Paul H. Brookes. 1993. 249p. This book presents eight premises underlying collaboration, stages in collaborative implementation, and specific steps need to stimulate interagency work. Differences between state and local efforts are surveyed.

The Cruelest Death: The Enigma of Adolescent Suicide. David Lester. Charles. 1993. 178p.

Dilemmas in Human Services Management: Illustrative Case Studies. Raymond Sanchez Mayers, Frederico Souffles, Jr., Dick J. Schoech. Springer. 1994. 130p. This text in human services presents case studies to strengthen for discussion in training, in-service, or personal skill-building.

Employment and Training Strategies to Reduce Family Poverty. Theodora Ooms. Family Impact Seminar. 1993. 41p.

Exemplary Social Intervention Programs for Members and Their Families. David Guttman, Marvin B. Sussman, eds. Haworth. 1994. 194p.

Interprofessional Care and Collaborative Practice. R. Michael Casto, Maria C. Julia, Larry J. Platt. Brooks/Cole. 1994. 179p.

Leadership Skills: Developing Volunteers for Organizational Success. Emily Kittle Morrison. Fisher. 1994. 223p.

Living on the Edge: The Realities of Welfare in

America. Mark Robert. Columbia University. 1994. 266p.

Losing Generations: Adolescents in a High Risk Setting. Shepherd Zeldin, ed. National Academy. 1993. 276p.

Making Sense of Federal Dollars: A Funding Guide for Social Service Providers. Madelyn DeWoody. Child Welfare League. 1994. 156p. After a clear introduction of basic information, this guide focuses on programs targeted at children, youth, and families.

Measuring Poverty: A New Approach. Constance F. Citro, Robert Michael, Nancy Maritato, eds. National Academy. 1994. 350p. This book responds to dissatisfaction with the 30-year-old system for measuring poverty by offering concrete alternatives.

Mental Health in Mental Retardation: Recent Advances & Practices. Nick Bouras, ed. Cambridge University Press. 1994. 300p. After an initial historical survey of the topic, this book devotes five chapters to examining identifying types of programs and describing their implementation.

Networking AIDS Services. Vincent Mor, John A. Fleishman, Susan M. Allen, John D. Piettle. Health Administration Press. 1994. 238p. The Robert Wood Johnson Foundation conducted this independent evaluation of the four-year operation of a grant-funded program to develop a community-based network of services needed for persons with AIDS.

Parallel Views: Education and Access for Deaf People in France and the U. S. French American Foundation. Gallaudet University Press. 1994. 262p.

Performance Review and Quality Assurance in Social Care. Anne Connor, Stewart Black, eds. Jessica Kingsley. 1994. 262p.

Person-in-Environment System: The PIE Classification System for Social Functioning Problems. James M. Karles, Karin E. Wandrei, eds. NASW. 1994. 288p. This manual shows how to use the PIE system to help understand clients in a variety of social service settings: health care, family services, welfare departments, mental health delivery, EAP programs, and case management.

Perverse Incentives: The Neglect of Social Technology in the Public Sector. Theodore Caplow. Praeger. 1994. 164p. The author identifies the hidden but powerful rewards and penalties that are built into the social system and hamper efforts to achieve genuine reform.

The Politics of Caring: Human Services at the Local Level. Alan J. Hahn. Westview. 1994. 256p.

Proceedings—Workshop on Needle Exchange and Bleach Distribution Programs. National Research Council and Institute of Medicine. National Academy Press. 1994. 360p. Research on and experience with programs is used to assess effects on rates of drug use, behavior of drug users, and the spread of HIV and other infections. International evaluations of needle exchange programs, legal issues, and U.S. data are presented.

The Professional Review Action Group (PRAG) Model: A User's Guide. Peg M. Hess, Gail Folaron. Child Welfare League. 1993. 57p. This guide offers practical recommendations for using the PRAG model to address problems with policy or programs.

Providing Community-Based Services to the Rural Elderly. John A. Krout, ed. Sage. 1994. 388p.

Serving and Surviving as a Human-Service Worker. 2nd. J. Robert Russo. Waveland Press. 1993. 182p.

Teamwork in Human Services: Models and Applications across the Life Span. Howard G. Garner, Fred P. Orelove, eds. Butterworth-Heinemann. 1994. 224p. This book uses actual programs providing services from early intervention to geriatric support to illustrate an in-depth analysis of the theory and down-to-earth practice of four types of teamwork in human services.

Understanding the Nature of Poverty in Urban America. James Jennings. Praeger. 1994. 209p.

Urban Sanctuaries: Neighborhood Organizations in the Lives and Futures of Inner-City Youth. Milbrey W. McLaughlin, Merita A. Irby, Juliet Langman. Jossey-Bass. 1994. 220p. The stories of six adolescents are used to illustrate programs that have successfully tapped the potential of inner-city youth.

Wasting America's Future: The Children's Defense Fund Report on the Costs of Child Poverty. Children's Defense Fund. Beacon. 1994. 192p.

The Work Alternative: Welfare Reform and the Realities of the Job Market. Demetra S. Nightingale, Robert H. Haveman. Urban Institute Press. 1994. 350p.

PERIODICALS

Administration in Social Work. (Q) Haworth.
Aging. (Q) U.S.Administration on Aging, GPO.
Aging Research and Training News. (BW) Business Publishers.
American Journal of Hospice and Palliative Care. (BM) Prime National Publishing.
Child Abuse and Neglect. (M) Pergamon.
Child Protection Report. (BW) Business Publishers.
Child Welfare. (BM) Transaction Publishing.
Families in Society. (10/yr) Families International.
Journal of Human Resources. (Q) Industrial Relations Research Institute.
Journal of Mental Health Administration. (BW) Sage.
Journal of Public Health Policy. (Q) Journal of Public Health Policy.
Journal of Rehabilitation. (Q) National Rehabilitation Association.
Journal of Social Service Research. (Q) Haworth.
Nutrition Week. (W) Community Nutrition Institute.
Public Welfare. (Q) American Public Welfare Association.

Social Service Review. (Q) University of Chicago.
Social Work Research and Abstracts. (Q) National Association of Social Workers.

DATABASE RESOURCES

AgeLine
Type: Bibliographic
Coverage: Social gerontology, with particular emphasis on the delivery of health care to older citizens. Public policy for all concerns of seniors. Citations, with abstracts, from journals, books, book chapters, and reports.
Scope: Updated bimonthly. 1978—, with selected coverage back to 1960.
Producer: American Association of Retired Persons.
Available: CDP, CompuServe, DIALOG. CD-ROM.

Social Work Abstracts
Type: Bibliographic
Coverage: Over 28,000 citations to journal articles, doctoral dissertations, and other materials covering social work, services, conditions and policy.
Scope: International. Updated quarterly. July 1977—.
Producer: National Association of Social Workers
Available: CDP. CD-ROM.

Sociological Abstracts
Type: Bibliographic.
Coverage: Citations, with abstracts, to articles in the field of sociology and related areas of the social and behavioral sciences. Topics include social welfare, planning and policy development both urban and rural
Scope: English language. 1963—. Updated bimonthly.
Producer: Sociological Abstracts
Available: CDP, CompuServe, Data-Star, DIALOG, DIMDI, OCLC. CD-ROM, magnetic tape.

INFORMATION TECHNOLOGIES

BOOKS, REPORTS, MONOGRAPHS, BIBLIOGRAPHIES, AND REFERENCE SOURCES

Computer Purchasing Practices in Municipalities. ICMA. 1994. 9p. Looks at purchasing technology through state contracts and blanket purchase agreements, compares the frequency of vendor and equipment problems among local governments, and describes the ups and downs of one city's purchasing experiences.

Computer Service Strategic Plan. ICMA. 1994. 58p. This report describes the comprehensive plan worked out by Portland, Oregon to monitor current usage and map future plans.

Computing Strategies of Reengineering Your

Organization. Currid & Company. Prima Publishing. 1994. 279p. Aimed primarily at businesses, this overview contains an insightful analysis of the impact of computer technology on people and work relationships.

Cost/Benefit Analysis for Information Technology Projects. ICMA. 1994. 112p.

Distribution of Information: How to Select the Appropriate Technology. Claude Fleury, Yvon Bernatchez. Canada Communication Group. 1993. 178p. Packed with practical information, this guide uses descriptions, charts, and graphics to compare strengths and weakness of various information technologies.

Don't Panic! It's Only Netware. Becky Campbell. New Riders. 1993. 408p.

Ethical Aspects of Information Technology. Richard A. Spinello. Prentice-Hall. 1994. 252p.

Fundamentals of Telecommunications Networks. Tarek N. Saadawi, et al. Wiley. 1994. 485p.

Guide to Municipally Owned Broadband Communications Highways. ICMA. 1994. 81p. The experience of Glasgow, Kentucky, is profiled. This municipality established a broadband cable network which provides voice, data and video transmission, serves as a competitive cable television service, and helps community members save money on electric bills.

Health Hazards and New Technology. Peter Glasner, David Travis. Routledge. 1994. 224p. The authors examine the new health problems which have followed the widespread introduction of microcomputers to the workplace. They describe the social context of scientists, managers, union leaders, and workers within which definitions of ''hazard'' evolve.

High Performance Computing Demystified. David S. Loshin. AP Professional. 1994. 261p.

Improving Mission Performance through Strategic Information Management and Technology: Learning from Leading Organizations. GAO. 1994. 48p.

Information Systems for Urban Management. OECD. 1993. 108p.

Information Systems Practice: The Complete Guide. Tony Gunton. Blackwell. 1993. 479p.

Information Technology in the Service Society: A Twenty-first Century Lever. National Research Council. National Academy Press, 1994. 270p.

Investing in Information Technology: Managing the Decision-Making Process. Geoff Hogbin. McGraw-Hill. 1994. 254p.

Leading Edge Computer Use in U. S. Municipalities. ICMA. 1994. 64p. Text, case studies, tables, and graphs document the results of a survey of U.S. cities on their use of current technologies such as CD-ROM, bar coding, and fingerprint identification systems.

Local Area Networks: New Technologies, Emerging Standards. 3rd. Thomas W. Madron. Wiley. 1994. 386p.

Local Government Information and Training Needs in the 21st Century. Jack P. DeSario. Quorum. 1994. 141p.

Metropolitan Area Networks. M. Conti, E.

Gregori, L. Lenzini. CRC Press. 1994. 352p. This is the first detailed description of the current status of MAN technology, networks that span greater distance than local area networks (LANs) and have integrated voice, video and data service capabilities.

Outside AutoCAD: A Non Programmer's Guide to Managing AutoCAD's Database. Dale Evans. ASCE. 1993. 345p.

Public Television for Sale: Media, the Market, and the Public Sphere. William Hoynes. Westview Press. 1994. 207p.

Realizing the Information Future: the Internet and Beyond. National Research Council. National Academy Press. 1994. 301p. This volume provides a readable but comprehensive discussion of the major issues opened up by the new Internet information highway.

Successful Information System Implementation: The Human View. Jeffrey K. Pinto. Project Management Institute. 1994. 220p.

Techno Vision: The Executive's Survival Guide to Understanding and Managing Information Technology. Charles B. Wang. McGraw-Hill. 1994. 198p.

Telecommuting Information Packet. ICMA. 1994. 25p. This brochure provides information and detailed guidelines developed by Montgomery County, Maryland, allowing employees to telecommute, or work at home.

Virtual Reality: Scientific and Technological Challenges. Nathaniel I. Durlach, Ann S. Mayor, eds. National Academy Press. 1994. 450p. This volume combines a look at the stateof-the-art of synthetic environments (SE) and poses thought provoking descriptions of a future where SE is commonplace.

Wireless Personal Communications: Trends and Challenges. Theodore S. Rappaport, et al. Kluwer Academic. 1994. 266p.

Writing Disaster Recovery Plans for Telecommunications Networks and LAN. Leo A. Wrobel. Artech House. 1993. 138p.

Effective Communication: A Local Government Guide. Kenneth M. Wheeler, ed. ICMA. 1994. 260p.

A Short Course on Computer Viruses. 2nd ed. Frederick B. Cohen. Wiley. 1994. 320p. Software comes with this volume which discusses LANs, international viruses, virus evolution, and safeguarding strategies.

PERIODICALS

Annual Review of Information Science & Technology. (A) Elsevier.

Records Management Quarterly. (Q) Association of Records Managers and Administrators.

Artificial Intelligence. (M) North Holland.

Business Communications Review. (M) BCR Enterprises.

Byte. (M) McGraw-Hill.

CIO: The Magazine for Information Executives. (18/yr) CIO.

Communication News. (M) Nelson.

Communicationsweek. (BW) CMP.

Computer Design. (M) PennWell (NH).

Computer Graphics World. (M) PennWell (NH).

Computers and Security. (8/yr) Elsevier.

Computerworld: Newsweekly for Information Systems Management. (W) IDG Communications.

Computing Reviews. (M) Association for Computing Machinery.

Data Based Advisor. (M) Data Based Solutions.

Data Communications. (SM) McGraw-Hill.

Datamation. (SM) Cahners, MA.

Government Computer News. (BW) Cahners, MD.

Information Today. (11/yr) Learned Information.

Information Week. (W) CMP.

Infoworld. (W) Infoworld.

Journal for the Association for Computing Machinery. (Q) Association for Computing Machinery.

Manage IT. (Q) CAUSE.

MicroSoftware News. (M) ICMA.

Office. (M) Penton Publishing.

Online: The Magazine of On-Line Information Systems. (BM) Online.

PC Week. (W) Ziff-Davis.

PC World. (M) P C World Communications.

Rural Communications. (BM) National Telephone Cooperative Association.

Software Digest Ratings Report. (12/yr) National Software Testing Laboratories.

State Telephone Regulation Report. (BW) Capitol.

Telecommunications. (M) Horizon House.

Trends in Communications Policy. (M) Economics and Technology.

DATABASE RESOURCES

ABI/INFORM
Type: Bibliographic.
Coverage: More than 790,000 citations, with abstracts, on articles on public administration and information technology from 1400 journals.
Scope: International. Updated weekly or monthly, depending upon online service schedules. 1972—.
Producer: UMI.
Available: Data-Star, Dialog, ESA-IRS, HRIN, OCLC, ORBIT. CD-ROM, magnetic tape.

Business Software Database
Type: Referral, bibliographic.
Coverage: Descriptions of over 50,000 software packages that are available for micro-, mini-, and mainframe computers.
Scope: U. S. Updated monthly or quarterly depending upon online service schedules. Currently available software.
Producer: Information Sources.
Available: CDP, CompuServe, Data-Star, DIALOG, ESA-IRS, HRIN.

Computer Database
Type: Bibliographic.
Coverage: Over 550,000 citations on articles on computers, electronics, telecommunications, and the computer industry. Full text of 80 of

the journals included is available in Computer ASAP.
Scope: International. Updated weekly. 1983—.
Producer: Information Access Company.
Available: CDP, CompuServe, Data-Star, DIALOG.

Computer Fraud and Security Bulletin
Type: Full text.
Coverage: Newsletter covering computer crime, prevention methods, and related commercial products.
Scope: U. S. Updated monthly, some weekly. 1988—.
Producer: Elsevier Advanced Technology.
Available: Newsletter Database.

FCC Report
Type: Full text.
Coverage: Regulatory activities of information-related governmental units, including the Federal Communications Commission, Congress, U. S. Departments of Justice and of Commerce.
Scope: U. S. Updated biweekly. 1985—.
Producer: Capitol Publications, Telecom Publishing Group.
Available: NewsNet.

ICCA Directory
Type: Directory.
Coverage: References to member firms of the Independent Computer Consultants Association, with information on their hardware, software, and subject specializations.
Scope: U.S. and Canada. Current. Updated monthly.
Producer: Independent Computer Consultants Association.
Available: CompuServe.

The Information Report
Type: Directory, full text.
Coverage: Sources of free or inexpensive government and private publications, including federal, state, local, international, professional, and trade information.
Scope: U. S. Updated monthly. 1985—.
Producer: Washington Researchers.
Available: NewsNet.

Management Information Service (MIS)
Type: Bibliographic.
Coverage: MIS is not a database per se. It is both a customized database search service of 13,000 documents held by ICMA, plus a loan service to members of documents on successful programs and ideas.
Scope: ICMA.
Producer: ICMA.
Available: ICMA by subscription.

Microcomputer Abstracts
Type: Bibliographic.
Coverage: Over 145,000 citations, with abstracts, to reviews and commentaries on the use and applications of microcomputers and software. Full text book reviews.
Scope: Australia, U. K., U. S. Updated monthly. 1981—.
Producer: Learned Information

Available: CompuServe, DIALOG, OCLC. Magnetic tape.

Online Today Daily Edition
Type: Directory, full text.
Coverage: Two files: the first contains the full text of a monthly periodical covering the computer, videotext, and information industry. The second covers legislation pertaining to computers and the computer industry.
Scope: Primarily U. S. Updated 6 times daily or, with legislation, as available. Current.
Producer: CompuServe.
Available: Producer.

Social SciSearch
Type: Bibliographic.
Coverage: Technological material of 1,500 social science journals and books and 3,000 science journals.
Scope: International. Updated weekly. 1972—.
Producer: Institute for Scientific Information.
Available: Data-Star, DIALOG, DIMDI. CD-ROM, magnetic tape.

A Guide to the Information Superhighway
Type: Full text.
Coverage: Includes a glossary defining key terms and concepts, results from ICMA's telecommunications survey, video clips from a national teleconference on local government's role in the National Information Infrastructure (NII), legislation identifying current and pending FCC regulations, and a bibliography of useful resources.
Scope: Current.
Producer: ICMA.
Available: CD-ROM.

INTERGOVERNMENTAL RELATIONS

BOOKS, REPORTS, MONOGRAPHS, BIBLIOGRAPHIES, AND REFERENCE SOURCES

Child Care: The Need for Federal-State-Local Coordination. ACIR. 1994. 72p.
City Hall Goes Abroad: The Foreign Policy of Local Politics. Heidi H. Hobbs. Sage. 1994. 128p.
Comparative Public Management: Putting U. S. Public Policy and Implementation in Context. Randall Baker. Praeger. 1994. 282p. In the contemporary interdependent world, these authors maintain, there is an international context and dimension to all public policy and administration, and even U.S. local developments can be examined from that perspective.
Directory of Intergovernmental Contacts. ACIR. 1993. 62p. This reference book is divided into three sections: state advisory councils on intergovernmental relations; federal departments or congressional committees that have an intergovernmental focus; and selected national organizations that represent state or local interests.
Disentangling Local Government Responsibili-

ties: International Comparisons. Canadian Urban Institute. 1993. 155p.
Factors Associated with the Growth of Local and Regional Economies: A Review of Selected Empirical Literature. Lorin D. Kusmin. U. S. Department of Agriculture. 1994. 75p.
From Columbus to ConAgra. Allesandro Bonanno, Lawrence Busch, William H. Friedland, Lourdes Gouveia, Enzo Mignione, eds. University Press of Kansas State. 1994. 294p. The rise of transnational corporations in agriculture provides the focus for this volume. The impact on both local farming and food industries such as meat packing in the U.S. are highlighted and discussed.
Economic Development Strategies for State and Local Governments. Robert P.McGowan, Edward J. Ottensmeyer, ed. Nelson-Hall. 1993. 194p.
Factors Associated with the Growth of Local and Regional Economies: A Review of Selected Empirical Literature. Lorin D. Kusmin. U.S. Dept. of Agriculture. 1994. 75p.
Intergovernmental Fiscal Relations in Canada. Robin W. Boadway, Paul A. R. Hobson. Canadian Tax Foundation. 1993. 168p. This book considers both the federal-provincial and provincial-local aspects of Canadian governmental practice. Both present issues and future projections are considered.
International Handbook of Local and Regional Government: A Comparative Analysis of Advanced Democracies. Alan Norton. Edward Elgar. 1994. 559p.
Interwoven Destinies: Cities and the Nation. Henry Cisneros, ed. Norton. 1993. 367p. This book examines the ways in which cities and the federal government are mutually affected by the numerous cultural and economic ties between them.
Issues Confronting City & State Governments: A Guide to Improving & Understanding Local Governments of All Shapes and Sizes from Towns to Counties to State Agencies. Andy Oakley. P.O. Publishing. 1994. 209p. The author draws together numerous of interviews and hundreds of stories from the Chicago-based national newspaper *City and State* into a compendium of concrete suggestions for problems at the local level.
Local Government Autonomy: Needs for State Constitutional, Statutory, and Judicial Clarification. Michael Liborati. ACIR. 1993. 60p.
Metropolitan Organization: Comparison of the Allegheny and St. Louis Case Studies. ACIR. 1993. 25p. These case studies were undertaken to highlight how organizational and governmental operation are affected by the complex interconnectedness of the contemporary large metropolitan area. Special attention is paid to how the two jurisdictions deal with the consequent fragmentation in service provision to individuals.
Multijurisdictional Drug Control Task Forces: A Five Year Review, 1988–1992. JRSA. 1993. 56p.
Municipal Consolidation in Canada and Its Alternatives. Allan O'Brien. ICURR. 1993.

119p. This book examines what is involved in political reorganization, amalgamation, and annexation with a view to aiding municipalities, provinces, or territories considering one of those steps. It also explores various alternative forms of interjurisdictional cooperation that have been used as alternatives.

Neighborhood Organizations and the Welfare State. Shlomo Hasson, David Ley. University of Toronto Press. 1994. 472p.

Readings on American Subnational Government: Diversity, Innovation, and Rejuvenation. John R. Baker, ed. HarperCollins Publishers. 1993. 422p.

State & Local Government Environmental Liability. Joel A. Mintz. Clark Boardman Callaghan. 1994. 185p.

State and Local Politics. Steven A. Peterson, Thomas H. Rasmussen. McGraw-Hill. 1994. 364p. This book discusses not only the challenges posed to local governments by other jurisdictions but the influence of subnational groups on the nation as well.

State-Tribal Relations: Into the 21st Century. James B. Reed, Judy A. Zelio. NCSL. 1994. 75p. Taxation, environmental management, waste disposal and transportation, education and health care, and gambling are issues which this book explores in examining in considering the interface between the sovereign powers of Native American tribes and the states. Both basic policy and successful approaches are discussed.

Urban America in Transformation: Perspectives on Public Policy an Development. Benjamin Kleinberg. Sage. 1995. 296p. This book looks at horizontal relationships (those between various organizations) and vertical relationships (those with federal, state, or local jurisdictions) as they shape, implement, and generate new policy.

Urban-regional Economics, Social System Accounts, and Eco-Behavioral Science: Selected Writing. Karl August Fox. Iowa State University Press. 1994. 276p.

Workforce Development: Building Statewide Systems. Karin McCarthy, Rebekah Lashman. NCSL. 1994. 24p.

PERIODICALS

From the State Capitals: Federal Action Affecting the States. (W) Wakeman-Walworth.

Government Finance. (SM) GFOA.

Intergovernmental Perspective. (Q) ACIR.

National Journal. (W) National Journal.

Nation's Cities Weekly. (W) National League of Cities.

State and Local Government Review. (3/yr) University of Georgia, Carl Vinson Institute of Government.

State Legislatures. (M) National Conference of State Legislatures.

DATABASE RESOURCES

No databases currently focus on intergovernmental relations. The resources listed in the Basic Information and the Local Government Organization and Management sections of the *Municipal Year Book* may provide some help on this topic.

LAW ENFORCEMENT AND CRIMINAL JUSTICE

BOOKS, REPORTS, MONOGRAPHS, BIBLIOGRAPHIES, AND REFERENCE SOURCES

Assessing the Effectiveness of Criminal Justice Programs: Assessment and Evaluation Handbook Series No. 1. JRSA. 1994. Various paging.

Beyond Convictions: Prosecutors as Community Leaders in the War on Drugs. APRI. 1994. 443p. The subtitle to this document reads "An overview of prosecutor-led programs in education, prevention, treatment, and enforcement."

Character and Cops: Ethics in Policing. 2nd ed. Edwin J. Delattre. AEI. 1994. 307p. Synthesizing his personal experiences with dedicated and moral law enforcement personnel, the author constructs a profile of the ethical police officer and uses it as a standard for evaluating practice and internal monitoring.

Civil Liability in Criminal Justice. 2nd ed. H. E. Barrineau III. Anderson. 1994. 150p.

Common Sense about Police Review. Douglas Perry. Temple University. 1994. 328p. Recognizing the often emotionally-charged reaction to this topic, the author lobbies for an openness to the potential usefulness of the process and for wise implementation.

Crime Control as Industry. Nils Christies. Chapman and Hall. 1993. 192p.

Crimes of the Criminal Justice System. Joel H. Henderson, David R. Simon. Anderson. 1994. 121p. This volume addresses the impact on the criminal justice system of illegal, immoral or "socially marginal" behavior by its professionals and examines various approaches to address the problem.

Effective Interviewing for Paralegals. 2nd ed. Fred E. Jandt. Anderson. 1994. 280p.

Female Offenders: Meeting Needs of a Neglected Population. Anderson. 1993. 111p. This book examines specific practical aspects of a wide range of topics from dealing with pregnant or older inmates or inmates with AIDS to addressing the spiritual needs of women in jail.

Handbook of Forensic Sexology: Biomedical and Criminological Perspectives. James J. Krivacsha, John Money. Prometheus. 1994. 594p.

Hate Crime: International Perspectives on Causes and Control. Mark S. Hamm. Anderson. 1994. 180p.

Interviewing: A Forensic Guide to Interrogation. 2nd ed. Charles L. Yeschke. Thomas. 1993. 259p.

An Introduction to Gangs. 2nd ed. George W. Knox. Anderson. 1994. 536p. An authoritative reference to the history and phenomenology of gangs, as well as to law enforcement efforts to control them, this revision includes the actual constitution and by-laws of a gang, updated research from the National Gang Crime Research Center, and transcripts of existing gang-targeted legal codes.

Multicultural Perspectives in Criminal Justice and Criminology. James E. Hendricks, Bryan Byers. Thomas. 1994. 534p.

Multicultural Training for Police. ICMA. 1994. 22p.

Neighborhood-Oriented Policing in Rural Communities. BJA. 1994. 129p.

Police Officer Selection: A Handbook for Law Enforcement Administrators. Anthony R. Moriarity. Thomas. 1994. 357p.

Police Response to Crime. Bureau of Justice Statistics. 1994. 15p. Data succinctly summarized in this brochure gives a profile of reported crime and police activity.

Prison Violence in America. 2nd ed. Michael Braswell, Reid H. Montgomery, Jr., Lucien X. Lombardo. Anderson. 1994. 426p. Riots, sexual violence, effects of overcrowding, prison size and determinate sentencing, and prison societies are among the topics addressed in the comprehensive look at prison violence. Both analysis and possible remedies are included.

Prisons in Crisis. William L. Selke. Indiana University Press. 1993. 201p. The author presents an overview of contemporary problems of overcrowding and administration as well as possible alternatives which may alleviate the situation without compromising public safety.

Privatization of Correctional Facilities. Diane. 1994. 69p. This monograph provides an overview of the relevant issues in the debate on this topic.

Psychological Services for Law Enforcement. Theodore H. Beau. Wiley. 1994. 453p. This book provides a comprehensive treatment of assessment and intervention strategies with individuals undergoing the stress of law enforcement duties. A special section examines the organization and training of peer counselors.

The Police Manager. Ronald G. Lynch. Anderson. 1994. 266p.

The Psychology of Criminal Conduct. D. A. Andrews, James Bonata. Anderson. 1994. 272p.

The Public Nature of Private Violence: Women and the Discovery of Abuse. Martha Albertson Fineman, Roxanne Mykitiuk, eds. Routledge. 1994. 416p. This volume uses a comprehensive definition of "domestic violence," encompassing such issues as battering, child abuse, non-physical violence, and incest. The authors argue that these crimes need to be seen and addressed in their public context, not merely as private problems.

Thieves' World: The Threat of the New Global Network of Organized Crime. Claire Sterling. Simon & Schuster. 1994. 304p. The author, an investigative reporter, examines the spread of the international crime network in the last decade and the impact of this development on local level.

Understanding Community Policing: A Framework for Action. BJA. 1994. 79p. This monograph discusses some of the rationale behind community policing experiments and details some of the steps in carrying out a program.

Unequal Justice: A Question of Color. Coramae Richey Mann. Indiana University Press. 1993. 320p. This book draws on historical background and contemporary experiences at each stage of the criminal justice system to argue that minorities receive disparate treatment. The experiences of African Americans, Asian Americans, Hispanic Americans, and Native Americans are used.

PERIODICALS

BJS National Update. (Q) U.S. Bureau of Justice Statistics.

Canadian Journal of Criminology. (Q) Canadian Criminal Justice Association.

Canadian Police Chief News. (Q) Canadian Association of Chiefs of Police.

Corrections Today. (BM) ACA.

Crime and Delinquency. (Q) Sage.

Criminal Justice and Behavior. (Q) Sage.

Criminal Justice Review. (SA) Georgia State University.

Criminology. (Q) American Society of Criminology.

Federal Probation. (Q) Administrative Office of United States Courts. GPO.

Fire and Police Personnel Reporter. (M) Public Safety Personnel Research Institute.

From the State Capitals: Justice Policies. (W)Wakeman/Walworth.

Journal of Criminal Justice. (6/yr) Pergamon.

Journal of Criminal Law and Criminology. (Q)Northwestern University School of Law.

Journal of Police Science and Administration. (Q) IACP.

Journal of Research in Crime and Delinquency. (Q) Sage.

Judicature. (BM) American Judicature Society.

Justice Quarterly. (Q) Academy of Criminal Justice Sciences.

Juvenile and Family Court Journal. (Q) National Council of Juvenile and Family Court Judges.

Police Chief. (M) IACP.

Prison Journal. (Q) Sage.

DATABASE RESOURCES

Criminal Justice Abstracts
Type: Bibliographic.
Coverage: Citations, with abstracts, to books, journal articles, reports, dissertations, and newspapers dealing with crime and criminal justice.
Scope: U.S. Updated quarterly. 1968—.
Producer: Willow Tree.
Available: WESTLAW. CD-ROM.

Criminal Justice Periodical Index
Type: Bibliographic.

Coverage: Index to sources on the administration of justice and law enforcement, including penology, criminal law, environmental and industrial crime, and security management.
Scope: U.S., Canada, and U.K. Updated monthly. 1975—.
Producer: University Microfilms International.
Available: DIALOG.

Law Enforcement and Criminal Justice Information Database
Type: Bibliographic, full text.
Coverage: Journal articles, reports, projects, standards, dissertations, and other database entries on criminal justice systems, criminology, forensics, and crime prevention.
Scope: International. Updated quarterly. 1954—.
Producer: International Research and Evaluation.
Available: Producer.

NCJRS (National Criminal Justice Reference Service)
Type: Bibliographic, directory.
Coverage: Citations to both print and nonprint materials on all aspects of law enforcement, crime prevention, security, criminal justice, and juvenile justice. This database is particularly valuable for access to materials not readily available elsewhere.
Scope: International. Updated monthly. 1972—.
Producer: U.S. National Institute of Justice.
Available: DIALOG.

WESTLAW Criminal Justice Library
Type: Full text.
Coverage: Articles and documents relating to federal criminal justice; federal sentencing guidelines from the *U.S. Code, Code of Federal Regulations,* and *Federal Register.*
Scope: U.S. Updating and time vary by sources used.
Producer: West.
Available: WESTLAW.

WESTLAW Topical Highlights Data Base
Type: Bibliographic, full text.
Coverage: Summaries of significant state and federal criminal justice decisions and summaries of relevant statutes, administrative rules, and news items
Scope: U.S. Current. Updated daily.
Producer: West.
Available: WESTLAW.

LOCAL GOVERNMENT ORGANIZATION AND MANAGEMENT

BOOKS, REPORTS, MONOGRAPHS, BIBLIOGRAPHIES, AND REFERENCE SOURCES

Agencies, Boards, and Commissions in Canadian Local Government. Dale Richmond, David Siegel. Institute of Public Administration of Canada. 1994. 138p.

Beyond Bureaucracy: A Blueprint and Vision for Government that Works. Kenneth B. Johnston. Irwin. 1993. 151p.

The Case for Bureaucracy: A Public Administration Polemic. 3rd ed. Charles T. Goodsell. Chatham House. 1994. 226p. Bureaucracy gets a bad press, according to the author. Extensive descriptions and evidence document his view that the American record of achievement and democratic responsibility is directly tied to its ability to operate a bureaucracy well.

Can Governments Learn? Comparative Perspectives on Evaluation and Organizational Learning. Frank L. Leeuw, Ray C. Rist, Richard Sonnichsen, eds. Transaction. 1993. 270p. The authors examine instances in the U.S. and Canada where evaluation has contributed to major policy revision or to concrete positive change.

The Craft of Public Administration. George E. Berkley. Brown & Benchmark. 1994. 437p.

Deregulating the Public Service: Can Government Be Improved? John J. DiIulio, Jr., ed. Brookings. 1994. 280p. This book recommends new and large scale deregulation of public service at all levels. Deregulation is described, analyzed, evaluated, and placed in the context of other contemporary approaches to public service reform.

Elements of Urban Management. Kenneth J. Davey. World Bank. 1993. 55p.

Excellence in Government: Total Quality Management in the 1990s. 2nd ed. David K. Carr. Coopers & Lybrand. 1993. 353p.

Facilitative Leadership in Local Government: Lessons of Successful Mayors and Chairpersons. James H. Svara and Associates, ed. Jossey-Bass. 1994. 263p.

Groupthink in Government: A Study of Small Groups and Policy Failure. Johns Hopkins University Press. 1994. 321p. This book gives concrete historical examples of situations in which the failure to think creatively had dire consequences.

Improving Government Performance: An Owner's Manual. John J. DiIulio, Jr., Gerald Garvey, Donald F. Kettl. Brookings. 1993. 90p. The authors highlight the problems and potential in "reinventing government," as articulated by the National Performance Review.

Improving Public Sector Productivity: Concepts and Practices. Ellen Doree Rosen. Sage. 1993. 280p.

Making Government Work: How Entrepreneurial Executives Turn Bright Ideas into Real Results. Martin A. Levin, Mary Bryna Sanger. Jossey-Bass. 1994. 240p. Case studies from a variety of public executives support the authors' thesis that innovative policy programs will be only as good as the managerial skills of the administrators who implement them.

Management in the Public Sector: Challenge and Change. Lester Isaac-Henry. Chapman and Hall. 1993. 209p.

Managing Chaos and Complexity in Government: A New Paradigm for Managing

Change, Innovation, and Organizational Renewal. L. Douglas Kiel. Jossey-Bass. 1994. 246p.

Managing Small Cities and Counties: A Practical Guide. James M. Banovetz, ed. ICMA. 1994. 366p. Over 90 practical examples from North America bring to life this book's overview of the structure and functioning of small jurisdictions. The broad range of topics spans budgeting to leisure services, cultural diversity to the use of volunteers.

Modern Organizations: Administrative Theory in Contemporary Society. Ali Farazmand. Greenwood. 1994. 257p.

Networking Smarts: How to Build Relationships for Personal and Organizational Success. Wayne E. Baker. McGraw-Hill. 1993. 256p.

New Paradigms for Government: Issues for the Changing Public Service. Patricia W. Ingraham, Barbara S. Romzek, eds. Jossey-Bass. 1994. 320p. If "reinventing government" is to happen, the authors maintain, public administrators must have a solid but understandable theoretical basis and a systemic analysis of the issues involved. This book provides those through academic research and policy overview.

Public Administration: Canadian Materials. Randy G. Hoffman, Victor S. MacKinnon, Janice Nicholson, James C. Simon. Captus. 1993. 477p. This work provides detailed case studies of administrative actions that have led to general policy change.

Public Sector Management: Theory, Critique and Practice. David McKevitt, Alan Lawton. Sage. 1994. 306p. Different views of the different stakeholders in the public arena lead to different perceptions of what accountability should mean. Innovative chapters examine what the impact is when constituents are viewed as equals and administrative focus switches from control to response to need.

Quality Management for Government: A Guide to Federal, State and Local Implementation. V. Daniel Hunt. ASQC Quality. 1993. 384p. This volume offers theory, case studies, and practical guidelines.

Resolving Conflict: Strategies for Local Government. Margaret S. Herrman, ed. ICMA. 1994. 232p. This book offers a practical how-to approach to dealing with conflict within the organization and between the organization and the community. Several innovative plans are presented, including a network of permanent, private-sector consensus councils.

Rethinking Government: Reform or Reinvention? F. Leslie Seidle, ed. Institute for Research on Public Policy. 1993. 221p.

Seamless Government: A Practical Guide to Reengineering in the Public Sector. Russel Matthew Linden. Jossey-Bass. 1994. 294p.

Strategic Planning for Local Government: A Handbook for Officials and Citizens. Roger L. Kemp. McFarland. 1993. 310p.

PERIODICALS

American City and County. (M) Communication Channels.

City and State. (BW) Crain Communications.

City Hall Digest. (M) City Hall Communications.

County News. (BW) National Association of Counties.

Current Municipal Problems. (Q) Clark-Boardman.

Downtown Idea Exchange. (SM) Alexander Research & Communications.

Guide to Management Improvement Projects in Local Government. (Q) ICMA.

Journal of Policy Analysis and Management. (Q) Wiley.

The Mayor. (SM) USCM.

NATaT's Reporter. (M) National Association of Towns and Townships,

Nation's Cities Weekly. (W) National League of Cities.

Public Management. (M) ICMA.

Spectrum: The Journal of State Government. (Q) Council of State Governments.

State and Local Government Review. (3/yr) Carl Vinson Institute of Government.

State Government News. (M) Council of State Governments.

State Legislatures. (M) National Conference of State Legislatures.

Urban League Review. (Q) Transaction Publishers.

DATABASE RESOURCES

Local Government Information Network (LOGIN)

Type: Full text, directory.

Coverage: An information exchange system, offering local government experience and expertise, technical data, how-to instructions, and information sources. Emphasis is on innovation and efficiency.

Scope: Updated daily. 1979—.

Producer: Login Services Corp.

Available: Producer.

Privatization Center

Type: Directory.

Coverage: A listing of privatized public services in the U.S.and the *Directory of Private Service Providers.*

Scope: Current.

Producer: Privatization Center.

Available: Producer.

Urban Data Service (UDS)

Type: Bibliographic, statistical.

Coverage: Subscription service package that includes six Special Data Issues each year with responses to survey data and The Municipal Year Book.

Scope: 1964—.

Producer: ICMA.

Available: Producer.

PERSONNEL AND LABOR RELATIONS

BOOKS, REPORTS, MONOGRAPHS, BIBLIOGRAPHIES, AND REFERENCE SOURCES

Bridging Differences: Effective Intergroup Communication. 2nd. William B. Gudykunst. Sage. 1994. 260p. Basic philosophy and techniques for communication are presented and applied to specific cases: differences in age, social class and physical ability; culture and ethnicity; stereotyping; community building; ethical issues and perceptions.

Building Teams and Teamwork: A Foundation for Organizational Success. ICMA. 1994. p. This monograph offers help in assessing whether a self-directed work team (SDWT) is right for an organization and in recruiting members, implementing, and nurturing the team.

Conflict and Consensus: A General Theory of Collective Decisions. Serge Moscovici. Sage. 1994. 240p. This work maintains that conflict can be a positive force leading to change and illustrates with numerous studies how consensus can be generated.

Creating Workplaces Where People Can Think. Phyl Smith, Lynn Kearny. Jossey-Bass. 1994. 192p. The authors encourage managers to focus on the work environment as a means of heightening performance and productivity.

Differences that Work: Organizational Excellence through Diversity. Mary C. Gentile, ed. Harvard Business School. 1994. 282p. In addition to the expected treatment of differences in race, gender, and sexual orientation, the book discusses how aging, AIDS, and differences in family make-up can be harnessed for positive organizational impact.

Drug and Alcohol Testing for Local Government Transportation Employees: The Public Employer's Guide. ICMA. 1994. p. Clearcut recommendations for achieving compliance to the Omnibus Transportation Employee Testing Act without incurring liability are set forth by an attorney and physician.

Effective Employee Assistance Programs: A Guide for EAP Counselors and Managers. Gloria Cunningham. Sage. 1994. 250p.

Everyday Frustration and Creativity in Government: A Personnel Challenge to Public Administration. Thomas E. Heinzen. ABLEX Publishing Corporation. 1994. 172p. The author conducted a psychological study of a portion of the New York State work force and highlights those practices which enabled employees to take a proactive stance.

A Force of Ones: Reclaiming Individual Power in a Time of Teams, Work Groups, and Other Crowds. Stanley M. Herman. Jossey-Bass. 1994. 175p. Guidelines and exercises are balanced with stories and poems to help individuals identify and hone individual strengths and self-empowerment.

Gender and Diversity in the Workplace: Learn-

ing Activities and Exercises. Gary N. Powell. Sage. 1994. 152p.

Genderflex: Men and Women Speaking Each Other's Language at Work. Judith C. Tingley. AMACOM. 199. 251p. The author builds on the recent studies of differences in men's and women's communication styles and recommends specific practices that can foster productive communication and work activity.

Handbook of Public Personnel Administration. Jack Rabin. Dekker. 1994. 1646p.

Handbook of Training and Development in the Public Sector. IPMA. 1993. 351p.

Healing the Wounds: Overcoming the Trauma of Layoffs and Revitalizing Downsized Organizations. IPMA. 1993. 215p. The focus here is on the "survivors" and the downsized organization, with strategies offered to re-establish personal and organizational growth.

Health Care for Municipal Employees: Plans, Options and Costs. ICMA. 1994. 107p. Describes the types of plans offered, the percentage of premiums paid by municipalities, retiree coverage, use of consortia, self insurance, and many other factors that affect cost.

Highwire Management: Risk-Taking Tactics for Leaders, Innovators, and Trailblazers. IPMA. 1993. 175p. The experience of successful managers is combined with a detailed how-to of managing the risk process and weighing the alternatives in taking risks.

Human Relations in Organizations. 5th ed. Dan L. Costley, ed. West. 1993. 680p.

Human Resource Management: A Contemporary Perspective. Ian Beardwell, Len Holden, eds. Trans-Atlantic. 1994. 554p.

Intercultural Communication Training. Richard Brislin, Tomoko Yoshida. Sage. 1994. 222p. This comprehensive manual outlines how to plan and set up intercultural communication training programs.

Leadership without Easy Answers. Ronald A. Heifetz. Belknap. 1994. 348p. Positive feedback from persons who have taken his workshop prompted the author to share rationale and techniques used to inspire both those in leadership roles and line employees who want to facilitate change in their workplace.

Managing Managers: Strategies and Techniques for Human Resource Management. Ed Snope, Tom Redman, Gregory J. Bamber. Blackwell. 1994. 240p.

National Association of Government Deferred Compensation Administrators 1993 Survey of 457 Plans. NASIRE. 1994. 52p. This monograph examines trends nationwide and interrelationships in the targeted plans. A directory for each plan gives contacts, addresses, plan assets, annual deferrals and investment providers.

Public Personnel Management: Contexts and Strategies. 3rd ed. Donald E. Klingner, John Nalbandian. Prentice-Hall. 1993. 356p. The relationship between pressure and productivity, legal questions and organizational justice are topics indicative of the fresh approach of the authors, who also consider such areas as performance appraisal, recognition and promotions, health and safety.

Qualified Retirement and Other Employee Benefit Plans. Michael J. Canan. West. 1994. 1552p.

Supervision for Success in Government: A Practical Guide for First Line Managers. Dalton S. Lee, N. Joseph Cayer. Jossey-Bass. 1994. 225p. Interviews with over 100 successful administrators contributed to this practical handbook which details supervisory skills such as decision-making, team building, and problem solving.

PERIODICALS

Benefits Law Journal. (Q) Executive Enterprises.

Compensation. (A) ICMA.

Creative Training Techniques. (M) Lakewood.

From the State Capitals: Employee Policy for the Private and Public Sector. (W) Wakeman/Walworth.

Government Employee Relations Report. (W) Bureau of National Affairs.

HR Report. (M) ICMA.

Journal of Collective Negotiations in the Public Sector. (Q) Baywood.

Journal of Individual Employment Rights. (Q) Baywood.

Labor and Employment Law Anthology. (A) International Library.

Labor Arbitration in Government. (M) American Arbitration Association.

Monthly Labor Review. (M) U.S. Bureau of Labor Statistics.

Personnel Journal. (M) A.C.C. Communications.

Public Administration Review. (BM) ASPA.

Public Management. (M) ICMA.

Public Personnel Management. (Q) IPMA,

Public Productivity and Management Review. (Q) Jossey-Bass.

SAM Advanced Management Journal. (Q) Society for Advancement of Management

DATABASE RESOURCES

ABI/INFORM
Type: Bibliographic.
Coverage: Citations with abstracts covering all phases of business management, including human resources and labor relations.
Scope: Updating varies. 1971—.
Producer: UMI/Data Courier.
Available: CDP, Data-Star, DIALOG, ESA/IRS, HRIN, NEXIS, ORBIT, STN International. CD-ROM.

Business Periodicals Index (BPI)
Type: Bibliographic.
Coverage: A general index to business and personnel administration articles found in trade and business research journals.
Scope: Varies. 1982—.
Producer: H. W. Wilson.
Available: CDP, OCLC, WILSONLINE. CD-ROM.

Employee Benefits Infosource (EBIS)
Type: Bibliographic.
Coverage: Online citations, with abstracts, to literature dealing with all facets of employee benefit plans drawn from periodicals, newspapers, newsletters, books, research reports, news releases, and proceedings.
Scope: Updated monthly. 1986—.
Producer: International Foundation of Employee Benefit Plans.
Available: DIALOG, WESTLAW.

Ethos
Type: Full text, interactive video.
Coverage: Ethics training. Includes case studies, interactive training modules.
Producer: ICMA.
Available: CD-ROM.

Government Manager
Type: Full text.
Coverage: Advice to federal government supervisors on all aspects of personnel management; judicial and National Labor Relations Board rulings.
Scope: Updated biweekly. 1985—.
Producer: Bureau of National Affairs.
Available: HRIN.

Human Resources Information Network (HRIN)
Type: Online service. Bibliographic, directory.
Coverage: A grouping of three resources: *HRIN Announcements Database* (current information updated daily), *HRIN Daily Developments Database* (updated daily), and *HRIN Special Reports Library* (updated as needed). Subjects of interest to human resources and/or personnel managers.
Scope: Updating varies. Years vary.
Producer: HRIN.
Available: Producer.

LABORLAW II
Type: Bibliographic.
Coverage: Separate entries on each U.S. federal, state, and administrative agency decision pertaining to labor relations; supportive details and summaries by BNA attorney/editors.
Scope: U.S. Updated monthly. 1980—. LABORLAW I, a closed file, covers 1938–1987.
Producer: Bureau of National Affairs.
Available: DIALOG, HRIN.

Management Contents
Type: Bibliographic.
Coverage: Citations to 130 international, English language business journals, newsletters, and tabloids.
Scope: Updated monthly. 1974—.
Producer: Information Access.
Available: Data-Star, DIALOG.

Salaries 95
Type: Full text.
Coverage: Individual salaries of thousands of public officials and police and fire personnel.
Scope: U.S. Updated annually. 1995—.
Producer: ICMA
Available: CD-ROM.

PLANNING AND DEVELOPMENT

BOOKS, REPORTS, MONOGRAPHS, BIBLIOGRAPHIES, AND REFERENCE SOURCES

After Lucas: Land Use Regulation and the Taking of Property without Compensation. David L. Callies, ed. ABA. 1993. 136p.

Basic Methods of Policy Analysis and Planning. 2nd ed. Carl V. Patton, David S. Sawicki. Prentice-Hall. 1993. 482p. The emphasis here is on a clear, pragmatic process that will enable managers to analyze and resolve policy issues quickly. An introduction to the literature and seven cases for reflection or discussion are also included.

A Better Place to Live: Reshaping the American Suburb. Phillip Langdon. University of Massachusetts. 1994. 270p. The author calls for a new vision of the suburb and proactive efforts to repair problems. He offers a thought-provoking argument for the "rediscovery of the town."

Common Groundwork: A Practical Guide to Protecting Rural and Urban Land. Institute for Environmental Education. 1993. 207p. This volume presents suggestions for land protection through private means such as land trusts and conservation easements and via public vehicles such as zoning ordinances and protection regulations.

Communities in the Lead: The Northwest Rural Development Sourcebook. Harold L. Fossum. Diane. 1993. 215p. In-depth case studies profile rural communities who have successfully used this book's strategies to revitalize their communities. How to build local capacity to produce goods, how to use state and federal assistance programs to their fullest, and how to develop value-added enterprises are among the practical guidelines offered.

Community Visioning: Citizen Participation in Strategic Planning. ICMA. 1994. 15p. Case studies provide six different models of grassroots participation in planning with detailed practical applications.

Contemporary Urban Planning. 3rd. John M. Levy. Prentice-Hall. 1994. 320p.

Development Agreements. Erin Johnson, Edward Ziegler, eds. Rocky Mountain Land Use Institute. 1993. 312p. Input from legal scholars, land-use attorneys, and experienced planners underlies the practical suggestions for using development agreements. Case studies, document examples, drafting checklist, and negotiation pointers are provided.

Forgotten Places: Uneven Development in Rural America. Thomas A. Lyson, William W. Falk. University Press of Kansas. 1993. 278p. The authors focus on ten specific areas, challenging policymakers to stimulate discussion on what can be done to bring them into the mainstream.

Information Sources in Urban and Regional Planning: A Directory and Guide to Reference Materials. Edward E. Duensing. Center for Urban Policy Research. 1994. 178p.

Land Conservation through Public/Private Partnerships. Eve Endicott, ed. Island Press. 1993. 364p.

Land Development. 8th ed. Linda D. Kone. Home Builder Press. 1994. 337p. Aimed primarily at commercial developers, this book presents a business perspective sensitive to environmental and other policy issues.

Landside Access to U. S. Ports. TRB. 1993. 198p.

Making America Competitive: A Policy Handbook. Barbara Puls. NCSL. 1994. 40p. This monograph examines key programs in economic competitiveness, educational reform, and job training. Case studies from the participants in the Invest in People Program, a state-by-state analysis of state participation in the project, and policy recommendations are also featured.

Modelling the City: Performance, Policy, and Planning. C. S. Bertuglia, G. P. Clarke, A. G. Wilson, eds. Routledge. 1994. 210p.

Paradise: Class, Commuters, and Ethnicity in Rural Ontario. Stanley R. Barrett. University of Toronto Press. 1994. 315p.

Planning and Programming, Land Use, Public Participation, and Computer Technology in Transportation. TRB. 1993. 112p.

The Political Culture of Planning. J. Barry Cullingworth. Routledge. 1993. 350p. The unique U.S. zoning system is the focus of much of this book: its history, objectives and legal grounding. Practical aids are also is offered on combatting exclusionary zoning to build affordable housing and on maintaining the quality of development.

Practical Manual of Land Development. 2nd ed. Barbara Colley. McGraw-Hill. 1993. 275p. Well-illustrated discussions provide an overview of site analysis, grading, parking lot and roadway design, and sewer and drainage facility design and placement. The book also design and drafting software and examines the role of geographic information systems.

Roadside Safety Features and Landscape and Environmental Design. TRB. 1994. 133p.

The Small Town Survival Guide Jack McCall. Morrow. 1993. 160p. Addressed to ordinary citizens, this book provides a plan for turning around negative thinking and setting up concrete programs to shore up the economy and development of the small town.

Stadiums, Professional Sports, and Economic Development: Assessing the Reality. Robert A. Baade. The Heartland Institute. 1994. 40p.

Sustainable Urban Development in Canada: From Concept to Practice. Virginia W. Maclaren. ICURR. 1993. 3 vols: 40p, 24p, 275p. The first volume in this series summarizes research, the second is a selected bibliography. Volume III details development initiatives either proposed or already undertaken. This work is also available in French.

Theories of Local Economic Development: Perspectives from Across the Disciplines. Richard D. Bingham, Robert Mier, eds. Sage. 1993. 319p. Both rural and inner city areas are examined in this multidisciplinary approach which provides illustrations and case studies in each chapter.

Urban Policy in Twentieth-Century America. Arnold Hirsch, Raymond A. Mohl, eds. Rutgers University Press. 1993. 238p.

The Urban West: Managing Growth and Decline. James Weatherby and Stephanie L. Witt. Praeger. 1994. 154p.

Urbanization of Rural Land in the United States. U.S. Department of Agriculture. 1994. 59p.

PERIODICALS

American Real Estate and Urban Economics Association Journal. (Q) AREUEA.

City and State. (BW) Crain Communications.

Economic Development and Law Center Report. (Q) National Economic Development and Law Center.

Economic Development Review. (Q) American Economic Development Council.

Journal of Architectural and Planning Research. (Q) Locke Science.

Journal of Planning Literature. (Q) Sage.

Journal of the American Planning Association. (Q) APA.

Journal of Urban and Contemporary Law. (SA) Washington University.

Journal of Urban Planning and Development. (Q) American Society of Civil Engineers.

Land Use Digest. (M) ULI.

Land Use Law and Zoning Digest. (M) APA.

Planning Magazine. (M) APA.

Planning and Zoning News. (M) Planning and Zoning Center.

Project Reference File. (Q) ULI.

Quality Cities. (M) Florida League of Cities.

The State Line. (BM) COSCDA.

Urban Affairs Abstracts. (W) NLC.

Urban Land. (M) ULI.

Zoning and Planning Law Report. (Ml Clark Boardman.

Zoning News. (M) APA.

DATABASE RESOURCES

Avery Architecture Periodicals
Type: Bibliographic.
Coverage: City planning, environmental studies, landscape architecture, and historic preservation. Citations to items appearing in the Avery Index.
Scope: International. English. 1979—. Updating varies.
Producer: Columbia University, Avery Architectural and Fine Arts Library.
Available: DIALOG, RLIN.

Civil Engineering Database
Type: Bibliographic.
Coverage: One division of this database is devoted to urban planning and development with citations to journal papers, discussions, feature articles, or books produced by the American Society of Civil Engineers.

Scope: Updated bimonthly. 1975—.
Producer: American Society of Civil Engineers.
Available: STN international.

Social Sciences Index
Type: Bibliographic.
Coverage: Planning at all levels, economic development, geography, and environmental sciences as part of general coverage of social sciences.
Scope: International. Updated weekly. 1983—.
Producer: H.W. Wilson.
Available: OCLC, Wilsonline. CD-ROM, magnetic tape.

PUBLIC FINANCE

BOOKS, REPORTS, MONOGRAPHS, BIBLIOGRAPHIES, AND REFERENCE SOURCES

Advanced Accounting for Governmental Units under GASB. Paul E. Glick. AICPA. 1993. Various paging. Numerous references to the codification of the Government Accounting and Financial Reporting Study highlight this practical accounting guide.

Audits of State and Local Governmental Units. Gary Giroux, Don Deis. AICPA. 1993. 54p.

Big-city Politics, Governance, and Fiscal Constraints. George E. Peterson, ed. University Press. 1994. 275p.

Budgetary Forecasting in Local Government: New Tools and Techniques. Howard A. Frank. Quorum. 1993. 213p.

Case Studies of City Spending: Explaining Differences in Per Capita City Expenditures. St. Paul, Minnesota, Office of the State Auditor. 1993. 41p. Tables, charts, and texts compare the operation of fifteen cities with a significant lower expenditure per capita.

Changing Public Attitudes on Governments and Taxes 1993. ACIR. 1993. 52p. Local governments place far ahead of the federal in the results of this ACIR poll which, along with other questions, asked Americans how they rated service returns on taxes levied, whether states should pressure for a balanced budget amendment, and whether tax income should be redistributed to equalize school spending.

Combating Fraud and Corruption in the Public Sector. Peter Jones. Chapman and Hall. 1993. 216p.

Essentials of Accounting for Governmental and Not-for-Profit Organizations. Leon Edwards Hay. Irwin. 1993. 351p.

Evaluating Financial Condition: A Handbook for Local Government. 3rd ed. ICMA. 1994. 202p.

Facing Choices Together: Response to Pre-Budget Consultations. Paul Martin. Department of Finance (Ottawa). 1994. 39p.

Financing State Government in the 1990s. Ronald K. Snell, ed. NCSL. 1993. 116p. This report examines the inadequacies currently inherent in state tax policy, future projections, and the impact of federal policy and makes recommendations to ameliorate current problems.

Fiscal Administration: Analysis and Applications for the Public Sector. 4th. John L. Mikesell. Wadsworth Publishing. 1994. 594p.

Governmental Accounting and Auditing Update. Allan B. Afterman, Rowna H. Jones. Warren Gorham Lamont. 1994. 60p. This single volume offers authoritative guidance for governmental units. It incorporates all currently effective pronouncements by major topic, regardless of date of issue, There are multiple illustrations and examples.

Governmental Accounting, Auditing and Financial Reporting. Stephen J. Gauthier. GFOA. 1994. 570p.

Governmental and nonprofit accounting: Theory and Practice. 4th ed. Robert J. Freeman, et al. Prentice-Hall. 1993. 823p.

The Handbook of Municipal Bonds and Public Finance. Robert Lamb, James Leigland, Stephen Rappaport, eds. New York Institute of Finance. 1993. 879p.

Impact of Unfunded Federal Mandates on U.S. Cities: A 314-City Survey. U. S. Conference of Mayors. Price Waterhouse. 1993. Various paging.

Information Systems Strategies for Public Financial Management. Hywel M. Davies. World Bank. 1993. 51p.

Little Budget Book: A Portable Budgeting Guide for Local Government. Len Wood. Training Shoppe. 1993. 184p.

Model Treasury Agreements. GFOA. 1993. 25p. Drafting tips and sample language illustrate this discussion of the various treasury agreements used by states and localities, covering aspects such as banking services, wire transfer, lockbox, and trust and escrow agreements.

Modern Public Finance. John M. Quigley, Eugene Smolensky. Harvard University Press. 1994. 352p.

Public Finance and the Price System. Edgar K. Browning. Macmillan. 1994. 566p.

Public Sector Financial Control and Accounting. 2nd. John J. Glynn. Blackwell. 1993. 301p.

Selected Readings in Governmental and Nonprofit Accounting and Auditing. Anna D. Gowans Young. AICP. 1993. p.

State and Local Travel Taxes. ACIR. 1994. 32p. This report examines the impact on state and local finance of "travel taxes," those items presumed to be purchased by tourists such as hotel room fees, food, entertainment, transportation, and car rentals. Theory and practice of these taxes are examined.

Tax-exempt Derivatives: A Guide to Legal Considerations for Lawyers, Finance Professionals, and Municipal Issuers. Steven D. Conlon. American Bar Association. 1994. 377p.

Tax-Exempt Financing: A Primer. APPA and GFOA. APPA. 1994. 30p. A question and answer format is divided into four sections: Fundamentals, Constitutional and Policy Issues, Congressional Actions and Their Effects, and Responses to Criticisms. A summary of 20 years of federal legislation relevant to tax-exempt bonds is also provided.

Washington Municipal Financing Deskbook. Roy J. Koegen. Lawyers Cooperative Publishing. 1993. 585p.

PERIODICALS

Assessment Journal. (BM) IAAO.
Financing Local Government. (BM) Government Information Services.
Fiscal Letter. (BM) NCSL.
From the State Capitals: Taxation and Revenue Policies. (W) Wakeman/Walworth.
Government Executive. (M) National Journal.
Government Finance Review. (BM) GFOA.
Journal of Finance. (5/yr) American Finance Association.
National Tax Journal. (Q) National Tax Association.
Property Tax Journal. (Q) IAAO.
Public Budgeting and Finance. (Q) Transaction.
Public Finance Quarterly. (Q) Sage.
Public Investor. (M) GFOA.
State and Local Government Review. (3/yr) University of Georgia, Carl Vinson Institute of Government.
Tax Notes. (W) Tax Analysts.

DATABASE RESOURCES

Financial Indicators Database
Type: Statistical.
Coverage: Data from award-winning annual financial reports made available to governments for comparative purposes. Reports are issued by municipalities, counties, and school districts.
Scope: U.S. 1989—.
Producer: GFOA.
Available: Producer. Diskette.

Grants
Type: Directory.
Coverage: Grants offered by local, state, and federal governments; commercial sources; private foundations; and associations.
Scope: International. Updated bimonthly. Current.
Producer: Oryx.
Available: DIALOG. CD-ROM.

Municipal Debt Database
Type: Numeric.
Coverage: Updates on issues of municipal debt, including public, limited, and private. Corresponds to *Monthly Survey of Municipal Debt.*
Scope: U.S. Updated daily. 1980—.
Producer: Securities Data.
Available: Producer.

MUNIWEEK
Type: Full text.
Coverage: Commentary and analyses of major issues of the municipal market: finance, economic indicators, government legislation, and debt problems of state and local government.

Scope: U.S. Updated weekly. 1991—.
Producer: American Banker/Bond Buyer.
Available: Online as part of The Bond Buyer full text, DataTimes.

Public Finance/Washington Watch
Type: Full text.
Coverage: Developments in the federal government that affect state and local finance, especially government bonds.
Scope: U.S. Updated weekly. 1989—.
Producer: American Banker/Bond Buyer.
Available: DataTimes, NewsNet, NEXIS.

PUBLIC WORKS AND UTILITIES

BOOKS, REPORTS, MONOGRAPHS, BIBLIOGRAPHIES, AND REFERENCE SOURCES

1994 Manual of Concrete Practice. ACI. 1994. 5 part set, 4616p. Included in this comprehensive reference work are both standards and analytical reports on all facets of concrete use. Individual parts may be purchased separately.

Alternatives for Overtopping Protection of Dams. ASCE. 1994. 139p.

Analytical Fleet Maintenance Management. John E. Dolce. SAE. 1994. 201p. Guidelines for cost-effective maintenance of parts, tires, vehicles, scheduled and unscheduled maintenance, replacement are covered by the author, who draws on 25 years of experience with fleets of up to 6000 vehicles in both the private and public sectors.

Benchmarking for Electric Utilities. APPA. 1994. 94p. This is a report of an APPA task force which conducted a benchmarking study of five processes in a cross-section of utilities. Descriptions of how to conduct a benchmarking study are provided.

Bridge Inspection and Rehabilitation: A Practical Guide. Louis G. Silano, ed. Parsons Brinckerhoff. 1993. 288p. The articles in this collection give practical advice for caring for the 33% of American bridges which are considered substandard or obsolete.

Business Planning and Performance Measurement: A Guide for Small Public Power Systems. APPA. 1993. 165p. In addition to outlining the process for generating a business plan, this book describes the successful small utility and lists the hallmarks by which utility performance can be measured.

Construction of Fills. 2nd ed. Edward J. Monaghan. Wiley. 1994. 224p. This practical overview of earthwork construction contains new material on environmental concerns, septic systems, artificial fills, and the use of waste materials as fills.

Economics of Water Resources: From Regulation to Privatization. Nicolas Spulber. Kluwer. 1994. 329p.

Emergency Planning Guide for Utilities. Samuel Mullen. PennWell Publishing. 1994. 148p.

Energy Efficiency: Challenges and Opportunities for Electric Utilities. GPO. 1993. 203p. Expansion of utility demand-side management and integrated resource planning programs are examined, along with a discussion of federal policy options.

Environmental Compliance: A Manual for Electric Utilities. Spiegel & McDiarmid and R.W. Beck and Associates. APPA. 1994. 900p. Purchasers of this comprehensive but easy-to-read reference book may purchase annual updates of page additions and substitutions.

The Federal Role in Funding State and Local Infrastructure: Two Reports on Public Works Financing. Institute for Water Resources. 1993. 191p.

Hazardous Materials and Hazardous Waste Management: A Technical Guide. Gayle Woodside. Wiley. 1993. 408p.

High Performance Public Works: A New Federal Infrastructure Investment Strategy for America. ACIR. 1993. 58p.

Integrated Stormwater Management. Marie L. O'Shea, Keek Chin, eds. Lewis. 1993. 383p.

The Lighting Management Handbook. Craig DiLouie. Fairmont. 1994. 300p.

New Perspectives in Water Supply. William Whipple. Lewis. 1994. 218p.

Planning and Design for Small Craft Harbors. Rev. ed. Task Committee on Marinas. ASCE. 1994. 111p.

Safety Manual for an Electric Utility. 10th ed. Richard King, Paul Weida, David Cahill. 1994. 171p. This newly revised guide covers all facets of safety for facilities, worker protective wear, and operations—from working on underground lines to tree trimming.

School Bus Fleet—Fact Book Issue. Frank DiGiacomo. Bobit. 1993. 230p.

SDWA Advisor. Frederick W. Pontius. AWWA. 1994. History, background, and detailed summaries of every regulation of the Safe Drinking Water Act make this a compendium of information on this legislation. Quarterly updates will be provided to the basic looseleaf document, making it a subscription service rather than a one-time purchase.

Snow Removal and Ice Control Technology: Papers Presented at a Symposium. National Academy Press. 1993. 235p.

Stormwater: Best Management Practices and Detention for Water Quality, Drainage, and CSO Management. Ben Urbonas. PTR Prentice-Hall. 1993. 449p.

Water Management in the '90's: A Time for Innovation. ASCE. 1993. 880p.

Water Quality: Prevention, Identification, and Management of Diffuse Pollution. Vladimir Novotny. Van Nostrand Reinhold. 1994. 1054p.

PERIODICALS

AASHTO Quarterly. (Q) AASHTO.
American City and County. (M) Communication Channels.
APWA Reporter. (M) APWA.
AWWA Journal. (M) AWWA.
Civic Public Works. (BM) MacLean Hunter, Ltd.
Civil Engineering. (M) ASCE.
ENR. (W) McGraw-Hill.
Facilities Manager. (Q) Association of Higher Education Facilities Officers.
Fleet Equipment. (M) Maple.
From the State Capitals: Waste Disposal and Environmental Control. (W) Wakeman/Walworth.
From the State Capitals: Public Utilities. (W) Wakeman/Walworth.
Garbage. (6/yr) Old House Journal.
Gas Industries Magazine. (M) Gas Industries.
Journal of Water Resources Planning and Management. (BM) ASCE.
Public Power. (BM) American Public Power Association.
Public Works. (M) Public Works Journal.
Recycling Canada. Sydenham.
Recycling Today. G.I.E.
Solid Waste Technologies. (BM) H.C.I. Publications.
Waste Age. (M) National Solid Wastes Management Association.
Water Environmental Research. (M) Water Environmental Research Control Federation.
World Wastes. (M) Argus.

DATABASE RESOURCES

Applied Science and Technology Index
Type: Bibliographic.
Coverage: A basic index to 390 science and technology journals, including entries on construction, waste disposal, water distribution, pollution control, and recycling.
Scope: International. Updated twice weekly. October 1983—.
Producer: H.W. Wilson.
Available: CDP, OCLC, Wilsonline. CD-ROM, magnetic tape.

COMPENDEX (Computerized Engineering Index)
Type: Bibliographic.
Cover: Citations with abstracts to over 2.1 million entries on civil, sanitary, and waste engineering; water and waterworks, construction; and materials testing.
Scope: International. Updated monthly. Years covered vary with services.
Producer: Engineering Information.
Available: ESA-IRS. Magnetic tape.

Local Government Information Network.
Type: Full text, directory
Coverage: An information exchange system, offering local government experience and expertise, technical data, how-to instructions, and information sources, Emphasis is on innovation and efficiency.
Scope: Updated daily. 1979—.
Producer: Login Services Corp.
Available: Producer.

Public Utilities Reports
Type: Full text.
Coverage: *Public Utilities Fortnightly* covering problems, trends, fiance, policy, legislation, and judicial decisions.
Scope: International. Updated monthly. 1953—.
Producer: Center for Public Service Communication.
Available: ORBIT. CD-ROM.

WasteInfo
Type: Bibliographic, directory.
Coverage: Nonradioactive waste management.
Scope: International. Updated monthly. 1973—.
Producer: Waste Management Information Bureau.
Available: ORBIT. CD-ROM.

Water Resources Abstracts
Type: Bibliographic.
Coverage: *Selected Water Resources Abstracts* covering water cycles, supply, augmentation, management of quantity and quality, planning, and related engineering activities.
Scope: International. Updated monthly. 1968—.
Producer: U.,S. Geological Survey. Water Resources Scientific Information Center.
Available: DIALOG. CD-ROM, magnetic tape.

RECREATION AND LEISURE

BOOKS, REPORTS, MONOGRAPHS, BIBLIOGRAPHIES, AND REFERENCE SOURCES

All Around the Year: Holidays and Celebrations in American Life. Jack Santino. University of Illinois Press. 1994. 256p.

Attitudes toward the Outdoors: An Annotated Bibliography of U.S. Survey and Poll Research Concerning the Environment, Wildlife, and Recreation. Dena Jones Joma. McFarland. 1994. 269p.

Designing Instructional Swim Programs for Individuals with Disabilities. Marcia Jean Carter, Mary A. Dolan, Stephen P. LeConey. AAHPERD. 1994. 115p.

Designing Your Community's Open Space: A Parks, Recreation, and Open Space Planning Guide. State of Washington, Dept. of Community Trade and Economic Development. 1993. 112p.

Facility Planning for Physical Education, Recreation, and Athletics. Richard B. Flynn, ed. AAHPERD. 1993. 256p.

Food Festival: The Guidebook to America's Best Regional Food Celebrations. 2nd. ed. Alice M. Geffen, Carole Berglie. Countryman. 1994. 296p.

The Handbook of Museums. Gary Edson, David Dean. Routledge. 1993. 302p.

Interpretive Master Planning: For Parks, Historic Sites, Forests, Zoos, and Related Tourism Sites, For Self-guided Interpretive Services, for Interpretive Exhibits, for Guided Programs and Tours. John A. Veverka. Falcon. 1994. 162p.

Leisure in Society: A Network Structural Perspective. Patricia A. Stokowski. Mansell Publishing. 1994. 141p.

Leisure Opportunities of Individuals with Disabilities: Legal Issues. Susan J. Grosse, Donna Thompson, eds. AAHPERD. 1993. 112p.

Leisure Site Guidelines for People over 55. George E. Fogg, Robert F. Fulton. NRPA. 1994. 236p. After an overview of the leisure wants, needs, and capabilities of older persons and of federal accessibility requirements, this volume devotes the bulk of its attention to specific guidelines and ample suggestions for how to apply them.

Library Programming for Families with Young Children. Sue McCleaf Nespeca. Neal-Schuman. 1994. 150p.

Marinas, Parks, and Recreation Developments: Proceedings of the International Conference. Marshall Flug, Fred A. Klancnik, eds. ASCE. 1994. 620p. Case studies and action plans are presented by environmentalists, developers, government personnel, and landscapers.

Museum Exhibiting: Theory and Practice. David Dean. Routledge. 1994. 224p.

Museums and Their Visitors. Eilean Hooper-Greenhill. Routledge. 1994. 224p.

New Challenges in Recreation and Tourism Planning. Hubert N. Van Lier, Pat D. Taylor. Elsevier. 1993. 240p. This work provides a philosophical as well as technological consideration of the worldwide changes in leisure planning which are developing in response to the changing desires of the public and the changing role of public agencies.

Outdoor Recreation Management Theory and Application. Alan Jubrenville, Ben W. Twight. Venture Publishing. 1993. 329p.

Park and Recreation Maintenance Management. Robert E. Sternloff, Roger Warren. Publishing Horizons. 1993. 295p.

Play and Recreation for Individuals with Disabilities: Practical Pointers. Susan J. Grosse, Donna Thompson. AAHPERD. 1993. 152p.

Points about Playgrounds. Monty L. Christiansern. NRPA. 1993. 232p. Information, resources, and step-by-step techniques are offered for designing new playgrounds or inspecting and renovating old ones.

The Productive Park: New Waterworks as Neighborhood Resources. Architectural League of New York. Princeton Architectural Press. 1994. 160p. Illustrations and descriptive text accompany projects submitted for a study of how the need for renovations to New York City's water supply infrastructure could be joined with a new system of neighborhood parks.

Race, Ethnicity, and Participation in the Arts. Paul DiMaggio, Francie Ostrower. Seven Locks Press. 1993. 201p.

Successful Parks and Recreation Public Relations. Barry D. Mangum, Robert D. Reed. NRPA. 1993. 40p. This booklet is a practical guide to all pertinent communications, including news media relations, community, special events, and employee communications.

Theme Parks, Leisure Centres, Zoos, and Aquaria. Anthony Wylson, Patricia W. Wylson. Wiley. 1994. 183p. Written primarily from a building perspective, this volume demonstrates the truth that good design is based on a clear understanding of the purpose of the structure and how it will be used.

Universal Access to Outdoor Recreation: A Design Guide. PLAE. MIG Communications. 1993. 240p. This volume presents an overview of the issues involved and offers a hands-on land management tool for facility planners.

Wildlife and Recreationists: Coexistence through Management and Research. Richard L. Knight, Kevin J. Gutewiller. Island Press. 1994. 384p.

Youth at Risk: Targeting in On Prevention. Paul Varnes, ed. AAHPERD. 1994. 140p.

Zoos and Animal Rights: The Ethics of Keeping Animals. Stephen St. C. Bostock. Routledge. 1993. 227p. The author believes that we need to listen to the critics and learn from them but ultimately argues for the positive aspects of zoos.

PERIODICALS

Cardoza Arts and Entertainment Law Journal. (SA) Cardozo School of Law.
Coastal Management. (Q) Taylor and Francis.
Curator. (Q) American Museum of Natural History.
Fairs and Expositions. (10/yr) International Association of Festivals and Expositions.
Festival Management and Event Tourism. (Q) Cognizant.
Journal of Leisure Research. (Q) NRPA.
Journal of Park and Recreation Administration. (Q) Sagamore.
Journal of Physical Education, Recreation and Dance. (M) AAHPERD.
Landmark. (BM) Charlton.
Leisure Sciences. (Q) Taylor and Francis.
National Parks. (BM) National Parks and Conservation Association.
Park and Grounds Management. (M) Madisen.
Parks and Recreation. (M) NRPA.
Public Art Review. (SA) Forecast.
Recreation and Parks Law Reporter. (Q) NRPA.
Recreation Canada. (5/yr) Canadian Parks-Recreation Association.
Research Quarterly for Exercise and Sport. (Q) AAHPERD.
Waterfront World. (5/yr) Waterfront Center.

DATABASE RESOURCES

CAB: Leisure, Recreation and Tourism
Type: Bibliographic.
Coverage: Citations with abstracts to 25,000 articles on every facet of leisure: theory, facilities design, sports, and culture.
Scope: International. Updated quarterly or monthly, depending upon online service.
Producer: C.A.B. International.

Available: Data-Star, DIMDI. CD-ROM, diskette, magnetic tape.

Schole
Type: Full text.
Coverage: *Disability Advocates Bulletin, Recreation and Parks Law Reporter, and Fitness and Disability Handbook,* along with general news items, travel writings, parks and recreation works, and references to the National Recreation and Parks Association publications.
Scope: U.S. Updating varies. Current.
Producer: Boston University, School of Education.
Available: DELPHI.

SPORT (SIRC)
Type: Bibliographic.
Coverage: More than 320,000 citations, some with abstracts, to scientific and practical literature on individual and team sports, sports medicine, physical fitness, and education.
Scope: International. Updated monthly. 1949—.
Producer: Sport Information Research Centre.
Available: CAN/OLE, CDP, CompuServe, Data-Star, DIALOG, DIMDI. CD-ROM.

TRANSPORTATION AND ROADS

BOOKS, REPORTS, MONOGRAPHS, BIBLIOGRAPHIES, AND REFERENCE SOURCES

Access to Over-the Road Buses for Persons with Disabilities. This monograph discusses access to buses with a high passenger deck, those commonly used for intercity transportation. GPO. 1993. 159p.

Accident Reconstruction: Technology and Animation IV. Society of Automotive Engineers. 1994. 505p. A set of proceedings from the conference of the same name, this book offers a look at cutting edge and future technologies to aid in accident analysis.

Advanced Public Transportation Systems: The State of the ArtUpdate '94. U.S. Dept. of Transportation. NTIS. 1994. 133p.

Airport Planning, Operation, and Management. TRB. 1994. 61p.

Compendium of Articles on Residential Street Traffic Control. ITE. 1994. 141p.

Design Guidelines for the Control of Blowing and Drifting Snow. TRB. 1994. 364p.

Eight Ways to Finance Transit: A Policymaker's Guide. Wayne Boyle. NCSL. 1994. 65p. Ways to access private-sector support are explored, each one supported by detailed plans, examples, and case studies.

Electric Vehicles: Technology, Performance, and Potential. OECD. 1993. 201p.

Environmental Impact Assessment of Roads. OECD. 1994. 186p. After giving an overview of traditional methods for assessing environmental impact, this review discusses procedures and future trends suggested by current research.

Freeway Management Strategies. Kevin A. Haborian. Parsons Brinckerhoff. 1993. 146p.

Freight Transportation Research. TRB. 1994. 243p.

The Impact of Transport Investment Projects upon the Inner City: A Literature Review. Margaret Greico. Avebury. 1994. 188p. Focusing largely on the British experience, this book contains observations and analysis that will be useful to a wide audience.

Implementing Effective Travel Demand Management Measures: Inventory of Measures and Synthesis of Experience. U.S. Department of Transportation. 1993.

Innovations in Travel Behavior Analysis, Demand Forecasting, and Modeling Networks. TRB. 1994. 44p.

Intelligent Vehicles Symposium. IEEE Service Center. 1993. 496p.

Linking Land Use and Transportation. APA. 1993. Various paging. These workshop materials examine the Intermodal Surface Transportation Efficiency Act (ISTEA) and the Clean Air Act, summarize proposed compliance legislation, and include a 500-page resource manual focused on implementation of the two acts.

Moving Urban America. TRB. 1993. 164p. The conference upon which this report draws explored methods for addressing urban transportation issues in the light of the Intermodal Surface Transportation Efficiency Act of 1991 and the Clean Air Act Amendments of 1990.

National Bicycling and Walking Study: Transportation Choices for a Changing America. GPO. 1994. 152p.

Parking: The Parking Handbook for Small Communities. John Edwards. ITE/National Trust for Historic Preservation. 1994. 107p. Written with an understanding of the needs of the professional with limited experience, this step-by-step plan touches on parking, design, and administrative considerations.

Pedestrian Malls and Skywalks: Traffic Separation Strategies in American Downtowns. Kent A. Robertson. Avebury. 1994. 146p. This book showcases the solutions of several major cities to the challenge of pedestrian use of downtown shopping areas.

Planning and Design of Airports. 4th ed. Robert Horonjeff, Francis X. McKelvey. McGraw-Hill. 1993. 358p.

Preferential Lane Treatments for High-occupancy Vehicles. Charles A. Fuhs. National Academy Press. 1993. 80p.

Railroad Freight Transportation Research Needs. TRB. 1994. 149p.

Saving Energy in U.S. Transportation. Office of Technology Assessment, U.S. Congress. GPO. 1994. 266p.

Training Resources Catalog: For Rural and Specialized Transit Systems. U.S. Dept. of Transportation. 1994. 292p. More than 200 programs and resources are included for managers and personnel of specialized systems.

Transit Planning and Research Reports: Annotated Bibliography. U.S. Dept. of Transportation. 1993. 53p.

Underwater Bridge Maintenance and Repair. National Cooperative Highway Research Project. TRB. 1994. 69p.

Urban Public Transport Today. Barry J. Simpson. E&FN Spon. 1994. 222p. From trolleys to light rail, this book explores contemporary solutions to public transportation in a wide range of metropolitan setting.

Workshop on Transit Fare Policy and Management Research Needs and Priorities. TRB. 1994. 77p.

PERIODICALS

Airport Services Management. (M) Lakewood.
Aviation Week & Space Technology. (W) McGraw-Hill.
Bus Ride. (9/yr) Friendship.
Business and Commercial Aviation. (M) McGraw-Hill.
Electric Vehicle Progress. (SM) Alexander Research and Communications.
Fleet Owner. (M) INTERTEC.
ITE Journal. (M) Institute of Transportation Engineers.
Journal of Transportation Engineering. (BM) ASCE.
Mass Transit. (M) PTN Publishing.
Passenger Transport. (W) American Public Transit Association.
Public Roads. (Q) U.S. Federal Highway Administration. GPO.
Railway Age. (M) Simmons-Boardman.
School Bus Fleet. (BM) Bobit.
TR News. (BM) TRB.
Traffic World. (W) Journal of Commerce.
Transport Topics. (W) American Trucking Association.
Transportation Journal. (Q) American Society of Transportation and Logistics.
Transportation Quarterly. (Q) Eno Foundation for Transportation. Transportation Research. Part A: General; Part B: Methodological. (BM) Pergamon.

DATABASE RESOURCES

Business Publishers
Type: Full text.
Coverage: More than 50 newsletters, including *Toxic Materials News, U.S. Rail News,* and *Urban Transport News.*
Scope: Varies with source publication.
Producer: Business Publishers.
Available: NewsNet, PTS, URBI.

DRI/McGraw-Hill. Data Products Division
Type: Statistical
Coverage: Not a database *per se,* but a service providing information such as economic data, analyses, forecasts, and simulations.
Scope: Varies with sources.
Producer: DRI/McGraw-Hill.
Available: Producer.

TRIS (Transportation Research Information Services)
Type: Bibliographic.
Coverage: Citations with abstracts from govern-

ment and private transportation organizations related to air, highway, rail, maritime, pipeline, and mass transportation. Policy, planning, administration, regulation, design construction, maintenance, control, and user concerns are covered, along with research in progress.

Scope: International. Updated monthly. 1968—.
Producer: National Academy of Science/Transportation Review Board.
Available: DIALOG.

LIST OF PUBLISHERS

AAHPERD *see* American Alliance for Health, Physical Education, Recreation, and Dance.

AASHTO *see* American Association of State Highway and Transportation Officials.

ABA *see* American Bar Association.

ABC-CLIO, Inc., 130 Cremona Dr., P.O. Box 1911, Santa Barbara, CA 93116-1911.

ABLEX Publishing Corporation, 355 Chestnut St., Norwood, NJ 07648.

ACA *see* American Correctional Association.

Academic Press, Inc., 525 B St., Ste. 1900, San Diego, CA 92101.

Academy of Criminal Justice Sciences, 402 Nunn Hall, Northern Kentucky University, Highland Heights, KY 41099-5998.

ACC Communications, Inc., P.O. Box 2440, Costa Mesa, CA 92628.

ACI *see* American Concrete Institute.

ACIR *see* U.S. Advisory Commission on Intergovernmental Relations

Administrative Office of United States Courts, 1 Columbus Circle, N.E., Washington, DC 20544.

AEI *see* American Enterprise Institute.

AICP *see* American Institute of Certified Planners.

AICPA *see* American Institute of Certified Public Accountants.

Alexander Research & Communications, Inc., 215 Park Ave. S., Ste. 1301, New York, NY 10003-1601.

AMACOM Books, (American Management Association), 135 W. 50th St., New York, NY 10020.

American Academy of Orthopaedic Surgeons, P.O. Box 75838, Chicago, IL 60675-5838.

American Alliance for Health, Physical Education, Recreation, and Dance, 1900 Association Drive, Reston, VA 22091-1599.

American Arbitration Association, 140 W. 51st St., New York, NY 10020-1203.

American Association of Retired Persons, 601 E St., N.W, Washington, DC 20049, (202)434-6231.

American Association of State Highway and Transportation Officials, 444 N. Capitol St., N.W., Ste. 225, Washington, DC 20001.

American Banker/Bond Buyer, One State St. Plaza, New York, NY 10004, (212)943-6304.

American Bar Association, 750 N. Lake Shore Drive, Chicago, IL 60611.

American Civil Defense Association, P.O. Box 1057, Starke, FL 32091.

American Concrete Institute, P.O. Box 19150, Detroit, MI 48219-0150.

American Correctional Association, 8025 Laurel Lakes Court, Laurel, MD 20707-5075.

American Economic Development Council, 9801 W. Higgins Road, Ste. 540, Rosemont, IL 60018-4726.

American Enterprise Institute for Public Policy Research, 1150 17th St., N.W., Washington, DC 20036.

American Finance Association, Stern School of Business, New York University, 100 Trinity Place, New York, NY 10006.

American Fire Sprinkler Association, 12459 Jupiter Rd., Ste. 142, Dallas, TX 75238-3200.

American Institute of Certified Planners, 1776 Massachusetts Ave., Ste. 400, Washington, DC 20036.

American Institute of Certified Public Accountants, 1211 Avenue of the Americans, New York, NY 10036-8775.

American Judicature Society, 25 E. Washington, Ste. 1600, Chicago, IL 60602-1805.

American Museum of Natural History, Central Park West at 79th St., New York, NY 10024-5192.

American Planning Association, 1313 E. 60th St., Chicago, IL 60637-2891.

American Prosecutors Research Institute, 99 Canal Center Plaza, Ste. 510, Alexandria, VA 22314.

American Public Power Association, 2301 M St., N.W., Washington, DC 20037-1484.

American Public Transit Association, 1201 New York Ave., N.W., Ste. 400, Washington, DC 20005.

American Public Welfare Association, 810 First St., N.E., Ste. 500, Washington, DC 20002-4205.

American Public Works Association, 106 W. 11th St., Ste. 1800 Kansas City, MO 64105-1806.

American Real Estate and Urban Economics Association, School of Business, Rm. 428, Indiana University, Bloomington, IN 47405.

American Society for Public Administration, 1120 G St., N.W., Ste. 700, Washington, DC 20005.

American Society of Civil Engineers, 345 E. 47th St., New York, NY 10017-2398, (212)705-7520.

American Society of Criminology, 1314 Kennear Rd., Columbus, OH 43212.

American Society of Transportation and Logistics, Inc., 3600 Chamberlain Ln., No. 232, Louisville, KY 40241-1989.

American Trucking Associations, 2200 Mill Road, Alexandria, VA 22314-4654.

American Water Works Association, 6666 W. Quincy Ave., Denver, CO 80325.

Anderson Publishing Co., P.O. Box 1576, Cincinnati, OH 45201-1576.

AP Professional, *see* Academic Press

APA *see* American Planning Association.

APPA *see* American Public Power Association.

APRI *see* American Prosecutors Research Institute.

APWA *see* American Public Works Association.

AREUEA *see* American Real Estate and Urban Economics Association.

Argus Publishing, 6151 Powers Ferry Rd., N.W., Atlanta, GA 30339.

Edward Arnold *see* Chapman and Hall.

Artech House, Inc., 685 Canton St., Norwood, MA 02062.

ASCE *see* American Society of Civil Engineers.

ASDSO *see* Association of State Dam Safety Officials.

Ashgate Publishing Company, Old Post Road, Brookfield, VT 05036.

ASPA *see* American Society for Public Administration.

ASQC Quality *see* Quality Press.

Association for Computing Machinery, 1515 Broadway, 17th Fl., New York, NY 10036-5701.

Association for Preservation Technology International, P.O. Box 8178, Fredericksburg, VA 22404.

Association of Bay Area Governments, P.O. Box 2050, Oakland, CA 94604-2050.

Association of Higher Education Facilities Officers, 1446 Duke St., Alexandria, VA 22314-3492.

Association of Records Managers and Administrators, 4200 Somerset Dr., P.O. Box 8540, Prairie Village, KS 66208.

Association of State Dam Safety Officials, 450 Old East Vine, Lexington, KY 40507.

Avebury Publications, Old Post Rd., Brookfield, VT 05036.

Avery Architectural and Fine Arts Library see Columbia University.

AWWA *see* American Water Works Association.

Barron's Educational Services, Inc., 250 Wireless Blvd., Hauppauge, NY 11788.

Basic *see* Harper/Collins.

Baywood Publishing Co., Inc., 26 Austin Ave., Box 337, Amityville, NY 11701.

BCR Enterprises, Inc., 950 York Rd., No. 203, Hinsdale, IL 605212939.

Beacon Press, 25 Beacon St., Boston, MA 02108.

Belknap *see* Harvard University Press.

Bernan Press, 4611-F Assembly Dr., Lanham, MD 20706-4391.

BJA *see* U.S. Bureau of Justice Assistance.

BJS *see* U.S. Bureau of Justice Statistics.

Blackie Academic *see* Chapman and Hall.

Blackwell Publishers, 238 Main St., Cambridge, MA 02142.

Basil Blackwell Ltd., 108 Cowley Rd., Oxford OX4 1JF, England.

Bobit Publishing Co., 2512 Artesia Blvd., Redondo Beach, CA 90278.

BOCA see Building Officials and Code Administrators International.

Booz-Allen & Hamilton, Inc., 8283 Greensboro Drive, McLean, VA 22102-3838.

Boston University, School of Education, 605 Commonwealth Ave., Boston, MA 02215, (617)353-3295.

Bowling Green State University, Philosophy Documentation Center, Bowling Green, OH 43403-0189.

BPI Communications, 1515 Broadway, 39th Ft., New York, NY 10036.

Brady Communications, 113 Sylvan Ave, Rt. 9W, Englewood Cliffs, NJ 07632.

Paul H. Brookes Publishing Co., P.O. Box 10624, Baltimore, MD 21285-0624.

Brookings Institution, 1775 Massachusetts Ave., N.W., Washington, DC 20036-2188.

Brooks/Cole, 511 Forest Lodge Rd., Pacific Grove, CA 93950.

Brown and Benchmark *see* Cooper Publishing.

Building Officials and Code Administrators International, 4051 Flossmoor Rd., Country Club Hills, IL 60478-5795.

Bureau of Emergency Services—Queensland, GPO Box 1425, Brisbane, Queensland 4001, Australia.

Bureau of National Affairs, Inc., 1231 25th St., N.W., Washington, DC 20037, (202)452-4132.

Business News Publishing, Box 2600, Troy, MI 48007.

Business Publishers, Inc., 951 Pershing Drive, Silver Spring, MD 20910-4464, (301)587-6300.

Butterworth-Heinemann, 80 Montvale Ave., Stoneham, MA 02180.

Butterworth Legal Publishers, 8 Industrial Way, Bldg. C, Salem, NH 03079.

C. A. B. International, Wallingford, Oxon, OX10 8DE, England, 0491 32111.

Cahners Publishing Co., 275 Washington St., Newton, MA 02158-1630.

Cahners Publishing Co., 8601 Georgia Ave., Silver Spring, MD 20910.

Cambridge Scientific Abstracts, 7200 Wisconsin Ave., Ste. 601, Bethesda, MD 20814, (301)961-6750.

Cambridge University Press, 40 W. 20th St., New York, NY 10011.

CAN/OLE *see* Canadian Institute for Scientific and Technical Information.

Canada Communication Group Publications, Supply and Service, #D2200, 45, boul. Sacre-Coeur, Hull, PQ K1A 0S9.

Canadian Almanac & Directory Publishing Co., Ltd., 134 Adelaide St. E., Ste. 207, Toronto, ON M5C 1K9.

Canadian Association of Chiefs of Police, 112 Kent St., Ste. 1908, Place de Ville, Tower ''B,'' Ottawa, ON K1P 5P2.

Canadian Centre for Philanthropy, 1329 Bay St., 2nd Fl., Toronto ON M5R 2C4.

Canadian Criminal Justice Association, 55 Parkdale Ave., Ottawa, ON K1Y 1E5.

Canadian Firefighter Publishing Co., Ltd., Box 95, Sta. D, Etobicoke ON M94 4X1.

Canadian Institute for Scientific and Technical Information, Montreal Rd., Ottawa, ON K1A 052, (613)993-1210.

Canadian Parks-Recreation Association, 1600 James Naismith Drive, Gloucester, ON KIB 5N4.

Canadian Scholars' Press, Inc., 1800 Bloor St., W, Ste. 402, Toronto ON M5S 2VG.

Canadian Tax Foundation, 1 Queen's Street, Ste. 1800, Toronto, ON M5C 2Y2.

Canadian Urban Institute *see* Urban Development Institute of Ontario.

Capitol Publications, Inc., Telecom Publishing Group, 1101 King St., Ste. 444, Box 1455, Alexandria, VA 22313-2055, (703)739-6400.

Captus Press, York University Campus, 4700 Keele St., North York, ON M3J 1P3.

Cardozo School of Law, 55 Fifth Ave., New York, NY 10003.

Carl Vinson Institute of Government *see* University of Georgia.

Cassell Publishing, 387 Park Ave. S., 5th Fl., New York, NY 10016.

CAUSE, 4840 Pearl E. Circle, Ste. 302E, Boulder, CO 80301.

Center for Public Service Communications, 1600 Wilson Blvd., Ste. 500, Arlington, VA 22209-2515.

Center for Research in Water Resources *see* University of Texas at Austin.

Center for Urban Policy Research, P.O. Box 489, Piscataway, NJ 08855-0489.

Center for Urban Research and Policy Studies *see* University of Chicago, 969 E. 60th St., Chicago, IL 60637.

Chapman and Hall, One Penn Plaza, 41st Fl., New York, NY 10119.

Charles Press, 3616 E. Cherry, Seattle, WA 98122.

Charlton Communications, 807 Manning Rd., N.E. Ste. 200, Calgary AB T2E 7418.

Chatham House Publications, Inc., Box 1, Chatham, NJ 07928.

Cher Amie Publishing, P.O. Box 3, Soda Springs, ID 83276.

Chevron Publishing Co., 5018 Dorsey Hall Dr., Ste. 104, Ellicott City, MD 21042.

Child Welfare League of America, Inc., 440 First St., N.W., Ste. 310, Washington, DC 20001-2085.

CIO Publishing, Inc., 492 Old Connecticut Path, P. O. Box 9208, Framingham, MA 01701-9208.

City Hall Communications, P. O. Box 910, Franklin, NC 28734-0919.

Clark Boardman Callaghan, 155 Pfingsten Rd. Deerfield, IL 60015.

CMP Publications, 600 Community Drive, Manhasset, NY 11030.

COGEL see Council on Governmental Ethics Laws.

Cognizant Communication Corporation, 3 Hartsdale Rd., Elmsford, NY 10523-3701.

Columbia University, Avery Architecture and Fine Arts Library, Broadway & 116th St., New York, NY 10027, (212)854-8404.

Columbia University, Graduate School of Architecture, Avery Hall, Broadway & 116th St., New York, NY 10027, (212)854-8404.

Columbia University Press, 562 W. 113th St., New York, NY 10025.

Commonwealth of Pennsylvania, Department of Aging, 400 Market St., Harrisburg, PA 17101-2301.

Communication Channels, Inc., 6151 Powers Ferry Rd., Atlanta, GA 30339-2941.

Community Nutrition Institute, 2001 S St., N.W., Ste. 530, Washington, DC 20009.

Community Services Society of New York, 105 E. 22nd St., New York, NY 10010.

CompuServe Information Service, 5000 Arlington Centre Blvd., Box 20102, Columbus, OH 43220, (614)457-8600.

Congressional Quarterly, Inc., 1414 22nd St., N.W., Washington, DC 20037.

Cooper Publishing Group, 701 Congressional Blvd., Ste. 340, Carmel, IN 46032.

Coopers and Lybrand, 1800 M St., N.W., Washington, DC 20036.

COSCDA *see* Council of State Community and Development Agencies.

Council of State Community and Development Agencies, Hall of States, 444 N. Capitol St., Ste. 224, Washington, DC 20001.

Council of State Governments, 3560 Iron Works Pike, P.O. Box 11910, Lexington, KY 40578-1910.

Council on Governmental Ethics Laws, 3560 Iron Works Pike, P.O. Box 11910, Lexington, KY 40578-1910.

The Countryman Press, Inc., Box 175, Woodstock, VT 05091-0175.

CQ Press *see* Congressional Quarterly.

Crain Communications, Inc., 740 N. Rush St., Chicago, IL 60611-2590.

CRC Press, Inc., 200 Corporate Blvd., N.W., Boca Raton, FL 33431.

Creative Age Publications, 7628 Dinsmore Ave., Van Nuys, CA 91406.

Data Based Solutions, Inc., 4010 Morena Blvd., Ste. 200, San Diego, CA 92117-4547.

Marcel Dekker, 270 Madison Ave., New York, NY 10016.

Department of Finance, 140 O'Connor St., Ottawa, ON K1A 0G5.

Diane Publishing Co., 600 Upland Ave., Upland, PA 19015.

Disaster Survival Planning, Inc., 669 Pacific Cove Dr., Port Hueneme, CA 93041.

DRI/McGraw-Hill, Data Products Division, 24 Hartwell Ave., Lexington, MA 02173, (617)863-5100.

E&FN Spon *see* Chapman and Hall.

Earthquake Engineering Research Institute, 499 14th St., Ste. 320, Oakland, CA 94612-1902.

Economics and Technology, Inc., One Washington Mall, Boston, MA 02108.

Edward Elgar *see* Ashgate Publishing Co.

EIS International, 1401 Rockville Pike, Ste. 500, Rockville, MD 20852, (301)424-2803.

Elsevier Science, Ltd., Mayfield House, 256 Banbury Road, Oxford OX2 7DH, England, 0865 512242.

Elsevier Science Publishers B. V., P.O. Box 211, 1000 AE Amsterdam, The Netherlands.

Elsevier Science Publishers, Ltd., Crown House, Linton Road, Barking, Essex 1G11 8JU, England.

Elsevier Science, Inc., P.O. Box 882, Madison Square Station, New York, NY 10159.

Emergency Preparedness Canada, 2nd Fl., Jackson Bldg., 122 Bank St. W., Ottawa, Ontario KIA OW6.

Engineering Information, Inc., Castle Point on

the Hudson, Hoboken, NJ 07030, (201)216-8500.

Eno Foundation for Transportation, 442211 Statestone Ct., Lansdowne, VA 22075.

EPA *see* U.S. Environmental Protection Agency.

ETSI, Human Resource Information Network, 1200 Quince Orchard Blvd., Gaithersburg, MD 288, (301)590-2300, (800)638-8094.

Executive Enterprises Publications, Co., Inc., 21-W. 21st St., New York, NY 10010-6904.

Facts on File, 460 Park Ave. S., New York, NY 10016.

The Fairmont Press, Inc., 700 Indian Trail, Liliburn, GA 30247.

Falcon Press Publishing Co., Inc., 48 N Last Chance Gulch, P.O. Box 1718, Helena, MT 59624.

Families International, 11700 W. Lake Park Drive, Milwaukee, WI 53224.

Family Impact Seminar, 1100 17th St., N.W., Washington, DC 20036.

Federal Emergency Management Agency, 500 C St., S. W., Rm. 429, Washington, DC 20472, (301)926-5376.

FEMA *see* Federal Emergency Management Agency.

Fire Buff House Publishers, P.O. Box 711, New Albany, IN 47151.

Fire Engineering Books & Videos, 8 W. Plaza II, Saddle Brook, NY 07662.

Fire Publications, Inc., c/o J. A. Ackerman, Pub., 9072 E. Artesia Blvd, Bellflower, CA 90706.

Fisher Publishing, 4239 West Ina Rd., Ste. 101, Tucson, AZ 85741.

Florida League of Cities, Inc., P.O. Box 1757, Tallahassee, FL 32302.

Forecast Public Artworks, 2324 University Ave. W, Ste. 102, St. Paul, MN 55114-1802.

The Foundation Center, 79 5th Ave., New York, NY 10003-3076, (212)620-4230.

Friendship Publications, Inc., P.O. Box 1472, Spokane, WA 99210-1472.

Gale Research, Inc., 835 Penobscot Building, Detroit, Ml 48226-4094.

GAO *see* U. S. General Accounting Office.

Gallaudet University Press, 800 Florida Ave., N.E. Washington, D.C. 20002-3695.

Garland Publishing, Inc., 717 Fifth Ave., Ste. 2500, New York, NY 10022-8102.

Gas Industries, P.O. Box 558, Park Ridge, IL 60068.

Geological Society of America, 3300 Penrose Place, P.O. Box 9140, Boulder, CO 80301.

Georgia State University, College of Public and Urban Affairs, Box 4018, Atlanta, GA 30302-4018.

GFOA *see* Government Finance Officers Association.

G.I.E. Publishing Co., 4012 Bridge Ave., Cleveland, OH 44113.

Government Finance Officers Association, 180 N. Michigan Ave., Ste. 800, Chicago, IL 60601, (312)977-9700.

Government Information Services, 4301 Fairfax Dr., Ste. 875, Fairfax, VA 2203-1627.

Government Research Services, 701 Jackson, Ste. 304, Topeka, KS 66603.

GPO *see* Superintendent of Documents, U.S. Government Printing Office.

Great Britain Department of the Environment, Building Research Establishment Library, Bucknalls Ln., Garston Watford, Herts, WD2 7JR, England.

Greenhaven Press, Box 289009, San Diego, CA 92198-9009.

Greenwood Press, 88 Post Road West, Box 5007, Westport, CT 068815007.

Grey House Publishing, Pocket Knife Square, Lakeville, CT 06039.

GTE, 5525 MacArthur Blvd., Ste 300, Irving, TX 75038, (214)518-8500.

Gulf Publishing Co., 3301 Allen Pkwy, Houston, TX 77019.

Halsted Press, 605 Third Ave., New York, NY 10158-0012.

Glenn Hare Publications, 6300 Yarrow Drive, Carlsbad, CA 92009-1597.

HarperCollins Publishers, Inc. 10 E. 53rd St., New York, NY 10225299.

Harvard Business School Publishing, Boston, MA 02163.

Harvard University Press, 79 Garden St., Cambridge, MA 02138.

Haworth Press, Inc., 10 Alice St., Binghamton, NY 13904-1580.

Hazardous Materials Control Resources Institute, 1 Church St., Ste 120, Rockville, MD 20850-4129.

Hazardous Materials Publishing, P.O. Box 204, Barre, VT 05641.

H.C.I. Publications, 410 Archibald St., Kansas City, MO 64111-3046.

Health Administration Press, 1021 E. Huron St., Ann Arbor, MI 48104-9990.

The Heartland Institute, 800 East Northwest Hwy., Ste. 1080, Palatine, IL 60067.

Highsmith Press, W5527 Hwy. 106, P.O. Box 800, Fort Atkinson, WI 53538-0800.

Home Builder Press, 1201 15th St., N.W., Washington, DC 20005.

Horizon House Publications, 685 Canton St., Norwood, MA 02062.

HRIN *see* ETSI, Human Relations Information Network.

Human Sciences Press, Inc., 233 Spring Street, NY 10013-1578.

IAAO *see* International Association of Assessing Officers.

IACP *see* International Association of Chiefs of Police.

IAFC *see* International Association of Fire Chiefs.

IAFF *see* International Association of Fire Fighters.

IAP *see* International Aviation Publishers.

ICMA *see* International City/County Management Association.

I.C.S. Books, Inc., 1370 E. 86th Pl. P.O. Box 10767, Merrillville, IN 46411-0767.

ICURR *see* Intergovernmental Committee on Urban and Regional Research.

IDG Communications, Inc., 375 Cochituate Rd., Box 9173, Framingham, MA 01701-9171.

IEEE *see* Institute of Electrical and Electronic Engineers.

Independent Computer Consultants Association, 933 Gardenview Office Parkway, St. Louis, MO 63141-5917, (314)997-4633.

Indiana University Press, 601 N. Morton St., Bloomington, IN 47404-3797.

Industrial Relations Research Institute, University of Wisconsin Press, Social Science Bldg., 1180 Observatory, Madison WI 53706.

Information Access Company, 362 Lakeside Dr., Foster City, CA 94404, (415)358-4643.

Information Sources, Inc., 1173 Colusa Ave., P.O. Box 7848, Berkeley, CA 94707, (510)525-6220.

Infoworld Publishing, 155 Bovet Rd., Ste. 800, San Mateo, CA 94402.

Institute for Environmental Education, 18554 Haskins Rd., Chagrin Falls, OH 44023-1823.

Institute for Research on Public Policy, 3771 Hare Rd., Victoria, BC V8P 5C3.

Institute for Scientific Information, 3501 Market St., Philadelphia, PA 19104, (215)386-0100.

Institute for Water Resources, 7701 Telegraph Rd., Alexandria, VA 22315-3868.

Institute of Behavioral Science *see* NHRAIC.

Institute of Public Administration of Canada, 150 Eglinton Ave., E., Ste. 305, Toronto, ON M4P 1E8.

Institute of Real Estate Management, 430 N. Michigan Ave., 7th Fl., Chicago, IL 60611-4002.

Institute of Transportation Engineers, 525 School St., S.W., Ste. 410, Washington DC 20024-2797.

Institute of Urban and Regional Development, 316 Wurster Hall, University of California, Berkeley 94720.

Intergovernmental Committee on Urban and Regional Research, 150 Eglinton Ave. E., Ste. 301, Toronto ON M4P 1E8.

International Association of Arson Investigators, P.O. Box 91119, Louisville, KY 40291.

International Association of Assessing Officers, 130 E. Randolph St., Ste. 800, Chicago, IL 60601.

International Association of Chiefs of Police, Inc. 515 N. Washington St., Ste. 400, Alexandria, VA 22314-2340.

International Association of Festivals and Exhibitions, Box 985, Springfield, MO 65801.

International Association of Fire Fighters, 1750 New York Ave., N.W., Washington, D.C. 20006-5395.

International Association of Fire Chiefs, 4025 Fair Ridge Dr., Fairfax VA 22033.

International Association of Wildland Fire, P.O. Box 328, Fairfield, WA 99012-0328.

International Aviation Publishers, P.O. Box 10000, Casper, WY 82602-1000.

International City/County Management Association, 777 North Capitol St., N.E., Ste. 500, Washington, DC 20002-4201, (202)289-4262.

International Consulting System, 1485 Paloma Pl., P.O. Box 199, Arroyo Grande, CA 9342.

International Fertilizer Development Center, P.O. Box 2040, Muscle Shoals, AL 35662.

International Foundation of Employee Benefit Plans, 18700 W. Bluemound Road, P.O. Box 69, Brookfield, WI 53008-0069, (414)786-6700.

International Library Law Book Publishers, 101 Lakeforest Blvd., Ste. 270, Gaithersburg, MD 20877.

International Personnel Management Association, 1617 Duke St., Alexandria, VA 22314.

International Research and Evaluation, 21098 IRE Control Center, Eagan, MN 55121, (612)888-9635.

International Society of Fire Service Instructors, 30 Main St., Ashland, MA 01721.

Intertec Publishing Corp., 707 Westchester Ave., Ste. 101, White Plains, NY 10604-3102.

Iowa State University Press, 2121 S. State Ave., Ames, IA 50010.

IPMA see International Personnel Management Association.

Richard D. Irwin, Inc., 1333 Burr Ridge Pkwy., Burr Ridge, IL 60521.

Island Press, 1718 Connecticut Ave., N.W., Ste. 300, Washington, DC 20009.

ITE see Institute of Transportation Engineers.

JEMS Publishing Co., P.O. Box 2789, Carlsbad, CA 92018.

Johns Hopkins University Press, 701 W. 40th St., Ste. 275, Baltimore, MD 21211-2190.

Joint Assistance Centre, H-65 South Extension 1, New Delhi 110049, India.

Jossey-Bass, Inc., 350 Sansome St., 5th Fl., San Francisco, CA 94104.

Journal of Commerce, 741 National Press Bldg., Washington, DC 20045.

Journal of Public Health Policy, 208 Meadowood Dr., South Burlington, VT 05403.

JRSA see Justice Research and Statistics Association.

Justice Research and Statistics Association, 444 N. Capitol St., N.W., Ste. 445, Washington, DC 20001.

Jessica Kingsley Publishing see Paul H. Brookes.

Kluwer Academic Publishers Group, P.O. Box 358, Accord Station, Hingham, MA 02108-0358.

Lakewood Publications, Inc., 50 S. Ninth St., Minneapolis, MN 55402.

Lawyers Cooperative Publishing, Aqueduct Bldg., Rochester, NY 14694.

Learned Information, 143 Old Marlton Pike, Medford, NJ 08055-8707.

Lewis Publishers, Inc., 121 S. Main St., P.O. Box 519, Chelsea, MI 48118.

LEXIS see Mead Data Central.

Little, Brown & Co., 34 Beacon St., Boston, MA 02108

Locke Science Publishing Co., Inc., 117 W. Harrison Bldg., Ste. 640-L221, Chicago, IL 60605

Login Services Corp., 125 Maint St., Ste. 311, Minneapolis, MN 55414-2143, (612)331-5672.

MacLean-Hunter, Ltd., 777 Bay St., Toronto, ON M5W 1A7.

Macmillan Publishing Co., 866 Third Ave., New York, NY 10022.

Madisen Publishing Division, P.O. Box 1936, Appleton, WI 54913.

Mansell see Cassell, Publishing.

Maple Publishing, 134 W. Slade St., Palatine, IL 60067.

McFarland & Co., Inc., Publishers, Box 611, Jefferson, NC 28640.

McGraw-Hill, Inc., 1221 Ave. of the Americas, New York, NY 10020.

McGraw-Hill, Inc., Byte Publications, One Phoenix Mill Lane, Peterborough, NH 03458.

Mead Data Central, Inc., 9443 Springboro Pike, P.O. Box 933, Dayton, OH 45401, (513)865-6800.

MIG Communications, 1802 Fifth St., Berkeley, CA 94710-1915.

Mosby-Year Book, Inc., 11830 Westline Industrial Dr., St. Louis, MO 63146.

William Morrow & Co., Inc., 1350 Avenue of the Americas, New York, NY 10009.

NAHB see National Association of Home Builders.

NAHRO see National Association of Housing and Redevelopment Officials

NASW see National Association of Social Workers.

NASIRE, P.O. Box 11910, Lexington, KY 40578-1910.

National Academy Press, 2101 Constitution Ave., N.W., Washington, DC 20418.

National Association of Counties, 440 First St., N.W., Washington, DC 20001-2023.

National Association of Home Builders, One Thomas Circle, N.W., Washington, DC 20005.

National Association of Housing and Redevelopment Officials, 1320 18th St., N.W., Washington, DC 20036-1811.

National Association of Search and Rescue Headquarters, P.O. Box 3709, Fairfax, VA 22038.

National Association of Social Workers, 750 First St., Ste. 70, N.E., Washington, DC 20002.

National Association of Towns and Townships, 1522 K St., N.W., Ste. 600, Washington, DC 20008.

National Civic League, 1445 Market St., Ste. 300, Denver, CO 80202-1728.

National Conference of State Legislatures, 1560 Broadway, Ste. 700, Denver, CO 80202-5140.

National Coordinating Council on Emergency Management, 7927 Lee Highway, Ste. N, Falls Church, VA 22042.

National Council of Juvenile and Family Court Judges, P.O. Box 8978, University of Nevada, Reno, NV 89507.

National Directory of Children, Youth and Family Services. Longmont, CO 80502-1837.

National Economic Development and Law Center, 2201 Broadway, Ste. 815, Oakland, CA 94612-3024.

National Emergency Training Center, 16825 S. Seton Ave., Emmitsburg, MD 21727, (301)447-1032, (800)638-1821.

National Fire Protection Association, 1 Batterymarch Park, Quincy, MA 02269-9101, (617)770-3000.

National Fire Sprinkler Association, Robin Hill Corporate Park, Rte. 22, P.O. Box 1000, Patterson, NY, 12563.

National Institute for Urban Search and Rescue, P.O. Box 91648, Santa Barbara, CA 93190-1648, (805)569-5066, (800)767-0093.

National Journal, 1730 M St., N.W., Ste. 1100, Washington, DC 20036.

National League of Cities, 1301 Pennsylvania Ave., N.W., Washington, DC 20004-1763.

National Oceanic and Atmospheric Administration, 14th and Constitution Ave., N.W., Rm. 5805, Washington, DC 20230-001.

National Parks and Conservation Association, 1776 Massachusetts Ave., N.W., Ste. 200, Washington, DC 20036.

National Recreation and Park Association, 2775 Quincy St., Ste. 300, Alexandria, VA 22206-2200.

National Rehabilitation Association, 4109 633 S. Washington St., Alexandria, VA 22314.

National Research Council, 2101 Constitution Ave., Washington, D.C. 20418.

National Search and Rescue Secretariat, 275 Slater St., 4th Fl., Ottawa, ON K1A 0K2.

National Software Testing Laboratory, Inc., Plymouth Corporation Center, Box 1000, Plymouth Meeting, PA 19462.

National Solid Wastes Management Association, 1730 Rhode Island Ave., N.W., Ste. 1000, Washington, D.C. 20036.

National Tax Association, Tax Institue of America, 5310 E. Main St., Ste. 104, Columbus, OH 43213.

National Technical Information Service, U.S. Department of Commerce, 5285 Port Royal Rd., Springfield, VA 22161.

National Telephone Cooperative Association, 2626 Pennsylvania Ave., N.W., Washington, D.C. 20037.

National Trust for Historic Preservation, 1785 Massachusetts Ave., N.W. Washington, D.C. 20036.

National Weather Service, Office of Hydrology, 1325 East-West Hwy., Ste. 1840, Silver Spring, MD 20910.

Natural Hazards Research and Applications Information Center, Campus Box 482, University of Colorado-Boulder, Boulder, CO 80309-0482.

Natural Phenomena Hazards Project (DOE), Lawrence Livermore National laboratory, P.O. Box 808, L-193, Livermore, CA 94551.

NCC Publishing, 222 Argyle Ave., Delhi, ON N4B 2Y2.

NCSL see National Conference of State Legislatures.

Neal-Schuman Publishers, Inc., 100 Varick St., New York, NY 10013-1506.

Nelson Publishing, 2504 N. Tamiami Trail, Nokomis, FL 34275.

Nelson-Hall Publishing, Inc., 111 N. Canal St., Chicago, IL 60606.

New Riders *see* Macmillan.

New York Institute of Finance, 2 Broadway, 5th Fl., New York, NY 10004.

NEXIS *see* Mead Data Central.

NFPA *see* National Fire Protection Association.

NHRAIC *see* Natural Hazards Research and Applications Information Center.

NIUSR *see* National Institute for Urban Search and Rescue.

NLC *see* National League of Cities.

Nolo Press, 950 Parker St., Berkeley, CA 94710.

North-Holland, P.O. Box 882, Madison Square Station, New York, NY 10159.

Northwestern University School of Law, 357 E. Chicago Ave., Chicago, IL 60611.

W. W. Norton & Co., 500 5th St. New York, NY 10110.

NRPA *see* National Recreation and Park Association.

NTIS *see* National Technical Information Service.

OECD/IEA Publications Office, 2 rue Andre Pascal, F-75775 Paris, CEDEX 16, France.

Office of Hydrology *see* National Weather Service.

Old House Journal Corp., 2 Main St., Gloucester, MA 01930-5726.

Omnigraphics, In., Penobscot Bldg., Detroit, MI 48226.

Online, Inc., 462 Danbury Rd., Wilton, CT 06897.

Oryx Press, 4041 N. Central Ave., Ste. 700, Phoenix, AZ 85012-3399, (602)265-2651.

Oxford University Press, 200 Madison Ave., New York, NY 10016.

PAIS International *see* Public Affairs Information Service, Inc.

Paramount Publishing, Ltd., 17-21 Shenley Rd., Borehamwood, Herts WD6 1RT, England.

Parsons Brinckerhoff *see* Wiley.

PennWell Publishing, Park 80 W., Plaza 2, Saddlebrook, NJ 07662-5812.

PennWell Publishing Co., Advanced Technology Group, 10 Tara Blvd., 5th Fl., Nashua, NH 03062-2801.

PennWell Publishing Co., 1421 S. Sheridan, Tulsa, OK 74112.

Penton Publishing, 400 Superior Ave., Cleveland, OH 44114-2543.

Pergamon Press, Inc., 660 White Plains Rd., Tarrytown, NY 10591-5153.

Phillips Publishing, Inc., 7811 Montrose Rd., Potomac, MD 20854.

Philosophy Documentation Center *see* Bowling Green University.

Planning and Zoning Center, Inc., 302 S. Waverly Rd., Lansing, MI 48917.Plenum Press, 233 Spring St., New York, NY 10013.

P. O. Publishing Co., Oakton Street Station, Skokie, IL 60076.

Police Foundation, 1001 22nd St., N.W., Ste. 200, Washington, D.C. 20037.

Political Woman, 276 Chatterton Pkwy., White Plains, NY 10606.

Praeger Publishers, Inc., 88 Post Road W., Box 5007, Westport, CT 06881-5007.

Praxis Publications, P.O. Box 9869, Madison, WI 53715.

Prentice-Hall, Inc., 15 Columbus Cir., New York, NY 10023.

Prima Publishing, Box 1260, Rocklin, CA 95677-1260.

Prime National Publishing Corp., 470 Boston Post Rd., Weston, MA 02193.

Princeton Architectural Press, 37 E. Seventh St., New York, NY 10003.

Privatization Center *see* Reason Foundation.

Professional Publications, Inc., 1250 Fifth Ave., Belmont, CA 94002.

Project Management Institute, P.O. Box 189, Webster, NC 28788.

Prometheus Books, 59 John Glenn Dr., Buffalo, NY 14228.

PTN Publishing Corp., 445 Broad Hollow Rd., Ste. 21, Melvill, NY 11747-4722.

Public Affairs Information Service, Inc., 521 W. 43rd St., New York, NY 10036-4396, (212)736-6629.

Public Safety Personnel Research Institute, Inc., 5519 N. Cumberland Ave., Ste. 1008, Chicago, IL 60656-1498.

Public Works Journal Corp., 200 S. Broad St., Box 688, Ridgewood, NJ 07451.

Publishing Horizons, 8233 Via Paseo del Norte, Ste. F-400, Scottsdale, AZ 85258.

Putnam Publishing Group, 200 Madison Ave., New York, NY 10016.

Quality Press, 611 E. Wisconsin Ave., P.O. Box 3005, Milwaukee, WI 53201-3005.

Quorum Books, 88 Post Rd. W., Box 5007, Westport, CT 06881-5007.

Rand Corporation, P.O. Box 2138, Santa Monica, CA 90406-2138.

Reason Foundation, 3415 S. Sepulveda Blvd., Ste. 400, Los Angeles, CA 90034, (310)391-2245.

RLIN *see* Research Libraries Group, Inc.

Rocky Mountain Land Institute, College of Law, University of Denver.

Routledge, 29 W. 35th St., New York, NY 10001-2291.

Rutgers University Press, 109 Church Street, New Brunswick, NJ 08901.

SAE *see* Society of Automotive Engineers.

Sagamore Publishing, Inc., 302 W. Hill St.,, Box 673, Champaign, IL 61824-0673.

Sage Publications, Inc., 2455 Teller Rd., Thousand Oak, CA 91320.

St. Paul, MN, Office of the State Auditor, Ste. 400, 525 Park St., St. Paul, MN 55103.

Santa Clara Council of Churches, 1229 Naglee Ave., San Jose, CA 95126.

Securities Data Co., 1180 Raymond Blvd., 5th Fl., Newark, NJ 07102, (201)622-3100.

Seven Locks Press, P.O. Box 68, Arlington, VA 22210.

SFPE *see* Society of Fire Protection Engineers.

Simon & Schuster, Inc., 1230 Avenue of the Americas, New York, NY 10020.

Simmons-Boardman Publishing Corp., 345 Hudson St., New York, NY 10014.

Society for Advancement of Management, P.O. Box 889, Vinton, VA 24179.

Society of Automotive Engineers, Inc., 400 Commonwealth Dr., Warrendale, PA 15096-0001.

Society of Fire Protection Engineers, 1 Liberty Sq., Boston, MA 02109-4825.

Sociological Abstracts, Inc., P.O. Box 22206, San Diego, CA 92192, (619)695-8803.

Solano Press Books, Box 773, Point Arena, CA 95468.

Specialized Publications Service, P.O. Box 1915, Madison Square Station, NY 10159.

Sport Information Resource Centre, 1600 James Naismith Dr., Gloucester, ON K1B 5N4, (613)748-5658.

Springer Publishing Co., Inc., 536 Broadway, 11th Fl., New York, NY 10012.

State University of New York Press (SUNY), State University Plaza, Albany, NY 12246-0001.

SUNY *see* State University of New York.

Superintendent of Documents, U.S. Government Printing Office, Washington, DC 20402-9371.

Sydenham Publishing, 344 23rd St. W., Owen Sound ON N4K 467.

State of Washington, Department of Community Trade and Economic Development, 900 Columbia, S.W., P.O. Box 48300, Olympia, WA 98504-8300.

Systems Research Institute, P.O. Box 86366, Los Angeles, CA 90086-0366.

Taft Group, Gale Research, Inc., 12300 Twinbrook Pkwy., Ste. 520, Rockville, MD 20852.

Tappi Technology Park, P.O. Box 105113, Atlanta, GA 30348-5113.

Tax Analysts, 6830 N. Fairfax Dr., Arlington, VA 22213.

Taylor and Francis, 1900 Frost Rd., Ste. 101, Bristol, PA 19007.

Technomic Publishing Co., 851 New Holland Ave., Box 3535, Lancaster, PA 17604.

Temple University Press, 1601 N. Broad St., University Services Bldg., Rm. 306, Philadelphia, PA 19122.

Thames and Hudson, 500 5th Ave., New York, NY 10110.

Charles C. Thomas, Publisher, 2600 S. First St., Springfield, IL 62794-9265.

Town and Country Planning Association, 17 Carlton House Terrace, London, SW1Y 5AS, England.

Training Shoppe, 4228 Palos Verdes, CA 90274.

Transaction Publishers, Dept. 3092, Rutgers University, New Brunswick, NJ 08903.

Trans-Atlantic Arts, Inc., 311 Bainbridge St., Philadelphia, PA 19147.

Transportation Research Board, 2102 Constitution Ave., N.W., Washington, D.C. 20418, (202)334-3250.

TRB *see* Transportation Research Board.

ULI *see* Urban Land Institute.

UMI 620 S. Third St., Louisville, KY 40202-2475, (502)538-4111, (800)628-2823.

University Microfilms International, 300 N. Zeeb Rd., Ann Arbor, MI 48106, (313)761-4700, (800)521-0600, Canada:(800)343-5299.

University of Chicago, Center for Urban Research and Policy Studies, 2969 E. 60th St., Chicago, IL 60637.

University of Chicago Journals Division, 5720 S. Woodlawn Ave., Chicago, IL 60637.

University of Georgia, Carl Vinson Institute of Government, Terrel Hall, Athens, GA 30602.

University of Illinois Press, 1325 S. Oak St., Champaign, IL 61820.

University of Massachusetts Press, Box 429, Amherst MA 01004-0429.

University of Pennsylvania Press, 418 Service Dr., Blockley Hall, 13th Fl., Philadelphia, PA 19104-6097.

University of Texas at Austin, Center for Research in Water Resources, Balcones Research Center, 10100 Burnet Rd., Austin, TX 78712.

University of Toronto Press, 340 Nagel Dr., Cheektowaga, NY 14225.

University Press of America, 4720 Boston Way, Lanham, MD 20706.

University Press of Kansas State University, 2501 W. 15th St., Lawrence, KS 66049.

Urban Development Institute of Ontario, 60 Bloor Street, W., Ste. 1203, P.O. B12, Toronto, ON M44 3B8.

Urban Institute Press, 2100 M St., N.W., Ste. 407, Washington, DC 20037.

Urban Land Institute, 625 Indiana Ave., N.W., Ste. 400 Washington, D.C. 20004-2930.

U.S. Advisory Commission on Intergovernmental Relations, 800 K St., N.W., Ste. 450-South, Washington, DC 20575.

U.S. Bureau of Justice Assistance, 1600 Research Blvd., Rockville, MD 20850.

U.S. Bureau of Justice Statistics, 633 Indiana Ave., N.W., Washington, DC 20531.

U.S. Bureau of Labor Statistics, 441 G. St., N.W., Washington, DC 20212.

U.S. Bureau of the Census, Data Users Service Division, Washington, DC 20233, (301)763-2074.

U.S. Bureau of the Census, U.S. Department of Commerce, Washington, DC 20233.

USCM *see* U.S. Conference of Mayors.

U.S. Conference of Mayors, 1620 Eye St., N.W., Washington, DC 20006.

U.S. Department of Agriculture, 14th St. and Independence Ave., S.W., Washington, DC 20250.

U.S. Department of Commerce, Herbert C. Hoover Building, 14th & Constitution Avenue, NW, Washington, DC 20230.

U.S. Department of Energy, Office of Scientific and Technical Information, P.O. Box 62, Oak Ridge, TN 37831, (615)576-1189.

U.S. Department of the Interior, 1849 C St., N.W., Washington, DC 20240.

U.S. Department of Transportation, 400 Seventh St., S.W., Washington, DC 20590.

U.S. Environmental Protection Agency, 401 M St., S.W. Washington, D.C. 20460-0001.

U.S. Federal Highway Administration, 400 Seventh St., N.W., Washington, DC 20590.

U.S. General Accounting Office, P.O. Box 6015, Gaithersburg, MD 20877.

U.S. Geological Survey, Box 25046 Federal Center Mail Stop 967, Denver Co 80225, (303)273-8500.

U.S. Geological Survey, Water Resources Scientific Information Center, 4125 National Center, Reston, VA 22092 (703)648-6820.

U.S. Government Printing Office *see* Superintendent of Documents.

U.S. National Institute of Justice, National Criminal Justice Research Service (NCJRS) P.O. Box 6000, Rockville, MD 20850 (301)251-5500, (800)851-3420.

U.S. National Institute of Standards and Technology, Building and Fire Research Laboratory, Bldg. 224, Rm. A252, Gaithersburg, MD 20899, (301)975-6862.

Van Nostrand Reinhold Co., 115 Fifth Ave., New York, NY 10003.

Venture Publishing, Inc., 1999 Cato Ave., State College, PA 16801.

Wadsworth Publishing Co., 10 Davis Dr., Belmont, CA 94002.

Wakeman/Walworth, Inc., 300 N. Washington St., Alexandria, VA 22314.

Warren, Gorham, & Lamont, 31 St. James Avenue, 4th Fl., Boston, MA 02116-4101.

Washington Post News Research Center, 1150 15th St., N.W., 5th Fl., Washington, D.C. 20002-0071, (202)334-7341.

Washington Researchers, Ltd. 2612 P St., N.W., P.O. Box 19005, Washington, D.C. 20007-3062, (202)333-3499.

Washington University, One Brookings Drive, Campus Box 1120, St. Louis, MO 63130-4999.

Waste Management Information Bureau, United Kingdom Atomic Energy Authority, AEA Environment and Energy, Bldg. 7.12, Harwell Laboratory, Didcot, Oxon, OX11 ORA, England, 0235-433442.

Water Environment Federation, 601 Wythe St., Alexandria, VA 22314-1994.

Waterfront Center, 1536 44th St., N.W., Washington, DC 20007.

Waveland Press, P.O. Box 400, Prospect Heights, IL 60070.

WEFA Group, 401 City Line Ave., Ste. 300, Bala Cynwyd, PA 19004-1780, (215)667-6000.

West Publishing Co., 620 Opperman Dr., Eagan, MN 55123, (612)6877000, (800)328-9352.

WESTLAW *see* West Publishing Co.

Westview Press, 5500 Central Ave., Boulder, CO 80301-2847.

John Wiley and Sons, One Wiley Dr., Somerset, NJ 08875-1272.

Willow Tree Press, Inc., 124 Willow Tree Rd., P.O. Box 249, Monsey, NY 10952, (914)362-8376.

H. W. Wilson, 950 University Ave., Bronx, NY 10452, (718)588-8400.

World Bank, 1818 H St., N.W., Washington, DC 20005.

Ziff-Davis Publishing Co., 10 Presidents Landing, Medford, MA 02155-5146.

List of Authors and Contributors

Authors and Contributors

Philip Benowitz is a senior manager with Deloitte & Touche's public sector consulting practice based in Parsippany, New Jersey. He specializes in providing financial and operational consulting services to state and local government clients, including the New Jersey Sports and Exposition Authority; the states of New Jersey, Florida, and Arizona; and the cities of Virginia Beach, Virginia, and Dallas, Texas. He holds bachelor's and master's degrees in public management from Carnegie Mellon University.

David R. Berman is a professor of political science at Arizona State University. He has written books and numerous articles on state and local government, politics, and public policy. Before coming to Arizona State, he was a research associate with the National League of Cities. Professor Berman holds a Ph.D and a master of arts degree from American University and a bachelor's degree from Rockford College.

Eugene P. Boyd is a public policy analyst with the Congressional Research Service of the Library of Congress where he conducts research and policy analysis of federal housing, community and economic development and related urban policy issues, legislation, and programs in support of members of Congress and congressional committees. He also has worked as a housing and information specialist for the Planning and Development Division of the Prince George's County Maryland Housing Authority. Mr. Boyd holds a bachelor's degree in urban studies from Virginia Commonwealth University and has undertaken graduate studies in city and regional planning at Howard University.

Glen Hahn Cope is associate dean of the Lyndon B. Johnson School of Public Affairs at the University of Texas at Austin and an associate professor of public affairs. She has also taught in the School of Public Affairs of the American University in Washington, DC. She served as a member of the Texas Interagency Performance Budgeting Panel in 1991–92. Prior to her academic career, she worked in the state governments of Michigan and Virginia in several capacities, including acting budget director of the Michigan Department of Social Services. Cope holds a bachelor's degree in economics from the University of Michigan, an MPA from the Maxwell School of Syracuse University, and a Ph.D. in public administration from Ohio State University. Her research and teaching interests include public management, budgeting, and financial management in state and local governments.

Anne Maura English is a freelance editor and researcher and a member of Washington Independent Writers. Her experience includes high school and college teaching, medical research and clinical work, and extensive social services and advocacy. She holds a bachelor's degree in English from the College of Notre Dame of Maryland and a master's from Catholic University. Currently, English is a doctoral candidate in religious studies at Catholic University and is completing an MSW in clinical mental health at the University of Maryland School of Social Work.

Gwen Hall is the publications assistant in ICMA's publications department. Prior to joining the ICMA staff, she was a project coordinator with the Triangle Coalition for Science and Technology Education. She holds a bachelor's degree in government and politics from the University of Maryland.

Rosemary O'Leary is an attorney and an associate professor at the School of Public and Environmental Affairs at Indiana University at Bloomington. O'Leary has served as an attorney and as the director of policy and planning for an environmental agency in the Midwest. She has published extensively in the areas of environmental policy, environmental law, and law and public policy and has won national research awards. Her book, *Environmental Change: Federal Courts and the EPA*, was published in 1993. She is a member of the board of editors of four national journals. O'Leary is the outgoing Chair of the Environment and Natural Resources Administration section of the American Society for Public Administration.

Adam Prager is a manager with Deloitte & Touche's economic development services practice, based in Chicago, Illinois. During his ten years in economic development, Prager has consulted and led consulting efforts on behalf of over fifty economic development related agencies in North America and Asia. He has advised organizations on the creation and enhancement of economic development strategies, aided with defense conversion strategies, performed community competitive assessments, devised marketing schemes, identified target industry opportunities, organized existing business assistance programs, conducted economic and fiscal impact analyses, and conducted many labor, real estate, and other location factor analyses. Prior to his consulting activities, Prager served as manager of marketing resources for the Maryland Department of Economic and Employment Development. He holds a bachelor's from the University of Delaware in Environmental Science and Agriculture and two master's—city and regional planning and public policy and management—from the Ohio State University.

Tari Renner is chair of the political science department at Illinois Wesleyan University. He was formerly an associate professor in the political science department at Duquesne University. Prior to his position at Duquesne, he was the senior statistical analyst for ICMA, where he was responsible for the design, data collection, and analysis of local government survey research projects. Renner holds a bachelor's degree from the University of South Florida and a master's and Ph.D. in political science from The American University.

Robert Schein is a senior consultant with Deloitte & Touche's public sector consulting practice. His areas of expertise include fiscal and economic analysis, organizational management, public sector service delivery, and legislative affairs. He was formerly an assistant legislative representative in the New York City Mayor's Office and a senior analyst with New York City's Office of Management and Budget. During that time, he was involved in several endeavors to shape economic development in New York City, including negotiations on the city's capital budget and efforts to implement the city's Business Improvement District program. Schein received a bachelor's from Northwestern University and a master's of public affairs from the Woodrow Wilson School of Public and International Affairs at Princeton University.

Craig M. Wheeland is assistant professor of political science at Villanova University, where he is coordinator of the public administration concentration in the Human Organization Science Graduate Program. He holds a bachelor's degree in history, an MPA from the University of South Carolina, and a Ph.D. in political science from Pennsylvania State University. Wheeland's research interests and publications focus on leadership in council-manager government and collaborative decision-making techniques. Prior to his appointment to the faculty of Villanova in 1990, Wheeland served on the faculty of Winthrop College for three years.

Charles R. Wise is professor of public affairs and associate dean for Bloomington in the School of Public and Environmental Affairs of Indiana University. Wise served in the U.S. Department of Justice as special assistant for policy analysis in the Office of Legislative Affairs and then as director of intergovernmental relations. Wise also served as research consultant with the U.S. Air Safety Commission.

Wise held numerous positions in the American Society of Public Administration and the National Association of Schools of Public Affairs and Administration. Wise was managing editor of *Public Administration Review* and has three times received the Mosher Award for best academic article to appear in that journal. Wise is the author of *The Dynamics of Legislation: Leadership and Policy Change in the Congressional Process* and has published extensively in professional journals.

Cumulative Index, 1991–1995

Cumulative Index, 1991–1995

The cumulative index comprises the years 1991 through 1995 of *The Municipal Year Book*.

Urban administrators and others involved in local government, as well as students, scholars, researchers, and others who refer frequently to *The Municipal Year Book*, should find this index a valuable tool.

Entries for the years 1991 through 1993 appear exactly as indexed in the Cumulative Index to *The Municipal Year Book 1993*. The years 1994 and 1995 are included in this Cumulative Index. Entries prior to 1991 are found in earlier editions of *The Municipal Year Book*.

How To Use This Index. Entries run in chronological order, starting with 1991. The **year** is in **boldface** numerals, followed by a colon (e.g., **94:**); the relevant page numbers follow. Years are separated by semicolons.

Page numbers followed by the words *table(s)* or *figure(s)* indicate that those particular pages contain table(s) and/or figure(s). The term *PICSs* refers to both *Profiles of Individual Cities* and *Profiles of Individual Counties*.

The Municipal Year Book 1995
  Volume 62

Composition by
  EPS Group
  Hanover, Maryland

Printing and binding by
  Quebecor Printing
  Kingsport, Tennessee